PCI

and

PCI-X

Hardware and Software

Architecture and Design

Fifth Edition

Edward Solari and George Willse

Annabooks

San Diego

PCI and PCI-X
Hardware and Software
by
Edward Solari and George Willse
Fifth Edition

PUBLISHED BY

Annabooks
12860 Danielson Court
Poway, CA 92064
USA

858-391-5600
http://www.annabooks.com

Printed in the United States of America

ISBN 0-929392-63-9

Fifth Edition

Ninth Printing, March 2001

Disclaimer and Corrections ... Please Read

New to the Fifth Edition

The first four editions of this book covered the PCI local bus specification and the changes due to Engineering Change Notices and Engineering Change Requests. This edition of the book includes everything relative to revision 2.2 and 3.0 (as of press time) of the PCI local bus specification, plus the most recent Engineering Change Notices and Engineering Change Requests. This fifth edition also includes the new information concerning revision 1.0a of the PCI-X addendum specification. PCI-X represents an enhancement to PCI; consequently, this book has retained the emphasis on PCI and provides the PCI-X information as incremental to PCI. Please see further discussion in the *Preface* relating to PCI 3.0, PCI 2.2, and PCI-X 1.0a.

This edition of the book references the power management and hot plug attributes of PCI and PCI-X. Due to the complexity of these topics, this book leaves complete discussion of these topics to other books. Please see *PCI Power Management* by George Willse *et. al.* and *PCI Hot-Plug Application and Design* by Alan Goodrum. Both of these books are available at www.annabooks.com.

This edition of the book also references PCI/PCI BRIDGES and PCI-X/PCI-X BRIDGES. Due to the complexity of these topics, this book leaves complete discussion of these topics to the actual specifications from the PCI SIG and to the specifications from the manufacturers of the actual bridge chips. The exact bridge characteristics can vary depending on the architecture of the bridge chip.

In addition, the authors and publisher appreciate the feedback we have received from alert readers, who are responsible for some of the corrections and clarifications that have been added to this edition. You are always welcome to contact us at *feedback@annabooks.com*.

Dedications

As with my previous books

The patience and understanding by my wife (who never sees me when I undertake a project like this) is greatly appreciated.

The education, discipline, and dedication imparted to me by my mother and father continues to be invaluable to projects like this.

Finally, working with George Willse on this and other projects continues to be a great pleasure. His dedication to a quality product is refreshing – it is very rare to find someone who is willing to do on-going work to maintain and update a published book in a timely fashion.

Ed

To Brigitte –
The best compass for my life this side of heaven.

To Travis and Tyler -
What a privilege to hear you call me "Dad". I am so proud of you.

And to Ed -
For the encouragement years ago to take the road less traveled, for which I shall always be grateful.

George

Contents

Preface
... Including "What is PCI 3.0 ?"

The major cause of low performance in computer systems is the time it takes to execute memory and I/O functions related to peripheral devices such as LAN, SCSI, and motion video. Low bus bandwidth adversely impacts data processing and screen output. In recent years, two independent approaches have been taken to solve this low bandwidth obstacle. First, peripheral device vendors have implemented new architectures to increase the data transfer rates between their devices and other system resources. The second approach is the movement of peripheral devices from lower to higher performance buses.

The PCI Bus (originally named Peripheral Component Interconnect, a name that is now inappropriate and that should no longer be used) was the first widely accepted bus architecture to address the performance issues associated with personal computers. The PCI bus also addresses multiple bus master support. The PCI bus resource and add-in card interface is also processor independent, allowing full support of present and future processors of different architectures.

The features of the PCI bus architecture also extend into the software realm. PCI devices incorporate registers that contain device-specific information. This information enables System BIOSs and operating system level software to automatically configure and manage PCI bus resources and add-in cards. Automatic device configuration eliminates the need for hardware jumpers and software configuration utilities. In addition, this feature reduces the possibility of system resource conflicts that can occur when two or more devices are assigned the same resource.

Recently, the PCI bus architecture has been enhanced by PCI-X. The purpose of PCI-X is to improve system performance by enhancing PCI with the inclusion of Split Transaction protocol and higher CLK signal line frequencies.

The major goal of this book is to document in one location both the hardware and software architectures of the PCI and PCI-X buses. This book is based on the PCI local bus specification Revision 2.2, PCI-to-PCI Bridge Architecture Specification Revision 1.1, PCI BIOS Specification Revision 2.1, PCI-X addendum specification 1.0a, and additional information not incorporated in any of these (and only available in this book). This enables you to quickly access ALL the information necessary to ensure the proper design of PCI and PCI-X based systems, components, or add-in cards.

The book is divided into three sections. Chapters 1 and 2 are introductory and provide a very general overview of the hardware and software for the PCI and

PCI-X buses. Chapters 3 through 15 are dedicated to the detailed specification and discussion of PCI and PCI-X bus hardware. Finally, Chapters 16 through 24 are dedicated to the detailed specification and discussion of PCI and PCI-X bus software.

What is PCI 3.0? ... Just prior to printing this book, the PCI SIG announced Revision 3.0 of PCI local addendum specification (PCI 3.0). As of this book's printing date, PCI 3.0 primarily consists of the merger of Revision 2.2 of the PCI local bus specification (PCI 2.2) and Revision 1.0a of the PCI-X addendum specification (PCI-X 1.0a). PCI 3.0 of course includes any ECNs (Engineering Change Notices) subsequent to PCI 2.2 and PCI-X 1.0a; this book includes all of the ECNs approved at the time of printing. PCI 3.0 also places one new requirement not part of PCI 2.2 and PCI-X 1.0a. This requirement allows the implementation only of add-in cards that are compliant to either the 3.3 volt only or the universal I/O signaling add-in card protocols. The purpose is to facilitate the adoption of PCI-X by removing the "design comfort" of 5 volt only signaling permitted by PCI 2.2. That is, PCI 3.0 compliant bus segments will not support add-in cards keyed for 5 volt only signaling. There has been a concern that the adoption of PCI-X (and thus the associated benefits) have been slow because bus segments operating in PCI-X mode require 3.3 volt signaling. Prior to PCI 3.0, bus segments operating in PCI mode only required support of 5 volt signaling. PCI 3.0 forces the PCI mode to move to 3.3 volt signaling and thus removes the "perceived" 3.3 volt signaling barrier of PCI-X 1.0a. See further discussion in Chapter 11: *Reset, Power, and Signal Line Initialization*, Chapter 13: *Connector, Platform, and Add-in Card Design*, and Chapter 15: *Mechanical Specification* for more information.

This book has retained the focus of PCI 2.2 while adding the incremental information relative to PCI-X 1.0a. This approach permits those of you working with the "traditional" PCI add-in cards and components to have a clear understanding of the PCI requirements. Those of you interested in designing add-in cards and components compliant to PCI-X 1.0a will also easily see the incremental design requirements. You are advised to periodically check with the PCI SIG web site (http://www.pcisig.com) and the errata sheet for this book (posted at http://www.annabooks.com.) for the latest information.

Annabooks and we are all interested in the continuing evolution, clarification, and corrections to this book. Please direct any related inputs to Annabooks at *feedback@annabooks.com.*

The publisher and authors would also like to thank Norm Rasmussen, Brad Hosler, Scott McMorrow, Laurie Fleisher, and Suba Vanka for taking the time to review the original PCI centric text prior to publication. We would also like to thank Mr. Nagumo and Mr. Fukushima of IDES Japan for their corrections made during their Japanese translation of this book. We are also grateful for the efforts extended by Tim Bohan of Annabooks during the production of both the Japanese and English editions of this work.

Of special note is the assistance rendered by Norman Rasmussen and Brad Hosler ... two of the key PCI experts on the planet. They dedicated excessive hours of their own time to this project. Their diligent review, comments, corrections, and insights were invaluable during the preparation of this book. We would also like to acknowledge the help provided by Alan Goodrum and Dwight Riley on the PCI-X portions of the book. Both of these gentlemen were instrumental in the technical definition and implementation of PCI-X.

We would also like to thank the PCI Special Interest Group and, in particular, David Schuler and Mike Bailey (the previous PCI SIG Steering Committee Chairman) for permission to extract and use portions of the PCI local bus specifications. Also thanks go to William Samaris for his help with the details of the electrical specifications. Most recently, relative to PCI-X, we would like to acknowledge the help we received from Dwight Riley and Roger Tipley (the current PCI SIG Steering Committee Chairman).

Last, but certainly not least, we would like to thank John Choisser for editing this and other editions of the book. A book of this size and technical detail requires a tremendous amount of quality editing ... which John provided.

Ed Solari and George Willse

Oregon

CHAPTER 1

ISA SYSTEM ARCHITECTURAL OVERVIEW

This chapter consists of the following subchapters:

1.0   ISA System Architecture
1.1   Layer 1-Platform Hardware
1.2   Layer 2-System ROM Bios
1.3   Layer 3-Operating System
1.4   Layer 4-Application Programs
1.5   Chapter Summary

1.0   ISA SYSTEM ARCHITECTURE

The architecture of ISA compatible systems can be viewed as four individual layers. Each layer has a defined interface between itself and the other layers. Utilizing this layered architecture permits each layer to be developed and modified independently of the others. It also translates into portability for the upper software layers.

> Even though not specifically mentioned, the architectural concepts described for an ISA system also apply to EISA and Micro Channel systems.

> The term "system" represents the entire hardware and software required to create an ISA compatible personal computer. The term "platform" represents the physical collection of hardware on a single circuit board. The platform usually contains connectors to support the attachment of add-in cards.

1.1   LAYER 1-PLATFORM HARDWARE

At the innermost layer of the architecture lies the platform hardware. This hardware consists of the platform with its integrated components and add-in cards that expand platform features. The simplest architecture of an ISA compatible platform is shown in Figure 1-1. The HOST CPU, cache, and memory (HDRAM) all reside on the HOST bus. The HOST bus is attached to an ISA bus (or EISA or Micro-Channel, depending on the platform) via a BRIDGE. The ISA bus contains ISA bus connectors and ISA compatible resources.

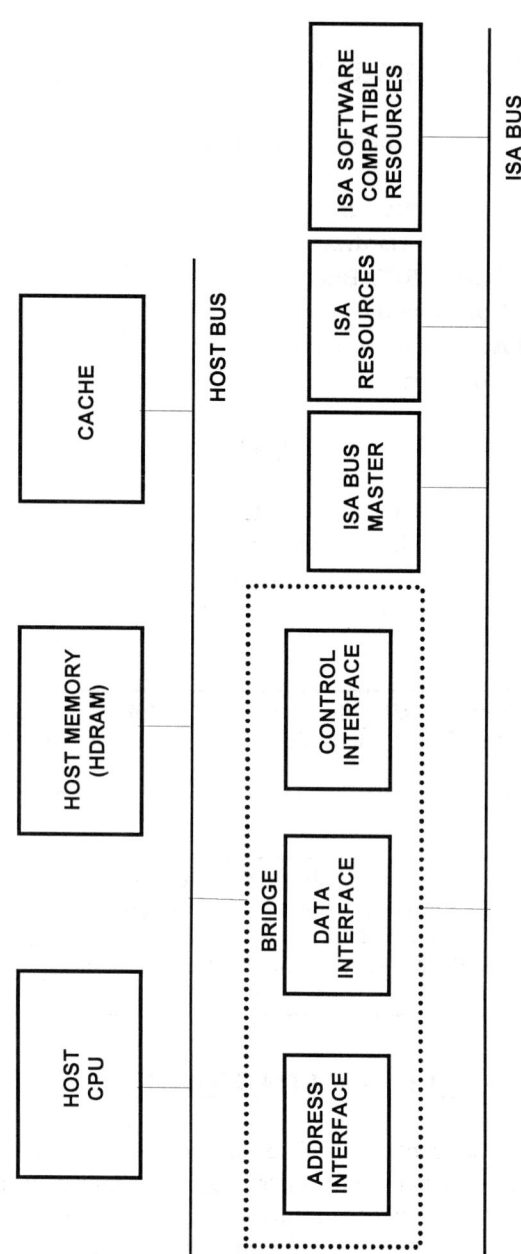

Figure 1-1: Generic ISA Platform Architecture

HOST BUS

The HOST bus supports the highest performance resources on the platform and is separated from the ISA bus. Newer platforms allow the HOST CPU to continue execution (with the cache and HDRAM) when the ISA bus is executing a bus transaction. The HOST bus is proprietary to the platform, but in most personal computers resembles the Intel 80386, 80486, or Pentium class of machines. The ISA bus provides a general-purpose bus that is of lower performance but continues to provide a wealth of add-in functions as a defacto standard. As will be discussed in Chapter 2, a third bus (PCI) has also become a defacto standard in personal computer platforms. This local bus blends the high performance of the HOST bus with the flexibility to attach a variety of functions with its standardized and documented protocol.

ISA BRIDGE

The ISA BRIDGE provides the link between the HOST and ISA buses. The three major components are ADDRESS, DATA, and CONTROL Interfaces.

The ADDRESS Interface translates the address memory space of the HOST bus (typically 32 bits or more) to the address space of the ISA bus (24 bits). In the case of the I/O address space, the conversion from HOST bus to ISA bus is from 16 to 10 address bits, respectively.

The DATA Interface matches the data size of the HOST bus (typically 32 bits or more) to the data size of the ISA bus (8 or 16 bits). This interface includes byte swapping and the execution of the multiple cycles (in conjunction with the CONTROL Interface). Multiple transaction support includes (for example) a 32 data bit access on the HOST bus to be translated to two 16 data bit transactions on the ISA bus. The DATA Interface may also post write DATA (under certain conditions) to allow the transactions on the two buses to complete at different times.

The CONTROL Interface translates the HOST bus protocol to the ISA bus protocol and vice versa. In the case of multiple transactions, the CONTROL Interface will generate the additional bus transactions required.

ISA RESOURCES

ISA Software Compatible Resources are required for compatibility with the ISA software. The ISA software requires certain resources with predefined registers to reside at specific addresses. The defacto resources required are: Interrupt Controller, Keyboard, Mouse, Video, Floppy Disk, Hard Disk, Refresh and DMA Controllers, System Timer, and the Real Time Clock.

Also attached to the ISA bus are the ISA bus masters and ISA resources. The ISA bus master can arbitrate (via the DMA Controller) to own the ISA bus and access ISA bus resources or the HOST memory. The ISA resource can consist of both memory and I/O types.

1.2 LAYER 2-SYSTEM ROM BIOS

The System ROM BIOS, or Basic Input Output System, is the layer directly above the platform hardware. The run-time function of the System ROM BIOS is to provide an interface between the layers of software above and the platform hardware below. The System ROM BIOS receives requests from the upper layers of software to manipulate the platform hardware.

Because the System ROM BIOS communicates directly with the platform hardware it is not usually portable between different computers. This is due in part to the difference in chip sets, microprocessor types, and bus architectures used in different computers. The software layers above the System ROM BIOS, such as the operating system, can remain hardware independent by using the System ROM BIOS's software interface to communicate with the platform hardware. The mechanism for this communication is through the use of software interrupts and is described in detail in Chapter 16, *System Resources.*

1.3 LAYER 3-OPERATING SYSTEM

The third layer in the architecture of an ISA compatible system is the operating system. An operating system is the computer's primary software program. An operating system controls application programs and computer hardware during the run-time operation of the system. Common operating systems compatible with ISA compatible systems includes MS-DOS, Microsoft Windows 2000 and NT 4.0, Linux, and several different flavors of Unix.

DOS BIOS

The DOS BIOS services the platform hardware-dependent components of the system. These functions include device drivers for the system date and time (CLOCK), serial port input or auxiliary interface (AUX), keyboard and video display (CON), line printer output (PRN or LPTx), serial port (COMx), and the disk drives that are accessed by the A, B, C, and so forth, disk drive designators. The DOS BIOS software is in a file that usually is named IO.SYS, IBMIO.SYS or IBMBIO.COM.

DOS KERNEL

The DOS Kernel services the platform hardware-independent components of the system. These functions include character input and output, file management, the execution of other software programs, and real-time clock services. As with the System ROM BIOS services, programmers also use software interrupts to access the DOS Kernel functions. The DOS Kernel is typically found in a file called IBMDOS.COM or MSDOS.SYS.

DOS COMMAND PROCESSOR

The DOS Command Processor is the software module that provides the user interface to the operating system. It is a program controlled by DOS that accepts the user's command line input, parses it, and then executes the commands. These commands usually include loading and executing other software programs. The DOS Command Processor is found in a file named COMMAND.COM.

1.4 LAYER 4-APPLICATION PROGRAMS

Application Programs are the software programs the user loads and executes under the control of an operating system. These include word processors, graphics packages, games, and telecommunications programs.

1.5 CHAPTER SUMMARY

Since the first versions of DOS (MS-DOS 1.0 and PC-DOS 1.0) were introduced in 1981, the operating systems have increased in power and flexibility. With each new version, the three software layers described above have been enhanced to accommodate new hardware features such as larger disk drives, networking, and more powerful microprocessors. With the more complex functionality of the systems has come a major emphasis on simplifying user interfaces for the software programs contained in each of the layers. As will be seen, PCI hardware and software has done much to enhance the ease of integration and use of the first layer of computer systems, the platform hardware itself.

CHAPTER 2

PCI AND PCI-X SYSTEM ARCHITECTURAL OVERVIEW

This chapter consists of the following subchapters:

2.0 INTRODUCTION

A major strength of any computer system is its expansion capability. This provides the ability to add new components to the system, typically through the use of expansion bus add-in cards, to increase the existing machine's functional capabilities. This concept, in conjunction with an open system architecture approach, is without a doubt the cornerstone behind the astonishing success of the IBM and IBM-compatible personal computers.

Despite its success, however, there are two cardinal omissions in the original design of the IBM personal computer that plagued the computer industry.

The first omission is that no formal hardware design specification was provided for the design of both the system platforms and the ISA expansion bus add-in cards. This lack of a uniform specification produced two major consequences. The first consequence affects the designers and manufactures of computer hardware: various vendors have spent untold man-hours of reverse engineering over the years to produce the various system components. The second consequence affects the consumer: the lack of a uniform hardware specification often results in an incompatibility between the system components. This in turn makes it difficult if not impossible to install and configure many of the hardware components in a computer system.

The second outstanding omission in the design of the original IBM personal computer is the lack of an architecture that coordinates the integration of the hardware and software components of the system. Installing and configuring new components such that the computer system remains resource conflict-free has been very troublesome. For example, assigning DMA, IRQ, memory, and I/O Port resources to older ISA expansion bus add-in cards and system platforms usually requires the reading of hardware manuals as well as the manipulation of jumpers or switches. Newer add-in cards and system platforms require the installer to run software setup utilities to configure the add-in cards for use in the system.

Neither of the above methods ensures a system that is resource conflict-free. The reason is that in order to assign unused resources to a previously uninstalled add-in card, the installer or the add-in card installation utility must be cognizant of all the system resources currently consumed by the system. This was impossible under the original IBM paradigm. Compounding the problem is the fact that expansion bus add-in cards may require specific resources already consumed by other devices in the system.

In addition, even when the system hardware was configured correctly, there was no consistent interface that permitted the software at the device driver/operating system level to reliably determine what devices were installed and what system resources these devices were consuming. This is particularly critical in those systems that permit hot insertion and removal of devices (such as PCMCIA) or hot docking of a mobile computer. Strict system resource management is required in such instances to ensure that system resources are allocated and de-allocated in a conflict-free manner when devices are added or removed from the system.

LEGACY DEVICES AND CARDS

Devices that fall into the class of not being fully identifiable and configurable without user intervention (other than simply installing the device), such as those discussed above, are referred to as LEGACY devices. ISA expansion bus add-in cards that are built with LEGACY devices are referred to as LEGACY cards. A major goal of the PCI local bus specification is to overcome the pitfalls inherited by system components designed according to the LEGACY architecture model. However, designing and implementing a new bus and device class are not enough to overcome the LEGACY of early devices. A new software methodology that coordinates the hardware configuration process at the System BIOS, device driver, and operating system levels is also required. This methodology, which exploits the hardware and software power of PCI and other device classes, is known as the Plug and Play architecture.

There is a strong emphasis in the industry to eliminate LEGACY devices and add-in cards from new computer systems. This will eliminate the need for an ISA Bridge as well as the need to preserve pre-defined system resources for legacy use only. System components such as serial and parallel ports will no longer be required or supported. In their place, devices that utilized these components, such as modems and printers, will employ hardware that resides on a PCI, USB, or other high-speed bus. In addition, the System BIOS, operating systems, device drivers, and application programs will also be coded to meet non-LEGACY system requirements.

SUMMARY

The major emphasis of this book is to aid in this goal with respect to the PCI architecture. However, prior to discussing actual specifics of the PCI hardware and software architectures, it is important to have an understanding of the general principles of the Plug and Play architecture. In addition, this edition of the book has been expanded to cover PCI-X. The attributes of Plug and Play as applied to PCI also apply to PCI-X.

2.1 OVERVIEW OF PLUG AND PLAY ARCHITECTURE

In 1993 an industry-wide group was formed. The common objective of this group was to resolve the deficiencies of the ISA bus architecture and to advance the usability of the personal computer. When this objective is achieved, the personal computer industry will possess an architecture for system configuration that encompasses all of the hardware and software components in the system. When this architecture is fully implemented in a given system, nothing will be required of the user except to add or remove the system hardware and software components. The system will automatically detect any hardware or software change and configure itself accordingly after any type of system reset. In addition, software executing at the operating system level will dynamically adapt to the new working environment without having to turn the system off first. To reach this level of integration, a set of design requirements was established for Plug and Play system hardware and software.

PLUG AND PLAY SYSTEM DESIGN REQUIREMENTS

A set of design requirements for Plug and Play is being specified to aid in the development of Plug and Play systems. These requirements encompass both the system hardware and software. Below is a summary of the current list of requirements for Plug and Play, as specified in the document *The Plug and Play Framework: Advancing the PC Architecture Backgrounder, September 1993, Microsoft Corporation*. These requirements are as applicable today as they were in 1993.

EASE OF INSTALLATION AND CONFIGURATION OF NEW DEVICES

For Plug and Play to be viable, software at all levels from the System BIOS to operating systems and device drivers require information about the devices in a system. This information includes the identity of the device's function, what services the device provides, and the system resources the device needs in order to function. For example, a graphics device will identify itself as such. In addition, if the video device requires a block of memory for a video frame buffer or a hardware interrupt, it should communicate this information to the controlling software.

With this information, software at the System BIOS level or higher can automatically detect the presence of the device. The software can assign system resources to the device while maintaining a computer system that is free of system resource conflicts. Operating system level software can also detect the presence of the device and automatically load its device drivers if required. The user simply has to install the device and perform a one-time load of the software associated with the device into the system. Thereafter the operating system will automatically detect the presence of the Plug and Play device and load its drivers without user intervention.

SEAMLESS DYNAMIC CONFIGURATION CHANGES

Another design requirement is to permit the hot insertion or removal of devices from a system. This includes add-in cards as well as the docking of a mobile computer. The operating system level software in conjunction with the System BIOS can configure the system automatically without requiring the user to power down the system.

There are many considerations to be addressed for this goal to be realized. For instance, software must be written to dynamically detect the system status change. Applications must be told about the change in order to start or stop using the device based on its insertion or removal. And again, system resources must be allocated or de-allocated while keeping the system resources conflict-free.

For example, assume a printer was just added to the system. The software would detect this change without user notification, assign system resources such as an available parallel port to the device, load any required printer drivers, and then notify all active applications that a new printer is available for printing documents.

For more information on this technology, refer to *PCI Hot-Plug Application & Design*, written by Alan Goodrum and reviewed by Edward Solari (available at www.annabooks.com).

BACKWARD COMPATIBILITY

As mentioned above, non-Plug and Play systems and peripherals cannot communicate information about what functions they perform or what their requirements are to successfully function in a system. This is unquestionably the greatest problem to overcome in the implementation of any Plug and Play system.

Certain methods of dealing with the problem involve some user intervention. For example, software programs such as the computer system's Setup (or Configuration) Utility allow the user to input information about LEGACY devices. This information is stored in the computer system and is used in the power-up and run-time configuration of the system components.

In addition, some companies have developed software utilities to aid in configuring systems with LEGACY add-in devices. These utilities allow the user to determine a working configuration for LEGACY devices in the system prior to adding the device to the system. These programs take into account both Plug and Play devices as well as LEGACY devices. Depending on the system, this information may or may not be stored in the computer system and then used in the power-up and run-time configuration of the system components.

EXTENSIBILITY

The Plug and Play architecture must accommodate both existing and future bus and device classes. PCI, along with ISA, EISA, and Micro Channel are types of existing device classes.

OPEN ARCHITECTURE

To fully realize the architectural goals of Plug and Play, both the computer software and hardware communities must agree to a defined set of interface specifications. These specifications have to be extensible to existing and future bus and device architectures.

This is a difficult (but not impossible) goal to achieve for several reasons. First, there are several different parties involved, each with their own market interests at heart. Creating a new standard that crosses so many boundaries at so many different technical levels does not come without paying the price of time to market and the redefining of some components that comprise the Plug and Play architecture.

There may also be confusion surrounding design specifications. For example, many vendors of PCI devices have entered the marketplace with non-compliant components. This is fueling confusion in the market as to what is compliant at the device hardware level as well as at the different levels of software.

ECONOMICAL

Plug and Play should be financially attractive to the market place. The cost of implementation should be minimal and the benefits maximized to provide the marketplace a competitive product. This means that hardware complexity must decrease. This in turn decreases the component cost of the device. In addition, hardware flexibility must increase. This allows the software to take full advantage of Plug and Play. To this end, design guidelines and standardized software and hardware interfaces must be defined and adhered to by all participating parties.

2.2   PCI AND PCI-X PLATFORM HARDWARE ARCHITECTURE

GENERIC PCI PLATFORM ARCHITECTURE

Figure 2-1 outlines the simplest generic platform architecture with three buses. The HOST bus is the high performance link between the primary platform resources. For a PC, the HOST bus is an Intel x86 bus. The LEGACY bus is a medium to low performance bus that allows multiple functions to be attached to the platform. A PC LEGACY bus includes the ISA, EISA, and Micro Channel buses. The medium to high performance local bus in this model is the PCI bus.

Each bus has its own unique purpose in a PC architecture. The HOST bus provides a high speed link between the HOST CPU, HOST MEMORY (typically dynamic RAM called HDRAM), and the cache (high speed static RAM). Typically these buses are lightly loaded and have very short backplanes (signal line length) to minimize bus losses (transmission line effects). The LEGACY bus provides complimentary resources to the primary resources on the HOST bus. It can contain other CPUs (bus masters), additional memory, and I/O. It allows for longer backplanes with connectors to support add-in cards. In a PC architecture, the I/O space of the LEGACY bus also contains the PC-compatible DMA, interrupt, and keyboard/mouse controllers. It also contains the real time clock, video interface, and, for EISA and Micro Channel, the configuration registers. The PCI bus provides additional complimentary resources to the HOST bus. Like the I/O buses, it contains other CPUs (bus masters), memory (typically dynamic RAM called PDRAM), and I/O. In the vernacular of the PCI, the memory and I/O resources are called "targets".

Many of the resources on the HOST and LEGACY buses can migrate to the PCI bus. The migration of resources between buses requires that address locations and software related functional attributes remain compatible to PC software.

Circuitry used to link these different buses are called BRIDGEs. BRIDGEs will be discussed in more detail later, but their primary purpose is to interface one bus protocol to another. The protocol includes the definition of the bus control signal lines, and data and address sizes. When a BRIDGE interfaces identical buses, the BRIDGE primarily limits the loading of each bus. As outlined in Figure 2-1, BRIDGEs link different bus levels.

A unique attribute of PCI based platforms is the ability to have multiple PCI buses. Each of these PCI buses operates independently of each other when the PCI bus master accesses a target on the same bus. The only interdependence that does occur is via the bridge when a PCI bus master accesses a target on the other side of a bridge (*i.e.*, on another bus). Similarly, it is possible to have multiple HOST buses and LEGACY buses. The possibility of multiple HOST buses is possible but does not affect the PCI bus protocol; consequently, it will not be discussed in this book. By convention established by the PCI local bus specification, only one LEGACY bus can exist in a platform and must be attached to a bridge to the HOST bus or to the PCI bus nearest the HOST bus (defined as PCI bus 0 later in this chapter).

In order to assist with the multiple bus focus, the term "bus segment" will be used for the balance of this book. The term "bus segment" refers to the mechanical and bus signal lines connected between PCI resources without bridges. By this definition, resources that reside on an add-in card behind a bridge at the connector interface are on an independent bus segment. The "bus segment" phrase will also be applied to HOST and LEGACY buses even though this book will only assume a single HOST bus segment and a single LECACY bus segment.

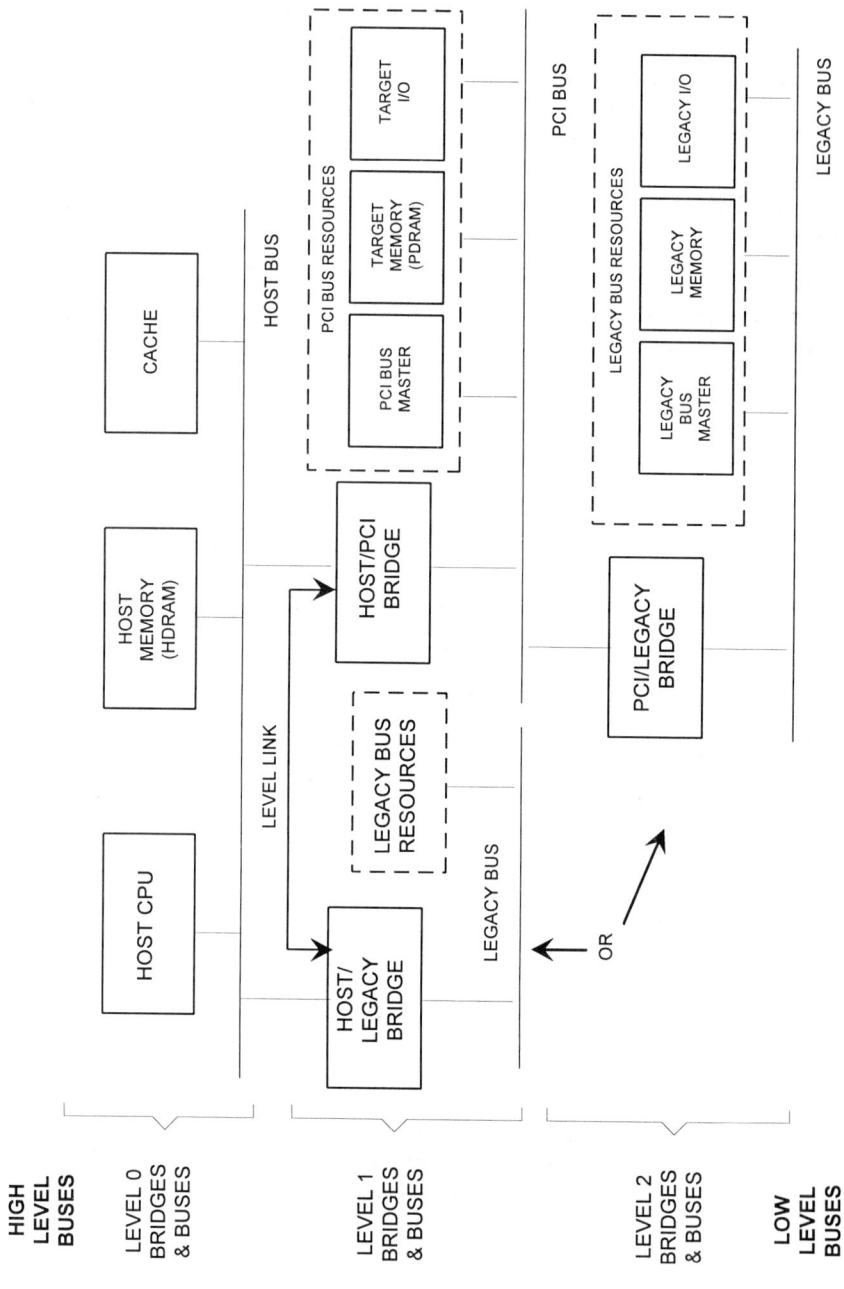

Figure 2-1: Generic Platform Architecture with Single PCI Bus

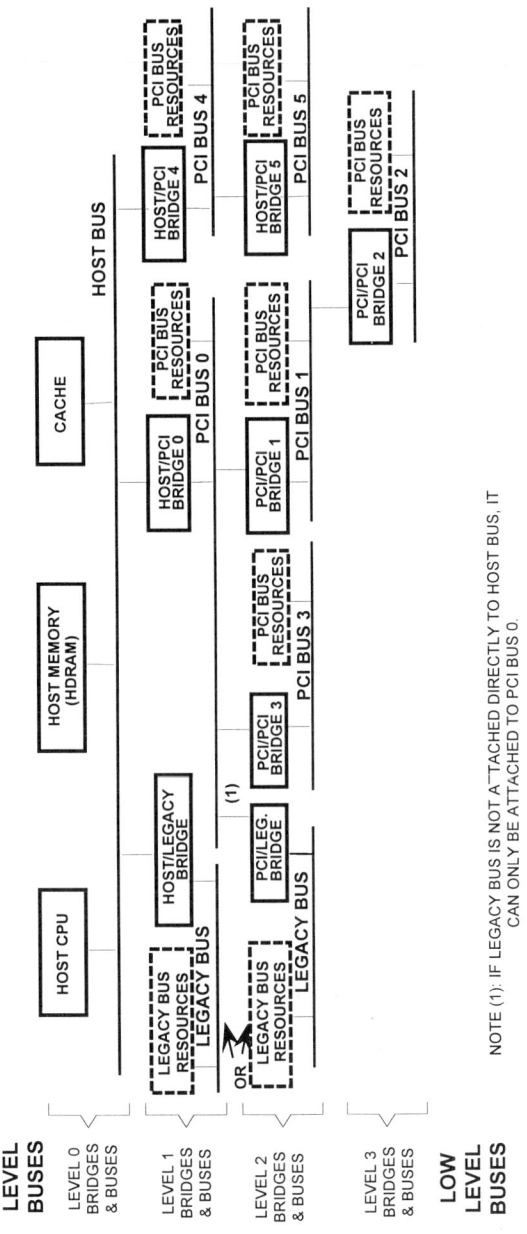

Figure 2-2: Generic Platform Architecture with Multiple PCI Buses

The focal point of the architecture is the HOST bus segment; consequently, the linkage of the LEGACY and PCI bus segments to the HOST bus segment is important. The HOST CPU is the primary bus master because it usually has the highest performance. In addition, the HOST bus services the interrupts and platform errors. The LEGACY and PCI bus segments can be connected directly to the HOST bus segment (defined as a LEVEL 0 bus segment) via a single BRIDGE level, and are defined as LEVEL 1 bus segments. The LEGACY bus segment could also be placed "under" the PCI bus segment on LEVEL 1 and be defined as a LEVEL 2 bus segment. Accesses between the HOST bus segment and a LEVEL 2 LEGACY bus segment must use the LEVEL 1 PCI bus segment. In some platforms, it is important for a LEVEL 1 PCI bus segment to communicate directly with a LEVEL 1 LEGACY bus segment; consequently, a LEVEL LINK is possible between the BRIDGEs. A LEVEL LINK is not part of the PCI bus segment protocol and is platform dependent.

As shown in Figure 2-2, additional PCI bus segments can be added to LEVEL 1. LEVEL 2 PCI bus segments can be added to LEVEL 1 PCI bus segments, LEVEL 3 PCI bus segments can added to LEVEL 2 PCI bus segments, and so forth. As shown in Figure 2-1, the LEGACY bus segment can be connected to the HOST bus segment or the primary PCI bus segment (PCI bus 0). Figure 2-2 also outlines the naming convention for the BRIDGEs and bus segments according to the PCI protocol. The "number" of the BRIDGE and of the lower level PCI bus segment immediately attached to it is the same. One of the LEVEL 1 HOST/PCI BRIDGEs is selected as "number 0" and the associated lower level PCI bus segment is "number 0". One of the LEVEL 2 PCI/PCI BRIDGEs is selected as "number 1", and the associated lower level PCI bus segment is "number 1". The next sequential numbers are assigned to PCI/PCI BRIDGEs that connect to LOWER LEVEL bus segments before numbers are assigned to PCI/PCI BRIDGEs on the same LEVEL. In this example, the "number 2" is assigned to the next lower level PCI bus segment and "number 3" is assigned to a PCI/PCI BRIDGE attached to a LEVEL 1 bus segment. If a PCI/PCI BRIDGE had been attached to a LEVEL 3 bus segment (PCI bus 2) or a LEVEL 2 bus segment (PCI bus 1), the number 3 would have been assigned that PCI/PCI BRIDGE instead.

Once all of the PCI bus segments associated with PCI/PCI BRIDGE 0 have been assigned numbers, the next HOST/PCI BRIDGE on LEVEL 1 is assigned the next sequential number (Number 4 in this example).

The LEGACY bus segment can either be attached through a bridge to the HOST bus segment or the PCI bus segment. In the case of a PCI bus segment, the bridge to the LEGACY bus segment must be attached to PCI bus 0. Any LEGACY bus segment resource that is moved from the LEGACY bus segment must reside either on the HOST or PCI bus segments. In the case of the PCI bus segment, it must be on PCI bus 0.

> The numbering protocol applies to BRIDGEs that connect to PCI bus segments and the associated PCI bus segments. BRIDGEs and bus segments associated with non-PCI bus segments are not numbered.

In order to limit the complexity of the architecture discussion, the platform outlined in Figure 2-3 will be used. The principles discussed relative to the architecture in Figure 2-3 are applicable to Figures 2-1, 2-2, and extensions.

> In Figures 2-1 to 2-3, the cache is shown as external to the HOST CPU. It is possible for an additional cache to be internal to the HOST CPU. The internal and external caches are behind the HOST/PCI BRIDGE; consequently, from the PCI bus segment viewpoint, the cache is simply behind the HOST/PCI BRIDGE.

> By convention, bus segments on the same LEVEL are called "peer bus segments" and buses on different levels are called "hierarchical buses". Peer PCI bus segments can access each other through two PCI/PCI BRIDGEs with a common PCI bus segment. A PCI bus segment that is a peer to LEGACY bus segment can access it with a LEVEL LINK and vice versa. Hierarchical bus segments on adjacent bus segment levels can directly access each other through a single BRIDGE. Hierarchical bus segments not on adjacent levels can access each other via multiple BRIDGEs and PCI bus segments. As will be discussed later in this book, there are some restrictions on accessing the configuration address space of targets on PCI bus segments on the same and different LEVELs than the PCI bus masters.

SOURCE (PRIMARY) AND DESTINATION (SECONDARY) BUS SEGMENTS

To describe bus transactions porting through a BRIDGE, the naming convention of "source bus segment" and "destination bus segment" will be used. The source bus segment is the one that contains the PCI bus master and the destination bus segment is the one that contains the target. For example, in Figure 2-3 a PCI bus master on PCI bus 0 (which could be HOST/PCI BRIDGE 0) is accessing a PCI resource (target) on PCI bus 1 via PCI/PCI BRIDGE 1. In this example, PCI bus 0 is the source bus segment and PCI bus 1 is the destination bus segment. Another example: In Figure 2-3, a PCI bus master on PCI bus 1 is accessing a PCI resource (target) on PCI bus 0 via PCI/PCI BRIDGE 1. Here, PCI bus 1 is the source bus segment and PCI bus 0 is the destination bus segment.

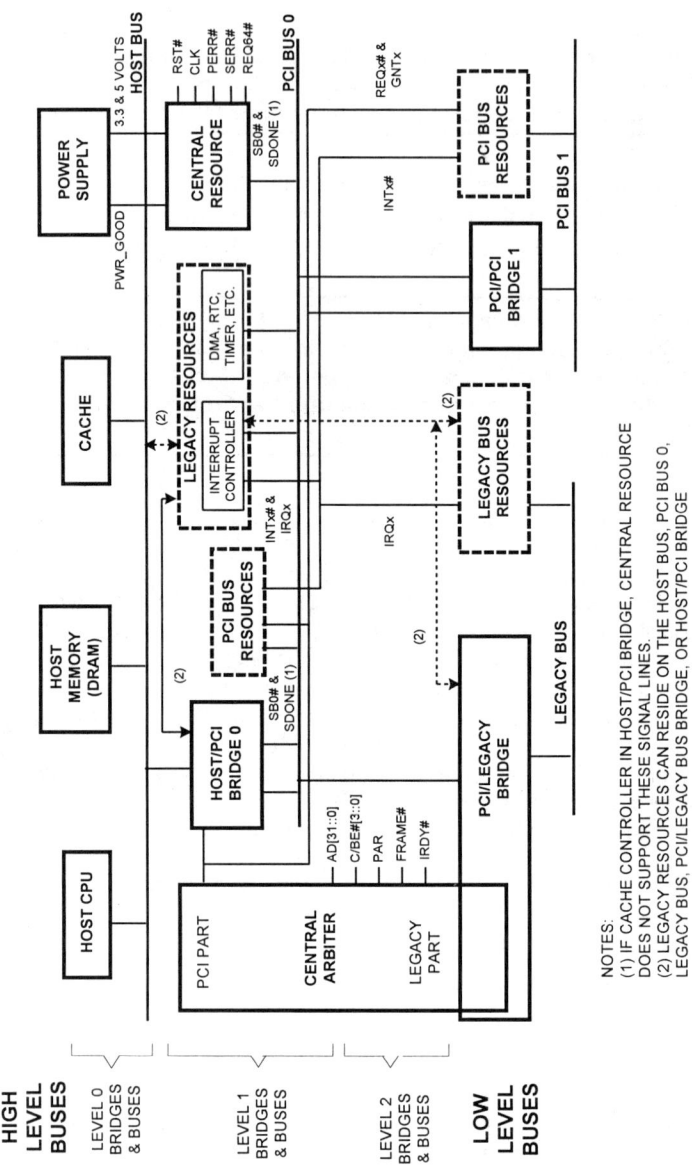

Figure 2-3: Discussion Platform Architecture with Multiple PCI Bus Segments

In some sections of this book the terms "primary" and "secondary" bus segments are used.. Either of these sets of terms is used as an aid in explaining the bi-directional nature of commands, data, and status of bus transactions porting through a PCI/PCI BRIDGE or an interface between PCI bus segments and internal circuitry of a PCI resource.

BUS SEGMENT OWNERSHIP

At any given time, a bus segment may be owned by a bus resource called the PCI bus master. Ownership allows the bus master to be the only resource executing bus transactions. A PCI bus master may be an intelligent resource that resides on the bus segment or it may be a BRIDGE acting on behalf of a bus master on another bus segment. The operation is the same whether the PCI bus master resides directly on the bus segment or if it is the BRIDGE representing a PCI bus master on another bus segment.

In the typical PCI architecture, the HOST CPU is a special bus master. It is the initial bus master of the HOST bus segment after platform power-up or RESET, it initializes all the resources in the platform, and it is the only bus master that services platform interrupts and errors.

PCI RESOURCES, DEVICES, AND BUS SEGMENT LOADING

Each PCI bus segment can support a total of ten "loads". A *load* is defined as an integrated circuit chip meeting the PCI electrical requirements. Whenever the integrated circuit is attached via a connector, the equivalent of one load must be assigned to the connector and one load assigned to the circuitry behind the connector. Consequently, each connector is assigned a limit of two loads. If more than one load is required behind the connector, a PCI/PCI BRIDGE with one load must be used behind the connector.

> More than ten loads at lower than the maximum CLK signal line frequency can be supported if the platform is properly designed, validated, and the effect of add-in cards is carefully considered.

Each integrated circuit chip on the PCI bus segment represents one load and each add-in card represents two loads. Collectively, the integrated circuits or add-in cards are viewed by the software as "devices". Each device contains between one and eight individual functions. Each PCI function contains its own set of configuration address space registers. These registers are used for configuring and controlling the function.

From the hardware viewpoint, all devices in a PCI system are a "PCI resource". The three types of PCI resources are PCI bus master, BRIDGE, and target. The PCI bus master is the PCI resource that owns the bus segment and executes the bus transaction. The BRIDGE is simply the circuitry that interconnects two bus segments (source and destination). When the bus transaction is ported to the destination bus segment, the BRIDGE becomes the PCI bus master of the bus segment. The target consists of memory or I/O resources that are being accessed by the bus transaction. In the case of an interrupt acknowledge transaction, it is the PCI resource that contains the interrupt controller. In the case of a special transaction, the target is potentially all PCI resources. When a configuration access cycle is executed, the configuration spaces of the PCI bus masters, BRIDGEs, and memory and I/O targets become the targets of the transaction. The HOST CPU, in conjunction with the HOST/PCI BRIDGE, is the primary PCI bus master.

As will be explained in Chapter 4, there are 21 individual signal lines (called IDSEL) used on each PCI bus segment to select a device (one IDSEL signal line per device) during configuration transactions. A "single-function" device is an integrated circuit chip on the platform or add-in card that requires one IDSEL signal line and has one configuration space. A "multi-function" device is an integrated circuit chip on the platform or add-in card that has one IDSEL signal line, but contains two to eight configuration spaces. The FUNCTION Number in the configuration access cycle is used to select one of the configuration spaces contained within a device.

If a PCI resource drives 10 loads (the limit at 33 MHz CLK signal line), and each load is an integrated circuit with eight configuration spaces (multi-function), the PCI bus segment can support eighty configuration spaces. In this example, only 10 IDSEL signal lines of the 21 possible were used. If a lower CLK signal line frequency is used, more loads (devices) can be supported.

CENTRAL RESOURCE

The central resource on the platform contains support circuitry not "assigned" to other platform resources. It typically contains the RESET circuitry (RST# signal line), the clock driver (CLK signal line), the error reporting circuitry (to communicate error to the HOST CPU, monitor PERR# and SERR# signal lines, and drive the SERR# signal line), and the support of memory transactions. Though not shown in Figure 2-3, it may also monitor and drive other PCI bus segment signal lines.

CENTRAL ARBITER

The central arbiter consists of platform circuitry that can be viewed as two distinct parts: PCI and LEGACY bus segment compliant. The PCI-compliant portion defines unique arbitration signal line pairs (REQ# = request bus segment ownership and GNT# = grant bus ownership) to each of the PCI resources that can potentially own the PCI bus segment (PCI bus master) (see Figure 2-3). The exact algorithm to determine the next PCI bus master is not defined by the PCI Local Bus Specification. However, whichever algorithm is selected it should provide "fairness" to all platform bus masters. "Fairness" can mean many things, but essentially should insure that the amount of time a PCI bus master must wait for the bus segment is appropriate. For example, high priority PCI bus masters should obtain the bus segment relatively quickly. However, two or three high priority PCI bus masters should not be awarded their respective bus segments at the detriment of lower priority PCI bus masters. Lower priority PCI bus masters must not be "starved"; they must not be denied sufficient bus segment ownership time or be forced to wait extremely long periods of time to obtain bus segment ownership.

The LEGACY bus segment compliant portion of the central arbiter is actually part of the PCI/LEGACY BRIDGE and its protocol is defined according to the protocol of the LEGACY bus segment. For example: if the LEGACY bus segment is ISA, arbitration for ISA bus segment ownership is via the DMA controller in the PCI/LEGACY BRIDGE, which must also support arbitration for refresh. If the LEGACY bus segment is EISA, arbitration for EISA bus segment ownership is via arbitration circuitry in the BRIDGE that accounts for unique arbitration signal line pairs (EISA-defined), bus segment time-out, refresh, and bus segment preemption. The LEGACY bus segment compliant portion can interface with the PCI compliant portion of the central arbiter via REQ# and GNT# signal lines or can use other non-PCI bus segment signal lines between the PCI and LEGACY compliant portions of the central arbiter.

> In the above discussion, the central arbiter was divided between PCI and LEGACY bus segment compliant portions, with the latter in the PCI/LEGACY BRIDGE. It is possible to build a central arbiter that contains both PCI and LEGACY bus segment compliant portions in the same physical location.

Finally, the central arbiter may have to act as the Park master. The PCI bus segment protocol insures that the float time of the signal lines is minimized. For most signal lines, this is achieved by being driven by a resource at all times or driven to a logical "1" by pull-up resistors. The AD[31::0], C/BE#[3::0], and PAR signal lines do not fall under any of these categories; consequently, they must be driven (parked) by a PCI resource when bus transactions are not executed. On some architectures, this resource may be the central arbiter.

> **Though not shown as such in Figure 2-3, it is possible that the central arbiter can be divided into multiple arbiters. That is, separate individual central arbiters may be assigned to each PCI bus segment.**

DEADLOCK ISSUES

By definition, deadlock is a fatal platform condition. Deadlock occurs when a bus segment resource is being accessed by two bus masters and one bus master cannot complete the access to a resource until the other bus master accesses the same bus segment resource. The second bus master cannot access the bus resource because it is being accessed by the first bus master. The PCI bus segment protocol provides mechanisms to prevent deadlock conditions within the PCI bus segment. Platforms that contain PCI and LEGACY bus segments (like ISA or EISA) must have carefully designed BRIDGEs to prevent deadlock conditions.

The PCI bus segment protocol prevents deadlocks by supporting bus segment termination without data access, commonly called "back off". The actual PCI bus segment protocols to achieve back off will be explained later in the book, but the concept can be understood from the following example: Assume that the HOST CPU is using a HOST bus memory resource (called HDRAM) (see Figure 2-3) and the HDRAM is cached by a write-back cache on the HOST bus segment. If the HOST CPU writes data to the cache, the HDRAM does not have correct data until the HDRAM is updated. Prior to updating the HDRAM, a PCI bus master on PCI bus 0 tries to read the same Cacheline in the HDRAM, but obviously the read access transaction cannot be completed because the data has not been updated. A deadlock condition would occur if the PCI bus master could not finish the read transaction with valid data because the cache controller (in this example assumed to be in the HOST/PCI BRIDGE) must gain access to the HDRAM in order to update it. The PCI bus segment protocol allows the cache controller in the HOST/PCI BRIDGE to request the PCI bus master to complete the bus transaction without reading data from the HDRAM (back off) and to try the access at another time (according to the PCI protocol, this is called Retry termination). The cache controller can now obtain access to the HDRAM and copy the Cacheline in the write-back cache to the HDRAM. When the PCI bus master repeats the transaction, the data in the HDRAM is correct and the bus transaction is allowed to complete with data being read from the HDRAM.

The above situation is completely different when the PCI bus master is actually a PCI/LEGACY BRIDGE. The PCI/LEGACY BRIDGE is acting on behalf of the LEGACY bus segment master; consequently, it is restricted by the LEGACY bus master protocol. For LEGACY buses like ISA or EISA, once a bus transaction has begun it must be completed with the actual accessing of data. If the LEGACY bus master (lacking a back off protocol) is accessing the HDRAM via the HOST/PCI and PCI/LEGACY BRIDGEs with the conditions outlined in the previous section, a deadlock condition will result. The PCI/LEGACY BRIDGE could be designed to actually back off its PCI read transaction and supply wait states to the LEGACY bus transaction. The LEGACY bus segment access can be completed when the PCI/LEGACY BRIDGE repeats the PCI read transaction after the HDRAM has been updated. Unfortunately, LEGACY bus segments like ISA and EISA require that LEGACY bus transactions be completed within a specific time. Unless the PCI/LEGACY BRIDGE knows that it can successfully repeat the PCI read transaction within a specific time (dependent on the central arbiter) LEGACY bus segment errors will occur. Another solution to this problem would be to disallow PCI resources that are accessible by LEGACY bus masters to be cached. Historically, some chip sets have provided side band signal lines that insure all memory is updated with cache information and all buffers are flushed prior to awarding PCI sub segment ownership to the PCI/LEGACY BRIDGE. This ensures immediate access to the HDRAM.

A similar deadlock condition occurs when write data is posted in the bridges attached to PCI bus 0. Until the buffers are written to the HDRAM (flushed), accesses to HDRAM cannot be completed. As with the cache example, the PCI /LEGACY BRIDGE can add wait states to the LEGACY bus transaction. The LEGACY bus transaction can be completed when the PCI/LEGACY BRIDGE repeats the PCI bus transaction after the HDRAM has been updated.

> **Notice that the PCI/LEGACY BRIDGE does not know what resources will be accessed when it awards LEGACY bus segment ownership to a LEGACY bus segment resource. There is no guarantee that the LEGACY bus master will access only LEGACY bus segment resources. The PCI/LEGACY BRIDGE does not know that an access is to a PCI bus segment resource until the LEGACY bus transaction has begun, which according to ISA and EISA protocols can only be completed with successfully accessing data.**

The existence of bus transaction ordering rules in the bridges can also cause deadlock conditions. As will be discussed later in this book, bus transactions porting through a bridge may be buffered inside the bridge. The porting of "other" bus transactions through a bridge are sometimes restricted by the buffered bus transactions in the bridge. The porting of the buffered bus transactions can be restricted by the non-porting of the "other" bus transactions ... which are restricted by the buffered bus transaction. PCI uses the Exclusive Hardware Access protocol to prevent this situation.

LIVELOCK ISSUES

By definition, a livelock is not a fatal platform condition.

Livelock occurs when PCI bus transactions can continue but with lower performance. An example is when a target requests a Disconnect termination because it was not available to complete the access in a reasonable amount of time. If the PCI bus master immediately accesses the same target, the target may still not be ready and respond with a Retry termination. Further "immediate accesses" may also result in Retry terminations that are effectively preventing other PCI bus master ownership of the bus segment. Another example: assume PCI resource (A) has both target and PCI bus master attributes. Assume that PCI bus master (A) does not allow access to its associated target (A) until the successful completion (no Retry, Disconnect, or Target Abort termination) of the bus transaction it had tried. Assume that PCI bus master (A) begins a bus transaction that results in a Retry termination. Under this protocol, if PCI bus master (B) accesses target (A), a Retry termination is also executed. At a later time, PCI bus master (A) is able to complete its bus transaction successfully. Subsequently, PCI bus master (B) can then successfully complete its access to target (A). Functionally, the bus transactions were completed, but the performance of PCI bus master (B) was lowered by the protocol of PCI bus master (A).

The PCI bus segment protocol avoids livelocks whenever possible. The two examples above would not occur in an actual PCI platform. In the first example, according to the actual PCI bus segment protocol, the execution of a Disconnect (also Retry or Target Abort) termination requires the present PCI bus master to relinquish bus segment ownership. Another PCI bus master can then become bus segment owner and execute a bus transaction. In the second example, the PCI bus segment protocol does not allow a PCI bus segment resource with PCI bus master and target attributes that are interdependent. The PCI bus master cannot prevent access to its associated target because a prior bus transaction as PCI bus master was not immediately completed.

Another interesting livelock example is when the post write buffers in a HOST/PCI BRIDGE are flushed. As data is written from the write buffers to the PCI bus segment, the HOST CPU may continue writing to the buffers. As the HOST/PCI BRIDGE is emptying the buffers, the HOST CPU is filing them. Unless the BRIDGE is specifically designed to address this situation, it will empty all the data originally in the buffers, and will continue the bus transaction with the new data written by the HOST CPU. Consequently, the HOST/PCI BRIDGE owns the PCI bus segment for a longer period of time than was necessary to flush the original data in the buffers. Other PCI bus masters are delayed in obtaining bus segment ownership and thus bus segment performance between multiple PCI bus masters is decreased.

INTERRUPT SIGNAL LINES

The interrupt structure of the PCI bus segment must be used in conjunction with Intel 8259 interrupt controllers to be fully compatible with personal computer software. Other architectures can use other interrupt controllers. ISA bus segment requirements define an edge-triggered interrupt line with a low to high transition to request interrupt service via the 8259. Even though the interrupt request on an ISA bus segment is defined as an edge-triggered signal line, the interrupt input must remain asserted (logical "1") until the software has begun the interrupt service routine. EISA bus segment requirements define both an edge-triggered input (for compatibility to ISA compatible add-in cards) and a level (logical "0") sensitive input to the interrupt controller circuit to allow interrupts to be shared via open collector outputs.

The concept of level sensitive interrupts has been applied to the PCI bus segment interrupt structure. Four interrupt signal lines have been defined (INTA#, INTB#, INTC#, and INTD#, collectively called INTx# signal lines). The INTx# signal lines are attached to Intel 8259 compatible circuitry via platform circuitry. The exact circuitry varies depending on the architecture of the platform. Compatibility to the ISA, EISA, and Micro Channel software does place some restraints on which personal computer (PC) compatible interrupts should be attached to the INTx# signal lines. The most obvious PC compatible interrupts are the four defined as bus segment interrupts (IRQ 9 to 11 and 15) and the one attached to the second parallel port (IRQ5). Any combination of the PCI INTx# signal lines can be combined or individually attached in any arrangement to the PC compatible interrupt lines. The exact implementation is the responsibility of the platform architect.

There are several protocol requirements for implementing the INTx# signal lines:

> **The three device types defined on a PCI bus segment are PCI bus master, target, and BRIDGE; collectively they are called *PCI resources.***

- Several devices (each with individual configuration registers) can be attached to each INTx# signal line; this is defined as interrupt sharing.

- A device is wire-ORed to an INTx# signal line.

- Once a device has asserted an INTx# signal line, it must keep it asserted until instructed to deassert by the appropriate interrupt service routine.

- A "single-device" integrated circuit chip on the platform or add-in card (see definitions in the Glossary) that requires only one interrupt must use the INTA# signal line. Each integrated circuit chip or add-in card with at least one device that requires an interrupt service must use the INTA# signal line before any of the other interrupt signal lines can be used. The additional devices in an integrated circuit chip or an add-in card can also use INTA# or use any one of the other INTx# signal lines (INTB#, INTC#, and INTD#).

■ Each individual device can only request service (assert) on one of the INTx# single lines. It can never request service on two or more INTx# signal lines.

> The interrupt acknowledge transaction protocol on the PCI bus segment is the only bus transaction that returns the interrupt vector. It is the responsibility of the HOST/PCI BRIDGE or similar circuitry to convert the dual cycle 8259 compatible interrupt acknowledge cycle on the HOST bus segment to a SINGLE cycle PCI interrupt acknowledge cycle. It also is the responsibility of the PCI resource that contains the 8259 to convert the SINGLE cycle PCI interrupt acknowledge cycle into the dual cycle required by the 8259.

SIDEBAND SIGNAL LINES

The PCI local bus specification allows signal lines to be defined between two or more PCI resources that are proprietary to these resources. These are defined as "sideband". Sideband signal lines are not part of the PCI local bus specification; consequently the sideband signal lines can only be defined for PCI resources on the same physical bus segment plane. That is, sideband signal lines cannot traverse a PCI connector. Similarly, sideband signal lines cannot be attached between two PCI bus segments (cannot traverse a PCI/PCI BRIDGE).

GENERIC PCI-X PLATFORM ARCHITECTURE

The PCI-X addendum specification built upon the work of the PCI local bus specification. A PCI-X bus segment provides greater performance than a PCI bus segment due to higher CLK signal line frequencies. The interaction performance between bus segments through a bridge has been improved with the PCI-X Split Transaction protocol replacing the PCI Delayed Transaction protocol. The architectural location of the HOST, PCI-X, and LEGACY bus segments are the same as in a platform with PCI bus segments. Also, as with a PCI platform, a PCI-X platform has the ability to have multiple PCI-X bus segments. The software that operated on PCI centric platforms also operates on PCI-X centric platforms. There are slight differences in the initialization and configuration software for PCI-X bus segments versus PCI bus segments that will be discussed in this book. The one uniquely new attribute is that each PCI-X bus segment can independently become a PCI bus segment. Either the platform has been designed with PCI only bus segments and PCI-X bus segments, or all PCI-X bus segments. Any PCI-X bus segment becomes a PCI bus segment if at initialization there is a PCI resource (*i.e.*, PCI add-in card) attached to the bus segment. A PCI-X bus segment that must operate as a PCI bus segment will follow all of the PCI bus segment protocols, and the CLK signal line will operate only at PCI compatible frequencies. When a PCI-X bus segment is interacting with a PCI bus segment through a bridge, the bridge must translate between the two protocols. Due to higher CLK signal line frequencies on a PCI-X bus segment, the permitted loads (number of resources) is lower than a PCI bus segment.

Otherwise, all of the architectural elements discussed earlier in this section for PCI centric platforms also apply to PCI-X centric platforms.

> As mentioned in other parts of this book, PCI and PCI-X are discussed independently. Revision 3.0 of the PCI local bus specification integrates PCI-X with PCI with the additional requirement that 5 volt only signaling connectors are no longer supported. See Chapter 11: *Reset, Power, and Signal Line Initialization*, Chapter 13: *Connector, Platform, and Add-in Card Design*, and Chapter 15: *Mechanical Specification* for more information

2.3 PCI AND PCI-X SOFTWARE AND THE PLUG AND PLAY ARCHITECTURE

> The PCI-X addendum specification has built upon the PCI Plug and Play architecture. Introduced below is the PCI centric Plug and Play, which is also applicable to PCI-X. Later in the book there will be further discussion of enhancements due to the PCI-X addendum specification.

INTRODUCTION

PCI compatible hardware and software has been the first architecture to incorporate true Plug and Play into ISA compatible computers. All compliant PCI devices can easily be identified by the system, along with the functions they provide. Also, PCI compliant devices identify their individual system resource requirements. These system resources can be dynamically assigned without user intervention.

In addition to the hardware capabilities of PCI devices, a software methodology that coordinates the hardware configuration process at the System BIOS, device driver, and operating system levels has also been implemented. This methodology exploits the hardware and software power of the PCI device class to bring Plug and Play capability to computers.

Figure 2-4 contains a view of a software architecture that encompasses software at all levels, from the System BIOS to the operating system and device drivers. This architecture is capable of configuring PCI and other device classes in true Plug and Play fashion. Refer to this figure as each component of the architecture is discussed below. Note that to be less confusing, non-PCI Plug and Play device classes are not specified by name. They are referred to as *other*.

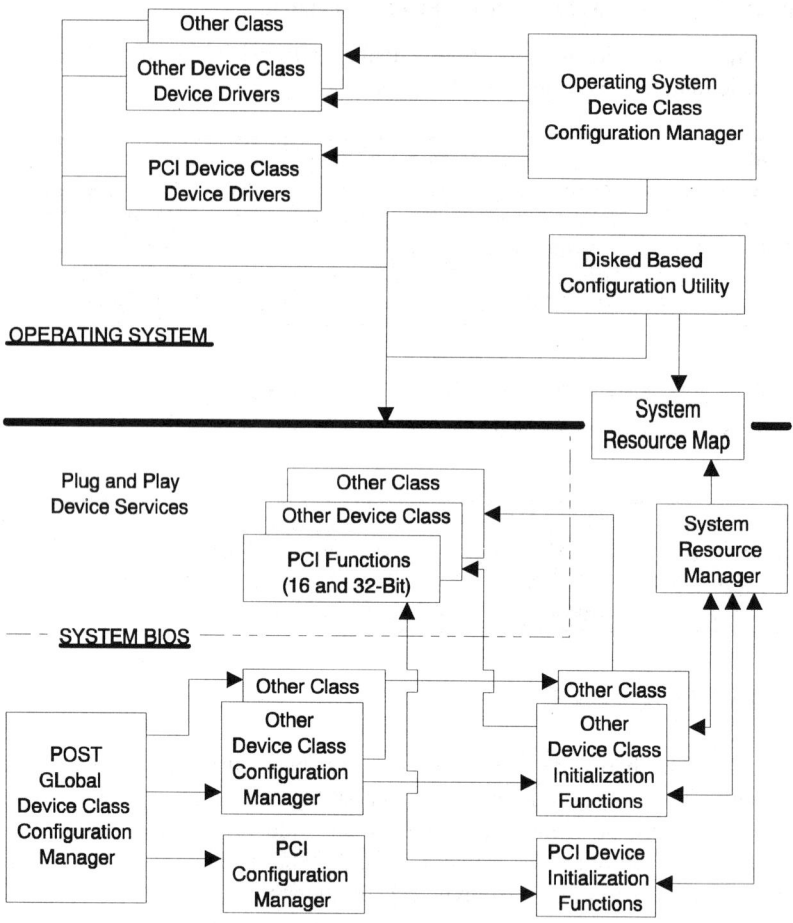

Figure 2-4: Plug and Play System

DEVICE CLASS MANAGEMENT

The System BIOS software is the first code executed when the computer system is powered on. One of its major functions is to test and configure devices. This function is accomplished during the execution of the System BIOS Power-On Self Test (POST). It is at this time that PCI devices are detected and configured along with the non-PCI components of the system.

While all System BIOS vendors perform basically the same tasks during the POST, the sequence in which the tasks are performed may vary significantly. For example, some vendors shadow and cache the System BIOS very early in the POST while other vendors may delay this function until just prior to bootstrapping an operating system. In addition, the functions provided by PCI devices may overlap with those supplied by non-PCI devices in the system. For instance, a VGA compatible video card installed on the ISA bus and a VGA compatible PCI video card may be installed in the same system at the same time. Both of these cards utilize identical industry compatible I/O ports. Which device has precedence during the boot sequence as well as when each device gets tested and initialized is of critical importance to maintaining a system that is resource conflict-free and guaranteed to boot. To solve these problems, a function known as the POST Global Device Class Configuration Manager is implemented in a typical System BIOS.

POST GLOBAL DEVICE CLASS CONFIGURATION MANAGER

The POST Global Device Class Configuration Manager is responsible for the overall testing and initializing of all Plug and Play device classes. The POST Global Device Class Configuration Manager can be viewed as a global dispatcher for initializing and testing Plug and Play devices. As Figure 2-4 shows, the System BIOS invokes the POST Global Device Class Configuration Manager. The POST Global Device Class Configuration Manager in turn invokes each individual Plug and Play device class configuration manager. Exactly when the POST Global Device Class Configuration Manager is invoked is System BIOS dependent. Also, the order in which each Plug and Play device class configuration manager is invoked is System BIOS dependent. The POST Global Device Class Configuration Manager is platform independent.

PCI CONFIGURATION MANAGER

The PCI Configuration Manager is responsible solely for the initialization of PCI devices in the system. This includes the identification each PCI device in the system as well as the individual functions provided by each device. In addition, the PCI Configuration Manager is responsible for determining the system resources each PCI device requests, obtaining the required resources from the System Resource Manager, and then assigning those resources to each PCI device. The PCI Configuration Manager is also platform independent. However, to accomplish its tasks, the PCI Configuration Manager requires access to platform dependent hardware. For example, the way in which PCI devices are programmed is platform specific. Device initialization functions are provided for each Plug and Play device class to permit access to the platform dependent hardware.

PCI DEVICE INITIALIZATION FUNCTIONS

PCI Device Initialization Functions allow the PCI device class platform independent software to access the platform dependent hardware. This minimizes the amount of Plug and Play software that has to be created for each new platform to those components that are unique to the platform. The PCI Device Initialization Functions access each PCI device to first determine the system resources required by each device, assign system resources to each PCI device and, depending on the function provided, initialize and test each PCI device.

SYSTEM RESOURCE MAP

The System Resource Map contains an encoded description of which system resources are currently consumed by devices in the system. Both the System BIOS System Resource Manager and certain run-time utilities can use the System Resource Map to monitor exactly which system resources have been allocated. Knowing which system resources have been allocated permits the easy identification of free system resources when an allocation request is serviced.

The medium that stores the System Resource Map depends on the implementation of the Plug and Play architecture. In addition, the specific information stored in the System Resource Map is platform specific.

NON-VOLATILE MEMORY STORAGE

In some systems, the System Resource Map is stored in non-volatile memory such as Flash memory or battery backed-up CMOS RAM. The information in the non-volatile memory is accessible by the System BIOS during system initialization and by Plug and Play configuration utilities during run-time operation. Having the System Resource Map contents accessible to the System BIOS prior to booting greatly increases the opportunity to configure the system so that no system resource conflicts occur.

SYSTEM RESOURCE MAP CONTENTS

The minimum implementation of a System Resource Map can be as basic as storing a bit-map of what hardware interrupts (IRQs) have been consumed by devices. On the other hand, the System Resource Map can be very exhaustive. Enhanced System Resource Maps may contain information such as the location and type of device that consumes a specific resource.

This information is especially important for Plug and Play disk based configuration utilities that have the ability to configure system resources for both LEGACY and Plug and Play devices at run-time. With this information, the software can make recommendations as to how to reconfigure the system to accommodate devices that may only be configured with a restricted set of system resources. For instance, the two standard ISA LEGACY serial port devices can only be assigned one of two different hardware interrupt lines. In contrast, a compliant PCI device can be assigned any hardware interrupt line and still function. Software can detect that a PCI device has been assigned the hardware interrupt line required by the ISA LEGACY device. It can de-allocate the interrupt line from the PCI device, allocate the interrupt line to the ISA LEGACY device, and then allocate a different hardware interrupt line to the PCI device. This process is known as system resource balancing.

SUMMARY

To increase the possibility of a system free of resource conflicts, locate the System Resource Map in non-volatile memory on the platform. This permits access to its contents during all phases of system operation. The amount and type of information stored has a direct impact on dynamically configuring the system as well as successfully achieving system resource balancing.

> With 8-slot ISA systems, 4K of non-volatile RAM is recommended; 8K of non-volatile RAM is recommended for 8 slot EISA systems.

31

BIOS SYSTEM RESOURCE MANAGER

The BIOS System Resource Manager is available only to pre-boot software. The System Resource Manager relieves each device class initialization function of having to maintain a list of free and consumed system resources. The System Resource Manager centralizes the task of allocating (assigning) and deallocating (freeing) system resources. This function is crucial for achieving a resource conflict-free system.

Device class initialization functions can request that system resources be allocated or de-allocated for their devices. In the case of allocating a system resource, the System Resource Manager will attempt to allocate resources that are free and not currently allocated to another device. One exception for PCI is hardware interrupts. PCI hardware interrupts are a shareable system resource.

Non-shareable system resources should only be assigned to one device. It is up to the discretion of the System Resource Manager how to assign shareable system resources.

Once the System Resource Manager either allocates or de-allocates the system resource, the device class initialization function making the request is responsible for configuring the Plug and Play device according to the type of request. For example, when a PCI device requests that a hardware interrupt be allocated to it, the hardware specific code is responsible for physically connecting the hardware interrupt line allocated by the System Resource Manager to the requesting device.

As stated in the previous section, the location of the System Resource Map has a direct impact on device configuration. If the System Resource Map is stored in non-volatile memory in the system, the System Resource Manager can use the information to configure the system with a high confidence level. When the System Resource Map is not available to the System Resource Manager, a dynamic map that contains the system resource consumption must be built during system initialization. This information is limited because many of the resources consumed by LEGACY devices cannot be detected.

Note that it is possible to dynamically configure Plug and Play devices such as PCI without requiring the user to execute the system Setup Utility. This is accomplished by doing the following:

1. During system initialization, the System Resource Manager is informed by the System BIOS what specific resources it can reliably detect that the platform consumes.

2. All dynamically configurable devices that are configured prior to POST must obtain their system resource assignments from the System Resource manager.

Note that functions such as setting the system time and date do require the user to execute a program such as the system Setup Utility in order to accomplish the task.

PCI PLUG AND PLAY DEVICE SERVICES

As Figure 2-4 shows, the PCI Device Initialization Functions that are available only during POST utilize PCI Plug and Play device services. These services are available for use during the POST and at run-time to software components such as an operating system. See Chapter 19: *PCI System BIOS Software Interface*, for a list of the defined PCI Plug and Play device services and how they are accessed. The PCI functions are typically used to read and write PCI device configuration registers.

OPERATING SYSTEM DEVICE CLASS CONFIGURATION MANAGER

The operating system is responsible for the run-time portion of the Plug and Play architecture. Like the System BIOS, it relies on special interfaces to accomplish the task of dynamically configuring the system so that there are no system resource conflicts.

A Plug and Play enabled operating system has the ability to dynamically configure the system in much the same way as the System BIOS. To do so, it must also have access to the platform hardware. To generically run on different types of hardware, the operating system also relies on the Plug and Play Device Services provided by the PCI and other device classes.

The Operating System Device Class Configuration Manager is decidedly more complex than its System BIOS counterpart. This is because of the nature of managing the run-time operation of the system in conjunction with the dynamics of Plug and Play. For example, in the case of hot-insertion, a device may be added to the system at any time. The Plug and Play operating system must detect the change in the system configuration, dynamically allocate system resources to the device if required, and load any device drivers associated with the device--all without user intervention.

PCI DEVICE DRIVERS

Operating system level device drivers provide application software with a common interface to the machine-dependent features of a system. Device drivers such as those that support PCI devices are written specifically for the hardware that they control. For instance, there are many PCI VGA compatible video devices. The VGA compatible functions that these devices provide are common to all VGA devices. However, there is no common method for accessing and configuring these devices at the hardware level. Without device drivers, applications programmers would be required to embed device-specific code to support each device in their software program. Code size and the constant introduction of new devices make this process unfeasible.

The operating system is required to load device drivers. When a device driver is loaded it usually determines the hardware configuration for its device and configures its environment accordingly. In the case of a PCI VGA device that supports a linear frame buffer, the associated device driver must interrogate the PCI component to determine the base address and length of the frame buffer that was allocated to the device. It does this by utilizing the appropriate Plug and Play Device Services. Once the device driver has determined the assigned resources of its device, it can configure the device and its own software for optimum performance.

2.4 CHAPTER SUMMARY

In an ideal computer system, the System BIOS and operating system level software automatically configure all devices so that no system resource conflicts exist. This includes devices located on the platform as well as those devices added via add-in cards. The successful operation of an add-in card in the ideal system requires no user intervention other than the physical installation of the card itself. In addition, the automatic configuration of the system also accounts for the removal of an add-in card; this insures that no system resource conflicts exist after the add-in card is extracted as well as optimizing the system for performance.

However, the possibility of system resource conflicts is greatly increased when a PCI based system is integrated with a LEGACY based system such as ISA. Because LEGACY devices are not dynamically configurable, the configuration software must obtain the LEGACY configuration information. In almost all cases this is accomplished with the aid of the user. Utilities are available to help in this task and make it easier for the user to configure a system.

The PCI Local Bus standard permits the design of a computer system that is fully capable of being automatically configured. For this to be achieved, an architecture that encompasses all aspects of the hardware and software of a system must be implemented. Interfaces must be crisply defined and strictly adhered to. Plug and Play provides such an architecture. While only a high level overview of the architecture is presented in this chapter, it can readily be seen that the task of providing users with a Plug and Play system is extremely complex and requires the participation of both hardware and software vendors to ensure success.

The remainder of this book addresses the fundamental hardware and software concepts of a PCI based computer system. The power of the PCI Local Bus hardware and software is explored in great detail. This will give the reader a thorough working knowledge of the PCI Local Bus standard.

Note that the discussion is limited to the Intel x86 architecture and certain Intel PCI chip sets. However, the guidelines and concepts presented are readily adaptable to other system types.

CHAPTER 3

GENERIC PCI HARDWARE OPERATION

This chapter consists of the following subchapters:

3.0   **Generic PCI and PCI-X Bus Transactions**

3.1   **Bridges and Interbus Segment Operations**

3.0   GENERIC PCI AND PCI-X BUS TRANSACTIONS

INTRODUCTION

The PCI bus specification defines the interaction between two PCI resources: the PCI bus master and target. The PCI bus master may be a processor or a HOST/PCI BRIDGE that represents a processor on a bus segment. The target may be a memory or I/O resource in addition to a PCI/PCI BRIDGE that ports bus transactions to resources on other bus segments. As with other bus specifications, the PCI local bus specification defines a protocol for the PCI bus master to read and write data from and to a target, respectively. Also, similar to other bus specifications, memory and I/O address spaces are defined.

The PCI bus specification defines other bus transactions that are more sophisticated than the simple bus transactions to memory or I/O resources. It also defines bus transactions to a configuration address space to identify and establish hardware requirements of PCI resources. In addition, it defines a special transaction to broadcast a message to all PCI resources, and an interrupt acknowledge transaction to return the interrupt vector to the platform CPU.

SINGLE read and write transactions are defined for memory, I/O, and configuration address spaces. SINGLE read and write transactions are also defined for interrupt acknowledge and special transactions, respectively. SINGLE bus transactions are defined as one data access per bus transaction.

BURST read and write transactions are defined for memory, I/O, and configuration (with some restrictions) address spaces. BURST write bus transactions are also defined for special transactions. BURST bus transactions are defined as multiple data accesses during one bus transaction.

The PCI bus protocol provides the memory resource with additional "insight" on how the bus transactions could be executed. The execution of the appropriate BURST transaction indicates to the memory resource that perhaps multiple cache lines or multiple bytes may be accessed in order to allow the memory resource to prepare. It also defines a BURST memory write transaction cache protocol to

37

indicate to the memory resource that an entire Cacheline will be overwritten to eliminate copy-back protocols for write-back caches.

Other important bus transaction attributes of the PCI bus specification include an extensive bus transaction termination protocol and parity protection over some of the signal lines.

The PCI local bus specification supports 32 data bit bus transactions for memory, I/O, and configuration address spaces. Special and interrupt acknowledge transactions are also defined as 32 data bit transactions. It defines 32 address bits for memory and I/O address spaces. The PCI local bus specification also defines 64 address bits for memory transactions. Finally, the PCI local bus specification supports 64 data bit memory transactions and 64 data bit (theoretically) for I/O transactions. This book assumes the use of only 32 data bit I/O transactions.

The PCI bus transaction protocol is defined as synchronous. All of the signal lines are referenced to the rising edge of the bus segment clock (CLK signal line) except for the SERR# (system error), RST# (RESET), PME# (Power Management Event), and INTx# (interrupt) signal lines.

The PCI-X addendum specification defines the interaction between two PCI-X resources the same as the PCI local bus specification does for PCI resources. The only differences are that BURST bus transactions are defined only for the memory address space, and 64 data bit I/O transactions are not defined (that is, not even theoretically). Additionally, the PCI-X addendum specification defines split completion transactions (32 or 64 data bits). These bus transactions are part of the Split Transaction protocol and are either executed with SINGLE or BURST bus transactions.

PCI AND PCI-X DRAWING PROTOCOL

A more detailed drawing protocol is outlined in Chapter 6: *Detailed Bus Transaction Operation*. For the purposes of discussing the generic bus transactions, the following protocol is adopted:

- ■ The drawing protocol for individual signal lines driven by a single PCI resource during the bus transaction and driven to a logical "1" by pull-up resistors some of the time is shown by the FRAME#, IRDY#, and TRDY# signal lines in Figure 3-0. The FRAME# (also STOP# and DEVSEL# (not shown)) signal line changes from logical "1" (deasserted) to a logical "0" (asserted) at only one transition point during the bus transaction, and remains asserted for the remainder of the bus transaction. The IRDY# and TRDY# signal lines may toggle between logical "1" (deasserted) to logical "0" (asserted) at one or several points during the bus transaction. The FRAME# and IRDY# signal lines are driven by the PCI bus master during the bus transaction. The TRDY#, DEVSEL#, and STOP# signal lines are driven by the target during the bus transaction.

■ The AD signal lines typify the protocol for signal lines not driven by pull-up resistors. The "A" and "D" between the parallel lines indicate that address and data are driven onto the signal lines, respectively. Non-labeled areas with parallel lines represent signal lines driven to a stable level, but do not always contain valid information. The unlabeled areas with the single horizontal line represent a tri-stated level; consequently, the signal lines are floating. Although not shown in Figure 3-0, the C/BE# and PAR signal lines also adhere to this protocol.

■ The C/BE# signal lines are marked with "C" and "BE" to indicate when COMMAND type versus valid byte lane information is driven onto the signal lines. The PAR signal line is marked with "PA" and "PD" for parity over the AD and C/BE# signal lines during the ADDRESS and DATA PHASES, respectively. The C/BE#, AD, and PAR signal lines are driven by the PCI bus master during a write transaction. For a portion of the read transaction, the AD and PAR signal lines are also driven by the target.

■ The CLK signal line shows the protocol for individual signal lines driven by a single source. These signal lines change from asserted to deasserted without the periods of float or being driven to logical "1" by pull-up resistors. The CLK signal line is driven by the central resource.

The figures in this chapter do not include all of the signal lines of the PCI bus transaction protocol. These figures only provide a general idea of the bus transaction protocol. See Chapter 6: *Detailed Bus Transaction Operation* for more information.

For the rest of this chapter, the changing states of the signal lines are referenced to the numbered CLK signal line period when the FRAME# signal line is asserted during the first CLK signal line period.

The generic PCI-X drawing protocol is the same as for PCI except for the dashed horizontal line in the AD, C/BE#, and PAR signal lines. The AD signal lines typify the protocol for signal lines not driven by pull-up resistors. Unlabeled areas with parallel solid lines and one dashed line represent signal lines driven to either a stable level or tri-stated. If driven stable, the signal lines do not always contain valid information.

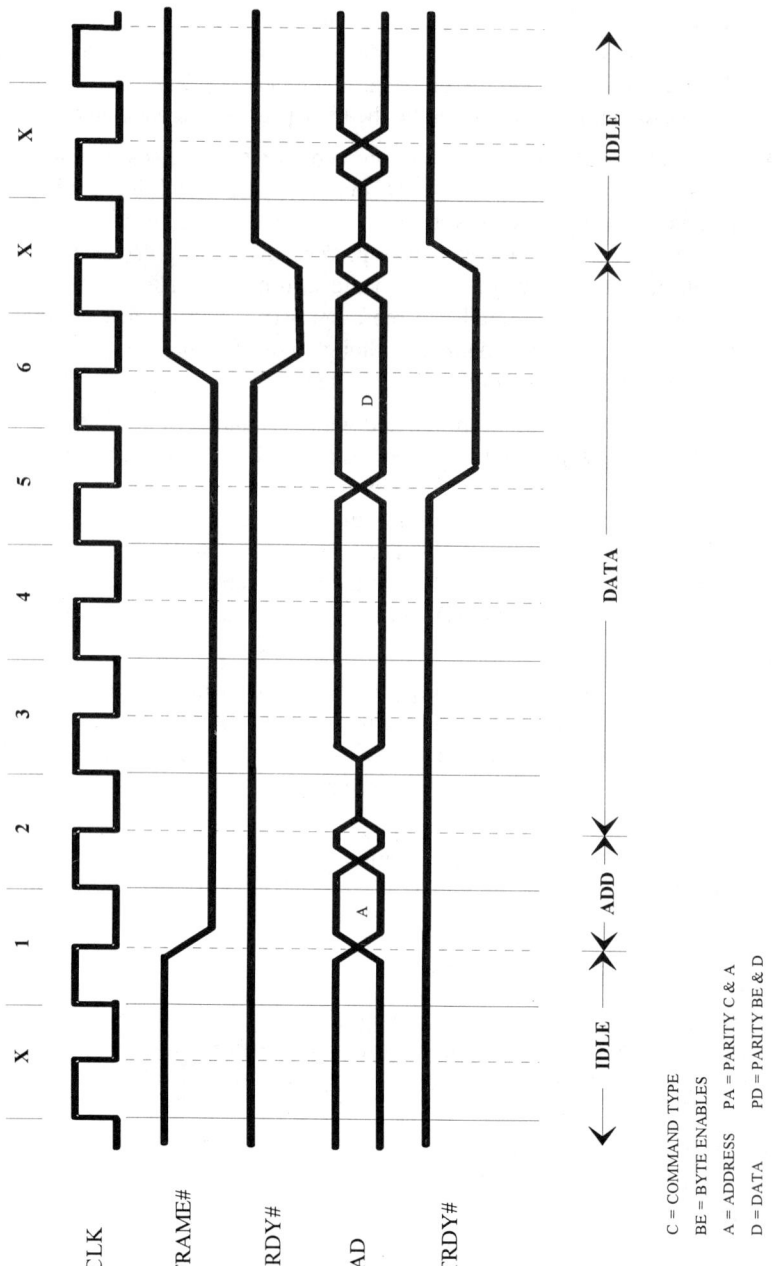

CLK

FRAME#

IRDY#

AD

TRDY#

C = COMMAND TYPE
BE = BYTE ENABLES
A = ADDRESS   PA = PARITY C & A
D = DATA   PD = PARITY BE & D

Figure 3-0: Drawing Protocol (Reading Example)

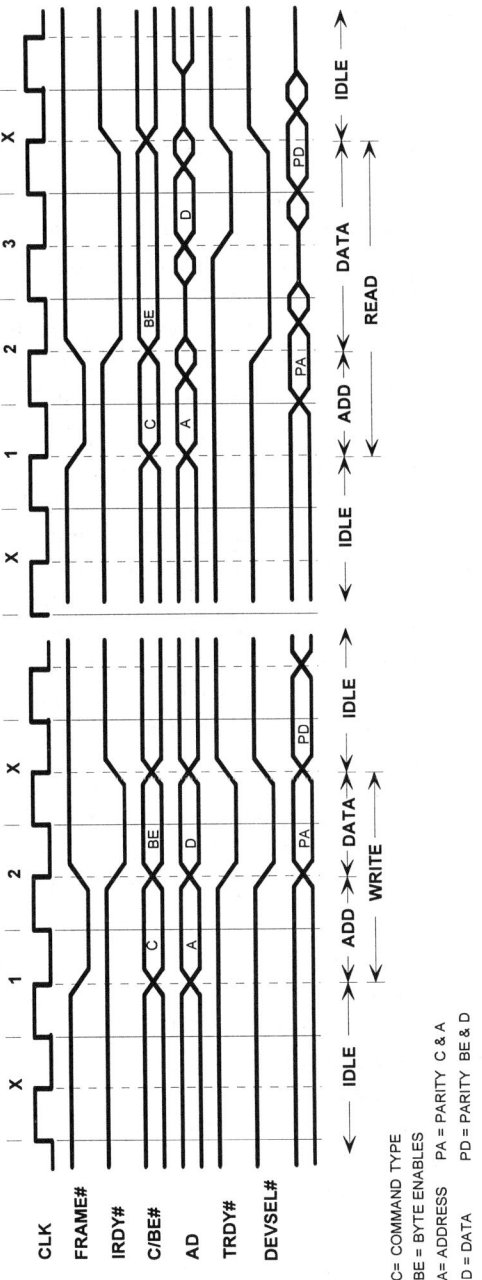

Figure 3-1: PCI Standard Single Write and Read Transaction

41

BUS TRANSACTIONS

PCI SPECIFIC

SINGLE BUS TRANSACTIONS ... MEMORY, I/O, & CONFIGURATION

Memory, I/O, and configuration address spaces are selected by the bus transaction. A bus transaction begins with the ADDRESS PHASE when the PCI bus master asserts the FRAME# signal line to indicate that a valid address and command exist on AD and C/BE# signal lines, respectively (see Figure 3-1). The PCI bus master drives the AD and C/BE# signal lines, and drives valid parity for these signal lines onto the PAR signal line one CLK signal line period later. The COMMAND type indicates the address space and whether the bus transaction is a read or write.

The bus transaction continues with the DATA PHASE, during which the data is actually accessed. All PCI targets decode the address, and the appropriate one claims the transaction by asserting the DEVSEL# signal line. For a write transaction, the PCI bus master drives the data to be written, the valid byte lane information, and the parity of these signal lines onto the AD, C/BE#, and PAR signal lines, respectively. For a read transaction, the PCI bus master drives valid byte lane information on the C/BE# signal lines. The target drives the data to be read onto the AD signal lines, and the parity of the AD and C/BE# signal lines onto to the PAR signal line. Due to multiplexing of the address and data, the AD signal lines are tri-stated for a CLK signal line period by the PCI bus master prior to the target driving data onto these signal lines. The access (also known as "transfer") of data occurs on the rising edge of the CLK signal line when both the IRDY# and TRDY# signal lines are asserted. The IDLE PHASE indicates that no bus transactions are being executed during the respective CLK signal line periods. The IDLE PHASE occurs whenever the FRAME# and IRDY# signal line are both deasserted.

The PCI bus protocol allows both the PCI bus master and the target to delay the completion of the bus transaction. Figure 3-1 outlines the STANDARD bus transaction that occurs when neither the PCI bus master nor target request any delay in the completion of the bus transaction. For a write transaction, the earliest possible assertion of the IRDY# and TRDY# signal lines is during the second CLK signal line clock period. For a read transaction, the earliest possible assertion of the IRDY# and TRDY# signal lines is during the second and third CLK signal line clock periods, respectively. The additional CLK signal line period is necessary to allow time to change the driving source of the AD signal lines; it is the responsibility of the target to delay the assertion of the TRDY# signal line.

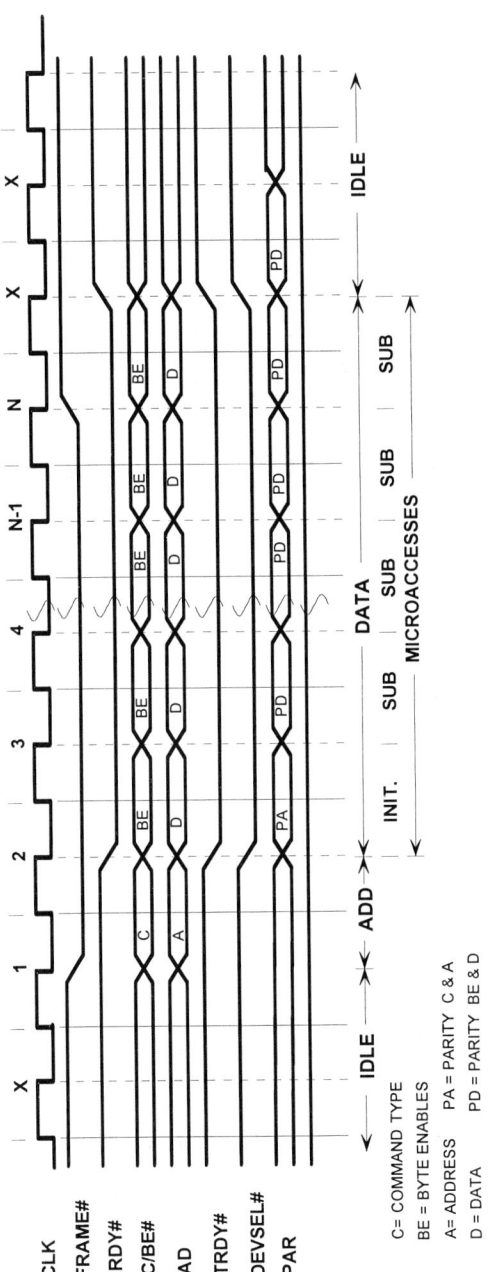

Figure 3-2: PCI Burst Write Transaction with all Standard Microaccesses

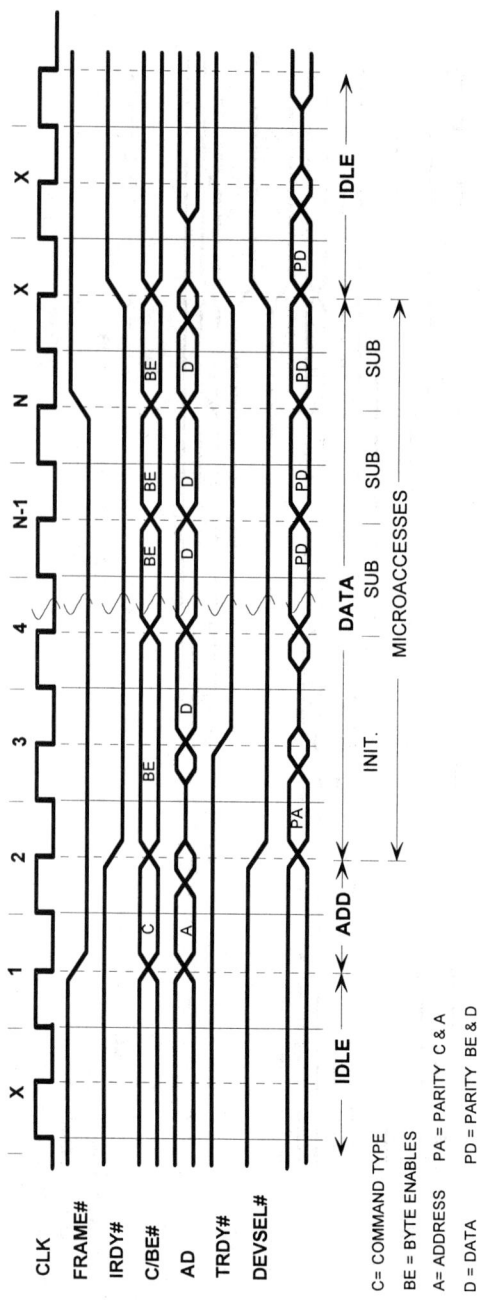

Figure 3-3: PCI Burst Read Transaction with all Standard Microaccesses

The AD signal lines may be translated into the IDSEL signal lines for configuration transactions. See Chapter 6: *Detailed Bus Transaction Operation*, for details.

BURST BUS TRANSACTIONS ... MEMORY, I/O, & CONFIGURATION

Figure 3-1 outlines STANDARD SINGLE bus transactions, in which data is accessed only once during the bus transaction. The PCI bus protocol also supports BURST bus transactions as shown in Figures 3-2 and 3-3. Unlike other bus protocols, the PCI bus segment does not use unique commands or signal lines to execute a BURST bus transaction. The assertion and deassertion of the FRAME# and IRDY# signal lines transform a SINGLE bus transaction into a BURST bus transaction. During the ADDRESS PHASE, the protocol of the signal lines is the same for both the SINGLE and BURST bus transactions. During the DATA PHASE, the IRDY# signal line is asserted when the PCI bus master is ready to access the data.

If the FRAME# signal line is deasserted simultaneously with the assertion of the IRDY# signal lines for the first data access, the bus transaction is completed as a SINGLE bus transaction. If the FRAME# signal line remains asserted after the assertion of the IRDY# signal line for the first transaction, the cycle continues as a BURST bus transaction. The BURST bus transaction continues until the FRAME# signal line is deasserted when the IRDY# signal line is asserted. The DATA PHASE of a BURST bus transaction consists of a series of microaccesses. Each microaccess consists of data when the IRDY# and TRDY# signal lines are both asserted. The first microaccess is defined as the "initial microaccess" (INIT) and remaining microaccesses are defined as "subsequent microaccesses" (SUB). The base address of the initial microaccess is established during the ADDRESS PHASE. The addresses for the subsequent microaccesses are incremental relative to the base address.

The entire BURST bus transaction is either all reads or all writes. The COMMAND type driven onto the C/BE# signal lines during the ADDRESS PHASE establishes the direction of data flow for all microaccesses.

STANDARD VERSUS READY BUS TRANSACTIONS ...MEMORY, I/O, & CONFIGURATION

Most bus protocols support extensions to the bus transaction length of the minimum bus transaction by the resource being accessed. The minimum bus transaction is called STANDARD and the extended bus transaction is called READY. The accessed resource on the typical bus extends the STANDARD bus transaction by deasserting a signal line defined as "ready". The assertion of the ready signal line allows the bus transaction to be completed.

The PCI local bus specification has adopted a similar protocol and has expanded it; both the resource executing the bus transaction (PCI bus master) and the resource being accessed (target) can extend the bus transaction. The STANDARD SINGLE bus transaction outlined in Figure 3-1 is executed when the IRDY# and TRDY# signal lines are both asserted at the beginning of the DATA PHASE. For a write transaction, the earliest possible assertion of the IRDY# and TRDY# signal lines is during the second CLK signal line clock period. For a read transaction, the earliest possible assertion of the IRDY# and TRDY# signal lines is during the second and third CLK signal line clock periods, respectively. Figures 3-4 and 3-5 outline the write and read READY SINGLE bus transactions, respectively. Either the PCI bus master (via the IRDY# signal line) or the target (via the TRDY# signal line) or both can extend the bus transaction length. The data access occurs on the rising edge of the CLK signal line when the IRDY# and TRDY# signal lines are both asserted.

During the DATA PHASE, the C/BE# signal lines are always driven with valid byte lane information while the AD and PAR signal lines may be driven to invalid values until the PCI bus master and target are ready to complete the bus transaction.

Each microaccess of a BURST bus transaction can be individually executed as STANDARD or READY using the same protocol as the STANDARD or READY SINGLE bus transactions, respectively. Figures 3-2 and 3-3 execute all of the microaccesses with the STANDARD protocol. The protocol of the initial microaccess is the same as the STANDARD SINGLE bus transaction. The subsequent microaccesses follow the STANDARD bus transaction protocol because both IRDY# and TRDY# signal lines are asserted to allow a data access on each rising edge of the CLK signal line.

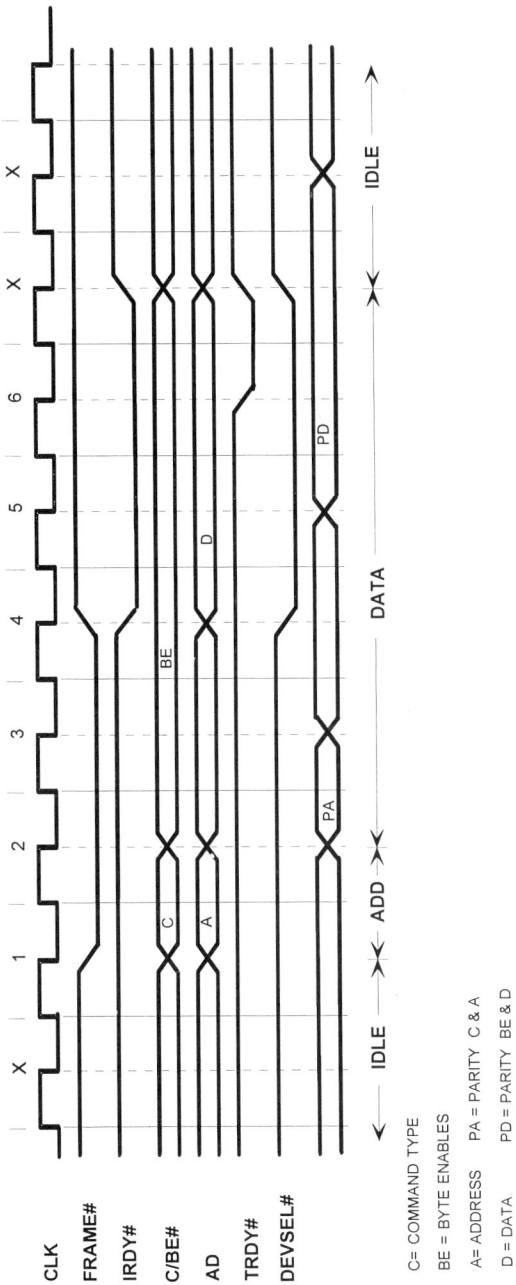

Figure 3-4: PCI Ready Single Write Transaction

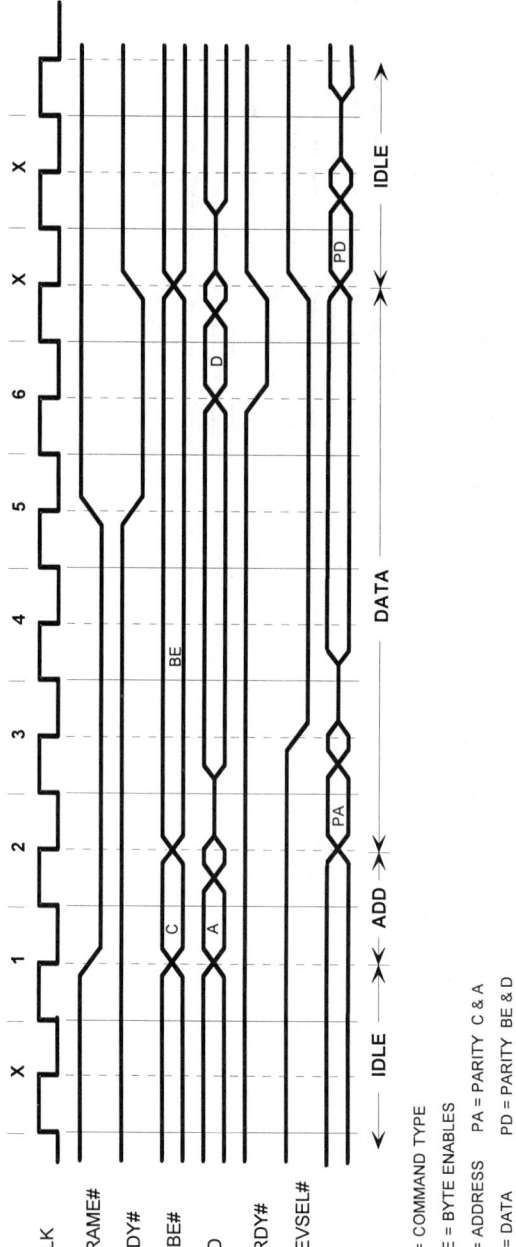

Figure 3-5: PCI Ready Single Read Transaction

Figures 3-6 and 3-7 show BURST bus transactions with a mixture of READY and STANDARD microaccesses. The mixture of READY and STANDARD microaccesses in these figures are examples; any microaccess can use either the READY or STANDARD protocol. In Figure 3-6, the initial microaccess and the first subsequent microaccess are extended by the PCI bus master and target, respectively. The initial microaccess would have been STANDARD if the PCI bus master asserted the IRDY# signal line during the second CLK signal line period. The first subsequent microaccess would have been STANDARD if the target did not deassert the TRDY# signal line during the fourth CLK signal line period. The second subsequent microaccess is STANDARD due to the continued assertion of the IRDY# and TRDY# signal lines during the sixth CLK signal line period.

In Figure 3-7 the initial microaccess and the first subsequent microaccess are extended by the target and PCI bus master, respectively. The initial microaccess would have been STANDARD if the target asserted the TRDY# signal line during the third CLK signal line period. The first subsequent microaccess would have been STANDARD if the PCI bus master did not deassert the IRDY# signal line during the fifth CLK signal line period. The second subsequent microaccess is STANDARD due the continued assertion of the IRDY# and TRDY# signal lines during the seventh CLK signal line period.

> For all bus transactions, the byte lane information on the C/BE# signal lines during the DATA PHASE indicates which AD signal lines contain valid data information. It is not required that any of the byte lanes contain any valid data.

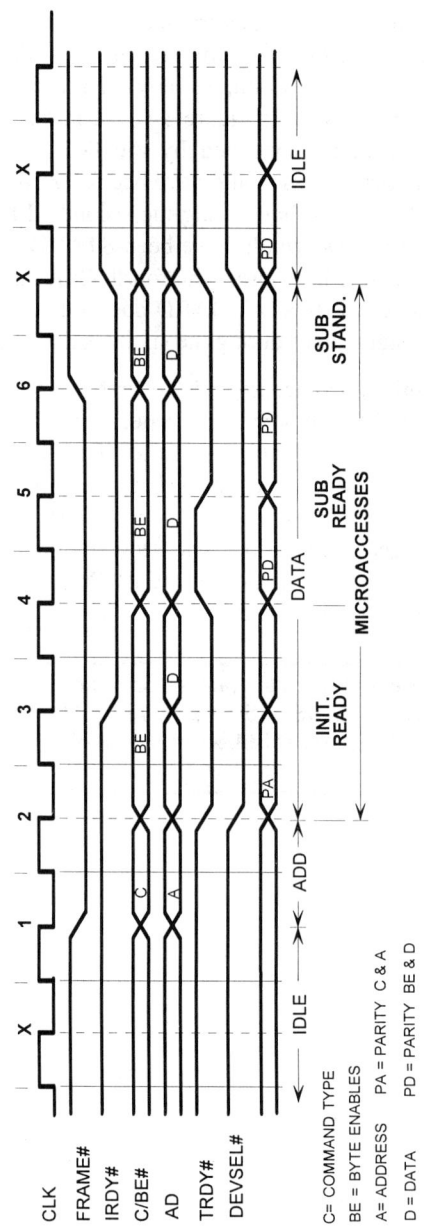

**Figure 3-6: PCI Burst Write Transaction with Standard and Ready
Microaccesses**

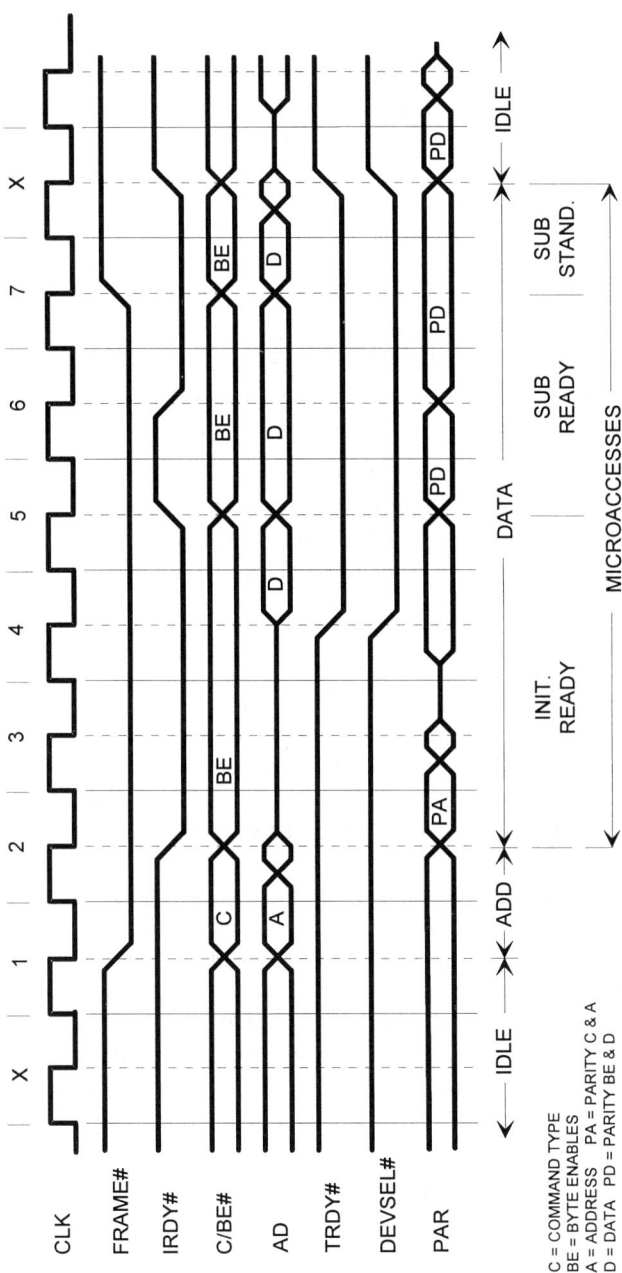

Figure 3-7: PCI Burst Read Transaction with Standard and Ready Microaccesses

INTERRUPT ACKNOWLEDGE TRANSACTIONS

The PCI bus protocol defines a version of a read transaction called interrupt acknowledge transaction. The interrupt acknowledge transaction operates with the same protocol as a SINGLE memory or I/O read transaction. The only PCI resource that can respond to this bus transaction is the one that contains the interrupt controller. This PCI resource must be attached to PCI Bus (0). The interrupt controller can reside in a PCI resource on PCI bus (0), the PCI/LEGACY BRIDGE on PCI bus (0), or in a resource on the LEGACY bus segment. The HOST/PCI BRIDGE, on behalf of the HOST CPU, is the only platform resource that can execute an interrupt acknowledge transaction on PCI bus (0). If the interrupt controller is on the LEGACY bus segment, a version of the interrupt acknowledge transaction will also be executed, according to the protocol of the LEGACY bus segment.

It is also possible for the interrupt controller to reside on the HOST bus segment or on a LEGACY bus segment that is directly attached to the HOST bus segment with a HOST/LEGACY BRIDGE. In these situations, no interrupt acknowledge transaction will be executed on PCI bus (0).

SPECIAL TRANSACTIONS

The PCI bus protocol defines a version of a write transaction called special transaction. The special transaction operates with the same protocol as memory or I/O write transactions (SINGLE or BURST), except none of the PCI resources (targets) claim the transaction. The DEVSEL#, TRDY#, and STOP# signal lines remain driven to a logical "1" by pull-up resistors. The AD signal lines during a special transaction do not contain a valid address. The special transaction allows data to be "broadcast" (simultaneously written) to all PCI bus resources on a specific PCI bus segment. The source of a special transaction is a PCI bus master or a bridge on the PCI bus segment. A PCI bus master can directly execute a special transaction to the PCI resources on the same PCI bus segment. When a special transaction is to be executed to PCI resources not on the same PCI bus segment as the PCI bus master, the request for a special transaction on another PCI bus segment is ported through PCI/PCI BRIDGE(s) by a Type 1 configuration transaction.

BUS TRANSACTION TERMINATION

As shown in the previous figures, the typical completion of a bus transaction is when the FRAME# signal line is deasserted and the IRDY# and TRDY# signal lines are asserted. This is followed by the deassertion of the FRAME#, TRDY#, and IRDY# signal lines (for the typical completion). This typical situation is called

Completion termination. Unlike other bus protocols, a PCI target does not have to respond to a bus transaction, and the bus transaction can be terminated early (atypically) by the PCI bus master or the target. After the PCI bus master asserts the FRAME# signal line and drives the address onto the AD signal lines, one of the targets can claim the bus transaction by asserting the DEVSEL# signal line within a predetermined number of CLK signal line periods. The non-assertion of the DEVSEL# signal line places the responsibility of bus transaction termination on the PCI bus master without any data being accessed. This situation is called Master Abort termination. The assertion of the DEVSEL# signal line places the responsibility of bus transaction termination on the target with or without data being accessed. In addition to Completion termination, the target can complete the bus transaction with three types of terminations: Retry, Disconnect, and Target Abort.

A Master Abort termination is executed by a PCI bus master when no PCI resource (target) claims the bus transaction by asserting the DEVSEL# signal line. The PCI bus master executes a Master Abort termination by asserting (for a minimum of one CLK signal line period if not already asserted) and subsequently deasserting the IRDY# signal line. The FRAME# signal line is deasserted for a minimum of one CLK signal line period when the IRDY# signal line is asserted. The Master Abort termination is completed with the deassertion of the FRAME# and IRDY# signal lines. See Chapter 8: *Master and Target Termination* for more information.

A Master Abort termination results when no PCI resource (target) has claimed the bus transaction. Consequently, the DEVSEL#, TRDY#, STOP#, and AD signal lines are not driven by a target. The DEVSEL#, TRDY#, and STOP# signal lines are driven to a logical "1" by pull-up resistors, and the AD signal lines are driven only by the PCI bus master.

A Retry, Disconnect, and Target Abort termination is executed by the target by asserting the STOP# signal line after it has claimed the bus transaction by asserting the DEVSEL# signal line. The Retry termination occurs when no data has been accessed during the bus transaction but the target can be accessed at a later time. The Disconnect termination occurs when data has been accessed during the bus transaction but further accesses during the present bus transaction are not possible. The Target Abort termination occurs regardless of whether data has been accessed in the associated bus transaction, the target cannot be accessed at a later time with the same bus transaction, and if data had been accessed it may not be valid. Once the target has requested one of these terminations, the PCI bus master must still complete the bus transaction as outlined above. The IRDY# signal line must be asserted for a minimum of one CLK signal line period when the FRAME# signal line is deasserted. Subsequently, the FRAME# and IRDY# signal lines are both deasserted. See Chapter 8: *Master and Target Termination* for more information.

64 DATA BIT PCI BUS MASTERS AND TARGETS

The generic PCI bus transactions described above apply to both 32 and 64 data bit bus transactions. The 32 data bit PCI bus protocol implements the AD[31::0], C/BE#[3::0] and PAR signal lines. The 64 data bit extension of the PCI bus protocol adds the AD[63::32], C/BE#[7::4], and PAR64 signal lines. The operation of the AD[63::32] and C/BE#[7::4] signal lines is almost identical to the operation of the AD[31::0] and C/BE#[3::0] signal lines.

The ability to actually execute 64 data bit bus transactions requires that both the PCI bus master and the target support 64 data bits as indicated by asserted REQ64# and ACK64# signal lines, respectively. The REQ64# signal line is asserted during the ADDRESS PHASE (using the same timing protocol as the FRAME# signal line) to indicate that the PCI bus master wants to read or write 64 data bits per bus transaction. The ACK64# signal line is asserted during the DATA PHASE (using the same timing protocol as the DEVSEL# signal line) to indicate that the target supports 64 data bit accesses. See Chapter 6: *Detailed Bus Cycle Operation*, for more information.

> PCI 64 data bit I/O targets can be implemented, but there is no benefit to requiring the increased complexity, and it is therefore strongly recommended that 64 data bit PCI I/O targets not be implemented. For the purposes of this book, PCI I/O targets are only 32 data bits in size. If a 64 data bit PCI I/O target is implemented, the 64 data bit protocol applied to memory targets would also apply to PCI I/O targets.

DUAL ADDRESS

The PCI bus protocol also supports a 64-bit address space. The typical bus transaction defines 32 address bits on the AD[31::0] signal lines when the FRAME# signal line is first asserted during the ADDRESS PHASE. If the DUAL ADDRESS command encoding is driven onto the C/BE# signal lines during the ADDRESS PHASE, the length of the ADDRESS PHASE is doubled (see Figure 3-8). The second CLK signal line period of the longer ADDRESS PHASE allows the upper order 32 address bits to be driven onto the AD[31::0] signal lines. Also, the COMMAND type (memory versus I/O, read versus write, etc.) are driven onto the C/BE#[3::0] signal lines during this second CLK signal line period of the ADDRESS PHASE. Figure 3-8 uses read transactions as examples, although the protocol is the same for a write transaction. See Chapter 6: *Detailed Bus Cycle Operation* for details.

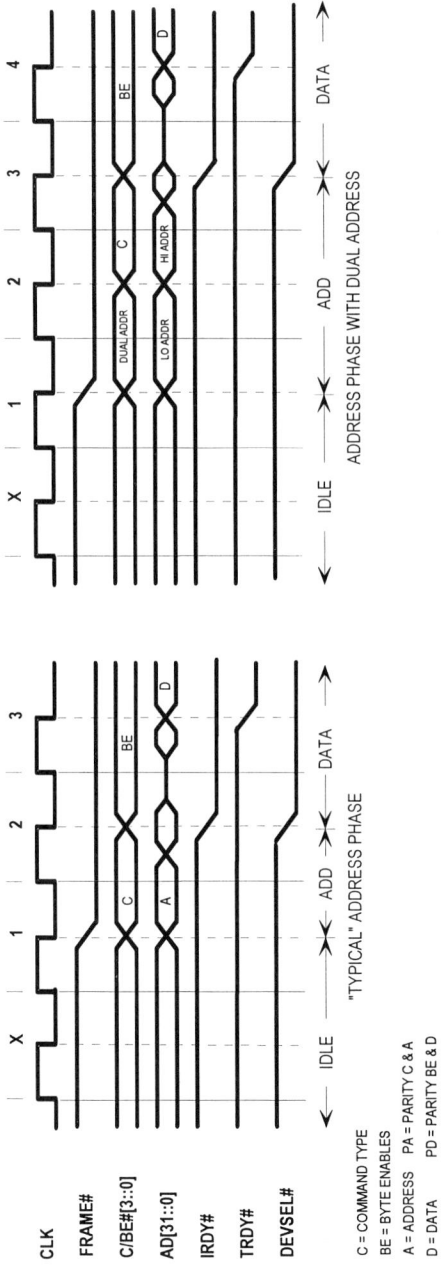

Figure 3-8: PCI DUAL ADDRESS (Read Example)

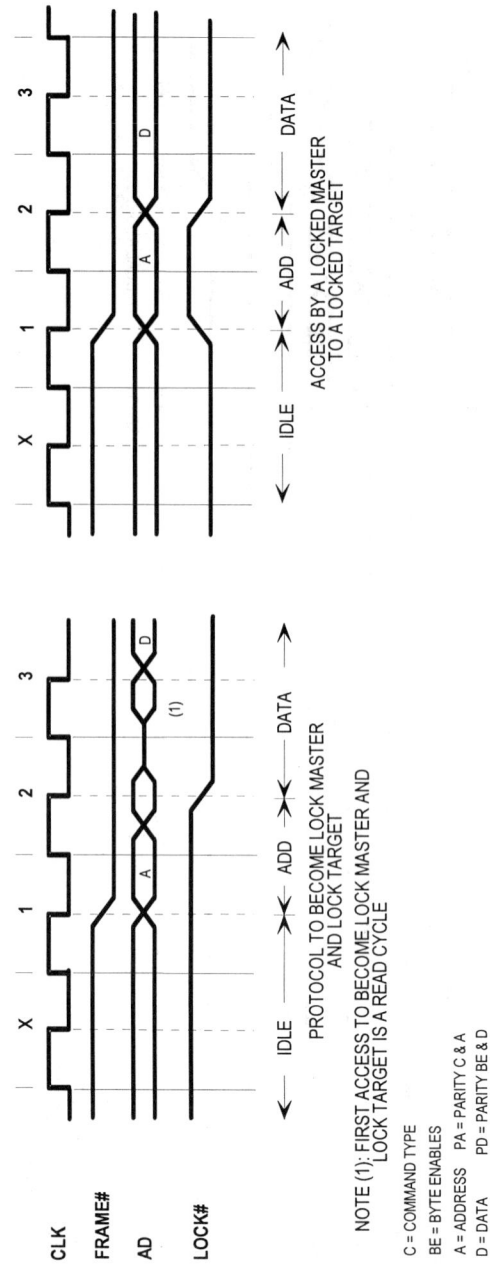

Figure 3-9: PCI Lock Protocol

The DUAL ADDRESS command is only defined for memory transactions. The DUAL ADDRESS command cannot be implemented for I/O, configuration, interrupt acknowledge, or special transactions.

If the PCI bus master asserts the REQ64# signal line, the upper order address and COMMAND type information on the AD[31::0] and C/BE#[3::0] signal lines are mirrored on the AD[63::32] and C/BE#[7::4] signal lines, respectively.

EXCLUSIVE ACCESS (LOCK)

According to Revision 2.2 of the PCI local bus specification, the HOST CPU and (through bridges) LEGACY bus masters can attain Exclusive Access (also known as LOCK) of certain system memory resources (targets) with hardware via the LOCK# signal line. The terms Lock master and locked target are defined for resources as viewed on each PCI bus segment. The use of "PCI bus master" or "locked target" refers to bridges, actual PCI bus masters, and actual PCI or LEGACY bus memory targets that support the LOCK# signal line. A locked target means that only the PCI bus master that locked it (Lock master) can access it, and can eventually unlock it. Other PCI bus masters cannot access a locked target. If the non-Lock master attempts an access, the target executes a Retry termination.

A PCI bus master can lock a target if no other PCI resource is presently locked (as indicated by the continued deassertion of the LOCK# signal line by pull-up resistors). At any given time, only one PCI bus master can be Lock master and only one target can be locked on each bus segment. When no Lock master presently exists on a bus segment, a PCI bus master begins the bus transaction to lock a target by deasserting the LOCK# signal line during the ADDRESS PHASE.

If the LOCK# signal line is asserted by the PCI bus master during the second CLK signal line period, the PCI bus master becomes the Lock master and the target is locked if data is successfully read (see Figure 3-9). The LOCK# signal line must remain asserted for the remainder of the bus transaction and after the bus transaction is completed for the PCI bus master to remain Lock master. The continued assertion of the LOCK# signal line after the bus transaction by the Lock master indicates to other PCI bus masters that a Lock master and locked target already exist.

The Lock master accesses a locked target by deasserting the LOCK# signal during the ADDRESS PHASE (see Figure 3-9). The LOCK# signal line is asserted for the remainder of the bus transaction if the Lock master wants to remain Lock master. The Lock master ceases to be Lock master when the LOCK# and FRAME# signal lines are both deasserted.

57

> When a DUAL ADDRESS is executed, the length of the ADDRESS PHASE is doubled. This has no effect on the LOCK# signal line protocol. The transition of the LOCK# signal line must be during the second CLK signal line period.

PCI-X SPECIFIC

The PCI-X bus transaction protocol is essentially the same as the PCI bus transaction protocol and includes the support of Exclusive Access and the DUAL ADDRESS command. PCI-X bus transactions can be executed as either STANDARD or READY SINGLE bus transactions, BURST bus transactions with a mixture of READY or STANDARD microaccesses, 32 and 64 data bit, and 64 address bits. There are some differences between the PCI-X bus transaction protocol and the PCI bus transaction protocol as follows:

- As shown in Figures 3-10 to 3-17, the generic PCI-X bus transaction protocol has two additional phases than the PCI bus transaction protocol. The ATTRIBUTE PHASE is after the ADDRESSS PHASE and is one CLK signal line period long. It contains information useful for the Split Transaction protocol, byte enable information for SINGLE bus transactions, and the byte count for BURST bus transactions. The TARGET RESPONSE PHASE is a formalization of the CLK signal line period used to change ownership of the AD and PAR signal lines as done for a PCI read transaction. PCI-X bus transaction protocol defines that both read and write transactions have the TARGET RESPONSE PHASE after the ATTTRIBUTE PHASE. Immediately after the TARGET RESPONSE PHASE is the DATA PHASE. Note: In the PCI-X addendum specification, the TARGET RESPONSE PHASE can be multiple CLK signal line periods in length. However, in this book it is defined as only one CLK signal line in length. See Chapter 4: *Functional Interaction Between PCI and PCI-X Resources* and Chapter 6: *Detailed Bus Transaction Operation* for more information

- The PCI-X bus transaction protocol allows only the target to add wait states (see Figures 3-14 to 3-17). That is, the PCI-X bus master is required to immediately assert the IRDY# signal line two CLK signal line periods after the ATTRIBUTE PHASE. For a PCI-X SINGLE READY transaction, only the target is allowed to delay data access by delaying the assertion the TRDY# signal line (see Figures 3-14 and 3-15). For a PCI-X BURST transaction, only the target is allowed to delay data access by delaying the assertion of the TRDY# signal line and only in the INITIAL microaccess (see Figures 3-16 and 3-17). The target is not permitted to deassert the TRDY# signal line to delay the data accesses in the SUBSEQUENT microaccesses.

■ PCI-X addendum specification has placed restrictions on SINGLE versus BURST bus transactions for certain commands. As previously discussed, the PCI local bus specification allows both SINGLE and BURST bus transactions for memory, I/O, configuration, and special commands. Also, the PCI local bus specification allows an interrupt acknowledge command to be executed with only a SINGLE bus transaction. The PCI-X addendum specification requires that all non-memory commands be executed only as SINGLE (STANDARD or READY) bus transactions. The PCI-X addendum specification allows memory commands to be executed as SINGLE (STANDARD or READY) and BURST (STANDARD or READY) bus transactions. The PCI-X addendum specification also requires that a DWORD memory read command be executed as a SINGLE (STANDARD or READY) bus transaction. The PCI-X addendum specification has defined the commands that can only be executed with a SINGLE (STANDARD or READY) bus transaction as DWORD COMMANDs. All other commands can be executed with SINGLE (STANDARD or READY) bus transactions or BURST bus transactions and are called BURST COMMANDs. See Chapter 4: *Functional Interaction between PCI and PCI-X Resources* for more information.

■ The distinction between PCI SINGLE and BURST bus transactions is the deassertion of the FRAME# signal line relative to the continued assertion or deassertion of the IRDY# signal line. For a PCI-X compliant bus transaction, the execution of SINGLE versus BURST is not dependent on the interaction of the FRAME# and IRDY# signal lines. For a PCI-X bus transaction, the command type and/or the byte count in the ATTRIBUTE PHASE defines the execution of a SINGLE versus a BURST bus transaction. Unlike a PCI bus transaction, the deassertion of the FRAME# signal line relative to the assertion or deassertion of the IRDY# signal line will vary depending on the number of microaccesses. For example, Figure 3-13 has two microaccesses and Figure 3-17 has three microaccesses. The FRAME# signal line is deasserted one CLK signal line period before the IRDY# signal line deassertion in Figure 3-17 and simultaneously with the IRDY# signal line deassertion in Figure 3-16.

■ The PCI-X addendum specification defines split completion transactions. The generic SINGLE split completion transaction protocol is shown in Figures 3-10 and 3-14. The generic BURST split completion transaction protocol is shown in Figures 3-12 and 3-16 with one difference: the C/BE# signal lines remain deasserted throughout the DATA PHASE.

■ For PCI-X BURST write transactions, the insertion of wait states by the target must be done in multiples of two CLK signal line periods as shown in Figure 3-16. Consequently, the values of the BE and AD signal lines are repeated in pairs. Similarly, the BURST split completion transactions also require wait states by the target to be done in multiples of two CLK signal line periods.

■ Both the PCI local bus specification and the PCI-X addendum specification support Retry, Master Abort, and Target Abort terminations. In addition to the above terminations, the PCI local bus specification supports Disconnect (with and without data) termination. The PCI-X addendum specification additionally supports Split Response, Disconnect at Next ADB, and Single Phase Disconnect terminations.

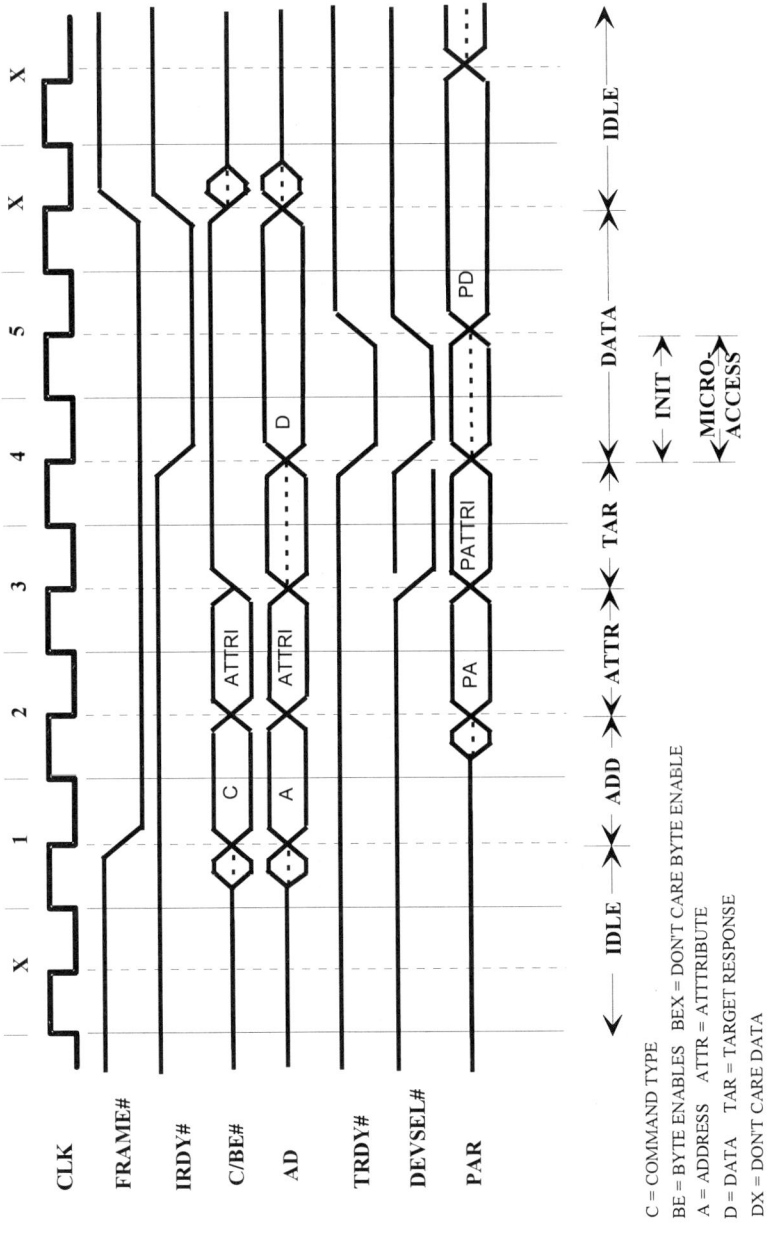

Figure 3-10: PCI-X Standard Single Write Transaction

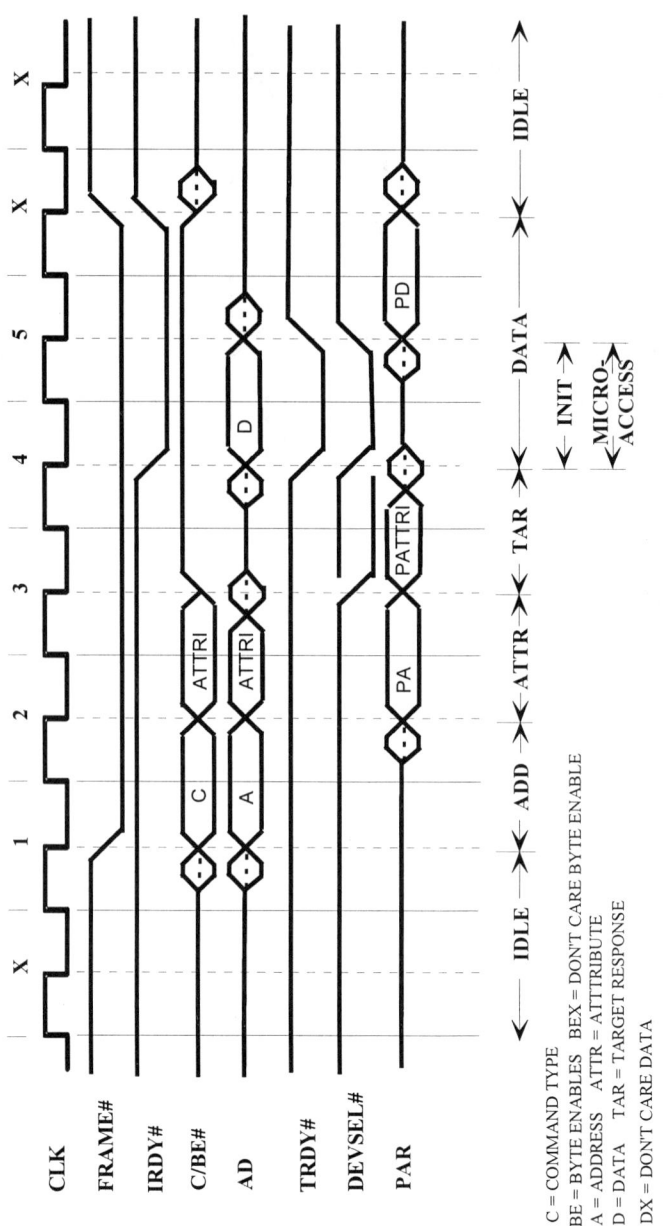

Figure 3-11: PCI-X Standard Single Read Transaction

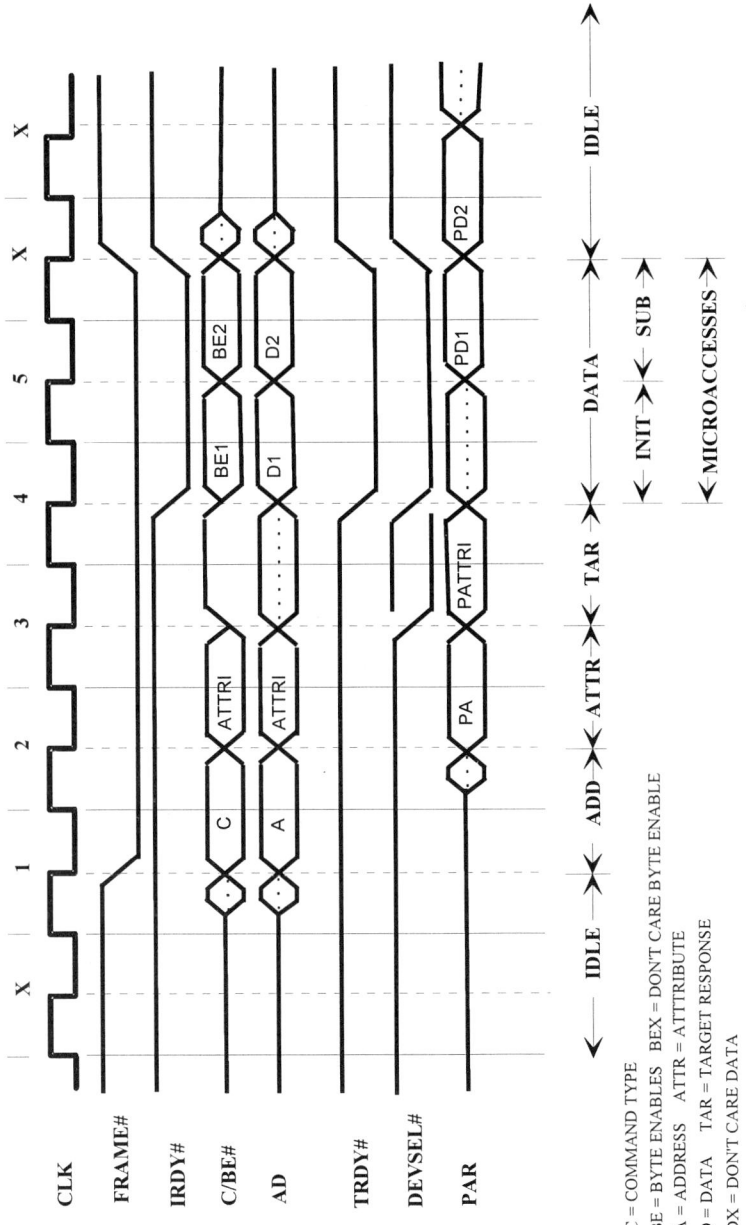

Figure 3-12: PCI-X Burst Write Transaction with all Standard Microaccesses

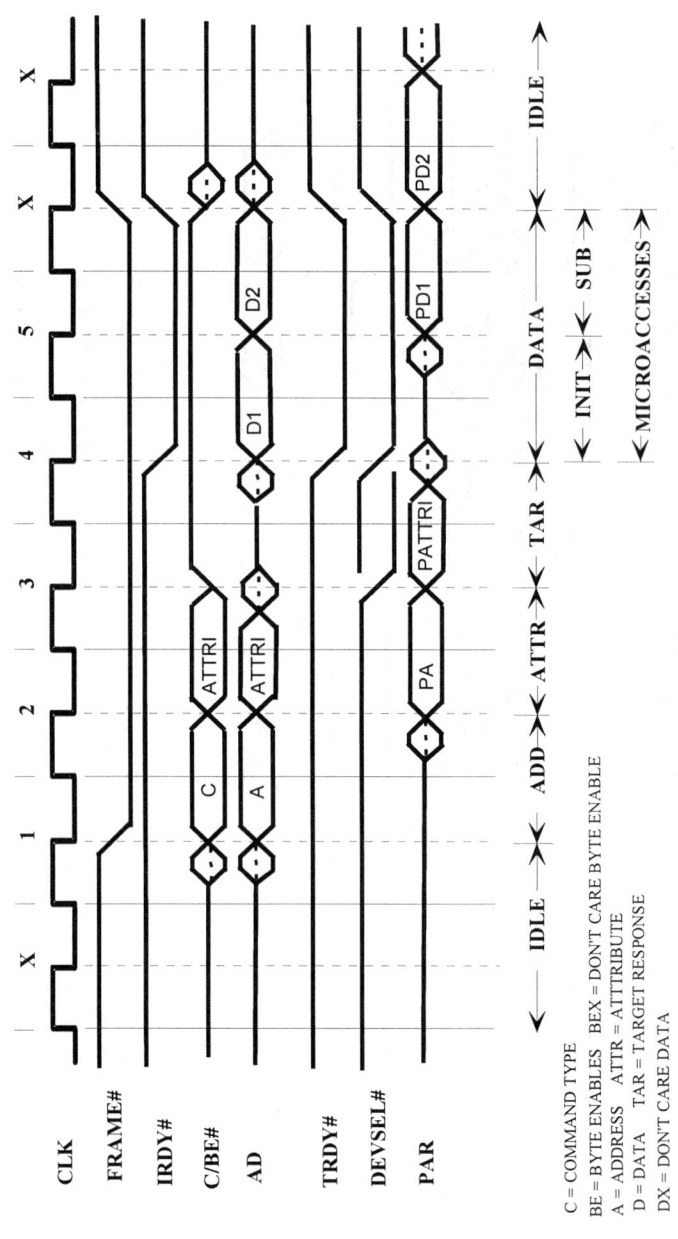

Figure 3-13: PCI-X Burst Read Transaction with all Standard Microaccesses

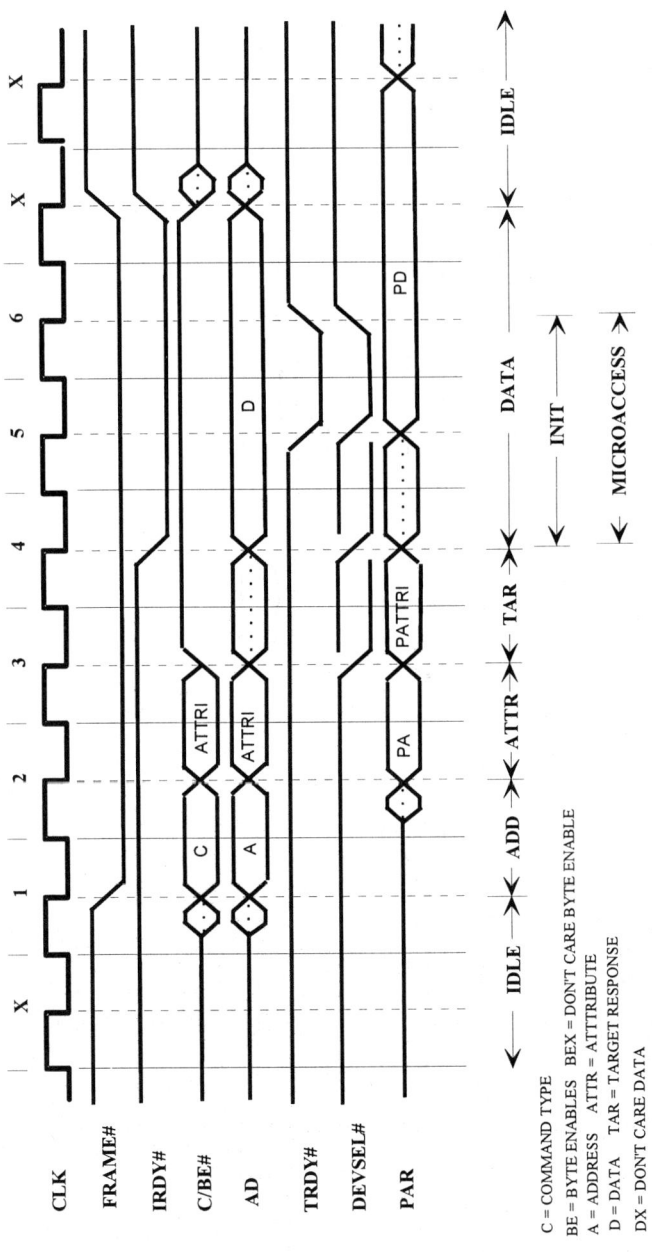

Figure 3-14: PCI-X Ready Single Write Transaction

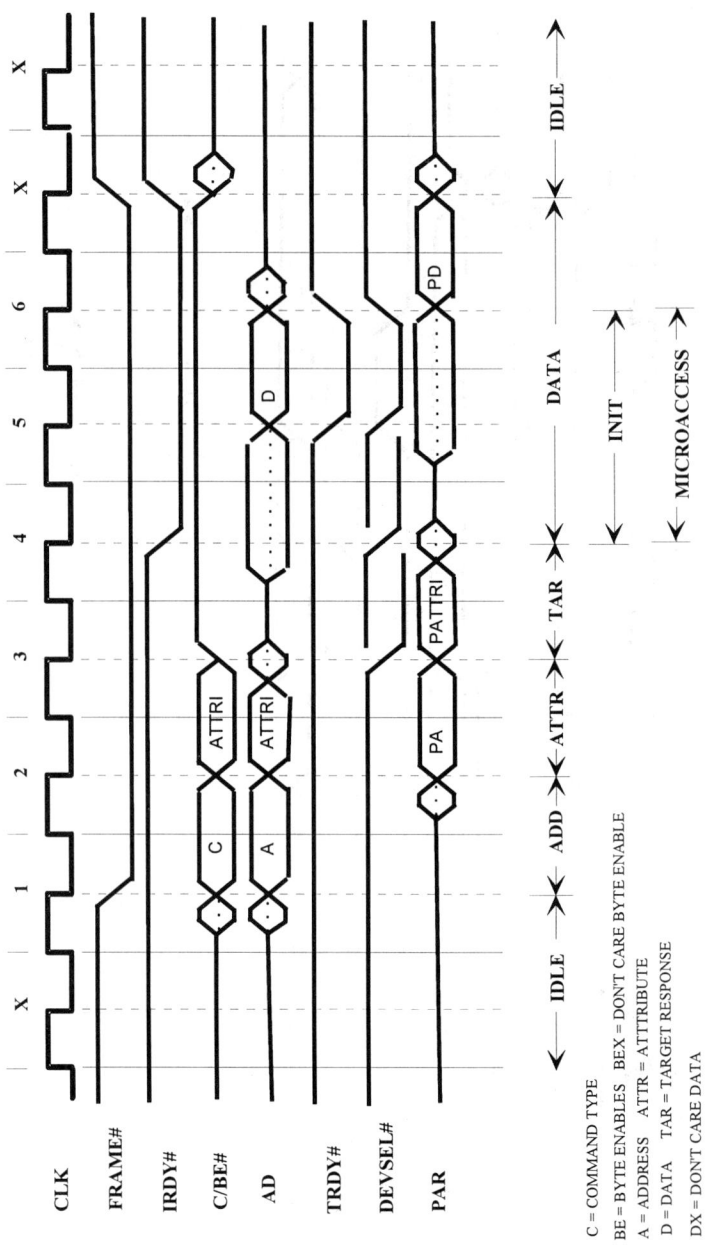

Figure 3-15: PCI-X Ready Single Read Transaction

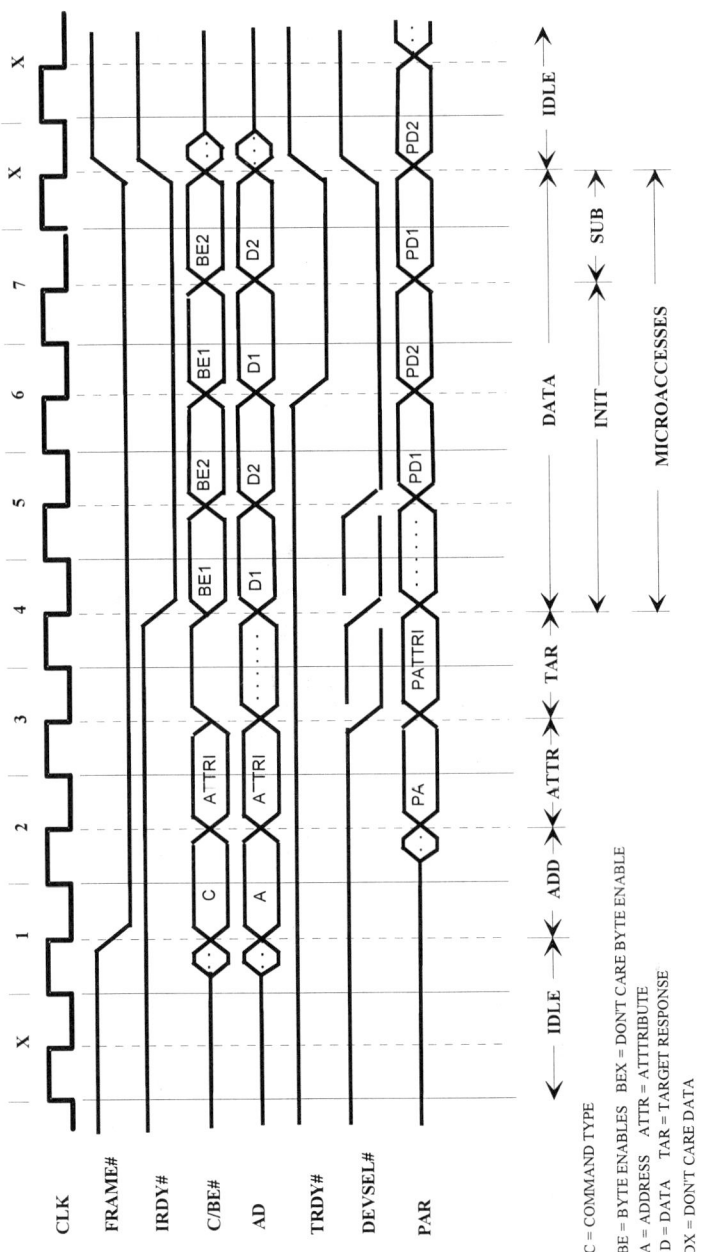

Figure 3-16: PCI-X Burst Write Transaction with Ready in Initial Microaccess

67

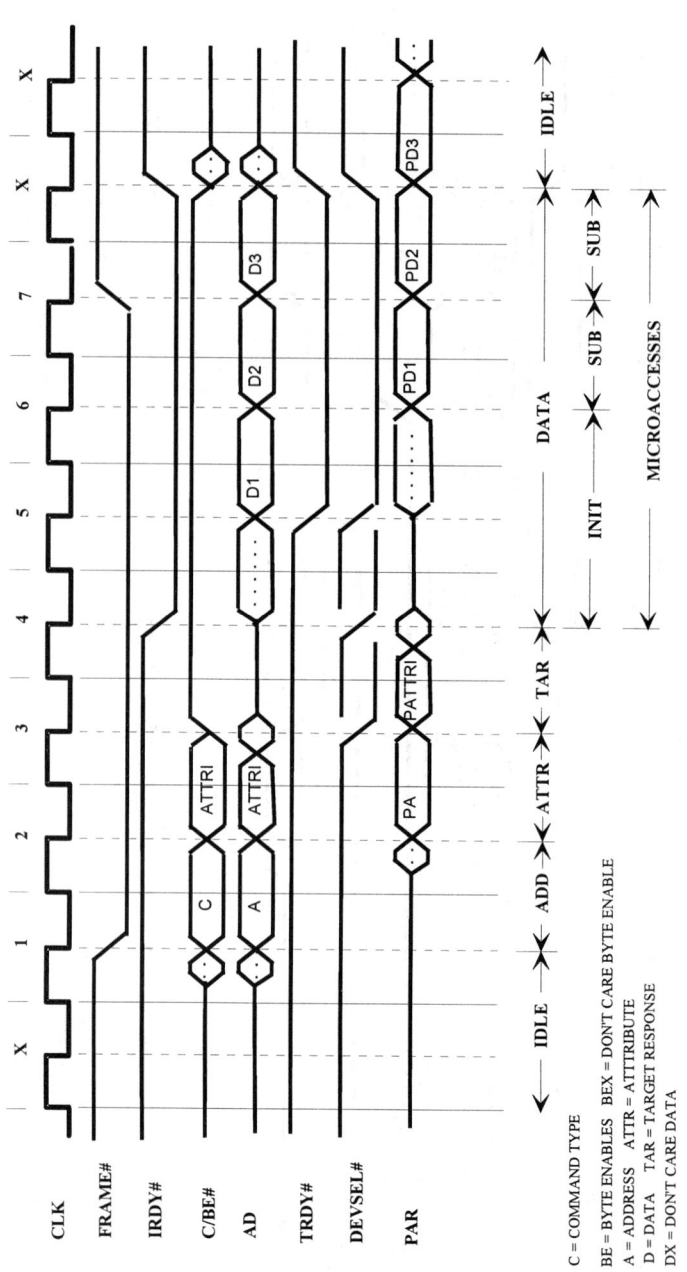

Figure 3-17: PCI-X Burst Read Transaction with Ready in Initial Microaccess

3.1 BRIDGES AND INTERBUS SEGMENT OPERATIONS

INTRODUCTION

Integral to the operations and features of the PCI and PCI-X bus segments are the bus transaction related protocols through a bridge and between independent PCI and PCI-X bus segments. As discussed in Chapter 2: *PCI and PCI-X System Architectural Overview*, there is a hierarchy of bus segments. The protocol, particularly the bus transaction termination protocol, permits the linking of bus segments with bridges. Even though the term "bridge" is used, the associated bridge protocol also applies to interconnect circuitry between the PCI or PCI-X bus segments and non-PCI buses or circuitry (*i.e.*, internal circuitry of an ASIC). The bus segments are usually PCI and PCI-X bus segments, but the protocol also applies to HOST and LEGACY bus segments. In order to avoid deadlock conditions or errors in bus transaction executions, the interface circuitry should follow the same protocols as bridges. Consequently, the information presented here for the different bridges and the interbus segment operation can also be applied to the operation of interfaces and the interaction between the PCI and PCI-X bus segments and non-PCI bus segments or circuitry.

OVERVIEW OF PCI DELAYED TRANSACTION AND PCI-X SPLIT TRANSACTION PROTOCOLS

Before providing an overview of bridge and interbus segment operation, there are two architectural considerations: Delayed Transactions and Split Transactions.

For porting through a bridge, the PCI local bus specification defines posting bus transactions and the Delayed Transaction protocol, and the PCI-X addendum specification defines posting bus transactions and the Split Transaction protocol. For both bus specifications, posting bus transactions only applies to memory write transactions, and Delayed Transaction and Split Transaction protocols only apply to read and non-memory write transactions. The Delayed Transaction and Split Transaction protocols do not apply to memory write transactions.

The purpose of each protocol is make large multiple bus segment platforms (also known as "systems") possible and to provide performance across multiple bus segments. In platforms with multiple bus segments, bus masters are interacting with targets on the same bus segment or with targets on other bus segments. It would be impractical to assume that a bus master executing a bus transaction going from one bus segment to another through a bridge will always find the destination bus segment immediately available. That is, a bus master on the destination bus segment may already be executing bus transactions on the destination bus segment that prevents the bridge from immediately porting a bus transaction from the source bus segment. Consequently, without the Delayed Transaction and Split Transaction protocols, it is very probable that a bus master executing a bus transaction going from one bus segment to another will have to repeat a bus transaction many times until the destination bus segment is available. The problem is further compounded when one considers that a bus master on the source bus segment may have to cross multiple bus segments to get to the destination bus segment containing the target. The probability that all bus segments between the source and destination bus segments are immediately available is extremely low; consequently, platform performance will be poor.

One of the simplest methods to address this problem is to post bus transactions in the bridge between the source and destination bus segments. A write transaction can provide address and data to the bridge. The bridge attached to the source bus can buffer the write transaction and proceed to process it on the destination bus segment when available. The bus master on the source bus segment assumes the write transaction will occur at the destination bus segment by the bridge on its behalf. Most importantly, the bus master can immediately release the source bus to other bus master. These other bus masters on the source bus segment can access other targets on the source bus segment or post other write transactions in the bridge. The bridge in parallel is completing to the target on the destination bus segment the previously posted write transaction. If the destination bus segment is multiple bus segments away from the source bus segment, each bridge can act on behalf of the bus master on the source bus segment. Most importantly, bus activity on each bus segment is not held up until the write transaction is actually completed at the target on the destination bus segment.

The posting of write transactions is only possible because write data is available simultaneously with the address. By convention, the memory address space is the only platform resource that can receive write data long after the source of the write data (bus master) assumes it has been received at the target (posted). Write data to an I/O or configuration address space cannot be posted. That is, whenever the source bus master completes a write transaction to the I/O or configuration address space, by convention the data has been actually written in real time at the target. If the posting of transactions cannot be applied to I/O and configuration address spaces, and of course posting of bus transactions cannot work for read transactions (no data), there is a need to provide solutions to maintain platform performance for non-memory write transactions across multiple bus segments. To address this problem that not all bus transactions can be posted, the PCI local bus specification defines the Delayed Transaction protocol, and the PCI-X addendum specification defines the Split Transaction protocol. Similar discussions apply to interrupt acknowledge and special transactions, neither of which can be posted in a bridge

> **The PCI local bus specification and PCI-X addendum specification permit I/O transactions to be posted in a bridge provided the platform designer understands the consequences. That is, the platform is either designed for or the software only implements a posted I/O write transaction when no negative side effects will occur. This book will assume that NO I/O transactions are posted.**

The Delayed Transaction protocol is defined only for PCI compliant bus segments and bridges, and relies on Retry termination of the source bus transaction. The Retry termination defined by the PCI local bus specification requires the repeat of the associated bus transaction and the execution of the bus transaction via Delayed Requests and Delayed Completions (elements of Delayed Transaction protocol) by the PCI/PCI BRIDGE. The elements of the Delayed Transaction protocol do not require any unique bus transactions. The key concept is that the address and data (information) of a bus transaction are latched by the PCI/PCI BRIDGE. The bus transaction is terminated with a Retry termination on the source bus segment and the PCI/PCI BRIDGE continues the execution of the associated bus transaction on the destination bus segment. The PCI bus master repeats the source bus transaction at a later time (or times) and the source bus transaction will be completed by the PCI/PCI BRIDGE (for example, when read data can be provided). The key concept is that a bus transaction is not defined as completed until it is terminated without a Retry termination by PCI/PCI BRIDGE. See Subchapter 3.2, Chapter 4: *Functional Interaction Between PCI, and PCI-X Resources*, and Chapter 7: *Bridge and Interface Protocol* for more information.

The Split Transaction protocol is only defined for PCI-X compliant bus segments and bridges, and relies on Split Response termination of a source bus transaction by the PCI-X/PCI-X BRIDGE. The Split Response termination defined by the PCI-X addendum specification is followed by the execution of unique bus transactions called split completion transactions (elements of the Split Transaction protocol) porting through the PCI-X/PCI-X BRIDGE. Split completion transactions are different than any other PCI or PCI-X bus transaction. The PCI-X bus master does not repeat the source bus transaction as in the case of the Delayed Transaction Protocol. The Split Transaction protocol requires the target (non-bridge) on the destination bus segment to source split completion transactions to return completion information to the PCI-X bus master of the source bus transaction (for example, data for the read transaction for the source bus transaction terminated by Split Response termination). Consequently, the Split Transaction protocol requires the source bus transaction to contain attributes (information about the PCI-X bus master of the source bus segment transaction). The attributes allow the target (non-bridge) on the destination bus segment that becomes the PCI-X bus master of split completion transactions (the split completion transactions contain source bus transaction completion information) to send the split completion transactions to the correct PCI-X bus master of the source bus transaction. See Subchapter 3.2, Chapter 4: *Functional Interaction Between PCI and PCI-X Resources,* and Chapter 7: *Bridge and Interface Protocol* for more information.

In addition to interbus segment operation as outlined above; the concepts of posting memory write transactions, the Delayed Transaction protocol, and Split Transaction protocol can be applied to interfaces between the bus segment and the internal circuitry of the target (ASIC for example). That is, accesses by a bus master to the actual target (non-bridge) can include the posted transactions (PCI and PCI-X), Delayed Transaction protocol (PCI), and Split Transaction protocol (PCI-X) in the same fashion as the access of a target (non-bridge) through a bridge. There are no restrictions in the PCI local bus specification and PCI-X addendum specification that prevent the interface of the target (non-bridge) to the bus segment to have bridge-like attributes. See Subchapter 3.2 and Chapter 4: *Functional Interaction between PCI and PCI-X Resources* for more information.

FUNCTIONAL INTERACTION BETWEEN PCI AND PCI-X RESOURCES

This chapter consists of the following subchapters:

4.0   GENERAL CONSIDERATIONS

INTRODUCTION

As outlined in Chapter 2, the PCI bus segment supports both PCI bus masters and targets. In platforms with multiple bus segments, a PCI/PCI BRIDGE can operate as a PCI resource on behalf of resources on other PCI bus segments. Similarly, different buses like HOST or LEGACY can attach to a PCI bus segment via the

HOST/PCI BRIDGE and PCI LEGACY BRIDGE, respectively. PCI/PCI BRIDGEs, the HOST/PCI BRIDGE, and the PCI LEGACY BRIDGE can be either a PCI bus master or a target attached to the PCI bus segment. PCI bus masters include PCI bus resources that become bus masters, the HOST CPU via the HOST/PCI BRIDGE, and LEGACY bus masters via the PCI/LEGACY BRIDGE. The targets are those PCI resources addressed by the PCI bus master, HOST memory via the HOST/PCI BRIDGE, and LEGACY resources via the PCI/LEGACY BRIDGE. The key concept is that a platform consists of multiple buses and bridges. For a given PCI bus segment, other PCI and non-PCI resources interact as PCI bus masters and targets via the use of bridges. Consequently, for the discussions in this chapter and other chapters, the focus is on the PCI bus master and targets that reside on PCI bus segments. The actual PCI bus masters and targets on a specific PCI bus segment may be non-PCI resources represented via bridges to that segment. Similarly, the actual PCI bus masters and targets on a specific PCI bus segment may be PCI resources on other PCI bus segments represented via bridges to that bus segment.

According to the PCI local bus specification, the PCI bus, when compared to more common LEGACY buses like ISA, has unique architecture attributes as follows:

- The address and data are multiplexed onto shared signal lines (AD), and the command and data size information are multiplexed onto shared signal lines (C/BE#). Consequently, the bus transaction is divided into ADDRESS and DATA PHASES. During the ADDRESS PHASE, the address and command are presented. During the DATA PHASE, the data and active byte lanes are presented.

- The address space is a full 32 bits with an option to extend it to 64 bits on a transaction-to-transaction basis.

- The data width of the bus is defined as 32 data bits with an option to extend it to 64 data bits on a transaction-to-transaction basis.

- The basic bus transaction to PCI resources is a BURST bus transaction. The BURST bus transaction allows multiple data accesses during the transaction. When a BURST bus transaction accesses the resource only once in the transaction it is defined as a SINGLE bus transaction.

- Between bus transactions the signal lines are driven to a logical "1" by pull-up resistors or to a stable level by a PCI bus master or central resource.

- There are several other bus activities besides bus transactions to memory, I/O, and configuration address spaces. These other activities include a non-specific message broadcast to all PCI targets (special transaction) and an interrupt acknowledge transaction. Other bus attributes include PCI bus master's ownership, and a target lock protocol to support LEGACY bus protocol and to prevent deadlock conditions within bridges.

■ Parity is supported across the address, data, and control signal lines. Also, a more complete error reporting structure is defined.

■ There is no byte swapping between byte lanes on the bus. PCI bus masters and targets must support a full 32 data bit interface. There are unique requirements for the optional 64 data bit extension.

■ A bus transaction can be terminated with or without data.

■ In addition to the target, the PCI bus master can prolong the completion of the bus transaction. The completion of the bus transaction requires a handshake between the bus master and the target.

■ The CLK signal line periods between bus transactions vary depending on bus ownership, the previous bus transaction, the type of bus transaction, and the targets involved in the bus transaction.

■ There is no central DMA (direct memory access) controller that transfers data between PCI memory and I/O targets.

■ Except for the SERR#, RST#, and INT# signal lines, the PCI signal lines are synchronous with the CLK signal line.

■ There is no memory refresh bus transaction across the PCI bus.

In the same fashion as discussed above, some of the bus segments in a system can be PCI-X bus segments. The architecture for a resource on one PCI-X bus segment to communicate to another resource on another PCI-X bus segment is similar to that of PCI resources. A PCI addendum bus specification defines PCI-X/PCI-X BRIDGEs. PCI-X/PCI-X BRIDGEs operate in the same fashion as PCI/PCI BRDIGEs. That is, both types of bridges represent resources on one bus segment on other bus segments as bus masters and targets. The PCI-X/PCI-X BRIDGEs also provide the interconnection between PCI-X and PCI bus segments. Under this operation, the PCI-X bus transactions are translated to PCI compliant transactions and vice versa.

The PCI-X bus segment can also be connected to HOST or Legacy buses via a HOST/PCI-X BRIDGE and PCI-X/LEGACY BRIDGE, respectively.

The comparison of PCI-X to the common LEGACY buses is the same as outlined above for the PCI comparison to common LEGACY buses.

There is an additional important consideration relating to a system containing multiple bus segments of different types (*i.e.*, HOST, PCI, PCI-X, and Legacy). The PCI-X addendum bus specification defines the operation of a PCI-X bus segment to be compliant to the PCI local bus specification if a single PCI-only compliant device resides on the bus segment. Consequently, all of the PCI-X devices that may reside on a bus segment with PCI complaint devices must be able to operate according to the PCI local bus specification. Please see further discussion on this topic later in the subchapter.

PCI DIFFERENCES BETWEEN BUS TRANSACTIONS

As outlined in the above introduction, there are several types of bus transactions executed on the PCI bus. In the following discussion, the interaction of the PCI resources will be described in terms of bus transactions to memory, I/O and configuration address spaces, special transactions, and interrupt acknowledge transactions. The bus transactions to memory, I/O, and configuration address spaces imply that the PCI bus master accesses data within a target by providing a specific address. These bus transactions are memory read and write, I/O read and write, and configuration read and write. The term "memory read transactions" relative to PCI includes memory read, Memory Read Multiple (MRM), and Memory Read Line (MRL) transactions. The term "memory write transactions" relative to PCI includes memory write and Memory Write and Invalidate (MWI) transactions. The memory and I/O transactions can be executed with either 32 data bit or 64 data bit bus transactions. The configuration transactions can only be executed as 32 data bit bus transactions and never as 64 data bit bus transactions. All PCI resources are required to support the configuration transactions; all other bus transactions are optional.

---

64 data bit I/O targets can be implemented, but there is no benefit to justify the increased complexity; it is therefore strongly recommended that 64 data bit I/O targets not be implemented. For the purposes of this book, I/O targets are only 32 data bits in size. If a 64 data bit PCI I/O target is implemented, the 64 data bit PCI protocol applied to memory targets would also apply to I/O targets.

The interrupt acknowledge transaction returns an interrupt vector to the HOST CPU only from the interrupt controller without the HOST CPU providing an address. It is executed by the HOST/PCI BRIDGE on behalf of the HOST CPU to the LEVEL 1 PCI bus (0). The target is the PCI bus resource that contains the interrupt controller, of which there is only one per platform. An interrupt acknowledge transaction is only defined as a 32 data bit bus transaction and never as a 64 data bit bus transaction.

The special transaction broadcasts a message to all targets on the same bus segment without providing a specific address (the special transaction cannot be ported through a PCI/PCI BRIDGE to another bus segment). The PCI bus master can be any PCI resource. The target can be any of the PCI bus resources on the same bus as the PCI bus master or via PCI/PCI BRIDGEs to PCI resources on other bus segments. A special transaction can only port through a bridge as a Type 1 configuration transaction. A special transaction is only defined as a 32 data bit bus transaction and never as a 64 data bit bus transaction.

Collectively, bus transactions to memory, I/O and configuration address spaces, special transactions, and interrupt acknowledge transactions are simply referred to as "bus transactions". The different types of bus transactions are encoded in the C/BE# signal lines during the address phase of the bus transaction. See Chapter 5: *Signal Line Definition* for more information.

As outlined in Chapter 3: *Generic PCI Bus Transactions* and summarized below, the PCI bus protocol seamlessly switches from a SINGLE bus transaction to a BURST bus transaction for accesses to memory and to I/O and configuration address spaces. A SINGLE bus transaction provides one specific address for a SINGLE access of data. It begins with the assertion of the FRAME# signal line in the ADDRESS PHASE. If the FRAME# signal line is asserted when the IRDY# signal line is asserted with the first data access during the DATA PHASE, the SINGLE bus transaction becomes a BURST bus transaction. Within the BURST bus transaction protocol, each of the data accesses during the DATA PHASE is called a microaccess. The address provided in the ADDRESS PHASE is used for the initial microaccess in the DATA PHASE. Addresses for subsequent microaccesses in the DATA PHASE are based on the address provided in the ADDRESS PHASE and incremented (linearly increasing or Cacheline wrap) for each subsequent microaccess. During the ADDRESS PHASE the AD signal lines contain the address of the target. During the DATA PHASE, these signal lines contain the accessed data. The type of bus transaction is encoded onto a binary pattern (command) driven onto the C/BE# signal lines during the ADDRESS PHASE. During the DATA PHASE, these signal lines identify the byte lanes on the AD signal lines to be accessed. A SINGLE bus transaction means that a single byte (8 data bits), word (16 data bits), triple byte (24 data bits), or double word (32 data bits) is accessed via the AD[31::0] signal lines. See the latter part of this chapter for the discussion of 64 data bit bus transactions.

For special bus transactions, the ability to switch from SINGLE to BURST bus transactions is similar to that described above except no address is provided. The interrupt acknowledge transaction can only be executed as a SINGLE bus transaction with no address provided. See Chapter 6: *Detailed Bus Transaction Operation* for more information.

PCI-X DIFFERENCES BETWEEN BUS TRANSACTIONS

PCI-X expands and modifies the definition of bus transactions. As outlined above, all of the PCI bus transactions (defined via the commands encoded in the C/BE# signal lines during the ADDRESS PHASE) can be executed as either SINGLE or BURST bus transactions with the exception of the SINGLE interrupt acknowledge transaction. The PCI-X local bus specification expanded and modified the definition of the commands and the associated bus transactions. Referring to Table 4-1, both PCI local bus and PCI-X addendum specifications support bus transactions to access memory, I/O, and configuration address spaces and the associated bus transactions. Also, both PCI local bus and PCI-X addendum specifications support interrupt acknowledge and special transactions. The PCI-X addendum specification has redefined the commands associated with the address spaces and has redefined the implementation of which commands can be executed by SINGLE versus BURST bus transactions as follows:

- ■ The PCI local bus specification commands of memory read multiple, memory read line, and memory write and invalidate are not defined in the PCI-X addendum specification. The PCI-X addendum specification added commands of DWORD memory read, memory write block, memory read block, alias memory write block, alias memory read block, and split completion. The term "memory read transactions" as used by the PCI-X addendum specification includes memory read, memory read block, and alias memory read block transactions (unless otherwise specifically noted). The term "memory write transactions" as used by the PCI-X addendum specification includes memory write, memory write block, and alias memory write block transactions (unless otherwise specifically noted).

- ■ The PCI-X addendum specification restricts the commands that can be implemented with BURST bus transactions. For all commands (see Table 4-1) defined as DWORD commands, only a SINGLE bus transaction (one DATA PHASE) can be executed. The commands defined as BURST commands execute as either a SINGLE bus transaction (one DATA PHASE) or BURST bus transaction (multiple DATA PHASES). See Chapter 6: *Detailed Bus Transaction Operation* for more information.

In Table 4-1, distinction is made between PCI and PCI-X SINGLE bus transactions, and PCI and PCI-X BURST bus transactions. This reflects the fact that the exact transaction protocol for similarly named transactions differ in exact transaction protocol.

> Table 4-1 focuses on SINGLE and BURST transactions on the same bus segment. The porting of commands through a bridge is more complex. In the case of PCI, as will be discussed later in this chapter, some of the commands cannot be ported through a bridge with BURST transactions. In the case of PCI-X, some commands ported through a bridge do not change the type of transaction that can be applied to a command. That is, as will be discussed later, all DWORD commands can only be implemented as SINGLE transactions whether executed on the same bus segment or ported through a bridge. BURST memory write commands can be implemented as SINGLE or BURST transactions whether executed on the same bus segment or ported through a bridge. BURST memory read commands can be implemented as SINGLE or BURST transactions on the same bus segment, but are required be terminated with split response termination when porting through a bridge, thus requiring both SINGLE and BURST memory read transactions to become SINGLE transactions.

■ As discussed above for the PCI local bus specification, the data size of certain commands is restricted. The PCI-X addendum specification has placed similar restrictions on data size for specific commands. Of particular note is that I/O transactions, configuration, special, interrupt acknowledge, and DWORD memory read transactions are required to be DWORD in size according to the PCI-X addendum bus specification. See Table 4-2.

■ Both the PCI local bus specification and the PCI-X addendum specification define specific address space size (number of valid address bits in the ADDRESS PHASE). The PCI-X addendum specification has placed an additional requirement on the memory address space. A PCI-X bus master that accesses the memory address space and the associated PCI-X memory targets are required support the full 64 address bits (support of DUAL ADDRESS command). When accessing the first four gigabytes of the memory address space, only 32 address bits are required. See Table 4-3.

C/BE# [3::0] ADDRESS PHASE Binary MSB to LSB	Name (PCI)	Name (PCI-X)	Bus Transaction Protocol Between Master and Target on Same Bus Segment Bus Transactions: PCI SINGLE = PST PCI BURST = PBT PCI-X SINGLE = PXST PCI-X BURST = PXBT	
	NO GROUP NAME	DWORD COMMANDS		
			PCI	PCI-X
0000	Interrupt Acknowledge	Interrupt Acknowledge	PST	PXST
0001	Special	Special	PST PBT	PXST
0010	I/O Read	I/O Read	PST PBT	PXST
0011	I/O Write	I/O Write	PST PBT	PXST
1010	Config. Read	Config. Read	PST PBT	PXST
1011	Config. Write	Config.Write	PST PBT	PXST
0110	Memory Read (2)	DWORD Memory Read (2)	PST PBT	PXST
	NO GROUP NAME	BURST COMMANDS		
0111	Memory Write (1)	Memory Write (1)	PST PBT	PXST PXBT
1000	Reserved	Alias Memory Read Block (2, 3)	na	PXST PXBT
1001	Reserved	Alias Memory Write Block (1)	na	PXST PXBT
1100	Memory Read Multiple (2)	Split Completion	PST PBT	PXST PXBT
1110	Memory Read Line (2)	Memory Read Block (2, 3)	PST PBT	PXST PXBT
1111	Memory Write Invalidate (1)	Memory Write Block (1)	PST PBT	PXST PXBT
	OTHERS	OTHERS		
1101	DAC	DAC	na	na
0100	Reserved	Reserved	na	na
0101	Reserved	Reserved	na	na

Table 4-1: Comparison of PCI and PCI-X Commands and Transactions on the Same Bus Segment

Notes: (1) Collectively called "BURST memory write" unless otherwise noted.
(2) Collectively called "memory read" unless otherwise noted.
(3) Collectively called "BURST memory read" unless otherwise noted.

C/BE# [3::0] ADDRESS PHASE Binary MSB to LSB	Name (PCI)	Name (PCI-X)	Data Size of Bus Transactions DW = 32 data bits QW = 64 data bits Bus Master can insert Wait States = BMW Target can insert Wait States = TW	
	NO GROUP NAME	**DWORD COMMANDS**		
			PCI	**PCI-X**
0000	Interrupt Acknowledge	Interrupt Acknowledge	DW BMW TW	DW BMW TW
0001	Special	Special	DW	DW
0010	I/O Read	I/O Read	DW BMW TW (QW is possible but not encouraged)	DW BMW TW
0011	I/O Write	I/O Write	DW BMW TW (QW is possible but not encouraged)	DW BMW TW
1010	Config. Read	Config. Read	DW BMW TW	DW BMW TW
1011	Config. Write	Config.Write	DW BMW TW	DW BMW TW
0110	Memory Read (2)	DWORD Memory Read (2)	DW QW BMW TW	DW BMW TW
	NO GROUP NAME	**BURST COMMANDS**		
0111	Memory Write (1)	Memory Write (1)	DW QW BMW TW	DW QW BMW TW (Pairs Only)
1000	Reserved	Alias Memory Read Block (2,3)	na	DW QW BMW TW
1001	Reserved	Alias Memory Write Block (1)	na	DW QW BMW TW (Pairs Only)
1100	Memory Read Multiple (2)	Split Completion	DW QW BMW TW	DW QW BMW TW (Pairs Only)
1110	Memory Read Line (2)	Memory Read Block (2,3)	DW QW BMW TW	DW QW BMW TW
1111	Memory Write Invalidate (1)	Memory Write Block (1)	DW QW BMW TW	DW QW BMW TW (Pairs Only)
	OTHERS	**OTHERS**		
1101	DAC	DAC	na	na
0100	Reserved	Reserved	na	na
0101	Reserved	Reserved	na	na

Table 4-2: Comparison of PCI and PCI-X Commands and Data Size and Wait State Support

Notes: (1) Collectively called "BURST memory write" unless otherwise noted.
(2) Collectively called "memory read" unless otherwise noted.
(3) Collectively called "BURST memory read" unless otherwise noted.

C/BE# [3::0] ADDRESS PHASE Binary MSB to LSB	Name (PCI)	Name (PCI-X)	Number of Address bits used for Address Space for a Specific Bus Transaction	
	NO GROUP NAME	**DWORD COMMANDS**		
			PCI	**PCI-X**
0000	Interrupt Acknowledge	Interrupt Acknowledge	na	na
0001	Special	Special	na	na
0010	I/O Read	I/O Read	32	32
0011	I/O Write	I/O Write	32	32
1010	Config. Read	Config. Read	8 plus IDSEL per PCI device	8 plus IDSEL per PCI-X device
1011	Config. Write	Config.Write	8 plus IDSEL per PCI device	8 plus IDSEL per PCI-X device
0110	Memory Read (2)	DWORD Memory Read (2)	32/64	64 (4)
	NO GROUP NAME	**BURST COMMANDS**		
0111	Memory Write (1)	Memory Write (1)	32/64	64 (4)
1000	Reserved	Alias Memory Read Block (2,3)	na	64 (4)
1001	Reserved	Alias Memory Write Block (1)	na	64 (4)
1100	Memory Read Multiple (2)	Split Completion	32/64	32
1110	Memory Read Line (2)	Memory Read Block (2,3)	32/64	64 (4)
1111	Memory Write Invalidate (1)	Memory Write Block (1)	32/64	64 (4)
	OTHERS	**OTHERS**		
1101	DAC	DAC	na	na
0100	Reserved	Reserved	na	na
0101	Reserved	Reserved	na	na

Table 4-3: Comparison of PCI and PCI-X Commands and Address Space

Notes: (1) Collectively called "BURST memory write" unless otherwise noted.
(2) Collectively called "memory read" unless otherwise noted.
(3) Collectively called "BURST memory read" unless otherwise noted.
(4) If the access is in first four gigabytes, only 32 address bits are needed (DUAL ADDRESS Command not implemented). The upper order 32 address bits are assumed to be a logical "0"

PCI SPECIFIC

PCI MEMORY MAPPED I/O

The PCI local bus specification does not define a unique bus transaction for memory mapped I/O. Unless otherwise specified, it is assumed that the memory address space contains memory mapped I/O. Memory mapped I/O can contain both regular DRAM type memory and I/O registers. The target defines the portion of memory address space associated with the Memory Base Address Register (MBAR) in the configuration address space as NOT memory mapped I/O when the Prefetchable bit is set to logical "1". Similarly, PCI/PCI BRIDGES define a portion of the memory address space as NOT memory mapped I/O via the Memory Base, Memory Limit, Prefetchable Memory Base, and Prefetchable Memory Limit registers in the configuration address space. A memory address range containing memory mapped I/O cannot be marked as prefetchable in the configuration address space. As will be discussed in detail later, a memory address can be identified as prefetchable if there are no negative side affects of multiple readings and possible discarding of the data read.

> As will be discussed later, if the PCI bus master executes an MRM or MRL transaction to a memory address, it is the responsibility of the PCI bus master to determine that there will be no negative side effects. The target and associated bridges will execute the MRM and MRL transactions independent of the value of the associated prefetchable bits and registers in the target and bridges for the associated memory address range.

PCI BYTE LANE OPERATION

The PCI local bus specification dynamically identifies the data size of each bus transaction. The central resource does not swap data between byte lanes; thus all AD[31::0] signal lines are required to be supported by all PCI resources. The AD[31::0] signal lines contain four byte lanes (AD[7::0] signal lines comprise the first byte lane, AD[15::8] signal lines are the second byte lane, and so forth.). The protocol for byte lane operation on the PCI bus backplane is as follows:

- Any combination of asserted and deasserted C/BE#[3::0] signal lines are allowed, including all of them deasserted. These signal lines are driven valid for the entire DATA PHASE of a bus transaction.

- No byte lane swapping occurs between the byte lanes of the AD[31::0] signal lines.

- A bus transaction does not always mean that data is read or written. During the DATA PHASE, the C/BE#[3::0] signal lines indicate which byte lanes contain valid data. If none of the C/BE#[3::0] signal lines are asserted, no data is driven onto the AD[31::0] signal lines during the bus transaction. Under this condition, the target of the bus transaction can immediately assert a TRDY# signal line, but immediate assertion is not required. No bus transaction error is indicated unless a parity error occurs.

■ The C/BE#[3::0] signal lines for a given microaccess of a BURST bus transaction can enable different bytes relative to previous and subsequent microaccesses. The byte lanes do not have to be continuous. This applies to byte lanes identified within a specific bus transaction or byte lanes identified from one bus transaction to another.

■ When the AD[31::0] signal lines are not driven with valid data per the assertion of the associated C/BE#[3::0] signal lines, they are required to be driven to a stable level throughout the bus transaction by the PCI bus master. When the AD[63::32] signal lines are not driven with valid data and the C/BE#[7::4] signal lines are not driven with valid information (REQ64# signal line not asserted), these signal lines are driven to a logical "1" by pull-up resistors throughout the bus transaction.

> The requirements for valid parity generation and checking over the AD[31::0] lines apply even when no data is accessed (*i.e.,* C/BE#[3::0] are deasserted).

See Subchapters 4.6 to 4.9 for the discussions of 64 data bit bus transactions and for bus transactions that begin as a 64 data bit bus transaction but are required to complete as 32 data bit bus transactions.

> The 32 data bits reflect a block of data addressed. It does not mean that 32 data bits are actually accessed.

PCI PARK

The PCI local bus specification defines a protocol that is not found in many other buses, such as ISA. Although most buses allow signal lines to float when no bus transactions are executed, the PCI bus specification defines a protocol that prevents the floating of signal lines by "parking" the signal line at a PCI resource. When the PCI bus master (REQ# and GNT# signal lines are both asserted) is between bus transactions, the bus is IDLE (FRAME# and IRDY# signal lines both deasserted). The AD[31::0], C/BE#[3::0], FRAME#, IRDY#, and PAR signal lines are driven to stable levels by the PCI bus master. The LOCK# signal line is asserted by the Lock master or driven to a logical "1" by a pull-up resistor. The other signal lines are driven by other resources, or are driven to logical "1" by pull-up resistors or to stable levels by the central resource. When the REQ# and GNT# signal lines of a PCI resource are both deasserted (by definition it is not a PCI bus master or Park master), it is required that no signal lines be driven (except for the LOCK# signal line and, if appropriate, the SERR# signal line). The central arbiter is required to assert the GNT# signal line of a PCI resource to request that it become Park master and drive the AD[31::0], C/BE#[3::0], and PAR signal lines to a stable level. The other signal lines are driven by other resources, or are driven to logical "1" by pull-up resistors or to stable levels by the central resource. By definition, a PCI bus resource with its associated REQ# signal line deasserted and GNT# signal line asserted is a Park master. See Chapter 9: *Bus Ownership*, for details.

> **The Park master may be any platform resource selected by the central arbiter. If all GNT# signal lines are deasserted, the central arbiter or possibly the central resource becomes the Park master.**

When a 32 data bit PCI bus master becomes a Park master, it drives the AD[31::0], C/BE#[3::0], and PAR signal lines to a stable level. The AD[63::32], C/BE#[7::4], and PAR64 signal lines are driven to a logical "1" by pull-up resistors.

"PCI 16 CLOCK" RULES

According to the PCI local bus specification, a target must complete a SINGLE bus transaction or the initial microaccess of a BURST bus transaction within sixteen CLK signal line periods ("PCI 16 clock" rule) from the assertion of the FRAME# signal line. If data access is not possible, the STOP# signal line must be asserted on the seventeenth rising edge of the CLK signal line measured from the first rising edge of the CLK signal line when the FRAME# signal line is asserted. For a write transaction, the data is either accepted by the target (with or without posting) or a Retry termination is executed within the confines of the "PCI 16 clock" rule. For a read transaction, the target must provide the data or execute Retry termination within the confines of the "16 clock" rule. The target is required to implement the "PCI 16 clock" rule relative for a SINGLE bus transaction or the initial microaccess of a BURST bus transaction. Adherence to the "PCI 16 clock" rule may require the target to execute a Retry termination. See Chapter 8: *Master and Target Termination* and Chapter 14: *Latency and Performance* for more information

> **The convention of this book is to use the term *"PCI 16 clock" rule* only as applied to PCI bus transactions and *"PCI-X 16 clock" rule* only applied to PCI-X bus transactions.**

"PCI 8 CLOCK" RULES

According to the PCI local bus specification, the target is required to implement the "8 clock" rule with the subsequent microaccesses of a BURST bus transaction. The net effect of the "PCI 8 clock" rule is to place limits on the length of a BURST bus transaction. The restrictions do not apply to a SINGLE bus transaction or to the initial microaccess of a BURST bus transaction. The "PCI 8 clock" rule simply forces the target to execute a Disconnect termination request under the following conditions:

- All subsequent microaccesses of a BURST bus transaction are governed by the "PCI 8 clock" rule.

- The initial microaccess is completed when the IRDY# and TRDY# signal lines are both asserted at a CLK signal line rising edge. The target will begin counting on the subsequent CLK rising edge and continues counting until one of the following occurs:

  - If the TRDY# signal line is asserted simultaneously with a count value of eight or less, the bus transaction is allowed to complete with Completion termination whenever the IRDY# signal line is asserted.

    OR

  - If the TRDY# signal line is not asserted when the count value reaches eight, the STOP# signal line must be asserted (TRDY# or STOP# signal line will be sampled asserted on the ninth rising edge of the CLK signal line relative to the first rising edge of the CLK signal line when the IRDY# and TRDY# signal lines are both asserted in the previous microaccess). The assertion of the STOP# signal line results in a Disconnect termination without data.

See Chapter 8: *Master and Target Termination* and *Chapter 14: Latency and Performance* for more information

The convention of this book is use the term *"PCI 8 clock" rule* to only apply to PCI bus transactions and *"PCI-X 16 clock" rule* to only apply to PCI-X bus transactions.

SUMMARY OF "PCI 16 CLOCK" AND "PCI 8 CLOCK" RULES

In summary, the "PCI 16 clock" rule *applies* to the SINGLE bus transactions and initial microaccess of BURST bus transactions of the following:

- Memory transactions
- I/O transactions

- Configuration transactions
- Interrupt acknowledge transactions (see shaded box below)

This is a brief summary. Please see Chapter 8: *Master and Target Termination* for more detailed information.

> The "PCI 16 clock" rule *DOES NOT apply* to the above PCI bus transactions during the initialization time (from RST# signal line deasserted to 2^{25} CLK signal line periods later), when executing from BOOT ROM, or when copying expansion ROM to memory. Note: If the device is accessing its expansion ROM after it has been hot inserted, the aforementioned "PCI 16 clock" rule relative to target termination *DOES* apply.
>
> The present revision of the PCI local bus specification states that only SINGLE interrupt acknowledge transactions are executed. Earlier reversions implied that a BURST interrupt acknowledge transaction was defined.
>
> The "PCI 16 clock" rule does not apply to special transactions, in that there is no specific target to assert the DEVSEL# signal line.

In summary, the "PCI 8 clock" rule *applies* to subsequent microaccesses of BURST bus transactions of the following:

- Memory transactions
- I/O transactions
- Configuration transactions
- Interrupt acknowledge transactions (see shaded box below)

> The "PCI 8 clock" rule *DOES NOT apply* to the above PCI bus transactions during the initialization time (from RST# signal line deasserted to 2^{25} CLK signal line periods later), when executing from BOOT ROM, or when copying expansion ROM to memory. Note: If the device is accessing its expansion ROM after it has been hot inserted, the aforementioned "PCI 16 clock" rule relative to target termination *DOES* apply.
>
> The present revision of the PCI local bus specification states that only SINGLE interrupt acknowledge transactions are executed. Earlier reversions implied that a BURST interrupt acknowledge transaction was defined.

> **The "PCI 8 clock" rule does not apply to special transactions because there is no specific target to assert the DEVSEL# signal line.**

PCI SIGNAL LINE OWNERSHIP DURING BUS TRANSACTIONS WITH 32 DATA BIT RESOURCES (PCI BUS MASTER AND TARGET)

During memory read and write (including memory read multiple, memory read line, and memory write and invalidate), I/O, configuration, interrupt acknowledge, and special transactions; the signal lines are owned by different PCI bus resources. A PCI resource owns the signal line when it is the only resource (other than pull-up resistors for some of the signal lines) that can drive the signal line during a portion of the bus transaction. In the following discussions, the PAR and PAR64 signal lines relative to a specific bus transaction PHASE are actually delayed from "that" specific bus transaction PHASE. The protocol is as follows:

- FRAME#, IRDY#, C/BE#[3::0], and REQx# signal lines are owned by the PCI bus master for any bus transaction.

- During memory write, I/O write, and configuration write transactions, the PCI bus master owns the AD[31::0] and PAR signal lines during both ADDRESS and DATA PHASES.

- During special transactions, the PCI bus master owns the AD[31::0] and PAR signal lines during both ADDRESS and DATA PHASES.

- During memory read, I/O read, and configuration read transactions, the PCI bus master owns the AD[31::0] and PAR signal lines during the ADDRESS PHASE. The target owns these signal lines during the DATA PHASE. The ownership of these signal lines changes from the PCI bus master to the target in the first CLK signal line period of the DATA PHASE.

- During interrupt acknowledge transactions, the PCI bus master owns the AD[31::0] and PAR signal lines during the ADDRESS PHASE. The target owns these signal lines during the DATA PHASE. The ownership of these signal lines changes from the PCI bus master to the target in the first CLK signal line period of the DATA PHASE.

- During memory, I/O, and configuration transactions, the TRDY#, DEVSEL#, and STOP# signal lines are owned by the target.

- During interrupt acknowledge transactions, the TRDY#, DEVSEL#, and STOP# signal lines are owned by the target.

- During special transactions, the TRDY#, DEVSEL#, and STOP# signal lines are not owned by the target because no target is addressed. They are driven to a logical "1" by pull-up resistors.

- The AD[63::32], C/BE#[7::4], REQ64#, ACK64#, and PAR64 signal lines are not owned by either the PCI bus master or the target and are driven to a logical "1" by pull-up resistors.

The remaining signal lines ownership is according to the following protocol:

- The CLK and RST# signal lines are owned by platform resources.
- The GNT# signal lines are owned by the central arbiter.
- The LOCK# signal line is owned by the Lock master.

PCI-X SPECIFIC

PCI-X MEMORY MAPPED I/O

The PCI-X addendum bus specification does not define a unique bus transaction for memory mapped I/O. Unless otherwise specified, it is assumed that the memory address space contains memory mapped I/O. Memory mapped I/O can contain both regular DRAM type memory and I/O registers. The target defines the portion of memory address space associated with the Memory Base Address Register (MBAR) in the configuration address space as NOT memory mapped I/O when the Prefetchable bit is set to logical "1". Similarly, PCI-X/PCI-X BRIDGES define a portion of the memory address space as NOT memory mapped I/O via the Memory Base, Memory Limit, Prefetchable Memory Base, and Prefetchable Memory Limit registers in the configuration address space. A memory address range containing memory mapped I/O cannot be marked as prefetchable in the configuration address space. As will be discussed in detail later, a memory address can be identified as prefetchable if there are no negative side affects of multiple readings and possible discarding of the data read.

As will be discussed later, the PCI-X bus master executes a DWORD memory read transaction to either prefetchable or non-prefetchable address space. BURST memory read block or alias memory read block transactions can only be executed to a prefetchable address space. It is the responsibility of the PCI-X bus master to determine that there will be no negative side effects if a BURST memory read block or alias memory read block transaction is executed. The target and associated bridges will execute these bus transactions independently from the value of the prefetchable bits and registers in the target and bridges for the associated memory address range.

PCI-X BYTE LANE OPERATION

The PCI-X addendum bus specification defines byte lane operation for a PCI-X bus segment in the same fashion as the PCI bus segment discussed above, with the following differences:

- The C/BE#[3::0] signal lines are driven to a logical "1" (deasserted) during the DATA PHASE of all DWORD COMMANDs, BURST memory read commands, and BURST alias memory write block and memory write block commands. For the DWORD COMMANDs, the value of the C/BE#[3::0] signal lines during the ATTRIBUTE PHASE define the valid byte lanes (in any combination of valid and not valid) of the AD[31::00] signal lines during the DATA PHASE of the bus transaction. The aforementioned BURST COMMANDs by definition indicate that all the byte lanes of the AD[31::00] signal lines are valid during the DATA PHASE. For the BURST memory write command, the C/BE[3::0] signal lines are valid for the entire DATA PHASE, and are defined in the same fashion as above for PCI . That is, any combination including defining non-continuous byte lanes is permitted.

See Subchapters 4.17 to 4.20 for the discussions of 64 data bit bus transactions and for bus transactions that begin as 64 data bit bus transactions but are required to complete as 32 data bit bus transactions.

PCI-X PARK

PCI-X addendum specification for the PARK protocol is same as discussed above for the PCI local bus specification.

"PCI-X 16 CLOCK" RULES

The PCI-X addendum specification defines the "PCI-X 16 clock" rule protocol like the PCI local bus specification defines the "PCI 16 clock" rule, EXCEPT it does not apply to the execution of Retry termination. The "PCI-X 16 clock" rule only applies to the execution of Disconnect at Next ADB and Single Phase Disconnect terminations. The "PCI-X 16 clock" rule measures the CLK signal line periods relative to FRAME# signal line assertion as is done according to the PCI "16 clock" rule. If the target is not able to terminate (encoded in the combination of DEVSEL#, TRDY#, and STOP# signal lines) on the seventeenth rising edge of the CLK signal line measured from the first rising edge of the CLK signal line when the FRAME# signal line is asserted, the target is required to terminate according to the "PCI-X 8 clock" rule or otherwise provide data access on or before the aforementioned seventeenth rising edge of the CLK signal line. See Chapter 8: *Master and Target Termination* for more information.

> **The convention of this book is use the term *"PCI 16 clock" rule* only when applied to PCI bus transactions and *"PCI-X 16 clock rule* only when applied to PCI-X bus transactions.**

"PCI-X 8 CLOCK" RULES

The PCI-X addendum specification defines the "PCI-X 8 clock" rule protocol differently than the PCI local bus specification defines the "PCI 8 clock" rule. As will be discussed later in the book, a PCI-X bus transaction only permits the target to insert wait states in the first DATA PHASE. No wait states can be inserted in the subsequent microaccesses of a BURST transaction. Consequently, the definition of the PCI "8 clock" rule does not apply to a PCI-X bus transaction. The PCI-X addendum specification requires the target to complete a SINGLE bus transaction or the initial microaccess of a BURST bus transaction within eight CLK signal line periods ("PCI-X 8 clock" rule) from the assertion of the FRAME# signal line. If the target is not able to terminate (encoded in the combination of DEVSEL#, TRDY#, and STOP# signal lines) on the ninth rising edge of the CLK signal line measured from the first rising edge of the CLK signal line when the FRAME# signal line is asserted, the target is required to terminate the bus transaction with a Retry, Target Abort, or Split Response termination according to the "PCI-X 8 clock" rule. Otherwise the target is required to provide data access on or before the aforementioned ninth rising edge of the CLK signal line or execute a bus transaction termination according to the "PCI-X 16 clock" rule. See Chapter 8: *Master and Target Termination* for more information.

> **The convention of this book is use the term "PCI 8 clock rule" applied only to PCI bus transactions and "PCI-X 16 clock rule" applied only to PCI-X bus transactions.**

SUMMARY OF "PCI-X 16 CLOCK" AND "PCI-X 8 CLOCK" RULES

In summary, the "PCI-X 16 clock" rule *applies* to the SINGLE bus transactions and initial microaccess of BURST bus transactions of the following:

- Memory transactions
- I/O transactions (only SINGLE bus transactions are defined)
- Configuration transactions (only SINGLE bus transactions are defined)

- Interrupt acknowledge transactions (only SINGLE bus transactions are defined)
- Split completion transactions

This is a brief summary. Please See Chapter 8: *Master and Target Termination* for more detailed information.

The "PCI-X 16 clock" rule *DOES NOT apply* for the above PCI-X bus transactions during the initialization time (from RST# signal line deasserted to 2^{27} CLK signal line periods later), when executing from BOOT ROM, or when copying expansion ROM to memory. Note: If the device is accessing its expansion ROM after it has been hot inserted, the aforementioned "PCI-X 16 clock" rule relative to target termination *DOES* apply.

The "PCI-X 16 clock" rule does not apply to special transactions in that there is no specific target to assert the DEVSEL# signal line.

In summary, the "PCI-X 8 clock" rule applies to the SINGLE bus transactions and initial microaccess of BURST bus transactions of the following:

- Memory transactions
- I/O transactions (only SINGLE bus transactions are defined)
- Configuration transactions (only SINGLE bus transactions are defined)
- Interrupt acknowledge transactions (only SINGLE bus transactions are defined)
- Split completion transactions

The "PCI-X 8 clock" rule DOES NOT apply for the above PCI-X bus transactions during the initialization time (from RST# signal line deasserted to 2^{27} CLK signal line periods later), when executing from BOOT ROM, or when copying expansion ROM to memory. Note: If the device is accessing its expansion ROM after it has been hot inserted, the aforementioned "PCI-X 16 clock" rule relative to target termination *DOES* apply.

The "PCI-X 8 clock" rule does not apply to special transactions in that there is no specific target to assert the DEVSEL# signal line.

PCI-X SIGNAL LINE OWNERSHIP DURING BUS TRANSACTIONS WITH 32 DATA BIT RESOURCES (PCI-X BUS MASTER AND TARGET)

During memory, I/O, configuration, interrupt acknowledge, split completion, and special transactions; the signal lines are owned by different PCI bus resources. A PCI-X resource owns the signal line when it is the only resource (other than pull-up resistors) that can drive the signal line during a portion of the bus transaction. In the following discussions, the PAR and PAR64 signal lines relative to a specific bus transaction PHASE is actually delayed from "that" specific bus transaction PHASE. The protocol is as follows:

- ■ FRAME#, IRDY#, C/BE#[3::0], and REQ#x signal lines are owned by the PCI-X bus master for any bus transaction.

- ■ During memory write, I/O write, and configuration write transactions, the PCI-X bus master owns the AD[31::0] and PAR signal lines during the ADDRESS, ATTRIBUTE, TARGET RESPONSE, and DATA PHASES.

- ■ During special and split completion transactions, the PCI-X bus master owns the AD [31::0] and PAR signal lines during the ADDRESS, ATTRIBUTE, TARGET, and DATA PHASES.

- ■ During memory read, I/O read, and configuration read transactions, the PCI-X bus master owns the AD[31::0] and PAR signal lines during the ADDRESS, and ATTRIBUTE PHASES. For these bus transactions, the PCI-X bus master does not own and tristates the AD[31::00] and PAR signal lines during the TARGET RESPONSE PHASE. The target owns these signal lines during the DATA PHASE. The ownership of these signal lines changes from the PCI-X bus master to the target during the TARGET RESPONSE PHASE.

- ■ During interrupt acknowledge transactions, the PCI-X bus master owns and drives the AD[31::0] and PAR signal lines during the ADDRESS and ATTRIBUTE PHASES. For this bus transaction the PCI-X bus master does not own and tristates the AD[31::00] and PAR signal lines during the TARGET RESPONSE PHASE. The target owns these signal lines during the DATA PHASE. The ownership of these signal lines changes from the PCI-X bus master to the target during the TARGET RESPONSE PHASE.

- ■ During memory, I/O, and configuration transactions, the TRDY#, DEVSEL#, and STOP# signal lines are owned by the target.

- ■ During split completion transactions, the TRDY#, DEVSEL#, and STOP# signal lines are owned the target.

■ During interrupt acknowledge transactions, the TRDY#, DEVSEL#, and STOP# signal lines are owned by the target.

■ During special transactions, the TRDY#, DEVSEL#, and STOP# signal lines are not owned by the target because no target is addressed. They are driven to a logical "1" by pull-up resistors.

■ The AD[63::32], C/BE#[7::4], REQ64#, ACK64#, and PAR64 signal lines are not owned by either the PCI-X bus master or the target and are driven to a logical "1" by pull-up resistors.

> The term "memory read" above includes DWORD memory read, memory read block, and alias memory read block. The term "memory write" above includes memory write, memory write block, and alias memory write block.

The remaining signal lines ownership obeys the following protocol:

■ The CLK and RST# signal lines are owned by platform resources.

■ The GNTx# signal lines are owned by the central arbiter.

■ The LOCK# signal line is owned by the Lock master.

PCI AND PCI-X BUS TRANSACTIONS RELATIVE BUS MASTER AND TARGET LOCATION

Both PCI local bus and PCI-X addendum bus specifications provide support of systems with multiple bus segments connected by bridges. Simpler bus protocols are focused on a single bus segment; consequently, the equivalent SINGLE and BURST transactions are simply defined. When a bus protocol includes bridges, the use of SINGLE and BURST transactions within a specific bus segment and between bus segments is different. Consider the following possible access paths in Figure 4-1 for a PCI system.

■ PATH A represents a direct access between two PCI resources on the same bus segment. This source of the access is the actual PCI bus master (non-bridge) and the destination is the actual target (non-bridge) that will receive or provide the data. Both SINGLE and BURST transactions can be supported. There are no concerns about transaction ordering. Table 4-4 summarizes the type of bus transactions between these two PCI resources. In the subsequent subchapters of this chapter, the term "same PCI bus segment" refers to PATH A. The same concepts apply to discussions relating to the PCI-X addendum bus specification.

The actual target in Figure 4-1 is labeled a "non-bridge". This implies that the interface between the bus segment and the internal circuitry of an ASIC (as an example target) is very simple and straightforward. However, for performance reasons, the interface may have more complexity and contain elements of posted write transaction FIFOs and Delayed Transaction buffers similar to a PCI/PCI BRIDGE. A more complex interface may place restrictions on the use of SINGLE versus BURST bus transactions similar to those discussed below for PATHs B and C. It is beyond the scope of this book to define all possible implementations of interfaces versus the support of SINGLE and BURST bus transactions. This book will assume that the interaction between the actual PCI bus master (non-bridge) and actual target (non-bridge) on the same bus segment will have simple and straightforward interfaces in the target. That is, the target (non-bridge) may or may not operate with posted memory write or Delayed Transaction protocol. According to the PCI local bus specification, a posted memory write also looks like a fast target and a Retry termination may or may not be part of a Delayed Transaction protocol. If more complex interfaces are implemented in the target, the designer will have to consider the restrictions to the application of SINGLE and BURST bus transactions as if a PCI/PCI BRIDGE (or elements thereof) is in the target interface.

For the PCI-X addendum bus specification implementations, the same concepts apply relative to posted memory write transactions and Split Transaction protocol. As with PCI, a posted memory write to a target (non-bridge) also looks like a fast target. However, unlike the Delayed Transaction protocol, the implementation of the Split Transaction protocol by the target (non-bridge) is obvious by the execution of the Split Response termination. Consequently, Split Transaction protocol will be discussed for both the target (non-bridge) and a bridge acting as a target on behalf of the target (non-bridge).

■ PATH B represents an access from the source of the access (*i.e.*, the actual PCI bus master (non-bridge)) through a PCI/PCI BRIDGE to the actual target (non-bridge). The target seen by the actual PCI bus master is the PCI/PCI BRIDGE (1 to 2). This bridge is representing the actual target of the access to the actual PCI bus master. PCI/PCI BRIDGE (1 to 2) is seen as the PCI bus master by the actual target (non-bridge). The SINGLE and BURST transactions that can be executed from the PCI/PCI BRIDGE as PCI bus master is restricted by the actual target (non-bridge). That is, the transactions used to access the actual target (non-bridge) by a PCI bus master (bridge or non-bridge) is restricted by the actual target (non-bridge) as defined by PATH A. However, the porting of a transaction through a PCI/PCI BRIDGE places additional restrictions on SINGLE versus BURST bus transactions. The type of bus transactions that can be executed in the portion of PATH B from the actual PCI bus master (non-bridge) to PCI/PCI BRIDGE (1 to 2) are outlined in Table 4-5. PCI/PCI BRIDGE (1 to 2) is defined as the target (bridge) and is only representing the actual target (non-bridge). For discussions relative to the PCI-X addendum bus specification, the same concepts apply.

■ PATH C presents an access from the actual PCI bus master (non-bridge) to memory. Typically there are no I/O or configuration address spaces accessible from the PCI bus segment to a HOST bus segment level. For purposes of this book it will be assumed that the HOST/PCI BRIDGE will operate as a target (bridge) representing memory in the same fashion as a PCI/PCI BRIDGE represents the actual target (non-bridge). It is also possible to design (but unlikely) a HOST/BUS BRIDGE that provides access to memory as if it is a target (non-bridge) with a simple and straightforward interface. For discussions relative to the PCI-X addendum bus specification the same concepts apply.

■ PATH D represents an access by the HOST CPU to the configuration address space of a PCI/PCI BRIDGE (1 to 2). In this example, the PCI/PCI BRIDGE (0 to 1) represents the actual target. The actual target is the configuration registers in PCI/PCI BRIDGE (1 to 2) bridge and are thus defined as the actual target (non-bridge). PCI/PCI BRIDGE (0 to 1) is representing the actual target (non-bridge) to the HOST/PCI BRIDGE that is the PCI bus master. For discussions relative to the PCI-X addendum bus specification the same concepts apply.

■ PATH E is the same as PATH B except it only applies to memory, I/O, and Type 1 configuration transactions (that convert to special transactions).

■ PATH F has the same restrictions as PATH E. See Chapter 7: *Bridge and Interface Protocol* for more information.

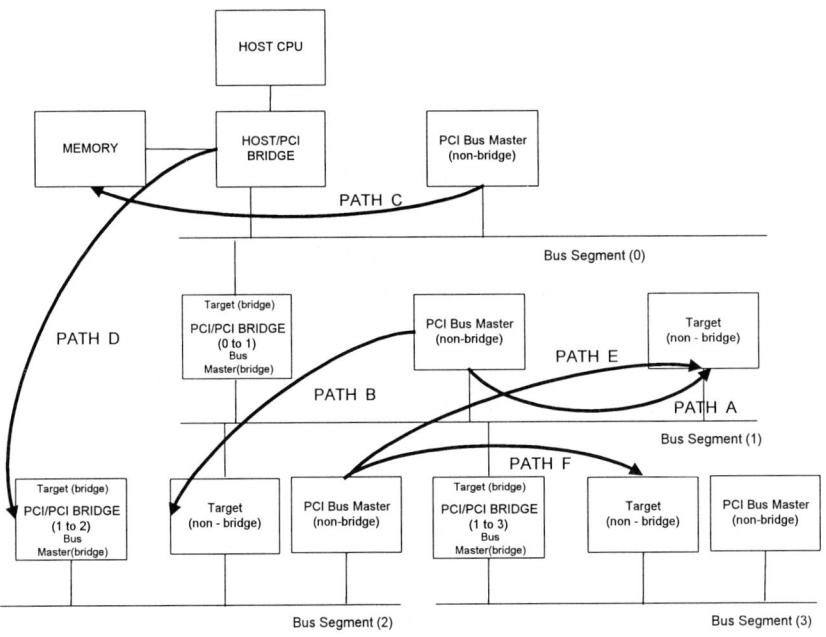

Figure 4-1: Possible Bus Transaction Paths

C/BE# [3::0] ADDRESS PHASE Binary MSB to LSB	Name (PCI)	Name (PCI-X)	Transaction Protocol Between Bus Master (bridge and non-bridge) and Target (non-bridge) on Same Bus Segment Bus Transactions: PCI SINGLE = PST PCI BURST = PBT PCI-X SINGLE = PXST PCI-X BURST = PXBT	
	NO GROUP NAME	DWORD COMMANDS		
			PCI	PCI-X
0000	Interrupt Acknowledge	Interrupt Acknowledge	PST	PXST
0001	Special	Special	PST PBT	PXST
0010	I/O Read	I/O Read	PST PBT	PXST
0011	I/O Write	I/O Write	PST PBT	PXST
1010	Config. Read	Config. Read	PST PBT	PXST
1011	Config. Write	Config.Write	PST PBT	PXST
0110	Memory Read	Memory Read DWORD	PST PBT	PXST
	NO GROUP NAME	BURST COMMANDS		
0111	Memory Write	Memory Write	PST PBT	PXST PXBT
1000	Reserved	Alias Memory Read Block	na	PXST PXBT
1001	Reserved	Alias Memory Write Block	na	PXST PXBT
1100	Memory Read Multiple	Split Completion	PST PBT	PXST PXBT
1110	Memory Read Line	Memory Read Block	PST PBT	PXST PXBT
1111	Memory Write Invalidate	Memory Write Block	PST PBT	PXST PXBT
	OTHERS	OTHERS		
1101	DAC	DAC	na	na
0100	Reserved	Reserved	na	na
0101	Reserved	Reserved	na	na

Table 4-4: Comparison of PCI and PCI-X Commands and Transactions on Same Bus Segment

C/BE# [3::0] ADDRESS PHASE Binary MSB to LSB	Name (PCI)	Name (PCI-X)	Transaction Protocol Between Bus Master and a PCI/PCI or PCI-X/PCI-X BRIDGE (representing the actual target (non-bridge)) Bus Transactions: PCI SINGLE = PST PCI BURST = PBT PCI-X SINGLE = PXST PCI-X BURST = PXBT Posted Write Req. = PWR Delayed Transaction Req. = DTR Split Transaction Req. = STR (Req. = Required)	
	NO GROUP NAME	**DWORD COMMANDS**		
			PCI/PCI BRIDGE	**PCI-X/PCI-X BRIDGE**
0000	Interrupt Acknowledge	Interrupt Acknowledge	na	na
0001	Special	Special	na	na
0010	I/O Read	I/O Read	PST DTR	PXST STR (2)
0011	I/O Write	I/O Write	PST DTR	PXST STR (2)
1010	Config. Read	Config. Read	PST DTR	PXST STR (2)
1011	Config. Write (3)	Config.Write (3)	PST DTR	PXST STR (2)
0110	Memory Read	DWORD Memory Read	PST PBT(1) DTR	PXST STR (2)
	NO GROUP NAME	**BURST COMMANDS**		
0111	Memory Write	Memory Write	PST PBT PWR	PXST PXBT PWR
1000	Reserved	Alias Memory Read Block	na	PXST PXBT STR(2)
1001	Reserved	Alias Memory Write Block	na	PXST PXBT PWR
1100	Memory Read Multiple	Split Completion	PST PBT DTR	PXST PXBT PWR
1110	Memory Read Line	Memory Read Block	PST PBT DTR	PXST PXBT STR(2)
1111	Memory Write Invalidate	Memory Write Block	PST PBT PWR	PXST PXBT PWR
	OTHERS	**OTHERS**		
1101	DAC	DAC	na	na
0100	Reserved	Reserved	na	na
0101	Reserved	Reserved	na	na

Table 4-5: Comparison of PCI and PCI-X Commands and Transactions Through a PCI/PCI BRIDGE or PCI-X /PCI-X BRIDGE

Notes: (1) When access is to a prefetchable memory address space, or MRL or MRM transactions are executed, BURST bus transactions through the bridge are supported.

(2) SINGLE and BURST transactions are terminated in the initial access of the DATA PHASE with a Split Response termination to implement Split Transaction protocol.

(3) Not all configuration transactions can port in both upstream and downstream directions.

TRANSLATION BETWEEN PCI AND PCI-X BUS TRANSACTIONS

The preceding discussion and the balance of this chapter are focused on either an all PCI system or an all PCI-X system. There has been no discussion of a system with a mix of PCI and PCI-X compliant bus segments. The PCI-X protocol is an addendum to the PCI local bus specification, and has defined that different bus segments can support either the PCI bus protocol or the PCI-X bus protocol but not both on the same bus segment. The key consideration is that a specific bus segment supports only one bus protocol and it is the responsibility of the bridge between bus segments to translate the bus transactions between a PCI complaint bus segment and a PCI-X compliant bus segment. The focus for the balance of this chapter will be a specific protocol applied to a specific bus segment. The translation of bus transactions through a bridge will be discussed in Chapter 7: *Bridge and Interface Protocol.*

PCI SPECIFC IMPLEMENTATION

4.1 PCI MEMORY AND I/O TRANSACTIONS

This is a brief introduction to PCI memory and I/O transactions. See Subchapter 4.5: *PCI 32 Data Bit Bus Master to 32 Data Bit Target* for more information.

Memory or I/O transactions executed between a PCI bus master (bridge or non-bridge) on the same PCI bus segment as the actual target (non-bridge) can be implemented as either SINGLE or BURST bus transactions. Only memory write transactions can be posted into a PCI/PCI BRIDGE and thus can be implemented as either SINGLE or BURST bus transactions with the PC/PCI BRIDGE representing the actual target (non-bridge). I/O write transactions cannot be posted into the PCI/PCI BRIDGE representing the actual target (non-bridge). Memory read transactions to non-prefetchable address space and all I/O transactions can only be implemented as SINGLE bus transactions with Immediate Transaction and Delayed Transaction protocols with the PCI/PCI BRIDGE representing the actual target (non-bridge). Memory read transactions to prefetchable address space can implement either SINGLE or BURST bus transactions with Immediate Transaction and Delayed Transaction protocols with the PCI/PCI BRIDGE representing the actual target (non-bridge). See Chapter 7: *Bridge and Interface Protocol* for more information.

The "PCI 16 clock" rule applies to all memory and I/O transactions. The "PCI 8 clock" rule applies to all BURST memory and I/O transactions. See Subchapter 4.0 for more information.

Please see a later portion of this subchapter on how ADDRESS/DATA STEPPING and PRE-DRIVE protocols operate. Only the ADDRESS/DATA STEPPING protocol applies to memory and I/O transactions.

As outlined in Chapter 7: *Bridge and Interface Protocol,* COMBINING, PREFETCHING, and MERGING can only be applied to memory transactions through a PCI/PCI BRIDGE. COLLAPSING cannot be applied to any memory transaction through a PCI/PCI BRDIGE. COMBINING, COLLAPSING, PREFETCHING, and MERGING cannot be applied to any I/O transactions through a PCI/PCI BRIDGE.

The Master and Target Fast Back-to-Back protocols apply to memory and I/O transactions. See Chapter 6: *Detailed Bus Transaction Operation* for more information.

ADDRESS DECODING FOR MEMORY AND I/O TRANSACTIONS

The address decoding protocol for PCI bus transactions is more extensive than other buses. Most bus protocols allow a bus master to begin a bus transaction and assume that a bus resource will respond to the address. A PCI bus resource can claim the bus transaction and become the target by asserting the DEVSEL# signal line. Because the address must be checked by all potential memory or I/O transaction targets, the decoding protocol is defined as distributed.

PCI resources decode the AD[31::02] signal lines (and AD[63::32] signal lines under the 64 data bit extension) and claim the bus transaction in the same number of CLK signal line periods. As shown in Figure 4-2, the fastest possible decode will respond one CLK signal line period after the FRAME# signal line is first sampled (identifies valid address on the AD signal lines and valid command on the C/BE# signal lines). The sampling point of the DEVSEL# signal line for a "FAST" decode is one CLK signal line period after the FRAME# signal line is sampled asserted. There are two additional DEVSEL# signal line sample points that follow at one CLK signal line period intervals, defined as "MEDIUM" and "SLOW". These three sampling points reflect a POSITIVE DECODING protocol.

If the DEVSEL# signal line is not asserted at any of the POSITIVE DECODING sample points, a single PCI resource can claim the bus transaction through SUBTRACTIVE DECODING by asserting the DEVSEL# signal line after the POSITIVE DECODING sample points. An example of a PCI resource that would use SUBTRACTIVE DECODING is a PCI/LEGACY BRIDGE. The resources on the PCI bus that contain the PCI bus master that began the bus transaction have the right of first refusal with POSITIVE DECODING. The bus "behind" the BRIDGE will have an opportunity to claim the bus transaction via the BRIDGE with SUBTRACTIVE DECODING. Subtractive decoding is particularly useful for targets with fragmented address space. If no PCI resource claims the bus transaction, a Master Abort termination is executed. See Chapter 8: *Master and Target Termination* for more information.

> For the I/O address space, AD[01::00] must be decoded in addition to the aforementioned address signal lines.

> When a RESERVED command is executed, no PCI resource may assert the DEVSEL# signal line for either POSITIVE or SUBTRACTIVE decoding.
>
> The POSITIVE and SUBTRACTIVE DECODING sample points (FAST, MEDIUM, SLOW, and SUB) for the DEVSEL# signal line to claim the bus transaction are delayed by one CLK signal line period (relative to the first rising edge of the CLK signal line when FRAME# signal line is asserted) if a DUAL ADDRESS command is executed. See the DUAL ADDRESS section in this chapter for more information.

> All bus transactions (except those implementing DUAL ADDRESS) can begin with ADDRESS/DATA STEPPING. Also, the configuration transaction can begin with a PRE-DRIVE PHASE. Consequently, the implementation of ADDRESS/DATA STEPPING or PRE-DRIVE PHASE results in the FRAME# signal line being asserted later in the bus transaction (not during #1 CLK signal line period as shown in Figure 4-2). Consequently, the decoding sampling points must be referenced to the first rising edge of the CLK signal line when the FRAME# signal line is asserted. See Chapter 6.0: *Detailed Bus Transactions Operation,* for more information.

> If all targets on a PCI bus segment have FAST DECODING according to their STATUS registers in the configuration address space, the PCI resource executing SUBTRACTIVE DECODING can assert the DEVSEL# signal line to be sampled asserted at the MEDIUM DECODING sampling point. Similarly, the PCI-X resource executing SUBTRACTIVE DECODING can assert the DEVSEL# signal line to be sampled asserted at the SLOW DECODING sampling point when all targets on the PCI-X bus segment have MEDIUM DECODING.

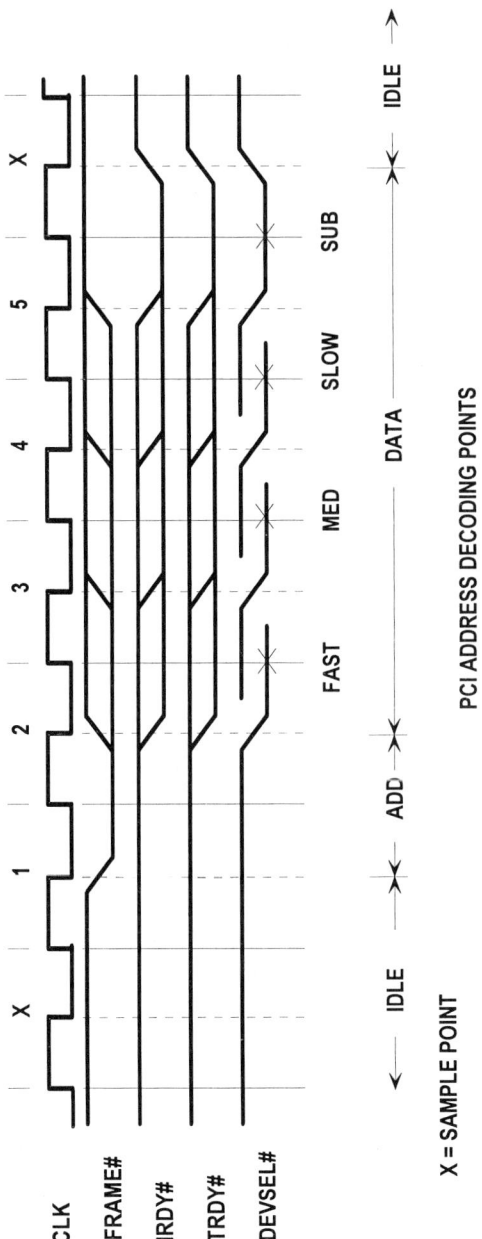

Figure 4-2: PCI ADDRESS Decoding Points

Targets that support FAST DECODING will indicate this information in their STATUS Register in the configuration address space. If all of the PCI resources that are potential targets support a FAST DECODE, the target that implements SUBTRACTIVE DECODING can assert the DEVSEL# signal line at the MEDIUM DECODING sample point. Consequently, the targets implementing "early" SUBTRACTIVE DECODING by asserting the DEVSEL# signal line at the MEDIUM DECODING sample point are required to "wait" (non-support of MEDIUM DECODING) until the SLOW DECODING sample point when the TARGET Back-to-Back bus transaction protocol is implemented.

Similarly, as previously mentioned, the execution of DUAL ADDRESS will "automatically" delay the POSITIVE DECODING sample points by one CLK signal line period. The aforementioned "non-support" of the MEDIUM DECODING for SUBTRACTIVE DECODING does not apply when the TARGET FAST Back-to-Back protocol is executed with a DUAL ADDRESS. In other words, when a DUAL ADDRESS is executed with TARGET FAST Back-to Back protocol, a target implementing SUBTRACTIVE DECODING can assert the DEVSEL# signal line at the MEDIUM DECODING sample point when all other targets support FAST DECODING as indicated in their STATUS Registers.

As previously stated, the PCI local bus specification permits a PCI resource to claim the bus transaction (assert the DEVSEL# signal line) before decoding the sampling point defined in its STATUS register in the configuration address space, if all of the other resources on the PCI bus segment indicate earlier decoding sampling points (according to their STATUS registers in the configuration address space). The PCI-X addendum specification does not implement this protocol. The decoding sampling points (DEC A, DEC B, DEC C, and SUBTRACTIVE DECODING) for a PCI-X resource to claim the bus transaction is fixed and independent of the decoding sampling points of other PCI-X bus segments on the PCI-X bus segment.

MEMORY AND I/O TRANSACTION COMPLETION

The memory and I/O transaction protocol includes completing these bus transactions with Completion, Completion with Timeout, Master Abort, Retry, Disconnect, and Target Abort terminations. See Chapter 8: *Master and Target Termination* for more information.

DUAL ADDRESS

The PCI local bus specification supports both 32 and 64 bit address spaces only for the memory address space. The support of 64 bits of address is in conjunction with the DUAL ADDRESS command. For memory transactions without DUAL ADDRESS, the AD[31::0] signal lines contain 32 address bits (30 bits for memory) during the ADDRESS PHASE. Also, during the ADDRESS PHASE the COMMAND type of the bus transaction is encoded into the C/BE#[3::0] signal lines.

To support a 64 bit address, the PCI bus master multiplexes a 64 bit address onto the AD[31::0] signal lines and adds an additional CLK signal line period to the ADDRESS PHASE (see Figure 4-3). To indicate a 64 bit address, the PCI bus master drives the binary pattern for DUAL ADDRESS onto the C/BE#[3::0] signal lines during the first CLK signal line period of the ADDRESS PHASE. The PCI bus master subsequently drives the binary pattern for the COMMAND type onto the C/BE#[3::0] signal lines during the second CLK signal line period of the ADDRESS PHASE. Note that Figure 4-3 is an example of a 64 data bit bus transaction. If a 32 data bit bus transaction is executed, the C/BE#[7::4] and AD[63::32] signal lines would not be driven with command and high address, respectively. See Chapter 6: *Detailed Bus Transaction Operation* for more information.

A PCI bus master that supports a 64 bit address space and only addresses the lower four gigabytes (in the present transaction) must execute a memory transaction without a DUAL ADDRESS. By definition the upper order address bits (AD[63::32] signal lines) are logical "0".

A PCI resource that does not support DUAL ADDRESS must not assert the DEVSEL# signal line to claim the bus transaction when DUAL ADDRESS is executed.

PCI bus masters cannot use ADDRESS/DATA STEPPING when executing a DUAL ADDRESS.

DUAL ADDRESS is not defined for I/O, configuration, special, or interrupt acknowledge transactions.

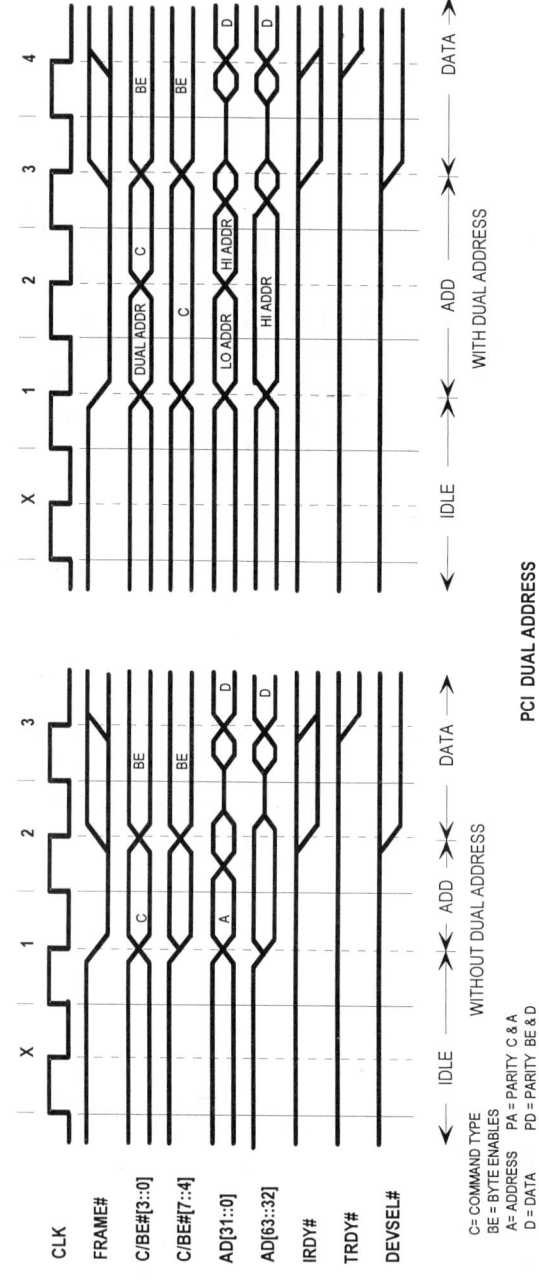

Figure 4-3: PCI DUAL ADDRESS

ADDRESS/DATA STEPPING AND PRE-DRIVE

When PCI was first developed there was a concern about the dual duty of a single AD signal line having a single load for address and data purposes, and a second load for the IDSEL. The concern was that the double load would prevent components from meeting all of the timing requirements. Once PCI systems were in production, it became clear that this was not an issue. Consequently, ADDRESS/DATA STEPPING and PRE-DRIVE have not been necessary for the successful implementation of PCI systems. Because of their inclusion in the PCI local bus specification, these topics are included in this book for historical completeness.

However, the introduction of the higher CLK signal line frequencies of PCI-X does require the use of PRE-DRIVE with configuration transactions, as will be discussed later in this chapter.

The majority of figures in this book assume that the CLK signal line periods are numbered (#) 1 to N with the FRAME# signal line asserted during CLK signal line period #1. There are two protocols in which the FRAME# signal line will not be asserted during CLK signal line period #1: ADDRESS/DATA STEPPING and PRE-DRIVE.

ADDRESS/DATA STEPPING protocol (A/D) allows the PCI bus master to drive some of the signal lines (AD, PAR, PAR64, and IDSEL) at different points within the bus transaction to lower the cost of implementing PCI compatible systems. Consider the three examples outlined in Figure 4-4. Without A/D, the AD signal lines are all driven at the same point at the beginning of the bus transaction. This requires strong drivers for integrated circuits and extra ground pins. These requirements may affect die size and package size, and therefore the cost. The A/D protocol allows the AD signal lines to be driven at different points; *i.e.*, staggered in time. These signal lines can implement the A/D protocol because they are qualified by the FRAME# signal line during the ADDRESS PHASE, and the IRDY# and TRDY# signal lines during the DATA PHASE.

Though not graphically shown in this section, the PAR and PAR64 signal lines follow the timing and qualification protocol of the AD signal lines, although delayed by one CLK signal line period. Thus, the PAR and PAR64 signal lines can also implement the A/D protocol. Similarly, the IDSEL signal lines follow the timing and qualification of the AD signal lines and can implement the A/D protocol.

The first example (Example 1) in Figure 4-4 shows the beginning of a bus transaction without the use of A/D. All of the AD signal lines (along with other signal lines) are simultaneously driven and the FRAME# signal line asserted during the #1 CLK signal line period. In the second example (Example 2), the AD signal lines are driven at different times. Subgroups of the AD signal lines can be driven at different times. In this example, the AD[15::0] and AD[31::16] signal lines are driven to stable levels, and subsequently with valid address information at different times. The assertion of the FRAME# signal line is delayed until the #3 CLK signal line period to allow the AD signal lines to contain valid address information. During the DATA PHASE, the driving of write data onto the AD signal lines can also be performed at different times by delaying the assertion of the IRDY# signal line. Though not shown, read data can also be driven at different times by the target by delaying the assertion of the TRDY# signal line.

- There are several important points about A/D to be considered: The signal lines that can use the A/D protocol are AD[63::0], PAR, PAR64, and IDSEL.

- In addition to reducing the number of signal lines simultaneously driven, the A/D protocol also allows the signal line drivers to be smaller and thus take more time to reach a stable level.

- A/D requires that the decoding sampling points (FAST, MEDIUM, SLOW, and SUBTRACTIVE) are referenced to the assertion of the FRAME# signal line.

- When the FRAME# signal line is asserted later in the bus transaction, other signal lines can also be driven at different points. In Example 2 of Figure 4-4, the FRAME# and C/BE# signal lines are driven at different points relative to the assertion of the FRAME# signal line. The range to drive these or similar signal lines are shown in the example. Even though these signal lines can be driven later in the bus transaction with the delayed assertion of the FRAME# signal line, there is still a requirement that the drivers be powerful enough to meet the driving requirements at other points later in the bus transaction. For example, the C/BE# signal lines can be driven later in the bus transaction at Point B (Circle B in Figure 4-3), but the change from COMMAND type to byte enables is required to occur instantaneously at Point C (Circle C) in Figure 4-4.

- The A/D protocol cannot be used by the PCI bus master when DUAL ADDRESS is executed. Example 3 in Figure 4-3 outlines the problem with applying the A/D protocol when DUAL ADDRESS is executed. At Point A (Circle A in Figure 4-4) ALL of the AD[31::0] signal lines must simultaneously change between low address to high address, thus requiring a powerful driver.

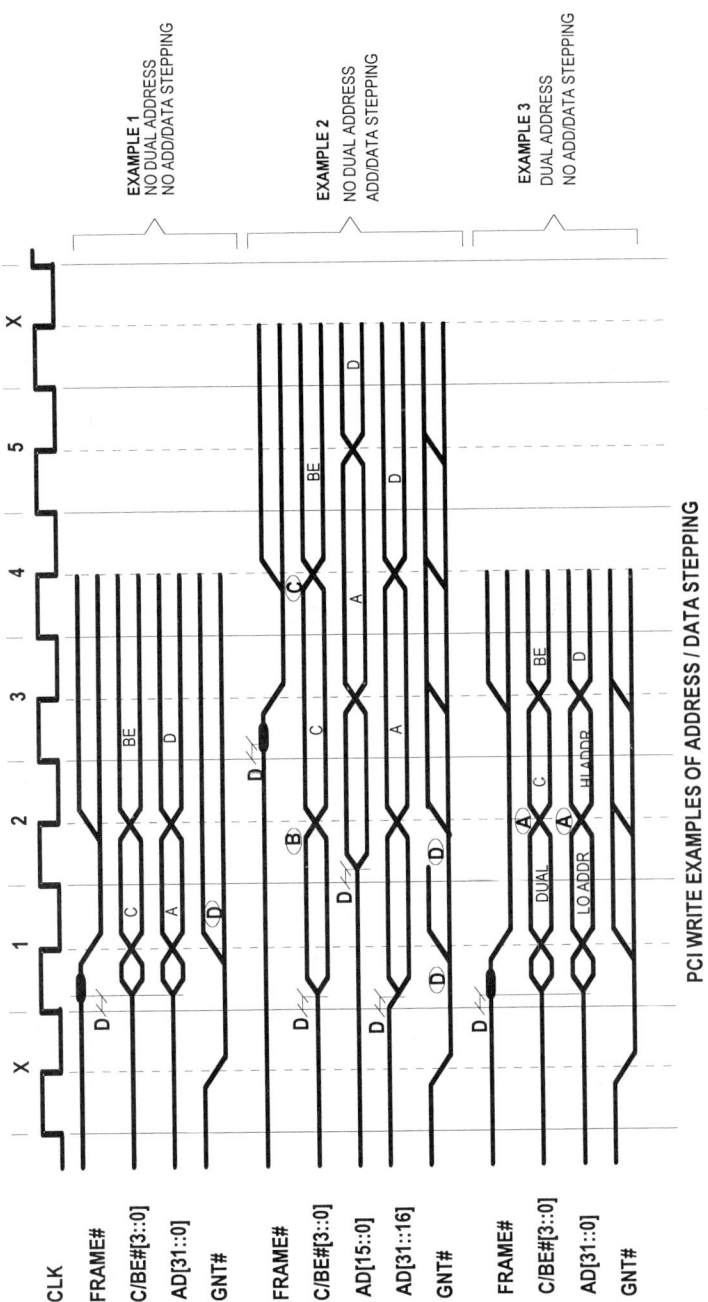

Figure 4-4: PCI Write Examples of ADDRESS/DATA STEPPING

- The PCI bus master that implements A/D risks losing bus ownership while delaying the assertion of the FRAME# signal line after the associated GNT# signal line is asserted. In Example 1 in Figure 4-4, the deassertion of the associated GNT# signal line at Point D (Circle D) still allows the PCI bus master to begin the bus transaction. In Example 2 in Figure 4-4, the deassertion of the associated GNT# signal line at Points D (Circle D) forces the PCI bus master not to begin the bus transaction and relinquish the bus.

Another consideration is the PRE-DRIVE protocol, which applies to only the configuration transaction. As with the A/D protocol, the FRAME# signal line is not asserted until a later point in the bus transaction. The difference is that the delay in asserting the FRAME# signal line is needed to allow the IDSEL signal line to reach a stable level. Thus, all of the AD signal lines are simultaneously driven valid several CLK signal line periods prior to the assertion of the FRAME# signal line. Unlike the ADDRESS/DATA STEPPING protocol, for the PRE-DRIVE protocol all AD signal lines are driven simultaneously.

4.2 PCI CONFIGURATION TRANSACTIONS

> This is a brief introduction to PCI configuration transactions. See Subchapter 4.5: *PCI 32 Data Bit Bus Master to 32 Data Bit Target* for more information.

Configuration transactions executed between a PCI bus master (bridge or non-bridge) on the same PCI bus segment as the actual target (non-bridge) can be implemented as either SINGLE or BURST bus transactions. Configuration transactions cannot be posted into the PCI/PCI BRIDGE representing an actual target (non-bridge). Configuration transactions can only be implemented as SINGLE bus transactions with Immediate Transaction and Delayed Transaction protocols with the PCI/PCI BRIDGE representing the actual target (non-bridge ... either directly or indirectly through other bridges). See Chapter 7: *Bridge and Interface Protocol* for more information.

The "PCI 16 clock" and "PCI 8 clock" rules only apply to configuration transactions during run time (*i.e.*, not during initialization, when not executing from BOOT ROM, or when not copying expansion ROM to memory). See Subchapter 4.0 for more information.

The ADDRESS/DATA STEPPING protocol does not apply to configuration transactions, but the PRE-DRIVE protocol does apply. Please see Subchapter 4.1 on how the PRE-DRIVE protocol is implemented.

As outlined in Chapter 7: *Bridge and Interface Protocol,* COMBINING, COLLAPSING, PREFETCHING, and MERGING cannot be applied to configuration transactions.

The Master and Target Fast Back-to-Back protocols that are defined for memory and I/O transactions also apply to configuration transactions. See Chapter 6: *Detailed Bus Transaction Operation* for more information.

ADDRESS DECODING AND OTHER ATTRIBUTES FOR CONFIGURATION TRANSACTIONS

Address decoding (*i.e.*, claiming the bus transaction by asserting the DEVSEL# signal lines) for configuration transactions is the same as for memory and I/O transactions. The configuration transactions protocol is the same as for memory and I/O transactions including completing configuration transactions with Completion, Master Abort, Retry, Disconnect, and Target Abort terminations. However, the configuration transaction protocol does not support the execution of the Completion with Timeout termination. See *Chapter 8: Master and Target Termination* for more information.

There are some additional exceptions for the protocol of configuration transactions versus the protocol of memory and I/O transactions:

- 32 data bits is the only size supported.

- 64 bit address extension is not defined for the configuration transaction — the AD[63::32] signal lines are never part of the decode.

- DUAL ADDRESS is not executed with configuration transactions.

- The AD[31::00] signal lines are reserved or can be used to drive IDSEL signal line values for Type 0 configuration transaction. For Type 1 configuration transaction, AD[23::16] signal lines select which PCI bus, and AD[15::11] contain the device number.

- The AD[01::00] signal lines are used for decoding to identify Type 0 or 1 configuration transactions.

- The IDSEL signal line of the resource must be asserted for Type 0 configuration transactions.

The PCI local bus specification supports configuration registers for each PCI resource (PCI bus master, target, or bridge defined as a "device"). Even though the configuration transaction follows the basic protocol of a memory or I/O transaction, there are some differences. See Chapter 7: *Bridge and Interface Protocol* for more information.

The definition of a configuration transaction places the following unique protocol requirements on this type of bus transaction:

■ Each device that is accessed by a configuration transaction has 256 byte registers.

■ Each PCI bus can have 21 individual devices with configuration registers by using the AD[31::11] signal lines as IDSEL signal lines, or the bridge can attach the IDSEL signal lines of the PCI resources to specific outputs of the bridge.

■ There are two types of configuration transactions: Types 0 and 1. A Type 0 configuration transaction is claimed (assertion of DEVSEL# signal line) by a device on the same PCI bus segment that the Type 0 configuration transaction is being executed. Type 1 can only be claimed by a PCI/PCI BRIDGE for the purpose of porting it to another PCI bus segment as a Type 1 configuration transaction, or a PCI/PCI BRIDGE converting it to Type 0 configuration or special transactions.

■ The configuration transaction executes with the same protocol as memory or I/O transactions.

  ■ The Type 0 configuration transaction can be executed as a SINGLE or BURST bus transaction.

  ■ Only a SINGLE Type 1 configuration transaction can be converted by a PCI/PCI BRIDGE to SINGLE special or Type 0 configuration transaction. Conversion by a PCI/PCI bridge of BURST Type 1 configuration transactions to BURST special or Type 0 configuration transactions is not allowed. Consequently, Type 1 configuration transactions cannot be executed as BURST bus transactions.

Consider the following four observations regarding flow direction of configuration transactions throughout a system:

One: A Type 0 configuration transaction originates with the HOST CPU (by definition the highest LEVEL bus) and is ported from PCI bus segment to PCI bus segment (lower LEVEL bus segments) with the bridges acting as the PCI bus master on behalf of the HOST CPU for each respective PCI bus segment. The side of each bridge attached to the lower LEVEL bus segment will drive the IDSEL# signal lines using the AD[31::11] signal lines, or discrete "chip select like" signal lines, to execute a Type 0 configuration transaction. A "specific" PCI bus master (not HOST/PCI BRIDGE) on a specific bus segment (other than the bridge acting on behalf of the HOST CPU) can only access the configuration address space of a device on the same bus segment if the IDSEL# signal lines are attached to the AD[31::11] signal lines of that bus segment. Because discrete "chip select like" signal lines attached to the bridge can be used, there is no way to consistently state that a "specific" PCI bus master can access the configuration address space of any device on the same bus segment.

Two: The "specific" PCI bus master on a specific bus segment (other than the bridge acting on behalf of the HOST CPU) can access the configuration address space of a device (target) on another bus segment only by a bridge translating a Type 1 configuration transaction to a Type 0 configuration transaction. This is possible when the target is on a lower LEVEL bus segment than that of the "specific" PCI bus master. That is, the actual bridge implementations are designed to claim Type 1 configuration transactions on the higher LEVEL bus segment side to port to the lower LEVEL bus segment as a Type 1 configuration transaction or to translate to a Type 0 configuration transaction. The architecture can be defined for either IDSEL signal line implementation: either shared with AD[31::11] signal lines or discrete "chip select like".

Three: Consistent with observations one and two above, Type 0 configuration transactions begun at the HOST CPU (minimal requirement for the operating system) can access the configuration address spaces of all devices in the system (via the PCI/PCI BRIDGEs designed to translate Type 1 configuration transactions on the higher LEVEL bus segment side to Type 0 configuration transactions on the lower LEVEL bus segment side). Also, per the above observations, there is no guarantee that a "specific" PCI bus master can access the configuration address space of devices on same bus segment. If a "specific" PCI bus master cannot even access the configuration space of devices on its own bus segment, there would be no reason to design PCI/PCI BRIDGEs to port Type 1 configuration transactions on the lower LEVEL bus segment side to the higher LEVEL bus segment side

Four: The "specific" PCI bus master on a specific bus segment (other than the bridge acting on behalf of the HOST CPU) can execute a special transaction to all devices on the same bus segment. The "specific" PCI bus master can execute a Type 1 configuration transaction that can port from the lower LEVEL bus segment side of a PCI/PCI BRIDGE to the higher LEVEL bus segment side of a PCI/PCI BRIDGE as a Type 1 configuration transaction or translated to a special transaction. Also, the "specific" PCI bus master can execute a Type 1 configuration transaction that can port from the higher LEVEL bus segment side of a PCI/PCI BRIDGE to the lower LEVEL bus segment side of a PCI/PCI BRIDGE as a Type 1 configuration transaction or translated to a special transaction. This latter direction also supports Type 1 configuration transactions from the HOST CPU being translated into special transactions on lower LEVEL bus segments. Consequently, only Type 1 configuration write transactions associated with special transactions from lower LEVEL to higher LEVEL bus segments will be ported through PCI/PCI BRIDGES. All Type 1 configuration write transactions from higher LEVEL to lower LEVEL bus segments will be ported through PCI/PCI BRIDGES.

The results of the above observations are as follows:

■ Only the HOST CPU can access the configuration address space of all devices. Due to system hierarchy, the flow for accesses from the HOST CPU to devices is always in a "downstream" direction.

■ A PCI bus master on a "specific" bus segment (not a bridge acting on behalf of the HOST CPU) cannot be guaranteed access to the configuration address space of a device on the same "specific" bus segment (chip select pins may be implemented for the IDSEL signal lines).

■ A PCI bus master on a "specific" bus segment ("specific" PCI bus master ... not a bridge acting on behalf of the HOST CPU) can only access the configuration address space of devices on lower LEVEL bus segments because a bridge can port or translate a Type 1 configuration transaction associated with a Type 0 configuration transaction from the higher LEVEL bus segment side to the lower LEVEL bus segment side of the bridge. This reflects the fact that PCI/PCI BRIDGE implementations are designed to claim Type 1 configuration transactions on the higher LEVEL bus segment side to translate to Type 0 configuration transactions on lower LEVEL bus segment side to support "downstream" accesses by the HOST CPU.

- PCI/PCI BRIDGEs port Type 1 configuration transactions from the lower LEVEL bus segment side to the higher LEVEL bus segment side (only Type 1 configuration write for special transactions) and from the higher LEVEL bus segment side to the lower LEVEL bus segment side. The porting also includes translation of Type 1 configuration transactions to special transactions. Consequently, the HOST CPU and PCI bus master on a "specific" bus segment ("specific" PCI bus master ... not a bridge acting on behalf of the HOST CPU) can generate special transactions on any bus segment. The "specific" PCI bus master can also generate a special transaction on the same "specific" bus segment.

4.3 PCI INTERRUPT ACKNOWLEDGE TRANSACTIONS

This is a brief introduction to PCI interrupt acknowledge transactions. See Subchapter 4.5: *PCI 32 Data Bit Bus Master to 32 Data Bit Target* for more information.

An interrupt acknowledge transaction originates with the HOST CPU and is ported to PCI bus (0) by the HOST/PCI BRIDGE. A typical platform will place the interrupt controller in a PCI resource on PCI bus (0). This PCI resource can be a "non-BRIDGE" component or a PCI/LEGACY BRIDGE. If the interrupt controller is on the LEGACY bus, the PCI/LEGACY BRIDGE will represent it on PCI bus (0).

The interrupt controller may be contained in a HOST bus resource, a HOST/LEGACY BRIDGE, or on a LEGACY bus attached to the HOST/ LEGACY bus BRIDGE. In this architecture, no interrupt acknowledge transaction is executed on PCI Bus (0).

Interrupt acknowledge transactions can only execute on PCI bus (0) segment as SINGLE bus transactions. Though it is possible to define a BURST interrupt acknowledge transaction generated by the HOST/PCI BRIDGE, the PCI local bus specification only defines a SINGLE bus transaction version. Interrupt acknowledge transactions are read only and thus cannot be posted into a bridge. Interrupt acknowledge transactions can only be implemented as SINGLE bus transactions with Immediate Transaction and Delayed Transaction protocols with the PCI/LEGACY BRIDGE (as the actual target or representing the actual target (non-bridge)). If the interrupt controller is directly attached to PCI bus (0), the SINGLE bus transaction Immediate Transaction and Delayed Transaction protocols can be executed. See Chapter 7: *Bridge and Interface Protocol* for more information.

The "PCI 16 clock" rule applies to interrupt acknowledge transactions. The "PCI 8 clock" rule does not apply because BURST interrupt acknowledge transactions are not defined. See Subchapter 4.0 for more information.

Please see Subchapter 4.1 on how ADDRESS/DATA STEPPING and PRE-DRIVE protocols operate. Only the ADDRESS/DATA STEPPING protocol can be applied interrupt acknowledge transactions. However, in that the address is not needed there is no reason to implement ADDRESS/DATA STEPPING protocol relative to the ADDRESS PHASE.

As outlined in Chapter 7: *Bridge and Interface Protocol* COMBINING, COLLAPSING, PREFETCHING, and MERGING cannot be applied to the interrupt acknowledge transactions through a bridge or interface.

The interrupt acknowledge transaction follows the protocol of a read transaction. Therefore, the Master and Target Fast Back-to-Back protocol cannot be applied to a subsequent bus transaction. See Chapter 6: *Detailed Bus Transaction Operation* for more information.

ADDRESS DECODING AND OTHER ATTRIBUTES FOR INTERRUPT ACKNOWLEDGE TRANSACTIONS

There is no address decoding (*i.e.*, claiming the bus transaction by asserting the DEVSEL# signal lines) for interrupt acknowledge transactions. Also, DUAL ADDRESS is not executed with interrupt acknowledge transactions. The PCI bus master (HOST/PCI BRIDGE) completes the interrupt acknowledge transaction with the same protocol as a memory or I/O transaction including Completion, Master Abort, Retry, Disconnect, and Target Abort terminations. The interrupt acknowledge transaction does not support the execution of the Completion with Timeout termination. See Chapter 8: *Master and Target Termination* for more information.

The PCI local bus specification supports discrete interrupt request signal lines (INTx#) that are not defined by bus transaction protocol. The purpose of the INTx# signal lines is to allow specific PCI resources to request service from the HOST CPU. In response to a request for service, the HOST CPU, in conjunction with the HOST/PCI BRIDGE, executes an interrupt acknowledge transaction. It is the responsibility of the interrupt controller to place the appropriate interrupt vector onto the AD[31::0] signal lines during the DATA PHASE of the interrupt acknowledge transaction.

The definition of an interrupt acknowledge transaction places the following unique protocol requirements on this type of bus transaction:

■ The interrupt acknowledge transaction is executed without an address; consequently, the PCI resource that contains the interrupt controller is the only device that "claims" the bus transaction by asserting the DEVSEL# signal line.

■ The PCI resource that claimed the interrupt acknowledge transaction uses the TRDY# signal line to lengthen the bus transaction. Like memory and I/O transactions, the TRDY# signal line, in conjunction with the IRDY# signal driven by the PCI bus master (HOST/PCI BRIDGE), controls the length of the bus transaction.

■ An interrupt acknowledge transaction can only perform data reads. No data writes are possible.

4.4 PCI SPECIAL TRANSACTIONS

This is a brief introduction to PCI special transactions. See Subchapter 4.5: *PCI 32 Data Bit Bus Master to 32 Data Bit Target* for more information.

A special transaction request originates with the HOST CPU or a PCI bus master on one of the PCI bus segments. The request is ported from the HOST CPU to lower LEVEL bus segments with the bridges acting as the PCI bus master for each respective PCI bus segment. A PCI bus master of a specific PCI bus segment can execute a special transaction to PCI resources on the same specific PCI bus segment or request a special transaction on another PCI bus segment. The request for special transactions is ported from a specific PCI bus segment to other higher or lower LEVEL bus segments via Type 1 configuration transactions, with the PCI/PCI BRIDGEs acting as the PCI bus master for each respective PCI bus segment.

The observations and results regarding flow direction of configuration transactions (and therefore special transactions) are discussed in the *PCI Configuration Transactions* section of Subchapter 4.2.

Special transactions executed between a PCI bus master (bridge or non-bridge) on the same PCI bus segment as the actual target (non-bridge) can be implemented as either SINGLE or BURST bus transactions. Special transactions cannot be posted into or ported through the PCI/PCI BRIDGE representing the actual target (non-bridge). Special transactions are ported through a PCI/PCI BRIDGE via Type 1 configuration transactions. See Chapter 7: *Bridge and Interface Protocol* for more information.

The "PCI 16 clock" and "PCI 8 clock" rules do not apply to special transactions because the application of "PCI 16 clock" and "PCI 8 clock" rules require a single PCI resource to claim (assert DEVSEL# signal line) the transaction. By protocol definition of special transaction, it is a broadcast write type of transaction and cannot be claimed by a singular PCI resource. See Subchapter 4.0 for more information.

Please see Subchapter 4.1 on how ADDRESS/DATA STEPPING and PRE-DRIVE protocols operate. Only the ADDRESS/DATA STEPPING protocol can be applied to special transactions. However, in that the address is not needed there is no reason to implement ADDRESS/DATA STEPPING protocol relative to the ADDRESS PHASE.

As outlined in Chapter 7: *Bridge and Interface Protocol* COMBINING, COLLAPSING, PREFETCHING, and MERGING cannot be applied to special transactions.

A special transaction guarantees a minimum of five CLK signal line periods between valid data and the beginning of the subsequent bus transaction. An IDLE PHASE is required between a special transaction and the subsequent bus transaction; consequently, the Master and Target Fast Back-to-Back protocols are not supported. See *Chapter 6. Detailed Bus Transaction Operation* for more information.

ADDRESS DECODING AND OTHER ATTRIBUTES FOR SPECIAL TRANSACTIONS

There is no address decoding (*i.e.*, claiming the bus transaction by asserting the DEVSEL# signal lines) for special transactions. Also, DUAL ADDRESS is not executed with special transactions.

The PCI bus specification allows for "physical" signal lines (called side bands), that are not defined by the PCI bus specification, to be connected between PCI resources. The PCI resources must be on the same circuit card, because side band signal lines are not defined on the PCI connector. The purpose of the side band signal lines is to allow specific information to be conveyed between PCI resources. The special transaction allows PCI bus masters to broadcast messages to all PCI resources on the same PCI bus segment. Similarly, through the use of Type 1 configuration transactions, a PCI bus master on a specific PCI bus segment can broadcast messages to PCI resources on other PCI bus segments. These messages can convey PCI bus master status and can also act as "logical" side band signal lines. The special transaction provides the PCI bus master the opportunity to broadcast information to all PCI resources without the use of physical side band signal lines. This information can be of any type, including the setting of flip flops in real time. It is the responsibility of each PCI resource to determine if the information is relevant to the resource and how it will be used. The PCI resource is required to immediately use the information. The completion of the special transaction guarantees that the information is acted on immediately.

The definition of a special transaction places unique protocol requirements on this type of bus transaction:

- The special transaction is broadcast to all PCI bus resources on a specific PCI bus segment; consequently, no individual target can claim a special transaction by asserting the DEVSEL# signal line.

- No PCI resource can claim the special transaction; consequently, the TRDY# signal line is not asserted and the length of the special transaction is controlled by the PCI bus master via the IRDY# signal line.

- A special transaction can only do data writes. No data reads are possible.

- A special transaction can only occur on the same bus as the PCI bus master that is executing the special transaction. A PCI/PCI BRIDGE cannot port a special transaction from one PCI bus segment to another.

- A PCI bus master can cause a bridge to execute a special transaction on any other PCI bus segment by executing a version of the Type 1 configuration transaction to the PCI/PCI BRIDGE(s).

- The special transaction is executed with the protocol of a SINGLE or BURST bus transaction.

- The PCI bus master completes the special transaction with a Master Abort termination. The other target transaction termination protocols are not supported for special transactions. See Chapter 8: *Master and Target Termination* for more information.

- Only SINGLE Type 1 configuration transactions can be converted by a PCI/PCI BRIDGE to SINGLE special transactions with Immediate Transaction or Delayed Transaction protocols. Conversion of a BURST Type 1 configuration transaction to a BURST special transaction is not allowed.

> The capability for a PCI bus master to execute a special transaction is optional. A HOST/PCI BRIDGE may support the special transaction to allow the HOST CPU to broadcast to PCI resources, but it is not required.

4.5 PCI 32 DATA BIT BUS MASTER TO 32 DATA BIT TARGET

The remainder of the PCI specific portion of this chapter will separately address 32 and 64 data bits relative to PCI resources. The first part will concentrate on 32 data bit PCI resources and the latter part will provide the incremental information relevant to the 64 data bit extension.

MEMORY TRANSACTIONS

> See Subchapter 4.1 for related information.

INTRODUCTION

The following discussions refer to the prefetchable address space that has been discussed in other sections of this book. It is repeated here for completeness.

- A prefetchable address space (or simply prefetchable address) is an address range within the memory address space. It can only reside in the memory address space. Multiple readings from a specific prefetchable address results in the same data (provided no write to this address has occurred). Also, PCI/PCI BRIDGES can merge memory write transactions. The multiple reading and possible discarding of data by the PCI bus master or bridge does not have negative side effects. Also, a prefetchable address space is required to support merging of bytes written to it within a DWORD (by a bridge) without any negative side effects. The Prefetchable bit in the Memory Base Address register in the configuration address space of the target must be set to "logical "1"" for the associated address range to be prefetchable. It is the responsibility of the PCI bus master to implement memory read line or memory read multiple commands only to a prefetchable address. That is, the target does not compare the value of the Prefetchable bit in the Memory Base Address register for bus transactions associated with the MRM and MRL commands. See Chapter 7: *Bridge and Interface Protocol* for more information.

> The reading of prefetchable address space requires all of the bytes being read and returned in the bus transaction independent of the byte enables specified in the bus transaction. (This is not part of the prefetchable address space definition of PCI-X bus transactions.)

> **The non-prefetchable address space of a memory resource behind a bridge must be located in the lower four gigabyte address space.**

A PCI bus master requests a 32 data bit memory transaction with the continued deassertion of the REQ64# signal line during the ADDRESS PHASE (deasserted by a pull-up resistor on the bus backplane). The target acknowledges executing a 32 data bit transaction with the continued deassertion of the ACK64# signal line during the DATA PHASE (deasserted by a pull-up resistor on the bus backplane). Once the respective bus transaction participants establish the transaction data size, it remains unchanged during the remainder of the bus transaction.

> **A memory transaction *can* be executed with DUAL ADDRESS.**

The signal line protocol during the ADDRESS and DATA PHASES are the same for the SINGLE and BURST memory transactions. The bus master executes a successful memory transaction as SINGLE versus BURST by the activity of the FRAME# and IRDY# signal lines. As outlined in Chapter 3: *Generic PCI and PCI-X Hardware Operation* and detailed in Chapter 6: *Detailed Bus Transaction Operation*, the simultaneous deassertion of the FRAME# signal line and assertion of the IRDY# signal line during the first data access of the DATA PHASE results in a SINGLE memory transaction. The assertion of the FRAME# signal line when the IRDY# signal line is asserted during the first data access in the DATA PHASE results in a BURST memory transaction.

BOUNDARY CONSIDERATIONS

There are several considerations relative to a BURST memory transaction crossing the following boundaries:

- ■ When a BURST memory transaction is executed it cannot exceed the address boundary of the target. The target is required to execute a Disconnect termination at its address boundary. See Chapter 8: *Master and Target Termination* for more information.

- ■ A PCI bus master is permitted to cross the lower four gigabyte address boundary. If the target straddles this boundary, the associated BURST bus transaction is permitted to continue. If the target does not straddle this boundary it is required to execute a Disconnect termination to prevent the BURST bus transaction from crossing the four gigabyte address boundary. The "actual" target (not a PCI/PCI BRIDGE) is not permitted to have an address range to cross (straddle) the four gigabyte address boundary. However, a PCI/PCI BRIDGE can be a target and its address range may represent two "actual" targets adjacent in the address space at the four gigabyte address boundary. See Chapter 8: *Master and Target Termination* for more information.

ADDRESS SPACE PER DEVICE

The PCI local bus specification allows a full 4K memory address space range to be assigned to each PCI device (or each function in a multiple function device), whether the full range is needed or not.

64 BIT ADDRESSING

The PCI local bus specification does not require all devices (either PCI bus masters or targets) that support the memory address space to also support the full 64 bit addressing. The address bits of the AD[31::00] signal lines define address from 0 to 4 gigabytes - 1. As previously discussed, the full 64 bits for the address is executed in conjunction with the DUAL ADDRESS command. However, the full 64 bit addressing (and thus the DUAL ADDRESS) is not required for all memory bus transactions according to the following:

■ If the memory address range is within the lower four gigabyte address range [0 to 4 gigabytes – 1], a memory bus transaction must not execute the DUAL ADDRESS command. Even though a PCI memory target may support a 64 bit address space, it must support non-DUAL ADDRESS command memory bus transactions for accesses if its memory address range is in the lower four gigabyte address space. See Chapter 7: *Bridge and Interface* for more information.

■ If the memory address range is within the upper four gigabyte address range (four gigabyte boundary included), a memory bus transaction with DUAL ADDRESS command must be executed.

■ Any memory address range of a target that cannot support prefetching must be located in the lower four gigabyte address range.

MEMORY TRANSACTIONS

During the ADDRESS PHASE of the memory transaction, the AD[31::2] signal lines select a 32 data bit double word, and the C/BE#[3::0] signal lines contain the encoded information of the COMMAND type. The 0110 ([3::0]) or 0111 ([3::0]) encoding indicates a memory read or a memory write transaction, respectively. The execution of a SINGLE or BURST memory transaction is not identified in the encoded information contained in the C/BE#[3::0] signal lines. The AD[1::0] signal lines during the ADDRESS PHASE are used to qualify the addressing order of the memory transaction. When the AD[1::0] signal lines are both logical "0", the addressing order for the BURST memory transaction is linear. For a SINGLE memory transaction, the AD[31::2] signal lines during the ADDRESS PHASE select the 32 data bits (double words) to be accessed during the DATA PHASE. For a BURST memory transaction, the AD[31::2] signal lines during the ADDRESS PHASE select the base address of the 32 data bits (double words) to be accessed during the DATA PHASE. The initial microaccess of a BURST memory transaction will access the double word selected by the AD[31::2] signal lines during the ADDRESS PHASE. The subsequent microaccesses will select the next double word located at the next sequential address (increasing) according to a linear addressing protocol.

> **Any PCI resource that supports BURST transactions must support linear address increasing as a minimum.**

The PAR signal line is driven by the PCI bus master and reflects the parity of the C/BE#[3::0] and AD[31::0] signal lines during the ADDRESS PHASE. The PAR signal line is driven with valid information with the same protocol as the AD signal lines, but with a one CLK signal line period delay from the actual CLK signal line periods associated with the ADDRESS PHASE.

> **During the ADDRESS PHASE, the target latches and decodes the AD[31::02] signal lines to determine if it will respond by asserting the DEVSEL# signal line; consequently, all AD[31::02] signal lines must be driven with valid information. Once the DEVSEL# signal line is asserted, it remains asserted until the completion of the memory transaction (except for Target Abort termination).**

There are two other interpretations of the AD[1::0] signal lines during the ADDRESS PHASE: Reserved and Cacheline Wrap (CLW). When the AD[0] signal line is logical "1" the burst address order is defined as Reserved. The target will allow a SINGLE memory transaction to be executed, but will prevent the continuation of a BURST memory transaction by requesting a Disconnect with data termination with the first data access or Disconnect without data termination with the second data access (first subsequent microaccess). When the AD[1::0] signal lines have a binary pattern of "10" (AD[1] = "1" and AD[0] = "0") the BURST memory transaction addressing order is CLW. The CLW simply means that the initial microaccess of a BURST memory transaction is to the address specified by the AD signal lines. If the address is in the "middle" of a Cacheline, the initial microaccess begins there and the next subsequent microaccess of the BURST memory transaction is to the next higher address in the Cacheline until the end of the Cacheline is encountered. Additional subsequent microaccesses address the beginning of the Cacheline and continue until the address of the initial microaccess is reached. At this point the subsequent microaccess is to the same "middle" location in the Cacheline with the next higher order addresses as the Cacheline of the initial microaccess.

> The reserved encoding may be defined in the future by the PCI Special Interest Group. The term "middle" of the Cacheline represents any location in the Cacheline, not necessarily the actual middle.

> If a target does not support the Cacheline Size register, the PCI bus master cannot access it with a Cacheline Wrap or Reserve burst order. If either of these burst modes is attempted, the target must execute a DISCONNECT with data termination on the initial microaccess or a DISCONNECT without data termination on the first subsequent microaccess.

> The switch from a SINGLE to a BURST memory transaction is controlled by the PCI bus master. Consequently, all memory targets are required to check the burst order encoded on the AD[1::0] signal lines during the ADDRESS PHASE. If the memory target cannot support the burst order requested, it must execute a Disconnect with data termination with the completion of the first access or a Disconnect without data termination with the second data access (first subsequent microaccess) which results in a SINGLE memory transaction, Chapter 8: *Master and Target Termination* for more information.

> The Rev. 2.0 of the PCI bus specification states that if the AD[0] signal line equals a logical "1" (deasserted) and the AD[1] signal line equals a logical "0" (asserted), the addressing order of the BURST memory transaction follows the Intel x86 and Pentium cache filling order. This protocol is no longer supported or applicable to the PCI local bus specification. This binary pattern is now reserved.

During the DATA PHASE of a SINGLE or BURST memory transaction, the C/BE#[3::0] signal lines will identify which bytes within the selected 32 data bits (double words) will be accessed. For a BURST memory transaction, the C/BE#[3::0] signal lines identify the bytes within the 32 data bits (double word) selected by each microaccess. It is possible that a different set of bytes get selected for each microaccess within the BURST memory transaction. As previously outlined in the "byte lane operation" section, the valid byte lanes for a given access or between accesses do not have to be continuous.

For the DATA PHASE of a read or write memory transaction, the PAR signal line is driven by the target or PCI bus master, respectively. It reflects the parity over ALL the C/BE#[3::0] and AD[31::0] signal lines. The PAR signal line is driven with valid information with the same protocol as the AD signal lines, but with a one CLK signal line period delay from the actual CLK signal line periods associated with the microaccess of the DATA PHASE. The byte lanes not valid (according to the C/BE#[3::0] signal lines) must be driven to a stable level, and parity is still computed on these byte lanes.

> **Parity is generated and valid parity is placed on the PAR signal line relative to the AD[31::00] and C/BE#[3::0] signal lines in the DATA PHASE independent of the value of the associated C/BE#[3::0] signal lines. That is, data parity generating and checking is defined for a data byte even though the associated C/BE# signal line is deasserted.**

For both SINGLE and BURST memory transactions, it is possible for none of the C/BE#[3::0] signal lines to be asserted during the DATA PHASE, and thus none of the associated byte lanes are valid. Under this condition the target should immediately assert the TRDY# signal line.

> **If a target is not able to support non-continuous byte accesses, it must execute a Target Abort termination. See Chapter 8:** *Master and Target Terminations* **for more information.**

The completion of a memory transaction requires the simultaneous deassertion of the FRAME# signal line and assertion of the IRDY# signal line, followed by the simultaneous deassertion of the FRAME# and IRDY# signal lines. Exceptions to these requirements occur due to termination (See Chapter 8: *Master and Target Termination* for more information) or Master and Target Fast Back-to-Back protocols. See Chapter 6: *Detailed Bus Transaction Operation* for more information.

MEMORY READ MULTIPLE (MRM) TRANSACTIONS

In the following discussions on MRM and MRL transactions, prefetchable address space is a consideration. The definition of the prefetchable address space is at the beginning of this section. Also, during the following discussions on MRM and MRL transactions remember that the associated BURST bus transaction cannot cross a natural 4096 byte address boundary. The target will execute a Disconnect termination if the PCI-X bus master tries to cross this boundary with MRM or MRL transactions.

The MRM (memory read multiple) transaction operates with the same protocol as a non-MRM SINGLE or BURST read memory transaction, including the support of DUAL ADDRESS. During ADDRESS PHASE, the C/BE#[3::0] signal lines contain the encoded information of the COMMAND type. The 1100 ([3::0]) encoding indicates an MRM transaction. The MRM transaction indicates to the PCI memory resource (target) that multiple Cachelines may potentially be read by the PCI bus master. In theory, an MRM transaction can be executed as a series of SINGLE memory transactions with the MRM COMMAND type encoding. But in practice, the MRM transaction should be performed as a BURST memory transaction with the MRM COMMAND type encoding.

The MRM transaction provides the best PCI bus performance for reading multiple Cachelines. A PCI memory resource implementing the MRM transaction will pre-read memory data before it is ported to the PCI bus. The Cacheline Size Register in the configuration address space provides the PCI memory resource with an indication of how many bytes of data should be pre-read. Support of the Cacheline Size Register by the PCI memory resource is not required for this COMMAND type. But if the Cacheline Size Register is supported, it should be used as an indicator for the optimum use of the MRM transaction. As defaults, 32 data bytes (for 32 data bit PCI buses) or 64 data bytes (for 64 data bit PCI buses) should be used.

According to Rev. 2.2 of the PCI local bus specification, a PCI memory resource can no longer be cached. However, the use of cache line size is a convenient unit of measurement for how much of the data should be pre-read. The use if Cacheline size does not imply in any way that the PCI resource is cached. The PCI memory resource is NOT REQUIRED TO BE CACHED OR CACHEABLE to be accessed by an MRM transaction. The reference to Cachelines simply provides a "size" relative to the number of bytes to be pre-read.

If the PCI memory resource does not support MRM transactions and the PCI bus master executes an MRM transaction, the target executes the transaction as a memory read or an MRL transaction. It still appears to the PCI bus segment as an MRM transaction because of the COMMAND type during the ADDRESS PHASE. The performance of the bus would be lower because a Cacheline pre-read does not occur.

126

> If the PCI memory resource supports MRM transactions and the PCI bus master completes an MRM or a non-MRM transaction by accessing less than a Cacheline, the bus transaction is successfully completed without an error related to accessing less than a Cacheline. The buffers in the target that contain the pre-read data are simply cleared (data discarded).

The execution of the MRM transaction to a PCI resource via a bridge is defined differently. A bridge should read an amount of data on the destination bus equal to a Cacheline of the source bus. The bridge should try to pre-read one Cacheline ahead of the source bus access in its access of the destination bus. See Chapter 7: *Bridge and Interface Protocol* for more information.

In the execution of an MRM transaction, a PCI resource (the actual target or a bridge) will be pre-reading data and will possibly discard it. Also, the PCI bus master may discard the data read via the MRM transaction. Because the data being read should be within a prefetchable address range, there will be no negative side effects in discarding it.

> MRM commands are limited to a 4K byte block on 4K address boundaries. If the PCI bus master attempts to cross this boundary (FRAME# signal line asserted for the last subsequent microaccess below the boundary) and the data is ready for access, the target must execute a Disconnect with data termination. Under this condition, if the data is not ready, the target executes a Disconnect without data termination.

MEMORY READ LINE (MRL) TRANSACTIONS

See the above section for the definition of prefetchable address space and discussions relative to crossing the four gigabyte address or natural 4096 byte address boundaries.

The MRL (memory read line) transaction operates with the same protocol as the non-MRL SINGLE or BURST read memory transaction, including the support of DUAL ADDRESS. During the ADDRESS PHASE, the C/BE#[3::0] signal lines contain the encoded information of the COMMAND type. The 1110 ([3::0]) encoding indicates an MRL transaction. The MRL transaction indicates to the PCI memory resource (target) that three or more 32 data bit words (double words) may potentially be read by the PCI bus master. In theory, an MRL transaction can be executed as a series of SINGLE memory transactions with the MRL COMMAND type encoding. But in practice, the MRL transaction should be performed as a BURST memory transaction with the MRL COMMAND type encoding.

If the PCI memory resource does not support MRL transactions and the PCI bus master executes an MRL transaction, the bus transaction completes as a memory read transaction. It still appears to the PCI bus as an MRL transaction because of the COMMAND type during ADDRESS PHASE. The performance will be poorer because the pre-read of the data does not occur.

If the PCI memory resource supports MRL transactions, and the PCI bus master completes an MRL or a memory read transaction by accessing only two or fewer 32 data bit words (double words), the bus transaction is successfully completed without an error related to accessing fewer than three double words. The buffers in the target that contain the pre-read data are simply cleared (data discarded).

The execution of the MRL transaction to a PCI resource via a bridge is defined differently. The bridge should try to pre-read one or two double words ahead of the source bus access in its access of the destination bus. See Chapter 7: *Bridge and Interface Protocol* for more information.

In the execution of an MRL transaction, a PCI resource (the actual target or a bridge) will be pre-reading data and will possibly discard it. Also, the PCI bus master may discard the data read via the MRL transaction. Because data being read should be within a prefetchable address range, there will be no negative side effects in discarding it.

MRL commands are limited to a 4K byte block on 4K address boundaries. If the PCI bus master attempts to cross this boundary (FRAME# signal line asserted for the last subsequent microaccess below the boundary) and the data is ready for access, the target must execute a Disconnect with data termination. Under this condition, if the data is not ready, the target executes a Disconnect without data termination.

MEMORY WRITE AND INVALIDATE (MWI) TRANSACTIONS

The MWI (memory write and invalidate) transaction operates with the same protocol as a non-MWI BURST memory write transaction, including the support of DUAL ADDRESS. During the ADDRESS PHASE, the C/BE#[3::0] signal lines contain the encoded information of the COMMAND type. The 1111 ([3::0]) encoding indicates an MWI transaction. The MWI transaction indicates to the cacheable PCI memory resource (PDRAM) that an entire Cacheline will be written. An MWI can only be executed as a single BURST write transaction within a Cacheline boundary. Support of the Cacheline Size Register is required for this COMMAND type.

> **If the PCI bus master is not going to write the entire Cacheline in a single BURST write transaction, it *cannot* use the MWI command. The MWI command can only be used with linear addressing order, and cannot be used with the Cacheline Wrap protocol.**
>
> **It is possible that a PCI bus master will begin execution of the MWI transaction with the intention to write an entire Cacheline, but the target may terminate the bus transaction (Retry, Disconnect, or Target Abort termination) prior to the PCI bus master writing the entire Cacheline. In this situation no error is generated. The bus transaction must be immediately terminated.**

> **A non-MWI transaction is defined as a memory write transaction with an encoding on the C/BE# signal lines of 0111 ([3::0]) during the ADDRESS PHASE.**

The use of the MWI transaction allows the cache controller in the HOST/PCI BRIDGE to mark a modified/valid Cacheline in a write-back cache invalid (after a cache hit) without executing a Retry termination. The Retry termination (if executed) requires the PCI bus master to repeat the bus transaction at another time, but provides the HOST/PCI BRIDGE the opportunity to "copy back" from cache to memory the modified/valid Cacheline. An MWI bus transaction indicates to the HOST/PCI BRIDGE that the "copy back" is not required because the Cacheline will be entirely written and thus can remain marked modified/valid after the execution of the MWI transaction.

When the MWI transaction is executed, a cache boundary in a write-back cache cannot be crossed unless all of the following conditions are met:

- The entire Cacheline addressed at the beginning of the BURST bus transaction must be written by the PCI bus master unless the target terminates the bus transaction with Retry, Disconnect, or Target Abort termination. In the case of a Retry termination the PCI bus master must repeat the MWI transaction.

- Whenever the Cacheline boundary is crossed, the entire new Cacheline must be written by the PCI bus master unless the target terminates the bus transaction with a Retry, Disconnect, or Target Abort termination. In the case of a Retry termination, the PCI bus master must repeat the MWI transaction.

If the above conditions are not met, the cache controller in the HOST/PCI BRIDGE must assert the SERR# signal line.

If the PDRAM does *not* support MWI transactions and the PCI bus master executes an MWI transaction, the target completes the bus transaction as if it received a non- MWI transaction.

If the PDRAM supports MWI transactions and the PCI bus master executes a non-MWI transaction, the target completes the bus transaction as a non-MWI transaction.

I/O TRANSACTIONS

See Subchapter 4.1 for related information.

A PCI bus master requests a 32 data bit access by deasserting the REQ64# signal line during the ADDRESS PHASE (deasserted by a pull-up resistor on the bus backplane). For an I/O transaction, the target can only respond by executing a 32 data bit transaction with the continued deassertion of the ACK64# signal line during the DATA PHASE (deasserted by a pull-up resistor on the bus backplane). Once the size of the respective bus transaction participants is established it remains unchanged during the remainder of the bus transaction.

An I/O transaction CANNOT be executed with DUAL ADDRESS.

The signal line protocol during the ADDRESS and DATA PHASES are the same for the SINGLE and BURST I/O transactions. The PCI bus master executes a successful I/O transaction as SINGLE versus by the activity of the FRAME# and IRDY# signal lines. As outlined in Chapter 3: *Generic PCI Hardware Operation* and detailed in Chapter 6: *Detailed Bus Transaction Operation*, the deassertion of the FRAME# signal line during the first data access of the DATA PHASE results in a SINGLE I/O transaction. The simultaneous assertion of the FRAME# signal line when the IRDY# signal line is asserted during the first data access in the DATA PHASE results in a BURST I/O transaction.

BOUNDARY CONSIDERATIONS

When a BURST I/O transaction is executed it cannot exceed the address boundary of target. The target must execute a Disconnect termination at its address boundary. See Chapter 8: *Master and Target Termination* for more information.

ADDRESS SPACE PER DEVICE

The size of the I/O address space assigned for each PCI device (or each function within a multiple function device) must be limited to a contiguous 256 bytes. The restriction to the contiguous address space insures compatibility to ISA-compatible I/O resources that may reside in the system. The total I/O address space for each PCI device (or each function within a multiple function device) can be larger than 256 bytes.

I/O TRANSACTIONS

During the ADDRESS PHASE of the bus transaction, the AD[31::0] signal lines identify a specific eight data bit byte and the C/BE#[3::0] signal lines contain the encoded information of the COMMAND type. The 0010 ([3::0]) or 0011 ([3::0]) encoding indicates an I/O read or an I/O write transaction, respectively. The execution of a SINGLE or BURST I/O transaction is not identified in the encoded information contained in the C/BE#[3::0] signal lines. The support of the AD[1::0] signal lines are according to a traditional addressing scheme which allows a PCI I/O resource (target) with a one byte size address space to claim the bus transaction by asserting the DEVSEL# signal line.

For example (as outlined on the next page), if the AD[1::0] signal lines are [0:1], the protocol between the AD[1::0] signal lines during the ADDRESS PHASE and the C/BE# signal lines during the DATA PHASE allows 8, 16, or 24 data bit only I/O resources to be accessed. In this case, the C/BE#[3::0] signal lines are required to be [X:X:0:1], and the target that claimed the bus transaction (DEVSEL# signal line asserted) can be accessed as an 8, 16, or 24 bit resource by the assertion of any or all of the C/BE#[3::1] signal lines. As a minimum, the least significant byte associated with C/BE#[1] = [0] is accessed. If another PCI resource owns the lowest order single byte, the byte can be individually accessed by AD[1:0] signal lines equaling [0::0] in the ADDRESS PHASE and the C/BE#[3::0] signaling lines equaling [1:1:1:0] in the DATA PHASE. The AD[1:0] signal lines contain data during the DATA PHASE.

The PAR signal line during the ADDRESS PHASE is driven by the PCI bus master and reflects the parity over the C/BE#[3::0] and AD[31::0] signal lines. The PAR signal line is driven with valid information with the same protocol as the AD signal lines, but with a one CLK signal line period delay. For an I/O transaction

the entire address must be supplied. Similarly, the C/BE#[3::0] signal lines must be driven by the PCI bus master with the complete COMMAND type encoding.

During the ADDRESS PHASE, the target decodes the AD[31::0] signal lines to determine if it will claim the bus transaction by asserting the DEVSEL# signal line. Consequently, all AD[31::0] signal lines must be driven with valid information. Once the DEVSEL# signal line is asserted, it remains asserted until the completion of the bus transaction, except for a Target Abort termination.

During the DATA PHASE of a SINGLE or BURST bus transaction, the C/BE#[3::0] signal lines will identify which bytes will be accessed. For a BURST I/O transaction, the C/BE#[3::0] signal lines identify the bytes selected by each microaccess. The C/BE#[3::0] signal lines during the DATA PHASE of a SINGLE bus transaction or the initial microaccess of a BURST bus transaction must also match the bytes that were addressed by the AD[1::0] signal lines during the ADDRESS PHASE. The allowed protocol for the AD[1::0] signal lines during the ADDRESS PHASE and the C/BE#[3::0] signal lines during the DATA PHASE follows:

AD[1]	AD[0]	C/BE#[3]	C/BE#[2]	C/BE#[1]	C/BE#[0]
0	0	X	X	X	0
0	1	X	X	0	1
1	0	X	0	1	1
1	1	0	1	1	1
x	x	1	1	1	1

Table 4-6: Relationship of AD signal lines (ADDRESS PHASE) with C/BE# signal lines (DATA PHASE) for I/O transactions (SINGLE bus transaction or initial microaccess of BURST bus transaction)

X = Don't care (asserted or deasserted)
1 = 3.3 or 5 volts (deasserted for C/BE#[3::0] signal lines)
0 = 0 volts (asserted for C/BE#[3::0] signal lines)

The I/O PCI target must monitor the AD[1::0] signal lines during the ADDRESS PHASE and compare their values with the C/BE#[3::0] signal lines during the DATA PHASE of a SINGLE bus transaction or initial microaccess of a BURST bus transaction. If the values do not support the same byte address, the target must execute a Target Abort termination. This protocol allows one to four different targets to own mutually exclusive portions of the 32 data bits (double words) being addressed by the bus transaction. This protocol DOES NOT apply if one target owns the entire double word. This protocol also does not apply to PCI/PCI or PCI/LEGACY BRIDGEs that implement subtractive decoding because there is no complete knowledge of resources on the destination PCI bus or the LEGACY bus, respectively.

> **Rev 2.0 of the PCI bus specification did not provide a "clear" protocol for BURST I/O transactions. Rev. 2.1 defines a BURST I/O transaction protocol. 64 data bit I/O targets can be implemented, but since there is no benefit that justifies the increased complexity, it is therefore strongly recommended that 64 data bit I/O targets not be implemented. For the purposes of this book, I/O targets are limited to 32 data bits in size. If a 64 data bit I/O target is implemented, the 64 data bit protocol applied to memory targets would also apply to I/O targets.**

As outlined above, the initial microaccess of a BURST I/O transaction must have the C/BE#[3::0] signal lines in the DATA PHASE agree with the AD[01::00] signal lines in the ADDRESS PHASE. The value of the C/BE#[3::0] signal lines in the subsequent microaccesses of the DATA PHASE do not have to agree with the AD[01::00] signal lines in the ADDRESS PHASE per Table 4-6.

Only a linear incrementing address sequence is allowed for a BURST I/O transaction. It is possible that a different set of bytes are selected for each microaccess within the BURST bus transaction. As previously outlined in the *Byte Lane Operation* section, valid byte lanes for a given or between accesses do not have to be continuous.

> **The switch from a SINGLE to a BURST bus transaction is controlled by the PCI bus master. If the I/O target cannot support BURST bus transactions, it must execute a Disconnect with data termination on completion of the first access (initial microaccess) or Disconnect without data termination after completion of the first access (initial microaccess). The aforementioned Target Abort is executed instead if the byte enables do not agree with address. See Chapter 8: *Master and Target Termination* for more information.**

> **For both SINGLE and BURST I/O transactions, it is possible for none of the C/BE#[3::0] signal lines to be asserted during the DATA PHASE of a SINGLE bus transaction or the initial microaccess of a BURST bus transaction.**

An I/O resource (target) can be re-mapped to the memory address space, can support up to 32 or 64 data bits, and can operate with the same protocol as any non-cacheable memory resource.

For the DATA PHASE of a read or write I/O transaction, the PAR signal line is driven by the target or PCI bus master, respectively. It reflects the parity over ALL the C/BE#[3::0] and AD[31::0] signal lines. The byte lanes not valid (according to the C/BE#[3::0] signal lines) must be driven to a stable level, and parity is still computed on these byte lanes.

> **Parity is generated and valid parity is placed on the PAR signal line relative to the AD[31::00] and C/BE#[3::0] signal lines in the DATA PHASE independent of the value of the associated C/BE#[3::0] signal lines. That is, data parity generating and checking is defined for a data byte even though the associated C/BE# signal line is deasserted.**

For both SINGLE and BURST I/O transactions, it is possible for none of the C/BE#[3::0] signal lines to be asserted during the DATA PHASE, and thus none of the associated byte lanes are valid. Under this condition the target should immediately assert the TRDY# signal line.

If the target is not able to support non-continuous byte accesses, it must execute a Target Abort termination. See Chapter 8: *Master and Target Terminations* for more information.

The completion of an I/O transaction requires the simultaneous deassertion of the FRAME# signal line and assertion of the IRDY# signal line followed by the simultaneous deassertion of the FRAME# and IRDY# signal lines. Exceptions to these requirements occur due to termination (see Chapter 8: *Master and Target Termination*, for more information) or Fast Back-to-Back protocol (Chapter 6: *Detailed Bus Transactions Operation* for more information).

CONFIGURATION TRANSACTIONS

> See Subchapter 4.2 and Chapter 7: *Bridge and Interface Protocol* for more information.
>
> The term "device" used in the following section is collectively the configuration address space (register sets) of the PCI resources. These PCI resources can be PCI bus masters (with configuration registers as a target), targets, or bridges. A device can have one to eight configuration address spaces.

> For a configuration transaction, only 32 data bit bus transactions can be executed. A configuration transaction *cannot* be executed with DUAL ADDRESS.

The signal line protocol during the ADDRESS and DATA PHASES of a configuration transaction is the same as a memory or I/O transaction, and both SINGLE and BURST (Type 0 executes with SINGLE and BURST ... Type 1 is SINGLE only) configuration transactions are supported. During the ADDRESS PHASE, the AD[7::2] signal lines select a double word (32 data bits) within a 256 byte address space of the configuration space. C/BE#[3::0] signal lines contain the COMMAND type: 1010 ([3::0]) or 1011 ([3::0]) encoding indicates a configuration read or configuration write transaction, respectively. The use of the AD[7::2] signal lines during the ADDRESS PHASE indicates that only 64 double words are available per configuration space. For a SINGLE bus transaction, the AD[7::2] signal lines during the ADDRESS PHASE select the double words to be accessed during the DATA PHASE of a Type 0. For a BURST bus transaction, the AD[7::2] signal lines during the ADDRESS PHASE select the base address of the double words to be accessed during the initial microaccess. The subsequent microaccesses will select the next double word located at the next sequential address (increasing) using a linear addressing protocol. The number contained within the AD[7::2] signal lines during the ADDRESS PHASE is defined as the REGISTER Number being accessed.

The PAR signal line is driven by the PCI bus master and reflects the parity of the C/BE#[3::0] and AD[31::0] signal lines during the ADDRESS PHASE. The PAR signal line is driven with valid information with the same protocol as the AD signal lines but with a one CLK signal line period delay. For a configuration transaction, all the AD[31::0] signal lines must be driven to a stable level by the PCI bus master.

During the DATA PHASE of a SINGLE or BURST configuration transaction, the C/BE#[3::0] signal lines will identify which bytes within the selected 32 data bits (double words) will be accessed. For a BURST configuration transaction, the C/BE#[3::0] signal lines identify the bytes within the 32 data bits (double word) selected by each microaccess. It is possible that a different set of bytes get selected for each microaccess within the BURST bus transaction. As previously outlined in the *Byte Lane Operation* section, the valid byte lanes for a given access, or between accesses, do not have to be continuous.

For the DATA PHASE of a read or write configuration transaction, the PAR signal line is driven by the device or PCI bus master, respectively. It reflects the parity over ALL the C/BE#[3::0] and AD[31::0] signal lines. The PAR signal line is driven with valid information with the same protocol as the AD signal lines, but with a one CLK signal line period delay from the actual CLK signal line periods associated with the microaccess of the DATA PHASE. The byte lanes not valid according to the C/BE#[3::0] signal lines are required to driven to a stable level, and parity is still computed on these byte lanes.

Parity is generated and valid parity is placed on the PAR signal line relative to the AD[31::00] and C/BE#[3::0] signal lines in the DATA PHASE independent of the value of the associated C/BE#[3::0] signal lines. That is, data parity generating and checking is defined for a data byte even though the associated C/BE# signal line is deasserted.

For both SINGLE and BURST memory transactions, it is possible for none of the C/BE#[3::0] signal lines to be asserted during the DATA PHASE, and thus none of the associated byte lanes are valid. Under this condition the target should immediately assert the TRDY# signal line.

The completion of a configuration transaction requires the simultaneous deassertion of the FRAME# signal line and assertion of the TRDY# signal, followed by the simultaneous deassertion of the FRAME# and IRDY# signal lines. Exceptions to these requirements occur either due to termination (see Chapter 8: *Master and Target Termination* for more information) or Master and Target Fast Back-to-Back protocol (see Chapter 6: *Detailed Bus Transaction Operation* for more information).

During ADDRESS PHASE, the AD[1::0] signal lines are used to select the configuration transaction type: Type 0 configuration transaction is selected when the AD[1::0] signal lines both = logical "0". Type 1 configuration transaction is selected when the AD[0] signal line = logical "1" and the AD[1] signal line = logical "0". A Type 0 configuration transaction is used to select (in conjunction with an asserted IDSEL signal line) the configuration address space of a device on the PCI bus segment when the configuration transaction is being executed (source bus). A Type 1 configuration transaction is used to port the configuration transaction through a PCI/PCI BRIDGE to a PCI resource behind the PCI/PCI BRIDGE (destination bus). The PCI/PCI BRIDGE converts the Type 1 configuration transaction on the source bus to a Type 0 configuration transaction on the destination bus.

During the ADDRESS PHASE of a Type 0 configuration transaction, the AD[31::11] signal lines are defined as reserved and the AD[10::8] signal lines contain the FUNCTION Number (see Figure 4-5). The definition of these signal lines is as follows:

- *RESERVED*: Must be driven to a stable level by the PCI bus master and may contain the IDSEL pattern. The parity for these signal lines is included in the PAR signal line.

- *FUNCTION number*: Used to select one of eight possible configuration spaces within the device.

> If the device being accessed contains only a single function, the device can either claim the Type 0 configuration transaction for any value of the AD[10::8] signal lines during the ADDRESS PHASE or only for function 0 (AD[10::8] signal lines = [1:1:0] during the ADDRESS PHASE).
>
> If the device being accessed contains multiple functions, the device must not claim the Type 0 configuration transaction if the AD[10::8] signal lines during the ADDRESS PHASE do not decode a specific function with a configuration address space.

During the ADDRESS PHASE of a Type 0 configuration transaction, the AD[31::11] signal lines may be individually mapped to the IDSEL signal lines to select one of 21 PCI resources (devices) on the bus. The HOST/PCI BRIDGE provides programmable registers that allow the HOST CPU to select the configuration transaction of a device on the lower LEVEL bus by programming the DEVICE number into these registers. When the HOST CPU begins a configuration transaction, the IDSEL signal lines reflect the encoded value of the DEVICE number into these programmable registers. The assertion of the IDSEL signal line requires the associated device to claim the bus transaction by asserting the DEVSEL# signal line. The REGISTER number is encoded in the AD[7::2] and addresses one of 64 DWORDS in the configuration address space. The device of a Type 0 configuration transaction cannot be on another bus connected by the PCI/PCI BRIDGE; consequently, negative decoding is not supported. If a BRIDGE claims a Type 0 configuration transaction, it is for the purpose of accessing the configuration registers within the PCI/PCI BRIDGE (which by definition is defined as the device). If the configuration transaction is not claimed, a Master Abort termination is executed.

> The mapping of the IDSEL signal lines to the AD[31::11] signal lines is one possible implementation. The IDSEL signal lines essentially function as chip selects and can be implemented by any platform circuitry that allows for the implementation of individual IDSEL signal lines.

During the ADDRESS PHASE of a Type 1 configuration transaction, the AD[31::24] signal lines are defined as reserved, the AD[23::16] signal lines contain the BUS Number, the AD[15::11] signal lines contain the DEVICE number, and the AD[10::8] signal lines contain the FUNCTION number (see Figure 4-6).

- ■ RESERVED: The AD[31::24] are driven to a logical "0" by the PCI bus master. Parity for these signal lines is encoded on the PAR signal line.

137

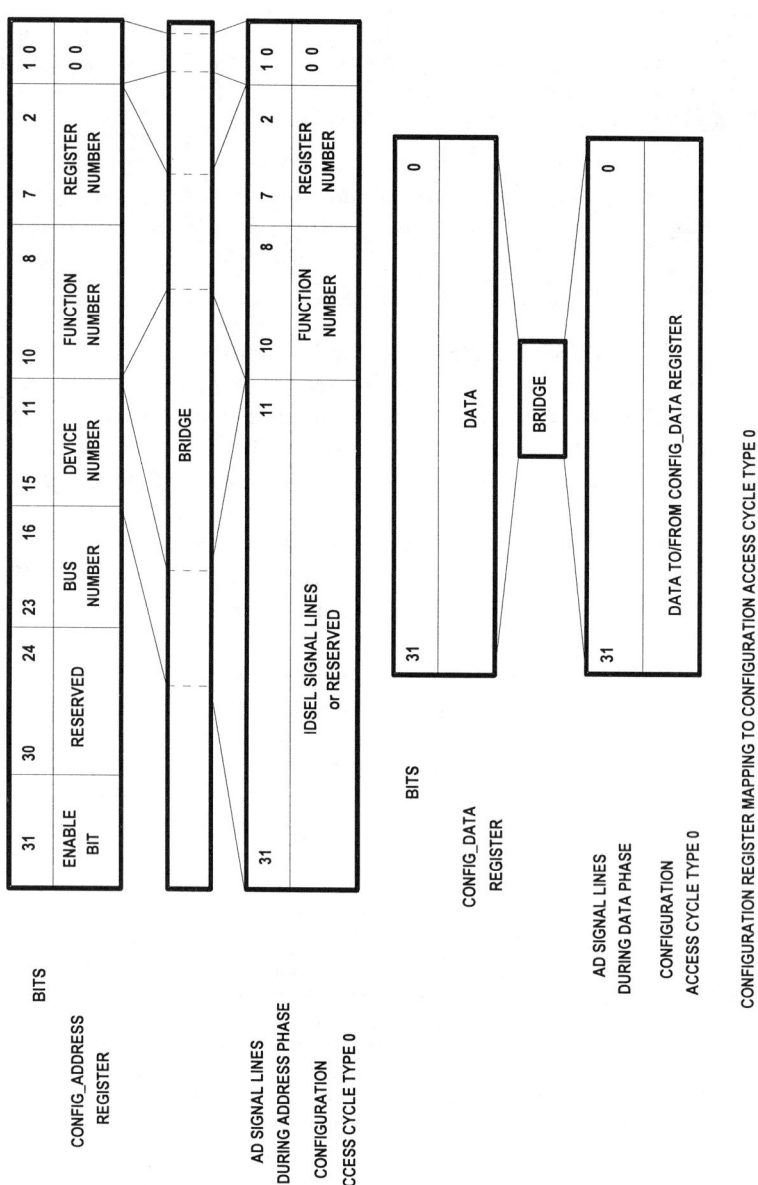

Figure 4-5: PCI Configuration Transaction Type 0

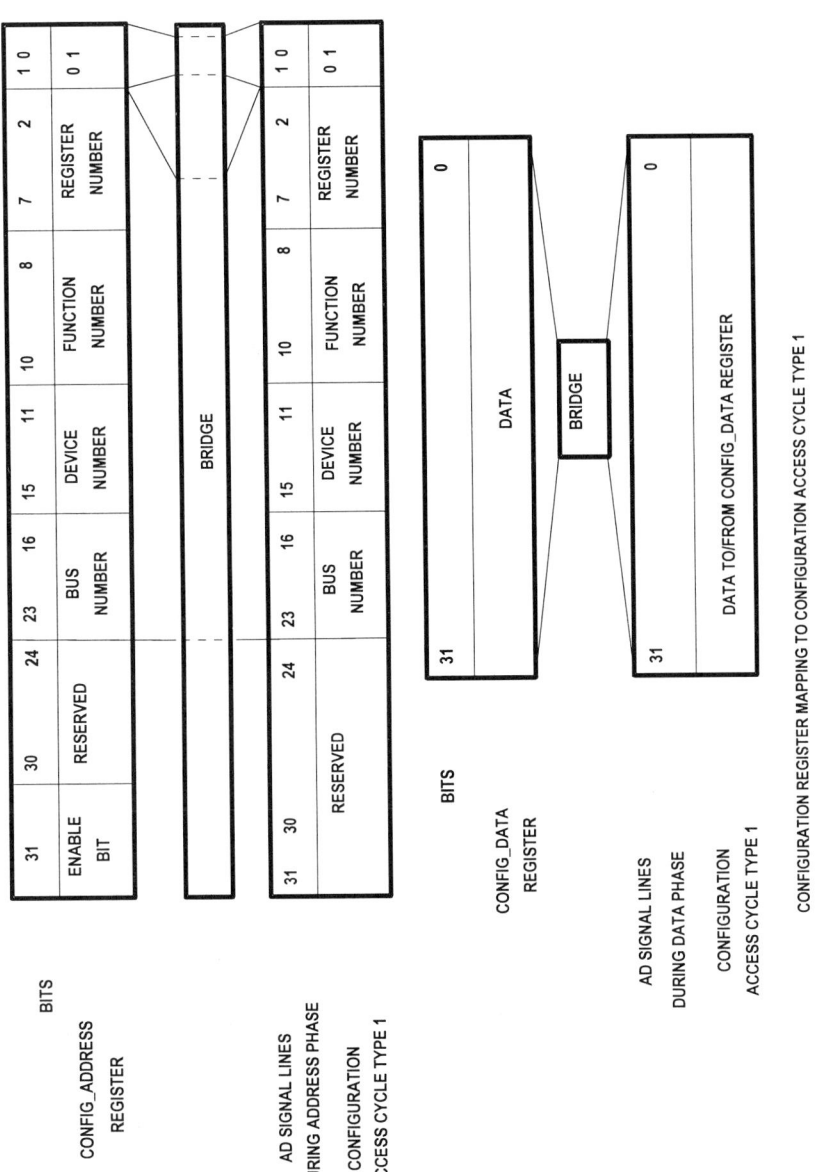

Figure 4-6: PCI Configuration Transaction Type 1

- BUS Number: Determines which one of a possible 256 bus segments is selected. The bus segments are numbered from 0 to 255 using the protocol outlined in Chapter 1.

- DEVICE Number: This selects 1 of 32 devices on the bus identified by the BUS Number. (Note: The IDSEL tied to the AD[31::11] signal lines allows up to 21 devices.)

- FUNCTION Number: Used to select one of eight possible configuration spaces (register sets) on each device.

During the ADDRESS PHASE of a Type 1 configuration transaction, the AD[23::16] signal lines contain the BUS number and the AD[15::11] signal lines contain the Device number. The PCI/PCI BRIDGE on the PCI bus segment executing the Type 1 configuration transaction claims the bus transaction if the BUS number matches a PCI bus segment behind the PCI/PCI BRIDGE. If the BUS number behind this PCI/PCI BRIDGE is directly attached to the BRIDGE (defined as "destination bus"), the Type 1 configuration transaction is repeated as a Type 0 configuration transaction on the destination bus with the binary pattern of the Device Number encoded onto the IDSEL (AD[31::11]) signal lines on the destination bus. If the BUS Number behind this PCI/PCI BRIDGE is not directly attached to this bridge (defined as the *non-destination bus*), the Type 1 configuration transaction is repeated as a Type 1 configuration transaction. If the Type 1 configuration transaction is passing from PCI bus segment to PCI bus segment for the purpose of executing a special transaction, all bits in the DEVICE and FUNCTION numbers in Type 1 configuration transaction equal logical "1" and all bits in the REGISTER number in the Type 1 configuration transaction equal logical "0".

INTERRUPT ACKNOWLEDGE TRANSACTIONS

See Subchapter 4.3 for related information.

For an interrupt acknowledge transaction, only 32 data bit bus transactions can be executed. An interrupt acknowledge transaction *cannot* be executed with DUAL ADDRESS.

The AD[31::0] and C/BE#[3::0] signal lines have the same protocol as that defined for a SINGLE memory transaction (BURST bus transactions are not defined for an interrupt acknowledge transaction). There are few differences between a SINGLE memory read transaction versus an interrupt acknowledge transaction as discussed below.

During the ADDRESS PHASE, the AD[31::0] signal lines are driven by the PCI bus master to a stable level, but contain no valid address information. The C/BE#[3::0] signal lines contain the binary pattern with the COMMAND type of an interrupt acknowledge transaction ([3::0] = [0000]). The PAR signal line contains parity information over the AD[31::0] and C/BE#[3::0] signal lines; consequently, a parity error during the ADDRESS PHASE can be reported by any PCI resource by asserting the SERR# signal line. During the DATA PHASE, the C/BE#[3::0] signal lines indicate the valid byte lanes and the AD[31::0] signal lines contain the interrupt vector. The PAR signal line contains parity information over the AD[31::0] and C/BE#[3::0] signal lines; consequently, a parity error during the DATA PHASE can be reported by the PCI bus master (BRIDGE) by asserting the PERR# signal line.

> Parity is generated and placed on the PAR signal line for the AD[31::00] and C/BE#[3::0] signal lines in the ADDRESS PHASE even though no valid address is encoded into the AD[31::0] signal lines. Parity is generated and placed on the PAR signal line for the AD[31::00] and C/BE#[3::0] signal lines in the DATA PHASE independent of the value of the associated C/BE#[3::0] signal lines. That is, data parity generating and checking is defined for a data byte even though the associated C/BE# signal line is deasserted.

> An 8259 interrupt-compatible vector requires only 8 data bits on the AD[7::0] signal lines.

> The fact that the PCI bus specification defines the size of the interrupt vector read from the PCI resource that contains the interrupt controller to be one byte (eight bits) in size is an example relative to Intel architectures. Consequently, the C/BE#[3::0] signal lines have a fixed binary pattern ([3::0] = [1110]). Larger data sizes with the appropriate C/BE#[3::0] signal lines asserted can also be used.

SPECIAL TRANSACTIONS

> See Subchapter 4.4 for related information.

> **For a special transaction, only a 32 data bit bus transaction can be executed. A special transaction *cannot* be executed with DUAL ADDRESS.**

AD[31::0] and C/BE#[3::0] signal lines have the same protocol as that defined for a SINGLE or BURST memory write transaction. There are a few differences between SINGLE and BURST memory write transactions versus SINGLE and BURST special transactions as discussed below.

During the ADDRESS PHASE, the AD[31::0] signal lines are driven by the PCI bus master to a stable level but contain no valid address information because no specific PCI resource is addressed. The C/BE#[3::0] signal lines contain the binary pattern with the COMMAND type of a special transaction (C/BE#[3::0] = [0001]). The PAR signal line contains parity information over the AD[31::0] and C/BE#[3::0] signal lines; consequently, a parity error during the ADDRESS PHASE can be reported by any platform resource by asserting the SERR# signal line. During the DATA PHASE, the C/BE#[3::0] signal lines indicate the valid byte lanes, and the AD[31::0] signal lines contain the special transaction encoded message and optional message-dependent data. The PAR signal line contains parity information over the AD[31::0] and C/BE#[3::0] signal lines; consequently, a parity error during the DATA PHASE can be reported by any platform resource by asserting the SERR# signal line.

> **Parity is generated and valid parity is placed on the PAR signal line relative to the AD[31::00] and C/BE#[3::0] signal lines in the ADDRESS PHASE even though no valid address is encoded into the AD[31::0] signal lines. Parity is generated and valid parity is placed on the PAR signal line relative to the AD[31::00] and C/BE#[3::0] signal lines in the DATA PHASE independent of the value of the associated C/BE#[3::0] signal lines. That is, data parity generating and checking is defined for a data byte even though the associated C/BE# signal line is deasserted.**

The information contained within the AD[31::0] signal lines during the DATA PHASE consists of two parts. The AD[15::0] signal lines are encoded with the message type. The AD[31::16] signal lines contain an optional data field relative to the message. The message type is defined by the PCI Special Interest Group steering committee. Any encoding that has been approved by this committee can be used by any manufacturer. The present list of four message types is shown below:

AD[15::0]	Message Type
0000h	SHUTDOWN
0001h	HALT
0002h	x86 architecture spec. (reserved for Intel)
0003h to FFFFh	Reserved

During the DATA PHASE, AD[15::0] signal lines contain the message type; consequently, C/BE#[3::0] signal lines are all logical "0" (asserted) to indicate valid byte lanes. The AD[31::16] signal lines contain the optional message-dependent data; the message type defines whether these signal lines have valid information even though the associated C/BE#[3::0] signal lines are asserted.

Because the special transaction completes with the Master Abort termination protocol, it is not possible to have a Master Abort termination as defined for other bus transactions (*e.g.*, a memory transaction). When a PCI bus master executes a special transaction, it terminates it with the Master Abort termination, but does not set the Received Master Abort bit of the Status Register in the configuration address space.

4.6   PCI 64 DATA BIT EXTENSION

INTRODUCTION

The 64 data bit extension only applies to memory transactions. Under all circumstances the configuration, interrupt acknowledge, and special transactions are executed only with 32 data bit transactions.

64 data bit I/O targets can be implemented, but there is no justification for the increased complexity, and it is therefore strongly recommended that 64 data bits I/O targets not be implemented. For the purposes of this book, I/O targets are only 32 data bits in size. If a 64 data bit I/O target is implemented, the 64 data bit protocol applied to memory transactions also applies to I/O transactions.

The PCI local bus specification supports both 32 and 64 data bit bus sizes. A 32 data bit implementation is all that is required to be compliant to the PCI local bus specification. The 64 data bit extension is optional, and 32 and 64 data bit resources can coexist on the same 64 data bit bus segment. The 64 data bit extension allows a 64 data bit PCI bus master to access a 64 data bit targets. A 32 data bit PCI bus master accessing a 64 data bit target or a 64 data bit PCI bus master accessing 32 data bit target does not require the 64 data bit extension. A 64 data bit PCI bus master or target is required to operate on a 32 data bit bus segment as a 32 data bit resource.

> **During the ADDRESS PHASE of a 64 data bit access the AD[2] signal line must be at logical "0". This value defines the address on 64 data bit (8 bytes) address boundaries. It is the value of the C/BE#[3::0] signal lines during the DATA PHASE that establishes which of the 8 bytes are being accessed.**

The support of the 64 data bit extension is accomplished with the addition of the AD[63::32], C/BE#[7::4], REQ64#, ACK64#, and PAR64 signal lines on the bus segment backplane. All of the bus transaction protocols outlined for platforms with the 32 data bit only PCI bus segments also apply to platforms with the 64 data bit extension. The 64 data bit extension does not apply to I/O, configuration, special, and interrupt acknowledge transactions. See Chapter 13: *Connector, Platform and Add-in Card Design, and Mechanical Considerations* for more information.

A SINGLE bus transaction or a microaccess of a BURST bus transaction with 32 data bit resources means that a single byte (8 data bits), word (16 data bits), triple bytes (24 data bits), or double words (32 data bits) are accessed via the AD[31::0] signal lines. A SINGLE bus transaction or a microaccess of a BURST bus transaction with 64 data bit resources means that the range from a single byte to quadruple words (64 data bits) can be accessed in 8 data bit increments via the AD[63::0] signal lines.

32 AND 64 DATA BIT PCI BUS MASTERS & 32 AND 64 DATA BIT TARGETS DETERMINATION

The PCI local bus specification supports 32 and 64 data bit PCI bus masters. The additional signal lines that support 64 data bit PCI bus masters are not required on all PCI bus segments; consequently, the 64 data bit bus masters must be able to reside on either 32 or 64 data bit bus segments. Platforms that support a 64 data bit PCI bus segment do not require that any device be a 64 data bit resource. For a PCI bus master to determine if it can request a 64 data bit bus transaction, it must monitor the REQ64# signal line when the RST# signal line is asserted (*i.e.*, during RESET). If the REQ64# and RST# signal lines are both asserted, the PCI bus master resides on a 64 data bit bus segment and can request a 64 data bit transaction; otherwise only 32 data bit transactions can be requested. See Chapter 11: *RESET, Power, and Signal Line Initialization*, for more information.

According to the PCI local bus specification, targets do not have to monitor the REQ64# signal line during RESET. The PCI bus master is responsible for asserting the REQ64# signal line only on a 64 data bit bus segment.

Due to the mixture of 64 data bit and non-64 data bit resources on 32 and 64 data bit bus segments, the PCI bus masters and targets must rely on the handshake of the REQ64# and ACK64# signal lines. A PCI bus master that samples the REQ64# signal line asserted during RESET asserts the REQ64# signal line during the ADDRESS PHASE to request a 64 data bit bus transaction. The bus transaction proceeds as a 64 data bit bus transaction if the target asserts the ACK64# signal line during the DATA PHASE in response to the asserted REQ64# signal line during the ADDRESS PHASE.

Only the memory address space supports 64 data bit bus transactions; consequently, only 64 data bit memory targets are required to monitor and drive the REQ64# and ACK64# signal lines, respectively. Targets that do not support 64 data bit bus transactions do not monitor or drive the REQ64# or ACK64# signal lines during bus transactions, respectively.

32 data bit PCI bus masters do not monitor (during RESET), drive (during bus transactions) the REQ64# signal line, or monitor the ACK64# signal line during bus transactions.

SIGNAL LINE OWNERSHIP DURING BUS TRANSACTIONS WITH 64 DATA BIT RESOURCES (PCI BUS MASTER AND TARGET)

See Subchapter 4.0 for associated information for 32 data bit resources.

A 64 data bit bus transaction and associated 64 data bit resources are only defined for the memory address space. During memory read and write transactions (including memory read multiple, memory read line, and memory write and invalidate), signal lines are owned by different PCI bus resources. A PCI resource "owns" the signal line when it is the only resource (other than a pull-up resistor) that can drive the signal line during a portion of the bus transaction. In the following discussions, the PAR and PAR64 signal lines relative to a specific bus transaction PHASE are actually delayed from that specific bus transaction PHASE. The protocol is as follows:

- FRAME#, IRDY#, and C/BE#[7::0], REQx#, and REQ64# signal lines are owned by the PCI bus master for any bus transaction.

- During a memory write transaction, the PCI bus master owns the AD[63::0], PAR, and PAR64 signal lines during both ADDRESS and DATA PHASES.

- During memory read transactions, the PCI bus master owns the AD[63::0], PAR, and PAR64 signal lines during the ADDRESS PHASE. The target owns these signal lines during the DATA PHASE. The ownership of these signal lines changes from the PCI bus master to the target in the first CLK signal line period of the DATA PHASE.

- During memory transactions, the TRDY#, DEVSEL#, STOP#, ACK64# signal lines are owned by the target.

Ownership of the remaining signal lines are defined according to the following protocol:

- The CLK and RST# signal lines are owned by platform resources.

- The GNTx# signal lines are owned by the central arbiter.

- The LOCK# signal line is owned by the Lock master.

DUAL ADDRESS

The DUAL ADDRESS protocol outlined in Subchapter 4.0 for 32 data bit resources applies to 64 data bit resources. As previously described, a 32 data bit PCI bus master can provide 64 address bits under the DUAL ADDRESS protocol without the use of the AD[63::32] signal lines. If the PCI bus master resides on a 64 data bit bus segment, requests a 64 data bit transaction (REQ64# signal line asserted during the ADDRESS PHASE), and executes a DUAL ADDRESS; the AD[63::32] signal lines contain the upper order address bit, and the C/BE#[7::4] signal lines contain the encoding for the COMMAND type.

BYTE LANE OPERATION

As outlined in Subchapter 4.0, the valid data of each bus transaction is dynamically identified by the C/BE# signal lines. As with the 32 data bit protocol, the central resource does not swap data between byte lanes. The AD[63::32] signal lines contain four byte lanes. (AD[39::32] signal lines make up the first byte lane, AD[47::40] signal lines comprise the second byte lane, and so forth.) The optional 64 data bit extension defines an additional 32 data bits (AD[63::32] signal lines) for memory transactions. The protocol for byte lane operation for the 64 data bit extension is the same as for 32 data bits with the following additions:

- No byte lane swapping occurs between the byte lanes of the AD[63::32] signal lines. Similarly, the central resource does not provide byte swapping between the byte lanes of the AD[31::0] and the AD[63::32] signal lines.

- If a 64 data bit PCI bus master accesses a 32 data bit target, the 32 data bit target can only reside on the AD[31::0] signal lines and the 64 data bit PCI bus master must internally swap the data between the AD[63::32] and AD[31::0] signal lines when the REQ64# signal line is asserted and the ACK64# signal line is deasserted.

- During the DATA PHASE of a memory write transaction, the AD[63::32] signal lines that do not have valid data (according to the C/BE#[7::4] signal lines) must be driven to a stable level by the PCI bus master when the REQ#64 and ACK64# signal lines are both asserted during the DATA PHASE. If the ACK64# signal line is deasserted during the DATA PHASE of a memory write transaction, the PCI bus master can drive the AD[63::32] and C/BE#[7::4] signal lines to logical "1", or optionally tristates these signal lines, relying on pull-up resistors to drive them to logical "1". During the DATA PHASE of a read transaction, the AD[63::32] signal lines that do not have valid data (according to the C/BE#[7::4] signal lines) are driven to a stable level by the target. If the ACK64# signal line is deasserted during the DATA PHASE of a memory read transaction, the AD[63::32] signal lines are driven to a logical "1" by pull-up resistors. A PCI bus master can drive the C/BE#[7::4] signal lines to logical "1" or optionally tristate these signal lines and rely on pull-up resistors to drive them to logical "1". See Subchapters 4.7 to 4.9 for boundary conditions prior to the assertion of the ACK64# signal line.

- The C/BE# signal lines for a given microaccess of a BURST bus transaction can enable different bytes relative to previous and subsequent microaccesses. The byte lanes do not have to be continuous. This applies to byte lanes identified within a specific bus transaction or byte lanes identified from one bus transaction to another.

The 64 data bits reflect the block of data addressed. It does not mean that 64 data bits are actually accessed.

PARK

The park protocol for 64 data bit PCI bus masters is the same as for a 32 data bit PCI bus master. When a 32 data bit PCI bus master becomes a Park master it drives the AD[31::0], C/BE#[3::0], and PAR signal lines to a stable level. The AD[63::32], C/BE#[7::4], and PAR64 signal lines are driven to a logical "1" by pull-up resistors. When a 64 data bit PCI bus master becomes a Park master it also drives the AD[31::0], C/BE#[3::0], and PAR signal lines to a stable level. The AD[63::32], C/BE#[7::4], and PAR64 signal lines are driven to a logical "1" by pull-up resistors.

4.7 PCI 32 DATA BIT BUS MASTER TO 64 DATA BIT TARGET

MEMORY TRANSACTIONS

A PCI bus master requests a 32 data bit bus transaction by the continued deassertion of the REQ64# signal line during the ADDRESS PHASE. The target can only respond by executing a 32 data bit bus transaction (ACK64# signal line deasserted). REQ64# and ACK64# signal lines are deasserted by pull-up resistors on the bus segment. The AD[63::32], C/BE#[7::4], and PAR64 signal lines are driven to a logical "1" by pull-up resistors for the entire bus transaction; consequently, the PAR64 signal line does not have valid parity information. Once the size of the respective bus transaction participants is established it remains unchanged during the remainder of the bus transaction.

Only a PCI memory resource (target) can be defined as a 32 or a 64 data bit resource. All memory transactions executed by a 32 data bit PCI bus master (REQ64# signal line deasserted) are independent of target data size and can only execute 32 data bit bus transactions.

See Chapter 6: *Detailed Bus Transaction Operation* for more information.

For a 64 data bit target, the memory transactions (including MRM, MRL and MWI) and DUAL ADDRESS operations, and Exclusive Access (LOCK) operation are supported with the same protocol as PCI bus transactions between a 32 data bit PCI bus master and a 32 data bit target.

I/O, CONFIGURATION, INTERRUPT ACKNOWLEDGE, AND SPECIAL TRANSACTIONS

These bus transactions are executed only with 32 data bit targets, and the REQ64# and ACK64# signal lines must be deasserted.

> 64 data bit I/O targets can be implemented, but there is no justification for the increased complexity and it is therefore not recommended that 64 data bit I/O targets be implemented. For the purposes of this book, I/O targets are only 32 data bits in size. If a 64 data bit I/O target is implemented, the 64 data bit protocol applied to memory targets will also apply to I/O targets.

4.8 PCI 64 DATA BIT BUS MASTER TO 64 DATA BIT TARGET

MEMORY TRANSACTIONS

A PCI bus master and a memory resource (target) are defined as 64 data bit resources when the REQ64# and ACK64# signal lines are asserted, respectively. The PCI bus master requests a 64 data bit bus transaction by asserting the REQ64# signal line during the ADDRESS PHASE, and the target acknowledges a 64 data bit bus transaction by asserting the ACK64# signal line during the DATA PHASE. The timing protocol of the FRAME# and REQ64# signal lines are the same and the timing protocol of the DEVSEL# and ACK64# signal lines are the same. The major difference between a 32 data bit and a 64 data bit bus transaction is that the AD[63::32], C/BE#[7::4], and PAR64 signal lines are used. The C/BE#[7::4], AD[63::32], and PAR64 signal lines operate with the same protocol as the C/BE#[3::0], AD[31::0], and PAR signal lines. The PAR64 signal line has valid parity information over the C/BE#[7::4] and AD[63::32] signal lines in the same fashion as the PAR signal line has valid parity information over the C/BE#[3::0] and AD[31::0] signal lines.

The addressing protocol of a 64 data bit BURST bus transaction is the same as for a 32 data bit BURST bus transaction, except that the address increments are 64 data bits (QWORDS). The AD[2] signal line is required to be logical "0" during the ADDRESS PHASE. The addressing order of the 64 data bit BURST bus transaction is defined by the AD[1::0] signal lines in the same fashion as a 32 data bit BURST bus transaction. The execution protocol of the 64 data bit SINGLE and BURST bus transactions is the same as for 32 data bit SINGLE and BURST bus transactions, except the AD[31::2] signal lines identify a 64 data bit QWORDS.

During the ADDRESS PHASE, when a 32 data bit PCI bus master (REQ64# signal line deasserted) begins a bus transaction, the AD[63::32], C/BE#[7::4], and PAR64 signal lines are driven to a logical "1" by pull-up resistors. The PAR64 signal line does not contain any valid parity information. When a 64 data bit PCI bus master (REQ64# signal line asserted) begins a bus transaction without DUAL ADDRESS it drives the AD[63::32] and C/BE#[7::4] signal lines to a stable level without any valid information. The PAR64 signal line is driven by the PCI bus master and will contain valid parity information over these signal lines during the ADDRESS PHASE with a one CLK signal line period delay. If a 64 data bit PCI bus master (REQ64# signal line asserted) begins a bus transaction with DUAL ADDRESS, it drives the upper order address and COMMAND type onto the AD[63::32] and C/BE#[7::4] signal lines, respectively. The PAR64 signal line is driven by the PCI bus master and will contain valid parity information over these signal lines during the ADDRESS PHASE with a one CLK signal line period delay.

> **See Chapter 6:** *Detailed Bus Transaction Operation* **for more information.**

For a 64 data bit target, the memory transactions (including MRM, MRL, and MWI), DUAL ADDRESS operation, and Exclusive Access (LOCK) operation are supported with the same protocol as bus transactions between a 32 data bit PCI bus master and a 32 data bit target

I/O, CONFIGURATION, INTERRUPT ACKNOWLEDGE, AND SPECIAL TRANSACTIONS

These PCI bus transactions are executed only with 32 data bit targets and the REQ64# and ACK64# signal lines must remain deasserted.

> **64 data bit I/O targets can be implemented, but there is no justification for the increased complexity and it is therefore not recommended that 64 data bit I/O targets be implemented. For the purposes of this book, I/O targets are only 32 data bits in size. If a 64 data bit I/O target is implemented, the 64 data bit protocol applied to memory targets will also apply to I/O targets.**

4.9 PCI 64 DATA BIT BUS MASTER TO 32 DATA BIT TARGET

MEMORY TRANSACTIONS

A PCI bus master and memory resource (target) are defined as 64 and 32 data bit resources when the REQ64# and ACK64# signal lines are asserted and deasserted, respectively. The PCI bus master requests a 64 data bit transaction by asserting the REQ64# signal line during the ADDRESS PHASE. A 32 data bit target responds without asserting the ACK64# signal line; a pull-up resistor on the backplane will deassert the ACK64# signal line during the DATA PHASE. The major difference between a PCI bus master request for a 64 data bit access to a 32 data bit target versus a 64 data bit target is the operation of the AD[63::32], C/BE#[7::4], and PAR64 signal lines during the DATA PHASE. For a write bus transaction, AD[63::32], C/BE#[7::4], and PAR64 signal lines during the ADDRESS PHASE and the initial microaccess of the DATA PHASE operate with the same protocol as outlined in the previous section for a 64 data bit bus transaction between a 64 data bit PCI bus master and a 64 data bit target. After the completion of the initial microaccess during the DATA PHASE, the AD[63::32], C/BE#[7::4], and PAR64 signal lines can be driven to a stable level by the PCI bus master, or tristated and driven to a logical "1" by pull-up resistors for the remainder of the BURST bus transaction. The PAR64 signal line will not contain valid parity information over these signal lines after the initial microaccess with a one CLK signal line period delay. For a read bus transaction, the AD[63::32], C/BE#[7::4], and PAR64 signal lines during the ADDRESS PHASE operate with the same protocol as outlined in the previous section for a 64 data bit transaction between a 64 data bit PCI bus master and a 64 data bit target. After the completion of the ADDRESS PHASE, the AD[63::32] and PAR64 signal lines are tristated and driven to logical "1" by pull up resistors. The C/BE#[7::4] signal lines can be driven to a stable level by the PCI bus master or tristated and driven to logical "1" by pull-up resistors for the remainder of the BURST bus transaction. The PAR64 signal line will not contain valid parity information over these signal lines after the ADDRESS PHASE with a one CLK signal line period delay.

> When a PCI bus master requests a 64 data bit bus transaction to a 32 data bit target, a SINGLE bus transaction cannot be executed. As explained in Chapter 6: *Detailed Bus Transaction Operation*, a request for a 64 data bit SINGLE bus transaction must be broken down into a BURST bus transaction with two 32 data bit microaccesses.

If the 64 data bit transaction (REQ64# signal line asserted) completes with Disconnect with data termination during the initial microaccess or Disconnect without data termination during the first subsequent microaccess with a 32 data bit target (ACK64# signal line deasserted), only the lower four bytes of the eight bytes (QWORD) of the 64 data bits have been accessed. The PCI bus master must subsequently execute a bus transaction as a 32 data bit PCI bus master (REQ64# signal line deasserted) to the upper four bytes of the original eight bytes (QWORD). See Chapter 8: *Master and Target Termination* for more information.

In the above discussion it is assumed that the 64 data bit accesses are attempted only to a memory resource (*i.e.*, memory address space) because a target with a memory address is the only resource that can potentially execute 32 data bit bus transactions. If for whatever reason the PCI bus master attempts a 64 data bit access to other address spaces, the target must respond as a 32 data bit resource.

Except as outlined above, the addressing protocol of a 64 data bit PCI bus master BURST bus transaction to a 32 data bit target is the same as for a 32 data bit PCI bus master BURST bus transaction to a 32 data bit target. Except as outlined above, a PCI bus master's request for a 64 data bit transaction to a 32 data bit target, the memory transactions (including MRM, MRL, and MWI), DUAL ADDRESS operation, and Exclusive Access (LOCK) operation use the same protocol as bus transactions between a 32 data bit PCI bus master and a 32 data bit target.

See Chapter 6: *Detailed Bus Transaction Operation* for more information.

I/O AND CONFIGURATION TRANSACTIONS, INTERRUPT ACKNOWLEDGE TRANSACTIONS, AND SPECIAL TRANSACTIONS

These PCI bus transactions are executed only with 32 data bit targets, and the REQ64# and ACK64# signal lines must remain deasserted.

64 data bit I/O targets can be implemented, but there is no justification for the increased complexity, and it is therefore strongly recommended that 64 data bit I/O targets not be implemented. For the purposes of this book, I/O targets are only 32 data bits in size. If a 64 data bit I/O target is implemented, the 64 data bit protocol applied to memory targets will also apply to I/O targets.

4.10   PCI MESSAGE SIGNALED INTERRUPT

INTRODUCTION

There are three methods to support interrupts: INTx# signal lines, polling, and message signaled interrupts. As previously described, the INTx# signal lines are active low, which permits sharing of a single INTx# signal line among several PCI resources that can request interrupt service. The receipt of a hardware interrupt request via a shared INTx# signal line requires the software to read the configuration address space and possibly other registers of the PCI resources sharing the associated INTx# signal line to determine the interrupt source. Another method of interrupt support is polling. This simply consists of the software reading the configuration address space and possibly other registers of PCI resources periodically to determine which resource requires interrupt service without the receipt of a hardware interrupt request via a shared INTx# signal line.

MSI

Revision 2.2 of the PCI bus specification has added an additional method to support interrupts called message signaled interrupt (MSI). MSI is entirely based on memory write transactions from the PCI resource requesting the interrupt (source) to the PCI resource that will service the interrupt (destination). Thus, MSI defines a protocol known as peer-to-peer. The MSI protocol permits the destination to be any appropriately designed PCI resource or the interrupt controller on PCI bus 0 (the PCI resource that receives the INTx# signal lines) if one is developed that supports MSI. MSI provides several advantages over using the INTx# signal lines or polling:

- Compared to the use of the INTx# signal line, MSI provides the following:

- The INTx# signal lines are attached to an interrupt controller on PCI bus 0. The interrupt request from the interrupt controller is connected to the interrupt request input of the HOST CPU. The assertion of the interrupt request by the interrupt controller requires software to read the configuration address space and possibly other registers of the PCI resources connected to the INTx# signal lines to determine the interrupt source. The reading activity by the HOST CPU requires arbitration for PCI bus ownership for each bus between the HOST/PCI BRIDGE and all PCI buses that contain the potential PCI interrupt sources. When a PCI / PCI BRIDGE(s) in the path between the HOST CPU and the potential PCI interrupt sources contains any posted memory write transactions (in either direction), the PCI /PCI BRIDGE(s) is required to complete all of the posted memory write transactions prior to porting the read transaction associated with the interrupt through the PCI/PCI BRIDGE(s). These requirements can cause excessive and unpredictable delay in servicing the interrupt. MSI operates with memory write transactions which at most are placed in the "Posted Memory Write Command FIFO" of the PCI/PCI BRIDGE(s) and only needs to maintain strong ordering with other posted memory write transactions in the same direction. Consequently, MSI reduces the level of unpredictable delay for servicing the interrupt request.

- According to the PCI bus specification, a single function PCI resource has one INTx# signal line and up to four INTx# signal lines for a multifunction PCI resource. However, there are only four INTx# signal lines available per connector. Consequently, if the PCI resources in a system require more than four hardware interrupts, at least one INTx# signal line must be shared. MSI removes this requirement because MSI does not rely on the INTx# signal lines. MSI is entirely based on memory write transactions from the PCI interrupt source to the PCI interrupt destination.

- With INTx# signal lines, the interrupt request is sent to the HOST CPU via the interrupt controller. Thus the HOST CPU must be involved in servicing the interrupt request. As previously stated, MSI is entirely based on memory write transactions from the PCI interrupt source to the PCI interrupt destination. Consequently, this peer-to-peer aspect of MSI does not need the intervention of the HOST CPU.

- Compared to polling, MSI provides the following advantage:
  - The use of polling in PCI to determine if an interrupt request is pending requires read transactions by the HOST CPU. The HOST CPU requires arbitration for PCI bus ownership for each bus segment between the HOST/PCI BRIDGE and all PCI bus segments that contain PCI resources that potentially may be requesting interrupt service. When a PCI/PCI BRIDGE(s) in the path between the HOST CPU and the potential PCI interrupt source contain posted memory write transactions (in either direction) the PCI/PCI BRIDGE(s) is required (following PCI ordering rules) to complete all posted memory write transactions prior to completing the read transaction associated with interrupt polling through the PCI/PCI BRIDGE(s). MSI operates with memory write transactions which at most are placed in the "Posted Memory Write Command FIFO" of the PCI/PCI BRIDGE(s) and only needs to maintain strong ordering with other memory write transactions in the same direction. Consequently,

MSI reduces the level of unpredictable delay for servicing the interrupt request via polling.

The MSI protocol cannot be implemented until the MSI is enabled (bit 0 of the Message Control Register set to logical "1"). After reset, MSI is disabled (default with bit 0 of the Message Control Register set to logical "0"), and interrupts from the PCI resource can only be done via the INTx# signal lines or by polling. Whenever MSI is enabled for a specific PCI resource, the resource cannot use the INTx# signal lines; however, interrupt support can still be done with polling even though MSI is enabled.

According to the MSI protocol, the PCI interrupt destination is responsible for servicing the interrupt with the most recent data. If the interrupt request was to alert the PCI interrupt destination that data had been written to memory on the same or higher LEVEL bus segment as the bus of the PCI interrupt destination, the PCI ordering protocol of the bridges ensures that data is written to memory before the completion of the MSI memory write transaction.

PCI-X SPECIFC IMPLEMENTATION

4.11   PCI-X MEMORY AND I/O TRANSACTIONS

> This is a brief introduction to PCI-X memory and I/O transactions. See Subchapter 4.16: *PCI-X 32 Data Bit PCI Bus Master to 32 Data Bit Target* for more information.

> The PCI-X addendum discourages the growth or continuation of the I/O address space. Access to the I/O address space is fully supported, but all registers accessible in the I/O address space must also be accessible in the memory address space.

Memory transactions executed between a PCI-X bus master (bridge or non-bridge) on the same PCI-X bus segment as the actual target (non-bridge) can be implemented as either SINGLE (with or without Split Transaction protocol) or BURST bus transactions. I/O transactions executed between a PCI-X bus master (bridge or non-bridge) on the same PCI-X bus segment as the actual target (non-bridge) can only be implemented as SINGLE bus transactions (with or without Spit Transaction protocol). Only memory write transactions can be posted in a PCI-X/PCI-X BRIDGE, and thus can implement either SINGLE or BURST bus transactions with the PCI-X/PCI-X BRIDGE representing the actual target (non-bridge ... either directly or indirectly through other bridges). I/O write transactions cannot be posted in a PCI-X/PCI-X BRIDGE. Memory read and I/O read and write transactions can only implement SINGLE bus transactions with the Split Transaction protocol with the PCI-X/PCI-X BRIDGE representing actual target (non-bridge ... either directly or indirectly through other bridges). See *Chapter 7: Bridge and Interface Protocol* for more information.

The "PCI-X 16 clock" and "PCI-X 8 clock" rules apply to all memory and I/O transactions. See Subchapter 4.0 for more information.

Please see a discussion in Subchapter 4.1 on how ADDRESS/DATA STEPPING and PRE-DRIVE protocols operate. Except for PRE-DRIVE of configuration transactions, these protocols do not apply to PCI-X bus transactions. The application of PRE-DRIVE to PCI-X configuration transactions will be discussed in Subchapter 4.12.

As outlined in Chapter 7: *Bridge and Interface Protocol* COMBINING, PREFETCHING, and MERGING can only be applied to memory write transactions of the "same sequence" through a bridge or interface. (Memory write includes the BURST memory write, memory write block, and alias memory write block commands.) The "same sequence" means a series of bus transactions with the same Requester ID and Tag. COLLAPSING cannot be applied to any memory transactions through a bridge or interface. COMBINING, COLLAPSING, PREFETCHING, and MERGING cannot be applied to any I/O transactions through a bridge or interface.

According to the PCI-X addendum specification, the MASTER and TARGET Fast Back to Back protocol DOES NOT apply to PCI-X memory or I/O transactions.

ADDRESS DECODING FOR MEMORY AND I/O TRANSACTIONS

The PCI-X addendum specification defines the decoding protocol in the same fashion as the PCI local bus specification. As will be discussed in detail in Chapter 6: *Detailed Bus Transaction Operation*, the PCI-X bus transaction protocol has added an ATTRIBUTE PHASE and a TARGET RESPONSE PHASE between the ADDRESS PHASE and first DATA PHASE. Consequently; the decoding sampling points have been moved and renamed as shown in Figure 4-7. The fastest possible decode will respond two CLK signal line periods after the FRAME# signal line is first sampled asserted (identifies valid address on the AD signal lines and command on the C/BE# signal lines). This sampling point of the DEVSEL# signal line is defined as "DEC A". As with PCI, there are two additional DEVSEL# signal line sample points that follow at one CLK signal line period intervals, defined as "DEC B" and "DEC C". These three sampling points reflect a POSITIVE DECODING protocol. Also, as defined for PCI bus transactions and for the same reasons, a PCI-X bus resource can claim the PCI-X bus transaction through SUBTRACTIVE DECODING by asserting the DEVSEL# signal line after the POSITIVE DECODING sample points. (Note that the "SUB" decoding sampling point is two CLK signal line periods after the "DEC C" sampling point.) If no PCI-X resource claims the bus transaction, a Master Abort termination is executed. See Chapter 8: *Master and Target Termination* for more information.

> For memory address space according to the PCI local bus specification, the AD[01::00] signal lines are not decoded as part of the address because they contain the addressing sequence for the bus transactions. For memory address space according to the PCI-X addendum bus specification, the AD[01::00] signal lines *are* decoded as part of the address.
>
> As with PCI, for the PCI-X I/O address space, the AD[01::00] signal lines must be decoded as part of the address in addition to the other aforementioned address signal lines.

> When a RESERVED command is executed, no PCI-X resource may assert the DEVSEL# signal line for either POSITIVE or SUBTRACTIVE decoding.
>
> The POSITIVE and SUBTRACTIVE DECODING sample points (DEC A, DEC B, DEC C, and SUB) of the DEVSEL# signal line to claim the bus transaction are delayed by one CLK signal line (relative to the first rising edge of the CLK signal line when FRAME# signal line is asserted) period if a DUAL ADDRESS command is executed. See the DUAL ADDRESS section in this chapter for details.

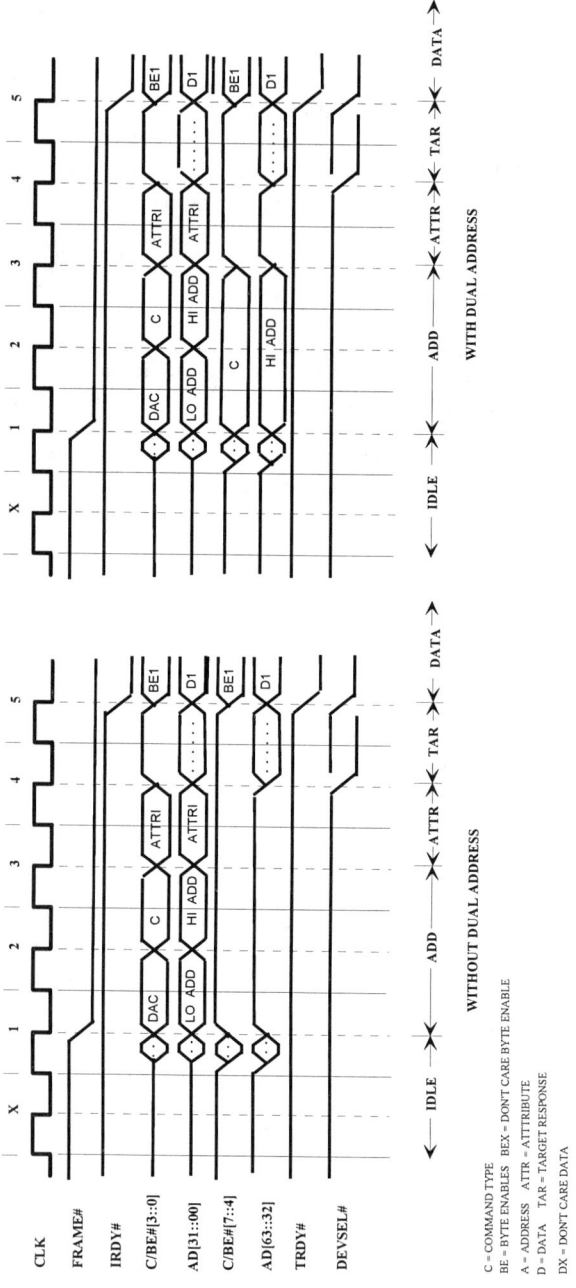

C = COMMAND TYPE
BE = BYTE ENABLES BEX = DON'T CARE BYTE ENABLE
A = ADDRESS ATTR = ATTTRIBUTE
D = DATA TAR = TARGET RESPONSE
DX = DON'T CARE DATA

Figure 4-7: PCI-X ADDRESS DECODING

As previously stated, the PCI local bus specification permits a PCI resource to claim the bus transaction (assert the DEVSEL# signal line) before the decoding sampling point defined in its STATUS register in the configuration address space if all of the other PCI resources on the PCI bus segment indicate earlier decoding sampling points (according to their STATUS register in the configuration address space). The PCI-X addendum specification does not implement this protocol. The decoding sampling points (DEC A, DEC B, DEC C, and SUBTRACTIVE DECODING) for a PCI-X resource to claim the bus transaction is fixed and independent of the decoding sampling points of other PCI-X resources on the PCI-X bus segment.

MEMORY AND I/O TRANSACTION COMPLETION

The memory and I/O transaction protocols include completing these bus transactions with Completion, Completion with Timeout, Master Abort, Retry, Split Response, Single Phase Disconnect, Disconnect at Next ADB, and Target Abort terminations. See Chapter 8: *Master and Target Termination* for more information.

DUAL ADDRESS

The PCI-X addendum specification implements the DUAL ADDRESS command protocol in the same fashion as PCI local bus specification. As with PCI, only PCI-X memory transactions implement the DUAL ADDRESS command.

All PCI-X bus masters that access the memory address space must support a 64 bit address space. The PCI-X compliant memory address space targets must also support a 64 bit address space. If the PCI-X bus master is addressing a PCI-X target located in the lower four gigabytes, it must execute the memory transaction without the DUAL ADDRESS command. By definition the upper order address bits (AD[63::32]) are logical "0".

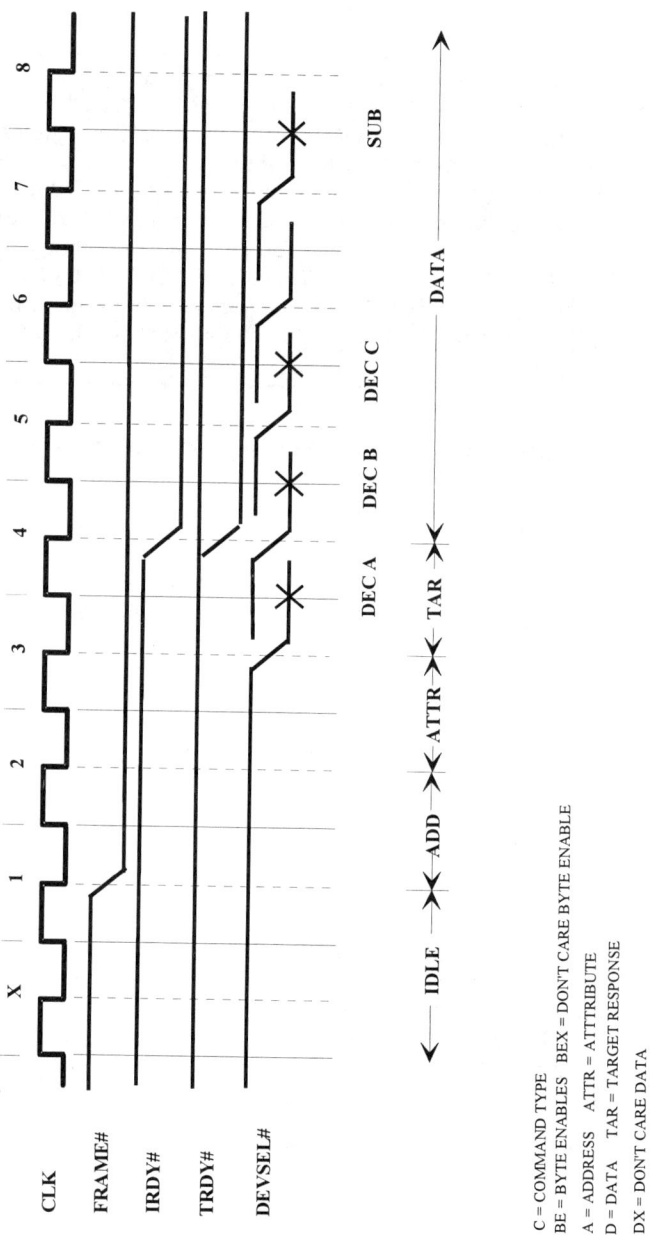

Figure 4-8: PCI-X DUAL ADDRESS

ADDRESS/DATA STEPPING AND PRE-DRIVE

Due to the higher CLK signal line frequencies of PCI-X, the PCI-X addendum specification defines the PRE-DRIVE protocol only for the configuration transactions. The PRE-DRIVE protocol is not defined for non-configuration bus transactions. The ADDRESS/DATA STEPPING protocol is not defined for any PCI-X bus transactions. See Subchapter 4.11 for more information about these protocols.

> Unless otherwise indicated, the figures in this book assume ADDRESS/DATA STEPPING and PRE-DRIVE (except for PCI-X configuration transactions) are not implemented for PCI and PCI-X; consequently, the FRAME# signal line is asserted during the #1 CLK signal line period. The one exception will be the use of PRE-DRIVE for PCI-X configuration transactions.

4.12 PCI-X CONFIGURATION TRANSACTIONS

> This is a brief introduction to PCI-X configuration transactions. See Subchapter 4.16: *PCI-X 32 Data Bit PCI Bus Master to 32 Data Bit Target* for more information.

Configuration transactions executed between a PCI-X bus master (bridge or non-bridge) on the same PCI-X bus segment as the actual target (non-bridge) can only be implemented with SINGLE bus transactions (with or without Spit Transaction protocol). Configuration transactions cannot be posted into a PCI-X/PCI-X BRIDGE. Configuration transactions can only implement SINGLE bus transactions with the Split Transaction protocol with a PCI-X/PCI-X BRIDGE representing the actual target (non-bridge ... either directly or indirectly through other bridges). See Chapter 7: *Bridge and Interface Protocol* for more information.

The "PCI-X 16 clock" and "PCI–X 8 clock" rules only apply to configuration transactions during run time (*i.e.*, not during initialization, when not executing from BOOT ROM, or when not copying expansion ROM to memory). See Subchapter 4.0 for more information.

The ADDRESS/DATA STEPPING protocol does not apply to configuration transactions, but the PRE-DRIVE protocol does apply. Please see Subchapter 4.1 on how the PRE-DRIVE protocol is implemented.

As outlined in Chapter 7: *Bridge and Interface Protocol,* COMBINING, COLLAPSING, PREFETCHING, and MERGING cannot be applied to configuration transactions.

According to the PCI-X addendum bus specification, the MASTER and TARGET Fast Back to Back protocol DOES NOT apply to PCI-X configuration transactions.

ADDRESS DECODING AND OTHER ATTRIBUTES FOR CONFIGURATION TRANSACTIONS

The PCI-X addendum specification defines the address decoding sampling points for configuration transactions the same as for memory and I/O transactions. The configuration transaction protocol is the same as memory and I/O transactions, including completing configuration transactions with Completion, Master Abort, Retry, Target Abort, Split Response, and Single Phase Disconnect terminations. However, the configuration transaction protocol does not support the execution of the Completion with Timeout and Disconnect at next ADB terminations. See Chapter 8: *Master and Target Termination,* for more information

The "additional exceptions for the protocol of configuration transactions versus the protocol of memory and I/O transactions" and the "unique protocol requirements" as outlined for PCI configuration transactions also apply to PCI-X configuration transactions. The only differences are as follows:

- The AD[31::11] signal lines are used for the IDSEL signal lines in PCI. For PCI-X, only the AD[31::11] signal lines are used for the IDSEL signal lines. See Subchapter 4.2 and 4.16 for more information.

- The AD[15::11] signal lines contain the Device Number.

- For PCI-X, both Type 0 and Type 1 configuration transactions can only be executed as SINGLE transactions.

The observations and results regarding flow direction of configuration transactions throughout PCI systems also apply to PCI-X systems. See Subchapter 4.2 for more information.

4.13 PCI-X INTERRUPT ACKNOWLEDGE TRANSACTIONS

> This is a brief introduction to PCI-X interrupt acknowledge transactions. See Subchapter 4.16: *PCI-X 32 Data Bit PCI Bus Master to 32 Data Bit Target* for more information.

> The placement of the interrupt controller in a PCI-X system is the same as described previously for a PCI system in this subchapter. See Subchapter 4.3 for more information.

Interrupt acknowledge transactions can only execute on PCI-X bus (0) segment as SINGLE bus transactions (with or without Spit Transaction protocol) to the actual target (non-bridge). Interrupt acknowledge transactions are read only and thus cannot be posted into a bridge. Interrupt acknowledge transactions can only be implemented as SINGLE bus transactions with Split Transaction protocol with the PCI-X/LEGACY BRIDGE (representing the actual target (non-bridge). See Chapter 7: *Bridge and Interface Protocol* for more information.

The "PCI-X 16 clock" and "PCI–X 8 clock" rules apply to interrupt acknowledge transactions. See Subchapter 4.0 for more information.

ADDRESS/DATA STEPPING and PRE-DRIVE protocols do not apply to interrupt acknowledge transactions.

As outlined in Chapter 7: *Bridge and Interface Protocol* COMBINING, COLLAPSING, PREFETCHING, and MERGING cannot be applied to interrupt acknowledge transactions.

According to the PCI-X addendum bus specification, the MASTER and TARGET Fast Back to Back protocol DOES NOT apply to PCI-X interrupt acknowledge transactions.

ADDRESS DECODING AND OTHER ATTRIBUTES FOR INTERRUPT ACKNOWLEDGE TRANSACTIONS

The PCI-X addendum specification defines the "no address decoding" for PCI-X interrupt acknowledge transactions the same as the PCI local bus specification for PCI interrupt acknowledge transactions. Also, the DUAL ADDRESS command is not executed with interrupt acknowledge transactions. The PCI-X bus master (HOST/PCI BRIDGE) completes the interrupt acknowledge transaction with the same protocol as a memory or I/O transaction including Completion, Master Abort, Retry, Split Response, Single Phase Disconnect, and Target Abort terminations. The interrupt acknowledge transaction does not support the execution of the Completion with Timeout and Disconnect at Next ADB terminations. See Chapter 8: *Master and Target Termination* for more information.

The PCI-X addendum specification supports discrete interrupt request signal lines (INT#) in the same fashion as described previously for the PCI local bus specification.

The "unique protocol requirements" as outlined for PCI interrupt acknowledge transactions also apply to PCI-X interrupt acknowledge transactions.

4.14   PCI-X SPECIAL TRANSACTIONS

This is a brief introduction to PCI-X special transactions. See Subchapter 4.16: *PCI-X 32 Data Bit PCI Bus Master to 32 Data Bit Target* for more information.

A special transaction request originates with the HOST CPU or a PCI-X bus master on one of the PCI bus segments. The request is ported from the HOST CPU to lower LEVEL bus segments with the bridges acting as the PCI bus master for each respective PCI-X bus segment. A PCI-X bus master of a specific PCI-X bus segment can execute a special transaction to PCI-X resources on the same PCI-X bus segment or request a special transaction on another PCI-X bus segment. The request for special transactions is ported from a specific PCI-X bus segment to other higher or lower LEVEL bus segments via Type 1 configuration transactions, with HOST/PCI-X or PCI-X/PCI-X BRIDGES acting as the PCI-X bus master for each PCI-X bus segment.

The observations and results regarding flow direction of configuration transactions (and therefore special transactions) are discussed in the PCI Configuration Transactions section of Subchapter 4.2.

Special transactions executed between a PCI-X bus master (bridge or non-bridge) on the same PCI-X bus segment as the actual target (non-bridge) can be implemented as SINGLE bus transactions (without Split Transaction protocol). Special transactions cannot be posted into or ported through the PCI-X/PCI-X BRIDGE representing the actual target (non-bridge). Special transactions are ported through a PCI-X/PCI-X BRIDGE via Type 1 configuration transactions. See Chapter 7: *Bridge and Interface Protocol* for more information.

The "PCI-X 16 clock" and "PCI-X 8 clock" rules do not apply to special transactions because the application of these rules require a single PCI-X resource to claim (assert DEVSEL# signal line) the transaction. By protocol definition of a special transaction, it is a broadcast write type of transaction and cannot be claimed by any PCI-X resource. See Subchapter 4.0 for more information.

ADDRESS/DATA STEPPING and PRE-DRIVE protocols do not apply to special transactions.

As outlined in Chapter 7: *Bridge and Interface Protocol,* COMBINING, COLLAPSING, PREFETCHING, and MERGING cannot be applied to special transactions.

According to the PCI-X addendum specification, the MASTER and TARGET Fast Back to Back protocol DOES NOT apply to PCI-X special transactions.

ADDRESS DECODING AND OTHER ATTRIBUTES FOR SPECIAL TRANSACTIONS

The PCI-X addendum specification defines the "no address decoding" for PCI-X special transactions the same as for the PCI local bus specification. Also, DUAL ADDRESS is not executed with special transactions. The PCI-X bus master (bridge or non-bridge) completes the special transaction with Master Abort termination because no target can claim (assert DEVSEL#) the bus transaction. Completion, Completion with Timeout, Retry, Split Response, Single Phase Disconnect, Disconnect at Next ADB, and Target Abort terminations do not apply to special transactions. See Chapter 8: *Master and Target Termination* for more information.

The PCI-X addendum specification supports side band signal lines in the same fashion as described previously for PCI local bus specification.

The "unique protocol requirements" as outlined for PCI special transactions also apply to PCI-X special transactions. The only difference is as follows:

- Special Transactions can only implement SINGLE bus transactions.

> A PCI-X bus master may have the capability to execute a special transaction. A HOST/PCI-X BRIDGE may support the special transaction to allow the HOST CPU to broadcast to PCI-X resources, but it is not required.

4.15   PCI-X SPLIT COMPLETION TRANSACTIONS

This is a brief introduction to PCI-X split completion transactions. See Subchapter 4.16: *PCI-X 32 Data Bit PCI Bus Master to 32 Data Bit Target* and Chapter 7: *Bridge and Interface Protocol* for more information.

Split completion transactions are part of the Split Transaction protocol. The concepts of this protocol are reviewed in Chapter 3: *Generic PCI and PCI-X Hardware Operation* and Chapter 7: *Bridge and Interface Protocol*. Terms that have been defined previously are repeated here for convenience:

- The PCI-X bus master that begins the access will be called the "original" PCI-X bus master. Each PCI-X/PCI-X BRIDGE may be a PCI-X bus master of the bus segment but is not the "original" PCI-X bus master.

- The target that is being accessed by the "original" PCI-X bus master is called the "original" target. Each PCI-X/PCI-X BRIDGE may be a target of the bus segment but is not the "original" target.

- The bus transaction executed by the "original" PCI-X bus master that is terminated with a Split Response termination by the "original" target or a PCI-X/PCI-X BRIDGE is called the "original" transaction.

- If the access is to the configuration address space of the PCI-X/PCI-X BRIDGE, the bridge is defined as the "original" target if the Split Transaction protocol is applied.

- The Split Transaction protocol can only be applied to non-memory write transactions. The term "non-memory write transactions" as it applies to the Split Transaction protocol is defined as follows:

    - A non-memory write transaction is defined as one of the following: I/O read and write, configuration read and write, interrupt acknowledge, DWORD memory read, memory read block, and alias memory read block transactions.

    - According to the PCI-X addendum specification, a split completion transaction CANNOT be terminated with a Split Response termination and is not defined as a "non-memory write transaction" for the purposes of the Split Transaction discussion. For all practical purposes, the split completion transaction operates as a memory write transaction but is not writing to memory in all cases.

    - The special transaction is a non-memory transaction but by definition it does not access a single target. Consequently, a Split Response termination CANNOT be executed because no single target can claim (assertion of the DEVSEL# signal line) the special transaction.

A special transaction is not defined as a "non-memory write transaction" for the purposes of the Split Transaction discussion.

Split completion transactions executed between a PCI-X bus master (bridge or non-bridge "original" target) on the same PCI-X bus segment as the "original" PCI-X bus master can be implemented with SINGLE and BURST bus transactions. Split completion transactions can be posted into a PCI-X/PCI-X BRIDGE. Split completion transactions can be implemented with SINGLE and BURST bus transactions with the Split Transaction protocol through the PCI-X/PCI-X BRIDGE representing the "original" PCI-X bus master (remember that the source of split completion transactions is the "original" target with the "original" PCI-X bus master as the destination). See *Chapter 7: Bridge and Interface Protocol* for more information.

The "PCI-X 16 clock" and "PCI–X 8 clock" rules apply to split completion transactions. See Subchapter 4.0 for more information.

ADDRESS/DATA STEPPING and PRE-DRIVE protocols do not apply to split completion transactions. See Subchapter 4.1 for more information.

As outlined in Chapter 7: *Bridge and Interface Protocol,* COMBINING and MERGING can be applied to split completion transactions of the same "sequence". The same "sequence" is a series of split completion transactions with the same Requester ID and Tag. COLLAPSING and PREFETCHING cannot be applied for split completion transactions.

According to the PCI-X addendum bus specification, the MASTER and TARGET Fast Back to Back protocol DOES NOT apply to PCI-X split completion transactions.

ADDRESS DECODING AND OTHER ATTRIBUTES FOR SPLIT COMPLETION TRANSACTIONS

The PCI-X addendum specification defines the address decoding sampling points for split completion transactions the same as for memory transactions. The split completion transaction protocol is similar to the memory transaction protocol in two ways:

- 32 and 64 data bit size is supported by split completion transactions.

- Fast Back-to-Back Master and Target protocols are not defined for split completion transactions.

The split completion transaction protocol differs from the memory transaction protocol as follows:

■ DUAL ADDRESS is not executed with split completion transaction.

■ 64 bit address extension is not defined for the configuration transaction - the AD[63::32] signal lines are never part of the decode.

Split completion transaction protocol relating to completing the transaction is not exactly the same as for memory transactions. The completion of the split completion transaction varies depending on whether a PCI-X/PCI-X BRIDGE is participating in the transactions:

■ When the split completion transaction is accessing the "original" PCI-X bus master (split completion transaction from "original" target or PCI-X/PCI-X BRIDGE (porting through) to "original" PCI-X bus master), Completion, Completion with Timeout, and Target Abort and Master Abort terminations are supported. The other types of terminations are not allowed for a split completion transaction because buffer space is available at the "original" PCI-X bus master. That is, a PCI-X bus master must not execute a bus transaction that can be terminated with a split response termination (and thus become the target of split completion transactions sourced from the "original" target) unless the PCI-X bus master has reserved sufficient buffer space for the entire "sequence" of split completion transactions associated with the "original" transaction. See Chapter 8: *Master and Target Termination* for more information.

■ When the split completion transaction is porting through a PCI-X/PCI-X BRIDGE (split completion transaction from "original" target to PCI-X/PCI-X BRIDGE representing the "original" PCI-X bus master), Completion, Completion with Timeout, and Target Abort and Master Abort terminations are supported. In addition, Retry and Disconnect at next ADB terminations are supported. Retry and Disconnect at next ADB terminations are supported because these terminations are only executed by the PCI-X/PCI-X BRIDGE acting as the target on the bus segment. It reflects the fact that a bridge will try to provide sufficient space for all bus transactions being posted (porting through) the bridge, but is not always able to do so because of the dynamics of the system. See Chapter 8: *Master and Target Termination* for more information.

A PCI-X bus transaction terminated with a Retry termination does not need to be repeated, but with two exceptions. One: if the split completion transaction is accessing a PCI-X/PCI-X BRIDGE, the execution of a Retry termination requires the PCI-X bus master that is the source of the split completion transaction on that bus segment to repeat the split completion transaction. Two: a PCI bus master is required to repeat a transaction terminated by Retry termination if it is part of an established sequence of transactions for BURST memory write, memory write block, or alias memory write block commands. See Chapter 8: *Master and Target Termination* for more information.

4.16 PCI-X 32 DATA BIT BUS MASTER TO 32 DATA BIT TARGET

The remainder of the PCI-X specific portion of the chapter will separately address 32 and 64 data bit PCI-X resources. The first part will concentrate on 32 data bit PCI-X resources and the latter portion will provide the incremental information relevant to the 64 data bit extension.

INTRODUCTION

The PCI local bus specification defined specific encoding for 32 data bit transactions in the AD[1::0] and C/BE#[3::0] signal lines during the ADDRESS and DATA PHASES. The PCI-X addendum bus specification implements some of the same protocols and has changed some protocols. In addition, the PCI-X bus transactions have two additional phases: ATTRIBUTE and TARGET RESPONSE PHASES. This subchapter will review these changes in the protocol for bus transactions for the different COMMANDS.

Tables 4-1 to 4-3 in Subchapter 4.0 show the bus transaction protocol (SINGLE versus BURST), data sizes for bus transactions, wait states for bus transactions, and number of address bits relative to the different PCI-X commands.

Tables 4-7 to 4-9 below summarize the encoding used in the aforementioned signal lines for the ADDRESS and ATTRIBUTE PHASES. The AD and C/BE# signal lines encoding will be detailed for all PHASES in the detailed discussion in this subchapter. PCI information is provided for comparison.

MEMORY TRANSACTIONS

See Subchapter 4.11 for related information.

INTRODUCTION

The following discussions use several definitions that have been discussed in other sections of the book but will be repeated here for convenience: prefetchable address space, ADB, "sequence" of bus transactions, and Tag.

A prefetchable address space (or simply prefetchable address) is an address range within the memory address space. It can only reside in the memory address space. Multiple readings from a specific prefetchable address results in the same data (provided no write to this address has occurred). The multiple reading and possible discarding of data by the PCI-X bus master or bridge does not have negative side effects. Also, a prefetchable address space must support merging of bytes written to it within a DWORD (by a bridge) without any negative side effects. The Prefetchable bit in the Memory Base Address register in the configuration address space must be set to "logical "1" for the associated address range to be prefetchable. It is the responsibility of the PCI-X bus master to implement a BURST memory read block or alias memory read block command correctly. By definition, these bus transactions are reading all bytes in the block. If a prefetchable address space is accessed by the DWORD memory read transaction, not all bytes will be read; only those bytes associated with valid byte lanes per the ATTRIBUTE PHASE will be read.

The reading of prefetchable address space requires only the bytes being read and returned according to the byte enables specified by the bus transaction (This is different than the definition of prefetchable address space definition for PCI bus transactions.)

The non-prefetchable address space of a memory resource behind a bridge must be located in the lower four gigabyte address space.

Name (PCI)	Name (PCI-X)	Encoding of AD [1::0] and C/BE#[3::0] Signal During ADDRESS PHASE Lowest Address of Byte to Be Accessed = LABA BURST Address Sequence = BAS COMMAND Type = CT Configuration Type = CONT			
NO GROUP NAME	DWORD COMMANDS	PCI		PCI-X	
		AD [1::0]	C/BE# [3::0]	AD [1::0]	C/BE# [3::0]
Interrupt Acknowledge	Interrupt Acknowledge	na	CT	na	CT
Special	Special	na	CT	na	CT
I/O Read	I/O Read	LABA	CT	LABA	CT
I/O Write	I/O Write	LABA	CT	LABA	CT
Config. Read	Config. Read	CONT	CT	CONT	CT
Config. Write	Config.Write	CONT	CT	CONT	CT
Memory Read	Memory Read DWORD	BAS	CT	LABA	CT
NO GROUP NAME	BURST COMMANDS				
Memory Write	Memory Write	BAS	CT	LABA	CT
Reserved	Alias Memory Read Block	na	na	LABA	CT
Reserved	Alias Memory Write Block	na	na	LABA	CT
Memory Read Multiple	Split Completion	BAS (1)	CT	LABA	CT
Memory Read Line	Memory Read Block	BAS (1)	CT	LABA	CT
Memory Write Invalidate	Memory Write Block	BAS (1)	CT	LABA	CT

Table 4-7: Comparison of AD [1::0] and C/BE#[3::0] Signal Lines in 32 Data Bit Bus Transactions during the ADDRESS PHASE

Note: (1) By defintion always linear increasing.

Name (PCI)	Name (PCI-X)	Encoding of AD [7::0] and C/BE#[3::0] Signal Lines During ATTRIBUTE PHASE Upper Byte Count = UBC Lower Byte Count = LBC Byte Enable for DATA PHASE = BEDP Reserved = RES = logical "0"			
NO GROUP NAME	DWORD COMMANDS	PCI		PCI-X	
		AD [7::0]	C/BE# [3::0]	AD [7::0]	C/BE# [3::0]
Interrupt Acknowledge	Interrupt Acknowledge	na	na	na	na
Special	Special	na	na	na	na
I/O Read	I/O Read	na	na	RES	BEDP
I/O Write	I/O Write	na	na	RES	BEDP
Config. Read	Config. Read	na	na	RES	BEDP
Config. Write	Config.Write	na	na	RES	BEDP
Memory Read	Memory Read DWORD	na	na	RES	BEDP
NO GROUP NAME	BURST COMMANDS				
Memory Write	Memory Write	na	na	LBC	UBC
Reserved	Alias Memory Read Block	na	na	LBC	UBC
Reserved	Alias Memory Write Block	na	na	LBC	UBC
Memory Read Multiple	Split Completion	na	na	LBC	UBC
Memory Read Line	Memory Read Block	na	na	LBC	UBC
Memory Write Invalidate	Memory Write Block	na	na	LBC	UBC

Table 4-8: Comparison of AD [7::0] and C/BE#[3::0] Signal Lines in 32 Data Bit Bus Transactions during the ATTRIBUTE PHASE

Name (PCI)	Name (PCI-X)	Encoding of C/BE#[3::0] Signal Lines During DATA PHASE Bus Master Drive Valid Byte Lane Info = Valid Bus Master Drives to Logical "1" = "1"	
NO GROUP NAME	**DWORD COMMANDS**	**PCI**	**PCI-X**
Interrupt Acknowledge	Interrupt Acknowledge	Valid	"1"
Special	Special	Valid	"1"
I/O Read	I/O Read	Valid	"1"
I/O Write	I/O Write	Valid	"1"
Config. Read	Config. Read	Valid	"1"
Config. Write	Config.Write	Valid	"1"
Memory Read	Memory Read DWORD	Valid	"1"
NO GROUP NAME	**BURST COMMANDS**		
Memory Write	Memory Write	Valid	Valid
Reserved	Alias Memory Read Block	na	"1"
Reserved	Alias Memory Write Block	na	"1"
Memory Read Multiple	Split Completion	Valid	"1"
Memory Read Line	Memory Read Block	Valid	"1"
Memory Write Invalidate	Memory Write Block	Valid	"1"

Table 4-9: Comparison of C/BE#[3::0] Signal Lines in 32 Data Bit Bus Transactions during the DATA PHASE

■ The allowed data boundary (ADB) is only defined for the memory address space and for split completion transactions. The ADB is naturally aligned to 128 byte address boundaries. It is the only address boundary at which a BURST COMMAND transaction can terminate if a Single Phase Disconnect termination is not executed or the total byte count of the bus transaction has not been reached.

■ A "sequence" of bus transactions is a series of memory bus transactions from a specific PCI-X bus master with the "same" Tag in the ATTRIBUTE PHASE. The specific PCI-X bus master is identified by the "same" Requester ID (requester bus number, requester device number, and requester function number in the ATTRIBUTE PHASE). The "same" sequence of memory transactions has the "same" Tag and "same" Requester ID. A sequence is also defined relative a series of split completion transactions. Thus, there are two names used: "sequence" of memory transactions versus "sequence" of split completion transactions.

■ The Tag is a unique five bit binary number that each PCI-X bus master assigns to each PCI-X bus transaction. A specific Tag number cannot be used again until a previous bus transaction assigned the same tag number has completed. If the bus transaction is terminated with a Split Response termination, the bus transaction is not completed until the associated "sequence" of split completion transactions is complete to the PCI-X bus master. Thus, each PCI-X bus master can have 32 bus transactions in execution at the same time.

> If the BURST memory command is executed as a "sequence", the bus transactions of the same "sequence" must be the same COMMAND type. That is, the bus transactions of the same "sequence" are all BURST memory write, all BURST memory write block, or all BURST alias memory write block transactions.

A PCI-X bus master requests a 32 data bit memory transaction with the continued deassertion of the REQ64# signal line during the ADDRESS PHASE (deasserted by a pull-up resistor on the bus backplane). The target acknowledges executing a 32 data bit transaction with the continued deassertion of the ACK64# signal line during the DATA PHASE (deasserted by a pull-up resistor on the bus backplane). For a 32 data bit bus transaction, the AD[63::32], C/BE#[7::4], and PAR64 signal lines are driven to logical "1" by pull-up resistors; consequently, the PAR64 signal line does not have valid parity information. Once the size of the respective bus transaction participants is established it remains unchanged during the remainder of the bus transaction.

A memory transaction *can* be executed with DUAL ADDRESS.

The signal line protocol during the ADDRESS, ATTRIBUTE, TARGET RESPONSE, and DATA PHASES are essentially the same for the SINGLE and BURST memory transactions, but there are minor differences that will be discussed below. The PCI-X bus master executes a successful memory transaction as SINGLE versus BURST bus transaction by the activity of the FRAME# and IRDY# signal lines and the type of command (DWORD versus BURST). As detailed in Chapter 6: *Detailed Bus Transaction Operation*, the type of command indicates the byte count. For a DWORD COMMAND the byte count is implied to be four. For a BURST COMMAND the byte count is provided in the ATTRIBUTE PHASE of the transaction. This information, in conjunction with the deassertion of the FRAME# and IRDY# signal lines, establishes SINGLE versus BURST memory transactions. Unlike a PCI bus transaction, the assertion and deassertion of the FRAME# and IRDY# signal lines to indicate a PCI-X BURST memory versus a SINGLE memory transaction is not as clean or simple as the protocol for a PCI BURST memory transaction versus a SINGLE memory transaction. See Chapter 6: *Detailed Bus Transaction Operation* for more information.

During the ADDRESS PHASE of the memory transaction, the AD[31::0] signal lines select address for the memory access and the C/BE#[3::0] signal lines contain the encoded information of the COMMAND type. For memory transactions, the COMMAND type defines either a DWORD COMMAND executed with a SINGLE bus transaction or a BURST COMMAND executed with either SINGLE or BURST bus transactions. The memory transaction that is defined as a DWORD COMMAND is DWORD memory read. The memory transactions that are defined as BURST COMMANDs are memory write, memory write block, memory read block, alias memory write block, and alias memory read block. The following discussion about memory bus transactions will be divided into DWORD COMMAND and BURST COMMAND types.

BOUNDARY CONSIDERATIONS

There are several considerations that relate to BURST memory transactions crossing the following boundaries:

- The starting address + total byte count of the bus transaction (defined below in the ATTRIBUTE PHASE) - 1 = an address of FFFF FFFF FFFF FFFFH or less.

- When a BURST memory transaction is executed, the ending address (defined in the ATTRIBUTE PHASE below) can exceed the address boundary of the target. The target must request a Single Phase

Disconnect, a Split Response, or a Disconnect at Next ADB termination at its address boundary. The PCI-X bus master will continue the "sequence" with another target (unless a Master Abort termination is executed).

- For a BURST memory read transaction, the PCI-X bus master must be prepared to receive a Split Response termination followed by a split completion transaction with a Split Completion Message containing the out of address range error.

- A PCI-X bus master may cross the lower four gigabyte address boundary defined by the starting address + total byte count of the bus transaction (defined below in the ATTRIBUTE PHASE). If the target straddles this boundary, the associated BURST bus transaction is permitted to continue. If the target does not straddle this boundary, it must request a Single Phase Disconnect, a Split Response, or a Disconnect at Next ADB termination to prevent the BURST bus transaction from crossing the four gigabyte address boundary. The "actual" target (not a PCI-X/PCI-X BRIDGE) is not permitted to have an address range that crosses (straddles) the four gigabyte address boundary. However, a PCI-X/PCI-X BRIDGE can be a target, and its address range may represent two "actual" targets adjacent in the address space at the four gigabyte address boundary. See Chapter 8: *Master and Target Termination* for more information.

ADDRESS SPACE PER DEVICE

The PCI local bus specification allows a full 4K memory address space range to be assigned to each PCI device (or each function within a multiple function device), whether the full range is needed or not. The PCI-X addendum specification requires the assignment of a memory address space range to reflect the actual needs of the PCI-X device (or each function within a multiple function device).

64 BIT ADDRESSING

The PCI-X addendum specification requires that all devices (both PCI-X bus master and target) that support the memory address space also support the full 64 bit addressing. The address bits of the AD[31::00] signal lines define addresses from 0 to 4 Gigabytes - 1. As previously discussed, the full 64 bits for the address is executed in conjunction with the DUAL ADDRESS command. However, the full 64 bits addressing (and thus the DUAL ADDRESS) is not required for all memory bus transactions:

- If the memory address range is within the lower four gigabyte address range [0 to 4 Gigabytes - 1], a memory bus transaction must be executed without the DUAL ADDRESS command. Even though a PCI-X memory target must support a full 64 bit address space, it must support non-DUAL ADDRESS command memory bus transactions for accesses if its memory address range is in the lower four gigabyte address space. The requirement for not executing the DUAL ADDRESS command permits the access of PCI compliant devices (translation though a bridge). See Chapter 7: *Bridge and Interface* for more information.

- If the memory address range is within the upper four gigabyte address range (four gigabyte boundary included), a memory bus transaction with DUAL ADDRESS command must be executed.

- Any memory address range of a PCI-X (or PCI) target that cannot support prefetching must be located in the lower four gigabyte address range.

DWORD MEMORY READ COMMANDS

> DWORD memory read commands can be executed to both prefetchable and non-prefetchable address spaces.

During the ADDRESS PHASE, the 0110 (C/BE#[3::0]) encoding indicates a memory read DWORD COMMAND (there is no DWORD COMMAND defined for a memory write access). This encoding identifies a DWORD COMMAND to the memory address space, and can only be executed as a SINGLE bus transaction (*i.e.*, DWORD memory read). The AD[31::00] signal lines during the ADDRESS PHASE define the memory address. The AD [1::0] signal lines define the lowest byte address. The minimum access of a memory bus transaction is 32 data bits (four bytes); consequently, the AD[1::0] signal lines during the ADDRESS PHASE define of the lowest order byte and the associated byte lane to be addressed in the DATA PHASE as follows:

- AD [1:0] = [0:0] address byte lane 0. Byte lane 0 is on AD[07::00] signal lines during the DATA PHASE.

- AD [1:0] = [0:1] address byte lane 1. Byte lane 1 is on AD[15::08] signal lines during the DATA PHASE.

- AD [1:0] = [1:0] address byte lane 2. Byte lane 2 is on AD[23::16] signal lines during the DATA PHASE.

- AD [1:0] = [1:1] address byte lane 3. Byte lane 3 is on AD[31::24] signal lines during the DATA PHASE.

During the ATTRIBUTE PHASE of the SINGLE bus transaction, the C/BE#[3::0] signal lines will identify which bytes will be accessed. The C/BE#[3::0] signal lines during the ATTRIBUTE PHASE of a SINGLE bus transaction must also match the bytes that were addressed by the AD[1::0] signal lines during the ADDRESS PHASE. The allowed protocol for the AD[1::0] signal lines during the ADDRESS PHASE and the C/BE#[3::0] signal lines during the ATTRIBUTE PHASE is as follows:

AD[1]	AD[0]	C/BE#[3]	C/BE#[2]	C/BE#[1]	C/BE#[0]
0	0	X	X	X	0
0	1	X	X	0	1
1	0	X	0	1	1
1	1	0	1	1	1
x	x	1	1	1	1

Table 4-10: Relationship of AD Signal Lines (ADDRESS PHASE) with C/BE# Signal Lines (ATTRIBUTE PHASE) for DWORD COMMAND Transactions

X = Don't care (asserted or deasserted)
1 = 3.3 or 5 volts (deasserted for C/BE#[3::0] signal lines)
0 = 0 volts (asserted for C/BE#[3::0] signal lines)

The PCI-X target must monitor the AD[1::0] signal lines during the ADDRESS PHASE and compare their values with the C/BE#[3::0] signal lines during the ATTTRIBUTE PHASE. If the values do not support the same byte address, the target must execute a Target Abort termination. This protocol allows one to four different targets to own mutually exclusive portions of the 32 data bits (double words) being addressed by the bus transaction. This protocol DOES NOT apply if one target owns the entire double word. This protocol also does not apply to PCI-X/PCI-X, PCI/PCI-X, or PCI/LEGACY BRIDGEs that implement subtractive decoding, because there is no complete knowledge of resources on the destination PCI bus or the LEGACY bus, respectively.

The requirement for the matching of the AD[1::0] signal lines with the C/BE#[3::0] signal lines as described above is necessary because of the requirement that all I/O registers are to be accessible in the memory address space. Also, this protocol only applies to the DWORD memory read transactions and not to BURST memory commands. By definition, the BURST COMMAND to memory is only used for a prefetchable memory address range. That is, the I/O registers can only be mapped (duplicated) in a non-prefetchable address space.

According to the PCI-X addendum bus specification, once the ADDRESS and the COMMAND type have been established in the ADDRESS PHASE, the next CLK signal line period is defined as the ATTRIBUTE PHASE. The information contained in the AD[31::00] and C/BE#[3::0] signal lines during the ATTRIBUTE PHASE for a DWORD memory read command is as follows:

- AD[07::00] = Reserved and required to be logical "0"

- AD[10::08] = Requester Function Number: This three bit number is the Function Number assigned by design of the component. The combination of Function, Device, and Bus numbers defines the Requester ID number.

- AD[15::11] = Requester Device Number: This five bit number is the Bus Device Number in the PCI-X Status Register in the configuration address space of the associated PCI-X bus master (on the bus segment associated with the Bus Number of AD[32::16]). The value 1FH indicates that these bits in the Status Register have not been initialized. The value 00H is reserved for bridge that connects the higher LEVEL bus segment to this bus segment. The combination of Function, Device, and Bus numbers defines the Requester ID number.

- AD[23::16] = Requester Bus Number: This eight bit number is the Bus Number in the PCI-X Status Register in the configuration address space of the associated PCI-X bus master. The value FFH indicates that these bits in the Status Register have not been initialized. The combination of Function, Device, and Bus numbers defines the Requester ID number.

- AD[28::24] = Tag: A unique number is assigned by the PCI-X bus master to each bus transaction of a sequence. The five bits permit a specific PCI-X bus master to have up to 32 different sequences at the same time.

- AD[29] = Relaxed Ordering: When this bit is set to logical "1", the programming model and the device driver guarantee that the order of read and write transactions to the associated memory address space does not (optional) have to maintain any ordering through a PCI-X/PCI-X BRIDGE (or a "bridge like" interface between the bus segment and other circuitry) relative to other bus transactions. If this bit is set to logical "0", bus transaction ordering relative to other bus transactions must be maintained. See Chapter 7: *Bridge and Interface Protocol* for more information.

  - The Relaxed Ordering bit must be set to logical "0" if the Enable Relaxed Ordering bit in the PCI-X Command register in the configuration address space is set to logical "0".

  - This bit is defined for all BURST COMMANDS (*i.e.*, accesses to memory address space ... see the later section in this chapter on Split Completion Transaction for application to this BURST COMMAND)

and for DWORD memory read. For all other bus transactions this bit must be set to logical "0". Also, for bus transactions associated with Message Signaled Interrupt; this bit must be set to logical "0".

- For a DWORD memory read, the Relaxed Ordering bit can be set to logical "1" only if strong ordering of the associated "sequence" of split completion transactions (if the bus transaction is terminated with a Split Response termination) relative to posted memory write transactions in the same direction as read commands does NOT have to be maintained. See Chapter 7: *Bridge and Interface Protocol* for more information.

- PCI-X/PCI-X BRIDGES port this bit through unmodified.

  - See the next section for how this bit is defined for BURST COMMANDS.

- AD[30] = No Snoop: When this bit is set to logical "1", the PCI-X bus master guarantees that there are no other resources in the system that need to snoop an access to the associated address (between and inclusive of starting and ending addresses). For example, this bit is set to logical 1 if the associated address space is not cached or if cached the associated address has been flushed.

  - This bit is defined for all BURST COMMANDS (except split completion transactions… *i.e.*, accesses to memory address space) and for DWORD memory read. For all other bus transactions, this bit must be set to logical "0". Also, for bus transactions associated with Message Signaled Interrupt; this bit must be set to logical "0".

  - PCI-X/PCI-X BRIDGES port this bit through unmodified.

  - See the next section for how this bit is defined for BURST COMMANDS.

- AD[31] = Reserved and required to be logical "0"

- C/BE#[3::0] = Byte Enables for the one DATA PHASE access.

Of particular note in the above bullets are the C/BE#[3::0] signal lines. As previously discussed, in the ADDRESS PHASE the AD [1::0] signal lines define the lowest level byte to be addressed in the DATA PHASE and define the associated byte lane. In the ATTRIBUTE PHASE the C/BE#[3::0] signal lines select which byte lanes will be accessed in the DATA PHASE and must match the address information as discussed in previous section and outlined in Table 4-10.

For a DWORD memory read transaction, the starting address is defined by the AD[31::0] signal lines, if no C/BE#[3::0] signal line is asserted in the ATTRIBUTE PHASE. The ending address is defined as any byte if no C/BE#[3::0] signal line is asserted in the ATTRIBUTE PHASE. If any C/BE#[3::0] signal line is asserted in the ATTRIBUTE PHASE, the lowest order byte accessed (by asserted C/BE#[3::0] signal line) defines the starting address and the highest order byte accessed (by asserted C/BE#[3::0] signal line) defines the ending address. Any combination of asserted and deasserted C/BE#[3::0] signal lines in the ATTRIBUTE PHASE is permitted (with the restrictions relative to the AD[1::0] signal lines previously discussed). In the case of a DWORD memory read transaction, the default total byte count for the DWORD memory read transaction is four (there is no Upper or Lower Byte Counts in the ATTRIBUTE PHASE as in a BURST bus transaction) independent of the number of byte enable bits asserted in the C/BE#[3::0] signal lines in the ATTRIBUTE PHASE. The value of the C/BE#[3::0] signal lines in the DATA PHASE are driven to logical "1" (deasserted) by the PCI-X bus master.

The ATTRIBUTE PHASE is a single CLK signal line period in length and is immediately followed by the TARGET RESPONSE PHASE. The TARGET RESPONSE PHASE is defined as the one CLK signal line period immediately after the ATTRIBUTE PHASE. The C/BE#[3::0] signal lines in the TARGET RESPONSE PHASE are driven to logical "1" by the PCI-X bus master. For a memory read, an alias memory read block, or a memory read block transaction, the AD[31::00] signal lines are tristated by the PCI-X bus master in the TARGET RESPONSE PHASE. Also, for the aforementioned bus transaction, the TARGET RESPONSE PHASE is the earliest point that the target can begin driving the AD[31::00] signal lines. For a memory write, an alias memory write block, or a memory write block transaction, the AD[31::00] signal lines are driven to logical "1" by the PCI-X bus master in the TARGET RESPONSE PHASE.

The definition of the TARGET RESPONSE PHASE according to the PCI-X addendum specification states that it is "one or more clocks after the attribute phase until the target claims the transaction by asserting the DEVSEL# signal line." According to the PCI-X bus transaction protocol, the DEVSEL# signal line may actually be asserted immediately after the ATTRIBUTE PHASE. Also, to be consistent with the PCI local bus specification, it would be cleaner to define the CLK signal line periods immediately after a singular CLK signal line period of the TARGET RESPONSE PHASE as the DATA PHASE. Consequently, the TARGET RESPONSE PHASE defined in the paragraph above will be used in this book and the definition described in this box by the PCI-X addendum specification will not be used.

Immediately after the TARGET RESPONSE PHASE is the DATA PHASE. The DATA PHASE is defined between the TARGET RESPONSE PHASE and the time when the FRAME# and IRDY# signal lines are both deasserted. The C/BE#[3::0] signal lines are driven to logical "1" by the PCI-X bus master throughout the DATA PHASE. During the DATA PHASE the AD[31::00] signal lines contain the memory read data per the C/BE#[3::0] signal lines encoding in the ATTRIBUTE PHASE.

The PAR signal line is driven by either the PCI-X bus master or the target and reflects the parity of the C/BE#[3::0] and AD[31::0] signal lines in the ADDRESS, ATTRIBUTE, and DATA PHASES. For the ADDRESS and ATTRIBUTE PHASES, the PAR signal line is tri-stated and driven by the PCI-X bus master with same protocol as the AD [31::00] signal lines, but with a one CLK signal line period delay from the actual CLK signal line periods associated with the ADDRESS and ATTRIBUTE PHASES of the AD [31::00] signal lines. The PAR signal line is tristated by the PCI-X bus master for one CLK signal line period after TARGET RESPONSE PHASE that is also earliest point that the target can begin driving the PAR signal line. Consequently, the PAR signal line has no valid parity information relative to the TARGET RESPONSE PHASE. For a DWORD memory read transaction, during the DATA PHASE the PAR signal line is driven by the target with valid parity information for the AD [31::00] signal lines (including parity of the deasserted C/BE#[3::0] signal lines) two CLK signal line periods after the TRDY# signal line is asserted The PCI-X bus master does not begin checking parity until two CLK signal line periods after the TRDY# signal line is asserted. Otherwise, the PAR signal line associated with the DATA PHASE is driven by the target with invalid information or a pull-up resistor and does not contain valid parity information. See Chapter 6: *Detailed Bus Transaction Operation* for more information.

> Parity is generated and valid parity is placed on the PAR signal line relative to the AD[31::00] and C/BE#[3::0] signal lines in the ADDRESS and ATTRIBUTE PHASES. Parity is generated and valid parity is placed on the PAR signal line relative to the AD[31::00] and C/BE#[3::0] signal lines in the DATA PHASE independent of the value of the associated C/BE#[3::0] signal lines in DATA PHASES. That is, data parity generating and checking is defined for a data byte even though the associated C/BE# signal line is deasserted. Also, during the ATTRIBUTE PHASE, any AD[31::00] signal line that is defined as RESERVED is still included in the generation and checking of parity.

BURST MEMORY COMMANDS

> BURST memory write, memory write block, and alias memory write block commands can be executed to both prefetchable and non-prefetchable address spaces. The BURST memory read, memory read block, and alias memory read block commands can be executed only to prefetchable address spaces.

During the ADDRESS PHASE, the 0111, 1000, 1001, 1110, and 1111(C/BE#[3::0]) encodings define the memory write, alias memory read block, alias memory write block, memory read block, and memory write block commands; respectively. The encoding identifies the BURST COMMANDs to the memory address space and can be executed as either a SINGLE or a BURST bus transaction. The AD[31::00] signal lines during the ADDRESS PHASE define the memory address. The AD[1::0] signal lines define the lowest byte address for the starting address of the 32 data bit (four bytes) address range for the initial microaccess of the DATA PHASE.

According to the PCI-X addendum specification, once the ADDRESS and the COMMAND type have been established in the ADDRESS PHASE, the next CLK signal line period is defined as the ATTRIBUTE PHASE. The information contained in the AD[31::00] and C/BE#[3::0] signal lines during the ATTRIBUTE PHASE for a BURST memory command is as follows:

- ■ AD[07::00] = Lower Byte Count: See discussion below.

- ■ AD[10::08] = Requester Function Number: This three bit number is the Function Number assigned by design of the component. The combination of Function, Device, and Bus numbers defines the Requester ID number.

- ■ AD[15::11] = Requester Device Number: This five bit number is the Bus Device Number in the PCI-X Status Register in the configuration address space of the associated PCI-X bus master (on the bus segment associated with the Bus Number of AD[32::16]). The value 1FH indicates that these bits in the Status Register have not been initialized. The value 00H is reserved for bridge that connects the higher LEVEL bus segment to this bus segment. The combination of Function, Device, and Bus numbers defines the Requester ID number.

- ■ AD[23::16] = Requester Bus Number: This eight bit number is the Bus Number in the PCI-X Status Register in the configuration address space of the associated PCI-X bus master. The value FFH indicates that the Status Register has not been initialized. The combination of Function, Device, and Bus numbers defines the Requester ID number.

- AD[28::24] = Tag: A unique number is assigned by the PCI-X bus master to each bus transaction. The five bits permit each PCI-X bus master to have up to 32 different bus transactions in execution at the same time.

- AD[29] = Relaxed Ordering: When this bit is set to logical "1", the programming model and the device driver guarantee that the order of read and write transactions to the associated memory address space does not (optional) have to maintain any ordering through a PCI-X/PCI-X BRIDGE (or a "bridge like" interface between the bus segment and other circuitry) relative to other bus transactions. If this bit is set to logical "0", bus transaction ordering relative to other bus transactions must be maintained. See Chapter 7: *Bridge and Interface Protocol* for more information.

  - The Relaxed Ordering bit must be set to logical "0" if the Enable Relaxed Ordering bit in the PCI-X Command register in the configuration address space is set to logical "0".

  - This bit is defined for all BURST COMMANDS (*i.e.*, accesses to memory address space ... see a later section in this chapter on Split Completion Transaction for application to this BURST COMMAND) and for DWORD memory read. For all other bus transactions this bit must be set to logical "0". Also, for bus transactions associated with Message Signaled Interrupt; this bit must be set to logical "0".

  - If a BURST COMMAND transaction is being executed, the execution of Disconnect at next ADB or Single Phase Disconnect terminations by the target, or if the PCI-X bus master terminates a transaction without completing the total byte count for the bus transaction; this bit must remain the same value for the subsequent transactions that are a continuation of the terminated bus transaction (*i.e.*, part of the same "sequence").

  - For a BURST memory write command (memory write, alias memory write block, and memory write block) the Relaxed Ordering bit can be set to logical "1" only if strong ordering relative to other posted memory write transactions of other "sequences" in the same direction does NOT have to be maintained. Strong ordering relative to the bus transactions of the same "sequence" must always be maintained. See Chapter 7: *Bridge and Interface Protocol* for more information.

  - For a BURST memory read command (alias memory read block or memory read block) the Relaxed Ordering bit can be set to logical "1" only if strong ordering of the associated "sequence" of split completion transactions relative to posted memory write transactions in the same direction as the BURST memory command does NOT have to be maintained. See *Chapter 7: Bridge and Interface Protocol* for more information.

■ PCI-X/PCI-X BRIDGES port this bit through unmodified.

■ See the previous section for how this bit is defined for the DWORD memory read command.

■ AD[30] = No Snoop: When this bit is set to logical "1", the PCI-X bus master guarantees that there are no other resources in the system that need to snoop an access to the associated address (between and inclusive of the starting and ending addresses). For example, this bit is set to logical 1 if the associated address space is not cached, or if cached, the associated address has been flushed.

■ This bit is defined for all BURST COMMANDS (except split completion transactions... *i.e.*, accesses to memory address space) and for DWORD memory read. For all other bus transactions this bit must be set to logical "0". Also, for bus transactions associated with Message Signaled Interrupt; this bit must be set to logical "0".

■ If a BURST COMMAND transaction is being executed, the execution of Disconnect at next ADB or Single Phase Disconnect terminations by the target, or if the PCI-X bus master terminates a transaction without transferring the total byte count of the transaction, this bit must remain the same value for the subsequent transactions that are a continuation of the terminated bus transaction (i.e., part of the same "sequence").

■ PCI-X/PCI-X BRIDGES port this bit through unmodified.

■ See the previous section for how this bit is defined for DWORD memory read command.

■ AD[31] = Reserved and required to be logical "0"

■ C/BE#[3::0] = Upper Byte Count: See discussion below.

Of particular note in the above bullets is that the Upper Byte Count and Lower Byte Counts (potential of total of 2^{12} bytes = 4096 total bytes) collectively define the total byte count of the bus transaction. The total byte count of the bus transaction in conjunction with the starting address defined in AD[31::0] in the ADDRESS PHASE establishes the ending address. The ending address = starting address + total byte count of the bus transaction −1. The total byte count of the bus transaction will vary for the bus transactions of a "sequence" as follows:

■ When the bus transaction is a BURST memory write (memory write, memory write block, and alias memory) command, the protocol relative to the total byte count of the bus transaction is as follows:

185

■ For the first bus transaction ("initial" transaction): The Upper and Lower Byte Counts collectively provide the total byte count of the bus transaction. The total byte count of the bus transaction is the total number bytes the PCI-X bus master of this bus transaction INTENDS to transfer. The PCI-X bus master or the target may terminate the bus transaction prior to the transfer of the total byte count of the bus transaction (see Chapter 8: *Master and Target Termination* for more information about termination protocol and requirements to continue). If the PCI-X bus master has not completed the transfer of the total byte count of the bus transaction, it may be required to continue the transfer by executing another bus transaction(s). That is, it may continue the "initial" bus transaction as a "sequence" of bus transactions with adjusted total byte counts of the bus transactions, and the same Requester ID and Tag. See Chapter 8: *Master and Target Termination* for more information.

■ For subsequent bus transactions that are part of a "sequence" of bus transactions relative to the "initial" transaction (defined above): The total byte count of the bus transaction (Upper and Lower Byte Counts) is the total byte count of the "initial" bus transaction minus the sum of the all bytes actually transferred as part of the "initial" and previous (subsequent to the "initial") bus transactions of the "sequence". The starting address of each subsequent bus transaction after the "initial" transaction of the "sequence" will be adjusted accordingly to reflect bytes transferred in the "initial" and previous (subsequent to "initial") bus transactions of the "sequence" with the same Requester ID and Tag.

■ When the bus transaction is for a BURST memory read command (memory read, memory read block, and alias memory read block), the protocol relative to the total byte count of the bus transaction is as follows:

■ For the first bus transaction ("initial" bus transaction): The Upper and Lower Byte Counts collectively provides the total byte count of the bus transaction. The total byte count of the bus transaction is the total number bytes the PCI-X bus master of the bus transaction INTENDS to transfer. The PCI-X bus master or the target may terminate the bus transaction prior to the transfer of the total byte count of the bus transaction (see Chapter 8: *Master and Target Termination* for more information about termination protocol and requirements to continue). If the PCI-X bus master has not completed the transfer of the total byte count of the bus transaction, it is not required to continue the transfer by executing another bus transaction. If the PCI-X bus master wants to continue the transfer, the total byte count of the subsequent bus transaction(s) will be adjusted as outlined for a BURST memory write command. However, because the subsequent bus transactions (to create a "sequence") for a BURST memory read command are not required, the total byte count and the Tag may or may not be the same (though the Requester ID is the same). See Chapter 8: *Master and Target Termination* for more information.

An important concept is to remember is that 4096 bytes is the maximum number of bytes that CAN be transferred in a BURST COMMAND transaction. The number of bytes INTENDED to be transferred is contained in the Upper and Lower Bytes Counts information provided in the ATTRIBUTE PHASE. The number of bits in the Upper and Lower Bytes Counts limits the number of bytes that can be transferred in a bus transaction.

For the "total byte count of the bus transaction", the value of 001H indicates one byte. The value FFFH indicates 4095 bytes. The value 000H indicates 4096 bytes.

In the discussion above relating to the total byte count of the bus transaction, the bytes transferred in any bus transaction are defined as those bytes associated with the bus transaction with or without the assertion of the associated C/BE#[3::0] signal lines.

In the case of a BURST memory write transaction, the C/BE#[3::0] signal lines during the DATA PHASE are valid. The count of bytes "actually" transferred in a BURST memory write transaction is defined by the bytes associated with both asserted and deasserted C/BE#[3::0] signal lines. It is required that the C/BE#[3::0] signal lines associated with the bytes below the starting address and above the ending address be deasserted. The bytes outside of the range of the starting and ending addresses are not written and are not included in the total byte count of the bus transaction (Upper and Lower Byte Counts that are INTENDED to be transferred) or the count of bytes "actually" transferred in the bus transaction.

In the case of a of BURST read (memory read, memory read block, and alias memory read block), BURST alias memory write block, and BURST memory write block transactions, the C/BE#[3::0] signal lines during the DATA PHASE are all deasserted. By definition, the count of bytes "actually" transferred in these bus transactions are defined as all the bytes of each microaccess. That is, these bus transactions by definition are accessing all of the bytes of each microaccess. The bytes outside of the range of the starting and ending addresses are not read or written and are not included in the total byte count of the bus transaction (Upper and Lower Byte Counts that are INTENDED to be transferred) or the count of bytes "actually" transferred in the bus transaction.

The ATTRIBUTE PHASE is a single CLK signal line period in length and is immediately followed by the TARGET RESPONSE PHASE. The TARGET RESPONSE PHASE is defined as the one CLK signal line period immediately after the ATTRIBUTE PHASE. The C/BE#[3::0] signal lines in the TARGET RESPONSE PHASE are driven to logical "1" by the PCI-X bus master. For a memory read, an alias memory read block, or a memory read block transaction, the AD[31::00] signal lines are tristated by the PCI-X bus master in the TARGET RESPONSE PHASE. Also, for the aforementioned bus transaction, the TARGET RESPONSE PHASE is the earliest point that the target can begin driving the AD[31::00] signal lines. For a memory write, an alias memory write block, or a memory write block transaction, the AD[31::00] signal lines are either driven to a stable value by the PCI-X bus master or float in the TARGET RESPONSE PHASE.

The definition of the TARGET RESPONSE PHASE according to the PCI-X addendum specification, states that it is "one or more clocks after the attribute phase until the target claims the transaction by asserting the DEVSEL#". According to the PCI-X bus transaction protocol, the DEVSEL# signal line may actually be asserted immediately after the ATTRIBUTE PHASE. Also, to be consistent with the PCI local bus specification, it would be cleaner to define the CLK signal line periods immediately after a singular CLK signal line period of the TARGET RESPONSE PHASE as the DATA PHASE. Consequently; the TARGET RESPONSE PHASE defined in the paragraph above will be used in this book and the definition outlined in this box by the PCI-X addendum specification will not be used.

Immediately after the TARGET RESPONSE PHASE is the DATA PHASE. The DATA PHASE is defined between the TARGET RESPONSE PHASE and the time when the FRAME# and IRDY# signal lines are both deasserted. For the BURST memory read (memory read, alias memory read block, and memory read block), BURST alias memory write block, or BURST memory write block transactions the C/BE#[3::0] signal lines are driven to logical "1" by the PCI-X bus master throughout the DATA PHASE. For these bus transactions, all of the bytes within the starting and ending address range (inclusively) of each microaccess are being accessed; consequently, the AD[31::00] signal lines are all driven with valid information.

For the BURST memory write transaction, the C/BE#[3::0] signal lines are driven with valid information to enable the writing of specific bytes within the starting and ending addresses range (inclusively) for each microaccess of the DATA PHASE. For BURST memory write transactions, the AD[31::00] signal lines associated with asserted C/BE[3::0] signal lines are driven with valid data. The AD[31::00] signal lines associated with deasserted C/BE#[3::0] signals must be driven by the PCI-X bus master to a stable level. As previously stated, the data accessed is within the starting and ending addresses and including the specific bytes of the starting and ending addresses of the 32 data bits addressed. A PCI-X bus master can drive any combination of asserted and deasserted C/BE#[3::0] signal lines in the DATA PHASE. If the target does not support the specific combination of C/BE#[3::0] signal lines, it must execute a Target Abort termination. See Chapter 8: *Master and Target Termination* for more information.

The PAR signal line is driven by the PCI-X bus master and reflects the parity of the C/BE#[3::0] and AD[31::0] signal lines in the ADDRESS, ATTRIBUTE, and DATA PHASES. For the ADDRESS and ATTRIBUTE PHASES, the PAR signal line is tristated and driven by the PCI-X bus master with same protocol as the AD[31::00] signal lines, but with a one CLK signal line period delay from the actual CLK signal line periods associated with the ADDRESS and ATTRIBUTE PHASES of the AD[31::00] signal lines. For BURST memory read, an alias memory read block, or memory read block transactions, the PAR signal line is tristated by the PCI-X bus master one CLK signal line period after TARGET RESPONSE PHASE (which is also the earliest point that the target can begin driving the PAR signal line).

For BURST memory write, alias memory write block, or memory write block transactions, the PAR signal line is driven to logical "1" by a the PCI-X bus master one CLK signal line period after the TARGET RESPONSE PHASE for the duration of one CLK signal line period. Consequently, the PAR signal line for all these bus transactions has no valid parity information relative to the TARGET RESPONSE PHASE. For BURST memory read, an alias memory read block, or memory read block transactions during the DATA PHASE, the PAR signal line is driven by the target with valid information two CLK signal line periods after the TRDY# signal line is asserted. The PCI-X bus master does not begin checking parity until two CLK signal line periods after the TRDY# signal line is asserted. Otherwise the PAR signal line associated with the DATA PHASE is driven by the target with invalid information or by a pull-up resistor and does not contain valid parity information.

For BURST memory write, alias memory write block, or memory write block transactions during the DATA PHASE the PAR signal line is driven by the PCI-X bus master with valid information two CLK signal line periods after the IRDY# signal line is asserted. The target does not begin checking parity until two CLK signal line periods after the IRDY# signal line is asserted. Otherwise the PAR signal line associated with the DATA PHASE is driven by the PCI-X bus master but does not contain valid parity information. See Chapter 6: *Detailed Bus Transaction Operation* for more information.

Parity is generated and valid parity is placed on the PAR signal line relative to the AD[31::00] and C/BE#[3::0] signal lines in the ADDRESS and ATTRIBUTE PHASES. Parity is generated and valid parity is placed on the PAR signal line relative to the AD[31::00] and C/BE#[3::0] signal lines in the DATA PHASE independent of the value of the associated C/BE#[3::0] signal lines in DATA PHASES. That is, data parity generating and checking is defined for a data byte even though the associated C/BE# signal line is deasserted. Also, during the ATTRIBUTE PHASE, any AD[31::00] signal line that is defined as RESERVED is still included in the generation and checking of parity.

The PCI-X addendum specification has defined the encoding patterns for BURST alias memory read block and alias memory write block commands. The exact protocol of these commands will be defined in a later version of the specification. According to Revision 1.0 if the PCI-X addendum specification, NO PCI-X bus master should execute these commands. If a target is accessed with a bus transaction for these commands, it should claim (assert the DEVSEL# signal line) the bus transaction and execute as if a memory read block or memory write block transaction was executed.

MEMORY BLOCK AND ALIAS MEMORY BLOCK COMMANDS

The BURST alias memory read block and alias memory write block commands encodings (C/BE#[3::0] signal lines in the ADDRESS PHASE) have been defined by the PCI-X addendum specification. At this time no specific information is available as to how the associated bus transactions are to be executed. If these commands are executed by a PCI-X bus master, targets must claim the bus transaction (DEVSEL# signal line asserted) and execute in the same fashion as BURST memory read block and memory write block commands. See further comments at the end of this section.

For this section the discussion will only focus on BURST memory read block and memory write block commands.

The BURST memory read block and memory write block commands execute transactions that are specifically going to access the entire block. The block being accessed is defined by the starting address and the total byte count of the bus transaction (*i.e.*, starting address to ending address, inclusively). By definition, all of the bytes in the block are accessed (the C/BE#3::0] signal lines are all deasserted in the DATA PHASE). It is the responsibility of the PCI-X bus master to execute these bus transactions only to prefetchable address spaces.

In the case of BURST memory read block transactions, the target knows that pre-reading of the entire block will provide performance enhancements.

The BURST memory write block command can be similar to the memory write and invalidate command of PCI. The starting address and block size can be aligned to a Cacheline boundary and multiples of Cachelines (defined by the Cacheline Size register in the configuration address space), respectively. Also, the NO SNOOP bit can be set to logical "0" in the ATTRIBUTE PHASE. One of the requirements of a BURST memory read block is that the entire block is written. That is, all of the bytes in the block are written and if the entire address range of the block is not written in a single BURST bus transaction, a "sequence" of bus transactions are required until the entire address range of the block is written. The Cacheline alignment as outlined above is by no means a requirement for execution of a BURST memory write block command unless cache coherency is a consideration.

A PCI-X memory resource as a target is required to support both BURST memory write and BURST memory write block commands. If the information that the entire block is to be written is of no use to the target, the target can treat the BURST memory write block command as if it was a BURST memory write command with all the bytes being written.

A PCI-X memory resource as a target is required to support both DWORD memory read and BURST memory read block commands. If the information that the entire block is to be read is of no use to the target, the target can treat the BURST memory read block command as if it was a DWORD memory read command with all the bytes being read.

See associated comments relative to BURST alias memory block commands at the beginning of this section.

I/O COMMANDS

See Subchapter 4.11 for related information.

INTRODUCTION

A PCI-X bus master requests a 32 data bit I/O transaction with the continued deassertion of the REQ64# signal line during the ADDRESS PHASE (deasserted by a pull-up resistor on the bus backplane). The target acknowledges executing a 32 data bit transaction with the continued deassertion of the ACK64# signal line during the DATA PHASE (deasserted by a pull-up resistor on the bus backplane). For a 32 data bit bus transaction, the AD[63::32], C/BE#[7::4], and PAR64 signal lines are driven to logical "1" by pull-up resistors; consequently, the PAR64 signal line does not have valid parity information. Once the size of the respective bus transaction participants is established it remains unchanged during the remainder of the bus transaction.

For an I/O transaction, only 32 data bit bus transactions can be executed. An I/O transaction *cannot* be executed with DUAL ADDRESS.

The PCI-X bus master executes a successful I/O transaction by the activity of the FRAME# and IRDY# signal lines. As outlined in Chapter 3: *Generic PCI and PCI-X Hardware Operation* and detailed in Chapter 6: *Detailed Bus Transaction Operation*, the type of command (DWORD) in conjunction with the deassertion of the FRAME# and IRDY# signal lines during the DATA PHASE defines a SINGLE I/O transaction. See Chapter 6: *Detailed Bus Transaction Operation* for more information.

During the ADDRESS PHASE of the I/O transaction, the AD[31::0] signal lines select the address for the I/O access and the C/BE#[3::0] signal lines contain the encoded information of the COMMAND type. An I/O transaction is defined as a DWORD COMMAND and can only be executed with a SINGLE bus transaction. There are no I/O transactions defined by a BURST COMMAND; consequently, no BURST bus transactions can be executed.

ADDRESS SPACE PER DEVICE

The size of the I/O address space assigned for each PCI-X device (or each function within a multiple function device) must be limited to a contiguous 256 bytes. The restriction to the contiguous address space insures compatibility to ISA-compatible I/O resources that may reside in the system. The total I/O address space for each PCI-X device (or each function within a multiple function device) can be larger than 256 bytes.

DWORD I/O COMMANDS

During the ADDRESS PHASE, the 0010 and 0011 (C/BE#[3::0]) encoding indicates an I/O read DWORD COMMAND and an I/O write DWORD COMMAND, respectively. These encodings identify a DWORD COMMAND to the I/O address space and can only be executed as a SINGLE bus transaction. The AD [31::00] signal lines during the ADDRESS PHASE define the I/O address. The AD [1::0] signal lines define the lowest byte address. The minimum access of an I/O bus transaction is 32 data bits (four bytes); consequently, the AD[1::0] signal lines during the ADDDRESS PHASE define of the lowest order byte and the associated byte lane to be addressed in the DATA PHASE as follows:

■ AD [1:0] = [0:0] address byte lane 0. Byte lane 0 is on AD[07::00] signal lines during the DATA PHASE.

■ AD [1:0] = [0:1] address byte lane 1. Byte lane 1 is on AD[15::08] signal lines during the DATA PHASE.

■ AD [1:0] = [1:0] address byte lane 2. Byte lane 2 is on AD[23::16] signal lines during the DATA PHASE.

■ AD [1:0] = [1:1] address byte lane 3. Byte lane 3 is on AD[31::24] signal lines during the DATA PHASE.

During the ADDRESS PHASE, the 0010 and 0011 (C/BE#[3::0]) encodings indicate an I/O read and an I/O write, respectively. These encodings identify a DWORD COMMAND to the I/O address space and can only be executed as a SINGLE bus transaction. The AD [31::00] signal lines during the ADDRESS PHASE define the I/O address. The AD [1::0] signal lines define the lowest byte address. The minimum access of an I/O bus transaction is 32 data bits (four bytes); consequently, the AD[1::0] signal lines during the ADDDRESS PHASE define the lowest order byte and the associated byte lane to be addressed in the DATA PHASE as follows:

■ AD [1:0] = [0:0] address byte lane 0. Byte lane 0 is on AD[07::00] signal lines during the DATA PHASE.

■ AD [1:0] = [0:1] address byte lane 1. Byte lane 1 is on AD[15::08] signal lines during the DATA PHASE.

■ AD [1:0] = [1:0] address byte lane 2. Byte lane 2 is on AD[23::16] signal lines during the DATA PHASE.

■ AD [1:0] = [1:1] address byte lane 3. Byte lane 3 is on AD[31::24] signal lines during the DATA PHASE.

During the ATTRIBUTE PHASE of the SINGLE bus transaction, the C/BE#[3::0] signal lines will identify which bytes will be accessed. The C/BE#[3::0] signal lines during the ATTRIBUTE PHASE of a SINGLE bus transaction must also match the bytes that were addressed by the AD[1::0] signal lines during the ADDRESS PHASE. The allowed protocol for the AD[1::0] signal lines during the ADDRESS PHASE and the C/BE#[3::0] signal lines during the ATTRIBUTE PHASE is as follows:

AD[1]	AD[0]	C/BE#[3]	C/BE#[2]	C/BE#[1]	C/BE#[0]
0	0	X	X	X	0
0	1	X	X	0	1
1	0	X	0	1	1
1	1	0	1	1	1
x	x	1	1	1	1

Table 4-11: Relationship of AD Signal Lines (ADDRESS PHASE) with C/BE# Signal Lines (ATTRIBUTE PHASE) for DWORD COMMAND Transactions

X = Don't care (asserted or deasserted)
1 = 3.3 or 5 volts (deasserted for C/BE#[3::0] signal lines)
0 = 0 volts (asserted for C/BE#[3::0] signal lines)

The PCI-X target must monitor the AD[1::0] signal lines during the ADDRESS PHASE and compare their values with the C/BE#[3::0] signal lines during the ATTTRIBUTE PHASE. If the values do not support the same byte address, the target must execute a Target Abort termination. This protocol allows one to four different targets to own mutually exclusive portions of the 32 data bits (double words) being addressed by the bus transaction. This protocol DOES NOT apply if one target owns the entire double word. This protocol also does not apply to PCI-X/PCI-X, PCI/PCI-X, or PCI/LEGACY BRIDGEs that implement subtractive decoding because there is no complete knowledge of resources on the destination PCI bus or the LEGACY bus, respectively.

According to the PCI-X addendum specification, once the ADDRESS and the COMMAND type have been established in the ADDRESS PHASE, the next CLK signal line period is defined as the ATTRIBUTE PHASE. The information contained in the AD[31::00] and C/BE#[3::0] signal lines during the ATTRIBUTE PHASE for an I/O DWORD COMMAND is defined as follows:

- AD[07::00] = Reserved and are required to be logical "0".

- AD[10::08] = Requester Function Number: This three bit number is the Function Number assigned by design of the component. The combination of Function, Device, and Bus numbers defines the Requester ID number.

- AD[15::11] = Requester Device Number: This five bit number is the Bus Device Number in the PCI-X Status Register in the configuration address space of the associated PCI-X bus master (on the bus segment associated with the Bus Number of AD[32::16]). The value 1FH indicates that these bits in the Status Register have not been initialized. The value 00H is reserved for the bridge that connects the higher LEVEL bus segment to this bus segment. The combination of Function, Device, and Bus numbers defines the Requester ID number.

- AD[23::16] = Requester Bus Number: This eight bit number is the Bus Number in the PCI-X Status Register in the configuration address space of the associated PCI-X bus master. The value FFH indicates that these bits in the Status Register have not been initialized. The combination of Function, Device, and Bus numbers defines the Requester ID number.

- AD[28::24] = Tag: A unique number is assigned by the PCI-X bus master to each bus transaction of a sequence. The five bits permit a specific PCI-X bus master to have up to 32 different sequences at the same time.

- AD[29] = Relaxed Ordering: This bit is defined only for memory and split completion transactions. For all other bus transactions this bit must be set to logical "0".

- AD[30] = No Snoop: This bit is defined only for memory transactions. For all other bus transactions this bit must be set to logical 0.

- AD[31] = Reserved and must be logical "0".

- C/BE#[3::0] = Byte Enables for the one DATA PHASE access.

Of particular note in the above bullets are the C/BE#[3::0] signal lines. In the ADDRESS PHASE, the AD [1::0] signal lines define the lowest level byte to be addressed in the DATA PHASE and define the associated byte lane. In the ATTRIBUTE PHASE, the C/BE#[3::0] signal lines select which byte lanes are accessed in the DATA PHASE and must match the address information as discussed in the previous section and outlined in Table 4-11.

For an I/O transaction, the starting address is defined by the AD[31::0] signal lines, if no C/BE#[3::0] signal line is asserted in the ATTRIBUTE PHASE. The ending address is defined as any byte if no C/BE#[3::0] signal line is asserted in the ATTRIBUTE PHASE. If any C/BE#[3::0] signal line is asserted in the ATTRIBUTE PHASE, the lowest order byte accessed (by asserted C/BE#[3::0] signal line) defines the starting address and the highest order byte accessed (by asserted C/BE#[3::0] signal line) defines the ending address. Any combination of asserted and deasserted C/BE#[3::0] signal lines in the ATTRIBUTE PHASE is permitted (with the restrictions relative to the AD[1::0] signal lines previously discussed). In the case of an I/O transaction, the default the total byte count for the I/O transaction is four (there is no Upper or Lower Byte Count in the ATTRIBUTE PHASE as in a BURST bus transaction), independent of the number of byte enable bits asserted in the C/BE#[3::0] signal lines in the ATTRIBUTE PHASE. The value of the C/BE#[3::0] signal lines in the DATA PHASE are driven to logical "1" (deasserted) by the PCI-X bus master.

The ATTRIBUTE PHASE is a single CLK signal line period in length and is immediately followed by the TARGET RESPONSE PHASE. The TARGET RESPONSE PHASE is defined as the one CLK signal line period immediately after the ATTRIBUTE PHASE. The C/BE#[3::0] signal lines in the TARGET RESPONSE PHASE are driven to logical "1" by the PCI-X bus master. For an I/O read transaction, the AD[31::00] signal lines are tristated by the PCI-X bus master in the TARGET RESPONSE PHASE, which is also the earliest point that the target can begin driving the AD[31::00][] signal lines. For an I/O write transaction, the AD[31::00] signal lines are driven to a to a stable level by the PCI-X bus master or floated in the TARGET RESPONSE PHASE.

The definition of the TARGET RESPONSE PHASE in the PCI-X addendum specification states that it is "one or more clocks after the attribute phase until the target claims the transaction by asserting the DEVSEL# signal line." According to the PCI-X bus transaction protocol, the DEVSEL# signal line may actually be asserted immediately after the ATTRIBUTE PHASE. Also, to be consistent with the PCI local bus specification, it would be cleaner to define the CLK signal line periods immediately after a single CLK signal line period of the TARGET RESPONSE PHASE as the DATA PHASE. Consequently; the TARGET RESPONSE PHASE defined in the paragraph above will be used in this book and the definition outlined in this box by the PCI-X addendum specification will not be used.

Immediately after the TARGET RESPONSE PHASE is the DATA PHASE. The DATA PHASE is defined between the TARGET RESPONSE PHASE and the time when the FRAME# and IRDY# signal lines are both deasserted. The C/BE#[3::0] signal lines are driven to logical "1" by the PCI-X bus master throughout the DATA PHASE. During the DATA PHASE, the AD[31::00] signal lines contain the I/O data to read or write according to the C/BE#[3::0] signal line encoding in the ATTRIBUTE PHASE.

The PAR signal line is driven by the PCI-X bus master and reflects the parity of the C/BE#[3::0] and AD[31::0] signal lines in the ADDRESS, ATTRIBUTE, and DATA PHASES. For the ADDRESS and ATTRIBUTE PHASES, the PAR signal line is tristated and driven by the PCI-X bus master with same protocol as the AD [31::00] signal lines, but with a one CLK signal line period delay from the actual CLK signal line periods associated with the ADDRESS and ATTRIBUTE PHASES of the AD [31::00] signal lines.

For I/O read transactions, the PAR signal line is tristated by the PCI-X bus master one CLK signal line period after the TARGET RESPONSE PHASE, which is also the earliest point that the target can begin driving the PAR signal line. For I/O write transactions, the PAR signal line is driven to logical "1" by the PCI-X bus master one CLK signal line period after the TARGET RESPONSE PHASE for the duration of one CLK signal line period. Consequently, the PAR signal line for all these bus transactions has no valid parity information relative to the TARGET RESPONSE PHASE.

For I/O read transactions during the DATA PHASE, the PAR signal line is driven by the target with valid information two CLK signal line periods after the TRDY# signal line is asserted. The PCI-X bus master does not begin checking parity until two CLK signal line periods after the TRDY# signal line is asserted. Otherwise the PAR signal line associated with the DATA PHASE is driven by the target with invalid information or by a pull-up resistor and does not contain valid parity information. For I/O write transactions during the DATA PHASE, the PAR signal line is driven by the PCI-X bus master with valid information two CLK signal line periods after the IRDY# signal line is asserted. The target does not begin checking parity until two CLK signal line periods after the IRDY# signal line is asserted. Otherwise the PAR signal line associated with the DATA PHASE is driven by the PCI-X bus master but does not contain valid parity information. See Chapter 6: *Detailed Bus Transaction Operation* for more information.

Parity is generated and valid parity is placed on the PAR signal line relative to the AD[31::00] and C/BE#[3::0] signal lines in the ADDRESS and ATTRIBUTE PHASES. Parity is generated and valid parity is placed on the PAR signal line relative to the AD[31::00] and C/BE#[3::0] signal lines in the DATA PHASE independent of the value of the associated C/BE#[3::0] signal lines in DATA PHASES. That is, data parity generating and checking is defined for a data byte even though the associated C/BE# signal line is deasserted. Also, during the ATTRIBUTE PHASE, any AD[31::00] signal line that is defined as RESERVED is still included in the generation and checking of parity.

An I/O resource (target) can be re-mapped to the memory address space, can support up to 32 or 64 data bits, and can operate with the same protocol as any memory resource.

BURST I/O COMMANDS

This COMMAND type is not defined for BURST transactions.

CONFIGURATION COMMANDS

See Subchapter 4.12 and Chapter 7: *Bridge and Interface Protocol* for more information.

The term "device" used in the following section collectively refers to the configuration address space (register sets) of the PCI-X resources. These PCI-X resources can be PCI-X bus masters (with configuration registers as a target), targets, or bridges. A device can have one to eight configuration address spaces.

INTRODUCTION

A PCI-X bus master requests a 32 data bit configuration transaction with the continued deassertion of the REQ64# signal line during the ADDRESS PHASE (deasserted by a pull-up resistor on the bus backplane). The target acknowledges executing a 32 data bit transaction with the continued deassertion of the ACK64# signal line during the DATA PHASE (deasserted by a pull-up resistor on the bus backplane). For a 32 data bit bus transaction, the AD[63::32], C/BE#[7::4], and PAR64 signal lines are driven to logical "1" by pull-up resistors; consequently, the PAR64 signal line does not have valid parity information. Once the size of the respective bus transaction participants is established it remains unchanged during the remainder of the bus transaction.

For a configuration transaction, only 32 data bit bus transactions can be executed. A configuration transaction *cannot* be executed with DUAL ADDRESS.

The PCI-X bus master executes a successful configuration transaction by the activity of the FRAME# and IRDY# signal lines. As outlined in Chapter 3: *Generic PCI and PCI-X Hardware Operation* and detailed in Chapter 6: *Detailed*

Bus Transaction Operation, the type of command (DWORD) in conjunction with the deassertion of the FRAME# and IRDY# signal lines during the DATA PHASE defines a SINGLE configuration transaction. See Chapter 6: *Detailed Bus Transaction Operation* for more information.

During the ADDRESS PHASE of the configuration transaction, the AD[31::0] signal lines select the address for the configuration access and the C/BE#[3::0] signal lines contain the encoded information of the COMMAND type. A configuration transaction is defined as a DWORD COMMAND and can only be executed with a SINGLE bus transaction. There are no configuration transactions defined by a BURST COMMAND; consequently, no BURST bus transactions can be executed.

ADDRESS SPACE PER DEVICE

The size of the configuration address space assigned for each PCI-X device (or each function within a multiple function device) must be limited to a contiguous 256 bytes. If a PCI-X device has multiple functions, each function is assigned a contiguous 256 bytes.

DWORD CONFIGURATION COMMANDS

During the ADDRESS PHASE, the 1010 and 1011 (C/BE#[3::0]) encoding indicates a configuration read and a configuration write, respectively. These encodings identify a DWORD COMMAND to the configuration address space and can only be executed as a SINGLE bus transaction. The AD [1::0] signal lines during the ADDRESS PHASE define the type of configuration (Type 0 or 1) as these signal lines do in the ADDRESS PHASE of a PCI configuration transaction. The AD [31::02] signal lines during the ADDRESS PHASE are defined the same as for a PCI configuration transaction. The only difference (relative to the ADDRESS PHASE) between a PCI-X and PCI configuration transaction is the definition of the AD[31::11] signal lines for a Type 0 configuration transaction. The differences are as follows:

- For PCI Type 0 configuration transactions, the AD [31::11] signal lines in the ADDRESS PHASE define the IDSEL signal line attachment for up to 21 devices on each PCI bus segment. As discussed in the previous section, the IDSEL signal lines are encoded in the Device Number of the Type 1 configuration transaction or the Config_Address Register of the HOST/PCI BRIDGE.

- For PCI-X Type 0 configuration transactions, the AD [31::16] signal lines in the ADDRESS PHASE define the IDSEL signal line attachment for up to 16 devices on each PCI-X bus segment. The AD [15::11] signal lines of the Type 0 configuration transaction contain the Device Number (the Device Number is also contained in the AD[15::11] of Type 1 configuration or bits [15::11] of the Config_Address Register of the HOST/PCI BRIDGE). Supplying the Device Number in the Type 0 configuration transaction permits the Device Number to be updated in the device's configuration address space (PCI-X Status register) every time a Type 0 configuration write transaction is executed to that device. The updating of the Device number in the device's configuration address space is required every time a Type 0 configuration write transaction is executed to the device. (Note: The Device Number is physically fixed by the IDSEL signal line asserted to the device and the assignment of an IDSEL signal line is fixed to a Device Number as outlined below.) The IDSEL signal lines are encoded in the Device Number of the Type 1 configuration transaction or the Config_Address Register of the HOST/PCI BRIDGE. The Device Number is five bits in size; consequently, "possibly" 32 devices are encoded. However, PCI-X addendum specification specifically maps only 16 encodings to 16 IDSEL signal lines. The IDSEL signal lines are shared one to one with the AD[31::16] signal lines. The mapping of the encoding is as follows:

- Device Number 0 0000 (AD[15::11] of Type 1 configuration or bits [15::11] of the Config_Address Register of the HOST/PCI BRIDGE) map to AD[31::16] = 0000 0000 0000 0001.

- Device Number 0 0001 (AD[15::11] of Type 1 configuration or bits [15::11] of the Config_Address Register of the HOST/PCI BRIDGE) maps to AD[31::16] = 0000 0000 0000 0010

- Device Number 0 0010 (AD[15::11] of Type 1 configuration or bits [15::11] of the Config_Address Register of the HOST/PCI BRIDGE) maps to AD[31::16] = 0000 0000 0000 0100

- Device Number 0 00011 (AD[15::11] of Type 1 configuration or bits [15::11] of the Config_Address Register of the HOST/PCI BRIDGE) maps to AD[31::16] = 0000 0000 0000 1000

- And so forth until .... Device Number 0 1111 (AD[15::11] of Type 1 configuration or bits [15::11] of the Config_Address Register of the HOST/PCI BRIDGE.) maps to AD[31::16] = 1000 0000 0000 0000

- Note that Device Number 1 XXXX (AD[15::11] of Type 1 configuration or bits [15::11] of the Config_Address Register of the HOST/PCI BRIDGE) maps to AD[31::16] = 0000 0000 0000 0000. That is ... no device is selected on the PCI-X bus segment

According to the PCI-X addendum specification, once the ADDRESS and the COMMAND type have been established in the ADDRESS PHASE, the next CLK signal line period is defined as the ATTRIBUTE PHASE. The information contained in the AD[31::00] and C/BE#[3::0] signal lines during the ATTRIBUTE PHASE for a configuration DWORD COMMAND is as follows:

For Type 0 configuration transactions

- AD[07::00] = Bus Number the Type 0 Configuration transaction is executing on. The Bus Number is updated in the device's configuration address space (PCI-X Status register) every time a Type 0 configuration write transaction is executed to that device. (Note: The Bus Number is inserted by the bridge and equals the secondary bus number.)

- AD[10::08] = Requester Function Number. This three bit number is the Function Number assigned by design of the component. The combination of Function, Device, and Bus numbers defines the Requester ID number.

- AD[15::11] = Requester Device Number. This five bit number is the Bus Device Number in the PCI-X Status Register in the configuration address space of the associated PCI-X bus master (on the bus segment associated with the Bus Number of AD[32::16]). The value 1FH indicates that these bits in the Status Register have not been initialized. The value 00H is reserved for bridge that connects the higher LEVEL bus segment to this bus segment. The combination of Function, Device, and Bus numbers defines the Requester ID number.

- AD[23::16] = Requester Bus Number: This eight bit number is the Bus Number in the PCI-X Status Register in the configuration address space of the associated PCI-X bus master. The value FFH indicates that these bits in the Status Register have not been initialized. The combination of Function, Device, and Bus numbers defines the Requester ID number.

- AD[28::24] = Tag: A unique number assigned by the PCI-X bus master to each bus transaction of a sequence. The five bits permit a specific PCI-X bus master to have up to 32 different sequences at the same time. For Split Completion transactions, the tag number is from the associated bus transaction that was terminated with a Split Response termination.

- AD[29] = Relaxed Ordering: This bit is defined only for memory and split completion transactions. For all other bus transactions this bit must be set to logical "0".

- AD[30] = No Snoop: This bit is defined only for memory transactions. For all other bus transactions this bit must be set to logical 0.

- AD[31] = Reserved and must be logical "0".

- C/BE#[3::0] = Byte Enables for the one DATA PHASE access.

For Type 1 configuration transactions

■ AD[07::00] = Reserved, and must be logical "0".

■ AD[10::08] = Requester Function Number: This three bit number is the Function Number assigned by design of the component. The combination of Function, Device, and Bus numbers defines the Requester ID number.

■ AD[15::11] = Requester Device Number: This five bit number is the Bus Device Number in the PCI-X Status Register in the configuration address space of the associated PCI-X bus master (on the bus segment associated with the Bus Number of AD[32::16]). The value 1FH indicates that these bits in the Status Register have not been initialized. The value 00H is reserved for bridge that connects the higher LEVEL bus segment to this bus segment. The combination of Function, Device, and Bus numbers defines the Requester ID number.

■ AD[23::16] = Requester Bus Number: This eight bit number is the Bus Number in the PCI-X Status Register in the configuration address space of the associated PCI-X bus master. The value FFH indicates that these bits in the Status Register have not been initialized. The combination of Function, Device, and Bus numbers defines the Requester ID number.

■ AD[28::24] = Tag: A unique number assigned by the PCI-X bus master to each bus transaction of a sequence. The five bits permit a specific PCI-X bus master to have up to 32 different sequences at the same time. For Split Completion transactions the tag number is from the associated bus transaction that was termination with a Split Response termination.

■ AD[29] = Relaxed Ordering: This bit is defined only for memory and split completion transactions. For all other bus transactions this bit must be set to logical "0".

■ AD[30] = No Snoop: This bit is defined only for memory transactions. For all other bus transactions this bit must be set to logical "0".

■ AD[31] = Reserved, and must be logical "0".

■ C/BE#[3::0] = Byte Enables for the one DATA PHASE access.

The encoding of the C/BE#[3:0] signal lines in the ATTRIBUTE PHASE define the lowest order byte and highest order byte accessed in the DATA PHASE. If any C/BE#[3::0] signal line is asserted in the ATTRIBUTE PHASE, the lowest order byte accessed (by asserted C/BE#[3::0] signal lines) defines the starting address and the highest order byte accessed (by asserted C/BE#[3::0] signal lines) defines the ending address. Any combination of asserted and deasserted C/BE#[3::0] signal lines in the ATTRIBUTE PHASE is permitted. In the case of a configuration transaction, the default total byte count of the configuration transaction is four (there is no Upper or Lower Byte Counts in the ATTRIBUTE PHASE as in a BURST bus transaction) independent of the number of byte enable bits asserted in the C/BE#[3::0] signal lines in the ATTRIBUTE PHASE. The value of the C/BE#[3::0] signal lines in the DATA PHASE are driven to logical "1" (deasserted) by the PCI-X bus master

The ATTRIBUTE PHASE is a single CLK signal line period in length and is immediately followed by the TARGET RESPONSE PHASE. The TARGET RESPONSE PHASE is defined as the one CLK signal line period immediately after the ATTRIBUTE PHASE. The C/BE#[3::0] signal lines in the TARGET RESPONSE PHASE are driven to logical "1" by the PCI-X bus master. For a configuration read transaction, the AD[31::00] signal lines are tristated by the PCI-X bus master in the TARGET RESPONSE PHASE, which is also the earliest point that the target can begin driving the AD[31::00] signal lines. For a configuration write transaction, the AD[31::00] signal lines are driven to a to a stable level by the PCI-X bus master or floated in the TARGET RESPONSE PHASE.

The definition of the TARGET RESPONSE PHASE according to the PCI-X addendum specification states that it is "one or more clocks after the attribute phase until the target claims the transaction by asserting the DEVSEL# signal line." According to the PCI-X bus transaction protocol, the DEVSEL# signal line may actually be asserted immediately after the ATTRIBUTE PHASE. Also, to be consistent with the PCI local bus specification, it would be cleaner to define the CLK signal line periods immediately after a singular CLK signal line period of the TARGET RESPONSE PHASE as the DATA PHASE. Consequently; the TARGET RESPONSE PHASE defined in the paragraph above will be used in this book and the definition outlined in this box by the PCI-X addendum specification will not be used.

Immediately after the TARGET RESPONSE PHASE is the DATA PHASE. The DATA PHASE is defined as being between the TARGET RESPONSE PHASE and the time when the FRAME# and IRDY# signal lines are both deasserted. The C/BE#[3::0] signal lines are driven to logical "1" (deasserted) by the PCI-X bus master throughout the DATA PHASE. During the DATA PHASE, the AD[31::00] signal lines contain the data to be read or written according to the C/BE#[3::0] signal line encoding in the ATTRIBUTE PHASE.

The PAR signal line is driven by the PCI-X bus master and reflects the parity of the C/BE#[3::0] and AD[31::0] signal lines in the ADDRESS, ATTRIBUTE, and DATA PHASES. For the ADDRESS and ATTRIBUTE PHASES, the PAR signal line is tristated and driven by the PCI-X bus master with same protocol as the AD[31::00] signal lines, but with a one CLK signal line period delay from the actual CLK signal line periods associated with the ADDRESS and ATTRIBUTE PHASES of the AD[31::00] signal lines.

For configuration read transactions, the PAR signal line is tristated by the PCI-X bus master one CLK signal line period after the TARGET RESPONSE PHASE, which is also earliest point that the target can begin driving the PAR signal line. For configuration write transactions, the PAR signal line is driven to logical "1" by the PCI-X bus master one CLK signal line period after TARGET RESPONSE PHASE for the duration of one CLK signal line period. Consequently, the PAR signal line for all these bus transactions has no valid parity information relative to the TARGET RESPONSE PHASE.

For configuration read transactions during the DATA PHASE, the PAR signal line is driven by the target with valid information two CLK signal line periods after the TRDY# signal line is asserted. The PCI-X bus master does not begin checking parity until two CLK signal line periods after the TRDY# signal line is asserted. Otherwise the PAR signal line associated with the DATA PHASE is driven by the target with invalid information or by a pull-up resistor and does not contain valid parity information. For configuration write transactions during the DATA PHASE, the PAR signal line is driven by the PCI-X bus master with valid information two CLK signal line periods after the IRDY# signal line is asserted. The target does not begin checking parity until two CLK signal line periods after the IRDY# signal line is asserted. Otherwise the PAR signal line associated with the DATA PHASE is driven by the PCI-X bus master but does not contain valid parity information. See Chapter 6: *Detailed Bus Transaction Operation* for more information.

Parity is generated and valid parity is placed on the PAR signal line relative to the AD[31::00] and C/BE#[3::0] signal lines in the ADDRESS and ATTRIBUTE PHASES. Parity is generated and valid parity is placed on the PAR signal line relative to the AD[31::00] and C/BE#[3::0] signal lines in the DATA PHASE independent of the value of the associated C/BE#[3::0] signal lines in DATA PHASES. That is, data parity generating and checking is defined for a data byte even though the associated C/BE# signal line is deasserted. Also, during the ATTRIBUTE PHASE, any AD[31::00] signal line that is defined as RESERVED is still included in the generation and checking of parity.

BURST CONFIGURATION COMMANDS

This COMMAND type is not defined for BURST transactions.

INTERRUPT ACKNOWLEDGE COMMANDS

See Subchapter 4.13 for related information.

INTRODUCTION

The PCI-X interrupt acknowledge transaction protocol is similar to the PCI interrupt acknowledge transaction protocol. That is, the interrupt acknowledge transaction is only executed on the PCI-X bus (0), does not provide a valid address, and is only claimed (assertion of the DEVSEL# signal line) by the PCI-X resource that contains the interrupt acknowledge logic. As with other PCI-X bus transactions, the bus transaction protocol has specific requirements for different phases of the transaction, as described in the following paragraphs.

A PCI-X bus master requests a 32 data bit interrupt acknowledge transaction with the continued deassertion of the REQ64# signal line during the ADDRESS PHASE (deasserted by a pull-up resistor on the bus backplane). The target acknowledges executing a 32 data bit transaction with the continued deassertion of the ACK64# signal line during the DATA PHASE (deasserted by a pull-up resistor on the bus backplane). For a 32 data bit bus transaction, the AD[63::32], C/BE#[7::4], and PAR64 signal lines are driven to logical "1" by pull-up resistors; consequently, the PAR64 signal line does not have valid parity information. Once the size of the respective bus transaction participants is established it remains unchanged during the remainder of the bus transaction.

For an interrupt acknowledge transaction, only 32 data bit bus transactions can be executed. An interrupt acknowledge transaction *cannot* be executed with DUAL ADDRESS.

The PCI-X bus master executes a successful interrupt acknowledge transaction by the activity of the FRAME# and IRDY# signal lines. As outlined in Chapter 3: *Generic PCI and PCI-X Hardware Operation* and detailed in Chapter 6: *Detailed Bus Transaction Operation*, the type of command (DWORD) in conjunction with the deassertion of the FRAME# and IRDY# signal lines during the DATA PHASE defines a SINGLE interrupt acknowledge transaction. See Chapter 6: *Detailed Bus Transaction Operation* for more information.

During the ADDRESS PHASE of the interrupt acknowledge transaction, the AD[31::0] signal lines do not contain any particular address (only one PCI-X resource can contain the interrupt controller) and the C/BE#[3::0] signal lines contain the encoded information of the COMMAND type. An interrupt acknowledge transaction is defined as a DWORD COMMAND and can only be executed with a SINGLE bus transaction. There is no interrupt acknowledge transaction defined by a BURST COMMAND; consequently, no BURST bus transactions can be executed.

DWORD INTERRUPT ACKNOWLEDGE COMMANDS

During the ADDRESS PHASE, the 0000 (C/BE#[3::0]) encoding indicates an interrupt acknowledge DWORD COMMAND (read data only, no write data is defined). This encoding identifies DWORD COMMAND to the interrupt acknowledge resource and can only be executed as a SINGLE bus transaction. The AD[31::00] signal lines during the ADDRESS PHASE do not define a specific address and are driven to a stable level by the PCI-X bus master.

According to the PCI-X addendum specification, once the ADDRESS and the COMMAND type have been established in the ADDRESS PHASE, the next CLK signal line period is defined as the ATTRIBUTE PHASE. The information contained in the AD[31::00] and C/BE#[3::0] signal lines during the ATTRIBUTE PHASE for an interrupt acknowledge DWORD COMMAND is as follows:

- AD[07::00] = Reserved, and must be logical "0".

- AD[10::08] = Requester Function Number: This three bit number is the Function Number assigned by design of the component. The combination of Function, Device, and Bus numbers defines the Requester ID number.

- AD[15::11] = Requester Device Number: This five bit number is the Bus Device Number in the PCI-X Status Register in the configuration address space of the associated PCI-X bus master (on the bus segment associated with the Bus Number of AD[32::16]). The value 1FH indicates that these bits in the Status Register have not been initialized. The value 00H is reserved for the bridge that connects the higher LEVEL bus segment to this bus segment. The combination of Function, Device, and Bus numbers defines the Requester ID number.

- AD[23::16] = Requester Bus Number: This eight bit number is the Bus Number in the PCI-X Status Register in the configuration address space of the associated PCI-X bus master. The value FFH indicates that these bits in the Status Register have not been initialized. The combination of Function, Device, and Bus numbers defines the Requester ID number.

- AD[28::24] = Tag: A unique number is assigned by the PCI-X bus master to each bus transaction of a sequence. The five bits permit a specific PCI-X bus master to have up to 32 different sequences at the same time.

- AD[29] = Relaxed Ordering: This bit is defined only for memory and split completion transactions. For all other bus transactions this bit must be set to logical "0".

- AD[30] = No Snoop: This bit is defined only for memory transactions. For all other bus transactions this bit must be set to logical 0.

- AD[31] = Reserved, and must be logical "0".

- C/BE#[3::0] = Byte Enables for the one DATA PHASE access.

> The encoding of the C/BE#[3:0] signal lines in the ATTRIBUTE PHASE define the lowest order byte and highest order byte accessed in the DATA PHASE. If any C/BE#[3::0] signal line is asserted in the ATTRIBUTE PHASE, the lowest order byte accessed (by asserted C/BE#[3::0] signal lines) defines the starting address and the highest order byte accessed (by asserted C/BE#[3::0] signal lines) accessed defines the ending address. Any combination of asserted and deasserted C/BE#[3::0] signal lines in the ATTRIBUTE PHASE is permitted. In the case of an interrupt acknowledge transaction, the default total byte count of the interrupt acknowledge transaction is four (there is no Upper or Lower Byte Counts in the ATTRIBUTE PHASE as in a BURST bus transaction) independent of the number of byte enable bits asserted in the C/BE#[3::0] signal lines in the ATTRIBUTE PHASE. The value of the C/BE#[3::0] signal lines in the DATA PHASE are driven to logical "1" (deasserted) by the PCI-X bus master

The ATTRIBUTE PHASE is a single CLK signal line period in length and is immediately followed by the TARGET RESPONSE PHASE. The TARGET RESPONSE PHASE is defined as the one CLK signal line period immediately after the ATTRIBUTE PHASE. The C/BE#[3::0] signal lines in the TARGET RESPONSE PHASE are driven to logical "1" by the PCI-X bus master. For an interrupt acknowledge transaction, the AD[31::00] signal lines are tristated by the PCI-X bus master in the TARGET RESPONSE PHASE. Also, the TARGET RESPONSE PHASE is the earliest point that the target (PCI-X interrupt acknowledge resource) can begin driving the AD[31::00[] signal lines.

The definition of the TARGET RESPONSE PHASE in the PCI-X addendum specification states that it is "one or more clocks after the attribute phase until the target claims the transaction by asserting the DEVSEL# signal line." According to the PCI-X bus transaction protocol, the DEVSEL# signal line may actually be asserted immediately after the ATTRIBUTE PHASE. Also, to be consistent with the PCI local bus specification, it would be cleaner to define the CLK signal line periods immediately after a single CLK signal line period of the TARGET RESPONSE PHASE as the DATA PHASE. Consequently; the TARGET RESPONSE PHASE defined in the paragraph above will be used in this book and the definition outlined in this box by the PCI-X addendum specification will not be used.

Immediately after the TARGET RESPONSE PHASE is the DATA PHASE. The DATA PHASE is defined between the TARGET RESPONSE PHASE and the time when the FRAME# and IRDY# signal lines are both deasserted. The C/BE#[3::0] signal lines are driven to logical "1" by the PCI-X bus master throughout the DATA PHASE. During the DATA PHASE, the AD[31::00] signal lines contain the data read per the C/BE#[3::0] signal lines encoding in the ATTRIBUTE PHASE.

The PAR signal line is driven by the PCI-X bus master and reflects the parity of the C/BE#[3::0] and AD[31::0] signal lines in the ADDRESS, ATTRIBUTE, and DATA PHASES. For the ADDRESS and ATTRIBUTE PHASES, the PAR signal line is tristated and driven by the PCI-X bus master with same protocol as the AD[31::00] signal lines, but with a one CLK signal line period delay from the actual CLK signal line periods associated with the ADDRESS and ATTRIBUTE PHASES of the AD[31::00] signal lines. For interrupt acknowledge transactions, the PAR signal line is tristated by the PCI-X bus master one CLK signal line period after TARGET RESPONSE PHASE, which is also earliest point that the target can begin driving the PAR signal line.

For interrupt acknowledge transactions during the DATA PHASE, the PAR signal line is driven by the target with valid information two CLK signal line periods after the TRDY# signal line is asserted. The PCI-X bus master does not begin checking parity until two CLK signal line periods after the TRDY# signal line is asserted. Otherwise the PAR signal line associated with the DATA PHASE is driven by the target with invalid information, or by a pull-up resistor, and does not contain valid parity information. See Chapter 6: *Detailed Bus Transaction Operation* for more information.

Parity is generated and valid parity is placed on the PAR signal line relative to the AD[31::00] (even though no valid address is encoded into the AD[31::0] signal lines) and C/BE#[3::0] signal lines in the ADDRESS and ATTRIBUTE PHASES. Parity is generated and valid parity is placed on the PAR signal line relative to the AD[31::00] and C/BE#[3::0] signal lines in the DATA PHASE independent of the value of the associated C/BE#[3::0] signal lines in the ATTRIBUTE or DATA PHASES. That is, data parity generating and checking is defined for a data byte even though the associated C/BE# signal line is deasserted. Also, during the ATTRIBUTE PHASE, any AD[31::00] signal line that is defined as RESERVED is still included in the generation and checking of parity..

The PCI-X addendum specification states that the protocol essentially follows the PCI local bus specification. Consequently, the size of the interrupt vector read from the PCI resource that contains the interrupt controller to be one byte (eight bits) in size is an example relating to Intel architectures. Consequently, the C/BE#[3::0] signal lines have a fixed binary pattern ([3::0] = [1110]). Larger data sizes with the appropriate C/BE#[3::0] signal lines asserted can also be used. Also, an 8259 interrupt-compatible vector requires only 8 data bits on the AD[7::0] signal lines.

BURST INTERRUPT ACKNOWLEDGE COMMANDS

This COMMAND type is not defined for BURST transactions.

SPECIAL COMMANDS

See Subchapter 4.14 for related information.

INTRODUCTION

The PCI-X special transaction protocol is similar to the PCI special transaction protocol. That is, the special transaction is only executed on a bus segment and is executed across bus segments via configuration transactions, does not provide a valid address, and is not claimed (no assertion of the DEVSEL# signal line) by any PCI-X resource (write broadcast). The PCI-X special transaction is unlike the PCI special transaction in that PCI-X special transactions cannot be executed with a BURST bus transaction. As with other PCI-X bus transactions, the bus transaction protocol has specific requirements for different phases of the transaction, as explained below.

A PCI-X bus master requests a 32 data bit special transaction with the continued deassertion of the REQ64# signal line during the ADDRESS PHASE (deasserted by a pull-up resistor on the bus backplane). The execution of a 32 data bit transaction is acknowledged with the continued deassertion of the ACK64# signal line during the DATA PHASE (deasserted by a pull-up resistor on the bus backplane). For a 32 data bit bus transaction, the AD[63::32], C/BE#[7::4], and PAR64 signal lines are driven to logical "1" by pull-up resistors; consequently, the PAR64 signal line does not have valid parity information. Once the size of the respective bus transaction participants is established it remains unchanged during the remainder of the bus transaction.

> For a special transaction, only a 32 data bit bus transaction can be executed. A special transaction *cannot* be executed with DUAL ADDRESS.

The PCI-X bus master executes a successful special transaction by the activity of the FRAME# and IRDY# signal lines. As outlined in Chapter 3: *Generic PCI and PCI-X Hardware Operation* and detailed in Chapter 6: *Detailed Bus Transaction Operation*, the type of command (DWORD) in conjunction with the deassertion of the FRAME# and IRDY# signal lines during the DATA PHASE defines a SINGLE special transaction. See Chapter 6: *Detailed Bus Transaction Operation* for more information.

During the ADDRESS PHASE of the special transaction, the AD[31::0] signal lines do not contain any particular address (only one PCI-X resource can contain the interrupt controller) and the C/BE#[3::0] signal lines contain the encoded information of the COMMAND type. A special transaction is defined as a DWORD COMMAND and can only be executed with a SINGLE bus transaction. There is no special transaction defined by a BURST COMMAND; consequently, no BURST bus transactions can be executed.

> Because the special transaction completes with the Master Abort termination protocol, it is not possible to have a Master Abort termination as defined for other bus transactions (*e.g.*, a memory transaction). When a PCI-X bus master executes a special transaction, it terminates it with the Master Abort termination, but does not set the Received Master Abort bit of the Status Register in the configuration address space.

DWORD SPECIAL COMMANDS

During the ADDRESS PHASE, the 0001 (C/BE#[3::0]) encoding indicates a special DWORD COMMAND (write data only, no read data is defined). This encoding identifies a DWORD COMMAND to the PCI-X resources on the bus segment and can only be executed as a SINGLE bus transaction. The AD [31::00] signal lines during the ADDRESS PHASE do not define a specific address and are driven to a stable level by the PCI-X bus master.

According to the PCI-X addendum specification, once the ADDRESS and the COMMAND type have been established in the ADDRESS PHASE, the next CLK signal line period is defined as the ATTRIBUTE PHASE. The information contained in the AD[31::00] and C/BE#[3::0] signal lines during the ATTRIBUTE PHASE for a special DWORD COMMAND is as follows:

- AD[07::00] = Reserved, and must be logical "0".

- AD[10::08] = Requester Function Number: This three bit number is the Function Number assigned by design of the component. The combination of Function, Device, and Bus numbers defines the Requester ID number.

- AD[15::11] = Requester Device Number: This five bit number is the Bus Device Number in the PCI-X Status Register in the configuration address space of the associated PCI-X bus master (on the bus segment associated with the Bus Number of AD[32::16]). The value 1FH indicates that these bits in the Status Register have not been initialized. The value 00H is reserved for the bridge that connects the higher LEVEL bus segment to this bus segment. The combination of Function, Device, and Bus numbers defines the Requester ID number.

- AD[23::16] = Requester Bus Number: This eight bit number is the Bus Number in the PCI-X Status Register in the configuration address space of the associated PCI-X bus master. The value FFH indicates that these bits in the Status Register have not been initialized. The combination of Function, Device, and Bus numbers defines the Requester ID number.

- AD[28::24] = Tag: A unique number assigned by the PCI-X bus master to each bus transaction of a sequence. The five bits permit a specific PCI-X bus master to have up to 32 different sequences at the same time.

- AD[29] = Relaxed Ordering: This bit is defined only for memory and split completion transactions. For all other bus transactions this bit must be set to logical "0".

- AD[30] = No Snoop: This bit is defined only for memory transactions. For all other bus transactions this bit must be set to logical 0.

- AD[31] = Reserved, and must be logical "0".

- C/BE#[3::0] = Byte Enables for the one DATA PHASE access.

The encoding of the C/BE#[3::0] signal lines in the ATTRIBUTE PHASE define the lowest order byte and highest order byte accessed in the DATA PHASE. For a special transaction, all of the C/BE#[3::0] signal lines are logical "0" (asserted) in the ATTRIBUTE PHASE. During the DATA PHASE, the AD[15::0] signal lines contain the message type. The AD[31::16] signal lines contain the optional message dependent data; the message type defines whether these signal lines have valid information even though the associated C/BE#[3::0] signal lines in the ATTRIBUTE PHASE are asserted. The lowest order byte accessed (by asserted C/BE#[3::0] signal lines) defines the starting address and the highest order byte accessed (by asserted C/BE#[3::0] signal lines) accessed defines the ending address. In the case of a special transaction, the default total byte count of the bus transaction is four (there is no Upper or Lower Byte Counts in the ATTRIBUTE PHASE as in a BURST bus transaction). The value of the C/BE#[3::0] signal lines in the DATA PHASE are driven to logical "1" (deasserted) by the PCI-X bus master

Similar to the PCI local bus specification, the PCI-X addendum specification defines the initialization of a device to include configuration write transactions to establish the Device Numbers and Bus Numbers. According to the Split Transaction protocol, it is possible for a device to execute a split completion transaction without the Bus Master bit in the Command Register of the configuration address space set to logical "1" (*i.e.*, the uninitialized value of the PCI-X bus master is "disabled"). If a device requests a Split Response termination for a configuration transaction (prior to the initialization of the Device Number and Bus Number by a prior configuration write transaction), the Completer ID for the split completion transaction uses the uninitialized values (*i.e.*, values after RESET) for the Device Numbers and Bus Numbers.

Another consideration is that the PCI-X resource that operates like a system management device may want to react if the initialization process fails. The PCI-X addendum specification states that the PCI-X resource may want to execute a bus transaction, and if the information for a Requestor ID (*i.e.*, initialization process fails) is the uninitialized values, the system management device will need to program values into itself and all devices on the bus segment to prevent ambiguous Requester IDs. As discussed in this book, the implementation of the IDSEL signal lines may not always be via the AD signal lines and the system management device cannot execute configuration transactions (*i.e.*, discrete signal lines from the PCI-X/PCI-X BRIDGE). Consequently, the alternative is for the system management device to assert the RST# signal line and force the bus segment into the PCI mode (which does not use Requester IDs).

The ATTRIBUTE PHASE is a single CLK signal line period in length and is immediately followed by the TARGET RESPONSE PHASE. The TARGET RESPONSE PHASE is defined as the one CLK signal line period immediately after the ATTRIBUTE PHASE. The C/BE#[3::0] signal lines in the TARGET RESPONSE PHASE are driven to logical "1" by the PCI-X bus master. The AD[31::00] signal lines are driven to a stable value by the PCI-X bus master in the TARGET RESPONSE PHASE.

> The definition of the TARGET RESPONSE PHASE in the PCI-X addendum specification states that it is "one or more clocks after the attribute phase until the target claims the transaction by asserting the DEVSEL# signal line." For a special transaction, the DEVSEL# signal line is never asserted. To be consistent with the PCI local bus specification, it would be cleaner to define the CLK signal line periods immediately after the single CLK signal line period of the TARGET RESPONSE PHASE as the DATA PHASE. Consequently; the TARGET RESPONSE PHASE defined in the paragraph above will be used in this book and the definition outlined in this box by the PCI-X addendum specification will not be used.

Immediately after the TARGET RESPONSE PHASE is the DATA PHASE. The DATA PHASE is defined between the TARGET RESPONSE PHASE and when the FRAME# and IRDY# signal lines are both deasserted. The C/BE#[3::0] signal lines are all driven to logical "1" by the PCI-X bus master throughout the DATA PHASE. During the DATA PHASE, the AD[31::00] signal lines consists of two parts. The AD[15::0] signal lines are encoded with the message type. The AD[31::16] signal lines contain an optional data field relative to the message. The message type is defined by the PCI Special Interest Group steering committee. Any encoding that has been approved by this committee can be used by any manufacturer. The present list of four message types is shown below:

AD[15::0]	Message Type
0000h	SHUTDOWN
0001h	HALT
0002h	x86 architecture spec. (reserved for Intel)
0003h to FFFFh	Reserved

The PAR signal line is driven by the PCI-X bus master and reflects the parity of the C/BE#[3::0] and AD[31::0] signal lines in the ADDRESS, ATTRIBUTE, and DATA PHASES. For the ADDRESS and ATTRIBUTE PHASES, the PAR signal line is tristated and driven by the PCI-X bus master with same protocol as the AD [31::00] signal lines, but with a one CLK signal line period delay from the actual CLK signal line periods associated with the ADDRESS and ATTRIBUTE PHASES of the AD [31::00] signal lines. For special transactions, the PAR signal line is driven to logical "1" by the PCI-X bus master one CLK signal line period after the TARGET RESPONSE PHASE for the duration of one CLK signal line period. Consequently, the PAR signal line has no valid parity information relative to the TARGET RESPONSE PHASE.

For special transactions during the DATA PHASE, the PAR signal line is driven by the PCI-X bus master with valid information two CLK signal line periods after the IRDY# signal line is asserted. The target does not begin checking parity until two CLK signal line periods after the IRDY# signal line is asserted. Otherwise the PAR signal line associated with the DATA PHASE is driven by the PCI-X bus master, but does not contain valid parity information. See Chapter 6: *Detailed Bus Transaction Operation* for more information.

> Parity is generated and valid parity is placed on the PAR signal line relative to the AD[31::00] (even though no valid address is encoded into the AD[31::0] signal lines) and C/BE#[3::0] signal lines in the ADDRESS and ATTRIBUTE PHASES. Parity is generated and valid parity is placed on the PAR signal line relative to the AD[31::00] and C/BE#[3::0] signal lines in the DATA PHASE independent of the value of the associated C/BE#[3::0] signal lines in the ATTRIBUTE or DATA PHASES. That is, data parity generating and checking is defined for a data byte even though the associated C/BE# signal line is deasserted. Also, during the ATTRIBUTE PHASE any AD[31::00] signal line that is defined as RESERVED is still included in the generation and checking of parity.

> Because the special transaction completes with the Master Abort termination protocol, it is not possible to have a Master Abort termination as defined for other bus transactions (*e.g.*, a memory transaction). When a PCI-X bus master executes a special transaction, it terminates it with the Master Abort termination, but does not set the Received Master Abort bit in its Status Register.

> Because a special transaction does not address a specific target, the bus transaction cannot be claimed by a specific target. Thus, the other terminations cannot be executed with a special transaction. Of particular note, a special transaction does not support Completion with Timeout termination.

BURST SPECIAL COMMANDS

The COMMAND type is not defined for BURST transactions.

PCI-X SPLIT COMPLETION COMMANDS

> See Subchapter 4.15 for related information. Also see this subchapter for definitions of "original" transaction, "original" PCI-X bus master, "original" target, and non-memory write transactions (as it applies to the Split Transaction protocol).

INTRODUCTION

The following discussions use several definitions (that have been discussed in other sections of the book): ADB, "sequence" of split completion transactions, and Tag.

- The allowed data boundary (ADB) is only defined for the memory address space and split completion transactions. The ADB is naturally aligned to 128 byte address boundaries. These are the only address boundaries where a BURST COMMAND transaction can terminate if a Single Disconnect termination is not executed or the total byte count of the bus transaction has not been reached (total byte count of the "original" transaction).

- A "sequence" of split completion transactions is a series of split completion transactions associated with each other in that they are sourced from the "original" target, are a response to a specific bus transaction terminated by Split Response termination ("original" transaction), and their destination is the "original" PCI-X bus master. The "same 'sequence'" consists of a series of split completion transactions with the "same" Requester ID (requester bus number, requester device number, and requester function number of the "original" PCI-X bus master) and "same" tag in the ADDRESS PHASE. A "sequence" is also defined relative to a series of memory bus transactions. Thus, there are two names used: "sequence" of memory transactions versus "sequence" of split completion transactions.

- The Tag is a unique five bit binary number that each PCI-X bus master assigns to each PCI-X bus transaction. A specific tag number cannot be used again until a previous bus transaction assigned the same tag number has completed. If the bus transaction is terminated with a Split Response termination, the bus transaction is not completed until the associated "sequence" of split completion transactions complete to the PCI-X bus master. Thus, each PCI-X bus master can have 32 bus transactions under execution at the same time. The "same" Tag in the ADDRESS PHASE of the split completion transaction is the tag of the "original" transaction provided in the ATTRIBUTE PHASE.

As previously discussed, the Split Transaction protocol is unique to the PCI-X addendum specification. Part of the protocol is the execution of split completion transactions. Split completion transactions are executed by the "original" target (completer) of an earlier non-memory write bus transaction ("original" transaction) that was terminated with a split response termination. The "original" target that executes (source) the split completion transaction is the PCI-X bus master for the split completion transactions. The target (destination) of the split completion transactions is the "original" PCI-X bus master (requester) of the bus transaction that was terminated with the Split Response termination. For the purposes of Split Transaction protocol, a non-memory write transaction is defined as one of the following: I/O read and write, configuration read and write, interrupt acknowledge, DWORD memory read, memory read block, and alias memory read block transactions. See Subchapter 4.5, Chapter 3: *Generic PCI and PCI-X Hardware Operation*, and Chapter 7: *Bridge and Interface Protocol* for more information.

> The "original" target can become the PCI-X bus master for the split completion transactions even when the Bus Master Control bit of the command register in its configuration address space is set to logical "0".

> As previously discussed, a PCI-X/PCI-X BRIDGE must terminate a non-memory write transaction (one side of the bridge) with a Split Response termination. It must repeat the non-memory write transaction (on the other side of the bridge). The repeating of the non-memory write transaction is assumed to be to another PCI-X/PCI-X BRIDGE or the actual non-bridge target that will terminate the bus transaction with a Split Response termination. In this situation, the "original" target is the not the PCI-X/PCI-X BRIDGE, but is the non-bridge target and will be the source of the split completion transactions. It is possible that one of the PCI-X/PCI-X BRIDGEs between the "original" PCI-X bus master and the non-bridge target repeats the non-memory write transaction to the non-bridge target that does not terminate it with Split Response termination. In this situation, this PCI-X/PCI-X BRIDGE will act on behalf of the non-bridge target and will be defined as the "original" target that is the source of the split completion transactions.

> For the balance of this discussion, the PCI-X bus master for the split completion transactions is the aforementioned "original" target (not a PCI-X/PCI-X BRIDGE acting on behalf of the non-bridge target as outlined in the previous shaded box) and the non-bridge target of the "original" PCI-X bus master ... unless otherwise noted.

A PCI-X bus master requests a 32 data bit split completion transaction with the continued deassertion of the REQ64# signal line during the ADDRESS PHASE (deasserted by a pull-up resistor on the bus backplane). The target acknowledges executing a 32 data bit transaction with the continued deassertion of the ACK64# signal line during the DATA PHASE (deasserted by a pull-up resistor on the bus backplane). Once the size of the respective bus transaction participants is established it remains unchanged during the remainder of the bus transaction.

> **When an "original" transaction is a 32 data bit transaction, the associated split completion transactions (with read data or Split Completion Message) must be executed as 32 data bit bus transactions.**
>
> **When an "original" transaction is a 64 data bit bus transaction, the associated split completion transactions with read data can be executed as either 32 or 64 data bit bus transactions.**
>
> **When an "original" transaction is a 64 data bit bus transaction, the associated split completion transactions with a Split Completion Message can be executed only as a 32 data bit bus transaction.**

> **A split completion transaction *cannot* be executed with DUAL ADDRESS.**

The signal line protocol during the ADDRESS, ATTRIBUTE, TARGET RESPONSE, and DATA PHASES are essentially the same as for the SINGLE and BURST memory transactions, but there are minor differences which will be discussed below. The PCI-X bus master executes a successful split completion transaction as SINGLE versus BURST by the activity of the FRAME# and IRDY# signal lines and the type of command (DWORD versus BURST). As detailed in Chapter 6: *Detailed Bus Transaction Operation*, the split completion transaction is defined as a BURST COMMAND. The BURST COMMAND provides the byte count in the ATTRIBUTE PHASE of the transaction. This information in conjunction with the deassertion of the FRAME# and IRDY# signal lines establishes SINGLE versus BURST split completion transactions. Unlike a PCI bus transaction, the assertion and deassertion of the FRAME# and IRDY# signal lines to indicate a PCI-X BURST split completion versus a SINGLE split completion transaction is not as clean or simple as the protocol for a PCI BURST memory transaction versus a SINGLE memory transaction. See Chapter 6: *Detailed Bus Transaction Operation* for more information.

The split completion transaction will contain either read data or a Split Completion Message. Whenever the split completion transaction contains a Split Completion Message, it can only be executed as a SINGLE bus transaction. When the "original" transaction is to write data, only a single split completion transaction with a Split Completion Message is returned. When the split completion transaction contains read data it may be executed either as a SINGLE or BURST bus transaction. If there are no error conditions relative to an "original" read transaction, the "sequence" of split completion transactions contain read data (SINGLE or BURST bus transaction). If there is an error condition relative to an "original" read transaction, the "sequence" will contain either only a split completion transaction with a Split Completion Message, or split completion transactions with read data and a final one with a Split Completion Message. For any "sequence" of split completion transactions, a split completion transaction with a Split Completion Message is the last one of the "sequence".

During the ADDRESS PHASE of the split completion transaction, the AD[31::0] signal lines identify the destination for the split completion data, and the C/BE#[3::0] signal lines contain the encoded information of the COMMAND type. For split completion transactions the COMMAND type only defines a BURST COMMAND executed with either SINGLE or BURST bus transactions.

An important concept to remember is that 4096 bytes is the maximum total byte count of the data that can be transferred to the "original" PCI-X bus master. The actual total number of bytes to be transferred from the "original" target to the "original" PCI-X bus master is limited by the total byte count specified in the "original" transaction. The "original" transaction executed by the "original" PCI-X bus master will not have been executed unless sufficient space was available in the "original" PCI-X bus master for the results. Consequently, the "original" PCI bus master must claim (assert the DEVSEL# signal line) the split completion transaction if the Requester ID and Tag in the ADDRESS PHASE of the split completion transaction match the "original" PCI-X bus master with the following considerations:

- With sufficient space available in the "original" PCI-X bus master, when it claims the split completion transaction it is NOT permitted to terminate it with a Split Response, Retry, Single Data Phase Disconnect, or Disconnect at next ADB termination. The "original" PCI bus master can only allow a split completion transaction to complete (with or without Timeout) or terminate it with Target Abort termination. The "original" PCI bus master can also not claim a split completion transaction resulting in a Master Abort termination. See Chapter 8: *Master and Target Termination* for more information.

■ If the PCI-X device receiving the split completion transaction is a PCI-X/PCI-X BRIDGE acting on behalf of the "original" PCI-X bus master, the bridge is permitted to terminate a split completion transaction as discussed above for the "original" PCI-X bus master. Additionally, the bridge can also terminate a split completion transaction with a Retry or Disconnect at the next ADB termination. See Chapter 7: *Bridge and Interface Protocol* and Chapter 8: *Master and Target Termination* for more information.

■ If the "original" PCI-X bus master has multiple Tags active, it must accept split completion transactions in any order. It is the responsibility of each "original" target for each specific "sequence" of split completion transactions to independently execute the split completion transactions of a specific "sequence" with linearly increasing address ordering.

■ See Chapter 8: *Master and Target Termination* for more information when the Tag of the split completion transaction does not match any active Tags of the "original" PCI-X bus master, or if the number of bytes of the "sequence" of split completion transactions exceeds the total byte count of the "original" transaction.

DWORD SPLIT COMPLETION TRANSACTIONS

This COMMAND type is not defined for split completion transactions.

BURST SPLIT COMPLETION TRANSACTIONS

During the ADDRESS PHASE, the 1100 (C/BE#[3::0]) encoding defines the split completion command. This encoding identifies the BURST COMMAND for a split completion transaction and can be executed as either a SINGLE or BURST bus transaction. The definition of the AD[31::00] signal lines during the ADDRESS PHASE is very different than the definition for bus transactions associated with access to the memory and I/O address spaces. The AD [31::00] signal lines during the ADDRESS PHASE of a split completion transaction are defined as follows:

■ AD [06::00] = Lower Address: See discussion below.

■ AD [07] = Reserved, and must be logical "0". (Note: If the split completion transaction ports through a PCI-X/PCI-X BRIDGE, this bit is set to logical "0" no matter what value was received by the bridge.)

■ AD [10::08] = Requester Function Number: This is the three bit number in the AD [10::08] signal lines during the ATTRIBUTE PHASE of the associated bus transaction terminated with a Split Response termination ("original" transaction as defined in other parts of the book). The requester in this case is the "original" PCI-X bus master. For a PCI-X/PCI-X BRIDGE these bits are ported through unmodified. The combination of Function, Device, and Bus numbers defines the Requester ID number.

■ AD [15:11] = Requester Device Number: This is the five bit number in the AD [15::11] signal lines during the ATTRIBUTE PHASE of the associated bus transaction terminated with a Split Response termination ("original" transaction as defined in other parts of the book). The requester in this case is the "original" PCI-X bus master. For a PCI-X/PCI-X BRIDGE these bits are ported through unmodified. The combination of Function, Device, and Bus numbers defines the Requester ID number.

■ AD [23:16] = Requester Bus Number: This is the eight bit number in the AD [23::16] signal lines during the ATTRIBUTE PHASE of the associated bus transaction terminated with a Split Response termination ("original" transaction as defined in other parts of the book). The PCI-X/PCI-X BRIDGE uses this number to determine whether it ports the split completion transaction to an attached higher or lower LEVEL bus segment. The requester in this case is the "original" PCI-X bus master. For a PCI-X/PCI-X BRIDGE, these bits are ported through unmodified. The combination of Function, Device, and Bus numbers defines the Requester ID number.

■ AD [28:24] = Tag: This is the five bit number in the AD [28::24] signal lines during the ATTRIBUTE PHASE of the associated bus transaction terminated with a Split Response termination ("original" transaction as defined in other parts of the book). The "original" PCI-X bus master uses the Tag number to identify which split completion transactions are associated with the same "sequence". For a PCI-X/PCI-X BRIDGE these bits are ported through unmodified.

■ AD [29] = Relaxed Ordering: This is the bit copied from the AD [29] signal line during the ATTRIBUTE PHASE of the associated bus transaction terminated with a Split Response termination ("original" transaction as defined in other parts of the book). The PCI-X/PCI-X BRIDGEs use this bit to determine if relaxed ordering is permitted.

■ When the "original" transaction is for a DWORD memory read or BURST memory read command (alias memory read block or memory read block), the Relaxed Ordering bit can be set (in the "original" transaction) to logical "1" only if strong ordering of the associated "sequence" of split completion transactions relative to posted memory write transactions in the same direction does NOT have to be maintained. See *Chapter 7: Bridge and Interface Protocol* for more information.

■ For a PCI-X/PCI-X BRIDGE this bit is ported through unmodified.

■ AD [30] = Reserved, and must be logical "0". (Note: If the split completion transaction ports through a PCI-X/PCI-X BRIDGE, this bit is set to logical "0" no matter what value was received by the bridge.)

■ AD [31] = Reserved and required to be logical "0". (Note: If the split completion transaction ports through a PCI-X/PCI-X BRIDGE, this bit is set to logical "0" no matter what value was received by the bridge.)

The address contained in the aforementioned AD[06:00] signal lines in the ADDRESS PHASE are passed through PCI-X/PCI-X BRIDGEs unmodified and are defined as follows:

■ If the associated bus transaction terminated with a Split Response termination ("original" transaction as defined in other parts of the book) was for a DWORD COMMAND or the split completion transaction contains a Split Completion Message, these signal lines are set to logical "0". By definition no address is defined because only a single 32 data bit transaction is being executed.

■ If the associated bus transaction terminated with a Split Response termination ("original" transaction as defined in other parts of the book) was for a BURST COMMAND and the previous split completion transaction associated with the same "sequence" was terminated at an ADB (Disconnect at next ADB), these signal lines are set to logical "0 when the "sequence" resumes. By definition, the previous split completion transaction of the "sequence" could only have been terminated at an ADB, which are naturally aligned on 128 byte address boundaries.

■ These signal lines are set equal to the AD[06::00] signal lines of the ADDRESS PHASE of the associated bus transaction terminated with a Split Response termination ("original" transaction as defined in other parts of the book) if ALL of the following conditions are met:

   ■ The "original" transaction was a BURST memory read command (memory block read or alias memory block read).

   ■ This is the first split completion transaction of the "sequence".

   ■ The split completion transaction does not contain a Split Completion Message.

The information outlined above for the ADDRESS PHASE allows the split completion transaction to include the Requester ID information which specifically defines the destination of the split completion transactions (*i.e.*, the Requester in this case is the "original" PCI-X bus master). The Tag information specifically identifies the "sequence" of split completion transactions associated with a specific "original" transaction from a specific "original" PCI-X bus master. The information outlined below for the ATTRIBUTE PHASE is focused on identifying the source of the split completion transactions, *i.e.*, "original" target.

According to the PCI-X addendum specification, once the ADDRESS (as defined above) and the COMMAND type have been established in the ADDRESS PHASE, the next CLK signal line period is defined as the ATTRIBUTE PHASE. The information contained in the AD[31::00] and C/BE#[3::0] signal lines during the ATTRIBUTE PHASE for a BURST split completion command is as follows:

■ AD[07::00] = Lower Byte Count: See discussion below.

■ AD[10::08] = Completer Function Number: This three bit number is the Function Number assigned by design of the component ("original" target). The Completer in this case is the "original" target. The combination of Function, Device, and Bus numbers defines the Completer ID number.

■ AD[15::11] = Completer Device Number: This five bit number is the Bus Device Number in the PCI-X Status Register in the configuration address space of the associated PCI-X bus master ("original" target) (on the bus segment associated with the Bus Number of AD[32::16]). The completer in this case is the "original" target. The value 1FH indicates that these bits in the Status Register have not been initialized. The value 00H is reserved for bridge that connects the higher LEVEL bus segment to this bus segment. The combination of Function, Device, and Bus numbers defines the Completer ID number.

■ AD[23::16] = Completer Bus Number: This eight bit number is the Bus Number in the PCI-X Status Register in the configuration address space of the associated PCI-X bus master ("original" target). The completer in this case is the "original" target. The value FFH indicates that the Status Register has not been initialized. The combination of Function, Device, and Bus numbers defines the Completer ID number.

■ AD[28::24] = Reserved, and must be set to logical "0". These bits are ignored by the "original" PCI-X bus master and are ported through PCI-X/PCI-X BRIDGES unmodified.

■ AD[29] = Split Completion Message (SCM): This bit is used in conjunction with the SCE bit as follows:

■ SCE = 0 and SCM = 0: This split completion transaction contains read data.

■ SCE = 0 and SCM = 1: This split completion transaction contains a Spilt Completion Message for a write completion of an "original" non-memory write transaction.

■ SCE = 1 and SCM = 0: Reserved.

■ SCE = 1 and SCM = 1: This split completion transaction contains a Spilt Completion Message for an error that occurred relative to the completion of the "original" transaction.

■ AD[30] = Split Completion Error (SCE): If this split completion transaction contains a Split Completion Message, this bit is set to logical "1" (see AD[29] above).

■ AD[31] = Byte Count Modified (BCM): If the total of the Upper and Lower Byte Counts byte count" for this split completion transaction is less than the total number of bytes needed to transfer to complete the "sequence" (that is, this split completion transaction does not complete the "total byte count" of the "original" transaction), this bit is set to logical "1". For all split completion transactions for "original" transactions of non-BURST memory read commands, this bit must be set to logical "0". (see discussion below)

■ C/BE#[3::0] = Upper Byte Count: See discussion below.

Of particular note in the above bullets is that the Upper and Lower Byte Counts (potential of total of 2^{12} bytes = 4096 total bytes) collectively define the actual total number of bytes the completer INTENDS to transfer in this split completion transaction. There is no requirement that the entire total byte count requested by the "original" transaction (other than for DWORD COMMAND "original" transactions or a split completion transaction containing a Split Completion Message) is serviced by a single split completion transaction. The protocol is as follows:

■ The Upper and Lower Byte Counts in the ATTRIBUTE PHASE of split completion transactions for a DWORD COMMAND transaction terminated with a Split Response termination or one that contains the Split Completion Message is always defined as 0004H.

■ The byte count modified (BCM) bit is always set to logical "0".

■ The Upper and Lower Byte Counts in the ATTRIBUTE PHASE of each split completion transaction for a BURST COMMAND transaction terminated with a Split Response termination varies as follows:.

■ When the split completion transaction is transferring data and not a Split Completion Message,

223

- The Upper and Lower Byte Counts are the total number of bytes the completer (target of "original" transaction terminated with Split Response termination) INTENDS to transfer in THIS bus transaction and is NOT ALWAYS the "remaining bytes to transfer". However, other than as outlined below, the completer must always INTEND to transfer in the present split completion transaction the "remaining bytes to transfer".

- When the bus transaction is the first split completion transaction, the completer has two options:

  - The total of Upper and Lower Byte Counts of the split completion transaction equals the "total byte count". The "total byte count" as defined by the "original" transaction terminated by Split Response termination. The "total byte count" equals the Upper and Lower Byte Counts in the ATTRIBUTE PHASE of the "original" transaction and is the total bytes the completer INTENDS to transfers in this transaction.

    OR

  - If the completer will terminate at the first ADB of the sequence, the Upper and Lower Byte Counts of the split completion transaction equals the number if bytes from the starting address to the first ADB. (NOTE: Unlike other items discussed here, this is not the number of bytes the completer INTENDS to transfer. It is the actual number of bytes to be transferred in that the completer can only terminate the transaction at the first ADB unless the requester ("original" PCI-X bus master) executes a Master Abort or a Target Abort termination.

- When the bus transaction is NOT the first split completion transaction of the "sequence", the total of the Upper and Lower Byte Counts are REQUIRED to equal the "remaining bytes to transfer". The "remaining bytes to transfer" equals the "total byte count" of the "original" transaction minus the number of bytes already transferred in previous spit completion transactions of the "sequence".

- The BCM bit set to logical "1" indicates that the total of the Upper and Lower Byte Counts of the present split completion transaction equals the number of bytes the completer INTENDS to transfer in this transaction and this number is not the "remaining byte count to transfer".

- The BCM bit is set to a logical "0" for the first split completion unless BOTH of the following conditions are met:

  - The completer will terminate at the first ADB.

- The first ADB address is less than the ending address of the "original" transaction.

- The BCM bit must be set to logical "0" for all split completion transactions after the first split completion transaction of the "sequence". The completer INTENDS to transfer the total of the Upper and lower Byte Counts in the present bus transaction and this number of bytes equals the "remaining bytes to transfer".

It should be noted that the completer INTENDS to transfer the entire total number of bytes identified by the Upper and Lower Byte Counts in the ATTRIBUTE PHASE. The target (requester or bridge) should prepare accordingly to accept the entire total number of bytes identified by the Upper and Lower Byte Counts or plan to terminate (force another the split completion traction to complete the transfer). When the requester is the "original PCI-X bus master, it must be prepared to accept the entire total of the Upper and Lower Byte Counts. There is no requirement that the completer ACTUALLY transfers the entire Upper and Lower Byte Counts in the single split completion transaction even if the target (requester or bridge) is willing (*i.e.*, target termination is not executed) to accept it. The completer can terminate the transaction at any ADB (See "NOTE:" in earlier bullet).

The above discussion focuses on split completion transactions between the "original" PCI-X bus master and the "original" target, which implies both participants are on the same bus segment. It is probable that these two participants are separated by one or more PCI-X/PCI-X BRIDGES. A bridge will request a Split Response termination to the "original" PCI-X bus master on the source bus segment and execute a BURST memory read transaction on the destination bus segment. It is possible for the target on the destination bus segment to immediately provide read data (but not all of it) to the bridge without using the Split Transaction protocol. The bridge will provide this data to the "original" PCI-X bus master on the source bus segment via split completion transactions it creates; consequently, the Completer ID in the split completion transactions will be that of the bridge. The bridge will continue the read transaction sequence to the target on the destination bus segment. If the target on the destination bus segment continues to provide data without the Split Transaction protocol (requesting a Split Response termination), the bridge will continue to receive the data and forward it to the "original" PCI-X bus master via split completion transactions created by the bridge.

It is also possible for the target to respond to the bridge by the Spit Transaction protocol with a Split Response termination on the first Burst memory read transaction from the bridge. Consequently, the target on the destination bus segment will be the source of all split completion transactions and are simply ported through the bridge to the "original" PCI-X bus master on the source bus segment. The Completer ID in the split completion transactions will be that of the target on the destination bus segment.

It is also possible for the target to initially provide data for the BURST read transaction from the bridge (but not all of it) and on a subsequent BURST read transaction of the "sequence" request a Split Response termination. With the request for a Split Response termination the bridge (which had been sourcing the split completion transactions) will begin porting the split completion transactions from the target on the destination bus segment and thus the Completer ID will become that of the target. Under this situation the requirements of the two participants are as follows:

- The "original" PCI-X bus master must be able to accept the continuance of the "sequence" split completion transactions with a different Completer ID than the "sequence" began with.

- If the target on the destination bus segment began with providing read data for BURST memory read transaction (but not all if it) from the bridge and "switches" to the Split Transaction protocol, it must meet the following requirements:

  - The target on the destination bus segment can only request a Split Response termination to "switch" to the Split Transaction protocol on the first ADB or a subsequent ADB.

- The memory read data to the first ADB has already been returned as a split completion transaction to the "original" PCI-X bus master by the bridge sourcing it. Consequently, if the target on the destination bus segment "switches" to the Split Transaction protocol the first split completion transaction has already been sourced from the bridge to the "original" PCI bus master. Consequently, when the target begins sourcing the split completion transactions, the BCM bit is required to be set to logical "0" and the target must INTEND to transfer the total of the Upper and lower Byte Counts in the present bus transaction. This number of bytes equals the "remaining bytes to transfer".

In the situations when the PCI-X/PCI-X BRIDGE that is creating the split completion transactions on behalf of the target on the destination bus segment that has not requested the Split Transaction protocol, the following are required:

- If the destination bus segment is upstream of the PCI-X/PCI-X BRIDGE, the bridge creates the Completer ID by using the bus number, device number, and function number from its PCI-X Bridge Status register.

- If the destination bus segment is downstream of the PCI-X/PCI-X BRIDGE; the bridge creates the Completer ID by using the bus number from its Secondary Bus number register, and sets the device number and function numbers to logical "0".

> **The BCM bit is to be used for debug and bus monitoring purposes (*e.g.*, bus analyzer). It is not intended to be used by PCI-X devices or bridges as part of actual PCI-X bus segment bus operation.**

> **The value of the Upper and Lower Byte Counts equals 0001H indicates one byte. The value of 0004H indicates 4 bytes. The value of FFFFH indicates 4095 bytes. The value 0000H indicates 4096 bytes.**

The ATTRIBUTE PHASE is a single CLK signal line period in length and is immediately followed by the TARGET RESPONSE PHASE. The TARGET RESPONSE PHASE is defined as the one CLK signal line period immediately after the ATTRIBUTE PHASE. The C/BE#[3::0] signal lines in the TARGET RESPONSE PHASE are driven to logical "1" by the PCI-X bus master. For a split completion transaction, the AD[31::00] signal lines are driven to a to a stable value by the PCI-X bus master or float in the TARGET RESPONSE PHASE.

> **The definition of the TARGET RESPONSE PHASE according to the PCI-X addendum specification states that it is "one or more clocks after the attribute phase until the target claims the transaction by asserting the DEVSEL# signal line". According to the PCI-X bus transaction protocol, the DEVSEL# signal line may actually be asserted immediately after the ATTRIBUTE PHASE. Also, to be consistent with the PCI local bus specification, it would be cleaner to define the CLK signal line periods immediately after a singular CLK signal line period of the TARGET RESPONSE PHASE as the DATA PHASE. Consequently, the TARGET RESPONSE PHASE defined in the paragraph above will be used in this book and the definition outlined in this box by the PCI-X addendum specification will not be used.**

Immediately after the TARGET RESPONSE PHASE is the DATA PHASE. The DATA PHASE is defined between the TARGET RESPONSE PHASE and when the FRAME# and IRDY# signal lines are both deasserted. For a split completion transaction the C/BE#[3::0] single lines are driven to logical "1" (deasserted) by the PCI-X bus master (completer) and thus provides no information as to which AD[31::00] signal lines (byte lanes) are valid. During the DATA PHASE the AD[31::00] signal lines contain either a Split Completion Message or the read data, and the valid bytes lanes are determined by different mechanisms. The details are as follows:

■ For read data relative to an "original" transaction that was a DWORD COMMAND, the only valid byte lanes are those defined in the ATTRIBUTE PHASE of the "original" transaction. Consequently, the requester ("original" PCI-X bus master) is required to retain this valid byte lane information.

■ For read data relative to an "original" transaction that was a BURST COMMAND, all of the byte lanes of the AD[31::00] signal lines of the split completion transaction are defined as valid. This is possible because the BURST COMMAND used can only be a memory read block or an alias memory read bock command to access memory address ranges that are prefetchable. Consequently, all of the data identified by the starting address in the ADDRESS PHASE and the Upper and Lower Bytes Counts in the ATTRIBUTE PHASE of the "original" transaction is being read and returned via the "sequence" of split completion transactions

■ For a Split Completion Message: Always a SINGLE bus transaction and always sent at the end of the "sequence". By definition, all of the byte lanes are valid (that is, only full 32 data bit wide Split Completion Messages are defined). If the complete "sequence" of read data is successfully sent there is NO split completion transaction with a Split Completion Message sent in the "sequence". When a Split Completion Message is contained in the split completion transaction, by definition this will be the last split completion transaction of the "sequence". See "Details of Split Completion Messages" at the end this section for more information.

The PAR signal line is driven by the "original" target as a PCI-X bus master and reflects the parity of the C/BE#[3::0] and AD[31::0] signal lines in the ADDRESS, ATTRIBUTE, and DATA PHASES. For the ADDRESS and ATTRIBUTE PHASES, the PAR signal line is tristated and driven by the PCI-X bus master with same protocol as the AD [31::00] signal lines, but with a one CLK signal line period delay from the actual CLK signal line periods associated with the ADDRESS and ATTRIBUTE PHASES of the AD [31::00] signal lines. The PAR signal line is driven to logical "1" by a the PCI-X bus master for one CLK signal line period after TARGET RESPONSE PHASE for the duration of one CLK signal line period. Consequently, the PAR signal line has no valid parity information relative to the TARGET RESPONSE PHASE. For a split completion transaction during the DATA PHASE, the PAR signal line is driven by the PCI-X bus master with valid parity information for the AD [31::00] signal lines (including parity of the deasserted C/BE#[3::0] signal lines) with a one CLK signal line period delay. The target ("original" PCI-X bus master) does not begin checking parity until one CLK signal line after the TRDY# signal line is asserted. See Chapter 6: *Detailed Bus Transaction Operation* for more information.

Parity is generated and valid parity is placed on the PAR signal line relative to the AD[31::00] and C/BE#[3::0] signal lines in the ADDRESS and ATTRIBUTE PHASES. Parity is generated and valid parity is placed on the PAR signal line relative to the AD[31::00] and C/BE#[3::0] signal lines in the DATA PHASE independent of the value of the associated C/BE#[3::0] signal lines in DATA PHASES. That is, data parity generating and checking is defined for a data byte even though the associated C/BE# signal line is deasserted. Also, during the ATTRIBUTE PHASE, any AD[31::00] signal line that is defined as RESERVED is still included in the generation and checking of parity.

A specific "original" target may have several "sequences" of split completion transactions at different levels of completion. The "original" target is permitted to execute "sequences" in any order and to intermix the execution of split completion transactions in any order. However, the linear increasing address order of the split completion transactions of each specific "sequence" (response to each specific BURST COMMAND) must be maintained.

If a specific "original" PCI-X bus master had a bus transaction terminated with a Split Response termination but has not received the entire "sequence", it cannot begin another bus transaction if it is dependent on the completion of the aforementioned bus transaction terminated with a Split Response termination. If the PCI-X bus master has internal buffer logic that will insure that the return of split completion transactions of one "sequence" are buffered until ALL split completion transactions of a "sequence" associated with an earlier "original" transaction are received, the PCI-X bus master software does not have to worry about the order of "original" transactions. But, from the viewpoint of the bus, the PCI-X bus master is responsible for transaction ordering.

USE OF SPLIT TRANSACTION PROTOCOL PRIOR TO INITIALIZATION

Just after RESET (RST# signal asserted to deasserted) and prior to initialization, the target ID (completer ID) is defined as follows:

- Function number: Established at design time of the resource
- Device number = 1FH
- Completer Bus Number = FFH

The PCI-X bus master is able to access a resource (target) via the configuration bus transactions. The target can terminate the configuration bus transaction with a Split Response termination. Even though the target ID contains default values, the address (Requester ID) and the Tag used by the split completion transaction are valid and derived from the "original" configuration transaction. This address identifies the PCI-X bus master of the configuration transaction and the Tag completes the information for the PCI-X bus master to uniquely identify the split completion transaction.

DETAILS OF SPLIT COMPLETION MESSAGES

As discussed above, a split completion transaction may contain a Split Completion Message (SCM). The SCM provides completion information (without error) for a write (I/O or configuration address spaces) "original" transaction, or error information for a write (I/O or configuration address spaces) or read (memory, I/O, or configuration address spaces) "original" transaction. The definition of the AD [31::00] signal lines during the DATA PHASE is as follows:

- AD[07::00] signal lines = Lower Remaining Bytes Count:
  - If the "original" transaction was a DWORD COMMAND, these signal lines are set to 04H.
  - If the "original" transaction was a BURST memory write (memory write, memory write block, or alias memory write block) command, these signal lines are set to 04H.
  - If the "original" transaction was a BURST memory read command (alias memory read block or memory read block), these signal lines contain the lower seven bits of the number of the remaining bytes to transfer (total number of bytes per the ATTRIBUTE PHASE of the "original' transaction minus the number of bytes transferred in the previous split completion transaction(s) of the "sequence").
  - Used by PCI-X/PCI-X BRIDGES to release reserved buffer space. The "original" PCI-X bus master (requester) must have sufficient buffer space for the total byte count of the "original" transaction; consequently, it already knows the number of bytes remaining.
- AD[11::08] signal lines = Upper Remaining Byte Count
  - If the "original" transaction was a DWORD COMMAND, these signal lines are set to 0H.
  - If the "original" transaction was a BURST memory write (memory write, memory write block, or alias memory write block) command, these signal lines are set to 0H.
  - If the "original" transaction was a BURST memory read command (alias memory read block or memory read block), these signal lines contain the upper four bits of the number of the remaining bytes to transfer (total number of bytes specified in the ATTRIBUTE PHASE

of the "original' transaction minus the number of bytes transferred in the previous split completion transaction(s) of the "sequence").

■ Used by PCI-X/PCI-X BRIDGES to release reserved buffer space. The "original" PCI-X bus master (requester) must have sufficient buffer space for the total byte count of the "original" transaction; consequently, it already knows the number of bytes remaining.

■ AD[18::12] signal lines = Remaining Lower Address:

   ■ If the "original" transaction was a DWORD COMMAND, these signal lines are set to logical "0".

   ■ If the "original" transaction was a BURST memory write (memory write, memory write block, or alias memory write block) command, these signal lines are set to logical "0".

   ■ If the "original" transaction was a BURST memory read command (alias memory read block or memory read block), these signal lines contain the lower seven bits of the address that represents the beginning address of the remaining bytes associated with the portion of the "sequence" that will not be sent due to error conditions. In that the previous (if any) split completion transactions can only terminate at an ADB, only seven bits is needed to identify the address within the subsequent 128 bytes.

   ■ Used by PCI-X/PCI-X BRIDGES to release reserved buffer space.

■ AD[19] signal line = Reserved: Required to be set to logical "0" and is ignored by the requester or bridges.

■ AD[27::20] signal lines = Message Index: See definition under Message Class in the following bullet:

■ AD[31::28] signal lines = Message Class: These bits are defined as follows:

   ■ [0000] = Write Completion:

      ■ The associated "original" transaction DWORD COMMAND for an I/O or configuration write was successful. The AD[27::20] signal lines contain the Message Index of 00H which is for normal completion (which is the only Message Index defined for this Message Class).

   ■ [0010] = Completer Error: After the "original" transaction is terminated with a Split Response termination, this message class indicates that there was an error at the "original" target.

      ■ The associated "original" transaction was a DWORD memory read command:

- When the AD[27::20] signal lines contain the Message Index of 00H: Indicates that the byte count is out of range. This does not apply to a DWORD COMMAND.

- When the AD[27::20] signal lines contain the Message Index of 01H: Does not apply to a read commands.

- When the AD[27::20] signal lines contain the Message Index of 8XH: Indicates that the "original" target had a error condition related to receipt of the "original" transaction received not covered by the other Message Index definitions. The value "X" is defined by the vendor of the "original" target.

- The associated "original" transaction was DWORD read or write commands to access I/O and configuration address spaces:

  - When the AD[27::20] signal lines contain the Message Index of 00H: Indicates that the byte count is out of range. This does not apply a DWORD COMMAND.

  - When the AD[27::20] signal lines contain the Message Index of 01H: Indicates that the "original" target received the write data with a parity error. Does not apply to a read commands.

  - When the AD[27::20] signal lines contain the Message Index of 8XH indicates that the "original" target had a error condition related to receipt of the "original" transaction received not covered by the other Message Index definitions. The value "X" is defined by the vendor of the "original" target.

- The associated "original" transaction was a BURST COMMAND for memory read (alias memory read block, memory read block):

  - When the AD[27::20] signal lines contain the Message Index of 00H: Indicates that the byte count is out of range. That is, the total byte count plus the starting address in the "original" transaction exceeds the address range of the "original" target. The completer ("original" target) will send to the requester ("original" PCI-X bus master) all of the bytes within the "original" target's address range via split completion transactions with data. The last split completion transaction contains this Split Completion Message. The "original" PCI-X bus master is required to report the receipt of this Split Completion Message to the device driver.

■   When the AD[27::20] signal lines contain the Message Index of 01H: Indicates that the "original" target received the write data with a parity error. Does not apply to a read command.

■   When the AD[27::20] signal lines contain the Message Index of 8XH (Device Specific Error): The "original" target had an error condition related to receipt of the "original" transaction received not covered by the other Message Index definitions. The value "X" is defined by the vendor of the "original" target.

  ■   It is possible for the completer to use this Message Index after it has begun a "sequence" of split completion transactions with valid data. It is assumed that the data associated with the earlier split completion transactions up to the ADB associated with the split completion transaction prior to the one containing the Split Completion Message is valid.

  ■   There are several possible methods for the requester to report the receipt of a Device Specific Error. Most typical is for the requester to store the "X" value of the error with the address of "original" target, and execute an interrupt to the device driver

■   [0001] = PCI-X/PCI-X BRIDGE Error: The other two Message Class encodings identified errors related to the "original" target. The assumption for the other two Message Class encodings is that there were no error conditions relative to the PCI-X/PCI-X BRIDGE between the "original" PCI-X bus master and the "original" target. If there was an error condition between the "original" PCI-X bus master and the "original" target, the encoding of 0001 is used.

■   The associated "original" transaction was a DWORD memory read command:

  ■   When the AD[27::20] signal lines contain the Message Index of 00H: Indicates that a PCI-X/PCI-X BRIDGE encountered a Master Abort termination. That is, the intended target did not claim the bus transaction (on the destination bus segment) associated with the bus transaction terminated with a Split Response termination on the other side (source bus segment) of the bridge.

  ■   When the AD[27::20] signal lines contain the Message Index of 01H: Indicates that a PCI-X/PCI-X BRIDGE encountered a Target Abort termination. That is, the intended target claimed the bus transaction (on the destination bus segment) associated with the bus transaction terminated with a Split Response termination on the other side (source bus segment) of the bridge. However, during the course of executing the transaction, the target on the destination bus segment executed a Target Abort termination.

- When the AD[27::20] signal lines contain the Message Index of 02H: Indicates that a PCI-X/PCI-X BRIDGE encountered a write data parity error. This is not defined for a DWORD read command.

- The associated "original" transaction was a DWORD read or write command to access I/O and configuration address spaces:

  - When the AD[27::20] signal lines contain the Message Index of 00H: Indicates that a PCI-X/PCI-X BRIDGE encountered a Master Abort termination. That is, the intended target did not claim the bus transaction (on the destination bus segment) associated with the bus transaction terminated with a Split Response termination on the other side (source bus segment) of the bridge.

  - When the AD[27::20] signal lines contain the Message Index of 01H: Indicates that a PCI-X/PCI-X BRIDGE encountered a Target Abort termination. The intended target claimed the bus transaction (on the destination bus segment) associated with the bus transaction terminated with a Split Response termination on the other side (source bus segment) of the bridge. However, during the course of executing the transaction the target on the destination bus segment executed a Target Abort termination

  - When the AD[27::20] signal lines contain the Message Index of 02H: Indicates that a PCI-X/PCI-X BRIDGE encountered a write data parity error. The intended target claimed the bus transaction (on the destination bus segment) associated with the bus transaction terminated with a Split Response termination on the other side (source bus segment) of the bridge. However, during the course of executing the transaction the target reported the receipt of a write data parity error to the bridge. This is not defined for a DWORD read command to access I/O and configuration address spaces.

- The associated "original" transaction was a BURST COMMAND for memory read (alias memory read block or memory read block):

  - When the AD[27::20] signal lines contain the Message Index of 00H: Indicates that a PCI-X/PCI-X BRIDGE encountered a Master Abort termination. The intended target did not claim the bus transaction (on the destination bus segment) associated with the bus transaction terminated with a Split Response termination on the other side (source bus segment) of the bridge.

  - When the AD[27::20] signal lines contain the Message Index of 01H: Indicates that a PCI-X/PCI-X BRIDGE encountered a Target Abort termination. The intended target claimed the bus transaction (on the destination bus segment) associated with the bus transaction terminated with a Split Response termination on the other side (source bus segment) of the bridge. However, during the course of executing the transaction (or one of a sequence in the case of a BURST read one of the transactions) the target on the destination bus segment executed a Target Abort termination. In this situation it is possible that previous Split Completion transactions of the "sequence" had been returned to the "original" PCI-X bus master without error.

  - When the AD[27::20] signal lines contain the Message Index of 02H: Indicates that a PCI-X/PCI-X BRIDGE encountered a write data parity error. This is not defined for a BURST COMMAND for memory read.

Note: If the target of the "original" transaction did not terminate it with a Split Response termination, the PCI-X/PCI-X BRIDGE becomes the "original" target. The PCI-X/PCI-BRIDGE as the "original" target will implement the aforementioned Message Class encodings ([0000], [0010]) as the "original" target. The actual target and the PCI-X/PCI-X BRIDGE are collectively viewed as the "original" target. The above encodings related to a bridge reporting an error can only be used by PCI/PCI-X and PCI-X/PCI-X BRIDGEs.

All other encodings not defined above are defined as reserved and cannot be used.

4.17 PCI-X 64 DATA BIT EXTENSION

INTRODUCTION

The PCI-X addendum specification supports both 32 and 64 data bit bus segments. The extension of the bus segment and transaction size is in the same fashion as the PCI local bus specification as outlined in the *Introduction* of Subchapter 4.6: *PCI 64 Data Bit Extension* section of the book. The PCI-X specific considerations related to which COMMANDS are restricted to use 64 data bits is outlined in Table 4-2 at the beginning of this chapter. A summary of 32 versus 64 data bit bus transactions relative to commands is as follows:

- The 64 data bit extension only applies to memory and split completion transactions (*i.e.*, BURST COMMANDs).

  - The DWORD memory read command is executed only with a 32 data bit bus transaction.

  - A split completion transaction must be executed with a 32 data bit bus transaction (SINGLE bus transaction) if it contains a Split Completion Message.

  - For split completion transactions not containing a Split Completion Message:

    - A split completion transaction associated with a 32 data bit "original" bus transaction must execute as a 32 data bit bus transaction.

    - A split completion transaction associated with a 64 data bit "original" bus transaction can be executed as either a 32 or 64 data bit bus transaction.

- Under all circumstances, the I/O, configuration, interrupt acknowledge, and special transactions are executed only with 32 data bit SINGLE bus transactions.

During the ADDRESS PHASE of a 64 data bit bus transaction, the AD[2] signal line is a required part of the actual address to define the lowest level byte of the starting address. It is not required to be [0] as is the case for PCI.

---

32 AND 64 DATA BIT PCI-X BUS MASTER & 32 AND 64 DATA TARGET DETERMINATION

The PCI-X addendum specification supports both 32 and 64 data bit PCI bus masters and targets in the same fashion as the PCI local bus specification, as outlined in the *32 and 64 Data Bit PCI Bus Masters & 32 and 64 Data Bit Targets Determination of Subchapter 4.6 PCI 64 Data Bit Extension* section of the book. The one exception is noted in the shaded box below.

According to the PCI local bus specification, targets do not have to monitor the REQ64# signal line during the assertion of the RST# signal line (RESET). According to the PCI-X addendum specification, a target that is a 64 data bit device and has a memory address space that may result in a Split Response termination if accessed (invoking the sourcing of split completion transactions), the target must monitor the REQ64# signal line during RESET. Thus, if the "original" transaction from a PCI-X bus master (as requester) is a 64 data bit bus transaction, the target (as the completer) may respond with a 64 data bit split completion transaction if it is residing on a 64 data bit bus segment.

SIGNAL LINE OWNERSHIP DURING BUS TRANSACTIONS WITH 64 DATA BIT RESOURCES (PCI-X BUS MASTER AND TARGET)

See Subchapter 4.0 for related information for 32 data bit resources.

A 64 data bit bus transaction and associated 64 data bit resources are only defined for the memory address space and BURST bus transactions. During BURST memory read and write transactions (including memory write, memory read block, memory write block, alias memory read block, and alias memory write block), and split completion transactions, signal lines are owned by different PCI-X bus resources. A PCI-X resource "owns" the signal line when it is the only resource (other than a pull-up resistor) that can drive the signal line during a portion of the bus transaction. In the following discussions, the PAR and PAR64 signal lines relative to a specific bus transaction PHASE is actually delayed from "that" specific bus transaction PHASE. The protocol is as follows:

- FRAME#, IRDY#, and C/BE#[7::0], REQ#x, and REQ64# signal lines are owned by the PCI-X bus master for any bus transaction.

- During BURST memory write transactions and split completion transactions; the PCI-X bus master owns the AD[63::0], PAR, and

PAR64 signal lines during ADDRESS, ATTRIBUTE, TARGET RESPONSE, and DATA PHASES.

- During BURST memory read transactions; the PCI-X bus master owns the AD[63::0], PAR, and PAR64 signal lines during the ADDRESS and ATTRIBUTE PHASES. For these bus transactions, the PCI-X bus master does not own and tristates the AD[63::00], PAR and PAR64# signal lines during the TARGET RESPONSE PHASE. The target owns these signal lines during the DATA PHASE. The ownership of these signal lines changes from the PCI-X bus master to the target during the TARGET RESPONSE PHASE.

- During BURST memory transactions and BURST split completion transactions, the TRDY#, DEVSEL#, STOP#, ACK64# signal lines are owned by the target.

Ownership of the remaining signal lines are defined according to the following protocol:

- The CLK and RST# signal lines are owned by platform resources.

- The GNTx# signal lines are owned by the central arbiter.

- The LOCK# signal line is owned by the Lock master.

DUAL ADDRESS

The PCI-X addendum specification supports the DUAL ADDRESS in the same fashion as the PCI local bus specification as outlined in the *Dual Address* of Subchapter 4.6: *PCI 64 Data Bit Extension* section of the book.

BYTE LANE OPERATION

The PCI-X addendum specification supports the byte lane operation in the same fashion as the PCI local bus specification as outlined in the *Byte Lane Operation of Subchapter 4.6 PCI 64 Data Bit Extension* section of the book There are some differences between PCI and PCI-X due to the differences in the bus transactions. The similarities and differences are as follows:

- No byte lane swapping occurs between the byte lanes of the AD[63::32] signal lines. Similarly, the central resource does not provide byte swapping between the byte lanes of the AD[31::0] and the AD[63::32] signal lines.

- If a 64 data bit PCI-X bus master accesses a 32 data bit target, the 32 data bit target can only reside on the AD[31::0] signal lines and the 64 data bit

PCI-X bus master is required to internally swap the data between the AD[63::32] and AD[31::0] signal lines when the REQ64# signal line is asserted and the ACK64# signal line is deasserted.

■ During the DATA PHASE of a memory write or a split completion transaction, the AD[63::32] signal lines that do not have valid data must be driven to a stable level by the PCI-X bus master when the REQ#64 and ACK64# signal lines are both asserted. If the ACK64# signal line is deasserted during the DATA PHASE of a memory write or a split completion transaction, the PCI-X bus master can drive the AD[63::32] signal lines to a stable level or optionally tri-state these signal lines and rely on pull-up resistors to drive them to logical "1". During the DATA PHASE of a memory read transaction, the AD[63::32] signal lines that do not have valid data are driven to a stable level by the target when the REQ#64 and ACK64# signal lines are both asserted during the DATA PHASE. If the ACK64# signal line is deasserted during the DATA PHASE of a memory read transaction, the AD[63::32] signal lines are driven to a logical "1" by pull-up resistors. See Subchapters 4.18 to 4.20 for boundary conditions prior to the assertion of the ACK64# signal line.

■ During the DATA PHASE, the C/BE#[7::4] signal lines for a given microaccess of bus transactions for BURST memory write (not including memory write block and alias memory write block) command can enable different bytes relative to previous and subsequent microaccesses. The byte lanes do not have to be continuous. For the other BURST COMMANDS (memory write block, alias memory write block, memory read block, alias memory read block, and split completion), and the DWORD memory read command, all of the C/BE#[7::4] signal lines are driven to logical "1" in the DATA PHASE. By definition all byte lanes are valid and continuous (except for qualifications by the REQ64# and ACK64# signal lines). This applies to byte lanes identified within a specific bus transaction or byte lanes identified from one bus transaction to another. If the ACK64# signal line is deasserted during the DATA PHASE, the PCI-X bus master can drive the C/BE#[7::4] signal lines to a stable level or optionally tri-state these signal lines and rely on pull-up resistors to drive them to logical "1".

> The term "64 data bits" reflects the block of data addressed. It does not mean that an actual 64 data bits are accessed.

PARK

The park protocol for 64 data bit PCI-X bus masters is the same as for a 32 data bit PCI-X bus master. When a 32 data bit PCI-X bus master becomes a Park master it drives the AD[31::0], C/BE#[3::0], and PAR signal lines to a stable level. The AD[63::32], C/BE#[7::4], and PAR64 signal lines are driven to a logical "1" by pull-up resistors. When a 64 data bit PCI-X bus master becomes a Park master it also drives the AD[31::0], C/BE#[3::0], and PAR signal lines to a stable level. Also, the AD[63::32], C/BE#[7::4], and PAR64 signal lines are driven to a stable level by the Park master.

4.18 PCI-X 32 DATA BIT BUS MASTER TO 64 DATA BIT TARGET

MEMORY AND SPLIT COMPLETION TRANSACTIONS

A PCI-X bus master requests a 32 data bit bus transaction by the continued deassertion the REQ64# signal line during the ADDRESS PHASE. The target can only respond by executing a 32 data bit bus transaction (ACK64# signal line deasserted). REQ64# and ACK64# signal lines are deasserted by pull-up resistors on the bus segment. AD[63::32], C/BE#[7::4], and PAR64 signal lines are driven to a logical "1" by pull-up resistors for the entire bus transaction; consequently, the PAR64 signal line does not have valid parity information. Once the size of the respective bus transaction participants is established it remains unchanged during the remainder of the bus transaction.

Only a PCI-X memory resource (target) that supports BURST COMMANDs can be defined as a 32 or a 64 data bit resource. All BURST memory transactions executed by a 32 data bit PCI-X bus master (REQ64# signal line deasserted) are independent of target data size and can only execute 32 data bit bus transactions.

The BURST split completion transaction protocol is the same as for a BURST memory write block or a BURST alias memory write block transaction. If the "original" transaction (terminated by the Split Response termination) is 32 data bits in size, the split completion transaction is required to be 32 data bits in size even though the "original" target can support 64 data bit bus transactions.

See Chapter 6: *Detailed Bus Transaction Operation* for more information.

For a 64 data bit target, the BURST memory transactions and DUAL ADDRESS operations, and Exclusive Access (LOCK) operation are supported with the same protocol as PCI-X bus transactions between a 32 data bit PCI-X bus master and a 32 data bit target.

DWORD MEMORY READ, I/O, CONFIGURATION, INTERRUPT ACKNOWLEDGE, AND SPECIAL TRANSACTIONS

These bus transactions are executed only with 32 data bit targets, and the REQ64# and ACK64# signal lines must be deasserted.

4.19 PCI-X 64 DATA BIT BUS MASTER TO 64 DATA BIT TARGET

MEMORY AND SPLIT COMPLETION TRANSACTIONS

A PCI-X bus master and a memory resource (target) are defined as 64 data bit resources when the REQ64# and ACK64# signal lines are asserted, respectively. The PCI-X bus master requests a 64 data bit bus transaction by asserting the REQ64# signal line during the ADDRESS PHASE and the target acknowledges a 64 data bit bus transaction by asserting the ACK64# signal line in the TARGET RESPONSE or DATA PHASES. The timing protocol of the FRAME# and REQ64# signal lines are the same and the timing protocol of the DEVSEL# and ACK64# signal lines are the same. The major difference between a 32 data bit and a 64 data bit bus transaction is that the AD[63::32], C/BE#[7::4], and PAR64 signal lines are used. The C/BE#[7::4], AD[63::32], and PAR64 signal lines operate with almost the same protocol as the C/BE#[3::0], AD[31::0], and PAR signal lines. The PAR64 signal line has valid parity information over the C/BE#[7::4] and AD[63::32] signal lines in the same fashion as the PAR signal line has valid parity information over the C/BE#[3::0] and AD[31::0] signal lines.

The addressing protocol of a 64 data bit BURST bus transaction is the same as for a 32 data bit BURST bus transaction, except that the address increments are 64 data bits (QWORDS). The execution protocol of the 64 data bit SINGLE and BURST transactions is the same as for 32 data bit SINGLE and BURST bus transactions except the AD[31::0] signal lines identify 64 data bit QWORDS.

There are some differences in the protocol of AD[63::32], C/BE[7::4], and PAR64 signal lines; and AD[31::00], C/BE[3::0], and PAR signal lines. During the ADDRESS PHASE when a 32 data bit PCI-X bus master (REQ64# signal line deasserted) begins a bus transaction, the AD[63::32], C/BE#[7::4], and PAR64 signal lines are driven to a logical "1" by pull-up resistors. The PAR64 signal line does not contain any valid parity information. When a 64 data bit PCI-X bus master (REQ64# signal line asserted) begins a bus transaction without DUAL ADDRESS it drives the AD[63::32], C/BE#[7::4], and PAR64 signal lines to a stable level without any valid information, or tristates them and relies on pull-up resistors to drive these signal lines to logical "1". The PAR64 signal line will not contain valid parity information over these signal lines during the ADDRESS PHASE with a one CLK signal line period delay. If a 64 data bit PCI-X bus master (REQ64# signal line asserted) begins a bus transaction with DUAL ADDRESS, it drives the upper order address and COMMAND type onto the AD[63::32] and C/BE#[7::4] signal lines, respectively. The PAR64 signal line is driven by the PCI-X bus master and will contain valid parity information over these signal lines during the ADDRESS PHASE with a one CLK signal line period delay.

During the ATTRIBUTE and TARGET RESPONSE PHASES, when a 32 data bit PCI-X bus master (REQ64# signal line deasserted) executes a bus transaction, the AD[63::32], C/BE#[7::4], and PAR64 signal lines are driven to a logical "1" by pull-up resistors. The PAR64 signal line does not contain any valid parity information. During the ATTRIBUTE PHASE, when a 64 data bit PCI-X bus master (REQ64# signal line asserted) executes a bus transaction, it drives the AD[63::32], and C/BE#[7::4] signal lines to logical "1". During the TARGET RESPONSE PHASE, the 64 data bit PCI-X bus master drives the AD[63::32] signal lines to a stable level or tristates and relies on pull-up resistors to drive these signal lines to logical "1". During the TARGET RESPONSE PHASE, the 64 data bit PCI-X bus master drives the CBE#[7::4] signal lines to logical "1". During the TARGET RESPONSE PHASE (with a one CLK signal line period delay), the 64 data bit PCI-X bus master drives the PAR64 signal line to a stable level or tristates it and relies on a pull-up resistor to drive this signal line to logical "1". During the ATTRIBUTE PHASE (with a one CLK signal line period delay), the 64 data bit PCI-X bus master drives the PAR64 signal line with valid parity.

During the DATA PHASE when both the PCI-X bus master and target support a 64 data bit bus transaction (REQ64# and ACK64# signal line both asserted), the AD[63::32] and PAR64 signal lines contain valid information. The C/BE#[7::4] signal lines contain valid byte enable information for BURST memory write (not including memory write block or alias memory write block) transactions. The C/BE#[7::4] signal lines are driven to logical "1" for BURST memory read, BURST memory write block, and BURST alias memory write block transactions.

See Chapter 6: *Detailed Bus Transaction Operation* for more information.

The BURST split completion transaction protocol is the same as for a BURST memory write block or a BURST alias memory write block transaction. If the "original" transaction (terminated by the Split Response termination) is 64 data bits in size, the split completion transaction can be executed as either a 32 data bit or a 64 data bit bus transaction.

For a 64 data bit target, the BURST memory transactions, DUAL ADDRESS operation, and Exclusive Access (LOCK) operation are supported with the same protocol as bus transactions between a 32 data bit PCI-X bus master and a 32 data bit target

DWORD, MEMORY READ, I/O, CONFIGURATION, INTERRUPT ACKNOWLEDGE, AND SPECIAL TRANSACTIONS

These bus transactions are executed only with 32 data bit targets and the REQ64# and ACK64# signal lines must be deasserted.

4.20 PCI-X 64 DATA BIT BUS MASTER TO 32 DATA BIT TARGET

MEMORY AND SPLIT COMPLETION TRANSACTIONS

A PCI-X bus master and memory resource (target) are defined as 64 and 32 data bit resources when the REQ64# and ACK64# signal lines are asserted and deasserted, respectively. The PCI-X bus master requests a 64 data bit transaction by asserting the REQ64# signal line during the ADDRESS PHASE. A 32 data bit target responds without asserting the ACK64# signal line; a pull-up resistor on the backplane will deassert the ACK64# signal line during the TARGET RESPONSE and DATA PHASES. The major difference between a PCI-X bus master request for a 64 data bit access to a 32 data bit target versus a 64 data bit target is the operation of the AD[63::32], C/BE#[7::4], and PAR64 signal lines during the DATA PHASES.

For a BRUST memory write bus transaction, the AD[63::32], C/BE#[7::4], and PAR64 signal lines during the ADDRESS PHASE, ATTRIBUTE PHASE, TARGET RESPONSE PHASE, and initial microaccess of the DATA PHASE operate with the same protocol as outlined in the previous section for a 64 data bit bus transaction between a 64 data bit PCI-X bus master and a 64 data bit target. After the completion of the initial microaccess of the DATA PHASE, the AD[63::32], C/BE#[7::4], and PAR64 signal lines can be driven to a stable level by the PCI-X bus master or tristated and driven to logical "1" by pull-up resistors for the remainder of the BURST bus transaction. The PAR64 signal line will not contain valid parity information over these signal lines after the initial microaccess of the DATA PHASE with a one CLK signal line period delay.

For a BURST memory read bus transaction, the AD [63::32], C/BE#[7::4], and PAR64 signal lines during the ADDRESS PHASE, ATTRIBUTE PHASE, and TARGET RESPONSE PHASE operate with the same protocol as outlined in the previous section for a 64 data bit bus transaction between a 64 data bit PCI-X bus master and a 64 data bit target. After completion of the TARGET RESPONSE PHASE, the AD[63::32] and PAR64 signal lines are tristated by the PCI-X bus master and driven to logical "1" by pull up resistors. The C/BE#[7::4] signal lines are driven to logical "1" in the initial microaccess of the DATA PHASE and after the initial microaccess these signal lines can be driven to a stable level by the PCI-X bus master or tristated and driven to logical "1" by pull-up resistors for the remainder of the BURST bus transaction. The PAR64 signal line will not contain valid parity information after the ATTRIBUTE PHASE with a one CLK signal line period delay.

> When a PCI-X bus master requests a 64 data bit bus transaction to a 32 data bit target, a SINGLE bus transaction cannot be executed. As explained in *Chapter 6: Detailed Bus Transaction Operation*, a request for a 64 data bit SINGLE bus transaction must be broken down into a BURST bus transaction with two 32 data bit microaccesses.

> If the 64 data bit transaction (REQ64# signal line asserted) completes with Single Phase Disconnect or Disconnect at Next ADB terminations with a 32 data bit target (ACK64# signal line deasserted), the PCI-X bus master must subsequently execute the bus transactions of the "sequence" as a 32 data bit PCI-X bus master (REQ64# signal line deasserted). See Chapter 8: *Master and Target Termination* for more information.

> In the above discussion it is assumed that the 64 data bit accesses are attempted only to a memory resource (*i.e.,* memory address space) because a target with a memory address is the only resource that can potentially execute 32 data bit bus transactions. If for whatever reason the PCI-X bus master attempts a 64 data bit access to the other address spaces, the target must respond as a 32 data bit resource.

> See Chapter 6: *Detailed Bus Transaction Operation* for more information.

The BURST split completion transaction protocol is the same as for a BURST memory write block or a BURST alias memory write block transaction. If the "original" transaction (terminated by the Split Response termination) is 64 data bits in size, the split completion transaction must be 32 data bits in size if the "original" target is only a 32 data bit resource.

DWORD, MEMORY READ, I/O, CONFIGURATION, INTERRUPT ACKNOWLEDGE, AND SPECIAL TRANSACTIONS

These bus transactions are executed only with 32 data bit targets, and the REQ64# and ACK64# signal lines must be deasserted.

4.21 PCI-X MESSAGE SIGNALED INTERRUPT

The PCI-X protocol for Message Signaled Interrupt (MSI) memory write transactions is the same as PCI. The BURST memory write bus transactions that can be used for MSI are BURST memory write, memory write block, and alias memory write block bus transactions. The No Snoop and Relaxed Ordering bits of the ATTRIBUTE PHASE must be set to logical "0". See Chapter 6: *Detailed Bus Transaction Protocol* for more information.

CHAPTER 5

SIGNAL LINE DEFINITION

This chapter consists of the following subchapters:

5.0   INTRODUCTION

The following discussions describe the definition of the signal lines on a PCI bus segment. The operation of the signal lines will vary depending on the type of bus transaction, the data size of the bus master, whether the DUAL ADDRESS command is being executed, whether the bus is IDLE (no bus transactions and not parked), and whether the bus is RESET or parked. The various types of bus transactions include access (memory, I/O, and configuration), special, and interrupt acknowledge transactions. The data size of a PCI resource can be either 32 or 64 data bits. When the bus is IDLE, the signal lines are driven to a stable level by the present PCI bus owner, Park master, or by pull-up resistors. The signal lines are driven to specific values when RESET or parked.

The following discussions also describe the definition of the signal lines on a PCI-X bus segment. Essentially the definition of the signal lines on a PCI-X bus segment and a PCI bus segment is the same. There are only minor enhancements to the definition of signal lines on a PCI-X bus segment as will be discussed below. Also, PCI-X has added one additional signal line: PCIXCAP.

The signal lines are all referenced to the rising edge of the CLK signal line (see Chapter 12 *Signal Line Timing and Electrical Requirements* for more information) with the following exceptions:

- The RESET signal line is asynchronous to the CLK signal line. See Chapter 11 *Reset, Power, and Signal Line Initialization* for more information.

- The SERR# signal line is asserted synchronously and deasserted asynchronously to the CLK signal line. See a latter portion of this chapter and Chapter 10 *Parity and Bus Errors* for more information.

- The INTx# signal lines are asserted and deasserted asynchronously to the CLK signal line.

- The PME# signal line is asserted and deasserted asynchronously to the CLK signal line.

- The PCIXCAP signal line is a constant logical "1", logical "0", or a voltage in between.

- The MEN66 signal line is a constant logical "1" or logical "0".

The PCI and PCI-X bus segment protocol does not require that every resource support all of the possible PCI bus signal lines. PCI bus masters, and targets that reside on the platform (not via a connector), require 47 and 45 signal lines, respectively. The PERR# and SERR# signal lines do not have to be supported by resources that do not attach to the bus segment via a connector. However, the PERR# and SERR# signal lines must be supported by each connector and by bus segments that support connectors. Additionally, the PRSNT[1::2]# pins must also be supported by bus segments that support connectors. These pins are not signal lines according to the bus protocol; consequently, they will not be discussed in this chapter (see Chapter 11 *Reset. Power, and Signal Line Initialization* for more information). Finally, a bus segment must support all of the REQ# and GNT# signal line pairs required for the support of all of the PCI and PCI-X resources to become PCI and PCI-X bus masters.

> The PCI Mobile Design Guide also defines an optional signal line called CLKRUN#. This signal line is not required for a non-mobile environment. See the PCI Mobile Design Guide for more information.

The **REQUIRED** signal lines must be supported by all PCI bus masters, PCI-X bus masters, and targets. The exception are the REQ# and GNT# (bus ownership arbitration) signal lines which are only required for PCI and PCI-X bus masters. The **OPTIONAL** signal lines can be supported individually by PCI bus masters, PCI-X bus masters, and targets.

The signal lines also have different electrical characteristics. These characteristics will be discussed in detail in Chapter 12: *Signal Line Timing and*

Electrical Requirements. In summary, the **ELECTRICAL ATTRIBUTES** of the signal lines are as follows:

- Input: Driven into the PCI or PCI-X resource and never tri-stated.

- Output: Driven by the PCI resource and never tri-stated.

- Bi-directional tri-state: Driven into and driven by the PCI or PCI-X resource. The signal line can also be tri-stated.

- Bi-directional drive tri-state: driven into and driven by the PCI resource. The signal line can also be tri-stated. When the PCI or PCI-X resource has driven this signal line low it must drive it high for one CLK signal line period prior to tri-state.

- Open drain: driven by the PCI or PCI-X resource as an output, and is an open drain device to allow for a wire-OR sharing of the signal line. The central resource is the only circuitry that receives it as an input.

The format of each entry is as follows:

Signal Name (Short)	Signal Name (Long)	Req./Opt.	I/O Pin Attributes	Resistors

Signal name (short): The name used in the text

Signal name (long): Full name

Req./Opt.: Distinguishes between required and an optional signal lines.

I/O pin attributes: Identifies the electrical attributes of the pins outlined above.

Resistors: Identifies the pull-up resistor value the bus segment provides to 3.3 or 5 volts. Resistors are mounted on the bus segment unless otherwise noted. See Chapter 12: *Signal Line Timing and Electrical Requirements* for more information.

> The use of the "#" suffix with the signal line name indicates that it is asserted with a logical "0" at 0 volts. A signal line without the "#" suffix is asserted when at a logical "1" at 3.3 or 5 volts.

BRIEF DESCRIPTION

This line will contain a brief description of the signal line(s), followed by a description of the following conditions:

RESET: Describes signal line operation during RESET. The RESET condition is when the RST# signal line is asserted. For a PCI-X bus segment, the RESET condition also provides information as to the frequency of the CLK signal line and whether the bus transaction protocol will be according to the PCI local bus specification or according to PCI-X addendum specification.

PARK: Describes the bus being parked under one of the following conditions: A PCI or PCI-X bus master is the Park master with its associated REQ# and GNT# signal lines deasserted and asserted, respectively, or the central arbiter is the Park master when all REQ# and GNT# signal lines are deasserted.

IDLE PHASE: Describes the signal line operation between bus transactions when the PCI or PCI-X bus master retains ownership of the bus segment (associated REQ# and GNT# signal lines are both asserted).

ADDRESS, DATA PHASES: Describes the signal line operation during the ADDRESS and DATA PHASE of bus transactions.

ATTRIBUTE PHASE: Describes the signal line operation during the ATTRIBUTE PHASE of bus transactions. The ATTRIBUTE PHASE is only defined for PCI-X bus segments.

TARGET RESPONSE PHASE Describes the signal line operation during the TARGET RESPONSE PHASE. The TARGET RESPONSE PHASE is only defined for PCI-X bus segments.

In this and other chapters, the phrase "driven to a logical '1' by pull-up resistor(s)" means that the signal line(s) reach a stable level by being pulled to logical "1" by the resistor(s). It does not represent an *active* driving of the signal line(s) to a logical "1".

In the following sections, Split Completion Transactions are discussed. These bus transactions are defined only for PCI-X bus segments.

5.1   ADDRESS, DATA, AND ASSOCIATED SIGNAL LINES

The AD[31::0] signal lines multiplex addresses and data. The C/BE#[3::0], FRAME#, and PAR signal lines are used to interpret and validate the signal lines that carry the addresses and data.

AD[31::0]	Address and Data	Req.	Bi-Directional Tri-state	No Pull-up Resistors

These signal lines contain the address and data bits for the bus transactions.

This section covers AD[31::0] where used by a 32 data bit PCI or PCI-X bus master (REQ64# deasserted by a pull-up resistor). See Subchapter 5.6: *64 Data Bit Signal Lines* for the case using 64 data bit PCI and PCI-X bus masters.

PCI SPECIFIC

RESET

Driven to stable level (logical "0" ... not logical "1") by central resource.

PARK

Driven to a stable level by Park master (logical "0" ... not logical "1" if central resource is PARK master).

IDLE PHASE

Driven to a stable level by PCI bus master if the bus segment ownership is retained. Otherwise these signal lines are tri-stated.

ADDRESS PHASE

MEMORY AND I/O TRANSACTIONS

For the memory address space, the AD[31::2] signal lines address a double word and the AD[1::0] signal lines provide the BURST sequence address order. For the I/O address space, the AD[31::0] signal lines contain the address of the least significant byte.

CONFIGURATON TRANSACTIONS

The AD[31::0] signals are divided into several groups. The definition of the signal lines in each group is dependent on the type of configuration transaction.

SPECIAL AND INTERRUPT ACKNOWLEDGE TRANSACTIONS

The AD[31::0] signal lines are driven to a stable level but contain no valid information.

DATA PHASE

MEMORY, I/O, AND CONFIGURATION TRANSACTIONS

The least significant data is on signal lines AD[7::0] with the most significant data in signal lines AD[31::24].

For a PCI bus transaction, only those AD signal lines indicated as valid by the C/BE#[3::0] signal lines have valid data. Those that are indicated as invalid do not contain data but must be driven to a stable level. For a write transaction, the bus master is responsible for driving the AD[31::0] signal lines, and for a read access transaction the target is responsible for driving the AD[31::0] signal lines. Under certain prefetchable memory conditions, all of the AD signal lines have valid read data independent of the C/BE# signal lines.

SPECIAL TRANSACTIONS

The AD[15::0] signal lines contain the message type. The AD[31::16] signal lines are driven to a stable level or contain an optional data field related to the message.

INTERRUPT ACKNOWLEDGE TRANSACTIONS

The AD[31::0] signal lines contain the interrupt vector.

PCI-X SPECIFIC

RESET, PARK, AND IDLE PHASE

Same as for PCI.

ADDRESS PHASE

MEMORY AND I/O TRANSACTIONS

For the memory address space, the AD[31::0] signal lines address a double word. For the I/O address space, the AD[31::0] signal lines contain the address of the least significant byte. These signal lines are driven by the PCI-X bus master.

SPLIT COMPLETION TRANSACTIONS

The AD[31::0] signal lines contain the destination ("original" PCI-X bus master) of the bus transaction. These signal lines are driven by the PCI-X bus master.

CONFIGURATION, SPECIAL, AND INTERRUPT ACKNOWLEDGE TRANSACTIONS

Same as for PCI.

ATTRIBUTE PHASE

MEMORY, I/O, SPLIT COMPLETION, SPECIAL, INTERRUPT ACKNOWLEDGE, AND CONFIGURATION TRANSACTIONS

The AD[31::00] signal lines contain general bus transaction information in conjunction with the C/BE#[3::0] signal lines including the source of the bus transaction. These signal lines are driven by the PCI-X bus master.

TARGET RESPONSE PHASE

MEMORY WRITE, I/O WRITE, SPECIAL, AND SPLIT COMPLETION TRANSACTIONS

The AD[31::00] signal lines are driven to a stable level or floated by the PCI-X bus master.

MEMORY READ, I/O READ, AND INTERRUPT ACKNOWLEDGE TRANSACTIONS

The AD[31::00] signal lines change ownership from PCI-X bus master to the target, and the PCI-X bus master will tri-state these signal lines.

DATA PHASE

MEMORY, I/O, SPLIT COMPLETION, AND CONFIGURATION TRANSACTIONS

The least significant data is on signal lines AD[7::0] with the most significant data on signal lines AD[31::24]. The AD[31::00] signal lines are driven by the PCI-X bus master for write and split completion transactions. The AD[31::00] signal lines are driven by the target for read transactions.

For PCI-X bus transactions for DWORD COMMANDs, only those AD[31::00] signal lines indicated as valid by the C/BE#[3::0] signal lines in the ATTRIBUTE PHASE have valid data. Those that are indicated as invalid do not contain data but must be driven to a stable level.

For PCI-X bus transactions for BURST memory write commands, only those AD [31::00] signal lines indicated as valid by the C/BE#[3::0] signal lines in the DATA PHASE have valid data. Those that are indicated as invalid do not contain data but must be driven to a stable level. For PCI-X bus transactions for BURST memory read commands, all of the AD[31::00] signal lines are defined as containing valid data and the C/BE#[3::0] signal lines are all driven to logcial"1" in the DATA PHASE.

For PCI-X bus transactions for BURST split completion commands, all of the AD[31::00] signal lines are defined as containing valid data and the C/BE#[3::0] signal lines are all driven to logical "1" in the DATA PHASE.

SPECIAL AND INTERRUPT ACKNOWLEDGE TRANSACTIONS

Same as PCI

> See Subchapter 5.6: *64 Data Bit Signal Lines* for information on the protocol of the AD[63::32] signal lines with 32 data bit PCI and PCI-X bus resources, and AD[31::0] and AD[63::32] signal lines with 64 data bit PCI and PCI-X resources.

C/BE#[3::0]	Bus Command and Byte Enables	Req.	Bi-Directional Tri-state	No Pull-up Resistors

These signal lines contain the COMMAND type for the bus transaction and the valid byte lanes of the ad signal lines.

This section covers C/BE#[3::0] where used by a 32 data bit PCI or PCI-X bus masters (REQ64# deasserted by pull-up resistor). See Section 5.6: *64 Data Bit Signal Lines*, for the case using a 64 data bit PCI or PCI-X bus masters.

PCI SPECIFIC

RESET

Driven to a stable level (logical "0" ... not logical "1") by central resource.

PARK

Driven to a stable level by Park master (logical "0" ... not logical "1" if central resource is PARK master).

IDLE PHASE

Driven to a stable level by PCI bus master if the bus segment ownership is retained. Otherwise these signal lines are tri-stated.

ADDRESS PHASE

MEMORY, I/O, AND CONFIGURATION TRANSACTIONS

These signal lines contain the COMMAND type for the access transaction and DUAL ADDRESS command.

SPECIAL TRANSACTIONS

These signal lines contain the COMMAND type for a special transaction.

INTERRUPT ACKNOWLEDGE TRANSACTIONS

These signal lines contain the COMMAND type for an interrupt acknowledge transaction.

DATA PHASE

MEMORY, CONFIGURATION, AND SPECIAL TRANSACTIONS.

The C/BE#[3::0] signal lines indicate which byte lanes of the AD[31::0] signal lines contain valid data.

I/O TRANSACTIONS

The C/BE#[3::0] signal lines indicate which byte lanes of the AD[31::0] signal lines contain valid data. The byte lanes identified by the asserted C/BE#[3::0] signal lines must agree with the byte address specified by the AD[1::0] signal lines during ADDRESS PHASE.

INTERRUPT ACKNOWLEDGE TRANSACTIONS

The C/BE#[3::0] signal lines indicate which byte lanes of the AD[31::0] signal lines contain valid interrupt vector information.

The COMMAND type encoding of the C/BE#[3::0] signal lines (and C/BE#[7::4] signal lines for 64 data bit PCI bus masters when DUAL ADDRESS command is executed) during the ADDRESS PHASE of a PCI bus transaction is as follows:

C/BE# Command Type

[3 2 1 0] ([7 6 5 4])	
0 0 0 0	Interrupt Acknowledge Command
0 0 0 1	Special Command
0 0 1 0	I/O Read Access Command
0 0 1 1	I/O Write Access Command
0 1 0 0	Reserved
0 1 0 1	Reserved
0 1 1 0	Memory Read Access Command
0 1 1 1	Memory Write Access Command
1 0 0 0	Reserved
1 0 0 1	Reserved
1 0 1 0	Configuration Read Access Command
1 0 1 1	Configuration Write Access Command
1 1 0 0	Memory Read Multiple Access Command
1 1 0 1	DUAL ADDRESS Access Command
1 1 1 0	Memory Read Line Access Command
1 1 1 1	Memory Write And Invalidate Access Command

PCI-X SPECIFIC

RESET, PARK, IDLE PHASE, AND ADRRESS PHASE

Same as PCI.

ADDRESS PHASE

MEMORY, I/O, SPECIAL, INTERRUPT ACKNOWLEDGE, AND CONFIGURATION TRANSACTIONS

Same as PCI except with different COMMAND type encoding (see below).

SPLIT COMPLETION TRANSACTIONS

These signal lines contain the COMMAND type (see below).

ATTRIBUTE PHASE

MEMORY, I/O, SPLIT COMPLETION, SPECIAL, INTERRUPT ACKNOWLEDGE, AND CONFIGURATION TRANSACTIONS

The C/BE#[3::0] signal lines contain general bus transaction information in conjunction with the AD[31::00] signal lines, including the source of the bus transaction.

TARGET RESPONSE PHASE

MEMORY, I/O, SPLIT COMPLETION, SPECIAL, INTERRUPT ACKNOWLEDGE, AND CONFIGURATION TRANSACTIONS

These signal lines are driven to a logical "1" by the PCI-X bus master.

DATA PHASE

ALL BUS TRANSACTIONS FOR DWORD COMMANDS

These signal lines are driven to a logical "1" by the PCI-X bus master.

ALL BUS TRANSACTIONS FOR BURST MEMORY WRITE COMMANDS

The C/BE#[3::0] signal lines indicate which byte lanes of the AD[31::0] signal lines contain valid data.

ALL BUS TRANSACTIONS FOR BURST MEMORY READ COMMANDS

These signal lines are driven to a logical "1" by the PCI-X bus master.

ALL BUS TRANSACTIONS FOR BURST SPLIT COMPLETION COMMANDS

These signal lines are driven to a logical "1" by the PCI-X bus master.

The COMMAND type encoding of the C/BE#[3::0] signal lines (and C/BE#[7::4] signal lines for 64 data bit PCI-X bus masters when DUAL ADDRESS command is executed) during the ADDRESS PHASE of a PCI-X bus transaction is as follows:

C/BE# Command Type

```
[3 2 1 0]
([7 6 5 4])
 0 0 0 0    DWORD Interrupt Acknowledge Command
 0 0 0 1    DWORD Special Command
 0 0 1 0    DWORD I/O Read Command
 0 0 1 1    DWORD I/O Write Command
 0 1 0 0    Reserved
 0 1 0 1    Reserved
 0 1 1 0    DWORD Memory Read Command
 0 1 1 1    BURST Memory Write Command
 1 0 0 0    BURST Alias Memory Read Block Command
 1 0 0 1    BURST Alias Memory Write Block Command
 1 0 1 0    DWORD Configuration Read Command
 1 0 1 1    DWORD Configuration Write Command
 1 1 0 0    BURST Split Completion Command
 1 1 0 1    DUAL ADDRESS Command
 1 1 1 0    BURST Memory Read Block Command
 1 1 1 1    BURST Memory Write Block Command
```

See Section 5.6: *64 Data Bit Signal Lines* for information on the protocol of the C/BE#[7::4] signal lines with 32 data bit PCI and PCI-X resources, and the C/BE#[3::0] and C/BE#[7::4] signal lines with 64 data bit PCI and PCI-X resources.

PAR	Parity	Req.	Bi-Directional Tri-state	No Pull-up Resistor

This signal line provides even parity across the AD and C/BE# signal lines

This section covers PAR where used by a 32 data bit PCI or PCI-X bus master (REQ64# deasserted by pull-up resistor). See Section 5.6: *64 Data Bit Signal Lines*, for the case using a 64 data bit PCI or PCI-X bus master.

PCI SPECIFIC

RESET

Driven to a stable level (logical "0" ... not logical "1") by central resource.

PARK

Driven to a stable state by the Park master (logical "0" ... not logical "1" if central resource is PARK master).

> This signal line lags the AD signal lines by one CLK signal line period. Consequently, what is defined for the ADDRESS and DATA PHASES below is actually one CLK signal period later.

IDLE PHASE

Driven to a stable level by the PCI bus master if the bus segment ownership is retained. Otherwise this signal line is tri-stated.

ADDRESS PHASE

MEMORY, I/O, CONFIGURATION, INTERRUPT ACKNOWLEDGE, AND SPECIAL TRANSACTIONS

The PAR signal line is driven by the PCI bus master to provide even parity over the AD[31::0] and C/BE#[3::0] signal lines. The total number of "1"s over these signal lines including the PAR signal line is an even number.

DATA PHASE

MEMORY, I/O, CONFIGURATION, INTERRUPT ACKNOWLEDGE, AND SPECIAL TRANSACTIONS

The PAR signal line is driven to provide even parity over the AD[31::0] and C/BE#[3::0] signal lines. The total number of "1"s over these signal lines including the PAR signal line is an even number. For memory, I/O, and configuration write transactions and special transactions, the PAR signal line is driven by the PCI bus master. For read and interrupt acknowledge transactions, the PAR signal line is driven by the target.

PCI-X SPECIFIC

RESET, PARK, AND IDLE PHASE

Same as PCI.

> This signal line lags the AD signal lines by one CLK signal line period. Consequently, what is defined for the IDLE (above), ADDRESS, ATTRIBUTE, TARGET RESPONSE, and DATA PHASES (below) is actually one CLK signal period later.

ADDRESS AND ATTRIBUTE PHASES

MEMORY, I/O, CONFIGURATION, SPLIT COMPLETION, INTERRUPT ACKNOWLEDGE, AND SPECIAL TRANSACTIONS

The PAR signal line is driven by the PCI-X bus master to provide even parity over the AD[31::0] and C/BE#[3::0] signal lines. The total number of "1"s over these signal lines including the PAR signal line is an even number.

TARGET RESPONSE PHASE

MEMORY WRITE, I/O WRITE, CONFIGURATION WRITE, SPECIAL, AND SPLIT COMPLETION TRANSACTIONS

The PCI-X drives the PAR signal line to stable level or floats it. Either way, there is no valid parity information.

MEMORY READ, I/O READ, CONFIGURATION READ, AND INTERRUPT ACKNOWLEDGE TRANSACTIONS

The C/BE#[3::0] signal lines exchange ownership from PCI-X bus master to the target.

DATA PHASE

MEMORY WRITE, I/O WRITE, CONFIGURATION WRITE, SPECIAL, AND SPLIT COMPLETION TRANSACTIONS

The PAR signal line is driven to provide even parity over the AD[31::0] and C/BE#[3::0] signal lines. The total number of "1"s over these signal lines, including the PAR signal line, is an even number. The PAR signal line is valid with a one CLK signal line delay from the AD[31::00] and C/BE#[3::0] signal lines.

MEMORY READ, I/O READ, CONFIGURATION READ, AND INTERRUPT ACKNOWLEDGE TRANSACTIONS

The PAR signal line is driven to provide even parity over the AD[31::0] and C/BE#[3::0] signal lines. The total number of "1"s over these signal lines, including the PAR signal line, is an even number with a one CLK signal line delay. The PAR signal line is valid with a one CLK signal line delay from the AD[31::00] and a two CLK signal line delay from the C/BE#[3::0] signal lines.

See Section 5.6: *64 Data Bit Signal Lines* for information on the protocol of the C/BE#[7::4] signal lines with 32 data bit PCI and PCI-X resources, and the PAR64 and PAR signal lines with 64 data bit PCI and PCI-X resources.

5.2 TRANSACTION CONTROL SIGNAL LINES

FRAME#	Frame	Req.	Bi-Directional Drive Tri-state	Pull-up Resistor

This signal line identifies the beginning of a bus transaction.

PCI SPECIFIC

RESET

Driven to a logical "1" (deasserted) by a pull-up resistor.

PARK

Driven to a logical "1" (deasserted) by a pull-up resistor.

IDLE PHASE

Driven to a logical "1" (deasserted) by the PCI bus master if the bus segment ownership is retained. Otherwise this signal line is tri-stated and driven to logical '1" by a pull-up resistor.

ADDRESS AND DATA PHASE

MEMORY, I/O, AND INTERRUPT ACKNOWLEDGE TRANSACTIONS

The PCI bus master asserts the FRAME# signal line to identify the ADDRESS PHASE and therefore the beginning of a memory, I/O, or interrupt acknowledge transaction. The asserted FRAME# signal line during the ADDRESS PHASE indicates that the AD and C/BE# signal lines contain valid address and COMMAND type information, respectively. When a DUAL ADDRESS is not executed, the minimum asserted pulse width is one CLK signal line period. When a DUAL ADDRESS is executed, the minimum asserted pulse width is two CLK signal line periods.

The PCI bus master uses the FRAME# signal lines during the DATA PHASE to control the length of the memory, I/O, or interrupt acknowledge transaction. If the FRAME# signal line is deasserted simultaneously with the first assertion of the IRDY# signal line, a SINGLE memory, I/O, or interrupt acknowledge transaction is executed. If the FRAME# signal line is deasserted after the first assertion of the IRDY# signal line, a BURST memory, I/O, or interrupt acknowledge transaction is executed.

A memory, I/O, or interrupt acknowledge transaction is complete, even if a Retry, Disconnect, Master Abort, or Target Abort termination is executed, when the FRAME# and IRDY# signal lines are simultaneously sampled deasserted (IDLE PHASE). Prior to the IDLE PHASE, the IRDY# signal line must be asserted for minimum of one CLK signal line period. The one exception is the execution of Fast Back-to-Back access transactions, because there is no IDLE PHASE after the completion of the memory, I/O, or interrupt acknowledge transaction. By convention, even in the case of Fast Back-to-Back protocol, the IRDY# signal line must be asserted for one CLK signal line period when the FRAME# signal line is deasserted at the completion of a memory, I/O, or interrupt acknowledge transaction.

CONFIGURATION TRANSACTIONS

The PCI bus master asserts the FRAME# signal line to identify the ADDRESS PHASE and therefore the beginning of a configuration transaction. The asserted FRAME# signal line during the ADDRESS PHASE indicates that the AD[31::0] contain valid IDSEL and address information. Also, the C/BE#[3::0] signal lines contain valid COMMAND type information. The minimum asserted pulse width is one CLK signal line period.

The PCI bus master uses the FRAME# signal lines during the DATA PHASE to control the length of the configuration transaction. If the FRAME# signal line is deasserted simultaneously with the first assertion of the IRDY# signal line, a

SINGLE configuration transaction is executed. If the FRAME# signal line is asserted with the first assertion of the IRDY# signal line, a BURST configuration transaction is executed.

A configuration transaction is complete even if a Retry, Disconnect, Master Abort, or target termination is executed, when the FRAME# and IRDY# signal lines are simultaneously sampled deasserted (IDLE PHASE). Prior to the IDLE PHASE the IRDY# signal line must be asserted for a minimum of one CLK signal line period.

SPECIAL TRANSACTIONS

The FRAME# signal line is defined with the same protocol as the memory and I/O write transactions, with a few exceptions. Fast Back-to-Back protocol cannot be applied.

PCI-X SPECIFIC

RESET, PARK, AND IDLE PHASE

Same as PCI.

ADDRESS, ATTRIBUTE, TARGET RESPONSE, AND DATA PHASES

MEMORY, I/O, CONFIGURATION, SPLIT COMPLETION, INTERRUPT ACKNOWLEDGE, AND SPECIAL TRANSACTIONS

The FRAME# signal line is driven asserted (logical "0") by the PCI-X bus master to identify the ADDRESS PHASE. It remains asserted during the bus transaction until the DATA PHASE. It is driven deasserted during the DATA PHASE by the PCI-X bus master according to the "General Deassertion" protocol. See Chapter 6: *Detailed Bus Transaction Operation* for more information on the "General Deassertion" protocol.

IRDY#	Initiator Ready	Req.	Bi-Directional Drive Tri-state	Pull-up Resistor

This signal line indicates when the PCI or PCI-X bus master (initiator) is ready to complete the bus transaction.

PCI SPECIFIC

RESET

Driven to a logical "1" (deasserted) by a pull-up resistor.

PARK

Driven to a logical "1" (deasserted) by a pull-up resistor.

IDLE PHASE

Driven to a logical "1" (deasserted) by PCI bus master if the bus segment ownership is retained. Otherwise this signal line is tri-stated and driven to logical "1" by a pull-up resistor.

ADDRESS PHASE

Driven to a logical "1" (deasserted) by PCI bus master or a pull-up resistor.

DATA PHASE

MEMORY, I/O, CONFIGURATION, AND INTERRUPT ACKNOWLEDGE TRANSACTIONS

The PCI bus master asserts the IRDY# signal line to indicate that it is ready to complete the access. For a memory, I/O, or configuration write transaction, it indicates that the bus master has driven valid data onto the AD signal lines. For a memory, I/O, configuration, or interrupt acknowledge transaction, it indicates that the PCI bus master is ready to retrieve data or an interrupt vector from the AD signal lines.

By convention, both the IRDY# and TRDY# signal lines must be asserted to complete the memory, I/O, configuration, or interrupt acknowledge transaction. The deassertion of the either of these signal lines prior to the completion of the memory, I/O, configuration, or interrupt acknowledge transaction results in the automatic insertion of wait states with a resolution of one CLK signal line period.

Once the IRDY# signal line is asserted it remains asserted for each data access until TRDY# (and/or STOP# signal line) signal line is asserted. When a Retry, Disconnect without data, Master Abort, or Target Abort termination is executed, the IRDY# signal line must be asserted a minimum of one CLK signal line period prior to the simultaneous deassertion of the FRAME# and IRDY# signal lines to complete a memory, I/O, configuration, or interrupt acknowledge transaction.

SPECIAL TRANSACTIONS

The IRDY# signal line operates with the same protocol as the memory, I/O, configuration, or interrupt acknowledge transaction, except that the TRDY# signal line is not asserted during a special transaction.

PCI-X SPECIFIC

RESET, PARK, AND IDLE PHASE

Same as PCI.

ADDRESS, ATTRIBUTE, TARGET RESPONSE, AND DATA PHASES

MEMORY, I/O, CONFIGURATION, SPLIT COMPLETION, INTERRUPT ACKNOWLEDGE, AND SPECIAL TRANSACTIONS

The IRDY# signal line is driven by the PCI-X bus master. It is driven deasserted (logical "1") during the ADDRESS, ATTRIBUTE, and TARGET RESPONSE PHASEs. Immediately after the single CLK signal line period TARGET RESPONSE it must be driven asserted to begin the DATA PHASE. It is deasserted during the DATA PHASE by the PCI-X bus master according to the "General Deassertion" protocol. See Chapter 6: *Detailed Bus Transaction Operation* for more information on the "General Deassertion" protocol.

TRDY#	Target Ready	Req.	Bi-Directional Drive Tri-state	Pull-up Resistor

This signal line indicates when the accessed PCI or PCI-X resource (target) is ready to complete the bus transaction.

PCI SPECIFIC

RESET

Driven to a logical "1" (deasserted) by a pull-up resistor.

PARK

Driven to a logical "1" (deasserted) by a pull-up resistor.

IDLE PHASE

Driven to a logical "1" (deasserted) by a pull-up resistor.

ADDRESS PHASE

Driven to a logical "1" (deasserted) by a pull-up resistor.

DATA PHASE

MEMORY, I/O, CONFIGURATION, AND INTERRUPT ACKNOWLEDGE TRANSACTIONS

The target asserts the TRDY# signal line to indicate that the target is ready to complete a memory, I/O, configuration, or interrupt acknowledge transaction. For a memory, I/O, or configuration read transaction, it indicates that the target has driven valid data onto the AD signal lines. For an interrupt acknowledge transaction, it indicates that the target has driven a valid interrupt vector onto the AD signal lines. For a memory, I/O, or configuration write transaction, it indicates that the target is ready to retrieve data from the AD signal lines.

By convention, both the IRDY# and TRDY# signal lines must be asserted to complete the memory, I/O, configuration, or interrupt acknowledge transaction. The deassertion of either of these signal lines prior to the completion of the memory, I/O, configuration, or interrupt acknowledge transaction results in the automatic insertion of wait states with a resolution of one CLK signal line period.

SPECIAL TRANSACTIONS

Due to the broadcast nature of the special bus transaction, the TRDY# signal line is driven deasserted by a pull-up resistor during the DATA PHASE.

During a memory, I/O, configuration read transaction, or interrupt acknowledge transaction, the TRDY# signal line must be asserted one CLK signal line period later than earliest possible point (after the DEVSEL# signal line is asserted) to allow the AD signal lines to be tri-stated by the PCI bus master.

266

The DEVSEL# signal line must be asserted simultaneously with or prior to the assertion of the TRDY# signal line. Once asserted, the TRDY# signal line remains asserted for each data access until the IRDY# signal line is asserted. See Subchapter 8.2 for a unique situation when the TRDY# signal line is deasserted earlier.

During Fast Back-to-Back access cycles, the assertion of the TRDY# signal line must be one CLK signal line period later (minimum) than the earliest possible point for a FAST decode versus a non-Fast Back-to-Back access cycle condition. Please see the *Fast Back-to-Back* portion of Subchapter 6.10 for details.

PCI-X SPECIFIC

RESET

The TRDY# signal line, in conjunction with the DEVSEL# and STOP# signal lines, establishes whether the bus segment is PCI or PCI-X, and the CLK signal line frequency. See Chapter 11: *Reset, Power, and Signal Line Initialization* for more information.

PARK AND IDLE PHASE

Same as PCI.

ADDRESS, ATTRIBUTE, AND TARGET RESPONSE PHASES

MEMORY, I/O, CONFIGURATION, SPLIT COMPLETION, INTERRUPT ACKNOWLEDGE, AND SPECIAL TRANSACTIONS

Driven to a logical "1" (deasserted) by a pull-up resistor. Except for the TARGET RESPONSE PHASE of a special transaction, the TRDY# signal line may be driven to logical "1" by either a pull-up resistor or the target.

DATA PHASE

MEMORY, I/O, CONFIGURATION, SPLIT COMPLETION. AND INTERRUPT ACKNOWLEDGE TRANSACTIONS

Driven deasserted (logical "1") by a pull-up resistor or the target. Driven asserted by the target when data is ready to transfer (simultaneously with or after the assertion of the DEVSEL# signal line). When the last data of the bus transaction is transferred, the TRDY# signal line is driven deasserted by the target. If a target is selected but no data is transferred, the target drives the TRDY# signal line deasserted for the entire bus transaction. It is also driven asserted for a minimum one CLK signal line period (then deasserted) for the Split Response termination protocol even though no data is transferred within the bus transaction.

If no target is selected, the TRDY# signal line is driven deasserted by a pull-up resistor.

SPECIAL TRANSACTIONS

Due to the broadcast nature of the special bus transaction, the TRDY# signal line is driven deasserted by a pull-up resistor during the DATA PHASE.

The DEVSEL# signal line must be asserted simultaneously with or prior to the assertion of the TRDY# signal line.

DEVSEL#	Device Select	Req.	Bi-Directional Drive Tri-state	Pull-up Resistor

This signal line indicates when a PCI or PCI-X resource (target) has decoded the address on the AD signal lines and claims the bus transaction.

PCI SPECIFIC

RESET

Driven to a logical "1" (deasserted) by a pull-up resistor.

PARK

Driven to a logical "1" (deasserted) by a pull-up resistor.

268

IDLE PHASE

Driven to a logical "1" (deasserted) by a pull-up resistor.

ADDRESS PHASE

Driven to a logical "1" (deasserted) by a pull-up resistor.

DATA PHASE

MEMORY, I/O, CONFIGURATION, AND INTERRUPT ACKNOWLEDGE TRANSACTIONS

The target asserts the DEVSEL# signal line to indicate it has decoded the address on the AD signal lines and will participate in (claim) the memory, I/O, or configuration transaction. For an interrupt acknowledge transaction, the assertion of the DEVSEL# signal line indicates that it is the PCI resource that contains the interrupt logic. The PCI bus master must monitor the DEVSEL# signal line to determine if a target has claimed the memory, I/O, configuration, or interrupt acknowledge transaction, or if a Master Abort termination will be executed. A bridge resource that utilizes SUBTRACTIVE DECODING must monitor the DEVSEL# signal line to determine if it should claim the transaction if not claimed by other PCI resources on the PCI bus segment.

> The DEVSEL# signal line must be asserted simultaneously with or prior to the assertion of the TRDY#, STOP#, and PERR# signal lines by the target. The DEVSEL# signal line is asserted simultaneously with the ACK64# signal line if a 64 data bit access is acknowledged.

> Once asserted, the DEVSEL# signal line remains asserted until the completion of the DATA PHASE, except when a Target Abort occurs.

> During Fast Back-to-Back bus transactions, the assertion of the DEVSEL# signal line must be one CLK signal line period later (minimum) than the earliest possible point for a FAST decode versus a non Fast Back-to-Back access transaction condition. Please see the *Fast Back-to-Back* portion of Subchapter 6.10 for details.

SPECIAL TRANSACTIONS

Due to the broadcast nature of the special bus transaction, the TRDY# signal line is driven deasserted by a pull-up resistor during the DATA PHASE.

PCI-X SPECIFIC

RESET

The DEVSEL# signal line, in conjunction with the STOP# and TRDY# signal lines, establishes whether the bus segment is PCI or PCI-X, and the CLK signal line frequency. See Chapter 11: *Reset, Power, and Signal Line Initialization* for more information.

PARK AND IDLE PHASE

Same as PCI.

ADDRESS, ATTRIBUTE, AND TARGET RESPONSE PHASES

MEMORY, I/O, CONFIGURATION, SPLIT COMPLETION, INTERRUPT ACKNOWLEDGE, AND SPECIAL TRANSACTIONS

Driven to a logical "1" (deasserted) by a pull-up resistor. If the target is claiming the bus transaction at the earliest decoding point ("A"), the DEVSEL# signal line can be asserted by the target in the TARGET RESPONSE PHASE.

DATA PHASE

MEMORY, I/O, CONFIGURATION, SPLIT COMPLETION. AND INTERRUPT ACKNOWLEDGE TRANSACTIONS

Driven deasserted (logical "1") by a pull-up resistor or the target. Driven asserted by the target when the address and command has been decoded and the target is claiming the bus transaction. When the last data of the bus transaction is transferred, the DEVSEL# signal line is driven deasserted by the target. For a Spilt Response, Target Abort, or Single Data Phase Disconnect termination request, the target asserts the DEVSEL# signal line for a minimum of one CLK signal line period (the one CLK signal line period may be either in the TARGET RESPONSE or the DATA PHASE). For a Spilt Response, Target Abort, or Single Data Phase Disconnect termination request, the DEVSEL# signal line is driven deasserted by the target at the end of the DATA PHASE as part of the protocol for these terminations.

If no target claims the bus transaction, the DEVSEL# signal line is driven deasserted by a pull-up resistor.

SPECIAL TRANSACTIONS

Due to the broadcast nature of the special bus transaction, the DEVSEL# signal line is driven deasserted by a pull-up resistor during the DATA PHASE.

> **The DEVSEL# signal line must be asserted simultaneously with or prior to the assertion of the TRDY#, STOP#, and PERR# signal lines by the target. The DEVSEL# signal line is asserted simultaneously with the ACK64# signal line if a 64 data bit access is acknowledged.**

STOP#	Stop	Req.	Bi-Directional Drive Tri-state	Pull-up Resistor

This signal line indicates that the accessed PCI or PCI-X resource (target) wants to end the bus transaction without the PCI or PCI-X bus master completing any or all accesses.

PCI SPECIFIC

RESET

Driven to a logical "1" (deasserted) by a pull-up resistor.

PARK

Driven to a logical "1" (deasserted) by a pull-up resistor.

IDLE PHASE

Driven to a logical "1" (deasserted) by a pull-up resistor.

ADDRESS PHASE

Driven to a logical "1" (deasserted) by a pull-up resistor.

DATA PHASE

MEMORY, I/O, CONFIGURATION, AND INTERRUPT ACKNOWLEDGE TRANSACTIONS

The target asserts the STOP# signal line to inform the PCI bus master that the current memory, I/O, configuration, or interrupt acknowledge transaction must be immediately terminated. The STOP# signal line is used in conjunction with the TRDY# and DEVSEL# signal lines to request a Retry, Disconnect, or Target Abort termination. The PCI bus master completes the memory, I/O, configuration, or interrupt acknowledge transaction with the protocol of the requested termination.

The DEVSEL# signal line must be asserted simultaneously with or prior to the assertion of the STOP# signal line. Once asserted, the STOP# signal line remains asserted until the completion of the memory, I/O, configuration, or interrupt acknowledge transaction.

During Fast Back-to-Back transactions, the assertion of the STOP# signal line must be one CLK signal line period later (minimum) than the earliest possible point for a FAST decode than for a non Fast Back-to-Back cycle condition. Please see the *Fast Back-To-Back* portion of Subchapter 6.10 for details.

SPECIAL TRANSACTIONS

Due to the broadcast nature of the special bus transaction, the STOP# signal line is driven deasserted by a pull-up resistor during the DATA PHASE.

PCI-X SPECIFIC

RESET

The STOP# signal line in conjunction with the DEVSEL# and TRDY# signal lines establish whether the bus segment is PCI or PCI-X, and the CLK signal line frequency. See Chapter 11: *Reset, Power, and Signal Line Initialization* for more information.

PARK AND IDLE PHASE

Same as PCI.

ADDRESS, ATTRIBUTE, AND TARGET RESPONSE PHASES

MEMORY, I/O, CONFIGURATION, SPLIT COMPLETION, INTERRUPT ACKNOWLEDGE, AND SPECIAL TRANSACTIONS

Driven to a logical "1" (deasserted) by a pull-up resistor. Except for the TARGET RESPONSE PHASE of a special transaction, the TRDY# signal line may be driven to logical "1" by either a pull-up resistor or the target.

DATA PHASE

MEMORY, I/O, CONFIGURATION, SPLIT COMPLETION, AND INTERRUPT ACKNOWLEDGE TRANSACTIONS

Driven deasserted (logical "1") by a pull-up resistor or the target. Driven asserted by the target for a Retry, Target Abort, Single Data Phase Disconnect, or Disconnect at Next ADB termination request. The STOP# signal line is driven deasserted by the target at the end of the DATA PHASE.

If no target is selected, the STOP# signal line is driven deasserted by a pull-up resistor.

SPECIAL TRANSACTIONS

Due to the broadcast nature of the special bus transaction, the STOP# signal line is driven deasserted by a pull-up resistor during the DATA PHASE.

> The DEVSEL# signal line must be asserted simultaneously with or prior to the assertion of the STOP# signal line.

IDSEL	Initialization Device Select	Req.	Input (1)	No Pull-up Resistor

Note (1): The AD[31::11] signal lines are used for the IDSEL signal lines for each PCI or PCI-X resource. To the resource, this is always an input pin.

These lines are driven by the PCI bus master to select the configuration space of a specific PCI resource.

In this book, the IDSEL signal lines are driven from the AD signal lines. Platform resources may also drive the IDSEL signal lines by any method independently of the AD signal lines. It is assumed that most every implementation will use the AD signal lines; consequently, this book will only assume this method.

PCI SPECIFIC

RESET

Driven to a stable level by central resource.

PARK

Driven to a stable level by Park master.

IDLE PHASE

Driven to a stable level by PCI bus master if the bus segment ownership is retained. Otherwise these signal lines are tri-stated.

ADDRESS PHASE

CONFIGURATION TRANSACTIONS

Used to select one of the PCI bus resource's configuration registers when the AD[1::0] signal lines = [0::0].

MEMORY, I/O, INTERRUPT ACKNOWLEDGE, AND SPECIAL TRANSACTIONS

These signal lines have no meaning during this phase of these bus transactions.

DATA PHASE

MEMORY, I/O, CONFIGURATION, INTERRUPT ACKNOWLEDGE, AND SPECIAL TRANSACTIONS

These signal lines have no meaning during this phase of these bus transactions.

PCI-X SPECIFIC

RESET, PARK, AND IDLE PHASE

Same as PCI.

ADDRESS PHASE

CONFIGURATION TRANSACTIONS

Same as PCI.

MEMORY, I/O, INTERRUPT ACKNOWLEDGE, SPLIT COMPLATION, AND SPECIAL TRANSACTIONS

These signal lines have no meaning during this phase of these bus transactions.

ATTRIBUTE, TARGET RESPONSE, AND DATA PHASES

MEMORY, I/O, CONFIGURATION, INTERRUPT ACKNOWLEDGE, SPLIT COMPLETION, AND SPECIAL TRANSACTIONS

These signal lines have no meaning during these phases of these bus transactions.

5.3 BUS CONTROL SIGNAL LINES

CLK	PCI or PCI-X Clock	Req.	Input (1)	No Pull-up

Note (1): Driven by central resource.

PCI SPECIFIC

RESET

Always driven by the central resource.

PARK

Always driven by the central resource.

IDLE, ADDRESS, AND DATA PHASES

MEMORY, I/O, CONFIGURATION, INTERRUPT ACKNOWLEDGE, AND SPECIAL TRANSACTIONS

The CLK signal line is driven by the central resource and acts as the synchronous reference point for all PCI bus signal line transitions. All signal lines are sampled on the rising edge of the CLK signal line except for the RST#, INT# A to D#, and the deassertion of the SERR# signal lines.

> The CLK signal line operates in two frequency ranges: 33 MHz and 66 MHz. The "33 MHz" name refers to a maximum frequency of 33.3 MHz. Similarly, the "66 MHz" name refers to a maximum frequency of 66.6 MHz.

The frequency of the 33 MHz CLK signal line can be dynamically changed during bus transactions from 0 (DC) to 33.3 MHz for components on the platform or add-in card. The dynamic change of frequency is required to provide clean clock edges, and the minimum low and high CLK signal line specification must be maintained. If the CLK signal line frequency is reduced to 0 MHz, the state of the signal line must be low. PCI compatible components can restrict the CLK signal line to a single frequency if the component will only be used in the platform and not on an add-in card. At CLK signal line frequencies below 16 MHz, a component can meet this requirement by design, but is not required to be physically tested.

The frequency of the 66 MHz CLK signal line can change from above 33.3 MHz. to 66.6 MHz. The change of frequency can only occur when the PCI bus segment is in reset (RST# signal line asserted). The frequency can also change using the spread spectrum clocking protocol (see Chapter 12: *Signal Line Timing and Electrical Requirements* for more information). As will be discussed in the next section, the assertion of the M66EN signal line will force a 66 MHz CLK signal line to operate at a frequency of 33.3MHz or below. Thus, the deassertion of the MM66EN signal line requires a 66MHz CLK signal line to operate according to the same protocol as a 33 MHz only CLK signal line.

Other specifications of the CLK signal relating to frequency tolerance over temperature changes must comply with the minimum low and high pulse times. See Chapter 12: *Signal Line Timing and Electrical Requirements* for more information.

> If the M66EN signal line is a logical "0", the CLK signal line's maximum frequency is 33 MHz. If the M66EN signal line is a logical "1", the CLK signal line's maximum frequency is 66 MHz.

PCI-X SPECIFIC

RESET

Always driven by the central resource.

PARK

Always driven by the central resource.

IDLE, ADDRESS, ATTRIBUTE, TARGET RESPONSE, AND DATA PHASES

MEMORY, I/O, CONFIGURATION, SPLIT COMPLETION, INTERRUPT ACKNOWLEDGE, AND SPECIAL TRANSACTIONS

Same basic application as a PCI bus segment with the exception of the frequency. The CLK signal line can be driven to a fixed maximum frequency of 33, 66, 100, and 133 MHz on a PCI-X bus segment. The change of frequency can only occur when the PCI-X bus segment is in reset (RST# signal line asserted). The frequency can also change using the spread spectrum clocking protocol (see Chapter 12: *Signal Line Timing and Electrical Requirements* for more information).

M66EN	66MHz ENABLE	Opt.	Input/Output	Pull-up Resistor 5K to Vcc

PCI SPECIFIC

Rev. 2.1 of the PCI bus specification has defined one of the previously reserved pins as M66EN to allow a 66 MHz CLK signal line on a PCI bus segment or platform. When this pin is grounded on a PCI bus segment or add-in card, it forces a 33 MHz CLK signal line operation. On a PCI bus segment that supports a 66 MHz CLK signal line, the M66EN signal line is pulled to V_{cc} with a 5K resistor and is bused to every chip and add-in connector. When a 33 MHz chip or add-in card is installed in a 66 MHz PCI bus, the M66EN pin is pulled to ground. This informs the central resource, any 66 MHz chips, and add-in cards on that specific PCI bus segment that they are required to operate at 33 MHz.

When a 66 MHz chip or add-on card is installed in a 66 MHz PCI bus, the M66EN is either a logical "1" or "0". Logical "1" (via a pull-up resistor) indicates that all PCI resources will operate at 66 MHz. Logical "0" (ground) indicates that at least one PCI resource is 33 MHz only; consequently, the bus must operate at 33 MHz.

> **Note: 66 MHz is only defined for 3.3 volt operation.**

PCI-X SPECIFIC

The PCI-X addendum specification has expanded the interpretation of the M66EN signal line. This signal line provides information to help (along with the PXICAP signal line) determine whether the bus segment is operating in accordance with the PCI local bus specification or the PCI-X addendum specification. See Chapter 11: *Reset, Power, and Signal Line Initialization* for more information.

PXICAP	PCI-X Capable	Req. (1)	Input/Output	Pull-up Resistor 5K to Vcc

Note (1): Required only for PCI-X bus segment.

PCI SPECIFIC

Not defined in the PCI local bus specification. The associated signal line is attached to ground in a PCI bus segment.

PCI-X SPECIFIC

This signal line is defined in the PCI-X addendum specification. The PXICAP signal line is pulled to Vcc with a 5K resistor and is bused to every chip and add-in connector. It is independent of any bus transaction and is sampled during RESET to identify if the bus segment is PCI-X capable. It also defines the CLK signal line frequency. See Chapter 11: *Reset, Power, and Signal Line Initialization* for more information.

RST#	RESET	Req.	Input (1)	No Pull-up Resistor

Note (1): Driven by central resource.

This signal line indicates a RESET of all PCI and PCI-X resources.

PCI SPECIFIC

RESET

Driven to a logical "0" (asserted) by central resource.

PARK

Driven to a logical "1" (deasserted) by central resource.

IDLE, ADDRESS, AND DATA PHASES

MEMORY, I/O, CONFIGURATION, INTERRUPT ACKNOWLEDGE, AND SPECIAL TRANSACTIONS

Driven to a logical "1" (deasserted) by central resource.

PCI-X SPECIFIC

RESET

Driven to a logical "0" (asserted) by central resource.

PARK

Driven to a logical "1" (deasserted) by central resource.

IDLE, ADDRESS, ATTRIBUTE, TARGET RESPONSE, AND DATA PHASES

MEMORY, I/O, CONFIGURATION, SPLIT COMPLETION, INTERRUPT ACKNOWLEDGE, AND SPECIAL TRANSACTIONS

Same basic application as PCI bus segment with the exception of the expanded initialization during RESET. See Chapter 11: *Reset, Power, and Signal Line Initialization* for more information.

LOCK#	Lock	Opt.	Bi-Directional Drive Tri-state	Pull-up Resistor

This signal line indicates that a PCI or PCI-X bus master has locked a PCI or PCI-X resource for its exclusive access.

PCI SPECIFIC

RESET

Driven to a logical "1" (deasserted) by a pull-up resistor.

PARK

Driven to a logical "1" (deasserted) by a pull-up resistor or to a logical "0" (asserted) by Lock master.

IDLE, ADDRESS, AND DATA PHASES

MEMORY AND I/O TRANSACTIONS

The LOCK# signal line can be used (for Exclusive Hardware Access) for memory read and I/O read transactions that originate from the HOST CPU or LEGACY bus master to address deadlock conditions. Under certain conditions, a PCI bus master can also use the LOCK# signal line for Exclusive Hardware Access. The LOCK# signal line can be used for the HOST CPU to access a LEGACY bus memory target. Finally, the LOCK# signal line can be used for the LEGACY bus master to access a PCI memory target.

CONFIGURATION, SPECIAL, AND INTERRUPT ACKNOWLEDGE TRANSACTIONS

The LOCK# signal line is not defined for these bus transactions; consequently, this signal line is ignored for these bus transactions.

PCI-X SPECIFIC

RESET

Driven to a logical "1" (deasserted) by a pull-up resistor.

PARK

Driven to a logical "1" (deasserted) by a pull-up resistor or to a logical "0" (asserted) by Lock master.

IDLE, ADDRESS, ATTRIBUTE, TARGET RESPONSE, AND DATA PHASES

MEMORY, SPLIT COMPLETION, AND I/O TRANSACTIONS

The LOCK# signal line can be used (for Exclusive Hardware Access) for memory read and I/O read transactions that originate from the HOST CPU or LEGACY bus master to address deadlock conditions. Under certain conditions, a PCI bus master can also use the LOCK# signal line for Exclusive Hardware Access. The LOCK# signal line can be used for the HOST CPU to access a LEGACY bus memory target. Finally, the LOCK# signal line can be used for the LEGACY bus master to access a PCI memory target.

CONFIGURATION, SPECIAL, AND INTERRUPT ACKNOWLEDGE TRANSACTIONS

The LOCK# signal line is not defined for these bus transactions; consequently, this signal line is ignored for these bus transactions.

PME# (1)	Power Management Event	Opt. (2)	Open Drain (3)	Pull-up Resistor (4)

Notes:
(1): Revision 2.2 of the PCI local bus specification has redefined a reserved pin to support power management events. The PCI-X addendum specification has also adopted the PME# signal line with the same consderations as the PCI local bus specification.

(2): Systems that do not support power management leave this signal line unconnected. Systems that do support power management connect this signal line between component(s) and/or slot(s) in a bus structure. It can optionally be routed around bridges.

(3): This signal is only an input to the central resource and an output from a PCI or PCI-X resource(s) on the bus segment.

(4): The pull-up resistor is only required in systems that support power management.

This signal line indicates to the central resource that a PCI or PCI-X resource(s) on the bus segment is requesting a power management event. The PME# signal line can only be asserted after the software has set the PME_EN bit in the (Power Management Control/Status (PMCSR) register in the configuration address space. See the books *PCI Bus Power Management* and *PCI Hot Plug Application and*

Design (available at www.annabooks.com), and the *PCI-X addendum bus specification* for more information.

The PME# signal line is unique relative to the other PCI signal lines. The design of the PME# signal line must take into account the following:

- If power is applied to the PME# signal line, the component will not be damaged regardless of the voltage on the V_{cc} signal line, or even if V_{cc} is not connected to any power source.

- A PCI or PCI-X resource must not assert the signal line (driven to V_{ol}) unless the resource is intentionally requesting a power management event.

- PCI or PCI-X resources powered by a battery or some other power source independent of the system power source are required to maintain the value of the PME_Status indication bit in the PMCSR register in the configuration address space through bus segment reset.

The PME# signal line is routed to all resources in the system that need to know about a power management event. The output from the central resource to identify a power management event may be an interrupt, a change in a register value, or some other event. The PCI and PCI-X resources on the bus segment should treat this signal line as an output from the PCI or PCI-X resource, but it is possible that the PME# signal line can also be an input to any PCI PCI-X resource.

The PME# signal line is asynchronous to the CLK signal line. The open drain characteristic allows multiple PCI or PCI-X resources to assert this signal line. Once this signal line is asserted it cannot be deasserted until software has cleared the PME_EN bit or the PME_Status bit in the PMCSR register in the configuration address space. See the *PCI Bus Power Management Interface Specification Revision 1.0* or *PCI Bus Power Management,* and *PCI Hot Plug Application and Design* books, and the PCI-X addendum bus specification for more information. The deassertion of the PME# signal line relies on a pull-up resistor and not a short active pulse; consequently, this signal line is considered asserted until sampled deasserted for two consecutive CLK signal line periods.

Note: The following definitions only apply to a system that supports power management events as defined by the *PCI Bus Power Management* and *PCI Hot Plug Application and Design* books (available at www.annabooks.com), and the *PCI-X addendum bus specification.*

PCI SPECIFIC

RESET

Driven to a logical "1" (deasserted) by a pull-up resistor.

PARK

Does not apply to a specific bus transaction. This signal line operates independently of bus transactions. PCI resource will assert when a power management event is requested.

IDLE PHASE

Does not apply to a specific transaction. This signal line operates independently of bus transactions. PCI resource will assert when a power management event is requested.

ADDRESS AND DATA PHASES

MEMORY, I/O, CONFIGURATION, INTERRUPT ACKNOWLEDGE, AND SPECIAL TRANSACTIONS

Does not apply to a specific bus transaction. This signal line operates independently of bus transactions. PCI resource will assert when a power management event is requested.

PCI-X SPECIFIC

RESET, PARK, AND IDLE PHASE

Same as PCI.

ADDRESS, ATTRIBUTE, TARGET RESPONSE, AND DATA PHASES

MEMORY, I/O, SPLIT COMPLETION,CONFIGURATION, INTERRUPT ACKNOWLEDGE, AND SPECIAL TRANSACTIONS

Does not apply to a specific bus transaction. This signal line operates independently of bus transactions. PCI resource will assert when a power management event is requested.

5.4 ERROR REPORTING SIGNAL LINES

PERR#	Parity Error	Req.	Bi-Directional Drive Tri-state	Pull-up Resistor

This signal line indicates a data parity error in the AD, C/BE#, PAR, and PAR64 signal lines during the DATA PHASE.

PCI SPECIFIC

RESET

Driven to a logical "1" (deasserted) by a pull-up resistor.

PARK

Driven to a logical "1" (deasserted) by a pull-up resistor.

IDLE PHASE

Driven to a logical "1" (deasserted) by a pull-up resistor.

ADDRESS PHASE

MEMORY, I/O, CONFIGURATION, INTERRUPT ACKNOWLEDGE, AND SPECIAL TRANSACTIONS

This signal line is not defined for the ADDRESS PHASE. Assertion of this signal line in the ADDRESS PHASE is reflective of the DATA PHASE of the preceding bus transaction.

DATA PHASE

MEMORY, I/O, CONFIGURATION, AND INTERRUPT ACKNOWLEDGE TRANSACTIONS

The PERR# signal line reports parity errors detected over the AD, C/BE#, PAR, and PAR64 signal lines during the DATA PHASE. The PCI bus master will drive this signal line during Memory, I/O, Configuration, and Interrupt Acknowledge Transactions. The target will drive this signal line during memory write, I/O write, and configuration write transactions. The PERR# signal line must be asserted for each data access (IRDY# and TRDY# signal lines asserted) for a minimum of one CLK signal line period whenever a parity error occurs. To report a parity error, the PERR# signal line must be asserted two CLK signal line periods after the data is accessed. If a BURST access cycle is being executed, the PERR# signal line is asserted for multiple CLK signal line periods provided a parity error occurred on the associated microaccesses.

The PERR# signal line is monitored by the central resource (and PCI bus master during a memory write, I/O write, or configuration write transactions). Parity errors can be reported by several means including the assertion of the SERR# signal line.

SPECIAL TRANSACTIONS

The PERR# signal line cannot be used to report parity errors on the AD[31::0], C/BE#[3::0], and PAR signal lines during the DATA PHASE of special transactions. The special transactions broadcast data to all target resources; consequently, no single target resource can claim the PERR# signal line.

The DEVSEL# signal line must be asserted two CLK signal line periods prior to the assertion of the PERR# signal line.

PCI-X SPECIFIC

RESET, PARK, AND IDLE PHASE

Same as PCI.

ADDRESS AND ATTRIBUTE RESPONSE PHASES

MEMORY, I/O, SPLIT COMPLETION, CONFIGURATION, INTERRUPT ACKNOWLEDGE, AND SPECIAL TRANSACTIONS

This signal line is not defined for these PHASES for these bus transactions. Assertion of this signal line is in the ADDRESS PHASE is reflective of the DATA PHASE of the preceding bus transaction.

TARGET RESPONSE PHASE

MEMORY, I/O, SPLIT COMPLETION, CONFIGURATION, INTERRUPT ACKNOWLEDGE, AND SPECIAL TRANSACTIONS

Parity is not checked for the TARGET RESPONSE PHASE.

DATA PHASE

MEMORY, I/O, SPLIT COMPLETION, CONFIGURATION, AND INTERRUPT ACKNOWLEDGE TRANSACTIONS

The PERR# signal line reports parity errors detected over the AD, C/BE#, PAR, and PAR64 signal lines during the DATA PHASE. The PCI-X bus master will drive this signal line during memory read, I/O read, configuration read, and interrupt acknowledge transactions. The target will drive this signal line during memory write, I/O write, configuration write, and split completion transactions. The PERR# signal line must be asserted for each data access (IRDY# and TRDY# signal lines asserted at each CLK signal line rising edge) for a minimum of one CLK signal line period whenever a parity error occurs. To report a parity error, the PERR# signal line must be asserted two CLK signal line periods after the data is accessed. If a BURST bus transaction is being executed, the PERR# signal line is asserted for multiple CLK signal line periods provided a parity error occurred on the associated microaccesses.

The PERR# signal line is monitored by the central resource (and PCI-X bus master during memory write, I/O write, configuration write, and split completions). Parity errors can be reported by several means including the assertion of the SERR# signal line.

SPECIAL TRANSACTIONS

The PERR# signal line cannot be used to report parity errors on the AD[31::0], C/BE#[3::0], and PAR signal lines during the DATA PHASE of special transactions. Special transactions broadcast data to all target resources; consequently, no single target resource can claim the PERR# signal line.

> The DEVSEL# signal line must be asserted two CLK signal line periods prior to the assertion of the PERR# signal line.

SERR#	System Error	Req.	Open Drain (1)	Pull-up Resistor

Note (1): This signal line is only an input to central resource.

This signal line indicates an address parity error in the AD, C/BE#, PAR, and PAR64 signal lines during the ADDRESS PHASE. It is also used for catastrophic PCI and PCI-X bus segment errors.

> SERR# is synchronous to the CLK signal line when asserted. However, the rise time of the open collector provides an asynchronous characteristic to this signal line. Consequently, this book defines this as an asynchronous signal line to emphasize the deassertion protocol.

> The SERR# signal line is asserted synchronously with the CLK signal line for one CLK signal line period and is then tri-stated. The open drain characteristic allows the central resource and multiple PCI resources to simultaneously assert this signal line. The deassertion of this signal line relies on a pull-up resistor and not on a short active pulse; consequently, the deassertion is asynchronous to the CLK signal line. Once the SERR# signal line is asserted it is considered asserted until sampled deasserted for two consecutive CLK signal line periods. The SERR# signal line can be asserted by the central resource or any of the PCI resources for any error condition. The platform's reaction to an asserted SERR# signal line is not specified by the PCI bus specification. However, a resource that asserts the SERR# signal line must assume that the HOST CPU NMI (non-maskable interrupt) will be asserted.

PCI SPECIFIC

RESET

Driven to a logical "1" (deasserted) by a pull-up resistor.

PARK

Driven to a logical "1" (deasserted) by a pull-up resistor.

IDLE PHASE

Driven to a logical "1" (deasserted) by a pull-up resistor.

ADDRESS PHASE

MEMORY, I/O, CONFIGURATION, INTERRUPT ACKNOWLEDGE, AND SPECIAL TRANSACTIONS

The SERR# signal line reports parity errors detected over the AD, C/BE#, PAR, and PAR64 signal lines during the ADDRESS PHASE. It can be asserted by the central resource or any PCI resource independently of the PCI bus master and target resources involved in the bus transaction. Also, the SERR# signal line may be asserted during the ADDRESS PHASE by any PCI resource for any error condition.

DATA PHASE

MEMORY, I/O, CONFIGURATION, AND INTERRUPT ACKNOWLEDGE TRANSACTIONS

This signal line is not defined for the DATA PHASE directly. Assertion of this signal line reflects other unrelated bus errors or the assertion of the PERR# signal line.

SPECIAL TRANSACTIONS

The SERR# signal line reports parity errors detected over the AD[31::0], C/BE#[3::0], and PAR signal lines during the DATA PHASE of special transactions. The PERR# signal line cannot be used to report this error during a special transaction because a target resource cannot claim the access cycle.

PCI-X SPECIFIC

RESET, PARK, AND IDLE PHASE

Same as PCI.

ADDRESS AND ATTRIBUTE PHASES

MEMORY, I/O, SPLIT COMPLETION, CONFIGURATION, INTERRUPT ACKNOWLEDGE, AND SPECIAL TRANSACTIONS

The SERR# signal line reports parity errors detected over the AD, C/BE#, PAR, and PAR64 signal lines during the ADDRESS PHASE. It can be asserted by the central resource or any PCI-X resource independently of the PCI-X bus master and target resources involved in the bus transaction. Also, the SERR# signal line may be asserted during the ADDRESS PHASE by any PCI-X resource for any error condition.

TARGET RESPONSE PHASE

MEMORY, I/O, SPLIT COMPLETION, CONFIGURATION, INTERRUPT ACKNOWLEDGE, AND SPECIAL TRANSACTIONS

Parity is not checked for the TARGET RESPONSE PHASE.

DATA PHASE

MEMORY, I/O, SPLIT COMPLETION, CONFIGURATION, AND INTERRUPT ACKNOWLEDGE TRANSACTIONS

This signal line is not defined for the DATA PHASE directly. Assertion of this signal line reflects other unrelated bus errors or the assertion of the PERR# signal line.

SPECIAL TRANSACTIONS

The SERR# signal line reports parity errors detected over the AD[31::0], C/BE#[3::0], and PAR signal lines during the DATA PHASE of special transactions. The PERR# signal line cannot be used to report this error during a special transaction because a target resource cannot claim the special transaction.

5.5   64 DATA BIT SIGNAL LINES

The PCI and PCI-X bus segments support 32 data bits as the standard data width. Accesses to memory resources have been extended to support a 64 bit data width. In addition to the REQ64# and ACK64# signal lines, a 64 data bit access also requires the AD[63::32], C/BE#[7::4], and PAR64 signal lines.

64 data bit I/O targets can be implemented for a PCI bus segment according to the PCI local bus specification. However, there are no benefits justifying the increased complexity, and it is therefore strongly recommended that 64 data bit I/O targets not be implemented. For a PCI-X bus segment specified by the PCI-X addendum specification, no 64 data bit I/O targets can be implemented. For the purposes of this book, I/O targets are only 32 data bits in size. If a 64 data bit I/O target is implemented on a PCI bus segment, the 64 data bit protocol applied to memory targets also applies to I/O targets.

AD[63::32]	ADDRESS and DATA	Opt.	Bi-Directional Tri-state	Pull-up Resistors

When PCI or PCI-X 64 data bit resources are attached to a 32 data bit PCI or PCI-X bus segment or connector, they must insure that 64 data bit related signal lines do not oscillate. Each PCI or PCI-X resource can drive the AD[63::32] signal lines as outputs (stable level), or if an input, can be biased to a stable level. These and other solutions are allowed, provided the input leakage current specification is not violated. External resistors on an add-in card are not allowed. PCI or PCI-X resources attached to a 64 data bit bus segment can rely on pull-up resistors to Vcc on the bus segment to drive these signal lines to a logical "1".

PCI SPECIFIC

AD[63::32] SIGNAL LINES WITH A 32 DATA BIT PCI BUS MASTER (REQ64# DEASSERTED BY PULL-UP RESISTOR)

RESET

Driven to a logical "1" by pull-up resistors.

PARK

Driven to a logical "1" by pull-up resistors.

IDLE PHASE

Driven to a logical "1" by pull-up resistors.

ADDRESS AND DATA PHASES

MEMORY, I/O, CONFIGURATION, INTERRUPT ACKNOWLEDGE, AND SPECIAL TRANSACTIONS

These signal lines are driven to a logical "1" by pull-up resistors.

AD[63::32] SIGNAL LINES WITH A 64 DATA BIT PCI BUS MASTER (REQ64# ASSERTED)

RESET

Driven to a logical "1" by pull-up resistors.

PARK

Driven to a logical "1" by pull-up resistors.

IDLE PHASE

Driven to a logical "1" (deasserted) by the PCI bus master if the bus segment ownership is retained. Otherwise these signal lines are tri-stated and driven to logical '1' by pull-up resistors.

ADDRESS PHASE

MEMORY TRANSACTIONS

These signal lines are driven to a stable level by the PCI bus master when DUAL ADDRESS command is not executed. Alternatively, the PCI bus master does not have to drive these signal lines and can rely on the pull-up resistors to drive these signal line to logical "1". When the DUAL ADDRESS command is executed, these signal lines are driven by the PCI bus master with the upper order address bits for a 64-bit address space.

I/O, CONFIGURATION, INTERRUPT ACKNOWLEDGE, AND SPECIAL TRANSACTIONS

An I/O, configuration, special, or interrupt acknowledge transaction is not defined for 64 data bit bus transactions. Consequently, the asserted REQ64# signal line is ignored and these signal lines operate as previously defined for a 32 data bit PCI bus master.

DATA PHASE

MEMORY TRANSACTIONS

The least significant data byte is on signal lines AD[39::32] with the most significant data byte on signal lines AD[63::56]. The data being accessed is the upper order double word (*i.e.*, AD[2] signal line = logical "0" during ADDRESS PHASE). If the ACK64# signal line is asserted, these signal lines contain valid data. For memory write transactions, these signal lines are driven by the PCI bus master. For memory read transactions, these signal lines are driven by the target.

If the ACK64# signal line is deasserted, these signal lines may or may not contain valid information. These signal lines contain valid data during the initial microaccess of a SINGLE or BURST bus transaction. During subsequent microaccesses for a BURST memory write transaction, the PCI bus master can drive these signal lines to a stable level or logical "1", or tri-state them (if tri-stated, driven to logical "1" by pull-up resistors). During subsequent microaccesses for a BURST memory read transaction, these signal lines are tri-stated and driven to a logical "1" by pull-up resistors.

If the ACK64# signal line is asserted, only those AD[63::32] signal lines indicated as valid by the C/BE#[7::4] signal lines have valid data. Those that are indicated as invalid do not contain data but must be driven to a stable level. For a memory write transaction, the PCI bus master is responsible for driving the AD[63::32] signal lines, and for a memory read transaction the target is responsible for driving the AD[63::32] signal lines. Under prefetchable memory conditions, all of the AD signal lines have valid read data independent of the C/BE# signal lines.

I/O, CONFIGURATION, INTERRUPT ACKNOWLEDGE, AND SPECIAL TRANSACTIONS

An I/O, configuration, special, or interrupt acknowledge transaction is not defined for 64 data bit bus transactions. Consequently, the asserted REQ64# signal line is ignored and these signal lines operate as previously defined for a 32 data bit PCI bus master.

ALSO CONSIDER:

AD[31::0] SIGNAL LINES WITH A 64 DATA BIT PCI BUS MASTER (REQ64# ASSERTED)

Same as a 32 data bit PCI bus master.

PCI-X SPECIFIC

AD[63::32] SIGNAL LINES WITH A 32 DATA BIT PCI-X BUS MASTER (REQ64# DEASSERTED BY PULL-UP RESISTOR)

RESET, PARK, AND IDLE PHASE

Same as PCI.

ADDRESS, ATTRIBUTE, TARGET RESPONSE, AND DATA PHASES

MEMORY, I/O, SPLIT COMPLETION, CONFIGURATION, INTERRUPT ACKNOWLEDGE, AND SPECIAL TRANSACTIONS

These signal lines are tri-stated and driven to a logical "1" by pull-up resistors.

AD[63::32] SIGNAL LINES WITH A 64 DATA BIT PCI-X BUS MASTER (REQ64# ASSERTED)

RESET, PARK, AND IDLE PHASE

Same as PCI.

ADDRESS AND ATTRIBUTE PHASES

MEMORY (EXCLUDING DWORD) AND SPLIT COMPLETION TRANSACTIONS

During the ADDRESS PHASE, these signal lines are driven to a stable level or tri-stated (if tri-stated, driven to logical "1" by pull-up resistors) by the PCI-X bus master when the DUAL ADDRESS command is not executed. When the DUAL

293

ADDRESS command is executed (not applicable to split completion), these signal lines are driven by the PCI-X bus master with the upper order address bits for a 64 bit address space in the ADDRESS PHASE. During the ATTRIBUTE PHASE, these signal lines are driven to a logical "1" by the PCI-X bus master.

DWORD, I/O, CONFIGURATION, INTERRUPT ACKNOWLEDGE, AND SPECIAL TRANSACTIONS

DWORD, I/O, configuration, special, or interrupt acknowledge transactions are not defined for 64 data bit bus transactions. Consequently, the asserted REQ64# signal line is ignored. These signal lines are driven to a stable level or tri-stated and driven to a logical "1" by pull-up resistors.

TARGET RESPONSE PHASE

MEMORY, I/O, SPLIT COMPLETION, CONFIGURATION, INTERRUPT ACKNOWLEDGE, AND SPECIAL TRANSACTIONS

These signal lines are driven to a stable level or tri-stated by the PCI-X bus master. If tri-stated, these signal lines are driven to logical "1" by pull-up resistors. For memory read transactions to 64 data bit targets, the TARGET RESPONSE PHASE is the exchange of ownership of these signal lines, and the PCI-X bus master will tri-state these signal lines.

DATA PHASE

MEMORY (EXCLUDING DWORD) AND SPLIT COMPLETION TRANSACTIONS

The least significant data byte is on signal lines AD[39::32] with the most significant data byte on signal lines AD[63::56]. The data being accessed is the upper order double word. If the ACK64# signal line is asserted, these signal lines contain valid data. For memory write and split completion transactions, these signal lines are driven by the PCI-X bus master. For memory read transactions, these signal lines are driven by the target.

If the ACK64# signal line is deasserted, these signal lines may or may not contain valid information. The AD[63::32] signal lines contain valid data driven by the PCI-X bus master during the initial microaccess of SINGLE or BURST bus transactions for BURST memory write and split completion commands. During subsequent microaccesses for BURST memory write or a split completion transaction, the PCI-X bus master can drive these signal lines to a stable level or tri-state them. (If tri-stated, they are driven to logical "1" by pull-up resistors.) The

AD[63::32] signal lines are tri-stated during all microaccesses of SINGLE or BURST bus transactions for BURST memory read commands. If not driven by the target, these signal lines are driven to a logical "1" by pull-up resistors.

If the ACK64# signal line is asserted for a memory write transaction (not including memory write block or alias memory write block), those AD[63::32] signal lines indicated as valid by the C/BE#[7::4] signal lines have valid data. Those that are indicated as invalid do not contain data but are required to be driven to a stable level. If the ACK64# signal line is asserted for a split completion transaction, a memory write block transaction, or an alias memory write block transaction, all of the AD[63::32] signal lines are defined as valid. If the ACK64# signal line is asserted for a memory read transaction, all of the AD[63::32] signal lines are defined as valid. For memory write or split completion transactions, the PCI-X bus master is responsible for driving the AD[63::32] signal lines, and for memory read transactions the target is responsible for driving the AD[63::32] signal lines.

DWORD, I/O, CONFIGURATION, INTERRUPT ACKNOWLEDGE, AND SPECIAL TRANSACTIONS

DWORD, I/O, configuration, special, or interrupt acknowledge transactions are not defined for 64 data bit bus transactions. Consequently, the asserted REQ64# signal line is ignored. These signal lines are tri-stated and driven to a logical "1" by pull-up resistors.

ALSO CONSIDER:

AD[31::0] SIGNAL LINES WITH A 64 DATA BIT PCI-X BUS MASTER (REQ64# ASSERTED)

Same as a 32 data bit PCI-X bus master

C/BE#[7::4]	Bus Command and Byte Enables	Opt.	Bi-Directional Tri-state	Pull-up Resistors

When PCI or PCI-X 64 data bit resources are attached to a 32 data bit PCI or PCI-X bus segment or connector they must insure that 64 data bit related signal lines do not oscillate. Each PCI or PCI-X resource can drive the C/BE#[7::4] signal lines as outputs (stable level), or as inputs, can be biased to a stable level. These and other solutions are allowed, provided that the input leakage current specification is not violated. External resistors on an add-in card are not allowed. PCI or PCI-X resources attached to a 64 data bit bus segment can rely on pull-up resistors to Vcc on the bus segment to drive them to a logical "1".

PCI SPECIFIC

C/BE#[7::4] SIGNAL LINES WITH A 32 DATA BIT PCI BUS MASTER (REQ64# DEASSERTED BY PULL-UP RESISTOR)

RESET

Driven to a logical "1" by pull-up resistors.

PARK

Driven to a logical "1" by pull-up resistors.

IDLE PHASE

Driven to a logical "1" by pull-up resistors.

ADDRESS PHASE

MEMORY, I/O, CONFIGURATION, INTERRUPT ACKNOWLEDGE, AND SPECIAL TRANSACTIONS

Driven to a stable logical "1" by pull-up resistors.

DATA PHASE

MEMORY, I/O, CONFIGURATION, INTERRUPT ACKNOWLEDGE, AND SPECIAL TRANSACTIONS

Driven to a stable logical "1" by pull-up resistors.

C/BE#[7::4] SIGNAL LINES WITH A 64 DATA BIT PCI BUS MASTER (REQ64# ASSERTED)

RESET

Driven to a logical "1" by pull-up resistors.

PARK

Driven to a logical "1" by pull-up resistors.

IDLE PHASE

Driven to a logical "1" (deasserted) by the PCI bus master if the bus segment ownership is retained. Otherwise these signal lines are tri-stated and driven to logical '1" by pull-up resistors.

ADDRESS PHASE

MEMORY TRANSACTIONS

These signal lines are driven to a stable level by the PCI bus master when a DUAL ADDRESS command is not executed. Alternatively, the PCI bus master does not have to drive these signal lines and can rely on the pull-up resistors to drive these signal lines to logical "1". When the DUAL ADDRESS command is executed these signal lines are driven by the PCI bus master and contain the COMMAND type of the memory transaction.

I/O, CONFIGURATION, INTERRUPT ACKNOWLEDGE, AND SPECIAL TRANSACTIONS

An I/O, configuration, special, or interrupt acknowledge transaction is not defined for 64 data bit bus transactions. Consequently, the asserted REQ64# signal line is ignored and these signal lines operate as previously defined for a 32 data bit PCI bus master.

DATA PHASE

MEMORY TRANSACTIONS

The C/BE#[7::4] signal lines indicate which byte lanes of the AD[63::32] signal lines contain valid data. If the ACK64# signal line is asserted, these signal lines contain valid byte lane information.

If the ACK64# signal line is deasserted, these signal lines may or may not contain valid information. These signal lines contain valid byte lane information during the initial microaccess of a SINGLE or BURST bus transaction. During subsequent microaccesses of a BURST bus transaction, the PCI bus master can drive these signal lines to a stable level or logical "1", or tri-state them (if tri-stated, they will be driven to logical "1" by pull-up resistors).

I/O, CONFIGURATION, SPECIAL, AND INTERRUPT ACKNOWLEDGE TRANSACTIONS

An I/O, configuration, special, or interrupt acknowledge transaction is not defined for 64 data bit bus transactions. Consequently, the asserted REQ64# signal line is ignored and these signal lines operate as previously defined for a 32 data bit PCI bus master.

ALSO CONSIDER:

C/BE#[3::0] SIGNAL LINES WITH A 64 DATA BIT PCI BUS MASTER (REQ64# ASSERTED).

Same as a 32 data bit PCI bus master.

PCI-X SPECIFIC

C/BE#[7::4] SIGNAL LINES WITH A 32 DATA BIT PCI-X BUS MASTER (REQ64# DEASSERTED BY PULL-UP RESISTOR)

RESET, PARK, AND IDLE PHASE

Same as PCI.

ADDRESS, ATTRIBUTE, TARGET RESPONSE, AND DATA PHASES

MEMORY, I/O, SPLIT COMPLETION, CONFIGURATION, INTERRUPT ACKNOWLEDGE, AND SPECIAL TRANSACTIONS

These signal lines are driven to a logical "1" by pull-up resistors.

C/BE#[7::4] SIGNAL LINES WITH A 64 DATA BIT PCI-X BUS MASTER (REQ64# ASSERTED)

RESET, PARK, AND IDLE PHASE

Same as PCI.

ADDRESS PHASE

MEMORY (EXCLUDING DWORD) AND SPLIT COMPLETION TRANSACTIONS

These signal lines are driven to a stable level or tri-stated (if tri-stated, driven to logical "1" by pull-up resistors) by the PCI-X bus master when the DUAL ADDRESS command is not executed. When the DUAL ADDRESS command is executed (not applicable to split completion), these signal lines are driven by the PCI-X bus master with the COMMAND type of the memory transaction in the ADDRESS PHASE. Also, when the DUAL ADDRESS command is executed, these signal lines are driven to logical "1" by the PCI-X bus master in the ATTRIBUTE PHASE.

DWORD, I/O, CONFIGURATION, INTERRUPT ACKNOWLEDGE, AND SPECIAL TRANSACTIONS

DWORD, I/O, configuration, special, or interrupt acknowledge transactions are not defined for 64 data bit bus transactions. Consequently, the asserted REQ64# signal line is ignored. These signal lines are driven to a stable level or tri-stated and driven to a logical "1" by pull-up resistors.

ATTRUBUTE AND TARGET RESPONSE PHASES

MEMORY (EXCLUDING DWORD), I/O, SPLIT COMPLETION, CONFIGURATION, INTERRUPT ACKNOWLEDGE, AND SPECIAL TRANSACTIONS

These signal lines are driven to logical "1" by the PCI-X bus master.

DWORD, I/O , CONFIGURATION, INTERRUPT ACKNOWLEDGE, AND SPECIAL TRANSACTIONS

DWORD, I/O, configuration, special, or interrupt acknowledge transactions are not defined for 64 data bit bus transactions. Consequently, the asserted REQ64# signal line is ignored. These signal lines are driven to a stable level or tri-stated and driven to a logical "1" by pull-up resistors.

DATA PHASE

MEMORY (EXCLUDING DWORD) AND SPLIT COMPLETION TRANSACTIONS

If the ACK64# signal line is asserted, these signal lines contain valid byte lane information of a bus transaction for a BURST memory write (not including memory write block or alias memory write block) command. The C/BE#[7::4] signal lines indicate which byte lanes of the AD[63::32] signal lines contain valid data. For bus transactions for BURST split completion, BURST memory write block, BURST alias memory write block, or BURST memory read commands, the C/BE#[7::4] signal lines are driven to logical "1" by the PCI-X bus master

If the ACK64# signal line is deasserted, these signal lines may or may not contain valid information. These signal lines contain valid byte lane information during the initial microaccess of a SINGLE or BURST bus transaction for a BURST memory write (not including memory write block or alias memory write block) command. During subsequent microaccesses of a BURST bus transaction for a BURST memory write (not including memory write block or alias memory write block) command, these signal lines are driven to a stable level or tri-stated (if tri-stated, driven to logical "1" by pull-up resistors) by the PCI-X bus master. During the initial microaccess, the C/BE#[7::4] signal lines are driven to logical "1" by the PCI-X bus master for the SINGLE and BURST bus transactions for BURST memory read, BURST memory write block, BURST alias memory write block, and BURST split completion commands. During subsequent microaccesses of a BURST bus transaction for a BURST memory read, BURST memory write block, BURST alias memory write block, and BURST split completion commands, these signal lines are driven to a stable level or tri-stated (if tri-stated, driven to logical "1" by pull-up resistors) by the PCI-X bus master.

DWORD, I/O , CONFIGURATION , INTERRUPT ACKNOWLEDGE, AND SPECIAL TRANSACTIONS

DWORD, I/O, configuration, special, or interrupt acknowledge transactions are not defined for 64 data bit bus transactions. Consequently, the asserted REQ64# signal line is ignored. These signal lines are tri-stated and driven to a logical "1" by pull-up resistors.

ALSO CONSIDER:

C/BE#[3::0] SIGNAL LINES WITH A 64 DATA BIT PCI-X BUS MASTER (REQ64# ASSERTED)

Same as a 32 data bit PCI-X bus master

PAR64	Parity 64	Opt.	Bi-Directional Tri-state	Pull-up Resistor

When PCI or PCI-X 64 data bit resources are attached to a 32 data bit PCI or PCI-X bus segment or connector, they must insure that the 64 data bit related signal lines do not oscillate. Each PCI or PCI-X resource can drive the PAR64# signal line as an output (stable level), or as inputs, can be biased to a stable level. These and other solutions are allowed, provided that the input leakage current specification is not violated. External resistors on an add-in card are not allowed. The PCI or PCI-X resources that are attached to a 64 data bit bus segment can rely on a pull-up resistor to Vcc on the bus segment to drive this signal line to a logical "1".

PCI SPECIFIC

PAR64 SIGNAL LINE WITH A 32 DATA BIT PCI BUS MASTER (REQ64# DEASSERTED BY PULL-UP RESISTOR).

RESET

Driven to a logical "1" by a pull-up resistor.

PARK

Driven to a logical "1" by a pull-up resistor.

> This signal line lags the AD signal lines by one CLK signal line period. Consequently, what is defined for the IDLE, ADDRESS, and DATA PHASES below is actually one CLK signal period later.

IDLE PHASE

Driven to a logical "1" by a pull-up resistor.

ADDRESS AND DATA PHASES

MEMORY, I/O, CONFIGURATION, INTERRUPT ACKNOWLEDGE, AND SPECIAL TRANSACTIONS

This signal line is tri-stated and driven to a logical "1" by a pull-up resistor.

PAR64 SIGNAL LINE WITH A 64 DATA BIT PCI BUS MASTER (REQ64# ASSERTED)

RESET

Driven to a logical "1" by a pull-up resistor.

PARK

Driven to a logical "1" by a pull-up resistor.

> This signal line lags the AD signal lines by one CLK signal line period. Consequently, what is defined for the IDLE, ADDRESS, and DATA PHASES below is actually one CLK signal period later.

IDLE PHASE

Driven to a logical "1" (deasserted) by PCI bus master if the bus segment ownership is retained. Otherwise this signal line is tri-stated and driven to logical '1" by a pull-up resistor.

ADDRESS PHASE

MEMORY TRANSACTIONS

The PAR64 signal line is driven to a stable level by the PCI bus master when a DUAL ADDRESS command is not executed. Alternatively, the PCI bus master does not have to drive this signal line and can rely on the pull-up resistor to drive this signal line to logical "1". When the DUAL ADDRESS command is executed, the PAR64 signal line is driven by the PCI bus master to provide even parity over the AD[63::32] and C/BE#[7::3] signal lines. The total number of "1"s over these signal lines including the PAR64 signal line is an even number.

I/O, CONFIGURATION, INTERRUPT ACKNOWLEDGE, AND SPECIAL TRANSACTIONS

Special or interrupt acknowledge transactions are not defined for 64 data bit bus transactions. Consequently, the asserted REQ64# signal line is ignored and these signal lines operate as previously defined for a 32 data bit PCI bus master.

DATA PHASE

MEMORY TRANSACTIONS

The PAR64 signal line is driven to provide even parity over the AD[63::32] and C/BE#[7::4] signal lines. The total number of "1"s over these signal lines including the PAR64 signal line is an even number.

If the ACK64# signal line is deasserted, the PAR64 signal line may or may not contain provide valid parity information. The PAR64 signal line contains valid parity during the initial microaccess of a SINGLE or BURST bus transaction. During subsequent microaccesses for a BURST memory write transaction, the PCI bus master can drive the PAR64 signal line to a stable level, or tri-state this signal line (if tri-stated, it is driven to logical "1" by a pull-up resistor). During

303

subsequent microaccesses for a BURST memory read transaction, this signal line is tri-stated and driven to a logical "1" by a pull-up resistor.

If the ACK64# signal line is asserted, the PAR64 signal line provides valid parity information. For memory write transactions, it is driven by the PCI bus master. For memory read transactions, it is driven by the target.

I/O, CONFIGURATION, INTERRUPT ACKNOWLEDGE, AND SPECIAL TRANSACTIONS

An I/O, configuration, special, or interrupt acknowledge transaction is not defined for 64 data bit bus transactions. Consequently, the asserted REQ64# signal line is ignored and these signal lines operate as previously defined for a 32 data bit PCI bus master.

ALSO CONSIDER:

PAR64 SIGNAL LINE WITH A 64 DATA BIT PCI BUS MASTER (REQ64# ASSERTED)

Same as a 32 data bit PCI bus master.

PCI-X SPECIFIC

PAR64 SIGNAL LINE WITH A 32 DATA BIT PCI-X BUS MASTER (REQ64# DEASSERTED BY PULL-UP RESISTOR)

RESET, PARK, AND IDLE PHASE

Same as PCI.

> This signal line lags the AD signal lines by one CLK signal line period. Consequently, what is defined for the IDLE (above), ADDRESS, ATTRIBUTE, TARGET RESPONSE, and DATA PHASES (below) is actually one CLK signal period later.

ADDRESS, ATTRIBUTE, TARGET RESPONSE, AND DATA PHASES

MEMORY, I/O, SPLIT COMPLETION, CONFIGURATION, INTERRUPT ACKNOWLEDGE, AND SPECIAL TRANSACTIONS

This signal line is tri-stated and driven to a logical "1" by a pull-up resistor.

PAR64 SIGNAL LINE WITH A 64 DATA BIT PCI-X BUS MASTER (REQ64# ASSERTED)

RESET, PARK, AND IDLE PHASE

Same as PCI.

> This signal line lags the AD signal lines by one CLK signal line period. Consequently, what is defined for the IDLE (above), ADDRESS, ATTRIBUTE, TARGET RESPONSE, and DATA PHASES (below) is actually one CLK signal period later.

ADDRESS AND ATTRIBUTE PHASES

MEMORY (EXCLUDING DWORD) AND SPLIT COMPLETION TRANSACTIONS

During the ADDRESS PHASE, this signal line is driven to a stable level or tri-stated (if tri-stated, driven to logical "1" by a pull-up resistor) by the PCI-X bus master when DUAL ADDRESS command is not executed. When the DUAL ADDRESS command is executed (not applicable to split completion), this signal line is driven by the PCI-X bus master with the parity information in the ADDRESS PHASE. During the ATTRIBUTE PHASE, this signal line is driven by the PCI-X bus master with valid parity.

DWORD, I/O, CONFIGURATION, INTERRUPT ACKNOWLEDGE, AND SPECIAL TRANSACTIONS

DWORD, I/O, configuration, special, or interrupt acknowledge transactions are not defined for 64 data bit bus transactions. Consequently, the asserted REQ64# signal line is ignored. This signal line is driven to a stable level or tri-stated and driven to a logical "1" by a pull-up resistor.

TARGET RESPONSE PHASE

MEMORY, I/O, SPLIT COMPLETION, CONFIGURATION, INTERRUPT ACKNOWLEDGE, AND SPECIAL TRANSACTIONS

This signal line is driven to a stable level or tri-stated. If tri-stated, this signal line is driven to logical "1" by a pull-up resistor. For memory read transactions to 64 data bit targets, the TARGET RESPONSE PHASE is the exchange of ownership of this signal line.

DATA PHASE

MEMORY (EXCLUDING DWORD) AND SPLIT COMPLETION TRANSACTIONS

The PAR64 signal line is driven to provide even parity over the AD[63::32] and C/BE#[7::4] signal lines. The total number of "1"s over these signal lines including the PAR64 signal line is an even number.

If the ACK64# signal line is deasserted, the PAR64 signal line may or may not contain valid parity information. The PAR64 signal line contains valid parity driven by the PCI-X bus master during the initial microaccess of SINGLE or BURST bus transactions for BURST memory write (including memory write block or alias memory write block) and split completion commands. During subsequent microaccesses for BURST memory write (including memory write block or alias memory write block) or split completion transactions, the PCI-X bus master can drive this signal line to a stable level or tri-state it. (If tri-stated, it is driven to logical "1" by a pull-up resistor.) The PAR64 signal line is tri-stated during all microaccesses of SINGLE or BURST bus transactions for BURST memory read commands and is driven to a logical "1" by a pull-up resistor.

If the ACK64# signal line is asserted for a memory write or a split completion transaction, the PAR64 signal line contains valid parity. If the ACK64# signal line is asserted for a memory read transaction, the PAR64 signal line contains valid parity. For memory write or a split completion transactions, the PCI-X bus master is responsible for driving the PAR64 signal line, and for memory read transactions the target is responsible for driving the PAR64 signal line.

DWORD, I/O, CONFIGURATION, INTERRUPT ACKNOWLEDGE, AND SPECIAL TRANSACTIONS

DWORD, I/O, configuration, special, or interrupt acknowledge transactions are not defined for 64 data bit bus transactions. Consequently, the asserted REQ64#

signal line is ignored. This signal line is tri-stated and driven to a logical "1" by a pull-up resistor.

ALSO CONSIDER:

PAR SIGNAL LINE WITH A 64 DATA BIT PCI-X BUS MASTER (REQ64# ASSERTED)

Same as a 32 data bit PCI-X bus master.

REQ64#	Request 64 Data Bit Access	Opt.	Bi-Directional Drive Tri-state	Pull-up Resistor

This signal line indicates that the PCI or PCI-X bus master can execute 64 data bit bus bus transactions.

PCI SPECIFIC

RESET

Driven to logical "1" (deasserted) by pull-up resistor. If the connector (for a slot) only supports the 32 data bit connector, there is an individual resistor to each REQ64# signal line for each connector on the platform backplane and these are not bussed together. If the connector supports the 64 data bit connector, the REQ64# signal line is bussed together to a single pull-up resistor on the platform backplane. This single bussed line is also attached to an open collector (or drain) of a transistor on the platform backplane. The bused REQ64# signal line is asserted (logical "0") during reset to indicate a 64 data bit connector. See Chapter 11: *Reset, Power, and Signal Initialization* for more information. If the connector and backplane support 64 data bits, the REQ64# signal line is deasserted during reset.

PARK

Driven to logical "1" (deasserted) by pull-up resistor. If the connector (for a slot) only supports the 32 data bit connector, there is an individual resistor to each REQ64# signal line for each connector on the platform backplane, and these are not bussed together. If the connector supports the 64 data bit connector, the REQ64# signal line is bussed together to a single pull-up resistor on the platform backplane.

IDLE PHASE

Driven to a logical "1" (deasserted) by 64 data bit PCI bus master or driven to a logical "1" (deasserted) by a pull-up resistor when a 32 data bit PCI bus master owns the bus segment.

ADDRESS PHASE

MEMORY TRANSACTION

The REQ64# signal line is asserted by the PCI bus master to request a 64 data bit bus transaction. Its timing is identical to the FRAME# signal line.

I/O, CONFIGURATION, INTERRUPT ACKNOWLEDGE, AND SPECIAL TRANSACTIONS

An access, special, or interrupt acknowledge cycle is not defined for 64 data bit bus transactions; consequently, this signal line is ignored.

DATA PHASE

MEMORY TRANSACTIONS

The assertion of the REQ64# signal line requests a 64 data bit bus transaction during the ADDRESS PHASE. Once this signal line is asserted it remains asserted throughout the DATA PHASE. Its timing protocol is identical to the FRAME# signal line.

I/O, CONFIGURATION, INTERRUPT ACKNOWLEDGE, AND SPECIAL TRANSACTIONS

An I/O, configuration, special, or interrupt acknowledge transaction is not defined for 64 data bit bus transactions; consequently, this signal line is ignored.

PCI-X SPECIFIC

RESET, PARK, AND IDLE PHASE

Same as PCI.

ADDRESS PHASE

MEMORY TRANSACTION

The REQ64# signal line is asserted by the PCI-X bus master to request a 64 data bit bus transaction. Its timing is identical to the FRAME# signal line.

I/O, CONFIGURATION, INTERRUPT ACKNOWLEDGE, AND SPECIAL TRANSACTIONS

An I/O, configuration, special, or interrupt acknowledge transaction is not defined for 64 data bit bus transactions; consequently, this signal line is ignored.

ATTRIBUTE,TARGET RESPONSE, AND DATA PHASES

MEMORY AND SPLIT COMPLETION TRANSACTIONS

The assertion of the REQ64# signal line requests a 64 data bit bus transaction during the ADDRESS PHASE. Once this signal line is asserted it remains until the end of the bus transaction. Its timing protocol is identical to the FRAME# signal line.

I/O, CONFIGURATION, INTERRUPT ACKNOWLEDGE, AND SPECIAL TRANSACTIONS

An I/O, configuration, special, or interrupt acknowledge transaction is not defined for 64 data bit bus transactions; consequently, this signal line is ignored.

ACK64#	Acknowledge 64 Data Bit Access	Opt.	Bi-Directional Drive Tri-state	Pull-up Resistor

This signal line indicates that the accessed PCI or PCI-X resource (target) supports 64 data bit bus transactions.

PCI SPECIFIC

RESET

Driven to a logical "1" (deasserted) by a pull-up resistor.

PARK

Driven to a logical "1" (deasserted) by a pull-up resistor.

IDLE PHASE

Driven to a logical "1" (deasserted) by a pull-up resistor.

ADDRESS PHASE

MEMORY TRANSACTION

Driven to a logical "1" (deasserted) by a pull-up resistor.

I/O, CONFIGURATION, INTERRUPT ACKNOWLEDGE, AND SPECIAL TRANSACTIONS

An I/O, configuration, special, or interrupt acknowledge transaction is not defined for 64 data bit bus transactions; consequently, this signal line is ignored. It is driven to a logical "1" (deasserted) by a pull-up resistor.

DATA PHASE

MEMORY TRANSACTION

The ACK64# signal line is asserted by the target to indicate that the target can support a 64 data bit bus transaction. The ACK64# signal line can only be asserted in response to the assertion of the REQ64# signal line during the ADDRESS PHASE. Once the ACK64# signal line asserted it remains asserted for the entire DATA PHASE. Its timing is identical to the DEVSEL# signal line.

I/O, CONFIGURATION, INTERRUPT ACKNOWLEDGE, AND SPECIAL TRANSACTIONS

An I/O, configuration, special, or interrupt acknowledge transaction is not defined for 64 data bit bus transactions; consequently, this signal line is ignored.

PCI-X SPECIFIC

RESET, PARK, AND IDLE PHASE

Same as PCI.

ADDRESS AND ATTRIBUTE PHASES

MEMORY AND SPLIT COMPLETION TRANSACTIONS

Driven to a logical "1" (deasserted) by a pull-up resistor.

I/O, CONFIGURATION, INTERRUPT ACKNOWLEDGE, AND SPECIAL TRANSACTIONS

An I/O, configuration, special, or interrupt acknowledge transaction is not defined for 64 data bit bus transactions; consequently, this signal line is ignored. It is driven to a logical "1" (deasserted) by a pull-up resistor.

TARGET RESPONSE AND DATA PHASES

MEMORY AND SPLIT COMPLETION TRANSACTIONS

The ACK64# signal line is asserted by the target to indicate that the target can support a 64 data bit bus transaction. The ACK64# signal line can only be asserted in response to the assertion of the REQ64# signal line during the ADDRESS PHASE. Once the ACK64# signal line asserted it remains asserted until the end of the bus transaction. Its timing is identical to the DEVSEL# signal line.

I/O, CONFIGURATION, INTERRUPT ACKNOWLEDGE, AND SPECIAL TRANSACTIONS

An I/O, configuration, special, or interrupt acknowledge transaction is not defined for 64 data bit bus transactions; consequently, this signal line is ignored.

5.6 ARBITRATION SIGNAL LINES

REQx#	Request	Req.	Bi-Directional Tri-state (1)	No Pull-up Resistor (2)

Notes:

(1): A PCI or PCI-X bus master uses this signal line only as an output. The signal line is defined as a bi-directional driver to take advantage of a standard PCI or PCI-X buffer that has tri-state attributes.

(2): To prevent the REQx# signal lines from floating, the central arbiter must attach a weak pull-up resistor to each line. These signal lines are individually attached (not bussed) between the central arbiter to each PCI or PCI-X resource.

Each PCI or PCI-X resource that can become a PCI or PCI-X bus master has an individual REQx# signal line to request ownership of the PCI or PCI-X bus segment, respectively. The PCI or PCI-X bus master must drive the REQx# signal line at all times (either asserted or deasserted).

PCI SPECIFIC

RESET

The central arbiter must ignore the REQx# signal line when the RST# signal line is asserted.

PARK

Does not apply to a specific bus transaction. These signal lines operate independently of bus transactions. A PCI resource will assert a REQx# signal line when bus ownership is requested.

IDLE PHASE

Does not apply to a specific bus transaction. These signal lines operate independently of bus transactions. A PCI resource will assert a REQx# signal line when bus ownership is requested.

ADDRESS PHASE

MEMORY, I/O, CONFIGURATION, INTERRUPT ACKNOWLEDGE, AND SPECIAL TRANSACTIONS

Does not apply to a specific bus transaction. These signal lines operate independently of bus transactions. A PCI resource will assert a REQx# signal line when bus ownership is requested.

DATA PHASE

MEMORY, I/O, CONFIGURATION, INTERRUPT ACKNOWLEDGE, AND SPECIAL TRANSACTIONS

Does not apply to a specific bus transaction. These signal lines operate independently of bus transactions. A PCI resource will assert a REQx# signal line when bus ownership is requested.

PCI-X SPECIFIC

RESET, PARK, AND IDLE PHASE

Same as PCI.

ADDRESS, ATTRIBUTE, TARGET RESPONSE, AND DATA PHASES

MEMORY, I/O, SPLIT COMPLETION, CONFIGURATION, INTERRUPT ACKNOWLEDGE, AND SPECIAL TRANSACTIONS

Does not apply to a specific bus transaction. These signal lines operate independently of bus transactions. A PCI resource will assert a REQx# signal line when bus ownership is requested.

GNTx#	Grant	Req.	Bi-Directional Tri-state (1)	No Pull-up Resistor

Note: (1) The PCI or PCI-X bus master uses this signal line only as an input. The signal line is defined as a bi-directional driver to take advantage of a standard PCI or PCI-X buffer that has tri-state attributes.

Each PCI or PCI-X resource that can become PCI or PCI-X bus master has an individual GNTx# signal line to allow the central arbiter to communicate to the

PCI or PCI-X resource that it now owns the bus segment, respectively. The central arbiter must drive the GNTx# signal line at all times (either asserted or deasserted), except as noted below. These signal lines are individually attached (not bussed) between the central arbiter to each PCI or PCI-X resource.

PCI SPECIFIC

RESET

These signal lines are tri-stated and floating. Each PCI bus master must ignore its associated GNT# signal line when the RST# signal line is asserted.

PARK

Does not apply to a specific bus transaction. These signal lines operate independently of bus transactions. Central arbiter will assert to indicate ownership.

IDLE PHASE

Does not apply to a specific bus transaction. These signal lines operate independently of bus transactions. Central arbiter will assert to indicate ownership.

ADDRESS PHASE

MEMORY, I/O, CONFIGURATION, INTERRUPT ACKNOWLEDGE ,AND SPECIAL TRANSACTIONS

Does not apply to a specific bus transaction. These signal lines operate independently of bus transactions. The central arbiter will assert to indicate bus segment ownership.

DATA PHASE

MEMORY, I/O, CONFIGURATION, INTERRUPT ACKNOWLEDGE, AND SPECIAL TRANSACTIONS

Does not apply to a specific bus transaction. These signal lines operate independently of bus transactions. The central arbiter will assert a GNTx# signal line to indicate bus segment ownership.

PCI-X SPECIFIC

RESET, PARK, AND IDLE PHASE

Same as PCI.

ADDRESS, ATTRIBUTE, TARGET RESPONSE, AND DATA PHASES

MEMORY, I/O, SPLIT COMPLETION,CONFIGURATION, INTERRUPT ACKNOWLEDGE, AND SPECIAL TRANSACTIONS

Does not apply to a specific bus transaction. These signal lines operate independently of bus transactions. The central arbiter will assert a GNTx# signal line to indicate bus segment ownership.

5.7 INTERRUPT SIGNAL LINES

INTx#	Interrupt	Opt.	Open Drain	Pull-up Resistor

These signal lines indicate a PCI or PCI-X resource needs service by the platform CPU. The platform CPU responds by executing an interrupt acknowledge cycle. Four interrupt signal lines are defined: INTA#, INTB#, INTC# and INTD#.

When an INTx# signal line is asserted, it remains asserted until the software device driver clears the interrupt request.

PCI SPECIFIC

RESET

Driven to a logical "1" (deasserted) by a pull-up resistor.

PARK

Does not apply to a specific bus transaction. These signal lines operate independently of bus transactions. PCI resource will assert when interrupt service is requested.

315

IDLE PHASE

Does not apply to a specific bus transaction. These signal lines operate independently of bus transactions. PCI resource will assert when interrupt service is requested.

ADDRESS PHASE

MEMORY, I/O, CONFIGURATION, INTERRUPT ACKNOWLEDGE, AND SPECIAL TRANSACTIONS

Does not apply to a specific bus transaction. These signal lines operate independently of bus transactions. A PCI resource will assert an INTx# when interrupt service is requested.

DATA PHASE

MEMORY, I/O, CONFIGURATION, INTERRUPT ACKNOWLEDGE, AND SPECIAL TRANSACTIONS

Does not apply to a specific bus transaction. These signal lines operate independently of bus transactions. A PCI resource will assert an INTx# when interrupt service is requested.

PCI-X SPECIFIC

RESET, PARK, AND IDLE PHASE

Same as PCI.

ADDRESS, ATTRIBUTE, TARGET RESPONSE, AND DATA PHASES

MEMORY, I/O, SPLIT COMPLETION,CONFIGURATION, INTERRUPT ACKNOWLEDGE, AND SPECIAL TRANSACTIONS

Does not apply to a specific bus transaction. These signal lines operate independently of bus transactions. A PCI-X resource will assert an INTx# when interrupt service is requested.

5.8   J-TAG SIGNAL LINES

> **Note: PRSNT1# and PRSNT2# are unique signal lines that are not specifically part of the bus transaction protocol. See Chapter 11:** *Reset, Power, and Signal Line Initialization* **for more information.**

These are not defined as part of the PCI or PCI-X bus segment protocol and are optional for PCI or PCI-X compliant integrated circuits (resources). The purpose of these signal lines is to support boundary scan in a PCI or PCI-X resource according to the IEEE Standard 1149.1. If a PCI or PCI-X resource supports boundary scan according to this standard, the TCK, TDI, TDO and TMS signal lines must be supported. Optional to the support of the IEEE Standard 1149.1 is the support of the TRST# signal line.

TCK	Test Clock	Opt.	Input	No Pull-up Resistor (2)

TCK is the J-TAG clock to reference the instructions and data in/out of the test signal lines.

TDI	Test DATA Input	Opt.	Input	No Pull-up Resistor (1)

TDI is the input port for the serial shifting of J-TAG instructions and data.

TDO	Test DATA Output	Opt.	Output	No Pull-up Resistor

TDO is the output port for the serial shifting of J-TAG instructions and data.

TMS	Test Mode Select	Opt.	Input	No Pull-up Resistor (1)

TMS is the input port to control the state of the TAP controller in the PCI resource.

TRST#	Test RESET	Opt.	Input	No Pull-up Resistor (2)

TRST# is the input port to initialize the TAP controller in the PCI or PCI-X resource.

Notes: (1) When boundary scan is not implemented on the platform (or independently on an add-in card), these signal lines should be independently connected and each driven to logical "1" by 5K pull-up resistors.

(2) When boundary scan is not implemented on the platform (or independently on an add-in card), these signal lines should be independently connected and each driven to logical "0" by 5K pull-down resistors.

The J-TAG signal lines are not active when the PCI or PCI-X resource is operating PCI or PCI-X bus transactions, but must meet the 3.3 and 5 volt electrical requirements, are part of the PCI or PCI-X connector specification, and are not required to have the same drive requirements of other PCI or PCI-X bus signal lines. The TCK, TMS, and TRST# signal lines of the PCI or PCI-X resources are all connected to common drivers. The TDI signal line of one PCI or PCI-X resource is connected to the TDO of another resource, and so forth in a daisy chain fashion. In addition to the IEEE standard, the *PCI System Design Guide* and the *PCI Local Bus Specification Rev. 2.2* suggest the following use of J-TAG test rings:

- Only use the test ring on the expansion board during manufacturing test.

- Create a test ring on the main platform and link with the test ring on the expansion boards.

- Integrated circuits can support hierarchical IEEE 1149.1 multi-drop addressability.

DETAILED BUS TRANSACTION OPERATION

This chapter consists of the following subchapters:

6.0   GENERAL CONSIDERATIONS

INTRODUCTION

As discussed in Chapter 3: *Generic PCI and PCI-X Hardware Operation*, there are several types of PCI bus transactions: memory, I/O, configuration, interrupt acknowledge, and special. This chapter will discuss the detailed operation of these bus transactions for 32 and 64 data bit PCI bus masters and targets. Also, as previously discussed, the PCI-X bus transactions consist of these PCI bus transactions plus split completion transactions.

A unique aspect of the PCI bus transaction protocol is that address and data are multiplexed onto the same signal lines: AD[31::0]. Under the 64 data bit extension option, address and data are also multiplexed onto the AD[63::32] signal lines. During a read transaction, an "extra CLK signal line period" must be added after the ADDRESS PHASE and at the beginning of the DATA PHASE portion of the transaction to change the resource driving the bus. This added CLK signal period allows the ASIC driving the address to tri-state the AD[63::0] signal lines before another ASIC (for example, the target) drives data onto the AD signal lines. Special and interrupt acknowledge transactions are write and read, respectively. Consequently, only the interrupt acknowledge transaction has the extra CLK signal line period. The PCI-X bus transaction protocol also implements multiplexed AD[31::0] signal lines with a multiplexing of the AD[63::32] signal lines for the 64 data bit extension option. Also, the PCI-X bus transactions have formalized the aforementioned "extra CLK signal line period" (called TARGET RESONSE PHASE) and has applied it to both read and write bus transactions.

> It is assumed in this book that the address and write data are driven by the same ASIC; consequently, there is no additional CLK signal line period required for the PCI bus transaction protocol. If the address and write data are provided from different ASICs, an additional CLK signal line period must be added as in the case of a read transaction in the PCI bus transaction protocol. The PCI-X bus transaction protocol always has a TARGET RESPONSE PHASE available for this situation for both read and write bus transactions.

According to the PCI local bus specification, the memory, I/O, and configuration address spaces can be accessed with SINGLE or BURST bus transactions. Each SINGLE or BURST bus transaction can be executed with STANDARD or READY microaccesses, sequential bus transactions may be executed with Fast Back-to-Back, any bus transaction can be prematurely terminated, and both the PCI bus master and the target can control the length of the bus transaction. Each bus transaction consists of three phases: ADDRESS,

DATA, and IDLE. The ADDRESS PHASE is one CLK signal line period in length at the beginning of the bus transaction and provides the address of the target of the bus transaction. If a DUAL ADDRESS executes, the ADDRESS PHASE will be two CLK signal line periods in length. The DATA PHASE can last for several CLK signal line periods and is the portion of the bus transaction where data is accessed. Between each bus transaction, when Fast Back-to-Back is not executed, the PCI bus segment enters the IDLE PHASE. Note: a DUAL ADDRESS cannot be executed as part of an I/O or a configuration transaction.

According to the PCI-X addendum specification, memory, I/O, and configuration address spaces can be accessed with SINGLE and BURST bus transactions. Also like the PCI bus transaction protocol, the PCI-X bus transaction protocol consists of ADDRESS, DATA, and IDLE PHASES. Both protocols support the DUAL ADDRESS command. Unlike the PCI bus transaction protocol, the PCI-X bus protocol does not support Fast Back-to-Back between bus transactions, and the PCI-X bus transaction protocol has added two more phases: ATTRIBUTE and TARGET RESPONSE.

> Rev. 2.0 of the PCI local bus specification did not specifically define the addressing protocol for a BURST I/O transaction, but Rev. 2.1 does define such a protocol. See Chapter 4: *Functional Interaction Between PCI and PCI-X Resources* for more information .

The interrupt acknowledge transaction in the PCI local bus specification does not have an address space associated with it. It is a SINGLE read transaction to the platform resource that contains the interrupt controller. Each SINGLE bus transaction can be executed with a STANDARD or READY microaccess. The length of the interrupt acknowledge transaction is controlled by the PCI bus master (HOST/PCI BRIDGE) and the target with the IRDY# and TRDY# signal lines, respectively. Each interrupt acknowledge transaction consists of three phases: ADDRESS, DATA, and IDLE (optional). The ADDRESS PHASE is one CLK signal line period in length at the beginning of the bus transaction without a target address. The DATA PHASE is the portion of the interrupt acknowledge transaction where the interrupt vector is read. The IDLE PHASE occurs between bus transactions unless the Fast Back-to-Back protocol is executed. The Fast Back-to-Back protocol can only be used under certain conditions when the interrupt acknowledge transaction is one of the bus transactions in the back-to-back sequence. See further discussions later in this chapter. Note: a DUAL ADDRESS cannot be executed as part of an interrupt acknowledge transaction protocol.

In the PCI-X addendum specification, the interrupt acknowledge transaction is implemented for the same reasons as in the PCI local bus specification. Like the PCI interrupt acknowledge transaction protocol, the PCI-X interrupt acknowledge transaction protocol consists of ADDRESS, DATA, and IDLE PHASES with a SINGLE bus transaction consisting of STANDARD or READY microaccesses. Unlike the PCI interrupt acknowledge transaction protocol, the PCI-X interrupt acknowledge transaction protocol supports only SINGLE bus transactions, does not support the Fast Back-to Back protocol, and adds two more phases: ATTRIBUTE and TARGET RESPONSE.

The special transaction in the PCI local bus specification does not have an address space associated with it. It is a "broadcast" SINGLE or BURST write transaction to all PCI resources. Each SINGLE or BURST bus transaction can be executed with STANDARD or READY microaccesses. The special transaction is a minimum of five CLK signal line periods, with only the PCI bus master controlling the length of the bus transaction with the IRDY# signal line. Each special transaction consists of three phases: ADDRESS, DATA, and IDLE. The ADDRESS PHASE is one CLK signal line period in length at the beginning of the bus transaction without a target address. The DATA PHASE can last for several CLK signal line periods and is the portion of the special transaction where information is broadcast. The IDLE PHASE occurs between bus transactions unless the Fast Back-to-Back protocol is executed. The Fast Back-to-Back protocol can be used under certain conditions when a special transaction is one of the bus transactions in the back-to-back sequence See further discussions later in this chapter. Note: a DUAL ADDRESS cannot be executed as part of a special transaction.

According to the PCI-X addendum specification, the special transaction is implemented for the same reasons as in the PCI local bus specification. Like the PCI special transaction protocol, the PCI-X special transaction protocol consists of ADDRESS, DATA, and IDLE PHASES with STANDARD and READY microaccesses. Unlike the PCI special transaction protocol, the PCI-X special transaction protocol supports only SINGLE bus transactions, does not support the Fast Back-to Back protocol, and adds two more phases: ATTRIBUTE and TARGET RESPONSE.

This book uses the convention of STANDARD and READY microaccesses. STANDARD microaccesses mean that no wait states are required by either the PCI or PCI-X bus master or target. Both resources are able to complete the bus transaction in the shortest period for a particular bus transaction. READY microaccesses mean that wait states are required by either the PCI or PCI-X bus master or the target or both. In the case of SINGLE bus transactions only one microaccess is defined; consequently, the overall SINGLE bus transaction is defined as either STANDARD or READY. This one microaccess is defined as "initial". In the case of BURST bus transactions there are one or more microaccesses; consequently, the overall BURST bus transaction is not defined in terms of STANDARD or READY bus transactions. The first microaccess is defined as "initial" and the others are defined as "subsequent". The wait states are defined in increments of CLK signal line periods. The PCI or PCI-X bus masters and targets request wait states by deasserting the IRDY# and TRDY# signal lines, respectively.

This book will address 32 and 64 data bit PCI resources in the first part of this chapter. 32 data bit PCI resources will be examined first, followed by the 64 data bit extension. In the last half of this chapter a similar discussion will cover PCI-X resources.

PCI SPECIFIC

SIGNAL LINE OWNERSHIP DURING BUS TRANSACTIONS WITH 32 DATA BIT RESOURCES

During memory, I/O, configuration, interrupt acknowledge, and special transactions; the signal lines are owned by different PCI bus segment resources. A PCI resource owns a signal line when it is the only resource (other than pull-up resistors) that can drive the signal line during a portion of the bus transaction. The protocol is as follows:

- During all bus transactions the PCI bus master owns the FRAME#, IRDY#, and C/BE#[3::0], signal lines throughout the entire bus transaction.

- During memory, I/O, and configuration write transactions; the PCI bus master owns the AD[31::0] and PAR signal lines throughout the entire bus transaction.

- During a special transaction, the PCI bus master owns the AD[31::0] and PAR signal lines.

- During memory, I/O, and configuration read transactions, the PCI bus master owns the AD[31::0] and PAR signal lines during the ADDRESS PHASE. The target owns these signal lines during the DATA PHASE.

- During an interrupt acknowledge transaction, the PCI bus master owns the AD[31::0] and PAR signal lines during the ADDRESS PHASE. The target owns these signal lines during the DATA PHASE.

- During memory, I/O, configuration, and interrupt acknowledge transactions; the TRDY#, DEVSEL#, and STOP# signal lines are owned by the target. During a special transaction, these signal lines are not owned by the target because no target is addressed.

During a configuration transaction, the protocol is the same as listed above with the following exceptions:

- The IDSEL signal lines are driven by a platform resource that is programmed by the PCI bus master. Typically it is the HOST/PCI or PCI/PCI BRIDGES acting as a PCI bus master that drives the IDSEL signal lines via the AD signal lines.

- The "target" in the above section is defined as the "device" according to the configuration transaction protocol. The device is defined as any PCI resource that has configuration registers; it includes PCI bus masters, targets, and bridges.

The remaining signal lines for all bus transactions are owned according to the following protocol:

- The CLK and RST# signal lines are owned by the central resource.

- The GNTx# signal lines are owned by the central arbiter.

- The LOCK# signal line is owned by the Lock master.

- The INTx# signal lines are owned by various PCI resources.

- The REQ64#, ACK64#, PAR64, C/BE#[7::4], and AD[63::32] signal lines are driven to logical "1" by pull-up resistors.

For further information, see Subchapters 6.2: *More Details of PCI Signal Line Protocol for 32 Data Bit Bus Transactions*, 6.4: *PCI 64 Data Bit Extension*, and 6.7: *More Details of PCI Signal Line Protocol for 64 Data Bit Bus Transactions*.

SIGNAL LINE PROTOCOL CONSIDERATIONS

The detailed figures in this and other chapters conform to the signal line protocol shown in Figures 6-0-A and 6-0-B for PCI bus transactions:

- The FRAME# and IRDY# signal lines show the protocol for individual signal lines driven by multiple sources. The signal line changes from logical "1" driven by a pull-up resistor to being driven by the PCI bus master and vice versa by the timing marks labeled "D" and "T", respectively. "D" represents driving and "T" represents tri-stating. Asserted and deasserted signal lines are the lower and upper signal line levels, respectively. The protocol for DEVSEL, TRDY# and STOP# signal lines is the same, except they are driven by the target. These signal lines represent those (not all are shown in Figures 6-0-A and 6-0-B) that are classified as "Bi-directional drive tri-state" in Chapter 5: *Signal Line Definition.*

- The AD[31::0] signal lines show the protocol for signal lines not driven by pull-up resistors. The AD[31::0] signal lines are driven by another PCI resource prior to the bus transaction; consequently, the signal lines are tri-stated (timing mark "T") and driven for the ADDRESS PHASE (for example) by the PCI bus master (timing mark "D"). The "A" and "D" between the parallel lines are labels that indicate address and data being driven onto the signal lines, respectively.

- In all of the figures for read transactions and interrupt acknowledge transactions, the protocol of the unlabeled areas between the parallel solid lines for the AD signal lines have two additional meanings:

  - Prior to the assertion of the DEVSEL# signal line, these signal lines are tri-stated.

  - With and after the assertion of the DEVSEL# signal line (but with the TRDY# signal line deasserted) these signal lines are driven to a stable level that may or may not contain valid data.

  - With and after the assertion of the TRDY# signal line, these signal lines are driven with valid data.

- In all of the figures for write transactions and special transactions, the protocol of the unlabeled areas between the parallel solid lines for the AD signal lines indicates the following:

  - Prior to the assertion of the IRDY# signal line, these signal lines are driven to a stable level that may or may not contain valid data.

- The single horizontal line that is neither logical "1" or logical "0" in between bus transactions indicates that the ownership of the AD[31::0] and C/BE#[3::0] signal lines is changing and these signal lines are tri-stated. This protocol applies to signal lines (not all are shown in Figs. 6-0-A and 6-0-B) that are classified as "Bi-directional tri-state" in Chapter 5: *Signal Line Definition.*

- The protocol between bus transactions for AD[63::32] signal lines is the same as the AD[31::00] signal line, except the AD[63::32] signal lines are driven to logical "1" by pull up resistors whenever these signal lines are tri-stated (except as noted in the next bullet for signal line ownership exchange). Consequently, the AD[63::32] signal lines signal lines are shown as a single logical "1" horizontal line. The AD[63::32] signal lines typify signal line groups with pull-up resistors such as the C/BE#[7::4] signal lines.

■ In a read transaction (shown in Figure 6-0-B), the AD[31::00] signal lines are tri-stated by the PCI bus master in the second CLK signal line period in preparation for the target driving these signal lines in the third CLK signal line period. The single horizontal line that is neither logical "1" or logical "0" in the DATA PHASE indicates that the ownership of the AD[31::0] signal lines is changing from the PCI bus master to the target and these signal lines are tri-stated. To emphasize the ownership change within the DATA PHASE of the bus transaction between PCI bus master and target, the AD[63::32] signal lines are represented by a single horizontal line that is neither logical "1" nor logical "0" as are the AD[31::00] signal lines. This is unlike ownership change between bus transactions where these signal lines are shown driven to logical "1" due to pull-up resistors.

■ A signal line changes from logical "1" driven by a pull-up resistor to being driven by the PCI bus master and vice versa by the timing marks labeled "D" and "T", respectively. The "D" represents "driving" and the "T" represents tri-stating.

Other considerations related to signal line protocol are ADDRESS/DATA STEPPING and PRE-DRIVE. These protocols were discussed in Chapter 4: *Functional Interaction Between PCI and PCI-X Resources,* and result in the assertion of the FRAME# signal line later in the bus transaction. For ease of understanding, these protocols are treated as extensions of the typical bus transactions; consequently, unless otherwise noted, all drawings in this book do not include ADDRESS/DATA STEPPING or PRE-DRIVE protocols. Thus, the FRAME# signal line is asserted during the first (#1) CLK signal line period of the bus transaction.

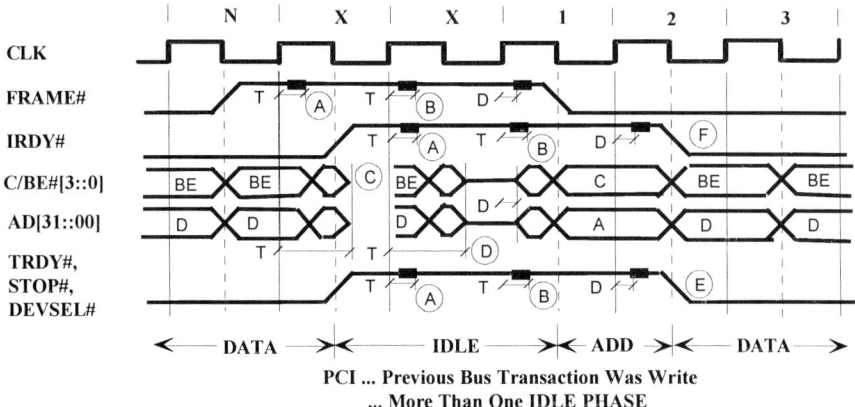

PCI ... Previous Bus Transaction Was Write
... More Than One IDLE PHASE

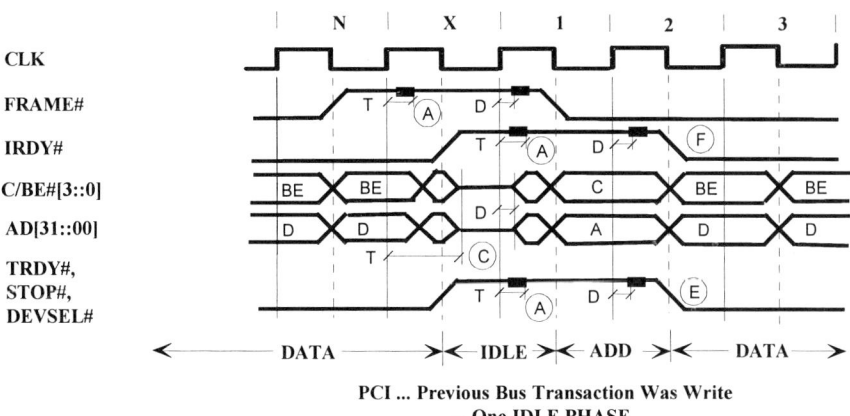

PCI ... Previous Bus Transaction Was Write
... One IDLE PHASE

Figure 6-0-A: PCI Drive and Tri-state Points in the Write Bus Transaction Protocol with Minimum IDLE PHASE

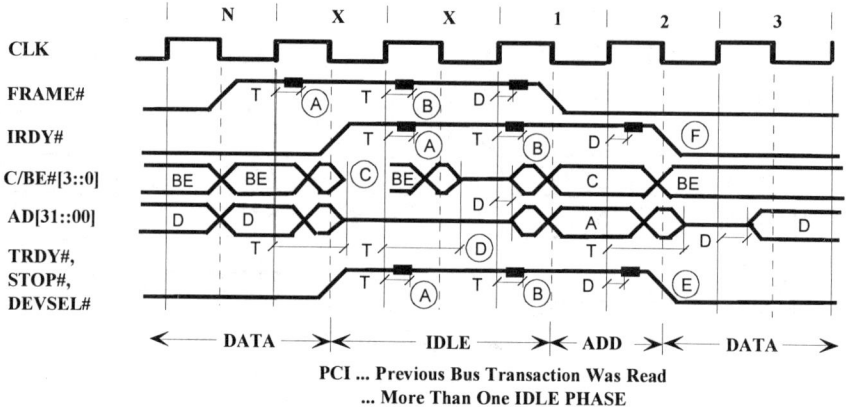

PCI ... Previous Bus Transaction Was Read
... More Than One IDLE PHASE

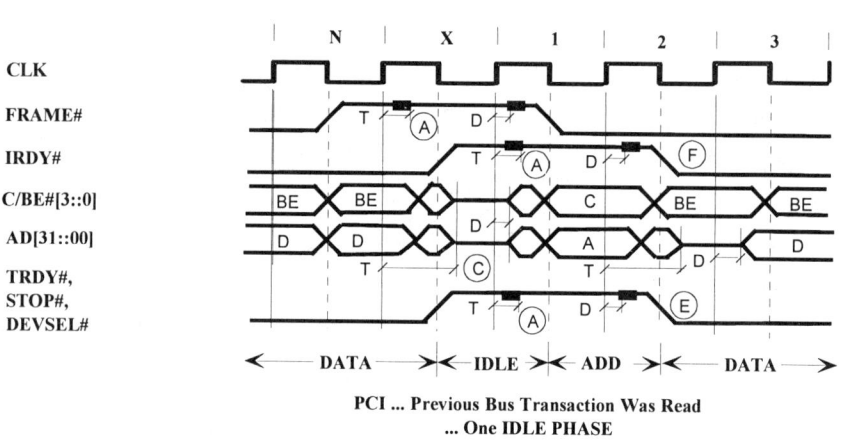

PCI ... Previous Bus Transaction Was Read
... One IDLE PHASE

**Figure 6-0-B: PCI Drive and Tri-state Points in the Read Bus Transaction
Protocol with Minimum IDLE PHASE**

The term "tri-state" is used in this book and assumes that no PCI resource is specifically driving the signal line. The definition is correct after the "T" timing mark in the figures. Prior to the "T" timing marks the signal lines represented by the unlabeled areas between the parallel solid lines indicate a driven stable level (but do not always contain valid information). The term "tri-state" as defined above still applies but the PCI local bus specification and this book uses the term "float". "Float" may not be the same output driver state as "tri-state", but as far as the bus transaction protocol is concerned, both terms indicate that the signal line is not being driven to logical "1'" or "0" by the output driver of the PCI resource. If the "floated" or "tri-stated" signal line is attached to a pull-up or pull-down resistor, the signal line will bias towards Vcc or ground, respectively.

Similarly, after the "D" timing marks the signal lines represented by the unlabeled areas between the parallel solid lines indicate a driven stable level (but do not always contain valid information). The "D" timing marks represent the earliest point a device output driver is activated, but does not mean that the signal line is actually being driven.

The other considerations for PCI signal line protocol for bus transactions are as follows:

- The PCI local bus specification assumes that between bus transactions the ownership of the bus segment can be retained. This is partly due to the support of Fast Back to Back protocol and by the extensive protocol for the change of bus segment ownership (See Chapter 9: *Bus Segment Ownership* for more information). Consequently, for the majority of the figures drawn for PCI bus transactions, the appropriate signal lines between bus transactions are driven by the PCI bus master of the previous bus transaction.

- The signal lines driven by a target must be tri-state signal lines relative to the end of the bus transaction as discussed below, except as noted by any Fast Back to Back considerations.

- The minimum number of CLK signal line periods (defined as IDLE PHASE) between two bus transactions (previous and present) is dependent on the Fast Back to Back protocol and the GNT# signal line protocol discussed in Chapter 9: *Bus Segment Ownership.*

- Independent of the retention of bus segment ownership issues, the points at the end of the bus transaction that the signal lines can be deasserted and tri-stated according to the PCI local bus specification are as follows (See Figures 6-0-A and 6-0-B):

  - As discussed later in this chapter, the FRAME# signal line is deasserted and IRDY# signal line asserted for one CLK signal line period to identify the end of the bus transaction. The FRAME# and IRDY# signal lines are required to be tri-stated one CLK signal line period (Circle A) after their deassertion with two exceptions:

■ If the GNTx# signal line protocol permits two IDLE PHASES, these signal lines can be tri-stated one additional CLK signal line period later (Circle B).

■ These signal lines do not have to be tri-stated until later if retention of bus segment ownership is anticipated. Figures 9-2 to 9-7 (in Chapter 9: *Bus Segment Ownership*) provides the boundary conditions for tri-stating given bus segment ownership change.

■ The REQ64# and ACK64# signal lines follow the protocol of the FRAME# and DEVSEL# signal lines, respectively. The LOCK# signal line tri-states one CLK signal line period after it is deasserted when the PCI bus master is relinquishes LOCK# signal line ownership.

■ Because targets do not necessarily monitor signal lines associated with bus segment ownership, the protocol for the deassertion and tri-stating of the TRDY#, STOP#, and DEVSEL# signal lines is as follows:

■ The TRDY#, STOP#, and DEVSEL# signal lines are deasserted (if not already) with the deassertion of the IRDY# signal line. These signal lines are tri-stated at one of the followings points:

■ One CLK signal line period after their deassertion.

OR

■ One CLK signal line period after the simultaneous sampling of FRAME# signal line deasserted and IRDY# signal line asserted (Circle A in Figures 6-0-A and 6-0-B).

■ For write transactions and special transactions, the AD[31::00] and C/BE#[3::0] signal lines are tri-stated simultaneously with the deassertion of the IRDY# signal line (Circle C in Figure 6-0-A). For write transactions and special transactions with two IDLE PHASES (dependent on the GNTx# signal line protocol ... See Chapter 9: *Bus Segment Ownership* for more information), the AD[31::00] and C/BE#[3::0] signal lines can optionally be tri-stated one CLK signal line later than the deassertion of the IRDY# signal line (Circle D in Figure 6-0-A).

■ For read transactions and interrupt acknowledge transactions, the AD[31::00] signal lines are tri-stated simultaneously with the deassertion of the IRDY# signal line (Circle C in Figure 6-0-B).

■ For read transactions and interrupt acknowledge transactions, the C/BE#[3::0] signal lines are tri-stated simultaneously with the deassertion of the IRDY# signal line (Circle C of Figure 6-0-B). For read transactions and interrupt acknowledge transactions with two IDLE PHASES (dependent on the GNTx# signal line protocol ... See Chapter 9: *Bus Segment Ownership* for more information), the C/BE#[3::0] signal lines can optionally be tri-stated one CLK signal line later than the deassertion of the IRDY# signal line (Circle D in Figure 6-0-B).

■ If the bus transaction terminates with Master Abort termination, the AD[31::00] and C/BE#[3::0] signal lines are tri-stated simultaneously with the deassertion of the IRDY# signal line or one CLK signal line period later.

■ The PAR signal line follows the protocol of the AD[31::00] signal lines except there is a one CLK signal line period delay. The PERR# signal line follows the PAR signal line protocol with an additional one CLK signal line period delay.

■ The points at the beginning of the bus transaction that signal lines can be driven and asserted are as follows (Note: The driving points discussed below are not the only possibilities. But they do identify "safe" driving points that will meet all of the conditions to avoid buffer fights between the previous bus transaction and the present bus transaction):

 ■ The latest point the FRAME# signal line can be driven is in the same CLK signal line period it is asserted.

 ■ The earliest point the IRDY# signal line can be driven is one CLK signal line period after the FRAME# signal line is asserted (Circle F in Figures 6-0-A and 6-0-B). The latest point the IRDY# signal line can be driven is in the same CLK signal line period it is asserted, which is dependent on the number of wait states inserted by the PCI bus master.

 ■ The earliest point the TRDY#, DEVSEL#, or STOP# signal lines can be driven is one CLK signal line period after the rising edge of the CLK signal line that samples the AD and C/BE# signal lines in the ADDRESS PHASE (Circle E in Figures 6-0-A and 6-0-B). The latest point the TRDY#, STOP#, or DEVSEL# signal lines can be driven is in the same CLK signal line period in which each respective signal line is asserted. The best protocol is to drive the STOP# and/or TRDY# signal lines simultaneously with or subsequent to driving the DEVSEL# signal line. The TRDY# and/or STOP# signal lines can only be asserted simultaneously with or after the assertion of the DEVSEL# signal line. The earliest driving and assertion points for the aforementioned signal lines are delayed by one CLK signal line period when DUAL ADDRESS command is executed.

- For all bus transactions, except configuration transaction, the latest the AD[31::00] or C/BE#[3::0] signal lines can be driven valid is the same CLK signal line period that the FRAME# signal line is asserted. For a configuration transaction the AD[31::00] or C/BE#[3::0] signal lines can be driven prior to the assertion of the FRAME# signal line according to the PRE-DRIVE protocol (see more information later in this chapter).

- The PAR signal line follows the same "driven" protocol as the AD[31::00] signal lines except there is a one CLK signal line period delay. The PERR# signal line follows the PAR signal line protocol with an additional one CLK signal line period delay.

- The REQ64# and ACK64# signal lines follow the protocol of the FRAME# and DEVSEL# signal lines, respectively. The LOCK# signal line is tri-stated one CLK signal line period after it is deasserted when the PCI bus master is relinquishes LOCK# signal line ownership.

- See Subchapter 6.6: *64 Data Bit PCI Bus Master to 64 Data Bit Target* for information about the AD[32::63], C/BE#[7::4], and PAR64 signal lines.

DUAL ADDRESS

The PCI bus segment supports both 32 and 64 bit address spaces for memory address space. The typical memory transaction supports 30 address bits encoded into the AD[31::2] signal lines with BURST sequence information encoded into the AD[1::0] signal lines (see Figures 6-1, 6-2-A, and 6-14-A and B). The typical I/O transaction supports 32 address bits encoded into the AD[31::0] signal lines. Also, during the ADDRESS PHASE, the COMMAND type of the bus transaction is encoded into the C/BE#[3::0] signal lines. For a SINGLE bus transaction not executing a DUAL ADDRESS, the minimum pulse width for an asserted FRAME# signal line is one CLK period.

To support a 64 bit address, the PCI bus master multiplexes the address onto the AD[31::0] signal lines with the following protocol:

- The PCI bus master drives the DUAL ADDRESS encoding (C/BE#[3::0] = [1011]) at the beginning of the ADDRESS PHASE (see Figures 6-1, 6-2-A, and 6-14-A and B). Simultaneously, the PCI bus master places the low order address onto the AD[31::2] signal lines for a memory transaction and the AD[31::0] signal lines for an I/O transaction.

- The DUAL ADDRESS encoding at the beginning of the ADDRESS PHASE requires the PCI bus master to subsequently drive the

COMMAND type onto the C/BE#[3::0] signal lines during the second CLK signal line period of the ADDRESS PHASE. Simultaneously, the AD[31::0] signal lines are driven with the high order 32 address bits.

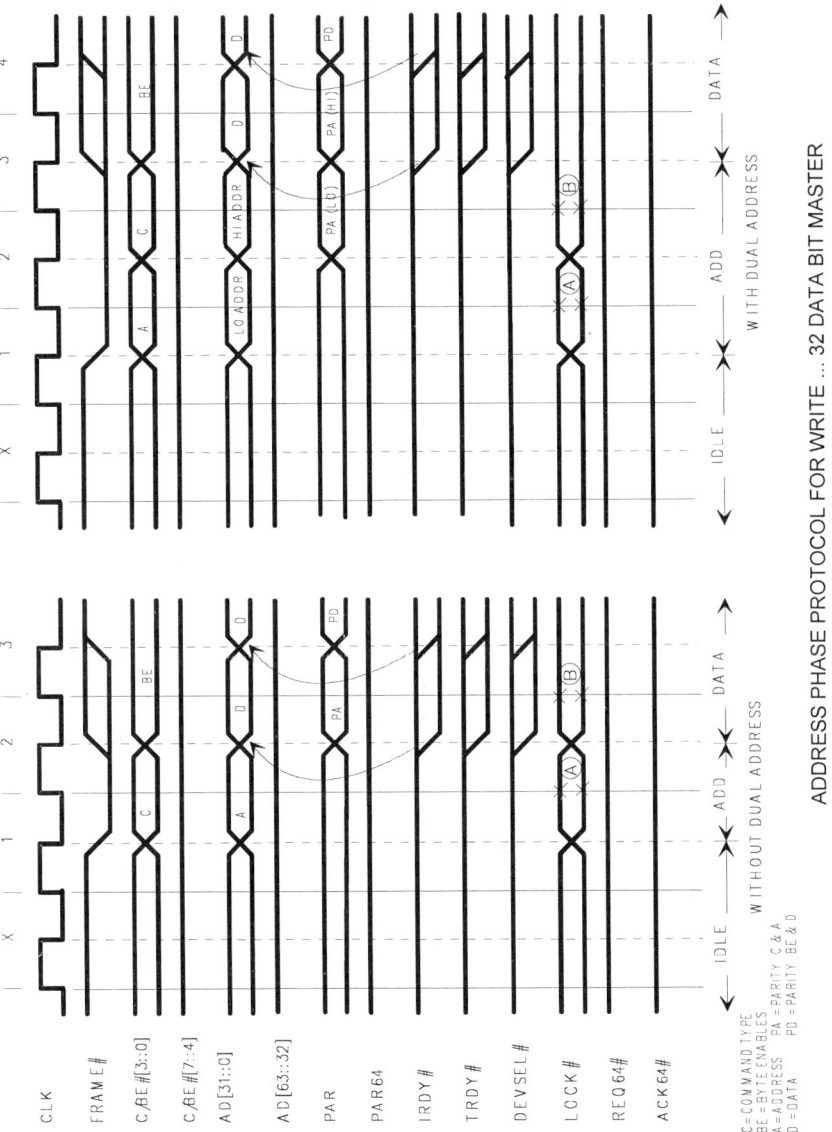

Figure 6-1: ADDRESS PHASE Protocol for Write Transaction, 32 Data Bit PCI Bus Master

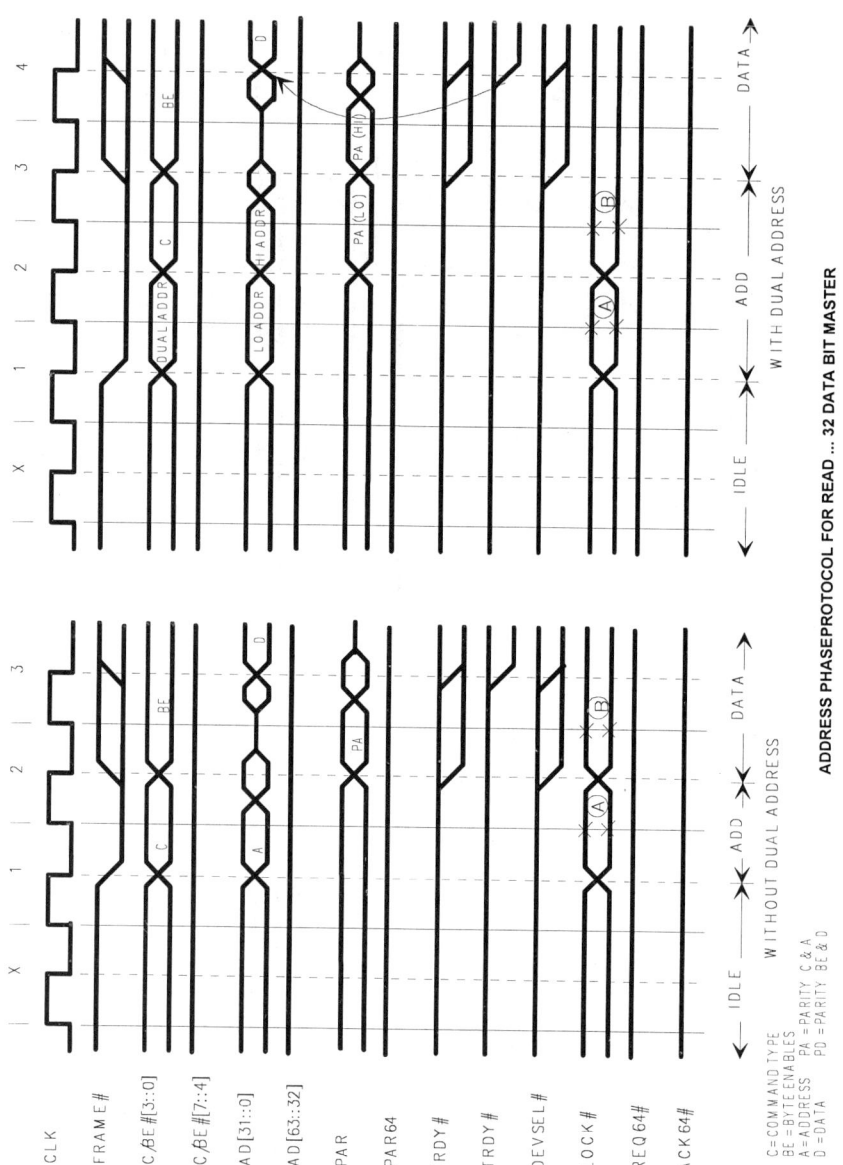

Figure 6-2-A: ADDRESS PHASE Protocol for Read Transaction, 32 Data Bit PCI Bus Master

The net effect of the two above items results in an ADDRESS PHASE that is two CLK signal line periods in length. For a SINGLE bus transaction with DUAL ADDRESS, the minimum pulse width for an asserted FRAME# signal line is two CLK signal line periods.

A PCI bus master that supports the 64 bit address space and only addresses the lower four gigabytes *cannot* execute bus transactions with DUAL ADDRESS. By definition, the upper order address bits are logical "0".

> **PCI bus masters that use ADDRESS/DATA STEPPING cannot use the DUAL ADDRESS protocol.**

> **The 64 bit address space (DUAL ADDRESS) is not defined for the I/O, configuration, interrupt acknowledge or special transactions. In the case of special and interrupt acknowledge transactions, there is no address involved in the protocol.**

> **In Figures 6-1, 6-2-A, and 6-14-A and B, the signal lines with parity and data are shown driven immediately with valid information. This was done for simplicity in these drawings. See the previous section for details.**

PCI-X SPECIFIC

SIGNAL LINE OWNERSHIP DURING BUS TRANSACTIONS WITH 32 DATA BIT RESOURCES

During memory, I/O, configuration, interrupt acknowledge, special, and split completion transactions, the signal lines are owned by different PCI-X bus segment resources. A PCI-X resource owns a signal line during a bus transaction with a similar protocol as discussed in the previous section for PCI bus transactions:

- During all bus transactions, the PCI-X bus master owns the FRAME#, IRDY#, and C/BE#[3::0] signal lines throughout the entire bus transaction.

- During memory write, configuration write, special, and split completion transactions, the AD[31::00] and PAR signal lines are owned by the PCI-X bus master throughout the entire bus transaction.

- During memory read, configuration read, and interrupt transactions, the AD[31::00] and PAR signal lines are owned by the PCI-X bus master during the ADDRESS and ATTRIBUTE PHASES. The target owns these signal lines during the DATA PHASE.

■ During configuration read or configuration write transactions, the AD[31::00] and PAR signal lines are owned by the PCI-X bus master for four CLK signal line periods prior to the assertion of the FRAME# signal line.

During a configuration transaction, the protocol is the same as listed above with the following exceptions:

■ The IDSEL signal lines are driven by a platform resource that is programmed by the PCI-X bus master. Typically it is the HOST/PCI-X or PCI-X/PCI-X BRIDGES acting as a PCI-X bus master, that drives the IDSEL signal lines via the AD signal lines.

■ The "target" in the above section is defined as the "device" according to the configuration transaction protocol. The device is defined as any PCI-X resource that has configuration registers; it includes PCI-X bus masters, targets, and bridges.

The remaining signal lines for all bus transactions are owned according to the following protocol:

■ The CLK and RST# signal lines are owned by the central resource.

■ The GNTx# signal lines are owned by the central arbiter.

■ The LOCK# signal line is owned by the Lock master.

■ The INTx# signal lines are owned by various PCI resources.

■ The REQ64#, ACK64#, PAR64, C/BE#[7::4], and AD[63::32] signal lines are driven to logical "1" by pull-up resistors.

For further information, see Subchapters 6.13: *More Details of PCI-X Signal Line Protocol for 32 Data Bit Bus Transactions*, 6.15: *PCI-X 64 Data Bit Extension*, and 6.18: *More Details of PCI-X Signal Line Protocol for 64 Data Bit Bus Transactions*.

SIGNAL LINE PROTOCOL CONSIDERATIONS

The signal line protocol according to the PCI-X addendum specification is essentially the same as defined by the PCI local bus specification earlier in this chapter. As discussed in the previous section, the signal lines are driven and tri-stated relative to the rising edge of the CLK signal line. As previously discussed for PCI bus transactions, the unlabeled areas between the parallel solid lines indicate that the signal lines are driven to a stable level but do not always contain valid information and under certain conditions will actually be tri-stated. Also, for PCI transactions, the single horizontal line has several meanings: Exchange signal line ownership in the bus transaction and between bus transactions, and when logical "1", are driven by the PCI resource or tri-stated by a pull-up resistor. The PCI-X bus transaction protocol is the same as the PCI bus transaction protocol with following DIFFERENCES (shown in Figures 6-1-A and 6-1-B):

- The dotted lines in the unlabeled areas between the parallel solid lines indicate that the signal lines are driven to a stable level (but do not always contain valid information) or are tri-stated. According to the PCI local bus specification, a dotted line between the solid parallel lines is not defined. Accoriding to the protocols adopted by this book, the parallel lines with a dotted line (no letter designation) in a PCI-X bus transaction is essentially the same as parallel lines without a dotted line (no letter designation) with the qualifications defined by the IRDY#, DEVSEL#, and TRDY# signal lines.

Note: The PCI-X addendum specification actually uses a different figure drawing protocol for bus transactions. The one adopted for PCI-X bus transactions in this book is visually simpler and more compatible in appearance with the previously published protocols for PCI bus transactions.

- In PCI-X bus transactions, the DATA PHASE for read transactions (including interrupt acknowledge transactions) has two interpretations for the dotted line in between the parallel solid lines:

  - The AD signal lines are tri-stated prior to the assertion (plus one CLK signal line period after assertion) of the DEVSEL# signal.

  - The AD signal lines are driven to a stable level (but do not always contain valid information) one CLK signal line period after the assertion of the DEVSEL# signal line.

Other considerations related to signal line protocol for a PCI-X bus segment are ADDRESS/DATA STEPPING and PRE-DRIVE. The ADDRESS/DATA STEPPING protocol does not apply to any PCI-X bus transaction. The PRE-DRIVE protocol does not apply to any PCI-X bus transaction except for configuration read and write transactions. See the discussion later in this chapter of the PRE-DRIVE protocol applied to configuration read and write transactions.

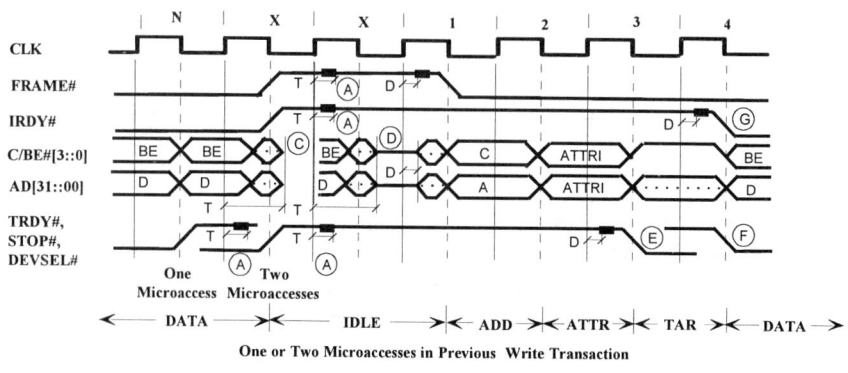

One or Two Microaccesses in Previous Write Transaction

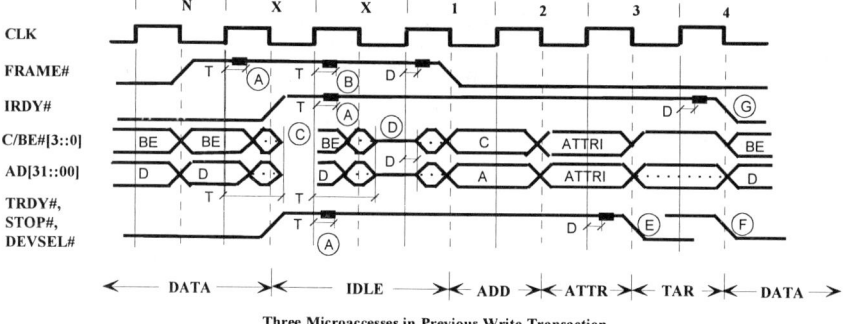

Three Microaccesses in Previous Write Transaction

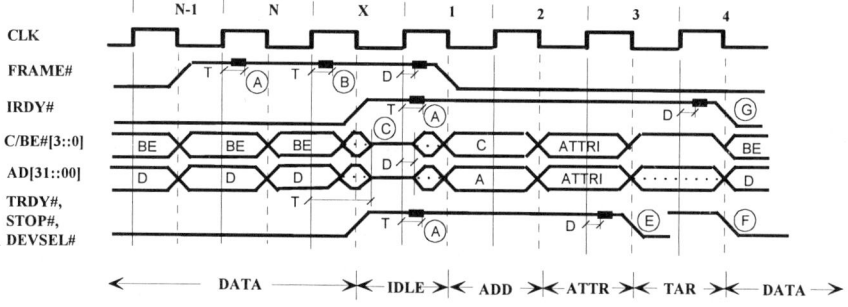

Four or More Microaccesses in Previous Write Transaction

C = COMMAND TYPE
BE = BYTE ENABLES   BEX = DON'T CARE BYTE ENABLE
A = ADDRESS   ATTR = ATTTRIBUTE
D = DATA   TAR = TARGET RESPONSE

Figure 6-1-A: PCI-X Drive and Tri-state Points in the Write Bus Transaction Protocol with Minimum IDLE PHASE

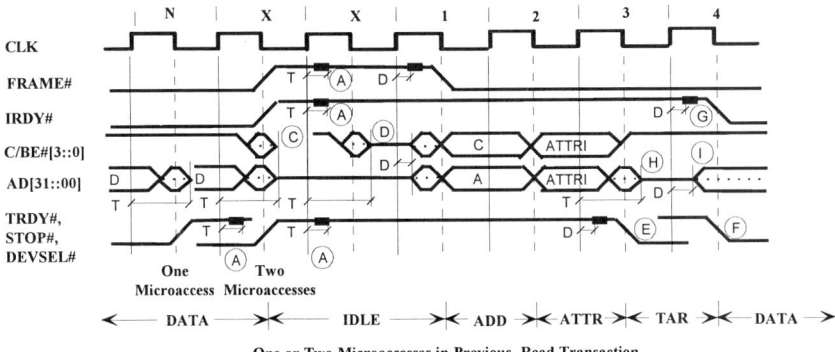

One or Two Microaccesses in Previous Read Transaction

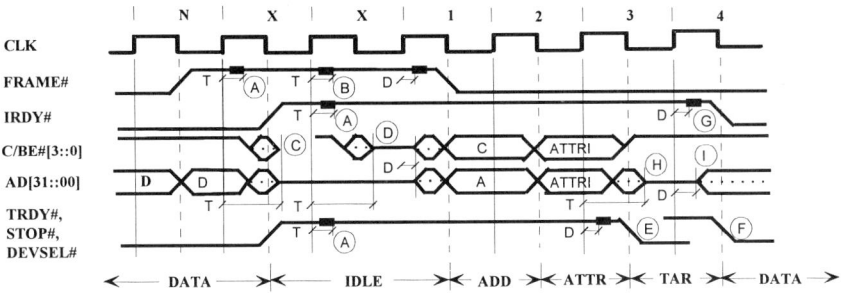

Three Microaccesses in Previous Read Transaction

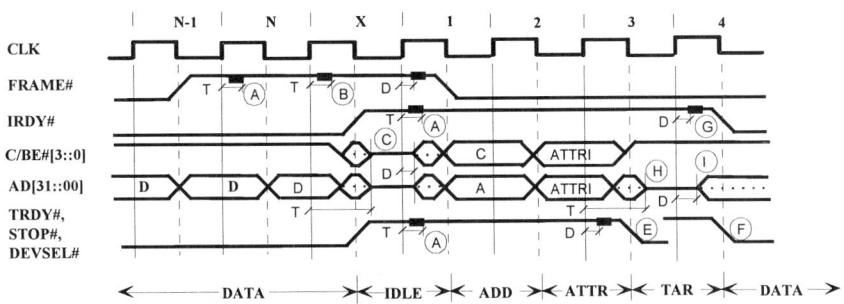

Four or More Microaccesses in Previous Read Transaction

C = COMMAND TYPE
BE = BYTE ENABLES   BEX = DON'T CARE BYTE ENABLE
A = ADDRESS   ATTR = ATTTRIBUTE
D = DATA   TAR = TARGET RESPONSE

**Figure 6-1-B: PCI-X Drive and Tri-state Points in the Read Bus Transaction
Protocol with Minimum IDLE PHASE**

> The term "tri-state" is used in this book and assumes that no PCI-X resource is specifically driving the signal line. The definition is correct after the "T" timing mark in the figures. Prior to the "T" timing marks, the signal lines represented by the dotted line in the unlabeled areas between the parallel solid lines indicate driven to a stable level (but do not always contain valid information) or are tri-stated. The term "tri-state" as defined above still applies, but the PCI-X addendum specification uses the term "float". "Float" may not be the same output driver state as "tri-state", but as far as the bus transaction protocol is concerned, both terms indicate that the signal line is not being driven to logical "1'" or "0" by the output driver of the PCI-X resource. If the "floated" or "tri-stated" signal line is attached to a pull-up or pull-down resistor; the signal line will bias towards Vcc or ground, respectively.
>
> Similarly, after the "D" timing marks, the signal lines represented by the dotted line in the unlabeled areas between the parallel solid lines indicate a driven stable level (but do not always contain valid information) or are tri-stated. The "D" timing marks represent the earliest point a device output driver is activated, but does not mean that the signal line is actually being driven.

The other considerations for the PCI-X signal line protocol for bus transaction are as follows:

■ Unlike the PCI local bus specification, the PCI-X addendum specification makes no assumption of bus segment ownership retention between bus transactions. One consideration is that the Fast Back to Back protocol is not defined for PCI-X bus transactions. Thus, the focus of PCI-X bus transactions is for the PCI-X bus master to tri-state signal lines at the end of each bus transaction. If the bus segment ownership is retained, the boundary conditions for tri-stating and driving are required to follow the GNTx# signal line deassertion by one PCI-X bus master relative to the assertion of the FRAME# signal line by another PCI-X bus master. See Chapter 9: *Bus Segment Ownership* for more information.

■ As with PCI bus transactions, a target must tri-state signal lines relative to the end of the bus transaction as discussed below. There is no Fast Back to Back transaction protocol defined for PCI-X bus transactions as in the case of PCI bus transactions.

■ The minimum number of CLK signal line periods (defined as IDLE PHASE) between two bus transactions (previous and present) is dependent on the number of microaccesses in the previous bus transactions as follows:

■ When the previous bus transaction contains one, two, or three microaccesses, the previous bus transition was a special transaction, or the previous bus transaction was terminated in a Master Abort termination; the minimum length of the IDLE PHASE after the previous bus transaction is two CLK signal line periods (identified with "X" in Figures 6-1-A and 6-1-B).

■ When the previous bus transaction has four or more microaccesses, the minimum length of the IDLE PHASE after the previous bus transaction is one CLK signal line period (identified with "X" in the Figures 6-1-A and 6-1-B).

■ The points at the end of the bus transaction that the signal lines can be deasserted and tri-stated according to the PCI-X addendum bus specification are as follows (see Figures 6-1-A and 6-1-B):

■ The FRAME# and IRDY# signal lines are deasserted following the "General Deassertion" protocol, as visually summarized in Figures 6-1-A and 6-1-B (see Subchapter 6.12: *32 Data Bit PCI-X Bus Master to 32 Data Bit Target* for more information on "General Deassertion" protocol). The FRAME# and IRDY# signal lines are required to be tri-stated one CLK signal line period (Circle A) after their deassertion with one exception: The FRAME# signal line can be tri-stated either one or two CLK signal line periods (Circles A or B) after their deassertion when the previous bus transaction has three or more microaccesses.

■ The REQ64# and ACK64# signal lines follow the protocol of the FRAME# and DEVSEL# signal lines, respectively. The LOCK# signal line tri-states one CLK signal line period after it is deasserted when the PCI-X bus master relinquishes LOCK# signal line ownership.

■ The TRDY#, STOP#, and DEVSEL# signal lines are deasserted (if not already) at the end of the last microaccess. These signal lines are tri-stated at the rising edge of a CLK signal line, one CLK signal line period after the last microaccess.

■ For write transactions and special transactions with four or more microaccesses, the AD[31::00] and C/BE#[3::0] signal lines are tri-stated simultaneously with the deassertion of the IRDY# signal line (Circle C in Figure 6-1-A). For write transactions and special transactions with three or fewer microaccesses, the AD[31::00] and C/BE#[3::0] signal lines are tri-stated simultaneously with the deassertion of the IRDY# signal line or one CLK signal line period later (Circles C and D in Figure 6-1-A).

■ For read transactions and interrupt acknowledge transactions, the AD[31::00] signal lines are tri-stated simultaneously with the last deassertion of one of the following that established the last microaccess: TRDY# signal line, DEVSEL# signal line, and STOP# signal line (Circle C in Figure 6-1-B).

■ For read transactions with four or more microaccesses, the C/BE#[3::0] signal lines are tri-stated simultaneously with the deassertion of the IRDY# signal line (Circle C of Figure 6-1-B). For read transactions with three or fewer microaccesses, and interrupt acknowledge transactions, the C/BE#[3::0] signal lines are tri-stated simultaneously with the deassertion of the IRDY# signal line or one CLK signal line period later (Circles C and D of Figure 6-1-B)

■ If the bus transaction terminates with Master Abort termination, the AD[31::00] and C/BE#[3::0] signal lines are tri-stated simultaneously with the deassertion of the IRDY# signal line or one CLK signal line period later.

■ The PAR signal line follows the protocol of the AD[31::00] signal lines except there is a one CLK signal line period delay. The PERR# signal line follows the PAR signal line protocol with an additional one CLK signal line period delay.

■ The points at the beginning of the bus transaction that signal lines can be driven and asserted are as follows (Note: The driving points discussed below are not the only possibilities. But they do identify "safe" driving points that will meet all of the conditions to avoid buffer fights between the previous bus transaction and the present bus transaction):

■ The latest point the FRAME# signal line can be driven is in the same CLK signal line period it is asserted.

■ The earliest point the IRDY# signal line can be driven is one CLK signal line period after the FRAME# signal line is asserted. The latest point the IRDY# signal line can be driven is in the same CLK signal line period it is asserted. The IRDY# signal line is required to be asserted one CLK signal line period after the end of the ATTRIBUTE PHASE (immediately after the TARGET RESPONSE) (Circle G in Figures 6-1-A and 6-1-B).

■ The earliest point the DEVSEL# signal line can be driven is one CLK signal line period after the rising edge of the CLK signal line that samples the AD and C/BE# signal lines in the ADDRESS PHASE (Circle E in Figures 6-1-A and 6-1-B). The earliest point the TRDY# and STOP# signal lines can be driven is two CLK signal line periods after the rising edge of the CLK signal line that samples the AD and C/BE# signal lines in the ADDRESS PHASE (Circle F in Figures 6-1-A and 6-1-B). The latest point the TRDY#, STOP#, or DEVSEL# signal lines can be driven is in the same CLK signal line period each respective signal line is asserted. The best protocol is to drive the STOP# and/or TRDY# signal lines simultaneously with or subsequent to driving the DEVSEL# signal line. The TRDY# and/or STOP# signal lines can only be asserted simultaneously with or after the assertion of the DEVSEL# signal line.

The earliest driving and assertion points for the aforementioned signal lines are delayed by one CLK signal line period when DUAL ADDRESS command is executed.

■ For all bus transactions, except configuration transaction, the latest the AD[31::00] or C/BE#[3::0] signal lines can be driven valid is the same CLK signal line period that the FRAME# signal line is asserted. For a configuration transaction, the AD[31::00] or C/BE#[3::0] signal lines are driven prior to the assertion of the FRAME# signal line following the PRE-DRIVE protocol (see more information later in this chapter).

■ The PAR signal line follows the same "driven" protocol as the AD[31::00] signal lines, except there is a one CLK signal line period delay. The PERR# signal line follows the PAR signal line protocol with an additional one CLK signal line period delay.

■ The REQ64# and ACK64# signal lines follow the protocol of the FRAME# and DEVSEL# signal lines, respectively. The LOCK# signal line is tri-stated one CLK signal line period after it is deasserted when the PCI-X bus master relinquishes LOCK# signal line ownership.

■ See Subchapter 6.17: *64 Data Bit PCI-X Bus Master to 64 Data Bit Target* for information about the AD[32::63], C/BE#[7::4], and PAR64 signal lines.

DUAL ADDRESS

Like the PCI bus segment, the PCI-X bus segment supports both 32 and 64 bit address spaces for the memory address space. Also like PCI, a PCI-X I/O transaction only supports 32 address bits encoded into the AD[31::0] signal lines. The only difference is that a PCI-X device that supports memory transactions is required to support both 32 and 64 bit addressing.

The previously discussed DUAL ADDRESS command protocol for PCI bus transactions is also implemented by PCI-X bus transactions. To support a 64 bit address, the PCI-X bus master multiplexes the address onto the AD[31::0] signal lines in the bus transaction in the same fashion as the PCI bus master does with its bus transaction. See the discussion in the previous section for a PCI bus transaction. Figure 6-1-C is an example of a 32 data bit PCI-X bus transaction.

A PCI-X bus master that supports the 64 bit address space and only addresses the lower four gigabytes *cannot* execute bus transactions with DUAL ADDRESS. By definition, the upper order address bits are logical "0".

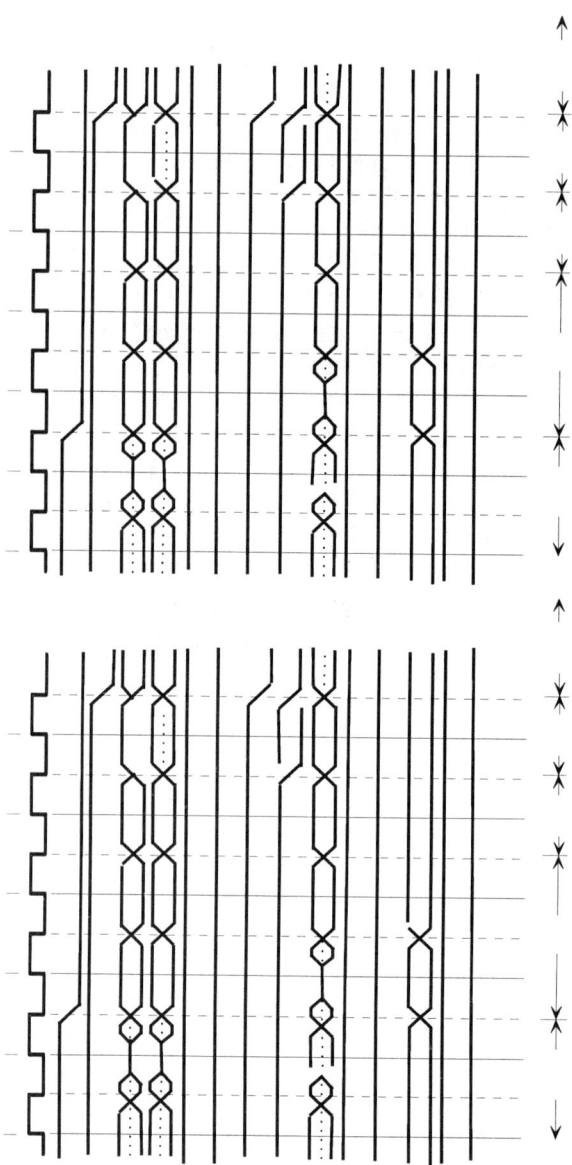

Figure 6-1-C: ADDRESS PHASE Protocol for Write Transaction, 32 Data Bit PCI-X Bus Master

> The 64 bit address space (DUAL ADDRESS) is not defined for the I/O, configuration, interrupt acknowledge, or special transactions. In the case of special and interrupt acknowledge transactions, there is no address involved in the protocol.

PCI SPECIFIC IMPLEMENTATION

6.1 32 DATA BIT PCI BUS MASTER TO 32 DATA BIT TARGET

SINGLE MEMORY OR I/O READ TRANSACTIONS

A SINGLE read transaction (to memory or I/O address space) begins with the PCI bus master asserting the FRAME# signal line, driving valid COMMAND type information onto the C/BE#[3::0] lines, and a valid address onto the AD[31::0] signal lines (see Figure 6-3). This activity comprises the ADDRESS PHASE of the bus transaction.

Immediately following the ADDRESS PHASE is the DATA PHASE. At the beginning of the DATA PHASE, the PCI bus master drives valid byte enable information onto the C/BE#[3::0] signal lines and tri-states the AD[31::0] signal lines (see Figure 6-3). Also during this transition period, the TRDY#, DEVSEL#, and STOP# signal lines are driven by the target.

For a STANDARD SINGLE read transaction, the IRDY# and DEVSEL# signal lines must be asserted in the second or third CLK signal line periods. The AD[31::0] signal lines must be tri-stated by the PCI bus master at the beginning of the second CLK signal line period. The tri-state of these signal lines allows the target to drive them at the beginning of the third CLK signal line period. The TRDY# signal line cannot be asserted until the third CLK signal line period for a read transaction. The STANDARD SINGLE read transaction is continued until the IRDY# and TRDY# are both asserted at the end of the third CLK signal line period, and the IRDY#, TRDY#, and DEVSEL# signal lines are subsequently deasserted. Also, at this time the AD[31::0] signal lines are tri-stated by the target, and the C/BE#[3::0] signal lines do not have valid byte enable information. One CLK signal line period later, the AD[31::0] signal lines are driven by the PCI bus master for the next bus transaction. The bus transaction is completed when the FRAME# and IRDY# signal lines are both deasserted.

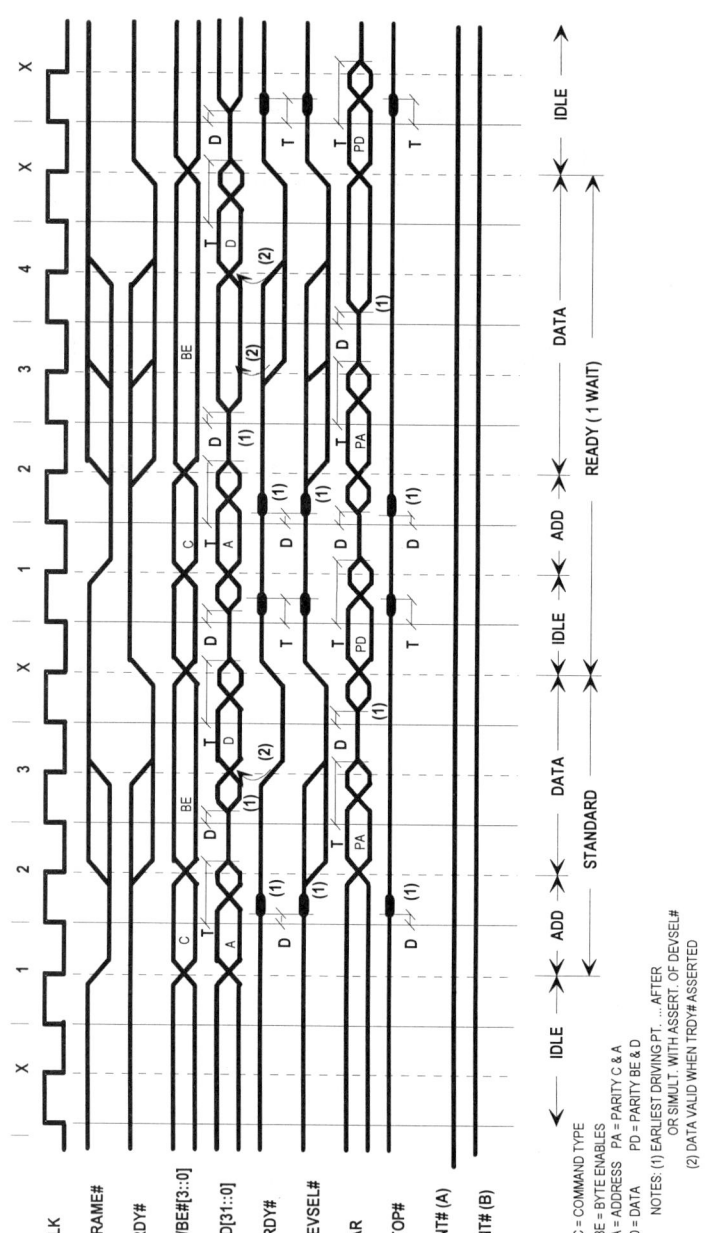

Figure 6-3: PCI Single Read Transaction without DUAL ADDRESS: Parked, Executed, and Retained by (A)

Ideally, all SINGLE read transactions should be STANDARD for maximum system performance; however, in reality not all resources can operate at maximum bus speed. Consequently, the PCI local bus specification also defines a protocol called READY to accommodate slower resources. For a READY SINGLE read transaction, the DEVSEL# signal line must be asserted within the first four CLK signal line rising edges of the DATA PHASE; if not, a Master Abort termination will be executed. The AD[31::0] signal lines must be tri-stated by the PCI bus master at the beginning of the second CLK signal line period. The tri-state of these signal lines allows the target to drive them at the beginning of the third CLK signal line period. The READY SINGLE read transaction continues until the IRDY# and TRDY# signal lines are both sampled asserted on a rising edge of the CLK signal line. The IRDY# signal lines can be asserted as early as the second CLK signal line period. The TRDY# signal line cannot be asserted until the third CLK signal line period for a read transaction. The bus transaction continues until the IRDY# and TRDY# signal lines are both asserted. Subsequently, the IRDY#, TRDY#, and DEVSEL# signal lines are subsequently deasserted. Also, at this time the AD[31::0] signal lines are tri-stated by the target, and the C/BE#[3::0] signal lines do not have valid information. One CLK signal line period later, the AD[31::0] signal lines are driven by the PCI bus master for a new bus transaction. The bus transaction completes when the FRAME# and IRDY# signal lines are both deasserted.

The PAR signal line provides even parity for the C/BE#[3::0] and AD[31::0] signal lines. The value of the PAR signal line reflects the value of these signal lines one CLK signal line period earlier. The points in the bus transaction where the PAR signal line are tri-stated and driven are same as the AD[31::0] signal lines but delayed by one CLK signal line period.

> The above discussion assumes data is accessed on the last CLK signal line rising edge prior to the IDLE PHASE. Accordingly, the TRDY# signal is asserted at this CLK signal line rising edge. Under certain conditions the TRDY# signal line may be deasserted at the last CLK signal line rising edge prior to the IDLE PHASE. See subchapter 6.2 for more information.

SINGLE MEMORY OR I/O WRITE TRANSACTIONS

A SINGLE write transaction (to memory or I/O address space) begins in the same fashion as the read transaction (see Figure 6-4). Unlike the read transaction shown in Figure 6-3, some of the signal lines in Figure 6-4 are initially parked at a PCI bus master. Prior to the ADDRESS PHASE, the Park master tri-states some of the signal lines and the PCI bus master will execute the bus transaction by driving these signal lines.

Immediately following the ADDRESS PHASE is the DATA PHASE. At the beginning of the DATA PHASE, the PCI bus master drives valid byte enable information onto the C/BE#[3::0] signal lines, and drives the AD[31::0] signal lines (see Figure 6-4). Valid data is not always available at the very beginning of the DATA PHASE. Also, during this period the TRDY#, DEVSEL#, and STOP# signal lines are driven by the target but may not be immediately asserted. The STOP# signal line may or may not be asserted during the DATA PHASE.

For a STANDARD SINGLE write transaction, the IRDY#, TRDY#, and DEVSEL# signal lines must be asserted in the second CLK signal line period. The STANDARD SINGLE write transaction is continued with the IRDY# and TRDY# signal lines both asserted at the end of the second CLK signal line period, and the IRDY#, TRDY#, and DEVSEL# signal lines subsequently deasserted. Also, during the completion of the bus transaction the AD[31::0] and the C/BE#[3::0] signal lines do not contain valid information. The bus transaction completes when the FRAME# and IRDY# signal lines both deasserted.

For a READY SINGLE write transaction, the DEVSEL# must be asserted within the first four CLK signal line rising edges of the DATA PHASE; if not, a Master Abort termination will be executed. The READY write transaction continues until the IRDY# and TRDY# signal lines are both asserted. The IRDY# and TRDY# signal lines can be asserted as early as the second CLK signal line period. Subsequently, the IRDY#, TRDY#, and DEVSEL# signal lines are deasserted. Also, during the completion of the bus transaction the AD[31::0] and C/BE#[3::0] signal lines do not have valid information. The bus transaction is completed when the FRAME# and IRDY# signal lines are both deasserted.

The PAR signal line provides even parity for the C/BE#[3::0] and AD[31::0] signal lines. The value of the PAR signal line reflects the value of these signal lines one CLK signal line period earlier. The points in the bus transaction where the PAR signal line are tri-stated and driven are the same as the AD[31::0] signal lines but delayed by one CLK signal line period.

> The above discussion assumes data is accessed on the last CLK signal line rising edge prior to the IDLE PHASE. Accordingly, the TRDY# signal line is asserted at this CLK signal line rising edge. Under certain conditions the TRDY# signal line may be deasserted at the last CLK signal line rising edge prior to the IDLE PHASE. See subchapter 6.2 for more information.

BURST MEMORY AND I/O READ AND WRITE TRANSACTIONS

BURST bus transactions (to memory or I/O address space) allow the PCI bus master to access the target as a sequence of microaccesses. The bus transaction begins with the PCI bus master asserting the FRAME# signal line, driving valid control bus transaction information onto the C/BE#[3::0] signal lines, and driving valid address onto the AD[31::0] signal lines (see Figures 6-5 and 6-6). This activity comprises the ADDRESS PHASE for the entire BURST bus transaction, and establishes the base address for all microaccesses. Just prior to the ADDRESS PHASE, the PCI bus master begins driving these signal lines if the bus was not parked at the PCI bus master that will execute the bus transaction.

Immediately following the ADDRESS PHASE is the DATA PHASE. At the beginning of the DATA PHASE, the PCI bus master drives valid byte enable bus transaction information onto the C/BE#[3::0] signal lines, and drives data onto the AD[31::0] signal lines for a write transaction, or tri-states the AD[31::0] signal lines for a read transaction (see Figures 6-5 and 6-6). Also, during this period the TRDY#, DEVSEL#, STOP# signal lines are driven by the target.

As previously discussed, a *microaccess* is a naming convention that identifies the individual data accesses within a BURST bus transaction. The *initial microaccess* begins at the end of the ADDRESS PHASE and ends when the IRDY# and TRDY# signal lines are first both asserted. *Subsequent microaccesses* begin with the end of the previous microaccess and end when the IRDY# and TRDY# signal lines are both asserted. The last microaccess of a BURST bus transaction completes the data access when the IRDY# and TRDY# signal lines are both asserted, but the under certain conditions the microaccess will complete in a later CLK signal line period. See Chapter 3: *Generic PCI and PCI-X Hardware Operation* and Chapter 8: *Master and Target Termination* for more information. In the case of a SINGLE bus transaction, the first and only access can also be defined as the intial microaccess.

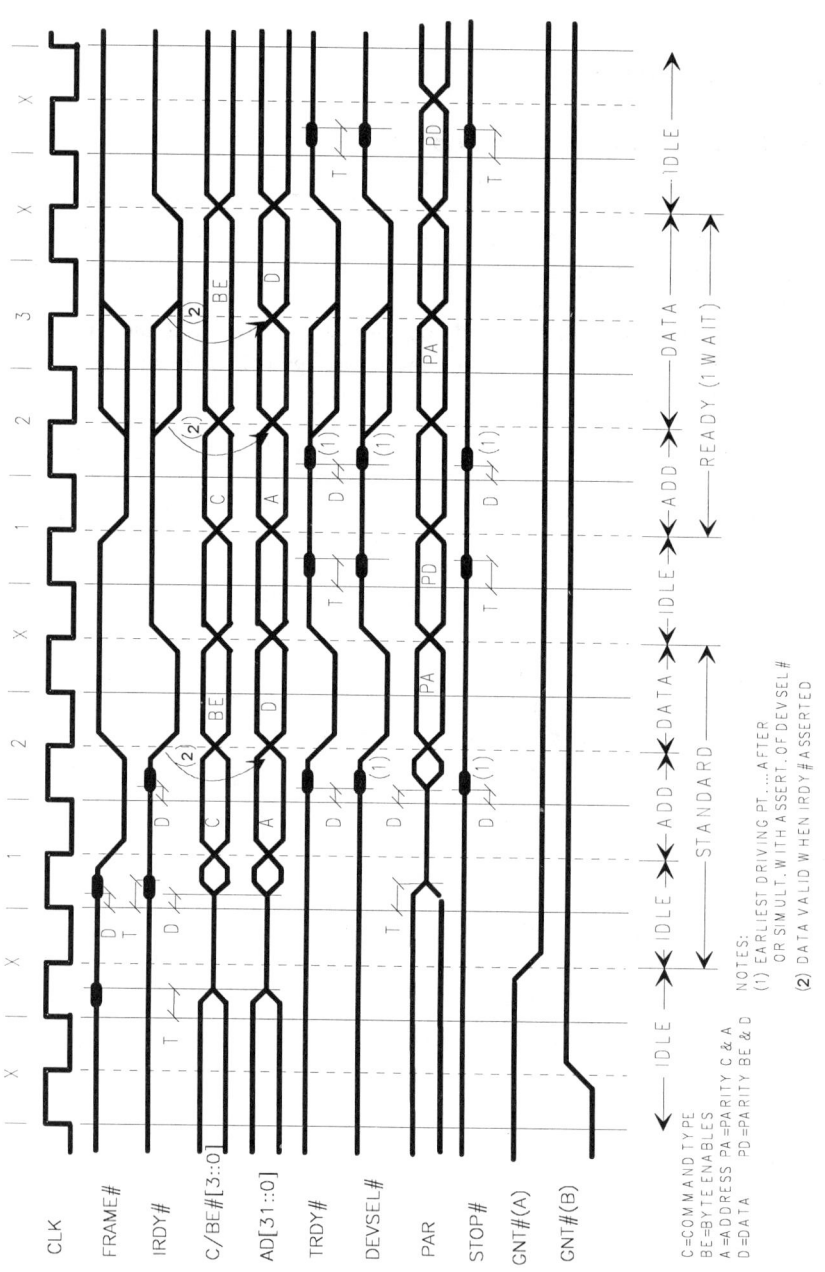

Figure 6-4: PCI Single Write Transaction without DUAL ADDRESS Parked at (B), Executed and Retained by (A), Non-Fast Back-to-Back

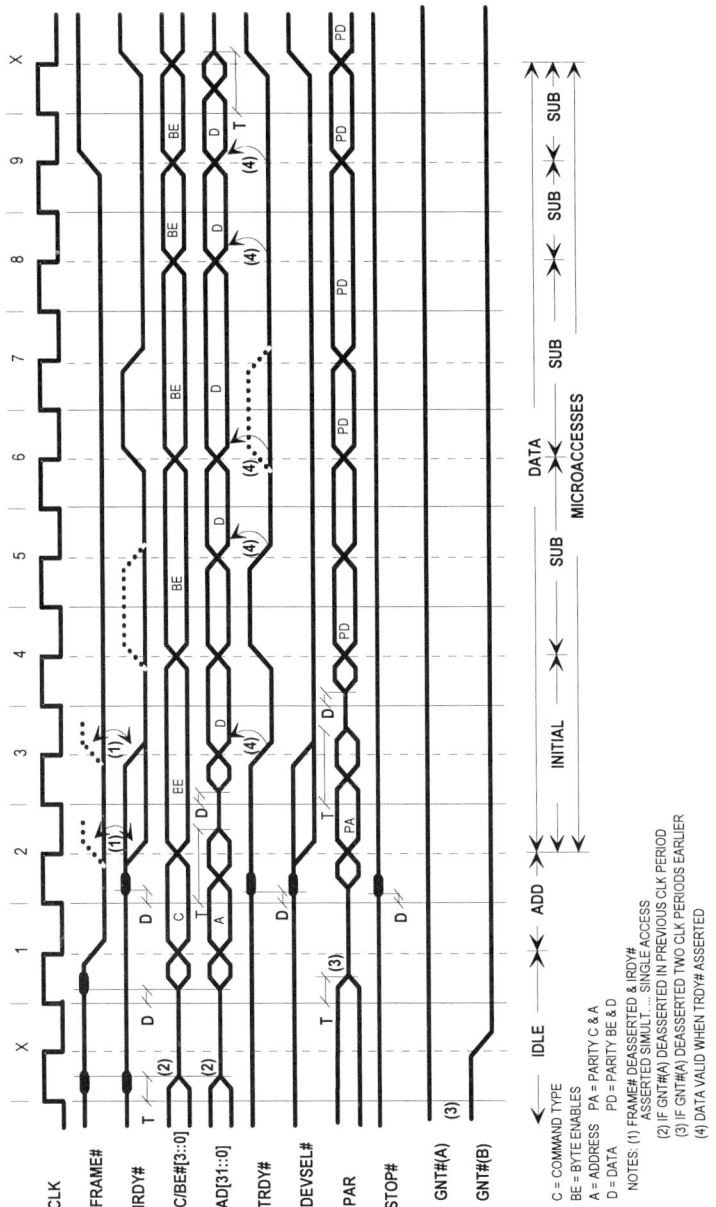

Figure 6-5: PCI Burst Read Transaction without DUAL ADDRESS Parked at (A), Executed and Retained by (B)

351

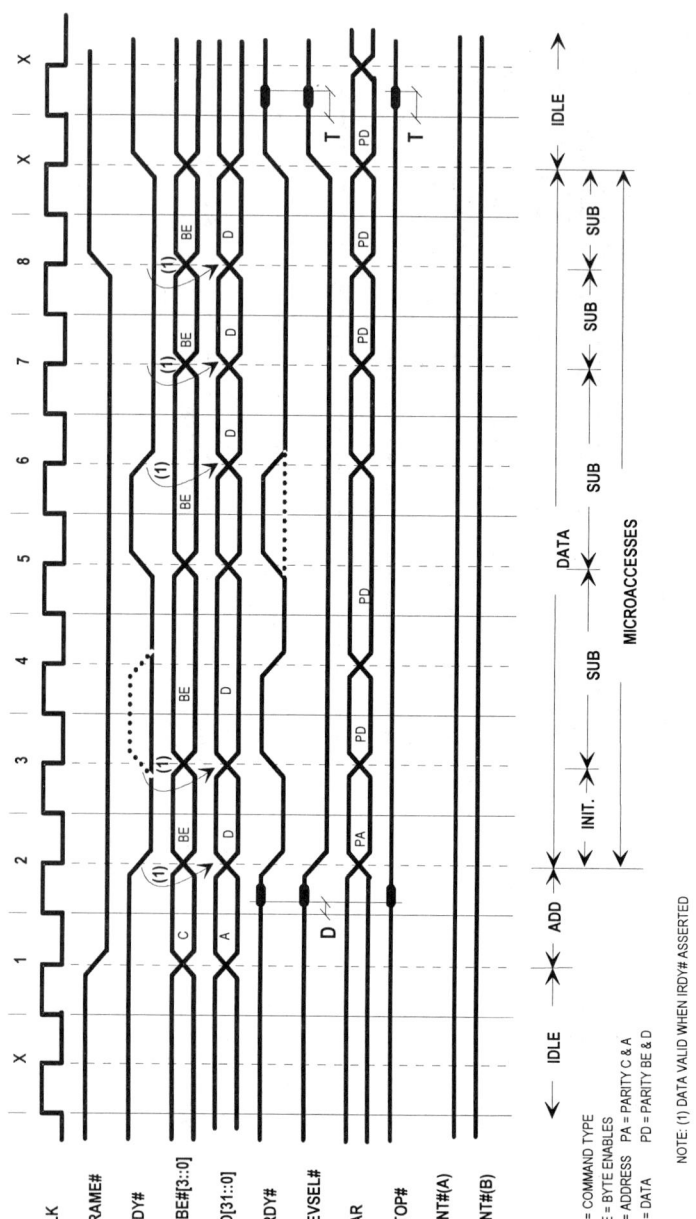

Figure 6-6: PCI Burst Write Transaction without DUAL ADDRESS Parked at (A), Executed and Retained by (A)

Unlike the SINGLE bus transaction in which the entire bus transaction can be defined as STANDARD or READY, the BURST bus transaction can consist of a mixture of microaccesses with or without added wait states. STARDARD microaccesses do not have wait states while READY microaccesses have wait states. The existence of a wait state is determined for each microaccess on a case by case basis and can be requested by either the PCI bus master or target.

The protocol to distinguish between a SINGLE bus transaction and a BURST bus transaction is the value of the FRAME# signal line when the IRDY# signal line is asserted. If the FRAME# signal line is deasserted at the first assertion of the IRDY# signal line, the bus transaction is completed as a SINGLE bus transaction. Otherwise, the bus transaction proceeds as a BURST bus transaction and is required to execute at least two microaccesses.

> **If the IRDY# signal line is asserted, the FRAME# signal line must be deasserted to insure a SINGLE bus transaction. This is because the TRDY# signal line can be asserted at any time.**

When the bus transaction is established as a BURST bus transaction, the data will be accessed according to the following protocol:

- The data will be accessed on each rising edge of the CLK signal line when the IRDY# and TRDY# signal lines are both asserted. DATA access will not occur on a rising edge of the CLK signal line when either the IRDY# or TRDY# signal line is deasserted.

- The values of the AD[31::0] signal lines establish the base address of the initial microaccess (see Figures 6-5 and 6-6). All subsequent microaccesses reflect the incremental address of four bytes from the previous microaccess for the linear addressing modes. For other address modes the order will be different. See Chapter 4: *Functional Interaction Between PCI Resources* for more information.

- The COMMAND type of the BURST bus transaction is established by the C/BE#[3::0] during the ADDRESS PHASE of the initial microaccess. The type of access remains the same for the entire BURST bus transaction.

- The values of the C/BE#[3::0] signal lines during the DATA PHASE reflect the byte lanes that are being accessed by the associated microaccess. For the initial microaccess, the C/BE#[3::0] signal line value changes to the first byte lane value at the transition from the ADDRESS and DATA PHASES. For the subsequent microaccesses, the values of the C/BE#[3::0] signal lines may change when the IRDY# and TRDY# signal lines are both asserted for the completion of the present microaccess.

353

■   The BURST bus transaction is completed when the FRAME# signal line
is deasserted and the IRDY# and TRDY# signal lines are both asserted;
subsequently, the FRAME# and IRDY# signal lines are both deasserted.

The above discussion assumes data is accessed on the last CLK signal
line rising edge prior to the IDLE PHASE. Accordingly, the TRDY# signal is
asserted at this CLK signal line rising edge. Under certain conditions the
TRDY# signal line may be deasserted at the last CLK signal line rising
edge prior to the IDLE PHASE. See subchapter 6.2 for more information.

For a SINGLE bus transaction it is possible for the FRAME# signal line to
be asserted for multiple CLK single line periods. For a SINGLE bus
transaction it is required that the FRAME# signal line is deasserted with
the simultaneous assertion of the IRDY# signal line.

The FRAME# signal line cannot be deasserted until the second to last data
is accessed, but must be deasserted before the last data is accessed.

The BURST bus transaction usually accesses data entirely within a single
target, but the PCI bus master may not know the actual boundary of a
specific target. Consequently, one microaccess would be to one target and
the next microaccess to another. The PCI bus protocol requires that when
the target boundary is crossed, the BURST bus transaction must be
terminated as outlined in the following example:

The PCI bus master is accessing target (A) with a BURST bus transaction
with increasing linear addressing. It accesses data at address (X) with
microaccess (N). Microaccess (N+1) accesses data in target (B) at address
(X+1). Target (B) has not claimed the BURST bus transaction (assertion of
the DEVSEL# signal line) and target (A) is required to execute a Disconnect
without data termination in microaccess (N+1). The PCI bus master has
successfully accessed data at address (X) in target (A) when the bus
transaction termination is executed, but no data has been accessed in
target (B). Consequently, when the PCI bus master accesses target (B)
with a new bus transaction, it can begin with accessing data at address
(X+1). If a Cacheline wrap addressing sequence is implemented, the
protocol is the same.

The above protocol is also applicable to the crossing of the 4K byte boundary limit within a single target for MRL and MRM transactions (see below). Also, the above protocol can apply as needed to the HOST/PCI BRDIGE relative to the Cacheline boundary issues.

For a 32 data bit bus transaction, the PCI bus master accessing 32 data bit increments to the targets (both targets (A) and (B)), the number "1" in the "address (x+1)" represents the incremental address of four bytes. For 64 data bit bus transaction, the number "1" represents the incremental address of eight bytes.

MEMORY READ LINE (MRL) TRANSACTIONS

The MRL transaction operates with the same protocol as the non-MRL SINGLE or BURST memory read transaction, including the support of DUAL ADDRESS. During ADDRESS PHASE, the C/BE#[3::0] signal lines contain the encoded information of the COMMAND type. The 1110 ([3::0]) encoding indicates an MRL transaction. The MRL transaction indicates to the PCI memory resource (target) that three or more 32 data bit (double) words will be read. In theory, an MRL transaction can be executed as a series of MRL SINGLE memory read transactions, but in practice the reading of multiple double words should be performed with a series of MRL BURST memory read transactions within Cacheline boundaries.

A non-MRL transaction is defined as a memory read transaction with an encoding on the C/BE# signal lines of 0110 ([3::0]) during the ADDRESS PHASE.

The use of the MRL transaction allows the memory resource to perform advance memory reads of double words and to pipeline the data. Proper use of this type of the bus transaction will improve system performance.

If the memory target supports MRL transactions and the PCI bus master completes an MRL or non- MRL read transaction by accessing only two or fewer 32 data bits (double words), the bus transaction is successfully completed without an error related to accessing fewer than three double words. If the PCI bus master uses the MRL transaction, it is responsible that no adverse side effects will occur when pre-read memory data is not used and the associated buffers are "cleared" by the target.

If the PCI memory resource (target) does not support MRL transactions and the PCI bus master executes an MRL transaction, the bus transaction completes as a non-MRL read transaction with in the target. It still appears to the PCI bus segments as an MRL transaction because of the COMMAND type during ADDRESS PHASE.

The PCI memory resource is NOT REQUIRED TO BE CACHED OR CACHEABLE to be accessed by an MRL transaction. The use of the Cacheline size is simply as a unit of measure of the "line size".

MRL transactions are limited to a 4K byte block on 4K address boundaries. If a PCI master attempts to cross this boundary (FRAME# signal line asserted for the last subsequent microaccess below the boundary) and the data is ready for access, the target must execute a Disconnect with data termination. Under this condition, if the data is not ready, the target executes a Disconnect without data termination.

MEMORY READ MULTIPLE (MRM) TRANSACTIONS

The MRM transaction operates with the same protocol as a non-MRM SINGLE or BURST memory read transaction, including the support of DUAL ADDRESS. During the ADDRESS PHASE, the C/BE#[3::0] signal lines contain the encoded information of the COMMAND type. The 1100 ([3::0]) encoding indicates an MRM transaction. The MRM transaction indicates to the PCI memory resource (target) that multiple Cachelines will be read. In theory, an MRM can be executed as a series of MRM SINGLE memory read transactions; but in practice, the reading of the Cachelines should be performed with a series of MRM BURST memory read transactions within Cacheline boundaries.

A non-MRM transaction is defined as a memory read transaction with an encoding on the C/BE# signal lines of 0110 ([3::0]) during the ADDRESS PHASE.

The use of the MRM transaction allows the memory resource to do advance memory reads of entire Cachelines and to pipeline the data. The proper use of this transaction will improve system performance.

If the memory target supports MRM transactions and the PCI bus master completes an MRM transaction on a non-cache boundary, the bus transaction completes without an error related to accessing less than an entire Cacheline. The intention of the MRM transaction is to provide the memory resource "advance information" such that additional Cachelines will be accessed. Consequently, the use of an MRM transaction for one Cacheline (or less) should be avoided. If the PCI bus master uses the MRM transaction, it is responsible that no adverse side effects will occur when pre-read memory data is not used and the associated buffers are "cleared" by the target.

If the PCI memory resource (target) does not support MRM transactions and the PCI bus master executes an MRM transaction, the target executes the transaction as a memory read or a MRL transaction. It still appears to the PCI bus segment as an MRM transaction because of the COMMAND type during the ADDRESS PHASE. The performance of the bus would be less because a Cacheline pre-read does not occur.

The PCI memory resource is NOT REQUIRED TO BE CACHED OR CACHEABLE to be accessed by an MRM transaction. The reference to cache lines simply provides a "size" relative to the number of bytes to be pre-read. The MRM transaction provides the best PCI bus performance for reading multiple Cachelines. Support of the Cacheline Size Register is not required for this COMMAND type, but if supported it should be used as an indicator for the optimum use of the MRM transaction. As the default, 32 data bytes (for 32 data bit PCI buses) or 64 data bytes (for 64 data bit PCI buses) should be used.

MRM transactions are limited to a 4K byte block on 4K address boundaries. If a PCI master attempts to cross this boundary (FRAME# signal line asserted for the last subsequent microaccess below the boundary) and the data is ready for access, the target must execute a Disconnect with data termination. Under this condition, if the data is not ready, the target executes a Disconnect without data termination.

MEMORY WRITE AND INVALIDATE (MWI) TRANSACTIONS

The MWI transaction operates with the same protocol as a non-MWI BURST memory write transaction, including the support of DUAL ADDRESS. During the

ADDRESS PHASE, the C/BE#[3::0] signal lines contain the encoded information of the COMMAND type. The 1111 ([3::0]) encoding indicates an MWI transaction. The MWI transaction indicates to the PCI memory resource (target) that the entire Cacheline will be written.

> A ncn-MWI transaction is defined as a memory write transaction with an encoding on the C/BE# signal lines of 0111 ([3::0]) during the ADDRESS PHASE.

The use of the MWI transaction allows the memory resource (HOST/PCI BRIDGE) to manage the copy back operation relative to the cache. See Chapter 4: *Functional Interaction between PCI and PCI-X Resources* for more information.

> If the PCI memory resource (target) does not support MWI transactions and the PCI bus master executes an MWI transaction, the target executes the bus transaction as a non-MWI memory write. It still appears to the PCI bus segment as a MWI transaction because of the COMMAND type during the ADDRESS PHASE.

> The PCI memory resource is NOT REQUIRED TO BE CACHED OR CACHEABLE to be accessed by a MWI transaction.

CONFIGURATION TRANSACTIONS

> IMPORTANT: The following discussion about PRE-DRIVE for configuration transactions is included for completeness in explaining the PCI Local Bus Specification Rev. 2.0. Simulations performed since the writing of the bus specification indicates that the timing delay due to the extra load of the IDSEL signal lines does not cause a timing problem; a resistor between AD and IDSEL signal lines is not required. Consequently, the use of address/data stepping and pre-drive as outlined in Chapter 4: *Functional Interaction Between PCI Resources* and discussed below is not needed.
>
> The following discussion should only be used to understand platforms that may have been built according to the original PCI local bus specification prior to Rev. 2.1. The configuration transactions should follow the same protocol as a memory or I/O transaction. PCI resources that become targets should have no problem decoding the address relative to the assertion of the FRAME# signal line.

A configuration transaction begins with the PCI bus master (HOST/PCI or PCI/PCI BRIDGE) asserting the FRAME# signal line, driving valid COMMAND type information onto the C/BE#[3::0] lines and driving the AD[31::0] signal lines to a stable level (see Figure 6-7-A). For a Type 0 configuration transaction, individual AD[31::11] signal lines are attached to the individual IDSEL signal lines that are attached to each device. During the ADDRESS PHASE, only one of the IDSEL (therefore AD[31::11]) signal lines is asserted to select only one device. According to the PCI Local Bus Specification Rev. 2.0, the additional load on each of these AD signal lines may cause timing problems; consequently, the individual IDSEL signal line may have to be attached to the individual AD signal lines with a resistor. If attached via resistors, the IDSEL signal lines are not driven to a stable level as quickly as the AD signal lines. Consequently, the ADDRESS PHASE may not begin until the second CLK signal line period of the configuration transaction. The additional CLK signal line period before the ADDRESS PHASE allows the PCI bus master (HOST/PCI or PCI/PCI BRIDGE) to pre-drive the IDSEL signal lines (via the AD[31::11] signal lines), and to overcome the resistor and capacitor effects (RC time constant). "PD" is the amount of time for the IDSEL signal line to reach a stable level. In the case of a configuration read transaction (or when a PCI bus master relinquishes the bus), the IDSEL signal lines will take longer to tri-state, and the time is identified by "RCT".

In the above discussion, the configuration read transaction outlined in Figure 6-7-A was used to exemplify the pre-drive protocol. In this example, one CLK signal line period was inserted between the beginning of the configuration transaction and the ADDRESS PHASE for the PRE-DRIVE PHASE. A PRE-DRIVE PHASE is *not* required if the type of driver buffer, load of backplane, etc., are such that resistors are not used to link the AD and IDSEL signal lines. Conversely, a PRE-DRIVE PHASE of more than one CLK signal line period may be required for the PRE-DRIVE PHASE to overcome the resistor and capacitor effects for buses with greater loads. When a PRE-DRIVE PHASE is not used, the configuration transactions operate with the same protocol as memory or I/O transactions. The same issues apply to a configuration write transaction.

The PRE-DRIVE PHASE is indistinguishable from an IDLE PHASE; consequently, the FRAME# signal line is the only indicator when the configuration transaction begins.

359

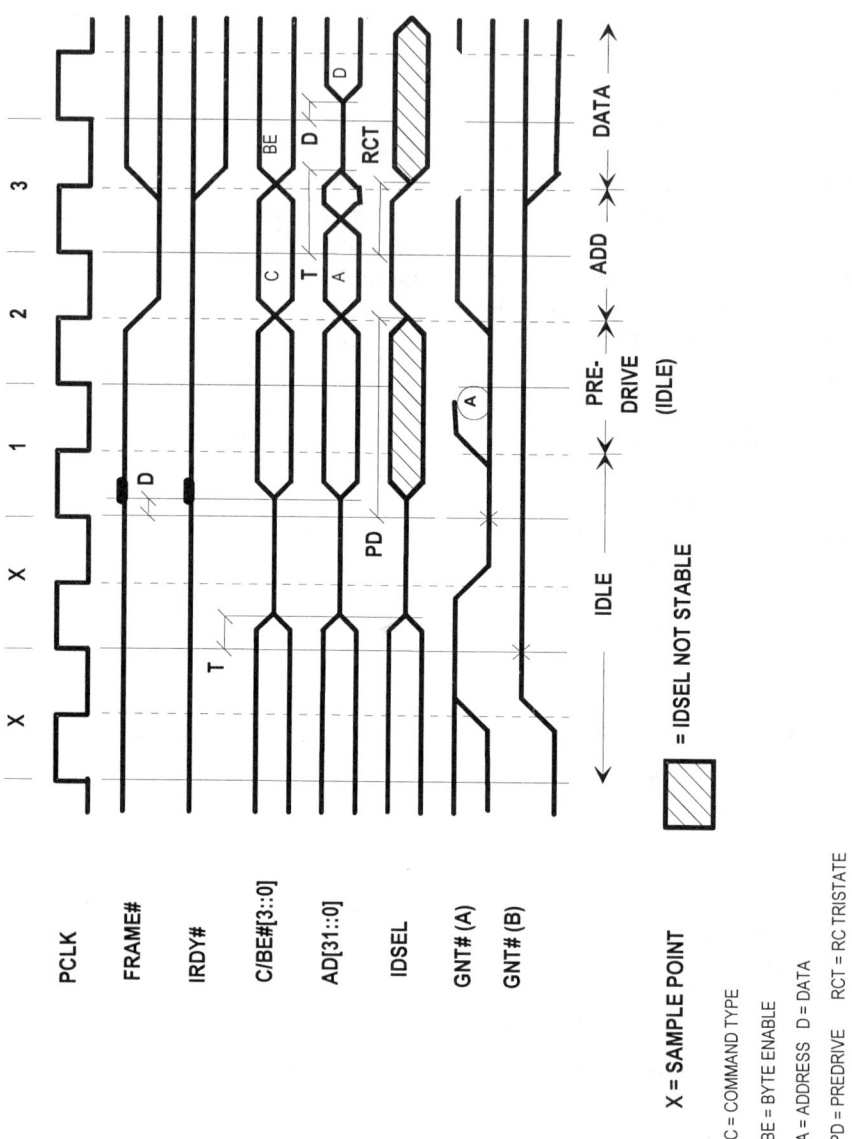

Figure 6-7-A: Beginning of Configuration Transaction (Read Example)

Other key considerations about the configuration transaction are as follows:

■ Immediately following the ADDRESS PHASE is the DATA PHASE. The DATA PHASE protocol for a SINGLE or BURST configuration transaction is the same as for a SINGLE or BURST memory or I/O transaction.

■ The sampling points of the DEVSEL# signal line for "FAST", "MEDIUM", and "SLOW" POSITIVE DECODINGs and SUBTRAC-TIVE DECODING are displaced (relative to the beginning of the transaction) by the number of CLK signal line periods in the PRE-DRIVE PHASE. The protocol for the sampling points relative to the assertion of the FRAME# signal line is the same as for the memory or I/O transactions.

■ The assertion of the FRAME# signal line occurs later in the configuration transaction than in the memory or I/O transactions and thus the tri-stating of signal lines by the previous target occurs earlier relative to the driving of these signal lines by the present target. This situation does not change the protocol for the back-to-back bus transactions and Fast Back-to-Back bus transactions for configuration transactions relative to other bus transactions. The protocols are still defined relative to the assertion of the FRAME# signal line.

■ The place where the PCI bus master that wishes to execute a configuration transaction can first drive the signal lines is defined relative to the assertion of the associated GNTx# signal line (see Figure 6-7-A). This is the same protocol as for other bus transactions. As with other bus transactions, the associated GNTx# signal line be must asserted on the rising edge of the CLK signal line just prior to the assertion of the FRAME# signal lines. Unlike other bus transactions, the PCI bus master may have already begun the PRE-DRIVE PHASE when the associated GNTx# signal line is deasserted. If the associated GNTx# signal line is deasserted at Point A (Circle A in Figure 6-7-A), the configuration transaction cannot be executed (The FRAME# signal line cannot be asserted).

A Type 1 configuration transaction does not have to provide valid IDSEL signal lines; therefore, the pre-drive protocol *does not* apply to Type 1.

As previously stated, the above discussion with the pre-drive protocol is according to the original PCI local bus specification. It is presented here for historical reasons. The actual transaction protocol for Type 0 and 1 configuration transactions is the same as memory or I/O transaction. The only difference is the use of the IDSEL signal lines by the Type 0 configuration transaction.

INTERRUPT ACKNOWLEDGE TRANSACTIONS

An interrupt acknowledge transaction executes with the protocol of a SINGLE bus transaction (BURST bus transactions are not defined) and begins with the PCI bus master (HOST/PCI BRIDGE) asserting the FRAME# signal line, driving valid COMMAND type information onto the C/BE#[3::0] lines and the AD[31::0] signal lines to a stable level. This activity comprises the ADDRESS PHASE of the interrupt acknowledge transaction.

Immediately following the ADDRESS PHASE is the DATA PHASE. The DATA PHASE protocol for a SINGLE interrupt acknowledge transaction is the same as a SINGLE memory or I/O transaction. At the beginning of the DATA PHASE, the PCI bus master drives valid byte enable information onto the C/BE#[3::0] signal lines and tri-states the AD[31::0] signal lines (see Figures 6-3 and 6-5). The PCI resource that contains the interrupt controller claims the interrupt acknowledge transaction by asserting the DEVSEL# signal line. This PCI resource (target) can also use the STOP# and TRDY# signal lines as needed.

For a STANDARD SINGLE interrupt acknowledge transaction, the IRDY# and DEVSEL# signal lines must be asserted in the second or third CLK signal line period. The AD[31::0] signal lines must be tri-stated by the PCI bus master at the beginning of the second CLK signal line period. The tri-state of these signal lines allows the PCI resource (target) to drive them at the beginning of the third CLK signal line period. The TRDY# signal line cannot be asserted until the third CLK signal line period for an interrupt acknowledge transaction. The STANDARD SINGLE interrupt acknowledge transaction is continued until the IRDY# and TRDY# are both asserted at the end of the third CLK signal line period, and the IRDY#, TRDY#, and DEVSEL# signal lines are subsequently deasserted. Also at this time, the AD[31::0] signal lines are tri-stated by the PCI resource (target), and the C/BE#[3::0] signal lines do not have valid byte enable information. One CLK signal line period later, the AD[31::0] signal lines are driven by the PCI bus master for the next bus transaction. The interrupt acknowledge transaction is completed when the FRAME# and IRDY# signal lines are both deasserted.

Ideally, all interrupt acknowledge transactions should be STANDARD for maximum system performance; however, in reality not all resources can operate at maximum bus speed. Consequently, the PCI local bus specification also defines a protocol to accommodate slower resources called READY. For a READY SINGLE interrupt acknowledge transaction, the DEVSEL# signal line is required to be asserted within the first four CLK signal line rising edges of the DATA PHASE; otherwise, a Master Abort termination will be executed. The AD[31::0] signal lines are required to be tri-stated by the PCI bus master at the beginning of the second CLK signal line period. The tri-state of these signal lines allows the target to drive them at the beginning of the third CLK signal line period. The READY SINGLE interrupt acknowledge transaction continues until the IRDY# and TRDY# signal lines are both sampled asserted on a rising edge of the CLK signal line. The IRDY# signal lines can be asserted as early as the second CLK signal line period. The earliest the TRDY# signal line can be asserted is the third CLK signal line period for an interrupt acknowledge transaction. The interrupt acknowledge transaction continues until the IRDY# and TRDY# signal lines are both asserted. Subsequently, the IRDY#, TRDY#, and DEVSEL# signal lines are subsequently deasserted. Also, at this time the AD[31::0] signal lines are tri-stated by the PCI resource (target), and the C/BE#[3::0] signal lines do not have valid information. One CLK signal line period later the AD[31::0] signal lines are driven by the PCI bus master for a new bus transaction. The interrupt acknowledge transaction completes when the FRAME# and IRDY# signal lines are both deasserted. The interrupt acknowledge transaction can also be executed using the BURST read interrupt acknowledge transaction protocol. It is unclear at this time if support of a BURST interrupt acknowledge transaction is useful, given the "normal" interrupt controller.

The PAR signal line provides even parity for the C/BE#[3::0] and AD[31::0] signal lines. The value of the PAR signal line reflects the value of these signal lines one CLK signal line period earlier. The points in the interrupt acknowledge transaction where the PAR signal line are tri-stated and driven are same as the AD[31::0] signal lines but delayed by one CLK signal line period.

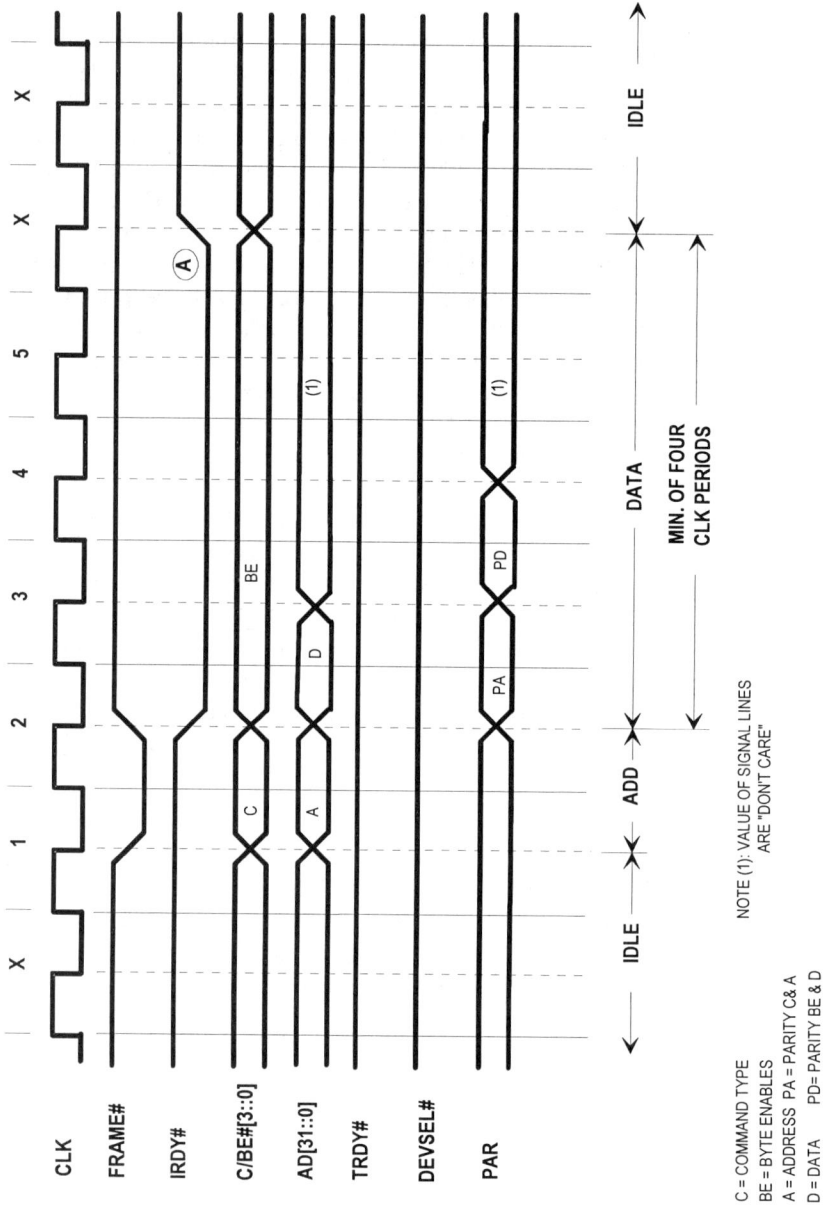

Figure 6-7-B: PCI Special Transaction (Single Standard Version)

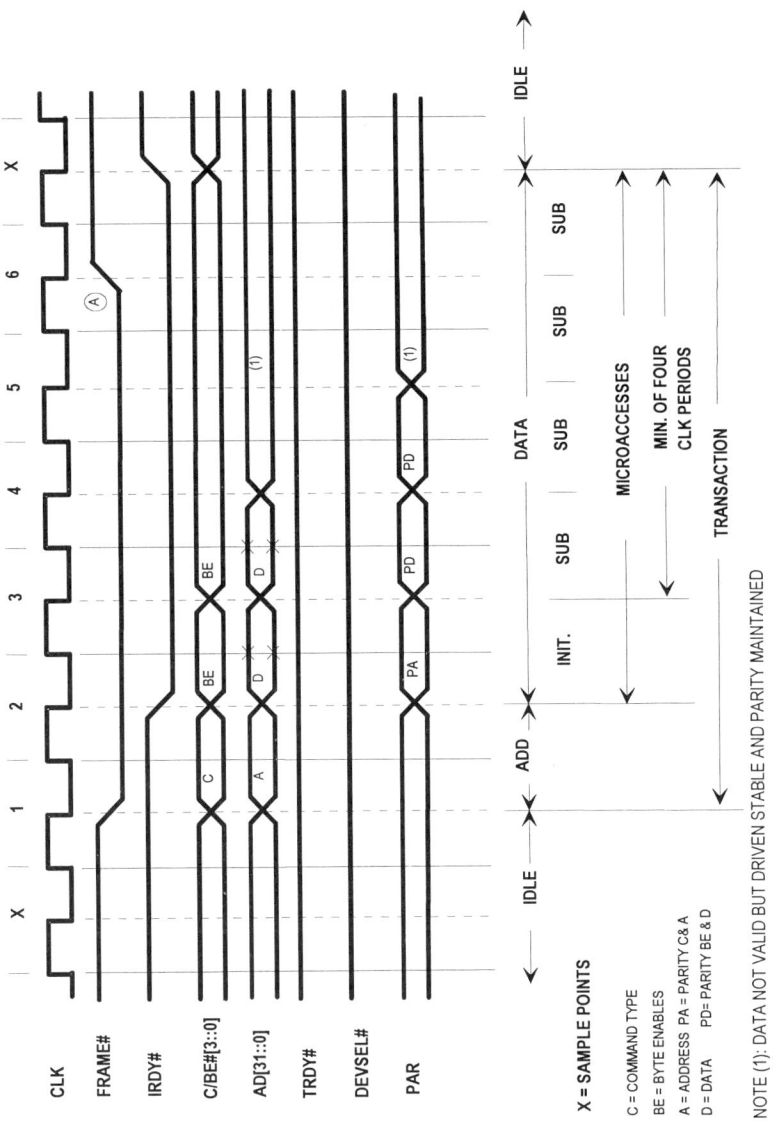

Figure 6-7-C: PCI Special Transaction (Minimum Burst)

365

> The above discussion assumes data is accessed on the last CLK signal line rising edge prior to the IDLE PHASE. Accordingly, the TRDY# signal is asserted at this CLK signal line rising edge. Under certain conditions, the TRDY# signal line may be deasserted at the last CLK signal line rising edge prior to the IDLE PHASE. See subchapter 6.2 for more information.

SPECIAL TRANSACTIONS

A special transaction begins with the PCI bus master asserting the FRAME# signal line, driving valid COMMAND type information onto the C/BE#[3::0] lines and the AD[31::0] signal lines to a stable level (see Figure 6-7-B). This activity comprises the ADDRESS PHASE of the special transaction.

Immediately following the ADDRESS PHASE is the DATA PHASE. The DATA PHASE protocol for a SINGLE or BURST special transaction is the same as a SINGLE or BURST memory or I/O transaction. At the beginning of the DATA PHASE, the PCI bus master drives valid byte enable information onto the C/BE#[3::0] signal lines, and provides the encoded message type and optional message dependent data (defined as primary data; see Figure 6-7-B). Unlike memory or I/O transaction, the TRDY#, DEVSEL#, and STOP# signal lines remain deasserted throughout the DATA PHASE.

The minimum length of a special transaction is five CLK signal line periods.

For a STANDARD SINGLE special transaction, the IRDY# signal line must be asserted in the second CLK signal line period and the IRDY# signal line must be asserted for four CLK signal line periods. There is no target that can claim the special transaction (assert the DEVSEL# signal line); consequently, the TRDY# signal line cannot be asserted and the protocol for the STANDARD SINGLE special transaction is as follows:

- The AD[31::0] signal lines contain valid data only at the first rising edge of the CLK signal line when the IRDY# signal line is first sampled asserted.

- For a STANDARD SINGLE special transaction, the IRDY# signal line is deasserted at the fifth CLK signal line period from the assertion of the IRDY# signal line. The IRDY# signal line must be asserted exactly four CLK signal line periods for a STANDARD SINGLE special transaction.

- To maintain minimum length of a special transaction, the IRDY# signal line is not deasserted until after the fifth CLK signal line period at Point A (Circle A in Figure 6-7-B). The special transaction completes when the FRAME# and IRDY# signal lines both deassert.

Special transactions that require PCI resources to do a more elaborate response than setting a flip flop may require the PCI bus master to execute a READY SINGLE special transaction. For a READY SINGLE special transaction, the protocol outlined in the above bullets applies. The READY SINGLE special transaction allows the IRDY# signal line to be asserted later than the second CLK signal line period and longer than four CLK signal line periods; consequently, it remains asserted beyond Point A (Circle A in Figure 6-7-B). According to the READY SINGLE write transaction protocol, the FRAME# signal line is deasserted during the last CLK signal line period. The special transaction completes when the FRAME# and IRDY# signal lines are both deasserted.

The special transaction can also be executed following the BURST write transaction protocol (exclusive of the assertion of the TRDY#, STOP#, and DEVSEL# signal lines). The non-assertion of the TRDY# signal line requires a slightly different interpretation of the microaccesses. When the IRDY# signal line is first asserted (initial microaccess), the special transaction primary data is available. The subsequent rising edge of the CLK signal line (subsequent microaccesses) provide secondary data associated with the primary data (provided the primary data indicated that more data would be available, and the amount). The minimum length of a special transaction is six CLK signal line periods; consequently, a minimum BURST special transaction provides the primary data and one sample point for the secondary data (see Figure 6-7-C). Not all of the secondary data bytes available at the sample points are required to be valid; the sample points with valid secondary data is determined by the assertion of the C/BE#[3::0] signal lines during the subsequent microaccesses. If the PCI bus master wants to provide additional secondary data or additional time for PCI resources to respond to a special transaction request, it can continue the BURST special transaction with the assertion of the FRAME# and IRDY# signal lines past Point A (Circle A in Figure 6-7-C). Wait states can be added to each microaccess by deasserting the IRDY# signal line when the FRAME# signal line is asserted. According to the BURST write transaction protocol, the FRAME# signal line is deasserted and the IRDY# signal line is asserted during the last CLK signal line period. The special transaction completes when the FRAME# and IRDY# signal lines both deassert.

The PAR signal line provides even parity for the C/BE#[3::0] and AD[31::0] signal lines. The value of the PAR signal line reflects the value of these signal lines one CLK signal line period earlier. The points in the special transaction where the PAR signal line are tri-stated and driven are same as the AD[31::0] signal lines but delayed by one CLK signal line period.

> **Fast Back-to-Back protocol between a special transaction and a subsequent bus transaction is not supported. The special transaction must always be followed by an IDLE PHASE.**

The STANDARD SINGLE special transaction provides a minimum of five CLK signal line periods between valid data and the beginning of the subsequent bus transaction (assertion of the FRAME# signal line). The READY SINGLE special transaction provides additional time to implement the data by the continued assertion of the IRDY# signal line (remember the primary data is valid only when the IRDY# signal line is first asserted). The BURST special transaction provides a minimum of five CLK signal line periods between valid last secondary data and the beginning of the subsequent bus transaction. If more time is required for implementing the primary or secondary data, the PCI bus master is required to execute additional subsequent microaccesses with the continued assertion of the IRDY# signal line. The number of valid subsequent microaccesses is defined in the primary data or message and is required to be present in the first set of valid (IRDY# signal line asserted) subsequent microaccesses. The continued assertion of the IRDY# signal line for subsequent microaccesses (after all of the secondary data has been written) is the method by which additional wait states can be added before the completion of the special transaction. Consequently, data for the subsequent microaccesses is only valid when the IRDY# signal is first asserted for each subsequent microaccess.

The special transaction completes according to the Master Abort termination protocol because the DEVSEL# signal line is not asserted.

6.2   MORE DETAILS OF PCI SIGNAL LINE PROTOCOL FOR 32 DATA BIT BUS TRANSACTIONS

Subchapter 6.0 outlined ownership of the signal lines during a bus transaction. Subchapter 6.1 outlined the bus transaction protocol when both the PCI bus master and target are 32 data bits in size. Chapter 8: *Master and Target Termination* details signal line operation, and signal line driving and tri-stating when Completion, Retry, Disconnect, Master Abort, or Target Abort terminations are executed. Chapter 9: *Bus Segment Ownership* covers the change of signal line ownership, and signal line driving and tri-stating between changes of bus ownership and between bus transactions. Chapter 10: *Parity and Bus Errors* explains the signal line ownership, and signal line driving and tri-stating of the SERR# and PERR# signal lines. This subchapter defines the signal line protocol for signal lines during the bus transaction and between bus transactions when the PCI bus master retains bus segment ownership:

In the following discussion, the terms "drive or tri-state" are different than the terms "assert or deassert". The former identifies when the signal line buffers are enabled or disabled. The latter reflects when signal lines change their logical state.

The signal line protocol outlined below is a general introduction to 32 data bit bus transaction operation with bus transaction completion when the FRAME# and TRDY# signal lines are simultaneously deasserted and asserted, respectively. Please note that bus transaction completion relative to the TRDY# signal line is slightly different under the protocol for special transaction and Master Abort, Retry, Disconnect, and Target Abort terminations. Also, there are slight differences in the interpretation of the AD signal lines during special and interrupt acknowledge transactions. Finally, details of additional signal lines like SERR#, PERR#, INTx#, and RST#, and other considerations relative to a 64 data bit bus transaction will be discussed in detail in other sections of the chapter.

- When a PCI bus master retains bus segment ownership, it .drives the FRAME# and IRDY# signal lines to a logical "1" (deasserted) between bus transactions (IDLE PHASE). Exception is the Fast Back-to-Back protocol.

- When the PCI bus master retains bus segment ownership, it drives C/BE#[3::0] and AD[31::0] signal lines to a stable level between bus transactions, and, with a one CLK signal line period lag, the PAR signal line to a stable level between bus transactions.

- The FRAME# signal line is required to be deasserted simultaneously with the assertion of the IRDY# signal line to indicate that this is a SINGLE bus transaction; otherwise, it is a BURST bus transaction. For a BURST bus transaction, the FRAME# signal line remains asserted and is not deasserted until after or simultaneously with the assertion of the IRDY# signal line. During bus transactions, the FRAME# and IRDY# signal lines are always driven by the PCI bus master.

- Once the FRAME# signal line is asserted and then deasserted, it remains deasserted until the completion of the bus transaction. By definition, the completion of any bus transaction is always identified by the TRDY# and STOP# signal lines, and the simultaneous deassertion of FRAME# signal line and assertion of the IRDY# signal line. The completion of the bus transaction is qualified by the TRDY# and STOP# signal lines as follows:

  - "Normal termination" Completion with data ... TRDY# and STOP# signal lines asserted and deasserted, respectively.

  - Disconnect with data termination ... TRDY# and STOP# signal lines are both asserted. See "Exception Note" in the shaded box below.

369

■ Disconnect without data termination ... STOP# and TRDY# signal lines asserted and deasserted, respectively.

■ Retry termination ... STOP# and TRDY# signal lines asserted and deasserted, respectively.

■ Target Abort termination ... STOP# and TRDY# signal lines asserted and deasserted, respectively. In addition, the DEVSEL# signal line is deasserted. See Chapter 8: *Master and Target Termination* for more information.

■ Master Abort termination ... STOP# and TRDY# signal lines are both deasserted.

■ During bus transactions, the TRDY# and STOP# signal lines are always driven by the target.

■ Once the FRAME# signal line is asserted, the PCI bus master drives the C/BE#[3::0] signal lines with valid information for the remainder of the bus transaction.

■ During a write transaction (memory, I/O, configuration and special), the PCI bus master drives the AD[31::0] and PAR signal lines with valid information or to a stable state. For the ADDRESS PHASE (when the FRAME# signal line is first asserted), these signal lines are driven with valid addresses and parity. For the DATA PHASE these signal lines are driven to a stable level when the IRDY# signal line is deasserted, and are driven with valid information when the IRDY# signal line is asserted. A lag of one CLK signal line period applies to the PAR signal line.

■ During a read transaction (memory, I/O, configuration and interrupt acknowledge), the PCI bus master drives the AD[31::0] and PAR signal lines with valid information during the ADDRESS PHASE (when the FRAME# signal line is first asserted). For the DATA PHASE, the target drives the AD[31::0] and PAR signal lines to a stable level when the TRDY# signal line is deasserted, and with valid information when the TRDY# signal line is asserted. At the end of the DATA PHASE, the PCI bus master will drive the AD[31::0] signal lines one CLK signal line period after the TRDY# and FRAME# signal lines are simultaneously sampled asserted and deasserted, respectively. The protocol applies to the PAR signal line with a one CLK signal line period delay.

> The above discussion assumes data is accessed on the last CLK signal line rising edge prior to the IDLE PHASE. Accordingly, the TRDY# signal is asserted at this CLK signal line rising edge. Under certain conditions, the TRDY# signal line may be deasserted at the last CLK signal line rising edge prior to the IDLE PHASE. See "Exception Note" in shaded box below.

Further details for the signal line protocol relative to the interaction of the PCI bus master and target during the bus transaction and between bus transactions follow:

- At the beginning of the bus transaction, the target begins driving the DEVSEL# signal line upon completion of the address decode. The earliest sampling point for address decode without DUAL ADDRESS is immediately after the FRAME# signal line is first sampled asserted. The earliest point for address decode with DUAL ADDRESS is one CLK signal line period after the FRAME# signal line is first sampled asserted. (There are certain exceptions to the first sampling point relative to address decode in the Fast Back to Back protocol.)

- The target that will participate in the bus transaction will assert the DEVSEL# signal line to claim the bus transaction. Only the target claiming the bus transaction can drive and deassert/assert the TRDY#, STOP#, AD, and PAR signal lines (AD[31::00] and PAR signal lines for read transactions and interrupt acknowledge transactions). The driving of these signal lines should be simultaneous with or subsequent to driving the DEVSEL# signal line. The assertion of the STOP# and TRDY# signal lines is required to be simultaneous with or subsequent to the assertion of the DEVSEL# signal line.

- Data is only transferred when the IRDY# and TRDY# signal lines are both asserted. The one exception is the special transaction.

- Once the IRDY# or TRDY# signal lines are asserted they cannot be deasserted until the completion of the SINGLE bus transaction or the completion of each microaccess of the BURST bus transaction. (See the "Exception Note" in the shaded box below.)

- The DEVSEL# signal line remains asserted until the completion of the transaction (see definition in the previous set of bullets). There are two exceptions to the protocol relative to DEVSEL# signal line: DEVSEL# signal line is deasserted for the entire bus transaction with Master Abort termination, and DEVSEL# signal line is deasserted for completion of the bus transaction with Target Abort termination. See Chapter 8: *Master and Target Termination* for more information.

- Once the STOP# signal line is asserted it cannot be deasserted until the completion of the bus transaction (used for Disconnect, Retry, and Target Abort terminations).

- For a Target Abort termination, the DEVSEL# signal line is asserted during the bus transaction but is required to be deasserted at the completion of the bus transaction. It must be deasserted subsequent to or simultaneously with the assertion of the STOP# signal line. See Chapter 8: *Master and Target Termination* for more information.

- If the STOP# signal line is asserted for a Disconnect with data termination, it must be subsequent to or simultaneous with the assertion of the TRDY# signal line. See Chapter 8: *Master and Target Termination* for more information.

- During a read transaction (memory, I/O, configuration, and interrupt acknowledge), the PCI bus master drives the AD[31::0] and PAR signal lines with valid information during the ADDRESS PHASE. The earliest a target can drive the AD[31::0] signal lines is relative to the second or third CLK signal line rising edge from first assertion of the FRAME# signal when DUAL ADDRESS (for memory transaction only) is not or is executed, respectively. For the DATA PHASE, the target drives the AD[31::0] signal lines to a stable level when the TRDY# signal line is deasserted and the DEVSEL# signal line is asserted, and drives these signal lines with valid information when the TRDY# signal line is asserted. Prior to the assertion of the DEVSEL# signal line, these signal lines are tri-stated. At the end of the DATA PHASE, the target will tri-state the AD[31::0] signal lines (per the completion of bus transaction protocol) when the IRDY# and FRAME# signal lines are simultaneously sampled asserted and deasserted, respectively. The AD signal lines protocol applies to the PAR signal line with a one CLK signal line period delay. Optionally, the STOP# signal line can be asserted during the bus transaction by the target. For a write transaction (memory, I/O, configuration, and special) the protocol is the same as the read transaction except the PCI bus master drives and tri-states the AD[31:0] and PAR signal lines during the DATA PHASE. Consequently, these signal lines are driven to a stable level when the IRDY# signal line is deasserted and driven with valid information when the IRDY# signal line is asserted. See Chapter 8: *Master and Target Termination* for more information.

See Subchapter 6.0 for more information about tri-stating the signal lines.

Exception Note: In the above discussion for a memory, I/O, configuration or interrupt acknowledge transaction, the simultaneous deassertion of the FRAME# signal line and the assertion of the TRDY# signal line identifies (in conjunction with IRDY# and STOP# signal lines) the Completion or Disconnect with data termination of the bus transaction. Once the TRDY# signal line is asserted for the last access of the bus transaction, it cannot be deasserted until the completion of the bus transaction (see the definition in the previous set of bullets). When the Disconnect with data termination is requested with the FRAME# signal line asserted, the TRDY# signal line is required to be deasserted before the completion of the bus transaction. (See Disconnect with and with out Data termination figures in Chapter 8: *Master and Target Termination* for more information.)

The protocol for the remaining signal lines for all bus transactions is as follows:

- The CLK and RST# signal lines are driven to valid levels by the central resource. For a typical bus transaction, the CLK signal line oscillates and the RST# signal line is deasserted.

- The GNTx# signal lines are driven to valid levels by the central resource. The REQx# signal lines are driven by the PCI bus masters or are driven to a logical "1" by pull-up resistors.

- The LOCK# signal line is driven to valid levels by the Lock master.

- An INTx# signal line is asserted when a PCI resource needs interrupt service.

- The REQ64#, ACK64#, PAR64, C/BE#[7::4], and AD[63::32] signal lines are driven to a logical "1" by pull-up resistors.

For further information, see Subchapters 6.0, 6.4, and 6.7.

6.3 PCI EXCLUSIVE ACCESS (LOCK) PROTOCOL

In the following discussions, the term "upstream" and "downstream" refer to the direction of the bus transaction flow. As explained in subchapter 2.2, accesses from PCI bus masters on higher LEVEL bus segments to targets on the same or lower LEVEL bus segments are defined as "downstream". Similarly, from PCI bus masters on lower LEVEL bus segment to targets on higher LEVEL bus segments are defined as "upstream".

INTRODUCTION

Prior to Rev 2.2 of the PCI local bus specification, a PCI bus master could insure Exclusive Access to a memory target with either the use of the LOCK# signal line (Exclusive Hardware Access) or by coordination among the different PCI bus masters (Exclusive Software Access) that could access a specific target. Exclusive Software Access could also be applied to an I/O target. In the case of Exclusive Hardware Access, the bus protocol insured a specific PCI bus master (Lock master) that no other PCI bus master could access a locked target with any bus transaction. If a PCI bus master that was not the Lock master tried to access a locked target, the locked target would request a Retry termination. The Exclusive Hardware Access required that the Lock master could access the locked target only with memory transactions. Also, to insure the minimal amount of time a memory resource was a locked target via Exclusive Hardware Access, the Lock master was not allowed to access any other target until it unlocked the locked target. According to the Exclusive Hardware Access protocol, the HOST CPU and PCI bus masters would drive the LOCK# signal line, the PCI memory targets would monitor it downstream PCI bus segments, and bridges would both monitor and drive the LOCK# signal line on the attached PCI bus segments. The support of an upstream Exclusive Hardware Access via the LOCK# signal line was not possible. The use of Exclusive Hardware Access was useful for such activities such as semaphore manipulation.

According to Rev. 2.2 of the PCI local bus specification, the protocol of Exclusive Software Access was retained. However, the Exclusive Hardware Access protocol has changed substantially from what was described above. Besides placing restrictions on the use of Exclusive Hardware Access for locking and accessing a target (in a non-deadlock condition), the protocol was expanded to address a deadlock condition that may occur in PCI/PCI BRIDGEs.

The balance of this subchapter will focus on the bus transaction protocol; see Chapter 7: *Bridge and Interface Protocol* for more information about the overall application of Exclusive Hardware Access across a platform (also known as "system").

Under the definition of Exclusive Hardware Access by the LEGACY bus master, the PCI memory target that can be locked is either HDRAM (HOST bus DRAM) or PDRAM (PCI DRAM). The PCI local bus specification requires a minimum of 16 bytes (aligned on 16 byte address multiples) to be locked at a time. The target can optionally lock a larger portion up to a maximum of the address range of the target. In the case of a bridge, the maximum portion can be the entire memory space range "behind" the bridge. The 16 byte block or continuous multiple block portion of the target (HDRAM or PDRAM) that is locked is the only portion of the target that follows the lock protocol when accessed by the Lock master, by the HOST CPU accessing HDRAM, or other processors via dual port memory (HDRAM or PDRAM). Accesses by other PCI bus masters (not Lock master) by HOST CPU accessing HDRAM, or other processors via dual port memory (HDRAM or PDRAM) to non-locked portions of the target MAY be affected by the lock protocol if the target had locked more than the portion required.

The Lock Function (LF) is defined when the target that has been locked (locked target) and a PCI bus master (Lock Master) controls the LOCK# signal line. The Lock Function is defined for each PCI bus segment; consequently, on each PCI bus segment only one PCI bus master and target at a time are the Lock master and locked target, respectively. A PCI bus master can lock a target if no other PCI resource is presently locked (as indicated by the continued deassertion of the LOCK# signal line by pull-up resistors) on the bus segment.

The PCI local bus specification permits the HOST/PCI-X BRIDGE (representing the HOST CPU) or a PCI bus master; and PCI/PCI BRIDGEs porting the Exclusive Hardware Access downstream to become a Lock master. Consequently, the Lock master on a specific bus segment may be a bridge representing an upstream Lock master. See Chapter 7: *Bridge and Interface Protocol* for more information about which resources can be locked.

For the balance of the Subchapter, the terms "Lock" and 'Lock Function" refer to Exclusive Hardware Access.

There are four basic considerations for the Lock Function: *Establishment of Lock, Continuance of Lock, Release of Target Lock and Lock Function Ownership,* and *Unsuccessful Bus Transaction Termination relative to Lock.*

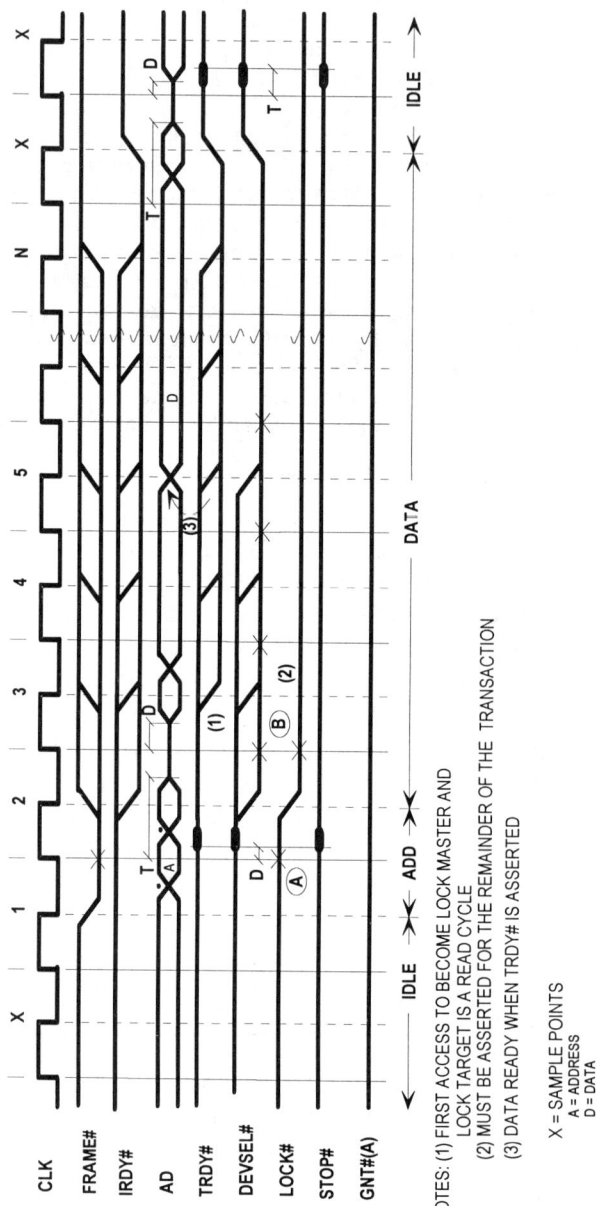

Figure 6-8: PCI Protocol to Become Lock Master

376

ESTABLISHMENT OF LOCK

Lock Function (LF) is established by the sequence of events outlined in Figure 6-8, showing the PCI bus master (A) becoming the Lock master. After PCI bus master (A) becomes the bus segment owner, it accesses the target it wants to lock. The LOCK# signal line has been deasserted by a pull-up resistor prior to the access. At the beginning of the access, PCI bus master (A) continues to deassert the LOCK# signal line during the ADDRESS PHASE, and then asserts it prior to the subsequent CLK signal line rising edge after the ADDRESS PHASE. The selected target of the access, according to a decode of the AD[31::2] (AD[63::2] signal lines for 64 data bits) signal lines, must respond by asserting the DEVSEL# signal line. The lock of the target and the establishment of PCI bus master (A) becoming Lock master is completed by a successful data access when the IRDY# and TRDY# signal lines are both asserted. An unsuccessful access of the target prevents it from becoming locked and bus master (A) from becoming Lock master. See *Unsuccessful Bus Transaction Termination Relative To Lock*, after the next section, for more information.

The sequence of sampling a deasserted LOCK# signal line at Point A during the ADDRESS PHASE and sampling it asserted at Point B (Circle A and B in Figure 6-8) is the protocol to create a Lock master and to lock the target. Once the LOCK# signal line is asserted at Point B, it must remain asserted for the duration of the bus transaction. If the target is a multi-ported resource (HDRAM accessible by HOST CPU or other processors on the HOST bus or dual port, or PDRAM accessible by processors via dual port), the HOST CPU and other processors cannot access the resource during the bus transaction. Consequently, a successful bus transaction results in a Lock master and a locked target *during* and *after* the bus transaction. If the LOCK# signal line had not been asserted at Point B, the present PCI bus master cannot become the Lock master and the target is not locked after completion of the bus transaction. If the LOCK# signal line is deasserted at Point B, it must remain deasserted for the duration of the bus transaction. If the target is a multi-ported resource (HDRAM accessible by HOST CPU or other processors on the HOST bus or dual port, or PDRAM accessible by processors via dual port), the HOST CPU and other processors can access the resource during the bus transaction.

> The first bus transaction used to establish PCI bus master ownership of an LF (become Lock master) and the target to be locked must be a memory read or I/O read transaction to a target.

The ability for a PCI bus master to begin an access and attempt to become Lock master is dependent upon the LF being available (LOCK# signal line deasserted) and the associated GNTx# signal line asserted. As outlined in Chapter 9: *Bus Ownership,* a PCI bus master can also begin a bus transaction without its associated REQx# signal line asserted, and thus can become Lock master.

The execution of a DUAL ADDRESS command does not change the sampling points for the LOCK# signal line (Circle A and B in Figures 6-1, 6-2, and 6-14-A and B, and Figure 6-8); Point B is always one CLK signal line period after the FRAME# signal line is first sampled asserted.

All targets that can be locked are required to latch the value of the LOCK# signal line during the ADDRESS PHASE at Point A and optionally Point B (circles A and B in Figures 6-1-A and B, 6-14-A and B, and 6-8). This requirement is needed because the decode to validate access may take several CLK signal line periods. Point B is optional because the value of the LOCK# signal line at Point B is required to be retained for the duration of the bus transaction. For a multi-port memory target, it will sample the LOCK# signal line at Point B to determine if it is locked. If the LOCK# signal line is asserted at Point B, no other processor can access the target. It is locked and can only be accessed by the PCI bus master (Lock master). If the LOCK# signal line is deasserted at Point B, other processors can access the target;. it is not locked and can be accessed by both the PCI bus master and other processors accessing through non-PCI bus ports. It is a "multi-port memory target" resource that can be accessed by means other than the PCI bus. The concern of multi-port access does not apply to I/O targets. The implementation of the LOCK# signal line relative to an I/O transactions is to prevent dead lock in a bridge and not to insure a hardware Exclusive Access to an I/O resource.

CONTINUANCE OF LOCK FUNCTION OWNERSHIP

The Lock master does not have to retain bus segment ownership to remain Lock master and for the target to remain locked. In Figure 6-8, the PCI bus master (A) retains the LF after the completion of the read transaction that established the LF by the continued assertion the LOCK# signal line. As shown in Figure 6-9, the asserted LOCK# signal line during the ADDRESS PHASE when PCI bus master (B) (not Lock master) accesses the target does not meet the criteria for becoming Lock master or locking the target by the PCI bus master (B). If the decode of the address selects a locked target and the locked target had sampled the LOCK#

signal line asserted at Point A (Circle A in Figure 6-9), the locked target must execute a Retry termination. The target remains locked and the Lock master retains the LF.

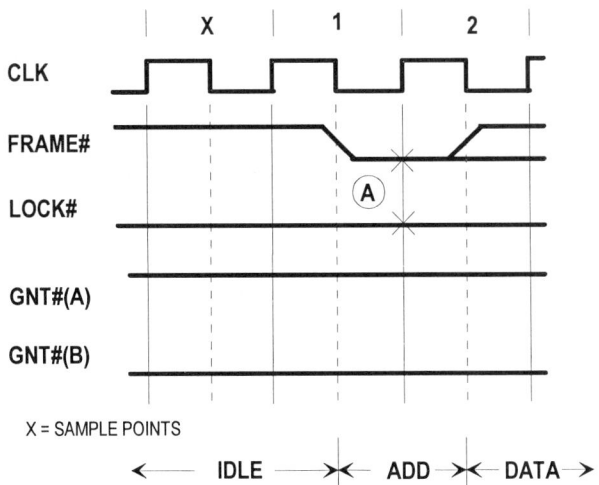

Figure 6-9: Access by Non-Lock PCI Bus Master to the Locked or a Non-Locked Target

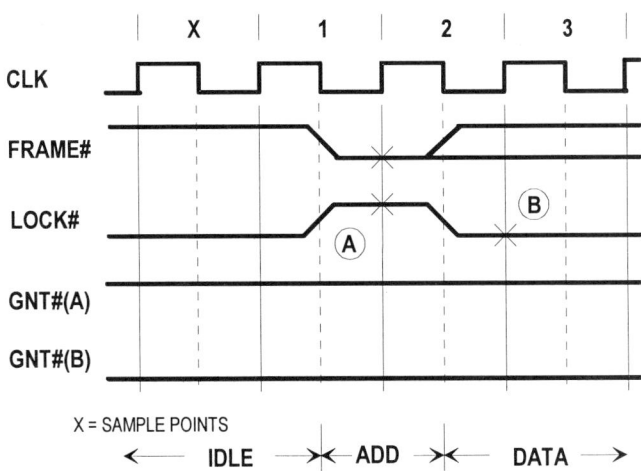

Figure 6-10: Access by the PCI Locked Master to the Locked Target

379

When the Lock master becomes the PCI bus master, the locked target can be accessed. Operation of the LOCK# signal is similar to the protocol that locked the target and established the Lock master. As shown in Figure 6-10, access to a locked target by the Lock master requires the sampling of a deasserted LOCK# signal line by the target at Point A (Circle A in Figure 6-10). If the LOCK# signal line is sampled asserted at Point B (the rising edge of the third CLK signal line period Circle B in Figure 6-10), the target remains locked and the Lock master remains Lock master during the entire bus transaction. If the LOCK# signal line is deasserted at Point B (Circle B in Figure 6-10 and shaded box below), the target ceases to be locked by the LF and the present Lock master ceases to be the Lock master whenever both the FRAME# and LOCK# signal lines are both sampled deasserted at the end of the bus transaction.

> The Lock master must not deassert the LOCK# signal line at Point B (Circle B in Figure 6-10). The Lock master is required to wait until after the end of the bus transaction that is transferring the last data of the LF. If it deasserted the LOCK# signal line at Point B and the target executes a Retry or Disconnect termination, the access of the final data of the LF cannot occur during the same lock period of the target as the other data.

> As previously noted, the execution of a DUAL ADDRESS command does not affect the sampling points outlined in Figure 6-10.

RELEASE OF TARGET LOCK AND RELINQUISHING OF LOCK FUNCTION OWNERSHIP

As introduced in the previous section, the Lock master relinquishes Lock Function ownership (ceases to be Lock master and the target is unlocked at the completion of the bus transaction) whenever both the LOCK# and FRAME# signal lines are sampled deasserted at a CLK signal line rising edge.

A target that has been locked can be unlocked by the Lock master by the procedure outlined in Figures 6-11, 6-12, and 6-13. As shown in Figure 6-11, the Lock master is completing its last access to the presently locked target. The LOCK# signal line must be asserted during the entire DATA PHASE of the bus transaction in case of Retry or Disconnect termination, as outlined in the previous section. At the successful completion of the bus transaction, the Lock master simultaneously deasserts the LOCK# and IRDY# signal lines. Because the FRAME# signal line must be deasserted one clock prior to the deassertion of the IRDY# signal line, the LF is immediately relinquished by the PCI bus master and the target is unlocked when the FRAME# and LOCK# signal lines are both sampled asserted.

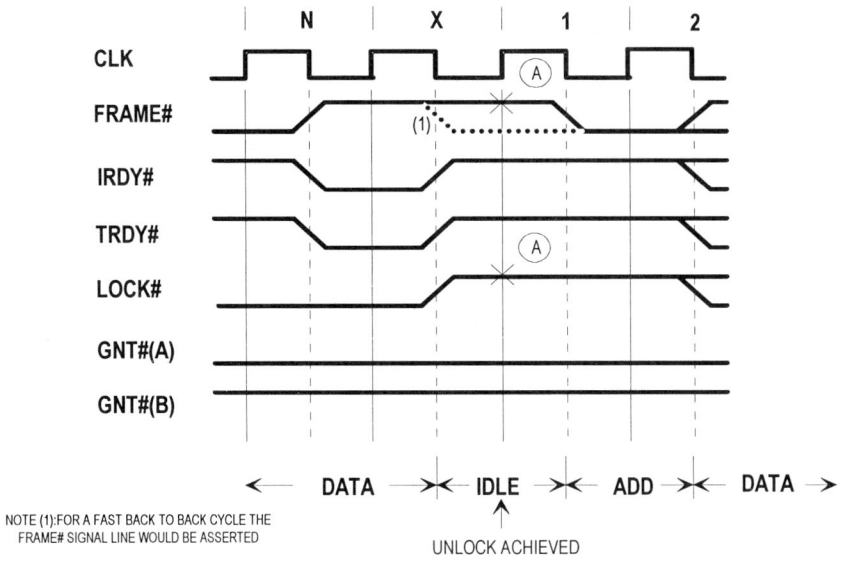

NOTE (1):FOR A FAST BACK TO BACK CYCLE THE
FRAME# SIGNAL LINE WOULD BE ASSERTED

UNLOCK ACHIEVED

X = SAMPLE POINTS

Figure 6-11: PCI Lock Master Unlocking Target

If the Lock master wants to unlock one target and immediately access another target to lock, at least one IDLE PHASE is required to occur. During this IDLE PHASE, the FRAME# and LOCK# signal lines are simultaneously sampled deasserted, thus the Lock master relinquishes LF ownership and the target is unlocked at Point A (Circle A in Figure 6-11). The FRAME# and LOCK# signal lines must be simultaneously deasserted prior to asserting the FRAME# signal line for the next access; consequently, a Fast Back-to-Back protocol between the last bus transaction of a LF and the first bus transaction of a LF cannot be executed.. A Fast Back-to-Back protocol can be executed between the last bus transaction of a LF and a subsequent bus transaction that is not he first bus transaction of an LF. The deassertion of the LOCK# signal line beginning at Point A (Circle A in Figure 6-11) will eventually coincide with a deasserted FRAME# signal line in one of the subsequent bus transactions. However, the preferred protocol is to have an IDLE PHASE between the two bus transactions.

The Lock master can relinquish the LF and the target can be unlocked when the Lock master does not own the bus. The Lock master relinquishing the LF and the unlocking of a locked target when the Lock master or another PCI bus master is not accessing the locked target is considered in greater detail in Figures 6-12 and 6-13. In Figure 6-12, the LOCK# signal line is sampled asserted at Point A during the ADDRESS PHASE (Circle A in Figure 6-12) when PCI bus master (B) (not the Lock master) is accessing a non-locked target. The continued assertion of the LOCK# signal line at Point B (Circle B in Figure 6-12) does not affect the locked target or the retention of the LF by the Lock master. The deassertion of the LOCK# signal line at Point B (Circle B in Figure 6-12) results in the relinquishing of the LF by the Lock master and the unlocking of the locked target when the FRAME# signal line is eventually deasserted.

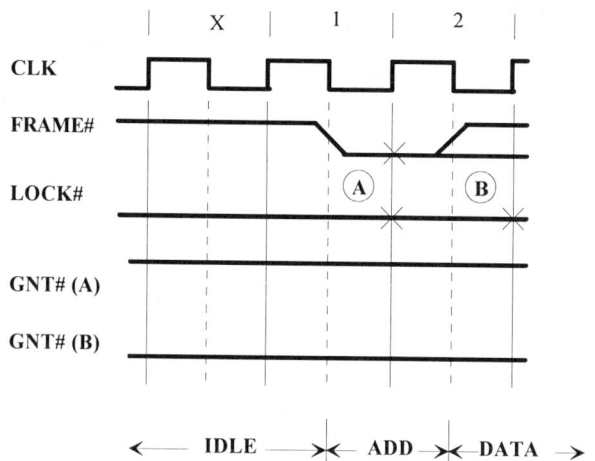

Figure 6-12: PCI Access by Non-Lock Master to Non-Locked Target, Lock Master Keeps LOCK# Signal Line Asserted

In Figure 6-13, the Lock master has deasserted the LOCK# signal line prior to Point A (Circle A in Figure 6-13) of the ADDRESS PHASE during the bus transaction executed by another PCI bus master to a non-locked target. The Lock master does not relinquish the LF and the locked target is not unlocked until the FRAME# and LOCK# signal lines are both sampled deasserted. The assertion of the LOCK# signal line at point A (Circle A in Figure 6-13) does not cause another PCI bus master to become Lock master because a successful read transaction has yet to be completed and the LOCK# signal line is deasserted at Point B and the duration of the bus transaction (Circle B in Figure 6-13). The existing Lock master retains the LF and the locked target remains locked until the FRAME# and LOCK# signal lines are both sampled deasserted. Thus, the existing Lock master has successfully relinquished the LF, the locked target is unlocked, and the present PCI bus master has not become Lock master.

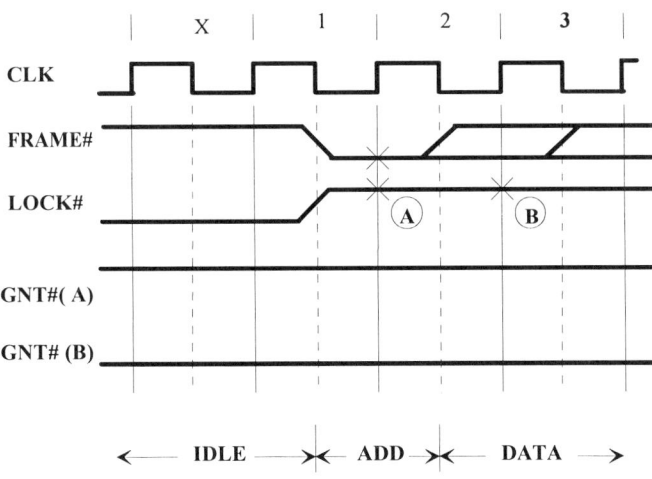

X = SAMPLE POINT

Figure 6-13: PCI Access by Non-Lock Bus Master to Non-Locked Target, Lock Master Deasserts LOCK# Signal Line

UNSUCCESSFUL BUS TRANSACTION TERMINATION RELATIVE TO LOCK

Certain conditions may occur during the memory read transaction to prevent a PCI bus master from obtaining ownership of the Lock Function (LF) (becoming Lock master and locking of a target). As previously discussed, for a PCI bus master to become Lock master and for the target to be locked after the completion of the bus transaction requires the successful reading of data in the memory or I/O address space. Data is not read and the bus transaction is not successfully completed if one of the following occurs: Master Abort, Retry, Disconnect without Data, or Target Abort termination. The LOCK# signal line must be immediately deasserted without regard to the end of the bus transaction. See Chapter 8: *Master and Target Termination* for more information.

Once a PCI bus master owns the LF (PCI bus master is Lock master and a target has been locked), the execution Retry termination has no effect on retaining ownership of the LF, but Master and Target Abort termination does affect LF ownership. If the non-Lock master is accessing the locked target, the execution of a Master or Target Abort termination does not affect the Lock master's retaining ownership of the LF. If the Lock master is accessing the locked target, the execution of a Master or Target Abort termination *forces* the Lock master to relinquish ownership of the LF (immediately deassert the LOCK# signal line without regard for the end of the bus transaction. See Chapter 8: *Master and Target Termination* for more information. The other target transaction termination types have no affect on a PCI-X bus master obtaining or retaining the LF and therefore keeping the target locked.

6.4 PCI 64 DATA BIT EXTENSION

INTRODUCTION

As outlined in Chapter 4: *Functional Interaction Between PCI and PCI-X Resources*, the PCI local bus specification is both a 32 and 64 data bit bus specification. A 32 data bit implementation is all that is required to be compliant. The 64 data bit extension is optional, and 32 and 64 data bit resources can coexist on the same PCI bus segment. A 32 data bit PCI bus master can access a 64 data bit target and vice versa.

The support of the 64 data bit extension is accomplished with the addition of the AD[63::32], C/BE#[7::4], REQ64#, ACK64#, and PAR64 signal lines. All of the bus transaction protocol outlined for platforms with the 32 data bit PCI bus segments also apply to platforms with the 64 data bit extension. Note: the 64 data bit extension does not apply to I/O, configuration, interrupt acknowledge, and special transactions.

See Chapter 4: *Functional Interaction between PCI and PCI-X Resources* for more information.

SIGNAL LINE OWNERSHIP DURING BUS TRANSACTIONS WITH 64 DATA BIT RESOURCES

For memory transactions to 64 data bit PCI resources, the signal lines are owned by different PCI bus resources. A PCI resource owns a signal line when it is the only resource (other than pull-up resistors) that can drive the signal line during a portion of the bus transaction. The protocol for 64 data bit accesses is as follows:

- The FRAME#, IRDY#, and C/BE#[7::0], REQx#, and REQ64# signal lines are owned by the PCI bus master.

- During a write transaction, the PCI bus master owns the AD[63::00], PAR, and PAR64 signal lines.

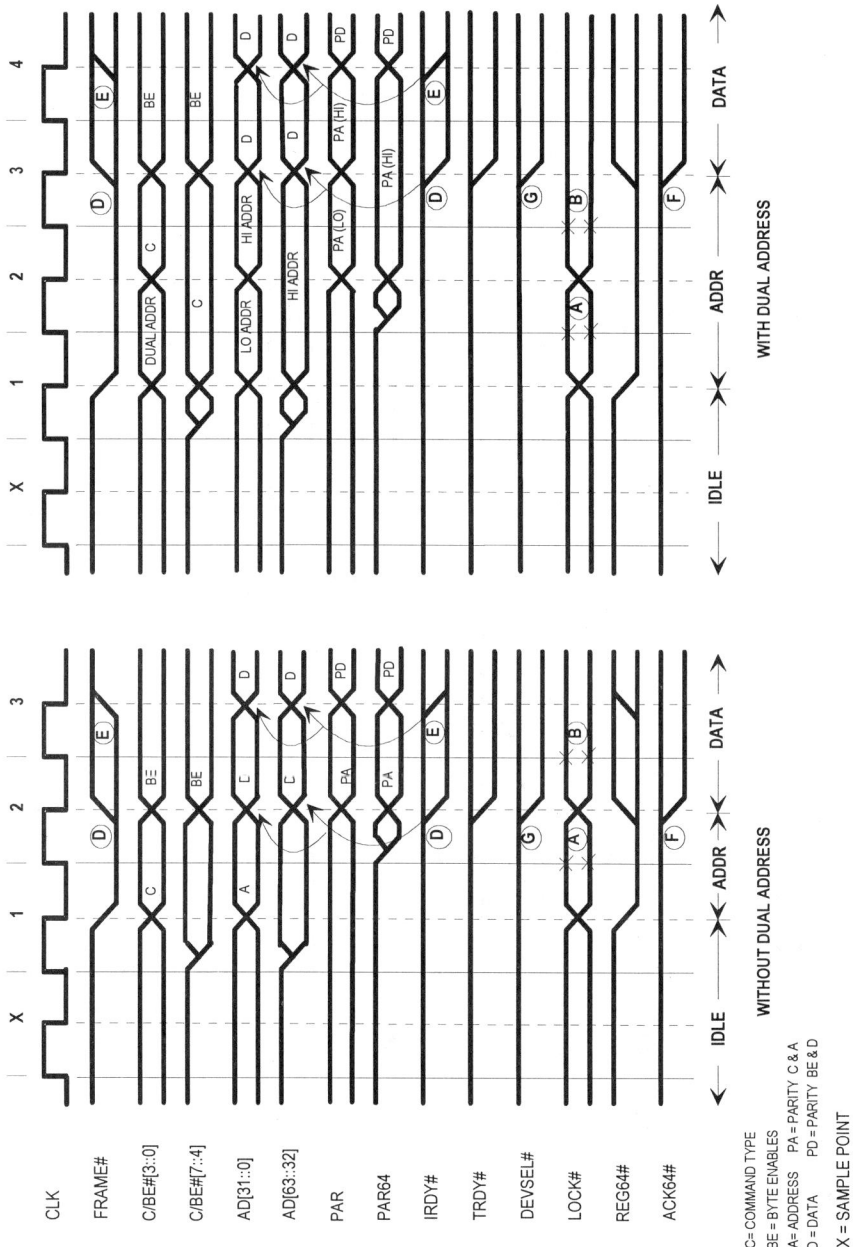

Figure 6-14-A: ADDRESS PHASE Protocol for Write by a 64 Data Bit PCI Bus Master

385

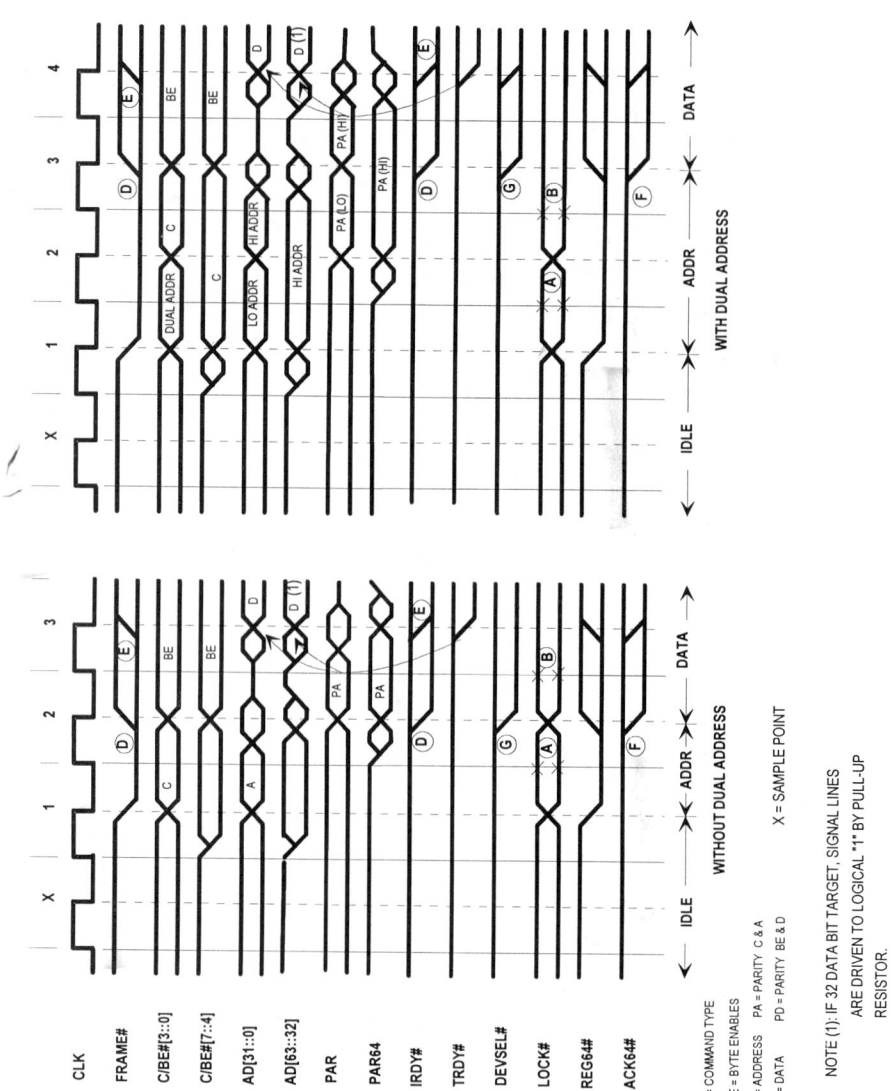

Figure 6-14-B: ADDRESS PHASE Protocol for Read by a 64-Data Bit PCI Bus Master

386

- During a read transaction, the PCI bus master owns the AD[63::00], PAR, and PAR64 signal lines during the ADDRESS PHASE. The target owns these signal lines during the DATA PHASE.

- The TRDY#, DEVSEL#, STOP#, ACK64# signal lines are owned by the target.

The remaining signal lines are owned according to the following protocol:

- The CLK and RST# signal lines are owned by the central resource.

- The GNTx# signal lines are owned by the central arbiter.

- The LOCK# signal line is owned by the Lock master.

- The INTx# signal lines are owned by various PCI resources.

The I/O, configuration,, interrupt acknowledge, and special transactions are defined as only 32 data bit transactions.

---

64 data bit I/O targets can be implemented, but there is no benefit to requiring the increased complexity and it is therefore strongly recommended that 64 data bit I/O targets not be implemented. For the purposes of this book, I/O targets are only 32 data bits in size. If a 64 data bit I/O target is implemented, the 64 data bit protocol applied to memory targets would also apply to I/O targets.

For further information, see Subchapters 6.0, 6.2, and 6.7.

The protocol for bus transaction to bus transaction operation and LOCK protocol when 64 data bit resources are involved are the same as outlined in the previous sections for 32 data bit resources. There are additional considerations about the DUAL ADDRESS protocol relative to the 64 data bit extension as outlined below.

DUAL ADDRESS

The protocol outlined in Subchapter 6.0 for 32 data bit resources provides 64 address bits without the use of AD[63::32] signal lines. If the PCI bus master resides on a 64 data bit bus segment (REQ64# signal line asserted during RESET), and requests a 64 data bit access (REQ64# signal line asserted during the ADDRESS PHASE), the additional information must be provided for a DUAL ADDRESS. When a DUAL ADDRESS is not requested, the AD[63::32] and C/BE#[7::4] signal lines are driven to a stable level during the ADDRESS PHASE but contain no valid information. The PAR64 signal line is also driven in the subsequent CLK signal line period to the ADDRESS PHASE with valid parity.

When a DUAL ADDRESS is requested, the AD[63::32] and C/BE#[7::4] signal lines are driven during the ADDRESS PHASE with the upper order address bits and the COMMAND type , respectively (see Figures 6-1, 6-2, and 6-14-A and B). The PAR64 signal line is also driven in the second CLK signal line period of the ADDRESS PHASE and the subsequent CLK signal line period with valid parity.

6.5   32 DATA BIT PCI BUS MASTER TO 64 DATA BIT TARGET

MEMORY TRANSACTIONS

A 32 data bit access by the PCI bus master to a 64 data bit target can be executed with SINGLE and BURST bus transactions using the same protocol as outlined above for a 32 data bit target. All bus transactions executed by a 32 data bit PCI bus master are the same independent of the data size of the target. Since the 64 data bit target cannot assert the ACK64# signal line, it appears to the PCI bus master as a 32 data bit target.

A PCI bus master requests a 32 data bit access by the deassertion of the REQ64# signal line during the ADDRESS PHASE. The target does not respond by asserting the ACK64# signal line. The REQ64# and ACK64# signal lines are kept deasserted by pull-up resistors. The AD[63::32], C/BE#[7::4], and PAR64 signal lines are driven to a logical "1" by pull-up resistors for the entire bus transaction; consequently, the PAR64 signal line does not have valid parity information.

A 64 data bit target memory transaction with DUAL ADDRESS operates with the same protocol as outlined for 32 data bit PCI bus masters accessing a 32 data bit target.

> The protocol of the memory read line (MRL), memory read multiple (MRM), and memory write and invalidate (MWI) transactions previously described for 32 data bit PCI bus masters accessing 32 data bit targets also apply to 64 data bit targets. The adjustments to these protocols are the same as the adjustments outlined above for simple memory transactions.

I/O, CONFIGURATION, INTERRUPT ACKNOWLEDGE, AND SPECIAL TRANSACTIONS

The I/O, configuration, interrupt acknowledge, and special transactions are executed only with 32 data bit resources. The deassertion of the ACK64# signal line makes the target always appear as a 32 data bit resource.

> 64 data bit I/O targets can be implemented, but there is no benefit to requiring the increased complexity and it is therefore strongly recommended that 64 data bit I/O targets not be implemented. For the purposes of this book, I/O targets are only 32 data bits in size. If a 64 data bit I/O target is implemented, the 64 data bit protocol applied to memory targets would also apply to I/O targets.

6.6 64 DATA BIT PCI BUS MASTER TO 64 DATA BIT TARGET

MEMORY TRANSACTIONS

A PCI bus master or a target is a defined as a 64 data bit resource when the REQ64# or ACK64# signal lines are asserted, respectively. The PCI bus master requests a 64 data bit transaction by asserting the REQ64# signal line, and the PCI target acknowledges a 64 data bit transaction by asserting the ACK64# signal line. The REQ64# and ACK64# signal lines are driven to a logical "1" by pull-up resistors when not driven by the PCI bus master and target resource, respectively. The execution of a 32 or 64 data bit transaction is determined on a bus transaction-by-bus transaction basis. During the ADDRESS PHASE, the REQ64# signal line is asserted and the AD[31::0], C/BE#[3::0], and PAR signal lines operate with the same protocol as a 32 data bit transaction (see Figure 6-15). During the DATA PHASE, the ACK64# signal line is asserted, and the AD[31::0], C/BE#[3::0], and PAR signal lines operate with the same protocol as a 32 data bits transaction. Also, during the DATA PHASE, the operation of the C/BE#[7::4], AD[63::32], and PAR64 signal lines operate with the same protocol as the C/BE#[3::0], AD[31::0], and PAR signal lines in a 32 data bits transaction.

Figure 6-15 outlines the SINGLE read transaction for a 64 data bit PCI bus master accessing a 64 data bit memory resource (target). The concepts outlined for a SINGLE read transaction are the same for SINGLE write, and BURST read and write transactions. As outlined above, the protocol for all signal lines during 64 and 32 data bit accesses are the same except for the AD[63::32], C/BE#[7::4], REQ64#, ACK64#, and PAR64 signal lines.

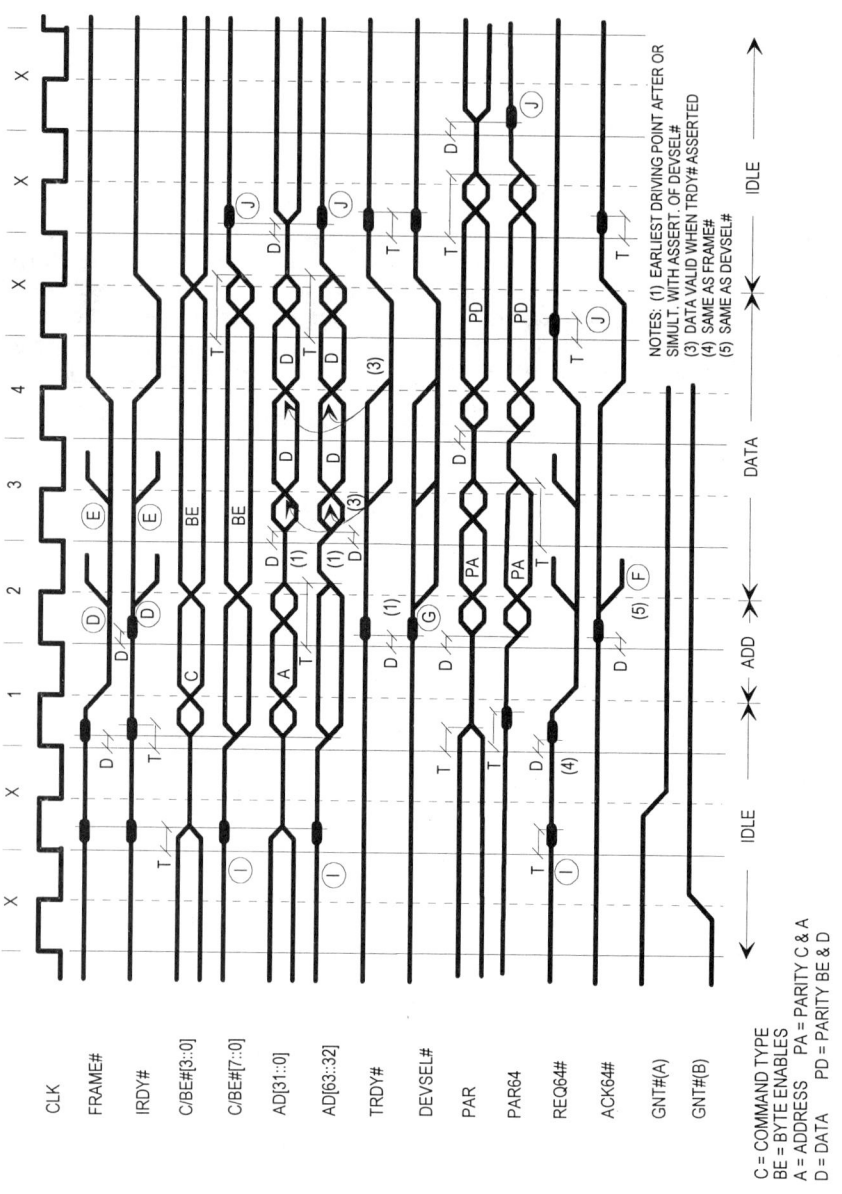

Figure 6-15: Ready Single Read Access Transaction, 64 Data Bit PCI Bus Master and Target, and One Wait State Over Standard without DUAL ADDRESS

The 64 data bit extension to the PCI bus protocol is optional. The operation of the AD[63::32], C/BE#[7::4], REQ64#, ACK64#, and PAR64 signal lines are slightly more complicated than the signal lines associated with 32 data bit bus transactions. Their unique operation during a bus transaction is outlined below.

In the following discussion, the activity of the PAR and PAR64 signal lines are referenced to the ADDRESS and DATA PHASES. In actuality, the PAR and PAR64 signal lines are delayed by one CLK signal line period; consequently, they do not exactly align with the ADDRESS and DATA PHASES as implied.

For a 64 data bit transaction, without DUAL ADDRESS, the protocol of the AD[63::32], C/BE#[7::4], REQ64#, ACK64#, and the PAR64 signal lines is as follows:

- The REQ64# signal line is asserted during the ADDRESS PHASE and deasserted at the end of the DATA PHASE by the PCI bus master with the same timing profile as the FRAME# signal line.

- The ACK64# signal line is asserted and deasserted by the target with the same timing profile as the DEVSEL# signal line during the DATA PHASE.

- During the ADDRESS PHASE, the AD[63::32] and C/BE#[7::4] signal lines are driven to a stable level by the PCI bus master. Due to the assertion of the REQ64# signal line, the PAR64 signal line contains valid parity information.

- Due to the assertion of the REQ64# signal line during the ADDRESS PHASE, the PCI bus master drives the C/BE#[7::4] signal lines during the DATA PHASE with the valid byte lane information for the AD[63::32] signal lines. This compliments the C/BE#[3::0] signal lines containing valid byte lane information for the AD[31::0] signal lines.

- During the DATA PHASE of a read transaction (see Figure 6-15), the AD[63::32] and PAR64 signal lines are tri-stated by the PCI bus master and driven by the target with the same time profile as the AD[31::0] and PAR signal lines, respectively. The target drives these signal lines with valid data and parity information simultaneously with or subsequent to the assertion of the DEVSEL# and ACK64# signal lines. Prior to being driven by the target, the AD[63::32] and PAR64 signal lines are driven to a logical "1" by pull-up resistors.

- During the DATA PHASE of a write transaction, the AD[63::32] and PAR64 signal lines are driven by the PCI bus master with the same timing profile as the AD[31::0] and PAR signal lines, respectively.

391

For a 64 data bit transaction with DUAL ADDRESS, the protocol of the AD[63::32], C/BE#[7::4], REQ64#, ACK64#, and the PAR64 signal lines is as follows:

- The REQ64# signal line is asserted during the ADDRESS PHASE and deasserted at the end of the DATA PHASE by the PCI bus master with the same timing profile as the FRAME# signal line.

- The ACK64# signal line is asserted and deasserted by the target with the same timing profile as the DEVSEL# signal line during the DATA PHASE.

- The ADDRESS PHASE is two CLK signal line periods in length (see Figures 6-14-A and B).

- During the ADDRESS PHASE, the assertion of the REQ64# signal line requires the PCI bus master to drive the AD[63::32] signal lines with valid upper order addresses (see Figures 6-14-A and B). Also, the PCI bus master drives the C/BE#[7::4] and PAR64 signal lines with COMMAND type and valid parity information, respectively.

- Due to the assertion of the REQ64# signal line during the ADDRESS PHASE, the PCI bus master drives the C/BE#[7::4] signal line during the DATA PHASE with the valid byte lane information for the AD[63::32] signal lines. This compliments the C/BE#[3::0] signal lines containing valid byte lane information for the AD[31::0] signal lines.

- During the DATA PHASE of a read transaction (see Figure 6-14-B), the AD[63::32] and PAR64 signal lines are tri-stated and driven by the target with the same timing profile as the AD[31::0] and PAR signal lines, respectively. The target drives these signal lines with valid data and parity information simultaneously with or subsequent to the assertion of the DEVSEL# and ACK64# signal lines.

- During the DATA PHASE of a write transaction (see Figure 6-14-A), the AD[63::32] and PAR64 signal lines are driven by the PCI bus master with the same timing profile as the AD[31::0] and PAR signal lines, respectively.

The addressing protocol of a 64 data bit BURST bus transaction is the same as for a 32 data bit BURST bus transaction except the address increments are in 64 data bit increments (QWORDS) (AD[2] signal line is logical "0" during the ADDRESS PHASE). The order of the BURST bus transaction is defined by the AD[1::0] signal lines in the same fashion as a 32 data bit transaction.

The protocol of the memory read line (MRL), memory read multiple (MRM), and memory write and invalidate (MWI) transactions previously described for 32 data bit PCI bus masters accessing 32 data bit targets also apply to 64 data bit PCI masters accessing 64 data bit targets. The adjustments to these protocols are the same as the adjustments outlined above for simple memory transactions.

I/O, CONFIGURATION, INTERRUPT ACKNOWLEDGE, AND SPECIAL TRANSACTIONS

The I/O, configuration, interrupt acknowledge, and special transactions are not defined for a 64 data bit transaction and can only be executed as 32 data bit transactions. A 64 data bit PCI bus master can only execute I/O, configuration, interrupt acknowledge, and special transactions as a 32 data bit PCI bus master; consequently, for these bus transactions the REQ64# signal line must be deasserted. If the REQ64# or ACK64# signal lines are asserted during one of these bus transactions, they are ignored by both the PCI bus master and target.

64 data bit I/O targets can be implemented, but there is no benefit to justify the increased complexity; it is therefore strongly recommended that 64 data bit I/O targets not be implemented. For the purposes of this book, I/O targets are only 32 data bits in size. If a 64 data bit I/O target is implemented, the 64 data bit protocol applied to memory targets would also apply to I/O targets.

6.7 MORE DETAILS OF PCI SIGNAL LINE PROTOCOL FOR 64 DATA BIT BUS TRANSACTIONS

Subchapter 6.4 outlines the ownership of the signal lines during a bus transaction. Subchapter 6.6 outlined the bus transaction protocol when both the PCI bus master and target are 64 data bits in size. Chapter 8: *Master and Target Termination* details the change of signal line ownership and signal line driving and tri-stating when Completion, Completion with Timeout, Retry, Disconnect, Master Abort, or Target Abort terminations are executed. Chapter 9: *Bus Ownership* explains the change of signal line ownership and signal line driving and tri-stating between changes of bus ownership. Chapter 10: *Parity and Bus Errors* covers the signal line ownership and signal line driving and tri-stating of the SERR# and PERR# signal lines. This subchapter defines the signal line protocol for the other signal lines during the bus transaction and between bus transactions when the PCI bus master retains bus segment ownership as follows:

> In the following discussion, the terms *drive or tri-state* are different from *assert or deassert*. The former identifies when the signal line buffers are enabled or disabled. The latter reflects when signal lines change their logical state.

- All of the signal lines used by a 32 data bit PCI bus master that are used by a 64 data bit PCI bus master with the same protocol have been previously outlined in Subchapters 6.1 and 6.2.

- The protocol for the signal lines associated with the 64 data bit extension in 64 data bit bus transactions is the same as the signal lines for 32 data bit transactions, which were discussed in Subchapter 6.6. Also, some additional protocol requirements for a 64 data bit PCI bus master accessing a 32 data bit target are discussed in Subchapter 6.8. Additionally, if the PCI bus master retains bus segment ownership between bus transactions, it can optionally drive the C/BE#[7::4], AD[63::32], REQ64#, and PAR64 signal lines to a stable level or tri-state them. If it tri-states these signal lines between bus transactions, it will tri-state in accordance with the end of a bus transaction protocol. In addition the target is required to tri-state the AD[63::32], ACK64#, and PAR64 signal lines

  - For all bus transactions, the protocol discussed in Subchapters 6.1 and 6.2 for AD[31::00], C/BE#[3::0], and PAR signal lines also applies to AD[63::32], C/BE#[7::4], and PAR64 signal lines; respectively (with some exceptions for DUAL ADDRESS). Any differences are summarized in Subchapters 6.6 and 6.8.

  - The REQ64# signal line is driven, tri-stated, asserted, and deasserted by the PCI bus master during the bus transaction with the same protocol as the FRAME# signal line..

  - The ACK64# signal line is driven, tri-stated, asserted, and deasserted by the target during the bus transaction with the same protocol as the DEVSEL# signal line.

  - If tri-stated, the AD[63::32], C/BE#[7::0], and PAR64 signal lines are driven to a logical "1" by pull-up resistors as identified by Point J (Circle J in Figures 6-15, 6-16 and 6-17) when bus segment ownership changes.

> The above discussion assumes data is accessed on the last CLK signal line rising edge prior to the IDLE PHASE. According to this discussion, the TRDY# signal is asserted at this CLK signal line rising edge. Under certain conditions the TRDY# signal line may be deasserted at the last CLK signal line rising edge prior to the IDLE PHASE. See "Exception Note" in subchapter 6.2 for more information.

6.8   64 DATA BIT PCI BUS MASTER TO 32 DATA BIT TARGET

MEMORY TRANSACTIONS

A PCI bus master and a target are defined as 64 and 32 data bit resources when the REQ64# and ACK64# signal lines are asserted and deasserted, respectively. The PCI bus master requests a 64 data bit transaction by asserting the REQ64# signal line and the PCI target acknowledges support of a 32 data bit transaction by not asserting the ACK64# signal line (deasserted by pull-up resistor).

The access of a 64 data bit PCI bus master to a 32 data bit target is determined on a bus transaction-by-bus transaction basis. During the ADDRESS PHASE, the REQ64# signal line is asserted, and the AD[31::0], C/BE#[3::0], and PAR signal lines operate with the same protocol as a 32 data bit PCI bus master executing a 32 data bit transaction (see Figures 6-16 and 6-17). Also, during the DATA PHASE, the operation of the C/BE#[7::4], AD[63::32], and PAR64 signal lines operate with the same protocol as the C/BE#[3::0], AD[31::0], and PAR signal lines in a 32 data bit transaction. Also, during the DATA PHASE, the ACK64# signal line remains deasserted to indicate that a 32 data bit access will be executed for the entire bus transaction.

> In the following discussion, the activity of the PAR and PAR64 signal lines are referenced to the ADDRESS and DATA PHASES. In actuality, the PAR and PAR64 signal lines are delayed by one CLK signal line period; consequently, they do not exactly align with the ADDRESS and DATA PHASES as implied.

> As will be outlined below, a 64 data bit PCI bus master does not usually access a 32 data bit target using a SINGLE bus transaction. Normally, a 64 data bit SINGLE bus transaction requested by the PCI bus master becomes a BURST bus transaction of two 32 data bit microaccesses. If the 64 data bit PCI bus master knows in advance (via configuration address space) that the target supports 64 data bit transactions, it executes a single 64 data bit transaction.

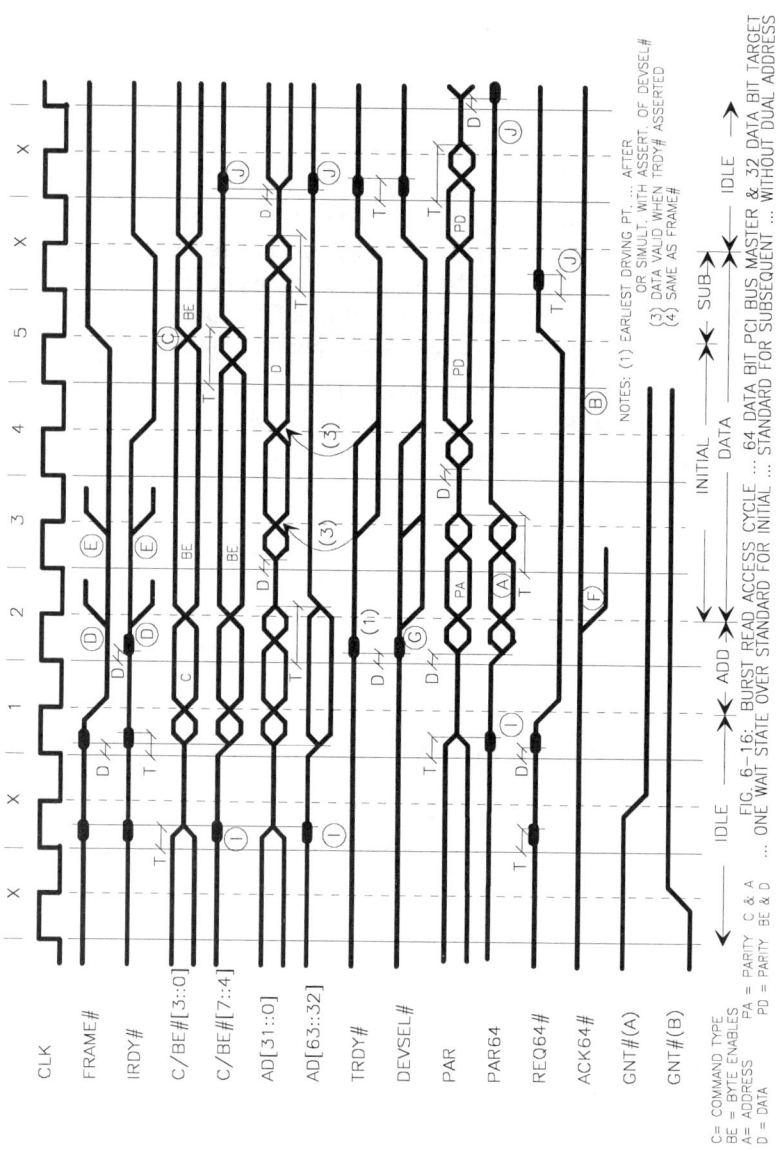

Figure 6-16: Burst Read Transaction, 64-Data Bit PCI Bus Master and 32 Data Bit Target, One Wait State Over Standard for Initial, Standard for Subsequent, and without DUAL ADDRESS

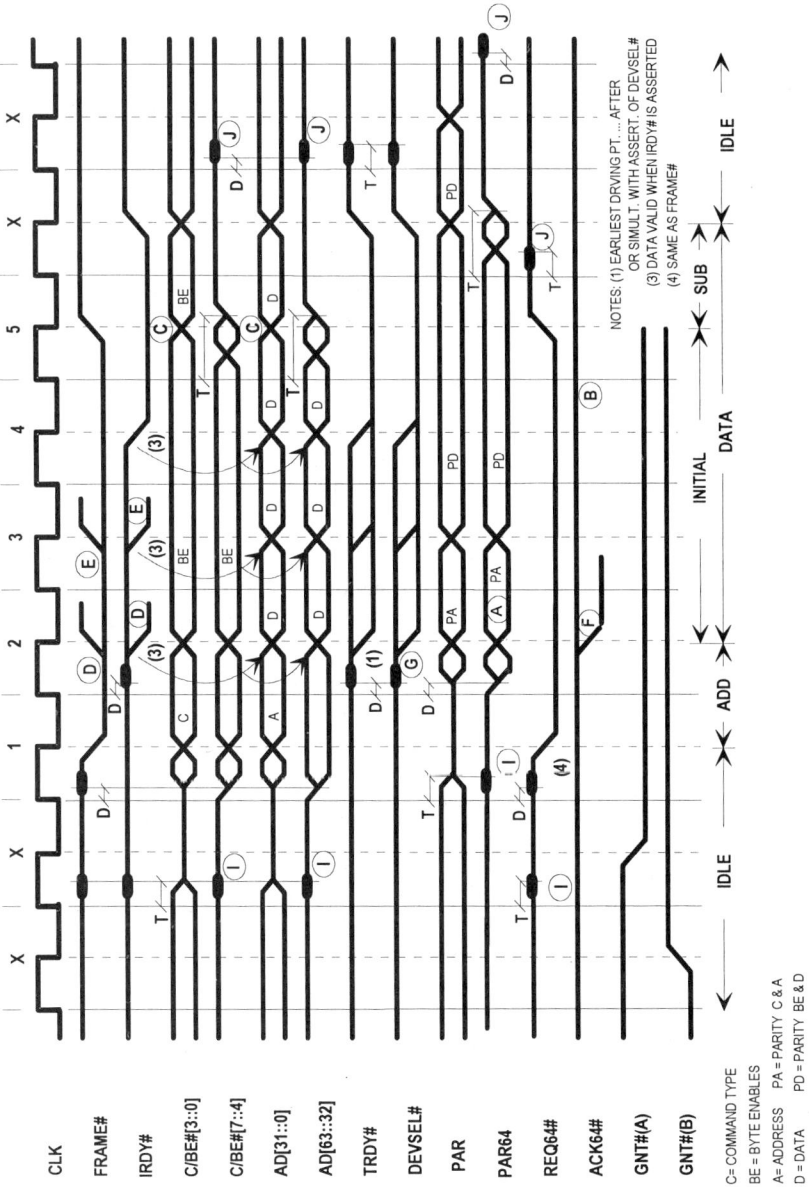

Figure 6-17: Burst Write Transaction, 64-Data Bit PCI Bus Master, 32 Data Bit Target, Two Wait States Over Standard for Initial, Standard for Subsequent, and without DUAL ADDRESS

For a 64 data bit PCI bus master's access to a 32 data bit target without DUAL ADDRESS, the protocol of the AD[63::32], C/BE#[7::4], REQ64#, ACK64#, and PAR64 signal lines is as follows:

- The REQ64# signal line is driven, tri-stated, asserted, and deasserted by the PCI bus master during the bus transaction with the same protocol as the FRAME# signal line.

- The ACK64# signal line remains deasserted (driven to logical "1" by pull-up resistors) throughout the bus transaction.

- During the ADDRESS PHASE, the AD[63::32], and C/BE#[7::4] signal lines are driven to a stable level by the PCI bus master. Due to the assertion of the REQ64# signal lines the PAR64 signal line contains valid parity information.

- Due to the assertion of the REQ64# signal line during the ADDRESS PHASE, the PCI bus master drives the C/BE#[7::4] signal lines during the DATA PHASE with the valid byte lane information for the initial microaccess (see Figures 6-16 and 6-17). After the completion of the initial microaccess, the C/BE#[7::4] signal lines are driven by the PCI bus master to a logical "1". Prior to the completion of the initial microaccess, the target has been identified as 32 data bits in size (TRDY# and DEVSEL# signal lines are asserted, and ACK64# signal line is deasserted). The byte information on the C/BE#[7::4] signal lines during the initial microaccess is repeated on the C/BE#[3::0] signal lines at Point C during the first of the subsequent microaccesses (Circle C in Figures 6-16 and 6-17).

> The above bullet states that the PCI bus master drives C/BE#[7::4] signal lines to a logical "1". Optionally, the PCI bus master can drive these signal lines to any stable level or tri-state them. The latter results in pull-up resistors driving them to a logical "1".

- During the DATA PHASE of a read transaction (see Figure 6-16), the AD[63::32] and PAR64 signal lines are tri-stated and driven to a logical "1" by pull-up resistors. The PAR64 signal line does not contain valid parity information due to the deasserted ACK64# signal line.

- During the initial microaccess of the DATA PHASE of a write transaction (see Figure 6-17), the AD[63::32] and PAR64 signal lines are driven with valid information by the PCI bus master with the same timing profile as the AD[31::0] and PAR signal lines, respectively. After the completion of the initial microaccess, the AD[63::32] and PAR64 signal lines are driven by the PCI bus master to a logical "1"; consequently, the PAR64 signal line does not contain valid parity information due to the deasserted

ACK64# signal line. Prior to the completion of the initial microaccess, the target has been identified as 32 data bits in size (TRDY# and DEVSEL# signal lines are asserted, and ACK64# signal line is deasserted). The valid information on the AD[63::32] and PAR64 signal lines during the initial microaccess is repeated on the AD[31::0] and PAR signal lines during the first subsequent microaccess, respectively.

> The above bullet states that the PCI bus master drives AD[63::32] and PAR64 signal lines to a logical "1". Optionally, the PCI bus master can drive these signal lines to any stable level or tri-state them. The latter results in pull-up resistors driving them to a logical "1". In any case the PAR64 signal line does not contain valid parity information.

> For the read transaction, the AD[63::32], C/BE#[7::4], and PAR64 signal lines are driven to a logical "1" by pull-up resistors during the DATA PHASE of the initial and the first subsequent microaccess. When the BURST bus transaction contains additional subsequent microaccesses, pull-up resistors hold these signal lines at logical "1".

> For the write transaction, the AD[63::32], C/BE#[7::4], and PAR64 signal lines are driven with valid information by the PCI bus master during the initial microaccess during the DATA PHASE. The operation of these signal lines during the first subsequent microaccess has been outlined above. If the BURST bus transaction contains other subsequent microaccesses, the PCI bus master can drive these signal lines to any stable level or tri-state them. The latter results in pull-up resistors driving them to a logical "1". In any case, the PAR64 signal line does not contain valid parity information.

For a 64 data bit PCI bus master's access to the 32 data bit target with DUAL ADDRESS, the protocol of the AD[63::32], C/BE#[7::4], REQ64#, ACK64#, and the PAR64 signal lines is as follows:

■ The REQ64# signal line is driven, tri-stated, asserted, and deasserted by the PCI bus master during the bus transaction with the same protocol as the FRAME# signal line.

■ The ACK64# signal line remains deasserted (driven to logical "1" by pull-up resistors) throughout the bus transaction.

■ The ADDRESS PHASE is two CLK signal line periods in length (see Figures 6-14-A and B).

■ During the ADDRESS PHASE, due to the assertion of the REQ64# signal line, the AD[63::32] signal lines are driven by the PCI bus master with a valid upper order address (see Figures 6-14-A and B). The PCI bus master also drives the C/BE#[7::4] and PAR64 signal lines with the COMMAND type and the parity information, respectively.

■ Due to the assertion of the REQ64# signal line during the ADDRESS PHASE, the PCI bus master drives the C/BE#[7::4] signal lines during the DATA PHASE with the valid byte lane information for the initial microaccess. After the completion of the initial microaccess, the C/BE#[7::4] signal lines are driven by PCI bus master to a logical "1". Prior to the completion of the initial microaccess, the target has been identified as 32 data bits in size (TRDY# and DEVSEL# signal lines are asserted, and ACK64# signal line is deasserted). The byte information on the C/BE#[7::4] signal lines during the initial microaccess is repeated on the C/BE#[3::0] signal lines at Point C during the first of the subsequent microaccesses (Circle C in Figures 6-16 and 6-17).

> The above bullet says that the PCI bus master drives the C/BE#[7::4] signal lines to a logical "1". Optionally, the PCI bus master can drive these signal lines to any stable level or tri-state them. The latter results in pull-up resistors driving them to logical "1".

■ During the DATA PHASE of a read transaction (see Figure 6-16), the AD[63::32] and PAR64 signal lines are tri-stated and driven to a logical "1" by pull-up resistors. The PAR64 signal line does not contain valid parity information due to the deasserted ACK64# signal line.

■ During the initial microaccess of the DATA PHASE of a write transaction (see Figure 6-17), the AD[63::32] and PAR64 signal lines are driven with valid information by the PCI bus master with the same timing profile as the AD[31::0] and PAR signal lines, respectively. After the completion of the initial microaccess, the AD[63::32] and PAR64 signal lines are driven by the PCI bus master to a logical "1"; consequently, the PAR64 signal line does not contain valid parity information due to the deasserted ACK64# signal line. Prior to the completion of the initial microaccess, the target has been identified as 32 data bits in size (TRDY# and DEVSEL# signal lines are asserted, and ACK64# signal line is deasserted). The valid information on the AD[63::32] and PAR64 signal lines during the initial microaccess is repeated on the AD[31::0] and PAR signal lines during the subsequent microaccess, respectively.

The above bullet states that the PCI bus master drives AD[63::32] and PAR64 signal lines to a logical "1". Optionally, the PCI bus master can drive these signal lines to any stable level or tri-state them. The latter results in pull-up resistors driving them to a logical "1". In any case the PAR64 signal line does not contain valid parity information.

For the read transaction, the AD[63::32], C/BE#[7::4], and PAR64 signal lines are driven to a logical "1" by pull-up resistors during the DATA PHASE of the initial and the first subsequent microaccesses. When the BURST bus transaction contains additional subsequent microaccesses, these signal lines remain at the logical "1" by pull-up resistors.

For the write transaction, the AD[63::32], C/BE#[7::4], and PAR64 signal lines are driven with valid information by the PCI bus master during the initial microaccess during the DATA PHASE. The operation of these signal lines during the first subsequent microaccess has been outlined above. If the BURST transaction contains other subsequent microaccesses, the PCI bus master can drive these signal lines to any stable level or tri-state them. The latter results in pull-up resistors driving them to a logical "1". In any case, the PAR64 signal line does not contain valid parity information.

The addressing protocol of a 64 data bit PCI bus master's request to a 32 data bit target BURST bus transaction is the same as for a 32 data bit BURST bus transaction. The address increments are 32 data bit (double word) increments. The order of the burst is defined by the AD[1::0] in the same fashion as a 32 data bit transaction.

The above assumes that the PCI bus master is requesting a 64 data bit SINGLE transaction. The 32 data bit target responded by allowing the SINGLE 64 data bit transaction to turn into a BURST bus transaction with an initial and subsequent microaccesses of 32 data bits each. If the PCI bus master was requesting a 64 data bit BURST bus transaction, the 64 data bit initial microaccess becomes a 32 data bit initial and subsequent microaccess. The BURST bus transaction continues with 32 data bit microaccesses. Alternatively, the target can execute a Disconnect with data termination with the data access of the SINGLE bus transaction or the initial microaccess of the BURST bus transaction. Under this protocol the PCI bus master is required to continue the access later as a 32 data bit PCI bus master (REQ64# signal line deasserted), if the PCI bus master decides to continue the access after the Disconnect termination.

> The protocol of the memory read line (MRL), memory read multiple (MRM), and memory write and invalidate (MWI) transactions previously described for 32 data bit PCI bus masters accessing 32 data bit targets also apply to 64 data bit PCI master accessing 32 data bit targets. The adjustments to these protocols are the same as the adjustments outlined above for simple memory transactions.

I/O, CONFIGURATION, INTERRUPT ACKNOWLEDGE TRANSACTIONS, AND SPECIAL TRANSACTIONS

These bus transactions are not defined for 64 data bit transactions and must be executed as 32 data bit transactions. If the REQ64# or ACK64# signal lines are asserted during one of these transactions, they are ignored.

> 64 data bit I/O targets can be implemented, but there is no benefit justifying the increased complexity; it is therefore strongly recommended that 64 data bit I/O targets not be implemented. For the purposes of this book, I/O targets are only 32 data bits in size. If a 64 data bit I/O target is implemented, the 64 data bit protocol applied to memory targets would also apply to I/O targets.

6.9   SPECIAL CONSIDERATIONS FOR A 64 DATA BIT PCI BUS MASTER TO A 32 DATA BIT TARGET

A PCI bus master asserts the REQ64# signal line at the beginning of the transaction without any assurance that the ACK64# signal line will be asserted. The target does not have to acknowledge a 64 data bit access (Point F) until the assertion of the DEVSEL# signal line at Point G (Circles F and G in Figures 6-14 A and B, and Figures 6-15 to 6-17). The protocol of a SINGLE bus transaction allows the FRAME# and IRDY# signal lines to be deasserted and asserted at Point D, respectively (Circle D in Figures 6-14-A and B, and Figures 6-15 to 6-17). The deassertion of the FRAME# signal line and the assertion of the IRDY# signal line at any point prior to Point F will prevent the proper completion of the bus transaction if the ACK64# signal line is not asserted. If the ACK64# signal line remains deasserted at Point B (Circle B in Figures 6-16 and 6-17) when the TRDY# and IRDY# signal lines are both asserted, a SINGLE bus transaction will become a BURST bus transaction because two 32 data bits (double words) must be accessed. The PCI bus master cannot deassert the FRAME# signal line until it is determined if the ACK64# signal line is asserted or remains deasserted; consequently, the FRAME# signal line must remain asserted until the DEVSEL#

signal line is asserted. The timing protocol of the DEVSEL# and ACK64# signal lines are the same; consequently, the DEVSEL# signal line can be used as a qualifier of the ACK64# signal and indicator when the FRAME# signal line can be deasserted. Points G and E (Circles G and E in Figures 6-14-A and B, and Figures 6-16 and 6-17) are the earliest assertion and deassertion points for the DEVSEL# and FRAME# signal lines, respectively.

If the ACK64# signal line is asserted when the DEVSEL# signal line is asserted, a SINGLE bus transaction will be executed; consequently, the FRAME# and IRDY# signal line can be immediately deasserted and asserted at Point E (Circle E in Figures 6-14-A and B, and Figures 6-16 and 6-17), respectively. The protocol of the FRAME# signal line requires it to be deasserted simultaneously with the assertion of the IRDY# signal line to execute a SINGLE bus transaction. If the ACK64# signal line is deasserted when the DEVSEL# signal line is asserted, the FRAME# signal line is required to remain asserted to allow a BURST bus transaction to be executed.

Once the first access is completed, the data size of the target is known; consequently, the requirements outlined above for the FRAME# and the DEVSEL# signal lines do not apply for the subsequent microaccesses of a BURST bus transaction.

If the PCI bus master knows (via the configuration address space) that the target size is 64 data bits, the above protocol of the FRAME# signal line deassertion and IRDY# signal line assertion after the assertion of the DEVSEL# and ACK64# signal lines is not required. This will allow the bus transaction to be executed as a single 64 data bit transaction in the minimum amount of time. Otherwise, the length of the bus transaction is longer due to the PCI bus master waiting for the assertion of the DEVSEL# signal line to determine when it can deassert the FRAME# signal line. The PCI bus master knows the size of the target via the device specific configuration space.

If the DUAL ADDRESS is executed, points D, E, F, and G (circles D, E, F, and G in Figures 6-14-A and B) are delayed by one CLK signal line period.

6.10   PCI BUS TRANSACTION TO BUS TRANSACTION OPERATION

INTRODUCTION

As shown in Figures 6-3 to 6-6 and Figures 6-15 to 6-17, the individual SINGLE and BURST bus transactions are preceded and followed by IDLE PHASES. IDLE PHASES occur whenever both the FRAME# and IRDY# signal lines are both deasserted. During the IDLE PHASES, the FRAME#, IRDY#, C/BE#[3::0], AD[31::0], and PAR signal lines are driven by a PCI bus master, and the C/BE#[7::4], AD[63::32], PAR64 (optional for 64 data bits), TRDY#, DEVSEL#, STOP#, and PERR# signal lines are driven by pull-up resistors. The PCI local bus specification outlines a protocol to change the resources responsible for driving the aforementioned signal lines. In addition, under certain circumstances IDLE PHASES do not occur between the individual SINGLE and BURST bus transactions. The following will first describe how the aforementioned signal lines are driven by different resources from bus transaction to bus transaction when IDLE is achieved. It will then describe how Fast Back-to-Back transactions occur without IDLE PHASES, and how the signal lines are driven by different resources during Fast Back-to-Back transactions.

> The LOCK# signal line is driven by the Lock master when other PCI bus masters own the bus; consequently, there is not always a change of Lock Function ownership between the bus transactions.

SIGNAL LINE DRIVING NON-FAST BACK-TO-BACK

TRANSACTIONS

Figure 6-3 outlines two SINGLE read transactions when a single PCI bus master (A) owns the PCI bus before and after the execution of the two bus transactions. The FRAME#, IRDY#, and C/BE#[3::0] signal lines are driven by the current PCI bus master throughout the execution of these two bus transactions because its associated GNTx# signal line remains asserted. The AD[31::0] and PAR signal lines are driven by both the PCI bus master and the target. During the IDLE PHASE prior to the first bus transaction, the AD[31::0] signal lines are driven by the current PCI bus master. Once the bus transaction has started (FRAME# signal line asserted), the PCI bus master must tri-state the AD[31::0] signal lines at the end of the ADDRESS PHASE in preparation for the target driving these signal lines with read data at the beginning of the DATA PHASE. The AD[31::0] signal lines are tri-stated by the target at the end of the first bus transaction when the

FRAME# and TRDY# signal lines are simultaneously deasserted and asserted, respectively. Subsequently, the AD[31::0] signal lines are driven by the current PCI bus master when the FRAME# and IRDY# signal lines are both deasserted because its associated GNTx# signal line remains asserted.

The PAR signal lines operate in exactly the same fashion as the AD[31::0] signal lines with a one CLK signal line period lag.

Figure 6-3 also outlines the protocol for the portion of the read transactions when the TRDY#, DEVSEL#, and STOP# signal lines are driven by the target. Whenever these signal lines are not driven by a target, they are driven by the pull-up resistors on the bus segment backplane. The target will drive the TRDY#, DEVSEL#, and STOP# signal lines at the beginning of the DATA PHASE of the first bus transaction. The target tri-states these signal lines when the FRAME# and IRDY# signal lines are both deasserted.

The tri-state and drive protocol of the second bus transaction in Figure 6-3 is identical to the first access because IDLE is achieved between the two bus transactions. The protocol is the same subsequent to the second bus transaction even though a third bus transaction will not immediately begin.

Figure 6-4 outlines two SINGLE write transactions when a single PCI bus master (A) owns the PCI bus segment during and after the execution of two bus transactions, but not before the first bus transaction. The FRAME#, IRDY#, C/BE#[3::0], AD[31::0], and PAR signal lines are driven by the current PCI bus master (B) while the GNT# (B) signal line is asserted. When the GNT# (B) signal line is deasserted, the aforementioned signal lines are tri-stated in anticipation of PCI bus master (A) driving these signal lines. Because the IDLE PHASE was achieved by PCI bus master (B), a CLK signal line period is inserted between the deassertion and assertion of the GNT# (B) and GNT# (A) signal lines, respectively. Until the GNT# (A) signal line is asserted, the FRAME# and IRDY# signal lines are driven by pull-up resistors, and the C/BE#[3::0], AD[31::0], and PAR signal lines are allowed to float. Once the GNT# (A) signal line is asserted, these signal lines are driven by the PCI bus master (A). The PCI bus master (A) executes the two write transactions in the same fashion as the two read transactions outlined in Figure 6-3. The only difference is that the AD[31::0] and PAR signal lines are not driven by the target.

The protocol for the portion of the write transactions when the TRDY#, DEVSEL#, and STOP# signal lines are driven by the target are outlined in Figure 6-4. The protocol is the same as for the read transactions as outlined in Figure 6-3.

Both Figures 6-3 and 6-4 outline the tri-state and drive protocol of the signal lines prior to, during, and after the two bus transactions. Obviously, this protocol applies for multiple sequential bus transactions. Figure 6-18 outlines the general case when more than one IDLE PHASE occurs between bus transactions when the

PCI bus master remains the same. During the IDLE PHASE the FRAME#, IRDY#, C/BE#, AD[31::0], and PAR signal lines are driven by the PCI bus master associated with the asserted GNTx# signal line. The TRDY#, DEVSEL#, and STOP# signal lines are driven by pull-up resistors. The PAR signal line is driven by the target during some portion of the IDLE PHASE subsequent to a read transaction.

The unmarked portions of the C/BE#, AD, PAR, and PAR64 signal lines in Figures 6-18 to 6-25 are driven to a stable level—but without valid information—during the IDLE PHASE (though not shown separately, for *reads*, the PAR64 signal line is driven to a logical "1" by a pull-up resistor). As previously mentioned, the PAR and PAR64 signal lines always lag by one CLK signal line period. As outlined in the *Signal Line Protocol Considerations* section, the AD[63::32], C/BE#[7::4], and PAR64 signal lines are driven to a logical "1" by either the PCI bus master or pull-up resistors. Consequently, for these signal lines, the shaded areas would appear as logical "1". Similarly, in these figures when the signal line is drawn with a single horizontal line to indicate *floating*, these signal lines are driven to a logical "1" by either the PCI bus master or pull-up resistors.

Figures 6-18 to 6-25 do not include LOCK# signal line. Because the operation of the LOCK# signal line transcends a specific bus transaction, its inclusion is not important to understanding Fast Back-to-Back transaction operation. Figures 6-18 to 6-25 show the data and parity (*D* and *PD*) valid for the entire bus transaction. As outlined in previous figures in this chapter, the assertion of the IRDY# and TRDY# signal lines qualifies when the AD, PAR, and PAR64 signal lines are valid. Consequently, the indication of valid data and parity is for simplification of Figures 6-18 to 6-25. Refer to previous figures for specific information about valid data and parity.

Figures 6-19 to 6-21 outline the tri-state and drive protocol for the signal lines between bus transactions when the ownership of the bus segment will change. Figure 6-19 shows the protocol when the GNT# (A) signal line is deasserted prior to the completion of the last bus transaction of the PCI bus master (A) but prior to an IDLE PHASE. The simultaneous sampling at Point A of deasserted FRAME# and GNT#(A) signal lines, and the asserted IRDY# and TRDY# signal lines indicates the completion of the bus transaction and the end of bus ownership by PCI bus master (A). The FRAME#, C/BE#, and AD signal lines are immediately tri-stated at Point A. For a read transaction, the target will tri-state the AD signal lines, and one CLK signal line period later the PAR signal line. For a write transaction, the PAR and PAR64 signal lines are tri-stated by the PCI bus master (A) one CLK signal line period later. The IRDY# signal line is tri-stated one CLK signal line period after Point A. In this example, the GNT# signal line (B) is asserted prior to IDLE PHASE being achieved by the last bus transaction of PCI bus master (A). The simultaneous sampling of the asserted GNT# (B) signal line and the IDLE ACHIEVED (FRAME# and IRDY# signal lines deasserted) at Point B allows the PCI bus master (B) to immediately drive the FRAME#, C/BE#, and AD signal lines (Circle B in Figure 6-19). The PCI bus master (B) drives the IRDY# signal line one CLK signal line period later, and the PAR (and PAR64 for 64 data bit transactions) signal line two CLK signal line periods later to avoid signal line contention with the PCI bus master (A). The TRDY#, DEVSEL#, STOP#, PAR, and PAR64 signal lines are tri-stated and driven with the same protocol used when bus ownership has not changed.

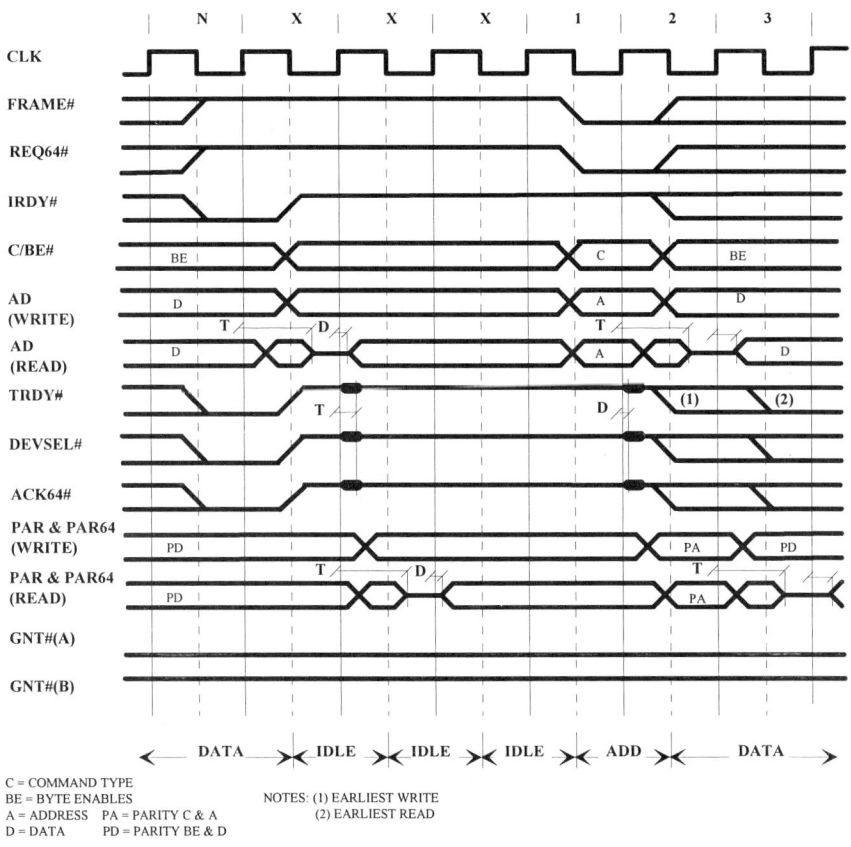

C = COMMAND TYPE
BE = BYTE ENABLES
A = ADDRESS   PA = PARITY C & A
D = DATA   PD = PARITY BE & D

NOTES: (1) EARLIEST WRITE
        (2) EARLIEST READ

Figure 6-18: PCI Bus Master (A) to IDLE to PCI Bus Master (A)

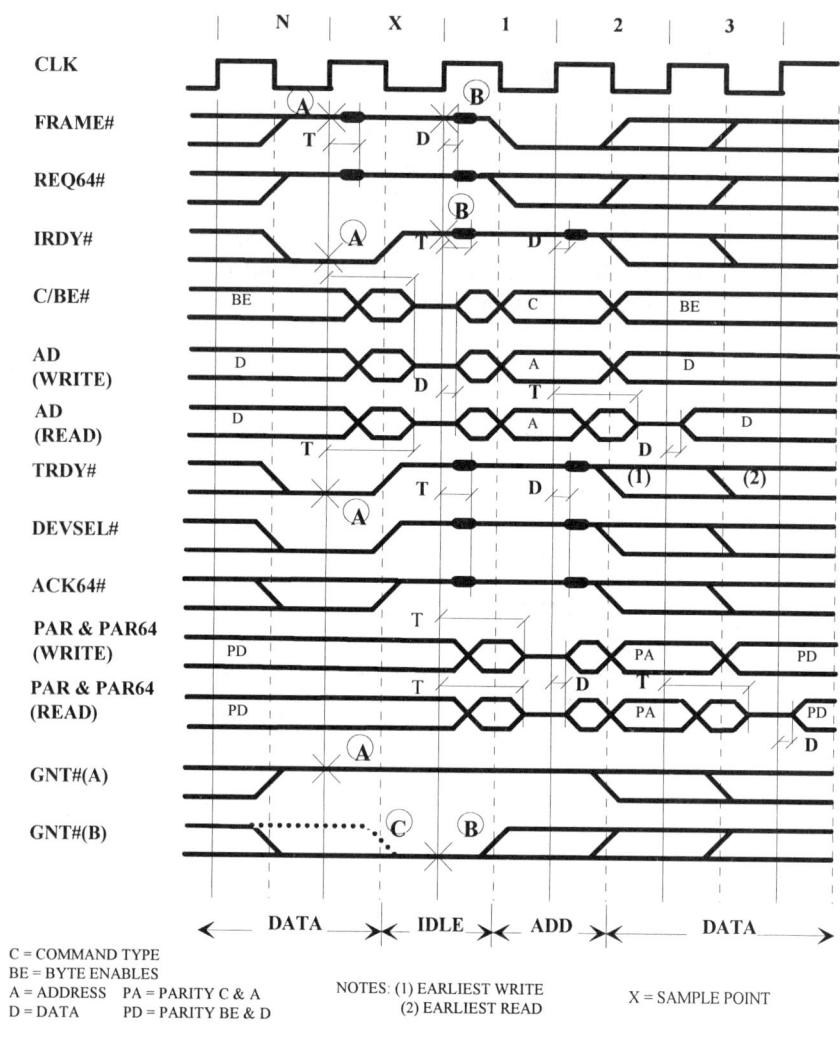

Figure 6-19: PCI Bus Master (A) to IDLE to PCI Bus Master (B)

In Figure 6-19, the GNT#(A) signal line is deasserted prior to IDLE ACHIEVED (FRAME# and IRDY# signal lines deasserted) occurring; consequently, the GNT#(B) signal line can be asserted immediately or at Point C (Circle C in Figure 6-19). The resulting bus transaction is the same for either point where the GNT#(B) signal line is asserted. See *Chapter 9: Bus Ownership* for more information.

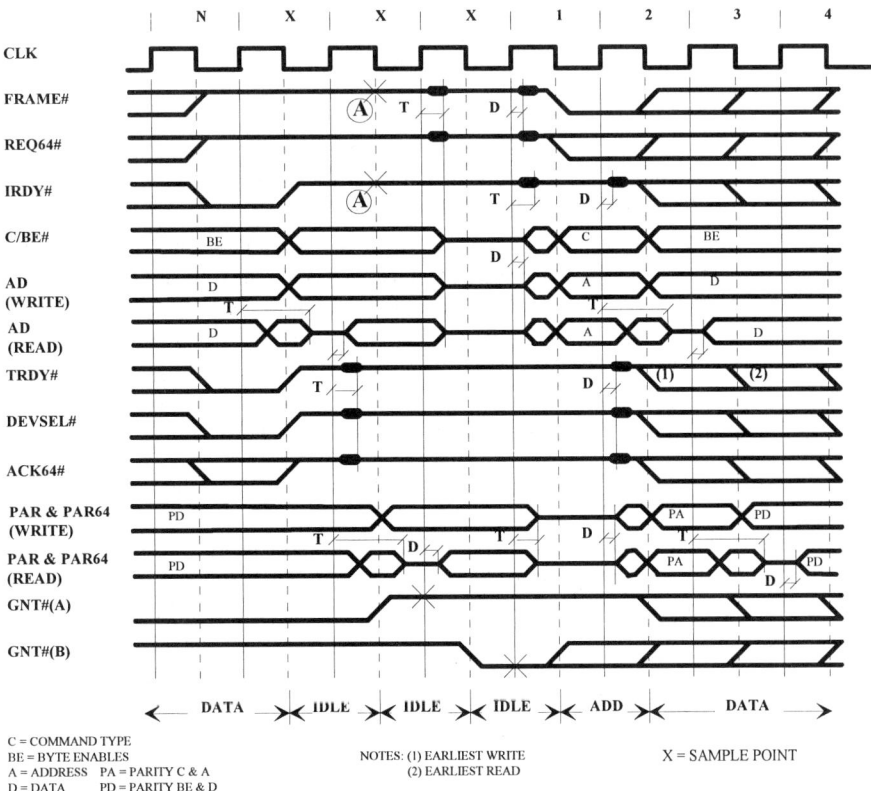

Figure 6-20: PCI Bus Master (A) to IDLE to PCI Bus Master (B)

Figure 6-20 shows the protocol when the GNT# (A) signal line is deasserted after IDLE ACHIEVED (FRAME# and IRDY# signal lines deasserted) at Point A has occurred for the last bus transaction of the PCI bus master (A)(Circle A in Figure 6-20). Prior to the deassertion of the GNT# (A) signal line, the PCI bus master (A) owns the bus segment and is required to continue to drive the FRAME#, C/BE#, AD, PAR, and PAR64 signal lines even if it does not intend to begin another bus transaction. Thus, after the completion of the bus transaction, the aforementioned signal lines are driven by the PCI bus master (A). In the case of C/BE#, AD, PAR, and PAR64 signal lines this is totally invalid information. If the last bus transaction read data, the PCI bus master (A) is required to wait until the IDLE PHASE before driving the AD signal lines to prevent contention with

409

the target. Similarly, the PAR and PAR64 signal lines are driven one CLK signal line period after the first IDLE PHASE period. When the GNT# (A) signal line is sampled deasserted, the PCI bus master (A) is required to immediately tri-state the FRAME#, IRDY#, C/BE#, and AD signal lines in anticipation that another PCI bus master will drive them. Similarly, the PAR and PAR64 signal lines are tri-stated one CLK signal line period later.

The PCI bus master (B) uses the IDLE condition in conjunction with an asserted GNT# B signal line to begin driving the FRAME#, IRDY#, C/BE#, and AD signal lines. The PAR signal line is driven one CLK signal line period later. In that the IDLE PHASE was achieved when the GNT# (A) signal line was still asserted, the central arbiter will assert the GNT# (B) signal line one CLK signal line after it deasserts the GNT# (A) signal line. This protocol allows the PCI bus master (A) to tri-state the aforementioned signal lines without contention with the PCI bus master (B). The TRDY#, DEVSEL#, and STOP# signal lines are tri-stated and driven with the same protocol used when bus segment ownership has not changed. See Chapter 9: *Bus Ownership* for more information.

Figure 6-21 outlines the protocol when the GNT# (A) signal line is deasserted simultaneously with IDLE ACHIEVED (FRAME# and IRDY# signal lines deasserted) at Point B for the last bus transaction of the PCI bus master (A) (Circle B of Figure 6-21). PCI bus master (A) will immediately tri-state the signal lines it was driving. In other examples (Figures 6-19 and 6-20) the PCI bus master that just completed a read transaction will re-drive the AD, PAR, and PAR64 signal lines that had been driven by the target. In this example (Figure 6-21), the PCI bus master knows it must relinquish bus segment ownership at the completion of the bus transaction; consequently, it does not re-drive the AD, PAR, and PAR64 signal lines at Point A (Circle A in Figure 6-21) in that the IDLE PHASE was achieved simultaneously with the deassertion of the GNT# (A) signal line. The central arbiter will assert the GNT# (B) signal line one CLK signal line after it deasserts the GNT# (A) signal line. This protocol allows PCI bus master (A) to tri-state these signal lines without contention with PCI bus master (B). The TRDY#, DEVSEL#, and STOP# signal lines are tri-stated and driven with the same protocol whether or not bus ownership has not changed. See Chapter 9: *Bus Ownership* for more information.

Even though the examples use only SINGLE bus transactions, the protocol also applies between BURST bus transactions, and between SINGLE and BURST bus transactions.

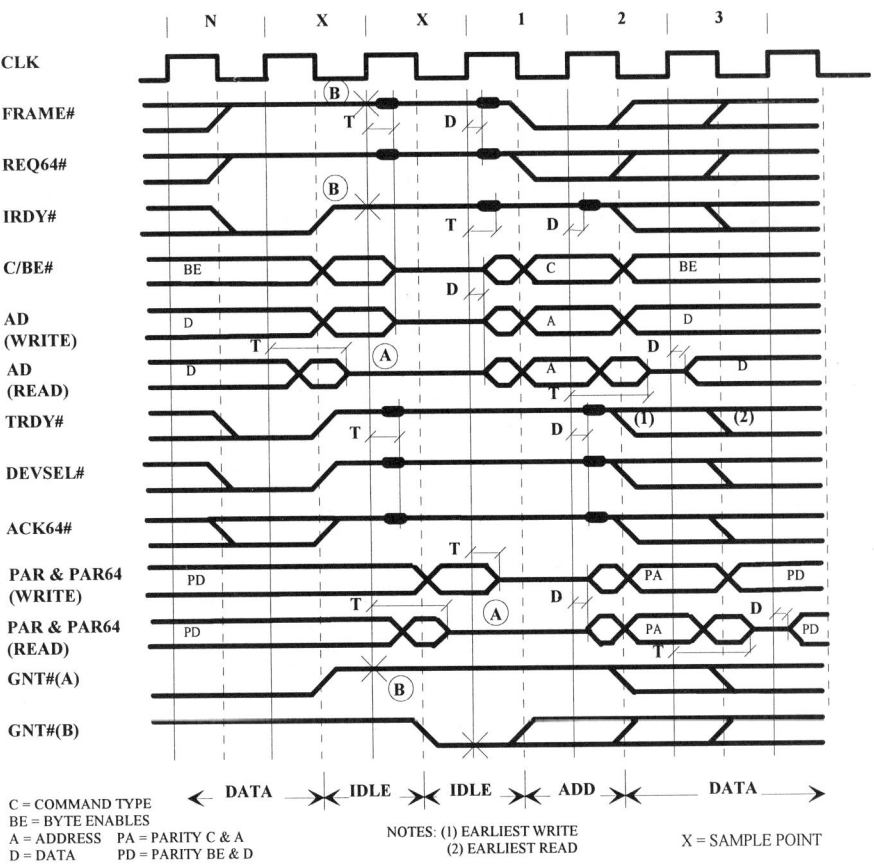

Figure 6-21: PCI Bus Master (A) to IDLE to PCI Bus Master (B)

INTERRUPT ACKNOWLEDGE TRANSACTIONS

The bus transaction to bus transaction protocol outlined above applies to interrupt acknowledge transaction to interrupt acknowledge transaction, interrupt acknowledge transaction to memory, I/O, configuration, or special transaction or special transaction, and memory, I/O, configuration, or special transaction to interrupt acknowledge transaction.

SPECIAL TRANSACTIONS

The bus transaction to bus transaction protocol outlined above applies to special transaction to special transaction, special transaction to memory, I/O, configuration, or interrupt acknowledge transaction, and memory, I/O, configuration, or interrupt acknowledge transaction to special transaction.

SIGNAL LINE DRIVING AND FAST BACK-TO-BACK BUS TRANSACTION

INTRODUCTION

The PCI local bus specification has specific requirements for back-to-back bus transactions by the same PCI bus master. As shown in Figure 6-19, the normal completion of a bus transaction includes achieving IDLE. By achieving IDLE, there is a minimum of one CLK signal line period between the DATA PHASE of the previous SINGLE bus transaction and the ADDRESS PHASE of the next SINGLE bus transaction. The achievement of IDLE would also occur between two BURST bus transactions, SINGLE and BURST bus transactions, and BURST and SINGLE bus transactions. Under certain situations, the IDLE PHASE between two bus transactions is not required. Specifically, there are two situations where IDLE is not required: Master Fast Back-to-Back and Target Fast Back-to-Back transactions. Either of these Fast Back-to-Back situations allow the DATA PHASE of the previous bus transaction to be immediately followed by the ADDRESS PHASE of the present bus transaction, thus providing higher bus performance.

Restrictions in the protocol of Fast Back-to-Back transactions are to eliminate contention (buffer fights) on the signal lines. The FRAME#, IRDY#, C/BE#, PAR, and PAR64 signal lines are driven by the PCI bus master between back-to-back transactions. The driving of these signal lines by the PCI bus master that owns the bus segment assures that no other resource is simultaneously driving these signal lines and causing contention between the back-to-back transactions. Because the previous bus transaction of Fast Back-to-Back bus transactions is required to always be a write, there is no contention on the AD, PAR, or PAR64 signal lines. That is, in the Fast Back-to-Back transaction protocol the following two sequences of bus transactions are permitted: write to write and write to read. The TRDY#, DEVSEL#, and STOP# signal lines can be driven by different targets from one bus transaction to another; consequently, these signal lines have a potential for contention. Contention on these signal lines is avoided by the protocol restrictions placed on Fast Back-to-Back transactions as will be discussed below.

The PAR and PAR64 signal lines can be driven by either the PCI bus master or the target. Except for a one CLK signal line period delay, the change of ownership for the PAR and PAR64 signal lines are patterned after the AD[31::0] and AD[63::32] signal lines, respectively. The requirement that the previous bus transaction is required to be a write transaction insures that only one PCI bus master drives the PAR and PAR64 signal lines between Fast Back-to-Back bus transactions.

In order to prevent contention on some of the signal lines, an IDLE PHASE exists between the last bus transaction of one PCI bus master and the first bus transaction of the next PCI bus master. (IDLE is achieved with the FRAME# and IRDY# signal lines simultaneously deasserted.) For bus transactions executed in a *non* Fast Back-to-Back fashion, the IDLE PHASE assures that there is no signal line contention.

Target unlocking cannot occur between Fast Back-to-Back transactions. See the *Lock* section.

A bus transaction that ends with a Retry, Disconnect, or Target Abort termination cannot be followed by a bus transaction in a Fast Back-to-Back fashion because the PCI bus master is required to deassert its REQx# signal line. One exception is when a Disconnect with data termination occurs when the IRDY# and FRAME# signal lines are asserted and deasserted, respectively. All of these terminations have the assertion of the STOP# signal line in common.

MASTER FAST BACK-TO-BACK TRANSACTIONS (ALSO KNOWN AS MASTER PROGRAMMED FAST BACK-TO-BACK)

A MASTER PROGRAMMED Fast Back-to-Back (MP-Back/Back) transaction can only occur when all of the following conditions are met:

- The MP-Back/Back transactions must be executed by the same PCI bus master.

- The bus transactions involved in the MP-Back/Back must be a write transaction followed by a write or read transaction. A read transaction followed by a read or write transaction is not allowed to be executed in a MP-Back/Back fashion.

- The bus transactions involved in MP-Back/Back must be to the same target.

■ The ASIC that drives the address onto the AD signal lines must be the same ASIC that drives the write data onto the AD signal lines.

■ All targets must be able to recognize the completion of the bus transaction with only the simultaneous deassertion of the FRAME# signal line and the assertion of the IRDY# signal line without a subsequent IDLE PHASE. A Disconnect with data termination requested when the FRAME# signal line is deasserted (see Figure 8-8-B) requires the TRDY# signal line to be asserted and does allow the Fast Back-to-Back protocol for the subsequent bus transaction.

■ A Master Abort termination (except when a special transaction is executed) allows a Fast Back-to-Back protocol for the subsequent bus transaction. Under this condition, the end of a bus transaction is the assertion and deassertion of the IRDY# and FRAME# signal line, respectively.

■ Completion of the bus transaction with the TRDY# signal line deasserted for Retry and Target Abort termination does not allow a subsequent Fast Back-to-Back bus transaction (REQx# signal line must be asserted under these conditions). Similarly, a Disconnect without data termination (see Figures 8-9-A and 8-9-B) and Disconnect with data termination requested when the FRAME# signal line is asserted (see Figure 8-8-A) require the TRDY# signal line to be deasserted and does not allow the Fast Back-to-Back protocol for the subsequent bus transaction.

The concept of MP-Back/Back is that the PCI bus master knows prior to the completion of the previous bus transaction the target and type of access of the present bus transaction. This knowledge, in conjunction with the requirements outlined in the bulleted items above, place the burden of preventing signal line contention on the PCI bus master.

> The explanation and examples in Figures 6-22 and 6-23 use SINGLE bus transactions. The protocol for MP-Back/Back when BURST bus transactions are involved is the same.

Figures 6-22 and 6-23 outline the protocol of MP-Back/Back. In Figure 6-22, the PCI bus master is first executing a STANDARD SINGLE write transaction. At the end of the previous bus transaction, the FRAME# signal line is sampled deasserted, and the IRDY# and TRDY# signal lines are both asserted. Under the MP-Back/Back protocol, the aforementioned pattern of these signal lines qualifies as the completion of the previous bus transaction and allows the PCI bus master to immediately assert the FRAME# signal line for the present bus transaction without an IDLE PHASE if its associated GNTx# signal line remains asserted. The completion of the present bus transaction (READY SINGLE WRITE) in Figure 6-

22 also follows the MP-Back/Back protocol, and the next bus transaction can begin as a Fast Back-to-Back transaction.

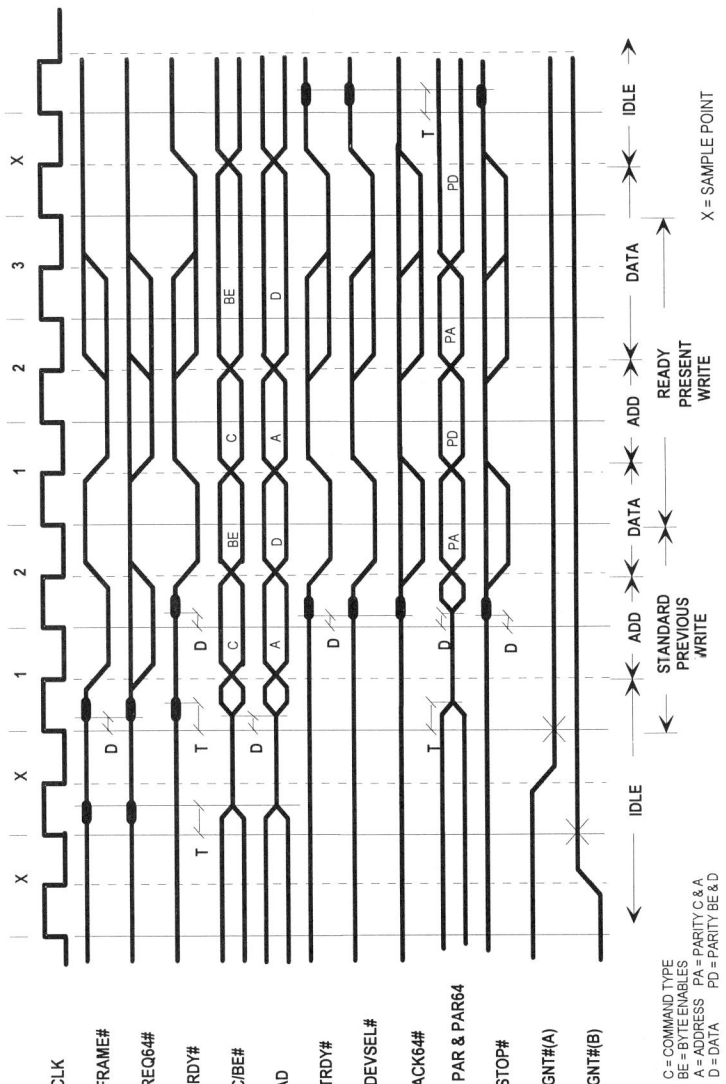

Figure 6-22: Same Target—SINGLE Bus Transaction, MASTER PROGRAMMED Fast Back-to-Back Parked at PCI Bus Master (B), Executed and Retained by PCI Bus Master (A)

415

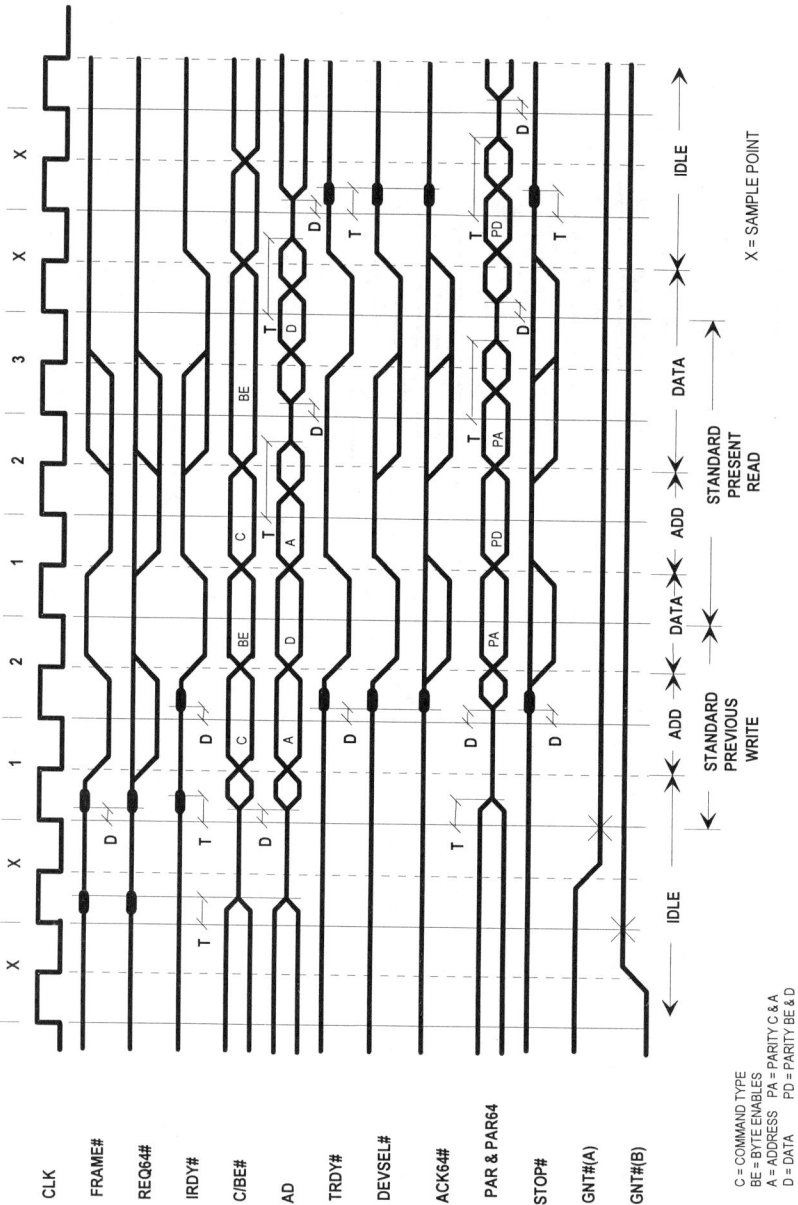

**Figure 6-23: Same Target—SINGLE Bus Transaction, MASTER
PROGRAMMED Fast Back-to-Back Parked at PCI Bus Master (B),
Executed and Retained by PCI Bus Master (A)**

Figure 6-23 shows the MP-Back/Back for a STANDARD SINGLE write transaction followed by a STANDARD SINGLE read transaction. The protocol to complete the write transaction and immediately begin the read transaction is the same as outlined in Figure 6-22. The completion of the read transaction clearly shows why a read transaction cannot be followed by a bus transaction under the MP-Back/Back protocol. The read data is driven onto the AD signal lines during the previous bus transaction, and sufficient time for the target to tri-state the AD signal lines prior to the PCI bus master driving the address onto the AD signal lines for the next bus transaction is required to prevent contention. Consequently, an extra CLK signal line clock period is needed, which results in an IDLE PHASE.

> The MP-Back/Back protocol requires that ALL targets are designed to operate with this protocol. Targets do not know in advance if an MP-Back/Back is going to occur for the next bus transaction unless the present bus transaction is a read transaction, or a Retry, Disconnect, or Target Abort termination is executed. With a read transaction or the aforementioned terminations, a Fast Back-to-Back will not occur. The aforementioned terminations require the PCI bus master to deassert its REQx# signal line. One exception is when a Disconnect with data termination occurs when the IRDY# and FRAME# signal lines are asserted and deasserted, respectively.

TARGET FAST BACK-TO-BACK

A Target Fast Back-to-Back (T-Back/Back) protocol removes the burden of preventing signal line contention from the PCI bus master and places it on the targets. All targets that potentially can be accessed by the same PCI bus master must be able to support T-Back/Back if the Fast Back-to-Back Capable bit is set in the targets' Status Register in the configuration address space. T-Back/Back can only occur when all of the following conditions are met:

- The T-Back/Back allows the same PCI bus master to access different targets without IDLE PHASES.

- In order for the PCI bus master to know that all potential targets can support the T-Back/Back protocol, the Fast Back-to-Back Enable bit must be set in the Command Register of the PCI bus master's configuration address space after the initialization software has determined that all potential targets have their respective Fast Back-to-Back Capable Status bits set in their respective Status Registers of the configuration address space.

■ The Fast Back-to-Back capable bit in the Status Register of each targets' configuration address space that will support T-Back/Back is must be set (logical "1"). To set the bit, the criteria outlined in the following two bullets must be met by the target.

■ All of the potential targets of the PCI bus master must be able to recognize the completion of the previous bus transaction as indicated by a deasserted FRAME# signal line and the asserted IRDY# and TRDY# signal lines. The potential targets must also be able to recognize when an IDLE PHASE does not occur (FRAME# and IRDY# signal lines both deasserted) prior to the assertion of the FRAME# signal line for the present bus transaction.

■ The target of the present bus transaction must delay the assertion of the DEVSEL#, TRDY#, STOP#, and ACK64# signal lines in the event that these signal lines are being asserted by the target of the previous bus transaction. To meet this requirement ONE of the following conditions must be met:

■ If the fastest possible decode is not supported by the target (DEVSEL# signal line is not asserted at the end of the second CLK signal line period.), by definition the DEVSEL#, TRDY#, STOP#, and ACK64# signal lines will not be in contention with the previous bus transaction. Point A (Circle A) in Figure 6-24 would be the earliest point for assertion of these signal lines would occur for the fastest decode. These signal lines is required to be asserted at or after Point B (Circle B). If a read transaction was used in this example, the present bus transaction would not have a contention on the TRDY# signal line for the fastest decode. There still remains a contention problem for the DEVSEL#, STOP#, and ACK64# signal lines.

OR

■ The target involved in the previous bus transaction is the same target involved in the present bus transaction. There is no contention with the DEVSEL#, TRDY#, STOP#, ACK64# signal lines in that these signal lines are driven by the same target. Under this condition, the fastest possible decode can be executed by the target. Point A (Circle A) in Figure 6-25 would be the earliest place of assertion of these signal lines would occur for the fastest decode.

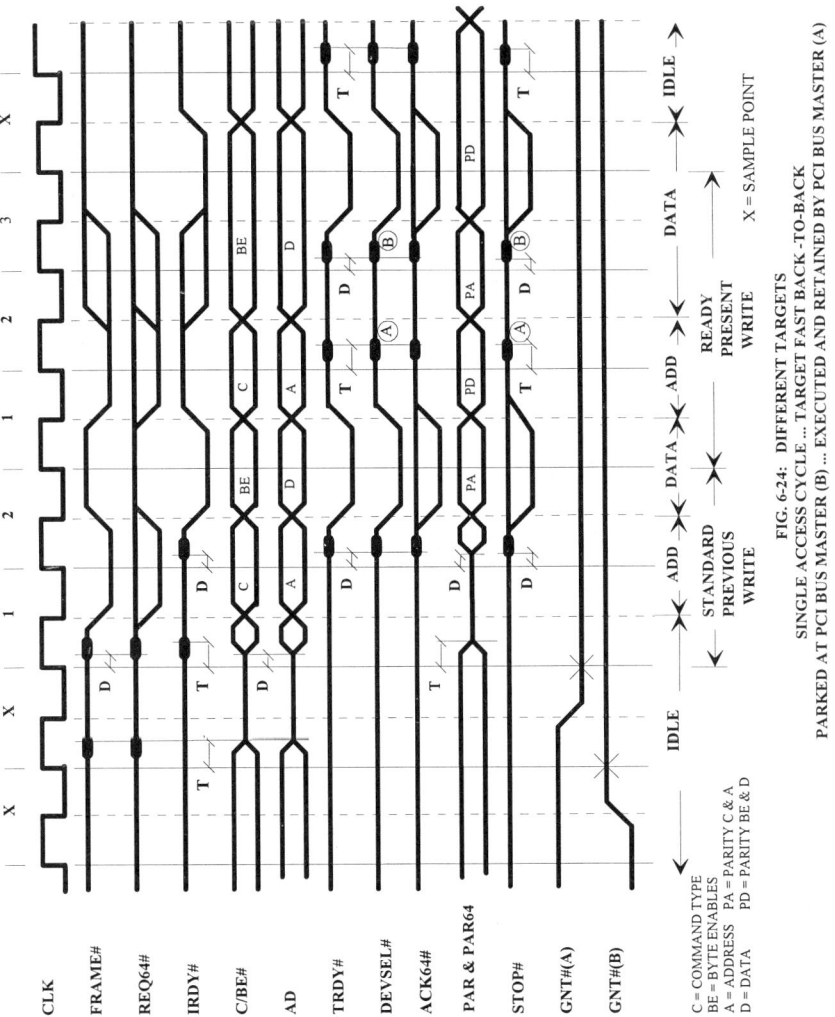

Figure 6-24: Different Targets--SINGLE Bus Transaction, Target Fast Back-to-Back Parked at PCI Bus Master (B), Executed and Retained by PCI Bus Master (A)

419

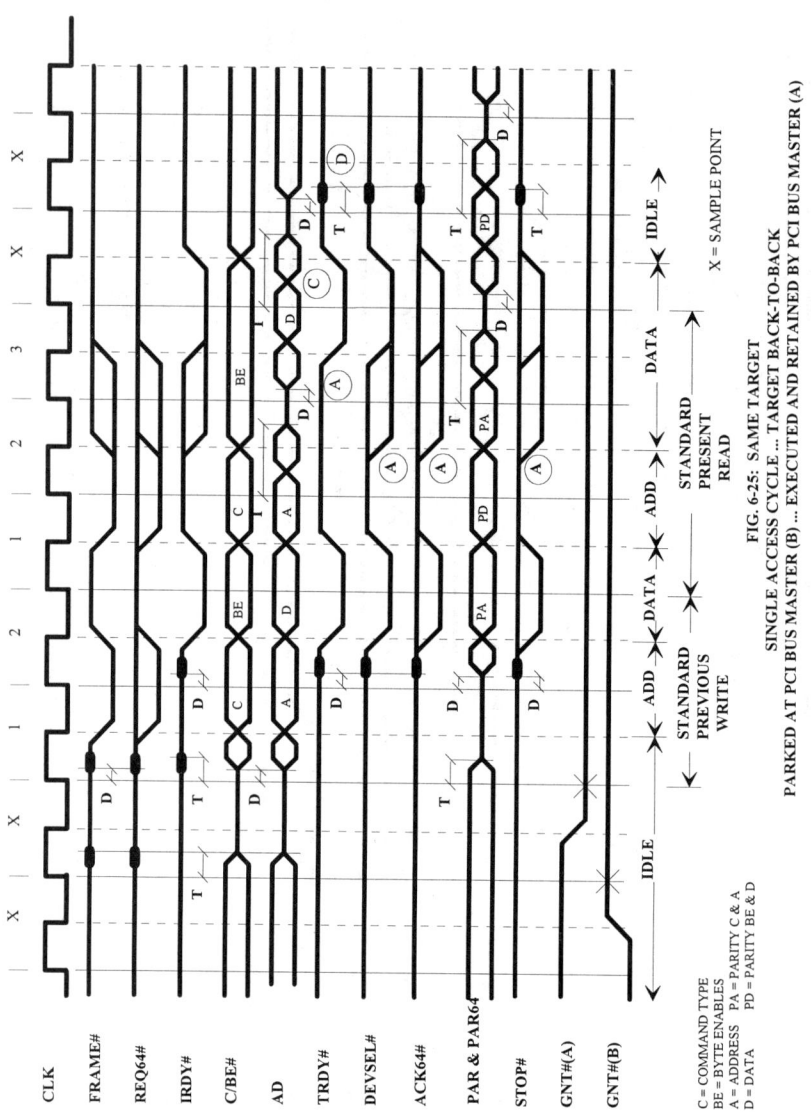

Figure 6-25: Same Target--SINGLE Bus Transaction, Target Back-to-Back Parked at PCI Bus Master (B), Executed and Retained by PCI Bus Master (A)

When a DUAL ADDRESS is executed, the ADDRESS PHASE is two CLK signal line periods in length. The earliest assertion point for the DEVSEL#, TRDY#, STOP#, and ACK64# signal lines for the fastest decode moves from the second to the third CLK signal line period (see Figures 6-1 A and B and 6-14-A and B). For a read transaction, the earliest assertion point of the TRDY# signal line moves from the third to the fourth CLK signal line period. Consequently, the use of DUAL ADDRESS on the present bus transaction allows the use of the fastest decode and in essence removes the restrictions outlined in this item.

■ The previous bus transaction is required to be a write transaction to allow a T-Back/Back to the present bus transaction

The concept of a T-Back/Back is that the burden to avoid contention on the signal lines when the IDLE PHASE is removed between back-to-back bus transactions is placed on all potential targets of the PCI bus master. By placing the burden of signal line contention on the targets, the restrictions of the MP-Back/Back protocol to do Fast Back-to-Back transaction to the same target is removed.

The design of a target should strive to support T-Back/Back to improve platform performance.

As will be explained in the following paragraphs, the T-Back/Back protocol prevents a Fast Back-to-Back situation following a read transaction as did the MP-Back/Back protocol. Thus, even in the T-Back/Back protocol, the PCI bus master is required to be aware of read transactions in the previous bus transactions.

The explanation and examples in Figures 6-24 to 6-25 use SINGLE bus transactions. The protocol for T-Back/Back when BURST bus transactions are involved is the same.

Figure 6-24 outlines the protocol of the T-Back/Back situation when different targets are accessed in two bus transactions. In Figure 6-24, the PCI bus master is executing a STANDARD SINGLE write transaction followed by a READY SINGLE write transaction. Simultaneously, the FRAME# signal line is deasserted, and the IRDY# and TRDY# signal lines are both asserted at the end of the bus transaction. In this example, under the T-Back/Back protocol the sampled signal line pattern qualifies as the completion of the previous bus transaction and allows the PCI bus master to immediately assert the FRAME# signal line for the present bus transaction without an IDLE PHASE. In that the targets in the two bus transactions are different, the target of the present access is required to delay driving the TRDY#, DEVSEL#, STOP#, and ACK64# signal lines until point B (Circle B). This delay reflects the fact that the target of the previous bus transaction does not tri-state the TRDY#, DEVSEL#, and STOP# signal lines until point A (Circle A). Figure 6-25 outlines the T-Back/Back protocol when the target is the same for both bus transactions. The only difference with the protocol outlined in Figure 6-24 is that the TRDY#, DEVSEL#, STOP#, and ACK64# signal lines can be driven as early as point A (Circle A) in Figure 6-25. This is possible because the ownership of these signal lines does not change between the bus transactions. The completion of the present bus transaction in Figure 6-24 also follows the T-Back/Back protocol; consequently, at the discretion of the PCI bus master, the bus transaction subsequent to the present bus transaction can also be a Fast Back-to-Back.

Figure 6-25 outlines the protocol of the T-Back/Back situation when the same target is accessed in the two bus transactions. In Figure 6-25, the PCI bus master is executing a STANDARD SINGLE write transaction followed by a STANDARD SINGLE read transaction. The protocol to complete the write transaction and immediately begin the read transaction is the same as outlined in Figure 6-24. The completion of the read transaction clearly shows why a read transaction cannot be followed by a Fast Back-to-Back situation under the T-Back/Back protocol even when the target is the same. The read data is driven onto the AD signal lines during the present bus transaction by the target and it is required to have sufficient time to tri-state the AD signal lines (Circle C in Figure 6-25) prior to the PCI bus master driving the address onto the AD signal lines (Circle D in Figure 6-25). Consequently, an extra CLK signal line clock period is needed which results in an IDLE PHASE.

Targets that support FAST decoding will indicate this information in their STATUS Registers. If all POSITIVE DECODING PCI resources that are potential targets support a FAST decode, the target that implements SUBTRACTIVE DECODING can assert the DEVSEL# signal line at the MEDIUM DECODING sample point. Consequently, the targets implementing "early" SUBTRACTIVE DECODING by asserting the DEVSEL# signal line at the MEDIUM DECODING sample point are required to "wait" (non-support of MEDIUM DECODING) until the SLOW DECODING sample point when the TARGET Back-to-Back protocol is implemented.

Similarly, as previously mentioned, the execution of DUAL ADDRESS will "automatically" delay the POSITIVE DECODING sample points by one CLK signal line period. The aforementioned "non-support" of the MEDIUM DECODING for SUBTRACTIVE DECODING does not apply when the TARGET Back-to-Back protocol is executed with a DUAL ADDRESS. In other words, when a DUAL ADDRESS is executed with TARGET Back-to-Back protocol, a target implementing SUBTRACTIVE DECODING can assert the DEVSEL# signal line at the MEDIUM DECODING sample point when it and all other targets support FAST DECODING as indicated by their STATUS Registers in their configuration address space.

SPECIAL TRANSACTIONS

The MASTER PROGRAMMED Fast Back-to-Back protocol outlined above applies for a memory, I/O, or configuration transaction to a special transaction. The protocol does not apply to a memory, I/O, configuration, or interrupt acknowledge transaction that follows a special transaction, because an IDLE PHASE is required after a special transaction.

The Target Fast Back-to-Back protocol outlined above applies for a memory, I/O, or configuration transaction to a special transaction. The protocol does not apply to a memory, I/O, configuration, or interrupt acknowledge transaction that follows a special transaction, because an IDLE PHASE is required after a special transaction.

INTERRUPT ACKNOWLEDGE TRANSACTIONS

The MASTER PROGRAMMED Fast Back-to-Back protocol outlined above does not apply for a memory, I/O, or configuration transaction to interrupt acknowledge transaction, because the PCI resources (targets) of the two transactions are not the same (assuming the PCI resource that contains the interrupt controller does not support other PCI resources that are accessed). If the PCI resources are the same, the MASTER PROGRAMMED Fast Back-to-Back protocol applies. The MASTER PROGRAMMED Fast Back-to-Back protocol does not apply for an interrupt acknowledge transaction to an interrupt acknowledge transaction, or interrupt acknowledge transaction to a memory, I/O, or configuration, special transactions; because the interrupt acknowledge transaction is a read transaction only.

The Target Fast Back-to-Back protocol outlined above can apply to a memory, I/O, or configuration transaction to an interrupt acknowledge transaction if the PCI resource that contains the interrupt controller supports this protocol. The Target Fast Back-to-Back protocol does not apply to an interrupt acknowledge transaction to an interrupt acknowledge transaction or an interrupt acknowledge transaction to a memory, I/O, configuration, or special transaction because the interrupt acknowledge transaction is a read transaction.

MASTER ABORT, RETRY, DISCONNECT, AND TARGET ABORT TERMINATION CONSIDERATIONS

Fast Back-to-Back protocol can be applied to the bus transaction subsequent to a bus transaction that completed with Master Abort termination with the exception of the special transaction. With the Master Abort termination, no PCI resource claimed the bus transaction; consequently, there is no bus contention with any of the signal lines. If the Master Abort is completing a special transaction, the Fast Back-to-Back protocol cannot apply because a special transaction is required to be followed by a IDLE PHASE.

The Fast Back-to-Back protocol cannot be applied to the bus transaction subsequent to a bus transaction that completed with a Retry, Disconnect, or Target Abort termination. When these terminations are executed, the PCI bus master is required to deassert its REQx# signal line; this results in the occurrence of an IDLE PHASE. One exception is when a Disconnect with data termination request occurs when the IRDY# and FRAME# signal lines are asserted and deasserted, respectively.

6.11 PCI MESSAGE SIGNALED INTERRUPT PROTOCOL

INTRODUCTION

As discussed in Chapter 4: *Functional Interaction Between PCI and PCI-X Resources*, revision 2.2 of the PCI local bus specification has added an additional method to support interrupts called message signaled interrupt (MSI). MSI is entirely based on memory write transactions from the PCI resource requesting the interrupt (source) to the PCI resource that will service the interrupt (destination). This protocol is called MSI peer-to-peer protocol ... or simply MSI protocol. The MSI protocol applies when a PCI resource is defined as a PCI interrupt source because the capability structure's bit 0 of the Message Control Register in the configuration address space is set to logical "1".

MSI PROTOCOL

The MSI protocol is implemented via memory write transactions with the following attributes:

■ The PCI interrupt source can address a PCI interrupt destination with either 32 address bits (the capability structure's bit 7 of the Message Control Register in the configuration address space is set to logical "0") or 64 address bits (Dual Address Command; the capability structure's bit 7 of the Message Control Register in the configuration address space is set to logical "1"). If the upper order address bits (according to the capability structure's Message Upper Address register) are all logical "0", the MSI memory write transaction will use 32 address bits (without the Dual Address Command) independent of the value of bit 7 of the Message Control Register. Implementing an MSI memory write transaction with 64 address bits (Dual Address Command) requires logical non-zero contents in the Message Upper Address register and bit 7 of the Message Control Register to be set to logical "1".

■ The MSI memory write transaction is only executed as a SINGLE memory write transaction and not a BURST memory write transaction.

■ Only 32 data bit memory write transactions are used for sending the MSI messages. In that the interrupt messages (contained in the message capability structure's Message Data register) are only 16 data bits, the following protocol applies:

   ■ AD[31::16] signal lines during the data phase must be driven to logical "0" and the C/BE[3::2]# signal lines both must be asserted during the DATA PHASE.

   ■ AD[15::0] signal lines during the data phase contain the entire contents of the Message Data Register; consequently, the C/BE[1::0]# signal lines both must be asserted during the DATA PHASE.

The protocol for an MSI memory write transaction is the same as other memory write transactions with the following special notes:

■ The PCI to PCI bridges cannot distinguish between an MSI memory write access transaction and other memory write transactions. Consequently the MSI memory write transaction must follow the posted write protocol.

■ The AD[01::00] signal must be driven to logical "0" during the address phase. The WORD contained in the MSI capability structure's Message Data register in the configuration address space is aligned on four byte (DWORD) address boundaries.

■ The completion of the memory write transaction used by the MSI protocol can be done with Completion; or by Retry, Disconnect with data, Master Abort, or Target Abort terminations. The termination protocol is the same as for any other memory write transaction.

Other considerations:

■ The initialization of the MSI capability structure's Message Data register in the configuration address space is accessing a register of only 16 bits. Consequently, only the 16 bit WORD aligned to the lower two bytes of the four byte (DWORD) address of the access is allowed and thus C/BE[3::2]# of the 32 data bit configuration transaction must both be deasserted in the data phase.

■ Configuration software cannot assume that a PCI resource that supports MSI also supports an INTx# signal line.

PCI-X SPECIFIC IMPLEMENTATION

6.12   32 DATA BIT PCI-X BUS MASTER TO 32 DATA BIT TARGET

INTRODUCTION

The PCI-X bus transaction protocol supports both SINGLE and BURST bus transactions, like the PCI bus transaction protocol. However, the application of the BURST bus transactions according to the PCI-X bus transaction protocol does not apply to all COMMANDs in the same fashion as in the case of the PCI bus transaction protocol. As summarized in Table 6-1, the PCI-X addendum specification defines the COMMANDs as either DWORD or BURST.

All COMMANDs used to access the I/O address space, configuration address space, or the interrupt controller are defined as DWORD commands. The DWORD memory read command is also defined as a DWORD command. Also, the broadcast of data via special transactions is defined as a DWORD command. By definition, a DWORD command can ONLY be executed as SINGLE bus transactions and can only be executed with 32 data bits.

BURST COMMANDs are defined for accesses to the memory address space and for the Split Transaction protocol. BURST commands can be executed as either SINGLE or BURST bus transactions and can be executed with either 32 or 64 data bits. See Chapter 4: *Functional Interaction between PCI and PCI-C Resources* for more information.

C/BE# [3::0] ADDRESS PHASE Binary MSB to LSB	Name According to PCI-X	PCI-X Bus Transaction Protocol Between Master and Target on Same Bus Segment Bus Transactions: PCI-X SINGLE = PXST PCI-X BURST = PXBT
	DWORD COMMANDS	
0000	Interrupt Acknowledge	PXST
0001	Special	PXST
0010	I/O Read	PXST
0011	I/O Write	PXST
1010	Config. Read	PXST
1011	Config.Write	PXST
0110	DWORD Memory Read (2)	PXST
	BURSTCOMMANDS	
0111	Memory Write (1)	PXST PXBT
1000	Alias Memory Read Block (2, 3)	PXST PXBT
1001	Alias Memory Write Block (1)	PXST PXBT
1100	Split Completion	PXST PXBT
1110	Memory Read Block (2, 3)	PXST PXBT
1111	Memory Write Block (1)	PXST PXBT
	OTHERS	
1101	DAC	N/A
0100	Reserved	N/A
0101	Reserved	N/A

Table 6-1: PCI-X Commands and Bus Transactions

Notes: (1) Collectively called "BURST memory write" unless otherwise noted.
(2) Collectively called "memory read" unless otherwise noted.
(3) Collectively called "BURST memory read" unless otherwise noted.

Like the PCI bus transaction protocol, the PCI-X bus transaction protocol consists of ADDRESS, DATA, and IDLE PHASES. The ADDRESS PHASE is one CLK signal line period in length. It is two CLK signal line periods in length when a DUAL ADDRESS COMMAND (DAC) is executed. The DATA PHASE consists of an initial and subsequent microaccesses. Unlike the PCI bus transaction protocol, the PCI-X bus transaction protocol does not support Fast Back-to-Back between bus transactions, and the PCI-X bus transaction protocol has added two more phases: ATTRIBUTE and TARGET RESPONSE.

The ATTRIBUTE PHASE is immediately after the ADDRESS PHASE and is one CLK signal line period in length. Immediately after the ATTRIBUTE PHASE is the TARGET RESPONSE PHASE and is also one CLK signal line period in length. See Chapter 4: *Functional Interaction between PCI and PCI-X Resources* for more information.

> The definition of the TARGET RESPONSE PHASE according to the PCI-X addendum specification states that it is "one or more clocks after the attribute phase until the target claims the transaction by asserting the DEVSEL#". According to the PCI-X bus transaction protocol, the DEVSEL# signal line may actually be asserted immediately after the ATTRIBUTE PHASE. Also, to be consistent with the PCI local bus specification it would be cleaner to define the CLK signal line periods immediately after a single CLK signal line period of the TARGET RESPONSE PHASE as the DATA PHASE. Consequently; the TARGET RESPONSE PHASE is defined as a single CLK signal line period after the ATTRIBUTE PHASE. The definition of the TARGET RESPONSE PHASE as stated in the PCI-X addendum specification will not be used.

The DATA PHASE in a PCI-X bus transaction is defined as the portion of the PCI-X bus transaction when the IRDY# signal line is asserted. It begins immediately after the TARGET RESPONSE PHASE (*i.e.*, two CLK signal line periods after the beginning of the ATTRIBUTE PHASE). The DATA PHASE contains the microaccesses. According to the PCI-X addendum specification, a microaccess is defined when data is actually transferred (with or without Single Phase Disconnect or Disconnect at Next ADB) or the microaccess that coincides with Retry or Target Abort termination. See Chapter 8: *Master and Target Termination* for more information. It is not necessarily the number of microaccesses the PCI-X bus master intended to execute prior to early bus transaction termination caused by the target termination. For a 32 or 64 data bit bus transaction, each microaccess transfers four bytes or eight bytes (not all byte lanes may be valid), respectively. The ADB is defined aligned to natural 128 byte address boundaries. Thus, the transfer between two ADBs is 32 microaccesses for 32 data bit bus transaction, and 16 microaccesses for 64 data bit bus transactions.

The initial microaccess, by definition, begins when the IRDY# signal line is asserted (by convention the IRDY# signal line must be asserted immediately after the TARGET RESPONSE PHASE ... *i.e.*, two CLK signal line periods (period 4 in the subsequent figures) after the ATTRIBUTE PHASE). The initial microaccess ends when the TRDY# or STOP# signal line is asserted. The subsequent microaccess (if there is one) begins at the end of the initial microaccess or at the end of the previous subsequent microaccess. Each subsequent microaccess is only one CLK signal line period in length.

The IDLE PHASE is defined when both FRAME# and IRDY# signal lines are both asserted.

The PCI-X bus transaction protocol also differs from the PCI bus transaction protocol in the implementation of wait states. The PCI-X bus master is NOT permitted to insert any wait states. As will be subsequently discussed, the IRDY# signal line must be asserted two CLK signal line periods after the beginning of the ATTRIBUTE PHASE. The IRDY# signal line cannot be deasserted until the end of the last microaccess. Thus, unlike PCI bus transactions, the PCI-X bus master can never insert wait states into any microaccess in the bus transaction. The target of a PCI-X bus transaction is permitted to insert wait states only in the initial microaccess of the bus transaction. Thus, unlike the PCI bus transaction protocol, the target of a PCI-X bus transaction cannot insert wait states in the subsequent microaccesses of the bus transaction. Also, as will be discussed in detail later, the wait states associated with BURST memory write and BURST split completion transactions can only be executed in pairs of CLK signal line periods.

This book uses the convention of STANDARD and READY microaccesses. STANDARD microaccesses mean that no wait states are required by either the PCI or PCI-X bus master or target. Both resources are able to complete the bus transaction in the shortest period for a particular bus transaction. READY microaccesses mean that wait states are required by either the PCI or PCI-X bus master, or the target, or both. In the case of SINGLE bus transactions only one microaccess is defined; consequently, the overall SINGLE bus transaction is defined as either STANDARD or READY. This one microaccess is defined as "initial". In the case of BURST bus transactions there is one or more microaccesses; consequently, the overall BURST bus transaction is not defined in terms of STANDARD or READY bus transactions. The first microaccess is defined as "initial" and the others are defined as "subsequent". The wait states are defined in increments of CLK signal line periods. PCI bus masters and targets request wait states by deasserting the IRDY# and TRDY# signal lines, respectively. PCI-X targets request wait states by deasserting the TRDY# signal line.

The following PCI-X bus transaction protocol discussions will reference specific elements of the "General Deassertion" protocol. The "General Deassertion" protocol defines the deassertion of the FRAME# and IRDY# signal lines.

1. For one or two actual microaccesses, the FRAME# and IRDY# signal lines are sampled deasserted two CLK signal line periods after the TRDY# or STOP# signal line is sampled asserted (whichever is first).

2. For three actual microaccesses, the FRAME# signal line is sampled deasserted two CLK signal line periods after the TRDY# or STOP# signal line is sampled asserted (whichever is first). Also, the IRDY# signal line is sampled deasserted one CLK signal line period after the last actual microaccess.

3. For four or more actual microaccesses, the FRAME# signal line is sampled deasserted one CLK signal line period after the last actual microaccess or two CLK signal line periods after the STOP# signal line is sampled asserted for a Disconnect at Next ADB termination. Also, the IRDY# signal line is sampled deasserted one CLK signal line period after the last actual microaccess.

The "General Deassertion" protocol outlined above DOES NOT APPLY to special transactions (see discussion of this transaction later in the chapter) or when a bus transaction is terminated by a Master Abort termination (See Chapter 8: *Master and Target Termination*).

"Valid information" in the following discussions indicates that the signal line are being driven by either the PCI-X bus master or the target. In some cases the valid information is simply "logical "1"" or "stable level" (logical "1" or "0" or combination) and will be so noted. "Pull-up resistor(s) to logical "1"" in the following discussion indicates that the signal line(s) is not driven by the PCI-X bus master or target, but by a resistor(s) on the bus segment backplane. The following discussions assume that there is a valid PCI-X bus master and target for the bus transaction.

The CLK signal line frequencies used with PCI-X bus transactions (compared with frequencies used with PCI bus transactions) requires that a device that receives a signal line state change (logical "0" to logical "1" and vice versa) clocks the change into a flip flop on one CLK signal line rising edge and drive another signal line (from another flip flop) with a response relative to the subsequent rising edge of the CLK signal line. Consequently, a key consideration with the PCI-X bus transaction protocol is that two rising edges of the CLK signal line is integral to a devices' response.

SINGLE MEMORY AND I/O READ TRANSACTIONS

The protocol for signal line assertion and deassertion for 32 data bit PCI-X bus transactions is similar to that for PCI bus transactions. This book will assume that Subchapter 6.1 (relating to PCI bus transaction protocol) is fully understood prior to reading this section relating to PCI-X bus transaction protocol. This section will focus on the specific differences of the PCI-X bus transaction protocol relative to the PCI bus transaction protocol.

The figures in the following section do not contain the "D" and "T" identifiers. The protocol for signal lines driving ("D") and tri-stating ("T") according to the PCI-X addendum specification is more rigid than the PCI local bus specification, the assertion of one GNTX# signal line and deassertion of another GNTX# signal line is not simultaneous, and the Fast Back to Back transaction protocol is not supported. Consequently, the PCI-X bus transaction protocol is simpler for "D" and "T" at the start and end of a bus transaction, respectively. See Subchapter 6.0 for more information.

The following discussions also assume complete understanding of the INTRODUCTION section of this subchapter.

According to the PCI-X addendum specification, memory and I/O address spaces can be accessed with SINGLE read transactions. Like the PCI bus transaction protocol, the PCI-X bus transaction protocol consists of ADDRESS, DATA, and IDLE PHASES. The DATA PHASE consists of the single initial microaccess. Also, like PCI bus transaction protocol, the PCI-X SINGLE read transaction can define the initial microaccess as a STANDARD or READY microaccess. Both PCI and PCI-X SINGLE read memory transactions support the DUAL ADDRESS command.

The assertion of the FRAME# signal line indicates the beginning of the SINGLE read transaction and thus the ADDRESS PHASE (see Figure 6-26). When the (DAC) DUAL ADDRESS COMMAND is not executed the ADDRESS

PHASE is one CLK signal line period and immediately followed by the ATTRIBUTE PHASE. When the (DAC) DUAL ADDRESS COMMAND is executed the ADDRESS PHASE is two CLK signal line periods and immediately followed by the ATTRIBUTE PHASE. Immediately after the ATTRIBUTE PHASE is the TARGET RESPONSE PHASE (See Chapter 4: *Functional Interaction between PCI and PCI-X Resources* for more about the information contained in the ATTRIBUTE PHASE.) The IRDY# signal line must be asserted subsequent to the TARGET RESPONSE PHASE at the beginning of the DATA PHASE.

One of the major differences between the PCI-X bus transaction protocol relative to the PCI bus transaction protocol is the deassertion of the FRAME# and IRDY# signal lines. As previously discussed, for the PCI bus transaction protocol, the deassertion of the FRAME# signal line with the assertion of the IRDY# signal line defines a SINGLE versus a BURST bus transaction. The PCI-X bus transaction protocol distinguishes between SINGLE and BURST bus transactions by a different mechanism. When the bus transaction is for a DWORD command, the default byte count of four is assumed. Consequently, a bus transaction for a DWORD command will be a SINGLE bus transaction with one microaccess (see Figure 6-26). Also, for bus transactions for DWORD commands the valid byte enable pattern is encoded in the ATTRIBUTE PHASE. Consequently, the C/BE# [3::0] signal lines are driven to a logical "1" by the PCI-X bus master in the TARGET RESPONSE and DATA PHASES. As outlined in Table 6-1, the DWORD commands include DWORD memory read and DWORD I/O read.

For a BURST command with a total byte count of four or less (defined in the Upper and Lower Byte Counts in the ATTRIBUTE PHASE), a SINGLE bus transaction is executed. When a SINGLE read transaction is for a BURST command it contains only one microaccess (see Figure 6-26). Also, BURST memory read valid byte enable pattern is defined as being all of the bytes. Consequently, the C/BE# [3::0] signal lines are driven to a logical "1" by the PCI-X bus master in the TARGET RESPONSE and DATA PHASES. As outlined in Table 6-1, the BURST commands include memory reads (alias memory read block and memory read block).

For a STANDARD SINGLE read transaction, there are no wait states inserted by the target. As shown in Figure 6-26, by definition the earliest point the TRDY# signal line can be asserted is after the TARGET RESPONSE PHASE (CLK signal line period 4). By definition the earliest point the DEVSEL# signal line can be asserted is after the ATTRIBUTE PHASE (CLK signal line period 3). The TRDY# signal line can only be asserted with or after the assertion of the DEVSEL# signal line. Consequently, the DEVSEL# signal line decoding points can be either A or B for a STANDARD SINGLE read transaction.

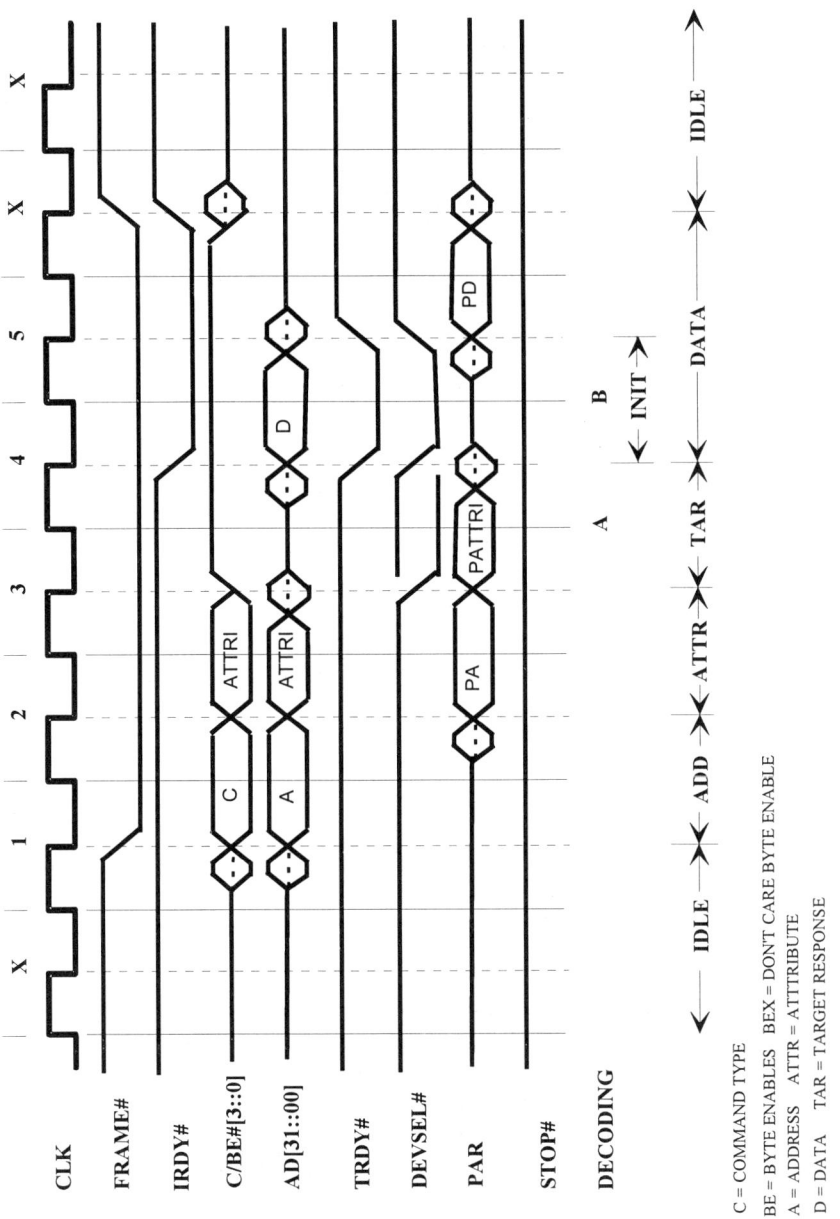

Figure 6-26: DWORD Memory Read, DWORD I/O Read, and BURST Memory Read Command Executed with a PCI-X STANDARD SINGLE Bus Transaction

As shown in Figure 6-26, the initial microaccess is defined with the assertion of the IRDY# signal line and ends with the assertion of the TRDY# signal line. The PCI-X bus master tri-states the AD[31::00] signal lines after the ATTRIBUTE PHASE (period 3 of the CLK signal line) and these signal lines will float until driven by the target. The earliest point the AD[31::00] signal lines can be driven by the target is period 4 of the CLK signal line. However, the AD[31::00] signal lines can only be driven by the target with or after the assertion of the DEVSEL# signal line. The AD[31:00] signal lines are required to have valid information whenever the TRDY# signal line is asserted. Once the TRDY# signal line is deasserted the AD[31::00] signal lines will either be floated or driven to a stable level by the target.

For a READY SINGLE read transaction, there are wait states inserted by the target. The protocol for a READY SINGLE read transaction is same as the STANDARD SINGLE read transaction with the following differences. As discussed for a STANDARD SINGLE read transaction and shown in Figure 6-26, by definition the earliest point the TRDY# signal line can be asserted is after the TARGET RESPONSE PHASE (CLK signal line period 4). Also, the earliest point the DEVSEL# signal line can be asserted is after the ATTRIBUTE PHASE (CLK signal line period 3). The TRDY# signal line can only be asserted with or after the assertion of the DEVSEL# signal line. For a READY SINGLE read transaction, the TRDY# signal line will be asserted after the fourth CLK signal period. Figure 6-27 shows one wait state inserted in the fourth CLK signal line period and the TRDY# signal line asserted in the fifth CLK signal line period. In the example shown in Figure 6-27, the DEVSEL# signal line decoding points can be asserted at either A, B, or C for a READY SINGLE read transaction with one wait state. Additional wait states can be inserted by the target delaying the assertion of the TRDY# signal line. The number of wait states that can be inserted is determined by the "PCI-X 16 clock" and "PCI-X 8 clock" rules. See Chapter 4: *Functional Interaction between PCI and PCI-X Resources* and Chapter 8: *Master and Target Termination* for more information.

As previously discussed, the "General Deassertion" protocol defines the point at which the FRAME# and IRDY# signal lines are deasserted, which is dependent on the number of microaccesses. According to Item 1 for the "General Deassertion" protocol, for a one microaccess bus transaction (which defines a SINGLE bus transaction) the PCI-X bus master is required to simultaneously deassert the FRAME# and IRDY# signal lines such they are sampled deasserted two CLK signal line periods after the TRDY# signal line is sampled asserted.

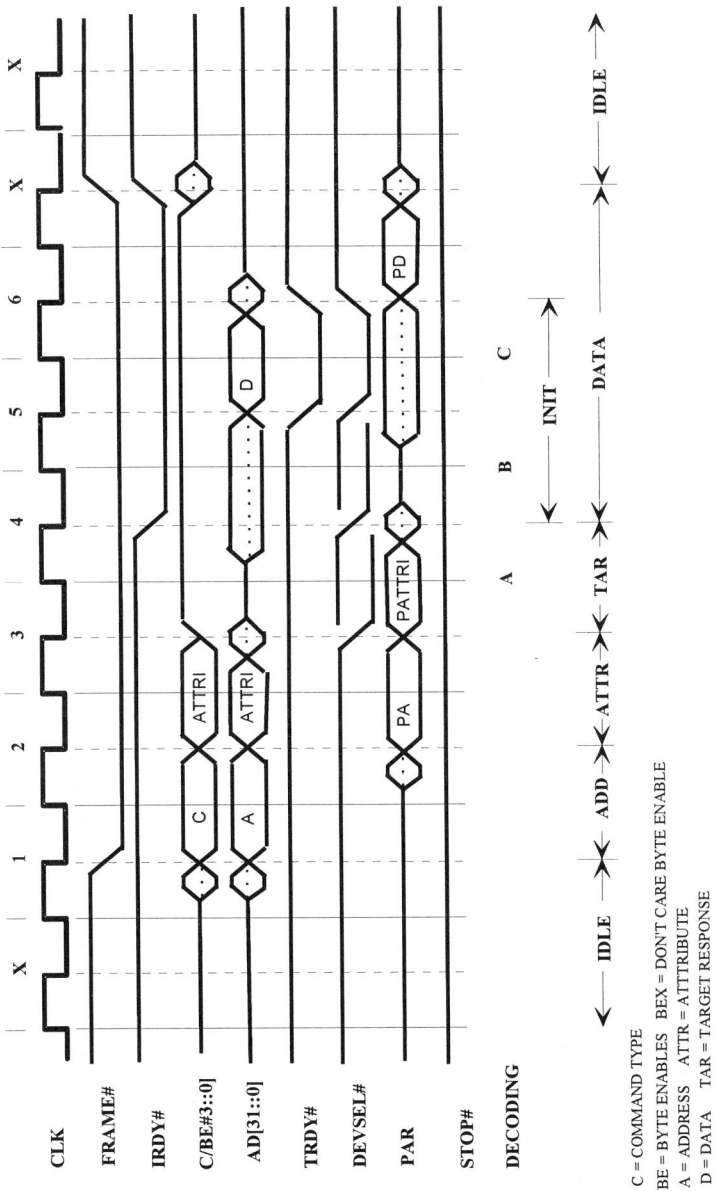

Figure 6-27: DWORD Memory Read, DWORD I/O Read, and BURST Memory Read Command Executed with a PCI-X READY SINGLE Bus Transaction (One Wait State)

435

The valid information, drive, and tri-stating protocol relative to the PAR signal line follows the protocol of the AD[31::00] signal lines but delayed by one CLK signal line period. Like the PCI bus transaction protocol, the PCI-X bus transaction protocol requires the target to drive the PAR signal line with correct parity over the AD[31::00] and the C/BE#[3::0] signal lines. In the case of a PCI bus transaction protocol, the PAR signal of a specific CLK signal line period is computed from the value of the AD[31::00] and C/BE#[3::0] signal lines of the previous CLK signal line period. This protocol also applies for the parity for the ADDRESS PHASE and the ATTRIBUTE PHASE of the PCI-X bus transaction because the AD[31::00], C/BE[3::0], and PAR signal lines are all driven by the PCI-X bus master (see Figures 6-26 and 6-27). During the DATA PHASE of a read transaction, the value of the C/BE#[3::0] signal lines is required to be read by the target from the bus segment; the target combines the associated parity value with the parity of the AD[31::00] signal lines it is driving. As previously stated, incoming signal lines are latched into one flip flop and in response other signal lines are driven from another flip flop. Consequently, for a PCI-X read transaction during the DATA PHASE, the value of the PAR signal line in period N (CLK signal line period) is based on the parity value of the AD[31::00] signal lines in period N-1 and the parity value of C/BE#[3::0] signal lines in period N-2. Note that the value of the C/BE#[3::0] signal lines for the purpose of parity generation in the DATA PHASE are all logical "1".

SINGLE MEMORY AND I/O WRITE TRANSACTIONS

The protocol for signal line assertion and deassertion for 32 data bit PCI-X bus transactions is similar to that for PCI bus transactions. This book will assume that Subchapter 6.1 (describing PCI bus transaction protocol) is fully understood prior to reading this section about PCI-X bus transaction protocol. This section will focus on the specific differences of the PCI-X bus transaction protocol relative to the PCI bus transaction protocol.

The figures in the following section do not contain the "D" and "T" identifiers. The protocol for signal lines driving ("D") and tri-stating ("T") according to the PCI-X addendum specification is more rigid than the PCI local bus specification, the assertion of one GNTX# signal line and deassertion of another GNTX# signal line is not simultaneous, and the Fast Back to Back transaction protocol is not supported. Consequently, the PCI-X bus transaction protocol is simpler for "D" and "T" at the start and end of a bus transaction, respectively. See Subchapter 6.0 for more information.

The following discussions also assume complete understanding of the INTRODUCTION section of this subchapter.

According to the PCI-X addendum specification, memory and I/O address spaces can be accessed with SINGLE write transactions. Like the PCI bus transaction protocol, the PCI-X bus transaction protocol consists of ADDRESS, DATA, and IDLE PHASES. The DATA PHASE consists of the single initial microaccess. Also like PCI bus transaction protocol, the initial microaccess of a PCI-X SINGLE write transaction can be defined as a STANDARD or READY microaccess. Both PCI and PCI-X SINGLE write memory transactions support the DUAL ADDRESS command.

The protocol for a STANDARD SINGLE write transaction is the same as the STANDARD SINGLE read transaction with the following differences. The first difference is that, as shown in Figures 6-28 and 6-29, the PCI-X bus master does not tri-state the AD[31::00] signal lines in the third CLK signal line period in order for the target to take ownership of these signal lines. The PCI-X bus master retains ownership of AD[31::00] signal lines and must drive these signal lines with valid write data when the IRDY# signal line is asserted. The AD[31::00] signal lines are driven to a stable level or floated during the TARGET RESPONSE PHASE. The second difference is that because the AD[31::00], C/BE#[3::0], and PAR signal lines are all driven by the PCI-X bus master, the protocol for parity generation is the same as for a PCI bus transaction. That is, for a PCI-X write transaction during the ADDRESS, ATTRIBUTE, TARGET RESPONSE, and DATA PHASES, the value of the PAR signal line in period N (CLK signal line period) is based on the parity value of the AD[31::00] and C/BE# [3::0] signal lines in period N-1.

The third difference between SINGLE write transactions and SINGLE read transactions is a little less obvious. The PCI-X addendum bus specification requires that DWORD commands apply to DWORD I/O write (see Figure 6-28). By the definition of bus transactions for DWORD commands, the valid byte enable pattern is contained in the ATTRIBUTE PHASE. Consequently, the C/BE# [3::0] signal lines are driven to a logical "1" by the PCI-X bus master in the TARGET RESPONSE and DATA PHASES. The PCI-X addendum bus specification defines that BURST commands apply to BURST memory write (alias memory write block and memory write block) (Figure 6-29). By the definition of bus transactions for BURST memory write commands, the valid byte enable pattern is driven onto the C/BE#[3::0] signal lines throughout the DATA PHASE.

For a READY SINGLE write transaction, there are wait states inserted by the target. The protocol for a READY SINGLE I/O write transaction is the same as the STANDARD SINGLE I/O write transaction with a *few* differences. However, the protocol for a READY SINGLE memory write transaction is the *almost the* same as the STANDARD SINGLE memory write transaction.

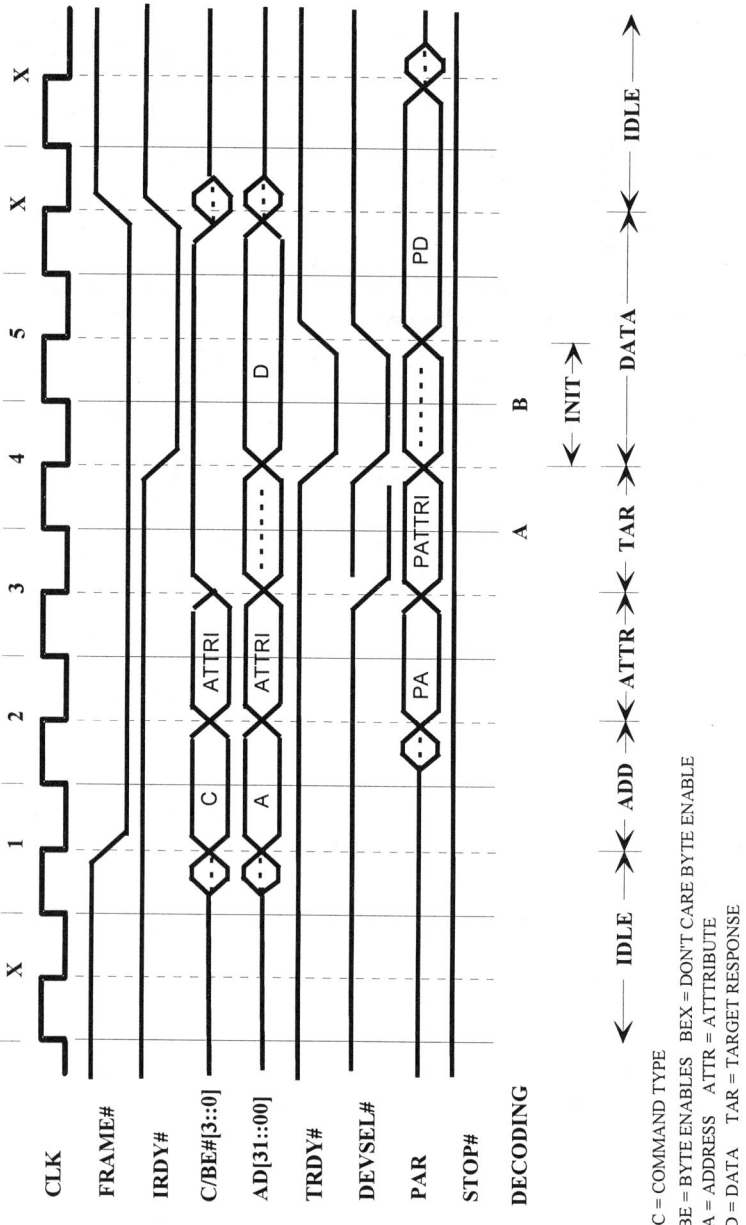

Figure 6-28: DWORD I/O Write Command Executed with a PCI-X STANDARD SINGLE Bus Transaction

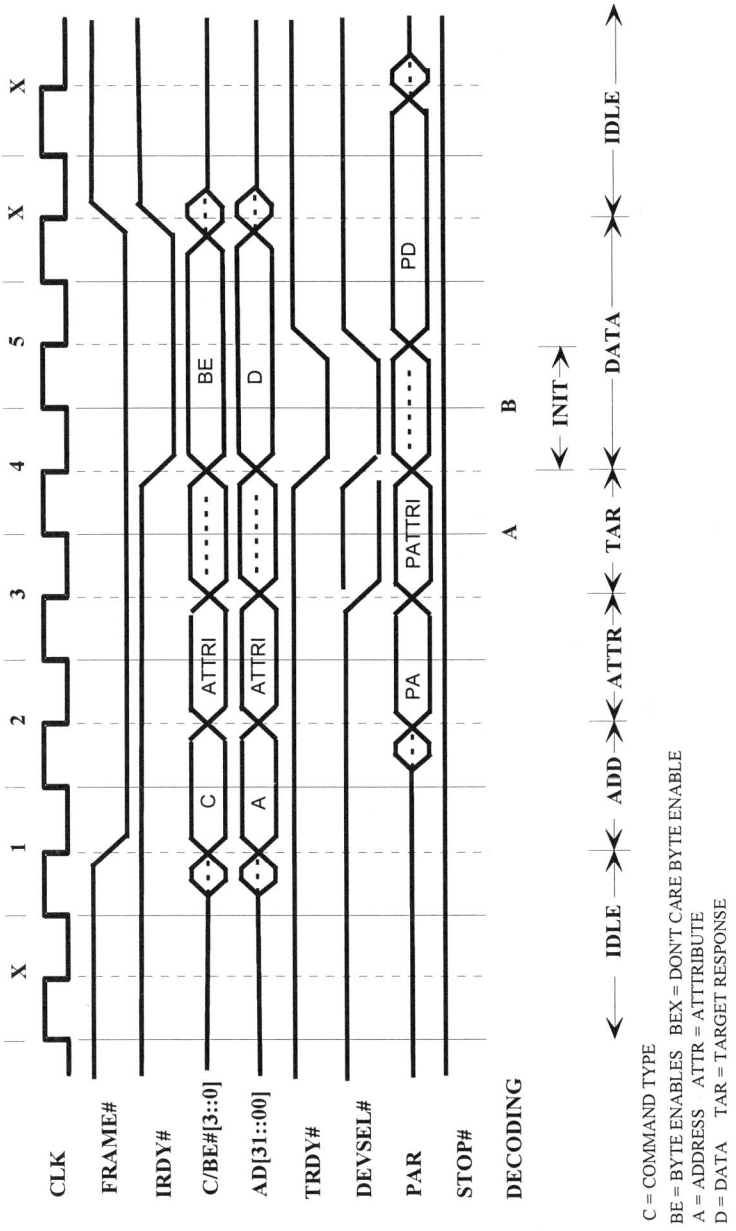

**Figure 6-29: BURST Memory Write Command Executed with a PCI-X
STANDARD SINGLE Bus Transaction**

439

As previously discussed, a STANDARD SINGLE I/O write transaction and as shown in Figure 6-28, by definition the earliest point the TRDY# signal line can be asserted is after the TARGET RESPONSE PHASE (CLK signal line period 4). Also, the earliest point the DEVSEL# signal line can be asserted is after the ATTRIBUTE PHASE (CLK signal line period 3). The TRDY# signal line can only be asserted with or after the assertion of the DEVSEL# signal line. For a READY SINGLE I/O write transaction, the TRDY# signal line will be asserted after the fourth CLK signal in period. Figure 6-30 shows one wait state inserted in the fourth CLK signal line period and the TRDY# signal line asserted in the fifth CLK signal line period. In the example shown in Figure 6-30, the DEVSEL# signal line decoding points can be asserted at either A, B, or C for a READY SINGLE I/O write transaction with one wait state. Additional wait states can be inserted by the target delaying the assertion of the TRDY# signal line. The number of wait states that can be inserted is determined by the "PCI-X 16 clock" and "PCI-X 8 clock" rules. See Chapter 4: *Functional Interaction between PCI and PCI-X Resources* and Chapter 8: *Master and Target Termination* for more information.

As previously discussed, in the case of a STANDARD SINGLE memory write transaction (shown in Figure 6-29), by definition the earliest point the TRDY# signal line can be asserted is after the TARGET RESPONSE PHASE (CLK signal line period 4). Also, the earliest point the DEVSEL# signal line can be asserted is after the ATTRIBUTE PHASE (CLK signal line period 3). The TRDY# signal line can only be asserted with or after the assertion of the DEVSEL# signal line. For a READY SINGLE memory write transaction, the TRDY# signal line will be asserted after the fourth CLK signal in period. A major difference with other bus transactions is that wait states for memory write (and split completion transactions as will be discussed later) are required to be done in pairs. Figure 6-31 shows the minimum of two wait states inserted in the fourth and fifth CLK signal line periods and the TRDY# signal line asserted in the sixth CLK signal line period. In the example shown in Figure 6-31, the DEVSEL# signal line decoding points can be asserted at either A, B, or C for a READY SINGLE I/O write transaction with two wait states. Additional wait states can be inserted by the target delaying the assertion of the TRDY# signal line by multiple increments of two wait states (associated with the "unique data write protocol" discussed below). Each wait state increment equals one CLK signal line period. The assertion of the DEVSEL# signal line can occur at single increments with CLK signal line periods (as with other transactions). The assertion of the TRDY# signal line must happen simultaneously with or after the assertion of the DEVSEL# signal line. The number of wait states that can be inserted is determined by the "PCI-X 16 clock" and "PCI-X 8 clock" rules. See Chapter 4: *Functional Interaction between PCI and PCI-X Resources* and Chapter 8: *Master and Target Termination* for more information.

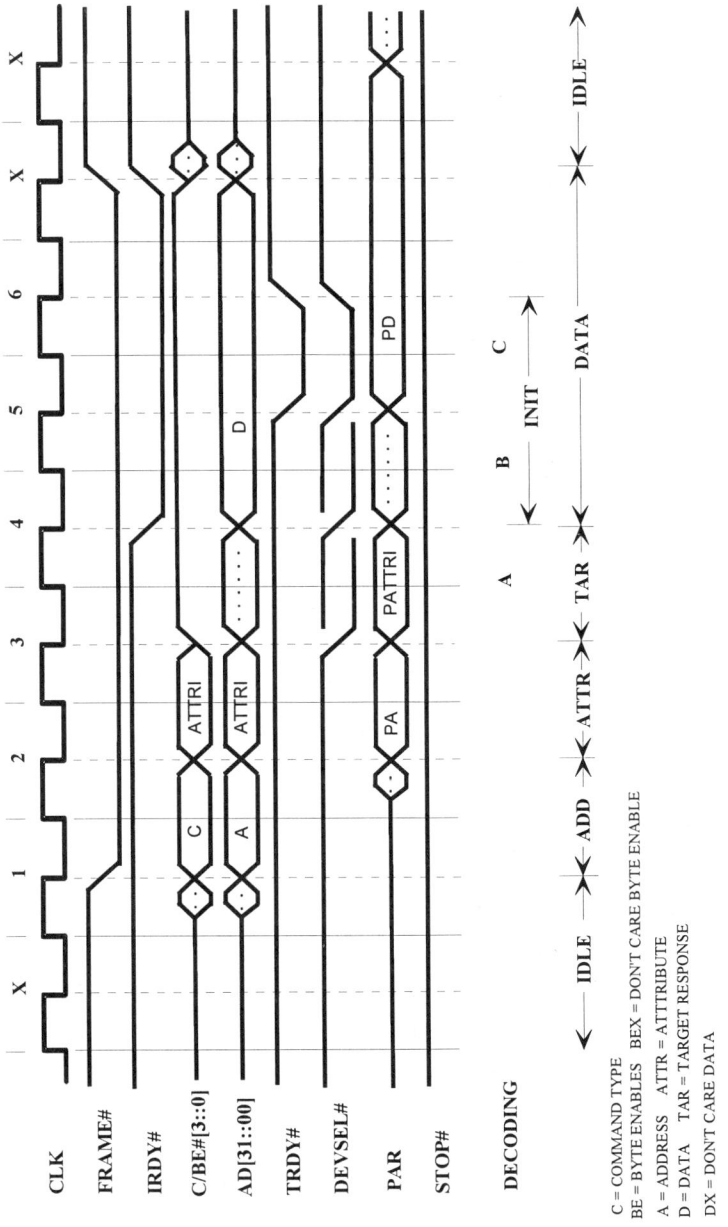

Figure 6-30: DWORD I/O Write Command Executed with a PCI-X READY SINGLE Bus Transaction (One Wait State)

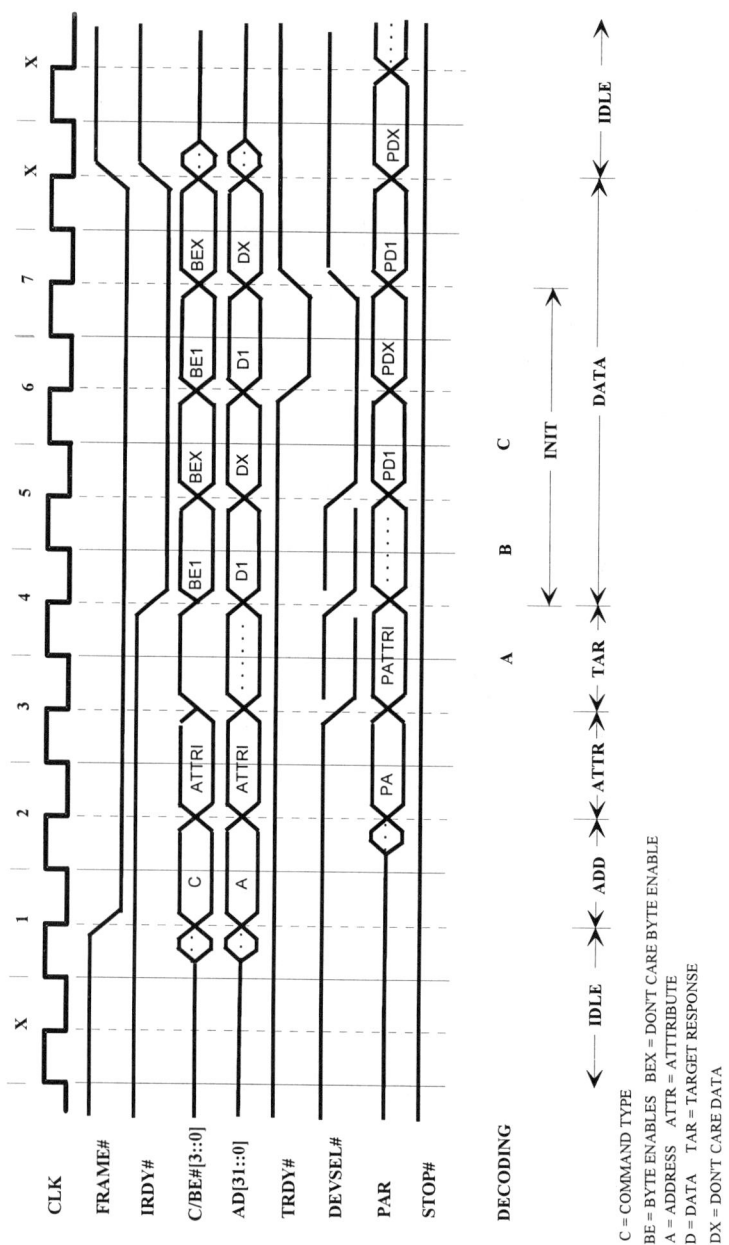

**Figure 6-31: BURST Memory Write Command Executed with a PCI-X
READY SINGLE Bus Transaction (Two Wait States)**

The concept of the "unique data write protocol" was introduced in the previous discussion for a READY SINGLE memory write transaction. As shown in Figure 6-31, the requirement that wait states are inserted in pairs for memory write (and split completion transactions) permits the data on the AD[31::00] signal lines to be driven according to the "unique data write protocol". The "unique data write protocol" simply states that memory write data (and split completion data, as will be discussed later) is written in pairs. The first data of the pair is the actual write data of address N. The second data of the pair is the next actual data of address N+1. For a READY SINGLE memory write, the second data of the pair is a *don't care* value. By definition, there is only one microaccess in a READY SINGLE memory write and thus no second data. As will be discussed for the BURST memory write transactions, the effect of the "unique data write protocol" is to toggle between the first actual write data and second actual write data.. Figure 6-32 is a further example of the toggling effect of the "unique data write protocol". As will be discussed later, this "unique data write protocol" also applies to BURST split completion transactions.

As shown in Figures 6-31 and 6-32, the "unique data write protocol" requires the PCI-X bus master to also toggle the value of the C/BE#[3::0] and PAR signal lines.

Even though the READY SINGLE memory write and split completion transactions for BURST memory write and split completion commands could have used the bus transaction protocol of the READY SINGLE I/O write transaction, and thus not implement the "unique write data protocol", the use of the "unique write data protocol" permits consistency with all BURST transactions (with one or more microaccesses) for BURST memory write and split completion commands.

Because the memory write and split completion commands are the only ones defined as BURST write commands, the "unique write data protocol" does not apply to bus transactions for the I/O, configuration, or special commands, which are all defined as DWORD write commands.

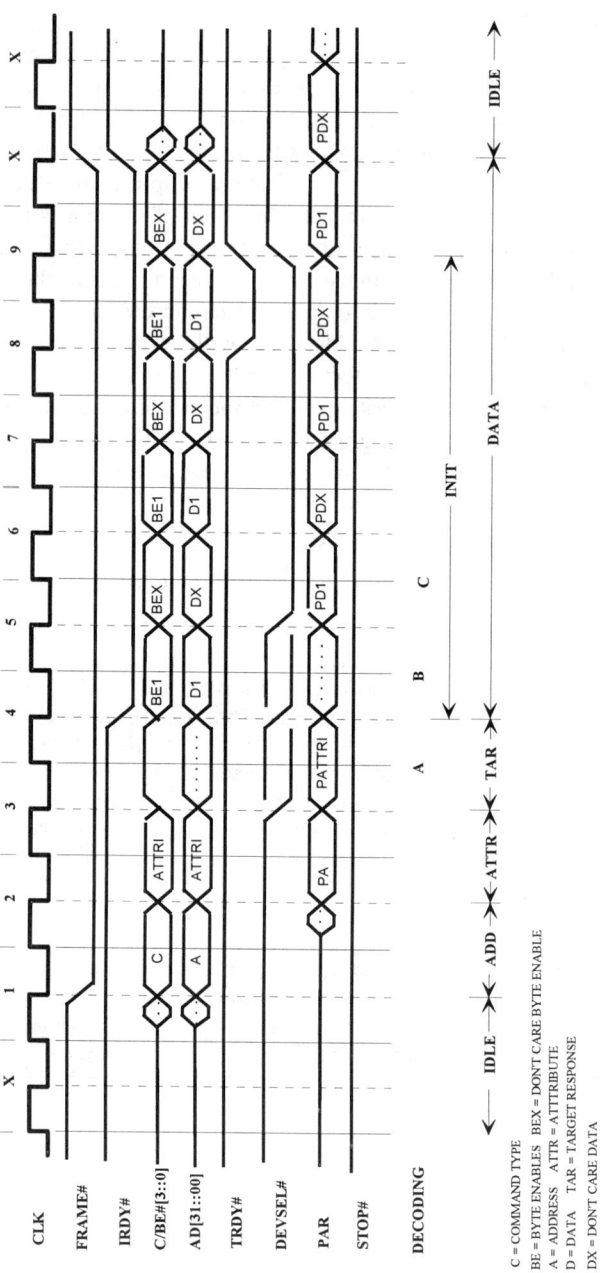

Figure 6-32: BURST Memory Write Command Executed with a PCI-X READY SINGLE Bus Transaction (Four Wait States)

BURST MEMORY READ AND WRITE MEMORY TRANSACTIONS

The protocol for signal line assertion and deassertion for 32 data bit PCI-X bus transactions is similar to that for PCI bus transactions. This book will assume that Subchapter 6.1 (describing PCI bus transaction protocol) is fully understood prior to reading this section on PCI-X bus transaction protocol. This section will focus on the specific differences of the PCI-X bus transaction protocol relative to the PCI bus transaction protocol.

The figures in the following section do not contain the "D" and "T" identifiers. The protocol for signal lines driving ("D") and tri-stating ("T") according to the PCI-X addendum specification is more rigid than the PCI local bus specification, the assertion of one GNTX# signal line and deassertion of another GNTX# signal line is not simultaneous, and the Fast Back to Back transaction protocol is not supported. Consequently, the PCI-X bus transaction protocol is simpler for "D" and "T" at the start and end of a bus transaction, respectively. See Subchapter 6.0 for more information.

The following discussions also assume complete understanding of the INTRODUCTION section of this subchapter.

As outlined in Table 6-1, the BURST commands are only defined for memory read and write, and split completion commands. Split completion commands will be discussed later. A BURST memory bus command transaction can be executed as a SINGLE bus transaction (one microaccess) or BURST bus transactions (two or more microaccess). The previous section discussed the protocol for a SINGLE bus transaction for a BURST memory command. The protocol for a BURST bus transaction for a BURST memory command is similar; however there are a few differences as follows.

BURST memory read transactions consist of two or more microaccesses. The first microaccess is defined as "initial" and the following are defined as "subsequent". The initial microaccess can be executed with (READY) or without (STANDAND) wait states. The subsequent microaccesses can only be executed without wait states. As shown in Figure 6-33 (example of a bus transaction with two microaccesses and no wait states), the protocol for the signal lines in the ADDRESS, ATTRIBUTE, TARGET RESPONSE PHASES, and the initial microaccess of the DATA PHASE is the same as the STANDARD SINGLE memory read transaction. As previously defined, the subsequent microaccess occur after the initial microaccess with a resolution of one CLK signal line period. The FRAME# and IRDY# signal lines assertion and deassertion protocol is the same as defined for SINGLE memory read transactions and follows Item 1 of the "General Deassertion" protocol. As with the STANDARD SINGLE memory read bus transaction, the deassertion of the TRDY# and DEVSEL# signal lines occur at the end of the last microaccess; in the case of the BURST memory read transaction shown in Figure 6-33, this is after the completion of the one subsequent microaccess.

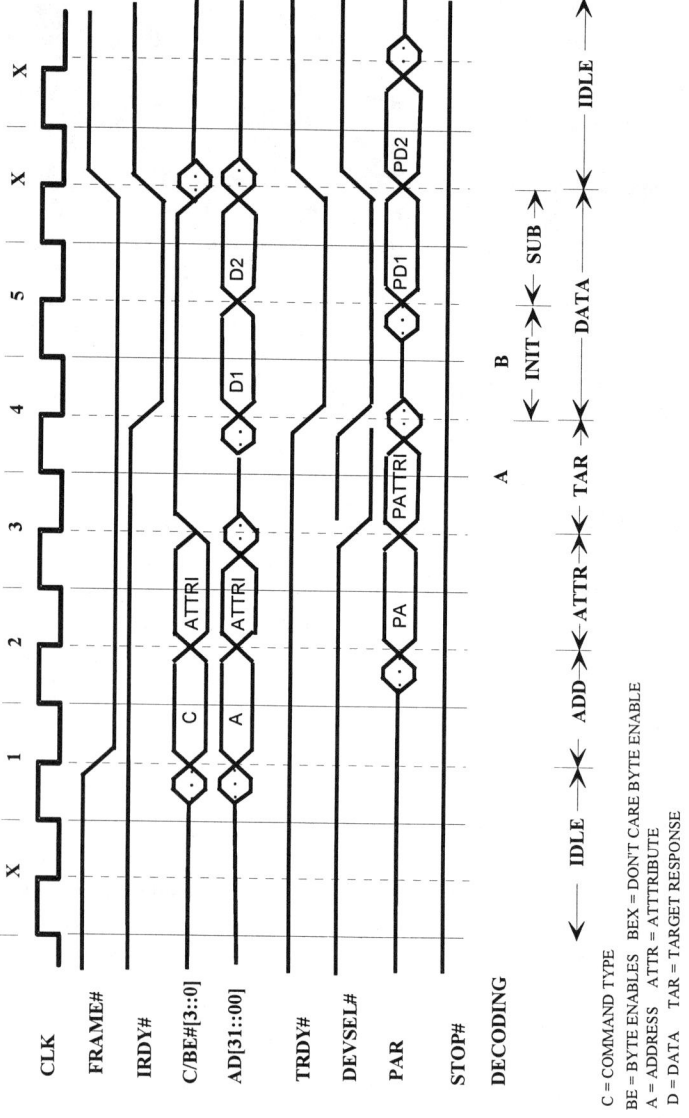

Figure 6-33: BURST Memory Read Command Executed with a PCI-X BURST Bus Transaction (Two Microaccesses and No Wait States)

Figure 6-34 shows a BURST memory read transaction with three microaccesses and no wait states The signal line protocol s the same as shown in the example of two microaccesses in Figure 6-33 except for the deassertion of the FRAME# and IRDY# signal lines. The deassertion of these two signal lines follows Item 2 of the "General Deassertion" protocol.

Figure 6-35 shows a BURST memory read transaction with four microaccesses. The signal line protocol is the same as shown in the example of two microaccesses in Figure 6-33 except for the deassertion of the FRAME# and IRDY# signal lines. The deassertion of these two signal lines follows Item 3 of the "General Deassertion" protocol. The signal line protocol shown in Figure 6-35 also applies to other BURST memory read transactions with five or more microaccesses.

The BURST memory read transactions shown in Figures 6-33 to 6-35 do not contain any wait states. As previously discussed, only the initial microaccess of a read transaction can have wait states in increments of one CLK signal line period in length. The protocol discussed for wait states in the initial (and only microaccess) for READY SINGLE memory read transactions applies to the initial microaccess of BURST memory read transactions. The deassertion protocol for the FRAME# and IRDY# signal lines remain dependent on the number of the microaccesses and the assertion of the TRDY# or STOP# signal lines as defined in the "General Deassertion" protocol. The balance of the bus transaction protocol for BURST memory read transactions with wait states is the same as previously discussed for BURST memory read transactions without wait states. Figure 6-36 shows BURST memory read transactions with multiple wait states and multiple microaccesses.

BURST memory write transactions consist of two or more microaccesses. The first microaccess is defined as "initial" and the following are defined as "subsequent". The initial microaccess can be executed with (READY) or without (STANDAND) wait states. The subsequent microaccesses can only be executed without wait states. As shown in Figure 6-37 (example of a bus transaction with two microaccesses), the protocol for the signal lines in the ADDRESS, ATTRIBUTE, TARGET RESPONSE PHASES, and the initial microaccess of the DATA PHASE is the same as the STANDARD SINGLE memory write transaction. As previously defined, the subsequent microaccess occurs after the initial microaccess with a resolution of one CLK signal line period. The FRAME# and IRDY# signal lines assertion and deassertion protocol is the same as defined for STANDARD SINGLE memory write transactions and follows Item 1 of the "General Deassertion" protocol. As with the STANDARD SINGLE memory write bus transaction, the deassertion of the TRDY# and DEVSEL# signal lines occur at the end of the last microaccess; in the case of the example in Figure 6-37, this is after the completion of the one subsequent microaccess.

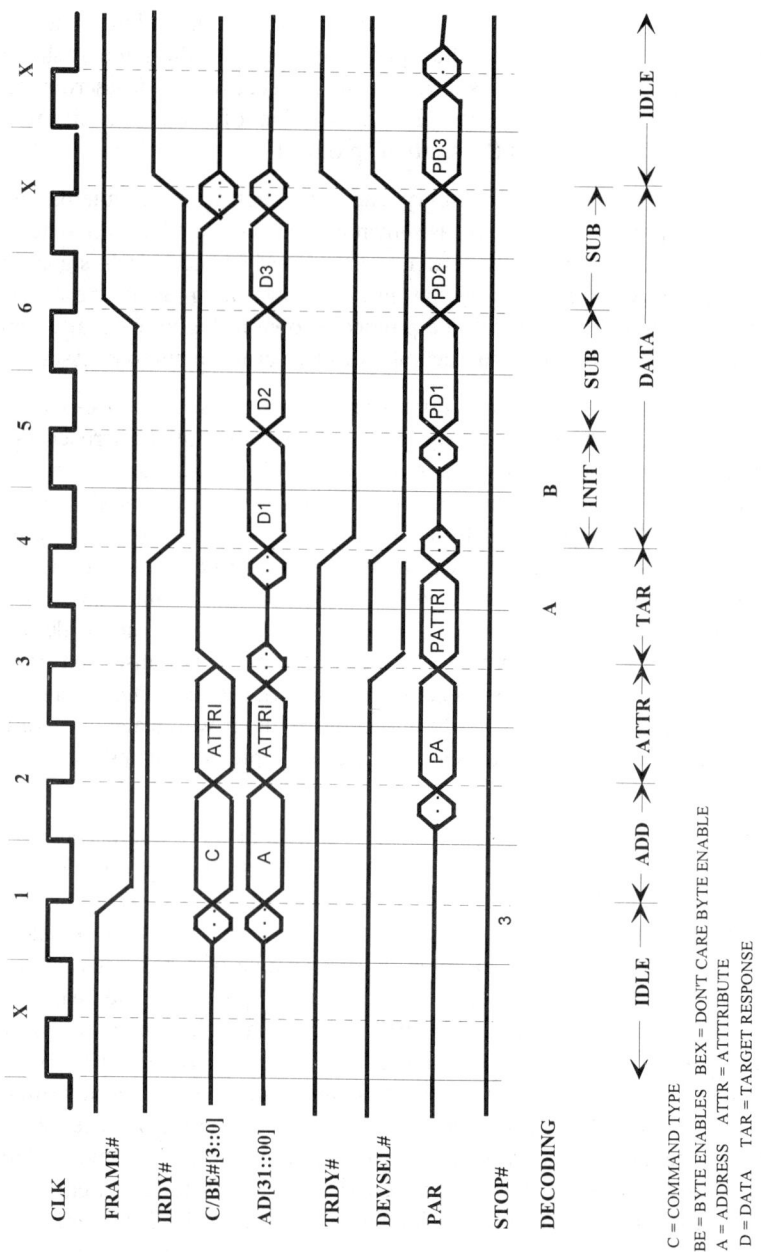

Figure 6-34: BURST Memory Read Command Executed with a PCI-X BURST Bus Transaction (Three Microaccesses and No Wait States)

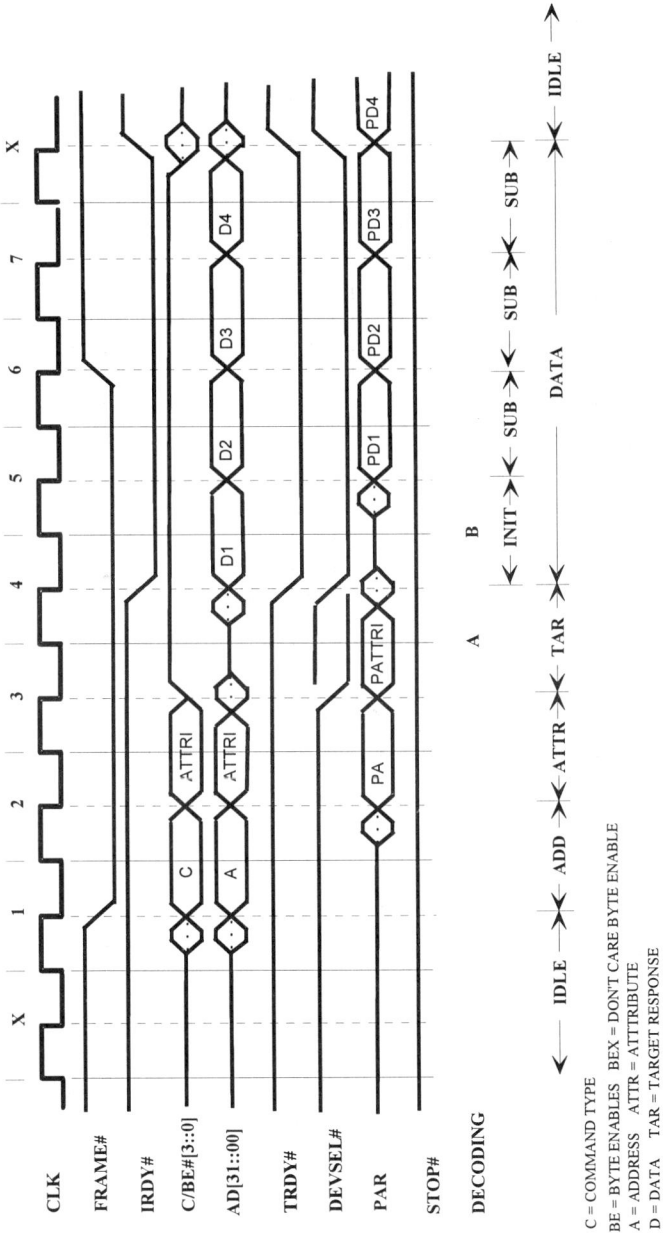

Figure 6-35: BURST Memory Read Command Executed with a PCI-X BURST Bus Transaction (Four Microaccesses and No Wait States)

449

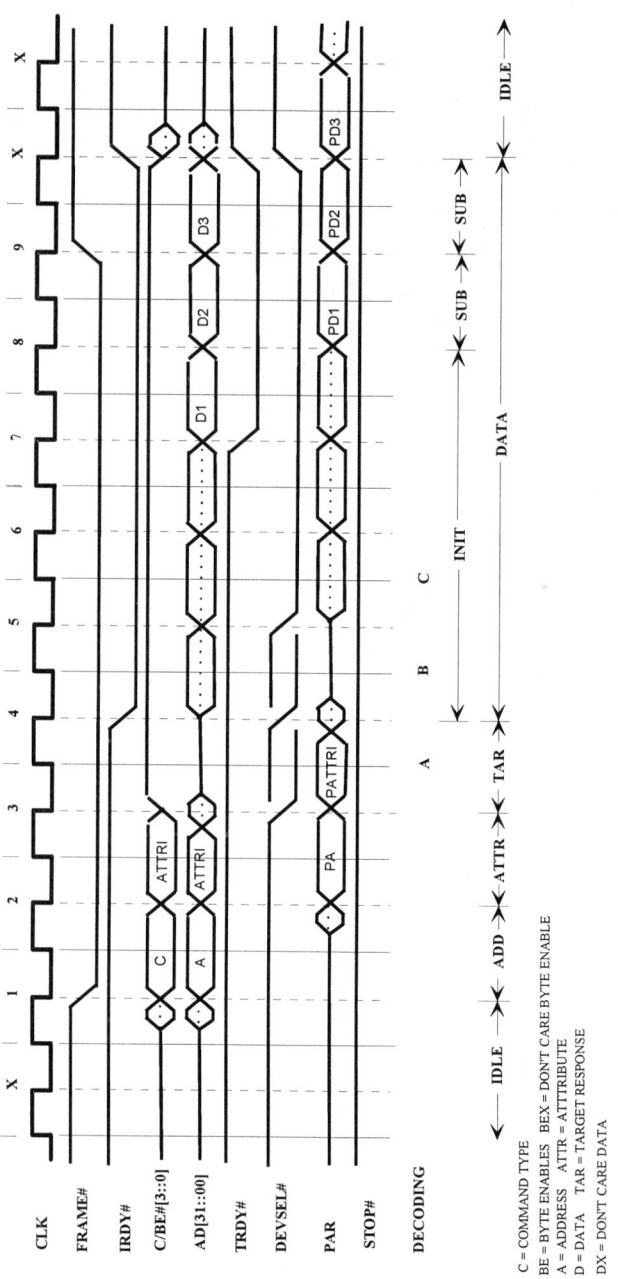

Figure 6-36: BURST Memory Read Command Executed with a PCI-X BURST Bus Transaction (Three Microaccesses and Three Wait States)

Figures 6-37 to 6-41 show the BURST memory write transaction for the BURST memory write command. The C/BE# signal line waveform for BURST bus transactions for memory write block and alias memory write block commands are identical except these signal lines are driven deasserted (logical"1") during the entire DATA PHASE. That is, the memory write block and alias memory write block commands write to all bytes. Consequently, BURST memory write block and alias memory write block transactions look like the BURST split completion transactions in Figures 6-45 and 6-46.

Figure 6-38 shows a BURST memory write transaction with three microaccesses and no wait states The signal line protocol ss the same as that shown in the example of two microaccesses in Figure 6-37, except for the deassertion of the FRAME# and IRDY# signal lines. The deassertion of these two signal lines follows Item 2 of the "General Deassertion" protocol.

Figure 6-39 shows a BURST memory write transaction with four microaccesses. The signal line protocol is the same as shown in the example of two microaccesses in Figure 6-37, except for the deassertion of the FRAME# and IRDY# signal lines. The deassertion of these two signal lines follows Item 3 of the "General Deassertion" protocol. The signal line protocol shown in Fig. 6-39 also applies to other BURST memory write transactions with five or more microaccesses.

The BURST memory write transactions shown in Figures 6-37 to 6-39 do not contain any wait states. As previously discussed, only the initial microaccess of a BURST write transaction can have wait states. In the case of a BURST memory write transaction, wait states must be executed in increments of two wait states; each wait state is one CLK signal line period in length. The protocol discussed for wait states in the initial (and only microaccess) for READY SINGLE memory write transactions applies to the initial microaccess of BURST memory write transactions. Also, the concepts of the "unique data write protocol" discussed for READY SINGLE memory write transactions extend to BURST memory write transactions with wait states.

Figures 6-40 and 6-41 show BURST memory write transactions with two microaccesses with two and four wait states, respectively. As shown in Figure 6-40 and according to the "unique data write protocol", the byte enable pattern and actual data toggle between the first and second. This toggle effect reflects the previously discussed concept of a how a device that receives a signal line state change (logical "0" to logical "1" and vice versa) will clock the change into a flip flop on one CLK signal line rising edge and drive another signal line (from another flip flop) with a response relative to the subsequent rising edge of the CLK signal line. Consequently, a key consideration with the PCI-X bus transaction protocol is that two rising edges of the CLK signal line is integral to a devices' response.

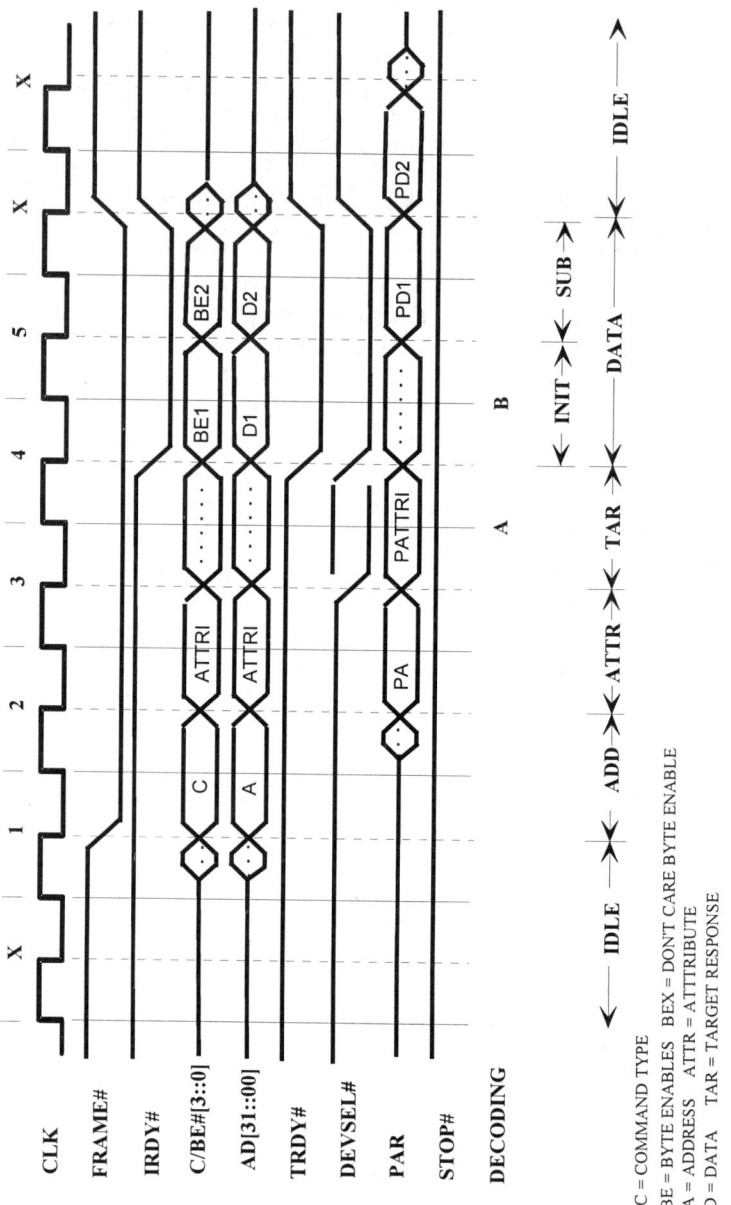

Figure 6-37: BURST Memory Write Command Executed with a PCI-X BURST Bus Transaction (Two Microaccesses and No Wait States)

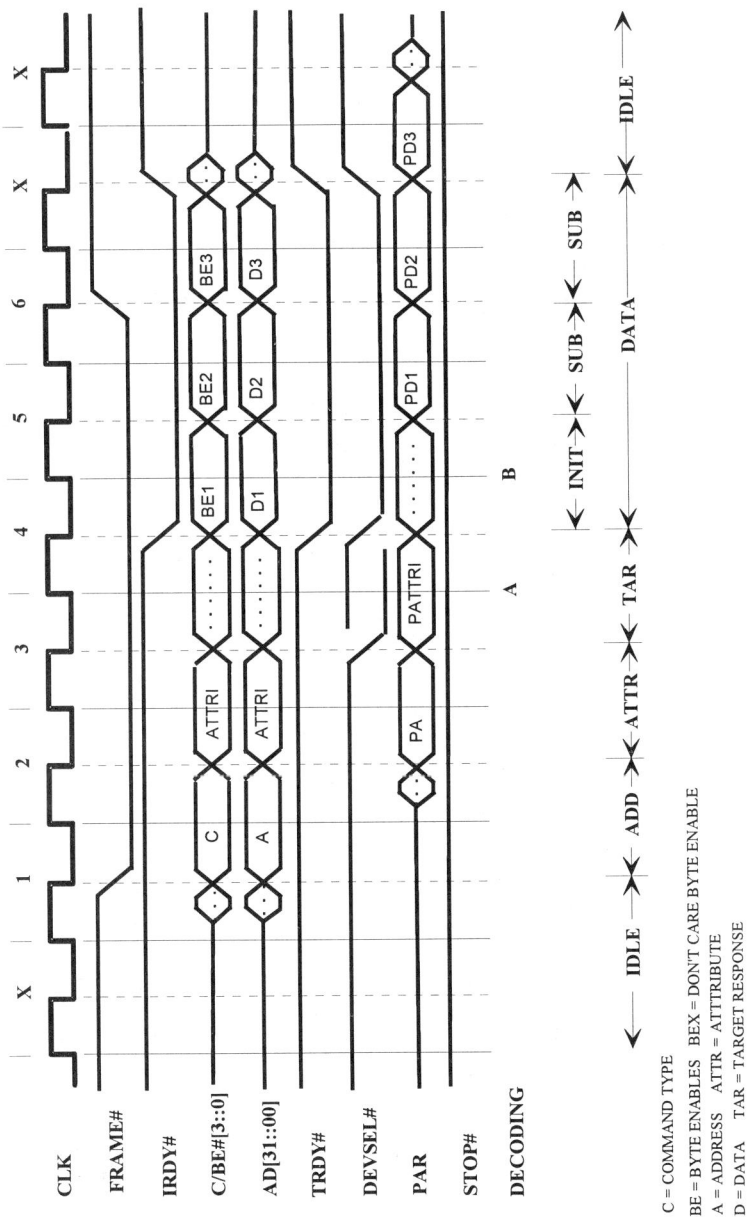

Figure 6-38: BURST Memory Write Command Executed with a PCI-X BURST Bus Transaction (Three Microaccesses and No Wait States)

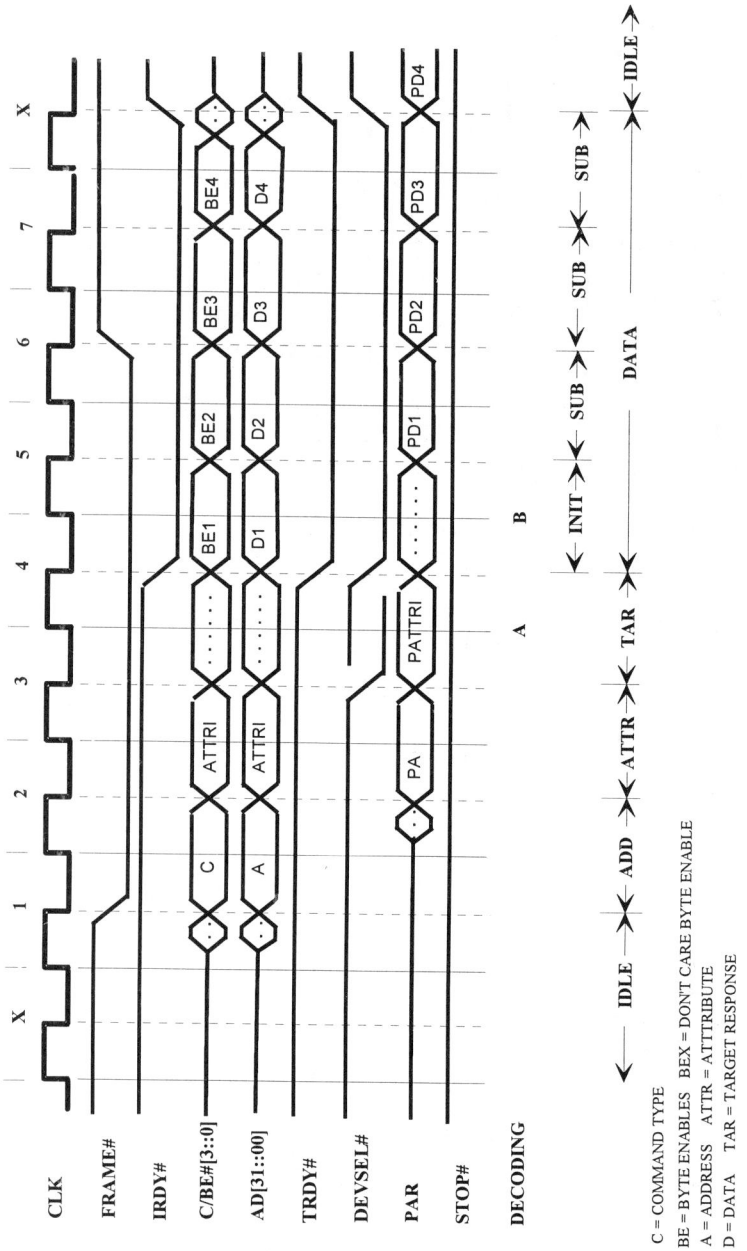

**Figure 6-39: BURST Memory Write Command Executed with a PCI-X
BURST Bus Transaction (Four Microaccesses and No Wait States)**

For a memory write transaction, the PCI-X bus master does not know that write data has been accepted by the target until the TRDY# signal is sampled asserted. If the PCI-X bus master waited for the first actual write data to be accepted by the target (assertion of the TRDY# signal line) before it drives the second actual write data, it would be impossible for the PCI-X bus master to have the second actual write data on the AD[31::00] signal lines on the subsequent CLK signal line period to the one where the TRDY# signal line is asserted. To simplify the hardware design the "unique data write protocol" is defined such that the memory write data is toggled and the wait states are executed in pairs.

CONFIGURATION READ AND WRITE TRANSACTIONS

The protocol for signal line assertion and deassertion for 32 data bit PCI-X bus transactions is similar to that for PCI bus transactions. This book will assume that Subchapter 6.1 (describing PCI bus transaction protocol) is fully understood prior to reading this section concerning PCI-X bus transaction protocol. This section will focus on the specific differences of the PCI-X bus transaction protocol relative to the PCI bus transaction protocol.

Figure 6-42 in this section does not contain all of the "D" and "T" identifiers. The protocol for signal lines driving ("D") and tri-stating ("T") according to the PCI-X addendum specification is more rigid than the PCI local bus specification, the assertion of one GNTX# signal line and deassertion of another GNTX# signal line is not simultaneous, and the Fast Back to Back transaction protocol is not supported. Consequently, the PCI-X bus transaction protocol is simpler for "D" and "T" at the start and end of a bus transaction, respectively. See Subchapter 6.0 for more information for all of the signal lines. Figure 6-42 does have a few of the identifiers included due to the unique nature of a configuration transaction.

The following discussions also assume complete understanding of the INTRODUCTION section of this subchapter.

According to the PCI-X addendum specification, the configuration address space can only be accessed with SINGLE read and write transactions. Like the PCI bus transaction protocol, the PCI-X bus transaction protocol consists of ADDRESS, DATA, and IDLE PHASES. The DATA PHASE consists of the single initial microaccess. Also, like PCI bus transaction protocol, the initial microaccess of the PCI-X SINGLE read and write transaction can be defined as a STANDARD or READY microaccess, and thus STANDARD SINGLE and READY SINGLE bus transactions are defined. Both PCI and PCI-X SINGLE read and write configuration transactions do not support the DUAL ADDRESS command.

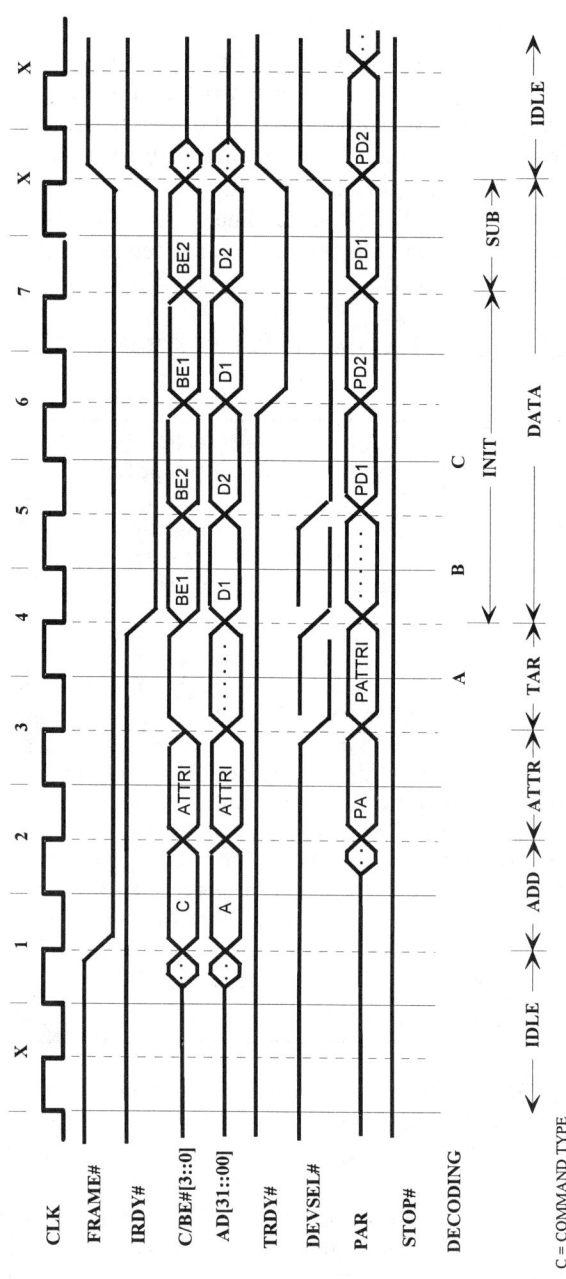

Figure 6-40: BURST Memory Write Command Executed with a PCI-X BURST Bus Transaction (Two Microaccesses and Two Wait States)

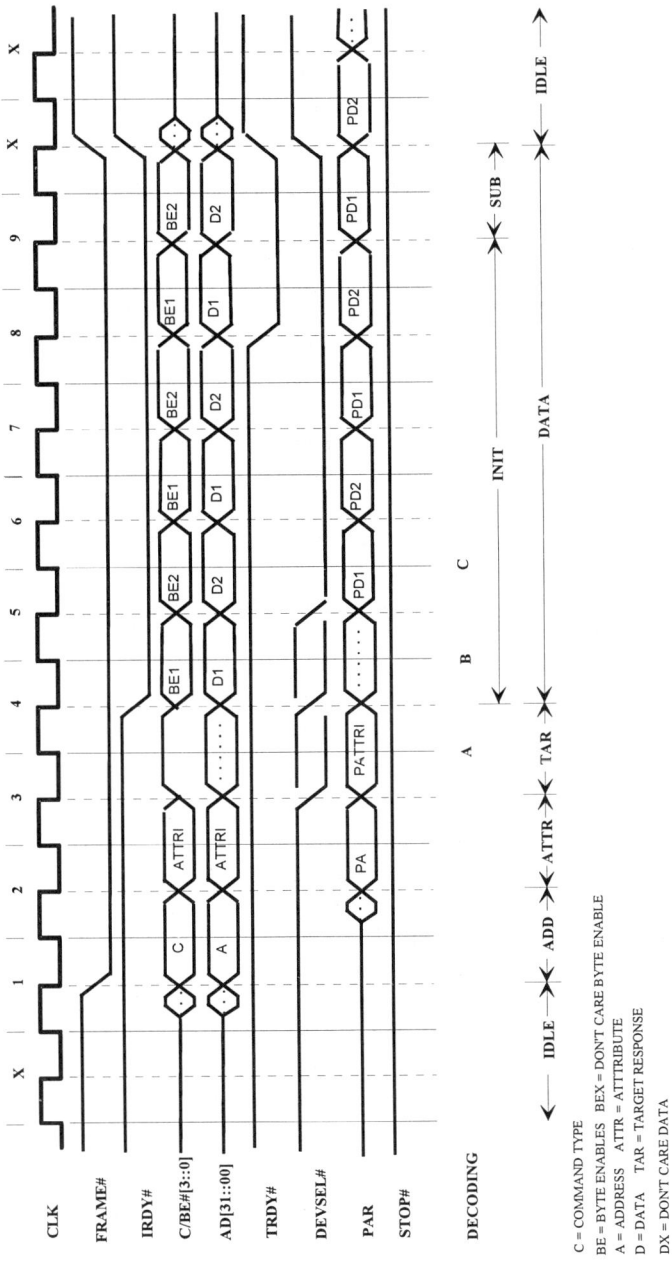

Figure 6-41: BURST Memory Write Command Executed with a PCI-X BURST Bus Transaction (Two Microaccesses and Four Wait States)

457

As outlined in Table 6-1, only DWORD configuration commands are defined; there are no BURST configuration commands and thus no BURST configuration transactions. Consequently, the configuration address space can only be accessed by STANDARD or READY SINGLE configuration read and write transactions.

The PCI-X bus transaction protocol for the STANDARD or READY SINGLE configuration read and write transactions is the same as the STANDARD or READY SINGLE I/O read and write transactions once the FRAME# signal line is asserted (except for the protocol of the IDSEL signal lines). That is, like I/O commands, DWORD commands are for the configuration address space. Prior to the assertion of the FRAME# signal line, the protocol of SINGLE configuration transactions (either read or write) is different than that of SINGLE I/O transactions. According to the PCI-X addendum specifications, the selection of a device with IDSEL signal lines is the same as under Rev. 2.2 of the PCI local bus specification. Earlier versions of the PCI local bus specification were concerned that the IDSEL signal lines attached to the AD signal lines would not be stable within a single CLK signal line period after being driven to a different logic state. Consequently, the PRE-DRIVE protocol was defined in the earlier versions of the PCI local bus specification for the AD[31::00] signal lines. Once it was determined that the load of the IDSEL signal lines on the AD signal lines did not require PRE-DRIVE, PRE-DRIVE was dropped from Rev 2.2 of the PCI local bus specification. The concept of PRE-DRIVE protocol has been reapplied to the AD[31::00] signal lines in the PCI-X addendum bus specification. This re-application relates to the higher CLK signal line frequencies of the PCI-X bus segments. See Subchapter 4.1 for more information.

The application of the PRE-DRIVE protocol on a PCI-X bus segment relative to configuration transactions is more complex than the PRE-DRIVE protocol defined in earlier PCI local bus specifications. One key consideration is the aforementioned requirement that a device's reaction to an input signal line change will take two CLK signal line periods for the device to change another signal line output in response. The other key consideration is that sufficient settling time is required for the IDSEL signal lines. The following discussion will use a configuration write transaction, but all of the elements of the PRE-DRIVE protocol also apply in the same fashion to SINGLE configuration read transactions. The PRE-DRIVE protocol is required for and only apples to configuration transactions.

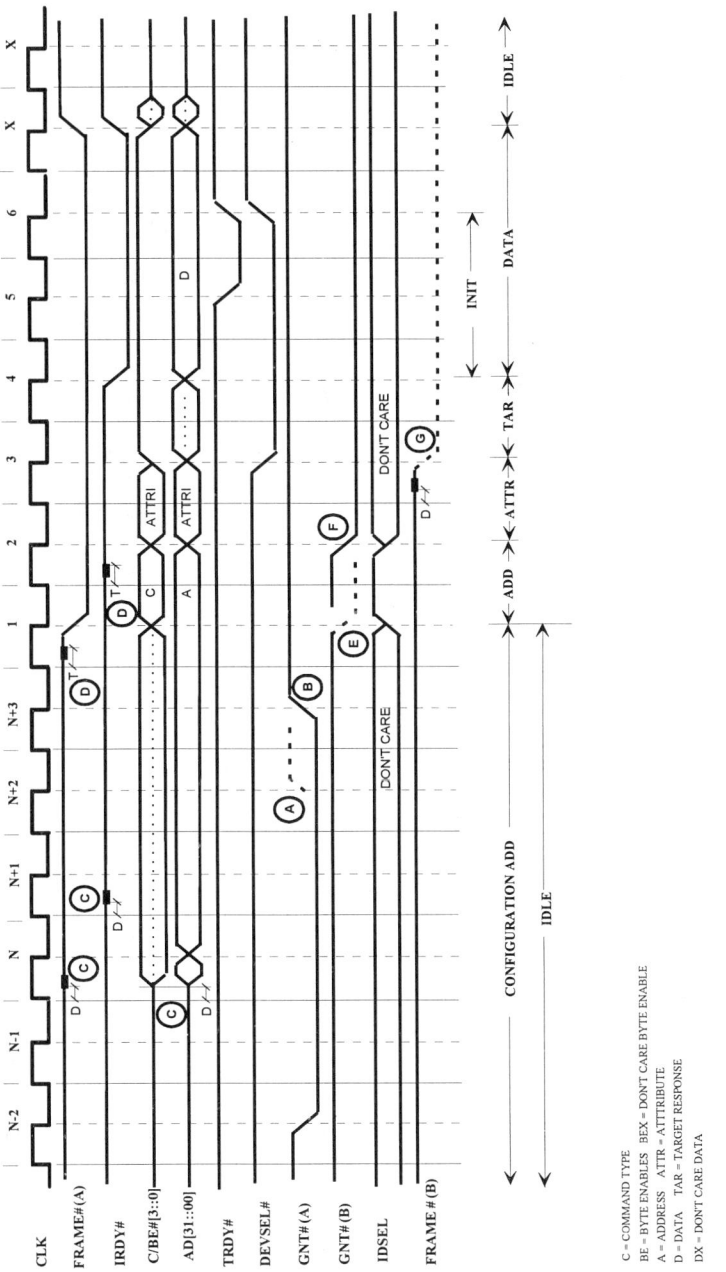

Figure 6-42: DWORD Configuration Write Command Executed with a PCI-X READY SINGLE Bus Transaction (One Wait State)

The bus transaction in Figure 6-42 shows the pre-drive protocol for both Type 0 and Type 1 configuration transactions. That is, the need for the pre-drive protocol is for the IDSEL signal lines attached to the AD signal lines to reach a stable level during Type 0 configuration transactions. The Type 1 configuration transactions do not use the IDSEL signal lines, but the transaction protocol is required to be the same as Type 0 configuration transactions for consistency. If the bridge does not use the AD signal lines to drive the IDSEL signal lines, it is still required to use the pre-drive protocol with all configuration transactions.

The use of the terms FRAME#(A) and FRAME#(B) in Figure 6-42 refer to the single FRAME# signal line driven by either PCI-X bus master (A) or (B), respectively. The signal line pattern of the IRDY#, TRDY#, DEVSEL#, C/BE#[3::0], and AD[31::00] signal lines relate to PCI-X bus master (A) executing the bus transaction, and does not represent a bus transaction executed by PCI-X bus master (B). The inclusion FRAME# (B) in Figure 6-42 is simply to illustrate the earliest point the FRAME# signal line can be driven by PCI-X bus master (B) instead of PCI-X bus master (A) if the latter loses bus segment ownership.

When a PCI-X bus master determines that it wants to execute a configuration transaction, it asserts its associated GNTx# signal line. As shown in Figure 6-42, PCI-X bus master (A) has previously asserted the REQ#(A) signal line, and in response the bus segment arbiter has asserted the GNT# (A) signal line. PCI-X bus master (A) drives the AD[31::00] signal lines a minimum of two CLK signal line periods later. For a configuration transaction, the PCI-X bus master (A) is required to drive a valid address onto the AD[31::00] signal lines for a minimum of four rising edges of the CLK signal line prior to the assertion of the FRAME# signal line. At the assertion of the FRAME# signal line, the configuration transaction proceeds in the same fashion as SINGLE I/O read or write transactions.

In CLK signal line periods N to N+3, the other PCI-X bus masters (such as PCI-X bus master (B) in this example) and the bus segment arbiter do not know that a PCI-X bus master (PCI-X bus master (A) in this example) has begun a configuration transaction. PCI-X bus master (A) does not indicate to the other PCI-X bus masters or arbiter the beginning of any bus transaction until the FRAME# signal line is driven asserted. Consequently, it is possible for the arbiter to grant the PCI-X bus segment to another PCI-X bus master after PCI-X bus master (A) has begun the PRE-DRIVE protocol but prior to the assertion of the FRAME# signal line. In Figure 6-42, if the GNT#(A) signal line is sampled asserted at the rising the of CLK signal line period N+3, PCI-X bus master (A) can assert the FRAME# signal line a minimum two CLK signal line rising edges later to retain bus segment ownership and begin the configuration transaction. The deassertion of the GNT#(A) signal at point B (Circle B) or later will not affect PCI-X bus master (A) in retaining bus segment ownership and begin the execution of the bus transaction, provided the FRAME#(A) signal line is asserted after two CLK signal line rising edges after the sampling the GNT#(A) signal line asserted.

If the GNT# (A) signal line is deasserted at point A (Circle A) or before, the PCI-X bus master (A) must not proceed forward with the bus transaction and must "get off the bus" (relinquish bus segment ownership). Even though PCI-X bus master (A) wanted to execute a configuration transaction and had begun the PRE-DRIVE protocol, it is required to "get off the bus". As previously mentioned, the arbiter and other PCI-X bus masters on the bus segment do not know that the bus transaction has begun until the FRAME#(A) signal line is asserted. As shown in Figure 6-42, the PCI-X bus master (A) should be designed to drive the AD[31::00] signal lines two CLK signal line periods after the assertion of the GNT#(A) signal line and to assert the FRAME#(A) signal line six CLK signal line periods after the assertion of the GNT#(A) signal line. Even if the protocol shown in Figure 6-42 is followed there is no assurance that the GNT#(A) signal will not be deasserted at a point that forces PCI-X bus master (A) "to get off" the bus segment. Consequently, similar to the arbitration fairness algorithm, the arbiter of each bus segment is required to insure that each PCI-X bus master gets an equal opportunity to begin a configuration transaction on a regular basis. That is, in order to insure that a specific PCI-X bus master can begin the execution of a configuration transaction, the associated GNTx# signal line is required to be asserted for a minimum of five CLK signal line periods. See Chapter 9: *Bus Ownership* for more information.

It is possible (as shown in Figure 6-42) for the bus segment arbiter to assert the GNT#(B) signal line one CLK signal line period after the deassertion of the GNT#(A) signal line (Circles B and E). The assertion of the GNT#(B) signal line at point E (Circle E) requires PCI-X bus master (B) to simultaneously sample the FRAME#(A) signal line to determine if it has been asserted at point F (Circle F). If the FRAME#(A) signal line has been asserted at point F (Circle F), PCI-X bus master (B) is required to wait until the IDLE PHASE of the associated bus transaction has occurred before the assertion of the FRAME#(B) signal line. If the FRAME#(A) signal line was deasserted at point F (Circle F), PCI-X bus master (B) can assert the FRAME#(B) signal line at point G (Circle G). See Chapter 9: *Bus Ownership* for more information.

As shown in the Figure 6-42, the earliest point at which PCI-X bus master (A) can drive the FRAME#(A), IRDY#, AD[31::00] and C/BE#[3::0] signal lines is point C (Circle C). If PCI-X bus master (A) is required to "get off the bus" due to the deassertion of the GNT#(A) signal line, it must tri-state the FRAME#(A) and IRDY# signal lines (Circle D) two and three CLK signal line rising edges after the GNT#(A) signal line is sample deasserted, respectively. Though not shown for

461

purposes of figure clarity, the AD[31::00] and C/BE[3::0] signal lines are also tri-stated simultaneously with the tri-stating of the FRAME#(A) signal line. Also, not shown for purposes of figure clarity is the driving of the TRDY# and DEVSEL# signal lines at the beginning of the configuration transaction and the tri-stating of all of the signal lines at the end of the configuration transaction. The protocol for driving and tri-stating the signal lines for configuration transactions is the same as discussed for SINGLE bus transactions for DWORD I/O commands. As with bus transactions for DWORD I/O commands, the C/BE#[3::0] signal lines are driven to logical "1" during the DATA PHASE of a configuration transaction. The valid byte enable pattern for configuration transactions is provided in the ATTRIBUTE PHASE. See Chapter 4: *Functional Interaction between PCI and PCI-X Resources* for more information.

INTERRUPT ACKNOWLEDGE TRANSACTIONS

The protocol for signal line assertion and deassertion for 32 data bit PCI-X bus transactions is similar to that for PCI bus transactions. This book will assume that Subchapter 6.1 (describing PCI bus transaction protocol) is fully understood prior to reading this section regarding PCI-X bus transaction protocol. This section will focus on the specific differences of the PCI-X bus transaction protocol relative to the PCI bus transaction protocol.

The figures in the following section do not contain the "D" and "T" identifiers. The protocol for signal lines driving ("D") and tri-stating ("T") according to the PCI-X addendum specification is more rigid than the PCI local bus specification, the assertion of one GNTX# signal line and deassertion of another GNTX# signal line is not simultaneous, and the Fast Back to Back transaction protocol is not supported. Consequently, the PCI-X bus transaction protocol is simpler for "D" and "T" at the start and end of a bus transaction, respectively. See Subchapter 6.0 for more information.

The following discussions also assume complete understanding of the INTRODUCTION section of this subchapter.

According to the PCI-X addendum specification, the DWORD interrupt acknowledge command is executed with SINGLE read transactions. Like the PCI bus transaction protocol, the PCI-X bus transaction protocol consists of ADDRESS, DATA, and IDLE PHASES. The DATA PHASE consists of the single initial microaccess. Also like PCI bus transaction protocol, the initial microaccess of the PCI-X SINGLE read transaction can be defined as a STANDARD or READY microaccess and thus STANDARD SINGLE and READY SINGLE bus transactions are defined. Both PCI and PCI-X SINGLE interrupt acknowledge read transactions do not support the DUAL ADDRESS command.

As outlined in Table 6-1, only DWORD interrupt acknowledge commands are defined; there are no BURST interrupt acknowledge commands and thus no BURST interrupt acknowledge transactions. Consequently, the interrupt controller can only be accessed by STANDARD or READY SINGLE interrupt acknowledge transactions. As with PCI interrupt acknowledge transactions, PCI-X interrupt acknowledge transactions only read data.

The PCI-X bus transaction protocol for STANDARD or READY SINGLE interrupt acknowledge transactions is the same as STANDARD or READY SINGLE I/O read transactions. The only difference is that during the ADDRESS PHASE, the AD[31::00] signal lines that do not contain a valid address are simply driven to a stable level. As with bus transactions for the DWORD I/O read command, the C/BE#[3::0] signal lines are driven to logical "1" during the DATA PHASE of interrupt acknowledge transactions. The valid byte enable pattern for interrupt acknowledge transactions is provided in the ATTRIBUTE PHASE. The PCI-X interrupt acknowledge transaction is shown in Figure 6-43. See Chapter 4: *Functional Interaction between PCI and PCI-X Resources* for more information.

SPECIAL TRANSACTIONS

The protocol for signal line assertion and deassertion for 32 data bit PCI-X bus transactions is similar to that for PCI bus transactions. This book will assume that Subchapter 6.1 (describing PCI bus transaction protocol) is fully understood prior to reading this section defining the PCI-X bus transaction protocol. This section will focus on the specific differences of the PCI-X bus transaction protocol relative to the PCI bus transaction protocol.

The figures in the following section do not contain the "D" and "T" identifiers. The protocol for signal lines driving ("D") and tri-stating ("T") according to the PCI-X addendum specification is more rigid than for the PCI local bus specification, the assertion of one GNTX# signal line and deassertion of another GNTX# signal line is not simultaneous, and the Fast Back to Back transaction protocol is not supported. Consequently, the PCI-X bus transaction protocol is simpler for "D" and "T" at the start and end of a bus transaction, respectively. See Subchapter 6.0 for more information.

The following discussions also assume complete understanding of the INTRODUCTION section of this subchapter.

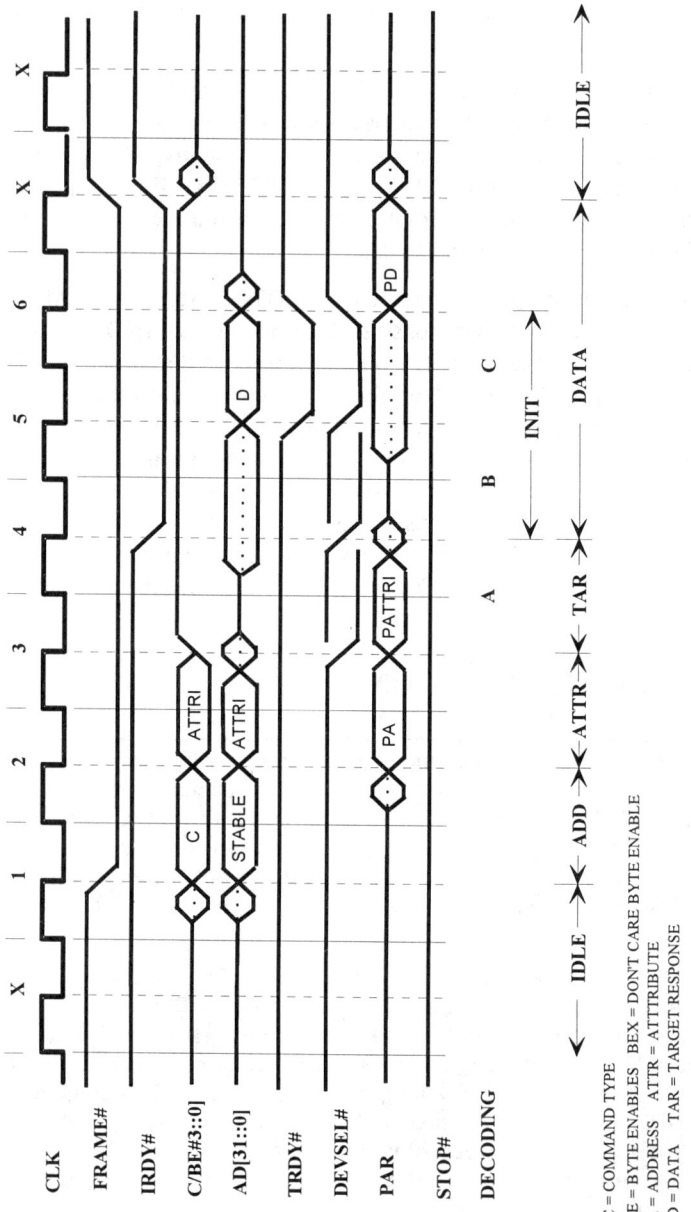

Figure 6-43: DWORD Interrupt Acknowledge Read Command Executed with a PCI-X READY SINGLE Bus Transaction (One Wait State)

According to the PCI-X addendum specification, the DWORD special command is executed with SINGLE write transactions. Like the PCI bus transaction protocol, the PCI-X bus transaction protocol consists of ADDRESS, DATA, and IDLE PHASES. The DATA PHASE consists of the single initial microaccess. Also like the PCI bus transaction protocol and as outlined in Table 6-1, the initial microaccess of the PCI-X SINGLE special transaction can be only be implemented as a STANDARD microaccess and thus only STANDARD SINGLE bus transactions are defined. Only DWORD special commands are defined; there are no BURST special commands and thus no BURST special transactions. This is unlike PCI special transactions, which are defined as both SINGLE and BURST bus transactions; PCI-X special transactions are only defined as SINGLE bus transactions. Consequently, the PCI-X bus master can only execute STANDARD SINGLE special transactions. As with PCI special transactions, PCI-X special transactions only write data. Both PCI and PCI-X SINGLE special transactions do not support the DUAL ADDRESS command.

The PCI-X bus transaction protocol for STANDARD SINGLE special transactions, shown in Figure 6-44, is the same as STANDARD SINGLE I/O write transactions with the following three differences:

■ During the ADDRESS PHASE, the AD[31::00] signal lines do not contain a valid address and are simply driven to a stable level.

■ For a STANDARD SINGLE special transaction, the IRDY# signal line must be asserted for exactly five CLK signal line periods and thus mimics the length of a bus transaction that terminates with a MASTER ABORT termination. (Note: In a PCI STANDARD SINGLE special transaction, the IRDY# signal line must be asserted exactly four CLK signal line periods.) There is no target that can claim the special transaction (assert the DEVSEL# signal line); consequently, the PCI-X special bus transaction completes with simultaneous deassertion of the FRAME# and IRDY# signal lines five CLK signal line periods after the IRDY# signal line is first asserted. The length of the initial microaccess is defined as the length of time that the IRDY# signal line is asserted. The DEVSEL#, TRDY#, and STOP# signal lines are not driven and thus are not tri-sated relative to the special transaction.

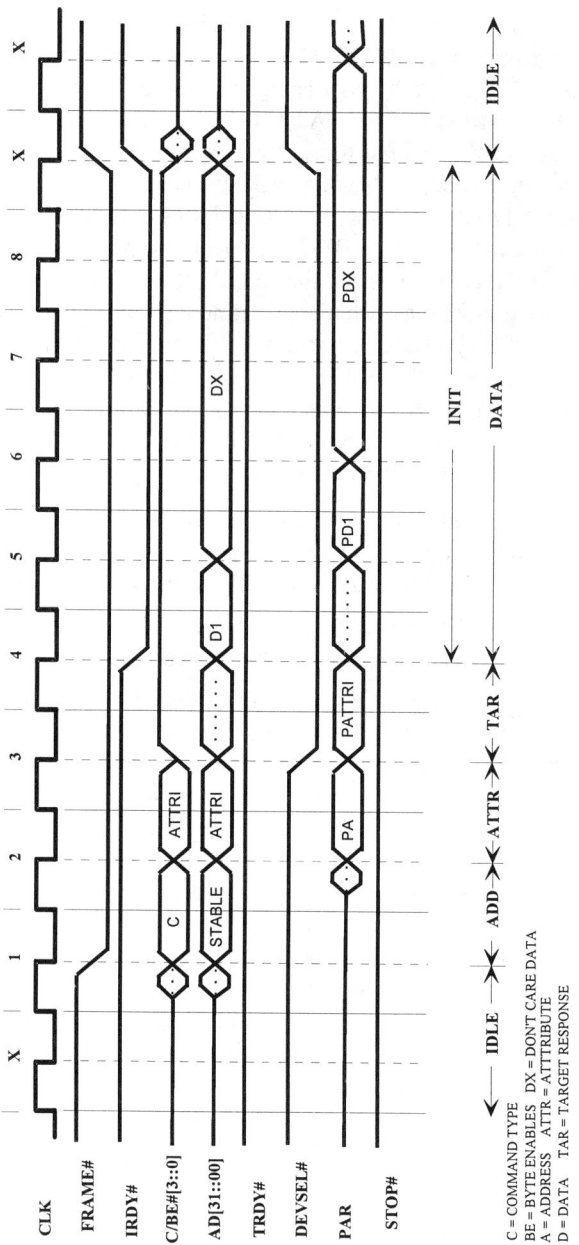

Figure 6-44: DWORD Special Command Executed with a PCI-X STANDARD SINGLE Bus Transaction

■ Like a PCI special transaction, in a PCI-X special transaction the data is only valid on first rising edge of the CLK signal line when the IRDY# signal line is first sampled asserted.

See Chapter 4: *Functional Interaction between PCI and PCI-X Resources* for more information.

SPLIT COMPLETION TRANSACTIONS

> The protocol for signal line assertion and deassertion for 32 data bit PCI-X bus transactions is similar to that for PCI bus transactions. This book will assume that Subchapter 6.1 (covering PCI bus transaction protocol) is fully understood prior to reading this section about PCI-X bus transaction protocol. This section will focus on the specific differences of the PCI-X bus transaction protocol relative to the PCI bus transaction protocol.
>
> The figures in the following section do not contain the "D" and "T" identifiers. The protocol for signal lines driving ("D") and tri-stating ("T") according to the PCI-X addendum specification is more rigid than the PCI local bus specification, the assertion of one GNTX# signal line and deassertion of another GNTX# signal line is not simultaneous, and the Fast Back to Back transaction protocol is not supported. Consequently, the PCI-X bus transaction protocol is simpler for "D" and "T" at the start and end of a bus transaction, respectively. See Subchapter 6.0 for more information.
>
> The following discussions also assume complete understanding of the INTRODUCTION section of this subchapter.

As previously discussed, the Split Transaction protocol is unique to the PCI-X addendum specification; consequently, the BURST split completion command and associated split completion transactions do not have any similar commands or bus transactions in the PCI local bus specification. Also as previously discussed, split completion transactions are in response to previous memory read transactions that were terminated by Split Response terminations. Split completion transactions only write data. See Chapter 3: *Generic PCI and PCI-X Bus Transactions* and Chapter 4: *Interaction between PCI and PCI-X Resources* for more information.

The PCI-X addendum specification defines only BURST split completion commands; there are no DWORD commands. Thus, SINGLE and BURST split completion transactions are defined and follow the bus transaction protocol of bus transactions for BURST memory write commands.

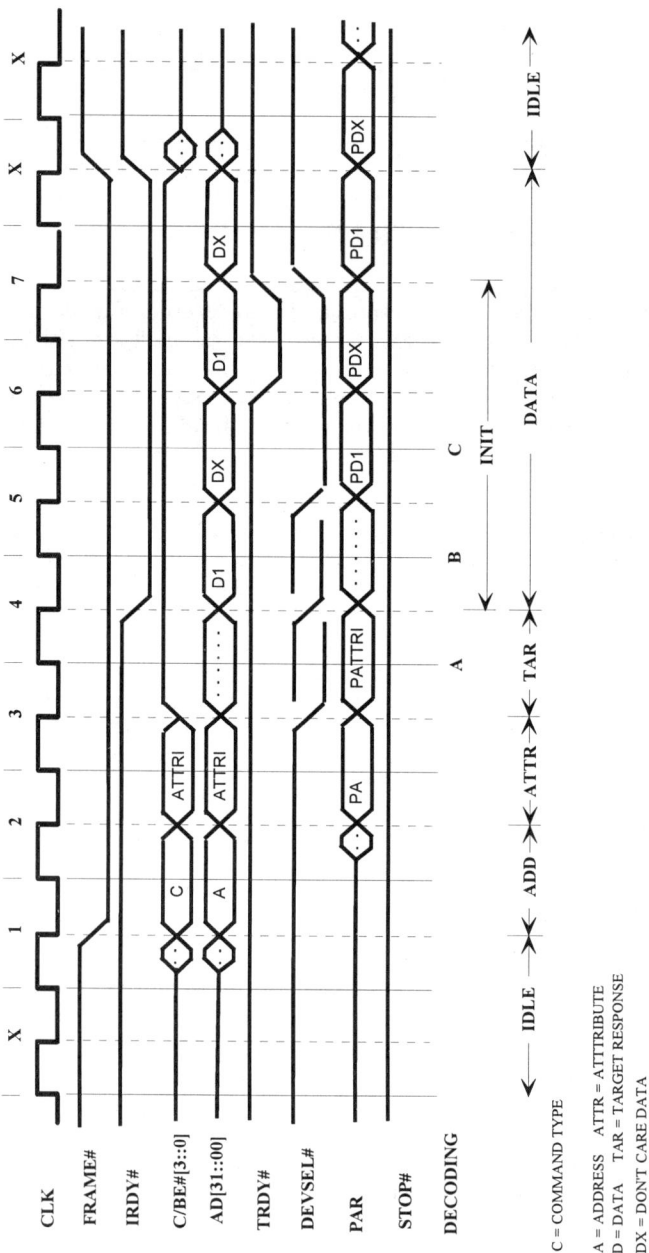

Figure 6-45: BURST Split Completion Command Executed with a PCI-X READY SINGLE Bus Transaction (Two Wait States)

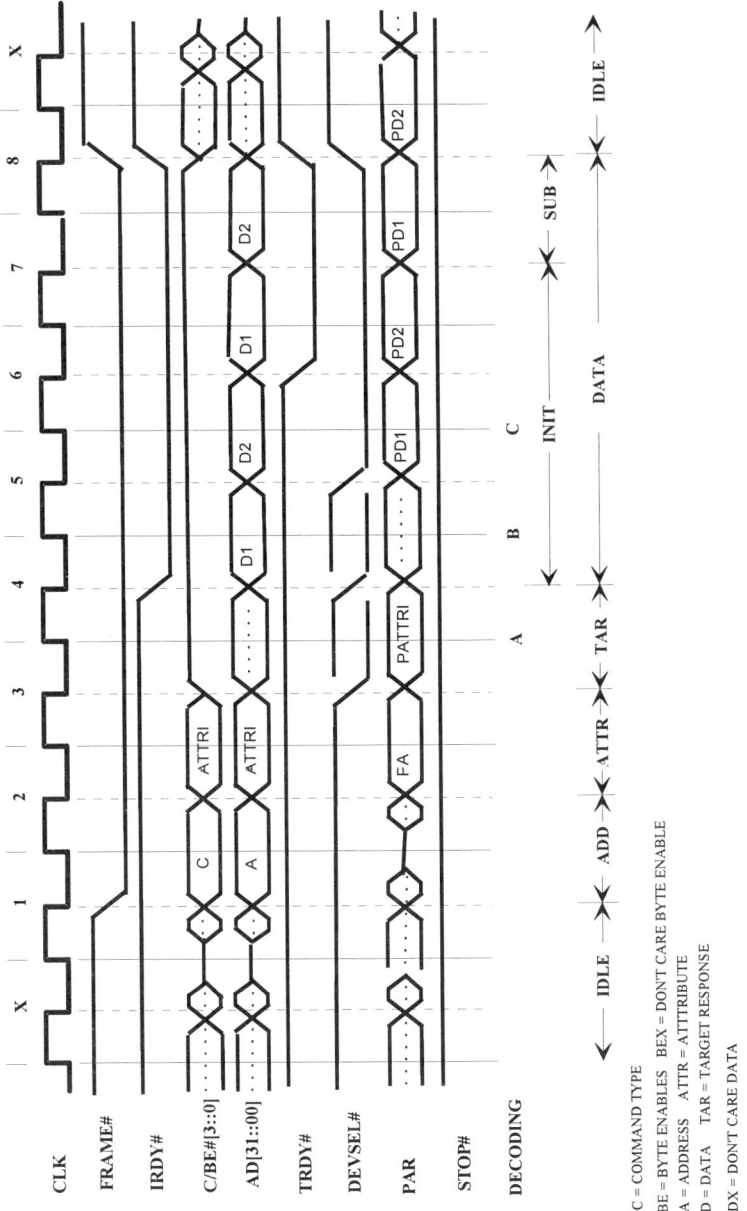

Figure 6-46-A: BURST Split Completion Command Executed with a PCI-X BURST Bus Transaction (Two Microaccesses and Two Wait States)

469

Figures 6-45 and 6-46-A show SINGLE and BURST split completion transactions. The protocol of SINGLE and BURST split completion transactions is the same for the previously discussed SINGLE and BURST memory write transactions, respectively. The only two differences are as follows:

■   The AD[31::00] signal lines in the ADDRESS PHASE of split completion transactions contain PCI-X resource destination, associated information, and not a memory address.

■   The C/BE#[3::0] signal lines are driven to logical "1" during the DATA PHASE.

In the DATA PHASE of SINGLE or BURST bus transactions for BURST memory write commands, the C/BE#[3::0] signal lines contain valid byte enable information. In the DATA PHASE of SINGLE or BURST bus transactions for BURST memory write block and alias memory write block commands, the C/BE#[3::0] signal lines are driven to logical "1". As previously stated, the C/BE#[3::0] signal lines during the DATA PHASE of split completion transactions are driven to logical "1". If the SINGLE split completion transaction is in response to a SINGLE bus transaction (for a DWORD memory read command) terminated with a Split Response termination, the PCI-X bus master of the a DWORD memory read command is required to remember the valid byte enable pattern. If the SINGLE or BURST split completion transaction is in response to a SINGLE or BURST bus transaction (for a BURST memory read command) terminated with a Split Response termination, the PCI-X bus master of the a BURST memory read command by definition is reading all of the bytes. Consequently the associated data in the split completion transaction is written with the assumption that all bytes are enabled in the DATA PHASE. When the split completion transaction contains a Split Completion Error Message, by definition all of the byte lanes are enabled. See Chapter 4: *Interaction Between PCI and PCI-X Resources* for more information.

The "unique data write protocol" previously discussed for bus transactions of BURST memory write commands also applies to bus transactions for BURST split completion commands.

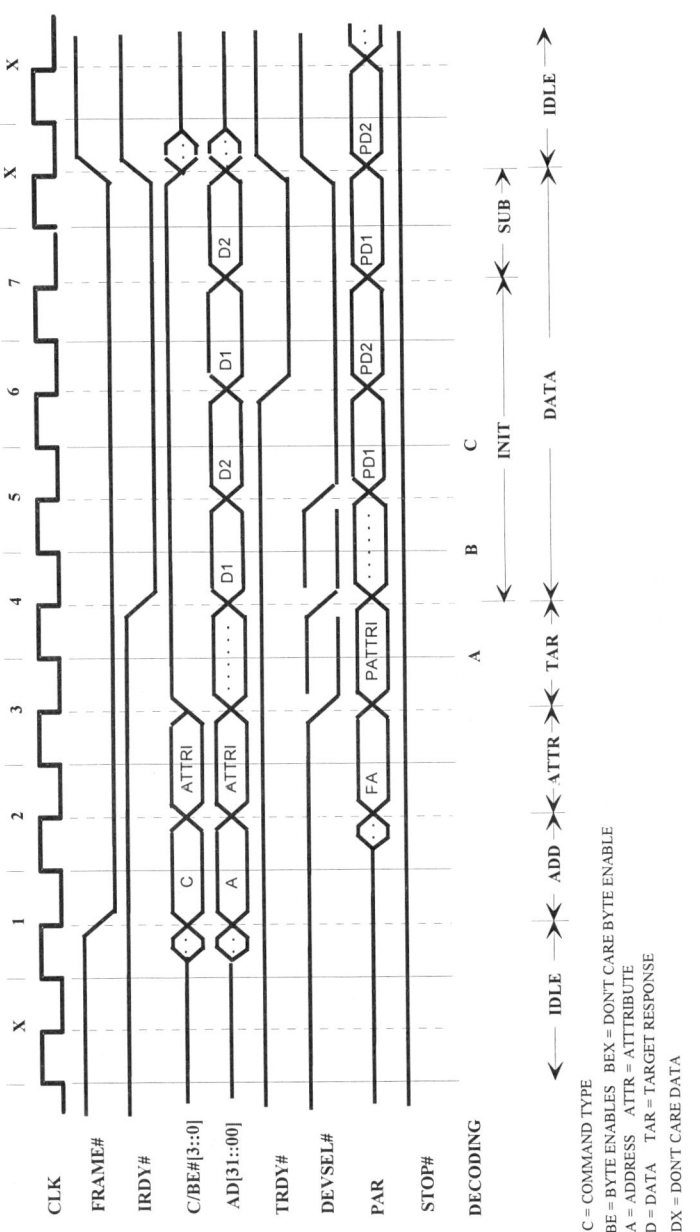

Figure 6-46-A: BURST Split Completion Command Executed with a PCI-X BURST Bus Transaction (Two Microaccesses and Two Wait States)

6.13 MORE DETAILS OF PCI-X SIGNAL LINE PROTOCOL FOR 32 DATA BIT BUS TRANSACTIONS

As previously discussed, the 'General Deassertion" protocol defines the deassertion of the FRAME# and IRDY# signal lines. Chapter 8: *Master and Target Termination* details signal line operation, and signal line driving and tri-stating when Completion, Completion with Timeout, Retry, Disconnect at Next ADB, Single Phase Disconnect, Master Abort, or Target Abort terminations are executed. Chapter 9: *Bus Segment Ownership* covers the change of signal line ownership, and signal line driving and tri-stating between changes of bus ownership and between bus transactions. Chapter 10: *Parity and Bus Errors* explains the signal line ownership, and signal line driving and tri-stating of the SERR# and PERR# signal lines. This subchapter defines the signal line protocol for signal lines during the bus transaction and between bus transactions when the PCI-X bus master retains bus ownership:

In the following discussion, the terms "drive or tri-state" are different than the terms "assert or deassert". The former identifies when the signal line buffers are enabled or disabled. The latter reflects when signal lines change their logical state.

The figures in the following section do not contain the "D" and "T" identifiers. The protocol for signal lines driving ("D") and tri-stating ("T") according to the PCI-X addendum specification is more rigid than the PCI local bus specification, the assertion of one GNTX# signal line and deassertion of another GNTX# signal line is not simultaneous, and the Fast Back to Back transaction protocol is not supported. Consequently, the PCI-X bus transaction protocol is simpler for "D" and "T" at the start and end of a bus transaction, respectively. See Subchapter 6.0 for more information.

The signal line protocol outlined below is a general introduction to 32 data bit bus transaction operation with bus transaction completion when the FRAME# and IRDY# signal lines are simultaneously deasserted. Please note there are slight differences in the interpretation of the AD signal lines during special and interrupt acknowledge transactions. Finally, details of additional signal lines like SERR#, PERR#, INTx#, and RST#, and other considerations relative to a 64 data bit bus transactions will be discussed in detail in other sections of this chapter.

- ■ The viewpoint of the PCI-X addendum specification is that the PCI-X bus master will tri-state the FRAME# and IRDY# signal lines between bus transactions even when it retains bus ownership.

■ The PCI-X addendum specification also assumes that the PCI-X bus master will tri-state the C/BE#[3::0] and AD[31::0] signal lines between bus transactions even when it retains bus segment ownership. The same protocol applies to the PAR signal line with a one CLK signal line period lag.

■ Unlike the PCI bus transaction protocol, the deassertion of FRAME# and IRDY# signal lines does not define SINGLE bus transactions due to a DWORD and BURST COMMANDS versus BURST bus transactions due to BURST COMMANDS. The command type and the byte count (for BURST COMMANDS) define the bus transactions as SINGLE or BURST bus transactions. As previously stated, the deassertion of the FRAME# and IRDY# signal lines is defined by the number of microaccesses according to the "General Deassertion" protocol. During bus transactions, the FRAME# and IRDY# signal lines are always driven by the PCI-X bus master.

   ■ Unlike a PCI bus transaction, the IRDY# signal line in a PCI-X bus transaction is required to be asserted two CLK signal line periods after the ATTRIBUTE PHASE information is driven onto the AD[31::00] and C/BE#[3::0] signal lines. According to the protocol defined by this book, the assertion of the IRDY# signal line is immediately after the single CLK signal line period of the TARGET RESPONSE PHASE and defines the beginning of the DATA PHASE.

■ Once the FRAME# signal line is asserted and then deasserted, it remains deasserted until the completion of the bus transaction. By definition, the completion of any bus transaction is always identified by the simultaneous deassertion of both FRAME# and IRDY# signal lines. The PCI-X bus transaction protocol defines microaccesses within the bus transaction, and the completion of a microaccess is defined by the DEVSEL#, TRDY#, and STOP# signal lines as follows:

   ■ "Normal termination" ... For SINGLE and BURST bus transactions the initial microaccess begins with the assertion of the IRDY# signal line and ends when the DEVSEL# signal line is asserted; and STOP# and TRDY# signal lines are deasserted and asserted, respectively. For a BURST bus transaction, subsequent microaccesses occur (begins and ends) on every CLK signal line period after the end of the initial microaccess. The last subsequent microaccess is defined by the byte count of the BURST bus transaction.

   ■ Split Response termination ... The initial microaccess begins with the assertion of the IRDY# signal line and ends when the DEVSEL# signal line is deasserted; and STOP# and TRDY# signal lines are deasserted and asserted, respectively.

- Disconnect at Next ADB termination ... The microaccesses as defined by the DEVSEL#, STOP#, and TRDY# signal lines are the same as for "Normal termination".

- Single Phase Disconnect termination ... The initial microaccess begins with the assertion of the IRDY# signal line and ends when the DEVSEL# signal line is deasserted; and STOP# and TRDY# signal lines are both asserted.

- Retry termination ... The initial microaccess begins with the assertion of the IRDY# signal line and ends when the DEVSEL# signal line is asserted; and STOP# and TRDY# signal lines are asserted and deasserted, respectively.

- Target Abort termination ... The initial microaccess begins with the assertion of the IRDY# signal line and ends when the DEVSEL# signal line is deasserted; and TRDY# and STOP# signal lines are deasserted and asserted, respectively. For a subsequent microaccess, a Target Abort termination ends it when the DEVSEL# signal line is deasserted; and TRDY# and STOP# signal lines are deasserted and asserted, respectively.

- Master Abort termination ... The initial microaccess begins with the assertion of the IRDY# signal line and ends when the FRAME# and IRDY# signal lines are both deasserted.

- During bus transactions, the DEVSEL#, IRDY# and STOP# signal lines are always driven by the target.

- Once the FRAME# signal line is asserted, the PCI-X bus master drives the C/BE#[3::0] signal lines with valid information or to logical "1" for the remainder of the bus transaction.

- During a write transaction (memory, I/O, configuration, split completion, and special), the PCI-X bus master drives the AD[31::0] and PAR signal lines with valid information, or to a stable level, or tri-stated (the stable level or tri-state is shown in the figures by the dotted line between two parallel lines). For the ADDRESS and ATTRIBUTE PHASEs (when the FRAME# signal line is first asserted), these signal lines are driven with valid information. For the TARGET RESPONSE PHASE these signal lines are driven to a stable level or tri-stated. For the DATA PHASE (IRDY# signal line is asserted) these signal lines are driven with valid information. This protocol applies to the PAR signal line with a one CLK signal line period delay.

- During a read transaction (memory, I/O, configuration and interrupt acknowledge), the PCI-X bus master drives the AD[31::0] and PAR signal lines with valid information, or to a stable level, or tri-stated (the stable level or tri-state is shown in the figures by the dotted line between two parallel lines). For the ADDRESS and ATTRIBUTE PHASEs (when the FRAME# signal line is first asserted), these signal lines are driven with valid information. For the TARGET RESPONSE PHASE the ownership of these signal lines is exchanged. For the DATA PHASE (IRDY# signal line is asserted) these signal lines are driven with valid information or tri-stated as follows:

■ These signal lines are tri-stated prior to the assertion of the DEVSEL# signal line.

■ These signal lines are driven to a stable level (but not necessarily valid) simultaneously with the assertion of the DEVSEL# signal line.

■ These signal lines are driven with valid data simultaneously with the assertion of the TRDY# signal line.

■ This protocol applies to the PAR signal line with a one CLK signal line period delay.

■ During a write transaction (memory, I/O, configuration, split completion, and special), the PCI-X bus master drives the C/BE#[3::0] signal lines with valid information, to a logical "1", to a stable level, or tri-stated (the stable level or tri-state is shown in the figures by the dotted line between two parallel lines). For the ADDRESS and ATTRIBUTE PHASEs (when the FRAME# signal line is first asserted), these signal lines are driven with valid information. For the TARGET RESPONSE PHASE these signal lines are driven to a logical "1". For the DATA PHASE (IRDY# signal line is asserted) these signal lines are driven with valid information for BURST memory write bus transactions. For the DATA PHASE (IRDY# signal line is asserted) these signal lines are driven as follows:

■ They are driven with valid byte enable information for BURST memory write bus transactions.

■ They are driven to logical "1" for BURST memory write block, BURST alias memory write block, and all NON-BURST memory write bus transactions.

■ During a read transaction (memory, I/O, and configuration), the PCI-X bus master drives the C/BE#[3::0] signal lines with valid information, to a logical "1", a stable level, or tri-stated (the stable level or tri-state is shown in the figures by the dotted line between two parallel lines). For the ADDRESS and ATTRIBUTE PHASEs (when the FRAME# signal line is first asserted), these signal lines are driven with valid information. For the TARGET RESPONSE PHASE these signal lines are driven to a logical "1". For the DATA PHASE (IRDY# signal line is asserted) these signal lines are driven to a logical "1".

475

Further details for the signal line protocol relative to the interaction of the PCI-X bus master and target during the bus transaction and between bus transactions follow:

- At the beginning of the bus transaction, the target begins driving the DEVSEL# signal line upon completion of the address decode. The earliest sampling point and the earliest point at which the DEVSEL# signal line can be asserted is immediately after the ATTRIBUTE PHASE. When a DUAL ADDRESS COMMAND is executed the ATTRIBUTE PHASE is delayed by one CLK signal line period.

- The target that will participate in the bus transaction will assert the DEVSEL# signal line to claim the bus transaction. Only the target claiming the bus transaction can drive or assert/deassert the TRDY#, STOP#, AD[31::00], and PAR signal lines (AD[31::00] and PAR signal lines for read transactions and interrupt acknowledge transactions). The driving of these signal lines should be simultaneous with or subsequent to driving of the DEVSEL# signal line. The assertion of the STOP# and TRDY# signal lines is required to be simultaneous with or subsequent to the assertion of the DEVSEL# signal line.

- Data is only transferred when the IRDY# and TRDY# signal lines are both asserted. The one exception is the special transaction.

- Once the IRDY# signal line is asserted it can only be deasserted according to the "General Deassertion" protocol or simultaneously with the deassertion of the FRAME# signal line for a special transaction or for a Master Abort termination. Once the TRDY# signal line is asserted it cannot be deasserted until the end of the initial microaccess of a SINGLE bus transaction or the end of last microaccess of a BURST bus transaction. The end of a microaccess depends on rather a "normal termination" occurs or if a target termination is executed (See the discussion above).

- The DEVSEL# signal line remains asserted until end of the last microaccess with four exceptions: Split Response, Single Phase Disconnect, Target Abort, and Master Abort terminations. For Split Response and Single Phase Disconnect the DEVSEL# signal line is asserted a minimum of one CLK signal line period. It is deasserted according to the "PCI-X 16 clock or 8 clock rules" protocol simultaneously with the assertion if the TRDY# or STOP# signal line. For a Target Abort termination the DEVSEL# signal line is asserted a minimum of one CLK signal line period. It is deasserted simultaneously with the assertion of the STOP# signal line. Once the DEVSEL# signal line is deasserted it remains deasserted for the duration of the bus transactions terminated by the aforementioned target terminations. For a bus transaction with a Master Abort termination the DEVSEL# signal line by definition is never asserted. See Chapter 8: *Master and Target Termination* for more information.

■ Once the TRDY# or STOP# signal line is asserted it cannot be deasserted until the end of the last microaccess.

A major difference between PCI and PCI-X bus transactions is how a bus transaction ends. The protocol according to the PCI local bus specification defines a single CLK single line period when the FRAME# signal line was deasserted and the IRDY# signal line was asserted. The ending of a bus transaction according to the PCI-X addendum bus specification is more complicated. As previously discussed, the "General Deassertion" protocol defines the deassertion points of the FRAME# and IRDY# signal lines relative to the number of microaccesses. For special transactions or any bus transaction that terminates with a Master Abort termination, the deassertion points of the FRAME# and IRDY# signal lines are simultaneous and at a fixed CLK signal line period relative to the beginning of the bus transaction. See Subchapter 6.0 for more information about the driving and tri-stating of the signal lines. This subchapter, in conjunction with Chapter 9: *Bus Segment Ownership*, defines the minimal length of the IDLE PHASE between bus transactions.

In the following discussion, the driving ("D") and tri-stating ("T") points within the bus transaction are described. Refer to the "D" and "T" of previous figures for a pictorial representation of these points. As outlined in Subchapter 6.0, these points are shown in the figures at the "earliest" occurrence and some of these points are shown in the figures at the "latest" occurrence.

The protocol for the remaining signal lines for all bus transactions is as follows:

■ The CLK and RST# signal lines are driven to valid levels by the central resource. For a typical bus transaction, the CLK signal line oscillates and the RST# signal line is deasserted.

■ The GNTx# signal lines are driven to valid levels by the central resource. The REQx# signal lines are driven by the PCI-X bus masters or are driven to a logical "1" by pull-up resistors.

■ The LOCK# signal line is driven to valid levels by the Lock master.

■ An INTx# signal line is asserted when a PCI-X resource needs interrupt service.

■ The REQ64#, ACK64#, PAR64, C/BE#[7::4], and AD[63::32] signal lines are driven to a logical "1" by pull-up resistors.

6.14   PCI-X EXCLUSIVE ACCESS (LOCK) PROTOCOL

> In the following discussions the term "upstream" and "downstream" refer to the direction of the bus transaction flow. As explained in Subchapter 2.2, accesses from PCI bus masters on higher LEVEL bus segments to targets on the same or lower LEVEL bus segments are defined as "downstream". Similarly, from PCI bus masters on lower LEVEL bus segment to targets on higher LEVEL bus segments are defined as "upstream".

INTRODUCTION

The PCI-X addendum specification defines both Exclusive Hardware Access and Exclusive Software Access in the same way as defined by Rev 2.2 of the PCI local bus specification (see Subchapter 6.3 for more information). The similarities and differences between a PCI bus transaction and a PCI-X bus transaction will be discussed below. The balance of this subchapter will focus on the bus transaction protocol; see Chapter 7: *Bridge and Interface Protocol* for more information about the overall application of Exclusive Hardware Access across a system.

As with a PCI bus transaction, a PCI-X bus transaction executed to implement the Exclusive Hardware Access protocol uses the LOCK# signal line. The Lock Function (LF) is defined when a target that has been locked (locked target) and a PCI-X bus master (Lock Master) controls the LOCK# signal line. The Lock Function is defined for each PCI-X bus segment; consequently, on each PCI-X bus segment only one PCI-X bus master and target at a time are the Lock master and locked target, respectively. A PCI-X bus master can lock a target if no other PCI-X resource is presently locked (as indicated by the continued deassertion of the LOCK# signal line by pull-up resistors) on the bus segment.

Unlike the PCI local bus specification, the PCI-X addendum bus specification only permits porting the Exclusive Hardware Access downstream via the PCI-X bus segment. The support of upstream Exclusive Hardware Access for a PCI-X/LEGACY BRIDGE and LEGACY bus master is defined for side band signals and are not via the PCI-X bus segment. See Chapter 7: *Bridge and Interface Protocol* for more information about which resources can be locked.

> For the balance of this subchapter the terms "Lock" and 'Lock Function" refer to Exclusive Hardware Access.

There are four basic considerations for the Lock Function: Establishment of Lock, Continuance of Lock, Release of Target Lock and Lock Function Ownership, and Unsuccessful Bus Transaction Termination relative to Lock.

ESTABLISHMENT OF LOCK

> **It is assumed that the Exclusive Hardware Access according to the PCI local bus specification in Subchapter 6.3 has been read and understood. Consequently, the discussion below will focus on the similarities and differences between the PCI-X addendum specification and the PCI local bus specification.**

The protocol to establish the Lock Function (LF) on a PCI-X bus segment is the same as the PCI bus segment with the following key similarities and differences:

- The PCI-X bus master is required to determine that the Lock Function is available (deasserted LOCK# signal line) prior to requesting bus ownership to execute the bus transaction that will establish lock.

- The sampling points for the deassertion and assertion if the LOCK# signal line in a PCI-X bus transaction are the same as for a PCI bus transaction (see Figure 6-46-B) That is, to implement the LF with a new Lock master ALL the following are required:

  - The LOCK# signal line is sampled deasserted on the rising edge of the CLK signal line when the FRAME# signal line is first sampled asserted (Circle A in Figure 6-46-B). The LOCK# signal line is required to be sampled asserted on the next subsequent rising edge of the CLK signal line (Circle B in Figure 6-46-B). Once the LOCK# signal line is sampled asserted at point B (Circle B in Figure 6-46-B) it must remain asserted until end of the bus transaction. Similarly, if the LOCK# signal line is sampled deasserted at point B (Circle B in Figure 6-46-B), it must remain deasserted until end of the bus transaction. The driving point for the LOCK# signal line is shown in Figure 6-46-B. The deassertion (if deasserted to end the LF) of the LOCK# signal line at the end the bus transaction is recommended to occur simultaneously with the deassertion of the IRDY# signal line. The tri-state point of the LOCK# signal line is also recommended to occur simultaneously with the tri-state point of the IRDY# signal line. See the shaded box just prior to the "Release of Target Lock and Relinquishing of Lock Function Ownership" section for further qualifications.

■ The bus transaction must complete with a successful memory read. For a PCI-X bus segment, successful read transactions are defined as bus transactions executed for DWORD memory read commands, and BURST memory block and alias memory read block commands that complete as follows:

■ A Completion (with or without timeout), Single Phase Disconnect, Disconnect at Next ADB, or Split Response termination.

> The execution of a DUAL ADDRESS command does not change the sampling points for the LOCK# signal line (Circles A and B in Figure 6-46-B). Point B is always the one CLK signal line period after the FRAME# signal line is first sampled asserted.

> The use of the Split Response termination presents a unique definition of when the target is actually locked. See Chapter 7: *Bridge and Interface Protocol* for more information.

CONTINUANCE OF LOCK

> It is assumed that the Exclusive Hardware Access according to the PCI local bus specification in Subchapter 6.3 has been read and understood. Consequently, the discussion below will focus on the similarities and differences between the PCI-X addendum specification and the PCI local bus specification.

The protocol of a PCI-X bus master retaining the Lock Function (LF) and remaining Lock master is the same as for a PCI bus master. Similarly, the operation of a locked target is the same for a PCI or PCI-X bus segment. The key similarities and differences are as follows:

■ The PCI-X bus master that is the Lock master remains the Lock master provided it retains ownership and asserts the LOCK# signal line after the bus transaction that established the Lock Function (LF).

■ The Lock master does not have to retain bus segment ownership, but is required to access only the locked target while it is Lock master

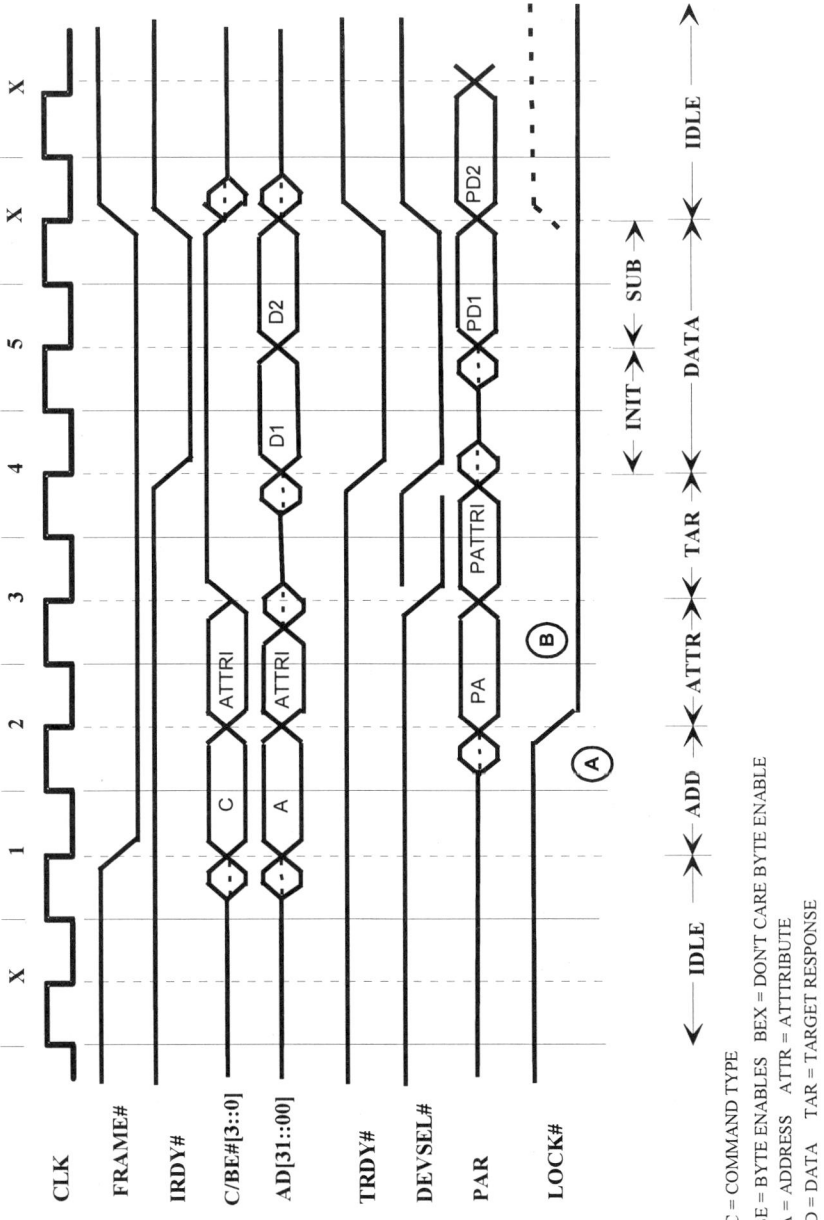

Figure 6-46-B: LOCK# Signal Line Sampling, Drive, and Tri-State Points in a PCI-X Bus Transaction

■ The locked target is only allowed to respond to bus transactions from non LOCK masters by requesting a Retry termination. As with the PCI local bus specification protocol, a target on a PCI-X bus segment knows the bus transaction is not being executed by the Lock master because the LOCK# signal line is asserted at the rising edge of the CLK signal line when the FRAME# signal line is first sampled asserted. When the Lock master is accessing the locked target, it will deassert the LOCK# signal line at the rising edge of CLK signal line when the FRAME# signal line is first sampled asserted. (Circle A in Figures 6-46-C and 6-46-D).

■ When the Lock master is accessing the locked target, the assertion of the LOCK# signal line at point B (Circle B of Figure 6-46-C) indicates that the LF will continue with the present Lock master. The LOCK# signal line asserted at point B must remain asserted for the remainder of the bus transaction.

■ When the Lock master is accessing the locked target for the final bus transaction that requires the LF, it must assert the LOCK# signal line until the end of bus transaction. The deassertion of the LOCK# signal line at point B (Circle B of Figure 6-46-C) indicates that the LF will not continue with the present Lock master. If the LOCK# signal line is deasserted at Point B (see Circle B in Figure 6-46-C and the shaded box below), the target ceases to be locked by the LF and the present Lock master ceases to be the Lock master whenever both the FRAME# and LOCK# signal lines are both sampled deasserted at the end of the bus transaction.

> **The Lock master must not deassert the LOCK# signal line at Point B (Circle B in Figure 6-46-C). The Lock master must wait until after the end of the bus transaction that is transferring the last data of the LF. If it deasserts the LOCK# signal line at Point B and the target executes a Retry, Single Phase Disconnect, Disconnect at Next ADB termination, or Split Response termination, the access of the final data of the LF cannot occur during the same lock period of the target as the other data.**

> **As previously noted, the execution of a DUAL ADDRESS command does not affect the sampling points outlined in Figure 6-46-C.**

482

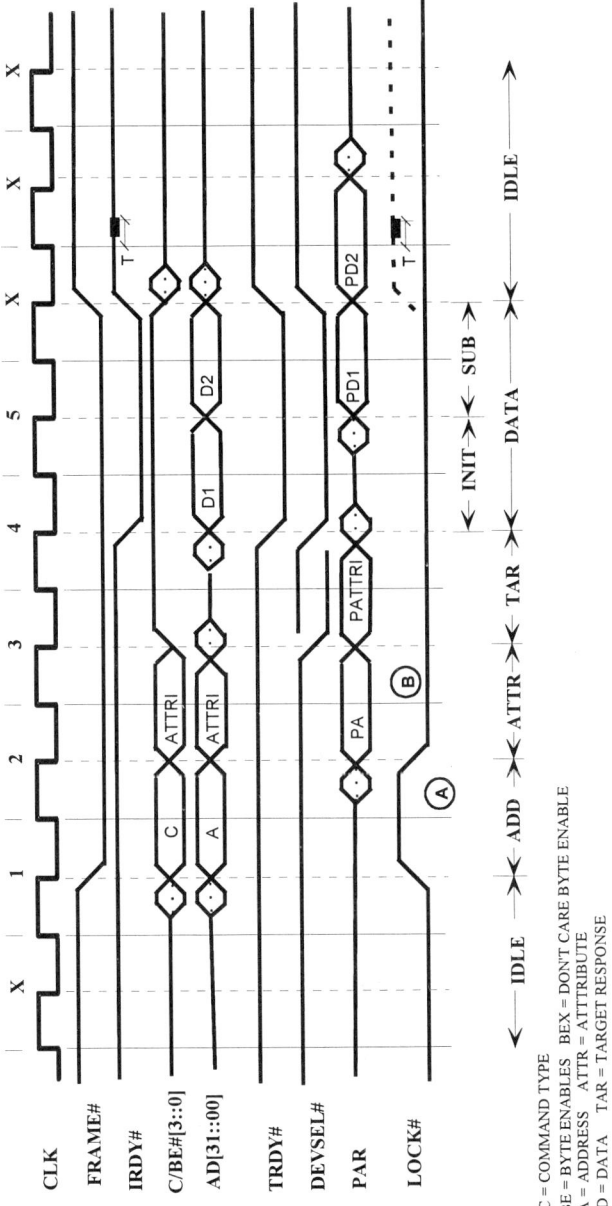

C = COMMAND TYPE
BE = BYTE ENABLES   BEX = DON'T CARE BYTE ENABLE
A = ADDRESS   ATTR = ATTTRIBUTE
D = DATA   TAR = TARGET RESPONSE

Figure 6-46-C: Access to Locked Target by Lock Master in a PCI-X Bus Transaction

483

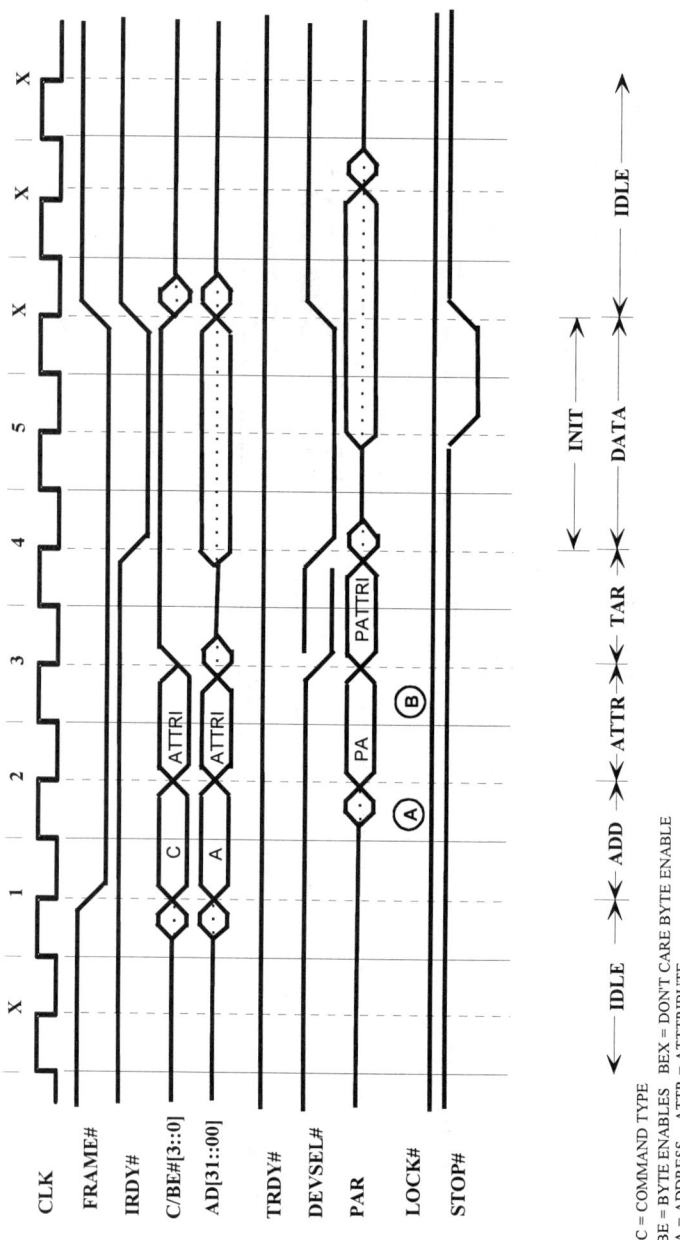

Figure 6-46-D: Access to a Locked Target by non Lock Master in a PCI-X Bus Transaction

RELEASE OF TARGET LOCK AND RELINQUISHING OF LOCK FUNCTION OWNERSHIP

It is assumed that the Exclusive Hardware Access according to the PCI local bus specification in Subchapter 6.3 has been read and understood. Consequently, the discussion below will focus on the similarities and differences between the PCI-X addendum specification and the PCI local bus specification.

The protocol of a PCI-X bus master relinquishing the Lock Function (LF) and target becoming unlocked is the same as for a PCI bus master with a few differences. The key similarities and differences are as follows:

- As introduced in the previous section, the Lock master relinquishes Lock Function ownership (ceases to be Lock master and the target is unlocked at the completion of the bus transaction) whenever both the LOCK# and FRAME# signal lines are sampled deasserted at a CLK signal line rising edge.

- The Lock master is required to assert the LOCK# signal line until after the last data of the LF is transferred. It is recommended that it deasserts the LOCK# signal line simultaneously with the deassertion of the IRDY# signal line for the last transaction. If a Split Response termination had been requested, the Lock master must assert the LOCK# signal line until the completion of all of the associated split completion transactions. It is recommended that the Lock master deasserts the LOCK# signal line simultaneously with the deassertion of the TRDY# signal line for the last split completion transaction. However, once the last data of the LF has transferred (by split completion transactions or other transactions) the Lock master can deassert the LOCK# signal line at any time. Whenever the LOCK# signal line and FRAME# signal line are both sample deasserted on a CLK signal line rising edge, the LF has completed and the target is unlocked.

- If the Lock master retains ownership of the bus segment and wants to unlock one target and immediately lock another target, it must deassert both the FRAME# and LOCK# signal line for a minimum of one CLK signal line rising edge to permit the locked target to "see" it has been unlocked.

- The tri-stating of the LOCK# signal line is the same as the IRDY# and TRDY# signal lines. That is, it tri-states the LOCK# signal line one CLK signal line period after it is sampled deasserted.

485

UNSUCCESSFUL BUS TRANSACTION TERMINATION RELATIVE TO LOCK

Certain conditions may occur during the memory read transaction to prevent a PCI-X bus master from obtaining ownership of the Lock Function (LF) (becoming Lock master and locking of a target). As previously discussed, for a PCI-X bus master to become Lock master and for the target to be locked after the completion of the bus transaction requires the successful reading of data in the memory address space. Data is not read and the bus transaction is not successfully completed if either Master Abort, Retry, or Target Abort termination occurs. The LOCK# signal line must immediately be deasserted without regard to the end of the bus transaction. See Chapter 8: *Master and Target Termination* for more information.

Once a PCI-X bus master owns the LF (PCI bus master is Lock master and a target has been locked), the execution Retry termination has no effect on retaining ownership of the LF, but Master and Target Abort termination does affect LF ownership. If the non-Lock master is accessing the locked target, the execution of a Master or Target Abort termination does not affect the Lock master's retaining ownership of the LF. If the Lock master is accessing the locked target, the execution of a Master or Target Abort termination *forces* the Lock master to relinquish ownership of the LF (immediately deasserting the LOCK# signal line without regard for the end of the bus transaction). See Chapter 8: *Master and Target Termination* for more information. The other target transaction termination types have no affect on a PCI-X bus master obtaining or retaining the LF and therefore keeping the target locked.

6.15   PCI-X 64 DATA BIT EXTENSIONS

The PCI-X addendum specification protocol for 64 data bit extensions is essentially the same as the Rev. 2.2 PCI local bus specification (please see Subchapters 6.0 and 6.4 for background information). The only differences between the PCI-X 64 data bit extension and PCI 64 data bit extension are as follows:

- ■ The PCI-X addendum specification requires that the 64 data bit extension only applies to the bus transactions accessing the memory address space. The PCI local bus specification does permit the I/O address space to be accessed with a 64 data bit bus transaction, though it is not recommended.

- ■ The PCI-X addendum specification also defines a 64 data bit split completion transaction.

486

As previously discussed, 64 data bit PCI I/O targets can be implemented, but there is no benefit to requiring the increased complexity and it is therefore strongly recommended that 64 data bits I/O targets not be implemented. For the purposes of this book, I/O targets are only 32 data bits in size. If a 64 data bit PCI I/O target is implemented, the 64 data bit protocol applied to memory targets would also be applied to PCI I/O targets.

DUAL ADDRESS

The protocol outlined in Subchapter 6.12 for 32 data bit resources provides 64 address bits without the use of the AD[63::32] signal lines. If the PCI-X bus master resides on a 64 data bit bus segment (REQ64# signal line asserted during RESET), and requests a 64 data bit access (REQ64# signal line asserted during the ADDRESS PHASE), the additional information must be provided for a DUAL ADDRESS. When a DUAL ADDRESS is not requested (see Figure 6-47), the AD[63::32] and C/BE#[7::4] signal lines are driven by the PCI-X bus master to a logical "1" during the ATTRIBUTE PHASE, and driven to a stable level or tri-stated during the ADDRESS PHASE. During the TARGET RESPONSE PHASE, the AD[63::32] signal lines are driven to a stable level or tri-stated, and the C/BE#[7::3] signal lines are driven to logical "1". The PAR64 signal line is also driven by the PCI-X bus master with a one CLK signal line period delay for a specific phase. The PAR64 signal line is driven to a stable level or tri-stated for the ADDRESS and TARGET RESPONSE PHASES, and is driven with valid parity for the ATTRIBUTE PHASE. When a DUAL ADDRESS is requested (see Figure 6-48), the AD[63::32] and C/BE#[7::4] signal lines are driven during the ADDRESS PHASE with the upper order address bits and the COMMAND type, respectively. The PAR64 signal line is also driven by the PCI-X bus master in the subsequent CLK signal line period to the ATTRIBUTE PHASE with valid parity. Whenever the AD[63::32], C/BE#[7::4], or PAR64 signal lines are floated, the associated pull-up resistors will drive them to logical "1".

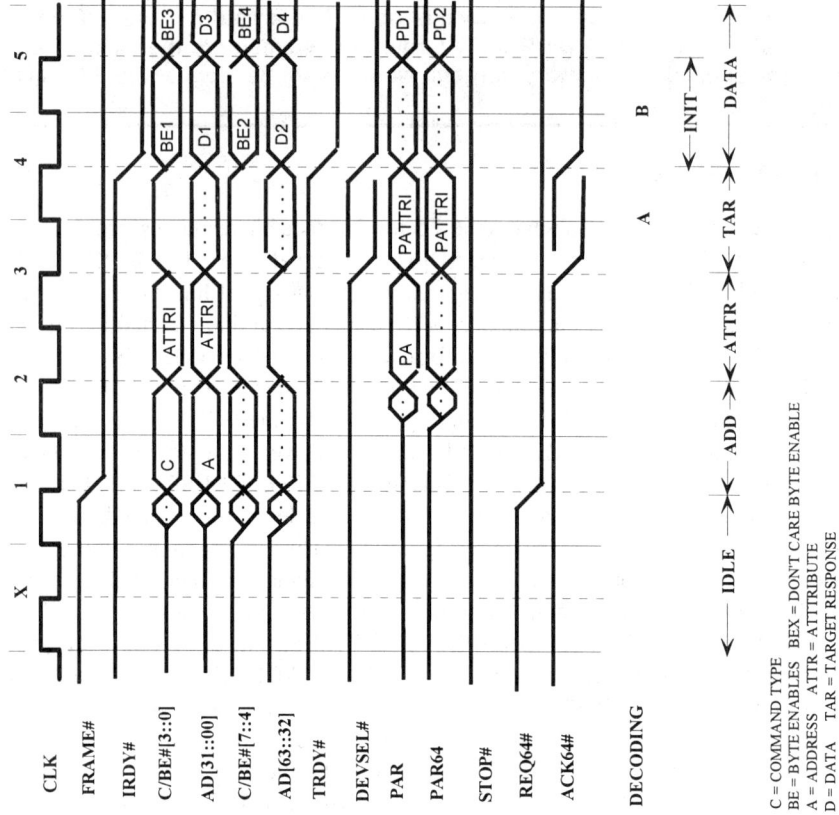

Figure 6-47: BURST Memory Write Command Executed with a PCI-X BURST Bus Transaction and NO DUAL ADDRESS COMMAND (No Wait States)

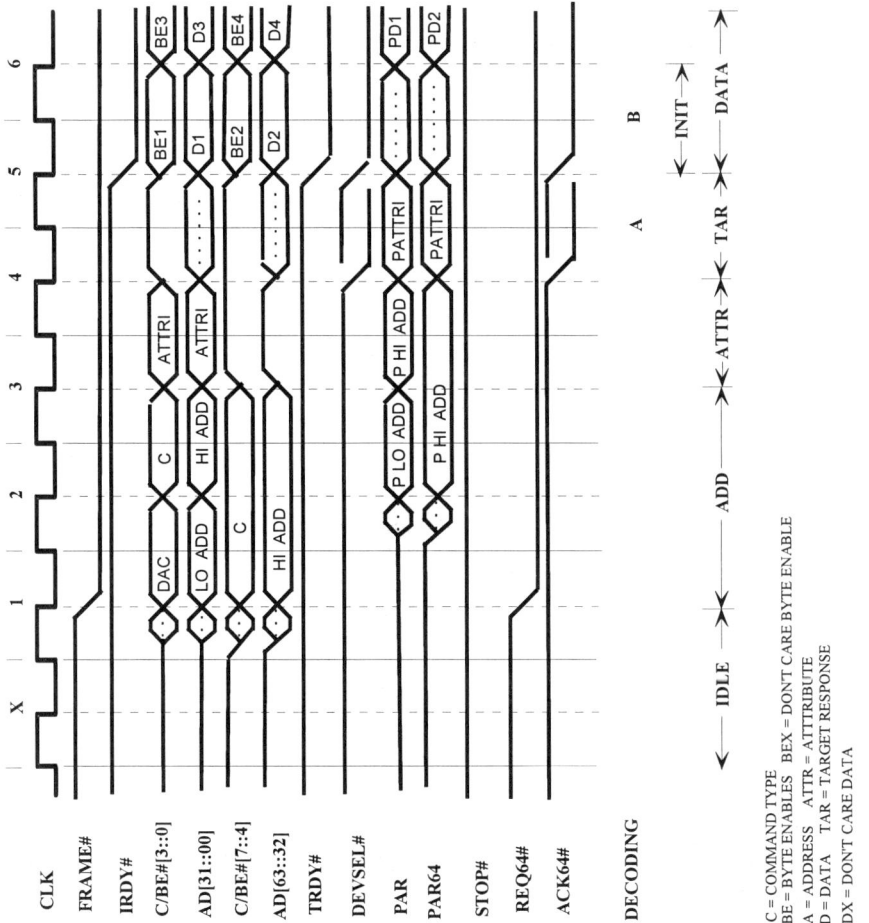

Figure 6-48: BURST Memory Write Command Executed with a PCI-X BURST Bus Transaction and DUAL ADDRESS COMMAND (No Wait States)

6.16   32 DATA BIT PCI-X BUS MASTER TO 64 DATA BIT TARGET

MEMORY TRANSACTIONS

The protocol for a PCI-X bus master executing a 32 data bit PCI-X memory transaction to a 64 data bit target is the same as for a PCI-X bus master executing 32 data bit PCI-X memory transaction to a 32 data bit target. The determination of a 32 data bit bus transaction is done on a transaction to transaction basis and is the is the same as that for a PCI bus transaction. The AD[63::32], C/BE[7::4], and PAR64 signal lines are driven to a logical "1" by pull-up resistors. See Subchapters 6.5 and 6.12 for more information.

I/O, CONFIGURATION, INTERRUPT ACKNOWLEDGE, AND SPECIAL TRANSACTIONS

The I/O, configuration, interrupt acknowledge, and special transactions are executed only with 32 data bit resources. The deassertion of the ACK64# signal line makes the target always appear as a 32 data bit resource.

SPLIT COMPLETION TRANSACTIONS

The protocol for a PCI-X bus master executing a 32 data bit PCI-X split completion transaction to a 64 data bit target is the same as for a PCI-X bus master executing 32 data bit PCI-X memory write transaction to a 64 data bit target. The only difference is that the C/BE#[3::0] signal lines are driven to a logical "1" by the PCI-X bus master during the DATA PHASE.

6.17   64 DATA BIT PCI-X BUS MASTER TO 64 DATA BIT TARGET

MEMORY TRANSACTIONS

The protocol for a PCI-X bus master executing a 64 data bit PCI-X memory transaction to a 64 data bit target is the same as for a PCI-X bus master executing 32 data bit PCI-X memory transaction to a 32 data bit target. The only differences or items of note are as follows (see Figures 6-49 to 6-52):

- The AD[63::32] signal lines are driven to a stable level or tri-stated by the PCI-X bus master during the ADDRESS PHASE except as follows:

490

■ For either memory write or read transactions, the AD[63::32] signal lines are driven with the high level address when a DUAL ADDRESS command is executed. See Subchapter 6.15 for more information.

■ For memory write transactions, the AD[63::32] signal lines are driven to a stable level or tri-stated by the PCI-X bus master during the TARGET RESPONSE PHASE. These signal lines are driven with valid data by the PCI-X bus master during the DATA PHASE. Otherwise, these signal lines follow the same bus transaction protocol as the AD[31::00] signal lines.

■ For memory read transactions, the AD[63::32] signal lines are tri-stated by the PCI-X bus master during the TARGET RESPONSE PHASE to change signal line ownership. These signal lines are driven with valid data, stable level, or floated by the target during the DATA PHASE. Otherwise, these signal lines follow the same bus transaction protocol as the AD[31::00] signal lines.

■ The AD[63::32] and C/BE#[7::4] signal lines are driven to logical "1" during the ATTRIBUTE PHASE.

■ For SINGLE and BURST bus transactions for BURST memory write commands, the C/BE#[7::4] signal lines are driven to a logical "1" by the PCI-X bus master during the TARGET RESPONSE PHASE. These signal lines are driven with valid byte enable information by the PCI-X bus master during the DATA PHASE for a BURST memory write command. These signal lines are driven to logical "1" for BURST memory write block or alias memory write block commands. Otherwise, these signal lines follow the same bus transaction protocol as the C/BE#[3::0] signal lines.

■ For SINGLE and BURST bus transactions for BURST memory read transactions, the C/BE#[7::4] signal lines are driven to a logical "1" by the PCI-X bus master during the TARGET RESPONSE and DATA PHASES. Otherwise, these signal lines follow the same bus transaction protocol as the C/BE#[3::0] signal lines.

■ The PAR64 signal line protocol follows the protocol of the AD[63::32] signal lines with a one CLK signal line period delay.

　■ As previously discussed, for write transactions the parity of the ADDRESS, ATTRIBUTE, and DATA PHASES provided by the PAR signal line is computed from the AD[31::00] and C/BE#[3::0] signal lines in the previous CLK signal line period. For write transactions, the parity of the ATTRIBUTE and DATA PHASES provided by the PAR64 signal line is computed from the AD[63::32] and C/BE#[7::4] signal lines in the previous CLK signal line period.

491

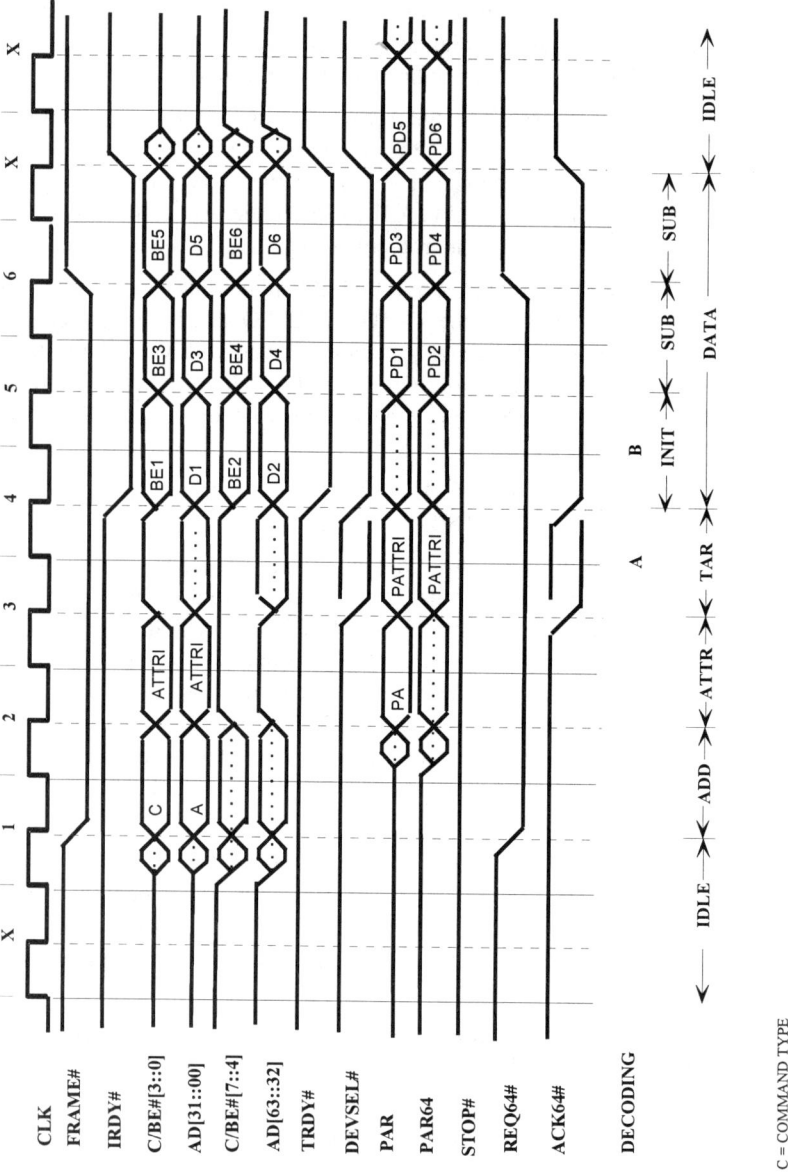

Figure 6-49: BURST Memory Write Command Executed with a PCI-X BURST Bus Transaction with Three Microaccesses (No Wait States) ... 64 Data Bit Transaction

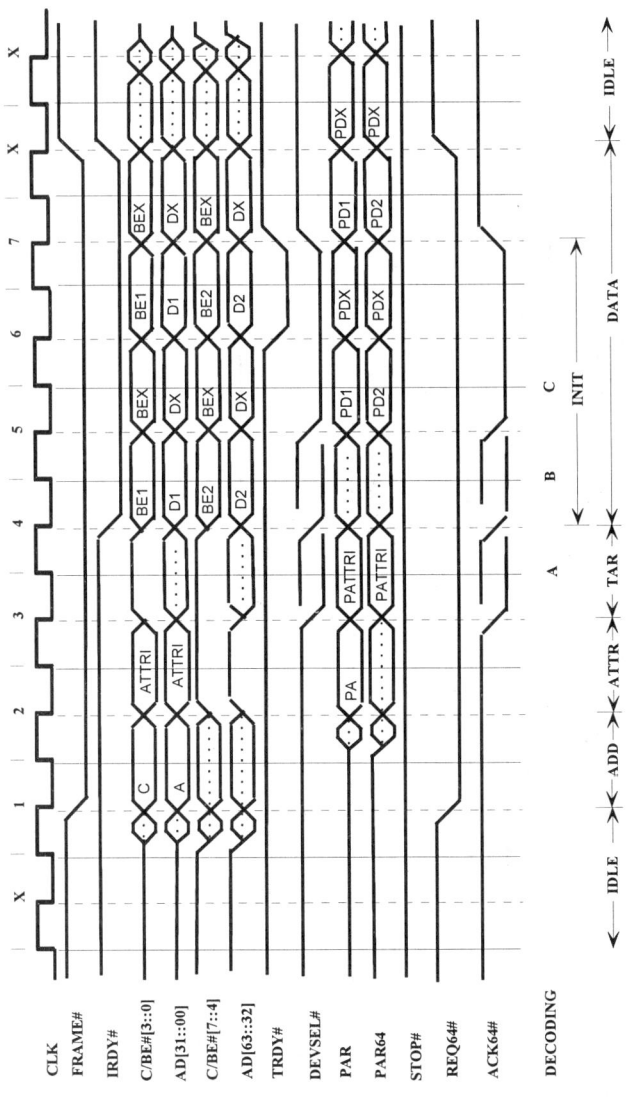

Figure 6-50: BURST Memory Write Command Executed with a PCI-X BURST Bus Transaction with One Microaccess (Two Wait States) ... 64 Data Bit Transaction

493

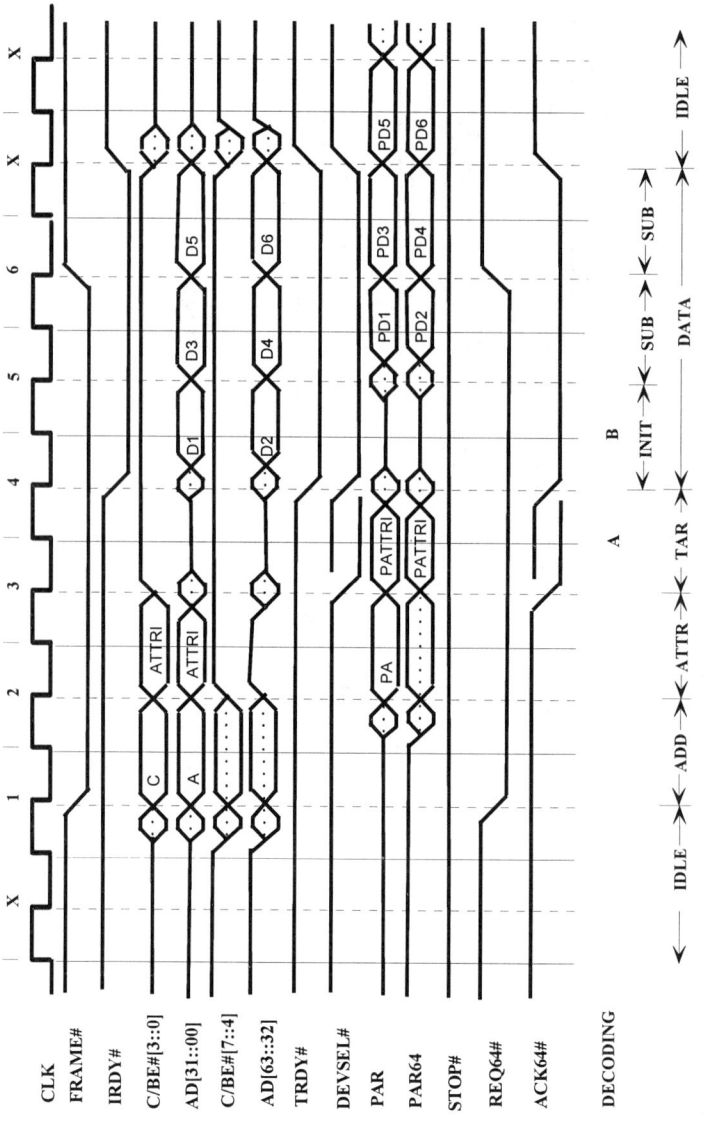

Figure 6-51: BURST Memory Read Command Executed with a PCI-X BURST Bus Transaction with Three Microaccesses (No Wait States) ... 64 Data Bit Transaction

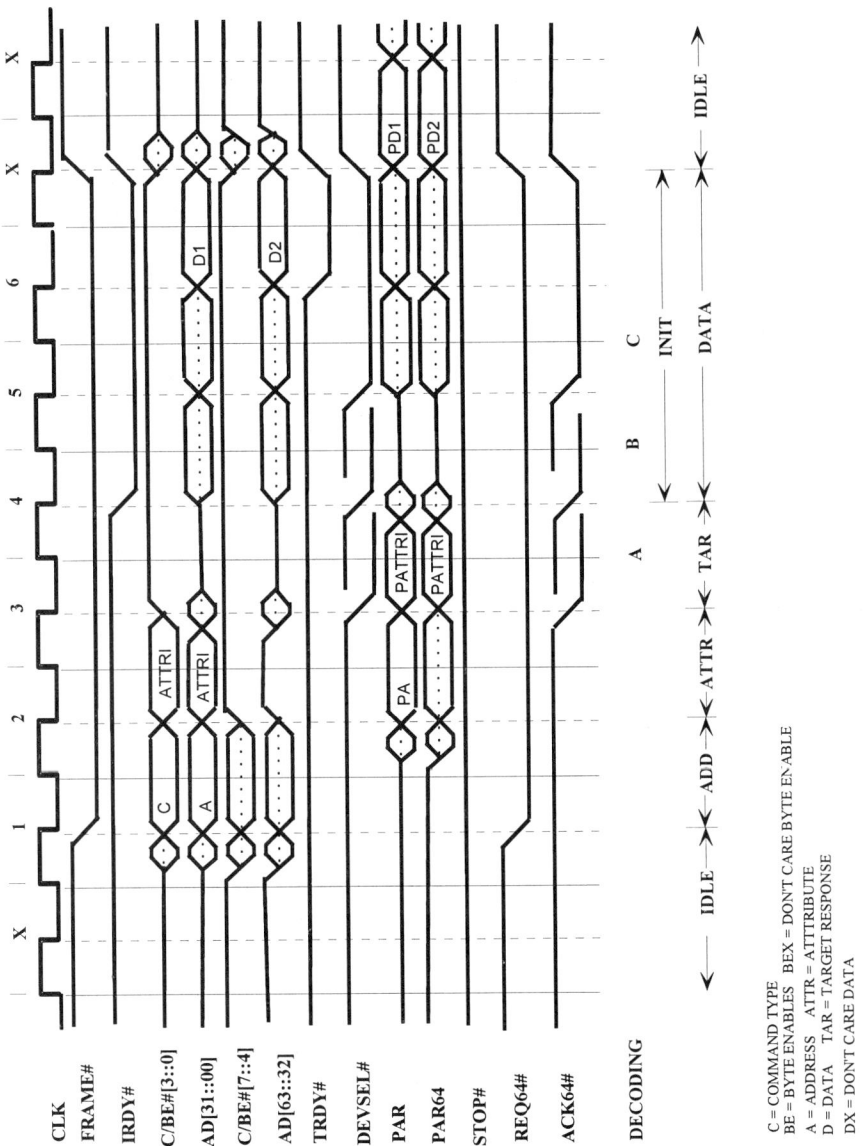

Figure 6-52: BURST Memory Read Command Executed with a PCI-X BURST Bus Transaction with One Microaccess (Two Wait States) ... 64 Data Bit Transaction

■ As previously discussed, for read transactions the parity of the ADDRESS, ATTRIBUTE, and DATA PHASES provided by the PAR signal line is computed from the AD[31::00] and C/BE#[3::0] signal lines in the previous CLK signal line period. For read transactions, the parity in the ATTRIBUTE PHASE is provided by the PAR64 signal line is computed from the AD[63::32] and C/BE#[7::4] signal lines in the previous CLK signal line period. The parity in the DATA PHASE is provided by the PAR64 signal line, which is computed from the AD[63::32] signal lines in the previous CLK signal line period and the C/BE#[7::4] signal lines in the second previous CLK signal line period.

■ For memory write transactions, the PAR64 signal line related to the TARGET RESPONSE PHASE is driven to a stable level or tre-stated. For memory read transactions, the exchange of ownership of the PAR64 signal line occurs in the TARGET RESPONSE PHASE.

The determination of a 64 data bit bus transaction is done on a transaction to transaction basis and is the same as that of a PCI bus transaction. The AD[63::32], C/BE[7::4], and PAR64 signal lines are driven to a logical "1" by pull-up resistors when not driven by the PCI-X bus master of the target. See Subchapters 6.6 and 6.12 for more information.

> **See Subchapter 6.0 for more information about signal lines "driven to a stable level" versus "tri-stating".**

Table 6-2 indicates that the data provided for a BURST memory write or a BURST split completion transaction in the AD[63::32] and AD [31::00] signal lines will differ for an ODD WORD versus an EVEN WORD starting address. The PCI-X bus master does not know if the ACK64# signal line will be deasserted when the DEVSEL# signal line is asserted (the configuration address space does provide information as to which targets are 64 data bits in size, but for the purposes of a bus transaction protocol this information is ignored). For BURST memory write or BURST split completion transactions, the Data N Hi is driven onto both the AD[63::32] and AD[31::00] signal lines in the initial microaccess for an ODD WORD address in case the target is a 32 data bit target. Once it has been established that the target has 64 data bits, the bus transaction proceeds forward in the first subsequent microaccess with the data naturally aligned to QUAD WORD address boundaries.

Table 6-3 indicates the data provided for a BURST memory read transaction in the AD[63::32] and AD [31::00] signal lines will not differ for an ODD WORD versus an EVEN WORD starting address. This is obviously due to the nature of a read transaction where the target has been established as using 64 data bits when the data transfer actually begins.

As previously discussed, the actual data associated bytes below the starting address within the QUAD WORD address boundary of BURST memory write transactions will be not be part of the transfer and the associated C/BE# signal lines are deasserted (*i.e.*, associated data is not written). For a BURST split completion transaction, the actual data associated with bytes within the QUAD WORD address boundary below the starting address will be transferred but discarded by the target. For a BURST read transaction, the actual data associated with bytes within the QUAD WORD address boundary below the starting address will be read but discarded by the PCI-X bus master.

Microaccess	ODD DWORD Starting Address		EVEN DWORD Starting Address	
	AD[63::32]	AD[31::00]	AD[63::32]	AD[31::00]
Initial	Data N Hi	Data N Hi	Data N Hi	Data N Lo
First Subsequent	Data N+1 Hi	Data N+1 Lo	Data N+1 Hi	Data N+1 Lo
Second Subsequent	Data N+2 Hi	Data N+2 Lo	Data N+2 Hi	Data N+2 Lo
Third Subsequent	Data N+3 Hi	Data N+3 Lo	Data N+3 Hi	Data N+3 Lo
Fourth Subsequent	Data N+4 Hi	Data N+4 Lo	Data N+4 Hi	Data N+4 Lo
Fifth Subsequent	Data N+5 Hi	Data N+5 Lo	Data N+5 Hi	Data N+5 Lo

Table 6-2: PCI-X BURST Memory Write or Split Completion Transactions 64 Data Bit PCI-X Bus Master to 64 Data Bit Targets

Microaccess	ODD DWORD Starting Address		EVEN DWORD Starting Address	
	AD[63::32]	AD[31::00]	AD[63::32]	AD[31::00]
Initial	Data N Hi	Data N Lo	Data N Hi	Data N Lo
First Subsequent	Data N+1 Hi	Data N+1 Lo	Data N+1 Hi	Data N+1 Lo
Second Subsequent	Data N+2 Hi	Data N+2 Lo	Data N+2 Hi	Data N+2 Lo
Third Subsequent	Data N+3 Hi	Data N+3 Lo	Data N+3 Hi	Data N+3 Lo
Fourth Subsequent	Data N+4 Hi	Data N+4 Lo	Data N+4 Hi	Data N+4 Lo
Fifth Subsequent	Data N+5 Hi	Data N+5 Lo	Data N+5 Hi	Data N+5 Lo

Table 6-3: PCI-X BURST Memory Read Transactions 64 Data Bit PCI-X Bus Master to 64 Data Bit Targets

DWORD, I/O, CONFIGURATION, INTERRUPT ACKNOWLEDGE, AND SPECIAL TRANSACTIONS

The DWORD, I/O, configuration, interrupt acknowledge, and special transactions are executed only with 32 data bit resources. The deassertion of the ACK64# signal line makes the target always appear as a 32 data bit resource.

SPLIT COMPLETION TRANSACTIONS

The protocol for a PCI-X bus master executing a 64 data bit PCI-X split completion transaction to a 64 data bit target is the same as for a PCI-X bus master executing 64 data bit PCI-X memory write transaction to a 64 data bit target. The only difference is that the C/BE#[7::0] signal lines are driven to a logical "1" by the PCI-X bus master during the DATA PHASE.

6.18   MORE DETAILS OF PCI-X SIGNAL LINE PROTOCOL FOR 64 DATA BIT BUS TRANSACTIONS

Subchapter 6.15 outlines the ownership of the signal lines during a bus transaction. Subchapter 6.17 outlined the bus transaction protocol when both the PCI-X bus master and target are 64 data bits in size. Chapter 8: *Master and Target Termination* details the change of signal line ownership and signal line driving and tri-stating when Completion, Completion with Timeout, Retry, Split Response, Single Phase Disconnect, Disconnect at Next ADB, Master Abort, or Target Abort terminations are executed. Chapter 9: *Bus Segment Ownership* explains the change of signal line ownership and signal line driving and tri-stating between changes of bus ownership. Chapter 10: *Parity and Bus Errors* covers the signal line ownership and signal line driving and tri-stating of the SERR# and PERR# signal lines. This subchapter defines the signal line protocol for the other signal lines during the bus transaction and between bus transactions when the PCI-X bus master retains bus ownership is as follows:

> In the following discussion, the terms *drive or tri-state* are different from *assert or deassert*. The former identifies when the signal line buffers are enabled or disabled. The latter reflects when signal lines change their logical state.

- All of the signal lines used by a 32 data bit PCI-X bus master that are used by a 64 data bit PCI-X bus master with the same protocol have been previously outlined in Subchapter 6.12 and 6.13.

- The protocol for the signal lines associated with the 64 data bit extension in 64 data bit bus transactions is the same as the signal lines for 32 data bit transactions, and were discussed in Subchapter 6.17. Also, some additional protocol requirements for a 64 data bit PCI-X bus master accessing a 32 data bit target are discussed in Subchapter 6.19. Additionally, if the PCI-X bus master can retain bus segment ownership between bus transactions it can optionally drive the C/BE#[7::4],

498

AD[63::32], and PAR64 signal lines to a stable level or tri-state them. If it tri-states these signal lines between bus transactions it will tri-state according to the end of a bus transaction protocol.

■ For all bus transactions, the protocol discussed in Subchapters 6.12 and 6.13 for AD[31::00], C/BE#[3::0], PAR64 signal lines also applies to AD[63::32], C/BE#[7::4], and PAR64 signal lines, respectively (with some exceptions with DUAL ADDRESS). Any differences are summarized in Subchapters 6.17 and 6.19.

■ The REQ64# signal line is driven, tri-stated, asserted, and deasserted by the PCI-X bus master during the bus transaction with the same protocol as the FRAME# signal line.

■ The ACK64# signal line is driven, tristated, asserted, and deasserted by the target during the bus transaction with the same protocol as the DEVSEL# signal line.

■ If tri-stated, the AD[63::32], C/BE#[7::4], and PAR64 signal lines are driven to a logical "1" by pull-up resistors.

6.19   64 DATA BIT PCI-X BUS MASTER TO 32 DATA BIT TARGET

MEMORY TRANSACTIONS

The bus transaction protocol for a 64 data bit PCI-X bus master accessing a 32 data bit target is similar to a 64 data bit PCI bus master accessing a 32 data bit target as discussed in Subchapter 6.8. Also, the bus transaction protocol for a 64 data bit PCI-X bus master accessing a 32 data bit target is similar to a 64 data bit PCI-X bus master accessing a 64 data bit target as discussed in Subchapters 6.17 and 6.18 (refer to Figures 6-53 and 6-56 during the following discussion). The key elements and differences are as follows:

In the following discussion, the activity of the PAR and PAR64 signal lines are referenced to the ADDRESS, ATTRIBUTE, TARGET RESPONSE, and DATA PHASES. In actuality, the PAR and PAR64 signal lines are delayed by one CLK signal line period; consequently, they do not exactly align with these PHASES as implied.

■ The access of a 64 data bit PCI-X bus master to a 32 data bit target without the DUAL ADDRESS command is the same as with the DUAL ADDRESS command. See Subchapter 6.17 for more information.

- The REQ64# signal line is driven, tri-stated, asserted, and deasserted by the PCI-X bus master during the bus transaction with the same protocol as the FRAME# signal line.

- The ACK64# signal line remains deasserted (driven to logical "1" by pull-up resistors) throughout the bus transaction.

- The PCI-X bus master drives the AD[63::32], C/BE#[7::4], and PAR64 signal lines during the ADDRESS, ATTRIBUTE, and TARGET RESPONSE PHASES with the same protocol as discussed in Subchapter 6.17 for 64 data bit bus transactions.

- For the DATA PHASE of write transactions prior to the assertion of the DEVSEL# signal line (*i.e.*, the ACK64# signal line is sample deasserted), the AD[63::32] and C/BE#[7::4] signal lines are driven by the PCI-X bus master with valid information. For these signal lines, the PAR64 signal line is driven by the PCI-X bus master with valid parity. Note: For a bus transaction for a BURST memory write command, valid information on the C/BE#[7:4] signal lines is the byte enable information. For a bus transaction for a BURST memory write block or alias memory write block command, valid information on the C/BE#[7:4] signal line is logical "1".

- For the DATA PHASE of write transactions, the PCI-X bus master samples the ACK64# signal line deasserted when the DEVSEL# signal line is first sampled asserted. The AD[63::32], C/BE#[7::4], and PAR64 signal lines will be driven by the PCI-X bus master to a stable level or tri-stated two CLK signal line periods after the assertion of the DEVSEL# signal line (if tri-stated, these signal lines are driven to logical "1" by pull-up resistors) (see Figures 6-53 and 6-54).

- For the DATA PHASE of read transactions prior and after the assertion of the DEVSEL# signal line (*i.e.*, the ACK64# signal line is sample deasserted), the AD[63::32] and PAR64 signal lines are tri-stated and driven to logical "1" by the pull-up resistors (see Figures 6-55 and 6-56).

- For the DATA PHASE of read transactions, the PCI-X bus master samples the ACK64# signal line deasserted when the DEVSEL# signal line is first sampled asserted. The C/BE#[7::4] signal lines will be driven by the PCI-X bus master to a stable level or tri-stated two CLK signal line periods after the assertion of the DEVSEL# signal line (if tri-stated, these signal lines are driven to logical "1" by pull-up resistors) (see Figures 6-55 and 6-56).

> **See subchapter 6.0 for more information about signal lines "driven to a stable level" versus "tri-stating".**

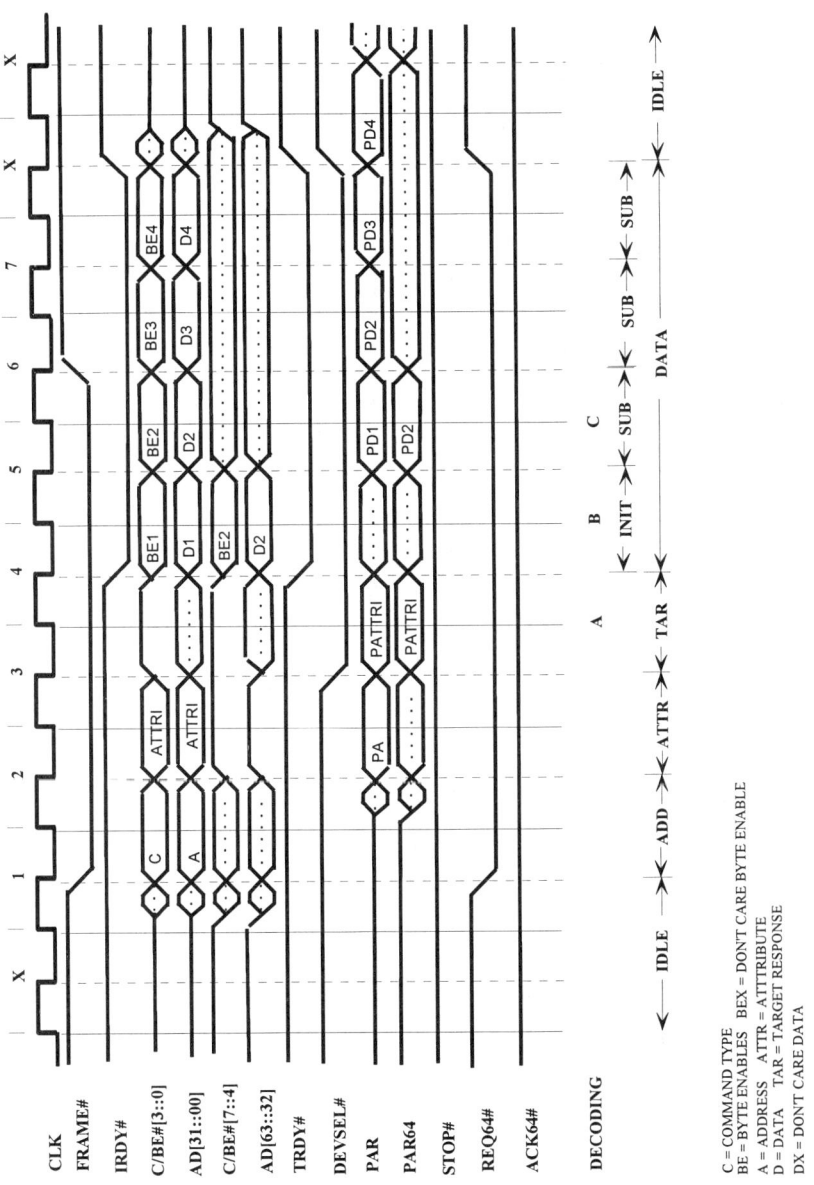

Figure 6-53: BURST Memory Write Command Executed with a PCI-X BURST Bus Transaction with Four Microaccesses (No Wait States) ... 64 Data Bit Transaction Requested by PCI-X Bus Master and Target Supports Only 32 Data Bits

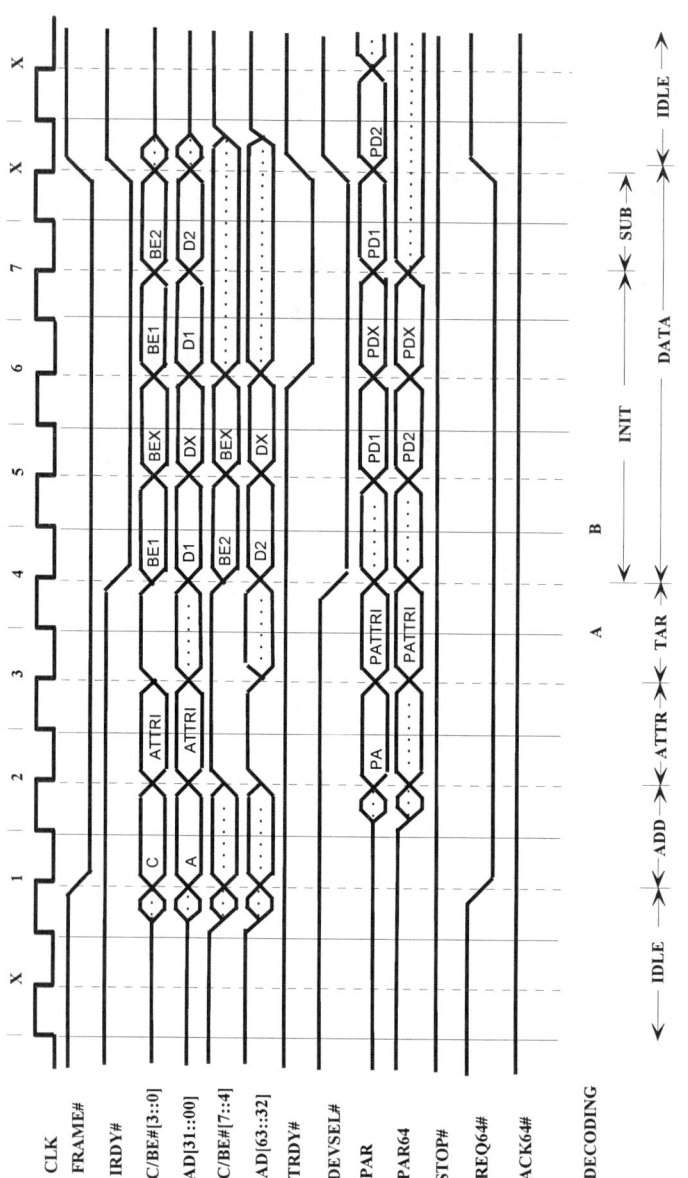

Figure 6-54: BURST Memory Write Command Executed with a PCI-X BURST Bus Transaction with Two Microaccesses (Two Wait States) … 64 Data Bit Transaction Requested by PCI-X Bus Master and Target Supports Only 32 Data Bits

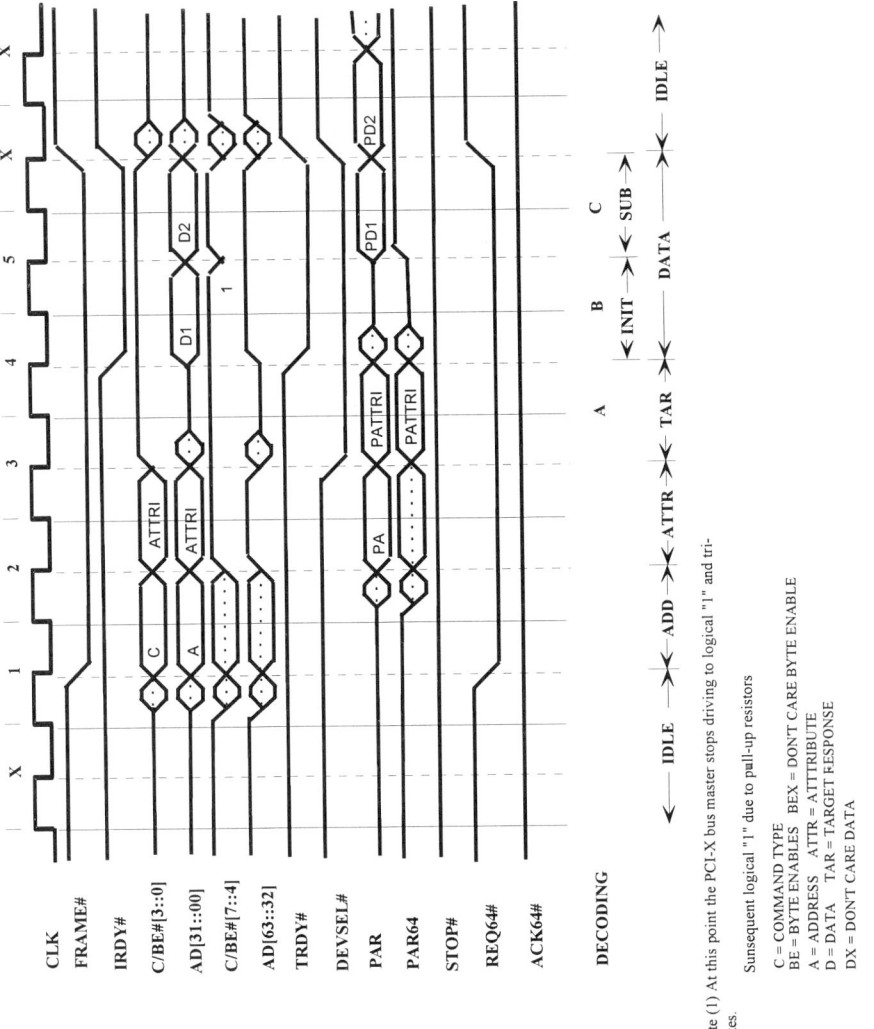

Figure 6-55: BURST Memory Read Command Executed with a PCI-X BURST Bus Transaction with Four Microaccesses (No Wait States) ... 64 Data Bit Transaction Requested by PCI-X Bus Master and Target Supports Only 32 Data Bits

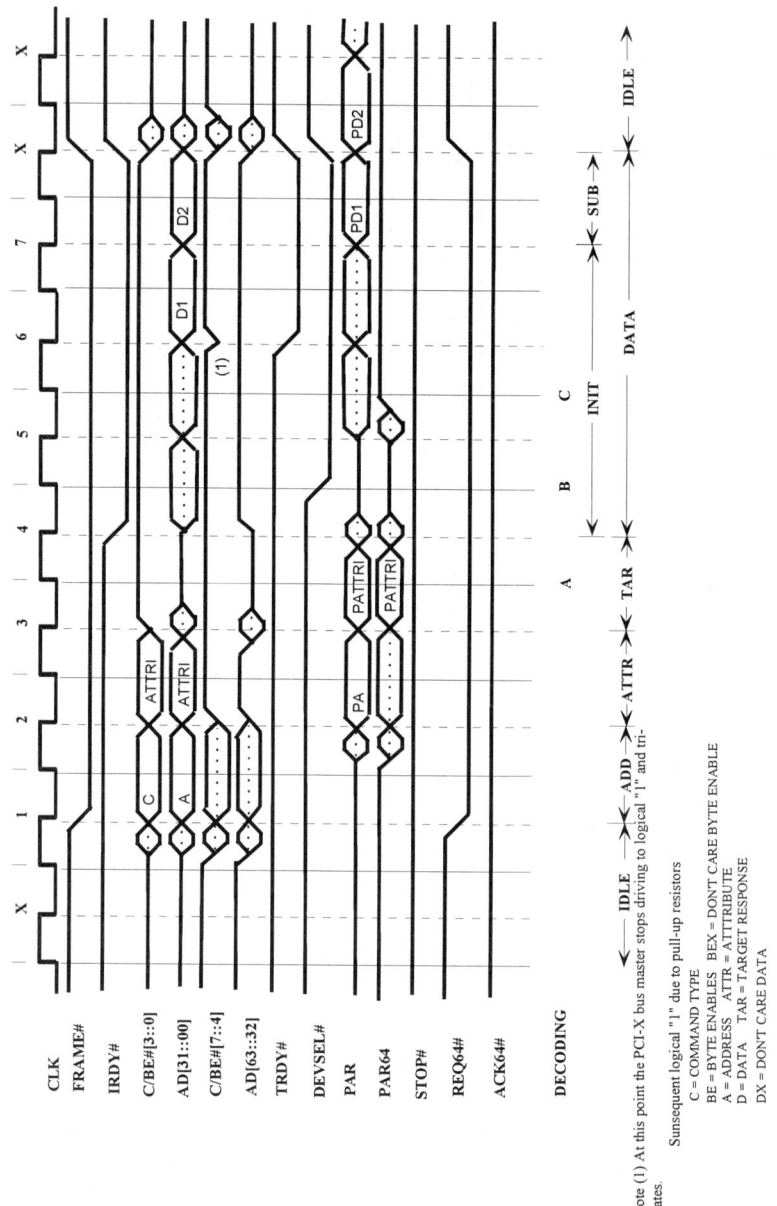

Figure 6-56: BURST Memory Read Command Executed with a PCI-X BURST Bus Transaction with Two Microaccesses (Two Wait States) ... 64 Data Bit Transaction Requested by PCI-X Bus Master and Target Supports Only 32 Data Bits

There are special considerations relating to the starting address of BURST memory read and write transactions. The sequence of data written or read is not always sequential address increasing. See Subchapter 6.20 for more information.

The access of a 64 data bit PCI-X bus master to a 32 data bit target with the DUAL ADDRESS command is same as discussed above for a bus transaction without the DUAL ADDRESS command. The only difference is the information driven onto the AD[63::32], C/BE#[7::4], and PAR64 signal lines by the PCI-X bus master for the DUAL ADDRESS command as discussed in Subchapter 6-15.

DWORD, I/O, CONFIGURATION, INTERRUPT ACKNOWLEDGE TRANSACTIONS, AND SPECIAL TRANSACTIONS

These bus transactions are not defined for 64 data bit transactions and must be executed as 32 data bit transactions. If the REQ64# or ACK64# signal lines are asserted during one of these transactions, they are ignored.

SPLIT COMPLETION TRANSACTIONS

The split completion transaction for a 64 data bit PCI-X bus master accessing a 32 data bit target is the same as discussed above for memory write transactions, with a few differences as outlined below. All of the other bus transactions for a 32 data bit split completion transaction applies.

- The C/BE#[7::4] signal lines are driven to logical "1" during the DATA PHASE.

- The DUAL ADDRESS command is not execute with split completion transactions.

There are special considerations regarding the starting address of BURST split completion transactions. The sequence of data written is not always sequential address increasing. See Subchapter 6.20 for more information.

6.20 SPECIAL CONSIDERATIONS FOR A 64 DATA BIT PCI-X BUS MASTER TO A 32 DATA BIT TARGET

The PCI local bus specification requires special consideration for 64 data bit PCI bus masters accessing 32 data bit targets (See Subchapter 6.9). As previously discussed, the following only applies to bus transactions for BURST memory and split completion commands. The key considerations are:

- When a PCI bus master begins 64 data bit bus transaction, it is required to convert to a 32 data bit bus transaction if the ACK64# signal line is sampled deasserted when the DEVSEL# signal line is asserted. The only exception is when the target executes a Disconnect with or without data termination on the initial microaccess. The PCI bus master proceeds with completion with the initial microaccess. According to the PCI-X addendum specification, the same situation requires the PCI-X bus master to convert to a 32 data bit bus transaction. The target may execute a target termination for some other reason, but a 32 data bit target does not execute a target termination when the PCI-X bus master begins the bus transaction as 64 data bits.

- When a PCI bus master begins a 64 data bit SINGLE bus transaction, it can't deassert the FRAME# signal line (to indicate a SINGLE transaction) until the DEVSEL# signal line is sampled asserted in order to determine if the ACK64# signal line is deasserted (for a 32 data bit bus transaction) or asserted (for a 64 data bit bus transaction). As previously discussed, this causes a very long bus transaction. According to the PCI-X addendum specification, the execution of BURST memory or split completion commands does not determine implementation by SINGLE versus BURST bus transactions. The byte count identified in ATTRIBUTE PHASE establishes if a SINGLE versus BURST bus transactions is implemented. The subsequent sampling of the ACK64# signal line asserted when the DEVSEL# signal line is asserted will modify a 64 data bit SINGLE into a 32 data bit BURST bus transaction.

One of the considerations for bus transactions that begin as a 64 data bit bus transaction is the starting address. Also as previously stated, for BURST bus transactions the address sequence is linear increasing. The starting address is provided in the ATTRIBUTE PHASE and is defined as N in Tables 6-4 and 6-5. N is defined on naturally aligned QUAD WORD address boundaries. Within each QUAD WORD is data associated with an ODD WORD address and an EVEN WORD address. In the following discussion, the PCI-X bus master defines the upper order bits ("Hi") in the QUAD WORD (64 data bits) normally associated with AD[63::32] signal lines in a 64 data bit bus transaction as the data associated with the EVEN WORD address. Similarly, the PCI-X bus master defines the lower order bits ("Lo") in the QUAD WORD (64 data bits) normally associated with AD[31::00] signal lines in a 64 data bit bus transaction as the ODD WORD address.

Table 6-4 indicates that the data provided for a BURST memory write or a BURST split completion transaction in the AD[63::32] and AD [31::00] signal lines will differ for an ODD WORD versus an EVEN WORD starting address. The PCI-X bus master does not know if the ACK64# signal line will be deasserted when the DEVSEL# signal line is asserted (the configuration address space does provide information as to which targets are 64 data bits in size, but for the purposes of a bus transaction protocol this information is ignored). For BURST memory write or BURST split completion transactions the Data N Hi is driven onto both the AD[63::32] and AD[31::00] signal lines in the initial microaccess for an ODD WORD address in case the target is 64 data bits. Once it has been established that the target is 32 data bits, the bus transaction proceeds forward in the first subsequent microaccess by transferring the all of the data on the AD[31::0] signal lines and driving the AD[63::32] signal lines a stable level or tri-stating them.

Table 6-5 indicates the data provided for a BURST memory read transaction in the AD[63::32] and AD [31::00] signal lines will not differ for an ODD WORD versus an EVEN WORD starting address. This is obviously due to the nature of a read transaction where the target has been established as 32 data bits when the data transfer actually begins.

As previously discussed, the actual data associated bytes below the starting address within the QUAD WORD address boundary of BURST memory write transactions will not be part of the transfer and the associated C/BE# signal lines deasserted (*i.e.*, associated data is not written). For a BURST split completion transaction the actual data associated bytes within the QUAD WORD address boundary below the starting address will be transferred but discarded by the target. For a BURST read transaction the actual data associated bytes within the QUAD WORD address boundary below the starting address will be read but discarded by the PCI-X bus master.

Also note as previously discussed, if the AD[63::32], C/BE[7::4], or PAR64 signal lines are tri-stated they will be driven to logical "1" by pull-up resistors.

Microaccess	ODD DWORD Starting Address		EVEN DWORD Starting Address	
	AD[63::32]	AD[31::00]	AD[63::32]	AD[31::00]
Initial	Data N Hi	Data N Hi	Data N Hi	Data N Lo
First Subsequent	Stable or Float	Data N+1 Lo	Stable or Float	Data N Hi
Second Subsequent	Stable or Float	Data N+1 Hi	Stable or Float	Data N+1 Lo
Third Subsequent	Stable or Float	Data N+2 Lo	Stable or Float	Data N+1 Hi
Fourth Subsequent	Stable or Float	Data N+2 Hi	Stable or Float	Data N+2 Lo
Fifth Subsequent	Stable or Float	Data N+3 Lo	Stable or Float	Data N+2 Hi

**Table 6-4: PCI-X BURST Memory Write or Split Completion Transactions
64 Data Bit PCI-X Bus Master to 32 Data Bit Targets**

Microaccess	ODD DWORD Starting Address		EVEN DWORD Starting Address	
	AD[63::32]	AD[31::00]	AD[63::32]	AD[31::00]
Initial	Float	Data N Hi	Float	Data N Lo
First Subsequent	Float	Data N+1 Lo	Float	Data N Hi
Second Subsequent	Float	Data N+1 Hi	Float	Data N+1 Lo
Third Subsequent	Float	Data N+2 Lo	Float	Data N+1 Hi
Fourth Subsequent	Float	Data N+2 Hi	Float	Data N+2 Lo
Fifth Subsequent	Float	Data N+3 Lo	Float	Data N+2 Hi

**Table 6-5: PCI-X BURST Memory Read Transactions
64 Data Bit PCI-X Bus Master to 32 Data Bit Targets**

6.21 PCI-X TRANSACTION-TO-TRANSACTION OPERATION

As previously discussed, the PCI local bus specification defines a minimum number of CLK signal line periods (defined as the IDLE PHASE) between bus transactions. The default minimum number of CLK signal line periods between bus transactions is two. Under the Fast Back to Back protocol, the number of CLK signal lines is defined as one. See Subchapter 6.10 for more information

Also as previously discussed, the PCI-X addendum specification does not support the Fast Back to Back protocol. However, as discussed in Subchapter 6.12 the minimum number of CLK signal line periods between two bus transactions is either one or two. The minimum number of CLK signal line periods is dependent on the number of actual microaccesses in the previous bus transaction. See Subchapter 6.12 for more information.

6.22 PCI-X MESSAGE SIGNALED INTERRUPT PROTOCOL

The PCI-X addendum specification implementation of Message Signaled Interrupt (MSI) is essentially the same as for the PCI local bus specification. See Subchapter 6.11 for more information. The items of particular note relative to PCI-X are as follows:

- MSI can only be implemented with BURST memory write transactions (which include memory write, memory write block, and alias memory write block).

- Only the SINGLE bus transaction version of BURST memory write commands can be use for MSI.

- Only 32 data bit bus transactions are defined for MSI.

- PCI-X devices that can generate an MSI are required to support a 64 data bit message address.

- PCI-X devices that require interrupt support and that do not support MSI are required to implement the INTx# signal lines.

- Software must assume that a PCI-X device that supports MSI does not have a connection to the INTx# signal lines.

- A PCI-X device that is supported by software polling is permitted to optionally implement MSI to improve performance.

- The NO Snoop and Relaxed Ordering bits in the ATTRIBUTE PHASE of the bus transaction are required to be set to logical "0".

- The completion of a SINGLE BURST memory transaction can only be by normal Completion (without Timeout); or by Retry, Single Phase Disconnect, Master Abort, or Target Abort terminations.

CHAPTER 7

BRIDGE AND INTERFACE PROTOCOL

This chapter consists of the following subchapters:

In the PCI/PCI BRIDGE, the Prefetchable Memory Base Address and Prefetchable Memory Limit registers (both are optional) are stored in the configuration address space. Also, there are the Prefetchable Base Upper 32 Bits register and Prefetchable Limit Upper 32 Bits register for 32 bit addressing. These registers define memory space address ranges that are prefetchable. See the PCI-to-PCI Bridge Architecture Specification Rev 1.1 for more information.

If a prefetchable memory address space or memory mapped I/O (essentially any memory that is not prefetchable) is not defined for the lower LEVEL bus by the Memory Space Enable bit set to logical "1" in the COMMAND register in the configuration address space, the PCI/PCI BRIDGE will not port any memory transactions from the upper LEVEL bus segment to the lower LEVEL bus segment. It will only port memory transaction from the lower LEVEL bus segment to the upper LEVEL bus segment

7.0   INTRODUCTION

The purpose of this chapter is not to replace the PCI/PCI BRIDGE or PCI-X/PCI-X BRIDGE information of the PCI-to-PCI Bridge Architecture Specification or the PCI-X Addendum Bus Specification. The purpose is to give insight on how bus transactions will propagate between bus segments. Also, it is to discuss key architectural issues for the design of interface circuitry in an ASIC (between a bus segment and internal circuitry), which essentially is a type of bridge. This provides the designer of PCI and PCI-X devices the appropriate information for compliance and performance. It does not provide the fully functional bridge designer all of the information required.

The operation of fully functional bridges between bus segments (not interface circuitry in an ASIC) is very complex and in many ways unique to the exact implementation by the various bridge chip vendors. Similarly, the operation of HOST/PCI, HOST/PCI-X, PCI/LEGACY, and PCI-X/LEGACY BRIDGES is very complex and in many ways unique to the exact implementation by the various chip set vendors.

Consequently, for the very detailed information about bridge operation please refer to the aforementioned standards specifications and the specifications of the bridge chip and chip set vendors.

The PCI local bus specification defines a bus protocol that is unique relative to other earlier buses, in that individual PCI bus segments are connected by bridges and can operate independently. The protocol of porting a bus transaction from one PCI bus segment to another through a bridge has several considerations. First, a bus transaction begun on one PCI bus segment (defined as "source bus segment") may have to wait to continue on another PCI bus segment (defined as "destination bus segment"). This wait may be due to full FIFOs or buffers in bridges, or other

PCI bus masters executing bus transactions on the destination bus segment. Second, once a bus transaction begun on a PCI bus segment continues on another PCI bus segment, there may be a requirement to port the PCI bus transactions through multiple bridges and PCI bus segments. Third, PCI bus protocol permits PCI bus masters to exist on any PCI bus segment; consequently, PCI bus transactions between bus segments can be ported simultaneously in opposite directions through the bridge(s). Similarly, a bridge can be porting multiple transactions from one or multiple PCI bus masters in the same or different directions. These considerations define the transaction ordering in a bridge, Delayed Transactions, and other bridge PCI bus transaction porting operations.

As previously stated many times in this book, a specific PCI to PCI (PCI/PCI) BRIDGE can operate as both a PCI bus master on one PCI bus segment (destination bus segment) and as a target (source bus segment). The HOST/PCI BRIDGE and PCI/LEGACY BRIDGEs operate as a PCI/PCI BRIDGE on the PCI side of the bridge but not on the opposite side. There is no requirement that the HOST and LEGACY side of these bridges operate as a PCI bus segment. However, the only safe implementation to prevent PCI related deadlocks and data errors within a PCI based platform is to operate all bridges according to the PCI/PCI BRIDGE protocol.

Also, the interface circuitry in an ASIC between the PCI bus segment and the ASIC circuitry is essentially a bridge. The ASIC circuitry behind interface circuitry can be viewed simply as another PCI bus segment with resources. For the same reasons outlined above for HOST/PCI and PCI/LEGACY BRIDGEs, the operation of the interface circuitry within ASICs should follow the PCI/PCI BRIDGE protocol to prevent PCI related deadlocks and data errors within a PCI based system

> Given the above considerations, the balance of this chapter defines the interaction of PCI bus segments relative to PCI/PCI BRIDGES. Collectively, interface circuitry in ASICs, HOST/PCI BRIDGES, and PCI/LEGACY BRIDGES will be represented by the PCI/PCI BRIDGES in this chapter. The operational principles of the PCI/PCI BRIDGES as discussed below can be applied to all of the interfaces in the ASICs and the other types of bridges unless otherwise noted.

> Similarly, on a PCI bus segment, the PCI resources that are being accessed include bridges, targets, and (via interface circuitry in ASICs) standalone PCI bus masters (for configuration address space). These will be collectively called "devices" in this chapter.

A PCI/PCI BRIDGE between two PCI bus segments *must* support the following:

- DC to 33 MHz operation
- PCI 8 and PCI 16 clock rules
- Configuration address space internal to the bridge
- Porting of configuration transaction between bus segments
- Memory mapped I/O address space
- Posting of all memory write transactions
- Delayed Transaction protocol for all non-memory write transactions
- Support of DAC (DUAL ADDRESS COMMAND) porting upstream
- Downstream Exclusive Hardware Access
- Bus Transaction Ordering

A PCI/PCI BRIDGE between two PCI bus segments *may also* support the following:

- 66 MHz operation
- I/O address space
- Prefetchable memory address space
- VGA addressing
- VGA color palette snooping
- 64 address bits on the side of the bridge attached to the upper LEVEL bus segment
- 64 data bits
- JTAG
- Arbitration support for lower LEVEL bus segment
- Expansion ROM
- Subtractive Decoding
- Support of DAC porting downstream

A PCI/PCI BRIDGE between two PCI bus segments *does not* support the following:

- Side band signals to port side band related operations from one bus segment to another

The PCI-X addendum specification also has a bus protocol that is unique relative to other earlier buses in that individual PCI-X bus segments are connected by PCI-X/PCI-X BRIDGES and can operate independently. The protocol of porting a bus transaction from one PCI-X bus segment to another through a bridge has the same required, optional, and not supported considerations as discussed above for a PCI/PCI BRIDGES. The only differences for PCI-X/PCI-X BRIDGES are as follows:

■ 66 MHz operation required, 66 MHz plus to 133.2 MHz operation optional.

■ The Delayed Transaction protocol defined for PCI bus transactions porting through bridges has been replaced for PCI-X bus transactions porting through bridges with the Split Transaction protocol.

■ DAC support in both upstream and downstream directions requires 64 address bits on both upper and lower LEVEL bus segment sides of the bridge.

■ A PCI-X bus segment can operate with both PCI and PCI-X bus transaction protocols. Consequently, a system can consist of all PCI bus segments (following the PCI local bus specification), all PCI-X bus segments (following the PCI-X addendum specification), or a combination of PCI and PCI-X bus segments (either pure PCI bus segments or PCI-X bus segments operating with PCI bus transactions). The PCI-X addendum specification defines PCI/PCI-X BRIDGEs (source/destination) and PCI-X/PCI BRDIGEs (source/destination). Not all elements of the PCI bus transaction protocol on a bus segment can be mapped to the PCI-X bus transaction protocol on another bus segment through a bridge and vice versa. Consequently, the bridge between a bus segment operating with PCI bus transactions and a bus segment operating with PCI-X bus transactions is more complex. This particular type of bridge (PCI/PCI-X BRIDGE and PCI-X/PCI BRIDGE) is required to convert between the two bus transaction protocols. The conversion requirements will be discussed in detail later in this chapter.

As previously defined for PCI bus segments, the balance of this chapter defines the interaction of PCI-X bus segments relative to PCI-X/PCI-X BRIDGEs. Collectively, interface circuitry in ASICs, HOST/PCI-X BRIDGEs, and PCI/LEGACY BRIDGEs will be represented by the PCI-X/PCI-X BRIDGEs in this chapter. The operational principles of the PCI-X/PCI-X BRIDGEs as discussed below can be applied to all of the interfaces in the ASICs and the other types bridges unless otherwise noted.

Similarly, on a PCI-X bus segment, the PCI-X resources that are being accessed include bridges, targets, and (via interface circuitry in ASICs) standalone PCI-X bus masters (for configuration address space). These will be collectively called "devices" in this chapter.

Before covering interbus segment transactions (*i.e.*, porting through bridges) the next subchapter will discuss transaction ordering relative to the source and destination of the bus transactions.

7.1   SUMMARY OF BUS TRANSACTION ORDERING

The balance of this chapter will focus on bus transactions porting through bridges. Part of this porting includes ordering of bus transactions through bridges. There are also bus transaction ordering considerations outside of those associated with bridges, reflecting the requirements imposed upon the PCI or PCI-X bus master (source) and the target (destination). The PCI or PCI-X bus master does not "know" if the target resides on the same bus segment on the other side of a bridge. Similarly, the target does not "know" if the PCI or PCI-X bus master is on the same or different bus segment. In both situations, one or more bridges may or may not exist between the actual source and actual destination of a bus transaction. Consequently, prior to discussing bus transaction porting through bridges and the associated bus transaction ordering, this subchapter will review non-bridge ordering. In other words, prior to a bus transaction porting through a bridge, the PCI or PCI-X bus master as the source of the bus transaction is required to follow certain bus transaction ordering rules. Similarly, a target that is the destination of the bus transaction has certain bus transaction ordering considerations.

OVERVIEW OF PCI BUS TRANSACTION ORDERING PROTOCOL

In the following discussion, the focus will be on PCI bus masters (non-bridge) and targets (non-bridges). All of the concepts discussed also apply to PCI/PCI BRIDGES operating as a master or target on a bus segment. A bridge may be the destination of a bus transaction (Example: configuration transaction to the setup registers within the bridge) or the bridge may be porting a bus transaction (Example: posting of a memory write transaction that will be ported through the bridge to a target on the destination bus segment).

According to the PCI local bus specification, the bus transaction ordering protocol (herein in this chapter called "transaction ordering") for PCI bus masters and targets is as follows:

■   If the bus transaction order is important to a PCI bus master, it may not begin a bus transaction until all dependent bus transactions are completed without Retry termination. A Disconnect termination indicates that further

516

access of data in the target is not required and it is optional for the PCI bus master to continue the access at a later time. Consequently, the PCI bus master is required to determine if the beginning of another bus transaction is dependent on the completion of a bus transaction terminated with a Disconnect termination. A Completion, Completion with Timeout, Master Abort, or Target Abort termination indicates that the bus transaction is done.

■ PCI bus masters on the same or different PCI bus segments independently access targets on the same or different PCI bus segments. If a device supports multiple functions, the associated PCI bus master attribute of one function is independent of the PCI bus masters and targets attributes of other functions. Similarly, the target of one function is independent of the PCI bus masters and targets of other functions. If the device contains multiple PCI bus masters within a multiple function device, these PCI bus masters must maintain ordering internally and must appear as a single PCI bus master on the PCI bus segment.

■ If the same target is accessed by HOST CPU, LEGACY bus masters, or other PCI bus masters; they are required to use Exclusive Software Access if the order of completion of the bus transactions is important. As will be discussed with more detail in a subsequent subchapter, the use of the LOCK# signal for Exclusive Hardware Access to lock a target only applies to the HOST CPU or a PCI bus master on PCI bus (0) accessing a LEGACY bus memory target, or a LEGACY bus master accessing a HOST memory target (memory behind the HOST/PCI BRIDGE). Otherwise, the Exclusive Hardware Access is used to prevent deadlock situations in the PCI/PCI Bridges.

■ A target on a PCI bus segment can complete all bus transactions in any order unless an Exclusive Software Access is implemented. For example, the PCI bus master may have an order of bus transaction "A" followed by bus transaction "B". The target may first execute a Retry termination on bus transaction "A" and complete or target terminate bus transaction "B" (Completion, Completion with Timeout, Master Abort, Target Abort, or Disconnect termination). The target may also complete or target terminate bus transaction "A" and then complete bus transaction "B".

■ If a device (as a single function or an individual function in a multifunction resource) contains both PCI bus master and target attributes, and operates as a PCI master and target on the same PCI bus segment; the following protocol applies:

　■ The operation of the device as a target is required to be independent of its operation as a PCI bus master.

517

- The device as a target must accept memory write transactions independently of the prior completion of non-memory write transactions (Immediate or Delayed Transactions) by the device as a PCI bus master. That is, the device as a target is not allowed to return a Retry termination (see exceptions in the bullet below) for a memory write transaction because it wants to first execute or is waiting for completion of non-memory write bus transactions as PCI bus master.

- The device as a target must accept a memory write transaction independent of any pending memory write transactions by the device as a PCI bus master. That is, the device as a target is not allowed to return a Retry termination (see exceptions in the bullet below) for a memory write transaction because it wants to execute or is waiting for the completion memory write transactions as a PCI bus master.

- In general, the completion of a bus transaction to device as target cannot be dependent on the completion of another bus transaction as a PCI bus master. But, there are certain restrictions relative to a PCI/PCI BRIDGE and interface circuitry in an ASIC. See Subchapters 7.12: *Transaction Ordering through a Bridge* and 7.19: *Simple Devices* for more information.

- The operation of the device as a PCI bus master does not need to be independent of its operation as a target.

- The device as a PCI bus master must not affect the operation of its internal arbiter for multiple PCI bus masters by how full or empty the device's different Posted Memory Write Command FIFOS are.

- The exceptions that allow a device as a target to request a Retry termination for all memory write transactions (including MWI) are as follows:

  - The Posted Memory Write Command FIFO of the target is full.

  - Internal to the device, an operation is being executed that has a guaranteed completion within a reasonable amount of time.

  - The device as a PCI bus master is presently the Lock master and has thus locked a target prior to the receipt of a memory write transaction as a target.

  - The device is presently a locked target.

See Subchapter 7.19: *Simple Devices* for more information

518

OVERVIEW OF PCI-X BUS TRANSACTION ORDERING PROTOCOL

In the following discussion, the focus will be on PCI-X bus masters (non-bridge) and targets (non-bridges). All of the concepts discussed also apply to PCI-X/PCI-X BRIDGES operating as a master or target on a bus segment. A bridge may be the destination of the bus transaction (Example: configuration transaction to the setup registers within the bridge), or the bridge may be porting a bus transaction (Example: posting of a memory write transaction that will be ported through the bridge to a target on the destination bus segment).

The protocol for the PCI-X bus transaction ordering protocol (in this subchapter called "transaction ordering") is conceptually the same as that protocol outlined above for the PCI bus transaction ordering. The similarities, differences, and additions are as follows:

■ As with the PCI bus transaction protocol, if the bus transaction order is important to a PCI-X bus master, it is not allowed to begin a bus transaction until all dependent bus transactions are completed without Retry termination. A Disconnect at Next ADB or a Single Phase Disconnect termination indicates that further access of data in the target is not required and the PCI-X bus master may continue the access at a later time. Consequently, the PCI-X bus master must determine whether the beginning of another bus transaction is dependent on the completion of a bus transaction terminated with a Disconnect at Next ADB or a Single Phase Disconnect termination. A Completion, Completion with Timeout, Master Abort, or Target Abort termination indicates that the bus transaction is done.

  ■ If a specific "original" PCI-X bus master had its bus transaction terminated with a Split Response termination but it has not received the entire "sequence" of split completion transactions, it cannot begin another bus transaction if it is dependent on the completion (receipt of all associated data according to the Split Transaction protocol) of the aforementioned bus transaction terminated with a Split Response termination.

■ PCI-X bus masters on the same or different PCI bus segments independently access targets on the same or different PCI-X bus segments. If a device supports multiple functions, the associated PCI-X bus master attribute of one function is independent of the PCI-X bus masters and targets attributes of other functions. Similarly, the target of one function is independent of the PCI-X bus masters and targets of other functions. If the device contains multiple PCI-X bus masters within a multiple function device, these PCI-X bus masters must maintain ordering internally and appear as a single PCI-X bus master on the PCI-X bus segment.

■ If the same target is accessed by HOST CPU, LEGACY bus masters, or other PCI-X bus masters; they must use Exclusive Software Access if the order of completion of the bus transactions is important. As will be discussed with more details in a subsequent subchapter, the use of the LOCK# signal for Exclusive Hardware Access to lock a target only applies to the HOST CPU or a PCI-X bus master on PCI-X bus (0) accessing a LEGACY bus memory target, or a LEGACY bus master accessing a HOST memory target (memory behind the HOST/PCI-X BRIDGE).

■ A target on a PCI-X bus segment can complete all bus transactions accessing it in any order unless an Exclusive Software Access is implemented. For example, the PCI-X bus master may have an order of bus transaction "A" followed by bus transaction "B". The target may first execute a Retry termination on bus transaction "A" and complete or target terminate bus transaction "B" (Completion, Completion with Timeout, Master Abort, Target Abort, Disconnect at Next ADB, Split Response, or Single Phase Disconnect termination). The target may also complete or target terminate bus transaction "A" and then complete bus transaction "B".

■ If a device (as a single function or an individual function in a multifunction resource) contains both PCI-X bus master and target attributes, and operates as a PCI-X master and target on the same PCI-X bus segment; the following protocol applies:

   ■ The operation of the target must be independent of the operation of the PCI-X bus master.

   ■ The device as a target must accept memory write and split completion transactions independently of the prior completion of non-memory write or non-split completion transactions by the device as a PCI-X bus master. That is, the device as a target is not allowed to return a Retry termination (see exceptions in the bullet below) for memory write or split completion transactions because it wants to execute or is waiting for the completion of non-memory write or non-split completion transactions as PCI-X bus master.

   ■ The device as a target must accept memory write and split completion transactions independently of prior completion of memory write or split completions transactions by the device as a PCI-X bus master. That is, the device as a target is not allowed to return a Retry termination (see exceptions in the bullet below) for memory write and split completion transactions because it wants to execute or is waiting for the completion of memory write or split completion transactions as a PCI-X bus master.

■ In general, the completion of a bus transaction to device as target cannot be dependent on the completion of another bus transaction as a PCI-X bus master. But there are certain restrictions relative to a PCI-X/PCI-X BRIDGE and interface circuitry in an ASIC. See Subchapters 7.12: *Transaction Ordering through a Bridge* and 7.19: *Simple Devices* for more information.

■ The operation of the device as a PCI-X bus master is not required to be independent as a target.

■ The device as a PCI-X bus master is not allowed to affect the operation of its internal arbiter for multiple PCI-X bus masters by how full or empty the device's different Posted Memory Write Command FIFOs are.

■ The exceptions that allow a device as a target to request a Retry termination for a memory write transaction (including memory write block and alias memory write block) are as follows:

   ■ The Posted Memory Write Command FIFO of the target is full.

   ■ Internal to the device, an operation is being executed that has a guaranteed completion within a reasonable amount of time.

   ■ The device as a PCI-X bus master is presently the Lock master and has thus locked a target prior to the receipt of a memory write transaction as a target.

   ■ The device is presently the locked target.

■ The exceptions that allow a device as a target to request a Retry termination (or Disconnect at Next ADB) for a split completion transaction are as follows:

   ■ The Split Completion Command FIFO of the target is full (or will be full at the next ADB). This only applies to PCI-X/PCI-X BRIDGES; the "original" PCI-X bus master must always have sufficient buffer space for split completion transactions.

   ■ Internal to the device, an operation is being executed that has a guaranteed completion within a reasonable amount of time.

   ■ The device as a PCI-X bus master is presently the Lock master and has thus locked a target prior to the receipt of a split completion transaction as a target.

   ■ The device is presently a locked target.

See Subchapter 7.19: *Simple Devices* **for more information**

- A specific "original" target (following Split Transaction protocol) may have several different "sequences" of split completion transactions at different levels of completion. The "original" target is permitted to execute different "sequences" of split completion transactions in any order and to intermix the execution of split completion transactions of different "sequences". However, the address order of split completion transactions of a same "sequence" of split completion transaction must be maintained.

- If the "original" PCI-X bus master has multiple Tags active, it is required to accept the different split completion transactions associated with the different Tags in any order. It is the responsibility of the "original" target to insure the addressing ordering of the split completion transactions of a same "sequence" is maintained.

7.2   BRIDGE AND INTERBUS SEGMENT PROTOCOL

As previously discussed, a "bridge" is defined for a connection between PCI source and destination bus segments, and the interface circuitry between a PCI bus segment and internal ASIC circuitry of a device. In order to prevent live lock and dead lock conditions the interface circuitry should follow that same protocol as a PCI/PCI BRIDGE. However, some elements of the protocol do not apply. For example, special transactions can not port through a PCI/PCI BRIDGE. However if the "bridge" is actually interface circuitry in an ASIC, the special transaction may need to port through this "bridge" to the internal circuitry of the ASIC.

INTRODUCTION

There are many architectural details that could be discussed relating to the interbus segment protocol and the associated protocols implemented by bridges to port the bus transactions from one bus segment to another. The details are so extensive that the discussion would be a book in itself. In Chapter 3: *Generic PCI and PCI-X Hardware Operation* a general overview was given on porting bus transactions through generic bridges. This chapter contains more detailed discussions that will focus on the protocol defined for PCI/PCI and PCI-X/PCI-X BRIDGEs to avoid deadlock conditions and data error conditions. An extension of these discussions also applies to PCI/PCI-X BRIDGEs. The detailed discussions in this subchapter will be as follows:

- Posting of Bus Transactions (PCI and PCI-X)

- Immediate Transactions versus Delayed Transaction Protocols (PCI only)

- Immediate Transactions versus Split Transaction Protocols (PCI-X only)

- Master Latency Rule, Maximum Completion Time Limit, and Latency Timer Protocol Relative to Bridges

- "16 Clock" and "8 Clock" Rules Relative to Bridges

Detailed in other subchapters of this chapter and associated with the above elements of bridge and interbus segment protocol are those topics identified at the beginning of this chapter for Subchapters 7.3 and higher.

> As previously stated, the interface circuitry in an ASIC between a bus segment and internal circuitry may also have attributes of a bridge; consequently, the concepts discussed below are also applicable. See the subsequent Subchapter 7.19: *Simple Devices* for more information.

POSTING OF BUS TRANSACTIONS (PCI AND PCI-X)

> In the following discussion, only bus transactions beginning on one source bus and porting to one destination bus are under consideration. See Subchapter 7.12: *Transaction Ordering Through a Bridge* for the relationship of bus transactions flowing in both directions simultaneously through the bridge.

POSTING OF BUS TRANSACTIONS (PCI)

According to the PCI local bus specification, posting is defined as placing a memory write transaction (including MWI) (associated address, data, etc.) into a PCI/PCI BRIDGE register bank and completing the bus transaction on the source bus segment before the bus transaction is completed on the destination bus segment. Consequently, a write transaction executed in the memory address space can be completed on the source bus segment before the associated bus transaction is completed on the destination bus segment. The execution order of memory write transactions on the destination bus segment is required to maintain the same transaction order (strong order) as executed on the source bus segment. Consequently, in Subchapter 7.12: *Transaction Ordering through a Bridge*, the mechanism for posting memory write transactions is the "Posted Memory Write Command FIFO" which includes all of the associated information of memory write transactions. Also, observe that a memory write transaction must be posted if the FIFO is not full. Otherwise, a Disconnect occurs on the source bus segment when FIFO is nearing capacity (full), or a Retry termination will occur if the FIFO is already full. Posting can only occur for memory write transactions.

The posting of memory write transactions is a fairly standard method even for non-bridge devices and in non-PCI systems. Consequently, the main focus of this book will assume posting of memory write transactions. See Subchapter 7.19: *Simple Devices* for more information.

I/O and configuration write transactions cannot be posted like a memory write transaction. These bus transactions can be ported through a bridge with a different protocol ... see Subchapter 7.5: *Delayed Transaction and Split Completion Transaction Protocols*. I/O and configuration write transactions begin on a source bus segment and cannot be completed on the source bus segment until the associated bus transaction is completed on the destination bus segment. Also, special transactions cannot be posted in PCI/PCI BRIDGE buffers because special transactions complete on the bus segment they originate on and cannot port through the PCI/PCI BRIDGE. The special transactions are only addressing internal registers in the PCI/PCI BRIDGE or other targets on the bus segment they originate on. As discussed in Chapter 6: *Detailed Bus Transaction Operation*, a special transaction can port through a PCI/PCI BRIDGE via a Type 1 configuration transaction.

> Posting of I/O write transactions in the HOST/PCI BRIDGE is permitted by the PCI local bus specification, the hardware and software designers must have a clear understanding of the consequences. For the purposes of this book it is assumed that I/O write transactions are not posted, which is the safest implementation.

By the nature of read transactions, the data cannot be posted into a buffer like a memory write transaction. If memory read, MRM, MRL, configuration read, or I/O read transactions occur on the source bus segment, the bus transaction on the source bus is not completed until the associated bus transaction is completed on the destination bus segment. These bus transactions are ported through the bridge with a different protocol. See the discussion in the next section and Subchapter 7.5: *Delayed Transaction and Split Completion Transaction Protocols* for more information.

Interrupt acknowledge transactions are only defined for PCI bus (0); consequently, this bus transaction is only defined for HOST/PCI and PCI/LEGACY BRIDGES. It has the same limitations as other read transactions.

POSTING OF BUS TRANSACTIONS (PCI-X)

The PCI-X addendum specification defines posting for memory write transactions (including memory write block and alias memory write block) in a PCI-X/PCI-X BRIDGE register bank ("Posted Memory Write Command FIFO"), and the strong order of completion on the destination bus segment is the same as defined for the PCI local bus specification, with two differences. First, a memory write transaction must be posted if the FIFO is not full. Otherwise, on the source bus segment, a Single Phase Disconnect or a Disconnect at Next ADB termination occurs when FIFO is nearing capacity (full), or a Retry termination will occur if the FIFO is already full. Second, the PCI-X addendum specification defines the Relaxed Order bit in the ATTRIBUTE PHASE of the memory write transactions, which changes the strong order of completion. See Subchapter 7.12: *Transaction Ordering through a Bridge* for more information.

The PCI-X addendum specification also defines posting for split completion transactions in a PCI-X/PCI-X BRIDGE register bank ("Posted Split Completion Command FIFO"), and the strong order of completion on the source bus segments (source bus segment contains the "original" PCI bus master) is the same as defined in the PCI-X addendum specification with two differences. First, a split completion must be posted if the FIFO is not full. Otherwise, on the source bus segment, a Disconnect at Next ADB termination occurs when FIFO is nearing capacity (full), or a Retry termination will occur if the FIFO is already full. In the case of the "original" PCI-X bus master, the aforementioned terminations are not defined in that the PCI-X bus master is required to have reserved sufficient buffer space. Second, the PCI-X addendum bus specification defines the Relaxed Order bit in the ATTRIBUTE PHASE of the split completion transactions which changes the strong order of completion. See Subchapter 7.12: *Transaction Ordering through a Bridge* for more information.

The posting of memory write transactions is a fairly standard method even for non-bridge devices and in non-PCI-X systems. Consequently, the main focus of this book will assume posting of memory write transactions. See Subchapter 7.19: *Simple Devices* for more information. Because the "original" PCI-X bus master is required to have sufficient buffer space for accepting all split completion transactions, the focus in this book for split completion transactions will be posting.

I/O and configuration write transactions cannot be posted in the PCI-X/PCI-X BRIDGE buffers. I/O and configuration write transactions begin on a source bus segment and cannot be completed on the source bus segment until the associated bus transaction is completed on the destination bus segment. These bus transactions are completed through a bridge with a different protocol ... see Subchapter 7.5: *Delayed Transaction and Split Completion Transaction Protocols*.

Also, special transactions cannot be posted in PCI-X/PCI-X BRIDGE buffers because special transactions complete on the bus segment they originate on and cannot port through the PCI-X/PCI-X BRIDGE. The special transactions are only addressing internal registers in the PCI-X/PCI-X BRIDGE or other targets on the bus segment they originate on. As discussed in Chapter 6: *Detailed Bus Transaction Operation*, a special transaction can port through a PCI-X/PCI-X BRIDGE via a Type 1 configuration transaction.

> Posting of I/O write transactions in the HOST/PCI-X BRIDGE is permitted by the PCI-X addendum specification, but the hardware and software designers must have a clear understanding of the consequences. For the purposes of this book it is assumed that I/O write transactions are not posted which is the safest implementation.

By the nature of read transactions, the data cannot be posted into a buffer like a memory write transaction. If memory read, configuration read, or I/O read transactions occur on the source bus segment, the bus transaction on the source bus is not completed until the associated bus transaction is completed on the destination bus segment. These bus transactions are ported through a bridge with a different protocol. See the discussion in the next section and Subchapter 7.5: *Delayed Transaction and Split Completion Transaction Protocols*.

Interrupt acknowledge transactions are only defined for PCI-X bus (0); consequently, this bus transaction is only defined for HOST/PCI-X and PCI-X/LEGACY BRIDGES. It has the same limitations as other read transactions.

IMMEDIATE TRANSACTIONS AND DELAYED TRANSACTION PROTOCOL (PCI ONLY)

> In the following discussion, only bus transactions beginning on one source bus and porting to one destination bus are under consideration. See the subsequent Subchapter 7.12: *Transaction Ordering through a Bridge* for the relationship of bus transactions flowing in both directions simultaneously through the bridge.

> The following discussion includes comments relative to Delayed Transaction protocol. It may be appropriate to review Subchapter 7.5: *Delayed Transaction and Split Transaction Protocols* prior to reading this section.

According to the PCI local bus specification, and as discussed in the previous section, PCI/PCI BRIDGES are required to post (if register space is available) a memory write transaction executed on the source bus segment into a PCI/PCI BRIDGE buffer. If the bus transaction is a memory read (including MRL and MRM), an I/O (read and write), or a configuration (read and write) transaction, the bridge could immediately port the bus transaction to the destination bus segment (Immediate Transaction) or place it into a buffer using the Delayed Transaction protocol. For either Immediate Transactions or bus transactions executed according to the Delayed Transaction protocol, the bus transaction on the source bus segment is not completed until the associated bus transaction is completed on the destination bus segment and the completion information is returned to the source bus segment.

When a PCI bus transaction attempts to port through a PCI/PCI BRIDGE as an Immediate Transaction, it may not be able to immediately complete on the source bus transaction with accessed (read or written) data relative to a resource on the destination bus segment. This is particularly true if the bus transaction has to transcend several bridges and/or bus segments, which is the typical situation. In order to minimize bus latency and maximize bus bandwidth, the PCI/PCI BRIDGE must terminate the bus transaction (non-memory write and non-special transactions) with Retry termination until the data is prepared to be accessed at a later time using the Delayed Transaction protocol. The use of an Immediate Transaction is only possible if the bridge knows that the target is on the attached destination bus segment and there are no other bus transaction ordering issues relative to the bridge. This is a highly unlikely situation unless the bridge is actually the interface circuitry within an ASIC (See Subchapter 7.19: *Simple Devices* for more information). According to the PCI local bus specification, the Delayed Transaction protocol must be applied to all non-memory write and non-special transactions porting through a bridge.

The Immediate Transaction protocol could also apply to memory write transactions if the PCI/PCI BRIDGE does not contain buffers and thus does not support posting. This would be an atypical bridge; consequently, for discussions in this book it is assumed that Immediate Transactions do not apply to memory write transactions. If Immediate Transactions did apply, the memory write transaction is still required to complete on the destination bus segment prior to its completion on the source bus segment. See Subchapter 7.19: *Simple Devices* for more information.

For all practical purposes, the implementation of Immediate Transactions is most appropriate for a bridge that is actually an interface between a PCI bus segment and internal circuitry of an ASIC.

As previously stated, special transactions cannot be ported though a PCI/PCI BRIDGE. However, special transactions can port through or directly access interface circuitry of an ASIC. Also, as previously stated, interrupt acknowledge transactions are only defined for PCI bus (0); consequently, this bus transaction is only defined for HOST/PCI and PCI/LEGACY BRIDGES. The concepts of Immediate Transactions and the Split Transaction protocol apply to interrupt acknowledge transactions as for other read transactions.

As will be discussed later in this chapter, BURST memory read (to non-prefetchable address space, non-MRL, and non-MRM), and BURST I/O (read and write), BURST configuration (read and write) cannot be ported through a PCI/PCI BRIDGE. As previously stated, special transactions cannot be ported though a PCI/PCI BRIDGE. However, special transactions can port through or directly access interface circuitry of an ASIC. Also, as previously stated, interrupt acknowledge transactions are only defined for PCI bus (0); consequently, this bus transaction is only defined for HOST/PCI and PCI/LEGACY BRIDGES. The concepts of Immediate Transactions and the Delayed Transaction protocol apply to interrupt acknowledge transactions the same as for other read transactions.

In summary, the Delayed Transaction protocol for bus transactions porting through a PCI/PCI BRIDGE APPLIES to the SINGLE bus transactions of the following commands:

- Memory read, MRM, and MRL
- I/O
- Configuration
- Interrupt acknowledge (HOST/PCI and PCI/LEGACY BRIDGES only)

In summary, the Delayed Transaction protocol for bus transactions porting through a PCI/PCI BRIDGE APPLIES to the BURST bus transactions of the following commands:

- MRL and MRM
- Memory read transactions if the target is within a prefetchable address range).

Table 7-1 below is a reprint of Table 4-5 (provided here for convenience). It summarizes which bus transactions of which commands are required to be posted as opposed to which are executed according to the Delay Transaction Protocol.

C/BE# [3::0] ADDRESS PHASE Binary MSB to LSB	Name (PCI)	Name (PCI-X)	Transaction Protocol Between Bus Master and a PCI/PCI or PCI-X/PCI-X BRIDGE (representing the actual target (non-bridge)) Bus Transactions: PCI SINGLE = PST PCI BURST = PBT PCI-X SINGLE = PXST PCI-X BURST = PXBT Posted Write Req. = PWR Delayed Transaction Req. = DTR Split Transaction Req. = STR (Req. = Required)	
	NO GROUP NAME	**DWORD COMMANDS**		
			PCI/PCI BRIDGE	**PCI-X/PCI-X BRIDGE**
0000	Interrupt Acknowledge	Interrupt Acknowledge	na	na
0001	Special	Special	na	na
0010	I/O Read	I/O Read	PST DTR	PXST STR (2)
0011	I/O Write	I/O Write	PST DTR	PXST STR (2)
1010	Config. Read	Config. Read	PST DTR	PXST STR (2)
1011	Config. Write (3)	Config.Write (3)	PST DTR	PXST STR (2)
0110	Memory Read	Memory Read DWORD	PST PBT(1) DTR	PXST STR (2)
	NO GROUP NAME	**BURST COMMANDS**		
0111	Memory Write	Memory Write	PST PBT PWR	PXST PXBT PWR
1000	Reserved	Alias Memory Read Block	na	PXST PXBT STR(2)
1001	Reserved	Alias Memory Write Block	na	PXST PXBT PWR
1100	Memory Read Multiple	Split Completion	PST PBT DTR	PXST PXBT PWR
1110	Memory Read Line	Memory Read Block	PST PBT DTR	PXST PXBT STR(2)
1111	Memory Write Invalidate	Memory Write Block	PST PBT PWR	PXST PXBT PWR
	OTHERS	**OTHERS**		
1101	DAC	DAC	na	na
0100	Reserved	Reserved	na	na
0101	Reserved	Reserved	na	na

Table 7-1: Comparison of PCI and PCI-X Commands and Transactions through a PCI/PCI BRIDGE or PCI-X/PCI-X BRIDGE

Notes: (1) When access is to a prefetchable memory address space, or MRL or MRM
           transactions are executed; BURST bus transactions through the bridge are
           supported.
       (2) SINGLE and BURST transactions are terminated in the initial access of the
           DATA PHASE with a Split Response termination to implement Split
           Transaction protocol.
       (3) Not all configuration transactions can port in both upstrean and downstream
           directions.

See Subchapter 7.5: *Delayed Transaction and Split Completion Transaction Protocols* for more information.

IMMEDIATE TRANSACTION AND SPLIT TRANSACTION PROTOCOLS (PCI-X ONLY)

In the following discussion, only bus transactions beginning on one source bus and porting to one destination bus are under consideration. See the subsequent Subchapter 7.12: *Transaction Ordering Through a Bridge* for the relationship of bus transactions flowing in both directions simultaneously through the bridge.

The following discussion includes comments relative to Split Transaction protocol. It may be appropriate to review Subchapter 7.5: *Delayed Transaction and Split Transaction Protocols* prior to reading this section.

According to the PCI-X addendum specification, and as discussed in the previous section, the PCI-X/PCI-X BRIDGES are required to post (if register space is available) a memory write or split completion transaction executed on the source or destination bus segment into a PCI-X/PCI-X BRIDGE buffer, respectively. If the bus transaction is a memory read (including DWORD memory read, memory read block, and alias memory read block), an I/O (read and write), or a configuration (read and write) transaction, the bridge could immediately port the bus transaction to the destination bus segment (Immediate Transaction), or execute it using the Split Transaction protocol. For Immediate Transactions, the bus transaction on the source bus segment is not completed until the associated bus transaction is completed on the destination bus segment and the completion information is returned to the source bus segment. For bus transactions executed under the Split Transaction protocol, the bus transaction on the source bus segment is not completed until the associated bus transaction is completed on the destination bus segment and the "sequence" of split completion transactions is completed on the source bus segment.

530

When an attempt is made to port a PCI-X bus transaction through a PCI-X/PCI-X BRIDGE as an Immediate Transaction, it may not be able to immediately complete on the source bus transaction with accessed (read or written) data relative to a resource on the destination bus segment. This is particularly true if the bus transaction has to transcend several bridges and/or bus segments, which is the typical situation. In order to minimize bus latency and maximize bus bandwidth, the PCI-X/PCI-X BRIDGE is required to terminate the bus transaction (non-memory write, non-split completion, and non-special transactions) with Split Response termination until the data or completion information is provided according to the Split Transaction protocol. The use of an Immediate Transaction is only possible if the bridge knows that the target is on the attached destination bus segment and there are no other bus transaction ordering issues relative to the bridge. This is a highly unlikely situation unless the bridge is actually the interface circuitry within an ASIC (See Subchapter 7.19: *Simple Devices* for more information). According to the PCI-X addendum specification, the Split Transaction protocol must be applied to all non-memory write, non-split completion, and non-special transactions porting through a bridge.

The Immediate Transaction protocol could also apply to memory write transactions if the PCI-X/PCI-X BRIDGE does not contain buffers and thus does not support posting. This would be an atypical bridge; consequently, for discussions in this book it is assumed that Immediate Transactions do not apply to memory write transactions. If Immediate Transactions did apply, the memory write transaction still must complete on the destination bus segment prior to its completion on the source bus segment. See Subchapter 7.19: *Simple Devices* for more information.

For all practical purposes, the implementation of Immediate Transactions is most appropriate for a bridge that is actually an interface between a PCI-X bus segment and internal circuitry of an ASIC.

As previously stated, special transactions cannot be ported though a PCI-I/PCI-X BRIDGE. However, special transactions can port through or directly access interface circuitry of an ASIC. Also, as previously stated, interrupt acknowledge transactions are only defined for PCI-X bus (0); consequently, this bus transaction is only defined for HOST/PCI-X and PCI-X/LEGACY BRIDGES. The concepts of Immediate Transactions and the Split Transaction protocol apply to interrupt acknowledge transactions as for other read transactions.

531

In summary, the Split Transaction protocol for bus transactions porting through a PCI-X/PCI-X BRIDGE APPLIES to the SINGLE bus transactions of the following commands:

- DWORD memory read
- I/O transactions
- Configuration
- Interrupt acknowledge transactions (HOST/PCI and PCI/LEGACY BRIDGES only)

In summary, the Split Transaction protocol for bus transactions porting through a PCI-X/PCI-X BRIDGE APPLIES to the SINGLE or BURST bus transactions of the following commands:

- Memory write, alias memory write block, and memory write block
- Alias memory read block and memory read block

Table 7-1 above in the previous section is a reprint of Table 4-5 (provided here for convenience). It summarizes which bus transactions of which commands are required to be posted versus executed according to the Split Transaction Protocol.

See Subchapter 7.5: *Delayed Transaction and Split Completion Transaction Protocols* for more information.

"MASTER LATENCY" RULE, MAXIMUM COMPLETION TIME LIMIT, AND LATENCY TIMER PROTOCOL RELATIVE TO BRIDGES

PCI SPECIFIC

A bridge operates as a PCI bus master on each specific PCI bus segment; consequently, the "Master Latency" rule and Latency Timer protocol applies to a PCI/PCI BRIDGE.

A PCI/PCI BRIDGE relies on the ability to access a resource on the destination bus segment in order to complete bus transactions from the source bus segment. Consequently, the Maximum Completion Time Limit does not apply to PCI/PCI BRIDGES; the limit only applies to non-bridge devices. However, if the PCI/PCI BRIDGE is the actual target (not porting the bus transaction), it is defined as a non-bridge for the associated bus transaction and is required to adhere to the Maximum Completion Time Limit.

See Chapter 14: *Latency and Performance* for more information.

PCI-X SPECIFIC

The "Master Latency" as defined in the PCI local bus specification does not apply to the PCI-X addendum specification. The bus transaction protocol for PCI-X bus transactions requires that the IRDY# signal line is asserted at a specific time in the bus transaction and remains asserted until the completion of the bus transaction.

The Latency Timer protocol and the Maximum Completion Time Limit as defined in the PCI local bus specification also applies to the PCI-X addendum specification.

See Chapter 14: *Latency and Performance* for more information.

"16 CLOCK" AND "8 CLOCK" RULES RELATIVE TO BRIDGES

PCI

As previously discussed, PCI/PCI BRIDGES are required to support the posting of memory write transactions and the Delayed Transaction protocol for certain other bus transactions. Also, some bus transactions are actually accessing a bridge as a target. In either case, the bridge is required to adhere to the "PCI 16 clock" and "PCI 8 clock" rules. See Chapter 4: *Functional Interaction between PCI and PCI-X Resources* for more information about the "PCI 16 clock" and "PCI 8 clock" rules.

Whenever possible, PCI/PCI BRIDGES should be designed to complete the posted memory write or execute a Retry termination for the Delayed Transaction protocol well before the time limitations of the "PCI 16 clock" and "PCI 8 clock" rules. See Chapter 8: *Master and Target Termination* for more information.

PCI-X

As previously discussed, PCI-X/PCI-X BRIDGES are required to support the posting of memory write transactions and the Split Transaction protocol for certain other bus transactions. Also, some bus transactions are actually accessing a bridge as a target. In either case, the bridge appears as a target and is required to adhere to the "PCI-X 16 clock" and "PCI-X 8 clock" rules. See Chapter 4: *Functional Interaction between PCI and PCI-X Resources* for more information about the "PCI-X 16 clock" and "PCI-X 8 clock" rules.

Whenever possible, PCI-X/PCI-X BRIDGES should be designed to complete the posted memory write or execute a Split Response termination for the Split Transaction protocol well before the time limitations of the "PCI-X 16 clock" and

"PCI-X 8 clock" rules. See Chapter 8: *Master and Target Termination* for more information.

7.3 HIERARCHICAL AND PEER PCI AND PCI-X BUS SEGMENTS, AND SIDE BAND AND INTX# SIGNAL LINES

PCI SPECIFIC

The protocol discussed in this chapter for the interaction of PCI bus segments and the operation of the PCI/PCI BRIDGES is a "safe" protocol. More elaborate and higher performance protocols can be defined, but there is a risk of incompatible operation with other devices following other protocols. Consequently, it is strongly suggested that all interfaces in ASICs and bridges follow the protocols discussed in this chapter.

There are certain PCI/PCI BRIDGE and PCI bus segment configurations that are NOT ALLOWED according to the PCI local bus specification. These are shown in Figure 7-1 as follows:

- Two or more PCI/PCI BRIDGES that interface from individual upper LEVEL bus segments to the same lower LEVEL bus segment (Circle A in Figure 7-1) are NOT ALLOWED. Similarly, a PCI/PCI BRIDGE between two PCI bus segments on the same LEVEL is NOT ALLOWED (Circle D in Figure 7-1). The same LEVEL definition for bus segments PCI bus (2) and PCI bus (4) in Figure 7-1 has been established by the existence of PCI/PCI BRIDGE (3 to 4).

- Two or more PCI/PCI BRIDGES that interface between the same upper LEVEL bus segment and the same lower LEVEL bus segment (Circle B in Figure 7-1) are NOT ALLOWED.

- Two or more PCI/PCI BRIDGES that are serially connected between two bus segments without a PCI bus segment between the bridges (Circle C in Figure 7-1) are NOT ALLOWED.

Other system hierarchies not shown in Figure 7-1 that are NOT ALLOWED:

- The PCI/LEGACY BRIDGE can only be attached to PCI bus (0); placement on any other bus segments is NOT ALLOWED.

  - A system is allowed to implement a HOST/LEGACY BRIDGE instead of a PCI/LEGACY BRIDGE.

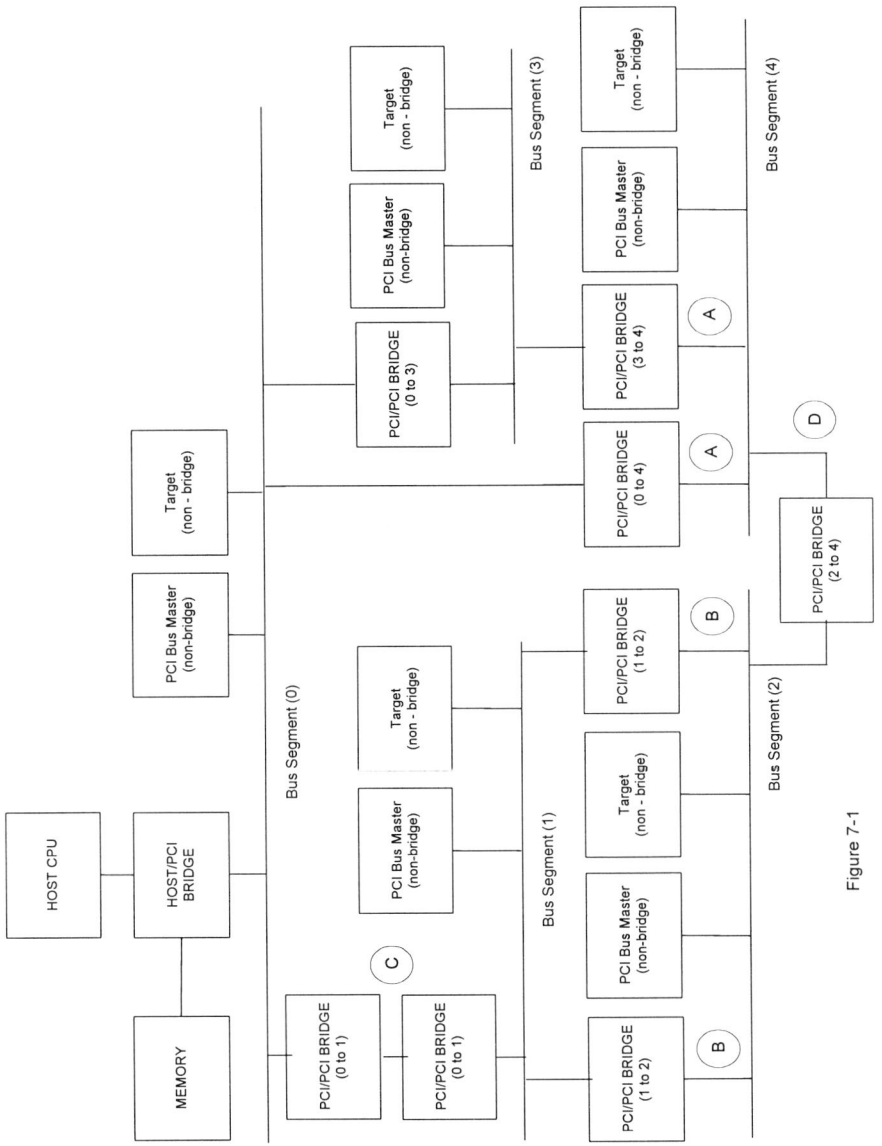

Figure 7-1: NOT ALLOWED Architecture and Hierarchy of Bridges and Bus Segments

- There is no requirement that a LEGACY bus segment or associated bridges exist in a system.

- The interrupt controller can only be attached to PCI bus (0), be placed in the HOST/LEGACY BRIDGE, be placed in the PCI/LEGACY BRIDGE, or attached to the LEGACY bus segment. The placement of the interrupt controller on any other PCI bus segments is NOT ALLOWED.

Figure 7-2 shows the ALLOWED architecture and hierarchy for a system with PCI bus segments. The ALLOWED architecture and hierarchy obviously avoids all of the items NOT ALLOWED in the above section. There are several items of interest relative to the ALLOWED architecture and hierarchy:

- The HOST bus segment can have more than one HOST/PCI BRIDGE.

- Each PCI bus segment can have an individual bus arbiter, or a collection of several PCI bus segments (including all of the PCI bus segments) can be serviced by one central arbiter.

- The interrupt signal lines (INTx#) are connected across the system (including add-on card connectors) from bus segment to bus segment independently of PCI/PCI BRIDGES. However, bridges can connect to them if the bridge needs interrupt service support.

- Side band signal lines (any non-PCI signal lines between two or more devices) can only operate within the confines of the bus segments on the system board plane. They are not part of the PCI local bus specification and cannot alter the associated definitions and protocols. The connectors to add-on cards do not contain side band signal lines and PCI/PCI BRIDGES do not port side band signal lines.

- The placement of the interrupt controller, and the LEGACY bus segments and associated bridges is as discussed in the previous section.

- The flow of memory and I/O bus transactions within the system is fairly unrestricted. In addition to the obvious interactions between PCI bus masters and targets on the same bus segment, there are also interactions between devices on different bus segments as follows:

  - PCI bus masters on upper LEVEL bus segments can access targets on lower LEVEL bus segments and PCI bus masters on lower LEVEL bus segments can access targets on upper LEVEL bus segments. The path of the access may be very straight forward (Circle A in Figure 7-2) or through an upper LEVEL bus segment (Circle B in Figure 7-2).

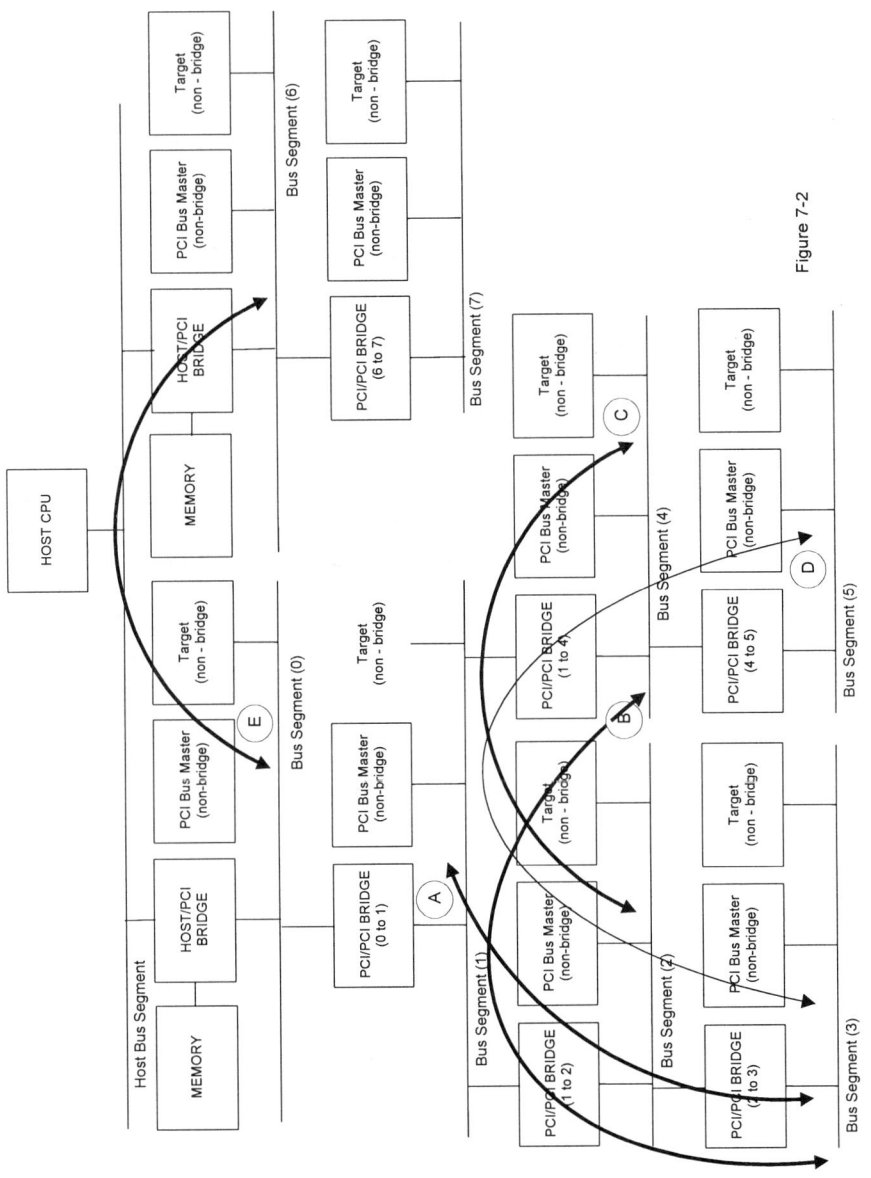

Figure 7-2: ALLOWED Architecture and Hierarchy of Bridges and Bus Segments

537

- PCI bus masters can access targets on the same LEVEL bus segment. The path of the access may be through only one upper LEVEL bus segment (Circle C in Figure 7-2) or through more than one upper LEVEL bus segments (Circle D in Figure 7-2). An access between PCI bus masters and targets on the same LEVEL bus segment is defined as a "peer bus segments" access.

- The paths described above must be supported by the system according to the PCI local bus specification. Optionally, the HOST/PCI BRIDGES can be designed to support a path for bus transactions through the HOST bus segment. (Circle E in Figure 7-2 shows a peer bus segment access via the HOST bus segment). Also optional, HOST/LEGACY BRIDGES can be designed to support an access to the same LEVEL PCI bus segment through a HOST/PCI BRIDGE.

- The possible paths in a system for memory transactions used for an Exclusive Hardware Access are more restrictive than the paths for memory and I/O transactions. See Subchapter 7.17: *Exclusive Access (Lock) Protocol and Deadlock Considerations* for more information.

The paths between PCI bus masters and targets for Type 1 configuration write transactions for porting special transactions are the same as above for memory and I/O transactions. The paths for Type 1 configuration transactions for porting Type 0 configuration transactions are more restrictive. Similarly, the interrupt acknowledge transaction is restricted to PCI bus (0). See Subchapter 7.9: *Porting I/O, Configuration, Interrupt Acknowledge, and Special Transactions through PCI/PCI or PCI-X/PCI-X BRIDGES* for more information.

PCI-X SPECIFIC

The NOT ALLOWED and ALLOWED architecture and hierarchy in the PCI-X addendum specification is the same as in the PCI local bus specification. In addition, the flow of split completion transactions in systems compliant to the PCI-X addendum specification is the same as the flow of memory transactions.

7.4   PCI TO PCI-X AND PCI-X TO PCI CONVERSION

The PCI-X addendum specification introduces the requirement that bridges are must convert PCI bus transactions on one bus segment to PCI-X bus transactions on another bus segment. The conversion through the bridge is symmetric. That is, the PCI-X addendum specification defines a conversion of PCI-X bus transactions on one bus segment to PCI bus transactions on another bus segment. The direction of translation can be either upstream or downstream. This discussion focuses on PCI/PCI BRIDGES, PCI-X/PCI-X BRIDGES, and PCI/PCI-X BRIDGEs.

From the PCI bus segment's point of view, the PCI/PCI-X BRIDGE provides the following functions:

- Memory write transactions (including memory write and invalidate (MWI)) are posted into the bridge. Memory write transactions can be executed as BURST bus transactions through the bridge as part of the posting protocol.

- Memory read transactions cannot be executed as BURST bus transactions through a bridge unless the bus transactions are addressing a prefetchable address space. Memory read transactions for memory read multiple and memory read line (MRM and MRL) commands can be executed as BURST bus transactions through a bridge according to the definition of MRM and MRL commands. These BURST bus transactions through a bridge can be executed as part of the Delayed Transaction protocol.

- The Delayed Transaction protocol applies to memory read transactions that are not being executed to prefetchable address space, I/O read and write transactions, and configuration read and write transactions.

- Interrupt acknowledge transactions (porting through HOST/PCI and PCI/LEGACY BRIDGES only) can be executed using the Delayed Transaction protocol if the HOST/PCI and PCI/LEGACY BRIDGES support such a protocol. Special transactions never port through a bridge.

From the PCI-X bus transaction point of view, the PCI/PCI-X BRIDGE provides the following functions:

- Memory write transactions (for BURST COMMANDs) are posted into the bridge. Memory write transactions can be executed as BURST bus transactions through the bridge as part of a posting protocol.

- Memory read transactions (for both DWORD and BURST COMMANDs) can only be ported through the bridge per the Split Transaction protocol.

- The Split Transaction protocol applies to I/O read and write transactions, configuration read and write transactions porting through a bridge.

- Interrupt acknowledge transactions (HOST/PCI and PCI/LEGACY BRIDGES only) can be executed using the Split Transaction protocol if the HOST/PCI and PCI/LEGACY BRIDGES support such a protocol. Special transactions never port through a bridge.

Table 7-2 below is a reprint of the Tables 4-5 and 7-1 and outlines bus transaction porting through a PCI/PCI BRIDGE or a PCI-X/PCI-X BRIDGE between bus segments. It is provided here to aid in the comparison of the contents of Tables 7-3 and 7-4.

C/BE# [3::0] ADDRESS PHASE Binary MSB to LSB	Name (PCI)	Name (PCI-X)	Transaction Protocol Between Bus Master and a PCI/PCI or PCI-X/PCI-X BRIDGE (representing the actual target (non-bridge)) Bus Transactions: PCI SINGLE = PST PCI BURST = PBT PCI-X SINGLE = PXST PCI-X BURST = PXBT Posted Write Req. = PWR Delayed Transaction Req. = DTR Split Transaction Req. = STR (Req. = Required)	
	NO GROUP NAME	DWORD COMMANDS		
			PCI/PCI BRIDGE	PCI-X/PCI-X BRIDGE
0000	Interrupt Acknowledge	Interrupt Acknowledge	na	na
0001	Special	Special	na	na
0010	I/O Read	I/O Read	PST DTR	PXST STR (2)
0011	I/O Write	I/O Write	PST DTR	PXST STR (2)
1010	Config. Read	Config. Read	PST DTR	PXST STR (2)
1011	Config. Write (3)	Config.Write (3)	PST DTR	PXST STR (2)
0110	Memory Read	Memory Read DWORD	PST PBT(1) DTR	PXST STR (2)
	NO GROUP NAME	BURST COMMANDS		
0111	Memory Write	Memory Write	PST PBT PWR	PXST PXBT PWR
1000	Reserved	Alias Memory Read Block	na	PXST PXBT STR(2)
1001	Reserved	Alias Memory Write Block	na	PXST PXBT PWR
1100	Memory Read Multiple	Split Completion	PST PBT DTR	PXST PXBT PWR
1110	Memory Read Line	Memory Read Block	PST PBT DTR	PXST PXBT STR(2)
1111	Memory Write Invalidate	Memory Write Block	PST PBT PWR	PXST PXBT PWR
	OTHERS	OTHERS		
1101	DAC	DAC	na	na
0100	Reserved	Reserved	na	na
0101	Reserved	Reserved	na	na

Table 7-2: Comparison of PCI and PCI-X Commands and Transactions through a PCI/PCI BRIDGE or PCI-X/PCI-X BRIDGE

Notes: (1) When access is to a prefetchable memory address space, or MRL or MRM transactions are executed; BURST bus transactions through the bridge are supported.

(2) SINGLE and BURST transactions are terminated in the initial access of the DATA PHASE with a Split Response termination to implement Split Transaction protocol.

(3) Not all configuration transactions can port in both upstrean and downstream directions.

Table 7-3 outlines the translation of a bus transaction on a PCI bus segment to an associated bus transaction on a PCI-X bus segment. The considerations are as follows:

■ A Delay Transaction protocol executed by the PCI/PCI-X BRIDGE on the PCI bus segment side of the bridge is executed as a read or write bus transaction on the PCI-X bus segment side of the bridge. The write or read transaction on the PCI-X bus segment may execute as an Immediate Transaction or according to the Split Transaction protocol depending on the PCI-X target.

Bus Transaction From PCI Bus Segment	Translated to Bus Transaction on PCI-X Bus Segment
NO GROUP NAME	**DWORD COMMANDS**
Interrupt Acknowledge	NA
Special	NA
I/O Read	I/O Read
I/O Write	I/O Write
Config. Read	Config. Read
Config. Write	Config. Write
Memory Read	Memory Read DWORD (1)
NO GROUP NAME	**BURST COMMANDS**
Memory Write	Memory Write or Memory Write Block (2)
Reserved	NA
Reserved	NA
Memory Read Multiple	Memory Read Block
Memory Read Line	Memory Read Block
Memory Write Invalidate	Memory Write Block

Table 7-3: Translation of PCI Bus Transactions to PCI-X Bus Transactions by a PCI/PCI-X Bridge

Notes:

(1) The BURST COMMAND of memory read block is required to be used, if the PCI bus segment side of the bridge has "pre-read" more than one DWORD.

(2) If the bus transaction for the PCI memory write command has ANY byte enables (C/BE#) deasserted, the PCI-X BURST memory write command is required. If the bus

transaction for the PCI memory write command has ALL the byte enables (C/BE#) asserted, either PCI-X BURST COMMAND listed can be used.

■ Memory write transactions on the PCI bus segment side of the PCI/PCI-X BRIDGE are posted into the bridge for subsequent execution on the PCI-X bus segment side of the bridge. Memory write transactions on the PCI-X bus segment may execute as Immediate Transactions or posted depending on the PCI-X target.

■ PCI ordering protocol applies to the ordering of the translated bus transaction on the PCI-X bus segment. No Relaxed Ordering can be applied to the associated PCI-X bus transactions.

■ Other considerations listed in Table 7-3 for PCI bus transactions translated to PCI-X bus transactions (Please carefully review the Notes associated with the table.)

Table 7-4 outlines the translation of a bus transaction on a PCI-X bus segment to an associated bus transaction on a PCI bus segment. The considerations are as follows:

■ A Split Transaction protocol executed by the PCI/PCI-X BRIDGE on the PCI-X bus segment side of the bridge is executed as a read or write bus transaction on the PCI bus segment side of the bridge. The write or read transaction on the PCI bus segment may either execute as an Immediate Transaction or according to the Delayed Transaction protocol, depending on the PCI target.

■ Memory write transactions on the PCI-X bus segment side of the bridge are posted into the bridge for subsequent execution on the PCI bus segment side of the bridge. Memory write transactions on the PCI bus segment may either execute as Immediate Transactions or posted, depending on the PCI target.

■ PCI-X ordering protocol applies to the ordering of the translated bus transaction on the PCI bus segment. No Relaxed Ordering applied to the PCI-X bus transactions can be applied to the associated PCI bus transactions.

■ Other considerations are listed in Table 7-4 for translating PCI-X bus transactions to PCI bus transactions (please carefully review the Notes associated with the table).

Bus Transaction from PCI-X Segment	Translated to Bus Transaction on PCI-X Bus Segment
DWORD COMMANDS	**NO GROUP NAME**
Interrupt Acknowledge	NA
Special	NA
I/O Read	I/O Read
I/O Write	I/O Write
Config. Read	Config. Read
Config. Write	Config. Write
Memory Read DWORD	Memory Read
BURST COMMANDS	**NO GROUP NAME**
Memory Write	Memory Write or Memory Write Invalidate (1)
Alias Memory Read Block	Not yet defined
Alias Memory Write Block	Not yet defined
Split Completion	Not yet defined
Memory Read Block	Memory Read or Memory Read Line or Memory Read Multiple (2)
Memory Write Block	Memory Write or Memory Write Invalidate (1)

Table 7-4: Translation of PCI-X Bus Transactions to PCI Bus Transactions by a PCI-X/PCI Bridge

Notes:

(1) If the bus transaction for the PCI-X memory write or memory write block command has all byte enables (C/BE#) asserted and begins and ends at a Cacheline boundary, the PCI memory write and invalidate command can optionally be executed. If the bus transaction for the PCI-X memory write or memory write block command has any byte enables (C/BE#) deasserted or does not begin and end at a Cacheline boundary, only the PCI memory write command can be executed.

(2) If the bus transaction for the PCI-X memory read block command has a byte count of fewer than four bytes, the PCI memory read command is required. If the bus transaction for the PCI-X memory read block command has a byte count of four bytes or more but less than a Cacheline size, either the PCI memory read command or the MRL (MRL is most recommended) command can be executed. If the bus transaction for the PCI-X memory read block command has a byte count equal to or more than a Cacheline size, either the PCI memeory read command, MRL, or the MRM (MRM is most recommended) can be executed. Note: In the above discussion the byte count was compared to four bytes. The comparison to four bytes assumed a 32 data bit bus transaction. The comparison is made relative to 8 bytes for a 64 data bit bus transaction.

It should be noted that any particular attribute of a PCI/PCI BRIDGE must be implemented on the PCI side of a PCI/PCI-X BRIDGE (for example, a Delayed Request Discard Timer). A similar statement applies to attributes specific to PCI-X/PCI-X BRDIGEs for the PCI-X side of a PCI/PCI-X BRIDGE.

7.5   DELAYED TRANSACTION AND SPLIT TRANSACTION PROTOCOLS

DELAYED TRANSACTION PROTOCOL (PCI ONLY)

The Delayed Transaction protocol only applies to a bus segment that complies with the PCI local bus specification, and does not apply to a bus segment compliant to the PCI-X addendum specification. As previously discussed, non-memory write transactions can be executed using the Delayed Transaction protocol.

For discussions relative to the Delayed Transaction protocol, the non-memory write bus transactions are memory read, MRM, MRL, configuration read and write, and I/O read and write transactions. Also, the interrupt acknowledge transaction can be executed using the Delayed Transaction protocol by a HOST/PCI BRIDGE and PCI/LEGACY BRIDGE. A non-memory write transaction does not include special transactions.

For the discussions relative to the Delayed Transaction protocol, the focus will be on a PCI/PCI BRIDGE. The Delayed Transaction protocol can also be executed by the PCI bus segment side of a PCI/PCI-X BRIDGE, and by the interface circuitry between a PCI bus segment and the internal circuitry of an ASIC.

The Delayed Transaction protocol is divided into two components: Delayed Request and Delayed Completion. The Delayed Transaction protocol begins and a Delayed Request occurs when a source bus segment transaction is completed with a Retry termination by the PCI/PCI BRIDGE. The Retry termination may be executed as a result of the "PCI 16 clock" rule (16 CLK signal line periods from FRAME# asserted) or when the PCI/PCI BRIDGE knows that the bus transaction on the source bus segment will definitely not be completed according to the "PCI 16 clock" and PCI 8 clock" rules ("Completed" as used in this discussion means a Disconnect, Completion, Completion with Timeout, Target Abort, or Master Abort termination). (See Chapter 8: *Master and Target Terminations* for more information). The Delayed Transaction protocol requires the PCI/PCI BRIDGE to latch the bus transaction information (command type, byte enables, REQ64#, etc.)

to create the Delayed Request. The Delayed Request is stored into the Delayed Request Buffer. A Delayed Request can only be discarded from the buffer prior to the first execution of the associated bus transaction on the destination bus segment. After the first execution on the destination bus segment transaction associated with the Delayed Request, the bridge is required to repeat the bus transaction until Delay Completion occurs on the destination bus segment or a reset is executed.

> For a read bus transaction, the PCI/PCI BRIDGE does not have to wait until the IRDY# signal line is asserted to request a Retry termination. For a write transaction, the PCI/PCI BRIDGE is required to wait for the IRDY# signal line to be asserted before requesting Retry termination (in order to latch in the data).
>
> The PCI bus master cannot distinguish a Retry termination due to a Delayed Transaction protocol from a Retry termination for other reasons (For example, presently no space in the Delayed Request Buffer).

When a source bus segment transaction has completed with a Retry termination, the PCI bus master must repeat the "exact same" source bus segment transaction until the PCI/PCI BRIDGE is able to complete it without Retry termination. If the PCI/PCI BRIDGE is not ready to complete the "exact same" source bus segment transaction, it will continue to execute a Retry termination (without re-latching the source bus transaction information) and the PCI bus master on the source bus segment will repeat the "exact same" source bus segment transaction. The bridge is able to complete the source bus segment transaction without Retry termination with the Delayed Completion component of the Delayed Transaction protocol. The Delayed Completion component occurs when the PCI/PCI BRIDGE completes the destination bus transaction for the associated Delayed Request without a Retry termination. The Delayed Completion information is stored in the Delayed Completion Buffer in the bridge and is ported to the source bus segment when the "exact same" bus segment transaction is repeated. Once the Delayed Completion has occurred (the source bus segment transaction is "completed" by the PCI/PCI BRIDGE) the PCI bus master does not repeat the "exact same" source bus segment transaction.

> The repeat of the "exact same" source bus segment transaction that was originally completed with Retry termination by the PCI/PCI BRIDGE transaction includes address, command, byte enables, REQ64#, LOCK#, and so forth.

For execution of memory read, MRM, or MRL transactions to an address space defined as prefetchable according to the registers in the bridge's configuration address space, the byte enables (according to the asserted C/BE# signal lines in the DATA PHASE) do not have to be the "same". Otherwise, the bytes enables are required to be the same.

The PCI bus master may execute other source bus segment transactions to the PCI/PCI BRIDGE (accessing the bridge or a device on the other side of the bridge) and other devices on the bus segment between repeating the "exact same" source bus segment transaction to the PCI/PCI BRIDGE. Also, other PCI bus masters may execute source bus segment transactions to the PCI/PCI BRIDGE (accessing the bridge or a device on the other side of the bridge) and other devices the bus segment between repeats of the "exact same" source bus transaction. The completion of the other source bus segment transactions is not required prior to the completion of the repeated "exact same" source bus segment transaction associated with the Retry termination from the PCI/PCI BRIDGE.

When a PCI/PCI BRIDGE is executing the Delayed Transaction protocol, there is a unique side effect to be considered. It is possible that when the PCI bus master (labeled "A") is repeating the aforementioned "exact same" source bus segment transaction, another PCI bus master (labeled "B") may coincidentally execute the "exact same" source bus segment transaction at the time the bridge is ready to complete the Delay Transaction protocol. Under this situation, the PCI/PCI BRIDGE believes that the Delayed Completion has occurred and PCI bus master (A) has completed its repeat of the "exact same" source bus segment transaction. PCI bus master (A) still believes that the Delayed Transaction protocol is still be executed and will continue to repeat the "exact same" source bus segment transaction. On the first repeat of the "exact same" bus transaction by PCI bus master (A) after PCI bus master (B) completed its bus transaction, the PCI/PCI BRIDGE will execute a Retry termination. The execution of the Retry termination re-establishes the Delayed Transaction protocol in the PCI/PCI BRIDGE. From PCI bus master (A) it appears as a continuation of the Delayed Transaction protocol.

In the above discussion, only one Delayed Transaction protocol was active at a time. It is possible for the PCI/PCI BRIDGE to have several Delayed Requests and Delayed Completions active simultaneously. Subchapter 7.5: *Transaction Ordering through a Bridge* of this book discusses mechanisms for supporting several Delayed Requests and Delayed Completions simultaneously in a PCI/PCI BRIDGE.

DISCARDING DELAYED REQUESTS AND DELAYED COMPLETIONS, AND DISCARD TIMER (PCI ONLY)

As previously mentioned, a Delayed Request can be discarded from the Delayed Request Buffer at any time prior to its first execution on destination bus. When discarded, the next subsequent repeat of the "exact same" source bus segment transaction will re-establish it in the Delayed Request Buffer (independent of which PCI bus master executed the source bus segment transaction).

As discussed above, once a destination bus segment transaction associated with a Delayed Request is completed, the result is stored in the Delayed Completion Buffer. The Delayed Completion Buffer is the mechanism for holding Delayed Completion(s) in the PCI/PCI BRIDGE until the associated "exact same" source bus segment transaction is repeated. A Delayed Completion stored in the Delayed Completion Buffer can be discarded under one of the following conditions:

- The source bus segment transaction is to a prefetchable address region per the associated registers in the bridge (defined only for memory read).

- The source bus segment transaction is an MRM or MRL transaction.

- The source bus segment PCI bus master has not repeated the "exact same" bus transaction for 2^{15} periods of the source bus segment CLK signal line (as recorded in the PCI/PCI BRIDGE's Discard Timer) since the associated Delay Completion was ready.

A separate Discard Timer is defined within each PCI/PCI BRIDGE for each Delayed Completion Buffer element. When a PCI bus transaction on the source bus segment is terminated with a Retry termination for purposes of the Delayed Transaction, the associated Discard Timer is reset. Upon completion of the associated destination bus segment transaction (Delayed Completion) the counting of the CLK signal line (on source bus segment) on each rising edge begins. The PCI/PCI BRIDGE is required to discard the Delayed Completion information when the Discard Timer expires. It is recommended that the Discard Timer be programmed for 2^{15} periods of the source bus segment CLK signal line. However, the Discard Timer may have to be programmed (optional) to as few as 2^{10} PCI clock periods to accommodate PCI bus masters that have been built to revisions of the PCI bus specification Rev 2.0 and earlier. In earlier bus specifications, PCI bus masters were not required to repeat the "exact same" bus transaction.

When a Delayed Completion has been discarded as defined above, an error can optionally be reported if one of the following occurred:

- The source bus segment transaction is to a non-prefetchable address range (memory read)
- The source bus segment transaction was an MRM or MRL transaction
- The source bus segment transaction was an I/O, configuration, or interrupt acknowledge transaction

If one of the above occurs, the PCI/PCI BRIDGE may (it is recommended but not required) assert the SERR# signal line. The assertion of the SERR# signal line occurs if the discard cannot be reported to a device driver or to the system (if a device driver does not exist) by some other means

If the source bus segment transaction was to a prefetchable address range (memory read), or was an MRM or MRL transaction; the PCI/PCI BRIDGE may (it is not recommended) assert the SERR# signal line.

The assertion of the SERR# signal line occurs if the discard of a Delayed Completion cannot be reported to a device driver or to the system (if device driver does not exist) by some other means.

The assertion of the SERR# signal line requires that the target or bridge has this signal line enabled for assertion and reports the assertion of this signal line. Both of the associated bits (enable and assertion) are in the PCI/PCI BRIDGE'S configuration address space. See Chapter 10: *Parity and Bus Errors* for more information

SPLIT TRANSACTION PROTOCOL (PCI-X ONLY)

The Split Transaction protocol only applies to a bus segment that is compliant to the PCI-X addendum bus specification, and does not apply to a bus segment in compliance with the PCI local bus specification. As previously discussed, non-memory write transactions can be executed using the Split Transaction protocol.

For discussions relating to the Split Transaction protocol, the non-memory write bus transactions are DWORD memory read, memory read block, alias memory read block, configuration read and write, and I/O read and write transactions. Also, the interrupt acknowledge transaction can be executed using the Split Transaction protocol by a HOST/PCI-X BRIDGE and PCI-X/LEGACY BRIDGE. For this discussion, non-memory write transactions do not include special transactions.

For the discussions relating to the Split Transaction protocol, the focus will be on a PCI-X/PCI-X BRIDGE. The Split Transaction protocol can also be executed by the PCI-X bus segment side of a PCI/PCI-X BRIDGE, and by the interface between a PCI–X bus segment and the internal circuitry of an ASIC.

As previously discussed, the Delayed Transaction protocol allows non-memory write transactions (as defined above for the Delayed Transaction protocol) to port between bus segments through bridges, and between a PCI bus segment and the internal circuitry of the target (ASIC for example). The ability for multiple PCI bus segments and bridges to operate with high effective system performance would be impossible without the Delayed Transaction protocol. For all of the benefits of the Delayed Transaction protocol, there are some drawbacks. Primary is the occurrence of multiple repetitions of the "exact same" source bus segment transaction terminated with Retry termination. The PCI bus master will repeat such a bus transaction without assurance that the target (in this discussion the PCI/PCI BRIDGE) will actually be able to complete the repeated bus transaction; consequently, the PCI bus master may receive many Retry terminations for the same bus transaction. Each bus transaction that ends with a Retry termination has used bus segment and system bandwidth without completing the bus transaction.

The Split Transaction protocol is specific to PCI-X bus segments and avoids the aforementioned drawbacks of the Delayed Transaction protocol. When the PCI-X bus master executes a non-memory write transaction (as defined above for the Split Transaction protocol) the PCI-X/PCI-X BRIDGE is required to invoke the Split Transaction protocol by executing a Split Response termination following the "PCI-X 8 CLK" rule. See Chapter 8: *Master and Target Terminations* for more information.

The PCI-X bus master is executing a source bus segment transaction to a target that may also be on the source bus segment or on the other side of a bridge on the destination bus segment. If the target is on the same source bus segment, it may complete the non-memory write transaction or execute a Split Response termination and invoke the Split transaction protocol. If the target is on the other side of PCI-X/PCI-X BRIDGE (destination bus segment) the PCI-X/PCI-X BRIDGE is required to execute a Split Response termination and invoke the Split Completion protocol. If the target on the destination bus segment completes the associated bus transaction from the PCI-X/PCI-X BRIDGE with a Split Response termination, the target is responsible for sourcing the Split Completion transactions (discussed below) and the bridge simply ports them to the source bus segment. If the target on the destination bus segment completes the associated bus transaction from the PCI-X/PCI-X BRIDGE without a Split Response termination, the PCI-X/PCI-X BRIDGE is responsible for sourcing the Split Completion transactions (discussed below) using information from the associated bus transaction on the destination bus segment

Also as previously outlined, PCI-X/PCI-X BRIDGEs may reside between the PCI-X bus master that began the access and the non-bridge target that it is accessing. On each PCI-X bus segment the PCI-X/PCI-X BRIDGE appears as the PCI-X bus master of that bus segment. Also, on each bus segment the PCI-X/PCI-X BRIDGE may appear as the target of the bus segment but not the actual target being accessed.

The invoking of the Split Transaction protocol is not required for the interface between a PCI-X bus segment and the internal circuitry of an ASIC if the ASIC can meet the requirements of the "PCI-X 8 CLK" rule. See Chapter 8: *Master and Target Terminations* for more information.

The PCI-X/PCI-X BRIDGE is permitted to execute a Retry termination of a non-memory write transaction on the source bus segment if there is no space in the bridge to store the information relevant to executing the Split Transaction protocol. Unlike the Delayed Transaction protocol for a PCI bus segment, the PCI-X bus master is not required to repeat the "exact same" bus transaction terminated by a Retry termination until it is completed.

The execution of the Split Response termination by the PCI-X/PCI-X BRIDGE requires completion of the bus transaction according to the Split Transaction protocol. In a similar situation in the Delayed Transaction protocol, the PCI/PCI BRIDGE would have executed a Retry termination and placed the burden to complete the bus transaction on the PCI bus master (The burden is to repeat the "exact same" bus transaction until completed). Using the Split Transaction protocol, the burden to complete the bus transaction is placed on the PCI-X/PCI-X BRIDGE. Consequently; instead of a PCI-X bus master "blindly" repeating the "exact same" bus transaction as with the Delayed Transaction protocol, the PCI-X/PCI-X BRIDGE will complete the bus transaction with split completion transaction(s) under the Split Transaction protocol when the data or bus transaction completion information is actually ready. If the PCI-X/PCI-X BRIDGE receives a Split Response termination from a downstream target (bridge or non-bridge) the responsibility for sourcing the split completion transactions moves downstream.

In order to provide a clear discussion of the Split Transaction protocol, the following example architecture and conventions will apply:

- The PCI-X bus master is on the source bus segment, the target is on the destination bus segment, the PCI-X/PCI-X BRIDGE is between the source and destination bus segments, and the target will not execute a Split Response termination in response to an access by the bridge.

- The PCI-X bus master that begins the access will be called "original" PCI-X bus master. The PCI-X/PCI-X BRIDGE is a PCI-X bus master of the destination bus segment but is not the "original" PCI-X bus master.

- The target that is being accessed by the "original" PCI-X bus master is called the "original" target. The PCI-X/PCI-X BRIDGE is a target on the source bus segment but is not the "original" target.

- The bus transaction executed by the "original" PCI-X bus master that is terminated with a Split Response termination by the PCI-X/PCI-X BRIDGE is called the "original" transaction.

- If the access is to the configuration address space of the PCI-X/PCI-X BRIDGE, the bridge is defined as the "original" target if the Split Transaction protocol is applied. Similar statements can be made if there are memory and I/O address space elements in the bridge that are being accessed as the actual target. These situations will not be part of the following discussion.

- The "original" target of a non-memory write transaction has the option to immediately complete the bus transaction or terminate it with the Split Response termination. For this discussion, the PCI-X/PCI-X BRIDGE will terminate the source bus segment transaction with a Split Response termination and the "original" transaction will also terminate the associated bus transaction on the destination bus segment with a Split Response termination. Consequently, as previously discussed, the source of the split completion transactions is the "original" target. The PCI-X/PCI-X BRIDGE will port the split completion transactions to the "original" PCI bus master on the source bus segment.

- The "original" transaction under consideration is one of the non-memory write transactions previously defined for the Split Transaction protocol.

- **According to the PCI-X addendum specification, a Split Completion transaction CANNOT be terminated with a Split Response termination. For all practical purposes, the Split Completion transaction is a form of writing to a memory address space without the normal address structure. See Chapter 4:** *Functional Interaction Between PCI and PCI-X Resources* **for more information.**

The Split Transaction protocol consists of two elements: Split Response termination and Split Completion transactions. A PCI-X bus transaction terminated by a Split Response termination will be completed by a "sequence" of split completion transactions according to the Split Transaction protocol. If the bus transaction was not terminated by the Split Response termination, the Split Transaction protocol does not apply. See Chapter 8: *Master and Target Terminations* for more information.

The "sequence" of split completion transactions is the series of split completion transactions associated with each other in that they are sourced from the "original" target, are a response to the "original" transaction, and their destination is the "original" PCI-X bus master. The source of split completion transactions is the "original" target; consequently, the "original" target is required to arbitrate to become the PCI-X bus master of the destination bus segment and to execute the "sequence" of split completion transactions. The "original" PCI-X bus master is NOT the device that executes the split completion transactions, but is the recipient of the "sequence" of split completion transactions.

A split completion transaction provides three types of information: data, completion, and/or error. If the "original" transaction was a read transaction, a split completion transaction will provide all the data and/or error information. Under normal operation, the "sequence" of split completion transactions will provide all of the read data without error. Not all or none of the bytes requested by the "original" transaction will be provided by the "sequence" of split completion transactions when an error occurs. If an error occurs, the last split completion transaction (which may be the first) of the "sequence" will contain the Split Completion Message. If the "original" transaction was a write transaction, a split completion transaction will provide completion confirmation of the "original" transaction" or error information. Consequently, the "sequence" of split completion transactions consists of only one split completion transaction that contains the Split Completion Message confirming successful write completion or an error. See Chapter 4: *Functional Interaction between PCI and PCI-X Resources* for more information.

> As discussed above, the "sequence" of split completion transactions may actually be a singular split completion transaction. For this discussion, the plural name of "split completion transactions" will be used even when the "sequence" may indeed be a single split completion transaction.

It is possible that multiple independent "original" transactions from the same or different PCI-X bus masters are terminated with Split Response terminations from the same or different targets ("original" targets or PCI-X/PCI-X BRIDGE on behalf of "original" targets per this discussion). Consequently, multiple independent "sequences" of split completion transactions will be executed. That is, one "sequence" of split completion transactions associated with an "original" transaction" is executing when another different "sequence" of split completion transactions associated with a different "original" transaction is executing. The Split Transaction protocol requires the "sequence" of split completion transactions for a specific "original" transaction maintain linear increasing addressing order independent of the "sequence" of split completion transactions associated with other "original" transactions. It is not possible for the Split Transaction protocol to control the completion of a "sequence" of split completion transactions for a specific "original" transaction. Consequently, a PCI-X bus master is not allowed to begin a new bus transaction that is dependent on the completion of the "sequence" of split completion transactions for an earlier "original" transactions. Similar protocol is required (via software or other means) between independent PCI-X bus masters. See Subchapter 7.1: *Summary of Bus Transaction Ordering* for more information.

Another consequence of multiple independent bus transactions from the same or different PCI-X bus masters being terminated with Split Response terminations (thus becoming "original" transactions) from the same or different targets is the requirement that each "original" transaction is required to be linked to a specific "sequence" of split completion transactions. Consequently, the Split Transaction protocol defines unique information in the ADDRESS and ATTRIBUTE PHASES of the split completion transactions that links these bus transactions to each other, the "original" transaction, the "original" PCI-X bus master, and the "original" target. See Chapter 4: *Functional Interaction between PCI and PCI-X Resources* for more information.

As part of the Split Transaction protocol, the PCI-X/PCI-X BRIDGE contains "Original" Transaction Buffers and Split Completion Command FIFOS. The information related to a source bus transaction terminated by Split Response termination is latched and stored into the "Original" Transaction Buffers. The contents of the "Original" Transaction Buffers cannot be discarded (as with Delayed Requests) and the bridge is required to execute the associated bus transactions on the destination bus segment. The bridge uses this information to execute destination bus segment transactions to the "original" targets. Once executed on the destination bus segment, the associated entry in the "Original" Transaction Buffer is deleted. Regarding this discussion, the "original" target requests a Split Response termination and becomes the source of the split completion transactions. The bridge stores the split completion transactions into the Split Completion Command FIFOS and subsequently ports the split completion transactions to the "original" PCI-X bus master on the source bus segment.

As mentioned above, the assumption for this discussion is that the "original" target is the source of the split completion transactions. If the "original" target had not requested a Split Response termination (*i.e.*, requested other terminations or completed the bus transaction), the PCI-X/PCI-X BRIDGE is responsible for creating the appropriate information to be placed into the Split Transaction Completion FIFOS. Consequently, the split completion transactions are ported to the "original" PCI-X bus master and are actually sourced by the bridge and not simply ported through from the "original" target.

DISCARDING "ORIGINAL" TRANSACTIONS AND SPLIT COMPLETION TRANSACTIONS (PCI-X ONLY)

Unlike the Delayed Requests in the PCI local bus specification, the "original" transactions in the "Original" Transaction Buffers cannot be discarded. According to the Split Transaction protocol, the request for Split Response termination by the PCI-X/PCI-X BRIDGE requires it to provide split completion transactions. In order to provide all of the split completion transactions to the PCI-X bus master, the bridge must port all "original" transactions to the destination bus segment.

Following the Split Transaction protocol, the split completion transactions are ported from the Split Completion Command FIFO. As previously discussed, the source of the split completion transaction is either the "original" target or created by the bridge. The "original" PCI–X bus master is required to have reserved sufficient buffer space to accept the split completion transactions. If the split completion transactions cannot be accepted by the "original" PCI-X bus master (Master Abort or Target Abort termination is requested), all split completion transactions in the Split Completion Command FIFO of the "same" sequence are discarded. Subsequent split completion transactions for the "same" sequence are also discarded. If the associated "original" transaction was a write transaction or a read transaction from a prefetchable address space region according to the associated registers in the bridge, no further action is required. If the associated "original" transaction was a read transaction from a non-prefetchable address space region according to the associated registers in the bridge, the SERR# signal

line must be asserted by the bridge once when the aforementioned Master Abort or
Target Abort termination is requested.

> The assertion of the SERR# signal line requires that the target or bridge
> has this signal line enabled for assertion and reports the assertion of this
> signal line. Both of the associated bits (enable and assertion) are in the
> PCI-X/PCI-X BRIDGE'S configuration address space. See Chapter 10: *Parity
> and Bus Errors* for more information

> The Discard Timer is not defined for the PCI-X/PCI-X BRIDGE in the Split
> Transaction protocol. It is only defined by the Delayed transaction
> protocol.

7.6   PORTING PCI MEMORY TRANSACTIONS THROUGH A BRIDGE (PCI ONLY)

INTRODUCTION

BURSTING THROUGH A BRIDGE

As previously discussed, not all bus transactions can be executed with the BURST
bus transaction protocol through a PCI/PCI BRIDGE. As described in Chapter 6:
Detailed Bus Transaction Operation, a BURST bus transaction is a sequence of
microaccesses. Each microaccess is required to contain valid byte enable
information on the C/BE# signal lines during the DATA PHASE. As shown in
Figure 7-3, the microaccess protocol requires the valid byte information for the
entire microaccess (Point A to Point B in Figure 7-3). That is, the C/BE# signal
lines change of byte enable information for the present microaccess change
relative to the sampling of asserted IRDY# and TRDY# signal lines on the rising
edge of the CLK signal line when (Point C in Figure 7-3). The byte enable
information of the C/BE# signal lines must remain unchanged until the assertion
of the IRDY# and TRDY# signal lines at the end of the present microaccess (Point
B in Figure 7-3). There is a physical delay in porting of the C/BE# signal lines
from the source bus segment to the destination bus segment through a PCI/PCI
BRIDGE. Obviously, it is impossible for the C/BE# signal lines on the destination
bus segment to contain valid byte enable information at beginning of the next
microaccess until this information is ported through the PCI/PCI BRIDGE from
the source bus segment. As previously stated, the change of the C/BE# signal lines
for the present microaccess on the source bus segment is simultaneous with the
completion of the present microaccess. Consequently, it is impossible for the

destination bus segment to contain the valid byte enable information at the beginning of the next microaccess due to the delay of porting the information from the source bus segment through the PCI/PCI BRIDGE.

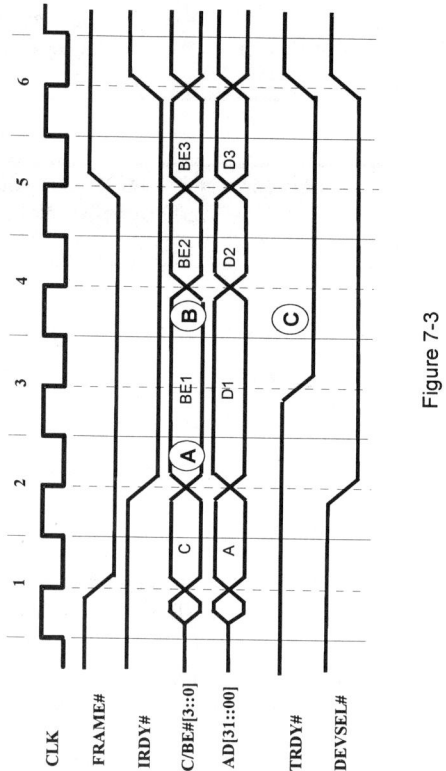

Figure 7-3: Valid C/BE# Signal Line Information

The inability for the destination bus segment to provide valid byte enable information at the beginning of the present microaccess causes problems for executing BURST bus transactions through a PCI/PCI BRIDGE. Three protocols in the PCI local bus specification address this problem: First, posting of memory write transactions (including memory write and invalidate (MWI)), Second, prefetchable address space relative to memory read transactions, and Third, The execution of memory read multiple (MRM) transactions and memory read line (MRL) transactions. These will be discussed in detail in subsequent sections.

PREFETCHABLE ADDRESS SPACE, MEMORY MAPPED I/O, AND BRIDGES

When the Prefetchable bit of the Memory Base Address register in the configuration address space of the target is set to logical "1", the associated memory address space is defined as prefetchable. A target's address range marked as prefetchable will return all bytes for memory read transactions (including MRM and MRL) independent of the bytes enabled by the asserted C/BE# signal lines during the DATA PHASE. If the Prefetchable bit of aforementioned Memory Base Address register is set to logical "0", the associated memory address space is defined as memory mapped I/O (MMI/O). A target's address range marked as MMI/O will return only the bytes enabled by the asserted C/BE# signal lines during the DATA PHASE for memory read transactions (including MRM and MRL). As previously discussed in Chapter 4: *Functional Interaction between PCI and PCI-X Resources*, the MMI/O address space may contain both regular DRAM memory and I/O type registers. For the MMI/O address space the multiple reading and discarding of data may have negative side effects (see below).

The PCI/PCI BRIDGES contain the Memory Base Address and Memory Limit registers in the configuration address space. These registers define the MMI/O address space that exists on the lower LEVEL bus segment relative to a bus transaction on the upper LEVEL bus segment. The PCI/PCI BRIDGES can optionally contain the Prefetchable Memory Base Address and Prefetchable Memory Limit registers in the configuration address space. These registers define the prefetchable address space that exists on the lower LEVEL bus segment relative to a bus transaction on the upper LEVEL bus segment. Also, there are optional Prefetchable Base Upper 32 Bits register and Prefetchable Limit Upper 32 Bits register for 32 bit addressing. These registers define memory address space ranges that are prefetchable. The existence in the PCI/PCI BRIDGE of these registers defines a prefetchable address space that affects how bus transactions are ported through the bridge, and are discussed below. See the PCI–to–PCI Bridge Architecture Specification Rev 1.1 for more information.

In order for any memory bus transaction to port through a PCI/PCI BRIDGE from an upper LEVEL bus segment to a lower LEVEL bus segment (downstream) a MMI/O address space and/or a prefetchable address space must be defined by the aforementioned registers in the bridge. By convention, it is assumed that all upstream memory bus transactions are accessing prefetchable address space. The only requirement is that the bridge provides a disabling bit in its configuration address space in the event the upstream memory read transaction (exclusive of MRM and MRL) is accessing a non-prefetchable memory resource. Upstream and downstream MRM and MRL transactions are always accessing prefetchable address space in accordance with the responsibility of the PCI bus master. That is, the PCI bus master is responsible for any negative side effects when it executes an MRM or a MRL transaction.

See Subchapter 7.7 for more information about prefetching.

> In the case of posting of memory write transactions, there is no distinction. That is, unlike the identification of prefetchable address space for memory read transactions, the posting of memory write transactions is applicable to the entire memory address space. The memory address space of a device must tolerate posted memory transaction activity in the PCI/PCI BRIDGE. This includes I/O registers that are mapped into the MMI/O address space.

MISCELLANEOUS

By convention, I/O, configuration, and interrupt acknowledge transactions are associated with address spaces that typically permit only a single data read or write. For example, once data is read from an I/O address space, the data typically is not available to be re-read from an external resource. That is, once data is read from an I/O input parallel register of a serial port interface, new data is ported into the register from the serial port. Similarly, once data is written to an I/O address space, the data may change the operation of the system (like enabling/disabling an interrupt to the HOST CPU in the interrupt controller). Thus, typically I/O writes cannot be posted in a PCI/PCI BRIDGE and BURST transactions are not possible. Consequently, I/O write and configuration write transactions cannot be posted in a PCI/PCI BRIDGE. Also, prefetchable address space is not defined for I/O read, configuration read, or interrupt acknowledge transactions. See Subchapter 7.9 for more information.

PORTING OF MEMORY WRITE TRANSACTIONS THROUGH A BRIDGE

The memory write transaction posting protocol has previously been discussed, and is applied across the memory address space. Because the C/BE# signal lines are posted in the PCI/PCI BRIDGE along with the other information of the memory write transaction, the PCI/PCI BRIDGE is prepared to begin the present microaccess on the destination bus segment immediately upon the completion of the previous microaccess. Consequently, the requirement that C/BE# signal lines having valid byte enable information throughout the entire microaccess is achieved and BURST bus transactions through the bridge are possible.

The posting and thus the bursting of bus transactions also applies to MWI transactions for the same reasons as for memory write transactions. PCI/PCI

BRIDGES can optionally implement a Memory Write and Invalidate Enable bit in the COMMAND register in its configuration address space.

- If not implemented or implemented and set to logical "0",

  - The bridge will port (with posting) MWI transactions provided the Cacheline Size Register in its configuration address space is implemented and has been set to a value. Otherwise an MWI transaction on the source bus segment will be executed as a memory write transaction on the destination bus segment.

  - The bridge will port memory write transactions (with posting), but will never convert them to MWI transactions.

- If implemented and set to logical "1".

  - The bridge will port (with posting) MWI transactions provided the Cacheline Size Register in the configuration address space is implemented and has been set to a value. Otherwise an MWI transaction on the source bus segment will be executed as a memory write transaction on the destination bus segment.

  - The bridge will port (with posting) memory write transactions from the source bus segment and execute them on the destination bus segment as MWI transactions provided both of the following requirements are met

    - The Cacheline Size Register in the configuration address space is implemented and has been set to a value.

    - The bridge can only translate the memory write transaction on the source bus segment to an MWI transaction on the destination bus segment provided that all of the linear increasing addressing, and beginning and ending on Cacheline boundaries can be maintained. All data in the memory write transaction on the source bus segment outside of the requirements for an MWI transaction are ported as part of additional memory write transactions (non-MWI) on the destination bus segment.

As previously discussed, the target on the destination bus segment can optionally implement the MWI transaction as a memory write transaction. See Chapter 4: *Functional Interaction between PCI and PCI-X Resources* for more information.

BURSTING OF MEMORY READ TRANSACTIONS THROUGH A BRIDGE

As discussed in the *Introduction* above, the bursting of a memory read (exclusive of MRL and MRM) transactions through a PCI/PCI BRIDGE requires all of the C/BE# signal lines to be asserted in the DATA PHASE on the destination bus segment. However, without the execution of an MRL or a MRM transaction, the bridge does not know if a memory read transaction on the source bus segment will have all of the C/BE# signal lines asserted for all microaccesses, and thus BURST memory read transactions through the bridge are not possible with one exception. The bridge can use the information in the aforementioned prefetchable address registers in the bridge to determine if a memory read transaction (with or without all C/BE# signal lines asserted in the DATA PHASE) on the source bus segment is within the prefetchable address space. If within the prefetchable address space, the bridge can translate the memory read transaction on the source bus segment to a memory read, MRM, or MRL transaction on the destination bus segment (with all C/BE# signal lines asserted in the DATA PHASE). Thus BURST read transactions can be ported through the bridge.

If the memory read transactions on the source bus segment are not within the prefetchable address space, or if the aforementioned prefetchable address registers are not implemented in the bridge, the memory read transaction on the source bus segment is ported through the bridge as a SINGLE bus transaction. There will be no change in the pattern of asserted C/BE# signal lines in the DATA PHASE, no BURST read transactions through the bridge will occur, and the memory read transaction on the source bus segment will not be translated to an MRL or MRM transaction on the destination bus segment.

BURSTING OF MRL AND MRM TRANSACTIONS THROUGH A BRIDGE

According to the PCI local bus specification definition, the MRL and MRM transactions can be executed as BURST bus transactions through a PCI/PCI BRIDGE. When a PCI bus master executes an MRM or MRL transaction on a source bus segment, all of the C/BE# signal lines of each microaccess may not be asserted. If the MRM or MRL transaction is within the prefetchable address space (according to the aforementioned prefetchable address space registers in the bridge's configuration address space), the bridge must execute the MRL or MRM bus transactions on the destination bus segment with all C/BE# signal lines asserted. Consequently, the PCI/PCI BRIDGE does not care about the value of the C/BE# signal lines in the present microaccess on the source bus segment before the completion of the previous microaccess on the source bus segment, and BURST bus transactions through a bridge can be executed.

If the MRM or MRL transaction on the source bus segment is not within the prefetchable address space (according to the aforementioned prefetchable address space registers in the bridge's configuration address space), the bridge can do one of the following:

- The bridge can translate an MRM or MRL transaction (not all C/BE# signal lines may be asserted in the DATA PHASE) on the source bus segment to a memory read transaction (not ported as an MRL or MRM transaction) on the destination bus segment. Consequently, a SINGLE bus transaction is ported through the bridge with no change in the pattern of asserted C/BE# signal lines (no bursting through the bridge will occur).

- The bridge can port the MRM transaction (not all C/BE# signal lines may be asserted in the DATA PHASE) on the source bus segment to a memory read or an MRM transaction on the destination bus segment executed as a BURST bus transaction with all C/BE# signal lines asserted in the DATA PHASE (bursting through the bridge).

- The bridge can port the MRL transaction (not all C/BE# signal lines may be asserted in the DATA PHASE) on the source bus segment to a memory read or an MRL transaction on the destination bus segment executed as a BURST bus transaction with all C/BE# signal lines asserted in DATA PHASE (bursting through the bridge).

> If the MRL and MRM transactions on the source bus segment are a SINGLE bus transaction (with or without all C/BE# signal lines asserted in the DATA PHASE), the PCI/PCI BRIDGE can optionally execute the bus transaction on the destination bus segment with same or all C/BE# signal lines asserted in the DATA PHASE.

As previously discussed, a target can execute an MRL or a MRM transaction if a memory read transaction has been executed. However the MRL or MRM transaction may have been ported through a bridge; consequently, the bridge will have asserted all of the C/BE# signal lines (the target will have no choice but to read all of the bytes). Thus, all bytes will be read even when the Prefetchable bit in the target's Memory Base Address register is set to logical "0". Consequently, the PCI bus master is required to be responsible that the execution of MRM and MRL transactions will have no negative side effects.

> A PCI memory target that has its Prefetchable bit set to logical "1" in its Memory Base Address Register in the configuration address space must execute MRM and MRL transactions without any negative side effects.

MRM and MRL transactions are limited to 4K byte blocks on 4K address boundaries by the target on the destination bus segment. Rev 1.1 of the PCI-to-PCI Bridge Architecture Specification removed the previous requirement for a PCI/PCI BRIDGE to terminate bus transactions at 4K address boundaries. The bridge will port the memory read, MRM, and MRL transactions to the destination bus segment without regard to the 4K address boundary.

7.7   PREFETCHING (PCI ONLY)

As discussed in the *Introduction* section of Subchapter 7.6, the target and PCI/PCI BRIDGES have registers that define the prefetchable address space. In the case of the target, the prefetchable address space defines an area of memory where multiple readings of data (without writes) and the discarding of data have no negative side effects. In some cases, the data read has been returned by the target and discarded by the PCI bus master or an intervening PCI/PCI BRIDGE. In other cases, the target may internally be prefetching portions of the prefetchable address space and does not get the opportunity to source the prefetched data back to the PCI bus master (*i.e.*, when executing MRM and MRL transactions). The target has limited buffer space and thus must discard data not returned to the PCI bus master.

In summary, for the target to have its Prefetchable bit set to logical "1" in the Memory Base Address Register in its configuration address space, all of the following requirements must be met for the associated prefetchable address space:

■ Multiple memory reads of the 32 data bits (or 64 data bits when REG64# and ACK64# signal lines are asserted) will result in the same data being read.

■ If the data read (all or part of a 32 or 64 data bit transaction) is discarded by the PCI bus master, PCI/PCI BRIDGE, or target, no negative side effects will occur.

■ The target must support byte merging in an intervening PCI/PCI BRIDGE.

■ All memory read, MRL, and MRM bus transactions to the target's prefetchable address space result in all bytes being returned by the target in each microaccess independent of the C/BE# signal lines asserted in each microaccess.

Other considerations relative to prefetching follow:

■ The PCI bus master using MRM and MRL transactions is responsible for no negative side effects. If the Prefetchable bit set to logical "0" in the Memory Base Address Register in the configuration address of the target it is not required to read and return all bytes. That is, the target returns the bytes enabled by the asserted C/BE# signal lines for each microaccess.

■ The target may prefetch data using MRM and MRL transactions, or not prefetch data as for memory read transactions.

■ The prefetching protocol must be executed within a 4K page on a 4K address boundary. If the PCI bus master tries to access across this boundary during BURST MRM or MRL bus transactions, the target must execute a Disconnect termination. Rev 1.1 of the PCI-to-PCI Bridge Architecture Specification has removed the requirement that the bridge monitor the prefetching across 4K address boundary. The associated bus transactions are ported through the bridge without a Disconnect termination. See Chapter 8: *Master and Target Termination* for more information.

7.8   PORTING PCI-X MEMORY AND SPLIT COMPLETION TRANSACTIONS THROUGH A BRIDGE (PCI-X ONLY)

INTRODUCTION

The PCI-X addendum specification defines the bus transactions in a different fashion than the PCI local bus specification. As previously discussed, the PCI-X COMMANDS are defined as DWORD and BURST. DWORD COMMANDS can only be executed as SINGLE bus transactions; consequently, porting through a PCI-X/PCI-X BRDIGE is only possible with SINGLE bus transactions. The BURST COMMANDS can be executed as either SINGLE or BURST bus transactions. The BURST COMMANDS executed as SINGLE bus transactions port through a bridge as SINGLE bus transactions. The BURST COMMANDS executed as BURST bus transactions in some cases can be ported through the bridge as BURST bus transactions.

BURSTING OF MEMORY WRITE AND SPLIT COMPLETION TRANSACTIONS THROUGH A BRIDGE

> The porting of memory write and split completion transactions through a bridge requires buffering (*i.e.*, FIFO). Section 8.4 of the PCI-X addendum specification has an extensive discussion of buffer sizing requirements. These requirements are not reviewed in this chapter in that they are more bridge-centric and not specific to the PCI-X bus segment protocol. If designing a bridge or an interface (with bridge-like features) between a PCI-X bus segment and internal circuitry in an ASIC, please review this section.

The protocol of BURST COMMANDS permit the bursting of memory write (including memory write block and alias memory write block) transactions through a PCI-X/PCI-X BRIDGE. The memory write transaction posting protocol in the PCI local bus specification also applies to bus transactions compliant to the PCI-X addendum bus specification. The ability for PCI-X bus transactions for BURST COMMANDS to burst through a bridge is dependent on the posting of the bus transaction. As previously discussed, the posting protocol is applied across the memory address space. In that the C/BE# signal lines are posted in the bridge along with the other information of the memory write transaction, the bridge is prepared to begin the present microaccess on the destination bus segment immediately upon the completion of the previous microaccess (see the discussion in the Introduction of Subchapter 7.6: *Porting PCI Memory Transactions through a Bridge (PCI Only)*). Consequently, the requirement that C/BE# signal lines have valid byte enable information throughout the entire microaccess is achieved and is available for the present microaccess at the end of the previous microaccess. In the case of BURST memory write block and alias memory write block transactions, all of the byte enables are defined as valid. Although all bytes are valid, the protocol for these bus transactions define the C/BE# signal lines to be deasserted throughout the DATA PHASE. Additionally, the Sequence ID in the ATTRIBUTE PHASE of a bus transaction for any of the BURST memory write commands is not modified as it is posted and ported through the PCI-X/PCI-X BRIDGE. See Section 8.4.3 of the PCI-X addendum specification for further clarification if the bridge is between PCI and PCI-X bus segments.

> The porting of a PCI-X BURST memory write transaction through a bridge is dependent on the available buffer space (*i.e.*, FIFO). The bridge is considered "full" if two ADB sized buffers are not available (with some exceptions). When the bridge is "full" it must request a Retry, a Single Phase Disconnect, or a Disconnect at Next ADB termination relative to available buffer space and if the bus transaction addresses are near an ADB. Also, in Rev. 1.0.a of the PCI-X addendum specification section 8.4.6 was added to reflect these considerations. If designing a bridge or an interface (with bridge-like features) between a PCI-X bus segment and internal circuitry in an ASIC, please review this "new" section.

Bus transactions for the BURST split completion command by definition provide all of the bytes requested by the associated memory read transaction terminated by Split Response termination. The C/BE# signal lines are driven deasserted in the DATA PHASE of the split completion transaction, but following split completion transaction protocol all of the bytes are read from the target and are being sourced in the "sequence" split completion transactions. Consequently, the bus transactions for a BURST split completion command can be posted and ported through the bridge as BURST bus transactions. See Chapter 4: *Functional Interaction between PCI and PCI-X Resources* for more information. Additionally, the Sequence ID in the ATTRIBUTE PHASE of a BURST split completion transaction can be modified as it is posted and ported through the PCI-X/PCI-X BRIDGE when it is decomposed into multiple split completion transactions. See section 8.4.2 of the PCI-X addendum specification for more information. Also, see section 8.4.3 of the PCI-X addendum specification for further clarification if the bridge is between PCI and PCI-X bus segments.

> The porting of a PCI-X BURST split completion transaction through a bridge is dependent on the available buffer space (*i.e.*, FIFO). The bridge is considered "full" if two ADB sized buffers are not available. The one exception when a bridge is not considered full is when fewer than two ADB sized buffers are not available and an alternative means is available to permit a split completion transaction that is too short to forward correctly.
>
> When the bridge is "full" it must request a Retry or a Disconnect at Next ADB termination relative to available buffer space (see Chapter 8: *Master and Target Termination* for more information). Also, in the PCI-X addendum specification, section 8.4 reflects these considerations. If designing a bridge or an interface (with bridge-like features) between a PCI-X bus segment and internal circuitry in an ASIC, please review this section.

BURSTING OF MEMORY READ TRANSACTIONS
THROUGH A BRIDGE

> The porting of BURST memory read transactions through a bridge requires buffering. Section 8.4 of the PCI-X addendum specification has a extensive discussion of buffer sizing requirements. These requirements are not reviewed in this chapter in that they are more bridge-centric and not specific to the PCI-X bus segment protocol. If designing a bridge or an interface (with bridge-like features) between a PCI-X bus segment and internal circuitry in an ASIC, please review this section.

The protocol for BURST transactions for the BURST memory read block and alias memory read block commands by definition are reading all of the bytes. The C/BE# signal lines are driven deasserted in the DATA PHASE of the BURST memory read block and alias memory read block transactions, but following BURST memory read transaction protocol, all of the bytes are being read from the target (in spite of the C/BE# signal lines being deasserted in the DATA PHASE). Consequently, in theory BURST memory read block and alias memory read block transactions can be ported through a PCI-X/PCI-X BRIDGE because indirectly valid byte enable information is available throughout the entire microaccess. For an interface (acting like a bridge) between the PCI-X bus segment and internal circuitry of an ASIC this is certainly true. However, the PCI-X addendum specification requires a PCI-X/PCI-X bridge to request a Split Response termination for the BURST memory read block and alias memory read block transactions to invoke the Split Transaction protocol.

According to the PCI-X addendum bus specification, a memory target can prefetch any data, provided there are no negative read side effects (*i.e.,* multiple reads, discarding, and merging of associated memory write transactions in an intervening bridge are not a problem). The PCI local bus specification requirements for prefetching of Cachelines and multiple Cachelines (MRL and MRM) do not apply, in that these commands are not defined in the PCI-X addendum specification. The PCI local bus specification requirement to return all bytes within the prefetchable address space (when requested via asserted C/BE# signal lines) is not required. That is, the bytes returned for a DWORD read transaction are only those defined by the bus transaction independent of the address space being prefetchable or not. The use of the Split Transaction protocol to complete BURST memory read block and alias memory read block transactions requires the return of all bytes address independent of the prefetchable address space. Similarly, the direct response to BURST memory read block and alias memory read block transactions requires the return of all bytes address independent of the prefetchable address space That is, following the bus transaction protocol of BURST memory read block, alias memory read block, and split completion transactions, a

ll bytes are being read.

> The porting of a PCI-X BURST memory read transaction through a bridge is dependent on the available buffer space. The bridge must have two ADB sized buffers available before porting forward. In the PCI-X addendum specification, section 8.4.1 reflects these considerations. If designing a bridge or an interface (with bridge-like features) between a PCI-X bus segment and internal circuitry in an ASIC, please review this section.

7.9 I/O, CONFIGURATION, INTERRUPT ACKNOWLEDGE, AND SPECIAL TRANSACTIONS THROUGH PCI/PCI OR PCI-X/PCI-X BRIDGES

PCI SPECIFIC

I/O TRANSACTIONS

I/O commands executed by a PCI bus master (non-bridge) to targets (non-bridge) on the same PCI bus segment can be executed as either SINGLE or BURST bus transactions. As previously stated, the porting of a BURST bus transaction through a PCI/PCI BRIDGE requires advance knowledge of the enabled byte via the asserted C/BE# signal lines in the DATA PHASE. One solution to having advance knowledge is to enable all of the byte enables on the destination bus segment and discarding the data that is read but not needed. The memory address space has the attribute of providing the same data for multiple reads. The I/O address space contains data that typically can be read only once. The reading of I/O data that may be discarded will obviously have negative side effects. Consequently, it is not possible to port a BURST I/O read transaction through a PCI/PCI BRIDGE. Only a SINGLE I/O read transaction can be ported through a PCI/PCI BRIDGE.

Similarly, the attribute of memory address space supporting the posting of write transactions in the PCI/PCI BRIDGE does not apply to the I/O address space. The completion of the memory write transaction on the source bus segment permits the associated bus transaction to be completed on the destination bus segment at a later time without negative side effects via the posting protocol. By convention, the I/O address space may have negative side effects if the bus transaction on the destination bus segment is completed after the completion of the associated bus transaction on the source bus segment. Consequently, I/O write transactions cannot be posted in the PCI/PCI BRIDGE. Without the posting of I/O write transactions in the bridge, BURST I/O write transactions through a PCI/PCI BRIDGE are not possible. Only a SINGLE I/O write transactions can be ported through a PCI/PCI BRIDGE.

If the hardware and software designers have a clear understanding of the consequences, posting of I/O write transactions in the HOST/PCI BRIDGE it is permitted by the PCI local bus specification. For the purpose of discussions in this book, the focus is on PCI/PCI BRIDGES; thus I/O write transactions are not posted.

CONFIGURATION AND SPECIAL TRANSACTIONS

As previously discussed, the PCI local bus specification supports configuration transactions to access registers for each device (PCI bus master, target, or PCI/PCI BRIDGE collectively defined as "device") and special transactions. Even though the configuration and special transactions follow the basic protocol of memory or I/O transactions, there are some differences relative to executing on a bus segment and porting through a PCI/PCI BRIDGE for SINGLE and BURST configuration and special transactions:

- A PCI bus master (non-bridge or bridge) can execute Type 1 configuration commands as SINGLE and BURST transactions to a target (non-bridge). In the case of Type 1 configuration transactions, the immediate target on a source bus segment may be the PCI/PCI BRIDGE that can port it to the destination bus segment of the target. For the same reasons as outlined above for I/O transactions, the bridge cannot port BURST Type 1 configuration transactions. A PCI/PCI BRIDGE would terminate a BURST Type 1 configuration transaction with a Disconnect termination and effectively force a SINGLE bus transaction. Consequently, this book will assume that the Type 1 configuration command can only be executed as a SINGLE bus transaction.

  - A Type 0 configuration transaction translated from a Type 1 configuration transaction (through a PCI/PCI BRIDGE) can only be executed as a SINGLE bus transaction.

  - A special transaction translated from a Type 1 configuration transaction (through a PCI/PCI BRIDGE) can only be executed as a SINGLE bus transaction.

- A SINGLE or BURST special transaction can occur when a PCI bus master (other than the PCI/PCI BRIDGE) is accessing a target (non-bridge) on the same PCI bus segment.

- A SINGLE or BURST special transaction can occur when a HOST/PCI BRIDGE is accessing a device on the attached PCI bus segment.

- A SINGLE or BURST Type 0 configuration transaction can occur when a HOST/PCI BRIDGE is accessing a device on the attached PCI bus segment.

- As previously discussed, a PCI bus master (non-bridge) cannot execute Type 0 configuration transactions. See Chapter 4: *Functional Interaction between PCI and PCI-X Resources* for more information

> **The PCI/PCI BRIDGE can only port upstream (lower LEVEL bus segment to upper LEVEL bus segment) the Type 1 configuration write transactions for purposes of executing special transactions; no other Type 1 configuration transactions can be ported upstream (*i.e.*, for porting Type 0 configuration transactions). Type 1 configuration transactions for purposes of executing special transactions or Type 0 configuration transactions can also be ported by the PCI/PCI BRIDGE downstream (upper LEVEL bus segment to lower LEVEL bus segment).**

In order for a PCI/PCI BRIDGE to determine if the Type 1 configuration transactions should be ported as a Type 1 configuration transaction or converted to a Type 0 configuration transaction or special transaction, three registers are required in the configuration address space of each PCI/PCI BRIDGE. These registers correlate the relative position of each PCI/PCI BRIDGE to the hierarchy of PCI bus segment. The PRIMARY BUS number register refers to the bus number of the upper LEVEL bus segment attached to the bridge. It is located at configuration register offset of 18h. The SECONDARY BUS number register refers to the bus number of the lower LEVEL bus segment attached to the bridge. It is located at configuration register offset of 19h. The SUBORDINATE BUS number register refers to the bus number of the lowest LEVEL bus segment accessible through the associated bridge. The assignment of a bus number for each PCI bus segment is done at platform initialization using a protocol outlined in Chapter 2: *PCI and PCI-X System Architecture Overview*. As a Type 1 configuration transaction moves from upper LEVEL to lower LEVEL bus segments, each PCI/PCI BRIDGE compares the BUS number in the bus transaction (AD[23::16] signal lines in the ADDRESS PHASE) to the values in the SECONDARY BUS and SUBORDINATE BUS registers of the bridge. Similarly, as a Type 1 configuration transaction moves from lower LEVEL to upper LEVEL bus segments, each PCI/PCI BRIDGE compares the BUS number in the transaction (AD[23::16] signal lines in the ADDRESS PHASE) to the values in the PRIMARY BUS, SECONDARY BUS, and SUBORDINATE BUS registers of the bridge.

The HOST/PCI BRIDGE also makes use of the SECONDARY BUS and SUBORDINATE BUS registers for a Type 1 configuration transaction moving from upper LEVEL to lower LEVEL bus segments, or to determine when to execute a Type 0 configuration transaction, Type 1 configuration transaction, or special transaction on a LEVEL 1 bus segment. The PRIMARY register is not required in the HOST/PCI BRIDGE because Type 1 configuration transaction from a lower LEVEL bus segment cannot be converted to a configuration transaction or special transaction on the HOST CPU bus segment (if this register address is read, all "0"s are returned). The SECONDARY BUS register is not required if only one HOST/CPU BRIDGE is attached to the HOST CPU bus segment (if this register address is read, all "0"s are returned). If multiple HOST/CPU BRIDGES are attached to the HOST CPU bus segment, the SECONDARY BUS register is required.

As shown in Figure 7-2, multiple HOST/CPU BRIDGEs (defined as peer bridges) result in different bus numbers (two individual bus segments in this example) for the LEVEL 1 bus. Consequently, there are multiple CONFIG_ADDRESS and CONFIG_DATA registers on the same HOST CPU bus. The platform is required to assign one of these bridges as the one responsible for handshaking ("main" bridge) with the HOST CPU bus segment for accesses to the CONFIG_ADDRESS register I/O address, and the other bridges are required to snoop the data written. By some method, the HOST CPU bus segment is required to individually address the CONFIG_DATA register of the HOST/CPU BRIDGE that is linked to the specific PCI bus segment of interest of all LEVEL 1 bus segments.

For a PCI/PCI BRIDGE to claim a Type 1 configuration transaction on its upper LEVEL bus segment side the following must be considered:

- The transaction can be claimed and ported to the lower LEVEL bus segment side as a Type 1 configuration transaction when the BUS number in the Type 1 configuration transaction is between the SECONDARY BUS number (exclusive) and the SUBORDINATE BUS number (inclusive). Type 1 configuration transaction is ported through the PCI/PCI BRIDGE for a special transaction or Type 0 configuration transaction to be executed on the eventual destination bus segment. During the ADDRESS PHASE of the Type 1 configuration transaction, the AD[1:0] signal lines = [0:1].

  - The information contained in the ADDRESS and DATA PHASE of the Type 1 configuration transaction on the upper LEVEL bus segment is ported unchanged to the information contained in the ADDRESS and DATA PHASE of the Type 1 configuration transaction on the lower LEVEL bus segment

- The transaction can be claimed and translated to a Type 0 configuration transaction on the lower LEVEL bus segment side when the BUS number in the Type 1 configuration transaction equals SECODARY BUS number. Also, NOT all bits in the DEVICE and FUNCTION numbers in the Type 1 configuration equal logical "1", and not all bits of the REGISTER number in the Type 1 configuration equal logical "0". That is, it is not a special transaction. Also, during the ADDRESS PHASE of the Type 1 configuration transaction, the AD[1::0] signal lines = [0::1]

■ The information contained in the DATA PHASE of the Type 1 configuration transaction on the upper LEVEL bus segment is ported unchanged to the information contained in the DATA PHASE of the Type 0 configuration transaction on the lower LEVEL bus segment. In the ADDRESS PHASE of the Type 0 configuration transaction AD[1::0] signal lines = [0::0], and AD[10::2] signal lines = AD[10::2] signal lines of the Type 1 configuration transaction in the ADDRESS PHASE. The AD[15::11] signal lines in the ADDRESS PHASE of the Type 1 configuration transaction is required (independent of how IDSEL signal lines are actually implemented) to be converted to the following values on the AD[31::16] signal lines in the ADDRESS PHASE of the Type 0 configuration transaction:

Type 1 Configuration Transaction AD[15::11] Signal Lines in ADDRESS PHASE	Type 0 Configuration Transaction AD[31::16] Signal Lines in ADDRESS PHASE
00000	0000 0000 0000 0001
00001	0000 0000 0000 0010
00010	0000 0000 0000 0100
00011	0000 0000 0000 1000
00100	0000 0000 0001 0000
00101	0000 0000 0010 0000
00110	0000 0000 0100 0000
00111	0000 0000 1000 0000
01000	0000 0001 0000 0000
01001	0000 0010 0000 0000
01010	0000 0100 0000 0000
01011	0000 1000 0000 0000
01100	0001 0000 0000 0000
01101	0010 0000 0000 0000
01110	0100 0000 0000 0000
01111	1000 0000 0000 0000
1xxxx	0000 0000 0000 0000

Table 7-5: ADDRESS PHASE IDSEL Mapping

The IDSEL signal line associated with the AD16 signal line is not permitted to be used because it is reserved for the PCI/PCI BRIDGE to which this downstream bus segment is attached.

> If the DEVICE number selects an IDSEL signal line not supported by the bridge, the bridge should either: NOT execute a Type 0 configuration transaction, and discard the write data or return all logical "1"s for a read transaction ... OR ... execute a Type 0 configuration transaction with no IDSEL signal lines asserted which will result in a Master Abort termination (no device on the attached bus segment claimed the bus transaction). The Master Abort termination results in a discard of write data and a read of all logical "1"s.

- The transaction can be claimed and translated to a special transaction on the lower LEVEL bus segment side when the BUS number in the Type 1 configuration transaction equals the SECODARY BUS number. Also, each bit of the DEVICE and FUNCTION numbers in the Type 1 configuration transaction equals logical "1", and each bit of the REGISTER number in the Type 1 configuration transaction equals logical "0 Also, during the ADDRESS PHASE of the Type 1 configuration transaction the AD[1::0] signal lines = [0::1].

  - The information contained in the DATA PHASE of the Type 1 configuration transaction on the upper LEVEL bus segment is ported unchanged to the information contained in the DATA PHASE of the special transaction on the lower LEVEL bus segment. In the ADDRESS PHASE of the special transaction, the AD[31::0] signal lines are driven to a stable logical level.

For a PCI/PCI BRIDGE to claim a Type 1 configuration transaction on its lower LEVEL bus segment side the following must be considered:

- The transaction can be claimed and ported to the upper LEVEL bus segment side as a Type 1 configuration transaction when the BUS number in the Type 1 configuration transaction is NOT between the SECONDARY BUS number (inclusive) and the SUBORDINATE BUS number (inclusive). The Type 1 configuration transaction is ported through the PCI/PCI BRIDGE for a special transaction on the eventual destination bus segment. The PCI/PCI BRIDGE can never claim a Type 1 configuration transaction on its lower LEVEL bus segment side if it is for a Type 0 configuration transaction on the destination bus segment. Also, during the ADDRESS PHASE of the Type 1 configuration transaction the AD[1::0] signal lines = [0::1]. The information contained in the ADDRESS and DATA PHASEs of the Type 1 configuration transaction on the lower LEVEL bus segment is ported unchanged to the information contained in the ADDRESS and DATA PHASEs of the Type 1 configuration transaction on the upper LEVEL bus segment.

  - The PCI/PCI BRIDGE will know the Type 1 configuration transaction is for a special transaction, because bits of the DEVICE number and

572

REGISTER number are all logical "1", and all the bits of the REGISTER number are logical "0". Otherwise, it is considered a Type 0 configuration transaction or a Type 1 configuration transaction containing a Type 0 configuration transaction, and is not claimed.

■ The transaction can be claimed and translated to a special transaction on the upper LEVEL bus segment side when the BUS number in the Type 1 configuration transaction equals the PRIMARY BUS number. Also, each bit in the DEVICE and FUNCTION numbers in the Type 1 configuration transaction equals logical "1", and each bit of the REGISTER number in the Type 1 configuration equals logical "0". Also, during the ADDRESS PHASE of the Type 1 configuration transaction, the AD[1::0] signal lines = [0::1]. The information contained in the DATA PHASE of the Type 1 configuration transaction on the lower LEVEL bus segment is ported unchanged to the information contained in the DATA PHASE of the special transaction on the upper LEVEL bus segment. In the ADDRESS PHASE of the special transaction, the AD[31::0] signal lines are driven to a stable logical level.

For a PCI/PCI BRIDGE to claim a Type 0 configuration transaction on its upper LEVEL bus segment side the following must be considered:

■ The transaction can be claimed when the access is to the configuration address space of the PCI/PCI BRIDGE. To claim a Type 0 configuration transaction requires the following conditions to be met:

　■ It is done in conjunction with the assertion of the associated IDSEL signal line on the upper LEVEL bus segment.

　■ During the ADDRESS PHASE AD[1::0] signal lines = [0:0].

　■ If the PCI/PCI BRIDGE contains only a single function, the PCI/PCI BRIDGE can either claim the Type 0 configuration transaction for any value of the AD[10::8] signal lines during the ADDRESS PHASE or only for function 0 (AD[10::8] signal lines = [1:1:0] during ADDRESS PHASE)

　■ If the PCI/PCI BRIDGE contains multiple functions, the PCI/PCI BRIDGE must not claim the Type 0 configuration transaction if the AD[10::8] signal lines during the ADDRESS PHASE does not decode a specific function with a configuration address space.

A PCI/PCI BRIDGE cannot claim a Type 0 configuration transaction on its lower LEVEL bus segment side.

As discussed previously in this book, a special transaction cannot port through a PCI/PCI BRIDGE. The special transaction can only port through a PCI/PCI BRIDGE via a configuration transaction.

> The protocol exception outlined above for posting of I/O transactions in a HOST/BRIDGE BRIDGE cannot be applied to configuration or special transactions.

INTERRRUPT ACKNOWLEDGE TRANSACTIONS

The protocol for interrupt acknowledge transactions is the same as for I/O transactions; however, there are a couple of issues to consider. An interrupt acknowledge is ported through HOST/PCI BRIDGES and PCI/LEGACY BRIDGES, and not ported through PCI/PCI BRIDGES. The present PCI local bus specification implies only SINGLE interrupt acknowledge transactions are executed. If a BURST interrupt acknowledge transactions are executed they can only be from the HOST/PCI BRIDGE.

Because the device containing the interrupt controller is defined as being only on PCI bus (0) (or attached in the PCI/LEGACY BRIDGE or the LEGACY bus segment), the flow of interrupt acknowledge transactions is only between the HOST and PCI bus (0) bus segments.

> The protocol exception outlined above for posting of I/O transactions in a HOST/BRIDGE BRIDGE cannot be applied to interrupt acknowledge transactions.

PCI-X SPECIFIC

I/O, CONFIGURATION, INTERRUPT ACKNOWLEDGE, AND SPECIAL TRANSACTIONS

The PCI-X addendum specification defines all I/O, configuration, interrupt acknowledge, and special commands as DWORD COMMANDS. DWORD COMMANDS can only be executed with SINGLE bus transactions. Consequently, I/O, configuration, and interrupt acknowledge commands can only port through a PCI-X/PCI-X BRIDGE as a SINGLE bus transaction.

The discussion above relative to the I/O, configuration, interrupt acknowledge, and special transactions flow for systems compliant to the PCI local bus specification also applies to the flow of these bus transactions in systems compliant to the PCI-X addendum specification.

The IDSEL mapping to the AD signal lines for a PCI-X addendum specification compliant system is the same as discussed above for a PCI local bus specification compliant system. The only differences are as follows:

- It is recommend that the IDSEL signal line for the first four add-on card slots be attached to AD [17] to AD[20] signal lines to minimize the trace length.

- The IDSEL signal lines in the Type 0 configuration transaction are mapped to the AD[31::16] signal lines, and the AD[15::11} signal lines contain the Device Number.

7.10   INTERACTION OF CONFIGURATION AND SPECIAL TRANSACTIONS WITH REGISTERS IN HOST/PCI AND HOST/PCI-X BRIDGES

PCI SPECIFIC

As previously outlined in this chapter, configuration transactions are executed on the PCI bus segment to provide access to the configuration space of devices. The bridges between PCI bus segments, and PCI bus segments and non-PCI buses play an important role in the execution of configuration transactions. Traditional HOST CPU and LEGACY buses define only memory and I/O address spaces. In the case of the x86 family of Intel CPUs (HOST CPU), no configuration transactions are defined. For LEGACY buses such as EISA, the equivalent of the configuration space is accessed via the I/O address space. The PCI local bus specification does not define the register protocol for the HOST/LEGACY or PCI/LEGACY BRIDGEs. Typically, the any configuration address space defined for the LEGACY bus is done via the I/O address space. Also, there are no special transactions defined for the LEGACY bus.

The PCI local bus specification does specify the operation of the HOST/PCI BRIDGE relative to configuration and special transactions. As previously stated, the typical HOST CPU bus does not support configuration or special transactions. Consequently, in this section the operation of registers within the HOST/PCI BRIDGE to generate configuration and special transaction is described.

> Relative to the HOST/PCI BRIDGE there are two unique issues. First, a HOST/PCI BRIDGE does not implement the PRIMARY BUS REGISTER because configuration or special transactions are not executed on the HOST CPU bus segment. If this register address is read, all "0"s are returned. Second, the SECONDARY BUS number register is not implemented in all HOST/PCI BRIDGEs. If only one HOST/PCI BRIDGE is attached to the HOST CPU bus segment, by definition the lower LEVEL bus segment attached to it is PCI bus (0). Consequently, whenever the BUS number bits in the CONFIG_ADDR register are all logical "0", only one LEVEL 1 bus segment is referenced and the SECONDARY BUS register is not required. If this register address is read, all "0"s are returned. If there are multiple HOST/PCI BRIDGEs on the HOST CPU bus segment, the SECONDARY BUS register is required. See the next section for more information.

As previously discussed, a Type 0 configuration transaction cannot be claimed (DEVSEL# signal line asserted) on the lower LEVEL bus segment side of the PCI/PCI BRIDGE. This protocol also applies to the HOST/PCI BRIDGE. Consequently, a PCI bus master on a LEVEL 1 bus segment (or any other lower LEVEL bus segment) cannot access the configuration address space of a HOST/PCI BRIDGE. Only the HOST CPU can access the configuration address space of the HOST/PCI BRIDGE. Similarly, because the HOST CPU bus segment does not support Type 0 configuration or special transactions, a Type 1 configuration transaction on a LEVEL 1 bus segment cannot be claimed by the HOST/PCI BRIDGE.

> The PCI Local Bus Specification Rev. 2.0 and 2.1 defines two "configuration mechanisms", #1 and #2. Configuration mechanism #2 was used on very early PCI bus implementations. All present and future implementations of the PCI bus should exclusively use configuration mechanism #1. The following discussion assumes that only configuration mechanism #1 is supported. For information on configuration mechanism #2, see the actual PCI Local Bus Specification Rev 2.1 or Rev 2.2.

The HOST CPU accesses two registers within the HOST/PCI BRIDGE: CONFIG_ADDRESS (at I/O address 0CF8h) and CONFIG_DATA (at I/O address 0CFCh). The protocols of these two registers are summarized in Figures 7-4 and 7-5.

Accesses to the CONFIG_ADDRESS Register must be in the form of 32 data bits (DWORD). An access to the CONFIG_ADDRESS Register of any other data size results in the access being passed to the I/O address space (0CF8h) of the PCI bus without affecting the CONFIG_ADDRESS Register. Accesses to the CONFIG_DATA Register can be 8 data bits (byte), 16 data bits (WORD), or 32 data bits (DWORD). The data size of configuration transactions reflects the data size of the access to the CONFIG_DATA Register.

The bits in the CONFIG_ADDRESS register and how they are translated to a type 0 configuration transaction on a LEVEL 1 bus segment in order to access the configuration address space of a PCI bus master, target, or any bridge (collectively called "device") directly attached to a LEVEL 1 PCI bus segment, is shown in the following bullets (see Figure 7-4):

- Bits 1 and 0 are defined as "00" and are ported directly to the AD[1::0] signal lines of a Type 0 configuration transaction during the ADDRESS PHASE. A logical "0" is returned for these bits if the register is read.

- Bits 7 to 2 are defined as the REGISTER number and are ported directly to the AD[7::2] signal lines of a Type 0 configuration transaction during the ADDRESS PHASE. The REGISTER number selects the 32 data bits (double word) to be accessed within the configuration address space of the selected device.

- Bits 10 to 8 are defined as the FUNCTION number and are ported directly to the AD[10::8] signal lines of a type 0 configuration transaction during the ADDRESS PHASE. The FUNCTION Number selects one of the possible eight configuration spaces within the selected device.

- Bits 15 to 11 are defined as the DEVICE number and are decoded by the HOST/PCI BRIDGE into the IDSEL signal lines. The IDSEL signal lines may be attached one-to-one to the AD[31::11] signal lines of a Type 0 configuration transaction during the ADDRESS PHASE. Only one IDSEL signal line can be asserted. The correlation between the IDSEL number (AD[31::11] signal lines) and the DEVICE number is not fixed by the PCI local bus specification. For example, DEVICE number 0 may be attached to AD[17] or AD[19] or AD[20] signal lines, etc. Another example: DEVICE numbers 0 to 16 can be assigned to signal lines AD[17] to AD[31] and each are attached to an actual device. If DEVICE numbers 17 to 31 are accessed, the HOST/PCI BRIDGE will execute the configuration transaction with the IDSEL (AD signal lines) deasserted resulting in a Master Abort termination. This is a method by which the HOST CPU can determine if an actual device is present on the PCI bus segment. If the DEVICE number selects an IDSEL signal line not supported by the bridge, the bridge should either: NOT execute a Type 0 configuration transaction, and discard the write data or return all logical "1"s for a read data ... OR ... execute a Type 0 configuration transaction with no IDSEL signal lines asserted, that will result in a Master Abort termination (no device on the attached bus segment claimed the bus transaction). The Master Abort termination results in a discard of write data and a read of all logical "1"s.

■ Bits 23 to 16 are defined as the BUS number and are NOT ported directly to the AD signal lines of a Type 0 configuration transaction during the ADDRESS PHASE. Their use will be explained in a later part of this section.

■ Bits 30-24 are defined as reserved and are NOT ported directly to the AD signal lines of a Type 0 configuration transaction during the ADDRESS PHASE. A logical "0" is returned for these bits if the register is read.

■ Bit 31 is defined as the ENABLE BIT and is NOT ported directly to the AD signal lines of a Type 0 configuration transaction during the ADDRESS PHASE. The HOST CPU sets this bit to a logical "1" to activate the configuration transaction mechanism. When this bit is set to "1" any read or write of the CONFIG_DATA register results in a configuration transaction. If this bit is "0", any accesses by the HOST CPU to the I/O address of the CONFIG_DATA register (0CFCh) is ported through the HOST/PCI BRIDGE as an access to the PCI bus I/O address space.

The bits in the CONFIG_DATA register and how they are translated to a Type 0 configuration transaction for an access to configuration address space in a selected device directly attached to a LEVEL 1 PCI bus is as follows:

■ Bits 31 to 0 are defined as data and are ported (read or write) directly to the AD[31::0] signal lines of a type 0 configuration transaction during the DATA PHASE. They reflect data in the configuration address space registers within the selected device.

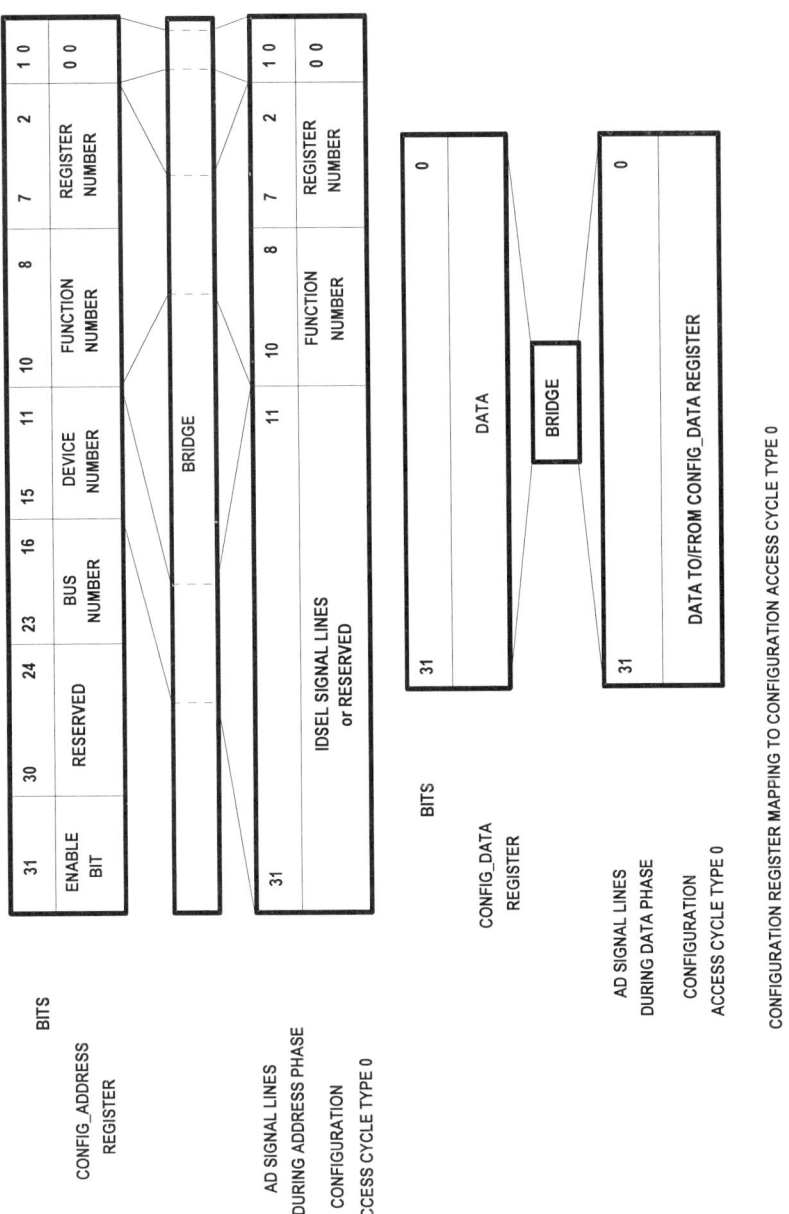

Figure 7-4: Configuration Register Mapping to Configuration Transaction Type 0

579

In the above discussion, it was assumed that the configuration address space being accessed was in a device that resided on a LEVEL 1 bus segment. When the HOST CPU reads or writes the CONFIG_DATA register (when the ENABLE BIT of the CONFIG_ADDRESS Register is set), a Type 0 configuration transaction is executed on the PCI bus segment attached to the HOST/PCI BRIDGE. If the configuration address space being accessed was in a device not on a LEVEL 1 PCI bus segment, the HOST/PCI BRIDGE must execute a Type 1 configuration transaction on a LEVEL 1 bus segment. The method by which a HOST/PCI BRIDGE determines where the device resides will be discussed later. A Type 1 configuration transaction can only be claimed by a PCI/PCI BRIDGE on the PCI bus segment. The PCI/PCI BRIDGE will port the Type 1configuration transaction to the next lower LEVEL bus segment as a Type 1 configuration transaction, or translated to a Type 0 configuration transaction or a special transaction.

The HOST/PCI BRIDGE will execute a special transaction on a LEVEL 1 bus when the BUS number (contained in bits 23 to 16 of the CONFIG_ADDRESS register) equals the value of the SECONDARY BUS register. To be distinguished as a special transaction versus a Type 0 configuration transaction (both will have the BUS number bits equaling the SECODARY BUS register), all the following conditions must be met:

- The DEVICE number and REGISTER number bits in the CONFIG_ADDRESS register are all logical "1"s.

- The REGISTER number bits in the CONFDIG_ADDRESS register are all logical "0"s.

The PCI local bus specification does not state that Bits 1-0 have any specific value if the requirements in the above two bullets are met. The CONFIG_DATA register contains the data associated with the special transaction.

The bits in the CONFIG_ADDRESS register and how they are translated to a Type 1 configuration transaction for a configuration address space of a device not directly attached to a LEVEL 1 bus segment is as follows (see Figure 7-5):

- Bits 1 and 0 are defined as "01" and are ported directly to the AD[1::0] signal lines of a Type 1 configuration transaction during the ADDRESS PHASE. A logical "01" is returned for these bits if the register is read.

- Bits 7 to 2 are defined as the REGISTER number and are ported directly to the AD[7::2] signal lines of a Type 1 configuration transaction during the ADDRESS PHASE. The REGISTER Number selects the 32 data bits (double word) to be accessed within the configuration address space of the selected device.

- Bits 10 to 8 are defined as the FUNCTION number and are ported directly to the AD[10::8] signal lines of a Type 1 configuration transaction during the ADDRESS PHASE. The FUNCTION number selects one of the possible eight configuration address spaces within the selected device.

■ Bits 15 to 11 are defined as the DEVICE number and are ported directly to AD[15::11] signal lines of a Type 1 configuration transaction during ADDRESS PHASE. The DEVICE number selects one of the possible 32 devices on a PCI bus segment when the Type 0 configuration transaction is translated from the Type 1 configuration transaction.

■ Bits 23 to 16 are defined as the BUS number and are ported directly to the AD[23::16] signal lines of a Type 1 configuration transaction during the ADDRESS PHASE. The BUS number selects one of the possible 256 PCI buses in a platform.

■ Bits 30-24 are defined as reserved and are ported directly to the AD[30::24] signal lines of a Type 1 configuration transaction during the ADDRESS PHASE. The associated signal lines will be driven to stable level but contain no valid information. A logical "0" is returned for these bits if the CONFIG_ADDRESS register in the HOST/PCI BRIDGE is read.

■ Bit 31 is defined as the ENABLE BIT and is NOT ported directly to the AD signal lines of a type 1 configuration transaction during the ADDRESS PHASE. The HOST/PCI BRIDGE drives the AD[31] signal line with a logical "0". The HOST CPU sets this bit to a logical "1" to activate the configuration transaction mechanism. When this bit is set to "1", any read or write of the CONFIG DATA register results in a configuration transaction. If this bit is "0", any accesses by the HOST CPU to the I/O address of the CONFIG_DATA register (0CFCh) is ported through the HOST/PCI BRIDGE as an access to the PCI bus I/O address space.

The bits in the CONFIG_DATA register and how they are translated to a Type 1 configuration transaction for a configuration address space of a device not directly attached to a LEVEL 1 bus segment follow:

■ Bits 31 to 0 are defined as data, and are ported (read or write) directly to the AD[31::0] signal lines of a type 1 configuration transaction during the DATA PHASE. They reflect data in the configuration space within the device selected.

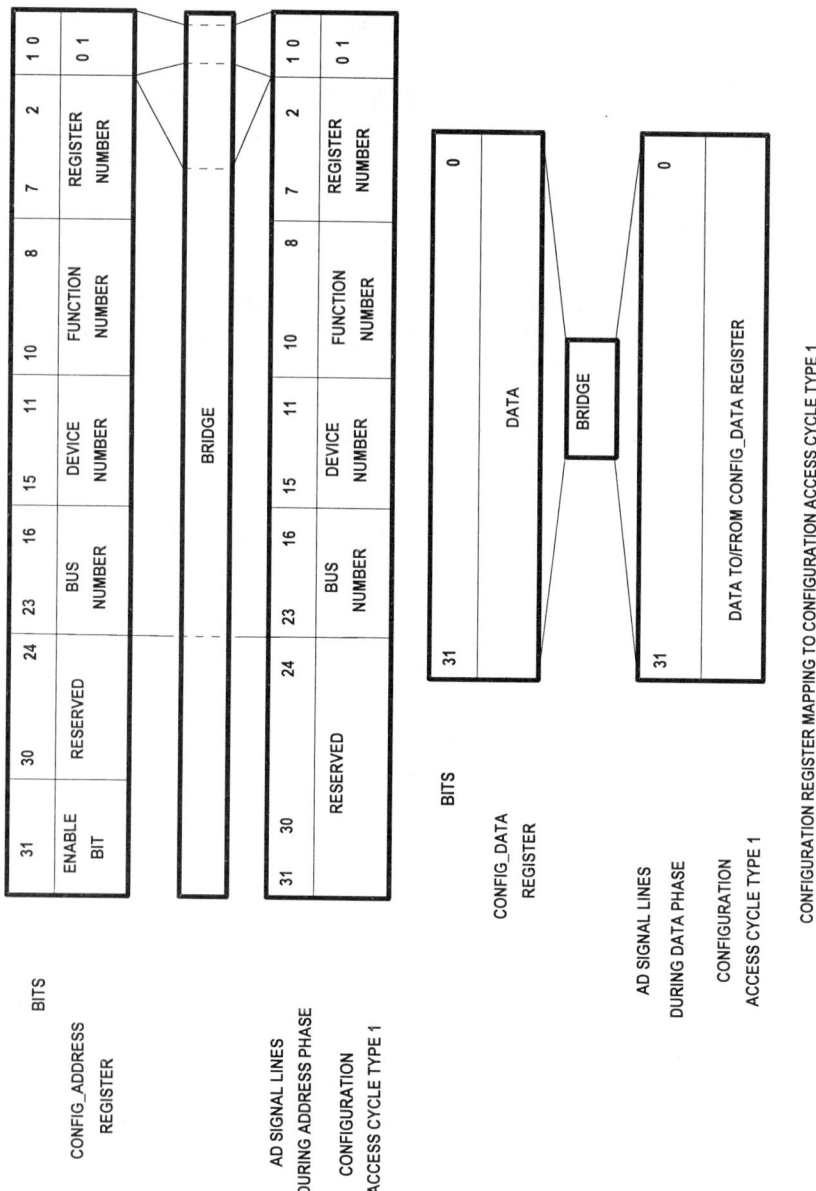

Figure 7-5: Configuration Register Mapping to Configuration Transaction Type 1

The HOST/PCI BRIDGE will cause a special transaction to be executed on a lower LEVEL bus segment bus when the BUS number (contained in bits 23 to 16 of the CONFIG_ADDRESS register) is between the value SECONDARY BUS number register (exclusive) and the SUBORDINATE BUS number register.(inclusive). The special transaction will be ported to a lower LEVEL bus segment via a Type 1 configuration transaction. The only differences that determine whether a Type 0 configuration transaction will be executed on the destination bus versus a special transaction is as follows:

- A special transaction requires the DEVICE number and REGISTER number bits in the CONFIG_ADDRESS register to be all logical "1"s, and the REGISTER number bits in the CONFIG_ADDRESS register to be all logical "0"s.

- The CONFIG_DATA register contains the data associated with the special transaction.

PCI-X SPECIFIC

The configuration and special transactions register requirements for HOST/PCI-X BRIDGES are the same as discussed above for HOST/PCI BRIDGES, with one exception. The IDSEL signal lines in the Type 0 configuration transaction are mapped to the AD[31::16] signal lines, and the AD[15::11] signal lines contain the Device Number.

7.11   BRIDGE AND BUS SEGMENT RESET PROTOCOL

PCI SPECIFIC

Reset of a specific PCI bus segment or associated PCI/PCI BRIDGES operates according to the following protocol:

- When the RST# signal line is asserted on the upper LEVEL bus segment (relative to the "base" PCI/PCI BRIDGE):
  - The lower LEVEL bus segments are reset.
  - PCI/PCI BRIDGES to lower LEVEL bus segments and "base" PCI/PCI BRIDGE (collectively called "all")
    - Resets internal registers to all PCI/PCI BRIDGES to default condition.

- All PCI/PCI BRIDGES discard contents of all Posted Memory Write Command FIFOS and Delayed Requests Buffers "moving towards" lower or upper LEVEL bus segments

- All PCI/PCI BRIDGES discard contents of the Delayed Completion Buffers with completion information and data "moving towards" upper or lower LEVEL bus segments.

- When the RST# signal line is asserted on a lower LEVEL bus segment (reset segment) due to setting to logical "1" the Secondary Bus Reset bit in the Bridge Control Register in the configuration address space in the "base" PCI/PCI BRIDGE:

  - This only resets lower LEVEL bus segments and lower LEVEL PCI/PCI BRIDGES relative to the "base" PCI/PCI BRIDGE

  - The upper LEVEL bus segments relative to "base" PCI/PCI BRIDGE are not reset

  - Specific to the "base" PCI/PCI BRIDGE to upper LEVEL bus segment

    - PCI/PCI BRIDGE registers are not reset to default condition.

    - PCI/PCI BRIDGE does not discard contents of Posted Memory Write Command FIFOS "moving toward" upper LEVEL bus segments.

    - PCI/PCI BRIDGE discards contents of Posted Memory Write Command FIFOS "moving toward" lower LEVEL bus segments.

    - PCI/PCI BRIDGE does not discard contents of Delayed Completion buffers "moving toward" upper LEVEL bus segments.

    - PCI/PCI BRIDGE discards contents of Delayed Request Buffers "moving toward" lower LEVEL bus segments.

    - PCI/PCI BRIDGE discards contents of Delayed Request Buffers "moving toward" upper LEVEL bus segments

    - PCI/PCI BRIDGE discards contents of Delayed Completion Buffers "moving toward" lower LEVEL bus segments.

PCI-X SPECIFIC

Reset of a specific PCI-X bus segment or associated PCI-X/PCI-X BRIDGES operates according to the following protocol:

- When the RST# signal line is asserted on upper LEVEL bus segment (relative to the "base" PCI-X/PCI-X BRIDGE):

■ Lower LEVEL bus segments are reset.

■ PCI-X/PCI-X BRIDGES to lower LEVEL bus segments and "base" PCI-X/PCI-X BRIDGE (collectively called "all")

   ■ Resets internal registers of all PCI-X/PCI-X BRIDGES to their default condition.

   ■ All PCI-X/PCI-X BRIDGES discard contents of all Posted Memory Write Command FIFOS and "Original" Transaction Buffers "moving towards" lower or upper LEVEL bus segments.

   ■ All PCI-X/PCI-X BRIDGES discard contents of all Posted Split Completion Command FIFOS "moving towards" lower or upper LEVEL bus segments.

■ When the RST# signal line is asserted on a lower LEVEL bus segment (reset segment) due to setting to logical "1" the Secondary Bus Reset bit in the Bridge Control Register in the configuration address space in a "base" PCI-X/PCI-X BRIDGE

   ■ Only resets lower LEVEL bus segments and lower LEVEL PCI-X/PCI-X BRIDGES relative "base" PCI-X/PCI-X BRIDGE

   ■ Upper LEVEL bus segments relative to "base" PCI-X/PCI-X BRIDGE are not reset

   ■ Specific to the "base" PCI-X/PCI-X BRIDGE to upper LEVEL bus segment

      ■ PCI-X/PCI-X BRIDGE registers are not reset to default condition.

      ■ PCI-X/PCI-X BRIDGE does not discard contents of Posted Memory Write Command FIFOS "moving toward" upper LEVEL bus segments.

      ■ PCI-X/PCI-X BRIDGE discards contents of Posted Memory Write Command FIFOS "moving toward" lower LEVEL bus segments.

      ■ PCI/PCI BRIDGE discards contents of "Original Transaction Buffers "moving toward" lower LEVEL bus segments.

      ■ PCI/PCI BRIDGE discards contents of "Original Transaction Buffers "moving toward" upper LEVEL bus segments

      ■ PCI-X/PCI-X BRIDGE discards contents of all Posted Split Completion Command FIFO "moving towards" lower LEVEL bus segments

■ PCI-X/PCI-X BRIDGE discards contents of all Posted Split Completion Command FIFO "moving towards" upper LEVEL bus segments

7.12 TRANSACTION ORDERING THROUGH A BRIDGE

PCI SPECIFIC

The discussion in this section of this subchapter focuses on the ordering protocol for PCI/PCI BRIDGES, though certain elements can be applied to other types of bridges and interface circuitry between the PCI bus segment and internal ASIC circuitry. Within a system, all bridges and interface circuitry in an ASIC should follow this protocol to eliminate deadlock and livelock conditions. As previously stated, other ordering protocols are possible, but all elements of a PCI system following the same conservative ordering protocol is the best overall design approach.

The discussion below addresses the ordering protocol for memory, I/O, and configuration transactions. Interrupt acknowledge transactions are only executed on PCI bus (0); consequently, it can be executed on PCI bus (0) by the HOST/PCI BRIDGE on behalf of the HOST CPU. For this book, a HOST/PCI BRIDGE is considered the only source for interrupt acknowledge transactions. Consequently, the ordering protocol discussed below for I/O and configuration read transactions can be applied to the architecture of the HOST/PCI BRIDGE relative to interrupt acknowledge transactions and other transactions.

Special bus transactions do not port though PCI/PCI BRIDGES; consequently, they are not part of ordering discussion below.

As previously discussed, PCI/PCI BRIDGES <u>are required</u> by the PCI local bus specification to post all memory write transactions (including MWI) into a Posted Memory Write Command FIFO. There are no Immediate write transactions that are ported through the bridge. Similarly, the all non-memory write transactions (as defined in Subchapter 7.6: *Porting PCI Memory Transactions through a Bridge (PCI Only)*) <u>are required</u> to be ported through the bridge with the Delayed Transaction Protocol via Delayed Request and Delayed Completion Buffers. There are no Immediate read transactions that are ported through the bridge.

The use of the word "FIFO" defines a register bank where the first contents placed into it are the first contents retrieved from it. The use of the word "buffer" defines a register bank where order of contents retrieved is not necessarily the same order as the contents are placed into it.

When applying bridge-like attributes to the interface between a PCI bus segment and internal circuitry, it is to be expected that all bus transactions are treated as Immediate Transactions. There are no transaction ordering issues for an interface that implements only Immediate Transactions. It is highly likely that the interface supports transaction posting but not the Delayed Transaction protocol.

The following discussion is divided into the two architectures (with and without Delayed Transaction Protocol) relative to the "Reference Event". The "Reference Event" is the established condition of the PCI/PCI BRIDGE prior to the specific "Subsequent Activity" under consideration. The use of the word "OR" between the following bullets indicates the possible "Subsequent Activities". Under normal PCI/PCI BRIDGE operation there may be more than one of these bullets that is applicable simultaneously.

The ordering of bus transactions porting through a PCI/PCI BRIDGE between two PCI bus segments can be viewed relative to the two architectures. One architecture only supports Posted Memory Write Command FIFOs without any Delayed Transaction Protocol (Delayed Request Buffers and Delayed Completion Buffers) (applicable to interface circuitry between the PCI bus segment and internal ASIC circuitry). The other architecture supports both Posted Memory Write Command FIFOs and Delayed Transaction Buffers (required implementation for PCI/PCI BRIDGES).

For the purposes of this discussion, a PCI/PCI BRIDGE will be used as an example. The use of PCI bus (0) with the PCI bus master and PCI bus (1) with the target is simply an example. The protocol outlined below also applies to PCI bus (0) with the target and PCI bus (1) with the PCI bus master. The source bus segment is PCI (0) and the destination bus segment is PCI (1). This designation is for purposes of discussion, and does not represent any special architectural requirements. Similarly, a destination bus segment contains the target under discussion and can also contain PCI bus masters. The source bus segment contains the PCI bus master under discussion and can also contain targets. The convention used in referencing PCI Bus (0) to (1) and PCI Bus (1) to (0) is as follows:

- "PCI bus (0) to (1)": for bus transactions originating on PCI bus (0).

- Transaction direction and address for Immediate Transactions, Delayed Requests, and Posted Memory Writes transactions originating on PCI bus (0). Also, the direction for write data originating on PCI bus (0).

■ The direction of Delayed Completions associated with Delay Requests (PCI bus (0) to (1)) is defined as "PCI bus (1) to PCI bus (0)". The Delayed Completions are returning read data and bus transaction completion from PCI bus (1). Also, the direction of read data associated with Immediate Transactions (PCI bus (0) to (1)) is defined as "PCI bus (1) to PCI bus (0)".

■ "PCI bus (1) to (0)": for bus transactions originating on PCI bus (1).

■ Direction of transaction, address, data, bus transaction completion, and status is opposite to the direction defined in the previous major bullet.

Note: The focus of the following section has PCI bus masters on PCI bus (0) and targets on PCI bus (1). The protocols also apply to PCI bus masters on PCI bus (1) and targets on PCI bus (0).

The ordering of Immediate Transactions, Delayed Requests, Delayed Completions, and Posted Memory Write Transactions flowing in opposite directions are independent of each other unless otherwise specifically noted in the following discussions.

ARCHITECTURE WITH POSTED MEMORY WRITE TRANSACTION FIFOS WITHOUT DELAYED TRANSACTION PROTOCOL

REFERENCE EVENT: POSTED MEMORY WRITE COMMAND FIFO CONTAINS TRANSACTIONS FROM PCI BUS (0) TO (1) AND/OR PCI BUS (1) TO (0)

SUBSEQUENT ACTIVITY

■ Additional memory write transactions (PCI bus (0) to (1)) are required to be posted into the Command FIFO (PCI bus (0) to (1)). It is required that transactions in the Posted Memory Write Command FIFO (PCI bus (0) to (1)) be completed on PCI bus (1) in the same order completed (received) on PCI bus (0) (See NOTE below).

OR

■ Immediate Transactions to execute reads (PCI bus (0) to (1)) are required to end with Retry termination until the Posted Memory Write Command FIFOS (PCI bus (0) to (1) and PCI bus (1) to (0)) are emptied of contents posted before the specific Immediate Transaction.

OR

■ Immediate Transactions to execute writes (PCI bus (0) to (1)) are required to end with Retry termination until the Posted Memory Write Command FIFO (PCI bus (0) to (1)) is emptied of posted contents posted before the specific Immediate Transaction (PCI bus (0) to (1)).

ARCHITECTURE WITH POSTED MEMORY WRITE COMMAND FIFOS AND DELAYED TRANSACTION PROTOCOL

REFERENCE EVENT: POSTED MEMORY WRITE COMMAND FIFOS CONTAIN TRANSACTIONS FROM PCI BUS (0) TO (1) AND/OR PCI BUS (1) TO (0)

SUBSEQUENT ACTIVITY

■ Additional memory write transactions and Immediate Transactions (PCI bus (0) to (1)) are executed with the same protocol as outlined above for architecture with only Posted Memory Write Command FIFOs.

OR

■ Delayed Requests (PCI bus (0) to (1)) can be buffered but cannot be executed on PCI bus (1) until the Posted Memory Write Commands FIFO (PCI bus (0) to (1)) is emptied of contents posted before the specific Delayed Request that was buffered.

OR

■ Buffered Delayed Completions FIFO (PCI bus (1) to (0) associated with Delayed Requests (PCI bus (0) to (1)) for reads cannot respond to repeated PCI bus (0) transactions until after the Posted Memory Write Command FIFO (PCI bus (1) to (0)) is emptied of contents posted before the bus transaction associated with a specific Delayed Completion was successfully completed on PCI bus (1) (See NOTE below).

REFERENCE EVENT: DELAYED REQUEST BUFFERS CONTAIN TRANSACTIONS FROM PCI BUS (0) TO (1) AND/OR PCI BUS (1) TO (0)

SUBSEQUENT ACTIVITY

■ Memory write transactions from PCI bus (0) that are completed by posting into the Posted Memory Write Command FIFO (PCI bus (0) to (1)) are required to be executed on the PCI bus (1) before executing transactions in the Delayed Request Buffer (PCI bus (0) to PCI (1)). This is independent of the Delayed Request being previously attempted on PCI bus (1).

OR

■ Buffered Delayed Completions (PCI-X bus (1) to (0)) associated with Delayed Requests (PCI bus (0) to (1)) are required to immediately complete on PCI bus (0) when the associated repeated bus transaction is executed on PCI bus (0). In other words, completion on PCI bus (0) of Delayed Completions associated with Delayed Requests (PCI bus (0) to (1)) is required to be completed independent of Delayed Requests (PCI bus (1) to (0)) (See NOTE below).

OR

■ Immediate Transactions to execute writes to memory (PCI bus (0) to (1)) are required to be executed on PCI bus (1) before executing any transactions in the Delayed Request Buffer (PCI bus (0) to PCI bus (1)). This is independent of the Delayed Request being previously attempted on PCI bus (1).

REFERENCE EVENT: DELAYED COMPLETION BUFFERS CONTAIN COMPLETION RESULTS OF EARLIER DELAYED REQUESTS OF PCI BUS (0) TO (1) AND/OR PCI BUS (1) TO (0):

SUBSEQUENT ACTIVITY

■ Buffered Delayed Completions (PCI-X bus (1) to (0)) that are results of earlier Delayed Requests of PCI bus (0) to (1) are completed to PCI bus (0) in the order of the repeated bus transactions on PCI bus (0) and not the order of completion on PCI bus (1) (See NOTE below).

OR

■ Memory write transactions from PCI bus (0) that are completed by posting into the Posted Memory Write Command FIFO (PCI bus (0) to (1)) are required to be executed on PCI bus (1) before the contents of the Delayed Completion Buffer that contains results of earlier Delayed Requests of PCI bus (1) to (0) can respond to a repeated bus transaction on PCI bus (1).

OR

■ Immediate Transactions to execute memory writes to (PCI bus (0) to (1)) are required to be executed on PCI bus (1) before the contents of the Delayed Completion buffer that contain results of earlier Delayed Requests (PCI bus (1) to (0)) can respond to associated repeated transaction on PCI bus (1).

NOTE:

"Successfully completed" means that the bus transaction completes with a Completion, Completion with timeout, or Disconnect, Master Abort, or Target Abort terminations.

The following table is a summary of the above discussion. As previously stated, PCI/PCI BRIDGES do not implement and port Immediate Transactions. The inclusion of Immediate Transactions is for possible implementations for the interface between the bus segment and internal circuitry of an ASIC. In Table 7-6, the notation "(0) > (1)" indicates the direction of the transaction or completion flow from PCI bus (0) to PCI bus (1). As previously implied, the table could also be applied for a flow of "(1) > (0)". Also as previously stated, the ordering of Immediate Transactions, Delayed Requests, Delayed Completions, and Posted Memory Write Transactions flowing in opposite directions are independent of each other unless otherwise specifically noted in the following table.

PCI-X SPECIFIC

The discussion in this section of this subchapter focuses on the ordering protocol for PCI-X/PCI-X BRIDGES, though certain elements can be applied to other types of bridges and interface circuitry between the PCI-X bus segment and internal ASIC circuitry. Within a system, all bridges and interface circuitry in an ASIC should follow this protocol to eliminate deadlock and livelock conditions. As previously stated, other ordering protocols are possible, but all elements of a PCI-X system following the same conservative ordering protocol is the best overall design approach.

> The discussion below addresses the ordering protocol for memory, I/O, and configuration transactions. Interrupt acknowledge transactions are only executed on PCI-X bus (0). They can be executed on PCI-X bus (0) by the HOST/PCI-X BRIDGE on behalf of the HOST CPU. For this book, a HOST/PCI-X BRIDGE is considered the only source for interrupt acknowledge transactions. Consequently, the ordering protocol discussed below for I/0 and configuration read transactions can be applied to the architecture of the HOST/PCI BRIDGE relative to interrupt acknowledge transactions and other transactions.
>
> Special bus transactions do not port though PCI-X/PCI-X BRIDGES; consequently, they are not part of ordering discussion below.

Reference Event >>>	Posted Memory Write (0) > (1)	Delayed Read Request (0) > (1)	Delayed Write Request (0) > (1)	Delayed Read Completion (0) > (1)	Delayed Write Completion (0) > (1)
Subsequent Activity vvv					
Posted Memory Write (0) > (1)	Cannot pass	Must pass	Must pass	Must pass	Must pass
Delayed Read Request (0) > (1)	Cannot pass	May pass	May pass	May pass	May pass
Delayed Write Request (0) > (1)	Cannot pass	May pass	May pass	May pass	May pass
Delayed Read Completion (0) > (1)	Cannot pass	Must pass	Must pass	May pass	May pass
Delayed Write Completion (0) > (1)	May pass	Must pass	Must pass	May pass	May pass
Immediate Memory Write (0) > (1)	Cannot pass (Note A)	Must pass	Must pass	Must pass	Must pass
Immediate I/O or Config. Write (0) > (1)	Cannot pass (Note A)	May pass	May pass	May pass	May pass
Immediate Read (0) > (1)	Cannot pass (Note B)	May pass	May pass	May pass	May pass

Table 7-6: PCI Transaction Ordering in PCI/PCI BRIDGEs

Notes: (A) Cannot pass because of the posted memory write and Delayed Write Request transactions cannot pass.
(B) Cannot pass because Delayed Read Completion transactions cannot pass.

As previously discussed, PCI-X/PCI-X BRIDGES are required by the PCI-X addendum specification to post all memory write transactions (including memory write block and alias memory write block) into a Posted Memory Write Command FIFO. Also, the bridge must post all split completion transactions into a Split Completion Command FIFO. There are no Immediate write transactions or Immediate split completion transactions that are ported through the bridge. Similarly, the all non-memory write and non-split completion transactions (as defined in Subchapter 7.8: *Porting PCI-X Memory and Split Completion*

592

Transactions through a Bridge (PCI-X Only)) are required to be ported through the bridge with the Split Transaction Protocol via "Original" Transaction Buffer and Split Completion Command FIFO. There are no Immediate read transactions that are ported through the bridge.

> The use of the word "FIFO" defines a register bank where the first contents placed into it are the first contents retrieved from it. The use of the word "buffer" defines a register bank where order of contents retrieved are not necessarily in the same order as the contents are placed into it.

The previous section for the PCI transaction ordering consisted of both text and table. The text was included as an aid to understanding the table. PCI-X transaction ordering is essentially the same as PCI transaction ordering. There are only two differences: One: Split Completion Transactions are specific to the PCI-X bus transaction protocol and mimics memory write transactions. Second: The PCI-X bus transaction protocol includes the Relaxed Ordering bit in the ATTRIBUTE PHASE. Consequently, the text description will not be repeated here for the PCI-X transaction ordering but the table will be provided.

For the purposes of this discussion, a PCI-X/PCI-X BRIDGE will be used as an example. The use of PCI-X bus (0) with the PCI-X bus master and PCI-X bus (1) with the target is simply an example. The protocol outlined below also applies to PCI-X bus (0) with the target and PCI-X bus (1) with the PCI-X bus master. The source bus segment is PCI-X (0) and the destination bus segment is PCI-X (1). This designation is for purposes of discussion, and does not represent any special architectural requirements. Similarly, a destination bus segment contains the target under discussion and can also contain PCI-X bus masters. The source bus segment contains the PCI-X bus master under discussion and can also contain targets. The convention used in referencing PCI-X Bus (0) to (1) and PCI-X Bus (1) to (0) is as follows:

- "PCI-X bus (0) to (1)": for bus transactions originating on PCI-X bus (0).

- Transaction direction and address for Immediate Transactions, Delayed Requests, and Posted Memory Writes transactions originating on PCI-X bus (0). Also, direction for write data originating on PCI-X bus (0).

- The direction of Delayed Completions associated with Delay Requests (PCI-X bus (0) to (1)) is defined as "PCI-X bus (1) to PCI-X bus (0)". The Delayed Completions are returning read data and bus transaction completion from PCI-X bus (1). Also, the direction of read data associated with Immediate Transactions (PCI-X bus (0) to (1)) is defined as "PCI-X bus (1) to PCI-X bus (0)".

- "PCI-X bus (1) to (0)": for bus transactions originating on PCI-X bus (1).

- Direction of transaction, address, data, bus transaction completion, and status is opposite to the direction defined in the previous major bullet.

> **Note: The focus of the following section has PCI-X bus masters on PCI-X bus (0) and targets on PCI-X bus (1). The protocols also apply to PCI-X bus masters on PCI-X bus (1) and targets on PCI-X bus (0).**

As previously mentioned, one of the differences in the PCI-X bus transaction protocol is the Relaxed Ordering (RO) bit. The implementation of the RO bit is as follows:

- The RO bit in the bus transactions for DWORD read and BURST read commands is defined only for purposes of setting the value of the RO bit in the associated split completion transactions. When the RO bit is set to logical "1" in a split completion transaction, the split completion transaction may pass previously posted memory write transactions (Posted Memory Write Command FIFO) moving in the same direction.

- The RO bit in the bus transactions for BURST memory write commands is set to logical "1" when these bus transactions may pass previously posted memory write transactions (Posted Memory Write Command FIFO) of the different "sequences" of memory write transactions moving in the same direction (Memory write transactions moving in different directions never have a ordering issues). Strong ordering must be maintained for the same "sequence" of memory write transactions independent of the value of the RO bit. This is only defined for the HOST/PCI-X BRIDGE receiving bus transactions for the system memory. PCI-X/PCI-X BRIDGES ignore this bit and maintain strong ordering for all memory write transactions

- The RO bit is not defined for the other PCI-X COMMANDS, and is set to logical "0" in the ATTRIBUTE PHASE of the associated bus transactions.

- The RO bit is not defined for the memory write transactions used for Message Signaled Interrupts, and is set to logical "0" in the ATTRIBUTE PHASE.

As previously stated, PCI-X/PCI-X BRIDGES do not implement and port Immediate Transactions. The inclusion of Immediate Transactions is for possible implementations for the interface between the bus segment and internal circuitry of an ASIC. In Table 7-7, the notation "(0) > (1)" indicates the direction of the transaction or completion flow from PCI-X bus (0) to PCI-X bus (1). As previously implied, the table can also be used for a flow of "(1) > (0)".

The ordering of Immediate Transactions, "Original" Transactions, Split Completion Transactions, and Posted Memory Write Transactions flowing in opposite directions are independent of each other unless otherwise specifically noted in the following table.

Reference Event >>> Subsequent Activity vvv	Posted Memory Write (0) > (1)	"Original" Transaction for Read (0) > (1)	"Original" Transaction for Write (0) > (1)	Split Completion Transaction for Read (0) > (1)	Split Completion Transaction for Write (0) > (1)
Posted Memory Write (0) > (1) Relaxed Bit = 0	Cannot pass	Must pass	Must pass	Must pass	Must pass
Posted Memory Write (0) > (1) Relaxed Bit = 1	May pass (A) (B)	Must pass	Must pass	Must pass	Must pass
"Original" Transaction for Read (0) > (1)	Cannot pass	May pass	May pass	May pass	May pass
"Original" Transaction for Write (0) > (1)	Cannot pass	May pass	May pass	May pass	May pass
Split Completion Transaction for Read > (1) Relaxed Bit = 0	Cannot pass	Must pass	Must pass	May pass (B)	May pass
Split Completion Transaction for Read > (1) Relaxed Bit = 1	May pass	Must pass	Must pass	May pass (B)	May pass

Split Completion Transaction for Write **(0) > (1)**	May pass	Must pass	Must pass	May pass	May pass
Immediate Memory Write **(0) > (1)** **Relaxed Bit = 0**	Cannot pass	Must pass	Must pass	Must pass	Must pass
Immediate Memory Write **(0) > (1)** **Relaxed Bit = 1**	May pass (A)	Must pass	Must pass	Must pass	Must pass
Immediate I/O or Config. Write **(0) > (1)**	Cannot pass	May pass	May pass	May pass	May pass
Immediate Read **(0) > (1)** **Relaxed Bit = 0**	Cannot pass	May pass	May pass	May pass	May pass
Immediate Read **(0) > (1)** **Relaxed Bit = 1**	Cannot pass	May pass	May pass	May pass	May pass

Table 7-7: PCI-X Transaction Ordering in PCI-XC/PCI-X BRIDGES

Notes: (A) Only aplies to HOST/PCI-X BRIDGE receiving bus transactions to system memory.
         (B) Cannot pass if part of same "sequence".

7.13   COMBINING TRANSACTIONS IN A BRIDGE

PCI SPECIFIC

For the following discussion, the "individual write transactions" are executed on the source bus segment and the "single BURST write transaction" is executed on the destination bus segment.

Any PCI/PCI BRIDGE can combine individual SINGLE and BURST write transactions (individual write transactions) to the memory address space into a single BURST write transaction. The addressing order of the single BURST write transaction must be linearly increasing and equal to the addressing order of the individual write transactions. The value of the C/BE# signal lines of the microaccess of the single BURST write transaction must match the value of the C/BE# signal lines during the microaccesses of the DATA PHASE for the DWORDS or QWORDS of the individual write transactions. For example, the individual write transactions that address DWORDS 0, 1, 2, and 3 (in this order) can be combined into a single BURST write transaction that maintains this order in the microaccess. Similarly, if the individual write transactions that address DWORDS 0, 1, and 3 (in this order) can be combined into a single BURST write transaction with following microaccesses: the initial microaccess is DWORD 0, the first subsequent microaccess is DWORD 1, the second subsequent microaccess has all of the associated C/BE#[3::0] signal lines deasserted, and the third subsequent microaccess is DWORD 3. If the individual write transactions address DWORDS 3, 0, 1 (in this order), combining is not allowed (it cannot be allowed because the resultant single BURST write transaction cannot maintain the exact addressing order with linear addressing). Finally, individual write transactions with all C/BE# signal lines deasserted during the DATA PHASE must be ported to the destination bus segment, either combined or individually.

An individual BURST write transaction or a series of individual SINGLE write transactions that execute a cache wrap or other non-linear address sequence cannot be combined. The combining of individual write transactions with non-linear addressing versus linear addressing would require the PCI/PCI BRIDGE to have extensive information on all memory targets.

The data size of the individual write transactions and the single BURST write transactions must be the same to be combined. The REQ64# signal line must be deasserted for all the individual write transactions of DWORDS and the single BURST write transaction of DWORDS. Similarly, the REQ64# signal line must be asserted for all the individual write transactions of QWORDS and the single BURST write transaction of QWORDS.

The PCI protocol allows any PCI/PCI BRIDGE to combine individual write transactions according to the protocol outlined above. A PCI memory resource that cannot support the addressing order of the resultant single BURST write transaction must execute a Disconnect termination to force the PCI/PCI BRIDGE to port the individual write transactions in the original sequence of individual SINGLE and BURST write transactions to the destination bus segment. A PCI memory resource is not optimally designed if it must execute a Disconnect termination of ANY single BURST write transaction.

Combining and/or merging is recommended when write posting.

Memory read, memory mapped I/O read, I/O, configuration, and interrupt acknowledge transactions cannot be combined. Memory write and memory mapped I/O write transactions can be combined. Also, combining cannot be applied to special transactions because the PCI/PCI BRIDGE can only port a request for a special transaction from PCI bus segment to PCI bus segment with a Type 1 configuration transaction.

The option of combining memory write transactions (including MWI) in a PCI/PCI bridge is always possible. The combining of these bus transactions is independent of the prefetchable address space as defined in the aforementioned related registers in the bridge. See *Introduction* section of Subchapter 7.6 for more information about prefetchable address registers in the PCI/PCI Bridge.

PCI-X SPECIFIC

The combining protocol in the PCI-X addendum specification is the same as for the PCI local bus specification, with the addition that split completion transactions of the "same" sequence can be combined with the same protocol as memory write transactions.

7.14 COLLAPSING TRANSACTIONS IN A BRIDGE

PCI SPECIFIC

For the following discussion, the "individual write transactions" are executed on the source bus and the "single BURST write transaction" is executed on the destination bus.

A PCI/PCI BRIDGE cannot collapse data. Consider individual write transactions on the source bus segment where the bytes, WORDS, DWORD, or QWORDS of data are placed in the PCI/PCI BRIDGE's buffer and prior to writing the buffer to the destination bus segment "new" data within the address range of the buffer arrives from the source bus segment. Collapsing occurs when the "new" data overwrites the data in the buffer and then the buffer is written to the destination bus segment.

> Memory, memory mapped I/O, I/O, configuration, and interrupt acknowledge transactions cannot be collapsed. Also, collapsing cannot be applied to special transactions because the PCI/PCI BRIDGE can only port a request for a special transaction from PCI bus to PCI bus with a Type 1 configuration transaction.

> The one exception that allows collapsing in a PCI/PCI BRIDGE is when the PCI/PCI BRIDGE "knows" that no negative side effects will occur.

PCI-X SPECIFIC

The collapsing protocol in the PCI-X addendum specification is the same as for the PCI local bus specification, with the addition that split completion transactions of the "same" or "different" sequences cannot be collapsed.

7.15 MERGING TRANSACTIONS IN A BRIDGE

PCI SPECIFIC

For the following discussion, the "individual write transactions" are executed on the source bus segment and the "single BURST write transaction" is executed on the destination bus segment.

A PCI/PCI BRIDGE can merge multiple individual SINGLE or BURST write transactions accessing the memory address space. Byte merging is defined as an optional function of a PCI/PCI BRIDGE by which data bytes, WORDS, multiple bytes (3, 5, 6, and 7 bytes), or DWORDS written in ANY order by multiple individual write transactions can be merged into a SINGLE write transaction of DWORD or QWORD by a PCI/PCI BRIDGE. The following conditions must be met for data to be merged:

■   The target must be a memory resource with an address space identified as prefetchable by the prefetchable address registers in the PCI/PCI BRIDGE. See *Introduction* section of Subchapter 7.6 for more information about prefetchable address registers in the PCI/PCI Bridge.

■ The entire address range of the merged SINGLE write transaction does not have to be written to by the multiple individual write transactions. For example, if the sequence of the multiple individual write transactions addresses bytes 3, 1, 0, and 2 with the associated C/BE# signal lines asserted, the bridges can merge this into a single DWORD write transaction. The PCI/PCI BRIDGE will not merge this into two WORD write transactions. Consider another example: the sequence of the multiple individual write transactions addresses bytes 3, 1, and 2 with the C/BE# signal lines associated with bytes 3 and 2 asserted, and the C/BE# signal line associated with byte 1 deasserted. The PCI/PCI BRIDGE will execute a single DWORD write transaction with the C/BE# signal lines associated with bytes 3 and 2 asserted, and the C/BE# signal lines associated with bytes 1 and 0 deasserted. Consider another example: the sequence of the multiple individual write transactions addresses bytes 3, 1, 1, 2, and 0 with the C/BE# signal lines associated with these bytes asserted and the other C/BE# signal lines deasserted. The PCI/PCI BRIDGE will first execute two single byte write transactions. The first bus transaction will write byte 3 of the original sequence with the C/BE# signal line associated with byte 3 asserted and the other C/BE# signal lines deasserted. The second bus transaction will write the first byte 1 of the original sequence with the C/BE# associated with byte 1 asserted and the other C/BE# signal lines deasserted. The PCI/PCI BRIDGE will then execute a single DWORD write transaction with the C/BE# signal lines associated with bytes 1, 2, and 0 asserted and the C/BE# signal line associated with byte 3 deasserted. As final example, consider the sequence of the multiple individual write transactions addressed bytes 3, 1, and 2 with the associated C/BE# signal lines deasserted and the REQ64# signal line deasserted. The BRIDGE will execute a single DWORD write transaction with all the C/BE# signal lines deasserted and the REQ64# signal line deasserted.

■ The merged data cannot include collapsed data. See the discussion of collapsed data in the previous section.

Merging and/or combining is recommended when write posting.

Inside of a PCI/PCI BRIDGE, combining improves platform performance more than merging. However, if the PCI/PCI BRIDGE is merging misaligned bytes into a SINGLE memory write, merging can reduce destination bus segment transactions by a factor of two.

Memory read, memory mapped I/O transactions (read or write), I/O, configuration, and interrupt acknowledge transactions cannot be merged. Also, merging cannot be applied to special transactions because the PCI/PCI BRIDGE can only port a request for a special transaction from PCI bus to PCI bus with a Type 1 configuration transaction.

Any PCI memory target whose Prefetchable bit in its Memory Base Address Register in the configuration address space is set to logical "1" must support merging in PCI/PCI BRIDGES.

PCI-X SPECIFIC

The merging protocol in the PCI-X addendum specification is the same as for the PCI local bus specification with the addition that split completion transactions of the "same" sequence can be merged with the same protocol as memory write transactions.

7.16 UNIQUE BRIDGE CONSIDERATIONS RELATING TO SNOOPING AND VGA

SNOOPING

PCI SPECIFIC

A general definition of snooping is simply one device (snoop device) monitoring a bus transaction of a PCI bus master accessing another device (target). The snoop device must be able to latch whatever data is read/written from/to to the target. The target being accessed is responsible for claiming the bus transaction (DEVSEL# signal line asserted). Only the PCI bus master and the target can control the data transfer (IRDY# and TRDY# signal lines asserted). Also, only the target can execute any type of target termination at any time. Consequently, the snoop device must be able to track the bus transaction for the fastest possible implementation of the PCI bus transaction protocol (unless the snoop device "knows" that the target is slower). According to the PCI local bus specification, snooping is only possible when the PCI bus master, snoop device, and the target are on the same PCI bus segment. This book also defines that snooping is possible with only the snoop device and target on the same PCI bus segment. The PCI bus master on another PCI bus segment is represented on the target's bus segment by the PCI/PCI BRIDGE.

PCI-X SPECIFIC

The snooping protocol in the PCI-X addendum specification is the same as described above for the PCI local bus specification, with the following differences:

- The Split Transaction protocol results in the data and completion information provided in split completion transactions be from the "original" target. Consequently, the snoop device must also monitor the split completion transactions.

> The SNOOP bit in the ATTRIBUTE PHASE of a bus transaction is not related to the general snooping discussed above. *See Chapter 4: Functional Interaction between PCI and PCI-X Resources.*

VGA

PCI SPECIFIC

A minimal requirement of a PC compatible PCI system is a VGA chip. In some cases the VGA chip may be attached on a PCI bus segment or LEGACY bus segment (or within the PCI/LEGACY BRIDGE with the appearance of being on the LEGACY bus segment). An enhancement is the installation of graphics card(s). (The graphics card in this discussion could also be a chip or another VGA chip. For this discussion, a graphics card will be assumed.) The PCI local bus specification requires that the graphics card(s) in the system can snoop the I/O write transaction updates of the color palette to the VGA chip. A graphics card must update its color palette every time the color palette is updated in the VGA chip. The PCI bus master and the VGA chip complete the I/O write transaction as the two bus transaction participants. The VGA chip as the target is the only device that can claim the transaction and drive the TRDY#, DEVSEL#, etc., signal lines. The graphics card is required to monitor and latch the color palette data simultaneously with or before the PCI bus master and the VGA chip terminate the write transaction (including when Master Abort termination occurs as outlined below). The graphics card cannot claim the bus transaction by asserting the DEVSEL# signal line; consequently, it cannot insert wait states, etc.

It is possible to configure the graphics card to claim the I/O write bus transactions the color palette and configure the VGA chip to snoop it. If so configured, the VGA snooping related roles of the VGA chip and graphics card as discussed below are reversed.

Also, if the VGA chip and graphics card in this discussion are actually implemented in the same chip and no other graphics cards or VGA chips are in the system, the support of VGA related snooping does not apply.

Unlike the general snooping discussed in the previous section, the VGA chip and the graphics card do not have to be on the same bus segment. The VGA and graphics card can be separated by PCI/PCI BRIDGES, and VGA color palate snooping (VGA snooping) is still possible provided both are on the same path. The same path means one of following architectures:

- The VGA chip and graphics card are on the same bus segment and the PCI/PCI BRIDGE does not have to support VGA related snooping.

- The sequence of bus segments traversed by bus transactions between the PCI bus master and the VGA chip includes the bus segment containing the graphics card.

- The sequence of bus segments traversed by bus transactions between the PCI bus master and the graphics card includes the bus segment containing the VGA chip.

See the PCI-to-PCI Bridge Architecture Specification for examples of the "same" path.

In order to support the VGA chips downstream of a PCI/PCI BRIDGE, the bridge must implement the VGA Enable (BVGA E) bit in the Bridge Control Register in its configuration address space. Its implementation is defined in more detail in later chapters, but is mentioned briefly here as a tie-in with the mechanics of VGA support

- The BVGA E bit is not related to the VGA BIOS memory address space. It is a requirement that the ROM containing the VGA BIOS has been copied to the system memory before execution.

- The implementation of the BVGA E bit for VGA support is optional (read-only value of 0 and write of the bit are ignored) and thus the associated unique support for VGA bus transactions across bus segments via porting by PCI/PCI BRIDGE is optional. The implementation of the BVGA E bit and setting its value to logical "1" enables the bridge to port the VGA related bus transactions downstream.

The BVGA E bit discussed above supports the porting of VGA chip related bus transactions downstream (otherwise the associated memory and I/O address range are ported upstream). The PCI/PCI BRIDGES between the PCI bus master and the VGA chip are porting all VGA related bus transactions in accordance with the BVGA E bit. As previously discussed, it is possible for a graphics card to snoop the VGA color palate write transaction. Because the graphics card may be downstream relative to the actual bus transaction path between the PCI bus master and the VGA chip, the PCI/PCI BRIDGE will be required to support VGA snooping on behalf of the graphics card. Consequently, the VGA Palate Snoop Enable (BVGE PSE) bit in the Bridge Control Register in the PCI/PCI BRIDGE'S configuration address space is defined. The BVGE PSE bit is defined as follows:

■ Similarly to the BVGE E bit, the BVGE PSE bit is not related to the VGA BIOS memory address space. It is a requirement that the ROM containing the VGA BIOS has been copied to the system memory before execution.

■ The implementation of the BVGA PSE bit for VGA snooping is optional (read-only value of 0 and write of the bit are ignored) and thus the associated unique support for VGA snooping across bus segments is optional. If a graphics card (the snooping device in this discussion) is on a lower LEVEL bus segment than the VGA chip and meets the "same" path requirements discussed above, the BVGA PSE bit implementation and setting its value to logical "1" is required.

The implementation of the BVGA E and BVGA PSE bits is as follows:

■ If both the BVGA E and BVGA PSE bits are set to a logical "0" (or not implemented), there is no activity by the bridge specific to VGA related snooping. The bridge may still respond in a "typical" fashion if a VGA related bus transaction is within the range of the Memory Base Address or I/O Base Address Registers. Also, the graphics card can still snoop VGA bus transactions if on the same bus segment and VGA chip.

■ When the BVGA E bit is set to logical "1" (independent of the value of the BVGA PSE bit), memory and I/O transactions related to VGA on the upper LEVEL bus segment must be claimed (DEVSEL# signal line asserted) by the PCI/PCI BRIDGE and ported to the lower LEVEL bus segment. Bus transactions on the lower LEVEL bus segment for the same address ranges are blocked from porting to the upper LEVEL bus segment. If the BVGA E bit is set to logical "1", the response to VGA related bus transactions on the upper LEVEL bus segment is independent of the values of the Memory Base and Limit registers, the I/O Base and Limit registers, ISA Enable bit, and the BVGA PSE bit in the bridge's configuration address space. However, the porting of the bus transactions is qualified by the Memory Enable and I/O Enable bits in the bridge's Command register in the configuration address space.

- For memory transactions on the upper LEVEL bus segment
  - All addresses encoded on the AD[31::00] signal lines are between 000A 0000h and 000B FFFFh (inclusively) when the AD[63::32] signal lines are all logical "0".
- For I/O transactions on the upper LEVEL bus segment
  - AD[31::16] signal lines are all logical "0" during ADDRESS PHASE of a bus transaction (if a 64 address bit I/O transaction is supported, it is also required that the AD [63::32] signal lines are all logical "0").
  - AD[15::10] signal lines can be any value
  - AD[9::0] signal lines equal one of the following addresses: 3B0h through 3BBh and 3C0h through 3DFh.
- When the BVGA E bit is set to logical "0" and the BVGA PSE bit is set to logical "1", the VGA color palette related I/O writes (reads are ignored) on the upper LEVEL bus segment (bus transactions on lower LEVEL bus segment are ignored) are only ported **(DEVSEL# signal line not asserted by bridge)** to the lower LEVEL bus segment by the PCI/PCI BRIDGE provided all of the following are met:
  - For I/O transactions on the upper LEVEL bus segment
    - AD[31::16] signal lines are all logical "0" during ADDRESS PHASE of a bus transaction (if a 64 address bit I/O transaction is supported, then AD[63::32] signal lines are all logical "0").
    - AD[15::10] signal lines can be any value
    - AD[9::0] signal lines equal one of the following addresses: 3C6h, 3C8h, and 3C9h.

The VGA chip and graphics card obviously have to be programmed to either claim (assert the DEVSEL# signal line) the VGA related bus transaction, or to only snoop VGA color palette bus transactions. See discussions later in this book about the VGA Palette Snoop bit in the Command Register in the configuration address space of the VGA and graphics card.

Subtractive decoding by a bridge is not related to the above bits for VGA access and snooping.

If the VGA chip (or graphics card) is on PCI bus (0) and if the PCI/LEGACY BRIDGE that links the graphics card on the Legacy bus (or VGA chip) to PCI bus (0) was attached to PCI bus (0) with subtractive decoding, the following protocol applies:

- The resource that is on PCI bus (0) is set to snoop and the PCI/LEGACY BRIDGE will claim the bus transaction with subtractive decoding.

- In general, any PCI/PCI BRIDGE (attached to upper LEVEL bus segment is PCI (X)) that links to a lower LEVEL bus segment with subtractive decoding, requires a VGA chip or graphics card on PCI bus (X) to be set to snoop mode.

PCI-X SPECIFIC

The protocol for porting VGA related bus transactions, VGA color palate snooping through a bridge, and the associated placement of the VGA chip and graphics card within a system in the PCI-X addendum specification is the same as described above for the PCI local bus specification.

7.17   EXCLUSIVE ACCESS (LOCK#) PROTOCOL AND DEADLOCK CONSIDERATIONS

In the following discussions the terms "upstream" and "downstream" refer to the direction of the bus transaction flow. Bus transactions from PCI bus masters on upper LEVEL bus segments to targets on the lower LEVEL bus segments are defined as "downstream". Similarly, bus transactions from PCI bus masters on lower LEVEL bus segment to targets on upper LEVEL bus segments are defined as "upstream".

PCI SPECIFIC

Prior to Rev 2.2 of the PCI local bus specification, a PCI bus master could insure Exclusive Hardware Access with the LOCK# signal line to control bus transaction completion by specific memory targets (HOST memory (HDRAM) and PCI memory (PDRAM)). In addition, coordination among the different PCI bus masters (Exclusive Software Access) could control bus transaction accesses to a specific target. Exclusive Software Access could also be applied to an I/O target. In the case of Exclusive Hardware Access, the bus protocol insured a specific PCI bus master (Lock master) that no other PCI bus master could access a locked target with any bus transaction. If a PCI bus master that was not the Lock master tried to access a locked target, the locked target would request a Retry termination. The Exclusive Hardware Access required that the Lock master could access the locked target only with memory transactions. Also, to insure the minimal amount of time that a memory resource was a locked target via Exclusive Hardware

Access, the Lock master was not allowed to access any other target until it unlocked the locked target.

> **Exclusive Software Access is entirely done with software. The different PCI bus masters are required to determine a software mechanism among each other relative to a specific target**

Prior to Rev. 2.2 of the PCI local bus specification per the Exclusive Hardware Access protocol, the HOST CPU and PCI bus masters would use Exclusive Hardware Access (LOCK# signal line) only in a downstream to PDRAM. The PCI/PCI BRIDGES would both monitor and drive the LOCK# signal lines to support downstream Exclusive Hardware Access. The support of an upstream Exclusive Hardware Access via the LOCK# signal line was not possible, except for one situation. The LOCK# signal line was monitored by the HOST/PCI BRIDGE for upstream Exclusive Hardware Accesses. This was done for both PCI bus masters becoming Lock masters and locking the HDRAM and for backward compatibility of a LEGACY bus master also locking the HDRAM. Also backward compatibility requires the PCI/LEGACY BRIDGE to support both upstream and downstream Exclusive Hardware Access. The use of Exclusive Hardware Access was useful for such activities such as semaphore manipulation.

According to Rev. 2.2 of the PCI local bus specification, the protocol for Exclusive Software Access was retained. However, the Exclusive Hardware Access protocol was substantially changed from what was described above for earlier revisions of the PCI local bus specification. The implementation of the Exclusive Hardware Access by definition is through the use of the LOCK# signal line and its associated protocol. Besides placing new restrictions on the use of Exclusive Hardware Access for locking and accessing a target (in a non-deadlock condition), the protocol was expanded to address deadlock conditions that may occur in PCI/PCI BRIDGES.

Before discussing the "new" additional focus of Exclusive Hardware Access (deadlock condition) specified by Rev. 2.2 of the PCI local bus specification, the key elements that were carried forward (those not mentioned were not carried forward) from previous versions of the specification as follows (for non-deadlock considerations):

■ The HOST CPU can use the LOCK# signal line for an Exclusive Hardware Access to a LEGACY memory target for backward compatibility. The LEGACY bus master can use the LOCK# signal line for an Exclusive Hardware Access to the HDRAM for backward compatibility. Consequently, the HOST/PCI and PCI/LEGACY BRIDGES are required to support both upstream and downstream Exclusive Hardware Accesses. The PCI/LEGACY BRIDGE by convention is attached to PCI bus (0) which is directly attached to the HOST/PCI BRIDGE. (The architecture of

607

a HOST/LEGACY BRIDGE is also possible but not part of the Exclusive Hardware Access discussion.) Consequently, the HOST/PCI and PCI/LEGACY BRIDGES support LOCK# signal line for the aforementioned accesses. The support of the LOCK# signal line by PCI/PCI BRIDGES is only to prevent deadlock conditions (see discussion below).

The above paragraphs focused on the HOST CPU as the source of bus transactions to a LEGACY memory target and the LEGACY bus master as the source of bus transactions to the HOST memory target. It is theoretically possible that a PCI memory device could also be a target instead of Host memory and a PCI bus master on PCI bus (0) could also be the source of bus transactions instead of the HOST CPU. According to Rev. 2.2 of the PCI local bus specification, these latter two devices are not part of the Exclusive Hardware Access discussion. For this book, the focus for Exclusive Hardware Access discussions (non-deadlock) will remain with the HOST memory as the target of the LEGACY bus master and LEGACY memory as the target of the HOST CPU.

As previously stated, in Rev 2.2 of the PCI local bus specification the Exclusive Hardware Access (LOCK# signal line) is also used to address deadlock conditions. The required protocol for a HOST/PCI BRIDGE (acting as a PCI bus master on behalf of a HOST CPU) is to accept memory write transactions as a target independent of the completion of any other bus transactions it is executing as a PCI bus master. Similarly, PCI/PCI BRIDGES are required to accept memory write transactions as a target independent of the completion of any other bus transactions it is executing as a PCI bus master. There are deadlock problems if a HOST/PCI BRIDGE executes a downstream read transaction through a PCI/PCI BRIDGE (Delayed Transaction protocol) and cannot accept an upstream memory write to the HOST memory behind the HOST/PCI BRIDGE.

A "real world" situation in which the above deadlock will occur is when a HOST CPU (via a HOST/PCI BRIDGE that does not accept all memory writes under all conditions) executes eight byte memory read transactions to an odd DWORD address boundary. The accessing of an odd DWORD address boundary will cause the PCI/PCI BRIDGE to execute a Delayed Transaction and the target to execute a Disconnect with data termination. The HOST/PCI BRIDGE could potentially receive an upstream memory write prior to the other part of the bus transaction for crossing the natural address boundary being accessed. If the PCI/PCI BRIDGE has an upstream posted memory write in the Posted Memory Write FIFO it is required to complete it before an upstream Delayed Read Completion can be ported upstream. If the HOST/PCI BRIDGE does not accept the upstream memory write because it is waiting for the bus transaction for the

Delayed Read Completion for the other part of the bus transaction across the address boundary, there is a deadlock.

When the HOST/PCI BRIDGE is reading data from a target though a PCI/PCI BRIDGE, a PCI bus master can potentially execute write transactions to the HOST memory and the HOST/PCI BRIDGE will not accept a memory write because of the pending completion of the read transaction. Whenever this situation might occur, the HOST/PCI BRIDGE must execute the read transactions with the Exclusive Hardware Access protocol to avoid a deadlock situation. The balance of this discussion will focus on Exclusive Hardware Access as it pertains to PCI/PCI BRIDGES.

> **Note: There have been discussions about deadlock conditions for four byte I/O read transactions to an odd DWORD address boundary in the earlier errata sheets. The final errata and Rev 2.2 of the PCI local bus specification have dropped this consideration. Consequently, this book will only focus on Exclusive Hardware Access as it relates to memory transactions.**
>
> **An eight byte (64 data bits) read of an I/O target on an ODD boundary can be executed, resulting in the same deadlock situation described above. However, there is no benefit that justifies the increased complexity for 64 data bit I/O transactions. It is therefore strongly recommended that 64 data bit I/O targets not be implemented. For the purposes of this book, I/O targets are only 32 data bits in size. If a 64 data bit I/O target is implemented, eight byte I/O read accesses to an ODD address boundary will also potentially cause a deadlock condition.**

The use of the LOCK# signal line using the Exclusive Hardware Access protocol will prevent the aforementioned deadlock condition. According to Rev 2.2 of the PCI local bus specification, a PCI/PCI BRIDGE must support Exclusive Hardware Access (LOCK# signal line) as follows:

■ PCI/PCI BRIDGES are required to support the LOCK# signal line only in the downstream direction to address the deadlock condition. That is, the PCI/PCI BRIDGE monitors the LOCK# signal line only on the upper LEVEL bus segment and only drives the LOCK# signal line on the lower LEVEL bus segment to which it is attached.

■ The Exclusive Hardware Access can be implemented with memory transactions. To establish Exclusive Hardware Access, a successfully memory read transaction with the LOCK# signal line asserted is required. See Chapter 6: *Detailed Bus Transaction Protocol* for more information.

■ **Unless otherwise noted in the bullets below**, the operation of the PCI/PCI BRIDGE relative to posted memory writes, Delayed Transaction protocol, and bus transaction ordering rules remain unchanged from the non-Exclusive Hardware Access situation.

> For the balance of this discussion and given the unidirectional nature of the Exclusive Hardware Access, the source bus segment will be defined as the upper LEVEL bus segment and the destination bus segment will be defined as the lower LEVEL bus segment. Source bus segment to destination bus segment is defined as downstream and destination bus segment to source bus segment is defined as upstream.

> In the following discussion the phrase "non-memory write transactions" means all memory read, I/O read, I/O write, configuration write, and configuration read transactions.

> The LOCK# signal line is only driven and monitored by HOST/PCI and PCI/PIC BRIDGES. PCI bus segment targets (non-bridges) do not monitor the LOCK# signal line.

> In the following discussion, a PCI resource (HOST/PCI BRIDGE or another PCI/PCI BRIDGE) on the source bus segment will be Lock master. The target is on the destination bus segment, and the "bridge" in the following discussion is between the source and destination bus segments.

- When the LOCK# signal line indicates an attempt to lock a target in conjunction with a PCI bus memory read transaction, the bus transaction is completed with Retry termination (Delayed Transaction protocol is applied) on the source bus segment and the bridge enters the Source Lock state. The PCI resource as Lock master will continue to assert the LOCK# signal line until the result of the Delayed Transaction protocol is returned. The PCI resource can also execute other bus transactions (not associated with the Exclusive Hardware Access) to the source bus segment as non-Lock master. In the Source Lock state the bridge operates as follows:

  - The bridge will no longer post downstream memory write transactions from the source bus segment into the downstream Posted Memory Write Command FIFO. Retry terminations are requested by the bridge for downstream memory write transactions.

  - The bridge will no longer buffer downstream non-memory write transactions from the source bus segment into the downstream

Delayed Request Buffer. Retry terminations are requested by the bridge for downstream non-memory write transactions.

■ The memory write and non-memory write transactions posting and buffering upstream from the destination bus segment and executing them on the source bus segment will continue. Also, executing previously (previous to Source Lock) posted and buffered memory write and non-memory write transactions downstream to the destination bus segment will continue.

■ The PCI resource as Lock master will repeat the memory read transaction on the source bus segment for the Exclusive Hardware Access according to the Delayed Transaction protocol. The PCI resource can also execute other bus transactions (not associated with the Exclusive Hardware Access) to the source bus segment as non-Lock master (LOCK# signal line asserted when FRAME# signal line first asserted).

■ The downstream Delayed Request Buffer (and execution of the contents on the destination bus segment) follows all of the normal ordering rules, including the entry associated with the Exclusive Hardware Access. When the bus transaction for the Delayed Request associated with the source bus segment Exclusive Hardware Access is executed on the destination bus segment, the LOCK# signal line is asserted on the destination bus segment.

■ If the destination bus segment transaction associated with the Exclusive Hardware Access completes with a Master Abort, a Target Abort, or a Disconnect without data (on first microaccess) termination on the destination bus segment the result is placed into the upstream Delayed Completion Buffer. The upstream Delayed Completion Buffer (and porting of the contents on the source bus segment) follows all of the normal ordering rules, including the entry associated with the Exclusive Hardware Access. The "repeat" of the bus transaction used for the Exclusive Hardware Access occurs on the source bus segment and is terminated with a Target Abort (for both Master Abort and Target Abort terminations on the destination bus segment) or Disconnect without data (on first microaccess) termination. Upon completion of the source bus segment transaction, the LOCK# signal line on the source bus segment is deasserted. The LOCK# signal line on the destination bus segment will subsequently be deasserted due to the deassertion of the LOCK# signal line on the source bus segment and the bridge exits the Source Lock state. See Chapter 6: *Detailed Bus Transaction Operation* for more information.

- If the bus transaction associated with the Exclusive Hardware Access completes without a Master Abort, a Target Abort, or a Disconnect without data (on first microaccess) termination on the destination bus segment the result is placed into the upstream Delayed Completion Buffer and the bridge enters the Destination Lock state.

- When the PCI/PCI BRIDGE is in the Destination Lock state, the protocol is as follows:

  - The bridge will continue to not post downstream memory write transactions from the source bus segment into the downstream Posted Memory Write FIFO. Retry terminations are requested by the bridge for downstream memory write transactions.

  - The bridge will continue to not buffer downstream non-memory write transactions from the source bus segment into the downstream Delayed Request Buffer. Retry terminations are requested by the bridge for downstream non-memory write transactions.

  - The bridge will no longer post upstream memory write transactions from the destination bus segment into the upstream Posted Memory Write FIFO. Retry terminations are requested by the bridge for upstream memory write transactions.

  - The bridge can (optionally) no longer buffer upstream non-memory write transactions from the destination bus segment into the upstream Delayed Request Buffer. Retry terminations (optionally) are requested by the bridge for upstream non-memory write transactions.

  - Executing previously (previous to Destination Lock) posted and buffered bus transactions upstream to the source bus segment will continue. Also, executing previously posted and buffered downstream bus transactions to the destination bus segment will continue. The bridge can execute bus transactions (not associated with the Exclusive Hardware Access) to the destination bus segment as non-Lock master (LOCK# signal line asserted when FRAME# signal line first asserted).

  - The repeat of the memory read transaction for the Exclusive Hardware Access according to the Delayed Transaction protocol from the PCI resource on the source bus segment as Lock master is required. The PCI resource can also execute other bus transactions (not associated with the Exclusive Hardware Access) to the source bus segment as non-Lock master (LOCK# signal line asserted when FRAME# signal line first asserted).

- When the repeat of the bus transaction used to establish Exclusive Hardware Access is completed (data read) on the source bus segment, the bridge enters the Full Lock state. The Full Lock state is the same as Destination Lock state except the source bus transactions from the PCI resource as LOCK master will now be executed and are ported through the bridge.

■ When the PCI/PCI BRIDGE is in the Full Lock state it will exit this state with the simultaneous deassertion of the FRAME# and LOCK# signal lines on the source bus segment. The LOCK# signal line on the destination bus segment will subsequently be deasserted due to the simultaneous deassertion of the LOCK# and FRAME# signal lines on the source bus segment and the bridge exits the Full Lock state. See Chapter 6: *Detailed Bus Transaction Operation* for more information.

> An I/O write transaction that straddles an odd DWORD address boundary can also create a deadlock condition similar to the above discussion for memory read and I/O read transaction. Because the Exclusive Hardware Access protocol requires a read transaction to establish a Lock master and to lock a target, the Exclusive Hardware Access protocol cannot address the I/O write deadlock situation.

PCI-X SPECIFIC

> In the following discussion the phrase "non-memory write transactions" means memory read, I/O read, I/O write, configuration write, and configuration read transactions. Split completion transactions are identified separately.

> The LOCK# signal line is only driven and monitored by HOST/PCI-X and PCI-X/PIC-X BRIDGES. PCI-X bus segment targets (non-bridges) do not monitor the LOCK# signal line.
>
> In the following discussion, a PCI-X resource (HOST/PCI-X BRIDGE or another PCI-X/PCI-X BRIDGE) on the source bus segment will be Lock master. The target is on the destination bus segment, and the "bridge" in the following discussion is between the source and destination bus segments.

The Exclusive Hardware Access protocol and the associated operation of the LOCK# signal line, and the Exclusive Software Access protocol according to the PCI-X addendum bus specification is the same as described above for Rev 2.2 of the PCI local bus specification. However, the PCI-X addendum specification does not address Exclusive Hardware Accesses that includes the PCI-X Legacy BRIDGE and the LEGACY bus segment. The PCI-X addendum specification specifically states that these accesses are addressed by side band signals outside the scope of the specification. Also, the PCI-X addendum specification only defines the Exclusive Hardware Access relative to memory transactions. Otherwise, the approach to the Exclusive Hardware Access by PCI-X/PCI-X BRIDGES versus the PCI/PCI BRIDGES are similar, with the only differences due to Split Completion versus Delayed Transaction protocols as follows:

■ When the LOCK# signal line indicates an attempt to establish a lock of the target in conjunction with a PCI-X bus memory read transaction, the bus transaction is completed with Split Response termination (Split Transaction protocol is applied) on the source bus segment and the bridge enters the Source Lock state. The PCI-X resource as Lock master will continue to assert the LOCK# signal line until the result of the Split Transaction protocol is returned. The PCI-X resource can also execute other bus transactions (not associated with the Exclusive Hardware Access) to the source bus segment as non-Lock master. In the Source Lock state the bridge operates as follows:

■ The bridge will no longer post downstream memory write transactions from the source bus segment into the downstream Posted Memory Write Command FIFO. Retry terminations are requested by the bridge for downstream memory write transactions.

■ The bridge will no longer buffer downstream non-memory write transactions from the source bus segment into the downstream "Original" Transaction Buffer. Retry terminations are requested by the bridge for downstream non-memory write transactions.

■ Upstream split completion transactions will continue to be posted and ported to the source bus segment. Downstream split completion transactions will continue to be posted and ported to the destination bus segment.

■ The memory write and non-memory write transactions porting and buffering upstream from the destination bus segment and executing them on source bus segment will continue. Also, executing previously (previous to Source Lock) posted and buffered memory write and non-memory write transactions downstream to the destination bus segment will continue.

■ The PCI-X resource as Lock master on the source bus segment will wait for the split completion transaction for the Exclusive Hardware Access per Split Transaction protocol. The PCI-X resource can also execute other bus transactions (not associated with the Exclusive

614

Hardware Access) to the source bus segment as non-Lock master (LOCK# signal line asserted when FRAME# signal line first asserted).

■ The downstream "Original" Transaction Buffer (and execution of the contents on the destination bus segment) follows all of the normal ordering rules, including the entry associated with the Exclusive Hardware Access. When the bus transaction for the "Original" Transaction associated with the source bus segment Exclusive Hardware Access is executed on the destination bus segment, the LOCK# signal line is asserted on the destination bus segment.

  ■ If the destination bus segment transaction associated with the Exclusive Hardware Access completes with a Master Abort or a Target Abort termination on the destination bus segment, the result is placed into the upstream Posted Split Completion Command FIFO. The upstream Posted Split Completion Command FIFO (and porting of the contents on the source bus segment) follows all of the normal ordering rules, including the entry associated with the Exclusive Hardware Access. Upon completion of split completion transaction associated with the Exclusive Hardware Access on the source bus segment, the LOCK# signal line on the source bus segment is deasserted. The LOCK# signal line on the destination bus segment will subsequently be deasserted due to the deassertion of the LOCK# signal line on the source bus segment and the bridge exits the Source Lock state. See Chapter 6: *Detailed Bus Transaction Operation* for more information.

  ■ If the bus transaction associated with the Exclusive Hardware Access completes without a Master Abort or a Target Abort termination on the destination bus segment, the result is placed into the upstream Split Completion Command FIFO and the bridge enters the Destination Lock state.

■ When the PCI-X/PCI-X BRIDGE is in the Destination Lock state, the protocol is as follows:

  ■ The bridge will continue to not post downstream memory write transactions from the source bus segment into the downstream Posted Memory Write FIFO. Retry terminations are requested by the bridge for downstream memory write transactions.

  ■ The bridge will continue to not buffer downstream non-memory write transactions from the source bus segment into the downstream "Original" Transaction Buffer. Retry terminations are requested by the bridge for downstream non-memory write transactions.

- The bridge will not post upstream memory write transactions from the destination segment into the upstream Posted Memory Write FIFO. Retry terminations are requested by the bridge for upstream memory write transactions.

- The bridge will not buffer upstream non-memory write transactions from the destination bus segment into the upstream "Original" Transaction Buffer. Retry terminations are requested by the bridge for upstream non-memory write transactions.

- Upstream split completion transactions will continue to be posted and ported to the source bus segment. Downstream split completion transactions will continue to be posted and ported to the destination bus segment. The bridge can execute split completion transactions (not associated with the Exclusive Hardware Access) to the destination bus segment as non-Lock master (LOCK# signal line asserted when FRAME# signal line first asserted).

  - Executing previously (previous to Destination Lock) posted and buffered memory write and non-memory write transactions upstream to the source bus segment will continue. Also, executing previously (previous to Destination Lock) posted and buffered memory write and non-memory write transactions downstream to the destination bus segment will continue. The bridge can execute bus transactions (not associated with the Exclusive Hardware Access) to the destination bus segment as non-Lock master (LOCK# signal line asserted when FRAME# signal line first asserted

- The PCI-X resource as Lock master will wait for the split completion transaction on the source bus segment for the Exclusive Hardware Access following the Split Transaction protocol. The PCI-X resource can also execute other bus transactions (not associated with the Exclusive Hardware Access) to the source bus segment as non-Lock master (LOCK# signal line asserted when FRAME# signal line first asserted).

- When the split completion transaction associated with the Exclusive Hardware Access is completed (data read) on the source bus segment, the bridge enters the Full Lock state. The Full Lock state is the same as Destination Lock state except the source bus transactions from the PCI resource as Lock master will now be executed and are ported through by the bridge.

- When the PCI-X/PCI-X BRIDGE is in the Full Lock state, it will exit this state with the simultaneous deassertion of the FRAME# and LOCK# signal lines on the source bus segment. The LOCK# signal line on the destination bus segment will subsequently be deasserted due to the simultaneous deassertion of the LOCK# and FRAME# signal lines on the source bus segment, and the bridge exits the Full Lock State. See Chapter 6: *Detailed Bus Transaction Operation* for more information.

7.18   MEMORY WRITE MAXIMUM COMPLETION TIME

PCI SPECIFIC

As previously discussed, the protocol for memory write transactions through a PCI/PCI BRIDGE is via posting. From time to time the Posted Memory Write Command FIFO may become full, which requires the bridge to terminate the memory write transaction source bus segment with a Retry termination. One way that a Posted Memory Write Command FIFO can become full is that targets (non-bridge) on the destination bus segment are not accepting memory write transactions. That is, if not posting the memory write transactions, the target may request Retry termination if it cannot immediate accept the data and complete a memory write transaction. The request of a Retry termination by either the bridge or the target results in the repeating of the memory write transaction. Excessive repeats of a bus transaction will result in a decrease in overall system performance. Of particular note are the strong ordering requirements of the Posted Memory Command FIFO in the bridge. The request for a Retry termination on the destination bus segment prevents forward movement of other bus transactions in the Posted Memory Write Command FIFO. Consequently, it is important for the target to be designed to accept the memory write transactions with a minimum amount of time wasted on repeating memory write transactions terminated by Retry termination. A target cannot indefinitely respond with Retry termination for repeats of memory write transactions.

A PCI resource as target that terminated a memory write transaction with Retry termination is required by design to complete the associated data phase of a repeat of the bus transaction within the Maximum Completion Time (MCT). The MCT limit is 334 periods of the CLK signal line at 33 MHz and 668 periods of the CLK signal line at 66 MHz. At the CLK signal line frequencies of 33 MHz and 66 MHz, the MCT limit is 10 microseconds. If the CLK signal line frequency is less than 33 MHz, the 334 periods of the CLK signal line still applies; the MCT limit is proportionally more than 10 microseconds.

There are several elements of the MCT protocol:

■   Compliance to the MCT protocol is by design; there are no timers for this purpose in the target.

- A target by design is required (whenever possible) to complete within the MCT limit the data phase (access without Retry termination ... *i.e.*, Completion, Completion with Timeout, or Disconnect termination) of a repeat of the memory write transaction associated with the initial Retry termination. The PCI bus master should be designed with the repeat of the memory transaction aligned with the MCT limit.

- A target that cannot achieve the aforementioned compliance to the MCT limit requires its device driver in the PCI bus master to compensate. The compensation can be in two forms: Limit the rate of memory write transactions to the target ... OR ... The PCI bus master determines if the target has buffer space for subsequent memory write transactions to minimize the number of Retry terminations.

- The MCT limit is also satisfied when a repeat of the memory write transaction associated with the Retry termination results in a Master Abort or a Target Abort termination by the target. Obviously, reset of PCI bus segment also satisfies the MCT limit.

- Whenever the MCT limit protocol is met or satisfied as outlined above, the subsequent Retry termination of a memory write transaction re-establishes the MCT limit requirements.

An extension of the MCT protocol is when a target may have multiple memory write transactions addressing it. The MCT limit is measured from the Retry termination of a memory write transaction to the very next completion of a data phase (access without Retry termination ... *i.e.*, Completion, Completion with Timeout, or Disconnect termination) of a subsequent memory write transaction. The subsequent memory write transaction may not be a repeat of the memory write transaction the MCT limit is referenced to. However, by definition the requirement of the MCT limit has been satisfied. Similarly, the MCT limit is satisfied by a Master Abort or Target Abort termination of a subsequent memory write transaction that is not a repeat of the memory write transaction the MCT limit is referenced to.

The MCT protocol also has the following considerations:

- MCT protocol does not apply to a PCI/PCI BRIDGE unless the memory write transaction is to a memory address internal to the bridge (*i.e.*, not ported through).

- The PCI bus master cannot assume that the MCT protocol will be met for all memory write access cycles for three reasons:

  - The target was designed pre-Rev. 2.2 of the PCI local bus specification.

- ■ The target was designed to Rev 2.2 of the PCI local bus specification but simply may not comply.
- ■ The target may have several buses and PCI/PCI BRIDGES between itself and the PCI bus master.

■ The MCT protocol limit does not apply to a target during PCI initialization (the first 2^{25} CLK signal line periods after the deassertion of the RST# signal line).

PCI-X SPECIFIC

The Maximum Completion Time (MCT) protocol also applies to PCI-X bus segments. The protocol is the same as discussed above for PCI with the obvious adjustments to the different terminations for bus transactions (other than Retry termination), initialization issues, etc. There are differences relative to the CLK signal line frequency range as following:

- ■ For a bus segment initialized to 133 MHz CLK signal line mode, the MCT limit is 267 CLK signal line periods.

- ■ For a bus segment initialized to 100 MHz CLK signal line mode, the MCT limit is 200 CLK signal line periods.

- ■ For a bus segment initialized to 66 MHz CLK signal line mode, the MCT limit is 133 CLK signal line periods.

7.19 SIMPLE DEVICES

PCI SPECIFIC

As previously discussed, a PCI/PCI BRIDGE as a target is required to support memory write transaction posting and the Delayed Transaction protocol. Similarly, a target (non-bridge) should be designed to operate such that if operating as a PCI bus master, memory write transactions are accepted (posted without Retry termination) as a target. In the case of a simple device, the aforementioned requirements also apply.

A simple device is defined as a PCI resource operating as a PCI bus master that does not post write transactions to be executed on the PCI bus segment. Also, a simple device as target will probably not post memory write transactions (though the specification encourages it to do so) and does not support Exclusive Hardware Access protocol.

As with all devices, a simple device (as a target) can not make the acceptance of any bus transaction contingent on the completion of another bus transaction (as a PCI bus master). Also, simple devices must adhere to the Maximum Completion Time protocol.

> **See Subchapter 7.1:** *Summary of Bus Transaction Ordering* **for more information.**

PCI-X SPECIFIC

The concept of a PCI-X simple device is the same as discussed above for a PCI simple device with additions made for the Split Transaction Protocol as follows:

- A simple device (as with any PCI-X device) as PCI-X bus master must initiate split completion transactions (when it requested a Split Response termination) independent of the simple device as target waiting for the entire "sequence" of split completion transaction.

- A simple device (as with any PCI-X device) as a target must accept memory write transactions between a simple device requesting a Split Response termination and beginning the "sequence" of split completion transactions as PCI-X bus master.

- A simple device (as with any PCI-X device) as a target must accept memory write transactions independent of the simple device as PCI-X bus master executing other bus transactions.

- A simple device as a target can optionally terminate memory read, I/O read or write, configuration read or write, special, and interrupt acknowledge transactions with Retry termination until it finishes any or all "sequences" of split completion transactions for which it is a PCI-X bus master.

  - For an I/O write transaction, the simple device as a target is required to terminate without Retry termination per the Maximum Completion Time protocol. If the Split Transaction protocol is applied, the simple device must begin the split completion transaction as PCI-X bus master according to the Maximum Completion Time protocol.

> **See Subchapter 7.1:** *Summary of Bus Transaction Ordering* **for more information.**

7.20 SMBUS INTERFACE

At the time this book was printed there was an engineering change <u>request</u> for a "new" auxiliary bus to the PCI and PCI-X bus segments. This bus is called SMBus, which stands for System Management bus. As proposed, it consists of a low power and low bandwidth serial bus of two signal lines. It is proposed that two of the PCI reserved pins be redefined as SMBCLK and SMDAT. The SMBus is envisioned to support system instrumentation for sensing (*e.g.*, temperature). See the PCISIG.com web site for the final specification and whether indeed it has been accepted as part of the specification.

CHAPTER 8

MASTER AND TARGET TERMINATION

This chapter consists of the following subchapters:

8.0   INTRODUCTION TO PCI AND PCI-X BUS TRANSACTION TERMINATION

Both the PCI local bus and the PCI-X addendum specifications define two types of bus transaction termination: master and target. For master termination, the present PCI or PCI-X bus master determines when the bus transaction will be terminated. The three master termination protocols are: Completion, Completion with Timeout, and Master Abort. For target termination, the current target determines when the bus transaction will be terminated. The three target terminations for PCI are Retry, Disconnect, and Target Abort. The five target terminations for PCI-X are Retry, Split Response, Single Phase Disconnect, Disconnect at Next ADB, and Target Abort.

The PCI bus master must complete a terminated bus transaction in an orderly manner. All PCI bus transactions that are terminated must be completed with a minimum of one CLK signal line period with the FRAME# signal line deasserted and the IRDY# signal line asserted. Subsequently, when the DATA PHASE completes, the FRAME# and IRDY# signal lines are both deasserted. When a bus transaction completes according to a Master or Target Fast Back-to-Back protocol, the FRAME# signal line is deasserted and the IRDY# signal line is asserted a minimum of one CLK signal line period. When the DATA PHASE subsequently completes, the IRDY# signal line is deasserted and the FRAME# signal line is asserted.

The PCI-X bus master is also required to complete a terminated bus transaction in an orderly manner. According to the PCI-X addendum protocol, the completion pattern is more complicated than that of the PCI local bus specification. The PCI-

X completion protocol is dependent on the type of bus transaction and the number of microaccesses in the DATA PHASE. There is no support of Master and Target Fast Back-to-Back protocol in PCI-X. See Chapter 6: *Detailed Bus Transaction Operation* for more information.

In a simple system, the majority of PCI and PCI-X bus transactions complete with either Completion or Completion with Timeout terminations. In more complex PCI systems, the bus transaction terminations are more dependent on Completion (for posted memory writes) and Retry termination (for support of Delayed Transaction protocol). Similarly, in more complex PCI-X systems, the bus transaction terminations are more dependent on Completion (for posted memory writes) and Split Response termination (for support of Spilt Transaction protocol). The support of the different terminations of the bus transactions by the different PCI and PCI-X resources are outlined in Tables 8-1 to 8-2.

As will be detailed later in this chapter and summarized in Tables 8-1 to 8-2, there are time limits within which a target must execute a target termination relative to the assertion of the FRAME# signal line ("8 Clock" and "16 Clock" rules). Similarly, there are time limits for the bus master to execute Completion with Timeout termination of the bus transaction. Not all bus masters and targets need to support all of the terminations (summarized in Tables 8-1 to 8-2). The operation and interpretation of the STOP#, DEVSEL#, SERR#, PERR#, PAR, and PAR64 signal lines vary for the different terminations and will be detailed in this chapter. (Note: SDONE# and SBO# signal lines are no longer supported by the latest revision (2.2) of the PCI local bus specification). See details below.

The balance of this chapter defines the interaction of PCI bus segments relative to PCI/PCI BRIDGEs. Collectively, interconnect circuitry in ASICs, HOST/PCI BRIDGES, and PCI/LEGACY BRIDGES will be represented by the PCI/PCI BRIDGE in this chapter. The operational principles of the PCI/PCI BRIDGEs as discussed below can be applied to all of the interconnects in ASICs and the other types of bridges unless otherwise noted. On a PCI bus segment, the PCI resources that are being accessed include bridges and (via interconnect circuitry in ASICs) standalone PCI bus masters (for configuration address space), and targets. These will be collectively called "devices" in this chapter.

Similar statements can be made relative to PCI-X bus segments and PCI-X/PCI-X, HOST/PCI-X, and PCI-X/LEGACY BRIDGES.

Name (PCI)	Name (PCI-X)	Applies to both PCI and PCI-X Bus Masters		
		Completion	Completion with Timeout	Master Abort
NO GROUP NAME	**DWORD COMMANDS**			
Interrupt Acknow.	Interrupt Acknow.	Y (1)	N	Y (1)
Special	Special	Y	N	(2)
I/O Read	I/O Read	Y	PCI = Y PCI-X = N	Y
I/O Write	I/O Write	Y	PCI = Y PCI-X = N	Y
Config. Read	Config. Read	Y	PCI = Y PCI-X = N	(2)
Config. Write	Config. Write	Y	PCI = Y PCI-X = N	(2)
Memory Read	DWORD Memory Read	Y	PCI = Y PCI-X = N	Y
	BURST COMMANDS			
Memory Write	Memory Write	Y	Y	Y
	Alias Memory Read Block	Y	Y	Y
	Alias Memory Write Block	Y	Y	Y
Memory Read Multiple	Split Completion	Y	Y	Y
Memory Read Line	Memory Read Block	Y	Y	Y
Memory Write Invalidate	Memory Write Block	Y	Y	Y

Table 8-1: Master Termination

Notes:
  (1) Only supported by the HOST/PCI or HOST/PCI-X BRIDGEs
  (2) Master Abort termination is the normal termination of successful special transactions. During system initialization a Master Abort termination is the normal termination for configuration transactions.

Name (PCI)	Name (PCI-X)	Applies to only PCI Targets	Applies to both PCI and PCI-X Targets	
		Disconnect PCI = 8 Clk Rule for Subsequent Microaccesses	Retry PCI = 16 Clk Rule PCI-X = 8 Clk Rule for Initial Microaccess	Target Abort PCI-X= 8 Clk Rule for Initial Microaccess
NO GROUP NAME	DWORD COMMANDS			
Interrupt Acknow.	Interrupt Acknow.	Y (1)	Y (1)	Y (1)
Special	Special	na	na	na
I/O Read	I/O Read	Y	Y	Y
I/O Write	I/O Write	Y	Y	Y
Config. Read	Config. Read	Y	Y	Y
Config. Write	Config. Write	Y	Y	Y
Memory Read	DWORD Memory Read	Y	Y	Y
	BURST COMMANDS			
Memory Write	Memory Write	Y	Y	Y
Reserved	Alias Memory Read Block	na	Y	Y
Reserved	Alias Memory Write Block	na	Y	Y
	Split Completion Received by "original bus master" not bridge	Y	N	Y
Memory Read Multiple	Split Completion Received by bridge	Y	Y	Y
Memory Read Line	Memory Read Block	Y	Y	Y
Memory Write Invalidate	Memory Write Block	Y	Y	Y

Table 8-2: Target Termination

Name	Applies to only PCI-X Targets		
(PCI-X)	Split Response PCI-X= 8 Clk Rule for Initial Microaccess	Disconnect at Next ADB PCI-X= 16 Clk Rule for Initial Microaccess	Single Phase Disconnect PCI-X= 16 Clk Rule for Initial Microaccess
DWORD COMMANDS			
Interrupt Acknowledge	Y (1)	Y (1) (3)	Y (2) (1)
Special	N	N	N
I/O Read	Y	Y (3)	Y (2)
I/O Write	Y	Y (3)	Y (2)
Config. Read	Y	Y (3)	Y (2)
Config. Write	Y	Y (3)	Y (2)
Memory Read DWORD	Y	Y (3)	Y (2)
BURST COMMANDS			
Memory Write	N	Y (3)	Y
Alias Memory Read Block	Y	Y (3)	Y
Alias Memory Write Block	N	Y (3)	Y
Split Completion Received by "original" PCI-X bus master" not bridge	N	N	N
Split Completion Received by bridge	N	Y (3)	N
Memory Read Block	Y	Y (3)	Y
Memory Write Block	N	Y (3)	Y

Table 8-2: Target Termination (continued)

Notes:

(1) Only supported by the PCI or PCI-X resource that contains the interrupt controller. If the interrupt controller is on the legacy bus segment, the termination is supported by the PCI/LEGACY or PCI-X/LEGACY BRIDGES.

(2) Even though redundant, this target termination applies to bus transaction for DWORD COMMANDS.

(3) The PCI-X addendum specification permits the Disconnect at Next ADB termination for a SINGLE bus transaction (for a DWORD or BURST COMMAND) even though it will not change the execution of the SINGLE bus transaction.

PCI SPECIFC IMPLEMENTATION

8.1 PCI MASTER TERMINATION

COMPLETION TERMINATION OF MEMORY, I/O, AND CONFIGURATION TRANSACTIONS

A Completion termination of memory, I/O, and configuration transactions occurs when the FRAME# signal line is deasserted and the IRDY# signal line is asserted simultaneously for one CLK signal line period. The other terminations to be discussed in this chapter must always incorporate Completion termination. That is, all bus transactions terminate with the FRAME# signal line deasserted and the IRDY# signal line asserted simultaneously for one CLK signal line period.

Completion termination is defined as the orderly completion of a bus transaction by the PCI bus master. When a bus transaction is terminated with a target termination, it is still the responsibility of the PCI bus master to complete the bus transaction in an orderly fashion. For purposes of this book, whenever a target termination is executed the PCI bus master actually completes the bus transaction according to the Completion termination protocol. That is, the target termination protocol is implemented by the target and is a request to the PCI bus master to terminate the bus transaction. The PCI bus master will proceed to terminate the bus transaction by implementing the protocol of a Completion termination to actually terminate the bus transaction.

If a BURST memory write and invalidate transaction is being executed, the Completion termination can only occur at Cacheline boundaries.

If a PCI bus master tries to execute a bus transaction past a natural 4K bytes address boundary with a BURST MRM or MRL transaction, the target must execute a Disconnect termination. There are also considerations for a PCI bus master executing across the four gigabyte address boundary. See Subchapter 4.5 for more information about bus transactions and these address boundaries.

628

The assertion of the PERR# signal line during a memory, I/O, or configuration transaction does not require the PCI bus master to execute a Completion termination any sooner than it would if the PERR# signal line was not asserted. The assertion of the SERR# signal line during a memory, I/O, or configuration transaction does not require the PCI bus master to execute a Completion termination any sooner than it would if the SERR# signal line was not asserted.

COMPLETION TERMINATION OF INTERRUPT ACKNOWLEDGE TRANSACTIONS

The protocol for a Completion termination of an interrupt acknowledge transaction is the same as for a Completion termination for a read memory, I/O, or configuration transaction. The PCI bus master is the HOST/PCI BRIDGE and the target is the PCI bus resource that contains the interrupt controller.

COMPLETION TERMINATION OF SPECIAL TRANSACTIONS

The special transaction only completes with a Master Abort termination.

COMPLETION WITH TIMEOUT TERMINATION OF MEMORY, I/O, AND CONFIGURATION TRANSACTIONS

The request for Completion with Timeout termination occurs when the GNTx# signal line for the current PCI bus master is deasserted when the internal Latency Timer has expired (see Figures 8-1 and 8-2). For memory, I/O, and configuration transactions, the data that has been accessed and is being accessed is valid, and the target can be accessed at a later time. The microaccess of a memory, I/O, or configuration transaction being executed when Completion with Timeout termination is requested is allowed to complete. The purpose of the Completion with Timeout termination is to terminate bus ownership by the present PCI bus master and provide a known latency to obtain bus ownership. See Chapter 14: *Latency and Performance* for more information.

The Latency Timer is a programmable counter (in the configuration address space) that counts (increments or decrements, depending on the timer) on each rising edge of the CLK signal line while the FRAME# signal line is asserted. The

Latency Timer is reloaded with its count value at the beginning of the memory, I/O, and configuration transactions when the FRAME# signal line is first sampled asserted and expires after a count of 256 or less. The counter reload value can be a fixed (hardware) or a programmable value. Only the PCI bus master knows when the Latency Timer expires. The request occurs when the Latency Timer expires or has expired when the associated GNTx# signal line is deasserted.

Latency Timer counting stops whenever the FRAME# signal line is deasserted because the memory or I/O transaction completion is forthcoming (*i.e.*, Completion termination). Consequently, a SINGLE bus transaction does not complete with Completion with Timeout termination. If the FRAME# signal line was asserted (prior to the assertion of the IRDY# signal line) for several CLK signal line periods to allow the LATENCY TIMER to expire, the subsequent deassertion of the FRAME# signal line for a SINGLE bus transaction makes the expiration meaningless. The Completion with timeout only applies to BURST bus transactions.

If the Latency Timer is not programmable, it is hard coded with a count of 16 or less. If it is programmable, the count is programmable with counts of from 1 to 256. The Latency Timer is required when a PCI bus master executes a BURST bus transaction containing more than two microaccesses. It is otherwise optional.

Figures 8-1 and 8-2 show the Completion with Timeout termination of a BURST memory, I/O, or configuration transaction. In Figure 8-1, the FRAME# signal line is asserted, and the GNTx#, TRDY#, and IRDY# signal lines are deasserted prior to the expiration of the Latency Timer. When the Latency Timer expires at the CLK signal line rising edge, BURST memory, I/O, and configuration transactions must be terminated as soon as possible.

Consequently, the FRAME# signal line must be deasserted at the completion of the present microaccess, and only one more microaccess can be executed at this time. In this example, only the initial microaccess was executed prior to the time the Latency Timer expires; obviously, the same protocol applies if several microaccesses occurred in place of the initial microaccess. In Figure 8-2, the Latency Timer expires when one of the microaccesses is completed. In this example, the asserted IRDY# signal line when the Latency Timer expires requires that two more microaccesses are executed in order for the FRAME# signal line to be deasserted correctly for the last microaccess.

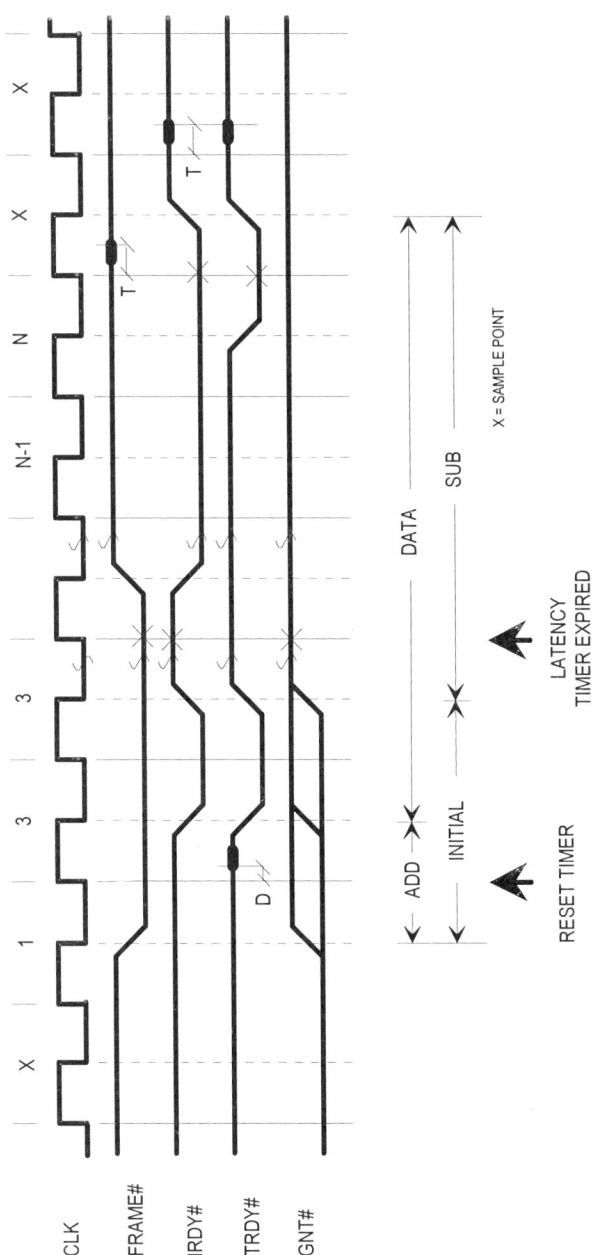

Figure 8-1: PCI Timeout Termination

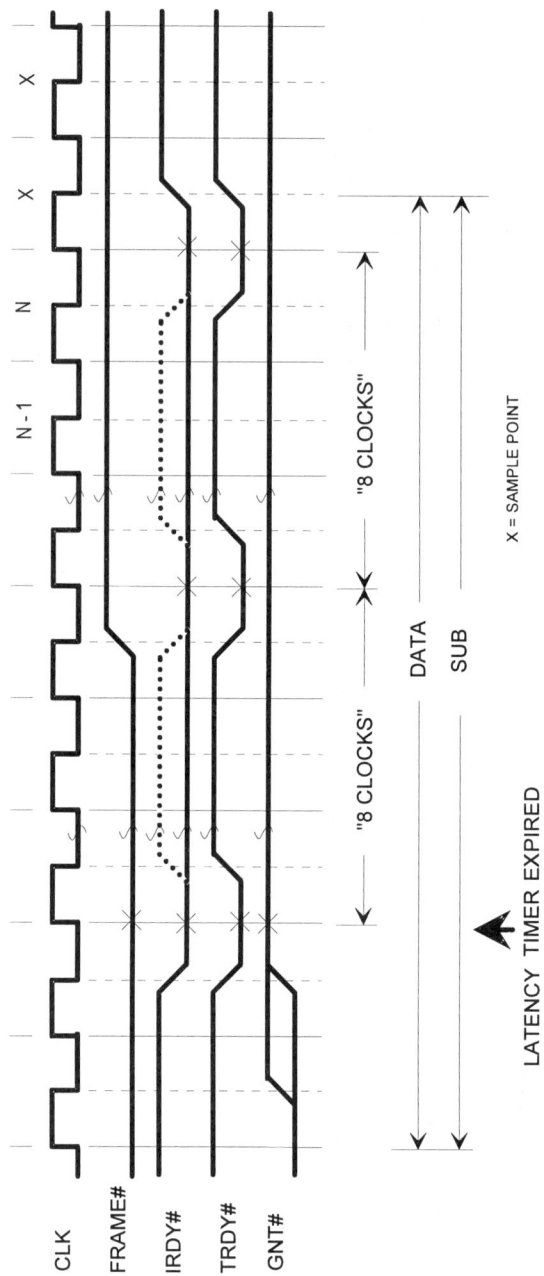

Figure 8-2: PCI Timeout Termination

> The LT is required for any PCI bus master than can burst more than two microaccesses. That is, more than an initial microaccess and a subsequent microaccess; consequently, the Completion with Timeout termination is only defined for BURST bus transactions.

> If a memory write and invalidate transaction is being executed, the Completion with Timeout termination can only occur at Cacheline boundaries.

The worst case number of CLK signal line periods until the completion of the BURST memory, I/O, or configuration transaction is 16 CLK signal line periods. This reflects two microaccesses in accordance with the "8 clock" rule (Chapter 14: *Latency and Performance* for more information). If the target was not able to complete the microaccess following the "8 clock" rule, it is required to execute a Disconnect termination. The BURST memory, I/O, or configuration transaction is completed under Completion termination (see *Completion termination* in this subchapter).

> In Figures 8-1 and 8-2, the FRAME# signal line is immediately deasserted. Due to the protocol of the IRDY# and FRAME# signal lines, the FRAME# signal line cannot be deasserted until the IRDY# signal line is asserted. The IRDY# signal line cannot be asserted until the PCI bus master is ready to access the data; consequently, the FRAME# signal line may not be immediately deasserted. According to the PCI bus specification, IRDY# should be asserted within 2-3 CLK signal line periods after the Latency Timer expires.

The Latency Timer is reloaded and counting starts at the beginning of each BURST memory, I/O, or configuration transaction when the FRAME# signal line is first asserted. If the GNTx# signal line of the present PCI bus master is asserted when the Latency Timer expires, the Completion with Timeout termination is not executed at that time. Subsequently, the PCI bus master can begin execution of another bus transaction if the GNTx# signal line is asserted just prior to asserting the FRAME# signal line.

> Execution of Completion with Timeout termination has no effect on the central arbiter because only the PCI bus master knows that it has been requested. A Completion with Timeout termination does not force the PCI bus master to deassert the associated REQx# signal line.

The request for Completion with Timeout termination (Latency Timer expires) is only recognized by the PCI bus master. The target termination requests (Retry, Disconnect, or Target Abort terminations) will take priority over the Completion with Timeout termination. When the Retry, Disconnect or Target Abort termination is requested, the memory, I/O, or configuration transaction is completed by the PCI bus master per the Completion termination protocol.

The execution of a Completion with Timeout termination appears to the PCI bus segment as a Completion termination once the PCI bus master determines that a Completion with Timeout termination is to be executed That is, the bus transaction is NOT being terminated as a target termination.

A Completion with Timeout termination has no affect on a PCI bus master obtaining or retaining the Lock Function and locking or the lock of a target.

The assertion of the PERR# signal line during a memory, I/O, or configuration transaction does not require the PCI bus master to execute a Completion with Timeout termination any sooner than it would if the PERR# signal line was not asserted. The assertion of the SERR# signal line during a memory or I/O transaction does not require the PCI bus master to execute a Completion with Timeout termination any sooner than it would if the SERR# signal line was not asserted.

COMPLETION WITH TIMEOUT TERMINATION OF INTERRUPT ACKNOWLEDGE AND SPECIAL TRANSACTIONS

The PCI local bus specification specifies that interrupt acknowledge transactions can only be executed as SINGLE bus transactions. Consequently, as defined above, the Completion with Timeout termination protocol DOES NOT apply.

Completion with Timeout termination protocol DOES NOT apply to the completion of special transactions in that the protocol for the special transaction requires a fixed quick completion.

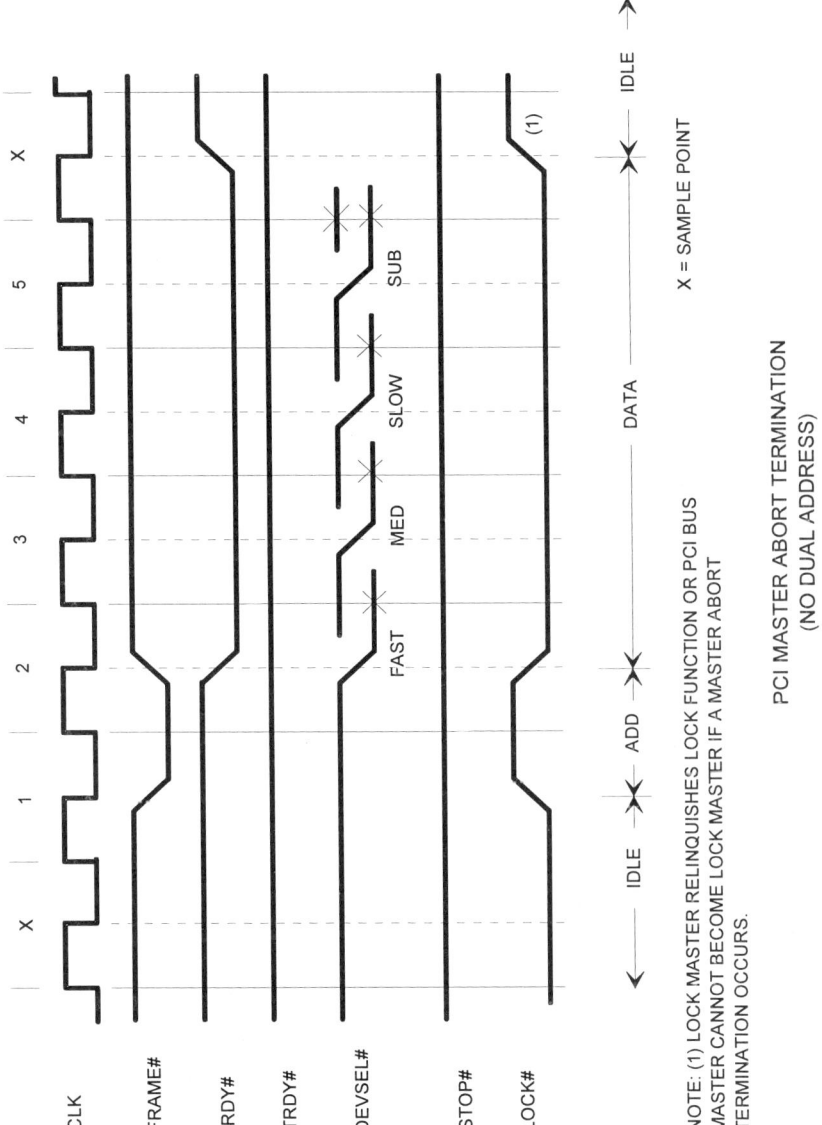

Figure 8-3: PCI Master Abort Termination (No DUAL ADDRESS)

MASTER ABORT TERMINATION OF MEMORY, I/O, CONFIGURATION, AND INTERRUPT ACKNOWLEDGE TRANSACTIONS

The Master Abort termination of memory, I/O, configuration, and interrupt acknowledge transactions occur when there is no potential for a device to claim the memory, I/O, configuration, or interrupt acknowledge transaction and become the target. The memory, I/O, configuration, or interrupt acknowledge transaction cannot be executed if not claimed by a target asserting the DEVSEL# signal line. The execution of a Master Abort termination requires a Completion termination; consequently, the IRDY# signal line must be asserted for a minimum of one CLK signal line period. As outlined in Figure 8-3, when the DEVSEL# signal line is sampled deasserted on the rising edge of the fourth CLK signal line period after the FRAME# signal line is first sampled asserted, the Master Abort termination must be executed.

The IRDY# signal line will be immediately deasserted if, prior to the sampling point of the deasserted DEVSEL# signal line, the FRAME# and IRDY# signal lines are deasserted and asserted, respectively. If the FRAME# and IRDY# signal lines are both asserted at the sample point of the deasserted DEVSEL# signal line, the FRAME# signal line is immediately deasserted and the IRDY# signal line is deasserted one CLK signal line period later (see Figure 8-4). Finally, Figure 8-5 outlines a third scenario for the FRAME# and IRDY# signal line at the sampling point of the deasserted DEVSEL# signal line. When the FRAME# signal line is asserted and the IRDY# signal line is deasserted, these signal lines are immediately driven to the opposite state. Subsequently, the IRDY# signal line is deasserted. The three examples outlined above all complete with Completion termination. For one CLK signal line period, the FRAME# and IRDY# signal lines are deasserted and asserted, respectively. Subsequently, the FRAME# and IRDY# signal lines are both deasserted.

In the above paragraph, the word *immediately* indicates the preferred protocol for the PCI bus master to complete the bus transaction. However, the PCI bus master may complete the bus transaction at a later time.

When the HOST/PCI BRIDGE or the PCI/LEGACY BRIDGE is executing a PCI bus transaction, a Master Abort termination requires the bridge to discard data for a write transaction and return all "1"s to the source bus for a read transaction. The bridge must set the Received Master Abort bit in the Status Register of its configuration space.

The Master Abort termination is defined for a memory, I/O, configuration, or interrupt acknowledge transaction (this is not a conclusive list ... other situations are possible) as follows:

- A target must not claim a bus transaction (NOT asserting the DEVSEL# signal line) if a Reserve Command is encoded in the C/BE# signal lines in the ADDRESS PHASE.

- A target must not claim a memory, I/O, configuration, or interrupt acknowledge transaction by asserting the DEVSEL# signal line if the DUAL ADDRESS is encoded in the C/BE# signal lines in the ADDRESS PHASE. The Master Abort termination occurs for accesses to a memory target when the target cannot decode 64 address bits (it is not a 64 data bit resource). The Master Abort occurs for accesses to the I/O, configuration, and interrupt acknowledge transactions because the associated address spaces do not support 64 address bits.

- A target may claim a memory, I/O, configuration, or interrupt acknowledge transaction by asserting the DEVSEL# signal line, if it detects an address parity error.

When the PCI bus master terminates a memory, I/O, configuration (during run time), or interrupt acknowledge transaction with a Master Abort termination, the Received Master Abort bit must be set in its Status Register in its configuration address space. This requirement does not apply for a Master Abort termination for execution of a configuration transaction during initialization (non-run time).

The PCI local bus specification does not prevent the PCI bus master from repeating the exact bus transaction that was terminated by a Master Abort termination.

The above discussion and Figures 8-3 to 8-5 do not consider DUAL ADDRESS, ADDRESS/DATA STEPPING or PRE-DRIVE. If a memory transaction is executing a DUAL ADDRESS, all of the sampling points for the DEVSEL# signal line are delayed by one CLK signal line period relative to when the FRAME# signal line is first sampled asserted. If a memory, I/O, or interrupt acknowledge transaction implements ADDRESS/DATA STEPPING or a configuration transaction implements ADDRESS/DATA STEPPING or PRE-DRIVE; the sampling points are the same relative to when the FRAME# signal line is first sampled asserted. However, under the ADDRESS/DATA STEPPING or pre-drive protocols, the FRAME# signal line will be asserted later in the bus transaction (not at CLK signal line period #1) than shown in Figures 8-3 to 8-5.

637

If the address is valid and the target is not broken, it is required to claim the bus transaction by asserting the DEVSEL# signal line.

The PERR# signal line cannot be asserted when a Master Abort termination is executed because no device claimed the memory, I/O, configuration, or interrupt acknowledge transaction, so no data was accessed. The PCI bus master may assert the SERR# signal line to report a Master Abort termination of a memory, I/O, configuration, or interrupt acknowledge transaction if not reported by other means. The assertion of the SERR# signal line can be used to report the error only if the System Error Control bit is set to logical "1" in the Command Register of the PCI bus master's Command Register. If the SERR# signal line is asserted, the PCI bus master must set the Signaled System Error Status in its Status Register in the configuration address space to logical "1". The PCI bus master does not assert the SERR# signal line to report a Master Abort termination of a special transaction or configuration transaction during initialization (non-run time).

If the Master Abort termination is due to a memory write transaction for a Message Signaled Interrupt, the associated PCI bus master must assert the SERR# signal line

Execution of the Master Abort termination has no affect on the central arbiter because it does not monitor the associated signal lines. Also, a Master Abort termination does not force the PCI bus master to deassert the associated REQx# signal line. An asserted STOP# signal line helps define Retry, Disconnect, or Target Abort termination requests. The STOP# signal line can only be asserted simultaneously with or after the assertion of the DEVSEL# signal line; consequently, the Master Abort termination has highest priority.

A PCI bus master cannot become Lock master and lock a target when a Master Abort termination is executed during the memory or I/O read transaction that the PCI bus master is using to lock the target. The LOCK# signal line is immediately deasserted.

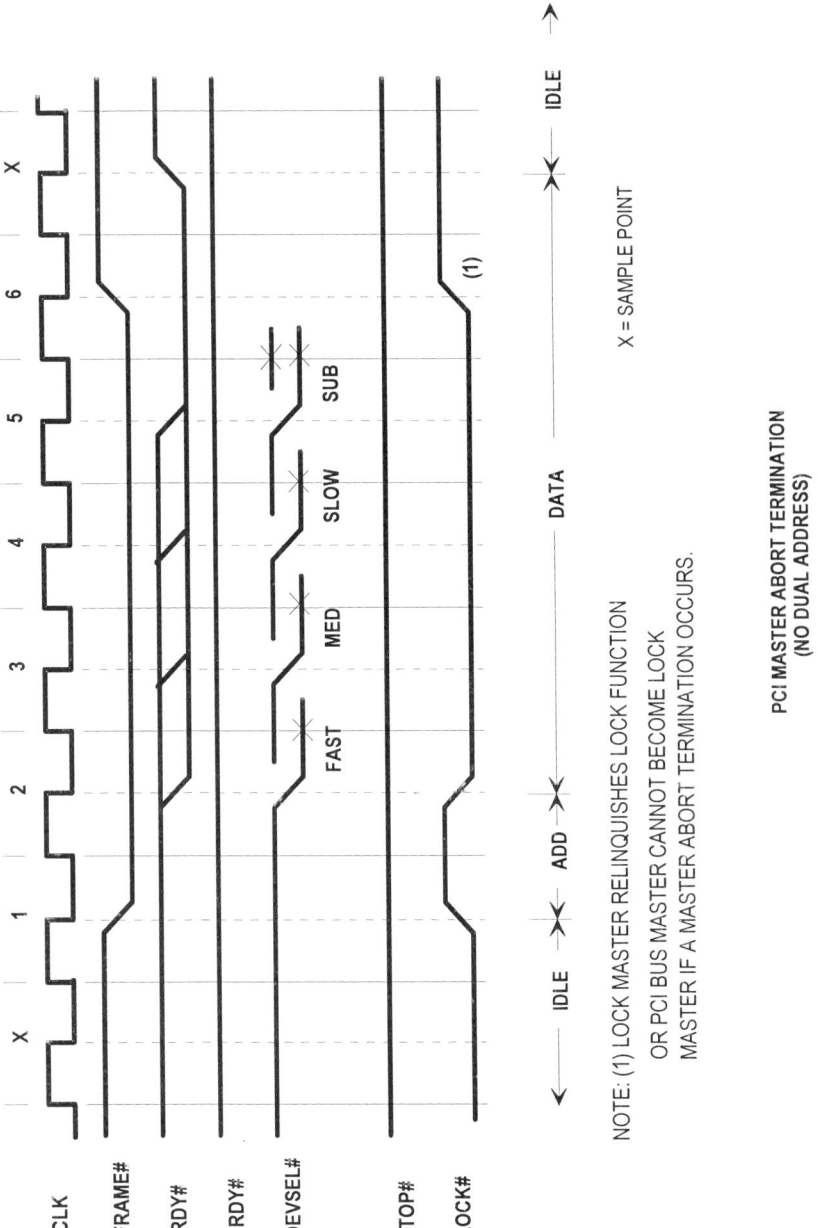

Figure 8-4: PCI Master Abort Termination (No DUAL ADDRESS)

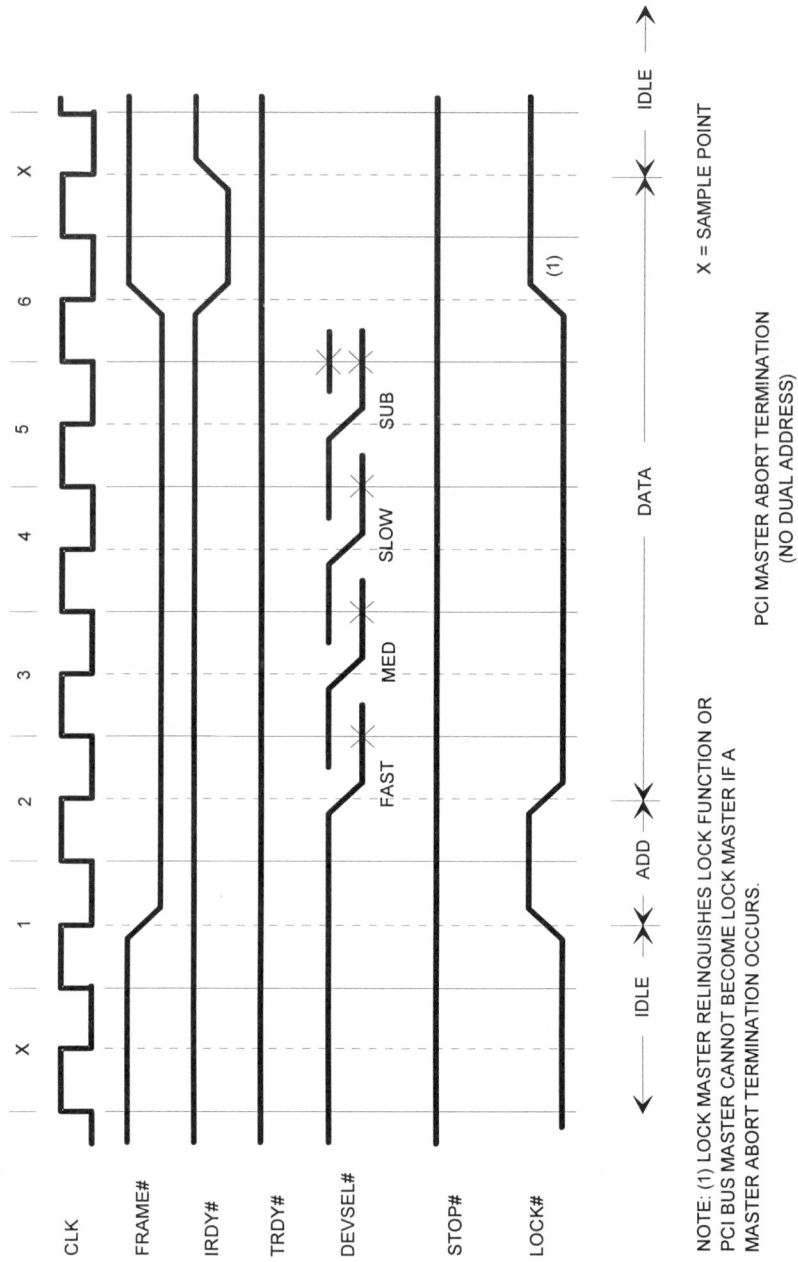

Figure 8-5: PCI Master Abort Termination (No DUAL ADDRESS)

If the Lock master is accessing the locked target with a memory, I/O, configuration, or interrupt acknowledge transaction, and a Master Abort termination occurs, the Lock master is required to relinquish the Lock Function. The LOCK# signal line is immediately deasserted and the target is immediately unlocked. If a non-Lock master accesses the locked target, the execution of a Master Abort termination does not force relinquishing of the Lock Function by the Lock master or the unlocking of the target.

The Master Abort is executed if no resource has claimed the memory, I/O, configuration, or interrupt acknowledge transaction (asserted the DEVSEL# signal line) by the SUBTRACTIVE DECODING sample point. When the Dual Address command is executed, this sampling point occurs one PCI clock period later.

PCI/PCI and PCI-X/PCI-X BRIDGES port bus transactions from the source bus segment to the destination bus segment without any advance knowledge of possible Master Abort or Target Abort terminations on the destination bus segment. Consequently, relative to the source bus segment, a bridge will post memory write transactions, post split completion transactions, apply Delayed Transaction protocol, and apply Split Completion protocol without knowledge of the pending Master Abort termination or Target Abort termination. Relative to Master Abort and Target Abort terminations on the destination bus segment, the bridge's response protocol to posted bus transactions is different than that for the bus transactions to the Delayed Transaction protocol or the Split Transaction protocol.

For the Master Abort termination and Target Abort termination protocols for PCI/PCI BRIDGES, see *PCI-to PCI Bridge Architecture Specification Rev 1.1* for more information. For the Master Abort termination and Target Abort termination protocols for PCI-X/PCI-X BRIDGES, see sections 8.7.1.5 and 8.7.1.6 of the *PCI-X Addendum Specification Rev 1.0a* for more information.

MASTER ABORT TERMINATION OF SPECIAL TRANSACTIONS

The special transaction can only be terminated with the Master Abort termination in conjunction with the Completion termination as outlined above for memory, I/O, configuration, and interrupt acknowledge transactions. When the PCI bus master terminates a memory, I/O, configuration (during run time), or interrupt acknowledge transaction with a Master Abort termination; the Received Master

Abort bit must be set in its Status Register in its configuration address space. If the bus transaction is a special transaction, the aforementioned bit is not set.

In that the Master Abort termination is the "normal" termination for a special transaction, the use of Master Abort termination by any target during a special transaction for DUAL ADDRESS encoding or address parity error is not possible.

> The PERR# signal line cannot be asserted when a Master Abort termination is executed, because no device claimed the special transaction so no data was accessed. The PCI bus master does not assert the SERR# signal line to report a Master Abort termination of a special transaction.

8.2 PCI TARGET TERMINATION

INTRODUCTION

The PCI local bus specification defines several conditions for terminating a bus transaction. These conditions vary from no buffer space available and compliance to "16 and 8 clock" rules, to a broken target. Please see the summary of target termination in Table 8-2 in Subchapter 8-0.

> The rest of this subchapter uses the phrase "forces the PCI bus master to deassert its associated REQx# signal line." The protocol for how long the REQx# signal line is deasserted is outlined in Subchapter 9.2.

RETRY TERMINATION OF MEMORY, I/O, CONFIGURATION, AND INTERRUPT ACKNOWLEDGE TRANSACTIONS

A Retry termination is requested when no data has been accessed in the memory, I/O, configuration, or interrupt acknowledge transaction, the TRDY# signal line is deasserted, and the DEVSEL# signal line is asserted when the STOP# signal line is first asserted in the memory, I/O, configuration, or interrupt acknowledge transaction (see Figures 8-6 and 8-7). Retry termination indicates that no memory, I/O, configuration, or interrupt acknowledge transaction is possible at this time for whatever reason, but the target is not broken and can be accessed at a later time. For example, a Retry termination will occur for an access to a locked target by a PCI bus master that is not the Lock master. Once Retry termination is requested, no other termination occurs except for Completion termination.

642

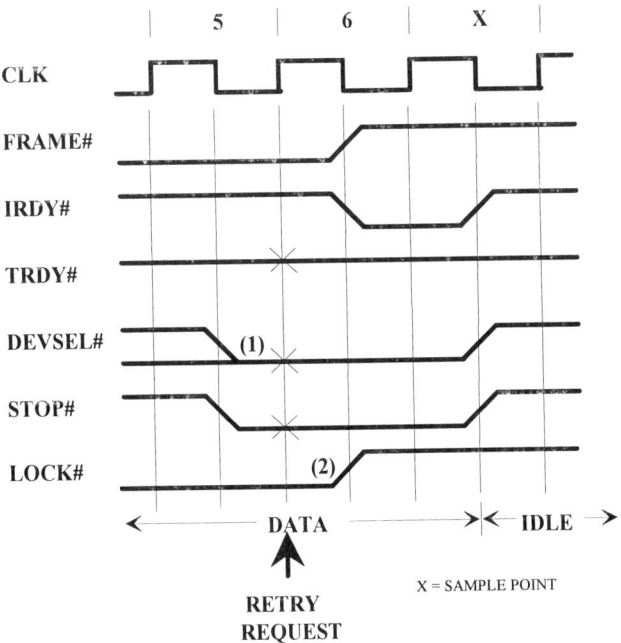

NOTES: (1) TO AVOID A MASTER ABORT TERMINATION
DEVSEL# MUST BE ASSERTED BY THE FOURTH
RISING EDGE OF THE CLK AFTER FRAME#
IS SAMPLED ASSERTED (FIFTH RISING EDGE
FOR DUAL ADDRESS)
(2) PCI BUS MASTER CANNOT BECOME LOCK
MASTER IF A RETRY TERMINATION OCCCURS

Figure 8-6: PCI Retry Termination

The Retry termination does not apply to special transactions; consequently, for this section the term "bus transactions" does not include special transactions.

The balance of this section will refer to memory, I/O, configuration, and interrupt acknowledge transactions collectively as "bus transactions".

The Retry termination is defined for the following bus transaction situations (this is not a conclusive list ... other situations are possible):

■   A Retry termination is required when a locked target is accessed by a PCI bus master that is not the Lock master.

■   A Retry termination is required per the "PCI 16 clock" rule (see the discussion below).

■   A Retry termination is required whenever the target will not be able to immediately respond to the bus transaction; for example, as part of Delayed Transactions or prior to the completion of a device's internal initialization. See Chapter 7: *Bridge and Interface Protocol* and Chapter 11: *Reset, Power, and Signal Line Initialization* for more information.

The Retry termination is NOT a response for an address or data parity error.

Retry termination must be executed by the target if it cannot complete a SINGLE bus transaction or the initial microaccess of a BURST bus transaction within sixteen CLK signal line periods ("PCI 16 clock" rule) from the assertion of the FRAME# signal line (STOP# signal line must be asserted on the seventeenth rising edge of the CLK signal line measured from the first rising edge of the CLK signal line when the FRAME# signal line is asserted). For a write transaction, the data is either accepted by the target (with or without posting) or a Retry termination is executed within the confines of the "PCI 16 clock" rule. For a read transaction, the target must provide the data or execute Retry termination within the confines of the "PCI 16 clock" rule.

A target that executes a Retry termination will accept or provide data when the bus transaction is repeated. A method by which the target accepts or provides data for the repeated bus transaction is to latch the address, COMMAND type, byte enables, REQ64# signal line, LOCK# signal line, etc., when it executes a Retry termination on a SINGLE bus transaction or the initial microaccess of a BURST bus transaction. The latched information is to identify the repeat of the "exact same" bus transaction. The target can proceed with the access independent of the PCI bus and prepare for a subsequent repeat of the bus transaction as defined by the aforementioned latched information.

In summary, the "PCI 16 clock" rule and the associated execution of the Retry termination due to this rule APPLIES to the SINGLE bus transactions and initial microaccess of BURST bus transactions of the following:

■   Memory transactions

■   I/O transactions

■   Configuration transactions

■   Interrupt acknowledge transactions

The "PCI 16 clock" rule DOES NOT apply for the above PCI bus transactions during the initialization time (RST# signal line deasserted to 2^{25} CLK signal line periods later), when executing from BOOT ROM, or when copying expansion ROM to memory. Note: If the device is accessing its expansion ROM after it has been hot-inserted, the aforementioned "PCI16 clock" rule relative to target termination DOES apply.

Rev. 2.0 of the PCI local bus specification did not require Retry termination per the "PCI 16 clock" rule, but Rev. 2.1 and later revisions do require Retry termination per the "PCI 16 clock" rule.

Rev. 2.1 of the PCI local bus specification requires the PCI bus master to repeat the "exact same" bus transaction that had resulted in a Retry termination(s) until it is completed with a Completion (with or without timeout) termination, Disconnect termination, Master Abort termination, Target Abort termination, or a reset of the bus segment occurs. Rev. 2.0 of the PCI local bus specification did not require the repeating of the aforementioned "exact same" bus transaction.

Some PCI bus masters are repeating an MRL or MRM transaction without the exact same command. Even though this violates the Rev. 2.1 PCI local bus specification, to insure operation the target should do the following:

• Assume that an "exact same" memory read transaction occurs when the command is either MRL, MRM, or memory read

The execution of a Retry termination requires the IRDY# signal line to be asserted for a minimum of one CLK signal line period. In Figure 8-6, Retry termination is requested by the target when the FRAME# signal line is asserted. The Retry termination request causes the immediate deassertion of the FRAME# signal line and assertion of the IRDY# signal line (if not previously asserted). Subsequently, the IRDY#, DEVSEL#, and STOP# signal lines are deasserted and the bus transaction is completed when the FRAME# and IRDY# signal lines are both deasserted. In Figure 8-7, Retry termination is requested when the FRAME# signal line is deasserted. The Retry termination request causes the immediate deassertion of the IRDY#, DEVSEL#, and STOP# signal lines to complete the bus transaction. The assertion of the DEVSEL# signal line when a Retry termination is requested distinguishes it from a Target Abort termination.

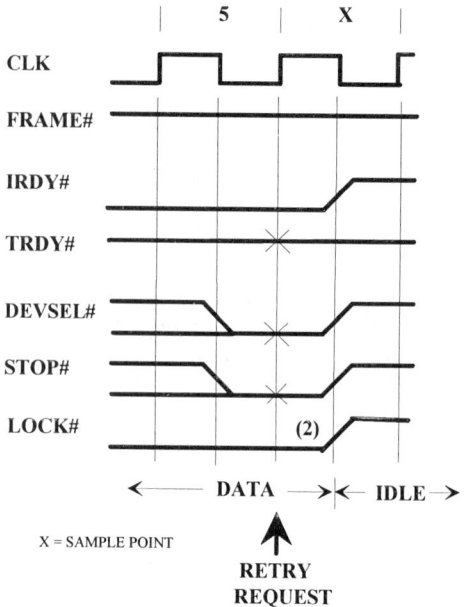

X = SAMPLE POINT

**RETRY
REQUEST**

NOTES: (1) TO AVOID A MASTER ABORT
TERMINATION DEVSEL# MUST BE
ASSERTED BY THE FOURTH RISING EDGE
OF THE CLK AFTER FRAME# IS SAMPLED
ASSERTED (FIFTH RISING EDGE FOR DUAL
ADDRESS)
(2) PCI BUS MASTER CANNOT BECOME LOCK
MASTER IF A RETRY TERMINATION OCCCURS

Figure 8-7: PCI Retry Termination

In the above paragraph, the word *immediate* indicates the preferred protocol for the PCI bus master to complete the bus transaction. If a Retry termination is executed during a read or write transaction, the PCI bus master is required to repeat the "exact same" bus transaction (same address, same addressing sequence, same C/BE# signal lines for byte lane enabling, etc.). The "exact same" bus transaction must be repeated until a Completion, Completion with Timeout, Target Abort, Master Abort, or Disconnect termination is executed. The assertion of the RST# signal line will also remove the requirement for the PCI bus master to repeat the "exact same" bus transaction.

The assertion of the SERR# signal line has no bearing on the aforementioned requirement to repeat the "exact same" bus transaction that completed with Retry termination. Similarly, the requirement to continue repeating the "exact same" bus transaction due to Retry termination is not affected by the assertion of the PERR# signal line.

The PCI bus master may execute other bus transactions to the target that executed the Retry termination or other targets between repeating the "exact same" bus transaction. Similarly, other PCI bus masters can execute bus transactions to the target that had executed a Retry termination. PCI bus masters that are executing the "exact same" bus transactions are required to respond to accesses by other PCI bus masters if it also has target attributes.

If the Lock master or a non-Lock master is accessing the locked target, the execution of a Retry termination does not force the Lock master to relinquish the Lock Function.

When the SERR# signal line is asserted by the target to indicate an address parity error on the AD, C/BE#, PAR, and PAR64 signal lines, the target cannot request a Retry termination due to this address parity error. A Retry termination can occur for other reasons, such as the bus and target are properly operating, but data cannot be accessed at this time. The PCI bus master cannot assert the SERR# signal line to report a Retry termination of a bus transaction. The PERR# signal line cannot be asserted when a Retry termination is requested because no data was accessed.

Once Retry termination is requested, the TRDY#, DEVSEL#, and STOP# signal lines cannot change state until Completion termination occurs. At Completion termination, the DEVSEL# and STOP# signal lines are deasserted simultaneously with the deassertion of the IRDY# and TRDY# signal lines

A Retry termination requires the PCI bus master to deassert its REQx# signal line. See Chapter 9: *Bus Ownership* for more information.

As previously discussed, when a bus transaction completes with a Retry termination, the PCI bus master must repeat the "exact same" bus transaction until the PCI bus segment is reset or the "exact same" bus transaction is completed without a Retry termination. If the target relative to the PCI bus master is "slow", there may be many repeats of the "exact same" bus transactions that will complete with Retry termination. When the repeats of the "exact same" bus transactions are memory write transactions, the effective bandwidth of the bus is lowered due to strong order rules for all memory write transactions posted in a bridge (See Chapter 7: *Bridge and Interface Protocol* for more information). To partly address this issue, the Maximum Completion Time (MCT) has been defined. MCT is a design goal of the target, and operates as follows:

- A device as target that terminated a memory write transaction with Retry termination must (by design) complete a microaccess (transfer data) of a repeat of the "exact same" memory write transaction within the Maximum Completion Time (MCT) limit. The MCT limit is 334 periods of the CLK signal line at 33 MHz and 668 periods of the CLK signal line at 66 MHz.

- At the CLK signal line frequencies of 33 MHz and 66 MHz the MCT limit is 10 microseconds. If the CLK signal line frequency is less than 33 MHz, the 334 periods of the CLK signal line still applies; thus the MCT limit is proportionally more than 10 microseconds.

- There are three elements to the MCT limit protocol:

  - A target by design is required (whenever possible) to complete within the MCT limit the data phase (access without Retry termination ... *i.e.*, Completion (including Completion with Timeout) or Disconnect termination) of the repeat of the "exact same" memory write transaction associated with the initial Retry termination.

  - A target that cannot achieve the aforementioned compliance to the MCT limit requires its device driver to compensate. The compensation can be in two forms: limit the rate of repeating the "exact same" memory write transactions to the target ... OR ... the PCI bus master executing the device driver software determines if the target has buffer space for a subsequent memory write transaction to minimize the number of Retry terminations.

  - The MCT limit is also satisfied when a repeat of the "exact same" memory write transaction associated with the Retry termination results in a Master Abort or a Target Abort termination by the target. Obviously, reset of PCI bus also satisfies the MCT limit.

- An extension of the MCT limit protocol is when a target may have multiple memory write transactions addressing it. The MCT limit is measured from the Retry termination of a memory write transaction to the very next completion of a microaccess (access without Retry termination ... *i.e.*, Completion (including Completion with Timeout) or Disconnect termination) of a memory write transaction even when it is not a repeat of the memory write transaction associated with the initial Retry termination that the MCT limit is referenced too.

■ When the target has multiple memory write transactions addressing it, the MCT limit is also satisfied when a memory write transaction that is or is not a repeat of the memory write transaction associated with the initial Retry termination, is terminated with a Master Abort or a Target Abort termination by the target. Obviously, reset of PCI bus segment also satisfies the MCT limit.

■ The MCT limit does not apply to PCI bus master, or a PCI/PCI BRIDGE Resource (Base Class = 0x06) under the following considerations:

   ■ The PCI bus master cannot assume that the MCT limit will be met for all memory write transactions for three reasons:

      ■ The target was designed pre-revision 2.2 of the PCI bus specification

      ■ The target was designed post-revision 2.2 of the PCI bus specification but simply may not comply.

      ■ The target may have several buses and PCI/PCI BRIDGES between itself and the PCI bus master.

   ■ The PCI/PCIBRIDGE as a target (memory write transaction to an internal register) must adhere to the MCT limit protocol. The MCT limit protocol does not apply to memory write transactions porting though the PCI /PCI BRIDGE.

   ■ Whenever MCT limit protocol is met or satisfied as outlined above, the subsequent Retry termination of a memory write transaction re-establishes the MCT limit protocol.

   ■ The MCT limit does not apply to a target during PCI initialization (the first 2^{25} CLK signal line periods after the deassertion of the RST# signal line) when executing from BOOT ROM, or when copying expansion ROM to memory. Note: If the device is accessing its expansion ROM after it has been hot-inserted, the MCT limit DOES apply.

■ A target cannot indefinitely respond with Retry termination for repeats of the "exact same" memory write transactions.

RETRY TERMINATION OF SPECIAL TRANSACTIONS

The special transaction does not address a specific target, so Retry termination and the "PCI 16 clock" rule do not apply to this transaction

DISCONNECT TERMINATION OF MEMORY, I/O, CONFIGURATION, AND INTERRUPT ACKNOWLEDGE TRANSACTIONS

The Disconnect termination does not apply to special transactions; consequently, for this section the term "bus transactions" does not include special transactions.

The balance of this section will refer to memory, I/O, configuration, and interrupt acknowledge transactions collectively as "bus transactions"

The Disconnect termination is similar to the Retry termination in that the STOP#, DEVSEL#, and TRDY# signals lines are involved in the bus transaction termination (see Figures 8-8-A and B and 8-9-A and B). The only difference between a Retry and a Disconnect termination is that with a Disconnect termination data has been accessed in a microaccess in a BURST bus transaction prior to the termination request or simultaneously with the access of data in a SINGLE bus transaction or microaccess in a BURST bus transaction. The Retry termination simply means no data access for the bus transaction. The Disconnect termination provides whatever data access is available and indicates that the target cannot respond to further accesses in the bus transaction within a reasonable amount of time. The target is not broken and can be accessed at a later time.

The Disconnect termination is defined for the following bus transaction situations (this is not a conclusive list ... other situations are possible):

- The target must execute a Disconnect termination if the target cannot provide data within eight CLK signal line periods from the beginning of each subsequent microaccess during a BURST bus transaction. The net effect of the "8 clock" rule is to place limits on the length of a BURST bus transaction. The restrictions do not apply to a SINGLE bus transaction or to the initial microaccess of a BURST bus transaction. The "8 clock" rule requires the target to execute a Disconnect termination request under the following conditions:

  - All subsequent microaccesses of a BURST bus transaction are governed by the "8 clock" rule.

■ The initial microaccess is completed when the IRDY# and TRDY# signal lines are both asserted at a CLK signal line rising edge. The target will begin counting on the subsequent CLK rising edge and continues counting until one of the following occurs:

  ■ If the TRDY# signal line is asserted simultaneously with a count value of eight or less, the bus transaction is allowed to complete with Completion termination whenever the IRDY# signal line is asserted

  OR

  ■ If the TRDY# signal line is not asserted by the time the count value reaches eight, the STOP# signal line must be asserted (TRDY# or STOP# signal line will be sampled asserted on the ninth rising edge of the CLK signal line relative to the first rising edge of the CLK signal line when the IRDY# and TRDY# signal lines are both asserted in the previous microaccess). The assertion of the STOP# signal line results in a Disconnect termination without data.

■ In summary, the "8 clock" rule and the associated execution of the Disconnect termination due to this rule APPLIES to the SINGLE bus transactions and initial microaccess of BURST bus transactions of the following:

  ■ Memory transactions

  ■ I/O transactions

  ■ Configuration transactions

  ■ Interrupt acknowledge transactions (see shaded box below)

> The "PCI 8 clock" rule DOES NOT apply for the above PCI bus transactions during the initialization time (RST# signal line deasserted to 2^{25} CLK signal line periods later), when executing from BOOT ROM, or when copying expansion ROM to memory. Note: if the device is accessing its expansion ROM after it has been hot-inserted, the aforementioned "PCI 8 clock" rule relative to target termination DOES apply.

■ The target must execute a Disconnect termination if the target cannot support the BURST bus transaction addressing sequence requested by the PCI bus master (Disconnect with data in initial microaccess or Disconnect without data in the first subsequent microaccess).

- The target may execute a Disconnect termination when the PCI bus master attempts a 64 data bit access to a 32 data bit target (See shaded box below).

- The target may execute a Disconnect termination when a data parity occurred in a previous microaccess of a BURST write transaction as part of the error reporting protocol. A target may execute a Disconnect with data termination when a data parity error occurs in the present microaccess of a BURST write transaction.

- The target must execute a Disconnect without data termination when a BURST bus transaction crosses out of the address space of the target.

- If the PCI bus master executed an MRM or MRL across a page boundary (4K page on a 4K address boundary), the target must execute a Disconnect without data termination.

- A PCI/PCI BRIDGE or the target executing prefetching for the PCI bus master (per Prefetchable Bit set in the Base Address register) must execute a Disconnect with data termination at the last access of the page or a Disconnect without data termination if the page boundary is crossed (4K page on a 4K address boundary).

The Disconnect termination is NOT a response for an address parity error.

There are two types of Disconnect termination: *with* and *without* data. The Disconnect with data termination occurs when the data of the present SINGLE bus transaction or microaccess of a BURST bus transaction is accessed. Disconnect without data termination occurs after data was accessed in previous microaccesses of the BURST bus transaction but no additional data will be accessed during the present microaccess. Once a Disconnect termination is requested, no other termination occurs except for Completion termination.

If the target termination request occurs without any data accessed (TRDY# signal line remains deasserted) for the SINGLE bus transaction or the initial microaccess of a BURST bus transaction, by definition it was a Retry termination.

The execution of a Disconnect termination does not require the PCI bus master to repeat the "exact same" bus transaction (same address, same addressing sequence, same C/BE# signal lines for byte lane enabling, etc.) per the protocol of the Retry termination.

The assertion of the SERR# or the PERR# signal line does not affect the execution of the Disconnect termination for other reasons.

Execution of Disconnect termination does not affect the central arbiter because it does not monitor the associated signal line. If the request for Disconnect with data termination request occurs when the IRDY# signal line is asserted and the FRAME# signal line is deasserted (last access, see Figure 8-8-B), then data is accessed and the PCI bus master is not required to deassert the associated REQx# signal line. Otherwise, a request for Disconnect with data termination, when the FRAME# signal line is asserted (see Figure 8-8-A), or a Disconnect without data, requires the PCI bus master to deassert the associated REQx# signal line. See *Chapter 9: Bus Ownership* for more information.

A Disconnect termination has no effect on a PCI bus master obtaining or retaining the Lock Function and therefore keeping a target locked.

Once Disconnect termination is requested, the TRDY#, DEVSEL#, and STOP# signal lines cannot change state until Completion termination occurs. At Completion termination, the DEVSEL# and STOP# (and TRDY# if Disconnect with data) signal lines are deasserted simultaneously with the deassertion of the IRDY# signal line. The one exception is the TRDY# signal line during Disconnect with data termination as shown in Figure 8-8-A. Once the IRDY# and TRDY# signal lines are simultaneously sampled asserted when the FRAME# signal line is asserted, the TRDY# signal line is required to immediately be deasserted prior to the deassertion of the IRDY# signal line. The immediate deassertion of the TRDY# signal line prevents another sampling point when the IRDY# and TRDY# signal lines are simultaneously asserted, which would indicate another data access.

MRL and MRM commands are limited to a 4K byte block on 4K address boundaries. If the master attempts to cross this boundary (FRAME# signal line asserted for the last subsequent microaccess below the boundary) and the data is ready for access, the target (or PCI/PCI BRIDGE) is required to execute a Disconnect with data termination. Under this condition, if the data is not ready, the target executes a Disconnect without data termination. Similar action is required by the target (or PCI/PCI BRIDGE) for the 4K byte block boundary of a prefetchable address range.

653

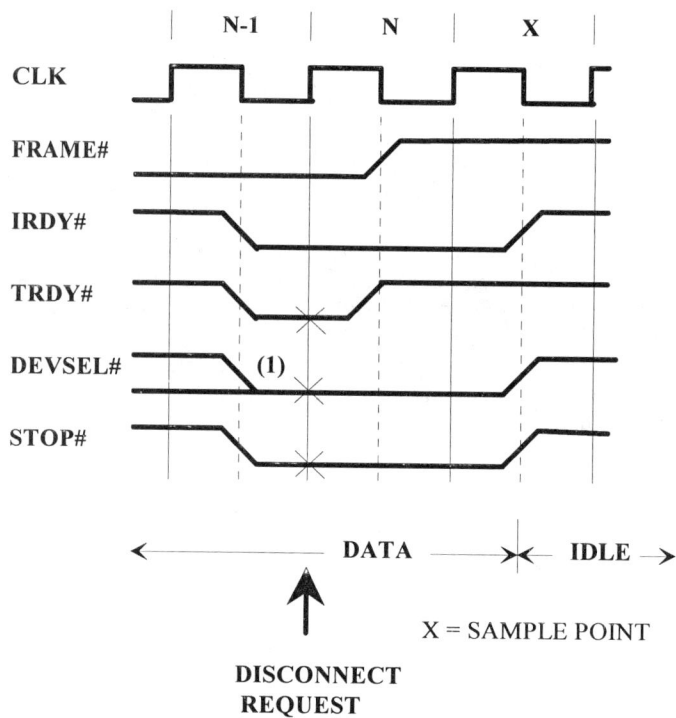

DISCONNECT
REQUEST

X = SAMPLE POINT

NOTE: (1) TO AVOID A MASTER ABORT TERMINATION
DEVSEL# MUST BE ASSERTED BY THE FOURTH
RISING EDGE OF THE CLK AFTER FRAME#
IS SAMPLED ASSERTED (FIFTH RISING EDGE
FOR DUAL ADDRESS)

Figure 8-8-A: Disconnect with Data Termination

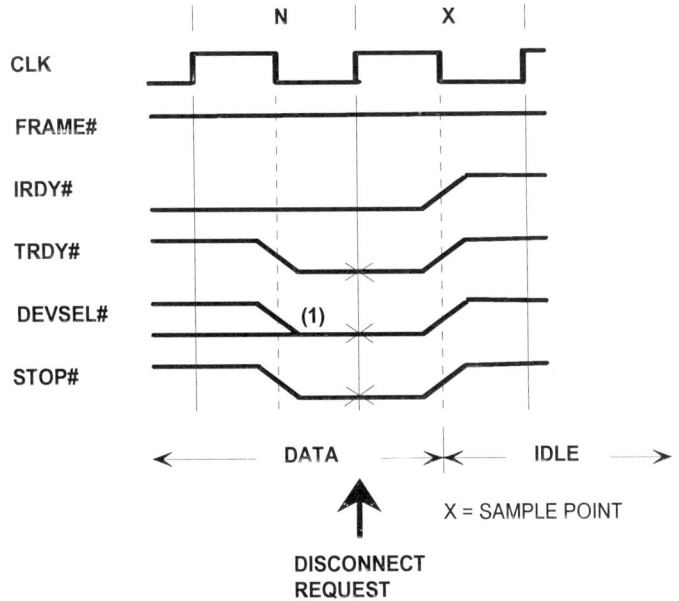

X = SAMPLE POINT

DISCONNECT
REQUEST

NOTES: (1) TO AVOID A MASTER ABORT TERMINATION
DEVSEL# MUST BE ASSERTED BY THE FOURTH
RISING EDGE OF THE CLK AFTER FRAME#
IS SAMPLED ASSERTED (FIFTH RISING EDGE
FOR DUAL ADDRESS)

Figure 8-8-B: Disconnect with Data Termination

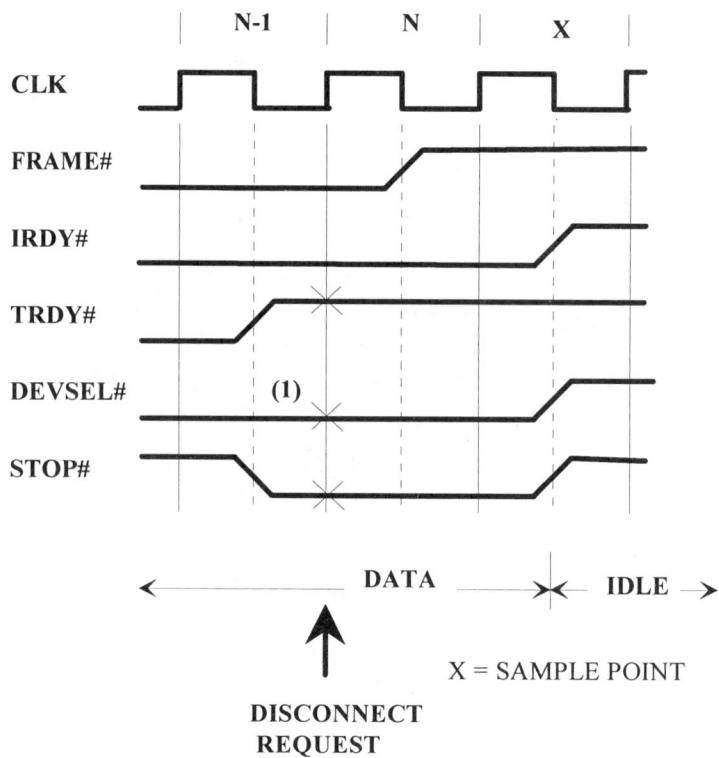

NOTE: (1) TO AVOID A MASTER ABORT TERMINATION
DEVSEL# MUST BE ASSERTED BY THE FOURTH
RISING EDGE OF THE CLK AFTER FRAME#
IS SAMPLED ASSERTED (FIFTH RISING EDGE
FOR DUAL ADDRESS)

Figure 8-9-A: Disconnect without Data Termination

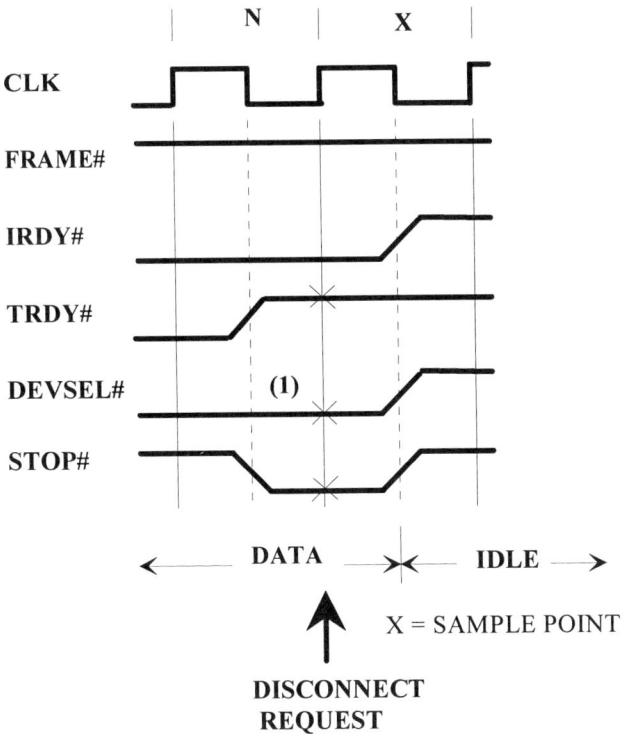

NOTES: (1) TO AVOID A MASTER ABORT TERMINATION
DEVSEL# MUST BE ASSERTED BY THE FOURTH
RISING EDGE OF THE CLK AFTER FRAME#
IS SAMPLED ASSERTED (FIFTH RISING EDGE
FOR DUAL ADDRESS)

Figure 8-9-B: Disconnect without Data Termination

DISCONNECT WITH DATA ACCESS

Figures 8-8-A and B and 8-9-A and B outline the different ways a Disconnect with data termination is executed. A Disconnect with data termination is requested when the STOP# signal line is first asserted in the bus transaction in which the TRDY# signal line is asserted. The Disconnect with data termination request indicates that the associated data is the last to be accessed at this time.

> When the STOP# signal line is first asserted to request a Disconnect with data termination, its assertion must be simultaneous with the assertion of the TRDY# signal line. If the STOP# signal line is asserted prior to the assertion of the TRDY# signal line, either a Retry or Disconnect without data termination is executed. (All of the above assume that the DEVSEL# signal line was asserted.)

In Figure 8-8-A, a Disconnect with data termination request occurs when the FRAME# signal line is asserted. The assertion of the TRDY# and STOP# signal lines indicates that the present access is the last access of data for this bus transaction. The Disconnect with data termination request causes the PCI bus master to immediately deassert the FRAME# signal line and assert the IRDY# signal line (if not already asserted) when it is ready to complete the access. The deasserted FRAME# signal line and asserted IRDY# signal line causes the IRDY#, STOP#, and DEVSEL# signal lines to be immediately deasserted. Data is accessed when the TRDY# and IRDY# signal lines are both asserted. The bus transaction is subsequently completed when the FRAME# and IRDY# signal lines are both deasserted.

> In Figure 8-8-A, the FRAME# signal line was immediately deasserted. Due to the protocol of the IRDY# and FRAME# signal lines, the FRAME# signal line cannot be deasserted until the IRDY# signal line is asserted. The IRDY# signal line cannot be asserted until the PCI bus master is ready to access the data; consequently, the FRAME# signal line may not be immediately deasserted. Also, once Disconnect with data termination is requested (IRDY#, STOP# and TRDY# signal lines all asserted), the TRDY# signal line is required to be immediately deasserted.

Figure 8-8-B outlines Disconnect with data termination when the FRAME# signal line is deasserted prior to the assertion of the TRDY# and STOP# signal lines. By definition, the IRDY# signal line will have been asserted when the FRAME# signal line was deasserted. The deasserted FRAME# and asserted IRDY# signal lines cause the IRDY#, TRDY#, STOP#, and DEVSEL# signal lines to be immediately deasserted. Data is accessed when the TRDY# and IRDY#

signal lines are both asserted. The bus transaction is completed when the FRAME# and IRDY# signal lines are both deasserted.

> A Disconnect with data termination indicates that the bus and target are properly operating, but additional data cannot be accessed at this time.

> If the 64 data bit transaction to a 32 data bit target (REQ64# and ACK64# signal lines asserted and deasserted, respectively) completes with Disconnect with data termination during the initial microaccess or Disconnect without data termination during the first subsequent microaccess, only the lower four bytes of the eight bytes (QWORD) of the 64 data bits has been accessed. The PCI bus master must subsequently execute a bus transaction as a 32 data bit PCI bus master (REQ64# signal line deasserted) to access the upper four bytes of the "original" eight bytes (QWORD). See *Chapter 6: Detailed Bus Transaction Operation* for more information.

> When the SERR# signal line is asserted by the target to indicate an address parity error on the AD, C/BE#, PAR, and PAR64 signal lines, the target cannot request a Disconnect with data termination due to this address parity error. A Disconnect with data termination can occur for other reasons, such as the bus and target are properly operating, but additional data cannot be accessed at this time. The PCI bus master cannot assert the SERR# signal line to report a Disconnect with data termination of a bus transaction. The PERR# signal line can be asserted by the target for a data parity error that occurs with a Disconnect with data termination because data was written in the present microaccess. A target may execute a Disconnect with data termination for a data parity error occurring in the present or a previous microaccess.

DISCONNECT WITHOUT DATA ACCESS

As previously discussed, a Disconnect termination can occur without data being simultaneously accessed. For example, in a BURST transaction data can be successfully accessed prior to the STOP# signal line being asserted (see Figures 8-9-A and 8-9-B). The transaction is terminated without the simultaneous access of data when the STOP# and DEVSEL# signal lines are both asserted, and the TRDY# signal line is deasserted. This type of transaction termination, Disconnect termination without data, completes in the same fashion as outlined for the Retry termination. The assertion of the DEVSEL# signal line when a Disconnect without data termination is requested distinguishes it from a Target Abort termination request.

A Disconnect without data termination indicates that the bus and target are operating properly, but data cannot be accessed at this time.

If the 64 data bit transaction to a 32 data bit target (REQ64# and ACK64# signal lines asserted and deasserted, respectively) completes with Disconnect with data termination during the initial microaccess or Disconnect without data termination during the first subsequent microaccess, only the lower four bytes of the eight bytes (QWORD) of the 64 data bits has been accessed. The PCI bus master is required to subsequently execute a bus transaction as a 32 data bit PCI bus master (REQ64# signal line deasserted) to access the upper four bytes of the "original" eight bytes (QWORD).

When the SERR# signal line is asserted by the target to indicate an address parity error on the AD, C/BE#, PAR, and PAR64 signal lines, the target cannot request a Disconnect with or without data termination due to this address parity error. A Disconnect with or without data termination can occur for other reasons, such as the bus and target are properly operating, but additional data cannot be accessed at this time. The PCI bus master cannot assert the SERR# signal line to report a Disconnect with or without data termination of a bus transaction. The PERR# signal line cannot be asserted for a data parity error that occurs with a Disconnect without data termination because no data was accessed. A target may execute a Disconnect without data termination for a data parity error occurring in the present or a previous microaccess.

DISCONNECT TERMINATION OF SPECIAL TRANSACTIONS

The special transaction does not address a specific target, so Disconnect termination and the "PCI 8 clock" rule do not apply to this bus transaction

TARGET ABORT TERMINATION OF MEMORY, I/O, CONFIGURATION, AND INTERRUPT ACKNOWLEDGE TRANSACTIONS

The balance of this section will refer to memory, I/O, configuration, and interrupt acknowledge transactions collectively as "bus transactions"

The Target Abort termination can only occur after the DEVSEL# signal line has been asserted for at least one CLK signal line period (see Figures 8-10 and 8-11). If the DEVSEL# signal line has not been asserted, a Master Abort termination will have occurred. Target Abort termination is requested by the target when the STOP# signal line is asserted and the DEVSEL# signal line is deasserted. Target Abort termination can be requested either after data has or has not been accessed. Target Abort termination request occurs without the simultaneous access of data (*i.e.*, the TRDY# signal line is required to be deasserted). This type of termination also indicates to the PCI bus master that the target cannot support the access requested for the related address and *no* further accesses of the (command) type with the same address should be attempted by the present PCI bus master. In order to distinguish the Target Abort termination from a Retry or Disconnect without data terminations, the DEVSEL# signal line is required to be deasserted when the STOP# signal line is asserted. Once Target Abort termination is requested, no other termination occurs except for Completion termination.

> **As discussed above, the present PCI bus master that was executing a bus transaction when a Target Abort termination occurs must not repeat the access (same COMMAND type) to the same address (i.e., target). The present PCI bus master can access the target with the same address, if a different COMMAND type is used. Target Abort termination does not affect accesses to the same target by other PCI bus masters. Other PCI bus masters may access this address (i.e., target) because they may not have monitored the Target Abort termination.**

The Target Abort termination is defined for the following bus transaction situations (this is not a conclusive list ... other situations are possible):

- The target must execute a Target Abort termination if it is broken or it detects a fatal error.

- The target must execute a Target Abort termination when the byte lane pattern in the C/BE# signal lines during the DATA PHASE (of a SINGLE I/O transaction or initial microaccess of a BURST I/O transaction) does not "match" the AD[01::00] signal lines during the ADDRESS PHASE. Target Abort termination cannot be executed if through subtractive decoding the bridge (PCI/LEGACY BRIDGE) claimed the bus transaction.

- If the target cannot support the non-continuous byte lanes enabled by the PCI bus master, it must execute a Target Abort termination.

- A target may execute a Target Abort termination as part of the reporting protocol for an address parity error.

■   The target may execute a Target Abort termination if it wants to restrict the data size of a memory transaction (not 32 data bits). A target cannot use Target Abort termination for an I/O, configuration, or interrupt acknowledge transaction to restrict data size. These bus transactions are always 32 data bits in size and the REQ64# signal line is ignored (the ACK64# signal line remains deasserted).

> 64 data bit I/O targets can be implemented, but there is no benefit to requiring the increased complexity and it is therefore strongly recommended that 64 data bit I/O targets not be implemented. For the purposes of this book, I/O targets are only 32 data bits in size. If a 64 data bit I/O target is implemented, the 64 data bit protocol applied to memory targets would also apply to I/O targets.

■   A target may execute a Target Abort termination as part of the reporting protocol for a data parity error in a previous microaccess.

■   The target may execute a Target Abort termination if it is accessed by an MRM or MRL command but does not support prefetching.

In Figure 8-10, the FRAME# signal line is asserted when a Target Abort termination (TRDY# and DEVSEL# signal lines deasserted and STOP# signal line asserted) is requested by the target. The Target Abort termination request causes the FRAME# and IRDY# signal lines to be immediately deasserted and asserted (if not already asserted), respectively. The deasserted FRAME# and asserted IRDY# signal lines cause the IRDY# and STOP# signal lines to be deasserted. The bus transaction is completed when the FRAME# and IRDY# signal lines are both deasserted.

In Figure 8-11, the FRAME# signal line is deasserted and the IRDY# signal line is asserted when the Target Abort termination (TRDY# and DEVSEL# signal lines deasserted and STOP# signal line asserted) is requested. The IRDY#, and STOP# signal lines are subsequently deasserted. The bus transaction is completed when the FRAME# and IRDY# signal lines are both deasserted.

> In both Figures 8-10 and 8-11, the TRDY# signal line will have been asserted in a previous microaccess(es) of a BURST bus transaction. In the microaccess of a BURST bus transaction in which a Target Abort termination is requested, the TRDY# signal line must be deasserted. The data of any microaccess of a BURST bus transaction is not considered valid. If the bus transaction was a SINGLE bus transaction, the TRDY# signal line cannot have been asserted in the bus transaction for a Target Abort termination. The completion of a bus transaction with Target Abort termination is dependent on the logical states of DEVSEL#, STOP#, and IRDY# signal lines.

In the above paragraphs the word *immediate* indicates the preferred protocol for the PCI bus master to complete the bus transaction. However, the PCI bus master may complete the bus transaction several CLK signal line periods later.

When a target terminates a bus transaction with a Target Abort termination, the Signaled Target Abort bit must be set in its Status Register of the configuration address space. When the PCI bus master detects a Target Abort termination, it must set the Received Target Abort bit in its Status Register of the configuration address space.

The STOP# signal line can be asserted simultaneously or prior to the deassertion of the DEVSEL# signal line. If the STOP# signal line is asserted prior to the deassertion of the DEVSEL# signal line, a Disconnect or Retry termination is executed. If the STOP# signal line is asserted simultaneously with the deassertion of the DEVSEL# signal line, a Target Abort termination is executed.

Once Target Abort termination is requested, the DEVSEL# and STOP# signal lines cannot change state until Completion termination occurs. At Completion termination the STOP# signal line is deasserted simultaneously with the deassertion of the IRDY# signal line.

For a read transaction, a Target Abort termination indicates that any data read in the earlier microaccesses of the BURST bus transaction may be invalid. For a write transaction, a Target Abort termination indicates that the data written in the earlier microaccess of the BURST bus transaction may not have been successfully written into the target.

Execution of Target Abort termination does not affect the central arbiter, because it does not monitor the associated signal lines. Target Abort termination forces the PCI bus master to deassert the associated REQx# signal line.

A PCI bus master cannot become Lock master and lock a target when a Target Abort termination is executed during the read transaction which the PCI bus master is using to lock the target. The LOCK# signal line is immediately deasserted.

If the Lock master is accessing the locked target and a Target Abort termination occurs, the Lock master must relinquish the Lock Function. The LOCK# signal line is immediately deasserted and the target is immediately unlocked. If a non-Lock master accesses the locked target, the execution of a Target Abort termination does not force relinquishing of the Lock Function by the Lock master or the unlocking of the target.

When the SERR# signal line is asserted by the target to indicate an address parity error on the AD, C/BE#, PAR, and PAR64 signal lines, the target can request a Target Abort termination due to this address parity error. The PCI bus master may assert the SERR# signal line to report a Target Abort termination of a bus transaction if there is no other mechanism to do so. The assertion of the SERR# signal line can be used to report the error only if the System Error Control bit is set to logical "1" in the Command Register of the PCI bus master's Command Register. If the SERR# signal line is asserted, the PCI bus master must set to logical "1" the Signaled System Error Status in its Status Register in the configuration address space. The PERR# signal line cannot be asserted when a data parity occurs with a Target Abort termination because no data was accessed. A target may execute a Target Abort termination for a data parity error occurring in a previous microaccess.

If the Target Abort termination is due to a memory write transaction for a Message Signaled Interrupt, the associated PCI bus master must assert the SERR# signal line.

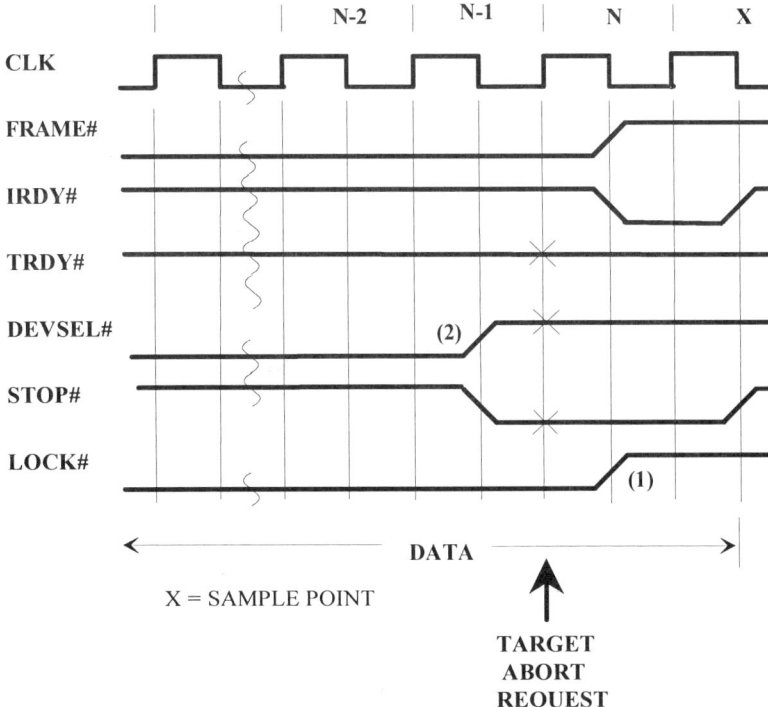

X = SAMPLE POINT

**TARGET
ABORT
REQUEST**

NOTE: (1) LOCK MASTER IS RELINGUISHES LOCK FUNCTION
          OR PCI BUS MASTER CANNOT BECOME LOCK
          MASTER IF A TARGET ABORT TERMINATION OCCURS
      (2) TO AVOID A MASTER ABORT TERMINATION DEVSEL#
          MUST BE ASSERTED BY THE FOURTH RISING EDGE OF CLK
          AFTER FRAME# IS SAMPLED ASSERTED (FIFTH RISING EDG
          FOR DUAL ADDRESS)

Figure 8-10: Target Abort Termination

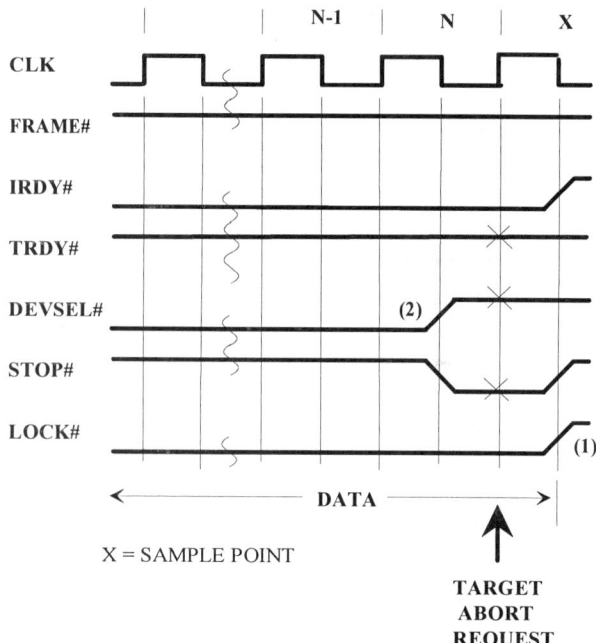

X = SAMPLE POINT

NOTE: (1) LOCK MASTER IS RELINGUISHES LOCK FUNCTION
OR PCI BUS MASTER CANNOT BECOME LOCK
MASTER IF A TARGET ABORT TERMINATION OCCURS
(2) TO AVOID A MASTER ABORT TERMINATION DEVSEL#
MUST BE ASSERTED BY THE FOURTH RISING EDGE OF CLK
AFTER FRAME# IS SAMPLED ASSERTED (FIFTH RISING EDG
FOR DUAL ADDRESS)

Figure 8-11: Target Abort Termination

TARGET ABORT TERMINATION OF SPECIAL TRANSACTIONS

The special transaction does not address a specific target, so Target Abort termination does not apply.

PCI-X SPECIFC IMPLEMENTATION

8.3   PCI-X MASTER TERMINATION

COMPLETION TERMINATION OF MEMORY, SPLIT COMPLETION, I/O, AND CONFIGURATION TRANSACTIONS

> The following discussions use two definitions: ADB and "sequence" of bus transactions. Please see these definitions in Subchapter 4.16.

A Completion termination of memory, split completion, I/O, and configuration transactions according to the PCI-X addendum specification is essentially the same as the PCI local bus specification, including the interaction with the PERR# and SERR# signal lines (See Subchapter 8.1). The differences are as follows:

- The FRAME# and IRDY# signal lines protocol for termination of a PCI-X bus transaction is more complex than for a PCI bus transaction. See Chapter 6: *Detailed Bus Transaction Operation* for specific information about how a bus transaction terminates.

    - Similar to PCI, all PCI-X bus transactions are required to terminate with Completion termination. That is, the target termination protocol is implemented by the target and is a request to the PCI-X bus master to terminate the bus transaction. The PCI-X bus master will proceed to terminate the bus transaction by implementing the protocol of a Completion termination to actually terminate the bus transaction.

- A PCI bus transaction protocol Completion termination (without a Retry termination) is not required to continue according to the Delayed Transaction protocol. Also, PCI BURST bus transactions have termination requirements relative to Cacheline boundaries. See subchapter 4.5 for more information specific to PCI. PCI-X bus transaction protocol does not follow the Cacheline boundaries and natural 4K byte address boundaries. See subchapter 4.16 for more information. The primary consideration is that PCI-X BURST bus transactions contain a total byte count (limit of 4096 bytes) and there is a certain requirement to transfer the total byte count dependent on the bus transaction as follows: (This is an overview; more detailed information follows relative for each type of bus transaction termination):

667

If the PCI-X bus master is not able to supply the correct data associated with the total byte count of the "sequence" due to some "internal problem" (non bus segment error), it still must complete the "sequence" unless Master Abort or Target termination is requested. For BURST memory write transactions, the C/BE# signal lines associated with the data written after the "internal problem" can be deasserted. For a BURST memory write block or a BURST alias memory write block transaction, there is no method defined by the PCI-X addendum specification to identify data written after the "internal problem". That is, for the bus transactions of the BURST memory write block and alias memory write block commands, the C/BE# signal lines are always deasserted and all data bytes are defined as written.

- PCI-X BURST memory write, memory write block, and alias memory write block transactions (collectively memory write transactions) all contain a starting address and a total byte count (Upper and Lower Byte Counts in the ATTRIBUTE PHASE ... maximum possible value of 4096 bytes). Ideally these memory write transactions should execute as a single BURST memory write transaction until the total byte count has been transferred. A PCI-X bus master that is not able to transfer the total bytes in a single BURST memory write transaction (due to a decision to terminate by PCI-X bus master, Timeout (see next section), or target termination except Retry) is required to do so in a "sequence" of bus transactions. A BURST memory write transaction that is the "first" bus transaction and terminated according to a Retry termination (that is a "sequence" of bus transactions has not been established), continuation (repeat) of the BURST memory write transaction is NOT required. If the "first" BURST memory write transaction is terminated with a Completion (with data transferred), Completion with Timeout, Disconnect at Next ADB, or Single Phase Disconnect termination; the PCI-X bus master must continue the transfer of bytes with a "sequence" of bus transitions until the total byte count identified (Upper and Lower Byte Counts in ATTRIBUTE PHASE) in the "first" bus transaction is transferred in the "sequence" of bus transactions. The BURST COMMAND encoded in the C/BE# signal lines in the ADDRESS PHASE of the bus transactions of the "sequence" must all be the same. Also, according to the definition of a "sequence", the Requester ID and Tag number in the ATTRIBUTE PHASE of each bus transaction of the "sequence" are the same. When a BURST memory write transaction of the "sequence" (not the "first") is terminated with Completion (with data transferred), Completion with Timeout, Disconnect at Next ADB, Retry, or Single Phase Disconnect terminations; the PCI-X bus master must continue the "sequence" of bus transitions until the total byte count identified (Upper and Lower Byte Counts in ATTRIBUTE PHASE) in the "first" bus transaction is transferred. For either the "first" BURST memory write transaction or a BURST memory write transaction of the "sequence" of bus transactions, a Master Abort or Target Abort termination requires the BURST memory write transaction to be terminated and the "sequence" to NOT continue.

■ PCI-X BURST memory read block and alias memory read block (collectively memory read transactions) transactions both contain a starting address and total byte count (Upper and Lower Byte Counts in the ATTRIBUTE PHASE). Ideally these memory bus transactions should execute as a single BURST memory read transaction until the total byte count has been transferred. A PCI-X bus master that is not able to transfer the total bytes in a single BURST memory read transaction (Completion (with data transferred), Completion with Timeout, Disconnect at Next ADB, Single Phase Disconnect, or Retry terminations) must NOT continue as a "sequence" of bus transactions. That is, a BURST memory read transaction that is the "first" bus transaction and terminated for any reason is not continued by the PCI-X bus master. If the PCI-X bus decides to continue, the targets will not assume any "sequence"; consequently, the PCI-X bus master can use the same or different Tag number. For the "first" BURST memory read transaction a Split Response termination will terminate the bus transaction and require that the PCI-bus master does not continue with the bus transaction. The Split Transaction protocol requires the target to complete the associated data read by executing split completion transaction to the PCI-X bus master. For the "first" BURST memory read transaction a Master Abort or Target Abort termination requires the BURST memory write transaction to NOT be continued.

■ PCI-X BURST split completion transactions contain a starting address (actually the lower seven bits to identify the beginning address relative to ADB ... or for when related to a DWORD or Split Completion Message) and a total byte count (Upper and Lower Byte Counts in the ATTRIBUTE PHASE ... maximum possible value of 4096 bytes). Ideally a single BURST split completion transaction until the total byte count has been transferred. A PCI-X bus master that is not able to transfer the total bytes in a single BURST split completion transaction (due to a decision to terminate by PCI-X bus master, Timeout (see next section), or Disconnect at Next ADB or Retry termination) is required to do so in a "sequence" of bus transactions. until the total byte count identified (Upper and Lower

Byte Counts in ATTRIBUTE PHASE) in the "first" bus transaction is transferred in the "sequence" of bus transactions. According to the definition of a "sequence" the Completer ID and Tag numbers in the ATTRIBUTE PHASE of each bus transaction of the "sequence" are the same. For any BURST split completion transaction Master Abort or Target Abort termination requires the BURST split completion transaction to be terminated and the "sequence" to NOT continue.

■ The Completion of a PCI-X DWORD COMMAND is not dependent on a byte count transfer. All transactions for DWORD COMMANDS are single 32 data bit bus transactions.

■ A BURST bus transaction terminated by a PCI-X bus master executing a Completion termination prior to the transfer of all of the associated bytes must terminate on an ADB (Allowed Disconnect Boundary).

The termination of a BURST bus transaction by the PCI-X bus master with Completion termination is a result of the conditions listed below. Alternatively, the bus transaction termination may be due to Completion with Timeout termination discussed in the next section. The ADB discussed below is aligned on a natural 128 byte address boundary. Consequently, the lower seven address bits of the starting address in the next BURST bus transaction of a "sequence" or the "first" BURST bus transaction beginning at an ADB are all logical "0". The lower seven address bits of the last byte of an ADB is 7FH. The ADB is defined independently of the data size of the bus transaction.

The PCI-X bus master executing a Completion termination is defined under the following conditions. That is, the other bus transaction terminations require the bus transaction to complete in an orderly fashion and relative to the FRAME# and IRDY# signal lines incorporate Completion termination. See Chapter 6: *Detailed Bus Transaction Operation* for more information.

- In response to arriving at the ending address (all of the bytes according to the total byte count have been transferred).

- At an ADB at which the PCI-X bus master wants to stop the present bus transaction for lack of further bytes to transfer at this time.

- Single Phase Disconnect, Disconnect at Next ADB, or Target Abort termination executed by the target.

> Whenever a large amount of data is to be transferred as a series of multiple sequences, the PCI-X bus master should align the transfers with ADB whenever possible for maximum system performance.

See Tables 8-1 and 8-2 in Subchapter 8.0 for a summary of Completion termination as it applies to the different PCI-X bus transactions.

COMPLETION TERMINATION OF INTERRUPT ACKNOWLEDGE TRANSACTIONS

The protocol for a Completion termination of an interrupt acknowledge transaction is the same as for a Completion termination for a bus transaction of a DWORD COMMAND. The PCI-X bus master is the HOST/PCI-X BRIDGE and the target is the PCI-X bus resource that contains the interrupt controller.

COMPLETION TERMINATION OF SPECIAL TRANSACTIONS

The special transaction only completes with a Master Abort termination.

COMPLETION WITH TIMEOUT TERMINATION OF MEMORY AND SPLIT COMPLETION TRANSACTIONS

The Completion with Timeout protocol only applies to BURST COMMANDS that execute with BURST bus transactions. Consequently, the Completion with Timeout termination protocol only applies to BURST memory transactions and BURST split completion transactions. Also, if the BURST bus transaction rule has one microaccess or two microaccesses, the Completion with Timeout termination does not apply. That is, the Completion with Timeout termination protocol can only apply to a bus transaction with more than an initial microaccess and a subsequent microaccess.

The PCI-X protocol for Completion with Timeout termination and the associated implementation of the Latency Timer is same as for PCI including the operation of PERR# and SERR# signal lines. See Subchapter 8.1 for more information. There are differences between the PCI-X's and PCI's implementations of Completion with Timeout termination as follows:

- As discussed above, the Completion with Timeout termination only applies to BURST memory transactions and BURST split completion transactions.

- The default value of the Latency Timer is 64 after RESET for a PCI-X bus segment (PCI-X initialization pattern on the DEVSEL#, STOP#, and TRDY# signal lines).

- The execution of Split Response, Single Phase Disconnect, and Disconnect at Next ADB terminations take priority over Completion with Timeout termination. This is in addition to Retry and Target Abort terminations, and the normal Completion by the PCI-X bus master like the protocol by the PCI bus master.

- Once the Latency Timer expires and GNTx# signal line is deasserted, the termination of the bus transaction is as follows:

  - The termination of a BURST memory bus transaction must be compliant to the ADB rule. The ADB rule is discussed later in this chapter in the Disconnect at Next ADB termination discussion (it would be beneficial to first understand the ADB rule before reading this section). There are several cases to consider:

    - Case A: The starting address and byte count (Upper and Lower Byte Counts in the ATTRIBUTE PHASE) indicates that four or more microaccesses will be executed to the next ADB. The Latency Timer expires with GNTx# signal line deasserted four or more microaccesses to the next ADB (exemplified by the BURST memory read transaction in Figure 8-12). The PCI-X bus master must terminate the BURST memory transaction at the next ADB unless the target requests a Retry, Single Phase Disconnect, Disconnect at the Next ADB, or Target Abort termination.

    - Case B: The starting address and byte count (Upper and Lower Byte Counts in the ATTRIBUTE PHASE) indicates that four or more microaccesses will be executed to the next ADB. The Latency Timer expires with the GNTx# signal line deasserted three or fewer microaccesses before the next ADB (exemplified by the BURST memory read transaction in Figure 8-13). The PCI-X bus master does not terminate the bus transaction at the next ADB due to the Latency Timer expiration with GNTx# signal line deasserted. The PCI-X bus master will continue the bus transaction until one of the following occurs (whichever occurs first):

      - The ending address is reached (which may be the next ADB).

      - The subsequent ADB is reached.

- The target requests a Retry, Single Phase Disconnect, Disconnect at the Next ADB, or Target Abort termination.

- The protocol outlined in the above cases also applies to BURST split completion transactions with the "lower address" replacing "starting address" in the discussion. Also, Single Phase Disconnect termination does not apply.

- The completion of the bus transaction must follow the FRAME# and IRDY# signal line protocol as defined by the "General Deassertion" protocol. See Chapter 6: *Detailed Bus Transaction Operation for* more information.

Figures 8-12 and 8-13 exemplify Completion with Timeout termination. The difference between three or fewer and four microaccesses to the ADB is an issue for a target termination, due to the response time for the PCI-X bus master to respond to the DEVSEL#, TRDY#, and STOP# signal lines. For a Completion with Timeout termination, the reaction to the GNTx# signal line and latency timer expires relative to the ADB is a finite minimum time.

COMPLETION WITH TIMEOUT TERMINATION OF DWORD MEMORY READ, I/O, CONFIGURATION, AND INTERRUPT ACKNOWLEDGE TRANSACTIONS

The Completion with Timeout protocol does not apply to DWORD COMMANDS because these commands can only be executed by a SINGLE bus transaction. That is, for Completion with Timeout to apply to a bus transaction, the transaction must have an initial microaccess and at least one subsequent microaccess.

COMPLETION WITH TIMEOUT TERMINATION OF SPECIAL TRANSACTIONS

Completion with Timeout termination protocol DOES NOT apply to the completion of special transactions in that the protocol for the special transaction requires a fixed quick completion.

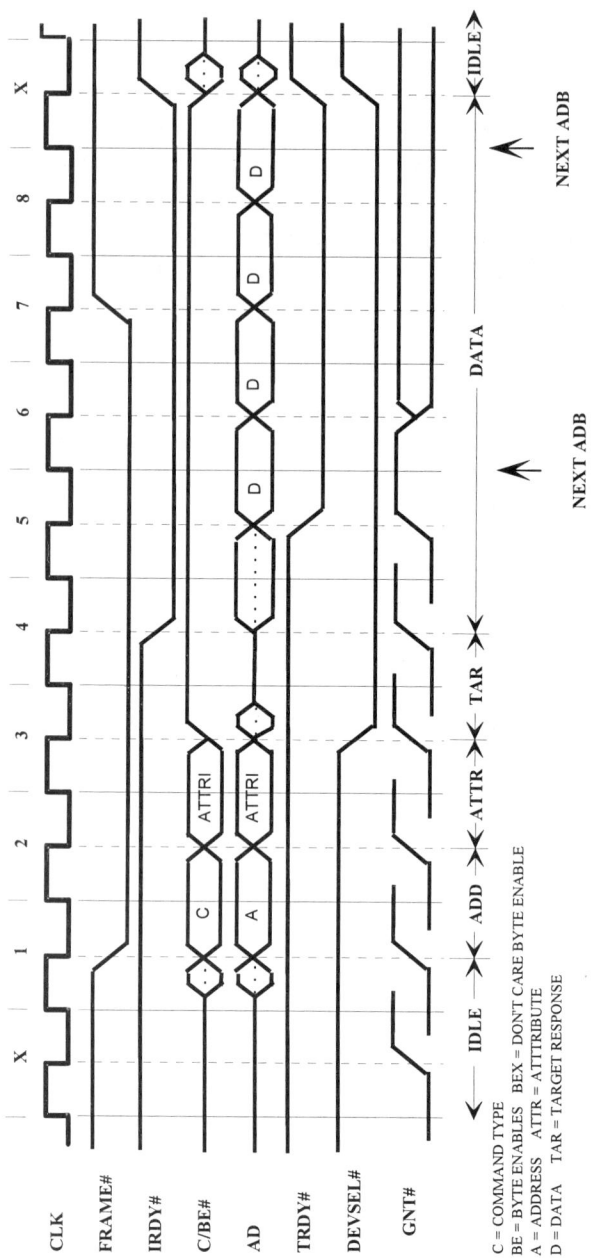

Figure 8-12: PCI-X Example of Completion Timeout Termination at Four or more Microaccesses to the ADB

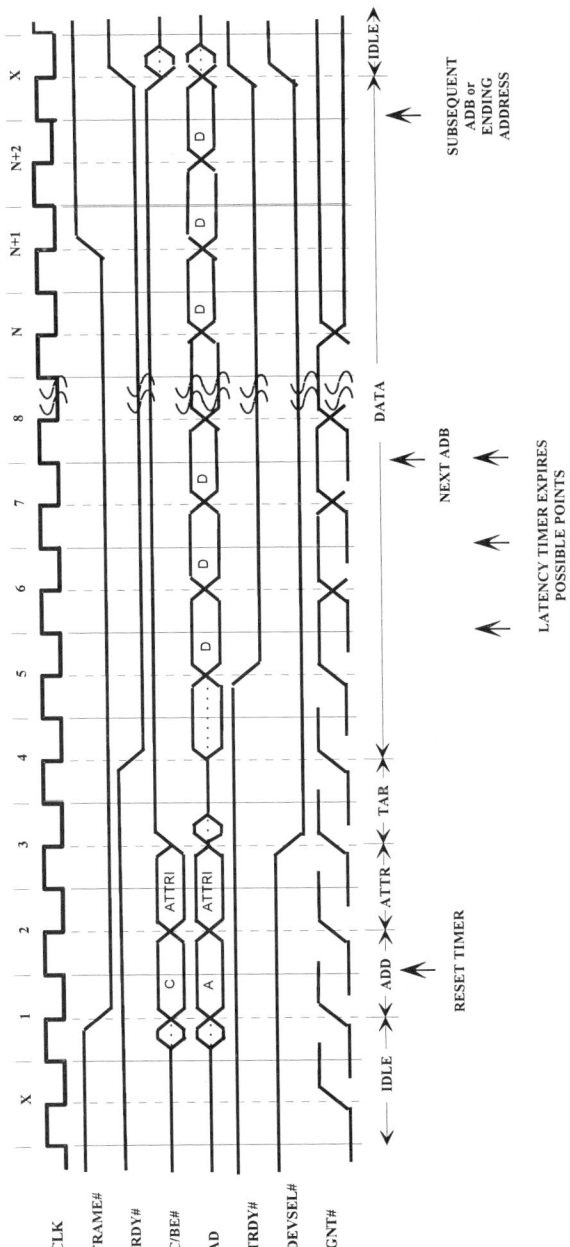

Figure 8-13: PCI-X Example of Completion Timeout Termination at Three or Fewer Microaccesses to the ADB

MASTER ABORT TERMINATION OF MEMORY, SPLIT COMPLETION, I/O, CONFIGURATION, AND INTERRUPT ACKNOWLEDGE TRANSACTIONS

The PCI-X protocol for Master Abort termination for memory, I/O, configuration, and interrupt acknowledge transactions is same as for PCI including the case when the Master Abort termination is appropriate, the setting to logical "1" of the Received Master Abort bit in the Status Register in the configuration address space, and the operation of the PERR# signal line. See Subchapter 8.1 for more information. There are differences between PCI-X's and PCI's implementations of Master Abort termination as follows:

- The PCI-X bus master that terminates the bus transaction with a Master Abort termination must notify the device driver via interrupt or some other suitable method. If notification of the device driver is not possible, the SERR# signal line must be asserted with the following qualifications: The assertion of the SERR# signal line can be used to report the error only if the System Error Control bit is set to logical "1" in the Command Register of the PCI-X bus master's Command Register. If the SERR# signal line is asserted, the PCI-X bus master must set to logical "1" the Signaled System Error Status bit in its Status Register in the configuration address space. The exception to this rule is configuration during initialization (non-run).

- All PCI-X devices that support memory address space must support 64 address bits; consequently, the receipt of a DUAL ADDRESS command by a target as part of a memory transaction cannot cause a Master Abort termination.

- As with PCI, a PCI-X target can optionally not claim the bus transaction if there is a parity error associated with the ADDRESS or ATTRIBUTE PHASE.

The protocol of the FRAME# and IRDY# signal lines to terminate the bus transaction differs from that of PCI. The FRAME# and IRDY# signal lines are simultaneously deasserted two CLK signal line rising edges relative to the SUB decode sample point. This protocol is outlined in Figure 8-14-A. This protocol also applies with DUAL ADDRESS, as shown in Figure 8-14-B.

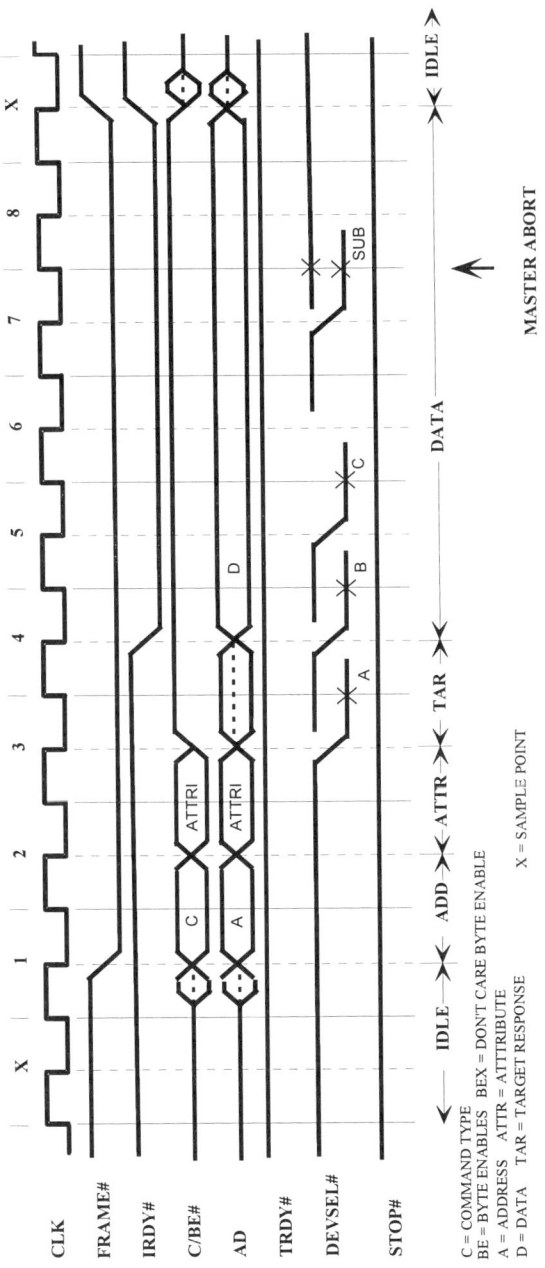

Figure 8-14-A: PCI-X Master Abort Termination DWORD Write Example

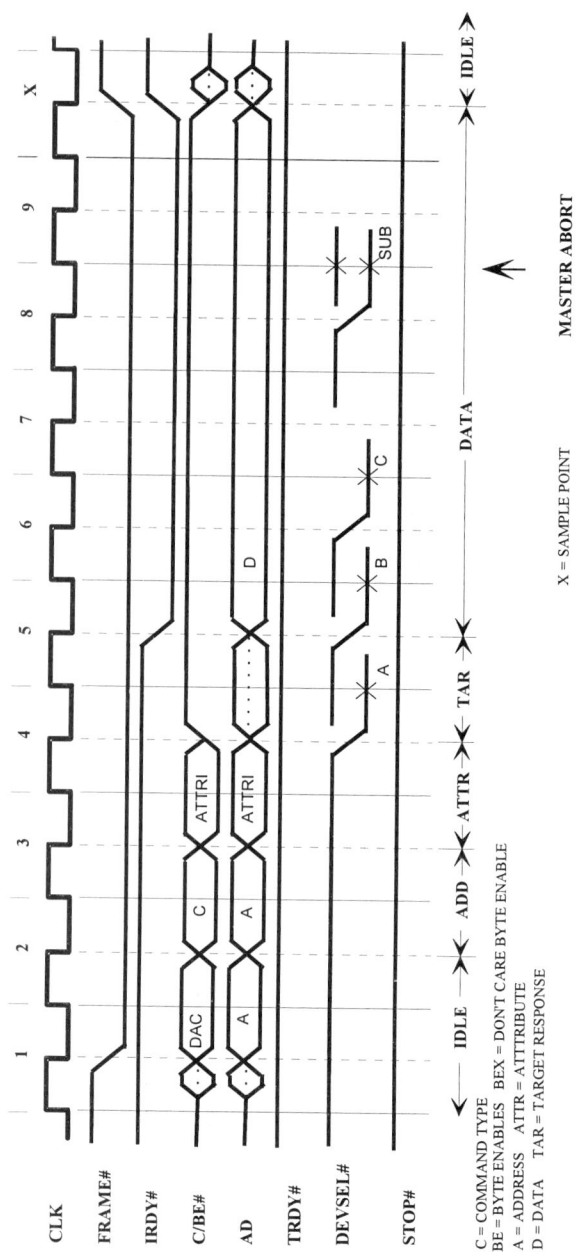

Figure 8-14-B: PCI-X Master Abort Termination with DUAL ADDRESS DWORD Write Example

The split completion transactions are unique to PCI-X and thus there are specific interpretations relative to Master Abort termination as follows (this is not a conclusive list ... other situations are possible):

- A Master Abort termination is appropriate for a split completion transaction as follows: (Remember, in the following discussion the "target" is the PCI-X bus master of the "original" transaction and the PCI-X bus master of the completion transaction is the target of the "original" transaction.)

  - The target may or may not claim the split completion transaction by asserting the DEVSEL# signal line if the Requester ID, Sequence ID, TAG number, byte count (Upper and Lower Byte counts), or Lower Address in the ADDRESS or ATTRIBUTE PHASES are not correct. (See Subchapter 10.6 for more information.) A Master Abort termination will occur if no PCI-X resource claims the bus transaction.

  - A target can optionally not claim a split completion by asserting the DEVSEL# signal line, if it detects a parity error associated with the ADDRESS or ATTRIBUTE PHASES.

- The protocol of the FRAME# and IRDY# signal lines to terminate the split completion transaction is the same as outlined above for the other PCI-X bus transactions.

> When the target (PCI-X bus master of the "original" transaction) terminates a split completion transaction with a Master Abort termination; the Received Master Abort bit must be set to logical "1" in its Status Register in its configuration address space.

> If the target (PCI-X bus master of the "original" transaction) is not broken, it must claim the bus transaction by asserting the DEVSEL# signal line.

The PERR# signal line cannot be asserted when a Master Abort termination is executed because no device claimed the memory, I/O, configuration, or interrupt acknowledge transaction so no data was accessed. The PCI-X bus master that terminates the bus transaction with a Master Abort termination must notify the device driver via interrupt or some other suitable method. If notification of the device driver is not possible, the SERR# signal line must be asserted with the following qualifications: The assertion of the SERR# signal line can be used to report the error only if the System Error Control bit is set to logical "1" in the Command Register of the PCI-X bus master's Command Register. If the SERR# signal line is asserted, the PCI-X bus master must set to logical "1" the Signaled System Error Status bit in its Status Register in the configuration address space.

Execution of the Master Abort termination has no affect on the central arbiter because it does not monitor the associated signal lines. Also, a Master Abort termination does not force the PCI-X bus master (target of "orginal" transaction) to deassert the associated REQx# signal line.

PCI/PCI and PCI-X/PCI-X BRIDGES port bus transactions from the source bus segment to the destination bus segment without any advance knowledge of possible Master Abort or Target Abort terminations on the destination bus segment. Consequently, relative to the source bus segment, a bridge will post memory write transactions, post split completion transactions, apply Delayed Transaction protocol, and apply Split Completion protocol without knowledge of the pending Master Abort termination or Target Abort termination. Relative to Master Abort and Target Abort terminations on the destination bus segment, the bridge's response protocol to posted bus transactions is different than that for the bus transactions to the Delayed Transaction protocol or the Split Transaction protocol.

For the Master Abort termination and Target Abort termination protocols for PCI/PCI BRIDGES, see *PCI-to PCI Bridge Architecture Specification Rev 1.1* for more information. For the Master Abort termination and Target Abort termination protocols for PCI-X/PCI-X BRIDGES, see sections 8.7.1.5 and 8.7.1.6 of the *PCI-X Addendum Specification Rev 1.0a* for more information.

MASTER ABORT TERMINATION OF SPECIAL TRANSACTIONS

The PCI-X protocol for Master Abort termination for special transactions is same as for PCI including when the Master Abort termination is appropriate, the setting of the Received Master Abort bit in the Status Register in the configuration address space, and the operation of PERR# and SERR# signal lines. See Subchapter 8.1 for more information.

8.4 PCI-X TARGET TERMINATION

INTRODUCTION

The PCI-X addendum specification defines several conditions for terminating a bus transaction. Some of these conditions are similar to those of PCI and others are unique to PCI-X. Please see the summary of target termination in Table 8-2 in Subchapter 8-0.

One of the major differences of target termination that is universal to PCI-X bus transactions relates to bus segment ownership. As discussed in a previous subchapter, under most target termination conditions, the REQx# signal line of the associated PCI bus master must be deasserted. For PCI-X bus transactions, the execution of a target termination does not require the REQx# signal line of the associated PCI-X bus master to be deasserted.

RETRY TERMINATION OF MEMORY, SPLIT COMPLETION, I/O, CONFIGURATION, AND INTERRUPT ACKNOWLEDGE TRANSACTIONS

The reasons for a Retry termination of memory, I/O, configuration, and interrupt acknowledge bus transactions according to the PCI-X addendum specification are essentially the same at the PCI local bus specification, including the interaction with the assertion of the PERR# and SERR# signal lines (see Subchapter 8.2 and Table 8.2 for more information). The differences are as follows:

- Retry termination is required according to the "PCI-X 8 clock" rule in the case of a PCI-X bus transaction in the same fashion as the "PCI 16 clock" rule applies to a PCI bus transaction. Retry termination is required if the other target terminations will not be executed or if the data transfer (according to the PCI-X 16 clock" rule for the initial microaccess and data transfer in subsequent microaccess with no wait states) will not occur. Once the Retry termination is executed, none of the other PCI-X target terminations can be executed.

■ For PCI bus transactions, the Retry termination is defined as part of the Delayed Transaction protocol. In the PCI-X addendum specification, the Split Transaction protocol has replaced the Delayed Transaction protocol and implements the Split Response termination. The Retry termination is not defined as part of the Split Transaction protocol.

■ The target can only execute a Retry termination in conjunction with the initial microaccess of the DATA PHASE.

■ As with PCI local bus specification, PCI-X addendum specification requires that the Retry termination NOT be used for an address or data parity error (ADDRESS and DATA PHASES). In addition, PCI-X addendum specification does not permit the use of Retry termination for parity error detected in the ATTRIBUTE PHASE. Similarly, if a parity error occurs in the ADDRESS, DATA, or ATTRIBUTE PHASES it does not prevent a Retry termination to be executed for other reasons.

The reasons for Retry terminations of split completion transactions is the same as discussed above (including the "PCI-X 8 clock" rule and relation to PERR# and SERR# signal lines discussed above) for PCI-X BURST memory write transactions with the following difference:

■ Retry termination can only be executed by a PCI-X/PCI-X BRIDGE between the "original" PCI-X bus master and the "original" target. The "original" PCI-X bus master (requester) cannot execute a Retry termination of a split completion transaction from the "original" target (completer). By definition, the "original" PCI-X bus master would not have begun a bus transaction that could terminate with Spit Response termination unless it has sufficient buffer space to accept the entire result as a "sequence" of split completion transactions.

As will be discussed in more detail in Chapter 6: *Detailed Bus Transaction Operation*, there is a protocol for the deassertion of the FRAME# and IRDY# signal lines. Parts of the deassertion protocols apply to target terminations. Summarized below is the "general deassertion" protocol that applies to the bus transaction operation in addition to the protocol specific to Retry termination.

■ "General Deassertion" protocol:

1. For one or two actual microaccesses the FRAME# and IRDY# signal lines are sampled deasserted two CLK signal line periods after the TRDY# or STOP# signal line is sampled asserted (whichever is first).

2. For three actual microaccesses the FRAME# signal line is sampled deasserted two CLK signal line periods after the TRDY# or STOP# signal line is sampled asserted (whichever is first). Also, the IRDY# signal line is sampled deasserted one CLK signal line period after the last actual microaccess.

3. For four or more actual microaccesses the FRAME# signal line is sampled deasserted one CLK signal line period after the last actual microaccess or two CLK signal line periods after the STOP# signal line is sampled asserted for a Disconnect at Next ADB termination. Also, the IRDY# signal line is sampled deasserted one CLK signal line period after the last actual microaccess.

In the above, "actual microaccess" is defined when data is actually transferred (with or without Single Phase Disconnect or Disconnect at Next ADB) or the microaccess that coincides with Retry or Target Abort termination. It is not necessarily the number of microaccesses the PCI-X bus master intended to execute prior to early bus transaction termination caused by the target termination. For a 32 or 64 data bit bus transaction each microaccess transfers four bytes or eight bytes (not all byte lanes may be valid), respectively. The ADB is defined aligned to natural 128 byte address boundaries. Thus, the transfer between two ADBs is 32 microaccesses for 32 data bit bus transactions, and 16 microaccesses for 64 data bit bus transactions. In the following examples a 32 data bit bus transaction is assumed.

Figures 8-15-A, 8-15-B, and 8-15-C show the Retry termination protocol. Retry termination is requested with the simultaneous assertion of the DEVSEL# and STOP# signal lines with the deassertion of the TRDY# signal line. The earliest point the STOP# signal line can be asserted is the CLK signal line period immediately after the TARGET RESPONSE PHASE or simultaneously with the assertion of the DEVSEL# signal line, whichever is later. In the case of BURST write transactions, the assertion of the STOP# signal line is with two wait state resolution. These figures do not include the change of signal line ownership. Please see Chapter 6: *Detailed Bus Transaction Operation* for detailed information for driving, tri-stating, and change of ownership of the signal lines. The Retry termination is only executed in the initial microaccess of a bus transaction according to the "PCI-X 8 clock" rule; consequently, item (1) of the "General Deassertion" protocol is the only one that applies. Figures 8-15-A and 8-15-C show that only the initial microaccess is executed and it coincides with the Retry termination. Figure 8-15-B shows that a BURST write transaction can only be

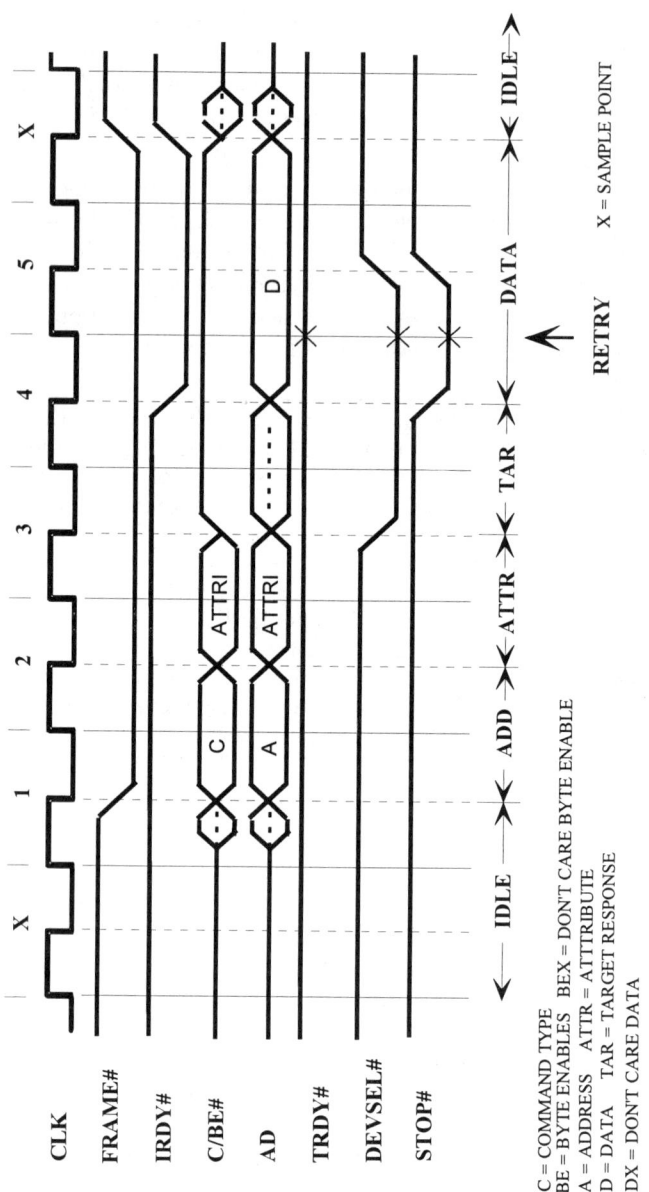

Figure 8-15-A: PCI-X Retry Termination for DWORD Write Transaction with NO Wait State and One Microaccess

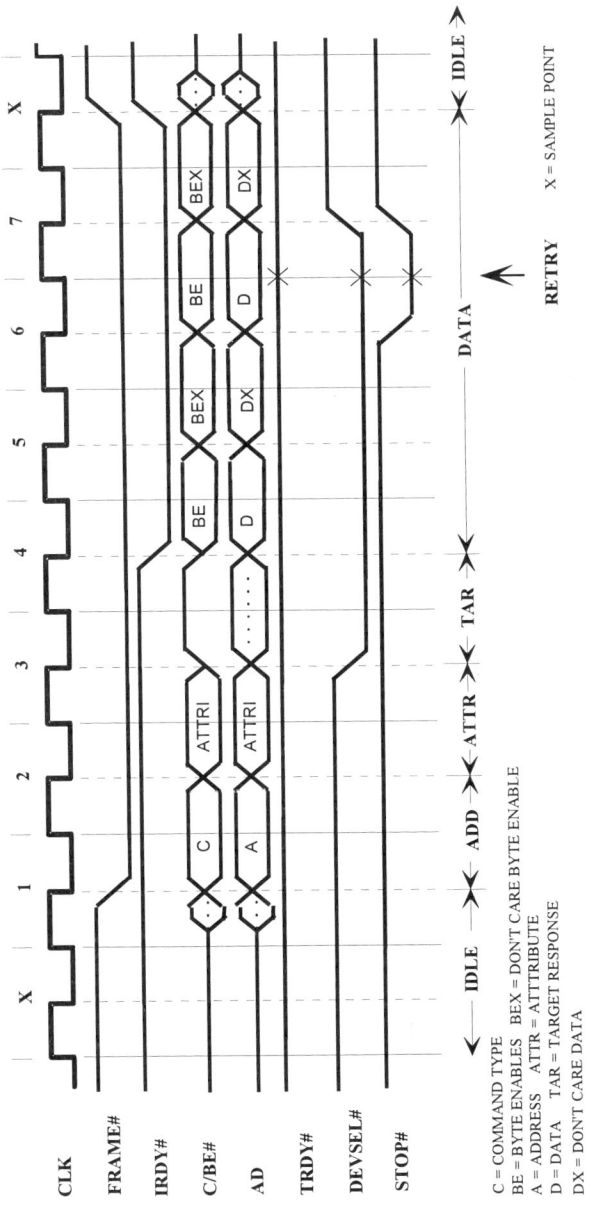

Figure 8-15-B: PCI-X Retry Termination for BURST Write Transaction with Two Wait States and One Microaccess

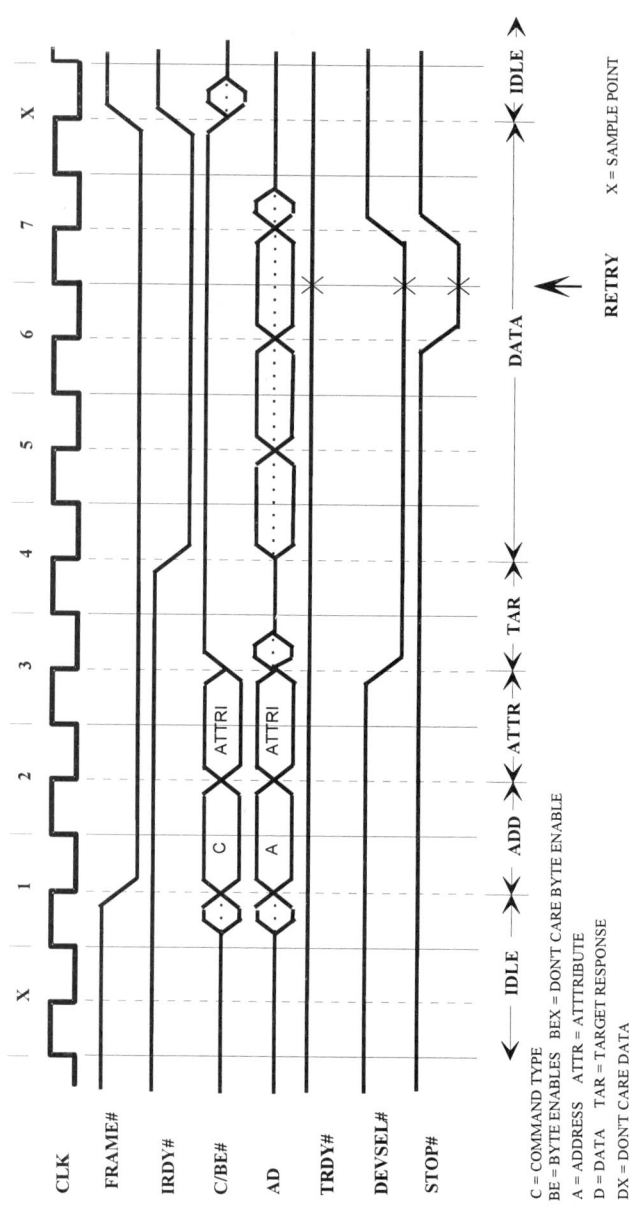

Figure 8-15-C: PCI-X Retry Termination for BURST Read Transaction with Two Wait States and One Microaccess

terminated on a microaccesses based on increments of two wait states. The two wait state increment requirement does not apply to DWORD transactions or to BURST write transactions with no wait states (That is, for BURST write transactions, the Retry termination is requested in the CLK signal line period immediately after the TARGET RESPONSE PHASE). The BURST write transaction also shows the Retry termination of BURST split completion transactions.

> Once Retry termination is requested, the DEVSEL# and STOP# signal lines cannot change state until the completion of the microaccess. The completion of the microaccess is defined as when the Retry termination is sampled. Once the microaccess completes the DEVSEL# and STOP# signal lines are deasserted, and the TRDY# signal line remains deasserted.

In summary, the "PCI-X 8 clock" rule and the associated execution of the Retry termination due to this rule APPLIES to the following SINGLE bus transactions and initial microaccess of the following BURST bus transactions. It gives the target the opportunity to terminate the bus transaction early if the other target terminations according to the "PCI-X 16" or "PCI-X 8" clock rules will not apply, and if the target will not be able to transfer data in the bus transaction.

- Memory transactions
- I/O transactions (only SINGLE bus transactions are defined)
- Configuration transactions (only SINGLE bus transactions are defined)
- Interrupt acknowledge transactions (only SINGLE bus transactions are defined)
- Split completion transactions

> The "PCI-X 8 clock" rule DOES NOT apply for Retry termination (or the "PCI-X 16 clock" rule for transferring data in the initial microaccess) of the above PCI-X bus transactions during the initialization time (RST# signal line deasserted to 2^{27} CLK signal line periods later), when executing from BOOT ROM, or when copying expansion ROM to memory. Note: If the device is accessing its expansion ROM after it has been hot-inserted, the aforementioned "PCI-X 8 clock and 16 clock" rules relative to target termination DO apply.

According to the PCI local bus specification, the execution of a Retry termination requires the associated bus transaction to be repeated. According to the PCI-X addendum specification, requirements to repeat a bus transaction or continue with the "sequence" of bus transactions relative to Retry termination differ depending on the COMMAND the bus transaction is executing. As previously discussed, a DWORD COMMAND can only be executed as a SINGLE bus transaction and a BURST COMMAND can be executed as either a SINGLE or BURST bus transaction (Note: The following discussion does not include split completion transactions. The split completion transaction is discussed in a later portion of this section).

- For a SINGLE bus transaction for a DWORD COMMAND, the execution of a Retry termination does not require the associated bus transaction to be repeated. No data has been transferred; consequently, no data has been discarded by the target for a write or by the PCI-X bus master for a read. The execution of the "exact same" bus transaction by a specific PCI-X bus master may or may not be associated with the previous executed bus transaction (by the same PCI-X bus master) terminated by Retry termination

- The BURST memory read command executed as either a SINGLE or BURST bus transaction follows the same repeat protocol (Retry termination without repeat of "exact same" bus transaction) as for a SINGLE bus transaction of a DWORD COMMAND. That is, a BURST memory read transaction that is terminated with Retry termination does not continue the transfer in a subsequent bus transaction and does not require the associated bus transaction to be repeated. If the PCI-X bus master executes the "exact same" bus transaction, that may or may not be coincidental as far as the target is concerned. Consequently, no "sequence" of bus transactions is established relative to a BURST read transaction.

- When a PCI-X bus master executes a BURST memory write command as a SINGLE bus transaction (only the initial microaccess is needed in the DATA PHASE), it follows the same protocol as for a SINGLE bus transaction of a DWORD COMMAND. That is, a BURST memory write transaction that is terminated with Retry termination does not continue the transfer in a subsequent bus transaction and does not require the associated bus transaction to be repeated. If the PCI-X bus master executes the "exact same" bus transaction; that may or may not be coincidental as far as the target is concerned.

- When a PCI-X bus master executes a BURST memory write command as a BURST bus transaction (more than one microaccess is needed in the DATA PHASE), it intends to transfer the total byte count (Upper and Lower Byte Counts in the ATTRIBUTE PHASE). If Retry termination is executed on the first bus transaction (that is, no "sequence" has been established) the repeat of the associated bus transaction is not required. If the PCI-X bus master executes the same bus transaction, that may or may not be coincidental as far as the target is concerned.

- A BURST memory write transaction has transferred a portion of the total byte count before termination if the "first" bus transaction (termination by other than Master Abort, Retry, or Target Abort termination) has established a "sequence" of memory write transactions. A Retry, Single Phase Disconnect, or Disconnect at the Next ADB termination of any subsequent bus (either SINGLE or BURST) transaction of the "sequence" requires the PCI-X bus master to repeat (for Retry) the "exact same" or continue (for Single Phase Disconnect or Disconnect at the Next ADB) the bus transaction (with the starting address and total byte count appropriately adjusted), until all of the bytes identified by the total byte count in the "first" bus transaction of the "sequence" has been transferred. Obviously, by definition the execution of a BURST memory write command as a SINGLE bus transaction as the "first" bus transaction that is terminated by Retry termination has not established a "sequence". This protocol also applies if a bus transaction part of a "sequence" is terminated by the PCI-X bus master prior to transferring all of the data.

> **The definition of the "exact same" bus transaction used above is defined as the PCI-X bus master executing the repeat bus transaction with the same COMMAND (according to the C/BE# signal lines in the ADDRESS PHASE), and the same values in the AD and C/BE# signal lines in the ATTRIBUTE PHASE (except as noted below). Also, the value of the REQ64# signal line is the same.**

The requirements for repeating a split completion transaction are more severe than for a BURST memory write transaction (discussed above):

- A BURST split completion command is in response to an "original" transaction terminated by a Split Response termination. The Split Transaction protocol requires that all of the data or information (completion or error) is sourced from the "original" target to the "original" PCI-X bus master via split completion transactions (via SINGLE and/or BURST bus transitions). That is, from the very "first" split completion transaction, a "sequence" has been established. The Retry termination of any (other than the "first" or a subsequent transaction of a sequence) split completion transaction requires the "exact same" bus transaction to be repeated.

  - Repeating of the BURST split completion command as a SINGLE transaction (rather the "first" or a subsequent transaction of a sequence) is required until the repeat of the "exact same" completes without Retry termination, *i.e.*, Completion (including Completion with Timeout) termination by PCI-X bus master or a Disconnect at Next ADB termination.

■ A BURST split completion command executed as a BURST bus transaction intends to transfer the total byte count (Upper and Lower Byte Counts in the ATTRIBUTE PHASE) associated with the "original" transaction that was terminated with Split Response termination. A Retry or Disconnect at the Next ADB termination of any SINGLE or BURST split completion transaction of the "sequence" requires the PCI-X bus master to repeat (or Retry) the "exact same" or continue (Disconnect at the Next ADB) the bus transaction (with the lower address and total byte count appropriately adjusted), until the transfer of all bytes identified by the total byte count in the "original" transaction or information (completion or error) occurs. Note: the execution of Disconnect at Next ADB termination of a split completion can only be executed by the PCI-X/PCI-X BRIDGE between the "original PCI-X bus master and "original" target.

> The definition of the "exact same" relative to a split completion transaction is defined as the PCI-X bus master executing the split completion transaction with the same COMMAND (according to the C/BE# signal lines in the ADDRESS PHASE), and the same values in the AD and C/BE# signal lines in the ATTRIBUTE PHASE. Also, the value of the REQ64# signal line is the same.

As previously stated, once a "sequence" of bus transactions associated with a BURST memory write or split completion commands has been established, the PCI-X bus master is required to complete the "sequence". However, there are several conditions that will REMOVE this requirement. The PCI-X bus master WILL NOT complete the "sequence" (which is defined as terminated) when any of the following occurs:

■ One of the bus transactions is terminated by a Master Abort or Target Abort termination.

■ The PCI-X bus segment is reset.

> When the aforementioned terminations or bus segment reset occurs the "sequence" does not continue and is defined as terminated. See the discussions in other later parts of this chapter for the continuance of a "sequence" for the other target terminations.

The assertion of the SERR# or the PERR# signal line has no bearing on the execution of a Retry termination.

The PCI-X bus master may execute other bus transactions to the target that executed the Retry termination or other targets between repeating the "exact same" bus transaction. Similarly, other PCI-X bus masters can execute bus transactions to the target that had executed a Retry termination. PCI-X bus masters that are executing the "exact same" bus transactions must respond to accesses by other PCI-X bus masters if it also has target attributes.

If the Lock master or a non-Lock master is accessing the locked target, the execution of a Retry termination does not force the Lock master to relinquish the Lock Function.

The porting of a PCI-X BURST memory write transaction through a bridge is dependent on the available buffer space (*i.e.*, FIFO). The bridge is considered "full" if two ADB sized buffers are not available (with some exceptions). When the bridge is "full" it must request a Retry, a Single Phase Disconnect, or a Disconnect at Next ADB termination relative to available buffer space and if the bus transaction addresses are near an ADB. Also, in Rev, 1.0.a of the PCI-X addendum specification section 8.4.6 was added to reflect these considerations.

The porting of a PCI-X BURST split completion transaction through a bridge is dependent on the available buffer space (*i.e.*, FIFO). The bridge is considered "full" if one ADB sized buffer is not available. When the bridge is "full" it must request a Retry or a Disconnect at Next ADB termination relative to available buffer space. Also, in the PCI-X addendum specification section 8.4 reflects these considerations.

If designing a bridge or an interface (with bridge-like features) between a PCI-X bus segment and internal circuitry in an ASIC, please review these sections.

As previously discussed, the Maximum Completion Time (MCT) had been defined relative to a PCI memory write transaction. The problem addressed by MCT was that a PCI bus master may be repeating the "exact same" memory write bus transaction (that was previously terminated by a Retry termination) with a frequency greater than the target can accept the write data. If the target relative to the PCI bus master is "slow", there may be many repeats of the "exact same" bus transactions that will complete with Retry termination. When the repeats of the "exact same" bus transactions are memory write transactions, the effective bandwidth of the system is lowered due to strong order rules for all memory write transactions posted in a bridge (See Chapter 7: *Bridge and Interface Protocol* and Subchapter 8.2 or more information). According to the PCI-X addendum specification, the requirement to repeat memory write transactions as part of a "sequence" has a similar effect. The PCI-X addendum specification has also expanded the MCT protocol to include I/O write transactions. In the following discussion both PCI-X memory write and I/O write transactions are referenced. They should be viewed as independent. That is, MCT limit protocol applies between memory write transactions and between I/O write transactions, not between memory write and I/O write transactions. The MCT protocol is defined as follows for PCI-X bus transactions:

- A device as target that terminated a memory write transaction or I/O write transaction with Retry termination must complete a microaccess (transfer) of a repeat of the "exact same" memory write transaction or I/O write transaction within the Maximum Completion Time (MCT) limit. (The repeat of a memory write transaction is required when a "sequence" is established and the repeat of an I/O write transaction is not required. The MCT applies if the PCI-X bus master wants to repeat the I/O write transaction). The MCT limit is 133 periods of the CLK signal line at 66 MHz, 200 periods of the CLK signal line at 100 MHz, and 267 periods of the CLK signal line at 133 MHz.

- At the CLK signal line frequencies of 66 MHz, 100 MHz, or 133 MHz (running at the limit of each) results in an MCT limit of two microseconds. If the CLK signal line frequency is less than 66 MHz the 133 periods apply, if the frequency is between 66+ and 100 MHz the 200 periods apply, and if the frequency is between 100+ and 133 MHz the 267 periods apply.

- There are three elements to the MCT limit protocol:

    - By design, a target must (whenever possible) complete the data phase within the MCT limit (access without Retry termination ... *i.e.*, Completion (including Completion with Timeout), Single Phase Disconnect, or Disconnect at Next ADB termination) of the repeat of the "exact same" bus transaction associated with the initial Retry termination

    - A target that cannot achieve the aforementioned compliance to the MCT limit requires its device driver to compensate. The compensation can be in two forms: limit the rate of repeating the "exact same" bus transactions to the target ... OR ... the PCI-X bus master executing the device driver software determines if the target has buffer space for a subsequent bus transactions to minimize the number of Retry terminations.

■ The MCT limit is also satisfied when a repeat of the "exact same" bus transaction associated with the Retry termination results in a Master Abort or a Target Abort termination by the target. Obviously, reset of PCI-X bus segment also satisfies the MCT limit.

■ An extension of the MCT limit protocol is when a target may have multiple memory write or I/O write transactions addressing it. The MCT limit is measured from the Retry termination of a memory write transaction of an established "sequence" to the very next completion of a microaccess (access without Retry termination ... *i.e.*, Completion (including Completion with Timeout), Single Phase Disconnect, or Disconnect at Next ADB termination) of a memory write transaction even when it is not a repeat of the memory write transaction associated with the initial Retry termination that the MCT limit is referenced to (i.e., not part of the same "sequence" and may or may not be part of another established "sequence"). Similarly, the MCT limit protocol for an I/O write transaction may indeed be satisfied by the target completing a microaccess of an I/O write transaction that is not associated with the I/O write transaction associated with the initial Retry termination.

■ When the target has multiple memory write transactions addressing it, the MCT limit is also satisfied when a memory write or I/O write transaction that is or is not a repeat of the bus transaction associated with the initial Retry termination (i.e. not part of the "sequence") is terminated with a Master Abort or a Target Abort termination by the target. Obviously, reset of PCI-X bus segment also satisfies the MCT limit.

■ The MCT limit does not apply to a PCI-X bus master, or a PCI-X/PCI-X BRIDGE Resource (Base Class = 0x06) under the following considerations:

■ The PCI-X bus master cannot assume that the MCT limit will be met for all memory write or I/O write transactions for three reasons:

■ The memory target was designed pre-revision 2.2 of the PCI bus specification (when the final target is on a PCI bus segment).

■ The memory target was designed post-revision 2.2 of the PCI bus specification but simply may not comply (when final target is on a PCI bus segment).

693

- The target may have several bus segments that includes bridges between itself and the PCI-X bus master.

- The PCI-X/PCI-X BRIDGE as a target (memory write or I/O write transaction to an internal register) is required to adhere to the MCT limit protocol. The MCT limit protocol does not apply to memory write or I/O write transactions porting though the PCI-X/PCI-X BRIDGE.

- Whenever MCT limit protocol is met or satisfied as outlined above, the subsequent Retry termination of a memory write or I/O write transaction re-establishes the MCT limit protocol.

- The MCT limit does not apply to a target during PCI initialization (the first 2^{26} CLK signal line periods after the deassertion of the RST# signal line), when executing from BOOT ROM, during diagnostics, or when copying expansion ROM to memory. Note: If the device is accessing its expansion ROM after it has been hot-inserted, the MCT limit DOES apply.

- The Maximum Completion Time (MCT) protocol does not apply to split completion transactions.

RETRY TERMINATION OF SPECIAL TRANSACTIONS

The special transaction does not address a specific target, so Retry termination and the "PCI-X 8 clock" rule do not apply to this transaction.

SPLIT RESPONSE TERMINATION OF MEMORY READ, I/O, CONFIGURATION, AND INTERRUPT ACKNOWLEDGE TRANSACTIONS

See Subchapter 4.15 for related information. Also see this subchapter for definitions of "original" transaction, "original" PCI-X bus master, "original" target, and non-memory write transactions (as it applies to the Split Transaction protocol).

The Split Response termination is unique to PCI-X and the Split Transaction protocol; thus there is no correlation to any other target terminations of PCI bus transaction. As previously discussed, the "sequence" of split completion transactions is sourced from the "original" target (completer) and is directed to the "original" PCI-X bus master (requester). Also, as previously discussed, a PCI-

X/PCI-X BRIDGE will execute a Split Response termination on behalf of a target on the other side of the bridge. The resulting split completion transaction may be from the "original" target or created by the bridge on behalf of the target that did not execute a Split Response termination. For the purposes of this section, assume that the "original" PCI-X bus master and the "original" target are on the same bus segment (i.e., there is no PCI-X/PCI-X BRIDGE) unless otherwise stated. For implementations with a PCI-X/PCI-X BRIDGE representing the "original" target and the "original" PCI-X bus master on the respective bus segments, the protocol outline below applies. See Chapter 7: *Bridge and Interface Protocol* for more information.

The Split Response termination is defined for bus transactions associated with all DWORD COMMANDS except the special command. Also, the Split Response termination is defined for bus transactions associated with BURST read (both memory read block and alias memory read block) COMMANDs. The Split Response termination is not defined for the BURST write (both memory write block and alias memory write block) or split completion COMMANDs. See the summary in Table 8-2 at the beginning of this chapter. For the purposes of this section, the term "non-memory write transactions" collectively refers to the aforementioned bus transactions that the Split response termination is defined for.

The Split Response termination is defined for the following non-memory write transactions situations (this is not a conclusive list ... other situations are possible):

- When the target is a bridge (*i.e.*, PCI-X/PCI-X bridge representing the "original" target) on a bus segment, the Split Response termination is required. The assumption is that there is no possible way for a bridge to port the transaction from the PCI-X bus master and receive an immediate response from the target on another bus segment. The bridge should execute the Split Response termination immediately; that is, it should not wait the full eight CLK signal lines periods per the "PCI-X 8 clock" rule.

- When the target is the "original" target and not a PCI-X/PCI-X BRIDGE, the Split Response termination is either required, optional, or not allowed according to the following:

  - If the target is going to execute a Disconnect at Next ADB or Single Phase Disconnect termination according to the PCI-X 16 clock" rule, data transfer (according to the PCI-X 16 clock" rule for the initial microaccess and data transfer in subsequent microaccess with no wait states), or Retry or Target Abort terminations according to the "PCI-X 8 clock" rule; the Split Response termination of the bus transaction is not permitted.

■ If the target is not planning to execute the target terminations or data transfers listed in the previous bullet for non-memory write transactions, the target must execute a Split Response termination according to the "PCI-X 8 clock" rule.

■ A BURST bus transaction with a starting address three or fewer microaccesses to the target's address range boundary and the total byte count (Upper and Lower Byte Counts in the ATTRIBUTE PHASE) indicates the address boundary range will be crossed; the target must execute a Single Phase Disconnect termination. That is, it is always the responsibility of the target to terminate a bus transaction that can potentially exceed its address range boundary prior to crossing the boundary. The three or fewer microaccesses requirement prevents the use of a Disconnect at Next ADB termination and requires the target to force bus transactions to ease towards the address range boundary with Single Phase Disconnect terminations.

■ A Split Response termination can also address this in a more efficient manner. It must be implemented, if possible, instead of relying on Single Phase Disconnect termination. The requirement that the Single Phase Disconnect termination applies is when Split Response termination is not possible

■ The target can only execute a Split Response termination in conjunction with the initial microaccess of the DATA PHASE. The protocol of a Split Response termination requires the target to drive (when the TRDY# signal line is asserted) the AD signal line to logical "1" (qualified by the ACK64# signal line).

■ The Split Response termination is NOT a response for a parity error in the ADDRESS, ATTRIBUTE, or DATA PHASES. Similarly, if a parity error occurs in the ADDRESS, DATA, or ATTRIBUTE PHASES it does not prevent a Split Response termination to be executed for other reasons.

As will be discussed in more detail in Chapter 6: *Detailed Bus Transaction Operation*, there is a protocol for the deassertion of the FRAME# and IRDY# signal lines. Parts of the deassertion protocols apply to target terminations. Summarized below is the "general deassertion" protocol that applies to the bus transaction operation in addition to the protocol specific to Split Response termination.

■ "General Deassertion" protocol:

1. For one or two actual microaccesses, the FRAME# and IRDY# signal lines are sampled deasserted two CLK signal line periods after the TRDY# or STOP# signal line is sampled asserted (whichever is first).

2. For three actual microaccesses the FRAME# signal line is sampled deasserted two CLK signal line periods after the TRDY# or STOP# signal line is sampled asserted (whichever is first). Also, the IRDY# signal line is sampled deasserted one CLK signal line period after the last actual microaccess.

3. For four or more actual microaccesses the FRAME# signal line is sampled deasserted one CLK signal line period after the last actual microaccess or two CLK signal line periods after the STOP# signal line is sampled asserted for a Disconnect at Next ADB termination. Also, the IRDY# signal line is sampled deasserted one CLK signal line period after the last actual microaccess.

In the above, "actual microaccess" is defined when data is actually transferred (with or without Single Phase Disconnect or Disconnect at Next ADB) or the microaccess that coincides with Retry, Split Response, or Target Abort termination. It is not necessarily the number of microaccesses the PCI-X bus master intended to execute prior to early bus transaction termination caused by the target termination. For a 32 or 64 data bit bus transaction, each microaccess transfers four bytes or eight bytes (not all byte lanes may be valid), respectively. The ADB is defined aligned to natural 128 byte address boundaries. Thus, the transfer between two ADBs is 32 microaccesses for 32 data bit bus transaction, and 16 microaccesses for 64 data bit bus transactions. In the following examples a 32 data bit bus transaction is assumed.

Figures 8-16-A and 8-16-B show the Split Response termination protocol. Split Response termination is requested with the simultaneous deassertion of the DEVSEL# and STOP# signal lines with the assertion of the STOP# signal line. The earliest point the TRDY# signal line can be asserted is the CLK signal line period immediately after the TARGET RESPONSE PHASE or simultaneously with the deassertion of the DEVSEL# signal line (previously asserted for a minimum of one CLK signal line period), whichever is later. These figures do not include the change of signal line ownership. Please see Chapter 6: *Detailed Bus Transaction Operation* for detailed information for driving, tri-stating, and change of ownership of the signal lines. The Split Response termination is only executed in the initial microaccess of a bus transaction according to the "PCI-X 8 clock" rule; consequently, item (1.) of the "General Deassertion" protocol is the only one that applies. Figures 8-16-A and 8-16-B show that only the initial microaccess is executed and it coincides with the Split Response termination.

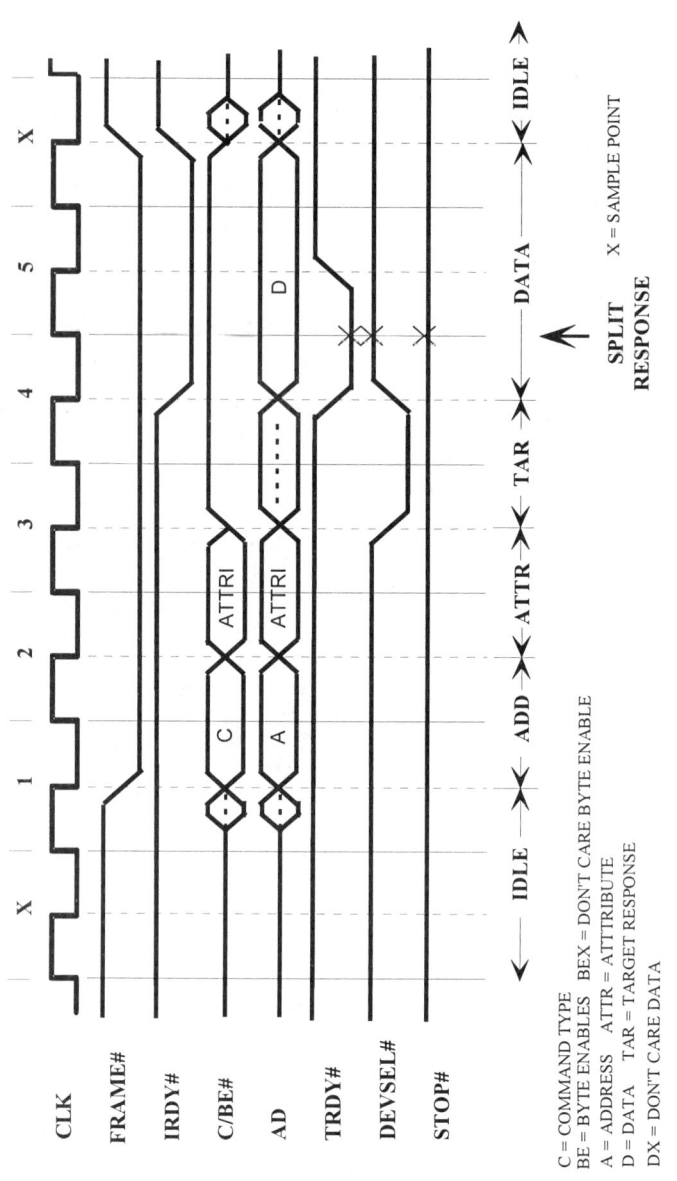

Figure 8-16-A: PCI-X Split Response Termination for DWORD Write Transaction with NO Wait State and One Microaccess

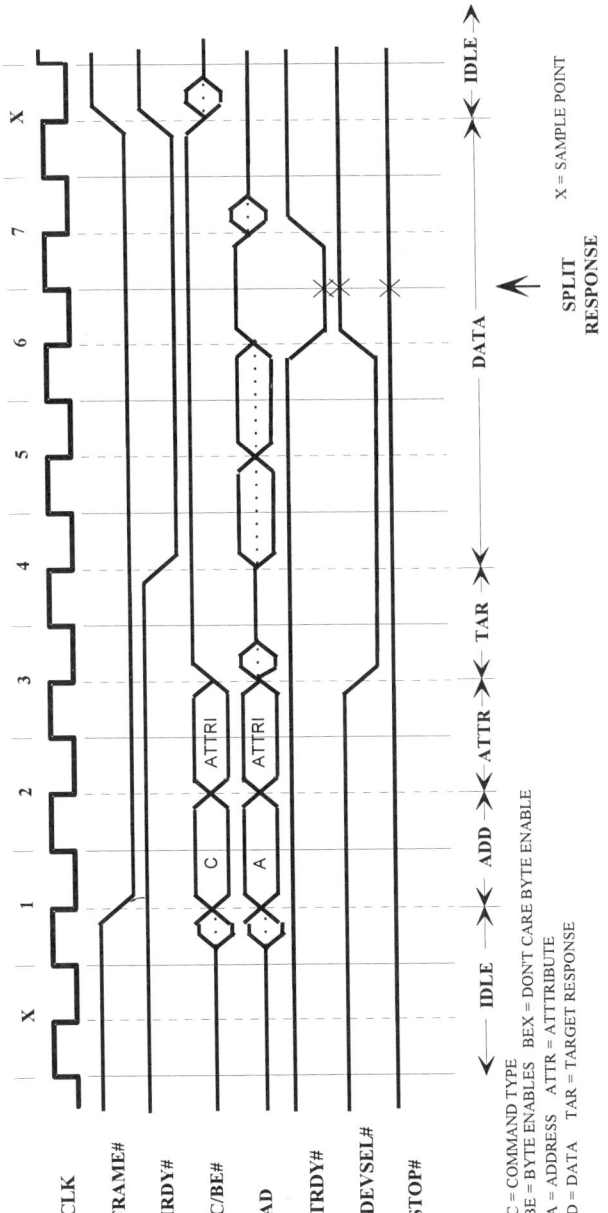

**Figure 8-16-B: PCI-X Split Response Termination for BURST Read
Transaction with Two Wait States and One Microaccess**

Once Split Response termination is requested, the TRDY# signal lines cannot change state until the completion of the microaccess. The completion of the microaccess is defined as when the Split Response termination is sampled. Once the microaccess completes, the TRDY# signal line is deasserted, and the DEVSEL# and STOP# signal lines remain deasserted.

In summary, the "PCI-X 8 clock" rule and the associated execution of the Split Response termination due to this rule APPLIES to the following SINGLE bus transactions and initial microaccess of the following BURST bus transactions. It gives the target the opportunity to terminate the bus transaction early if the other terminations following the "PCI-X 16" or "PCI-X 8" clock rules will not apply, and if the target will not be able to transfer all of the data of the bus transaction.

- Memory read transactions

- I/O transactions (Only SINGLE bus transactions are defined)

- Configuration transactions (Only SINGLE bus transactions are defined)

- Interrupt acknowledge transactions (Only SINGLE bus transactions are defined)

The "PCI-X 8 clock" rule for Split Response termination (or the "PCI-X 16 clock" rule for transferring data in the initial microaccess) DOES NOT apply to the above PCI-X bus transactions during the initialization time (RST# signal line deasserted to 2^{27} CLK signal line periods later), when executing from BOOT ROM, or when copying expansion ROM to memory. Note: If the device is accessing its expansion ROM after it has been hot-inserted, the aforementioned "PCI-X 8 clock and 16 clock" rules relative to target termination DO apply.

The execution of a Split Response termination is only executed for the "first" bus transaction (see the Retry termination section for discussion of the "first" bus transaction) as follows:

- For a SINGLE bus transaction for DWORD or BURST memory read commands, the execution of a Split Response termination immediately terminates the bus transaction. For a DWORD write transaction, data is ported to the target. A subsequent split completion transaction will only return a Split Completion Message for completion or error information. For a DWORD or BURST memory read transaction, no data is ported until the associated split completion transaction. The subsequent split completion transaction will return either the data or a Split Completion Message for write completion or error information. In either case, the PCI-X bus master must not repeat the "exact same" bus transaction as defined in the Retry termination section. That is, the PCI-X bus master (requester) must rely on the split completion transactions from the target (completer) to complete the execution of the COMMAND. The COMMAND is not defined as completed until the completion of the associated "sequence" of split completion transactions according to the Split Transaction protocol. See other sections of this chapter for definition of completion of a "sequence" of split completion transactions.

■ For a BURST bus transactions or a BURST memory read command, the execution of the split response termination by the target immediately terminates the bus transaction. That is, even though the total byte count (Upper and Lower Byte Counts) in the ATTRIBUTE PHASE indicated a bus transaction with multiple microaccesses, the Split Response termination immediately terminates the bus transaction. For a read transaction, no data is ported until the associated "sequence" of split completion transactions. The subsequent split completion transaction will return either the data or a Split Completion Message for error information. In either case, the PCI-X bus master must not repeat the "exact same" bus transaction as defined in the Retry termination section. That is, the PCI-X bus master (requester) must rely on the split completion transactions from the target (completer) to complete the execution of the COMMAND. The COMMAND is not defined as completed until the completion of the associated "sequence" of split completion transactions per the Split Transaction protocol. See other sections of this chapter for definition of completion of a "sequence" of split completion transactions.

> The assertion of the SERR# or the PERR# signal lines have no bearing on the execution of a Spit Response termination.

> PCI-X bus masters may execute other bus transactions to a target (completer) that has executed a Split Response termination to a previous bus transaction. The target must execute a "sequence" of split completion transactions independently of other bus transactions it is receiving. Also, it must execute different "sequences" of split completion transactions independently of each other. The target must maintain strong ordering relative to the bus transactions of the same "sequence" of split completion transactions. See Chapter 7: *Bridge and Interface Protocol* for more information.

> If the Lock master or a non-Lock master is accessing the locked target, the execution of a Split Response termination does not force the Lock master to relinquish the Lock Function.

> When a BURST memory read transaction has a starting address and ending address (address range) between two adjacent ADBs there is a requirement on the target requesting a Single Phase Disconnect termination. If a target is designed to request a Single Phase Disconnect termination for the aforementioned BURST memory read transaction address range, it is required to NEVER request a Split Response termination for another BURST memory read transaction with a starting address within the aforementioned address range (inclusively) or a DWORD memory read transaction with an address within the aforementioned address range (inclusively). See Rev 1a of the PCI-X addendum specification for the rationale for this requirement.

SPLIT RESPONSE TERMINATION OF MEMORY WRITE, SPLIT COMPLETION, AND SPECIAL TRANSACTIONS

The split completion transaction is a specific response to a Split Response termination and the associated "PCI-X 8 clock" rule of the previously defined non-memory write transactions. According to the PCI-X addendum specification, the purpose of a split completion transaction is to provide read data, write completion information (for non-memory write transaction), or error information for the "original" transaction. As previously discussed, split completion transactions must be posted and do not implement the Split Transaction Protocol. Consequently, memory write and split completion transactions cannot be terminated by a Split Response termination. The data for these transactions must be posted whenever possible.

As previously discussed, memory write transactions (including memory write block and alias memory write block) must be posted and do not implement the Split Transaction Protocol. Consequently, memory write transactions (including memory write block and alias memory write block) cannot be terminated by a Split Response termination.

The special transaction does not address a specific target, so Split Response termination and the associated "PCI-X 8 clock" rule do not apply to this bus transaction.

SINGLE PHASE DISCONNECT TERMINATION OF MEMORY, I/O, CONFIGURATION, AND INTERRUPT ACKNOWLEDGE TRANSACTIONS

The Single Phase Disconnect termination is unique to PCI-X, though it is similar to Disconnect with data termination of PCI. Once data is successfully transferred (or planned to be transferred in the initial microaccess according to the PCI-X "16 clock" rule) in the bus transaction, the bus transaction can only terminate when all of the associated data is transferred (SINGLE bus transactions = four bytes or eight bytes, or BURST bus transaction = ending address) or ADB for a BURST bus transaction has been reached. That is, no target termination in the initial microaccess was executed. The Single Phase Disconnect termination is the only exception to this rule; it permits the target to transfer the data in the initial microaccess of a bus transaction and to immediately terminate the bus transaction not at an ADB or the ending address. See the summary in Table 8-2 at the beginning of this chapter.

> The bus transactions for DWORD COMMANDs only have one microaccess according to the SINGLE bus transaction protocol. Similarly, a bus transaction for a BURST COMMAND may only consist of a single microaccess (*i.e.*, SINGLE bus transaction). In these situations, the execution of a Single Phase Disconnect termination by the target would seem redundant. However, according to the PCI-X addendum specification, the Single Phase Disconnect termination can be executed for any SINGLE bus transaction. There is no difference in the results of a SINGLE bus transaction with or without a Single Phase Disconnect termination.

The Single Phase Disconnect termination is defined for the following memory, I/O, configuration, and interrupt acknowledge bus transactions (this is not a conclusive list ... other situations are possible):

■ When the target is only able to transfer the data of the initial microaccess of the BURST bus transaction and not the subsequent microaccess (following the PCI-X 16 clock" rule for the initial microaccess and data transfer in subsequent microaccess with no wait states), it must execute a Single Phase Disconnect termination. Once the Single Phase Disconnect termination is executed, none of the other PCI-X target terminations can be executed.

■ When the target prefers to not support BURST bus transactions, it may execute a Single Phase Disconnect termination. For example, due to a bridge combing memory writes, it is possible that control registers that are normally accessed by SINGLE bus transactions will be accessed by a BURST bus transaction with multiple microaccesses.

- A BURST bus transaction with a starting address three or fewer microaccesses to the target's address range boundary and the total byte count (Upper and Lower Byte Counts in the ATTRIBUTE PHASE) indicates that the address boundary range will be crossed; the target must execute a Single Phase Disconnect termination. That is, it is always the responsibility of the target to terminate a bus transaction that can potentially exceed its address range boundary prior to crossing the boundary. The three or fewer microaccesses requirement prevents the use of a Disconnect at Next ADB termination and requires the target to force bus transactions to ease towards the address range boundary with Single Phase Disconnect terminations.

  - A Split Response termination can also address this in a more efficient manner. It must be implemented, if possible, instead of relying on Single Phase Disconnect termination. Single Phase Disconnect termination is appropriate only when Split Response termination is not possible.

- The target can only execute a Single Phase Disconnect termination in conjunction with the initial microaccess of the DATA PHASE.

- The Single Phase Disconnect termination is NOT a response for a parity error in the ADDRESS or ATTRIBUTE PHASES. Similarly, if a parity error occurs in the ADDRESS or ATTRIBUTE PHASES it does not prevent a Single Phase Disconnect termination to be executed for other reasons.

- A target may execute a Single Phase Disconnect termination when a parity error occurs in the initial microaccess of the DATA PHASE of a write transaction.

> When a BURST memory write transaction has a starting address (qualified by the REQ64# and ACK64# signal lines) that is four or less microaccesses to the next ADB, there is a requirement on the target for requesting a Single Phase Disconnect termination. If a target is designed to request a Single Phase Disconnect termination for the aforementioned BURST memory write transaction, it must ALWAYS request a Single Phase Disconnect termination for such a bus transaction. That is, for such a bus transaction the target cannot mix Single Phase Disconnect termination (some of the time) and allow the bus transaction to complete (other times). See Rev 1a of the PCI-X addendum specification for the rationale for this requirement.

When a BURST memory read transaction has a starting address and ending address (address range) between two adjacent ADBs there is a requirement on the target requesting a Single Phase Disconnect termination. If a target is designed to request a Single Phase Disconnect termination for the aforementioned BURST memory read transaction address range, it must NEVER request a Split Response termination for another BURST memory read transaction with a starting address within the aforementioned address range (inclusively) or a DWORD memory read transaction with an address within the aforementioned address range (inclusively). See Rev 1a of the PCI-X addendum specification for the rationale for this requirement.

As will be discussed in more detail in Chapter 6: *Detailed Bus Transaction Operation*, there is a protocol for the deassertion of the FRAME# and IRDY# signal lines. Parts of the deassertion protocols apply to target terminations. Summarized below is the "general deassertion" protocol that applies to the bus transaction operation in addition to the protocol specific to Single Phase Disconnect termination.

■ "General Deassertion" protocol:

1. For one or two actual microaccesses, the FRAME# and IRDY# signal lines are sampled deasserted two CLK signal line periods after the TRDY# or STOP# signal line is sampled asserted (whichever is first).

2. For three actual microaccesses, the FRAME# signal line is sampled deasserted two CLK signal line periods after the TRDY# or STOP# signal line is sampled asserted (whichever is first). Also, the IRDY# signal line is sampled deasserted one CLK signal line period after the last actual microaccess.

3. For four or more actual microaccesses, the FRAME# signal line is sampled deasserted one CLK signal line period after the last actual microaccess or two CLK signal line periods after the STOP# signal line is sampled asserted for a Disconnect at Next ADB termination. Also, the IRDY# signal line is sampled deasserted one CLK signal line period after the last actual microaccess.

In the above, "actual microaccess" is defined when data is actually transferred (with or without Single Phase Disconnect or Disconnect at Next ADB) or the microaccess that coincides with Retry, Split Response, or Target Abort termination. It is not necessarily the number of microaccesses the PCI-X bus master intended to execute prior to early bus transaction termination caused by the target termination. For a 32 or 64 data bit bus transaction, each microaccess transfers four bytes or eight bytes (not all byte lanes may be valid), respectively. The ADB is defined aligned to natural 128 byte address boundaries. Thus, the transfer between two ADBs is 32 microaccesses for 32 data bit bus transactions, and 16 microaccesses for 64 data bit bus transactions. In the following examples, a 32 data bit bus transaction is assumed.

Figures 8-17-A, 8-17-B, and 8-17-C show the Single Phase Disconnect termination protocol. Single Phase Disconnect termination is requested with the simultaneous assertion of the TRDY# and STOP# signal lines with the deassertion of the DEVSEL# signal line. The earliest point the TRDY# and STOP# signal lines can be asserted is the CLK signal line period immediately after the TARGET RESPONSE PHASE or simultaneously with the deassertion of the DEVSEL# signal line (previously asserted for a minimum of one CLK signal line period), whichever is later. In the case of BURST write transactions, the assertion of the TRDY# and STOP# signal lines and the deassertion of the DEVSEL# signal line is with two wait state resolution. These figures do not include the change of signal lines ownership. Please see Chapter 6: *Detailed Bus Transaction Operation* for detailed information for driving, tri-stating, and change of ownership of the signal lines. The Single Phase Disconnect termination is only executed in the initial microaccess of a bus transaction according to the "PCI-X 16 clock" rule; consequently, item (1.) of the "General Deassertion" protocol is the only one that applies. Figures 8-17-A and 8-17-C show that only the initial microaccess is executed and it coincides with the Single Phase Disconnect termination. Figure 8-17-B shows that a BURST write transaction can only be terminated on a microaccess based on increments of two wait states. The two wait states increment requirement does not apply to DWORD transactions or to BURST write transactions with no wait states (that is, for BURST write transactions, the Single Phase Disconnect termination is requested in the CLK signal line period immediately after the TARGET RESPONSE PHASE).

Once Single Phase Disconnect termination is requested, the TRDY# and STOP# signal lines cannot change state until the completion of the microaccess. The completion of the microaccess is defined as when the Single Phase Disconnect termination is sampled. Once the microaccess completes, the TRDY# and STOP# signal lines are deasserted, and the DEVSEL# signal line remains deasserted.

706

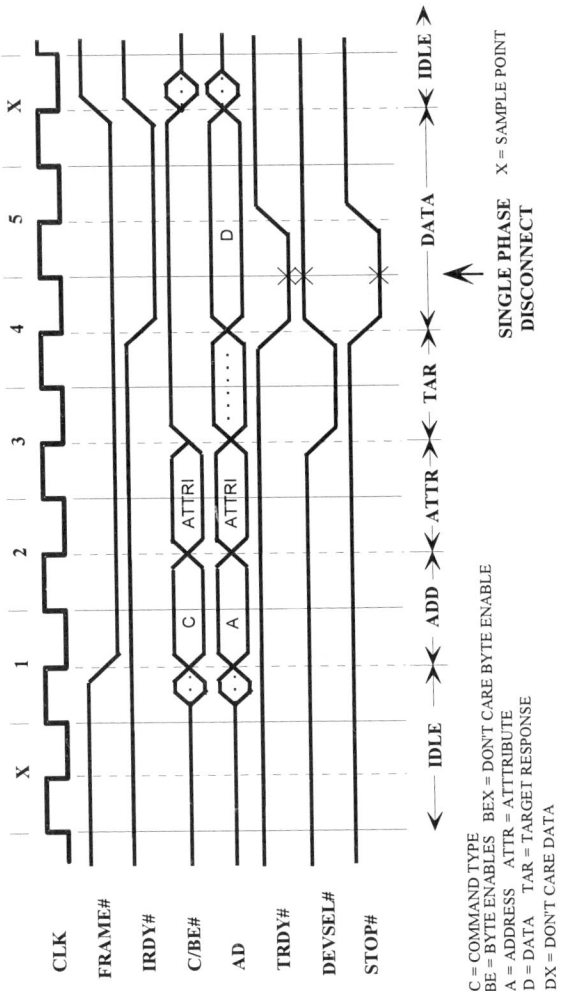

**Figure 8-17-A: PCI-X Single Phase Disconnect Termination for DWORD
Write Transaction with NO Wait State and One Microaccess**

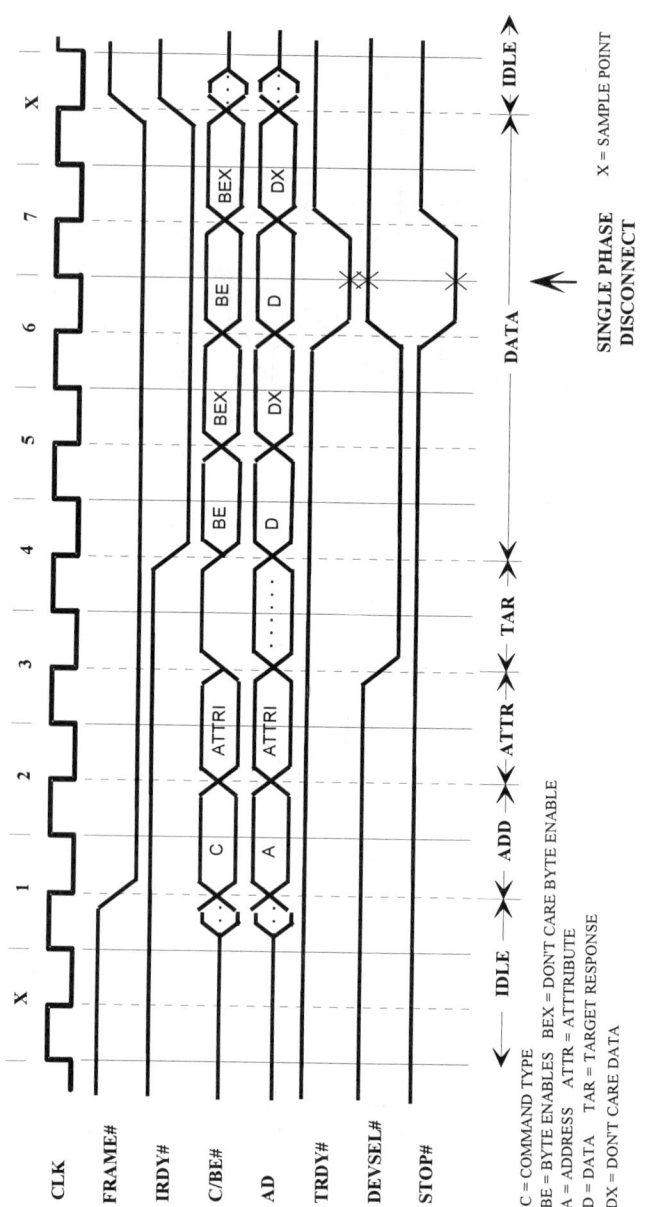

Figure 8-17-B: PCI-X Single Phase Disconnect Termination for BURST Write Transaction with Two Wait States and One Microaccess

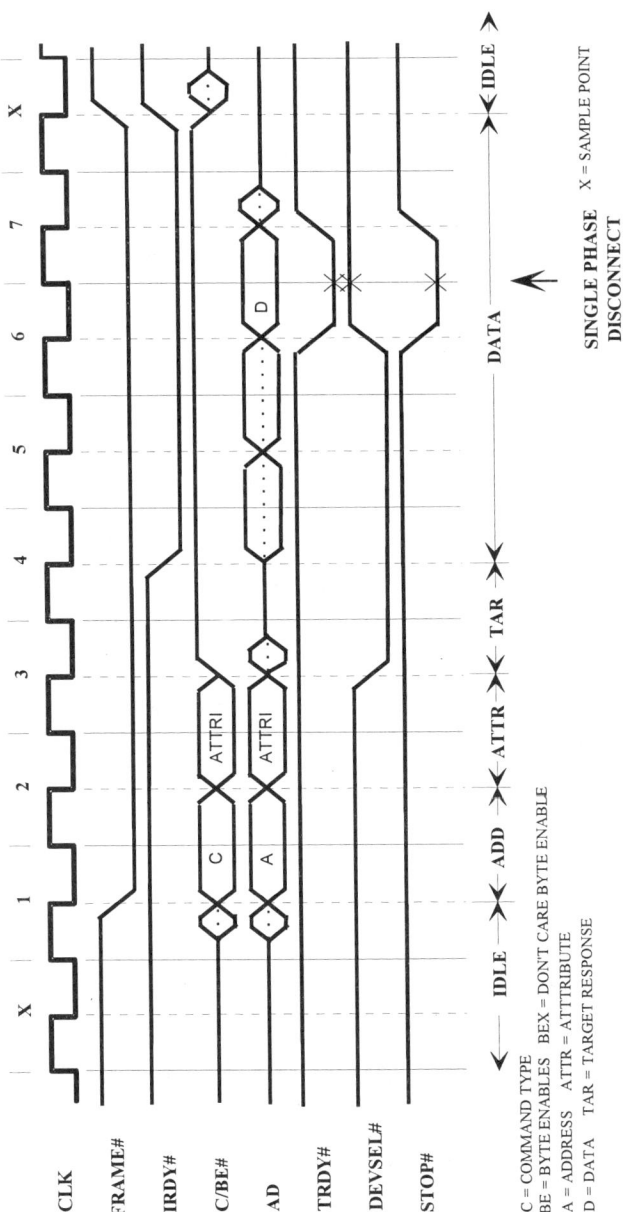

Figure 8-17-C: PCI-X Single Phase Disconnect Termination for BURST Read Transaction with Two Wait States and One Microaccess

In summary, the "PCI-X 16 clock" rule and the associated execution of the Single Phase Disconnect termination due to this rule APPLIES to the following SINGLE bus transactions and initial microaccess of the following BURST bus transactions. It gives the target the opportunity to terminate the bus transaction early if the other terminations according to the "PCI-X 16 clock" rule will not apply, and if the target will not be able to transfer all of the data of the bus transaction. Ideally, the termination should be at a minimum at the next ADB (see Disconnect at Next ADB termination) if possible, whenever all of the data cannot be transferred in the bus transaction or a Split Response termination cannot be executed.

- Memory transactions

- I/O transactions (only SINGLE bus transactions are defined)

- Configuration transactions (only SINGLE bus transactions are defined)

- Interrupt acknowledge transactions (only SINGLE bus transactions are defined)

> The "PCI-X 16 clock" rule for a Single Phase Disconnect termination (or the "PCI-X 16 clock" rule for transferring data in the initial microaccess) DOES NOT apply for the above PCI-X bus transactions during the initialization time (RST# signal line deasserted to 2^{27} CLK signal line periods later), when executing from BOOT ROM, or when copying expansion ROM to memory. Note: If the device is accessing its expansion ROM after it has been hot-inserted, the aforementioned "PCI-X 16 clock" rule relative to target termination DOES apply.

According to the PCI-X addendum specification, the requirements to repeat a bus transaction or continue with the "sequence" of bus transactions relative to Single Phase Disconnect termination differ depending on the COMMAND the bus transaction is executing. As previously discussed, a DWORD COMMAND can only be executed as a SINGLE bus transaction, and a BURST COMMAND can be executed as either a SINGLE or BURST bus transaction.

- For a SINGLE bus transaction for a DWORD COMMAND, the execution of a Single Phase Disconnect termination does not require the associated bus transaction to be repeated. By definition, the SINGLE bus transaction only consists of one microaccess in the DATA PHASE that aligns with the Single Phase Disconnect termination.

- The BURST memory read command executed as either a SINGLE or BURST bus transaction and terminated by a Single Phase Disconnect termination, must not be continued. That is, a BURST read transaction that is target terminated prior to transferring the total byte count (Upper and Lower Byte Counts in the ATTRIBUTE PHASE) does not continue the transfer in a subsequent bus transaction. The PCI-X bus master executing a bus transaction that appears to be a continuance may or may not be coincidental as far as the target is concerned. Consequently, no "sequence" of bus transactions is established relative to a BURST memory read command.

■ When a PCI-X bus master executes a BURST memory write command as a SINGLE bus transaction (only the initial microaccess is needed in the DATA PHASE) and terminated by a Single Phase Disconnect termination, the associated bus transaction does not need to be repeated. By definition, the SINGLE bus transaction only consists of one microaccess in the DATA PHASE which aligns with the Single Phase Disconnect termination.

■ When a PCI-X bus master executes a BURST memory write command as a BURST bus transaction (more than one microaccess is needed in the DATA PHASE), it intends to transfer the total byte count (Upper and Lower Byte Counts in the ATTRIBUTE PHASE). If Single Phase Disconnect termination is executed on the "first" bus transaction, the continuance of the bus transactions is required. That is, the execution of the Single Phase Disconnect termination has established a "sequence". For a BURST memory write command that has established a "sequence" of memory write transactions, the following applies:

   ■ A Retry, Single Phase Disconnect, or Disconnect at the Next ADB termination by the target of any subsequent bus (either SINGLE or BURST) transaction of the "sequence" requires the PCI-X bus master to repeat the "exact same" bus transaction like a Retry termination, or continue the bus transaction for Single Phase Disconnect, or Disconnect at the Next ADB termination (with the starting address and total byte count appropriately adjusted). These requirements apply until all of the bytes identified by the total byte count in the first bus transaction of the "sequence" has been transferred. This protocol also applies if a bus transaction part of a "sequence" is terminated by the PCI-X bus master prior to transferring all of the data.

> The definition of the "exact same" bus transaction (except split completion) referred to above is defined as the PCI-X bus master executing the repeat bus transaction with the same COMMAND (according to the C/BE# signal lines in the ADDRESS PHASE), and the same values in the AD and C/BE# signal lines in the ATTRIBUTE PHASE. Also, the value of the REQ64# signal line is the same.

711

As previously stated, once a "sequence" of bus transactions associated with a BURST memory write command has been established, the PCI-X bus master must complete the "sequence". However, there are several conditions that will REMOVE this requirement. The PCI-X bus master WILL NOT complete the "sequence" (and is defined as terminated) when any of the following occurs:

- One of the bus transactions is terminated by a Master Abort or Target Abort termination.

- The PCI-X bus segment is reset.

> When the aforementioned terminations or bus segment reset occurs, the "sequence" does not continue and is defined as terminated. See the discussions in other later parts of this chapter for the continuance of a "sequence" for the other target terminations.

> The assertion of the SERR# or the PERR# signal lines have no bearing on the execution of a Single Phase Disconnect termination, except when used in conjunction with the reporting of a data parity error.

> PCI-X bus masters may execute other bus transactions to a target that has executed a Single Phase Disconnect termination to a previous bus transaction. See Chapter 7: *Bridge and Interface Protocol* for more information.

> If the Lock master or a non-Lock master is accessing the locked target, the execution of a Single Phase Disconnect termination does not force the Lock master to relinquish the Lock Function.

> The porting of a PCI-X BURST memory write transaction through a bridge is dependent on the available buffer space (*i.e.*, FIFO). The bridge is considered "full" if two ADB sized buffers are not available (with some exceptions). When the bridge is "full" it must request a Retry, a Single Phase Disconnect, or a Disconnect at Next ADB termination relative to available buffer space and if the bus transaction addresses are near an ADB. Also, in Rev, 1.0.a of the PCI-X addendum specification, section 8.4.6 was added to reflect these considerations. If designing a bridge or an interface (with bridge-like features) between a PCI-X bus segment and internal circuitry in an ASIC, please review this section.

SINGLE PHASE DISCONNECT TERMINATION OF SPLIT COMPLETION AND SPECIAL TRANSACTIONS

According to the PCI-X addendum specification, the Single Phase Disconnect termination is not defined for a split completion transaction.

The special transaction does not address a specific target, so Single Phase Disconnect termination and the "PCI-X 8 clock" rule do not apply to this transaction.

DISCONNECT AT NEXT ADB TERMINATION OF BUS TRANSACTIONS FOR BURST MEMORY AND SPLIT COMPLETION COMMANDS

INTRODUCTION

The Disconnect at Next ADB termination is unique to the PCI-X addendum specification, though it is similar to Disconnect with data termination of the PCI local bus specification. If a Retry, Single Phase Disconnect, or Target Abort termination is not executed in the initial microaccess of a BURST bus transaction; the bus transaction will continue until all of the associated data is transferred (Upper and Lower Byte Counts in the ATTRIBUTE PHASE), until an ADB is reached and the PCI-X bus master wishes to terminate, or a Target Abort termination is executed. The ADB is the allowed disconnect point chosen by the PCI-X bus master or required by the target executing a Disconnect at Next ADB termination. See the summary in Table 8-2 at the beginning of this chapter.

It is important to remember that BURST memory or split completion commands can be executed as either SINGLE or BURST bus transactions. The Disconnect at next ADB termination by definition can be executed on any microaccess. For a SINGLE bus transaction or any BURST bus transaction where the address (starting for memory or lower address for split completion) and the total byte count (Upper and Lower Byte Counts in the ATTRIBUTE PHASE) defines the last transfer (ending address). The PCI-X bus master can terminate the bus transaction on any ADB the bus transaction crosses or at the ending address. As will be discussed below, there are unique bus transaction protocol requirements whenever the starting address is three or fewer microaccesses away from the next ADB (defined as the "ADB rule"). That is, special considerations are required for a SINGLE or BURST bus transaction with a starting or lower address near an ADB.

Note: In the following discussion only the terms BURST memory transactions and BURST split completion transactions are discussed for the bus transactions for BURST memory and split completion commands. As previously discussed, the existence of one microaccess for a bus transaction for BURST COMMAND is defined as a SINGLE bus transaction. Because a SINGLE bus transaction is a one microaccess version of the BURST bus transaction, the following discussion of BURST bus transactions with "three or fewer microaccesses" also apply to the SINGLE bus transactions. That is, when applicable due to nearness of an ADB, the SINGLE bus transaction for a BURST COMMAND will have to be executed as a BURST transaction with more than one microaccess.

The Disconnect at Next ADB termination is defined for the following BURST memory bus transaction situations (this is not a conclusive list ... other situations are possible). The Disconnect at Next ADB termination is also defined for split completion transactions and will be discussed in a later section.

■ When the target is only able to transfer the data up to the next ADB, it must execute a Disconnect at Next ADB termination. Once the Disconnect at Next ADB termination is executed, the only terminations permitted upon reaching the next ADB are completion due to transferring all of the data for the bus transaction or a Target Abort termination. The ability to transfer data up to an ADB can be dependent on either data or buffer space available, or due to the address range boundary of the target.

■ A BURST memory bus transaction with a starting address three or fewer microaccesses from the target's address range boundary and the total byte count (Upper and Lower Byte Counts in the ATTRIBUTE PHASE) indicates the address boundary range will be crossed (address boundary is aligned to the ADB by definition); the target can execute either a Single Phase Disconnect or a Split Response termination. That is, it is always the responsibility of the target to terminate a bus transaction that can potentially exceed its address range boundary prior to crossing the boundary. The three or fewer microaccess situation prevents use of a Disconnect at Next ADB termination (with the exception noted in the sub-bullet below) and requires the target to either force bus transactions to ease towards the address range boundary with the following considerations:

■ A Split Response termination can also address this in a more efficient manner. It is must be implemented if possible, instead of relying on Single Phase Disconnect termination. The Single Phase Disconnect termination applies when Split Response termination is not possible.

- As will be discussed below, a Disconnect at Next ADB termination is requested (instead of Single Phase Disconnect or Split Response terminations on one of the three or fewer microaccesses) on the FIRST microaccess of a bus transaction when the starting address is three or fewer microaccesses from the next ADB, the PCI-X bus master must terminate the bus transaction at the next ADB.

- The Disconnect at Next ADB termination is NOT a response for a parity error in the ADDRESS or ATTRIBUTE PHASES. Similarly, if a parity error occurs in the ADDRESS or ATTRIBUTE PHASES it does not prevent a Disconnect at Next ADB termination to be executed for other reasons.

- A target may execute a Disconnect at Next ADB termination when parity error occurs in a previous microaccess of the DATA PHASE of a write or a split completion transaction provided the aforementioned three or fewer microaccesses protocol is followed.

The Disconnect at Next ADB termination is also defined for BURST split completion transactions and is executed for the same situations discussed above for BURST memory transactions with the following differences:

- When the target of the split completion transactions is the "original" PCI-X bus master, the execution of the Disconnect at Next ADB termination is not permitted. Only a PCI-X/PCI-X bridge between the "original" PCI-X bus master and the "original" target of the bus transaction is permitted to execute a Disconnect at Next ADB termination.

  - If the PCI-X/PCI-X BRIDGE is between the "original" PCI-X bus master and the "original" target of the bus transaction, it cannot request a Disconnect at Next ADB termination on the FIRST microaccess of split completion transaction when the conditions of all three sub-bullets are met:

    - The bridge has fewer than two ADB sized buffers available for the split completion transaction.

    - The split completion transaction will otherwise cross the next ADB.

    - The starting address is three or fewer microaccesses to the next ADB.

- For split completion transactions, the "starting address" defined for memory transactions is replaced by "lower address".

ADB RULE

Before continuing the discussion of Disconnect at Next ADB Termination, it is important to understand bus transaction operation near an ADB. As discussed in more detail in Chapter 6: *Detailed Bus Transaction Operation*, there is a protocol for the deassertion of the FRAME# and IRDY# signal lines. Parts of the deassertion protocols apply to target terminations. Summarized below is the "general deassertion" protocol that applies to the bus transaction operation in addition to the protocol specific to Disconnect at Next ADB termination.

- "General Deassertion" protocol:

  1. For one or two actual microaccesses, the FRAME# and IRDY# signal lines are sampled deasserted two CLK signal line periods after the TRDY# or STOP# signal line is sampled asserted (whichever is first).

  2. For three actual microaccesses, the FRAME# signal line is sampled deasserted two CLK signal line periods after the TRDY# or STOP# signal line is sampled asserted (whichever is first). Also, the IRDY# signal line is sampled deasserted one CLK signal line period after the last actual microaccess.

  3. For four or more actual microaccesses, the FRAME# signal line is sampled deasserted one CLK signal line period after the last actual microaccess or two CLK signal line periods after the STOP# signal line is sampled asserted for a Disconnect at Next ADB termination. Also, the IRDY# signal line is sampled deasserted one CLK signal line period after the last actual microaccess.

In the above, "actual microaccess" is defined when data is actually transferred (with or without Single Phase Disconnect or Disconnect at Next ADB), or the microaccess that coincides with Retry, Split Response, or Target Abort termination. It is not necessarily the number of microaccesses the PCI-X bus master intended to execute prior to early bus transaction termination caused by the target termination. For a 32 or 64 data bit bus transaction, each microaccess transfers four bytes or eight bytes (not all byte lanes may be valid), respectively. The ADB is defined aligned to natural 128 byte address boundaries. Thus, the transfer between two ADBs is 32 microaccesses for 32 data bit bus transactions, and 16 microaccesses for 64 data bit bus transactions. In the following examples a 32 data bit bus transaction is assumed.

Whenever the PCI-X bus master begins a BURST memory transaction with a starting address and byte count (defined by the Upper and Lower Byte Counts in the ATTRIBUTE PHASE) near an ADB, the graceful completion of the bus transaction due to Disconnect at Next ADB termination is a consideration. That is, if the starting address is three or fewer microaccesses to the next ADB, the target potentially may request a Disconnect at the Next ADB termination when the PCI-X bus master is simultaneously terminating the bus transaction (due to byte count) prior to the next ADB. Also, the byte count may indicate that the bus transaction will terminate after the next ADB; but the PCI-X bus master can optionally terminate at the next ADB. Both of these situations will cause a problem in the graceful termination of the DEVSEL#, TRDY#, and STOP# signal lines by the target. Also, even when the target is not executing a Disconnect at Next ADB termination, the termination by the PCI-X bus master at an ADB prior to the byte count being reached will result in a non-graceful termination by the target of the DEVSEL# and TRDY# signal lines. To prevent this situation from causing a problem, the bus transaction termination protocol has the following requirements for all bus transactions for BURST memory and split completion commands near an ADB. The following discussion of the ADB Rule (collectively Subrules 1 to 5) is focused on the BURST memory transaction. As previously stated, the ADB rule also applies to split completion transactions, except the word "starting address" is replaced by "lower address".

■ Subrule 1: If the starting address of the BURST memory transaction (for the size of the bus transaction requested by the PCI-X bus master) is three microaccesses or fewer away from the next ADB and the byte count is such that the PCI-X bus master WILL terminate the bus transaction at or prior to the next ADB, the PCI-X bus master must not execute the bus transaction. Instead the PCI-X bus master executes a different BURST bus transaction as follows ("at" means the ending address equals the last address of the next ADB block. "prior" means that the total bytes to transfer per the byte count has been reached):

  ■ The PCI-X bus master adjusts the starting address and byte count of the memory transaction (for the size of the transaction requested by the PCI-X bus master) such that the bus transaction will have a starting address four microaccesses to the next ADB and the byte count will complete at the next ADB. For a BURST memory write transaction the byte enables (C/BE#) asserted control the actual bytes that are written. For a BURST memory read all of the bytes are read but all may not be used by the PCI-X bus master.

    ■ For a BURST split completion transaction, all of the bytes are assumed valid and transferred from the "original" target to the "original" PCI-X bus master. Similar to the BURST memory read transaction, the extra bytes may be transferred on the BURST split completion transaction thus may be discarded by the "original" PCI-X bus master acting as split completion target.

- Under all these situations, the bytes transferred may be more than just what the PCI-X bus master needed to actually transfer.

- When the starting address (or lower address for split completion) and byte count has been adjusted to achieve the conditions in the preceding bullet, the PCI-X bus master must terminate only at the next ADB unless a Retry, Single Phase Disconnect, or Target Abort termination is requested by the target. If the target requests a Disconnect at Next ADB termination, the PCI-X bus master will of course still terminate the bus transaction at the next ADB.

- Subrule 2: If the starting address of the BURST memory bus transaction (for the size of the bus transaction requested by the PCI-X bus master) is three microaccesses or closer to the ending address (as defined by the starting address and byte count) and an ADB is not between the starting address and the ending address (the ending address is not the last address of an ADB block), the aforementioned execution of a different "bus transaction" as discussed above is not implemented. The bus transaction is executed "normally" with the following considerations:

  - The PCI-X bus master must terminate the bus transaction at the ending address unless the target requests a Retry, Single Phase Disconnect, or Target Abort termination.

  - As previously stated, this protocol also applies to BURST split completion transactions with the "lower address" replacing "starting address" in the discussion. Also, Single Phase Disconnect termination does not apply.

- Subrule 3: If the starting address of the BURST memory transaction (for the size of the bus transaction requested by the PCI-X bus master) is three microaccesses or fewer to the next ADB and the byte count is such that the PCI-X bus master WILL terminate the bus transaction after the next ADB, the bus transaction is executed "normally" with the following considerations:

  - The PCI-X bus master is required to terminate the BURST memory transaction at the ending address or a subsequent ADB unless the target requests a Retry, Single Phase Disconnect, Disconnect at the Next ADB (see "3 microaccesses issue" below), or Target Abort termination.

  - In this situation, the ending address (defined by the starting address and the byte count) identifies to the target when the BURST memory transaction is to be terminated. It is possible for the PCI-X bus master to terminate the bus transaction at the next ADB and not the ending address. The PCI-X bus master is required to cross the next ADB unless the aforementioned target terminations are requested.

- Independently of the target requesting Retry, Single Phase Disconnect, Disconnect at the Next ADB, or Target Abort, if the PCI-X bus master does not intend to follow the starting address and byte count such that the bus transaction would terminate at the next ADB, Subrule 1 will apply.

- As previously stated, this protocol also applies to BURST split completion transactions with the "lower address" replacing "starting address" in the discussion. Also, Single Phase Disconnect termination does not apply.

- Subrule 4: If the starting address of the BURST memory transaction (for the size of the bus transaction requested by the PCI-X bus master) is four or more microaccesses to the next ADB the bus transaction is executed "normally" with the following considerations:

  - The PCI-X bus master must terminate the bus transaction at the ending address or at an ADB unless the target requests a Retry, Single Phase Disconnect, Disconnect at the Next ADB, or Target Abort termination.

As previously stated, this protocol also applies to BURST split completion transactions with the "lower address" replacing "starting address" in the discussion. Also, for BRUST split completion transactions, the Single Phase Disconnect termination does not apply.

The above requirements for the PCI-X bus master relative to an ADB rule establish bus transactions that will operate with the proper number of microaccesses to permit the target to gracefully terminate the STOP#, TRDY, and DEVSEL# signal lines. Though not specially outlined above, the ownership of the AD signal lines also gracefully transfer to the PCI-X bus master. The target assumes that the bus transaction will terminate at the ending address (defined by the starting address and the byte count) or possibly on an ADB (if the transaction crosses an ADB or the ending address is the last address of an ADB block). The other part of the ADB rule for the target that complements the part of the ADB rule outlined above for the PCI-X bus master is as follows:

- Subrule 5: "3 microaccesses issue": There are two issues related to the number of microaccesses to the next ADB and when the target requests a Disconnect at Next ADB termination.

  - When the starting address of the BURST memory or split completion transaction is three microaccesses or fewer to the next ADB, the target IS REQUIRED to request a Disconnect at Next ADB termination on the first data phase of the bus transaction to insure termination at the next ADB unless a Target Abort termination is subsequently requested. Otherwise, when the execution of the Disconnect at Next ADB termination not at the first microaccess the bus transaction will be terminated at the subsequent ADB or at the ending address before the subsequent ADB (as defined by the starting address and the byte count) unless a Target Abort termination is subsequently requested.

■ When the starting address of the BURST memory or split completion transaction is four or more microaccesses to the next ADB, the target can request a Disconnect at Next ADB termination on any microaccess. If the Disconnect at Next ADB termination is requested at four or more microaccesses to the next ADB, the bus transaction is terminated at the next ADB or at the ending address before the next ADB (as defined by the starting address and the byte count) unless a Target Abort termination is also executed. If the Disconnect at Next ADB termination is requested at three or fewer data phases to the next ADB, the bus transaction will terminated at the subsequent ADB or at the ending address before the subsequent ADB (as defined by the starting address and the byte count) unless a Target Abort termination is subsequently requested.

In the above bullets, if the requested number of data phases by the PCI-X bus master is based on a 64 data bit bus transaction (REQ64# signal line asserted) the actual number of microaccesses will be twice that number if the target forces a 32 data bit bus transaction (ACK64# signal line deasserted). There is no change in the operation of the bus transaction by the PCI-X bus master or target. If the PCI-X bus master has adjusted the microaccesses and byte count to achieve four microaccesses to end the bus transaction at the next ADB, the implementation of the bus transaction as a 32 data bit bus transaction (as forced by the target not asserting the ACK64# signal line) does not change the byte count and the ending address.

IMPLEMENTATION OF DISCONNECT AT NEXT ADB TERMINATION OF BURST MEMORY AND SPLIT COMPLETION TRANSACTIONS

Figures 8-18-A to 8-18-L show the Disconnect at Next ADB termination protocol. The Disconnect at Next ADB termination is requested with the simultaneous assertion of the TRDY#, STOP#, and DEVSEL# signal lines. The earliest point the TRDY# and STOP# signal lines can be asserted is the CLK signal line period immediately after the TARGET RESPONSE PHASE or simultaneously with the assertion of the DEVSEL# signal line, whichever is later. In the case of BURST write transactions, the assertion of the TRDY# and STOP# signal lines is with two wait state resolution. Once the wait states have occurred (if any) the STOP# signal line can be asserted on any microaccess. These figures do not include the change of signal lines ownership. Please see Chapter 6: *Detailed Bus Transaction Operation* for detailed information for driving, tri-stating, and change of ownership of the signal lines. Unlike some of the other target terminations, the Disconnect at Next ADB termination can be executed at any microaccess of the bus transaction. As discussed above and will be described below, the specific microaccess the Disconnect at Next ADB termination is requested versus the number of microaccesses to the next ADB yields different results. There are four cases to consider:

■ Case A: The Disconnect at Next ADB termination can be executed with four or more microaccesses to the next ADB. In this case, Item (3) of the "General Deassertion" protocol applies as shown in Figures 8-18-A and 8-18-B. The request for a Disconnect at Next ADB termination with four or more microaccesses to the next ADB insures that the bus transaction will terminate at the next ADB. Figure 8-18-C shows how the assertion of the TRDY# and STOP# signal lines must occur with two wait state resolution if the Disconnect at Next ADB termination is requested on the initial microaccess.

■ Case B: The Disconnect at Next ADB termination can be executed with three or fewer microaccesses to the next ADB. In this case, the request for a Disconnect at Next ADB termination that occurs on the INITIAL microaccess where data is transferred insures that the bus transaction will terminate at the next ADB. Items (1) and (2) of the "General Deassertion" protocol apply as shown in Figures 8-18-D to 8-18-G.

■ Case C: The Disconnect at Next ADB termination can be executed with three or fewer microaccesses to the next ADB. In this case the request for a Disconnect at Next ADB termination does NOT occur on the INITIAL microaccess where data is transferred; thus the bus transaction will terminate at the subsequent and not next ADB. Item (3) of the "General Deassertion" protocol applies as shown in Figure 8-18-H.

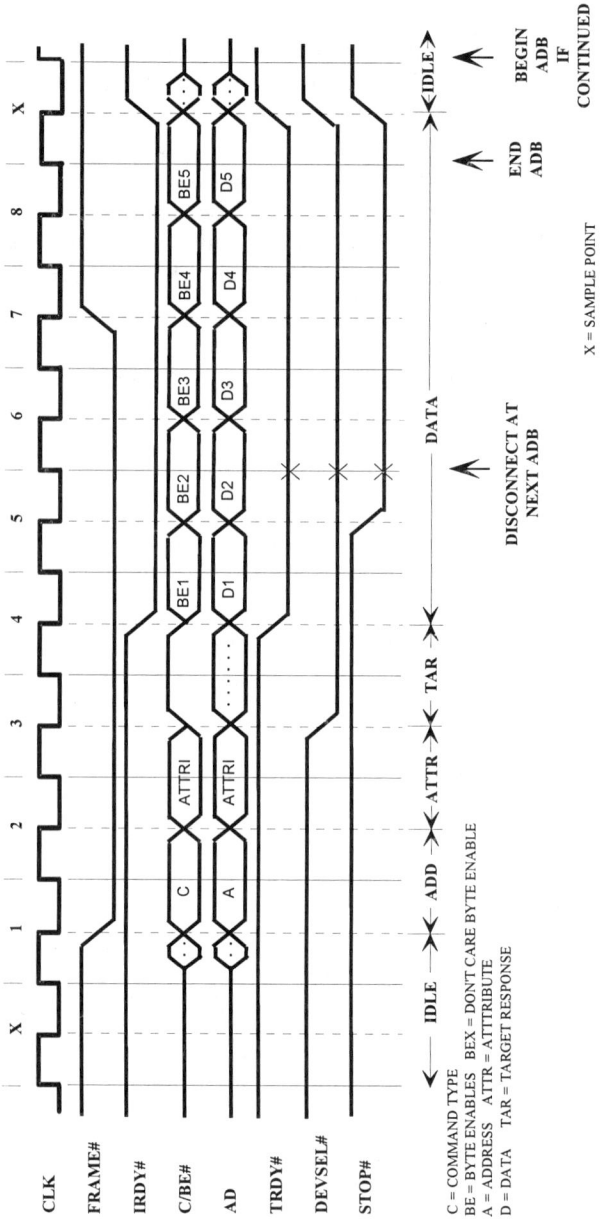

Figure 8-18-A: PCI-X Disconnect at Next ADB Termination for BURST Write Transaction with No Wait States and Four Microaccesses to ADB

722

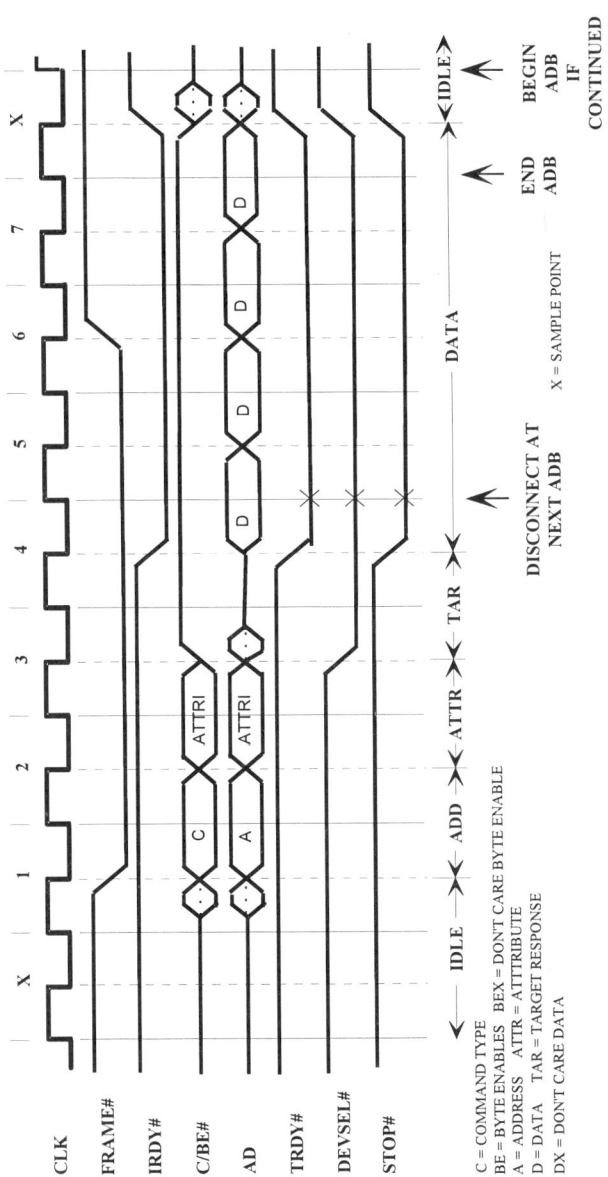

Figure 8-18-B: PCI-X Disconnect at Next ADB Termination for BURST Read Transaction with No Wait States and Four Microaccesses to ADB

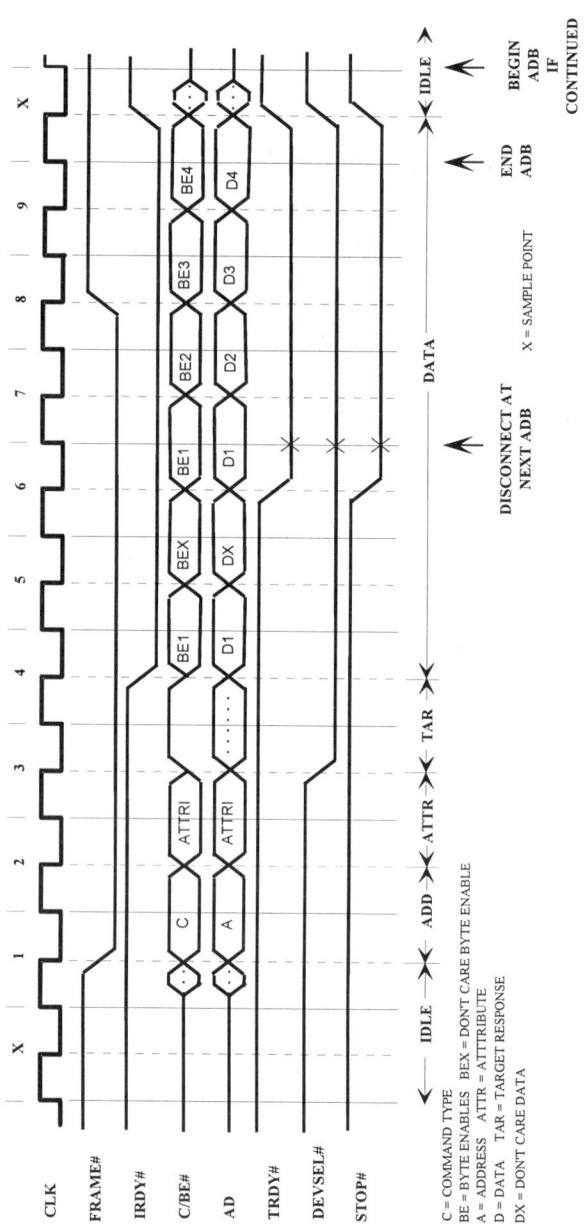

Figure 8-18-C: PCI-X Disconnect at Next ADB Termination for BURST Write Transaction with Two Wait States and Four Microaccesses to ADB

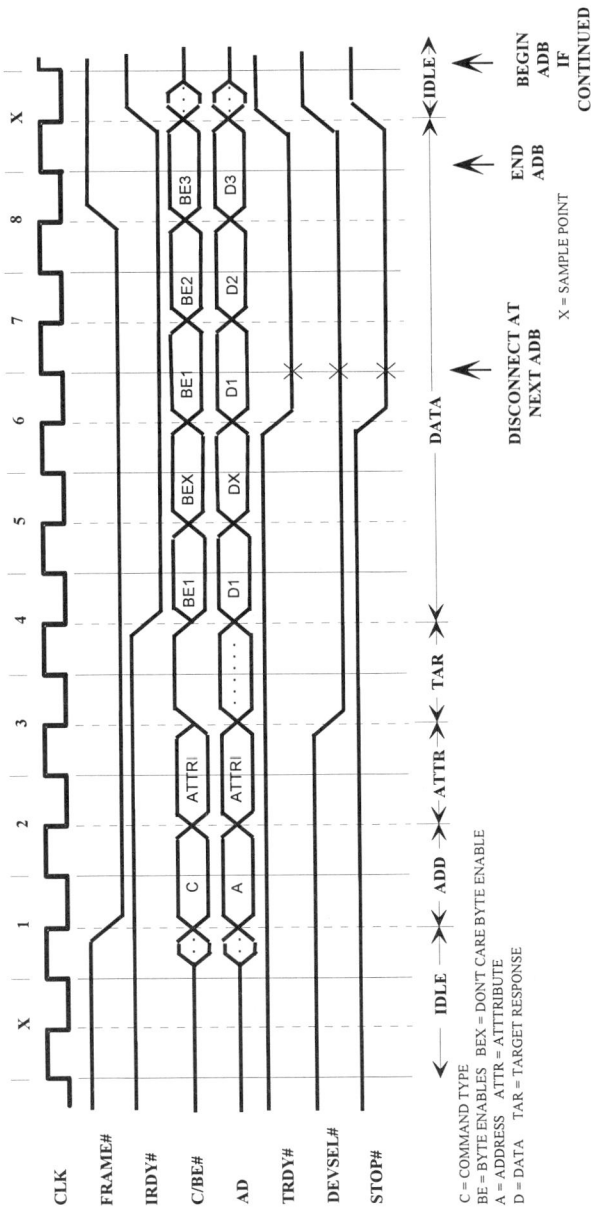

Figure 8-18-D: PCI-X Disconnect at Next ADB Termination for BURST Write Transaction with Two Wait States and Three Microaccesses to ADB

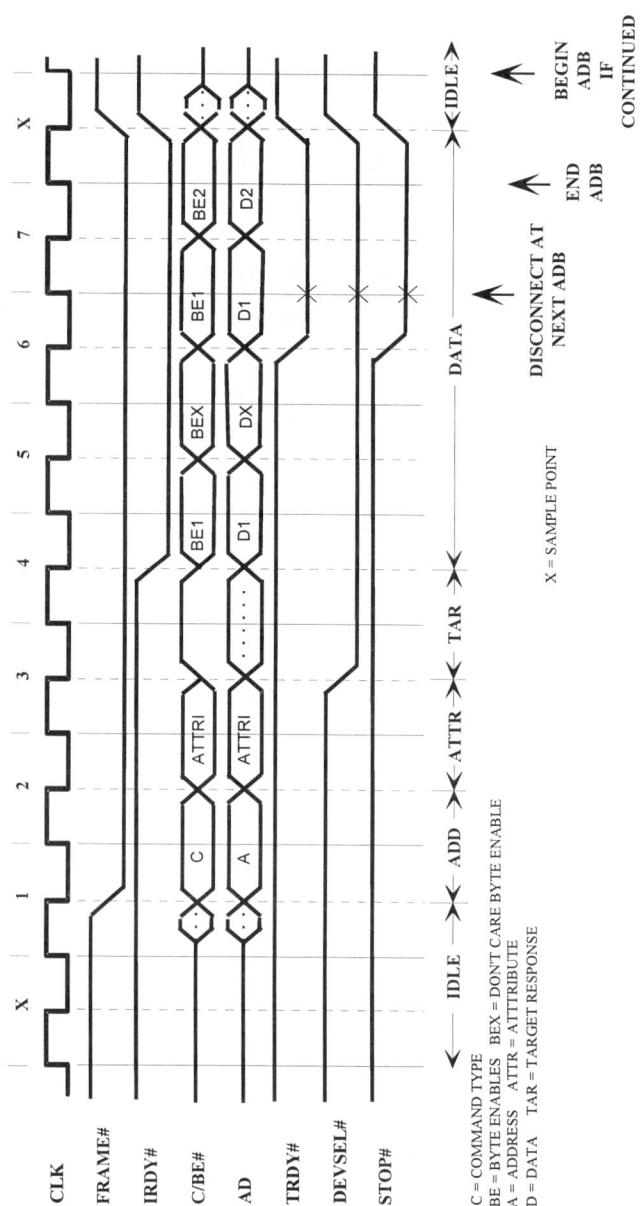

**Figure 8-18-E: PCI-X Disconnect at Next ADB Termination for BURST
Write Transaction with Two Wait States and Two Microaccesses to ADB**

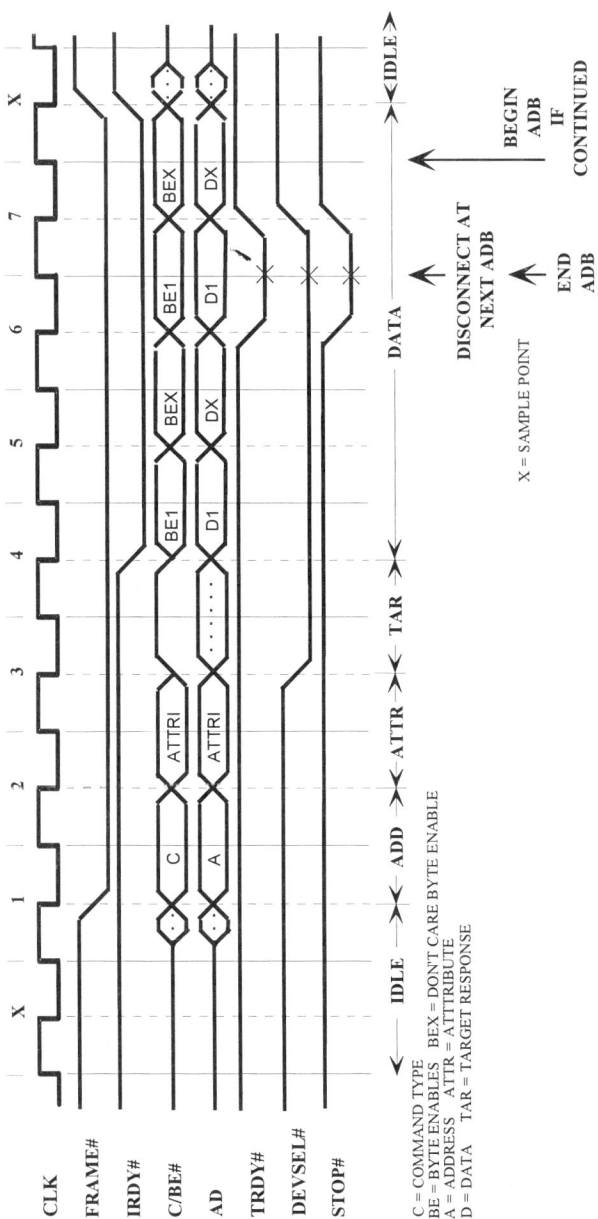

Figure 8-18-F: PCI-X Disconnect at Next ADB Termination for BURST Write Transaction with Two Wait States and One Microaccess to ADB

727

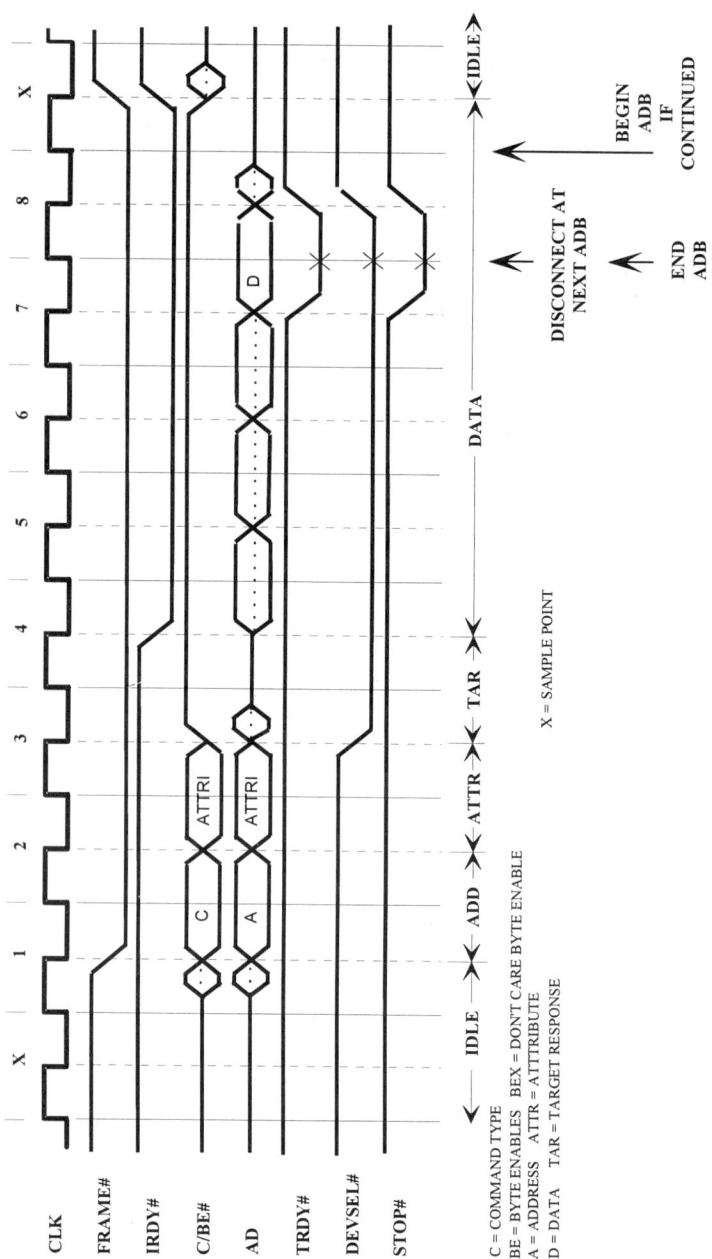

Figure 8-18-G: PCI-X Disconnect at Next ADB Termination for BURST Read Transaction with Three Wait States and One Microaccess to ADB

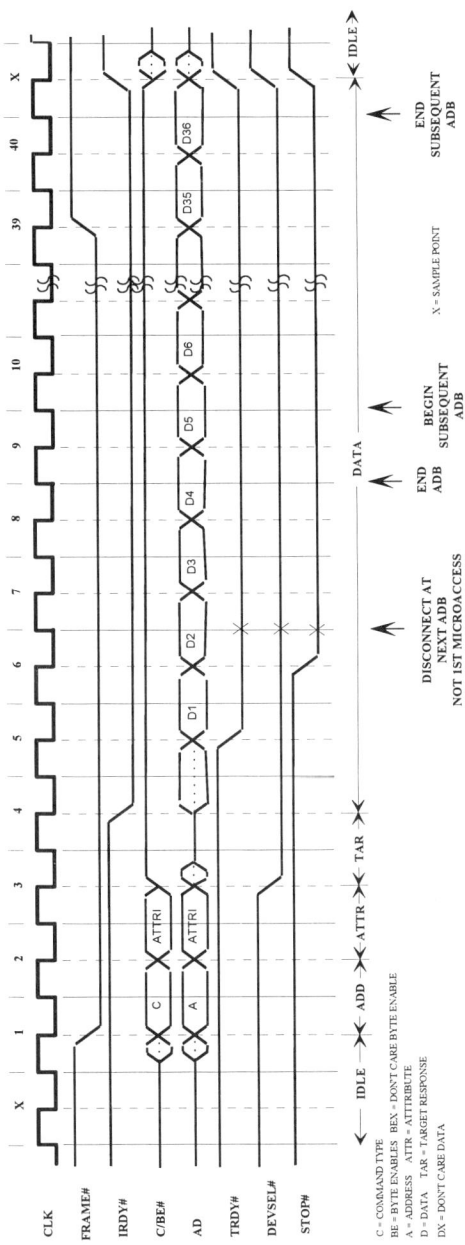

Figure 8-18-H: PCI-X Disconnect at Next ADB Termination for BURST Read Transaction with One Wait State and Three Microaccesses to ADB

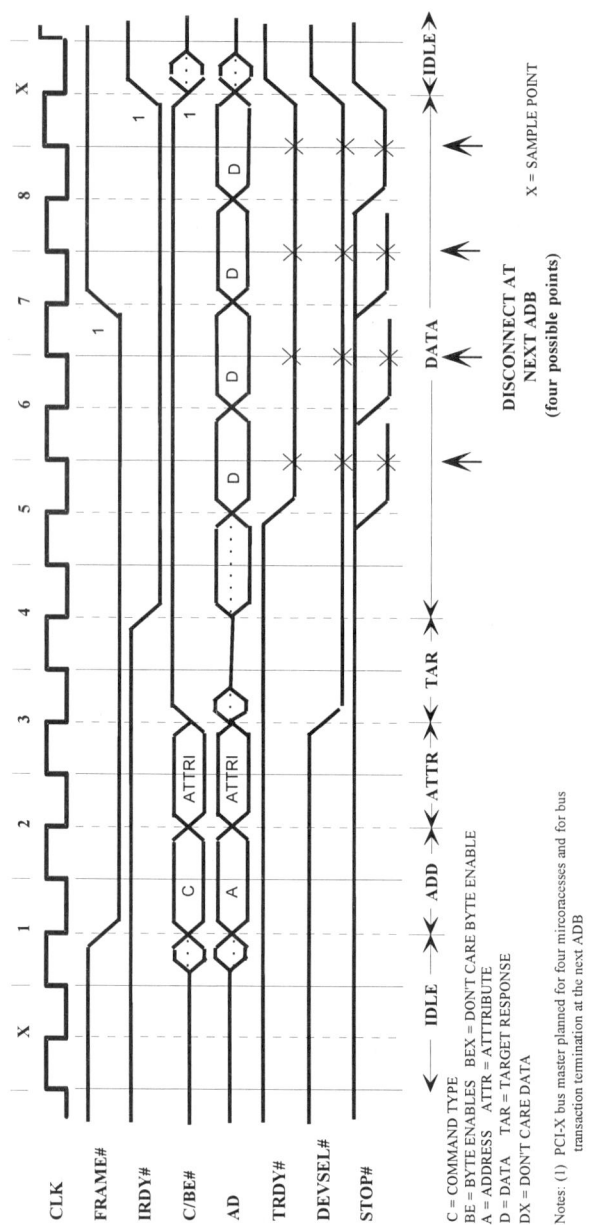

Figure 8-18-I: PCI-X Disconnect at Next ADB Termination for BURST Read Transaction with One Wait State and Disconnect at Next ADB on 4th Microaccess

■ Case D: The Disconnect at Next ADB termination can be executed, but the PCI-X bus master intended to terminate the bus transaction at the next ADB independently of the termination at an ADB in accordance with the target termination. In this case, the bus transaction termination occurs at the same point whether the Disconnect at Next ADB termination had been requested or not. Item (3) of the "General Deassertion" protocol applies as shown in Figure 8-18-I.

> Once Disconnect at Next ADB termination is requested, the TRDY#, STOP#, and DEVSEL# signal lines cannot change state until the completion of the last microaccess. Once the last microaccess completes, the TRDY#, STOP#, and DEVSEL# signal lines are deasserted. The one exception is that the target may change the termination to a Target Abort termination. The request of a Target Abort termination supercedes any bus transaction operation for a Disconnect at Next ADB termination.

In summary, the "PCI-X 16 clock" rule and the associated execution of the Disconnect at Next ADB termination due to this rule APPLIES to the following SINGLE bus transactions and the initial microaccess of the following BURST bus transactions. It gives the target the opportunity to terminate the bus transaction with this termination in preference to the other terminations according to the "PCI-X 16 clock" rule if the target will not be able to transfer all of the data of the bus transaction or a Split Response termination cannot be executed. The Disconnect at Next ADB termination is different than the Retry, Split Response, or Single Phase Disconnect terminations in that it can also be executed in any microaccess of a BURST bus transaction. The "PCI-X 16 clock" rule only applies to the SINGLE bus transactions or the initial microaccess of the BURST bus transaction.

■ Memory transactions

■ Split completion transactions

> The "PCI-X 16 clock" rule for a Disconnect at Next ADB termination (or the "PCI-X 16 clock" rule for transferring data in the initial microaccess) DOES NOT apply for the above PCI-X bus transactions during the initialization time (RST# signal line deasserted to 2^{27} CLK signal line periods later), when executing from BOOT ROM, or when copying expansion ROM to memory. Note: If the device is accessing its expansion ROM after it has been hot-inserted, the aforementioned "PCI-X 16 clock" rule relative to target termination DOES apply.

According to the PCI-X addendum specification, the requirements to repeat a bus transaction or continue with the "sequence" of bus transactions relative to Disconnect at Next ADB termination differs depending on the COMMAND the bus transaction is executing. As previously discussed, this termination only applies to BURST COMMANDs executed as either SINGLE or BURST bus transactions.

■ The BURST memory read command executed as either a SINGLE or BURST bus transaction and terminated by a Disconnect at Next ADB termination must not be continued. That is, a BURST read transaction that is target terminated prior to transferring the total byte count (Upper and Lower Byte Counts in the ATTRIBUTE PHASE) does not continue the transfer in a subsequent bus transaction. If the PCI-X bus master executes a bus transaction that appears to be a continuance, it may or may not be coincidental as far as the target is concerned. Consequently, no "sequence" of bus transactions is established relative to a BURST read command.

■ When a PCI-X bus master executes a BURST memory write or split completion command as a SINGLE bus transaction (only the initial microaccess is needed in the DATA PHASE) and terminated by a Disconnect at Next ADB termination, by definition does not require the associated bus transaction to be repeated or continued. By definition, the SINGLE bus transaction only consists of one microaccess in the DATA PHASE which aligns with the Disconnect at Next ADB termination.

■ When a PCI-X bus master executes a BURST memory write command as a BURST bus transaction (more than one microaccess is needed in the DATA PHASE), it intends to transfer the total byte count (Upper and Lower Byte Counts in the ATTRIBUTE PHASE). If Disconnect at Next ADB termination is executed on the "first" bus transaction, the continuance of the bus transaction is required. That is, the execution of the Disconnect at Next ADB termination has established a "sequence". For a BURST memory write command that has established a "sequence" of memory write transactions and the following applies:

■ A Retry, Single Phase Disconnect, or Disconnect at the Next ADB termination by the target of any subsequent bus (either SINGLE or BURST) transaction of the "sequence" requires the PCI-X bus master to repeat the "exact same" bus transaction according to Retry termination, or continue the bus transaction for Single Phase Disconnect or Disconnect at the Next ADB termination (with the starting address and total byte count appropriately adjusted). These requirements apply until all of the bytes identified by the total byte count in the first bus transaction of the "sequence" has been transferred. This protocol also applies if a bus transaction part of a "sequence" is terminated by the PCI-X bus master prior to transferring all of the data.

■ When a PCI-X bus master executes a BURST split command as a BURST bus transaction (more than one microaccess is needed in the DATA PHASE), it intends to transfer the total byte count (Upper and Lower Byte Counts in the ATTRIBUTE PHASE). If Disconnect at Next ADB termination is executed on the "first" bus transaction, the continuance of the bus transaction is required. That is, the Split Transaction protocol by definition is an established a "sequence". For a BURST split completion transaction following applies:

   ■ A Retry or Disconnect at the Next ADB termination by the target of any subsequent bus (either SINGLE or BURST) transaction of the "sequence" requires the PCI-X bus master to repeat the "exact same" bus transaction per Retry termination or continue the bus transaction for a Disconnect at the Next ADB termination (with the lower address and total byte count appropriately adjusted). These requirements apply until all of the bytes identified by the total byte count in the "original" transaction has been transferred. This protocol also applies if a bus transaction part of a "sequence" is terminated by the PCI-X bus master prior to transferring all of the data.

> The definition of the "exact same" bus transaction (except split completion) according to the above is defined as the PCI-X bus master executing the repeat bus transaction with the same COMMAND (according to the C/BE# signal lines in the ADDRESS PHASE), and the same values in the AD and C/BE# signal lines in the ATTRIBUTE PHASE. Also, the value of the REQ64# signal line is the same. The definition of the "exact same" relative to a split completion transaction is defined as the PCI-X bus master executing the split completion transaction with the same COMMAND (according to the C/BE# signal lines in the ADDRESS PHASE), and the same values in the AD and C/BE# signal lines in the ATTRIBUTE PHASE. Also, the value of the REQ64# signal line is the same.

As previously stated, once a "sequence" of bus transactions associated with a BURST memory write or split completion commands has been established, the PCI-X bus master must complete the "sequence". However, there are several conditions that will REMOVE this requirement. The PCI-X bus master WILL NOT complete the "sequence" (and is defined as terminated) when any of the following occurs:

■ One of the bus transactions is terminated by a Master Abort or Target Abort termination.

■ The PCI-X bus segment is reset.

When the aforementioned terminations or bus segment reset occurs, the "sequence" does not continue and is defined as terminated. See the discussions in other later parts of this chapter for the continuance of a "sequence" for the other target terminations.

The PCI-X addendum specification defines a special case for the use of the Disconnect at Next ADB termination relative to PCI-X/PCI-X BRIDGES. A PCI-X/PCI-X BRIDGE must not request a Disconnect at Next ADB termination of a BURST memory write transaction (including BURST memory write block and BURST alias memory write block) if both of the following apply:

- The bus transaction's Upper and Lower Bytes Counts in the ATTRIBUTE PHASE indicates that the PCI-X bus master intends to write past the next ADB.

- If the PCI-X/PCI-X BRIDGE will execute the bus transaction on the destination bus segment with fewer than four microaccesses.

The assertion of the SERR# or the PERR# signal lines have no bearing on the execution of a Disconnect at Next ADB termination, except when used in conjunction reporting a data parity error.

PCI-X bus masters may execute other bus transactions to a target that has executed a Disconnect at Next ADB termination to a previous bus transaction. See Chapter 7: *Bridge and Interface Protocol* for more information.

If the Lock master or a non-Lock master is accessing the locked target, the execution of a Disconnect at Next ADB termination does not force the Lock master to relinquish the Lock Function.

The porting of a PCI-X BURST memory write transaction through a bridge is dependent on the available buffer space (*i.e.*, FIFO). The bridge is considered "full" if two ADB sized buffers are not available (with some exceptions). When the bridge is "full" it must request a Retry, a Single Phase Disconnect, or a Disconnect at Next ADB termination relative to available buffer space and if the bus transaction addresses are near an ADB. Also, in Rev. 1.0.a of the PCI-X addendum specification, section 8.4.6 was added to reflect these considerations.

> The porting of a PCI-X BURST split completion transaction through a bridge is dependent on the available buffer space (*i.e.*, FIFO). The bridge is considered "full" if one ADB sized buffer is not available. When the bridge is "full" it must request a Retry or a Disconnect at Next ADB termination relative to available buffer space. Also, in the PCI-X addendum specification, section 8.4 reflects these considerations.
>
> If designing a bridge or an interface (with bridge-like features) between a PCI-X bus segment and internal circuitry in an ASIC, please review these sections.

DISCONNECT AT NEXT ADB TERMINATION OF DWORD MEMORY READ, I/O, CONFIGURATION, INTERRUPT ACKOWLEDGE, AND SPECIAL TRANSACTIONS

According to the PCI-X addendum specification, the Disconnect at Next ADB termination is defined for DWORD memory read, I/O, configuration, and interrupt acknowledge commands. The bus transactions for these commands only have one microaccess like the SINGLE bus transaction protocol. Similarly, a bus transaction for a BURST COMMAND may only consist of one microaccess (*i.e.*, SINGLE bus transaction). In these situations the execution of a Disconnect at Next ADB termination by the target would seem redundant. However, according to the PCI-X addendum specification, a Disconnect at Next ADB termination can be executed for any SINGLE bus transaction. There is no difference in the results of a SINGLE bus transaction with or without a Disconnect at Next ADB termination.

The special transaction does not address a specific target, so Disconnect at Next ADB termination and the "PCI-X 16 clock" rule do not apply to this transaction.

TARGET ABORT TERMINATION OF MEMORY, SPLIT COMPLETION, I/O, CONFIGURATION, AND INTERRUPT ACKNOWLEDGE TRANSACTIONS

The PCI-X addendum specification Target Abort termination protocol for memory, I/O, configuration, and interrupt acknowledge transactions is the same as the PCI local bus specification (for the same bus transactions). This protocol similarity includes the case when the Target Abort termination is appropriate, the setting to logical "1" of the Received Target Abort termination (PCI-X bus master), and Signaled Target Abort termination (target) bit in the associated Status

Register in the configuration address space, and the operation of the PERR# signal line. See Subchapter 8.2 for more information. There are differences between the PCI-X's and PCI's implementations of Target Abort termination for memory, I/O, configuration, and interrupt acknowledge transactions as follows: (In addition, for PCI-X bus segments, the Target Abort termination protocol also applies in similar fashion to split completion transactions and will be discussed later).

■ The PCI-X bus master that terminates the bus transaction with a Target Abort termination must notify the device driver via either an interrupt or some other suitable method. If notification of the device driver is not possible, the SERR# signal line must be asserted with the following qualifications. The assertion of the SERR# signal line can be used to report the error only if the System Error Control bit is set to logical "1" in the Command Register of the PCI-X bus master's Command Register. If the SERR# signal line is asserted, the PCI-X bus master must set to logical "1" the Signaled System Error Status in its Status Register in the configuration address space. The exception to this rule is configuration during initialization (non-run).

■ A target can optionally execute a Target Abort termination as part of the reporting protocol for an address or attribute parity error. The exception is when the address or attribute parity error occurs with a read transaction with a request for Split Response termination. See Subchapter 10.7 for more information.

■ According to the PCI local bus specification protocol, the target must execute a Target Abort termination when the byte lane pattern in the C/BE# signal lines during the DATA PHASE (of a SINGLE I/O transaction or initial microaccess of a BURST I/O transaction) does not "match" the AD[01::00] signal lines during the ADDRESS PHASE. This protocol extends to DWORD memory commands executed as a SINGLE memory transaction.

■ A target can optionally execute a Target Abort termination for an error on the byte count.

■ A target can optionally execute a Target Abort termination as part of the reporting protocol for a parity error in the ADDRESS or ATTRIBUTE PHASES. Similarly, if a parity error occurs in the ADDRESS or ATTRIBUTE PHASES it does not prevent a Target Abort termination to be executed for other reasons.

The split completion transactions are unique to PCI-X; thus there are specific implementation requirements (in addition to the above for other bus transactions) relative to Target Abort termination as follows (this is not a conclusive list ... other situations are possible). (Remember, in the following discussion the "target" is the PCI-X bus master (requester) of the "original" transaction and the "PCI-X

736

bus master" of the split completion transaction is the target (completer) of the "original" transaction terminated by Split Response termination:)

- Either a 64 or 32 data bit split completion transaction can be executed in response to a 64 data bit "original" transaction. Only a 32 data bit split completion transaction can be executed as a response to a 32 data bit "original" transaction. In the latter case, the target may execute a Target Abort termination if it cannot accept 64 data bit split completion transactions.

- A target may execute a Target Abort termination as part of the reporting protocol for a data parity error in a previous microaccess.

A Target Abort termination requested during a split completion transaction can cause severe reactions by other PCI-X resources in the platform, including the assertion the SERR# signal line. Consequently, the request of a Target Abort termination for a split completion transaction can only be for error conditions in which integrity of the data can be guaranteed. It must always be assumed by the "target" (PCI-X bus master (requester) of the "original" transaction) that the request for Target Abort termination during a split completion transaction will result in the platform halting execution.

A PCI-X bus master that was executing a bus transaction when a Target Abort termination occurs must not repeat the access (same COMMAND type) to the same address (*i.e.*, target). The present PCI-X bus master can access the target with the same address, if a different COMMAND type is used. Target Abort termination does not affect accesses to the same target by other PCI-X bus masters. Other PCI-X bus masters may access this address (*i.e.*, target) because they may not have monitored the Target Abort termination. In the case of split completion transactions, the execution of a Target Abort termination requires the split completion transaction to not be repeated and, if part of a "sequence", for the sequence not to continue.

As will be discussed in more detail in Chapter 6: *Detailed Bus Transaction Operation*, there is a protocol for the deassertion of the FRAME# and IRDY# signal lines. Parts of the deassertion protocols apply to target terminations. Summarized below is the "general deassertion" protocol that applies to the bus transaction operation in addition to the protocol specific to Target Abort termination.

- "General Deassertion" protocol:

1. For one or two actual microaccesses, the FRAME# and IRDY# signal lines are sampled deasserted two CLK signal line periods after the TRDY# or STOP# signal line is sampled asserted (whichever is first).

2. For three actual microaccesses, the FRAME# signal line is sampled deasserted two CLK signal line periods after the TRDY# or STOP# signal line is sampled asserted (whichever is first). Also, the IRDY# signal line is sampled deasserted one CLK signal line period after the last actual microaccess.

3. For four or more actual microaccesses, the FRAME# signal line is sampled deasserted one CLK signal line period after the last actual microaccess or two CLK signal line periods after the STOP# signal line is sampled asserted for a Disconnect at Next ADB termination. Also, the IRDY# signal line is sampled deasserted one CLK signal line period after the last actual microaccess.

In the above, "actual microaccess" is defined when data is actually transferred (with or without Single Phase Disconnect or Disconnect at Next ADB) or the microaccess that coincides with Retry, Split Response, or Target Abort termination. It is not necessarily the number of microaccesses the PCI-X bus master intended to execute prior to early bus transaction termination caused by the target termination. For a 32 or 64 data bit bus transaction each microaccess transfers four bytes or eight bytes (not all byte lanes may be valid), respectively. The ADB is defined aligned to natural 128 byte address boundaries. Thus, the transfer between two ADBs is 32 microaccesses for 32 data bit bus transactions, and 16 microaccesses for 64 data bit bus transactions. In the following examples, a 32 data bit bus transaction is assumed.

Figures 8-19-A to 8-19-F show the Target Abort Disconnect termination protocol. Target Abort termination is requested with the simultaneous assertion of the STOP# signal line with the deassertion of the DEVSEL# and TRDY# signal line. The earliest point the TRDY# signal line can be deasserted and STOP# signal lines can be asserted is during the CLK signal line period immediately after the TARGET RESPONSE PHASE or simultaneously with the deassertion of the DEVSEL# signal line (previously asserted for a minimum of one CLK signal line period), whichever is later. In the case of BURST write transactions, the assertion of the STOP# signal line and the deassertion of the TRDY# and DEVSEL# signal lines is with two wait state resolution. Please see Chapter 6: *Detailed Bus Transaction Operation* for detailed information for driving, tri-stating, and change of ownership of the signal lines. The two wait state increment requirement does not apply to DWORD transactions or to BURST write transactions with no wait states (that is, for BURST write transactions, the Target Abort termination is requested in the CLK signal line period immediately after the TARGET

RESPONSE PHASE). Unlike some of the other target terminations, the Target Abort termination can be executed at any microaccess of the bus transaction. There are two cases to consider:

■ Case A: The Target Abort termination request can be executed in the initial microaccess according to the "PCI-X 8 clock" rule. In this case, item (1) of the "General Deassertion" protocol applies as shown in Figures 8-19-A to 8-19-C. The request for a Disconnect at Next ADB termination with four or more microaccesses to the next ADB insures that the bus transaction will terminate at the next ADB. Figure 8-19-B shows how the assertion of the STOP# signal line and the deassertion of the TRDY# (if not already deasserted) and DEVSEL# signal lines occur with two wait state resolution if the Target Abort termination is requested on the initial microaccess.

■ Case B: The Target Abort termination request can occur on any microaccess. When it a occurs after the initial microaccess, the protocol for the deassertion of the FRAME# and IRDY# signal lines must react to the Target Abort termination within two CLK signal line periods. However, there are boundary conditions controlling when the Target Abort termination is requested relative to the planned number of microaccesses the PCI-X bus master planned prior to the receipt of the Target Abort termination. These are shown in Figures 8-19-D to 8-19-F.

> Once Target Abort termination is requested, the STOP# signal lines cannot change state until the completion of the microaccess. The completion of the microaccess is defined as the time the Target Abort termination is sampled. Once the microaccess completes, the STOP# signal line is deasserted, and the TRDY# and DEVSEL# signal lines remain deasserted.

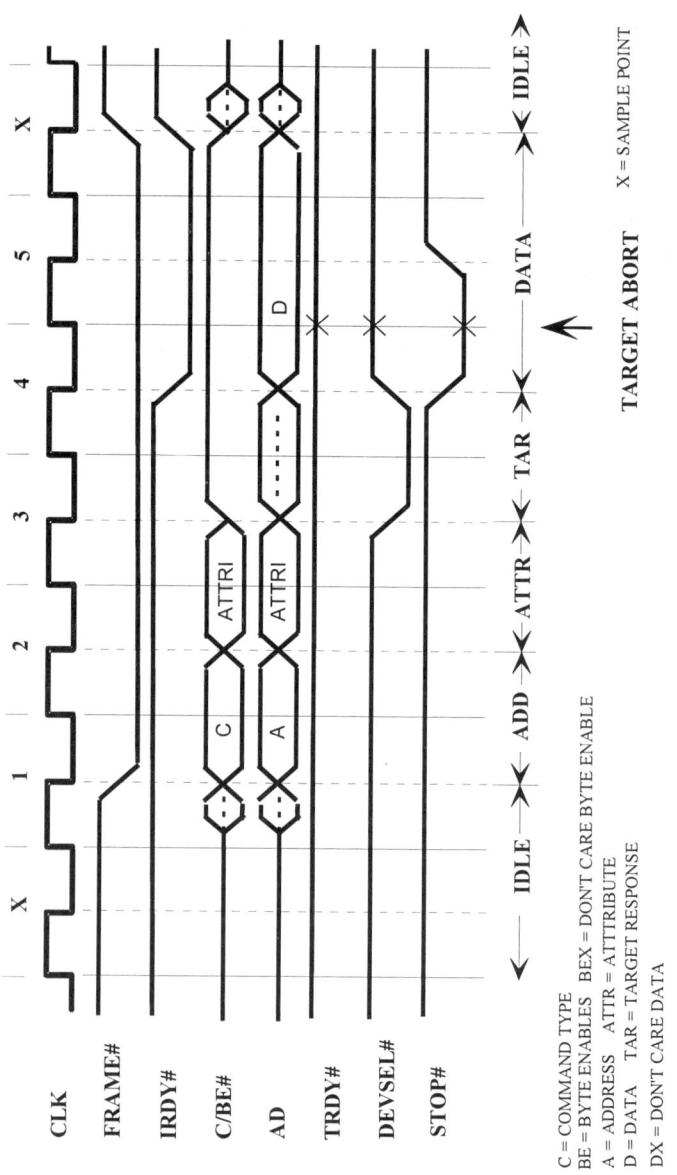

Figure 8-19-A: PCI-X Target Abort Termination for DWORD Write Transaction with No Wait States and One Microaccess

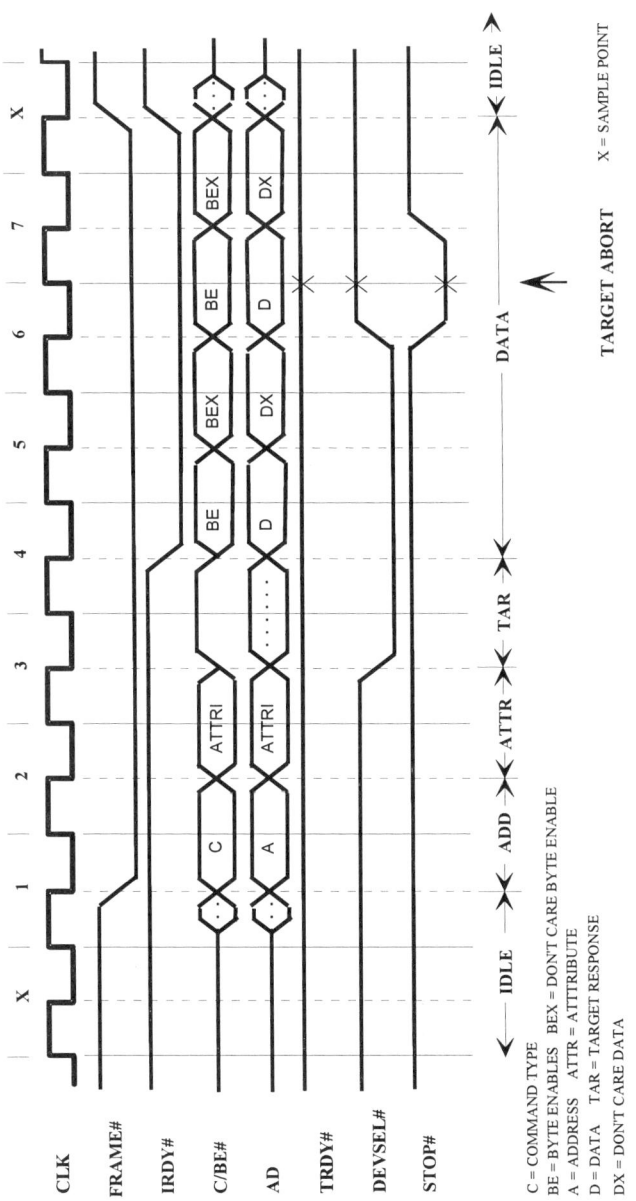

Figure 8-19-B: PCI-X Target Abort Termination for BURST Write Transaction with Two Wait States and One Microaccess

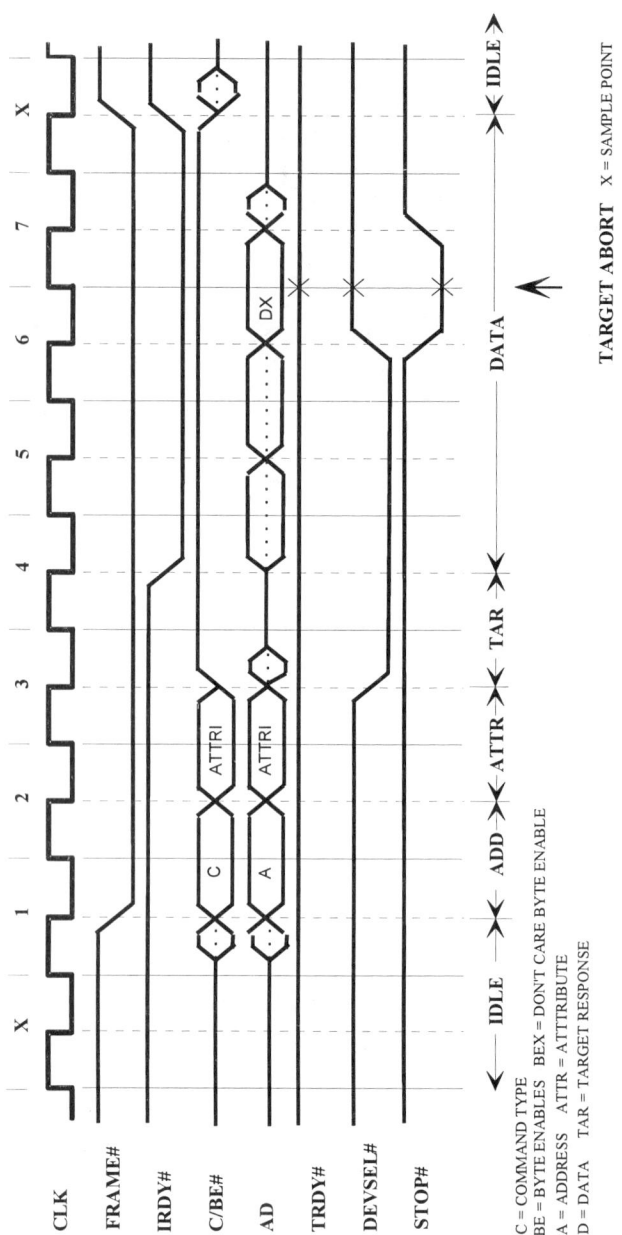

**Figure 8-19-C: PCI-X Target Abort Termination for BURST Read
Transaction with Two Wait States and One Microaccess**

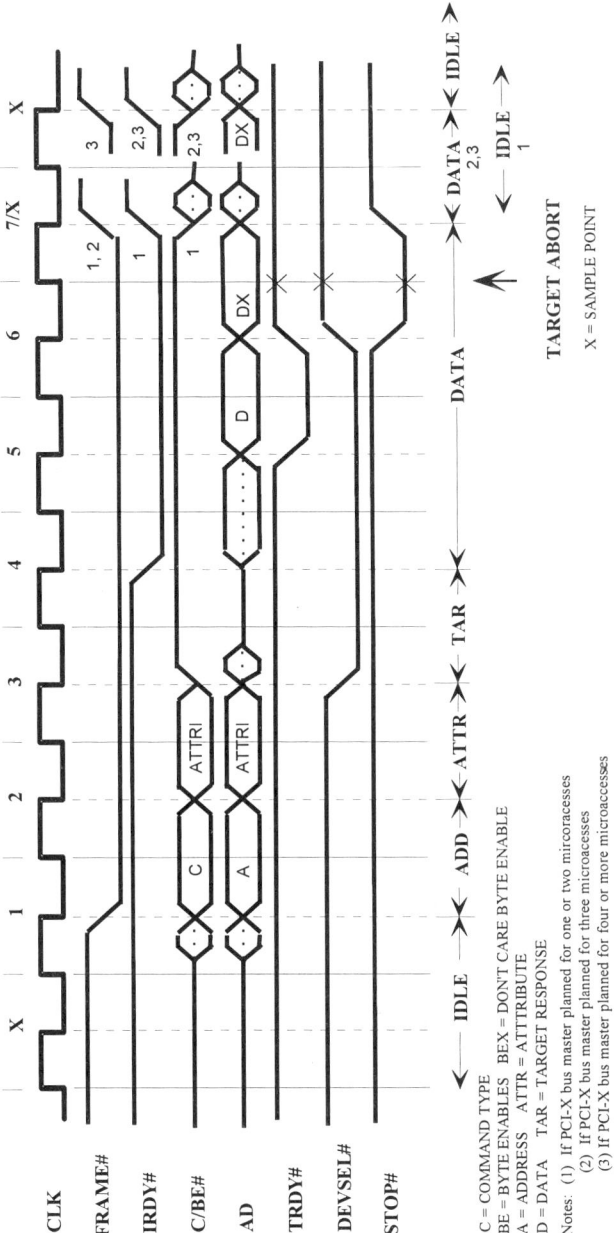

Figure 8-19-D: PCI-X Target Abort Termination for BURST Read Transaction with One Wait State and Target Abort on 2nd Microaccess

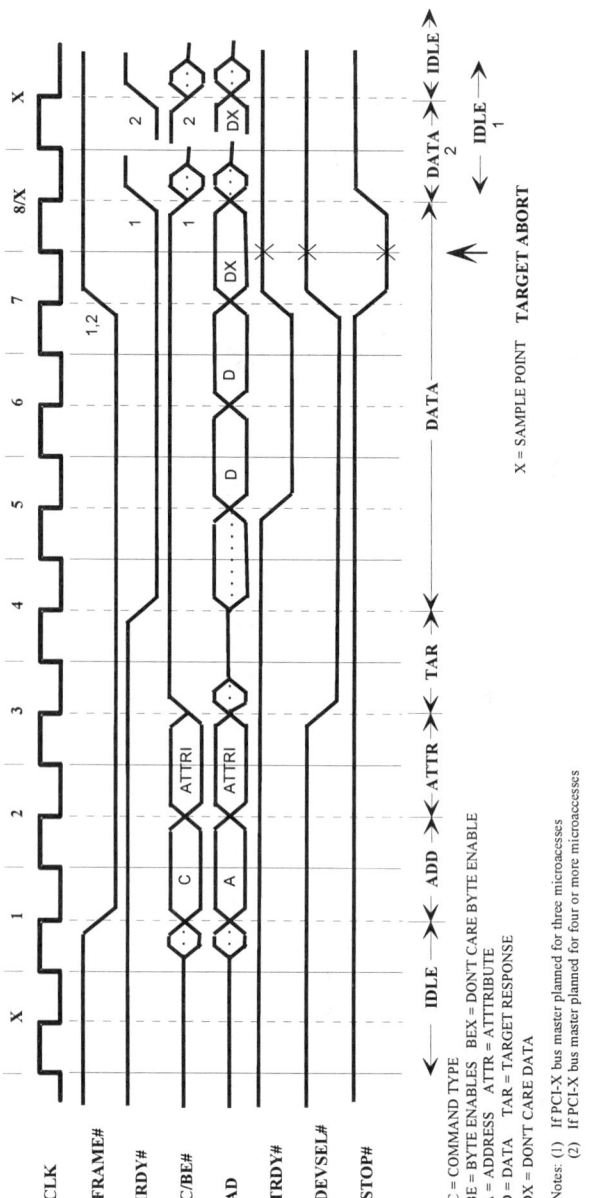

**Figure 8-19-E: PCI-X Target Abort Termination for BURST Read
Transaction with One Wait State and Target Abort on 3rd Microaccess**

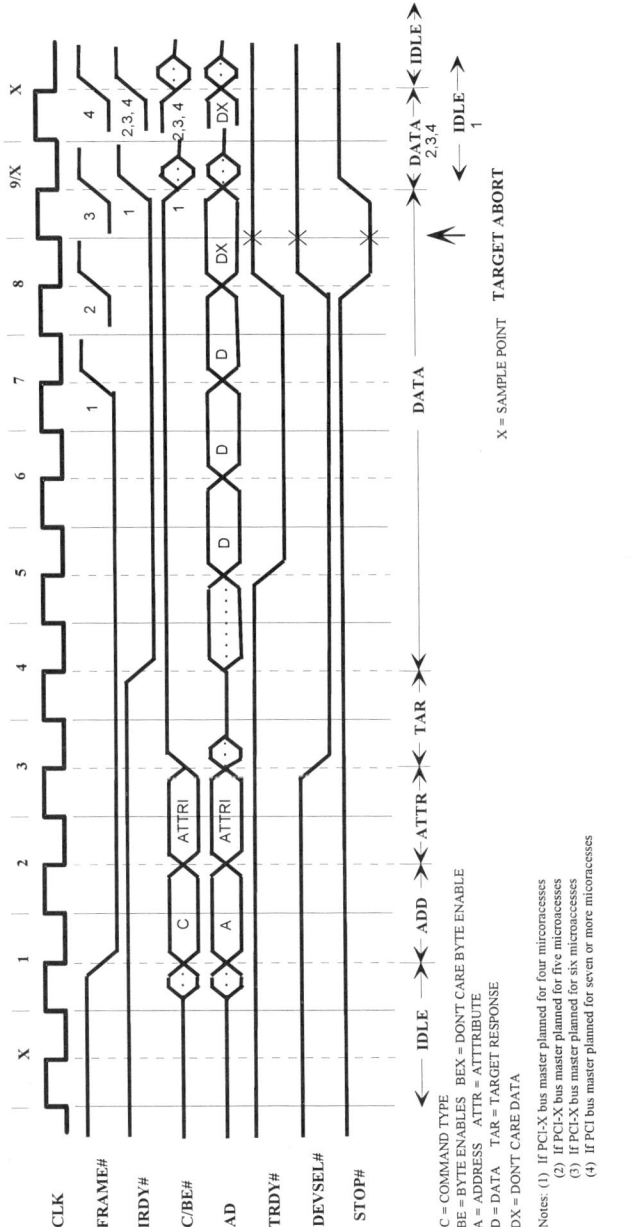

**Figure 8-19-F: PCI-X Target Abort Termination for BURST Read
Transaction with One Wait State and Target Abort on 4th Microaccess**

In summary, the "PCI-X 8 clock" rule and the associated execution of the Target Abort termination due to this rule APPLIES to the following SINGLE bus transactions and the initial microaccess of the following BURST bus transactions. The Target Abort termination is also permitted for any microaccess of a BURST bus transaction. It gives the target the opportunity to terminate the bus transaction with this termination if the target is "broken" or if the bus transaction is absolutely incompatible to the target. Target Abort termination is not an appropriate response simply because the target is not ready to transfer data.

- Memory transactions

- I/O transactions (only SINGLE bus transactions are defined)

- Configuration transactions (only SINGLE bus transactions are defined)

- Interrupt acknowledge transactions (only SINGLE bus transactions are defined)

- Split completion transactions

> **The "PCI-X 8 clock" rule for a Disconnect at Next ADB termination (or the "PCI-X 8 clock" rule for transferring data in the initial microaccess) DOES NOT apply for the above PCI-X bus transactions during the initialization time (RST# signal line deasserted to 2^{27} CLK signal line periods later), when executing from BOOT ROM, or when copying expansion ROM to memory. Note: If the device is accessing its expansion ROM after it has been hot-inserted, the aforementioned "PCI-X 8 clock" rule relative to target termination DOES apply.**

According to the PCI-X addendum specification, the requirements to repeat a bus transaction or continue with the "sequence" of bus transactions relative to Target Abort termination is similar to the PCI local bus specification. The execution of the Target Abort termination requires the "exact same" sequence not to be repeated and for the "sequence" of bus transaction not to be continued.

When a target terminates a bus transaction with a Target Abort termination, the Signaled Target Abort bit must be set in its Status Register of the configuration address space. When the PCI-X bus master detects a Target Abort termination, it must set the Received Target Abort bit in its Status Register of the configuration address space.

The STOP# signal line can be asserted simultaneously with or prior to the deassertion of the DEVSEL# signal line. If the STOP# signal line is asserted prior to the deassertion of the DEVSEL# signal line, a Disconnect at Next ADB or Retry termination is executed. If the STOP# signal line is asserted simultaneously with the deassertion of the DEVSEL# signal line and the TRDY# signal line is deasserted, a Target Abort termination is executed. If the STOP# signal line is asserted simultaneously with the deassertion of the DEVSEL# signal line and the TRDY# signal line is asserted, a Single Phase Disconnect termination is executed.

For a read transaction, a Target Abort termination indicates that any data read in the earlier microaccesses of the BURST bus transaction may be invalid. For a write transaction, a Target Abort termination indicates that the data written in the earlier microaccess of the BURST bus transaction may not have been successfully written into the target.

Execution of Target Abort termination does not affect the central arbiter, because it does not monitor the associated signal lines. Target Abort termination forces the PCI-X bus master to deassert the associated REQx# signal line.

A PCI-X bus master cannot become Lock master and lock a target when a Target Abort termination is executed during the read transaction that the PCI bus master is using to lock the target. The LOCK# signal line is immediately deasserted. If the Lock master is accessing the locked target and a Target Abort termination occurs, the Lock master must relinquish the Lock Function. The LOCK# signal line is immediately deasserted and the target is immediately unlocked. If a non-Lock master accesses the locked target, the execution of a Target Abort termination does not force relinquishing of the Lock Function by the Lock master or the unlocking of the target.

When the SERR# signal line is asserted by the target to indicate a parity error in the ADDRESS and ATTRIBUTE PHASES on the AD, C/BE#, PAR, and PAR64 signal lines, the target can request a Target Abort termination due to this error. The PCI-X bus master may assert the SERR# signal line to report a Target Abort termination of a bus transaction if there is no other mechanism to do so. The assertion of the SERR# signal line can be used to report the error only if the System Error Control bit is set to logical "1" in the Command Register of the PCI-X bus master's Command

Register. If the SERR# signal line is asserted, the PCI-X bus master must set to logical "1" the Signaled System Error Status in its Status Register in the configuration address space. The PERR# signal line cannot be asserted when a data parity occurs with a Target Abort termination because no data was accessed. A target may execute a Target Abort termination for a data parity error occurring in a previous microaccess.

If the Target Abort termination is due to a memory write transaction for a Message Signaled Interrupt, the associated PCI-X bus master must assert the SERR# signal line.

PCI/PCI and PCI-X/PCI-X BRIDGES port bus transactions from the source bus segment to the destination bus segment without any advance knowledge of possible Master Abort or Target Abort terminations on the destination bus segment. Consequently, relative to the source bus segment, a bridge will post memory write transactions, post split completion transactions, apply Delayed Transaction protocol, and apply Split Completion protocol without knowledge of the pending Master Abort termination or Target Abort termination. Relative to Master Abort and Target Abort terminations on the destination bus segment, the bridge's response protocol to posted bus transaction is different than that for the bus transactions due the Delayed Transaction protocol or the Split Transaction protocol.

For the Master Abort termination and Target Abort termination protocols for PCI/PCI BRIDGES, see *PCI to PCI Bridge Architecture Specification Rev 1.1* for more information. For the Master Abort termination and Target Abort termination protocols for PCI-X/PCI-X BRIDGES, see sections 8.7.1.5 and 8.7.1.6 of the *PCI-X Addendum Specification Rev 1.0a* for more information.

TARGET ABORT TERMINATION OF SPECIAL TRANSACTIONS

The special transaction does not address a specific target, so Target Abort termination and the "PCI-X 8 clock" rule do not apply to this transaction.

CHAPTER 9

BUS SEGMENT OWNERSHIP

This chapter consists of the following subchapters:

9.0   Arbitration Protocol

9.1   Parking

9.2   Change of Bus Segment Ownership

9.0   ARBITRATION PROTOCOL

PCI SPECIFIC

All PCI resources that can potentially own a PCI bus segment are defined as PCI bus masters. Only one PCI bus master can own a PCI bus segment at a time, controlling some of the signal lines during and between bus transactions that it is executing. In platforms with multiple PCI bus segments, potentially there can be multiple PCI bus masters simultaneously. Arbitration must occur among all of the PCI bus masters that want to own the PCI bus segment through the use of the central arbiter. The potential PCI bus masters are individually linked to the central arbiter by individual Request (REQx#) and Grant (GNTx#) signal lines. It is the responsibility of the central arbiter to determine which PCI resource will become the master for each PCI bus segment.

It must be noted that a PCI bus master only asserts its associated REQx# signal line when it is ready to immediately begin a bus transaction. Once its associated GNTx# signal line is asserted, the PCI bus master must assert the FRAME# signal line as soon as possible to begin the bus transaction. If the asserted GNTx# signal line is deasserted prior to the assertion of the FRAME# signal line, the PCI bus master loses PCI bus segment ownership and must re-arbitrate.

The central arbiter must determine whether the present PCI bus master will retain the PCI bus segment after the present bus transaction is completed, whether the PCI bus segment will be awarded to another PCI resource, whether the Lock master will be awarded complete bus lock, and where the PCI bus segment will be parked. See Chapter 4: *Functional Interaction between PCI and PCI-X Resources* and Chapter 6: *Detailed Bus Transaction Operation* for more Lock master information. See more information below regarding "parked".

The protocol for distinguishing the REQx# and GNTx# signal lines of different PCI bus masters is to append a letter in parentheses. Example REQ#(A) is the request signal line for the PCI bus master labeled *A*.

The REQx# signal lines are individually routed point-to-point between a PCI resource and the central arbiter. The assertion and deassertion of a REQx# signal line is synchronized to the CLK signal line, and must follow the setup and hold times outlined in Chapter 12: *Signal Line Timing and Electrical Requirements*. The same considerations apply to the GNTx# signal lines. The assertion and deassertion of the GNTx# signal lines will be outlined in the figures in this chapter because of their relationship to bus transaction operation.

The PCI local bus specification does not establish the exact protocol for the central arbiter to grant PCI bus segment ownership. It does require the central arbiter to support a fairness algorithm in order to establish a known PCI bus segment ownership latency for each PCI bus master. See Chapter 14: *Latency and Performance* for more information.

General arbitration protocol for personal computer-like buses (not simply specific to PCI bus segments) have been documented in other texts and specifications for other buses. In its simplest form, the central arbiter should grant PCI bus segment ownership on a rotating basis. For example, presume that the platform has three potential PCI bus masters (A, B, and C). The central arbiter will first grant the PCI bus segment ownership to (A) if it is requesting the PCI bus segment ownership. After (A) uses the PCI bus segment or if (A) had not requested the PCI bus segment, the central arbiter will grant it to (B). After (B) uses the PCI bus segment, or if (A) or (B) had not requested it, the central arbiter will grant it to (C). After the central arbiter has given each bus master the chance to own the PCI bus segment, the process begins again with (A).

Another simple arbitration protocol is for the PCI bus masters to be assigned a priority. Whenever two PCI bus masters simultaneously request the same PCI bus segment, the one with higher priority is granted the PCI bus segment. To prevent always granting it to the bus master with higher priority and starving the others, central arbiters that follow this protocol cannot again grant the bus to the highest priority PCI bus master until all others have been serviced, or a minimum amount of time has elapsed.

There are many other protocols that can be implemented; the important considerations are: to not starve any PCI bus master (excessively long latency), to establish a maximum time period from a PCI bus segment request to grant for a specific PCI bus master (latency guaranteed), and the granting of bus segment ownership to a specific PCI bus master (to support the previous two items) independent of other requests (fairness).

A central arbiter on a PCI bus segment must consider an additional item: If a low priority PCI bus master has locked a target that is also accessed by a high priority PCI bus master, accesses by the high priority PCI bus master will end with an excessive amount of Retry terminations. In order to improve platform performance, it is important to minimize Retry terminations.

A strict priority type of arbitration algorithm may lead to livelock conditions that will decrease performance. Other arbitration protocols may lead to deadlock conditions that are fatal to the system. See Chapter 2: *PCI System Architectural Overview* for more information.

The platform designer must select an algorithm that takes into consideration these lock situations.

PCI-X SPECIFIC

The PCI-X addendum specification requirements for arbitration are the same as discussed above regarding the PCI local bus specification.

9.1 PARKING

PCI SPECIFIC

A PCI bus segment has an attribute that is unique relative to other buses. Other buses traditionally have not considered the secondary affects of floating signal lines. For example, the protocol for an ISA bus segment traditionally lets the address signal lines float between bus transactions. Sometimes the address buffers have floated into unstable oscillations; consequently, some of the better ISA platforms have added pull-up resistors to the address signal lines. The PCI local bus specification took a very proactive approach to this situation. Between PCI bus transactions, the signal lines are either actively driven at all times by a single resource, are driven to a logical "1" by pull-up resistors on the platform, or are driven by a PCI bus master.

Chapter 6: *Detailed Bus Transaction Operation* explains the protocol for driving and tri-stating the signal lines during bus transactions. The information contained in the current section relates only to signal line protocol between the bus transactions.

In this section, the term "central resource" may be the central arbiter or any other platform resource. Typically, it is the central arbiter. For the purposes of this discussion, the central resource will have a virtual GNTx# signal line. That is, if a PCI bus master is not the Park master, the central resource is required to follow the same protocol as any PCI bus master for driving and tri-stating signal lines between bus transactions as the Park master.

Between bus transactions, the signal lines that are driven by a single resource or by pull-up resistors are not floating. The signal lines that can potentially float during the exchange of PCI bus segment ownership are AD[31::0], C/BE#[3::0], and PAR signal lines. To limit the amount of float time, the PCI bus master completing a bus transaction drives these signal lines to a stable level.

At the completion of a bus transaction, the present PCI bus master will continue to drive the AD[31::0], C/BE#[3::0], FRAME#, IRDY#, and PAR signal lines if the associated GNTx# signal line is asserted. If the associated REQx# signal line is asserted, by definition the PCI bus master is between bus transactions. If the associated REQx# signal line is deasserted, by definition the PCI bus master is defined as the Park master (see Figure 9-1). If the central arbiter has deasserted all GNTx# signal lines, it is the responsibility of the central arbiter to act as a Park master. A Park master is simply any resource that is actively driving the AD[31::0], C/BE#[3::0], and PAR signal lines to a stable level between PCI bus transactions when all REQx# signal lines of the PCI bus segment are deasserted. The Park master will tri-state and rely on pull-up resistors to drive the FRAME# and IRDY# signal lines to logical "1". As shown in Figures 9-2-A to 9-2-C and 9-3, a Park master will immediately tri-state the aforementioned signal lines when the associated GNTx# signal line is deasserted.

A Park master is defined as only a 32 data bit resource; consequently, the signal lines associated with 64 data bits (AD[63::32], C/BE#[7::4], REQ64#, ACK64#, and PAR64 signal lines) are not driven by the Park master. These signal lines are driven to a logical "1" level by pull-up resistors when the PCI bus segment is parked. The tri-stating and driving protocol of the 64 data bit signal lines AD[63::32], C/BE#[7::4], REQ64#, ACK64#, and PAR64 signal lines is the same as the AD[31::0], C/BE#[3::0], FRAME#, DEVSEL#, and PAR signal lines, respectively.

A PCI resource must not request to become Park master by asserting its REQx# signal line. When a PCI resource asserts its REQx# signal line, it must have the intention to begin a bus transaction once OWNERSHIP ACHIEVED has occurred.

When the central arbiter parks the PCI bus segment at a PCI bus master or central resource, either must drive the AD[31::0] and C/BE#[3::0] signal lines to a stable level within eight (inclusively; two to three is recommended) CLK signal line periods after the GNTx# signal line is asserted. The PCI bus master or central resource must drive the PAR signal line to a stable level within nine (inclusively; three to four is recommended) CLK signal line periods after the GNTx# signal line is asserted.

The central arbiter can assume the PCI bus master is broken if the REQx# signal line is not deasserted or the FRAME# signal line is not asserted by the ninth CLK line signal period after the associated GNTx# signal line was asserted (and remained asserted). If the PCI bus master is assumed broken, the central arbiter is not required to grant bus segment ownership to that PCI bus master again.

The central arbiter should typically park the bus segment with the present PCI bus master. This allows the present PCI bus master to continue with additional bus transactions without arbitration when no other PCI bus resource is requesting PCI bus segment ownership.

PCI-X SPECIFIC

The bus segment parking requirements according to the PCI-X addendum specification are the same as in the PCI local bus specification, with the following differences:

- When the central arbiter parks the PCI-X bus segment at a PCI-X bus master or central resource, either is required to drive the AD[31::0] and C/BE#[3::0] signal lines to a stable level within six (inclusively) CLK signal line periods after the GNTx# signal line is asserted. The PCI-X bus master or central resource is required to drive the PAR signal line to a stable level within seven (inclusively) CLK signal line periods after the GNTx# signal line is asserted.

The central arbiter can assume the PCI-X bus master is broken if the REQx# signal line is not deasserted or the FRAME# signal line is not asserted by the seventh CLK line signal period after the associated GNTx# signal line was asserted (and remained asserted). If the PCI-X bus master is assumed broken, the central arbiter is not required to grant bus segment ownership to that PCI-X bus master again.

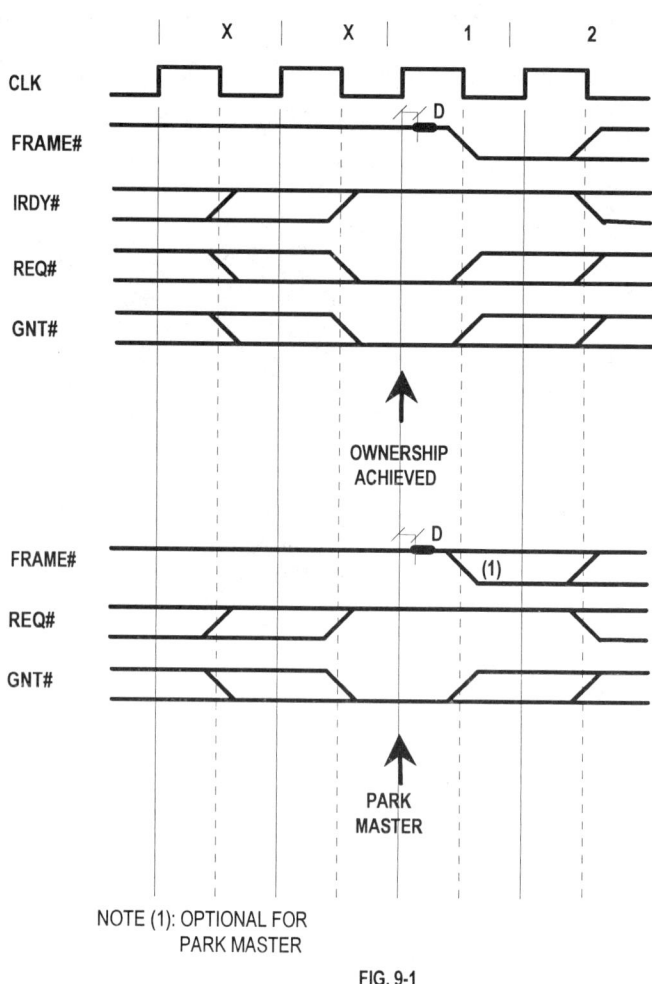

NOTE (1): OPTIONAL FOR
PARK MASTER

FIG. 9-1

Figure 9-1: PCI Bus Segment Ownership

9.2   CHANGE OF BUS SEGMENT OWNERSHIP

PCI SPECIFIC

REQUEST FOR BUS SEGMENT OWNERSHIP

There are two methods by which a PCI bus master can request a PCI bus segment ownership. One method is for a PCI bus master to assert the associated REQx# signal line and wait until the associated GNTx# signal line is asserted to become the next PCI bus master (new PCI Bus Master). The central arbiter must decide which PCI resource becomes the next PCI bus master. The second method is for the PCI bus master that has been parked (Park master) to simply begin the bus cycle. These two methods are outlined in the subsequent text.

Prior to the discussion of the new PCI Bus Master and Park master, other considerations about PCI bus segment ownership must be reviewed. A PCI resource is considered a PCI bus master between bus transactions when the FRAME# and IRDY# signal lines are both deasserted, and has its associated REQx# and GNTx# signal lines asserted. When the central arbiter wants to award the PCI bus segment ownership to another PCI resource, it must deassert the GNTx# signal line of the present PCI bus master (if the Park master is not a central resource). If the PCI bus master has already asserted the FRAME# and is executing a bus transaction when its associated GNTx# signal line is deasserted, the protocol outlined for a Completion with Timeout termination applies (see Chapter 8: *Master and Target Termination*, for more information). If the PCI bus master is between bus transactions (IDLE PHASES) when the GNTx# signal line is deasserted, the protocol outlined in Figure 9-3 for a Park master applies. The only difference is that some of the signal lines must be tri-stated by the PCI bus master when the associated GNTx# signal line is deasserted. The FRAME# and IRDY# signal lines must be tri-stated by the PCI bus master; for a Park master, these signal lines are already tri-stated and are driven to logical "1" by pull-up resistors. Also, for a 64 data bit PCI bus master, the REQ64#, AD[63::32], C/BE#[7::4], and PAR64 signal lines must be tri-stated; for a Park master, these signal lines are already tri-stated and are driven to logical "1" by pull-up resistors.

Any PCI bus master can assert its REQx# signal line whenever it wishes to own the PCI bus segment. It is the responsibility of the central arbiter to determine which PCI bus master is awarded the bus. Once the REQx# signal line is asserted, it can be deasserted at any time. When the REQx# and GNTx# signal lines are both asserted, and FRAME# and IRDY# signal lines are both deasserted (OWNERSHIP ACHIEVED), the new PCI bus master can begin the bus transaction with the assertion of the FRAME# signal line (see Figure 9-1). After OWNERSHIP ACHIEVED has occurred, the GNTx# and REQx# signal lines can be deasserted simultaneously with the assertion of the FRAME# signal line. The bus transaction completes according to the Completion with Timeout termination protocol if the GNTx# signal line is deasserted during the bus transaction. After completion of the bus transaction, the continued assertion of the GNTx# and REQx# signal lines allows the PCI bus master to execute an additional bus transaction. After the completion of a bus transaction, the continued assertion of the GNTx# signal line and deassertion of the REQx# signal line (during the bus transaction) simply turns the PCI bus master into a Park master.

> The discussion in this section uses a Completion with Timeout termination to illustrate the principle that a minimum amount time of PCI bus segment ownership is provided to the PCI bus master. It should be obvious that for those bus transactions that do not implement a Completion with Timeout or are terminated by other bus transaction terminations, a Completion with Timeout will not occur, It does not change the concept of the protocol of PCI bus segment ownership that is being discussed.

> The determination of which PCI resource becomes PCI bus master or Park master is determined entirely by the central arbiter. The PCI local bus specification does not specify a protocol for the central arbiter to award the PCI bus segment ownership.

> The deassertion of the REQx# signal line does not require the associated GNTx# signal line to be deasserted.

The PCI bus master can assert and deassert the REQx# signal line at any time. The only situation where an REQx# signal line is required to be deasserted is when a PCI bus master's transaction is terminated with a Retry, Disconnect, or Target Abort termination. These bus transaction terminations are all partly identified by the assertion of the STOP# signal line. The execution of one these bus transaction terminations requires that the associated REQx# signal line be deasserted, as outlined in the following section.

> There is one exception to the protocol outlined in the above paragraph. The deassertion of the REQx# signal line is not required (but is permitted) for a Disconnect with data termination if the FRAME# signal line is deasserted and the IRDY# signal line is asserted when the termination is requested (Figure 9-2-A). See Chapter 8: *Master and Target Termination* for more information.

The central arbiter does not monitor the PCI bus segment signal lines other than the REQx#, FRAME#, and IRDY# signal lines. There is no method for the central arbiter to determine that one of these terminations has been executed. In order to prevent a PCI bus master from continuing to access a target that caused the termination and provide PCI bus segment ownership to other PCI bus masters, the PCI bus segment ownership must be granted to another PCI bus master that has requested the PCI bus segment. In order to grant the PCI bus segment to another PCI bus master, the present PCI bus master must relinquish the PCI bus segment. As shown in Figures 9-2-A to 9-2-C, the REQ#(A) signal line is immediately deasserted when the STOP# signal line is sampled asserted and the central arbiter responds with the deassertion of the GNT#(A) signal line. The three versions of Figure 9-2 show the completion of the bus transaction with the STOP# signal line asserted relative to the value of the FRAME# and IRDY# signal lines. Also, note that the three versions use the Disconnect with data termination as the example. As explained later, when IDLE ACHIEVED occurs prior to or simultaneously with the deassertion of the GNT#(A) signal line, the GNT#(B) signal line cannot be asserted until one CLK signal line period later (see Figures 9-2-A and 9-2-B). Also, as explained later, when IDLE ACHIEVED occurs after the deassertion of the GNT#(A) signal line, the GNT#(B) signal line can be simultaneously asserted (see Figure 9-2-C). The protocol (Figures 9-2-A to 9-2-C) for the REQx# signal lines when a Retry, Disconnect or Target Abort Termination occurs is summarized as follows:

- REQx# signal line is asserted immediately when the STOP# signal line is sampled asserted.

- REQ# (A) signal line must remain deasserted for a minimum of two CLK signal line periods. If IDLE ACHIEVED has not occurred within the two CLK signal line periods, then the REQx# signal remains deasserted until IDLE Achieved has occurred (see Figure 9-2-C).

- PCI bus master (A) can reassert REQ# (A) after the conditions in the above bullet have been met as noted by Point A (Circle A in Figures 9-2-A to 9-2-C).

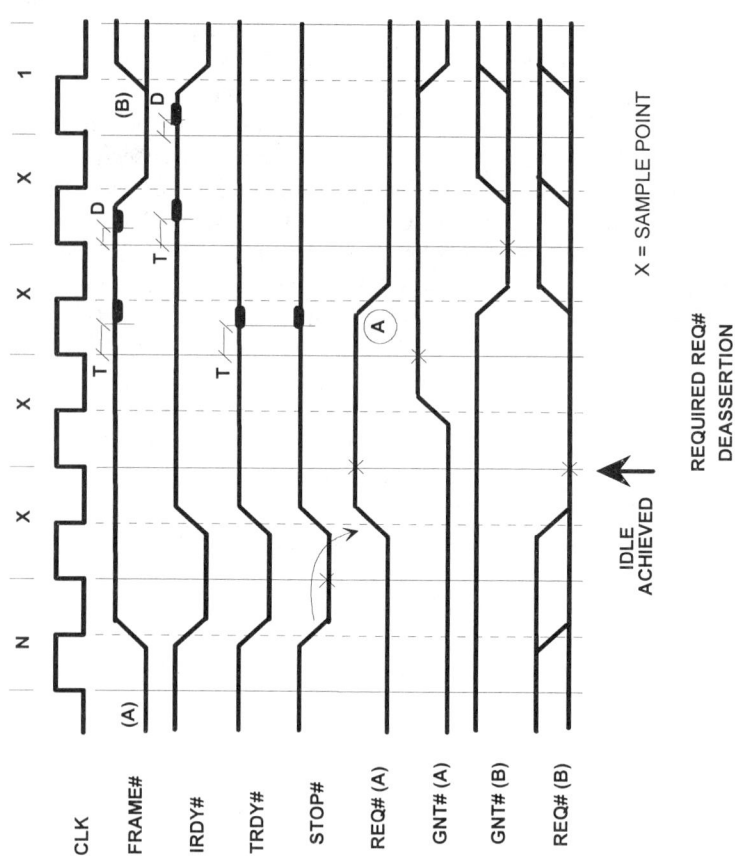

Figure 9-2-A: Not Required (but Permitted) REQx# Deassertion

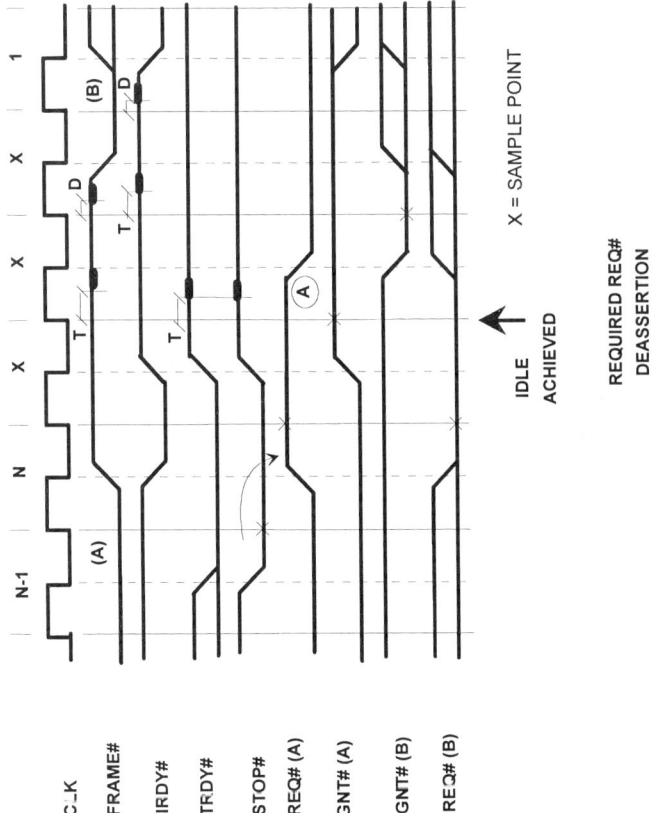

Figure 9-2-B: Required REQx# Signal Line Deassertion

NEW PCI MASTER

GRANT OF PCI BUS SEGMENT OWNERSHIP

Once the central arbiter has determined that another PCI resource will be awarded PCI bus segment ownership, the termination of the present PCI bus segment ownership must be accomplished. When the present PCI bus master is the Park master that is not executing a bus transaction, termination of PCI bus segment ownership is immediate. The GNTx# signal line for the Park master is deasserted and the GNTx# signal line for the new PCI bus segment owner is asserted one CLK signal line period later. If the present PCI bus master is executing a bus transaction, the central arbiter requests it to relinquish PCI bus segment ownership at the end of the bus transaction by deasserting the associated GNTx# signal line.

759

The bus transaction completes with appropriate termination. See Chapter 8 *Master and Target Termination* for more information.

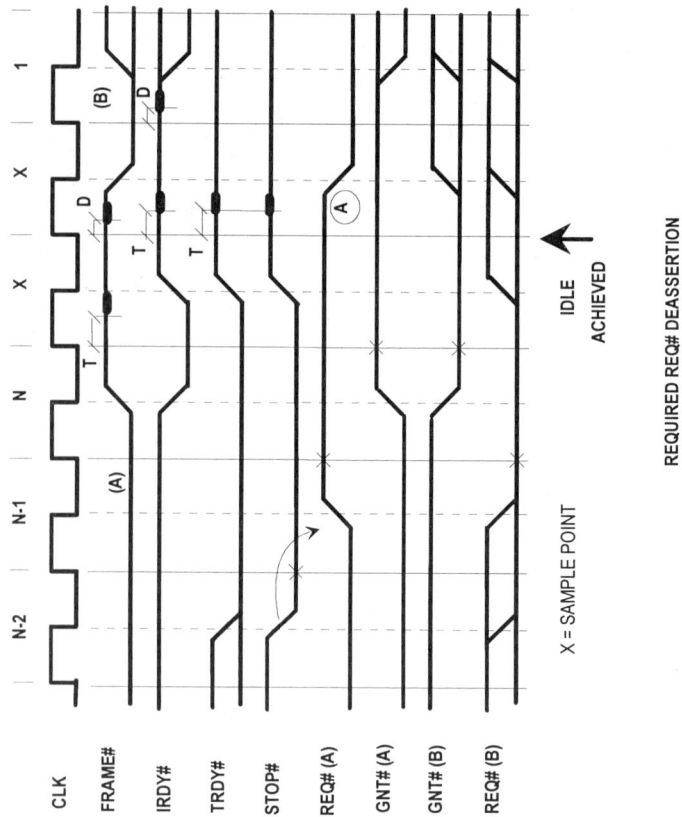

Figure 9-2-C: Required REQx# Deassertion

Figure 9-3 outlines how PCI bus master (B) exchanges PCI bus segment ownership with PCI bus master (A) (Park master) after IDLE ACHIEVED occurs (FRAME# and IRDY# signal lines both deasserted). To prevent signal line contention, the GNT# (A) signal line must be deasserted a minimum of one CLK signal line period prior to the assertion of the GNT# (B) signal line for the new PCI bus segment owner once IDLE is achieved. The deassertion of the GNT# (A) signal line forces the Park master to immediately tri-state the C/BE#[3::0], AD [31::0], and PAR signal lines. The assertion of the GNT# (B) signal line indicates to the PCI bus master (B) that it can begin a bus transaction.

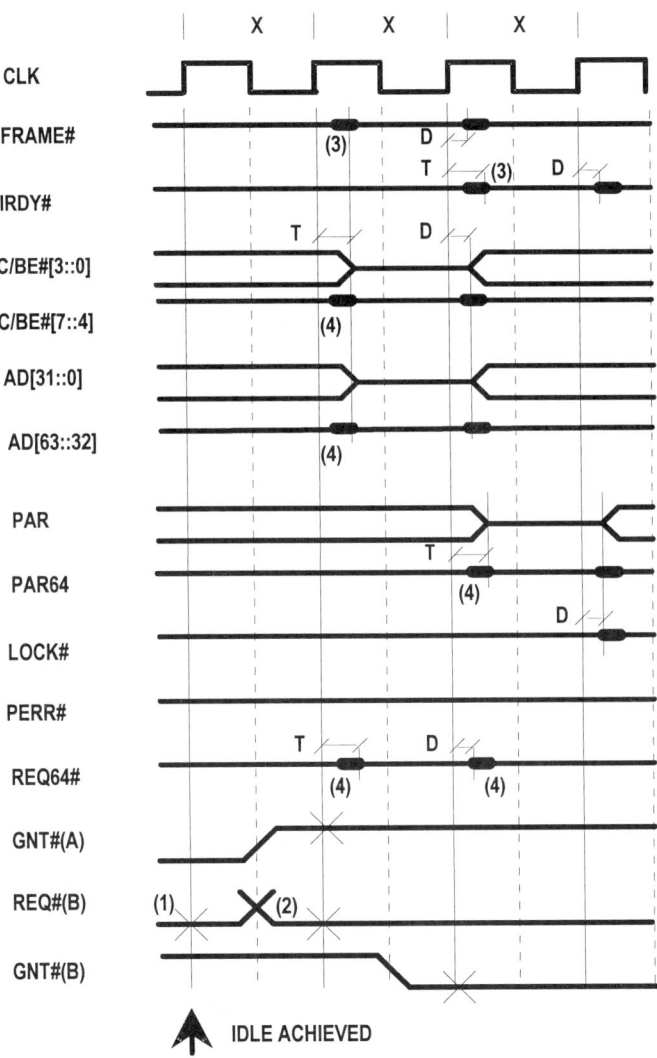

Figure 9-3: PCI Bus Segment Ownership Change

NOTES: (1) TYPICAL REQUEST
(2) COINCIDENTAL REQUEST
(3) IF NOT PARK MASTER, THEN NOT PREVIOUSLY DRIVEN
(4) OPTIONALLY 64 DATA BIT PCI BUS MASTERS CAN
PREVIOUSLY DRIVE THESE SIGNAL LINES

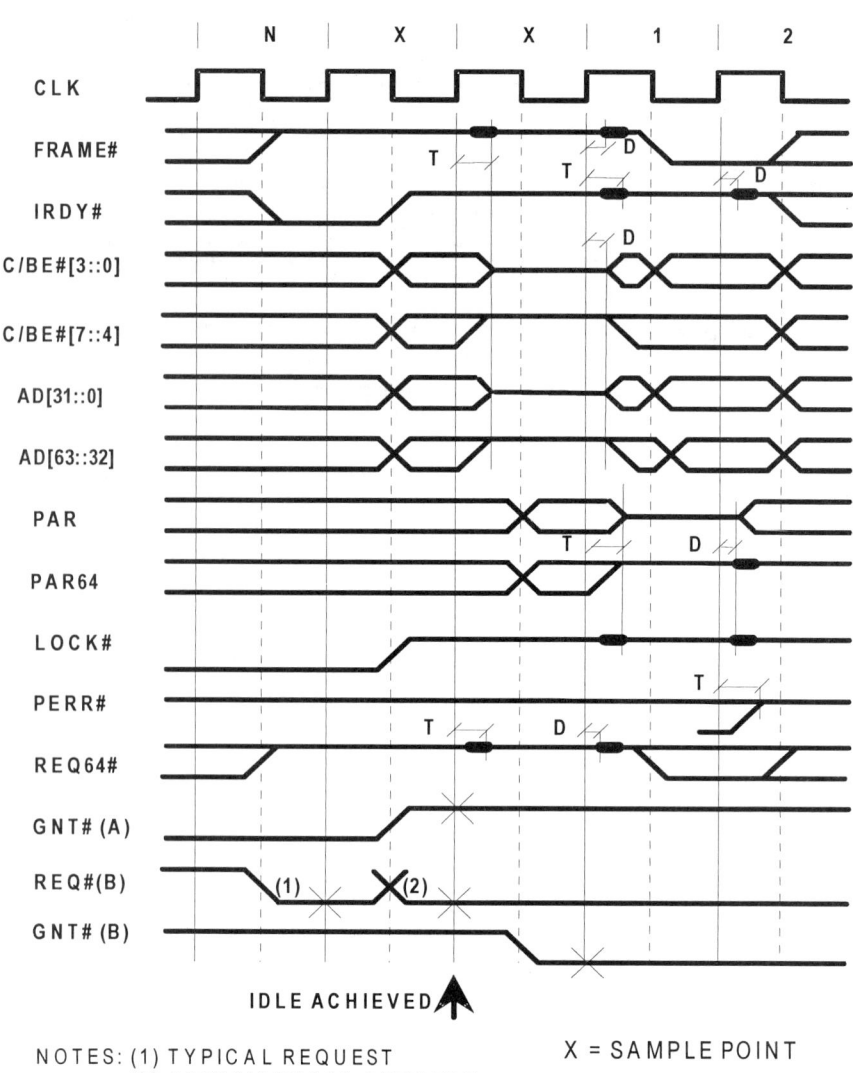

Figure 9-4: PCI Bus Segment Ownership Change, Previous Bus Transaction Was a Write

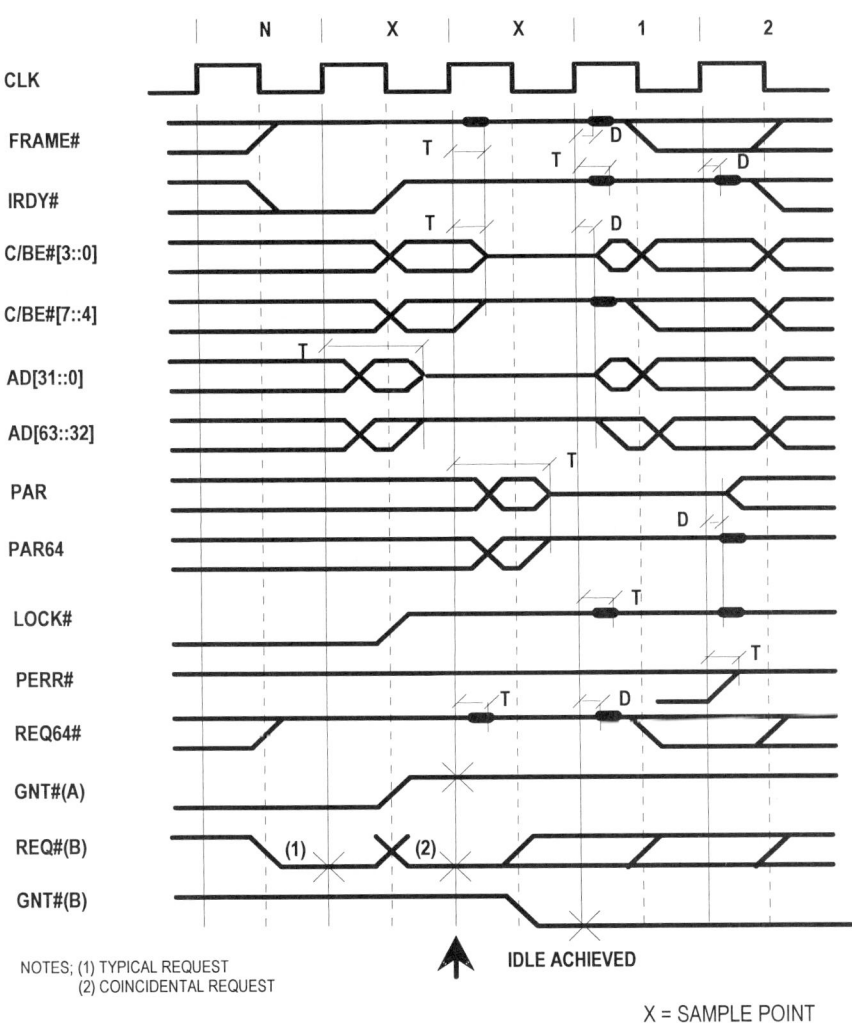

Figure 9-5: PCI Bus Segment Ownership Change, Previous Cycle Was a Read

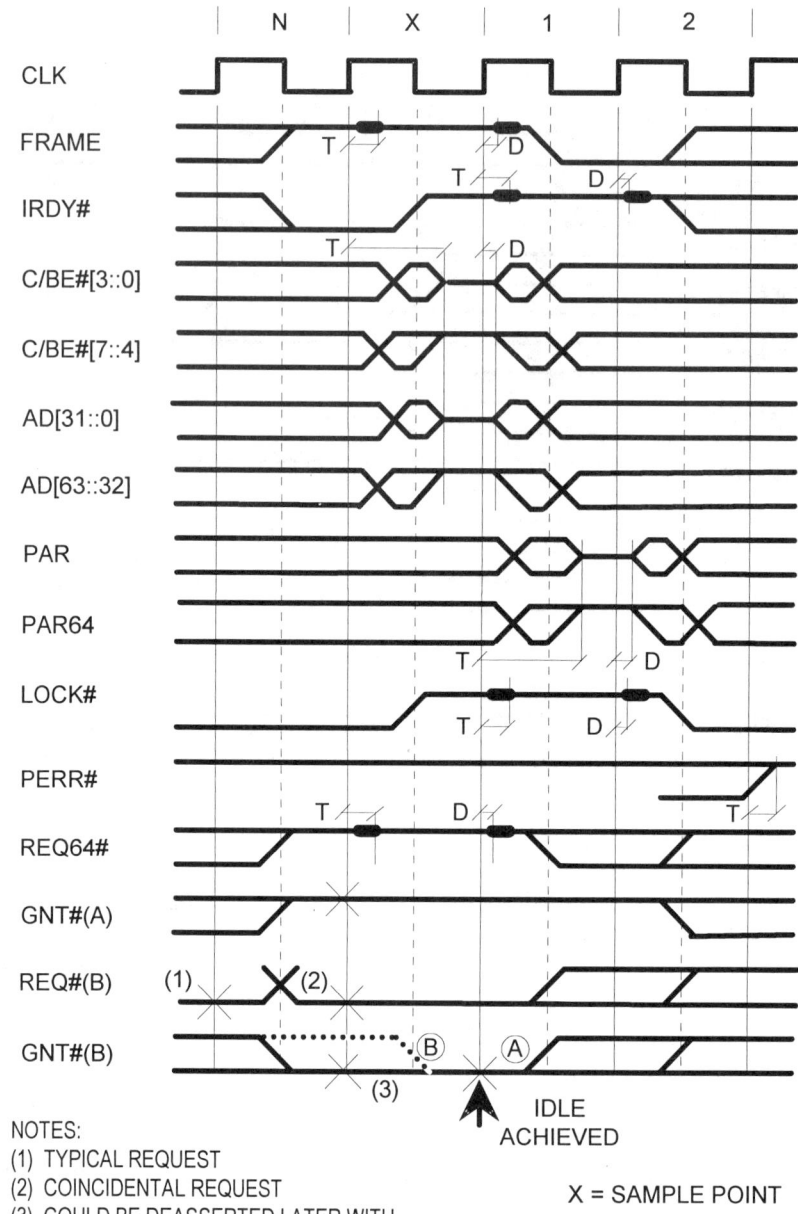

Figure 9-6: PCI Bus Segment Ownership Change, Previous Cycle Was a Write

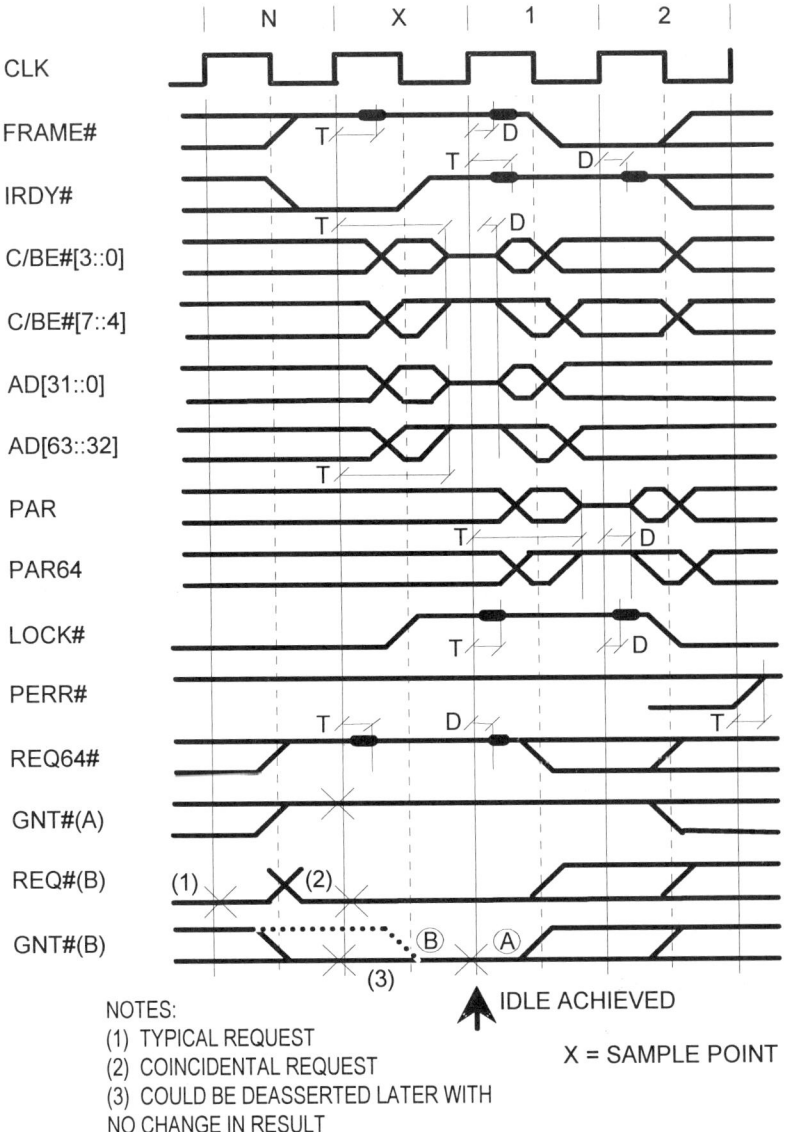

NOTES:
(1) TYPICAL REQUEST
(2) COINCIDENTAL REQUEST
(3) COULD BE DEASSERTED LATER WITH
NO CHANGE IN RESULT

IDLE ACHIEVED

X = SAMPLE POINT

Figure 9-7: PCI Bus Segment Ownership Change, Previous Cycle Was a Read

The PCI bus master (B) is not required to immediately drive the C/BE#[3::0], AD[31::0], and PAR signal lines as outlined above, although PCI bus master (A) immediately tri-states them. PCI bus master (B) must assert the FRAME# signal line by the sixteenth CLK signal line rising edge after OWNERSHIP ACHIEVED (the appropriate REQx# and GNTx# signal lines both asserted) has occurred. See further information at the end of this section.

When the PCI bus segment is parked at a 32 data bit Park master, the AD[63::32], C/BE#[7::4], and PAR64 signal lines are driven to a logical "1" by pull-up resistors. Similarly, when the PCI bus segment is awarded to a new 32 data bit PCI bus master (PCI bus master (B) in this example), these signal lines remain at logical "1" by pull-up resistors. If the PCI bus segment is awarded to a 64 data bit PCI bus master, these signal lines could optionally be driven to a logical "1" by the PCI bus master (B) as outlined in Figure 9-3.

The protocol outlined above for Figure 9-3 also applies when the central arbiter is simply changing the Park master from PCI bus master (A) to PCI bus master (B).

Figures 9-4 to 9-7 outline how PCI bus master (B) changes PCI bus segment ownership with PCI bus master (A) immediately after PCI bus master (A) has completed a bus transaction. The protocol for signal line tri-stating and driving relative to the GNTx# signal lines is the same as discussed for Figure 9-3. The distinction between Figures 9-4 and 9-5 and Figures 9-6 and 9-7 is the staggering of the deassertion and assertion of the GNT# (A) and GNT# (B) signal lines, respectively.

In Figures 9-4 and 9-5, PCI bus segment ownership is removed (GNT# (A) signal line is deasserted) simultaneously when IDLE ACHIEVED has occurred (FRAME# and IRDY# signal lines both deasserted). To prevent signal line contention, the PCI local bus protocol requires the central arbiter to insert one CLK signal line period between the deassertion and assertion of the GNT# (A) and GNT# (B) signal lines, respectively. When the previous bus transaction is a write, the target tri-states the PERR# signal line indicating the completion of the bus transaction; the line is not driven by PCI bus master (A) (see Figure 9-4). When the previous bus cycle is a read, the target will tri-state the AD, PAR, and PAR64 signal lines indicating the completion of the access cycle; the lines are not driven by PCI bus master (A) reflective of the change of PCI bus segment ownership (see Figure 9-5). In both cases, the driving of the PERR# signal line by PCI bus master (B) or the target is reflective of the forthcoming bus transaction and not the change of PCI bus segment ownership. The protocol for asserting the GNT# (B) signal line is the same if IDLE ACHIEVED (FRAME# and IRDY# signal lines deasserted) occurred prior to the deassertion of the GNT# (A) signal line.

In Figures 9-6 and 9-7, PCI bus segment ownership is removed (GNT#(A) signal line is deasserted) prior to IDLE ACHIEVED (FRAME# and IRDY# signal lines deasserted) occurring. In the situations outlined in Figures 9-4 to 9-5, the PCI bus master determines when to tri-state and drive the signal lines relative to IDLE ACHIEVED occurring and the value of the GNTx# signal lines. The PCI bus master that is relinquishing PCI bus segment ownership tri-states the signal lines when the associated GNTx# signal line is deasserted and IDLE ACHIEVED has occurred. The PCI bus master that will become the new PCI bus segment owner begins driving the signal lines when IDLE ACHIEVED occurs and the associated GNTx# signal line is asserted. Figures 9-6 and 9-7 outline situations when prior to IDLE ACHIEVED occurring the GNT#(A) and GNT#(B) signal lines are deasserted and asserted, respectively. PCI bus master (A) will implement a different protocol than in the situations outlined in Figures 9-4 to 9-5. The deassertion of the GNT#(A) prior to IDLE ACHIEVED occurring allows PCI bus master (A) to anticipate tri-stating the signal lines relative to the completion of the bus transaction. At the completion of the bus transaction, PCI bus master (A) can begin tri-stating the signal lines a CLK signal line period earlier than in Figures 9-4 to 9-5. The central arbiter is aware that it deasserted GNT#(A) prior to IDLE ACHIEVED occurring; consequently, it will assert the GNT#(B) signal line prior to IDLE ACHIEVED occurring. The net result is that a one CLK signal line period between the deassertion of the GNT#(A) signal line and the assertion of the GNT# (B) signal line is not required; consequently, the change of PCI bus segment ownership is quicker.

Figures 9-6 and 9-7 show a couple of important protocols relative to the GNTx# signal line. First, when the GNTx# signal line is deasserted prior to IDLE ACHIEVED (FRAME# and IRDY# signal lines deasserted) occurring (GNT# (A) in this example) the GNTx# signal line can be asserted (GNT# (B) in this example) immediately or at Point B (Circle B in Figures 9-6 and 9-7. The resulting bus transaction is the same for either point where the GNT# (B) signal line is asserted. Second, when the central arbiter has granted the PCI bus segment to a PCI resource, it does not know whether the PCI resource had begun a bus transaction until the FRAME# signal line is asserted. In Figures 9-6 and 9-7, the PCI resource samples the GNT# (B) signal line asserted at Point A (Circle A) and IDLE ACHIEVED (FRAME# and IRDY# signal lines) occurred; subsequently, it becomes PCI bus master (B) by asserting the FRAME# signal line. The central arbiter can deassert the GNTx# signal line at any time at Point A (Circle A in Figures 9-6 and 9-7). If the central arbiter deasserts a GNTx# signal line when the PCI bus segment is in an IDLE PHASE, it must wait one CLK signal line period before asserting another GNTx# signal line for another PCI bus master in case the FRAME# signal line is asserted. If the FRAME# signal line is asserted, the

GNTx# signal line cannot grant the PCI bus segment to another PCI bus master on that PCI bus segment.

> The new PCI bus master does not have to begin driving the signal lines or the bus transaction (FRAME# signal line asserted) immediately after OWNERSHIP ACHIEVED has occurred. The PCI bus master must drive the signal lines by the sixteenth CLK signal rising edge after OWNERSHIP ACHIEVED (the appropriate REQx# and GNTx# signal lines are asserted) occurred. Otherwise, the central arbiter may declare the PCI bus master "dead" and never grant it the PCI bus segment again. Prior to the assertion of the FRAME# signal line, the output buffers of the PCI bus master can be enabled simultaneously or in a sequential fashion using ADDRESS/DATA STEPPING or pre-driving.

> When the central arbiter grants the PCI bus segment to a new PCI bus master that requested it, the latter must drive the AD[31::0] and C/BE#[3::0] signal lines to a stable level within eight (two to three is recommended) CLK signal line periods after the GNTx# signal line is asserted. The PCI bus master must drive the PAR signal line to a stable level within nine (three to four is recommended) CLK signal line periods after the GNTx# signal line is asserted.
>
> Prior to the assertion of the FRAME# signal line, the output buffers of the PCI bus master can be enabled in a sequential fashion using ADDRESS/DATA STEPPING or PRE-DRIVING.

CONVERSION OF PARK MASTER TO NEW PCI BUS MASTER

When the Park master is not a central resource, the PCI bus master (that is Park master) at which the central arbiter has parked the PCI bus segment is not required to assert its REQx# signal line to execute a bus transaction. By definition, a Park master is a PCI resource with its REQx# and GNTx# signal lines deasserted and asserted, respectively. Once the Park master begins the bus transaction while its REQx# signal line is deasserted, it executes with the same protocol used by a PCI bus master. If, during the bus transaction its associated REQx# signal line is asserted, the Park master becomes a normal PCI bus master by definition.

> If the Park master is only executing one SINGLE or one BURST bus transaction, it should not assert the REQx# signal line.

A Park master begins its bus transaction when the associated GNTx# signal line is sampled asserted on the previous CLK signal line rising edge, prior to the rising edge to which the driving of the FRAME# signal line is referenced.

PCI-X SPECIFIC

REQUEST AND GRANT FOR PCI-X BUS SEGMENT OWNERSHIP, AND CONVERSION OF PARK MASTER TO NEW PCI-X BUS MASTER

Like the PCI local bus specification, the PCI-X addendum specification supports a PCI-X resource becoming bus master by requesting (REQx# signal line asserted) and being granted the ownership of the bus segment (GNTx# signal line asserted). If the PCI-X resource is the Park master, it simply begins the bus transition by asserting the FRAME# signal line like a PCI resource. The only major differences between the PCI local bus specification and the PCI-X addendum specification are as follows:

■ The REQx# and GNTx# signal lines are registered on the PCI–X bus segment. Consequently, there are more CLK signal line periods between the assertion and deassertion of the REQx#, GNTx#, and FRAME# signal lines.

■ The PCI-X bus master is not required to relinquish bus segment ownership when a Retry or Target Abort termination is requested. Also, The PCI local bus specification defines Disconnect termination as a condition to relinquish bus segment ownership; no such termination exists in the PCI-X addendum specification. Consequently, the boundary conditions discussed relative to Figures 9-2-A to 9-2-C do not apply for a PCI-X bus master.

■ Periodically, the GNTx# signal line is required to remain asserted for several CLK signal line periods to support configuration transactions.

Given the above differences, the protocol for requesting and granting of PCI-X bus segment ownership is as follows:

■ In anticipation that a PCI-X bus master is going to execute a configuration transaction, the arbiter must assert a GNTx# signal line for a minimum of five CLK signal line periods whenever the bus segment is in the IDLE PHASE (FRAME# and IRDY# signal lines both deasserted) and no REQx# signal lines are asserted. See Subchapter 6.12: *32 Data Bit PCI-X Bus Master to 32 Data Bit Target* for more information.

■ To grant the bus segment ownership and begin a bus transaction for a non-Park master, the protocol is as follows:

- A REQx# signal line can be asserted and deasserted on any CLK signal line period.

- A GNTx# signal line can be deasserted on any CLK signal line period.

- A GNTx# signal line can be asserted on any CLK signal line period if no other GNTx# signal line is asserted. If a GNTx# signal line is asserted it must be deasserted before another GNTx# signal line can be asserted (see the next bullet for minimum wait time).

- When a PCI-X bus master has asserted its REQx# signal line and the associated GNTx# signal line is sampled asserted (and remains asserted); the PCI-X bus master is required to do one of the folowing two sub-bullets. If one of the two sub-bullets does not occur, the central arbiter assumes that the PCI-X bus master is broken and keeps the associated GNTx# signal line deasserted.

  - The FRAME# signal line is driven such that it is sampled asserted prior to or on the seventh rising edge of the CLK signal line (maximum delta of six CLK signal line periods relative to the asserted associated GNTx# signal line).

    OR

  - The associated REQx# signal line is sampled deasserted prior to or on the seventh rising edge of the CLK signal line (maximum delta of six CLK signal line periods relative to the asserted associated GNTx# signal line).

- The arbiter must wait two CLK signal lines periods between the sampling of deassertion of one GNTx# signal line to the sampling of assertion of another GNTx# signal line (*i.e.*, one CLK signal line period between deassertion and assertion). For an example, see Circle A for the GNT# (A) and GNT# (B) signal lines in Figure 9-8. (Note: This requirement per the PCI-X addendum specification in conjunction with the shaded box below reduces the possible boundary conditions as discussed for Figures 9-3 to 9-7 per the PCI local bus specification.)

- A PCI-X bus master must assert the FRAME# signal line only when the associated GNTx# signal line is sampled asserted two CLK signal line periods before the FRAME# signal line is sampled asserted (*i.e.*, one CLK signal line period between assertion and assertion). This requirement is due to the fact that the GNTx# signal line is a registered input. For an example, see Circle B for GNT#(A) signal line to FRAME# signal line driven by PCI-X bus master (A) in Figure 9-8.

The PCI local bus specification permits the FRAME#, REQ64#, and IRDY# signal lines to be tri-stated one CLK signal line period after their deassertion or later if retention of bus segment ownership is anticipated. Figures 9-2 to 9-7 show the boundary conditions for tri-stating during bus segment ownership change.

The PCI-X addendum specification has placed more stringent requirements on the tri-stating of the aforementioned signal lines. The FRAME#, IRDY#, and REQ64# signal lines are required to be tri-stated one CLK signal line period after their deassertion with one exception: The FRAME# and REQ64# signal lines can be tri-stated either one or two CLK signal line periods after their deassertion when the previous bus transaction has three or more microaccesses. There is no anticipation of retaining bus segment ownership. The TRDY#, STOP#, LOCK#, DEVSEL#, PERR#, and ACK64# signal lines must be tri-stated one CLK signal line period after the last microaccess. The PERR# signal line follows this protocol with a delay of two CLK signal line periods.

See Chapter 6: *Detailed Bus Transaction Operation* for more information.

Note: In Figure 9-8, when the FRAME# signal line is driven by PCI-X bus master (A), it is labeled "FRAME# (A)". Similarly, to represent when the FRAME# signal line is driven by PCI-X bus master (B), it is labeled "FRAME# (B)". There is only one FRAME# signal line on each bus segment.

- Given the above two bullets, the assertion of the FRAME# (A) signal line by PCI-X bus master (A) will be simultaneous with the assertion of GNT# (B) signal line. Consequently, PCI-X bus master (B) can simultaneously sample both the FRAME# (A) and GNT# (B) signal lines (rising edge of CLK signal line period N+2). This provides information to PCI-X bus master (B) that another bus master has begun a bus transaction; consequently, PCI bus master (B) is required to wait for the completion of the bus transaction by PCI-X bus master (A). See following bullet.

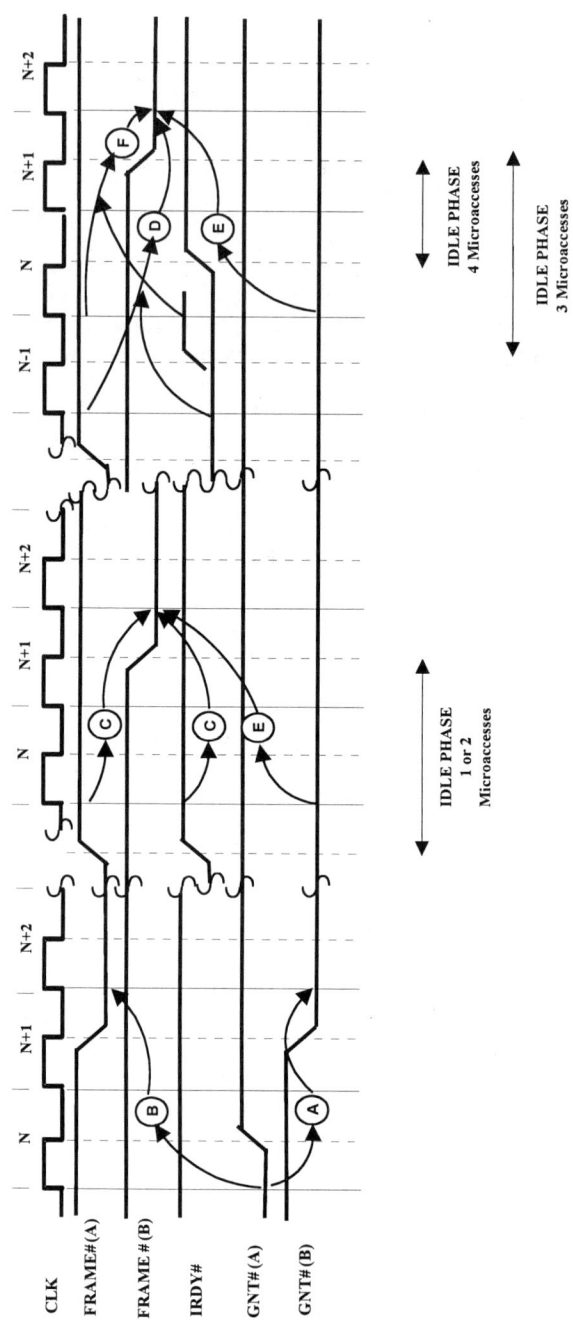

Figure 9-8: PCI-X Bus Segment Ownership Change

■ The completion of a bus transaction is identified by the deassertion of the FRAME# and IRDY# signal lines. A PCI-X bus master begins its bus transaction via FRAME# signal line sampled asserted one or two CLK signal line periods after the completion of the present bus transaction. The requirement that the associated GNTx# signal line is sampled asserted two CLK signal line periods prior to sampling asserted the FRAME# signal line (*i.e.*, one CLK signal line period between assertion and assertion) (Circle E in Figure 9-8) remains. The need for the aforementioned one or two CLK signal line periods between bus transactions is due to the following requirements:

■ As discussed in Chapter 6: *Details of Bus Transaction Operation,* one, two, and three microaccess bus transactions, special transactions, and bus transactions terminated by Master Abort termination will be completed with the simultaneous deassertion of the FRAME# and IRDY# signal lines. As shown in Figure 9-8, the FRAME# (B) signal line is sampled asserted two CLK signal line periods after the end of the PCI-X bus master (A)'s bus transaction (Circles C and F in Figure 9-8). Circle C is one or tow microaccesses, special transactions, and bus transactions terminated by Master Abort terminations, and Circle F is for three microaccesses. This results in an IDLE PHASE of two CLK signal periods in length.

■ As discussed in Chapter 6: *Details of Bus Transaction Operation,* bus transactions of four or more microaccesses will be completed with the first sampling (CLK signal line rising edge of N-1) of a deasserted FRAME# signal line with an asserted IRDY# signal line (Circle D in Figure 9-8). As shown in Figure 9-8, the FRAME# (B) signal line is asserted one CLK signal line period after the end of the PCI-X bus master (A) bus transaction. This results in an IDLE PHASE one CLK signal period in length.

> The assertion of the FRAME# signal line by the new bus segment owner relative to the completion of the bus transaction by the previous bus segment owner (Circles C, D, and F in Figure 9-8) as shown in Figure 9-8 is shown as a minimum. However, the ability to assert the FRAME# signal line requires the new bus segment master to check that the associated GNTx# signal line is sampled asserted two CLK signal line periods before the FRAME# signal line is sampled asserted (*i.e.*, one CLK signal line period between assertions) (Circle E in Figure 9-8).

CONVERSION OF PARK MASTER TO NEW PCI-X BUS MASTER

When the Park master is not a central resource, the PCI-X bus master (that is Park master) at which the central arbiter has parked the PCI-X bus segment is not required to assert its REQx# signal line to execute a bus transaction. By definition, a Park master is a PCI-X resource with its REQx# and GNTx# signal lines deasserted and asserted, respectively. Once the Park master begins the bus transaction while its REQx# signal line is deasserted, it executes with the same protocol used by any PCI-X bus master. If, during the bus transaction its associated REQx# signal line is asserted, the Park master becomes a "normal" PCI-X bus master by definition.

If the Park master is only executing one SINGLE or one BURST bus transaction, it should not assert the REQx# signal line.

A Park master begins its bus transaction when the associated GNTx# signal line is sampled asserted two CLK signal line periods prior to sampling asserted the FRAME# signal line (Circle E in Figure 9-8).

CHAPTER 10

PARITY AND BUS ERRORS

This chapter consists of the following subchapters:

10.0 INTRODUCTION

The PCI local bus specification supports a limited error reproting protocol. The C/BE# and AD signal lines are protected with even parity by the PAR and PAR64 signal lines. The PERR# and SERR# signal lines are used to report parity and other errors within a system. The level of support of these error signal lines by various PCI resources varies widely. Error information is reported in registers in the configuration address space that can be read by the BIOS, the operating system, and application software.

The PCI-X addendum specification supports essentially the same error reporting protocol as defined by the PCI local bus specification. The major difference is the expansion of support for split completion transactions, and will be discussed in greater detail later.

10.1 PCI PAR AND PAR64 SIGNAL LINES OPERATION IN BUS TRANSACTIONS

INTRODUCTION

Parity is used on all bus transactions and protects the integrity of the AD and C/BE# signal lines. The generation of parity is not optional and must be computed and driven onto the PAR and PAR64 signal lines by all PCI resources. Similarly, for 64 data bit resources, the generation of parity is not optional and must be computed and driven onto the PAR64 signal line (according to the assertion of the REQ64# and ACK64# signal lines).

However, the parity does not have to be checked by all PCI segment bus resources. The PCI bus segment resources that do not check and report parity errors must meet one of the following conditions:

- ■ Resources that are only used on the platform and not add-in cards.

- ■ Resources that do not affect or process permanent data, *e.g.*, video display. In other words, resources that will not cause a loss of platform integrity when a parity error occurs do not need to support parity checking.

The operation of the PAR signal line during bus transactions is identical to the operation of the AD[31::0] signal lines except for a one CLK signal line period delay. The operation of the PAR64 signal line during bus transactions is identical to the operation of the AD[63::32] signal lines except for a one CLK signal line period delay.

Address parity error includes error in the address and COMMAND type. Data parity error includes the data and byte enables.

In the following discussions, the operation of the PAR and PAR64 signal lines are referenced to the ADDRESS and DATA PHASES. As previously mentioned, there is a one CLK signal line period delay of these signal lines relative to the AD signal lines. The AD signal lines are aligned with the ADDRESS and DATA PHASES; consequently, the use of these PHASES to define the PAR and PAR64 signal lines actually refer to the time line of the associated AD signal lines

PAR AND PAR64 SIGNAL LINES OPERATION IN MEMORY, I/O, AND CONFIGURATION TRANSACTIONS

The PAR and PAR64 signal lines are driven by both the PCI bus master and the target. The C/BE#[3::0] and AD[31::0] signal lines are protected with even parity by the PAR signal line. Similarly, the C/BE#[7::4] and AD[63::32] signal lines are protected with even parity by the PAR64 signal line.

The existence of valid parity information on the PAR and PAR64 signal lines is dependent on the type of memory, I/O, or configuration transaction (read versus write) and the data size of the PCI bus master and target.

The balance of this section will refer to memory, I/O, and configuration transactions collectively as "bus transactions", "write transactions", or "read transactions".

The generation and checking of the parity does not happen continuously throughout the bus transaction. The protocol for PCI bus transactions is as follows:

- For write transactions the parity is generated:

- Throughout the entire bus transaction, the parity of the AD and C/BE# signal lines in CLK signal line period N is driven onto the PAR and PAR64 (when applicable) signal lines on CLK signal line period N+1.

- For write transactions, the parity is checked (optionally):

- In the entire ADDRESS PHASE, the parity is checked for the AD and C/BE# signal lines in CLK signal line period N, and PAR and PAR64 (when applicable) signal lines on CLK signal line period N+1.

- In the DATA PHASE, when the DEVSEL# single line is asserted, the parity is checked for the AD and C/BE# signal lines in CLK signal line period N (when DEVSEL# signal line asserted in period N), and PAR and PAR64 (when applicable) signal lines on CLK signal line period N+1.

- For read transactions parity is generated:

- Throughout the entire ADDRESS PHASE of the bus transaction, the parity of the AD and C/BE# signal lines in CLK signal line period N is driven onto the PAR and PAR64 (when applicable) signal lines on CLK signal line period N+1.

- Throughout the DATA PHASE, only when the DEVSEL# signal line is asserted (except for when the AD signal lines ownership changes at the beginning of the DATA PHASE), the parity of the AD and C/BE# signal

777

lines in CLK signal line period N is driven onto the PAR and PAR64 (when applicable) signal lines on CLK signal line period N+1.

■ For read transactions, the parity is checked (optionally):

■ In the entire ADDRESS PHASE, the parity is checked for the AD and C/BE# signal lines in CLK signal line period N, and PAR and PAR64 (when applicable) signal lines on CLK signal line period N+1.

■ In the DATA PHASE, when the DEVSEL# single line is asserted, the parity is checked for the AD and C/BE# signal lines in CLK signal line period N (when DEVSEL# signal line asserted in period N), and PAR and PAR64 (when applicable) signal lines on CLK signal line period N+1.

Also, in the following discussion it is assumed that the PCI resources are used only on the system, or do not affect or process permanent data; thus, checking for parity errors is "optional". As stated above, PCI resources that are used on an add-in card or affect or process permanent data are required to check for parity errors

---

32 DATA BIT PCI BUS MASTER AND TARGET (REQ64# SIGNAL LINE = DEASSERTED)

■ During the ADDRESS PHASE, the PAR signal line contains valid parity information, and any PCI resource on the PCI bus segment optionally checks the parity. During the DATA PHASE of a write transaction, the PCI bus master drives valid parity onto the PAR signal line because the C/BE#[3::0] and AD[31::0] signal lines contain valid information (see Figures 10-1 and 10-2). The target optionally checks the parity. During the DATA PHASE of a read transaction, the PCI bus master drives the C/BE#[3::0] signal lines with byte enable information, and the target drives the AD[31::0] signal lines with valid data; consequently, it drives the PAR signal line with valid parity. The PCI bus master optionally checks parity (see Figures 10-3 and 10-4.).

During the DATA PHASE of a read transaction, the PCI bus master drives the byte enables onto the C/BE# [3::0] signal lines; consequently, the target generates parity for these signal lines, combines it with the parity of the AD[31::0] signal lines, and drives the PAR signal line.

■ The operation of the PAR signal line between bus transactions also follows the operation of the AD[31::0] signal lines. If the PCI bus master is retaining bus segment ownership (REG# and GNTx# both asserted) between bus transactions, it drives the PAR signal line to a stable level. If the PCI bus master does not retain bus segment ownership (REQx# and GNTx# both deasserted), the Park master drives the PAR signal line to a stable level.

■ The PAR signal line supports even parity. The total number of "1"s on the AD[31::0], C/BE#[3::0], and PAR signal lines must be an even number.

■ During the ADDRESS and DATA PHASES, the AD[31::0], C/BE#[3::0], and PAR signal lines must contain valid information or be driven to a stable level. During the DATA PHASE, the C/BE#[3::0] signal lines indicate which AD[31::0] signal lines contain valid information. Parity is computed on both types of signal lines; those that are stable, and those that contain valid information.

When the PCI bus master is requesting a 32 data bit access (REQ64# is deasserted), the AD[63::32], C/BE#[7::4], and PAR64 signal lines are driven to a logical "1" by pull-up resistors. The PAR64 signal line does not contain valid parity information. This is independent of the execution of DUAL ADDRESS (see Figures 10-5-A to 10-5-B).

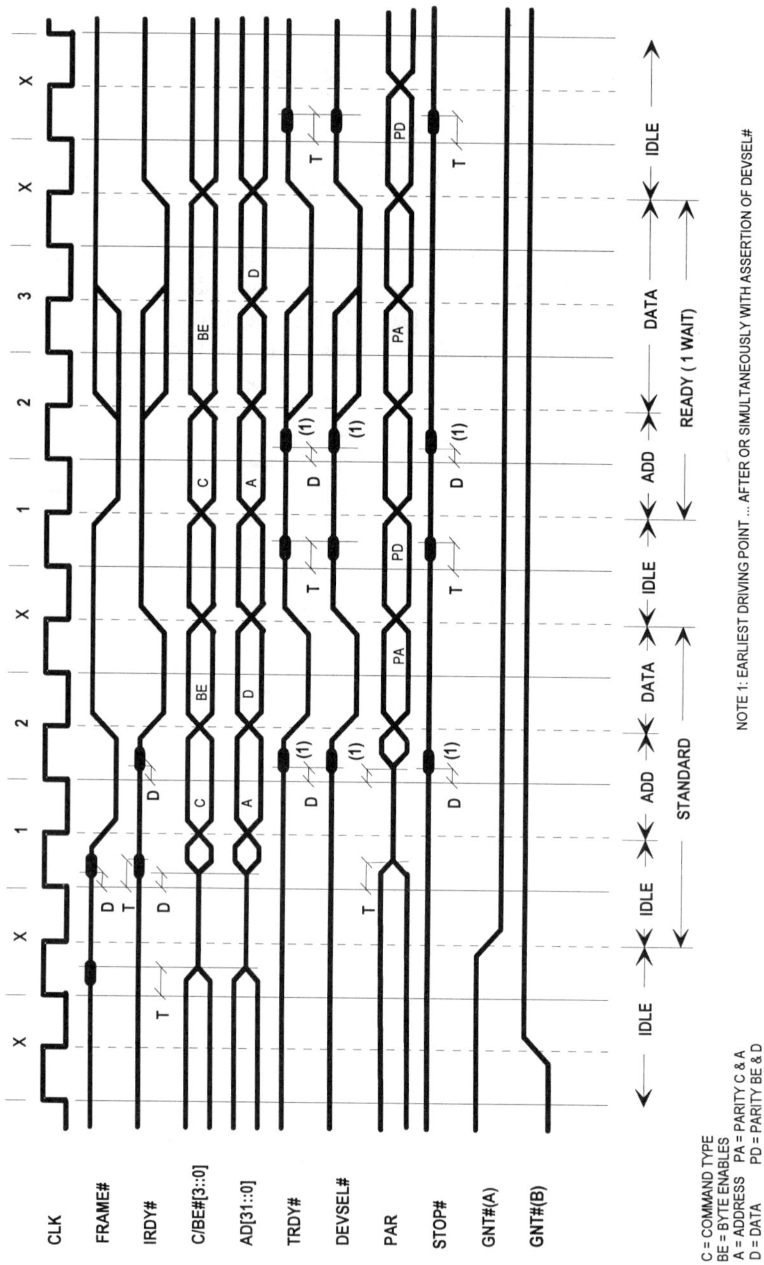

Figure 10-1: PCI Single Write Transaction without DUAL ADDRESS Parked at (A), Executed and Retained by (B), Non-Fast Back-to-Back

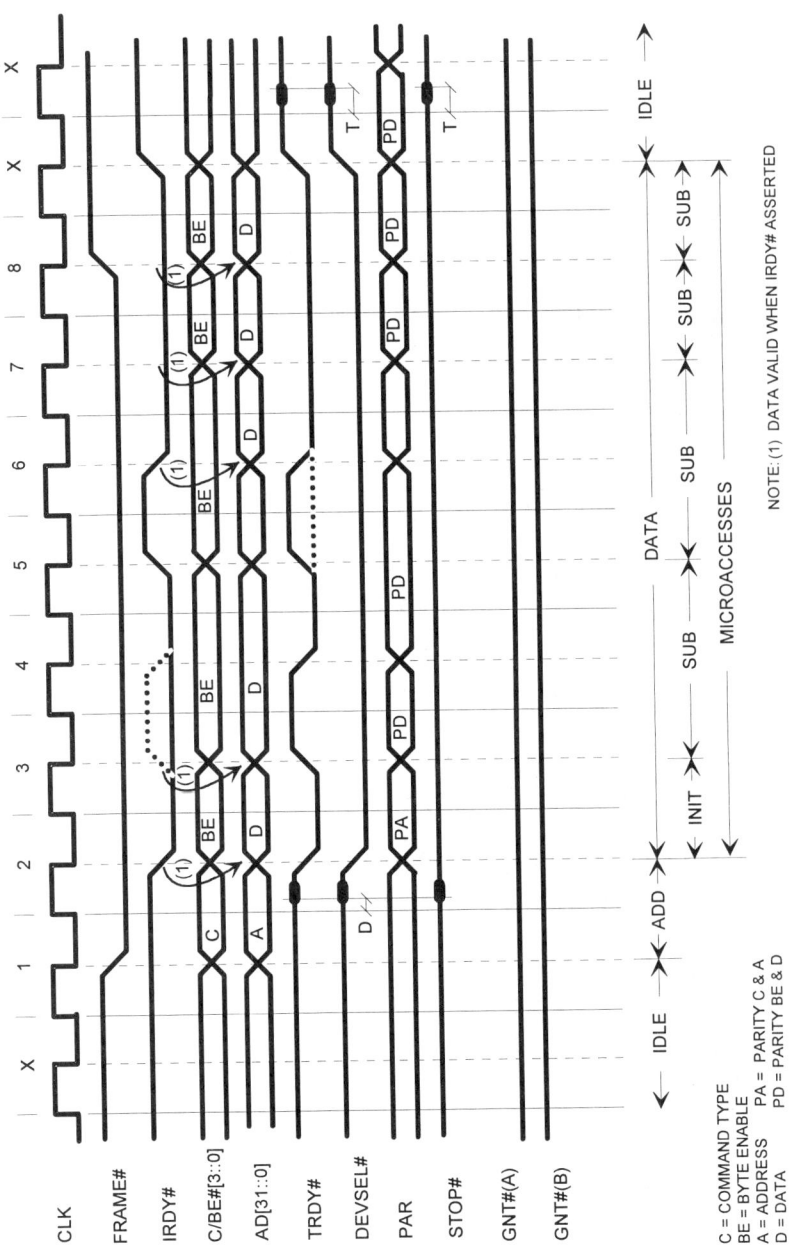

Figure 10-2: PCI Burst Write Transaction without DUAL ADDRESS Parked, Executed, and Retained by (A)

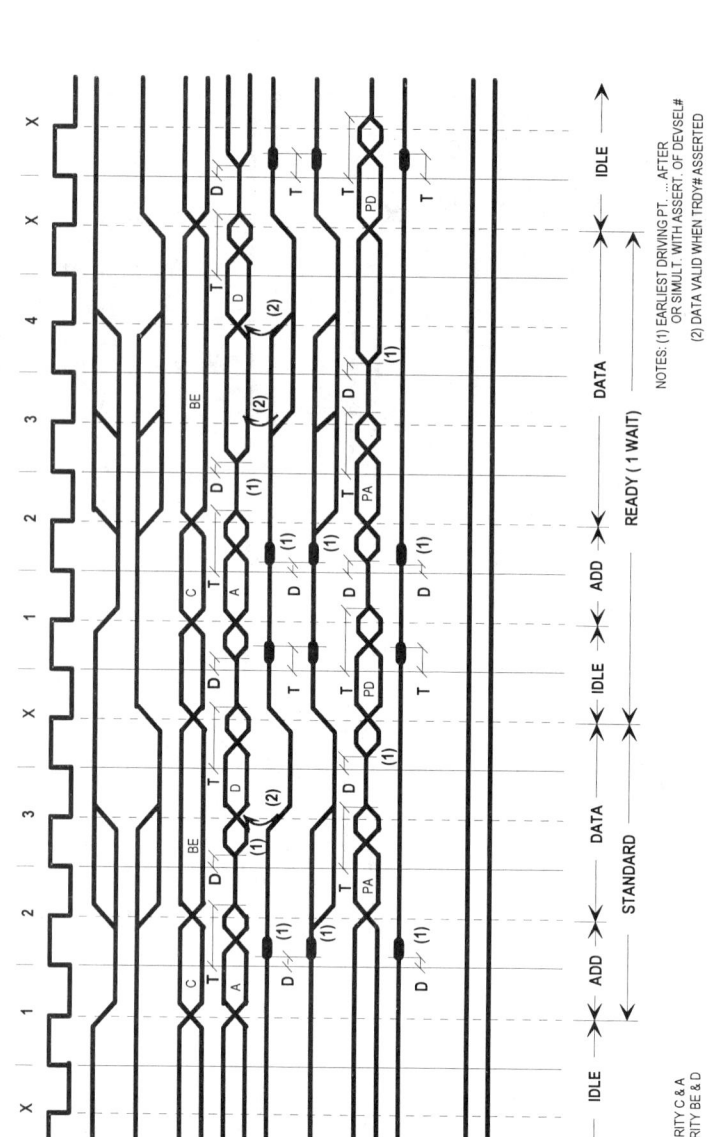

Figure 10-3: Single Read Bus Transaction without DUAL ADDRESS Parked, Executed, and Retained by (A)

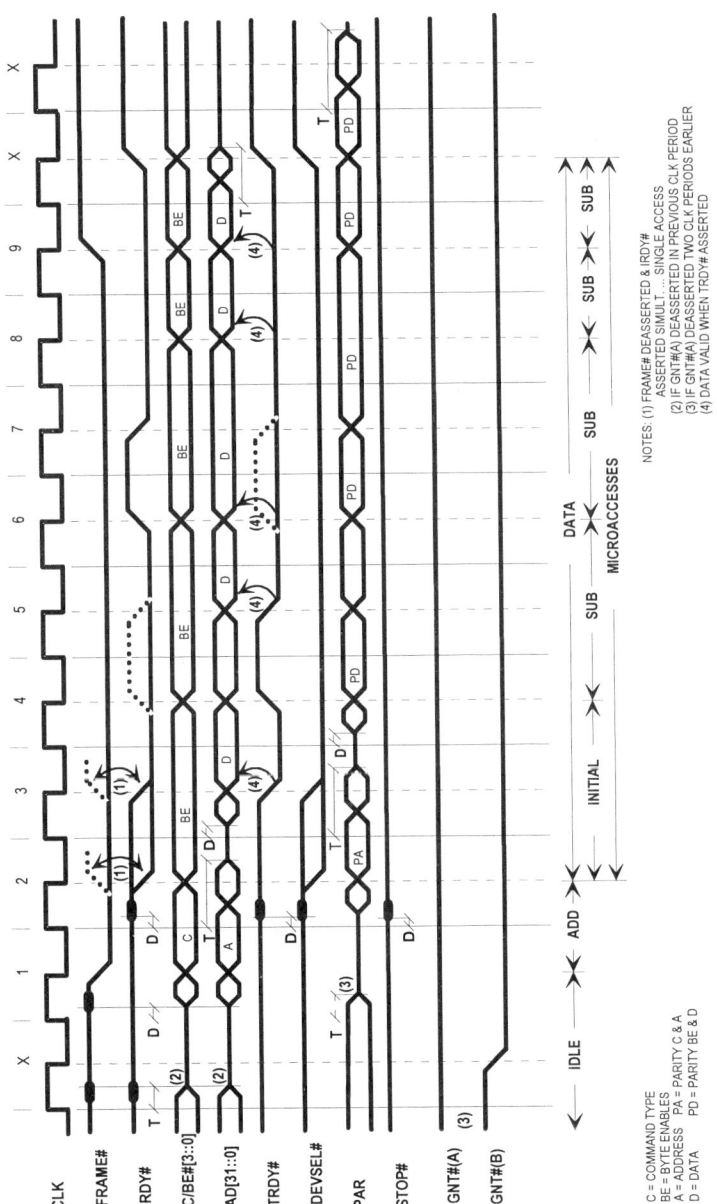

Figure 10-4: Burst Read Bus Transaction without DUAL ADDRESS Parked at (A), Executed, and Retained by (B)

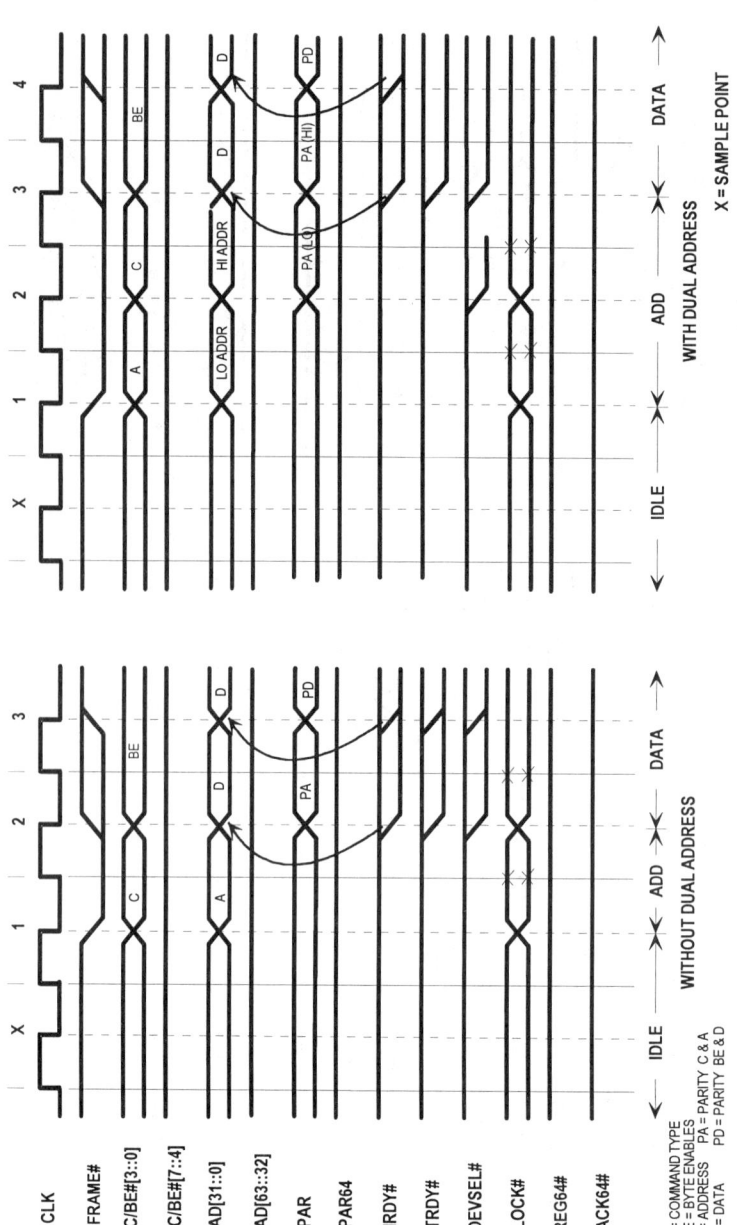

Figure 10-5-A: ADDRESS PHASE Protocol for Write, 32-Data Bit PCI Bus Master.

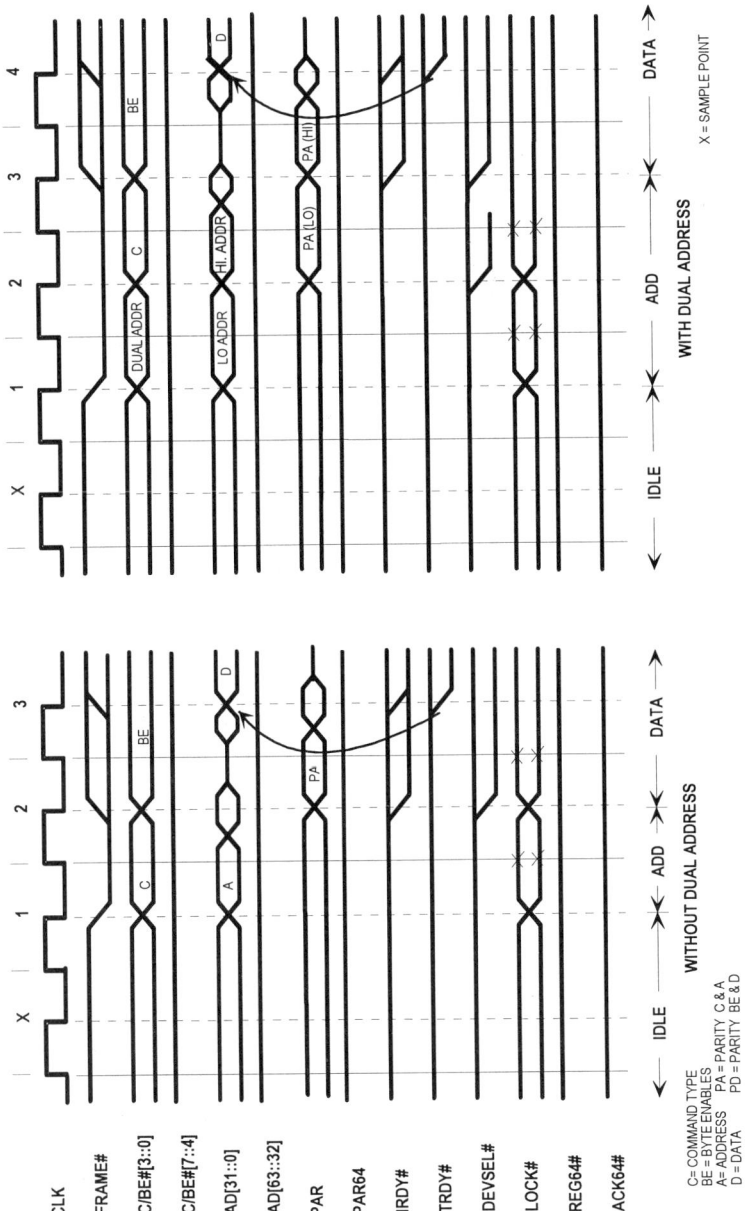

Figure 10-5-B: ADDRESS PHASE Protocol for Read, 64 Data Bit PCI Bus Master

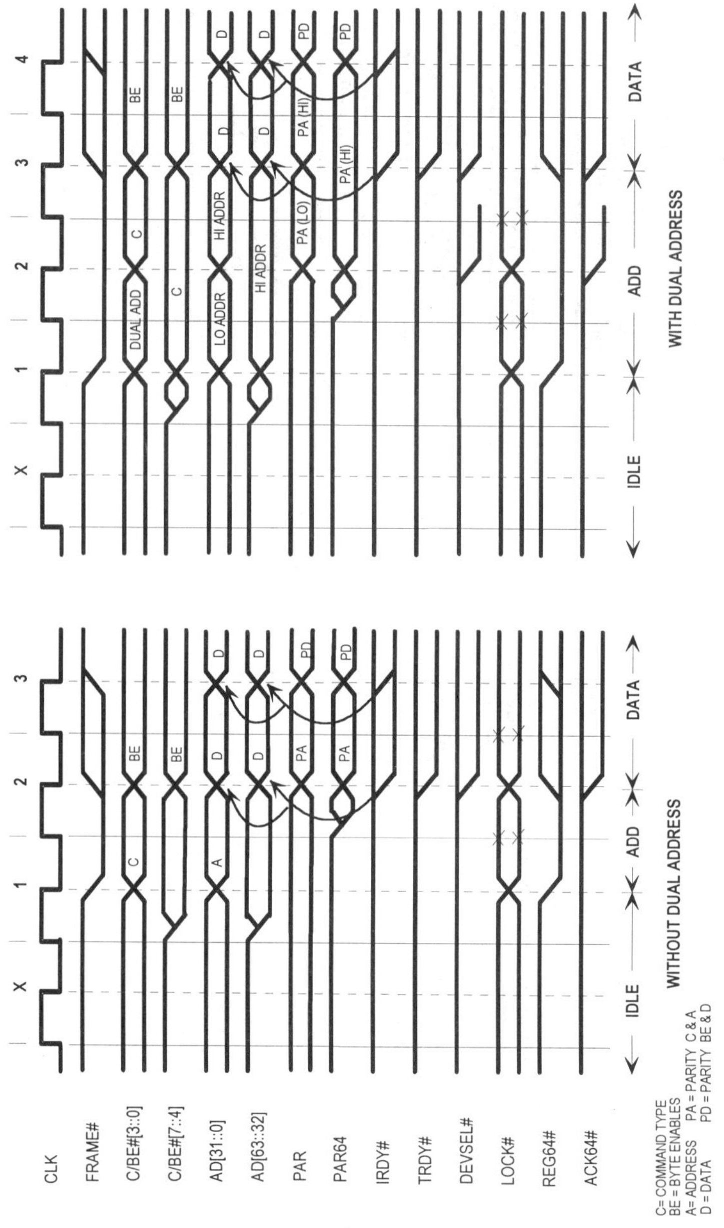

Figure 10-5-C: ADDRESS PHASE Protocol for Write, 64 Data Bit PCI Bus Master

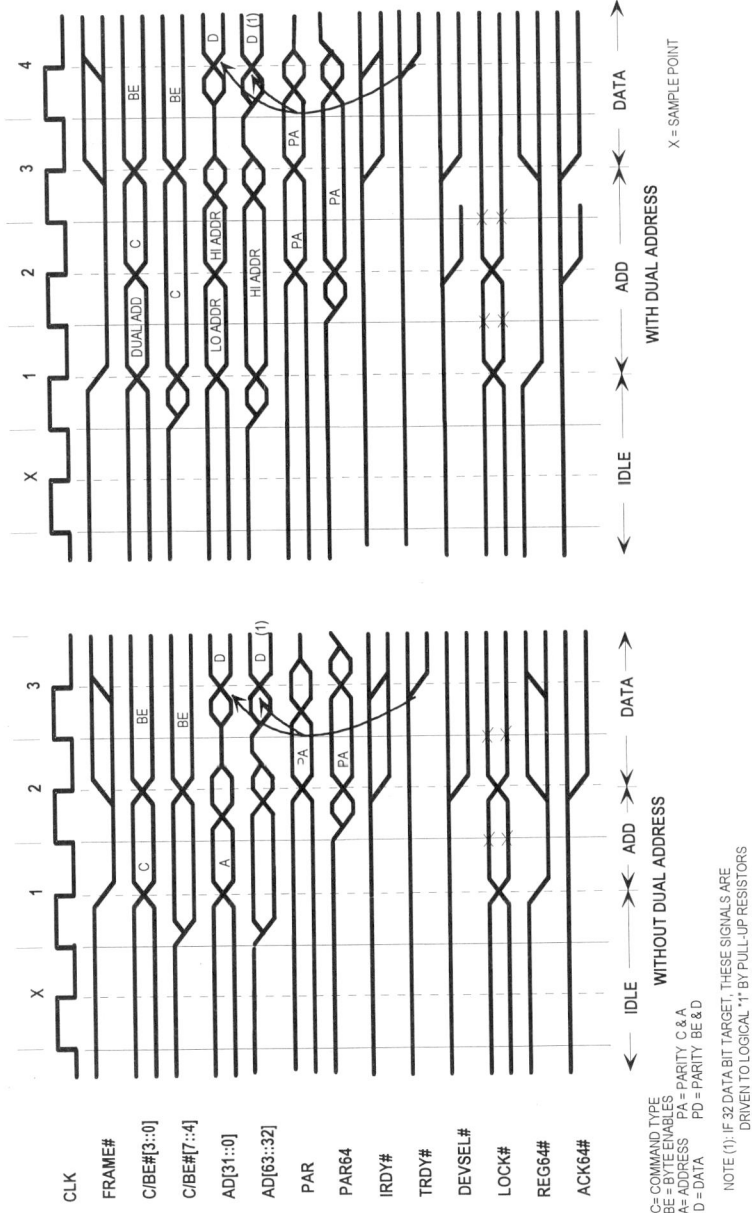

Figure 10-5-D: ADDRESS PHASE Protocol for Read, 64 Data Bit PCI Bus Master

64 DATA BIT PCI BUS MASTER AND
32 AND 64 DATA BIT TARGET (REQ64# = ASSERTED)

> 64 data bit I/O targets can be implemented, but there is no benefit to justify the increased complexity, and it is therefore strongly recommended that 64 data bit I/O targets not be implemented. For the purposes of the following discussion, the assertion of the REQ64# signal line is ignored by targets for I/O and configuration transactions. For I/O and configuration transactions, only 32 data bit target protocol applies.

- The operation of the PAR signal line relative to the AD[31::0] and C/BE#[3::0] for a 64 data bit PCI bus master is the same as outlined for a 32 data bit PCI bus master. The operation of PAR64 signal line relative to the AD[63::32] and C/BE#[7::4] signal lines varies, depending on the execution of DUAL ADDRESS and the value of the ACK64# signal line as follows (see Figures 10-5-C and D):

  - Dual address is not executed with a 32 data bit target (ACK64# is deasserted):

    During the ADDRESS PHASE, the PAR64 signal line contains valid parity because the C/BE#[7::4] and AD[63::32] signal lines are driven to a stable level (parity is computed even though no actual information is contained in the C/BE#[7::4] and AD[63::32] signal lines). Any PCI resource on the PCI bus segment (64 data bits in size) can optionally check the parity of these signal lines and optionally assert the SERR# signal line if an error is detected. During the DATA PHASE of a SINGLE write transaction and the initial microaccess of a BURST write transaction, the PCI bus master drives valid parity onto the PAR64 signal line because the C/BE#[7::4] and AD[63::32] signal lines contain valid information. The target is only 32 data bits; consequently, parity is not checked on the C/BE#[7::4], AD[63::32], and PAR64 signal lines. The PAR64 signal line may or may not contain valid parity information during the subsequent microaccesses of the BURST transaction; as mentioned before, a 32 data bit target cannot check the parity of the C/BE#[7::4], AD[63::32], and PAR64 signal lines. During the DATA PHASE of a SINGLE read transaction or the initial microaccess of a BURST read transaction, the PCI bus master drives the C/BE#[7::4] signal lines with byte enable information but the AD[63::32] and PAR64 signal lines are driven to a logical "1" by pull-up resistors; consequently, the latter does not contain valid parity. The PAR64 signal line does not contain valid parity during the subsequent microaccesses of the BURST bus transaction;

consequently, the PCI bus master does not check parity on the C/BE#[7::4], AD[63::32], and PAR64 signal lines.

■ DUAL ADDRESS is executed with a 32 data bit target (ACK64# is deasserted):

During the ADDRESS PHASE, the PAR64 signal line contains valid parity because the C/BE#[7::4] and AD[63::32] signal lines contain valid information. Any PCI resource on the PCI bus segment (64 data bits in size) can optionally check the parity of these signal lines and assert the SERR# signal line if an error is detected. During the DATA PHASE of a SINGLE write transaction and the initial microaccess of a BURST write transaction, the PCI bus master drives valid parity onto the PAR64 signal line because the C/BE#[7::4] and AD[63::32] signal lines contain valid information. The target is only 32 data bits; consequently, parity is not checked on the C/BE#[7::4], AD[63::32], and PAR64 signal lines. The PAR64 signal line may or may not contain valid parity information during the subsequent microaccesses of the BURST bus transaction; as mentioned before a 32 data bit target cannot check the parity of the C/BE#[7::4], AD[63::32], and PAR64 signal lines. During the DATA PHASE of a SINGLE read access cycle or the initial microaccess of a BURST read transaction, the PCI bus master drives the C/BE#[7::4] with byte enable information, but the AD[63::32] and PAR64 signal lines are driven to a logical "1" by pull-up resistors; consequently, the latter does not contain valid parity. The PAR64 signal line does not contain valid parity during the subsequent microaccesses of the BURST bus transaction; consequently, the PCI bus master does not check parity on the C/BE#[7::4], AD[63::32], and PAR64 signal lines.

■ Dual address is not executed with a 64 data bit target (ACK64# is asserted):

During the ADDRESS PHASE, the PAR64 signal line contains valid parity because the C/BE#[7::4] and AD[63::32] signal lines contain valid information. Any PCI resource on the PCI bus segment (64 data bits in size) can optionally check the parity of these signal lines and optionally assert the SERR# signal line if an error is detected. During the DATA PHASE of a write transaction, the PCI bus master drives valid parity onto the PAR64 signal line because the C/BE#[7::4] and AD[63::32] signal lines contain valid information. The target optionally checks the parity on the C/BE#[7::4], AD[63::32], and PAR64 signal lines. During the DATA PHASE of a read transaction, the PCI bus master drives the C/BE#[7::4] signal line with byte enable information, and the target drives the AD[63::32] signal lines with valid data; consequently, the PAR64 signal line is driven with valid parity. The PCI bus master optionally checks the parity on the C/BE#[7::4], AD[63::32], and PAR64 signal lines.

■ DUAL ADDRESS is executed with a 64 data bit target (ACK64# is asserted):

During the ADDRESS PHASE, the PAR64 signal line contains valid parity because the C/BE#[7::4] and AD[63::32] signal lines are driven to a stable level (parity is computed even though no actual information is contained in the C/BE#[7::4] and AD[63::32] signal lines). Any PCI resource on the PCI bus segment (64 data bits in size) can optionally check the parity of these signal lines and optionally assert the SERR# signal line if an error is detected. During the DATA PHASE of a write transaction, the PCI bus master drives valid parity onto the PAR64 signal line because the C/BE#[7::4] and AD[63::32] contain valid information. The target optionally checks the parity on the C/BE#[7::4], AD[63::32], and PAR64 signal lines. During the DATA PHASE of a read bus transaction, the PCI bus master drives the C/BE#[7::4] with byte enable information, and the target drives the AD[63::32] signal lines with valid data; consequently, the PAR64 signal line is driven with valid parity. The PCI bus master optionally checks the parity on the C/BE#[7::4], AD[63::32], and PAR64 signal lines.

> **During the DATA PHASE, the PCI bus master is driving the byte enables onto the C/BE# [7::4] signal lines during a read bus transaction; consequently, the target must sample these signal lines and combine the parity with the AD[63::32] signal lines to drive the PAR64 signal line.**

■ The operation of the PAR64 signal line between bus transactions also follows the operation of the AD[63::32] signal lines. If the PCI bus master is retaining bus segment ownership (REG# and GNTx# both asserted) between bus transactions, it drives the PAR64 signal line to a stable level or tri-states it and a pull-up resistor drives the PAR64 signal line to a logical "1". If the PCI bus master does not retain bus segment ownership (GNTx# signal line deasserted), the PAR64 signal line is driven to a logical "1" by a pull-up resistor. The Park master also does not drive the PAR64 signal line.

■ The PAR64 signal line supports even parity. The total number of "1"s on the AD[63::32], C/BE#[7::4], and PAR64 signal lines must be an even number when valid.

■ During the ADDRESS and DATA PHASES, the AD[63::32], C/BE#[7::4], and PAR64 signal lines must contain valid information or be driven to a stable level. Parity is computed over both types of signal lines; those that are stable, and those that contain valid information.

PAR AND PAR64 SIGNAL LINES OPERATION IN INTERRUPT ACKNOWLEDGE TRANSACTIONS

The interrupt acknowledge transaction does not generate a valid address during the ADDRESS PHASE, but does provide valid COMMAND type. The PCI bus master will drive the AD[31::0] to a stable level, the C/BE#[3::0] signal lines with valid COMMAND type, and the PAR signal with valid parity information. Consequently, any PCI resource on the PCI bus segment can optionally check the parity on the AD[31::0], C/BE#[3::0], and PAR signal lines. During the DATA PHASE, the PAR signal line will be driven by the target and will contain the parity over the AD[31::0] and C/BE#[3::0] signal lines. Consequently, the PCI bus master (HOST/PCI BRIDGE) can optionally check the parity on the AD[31::0], C/BE#[3::0], and PAR signal lines.

An interrupt acknowledge transaction is not defined for a 64 data bit bus transaction; consequently, during the ADDRESS and DATA PHASES, the AD[63::32], C/BE#[7::4], and PAR64 signal lines PAR64 signal lines do not contain valid parity and are not checked. If the REQ64# signal has been asserted, it is ignored by the target.

The interrupt controller may also reside in a resource on the HOST bus segment not associated with the PCI bus segment (the HOST/LEGACY BRIDGE, for example), in the HOST/PCI BRIDGE, in the PCI/LEGACY BRIDGE, or on the LEGACY bus segment. The use of this phrase represents an interrupt controller in a resource on the PCI Bus (0), in the PCI/LEGACY BRIDGE, or in a resource on the LEGACY bus segment attached via the PCI/LEGACY BRIDGE. When the interrupt controller resides in a resource on the HOST bus segment, in the HOST/PCI BRIDGE, or in a resource on the LEGACY bus segment attached by a HOST/LEGACY BRIDGE, no interrupt acknowledge transaction is executed on PCI bus (0).

PAR AND PAR64 SIGNAL LINES OPERATION IN SPECIAL TRANSACTIONS

The special transaction does not generate a valid address during the ADDRESS PHASE, but does provide a valid COMMAND type. The PCI bus master will drive the AD[31::0] signal lines to a stable level, the C/BE#[3::0] signal lines with valid COMMAND type, and the PAR signal with valid parity information. A special transaction broadcasts to more than one target; a singular target cannot claim the transaction and check the parity on the AD[31::0], C/BE#[3::0], and PAR signal lines. During the ADDDRESS PHASE, any PCI resource on the PCI bus segment can check for parity on the AD[31::0], C/BE#[3::0], and PAR signal lines and assert the SERR# signal line if there is a parity error. During the DATA PHASE, the PAR signal line will be driven by the PCI bus master and will contain the parity over the AD[31::0] and C/BE#[3::0] signal lines. Any PCI resource on the PCI bus segment can check for parity on the AD[31::0], C/BE#[3::0], and PAR signal lines and assert the SERR# signal line (not the PERR# signal line, which requires a single target to claim the special transaction).

> A special transaction is not defined for a 64 data bit bus transaction; consequently, during the ADDRESS and DATA PHASES, the AD[63::32], C/BE#[7::4], and the PAR64 signal line do not contain valid parity and are not checked. If the REQ64# signal has been asserted, it is ignored by the target.

10.2   PCI PERR# SIGNAL LINE OPERATION

INTRODUCTION

> The parity error discussed in the previous section for the AD, C/BE#, PAR, and PAR64 signal lines during the ADDRESS and DATA PHASES are also commonly known as "address parity error" and "data parity error", respectively.

The PERR# signal line is driven by the PCI resource receiving data on the AD signal lines during a bus transaction. It reflects the detection of a parity error on the AD, C/BE#, PAR, and PAR64 signal lines.

During a write transaction, the PERR# signal line is asserted by the target to report a parity error first to the PCI bus master. If the PCI bus master cannot resolve the data parity error, it can be reported to the device driver software by an interrupt or some other mechanism. If no interrupt or other mechanism is available to report the error, the SERR# signal line must be asserted by the PCI bus master. For a read transaction, the parity error reporting sequence is same except the assertion of the PERR# signal line is by the PCI bus master to indicate to the system that a data parity error had occurred. The PCI bus master still retains the opportunity to resolve the parity problem before reporting to the device driver software or asserting the SERR# signal line.

Not all of the PCI bus segment resources are required to support the PERR# signal line. The PCI bus segment resources that do not support the PERR# signal line must meet one of the following conditions:

- Resources that are only used on the platform and not add-in cards

- Resources that do not affect permanent data; *e.g.*, video display. In other words, resources that will not cause a loss of system integrity when the parity error occurs do not need to support parity checking.

PERR# SIGNAL LINE OPERATION DURING MEMORY, I/O, CONFIGURATION, AND INTERRUPT ACKNOWLEDGE TRANSACTIONS

> The balance of this section will refer to memory, I/O, configuration, and interrupt acknowledge transactions collectively as "bus transactions", "write transactions", or "read transactions".

> In the following discussion, the PERR# signal line can only be asserted by a PCI resource provided the associated Parity Error Response bit in its Command Register in the configuration address space is set to logical "1".

The PERR# signal line is asserted with the detection of a data parity error during the DATA PHASE on the AD[31::0], C/BE#[3::0], and PAR signal lines. The detection of a data parity error only occurs when the parity is checked as discussed in the previous subchapter. If it is a 64 data bit bus transaction (REQ64# and ACK64# both asserted), the PERR# signal line also includes a parity error in the AD[63::32], C/BE#[7::4], and PAR64 signal lines. Whenever the ACK64# signal line is deasserted during a bus transaction (32 data bit transaction) the parity error is not checked on the AD[63::32], C/BE#[7::4], and PAR64 signal lines.

> 64 data bit I/O targets can be implemented, but there is no justification requiring the increased complexity, and it is therefore strongly recommended that 64 data bit I/O targets not be implemented. For the purposes of the following discussion, the assertion of the REQ64# signal line is ignored by targets for I/O, in addition to configuration and interrupt acknowledge transactions. For I/O, configuration, and interrupt acknowledge transactions, only 32 data bit target protocol applies. If a 64 data bit I/O target is implemented, the 64 data bit protocol discussed below applies.

The PERR# signal line is asserted only to report data parity errors. The PERR# signal line must be asserted by the resource receiving the data on the AD signal lines two CLK signal line periods after the data is accessed when a parity error occurs. For a write transaction, the target asserts the PERR# signal line (subsequent to the assertion of the IRDY# and TRDY# signal lines) when a parity error is detected during the DATA PHASE. For a read transaction, the PCI bus master asserts the PERR# signal line (subsequent to the assertion of the IRDY# and TRDY# signal lines) when a parity error is detected during the DATA PHASE. When not driven by a PCI resource, the PERR# signal line is driven to a logical "1" by a pull-up resistor.

The PERR# signal line may be asserted and valid before IRDY# and TRDY# are both sampled asserted, provided a minimum of two CLK signal line periods have occurred since the FRAME# signal line was first sampled asserted. For a read transaction, the PERR# signal line is valid two CLK signal line periods after the TRDY# signal line is sampled asserted. For a write transaction, the PERR# signal line is valid two CLK signal line periods after the IRDY# signal line is sampled asserted. The sampling points (rising edge of the CLK signal line) at which the PERR# signal line must be valid (valid sample points) is two CLK signal line periods after the IRDY# and TRDY# signal lines are both sampled asserted (rising edge of the CLK signal line).

> In the following discussion, there is a difference between *drive* and *asserted*. When the PERR# signal line is *driven* it means that the signal line buffer is enabled but the signal line may remain deasserted. When the PERR# signal line is *asserted*, it is driven to a logical "0".

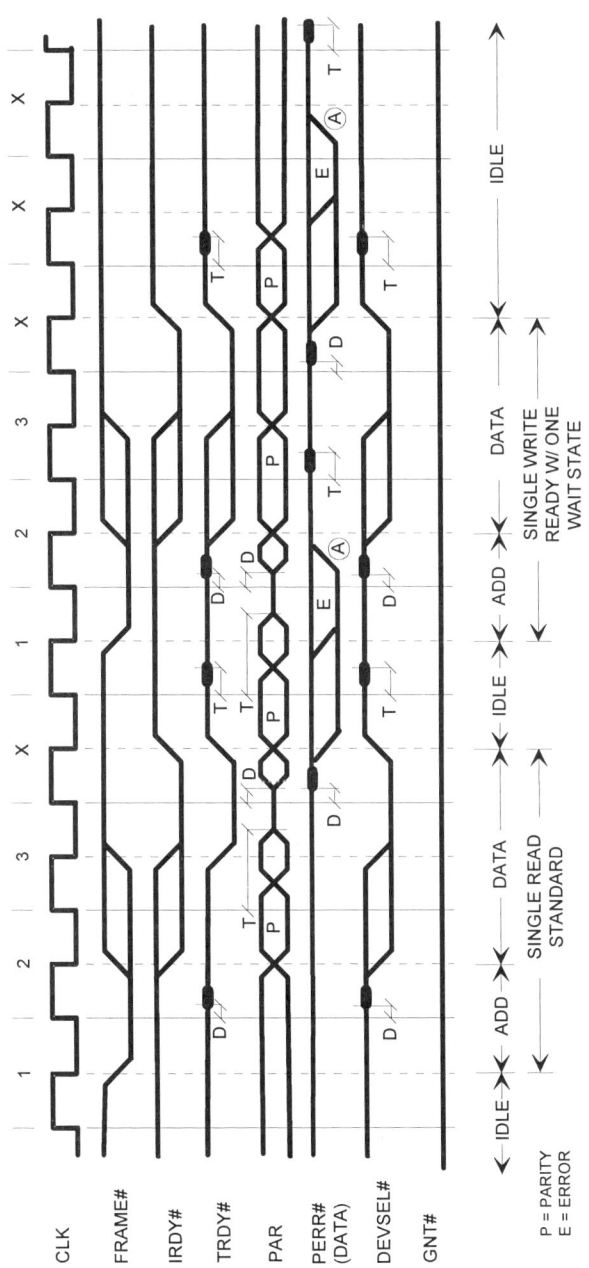

Figure 10-6: PERR# Protocol

Figure 10-6 outlines the operation of the PERR# signal line for SINGLE bus transactions, and has the following protocol:

The protocol for data parity error as reported by the PERR# signal line during a read transaction is as follows:

- The PERR# signal line initially can optionally be driven two CLK signal line periods after the FRAME# signal line is first sampled asserted at the beginning of the bus transaction. The PERR# signal line can optionally be driven at a later time prior to the assertion for the valid sample point.

- The PERR# signal line can optionally be asserted when both a minimum of two CLK signal line periods after the FRAME# signal line is first sampled asserted at the beginning of the bus transaction and after the TRDY# signal line is asserted.

- The PERR# signal line must be valid two CLK signal line periods after the IRDY# and TRDY# signal lines are both sampled asserted (rising edge of the CLK signal line).

- The PERR# signal line must be tri-stated three CLK signal line periods after the IRDY# and TRDY# signal lines are both asserted (rising edge of the CLK signal line).

The protocol for data parity error as reported by the PERR# signal line during a write transaction is as follows:

- The PERR# signal line can optionally be initially driven two CLK signal line periods after the FRAME# signal line is first sampled asserted at the beginning of the bus transaction. The PERR# signal line can optionally be driven at a later time prior to the assertion for the valid sample point.

- The PERR# signal line can optionally be asserted when both a minimum of two CLK signal line periods after the FRAME# signal line is first sampled asserted at the beginning of the bus transaction simultaneously with or after the DEVSEL# signal line is asserted, and after the IRDY# signal line is asserted.

- The PERR# signal line must be valid two CLK signal line periods after the IRDY# and TRDY# signal lines are both asserted (rising edge of the CLK signal line).

- The PERR# signal line must be tri-stated three CLK signal line periods after the IRDY# and TRDY# signal lines are both asserted (rising edge of the CLK signal line).

Other PERR# signal line protocol considerations are as follows:

- The above protocol relative to the assertion of the PERR# signal line applies to all bus transactions including Fast Back-to-Back protocol. For

796

TARGET Fast Back-to-Back protocol, the PERR# signal line is driven from a previous bus transaction until the end of the third CLK signal line period of the subsequent bus transaction. The tri-stating of the PERR# signal line driven from the previous bus transaction is at the beginning of the third CLK signal line period of the subsequent bus transaction. This coincides with the earliest possible point (two clock signal line periods from when the FRAME# signal line is first sampled asserted) when the target of the subsequent bus transaction drives the PERR# signal line. This results in a minor buffer fight on the PERR# signal line for the TARGET Fast Back-to-Back protocol. The ability to retain the same protocol during a Fast Back-to-Back reflects the fact that the PERR# signal line only reports data parity, does not have to be asserted during the ADDRESS PHASE, *i.e.*, the earliest possible point.

■ Once the PERR# signal line is asserted, it cannot be deasserted until two CLK signal line periods after the IRDY# and TRDY# signal lines are both asserted (Circle A in Figure 10-6).

■ For a BURST bus transaction, the PERR# signal line protocol is the same as that outlined above for the SINGLE bus transaction. The only difference is the PERR# signal line protocol for each microaccess is relative to the individual assertion of the IRDY# and TRDY# signal lines for each microaccess. If data is accessed with parity error on continuous rising edges of the CLK signal line, the PERR# signal line remains asserted for the associated continuous CLK signal line periods.

> The above discussion uses only a 32 data bit bus transaction as an example. The operation of the PERR# signal line relative to the PAR64 signal line uses the same protocol.

> The PCI bus master and target do not know that a SINGLE bus transaction was successful relative to errors until two CLK signal line periods after the data was accessed.

The assertion of the PERR# signal line by the PCI bus master or target (provided the Parity Error Response bit the Command Register in the configuration address space is set to logical "1) is only a portion of the data parity protocol. Consider the following:

■ During a write transaction, if the target detects a data parity error, it must set to logical "1" the Detected Parity Error bit in its Status register in the configuration address space. If the Parity Error Response bit in its Command register in the configuration address space is set to logical "0", the target must allow the bus transaction to continue and any target terminations will be for other reasons. If the Parity Error Response bit in its Command register in the configuration address space is set to logical "1", the target must assert the PERR# signal line to report a data parity error to the PCI bus master. On detection of the asserted PERR# signal line, the PCI bus master must set to logical "1" the Master Data Parity Error bit in its Status register in the configuration address space. The target can either allow the bus transaction to continue and any target terminations will be for other reasons, or immediately terminate the bus transaction by executing a Disconnect or a Target Abort termination for a BURST bus transaction (a SINGLE bus transaction by definition will be immediately "terminated" anyway).

- The most typical response is for the target to assert the PERR# signal line and the PCI bus master to execute a Completion, a Completion with timeout, or a completion in response to an independent target termination (as it would have if the PERR# signal line had not been asserted).

- During a read transaction, if the PCI bus master detects a data parity error, it must set to logical "1" the Detected Parity Error bit in its Status register in the configuration address space. If the Parity Error Response bit in its Command register in the configuration address space is set to logical "0", the PCI bus master must allow the bus transaction to continue and any bus transaction terminations will be for other reasons. If the Parity Error Response bit in its Command register of the configuration address space is set to logical "1"; the PCI bus master must assert the PERR# signal line and to set to logical "1" the Master Data Parity Error bit in its Status register of the configuration address space. The target can either allow the bus transaction to continue and any bus transaction terminations will be for other reasons, or immediately terminate the bus transaction for a BURST bus transaction (a SINGLE bus transaction by definition will be immediately "terminated" anyway).

  - The most typical response is for the PCI bus master to assert the PERR# signal line and execute a Completion, a Completion with timeout, or a completion in response to an independent target termination (as it would have if the PERR# signal had not been asserted).

Only the PCI bus master will have Data Parity Reported bit set to assert the PERR# signal line for a read or sense the PERR# signal line for write.

The addressed target cannot assert (for a SINGLE write transaction or the initial microaccess of a BURST write access cycle) the PERR# signal line for a data parity error detected with a Retry, Target Abort, or Disconnect without data termination because no data was accessed. A Disconnect without data, Disconnect with data, or Target Abort termination may be executed for a data parity error of an earlier microaccess of a Burst write transaction when the PERR# signal line is asserted. Finally, a Disconnect with data termination may be executed for a data parity error in the present microaccess of a Burst write transaction

For bus transactions the PCI bus master can attempt data parity error recovery as follows:

When a data parity error occurs and the PERR# signal line is asserted, the PCI bus master should repeat the bus transaction provided no negative side effects will result. If the bus transaction repeats without a data parity error, the PCI bus master does not have to report the occurrence of a data parity error to the system, as outlined below. If the repeated access cycle generates a data parity error or if the PCI bus master cannot repeat the bus transaction, the PCI bus master must report it to the system as follows:

- If the PCI bus master is supported by device driver software, the device driver software is informed of the data parity error via an interrupt, Status Register information, flags, or other means. The device driver software can try other methods for recovering from a data parity error. If the device driver is successful without any negative side effects, no further action is required. If the device driver is unsuccessful or is unable to correct the parity error due to the negative side effects, it must report it to the operating system software.

- If the PCI bus master does not have device driver software support, it must report the data parity error by asserting the SERR# signal line (provided the SERR# Enable bit in its Command register in the configuration address space is set to logical "1") as a method to report the error to the operating system. If the PCI bus master asserts the SERR# signal line, it must set to logical "1" the Signal System Error bit in its Status register in the configuration address space.

- Once the data parity error has been reported to the operating system, the exact method for addressing it is operating system dependent.

799

An exception to the above bullets occurs if the PCI bus master is the PCI interrupt source and is executing a message signaled interrupt (MSI) memory write transaction. If a data parity error occurs during the execution of an MSI memory write transaction, the PCI interrupt source must assert the SERR# signal line immediately. The PCI interrupt source does not try to repeat the access cycle, alert device driver software, or try other alternative activities previously outlined.

For the PCI interrupt source to assert the SERR# signal line for the above situation requires the SERR# Enable bit in its Command register of the configuration address space set to logical "1" by the software. If the SERR# signal line is asserted, the PCI interrupt source must also set to logical "1" the Signal System Error in its Status register of the configuration address space.

The system designer can use the central resource to assert the SERR# signal line to reflect the assertion of the PERR# signal line for a data parity error.

PERR# SIGNAL LINE OPERATION DURING SPECIAL TRANSACTIONS

The PERR# signal line is not used during special transactions because data is broadcast (written by PCI bus master) to all PCI resources without a specific address. Resources that receive the data can check data parity on the AD[31::0], C/BE#[3::01], and PAR signal lines. However, the lack of a specific address does not allow a specific target to claim ownership of the PERR# signal line; consequently, the data parity error cannot be reported to the PCI bus master with this signal line. Any PCI resource that detects a data parity error in the AD[31::0], C/BE#[3::0], and PAR signal lines during the DATA PHASE can report it by asserting the SERR# signal line.

A PCI resource that detects a data parity error must:

- Set the Detected Parity Error bit in its Status register in the configuration address space to logical "1".

- If the Parity Error Response and SERR# Enable bits are both set to logical "1" in its Command register in the configuration address, the PCI resource must also assert the SERR# signal line. If the SERR# signal line is asserted, the PCI resource must also set the Signaled System Error bit in its Status Register in the configuration address space to logical "1".

A special transaction is not defined for a 64 data bit bus transaction; consequently, during the ADDRESS and DATA PHASES, the AD[63::32], C/BE#[7::4], and PAR64 signal lines do not contain valid parity and are not checked. If the REQ64# signal has been asserted, it is ignored by the target.

10.3 PCI SERR# SIGNAL LINE OPERATION

INTRODUCTION

The parity error in the AD, C/BE#, PAR, and PAR64 signal lines during the ADDRESS and DATA PHASES are also commonly known as address parity error and data parity error, respectively.

The SERR# signal line can be asserted by any PCI resource independent of which PCI bus master or target is involved in the bus transaction or where the PCI bus segment is parked. The SERR# signal line is an open collector signal line that is deasserted by a pull-up resistor and can be driven by multiple PCI resources. The SERR# signal line is used to directly report an address parity error during any bus transaction, to report a data parity error during special transactions, or to report any error to the platform independent of the bus transaction.

Not all of the PCI bus segment resources are required to support the SERR# signal line. The PCI bus segment resources that are not required to support the SERR# signal line must meet one of the following conditions:

- Resources that are used only on the system and never on add-in cards
- Resources that do not affect permanent data, *i.e.*, video display. In other words, resources that do not support parity checking are those that will not cause a loss of system integrity when the parity error occurs.

There are no specific timing requirements for the assertion of the SERR# signal line. It should be asserted soon after the error is detected. There are two basic requirements for the assertion of the SERR# signal line. First, if reporting a data parity error for special transactions or an address parity error for all bus transactions, the PCI resource's Parity Error Response and SERR# Enable bits in its Command Register in the configuration address space must both be set to logical "1". Second, if a PCI resource is reporting some other catastrophic error condition, only the SERR# Enable bit in its Command Register in the configuration address space must be set to logical "1". For either situation, the assertion of the SERR# signal line requires the PCI resource to also set the Signal

System Error in its Status register in the configuration address space to logical "1".

> The SERR# signal line is asserted synchronously and deasserted asynchronously with the CLK signal line; consequently, once asserted the SERR# signal line is considered active until sampled deasserted for two consecutive CLK signal line periods. The SERR# signal line is asserted for one CLK signal line period and is then immediately tri-stated.

The system circuitry will monitor the SERR# signal line to report errors to the operating system (*i.e.*, the HOST CPU). The resulting system activity when a SERR# signal line is asserted is not defined by the PCI local bus specification. Alternatively, a PCI resource can notify a device driver or the system about an error via interrupts, NMI, polling of registers, etc. See further discussions later in this chapter.

SERR# SIGNAL LINE OPERATION DURING MEMORY, I/O, CONFIGURATION, AND INTERRUPT ACKNOWLEDGE TRANSACTIONS

> The balance of this section will refer to memory, I/O, configuration, and interrupt acknowledge transactions collectively as "bus transactions", "write transactions", or "read transactions".

The SERR# signal line can be asserted by any PCI resource independently of which PCI bus master or target is involved in the bus transaction. The SERR# is asserted after an address parity error is detected on the AD[31::0], C/BE#[3::0], and PAR signal lines during the ADDRESS PHASE. If it is a 64 data bit access (REQ64# signal line asserted) and a DUAL ADDRESS is executed, the SERR# is asserted for an address parity error in the AD[63::32], C/BE#[7::4], and PAR64 signal lines during the ADDRESS PHASE.

> When a bus transaction is not a 64 data bit transaction, the AD[63::32], C/BE#[7::4], and PAR64 signal lines do not contain valid parity and are not checked. If the REQ64# signal has been asserted, it is ignored by the target.

The SERR# signal line is asserted or not asserted during an access cycle by the PCI bus master or the addressed target as follows:

■ One of the following three bullets must be executed when an address parity error is detected:

■ When an addressed target detects an address parity error, it may (optionally) claim the bus transaction (assert DEVSEL# signal line) and assert the SERR# signal line, and allow a Disconnect, Retry, Completion, or Completion with timeout termination as if an address parity error had not occurred. The SERR# signal line can only be asserted by the target provided the associated Parity Error Response and SERR# Enable bits in its Command Register in the configuration address space are both set to logical "1". If a target asserts the SERR# signal line, it must set the Signal System Error bit in its Status register in the configuration address space to logical "1".

OR

■ When an addressed target detects an address parity error it may (optionally) claim the bus transaction (assert DEVSEL# signal line), and execute a Target Abort termination. This will place the responsibility on the PCI bus master to assert the SERR# signal line. However, the PCI bus master is not required to assert SERR# signal line if it can report the Target Abort termination to the system by other means. Otherwise, the SERR# signal line must be asserted by a PCI bus master provided the associated SERR# Enable bit in its Command Register in the configuration address space is set to logical "1". If a PCI bus master asserts the SERR# signal line, it must set the Signal System Error bit in its Status register in the configuration address space to logical "1".

OR

■ When an addressed target detects an address parity error it may (optionally) not claim the bus transaction (keep the DEVSEL# signal line deasserted); this will cause a Master Abort to occur and make it the responsibility of the PCI bus master to assert the SERR# signal line. However, the PCI bus master is not required to assert the SERR# signal line if it can report the Master Abort termination to the system by other means. Otherwise, the SERR# signal line must be asserted by a PCI bus master provided the associated SERR# Enable bit in its Command Register in the configuration address space is set to logical "1". If a PCI bus master asserts the SERR# signal line it must set the Signal System Error bit in its Status register in the configuration address space to logical "1".

■ A Master Abort termination is not an abnormal condition for a configuration transaction during initialization. Consequently, the SERR# signal line must not be asserted.

■ For a read transaction, the PCI bus master must assert the SERR# signal line if a data parity error is not reported to the operating system by other means and the data parity cannot be fixed by the PCI bus master (see previous section). The SERR# signal line can only be asserted by a PCI bus master provided the associated SERR# Enable and Parity Error Response bits in its Command Register in the configuration address space are both set to logical "1". The PCI bus master is also required to set the Master Data parity Error bit in the Status register of the configuration address space to logical "1" if the Parity Error Response bit in its Command register of the configuration address space is set to logical '1". If a PCI bus master asserts the SERR# signal line it must set the Signal System Error bit in its Status register in the configuration address space to logical "1".

■ For a write transaction, the PCI bus master must assert the SERR# signal line if a data parity error (as reported by the target asserting the PERR# signal line) is not reported to the operating system by other means and the data parity cannot be fixed by the PCI bus master (see previous section). The SERR# signal line can only be asserted by a PCI bus master provided the associated SERR# Enable and Parity Error Response bits in its Command Register in the configuration address space are both set to logical "1". The PCI bus master is also required to set the Master Data parity Error bit in the Status register of the configuration address space to logical "1" if the Parity Error Response bit in its Command register of the configuration address space is set to logical '1". If a PCI bus master asserts the SERR# signal line it must set the Signal System Error bit in its Status register in the configuration address space to logical "1".

■ When an addressed target cannot support the byte pattern requested by the PCI bus master, it may (optionally) assert the SERR# signal line. The SERR# signal line can only be asserted by a target provided the associated SERR# Enable bit in its Command Register in the configuration address space is set to logical "1". If a target asserts the SERR# signal line, it must set the Signal System Error bit in its Status register in the configuration address space to logical "1".

An exception to the above bullets occurs if the PCI bus master is the PCI interrupt source and is executing a message signaled interrupt (MSI) memory write transaction. If a data parity error occurs during the execution of an MSI memory write transaction, the PCI interrupt source must assert the SERR# signal line immediately in response to the assertion of the PERR# signal line. The PCI interrupt source does not try to repeat the memory write transaction, alert device driver software, or the other alternative activities previously outlined.

As discussed above, if an address parity error occurs during a bus transaction, the SERR# signal line is asserted by the target, or a Target Abort or a Master Abort termination is requested. If the bus transaction is an MSI memory write transaction, the occurrence of a Master Abort or a Target Abort termination requires the PCI interrupt resource to assert the SERR# signal line without considering reporting the error to the operating system by other means.

For the PCI interrupt source to assert the SERR# signal line for the above situations requires the SERR# Enable bit in its Command register of the configuration address space set to logical "1" by the software. If the SERR# signal line is asserted, the PCI interrupt source is also required to set the Signal System Error in its Status register of the configuration address space to logical "1".

SERR# SIGNAL LINE OPERATION DURING SPECIAL TRANSACTIONS

The SERR# signal line reports parity errors during the ADDRESS and DATA PHASES of special transactions. By definition, the special transaction broadcasts data to all PCI resources without a specific address. During the ADDRESS PHASE of the special transaction, the PCI bus master drives the AD[31::0] signal lines to a stable level and valid information onto the C/BE#[3::0] signal lines. It also drives valid parity information onto the PAR signal line (one CLK signal line period later); consequently, the system circuitry or any PCI resource is able to check parity and assert the SERR# signal line if an address parity error is detected. During the DATA PHASE, PCI resources that receive the data can check data parity on the AD[31::0], C/BE#[3::0], and PAR signal lines, but the lack of a specific address does not allow a specific PCI resource to claim ownership of the PERR# signal line. Consequently, parity can be checked by the system circuitry or any PCI resource, and may assert the SERR# signal line.

The SERR# signal line is asserted or not asserted during a special transaction by the PCI bus master or the other PCI bus segment resources as follows:

- At least one PCI resource on the bus segment must assert the SERR# signal line to indicate an address or data parity error if these errors are not reported by other means.

- The PCI bus master cannot assert the SERR# signal line to report a Master Abort termination to the system for a special transaction. A

Master abort termination is not an abnormal condition for a special transaction.

■   The SERR# signal line may (optionally) be asserted if the C/BE#[3::0] signal line pattern (byte lanes active) is not supported by one of the targets receiving the special transaction.

> A special transaction is not defined as a 64 data bit transaction; consequently, the AD[63::32], C/BE#[7::4], and PAR64 signal lines do not contain valid parity and are not checked. If the REQ64# signal has been asserted, it is ignored by the target.

SERR# SIGNAL LINE OPERATION FOR NON-BUS TRANSACTION RELATED ERRORS

As previously discussed, the SERR# signal line can also be used to report any catastrophic error; consequently, the SERR# signal line can be asserted at any time by any PCI resource. The use of the SERR# signal for catastrophic errors other than address parity error (and data parity for special transactions) is optional. The only requirement for non-address and non-data parity errors is that the SERR# Enable bit in the PCI resource's Command register of the configuration address space is set to logical "1" for the SERR# signal line to be asserted. When the PCI resource asserts the SERR# signal line it must set the Signal System Error bit in its Status register in the configuration address space to logical "1".

The SERR# signal line may or may not be asserted as follows:

■   There are no other means to report the catastrophic error to the operating system.

■   Discarding of the data and bus transactions according to the Discard Timer as part of the Delayed Transaction protocol. See Subchapter 7.5 for more information.

10.4   PCI-X PAR AND PAR64 SIGNAL LINES OPERATION IN BUS TRANSACTIONS

The PCI-X addendum specification's protocol for parity generating and checking (operation of PAR and PAR64 signal lines) is essentially the same as as defined by the PCI local bus specification. However, there a several additions and differences as follows:

■   Parity for the ATTRIBUTE PHASE is generated and checked with the same protocol as for the ADDRESS PHASE. As with the ADDRESS

PHASE, parity checking in the ATTRIBUTE PHASE is optionally checked by PCI-X resources on the bus segment.

■ No parity is generated or checked for the TARGET RESPONSE PHASE.

■ Throughout the entire ADDRESS and ATTRIBUTE PHASES, the parity is generated and checked (optionally) for the AD and C/BE# signal lines in CLK signal line period N, and PAR and PAR64 (when applicable) signal lines on CLK signal line period N+1.

■ For write and split completion transactions, the parity is checked (optionally) throughout the DATA PHASE only when the TRDY# signal line is asserted.

■ For read transaction, the parity is generated and checked (optionally) throughout the DATA PHASE only when the TRDY# signal line is asserted.

■ For read transaction, the parity is generated and checked (optionally) throughout the DATA PHASE only when the TRDY# signal line is asserted.

■ For read transactions during the DATA PHASE, the parity is generated and checked (optionally) for the AD signal lines in CLK signal line period N, C/BE# signal lines on CLK signal line period N-1, and PAR and PAR64 (when applicable) signal lines on CLK signal line period N+1.

■ The parity checking and generation protocol for split completion transactions is the same as for memory write transactions.

■ Some of the PCI-X bus transactions drive the C/BE# signal lines deasserted throughout the DATA PHASE. The parity is still generated and checked (optionally) during the DATA PHASE.

10.5 PCI-X PERR# SIGNAL LINE OPERATION

The PCI-X addendum specification defines the PERR# signal line protocol and the setting to logical "1" of data parity error related bits in the configuration address space in the same fashion as the PCI local bus specification with the following differences:

■ The PERR# signal line in a PCI-X bus transaction is valid one CLK signal line later than when it is valid in a PCI bus transaction. That is, PERR# signal line is valid two CLK signal line periods after the PAR (and PAR64 signal line for 64 data bit bus transaction) signal line is valid.

■   Split completion transactions are defined only as defined by the PCI-X addendum specification. The data parity error is defined and reported in the same fashion as a memory write transaction. The PCI-X bus transaction protocol for memory write is the same as the protocol as defined by the PCI bus transaction. However, the PCI-X resource that sets the Master Data Parity Error bit to logical "1" is different. See Tables 10-1-A to 10-1-C.

   ■   Table 10-1-A is the simplest viewpoint with no intermediate PCI-X/PCI-X BRIDGE between PCI-X bus master and target. Tables 10-1-B and 10-1-C are from the viewpoint of an intermediate PCI-X/PCI-X BRIDGE that represents the PCI-X bus master or target, and acts as either a PCI-X bus master or target on the bus segment, respectively. All the tables assume that the data parity error occurs in the bus transaction execution between PCI-X bus master and target as defined in the tables.

■   When a PCI-X DWORD write bus transaction is terminated by a split response termination and a data parity error occurs, the target must assert the PERR# signal line (if the Parity Error Response bit is set to logical "1" in its Command register in the configuration address space) and to respond with a split completion transaction containing a Split Completion Message. See the summary of Split Completion Error messages in the next subchapter.

■   In addition to the data parity error related bits in the registers defined as defined by both the PCI local bus specification and the PCI-X addendum bus specification, the PCI-X addendum specification defines an additional data parity error related bit. The Data Parity Error Recovery Enable bit is defined in the PCI-X Command Register in the configuration address space. This bit is set to logical "1" by the device driver software to require the PCI-X resource to attempt data error recovery. If this bit is set to logical "0", the PCI-X resource must assert the SERR# signal line if both of the following conditions are met:

   ■   Both the Parity Error Response and SERR# Enable bits in the PCI-X resource's Command register in the configuration address space are set to logical "1". (Note: If the SERR# signal line is asserted, the Signal System Error bit in the Status register of the configuration address space must be set to logical "1".)

   ■   The Master Data Parity Error bit in the PCI-X resource's Status register has been set to logical "1".

   ■   See Subchapter 10.7 for additional considerations when data parity is detected in a read transaction when a Split Response termination is requested.

The PCI-X resource that sets the Master Parity Error bit (See Tables 10-1-A to 10-1-C) is also the PCI-X resource that will either execute data parity error recovery or will assert the SERR# signal line as defined by the aforementioned Data Parity Error Recover bit.

There will be more discussion about data error recovery later in this subchapter.

In Tables 10-1-A to 10-1-C the activities listed for the master and target will occur in addition to the activity discussed in the tables' notes ... unless SPECIFICALLY stated otherwise in the notes.

PCI-X Bus Master That Executed Bus Transactions	Target Reaction	PERR# Driven by	Master Data Parity Error set by	Detected Parity Error set by
Memory Write	Immed/Posted	Target	Master	Target
Read	Immed	Master	Master	Master
Non-Memory Write	Split Response	Target	Master	Target
Read	Spit Response	Master	Master	Master
Split Completion in response to a write and read (1)	Immed/Posted	Target	Target	Target

Table 10-1-A: PCI-X Data Parity Error In Bus Transaction ... No Intermediate PCI-X/PCI-X BRIDGE

Note (1) For split completion transactions, the PCI-X bus master in the table is the "original" target and is sourcing the split completion transactions. The target is the "original" PCI-X bus master that executed the bus transaction that was terminated with Split Response termination.

PCI-X Bus Master That Executed Bus Transaction on Source Bus Segment	Bridge as Target on Source Bus Segment Reaction	PERR# on Source Bus Segment Driven by	Master Data Parity Error set by	Detected Parity Error set by
Memory Write (6)	Posted	Bridge as Target	PCI-X Bus Master	Bridge as Target
Read (2)	-	-	-	-
Non-Memory Write (3)	Split Response	Bridge as Target	PCI-X Bus Master	Bridge as Target
Read (4)	Split Response	Bridge as Target	PCI-X Bus Master	Bridge as Target
Split Completion in response to a write or read (1) (5)	Posted	Bridge as Target	Bridge as Target	Bridge as Target

Table 10-1-B: PCI-X Data Parity Error In Bus Transaction ... Data Parity Error at Intermediate PCI-X/PCI-X BRIDGE as Target

Notes:

(1) For split completion transactions, the PCI-X/PCI-X BRIDGE is the target representing the "orginal" PCI-X bus master that is now the target of the split completion transactions. The PCI-X bus master is now the source of the split completion transactions and was the "orginal" target.

(2) All read transactions to a PCI/PCI-X Bridge must end in a Split Response termination.

(3) If the PCI-X/PCI-X BRIDGE receives a non-postable write transaction with a data parity error on the source bus segment, it has two options: One option is to not request a Split Response termination, complete the bus trasnaction, discard the data, and do not port the bus transaction to the destiantion bus segment. The other option is for the bridge to request the Split Response termination and execute the write bus transaction on the destination bus segment with bad data pariiy.

(4) The PCI-X bus master may receive a data parity error when the Split Response termination is requested by the PCI-X/PCI-C BRIDGE as the target on the source bus segment because the protocol is for the PCI-X/PCI-X BRIDGE as the target to drive the AD signal lines with logical "1" in the DATA PHASE.

(5) When the PCI-X/PCI-X BRIDGE detects a data parity error for a split completion transaction (without a Split Completion Message), the PCI-X/PCI-X BRIDGE will forward the split completion transaction to the source bus segment with bad data parity. If the aforementioned split completion transaction contains a Split Completion Message, the PCI-X/PCI-X BRIDGE discards the split completion transaction, DOES NOTexecute the activities in the table, and asserts the SERR# signal line (the assertion of the SERR# signal line requires the appropriate bits to be enabled and set in the bridge configuration address space).

(6) If the PCI-X/PCI-X BRIDGE detects a data parity error on the source bus segment for the posted memory write transaction, it will port the bus transaction to the destination bus segment with bad data parity.

BRIDGE as PCI-X Bus Master That Executed Bus Transactions on Destination Bus Segment	Target Reaction on Destination Bus Segment	PERR# on Destination Bus Segment Driven by	Master Data Parity Error set by	Detected Parity Error set by
Memory Write (4)	Immed/Posted	Target	Bridge as Master	Target
Read (2)	Immed	Bridge as Master	Bridge as Master	Bridge as Master
Non-Memory Write (5)	Immed./Split Response	Target	Bridge as Master	Target
Read (3)	Split Response	Target	Bridge as Master	Target
Split Completion in response to a write or read (1)	Immed/Posted	Target	Bridge as Master	Target

Table 10-1-C: PCI-X Data Parity Error In Transaction … Data Parity Error at Target with Intermediate PCI-X/PCI-X BRIDGE as PCI-X Bus Master

Notes:

(1) For split completion transactions, the PCI-X/PCI-X BRIDGE is the PCI-X bus master representing the "original" target which is now the source of the split completion transactions. It is also possble for the PCI-X/PCI-X BRIDGE to be sourcing the split competion transaction and not simply passing them through from the "original" target. The target in the above table is the "original" PCI-X bus master.

(2) The PCI-X/PCI-X BRIDGE will have requested a Split Response termination to the PCI-X bus master on the source bus segment. The data parity error from the target on the destination bus segment will cause the bridge to create the split completion transaction (per the Split Transaction protocol) to source to the PCI-X bus master on the source bus segment and purposely drive bad data parity. If the read is part of a BURST read transaction, the bridge will continue the read of the target on the destination bus segment as if no data parity had occurred.

(3) The PCI-X/PCI-X BRIDGE may receive a data parity error when the Split Response termination is requested by the target on the destination bus segment because the protocol is for the target to drive the AD signal lines with logical "1" in the DATA PHASE.

(4) If the PCI-X/PCI-X BRIDGE detects the assertion of the PERR# signal line on the destination bus segment for a memory write transaction it ported but had driven with bad data parity in reaction to the data parity error it detected as a target on the source bus segment, it will take no futher action than that listed in the table. If the PCI-X/PCI-X BRIDGE detects the assertion of the PERR# signal line on the destination bus segment for a memory write transaction it ported that did not have

a data parity error on the source bus segment, it will take action as listed in the table and assert the SERR# signal line (provided the appropriare SERR# enable bits permit it).

(5)   If the PCI-X/PCI-X BRIDGE detects the assertion of the PERR# signal line on the destination bus segment, it will do one of the following: If the target on the destination bus segment does not request a Split Response termination (*i.e.*, Immediate Transaction) the bridge will source back to the source bus segment a split completion transaction with the Split Completion Message reflecting the error. If the target on the destination bus segment requests a Split Response termination, the bridge takes no further action (*i.e.*, it will forward to the source bus segment the split completion transaction from the target).

The protocol as defined by the PCI-X addendum specification for data error recovery is different then the protocol as defined by the PCI local bus specification. For data parity errors that occur in bus transactions the recovery as follows:

■   As outlined earlier in this subchapter, the Data Parity Error Recovery Enable bit set to logical "1" in a PCI resource's configuration address space indicates that the device driver includes data parity error recovery features. As previously stated, the PCI-X resource that sets the Master Parity Error bit to logical "1" (See Tables 10-1-A to 10-1-C) is also the PCI-X resource that will attempt data parity error recovery.

    ■   The recovery from a data parity error must be controlled by device driver software. It is also required that the operating system API specifies to the device driver software how recovery is to be accomplished, and how all of the previously defined error related bits in the configuration address space are set and reset.

    ■   As previously stated, if the Data Parity Error Recovery Enable bit is set to logical "0" in a PCI resource's configuration address space, it will assert the SERR# signal line (if enabled by the related bits) when a data parity error occurs. As defined by the PCI local bus specification, the assertion of the SERR# signal line ASSUMES a catastrophic reaction by the system. The PCI-X addendum specification does NOT ASSUME a catastrophic reaction by the system for the assertion of the SERR# signal line. However, this assumption does NOT ELIMINATE a catastrophic reaction by the system.

■   If the PCI-X resource's device driver software supports data error recovery (as identified in the previous bullets), the device driver software is informed of the data parity error via an interrupt, Status Register information, flags, or other means. The device driver software can try other methods for recovering from a data parity error. If the device driver is successful without any negative side effects, no further action is required. If the device driver is unsuccessful or is unable to correct the data parity error due to the negative side effects, it must report it to the operating system software.

An exception to the above bullets occurs if the PCI-X bus master is the PCI-X interrupt source and is executing a message signaled interrupt (MSI) memory write transaction. If a data parity error occurs during the execution of an MSI memory write transaction, the PCI-X interrupt source must assert the SERR# signal line immediately. The PCI-X interrupt source does not try to repeat the memory write transaction, alert device driver software, or try any of the other alternative activities previously outlined.

For the PCI-X interrupt source to assert the SERR# signal line for the above situations requires the SERR# Enable bit in its Command register of the configuration address space set to logical "1" by the software. If the SERR# signal line is asserted, the PCI-X interrupt source is also required to set the Signal System Error in its Status register of the configuration address space to logical "1".

10.6 PCI-X SPLIT COMPLETION ERROR MESSAGES

As previously discussed, the PCI-X addendum specification defines the Split Transaction Protocol; part of the protocol includes split completion transactions. Data parity errors in split completion transactions were discussed in the previous subchapter. Address or attribute parity errors in split completion transactions will be discussed in the next subchapter. One of the unique features of the Split Transaction protocol is that errors can occur "outside" of those defined specifically during the execution of PCI and PCI-X bus transactions. These "outside" errors occur internal to a target or PCI-X/PCI-X BRIDGE executing the split transaction protocol. That is, the target or PCI-X/PCI-X BRIDGE has requested Split Response termination of a bus transaction and is in the process of executing the Split Transaction protocol when an error condition is encountered. Consequently, the error condition must be reported via a Split Completion Error Message in the split completion transaction. Consider the following:

- Case A: When a PCI-X bus master is directly writing data to a target (that is not through a PCI-X/PCI-X BRIDGE), address or attribute parity errors, Master Abort terminations, and Target Abort terminations are handled as discussed in other subchapters. But, when a PCI-X write transaction is terminated by a Split Response termination ("original" transaction), it is possible for a data parity error to have occurred in the bus transaction. This write data parity error is reported via Split Completion Error Messages within a split completion transaction. See Split Completion Error reporting requirements below.

- Case B: When a PCI-X bus master is directly reading from a target (that is not through a PCI-X/PCI-X BRIDGE), address or attribute parity errors, Master Abort terminations, and Target Abort terminations are handled as discussed in other subchapters. But, when a PCI-X read transaction is terminated by a Split Response termination ("original" transaction), it is possible for a data parity error to occur in the target ("original" target) is preparing for sourcing data in the split completion transactions. This read data parity error is reported via Split Completion Error Message within a split completion transaction. See Split Completion Error reporting requirements below.

- Case C: It is possible that a PCI-X/PCI-X BRIDGE will request a Split Response termination on the source bus segment side of the bridge with no parity errors (and by definition of Split Response termination no Master Abort or Target Abort termination is requested). On the destination bus segment side of the bridge, a parity error, Target Abort termination, or Master Abort termination may occur in the bus transaction on the destination bus segment associated with bus transaction terminated with Split Response termination on the source bus segment. Consequently, the PCI-X/PCI-X BRIDGE attached to the source bus segment containing the "original" PCI-X bus master will source the split completion transaction with a Split Completion Error Message. See Split Completion Error reporting requirements below.

  - Similarly, on another bus segment not attached to the aforementioned bridge, another PCI-X/PCI-X BRIDGE or the "original" target may detect parity error, Master Abort termination, or Target Abort termination. Consequently, the PCI-X resource will source the split completion transaction with a Split Completion Error Message. The PCI-X/PCI-X BRIDGE attached to the bus segment of the "original" PCI-X bus master (in addition to other bridges in the path) will be passing through a split completion transaction with Split Completion Error Message.

- Case D: It is possible that a PCI-X/PCI-X BRIDGE will request a Split Response termination on the source bus segment side of the bridge with no parity errors (and by definition of Split Response termination, no Master Abort or Target Abort termination is requested). On the destination bus segment side of the bridge, the target determines that the bus transaction is requesting a byte count out of range or some other device specific error has occurred. Consequently, the target will source the split completion transaction with a Split Completion Error Message. The target may indeed be behind several PCI-X/PCI-X BRIDGES. The PCI-X/PCI-X BRIDGE attached to the bus segment of the "original" PCI-X bus master (in addition to other bridges in the path) will be passing through a split completion transaction with Split Completion Error Message.

In the above four cases (A to D), the split completion transaction is executed without a parity error, Master Abort termination, or Target Abort termination associated with the execution of the split completion transaction. The split completion transaction is reporting back to the "original" PCI-X bus master one of the errors defined in Table 10-5 occurred during the execution of the Split Transaction protocol for these four cases. The "original" PCI-X bus master as defined by the Split Transaction protocol that receives a Split Completion Error Message must set the Received Split Completion Error bit in its Status register of the configuration address space to logical "1". In Case B there is no specific Message Index for the occurrence of a read data parity error at the "original" target. This case can be handled by the device specific definition of "8X" in the Message Index.

Message Class	Message Index	Message Description	Bits Set to Logical "1" in the Status Register of PCI-X Resource
1 (Used by PCI-X/PCI-X BRIDGES)	00h	Master Abort	Received Master Abort
1 (Used by PCI-X/PCI-X BRIDGES)	01h	Target Abort	Received Target Abort
1 (Used by PCI-X/PCI-X BRIDGES)	02h	Write data parity error	Master Data Pariy Error bit
2 (Used by "orignal" target)	00h	Byte Count out of range	None
2 (Used by "orignal" target)	01h	Split Write Data parity Error (2)	Master Data Pariy Error bit
2 (Used by "orignal" target)	8Xh (1)	Device Specific	None

Table 10-2: Split Completion Error Messages

Notes: (1) "X" is device specific and is defined outside of the PCI-X addendum specification.
(2) Write data parity error occurred at the "orginal" target simultaneous with the Split Response termination request.

As defined for Table 10-2, the Status register of the PCI-X resource is the Status register of the configuration address space of the "original" PCI-X bus master. Similarly, these bits exist in the Secondary Status Register of a PCI-X/PCI-X BRIDGE. See Subchapter 4.16: *PCI-X 32 Data Bit Bus master to 32 Data Bit Target* for more information.

If a PCI-X/PCI-X BRIDGE is forwarding a split completion transaction upstream with a Split Completion Error Message for a Target Abort termination (Message Class 01h and Message Index 01h), it must set the Signaled Target Abort bit in the Status register of the configuration address space to logical "1". If a PCI-X/PCI-X BRIDGE is forwarding a split completion transaction downstream with a Split Completion Error Message for a Target Abort termination (Message Class 01h and Message Index 01h), it must set the Signaled Target Abort bit in the Secondary Status register of the configuration address space to logical "1".

In addition to the error conditions discussed above, the PCI-X addendum specification has two other error conditions to be considered:

- A PCI-X bus master that is sourcing a split completion transaction ("original" target or a PCI-X/PCI-X BRIDGE representing the "original" target) may receive a Master Abort or Target Abort termination. The PCI-X bus master must discard the split completion transaction. The PCI-X bus master does not set the Received Master Abort or Received Target Abort termination bits in its Status register of the configuration address space to logical "1". If the "original" transaction was a write transaction or a read transaction to a prefetchable address space (no negative side affects for reading and discarding data), no further action is taken. If the "original" transaction was a read transaction to a non-prefetchable address space (negative side affects for reading and discarding data), the PCI-X bus master must set the Split Completion Discard bit in its Status register of the configuration address space to logical "1". The PCI-X bus master is also required to assert the SERR# signal line if the SERR# Enable bit in its Command register of the configuration address space is set to logical "1". If the SERR# signal line is asserted, the PCI-X bus master is also required to set the Signal System Error in its Status register of the configuration address space to logical "1".

- The Master Abort termination may be requested for many reasons. These reasons include the "original" PCI-X bus master as the target receiving a split completion transaction with corrupted Requester ID, TAG number, Sequence ID, byte count (Upper and Lower Byte Count), and/or Lower Address. Consider the following:

■ A target ("original" PCI-X bus master) may receive a split completion transaction that contains a corrupted Requester ID. The corrupted Requestor ID may coincidentally match the Requester ID of an active PCI-X bus master but the TAG number and/or the Sequence ID does not match. Similarly, the Requester ID may be correct but the TAG number or Sequence ID may be corrupted and not match an active TAG number and Sequence ID. The target can execute one of the following:

■ The target can ignore the split completion transaction (not assert DEVSEL# signal line and thus cause a Master Abort termination). This is the preferred solution of the target that does not have any outstanding responses of split completion transactions.

OR

■ The target can claim the split completion transaction (assert DEVSEL# signal line). The target is then required to accept all of the split completion transaction and discard the data.

■ A target ("original" PCI-X bus master) may receive a split completion transaction that contains a corrupted byte count and/or Lower address. If the Requestor ID, Sequence ID, and TAG numbers all match valid numbers, the target is required to claim the split completion transaction (assert DEVSEL# signal line). The target is then required to accept all of the split completion transaction and discard the data.

■ When the bus transaction is claimed and the data is discarded per the above bullets, the target must set the Unexpected Split Completion bit in the Status register of the configuration address space to logical "1". See Chapter 8: *Master and Target Termination* for more information.

■ The Target Abort termination may be requested for many reasons. These reasons include the "original" PCI-X bus master receiving a split completion transaction with corrupted address or byte count. See Chapter 8: *Master and Target Termination* for more information.

In general, when a PCI/PCI-X BRIDGE is porting a split completion transaction containing a Split Completion Error Message, it must set the appropriate error related bits in its Status and Secondary registers of the configuration address space to logical "1".

10.7   PCI-X SERR# SIGNAL LINE OPERATION

The PCI-X addendum specification defines the implementation of the SERR# signal line protocol the same as the PCI local bus specification (for both bus transactions and non-bus transactions). Also, a PCI-X resource that can also be the PCI-X interrupt source (for MSI protocol) must assert the SERR# signal line for data parity, Master Abort termination, and Target Abort termination in the same fashion as discussed in the previous subchapters for a PCI interrupt source

The differences between the PCI-X addendum specification's implementation of the SERR# signal line and the PCI local bus specification's implementation is as follows:

- All PCI-X bus transactions contain an ATTRIBUTE PHASE; consequently, in addition to an address parity error, there is defined an attribute parity error. The attribute parity error follows the same protocol as an address parity error including the use of the SERR# signal line. All of the options for how to use the SERR# signal line as it applies to the address parity error also applies on the attribute parity error with one exception. If the attribute error occurred in a bus transaction and the target requests a Split Response termination, the target must discard the associated bus transaction and assert the SERR# signal line. (if enabled). The target is also required to assert the SERR# signal line if both the Parity Error Response and SERR# Enable bits are set to logical "1" in its Command register of the configuration address space. That is, the PCI-X resource does not execute the bus transaction and no split completion transactions are sourced. If the SERR# signal line is asserted, the PCI-X resource also must set to logical "1" the Signal System Error bit in its Status register of the configuration address space.

- The assertion or non-assertion of the SERR# signal line for PCI-X bus transactions related to parity errors (collectively the address, attribute, and data parity errors), Master Abort terminations, and Target Abort terminations sometimes differs from PCI bus transactions:

  - For NON-SPLIT COMPLETION PCI-X BUS TRANSACTIONS, the response by PCI-X resources for address parity and attribute errors is the same as the response by PCI resources for address parity errors (with the exception noted above for Split Response termination for attribute error). The only difference is that the phrase "Disconnect, Retry, Completion, or Completion with timeout terminations" applied to PCI bus transactions is replaced by the phrase "Single Phase Disconnect, Disconnect at Next ADB, Split Response, Retry, Completion, or Completion with timeout terminations" for PCI-X bus transactions.

■ For NON-SPLIT COMPLETION PCI-X BUS TRANSACTIONS, the protocol for assertion of the SERR# signal line for data party errors, Master Abort terminations, and Target Abort terminations is essentially the same as for PCI bus transactions. The only differences are as follows:

  ■ As previously discussed, the assertion of the SERR# signal line for a data parity error (in addition to PCI local bus specification requirements) requires that the Data Parity Error Recovery Enable bit in the Status register of the configuration address space to be set to logical "0". See Subchapter 10.5 for more information.

  ■ If the data parity is detected in a read transaction when a Split Response termination is requested, the PCI-X bus master must report a data parity as defined for a read transaction without a Split Response termination (see Subchapter 10 for more information) with the following additional considerations: (Note: Even though no data is available the target is required to drive all AD signal lines (qualified by ACK64# signal line) to logical "1" during the DATA PHASE).

    ■ The PCI-X bus master must assert the SERR# signal line (if the SERR# signal line is enabled as previously discussed) if the Data Parity Error Recovery bit in the COMMAND register of the configuration address space is set to logical "0" (*i.e.*, the PERR# signal line is asserted but data recovery is not supported).

    ■ The PCI-X bus master does not assert the SERR# signal line if the Data Parity Error Recovery bit in the COMMAND register of the configuration address space is set to logical "1" (*i.e.*, the PERR# signal line is asserted and data recovery by the PCI-X bus master is supported). The PCI-X bus master can optionally report the data parity by setting a unique status bit in a device-specific register. If the PCI-X bus master optionally requests an interrupt, it is recommended that the interrupt occurs after the completion of the associated "sequence" of split completion transactions.

    ■ The data error recovery protocol for a read bus transaction with a Split Response termination does not have to be the same protocol as for data parity errors for the associated Split Completion transactions

- ■ A data parity error in the read bus transaction with a Split Response termination does not imply that the associated Split Completion transactions will have an error.

■ For SPLIT COMPLETION PCI-X BUS TRANSACTIONS, the response by PCI-X resources for address parity and attribute errors is the same as the response by PCI resources for address parity errors. The only difference is that the phrase "Disconnect, Retry, Completion, or Completion with timeout terminations" applied to PCI bus transactions is replaced by the phrase "Disconnect at Next ADB, Retry, Completion, or Completion with timeout terminations" for PCI-X bus transactions.

■ For SPLIT COMPLETION PCI-X BUS TRANSACTIONS, the protocol for assertion of the SERR# signal line for data party errors, Master Abort terminations, and Target Abort terminations is essentially the same as for PCI bus transactions. The only differences are as follows:

- ■ As previously discussed, the assertion of the SERR# signal line for a data parity error (in addition to PCI local bus specification requirements) requires that the Data Parity Error Recovery Enable bit in the Status register of the configuration address space to be set to logical "0". See Subchapter 10.5 for more information.

- ■ As discussed in the previous subchapter, the SERR# signal line (if the SERR# Enable bit in its Command register of the configuration address space is set to logical "1") must be asserted (under certain conditions) for a Master Abort or Target Abort terminations of split completion transactions. If the SERR# signal line is asserted, the PCI-X bus master is also required to set the Signal System Error in its Status register of the configuration address space to logical "1". See the previous subchapter for more information.

■ The assertion of the SERR# signal line for discarding of the data and bus transactions according to the Discard Timer as part of the Delayed Transaction protocol is not defined by PCI-X addendum specification.

CHAPTER 11

RESET, POWER, AND SIGNAL LINE INITIALIZATION

This chapter consists of the following subchapters:

11.0   RESET
11.1   Power
11.2   Signal Line Initialization
11.3   Bus Segment Interoperability

11.0 RESET

The PCI bus local bus specification and PCI-X addendum define a RESET protocol that is typical for most platforms. In addition, unlike other buses, the PCI and PCI-X bus segments require a central resource to monitor certain PCI and PCI-X signal lines during RESET.

The RESET protocol (RESET) discussed below is relative to each specific bus segment. The reset across a platform is required to consider how the reset is ported through a bridge. See Chapter 7: *Bridge and Interface Protocol* for more information.

RESET on a bus segment occurs when the RST# signal line is asserted. This signal line changes states asynchronously to the CLK signal line, and must transition in a clean fashion without spikes between the minimum V_{ih} and maximum V_{il} (see Chapter 12: *Signal Line Timing and Electrical Requirements*, for more information). When the power good signal line (PWR_GOOD# in Figure 11-1) from the power supply indicates the voltage levels are above the minimums outlined in Table 11-1, the RST# signal line is asserted. The RST# signal line remains asserted until the following three events occur (see Figure 11-1):

- The RST# signal line is asserted for a minimum of 1 millisecond (T2).

- The CLK signal line has been oscillating a minimum of 100 microseconds (T3).

- Voltage levels outlined in Table 11-1 have remained above the minimum levels (PWR_GOOD# asserted) for about 100 milliseconds (T1).

VOLTAGE NAME	MINIMUM	MAXIMUM
5.0	4.75	5.25
3.3	3.00	3.60
12.0	11.40	12.60
−12.0	−11.80	−13.20

Table 11-1: Minimum and maximum voltage levels

The RST# signal line timings relative to other signal lines and platform events are outlined in Table 11-2 and pictured in Figure 11-1.

An important consideration is when the voltage levels fall below the minimum levels. For many power supplies, the PWR_GOOD# signal line may only reflect the status of the 5 or 3.3 volt supplies. Therefore the PWR_GOOD# signal line does not necessarily reflect the integrity of all voltages. If the 3.3 or 5 volt power rails fail to meet the values listed in Table 11-1, the RST# signal line must be asserted. However, the power supply (via the PWR_GOOD# signal line) may not be monitoring both the 5 and 3.3 volts. According to the PCI local bus specification and PCI-X addendum specification, the criteria for RESET are as follows:

- The smaller T5 of the following two conditions:

  - The RST# signal line must be asserted within 500 nanoseconds (T5) (see Figure 11-1) from when 3.3 or 5 volts exceeds (by 500 millivolts) the minimum and maximum values in Table 11-1.

  OR

  - The RST# signal line must be asserted within 100 nanoseconds (T5) (see Figure 11-1) from when the 5 volt rail falls below the 3.3 volt rail by 300 millivolts or more.

- The RST# signal line must be asserted during power up or during a power fail situation. The PCI and PCI-X resources are not considered RESET until the times of both T2 and T3 have been met (see Figure 11-1).

- The assertion of the RST# signal lines require all PCI and PCI-X resources on the bus segments to tri-state the signal lines within 40 nanoseconds (T6) (see Figure 11-1).

> When the RST# signal line is asserted, all of the output drivers (except for the CLK signal line) must be tri-stated.

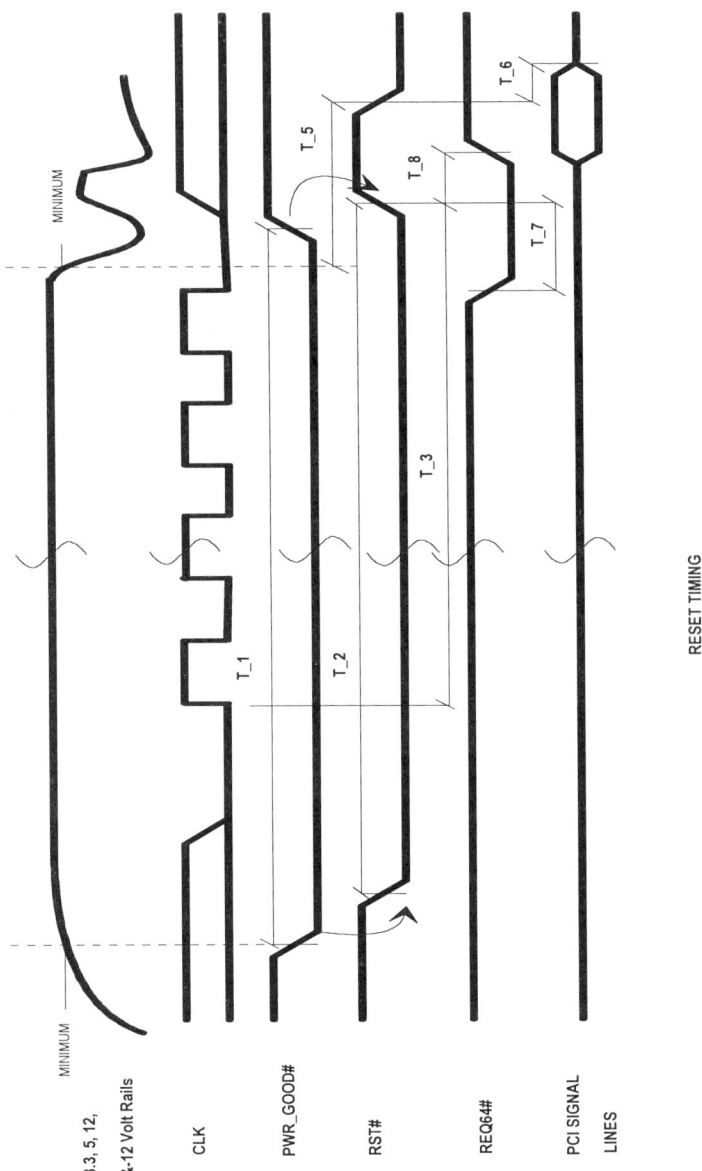

Figure 11-1: RESET Timing

The above figure is copied from *PCI Local Bus Specification Rev. 2.2*. Reprinted with the permission of the PCI Special Interest Group.

823

RST# signal line change of states do not have to be synchronous with the CLK signal line. Therefore, the 40 nanosecond requirement (T6) must be met independently of the CLK signal line.

The power up sequence for the power pins (3.3 V, 5.0V, +5V (I/O), and +3.3V (I/O) is not defined in Rev. 2.2 and earlier revisions of the PCI bus specification. If the system supports 3.3Vaux it is required to execute the power up sequence for the power pins and 3.3Vaux according to power management requirements. See the *PCI Bus Power Management* and *PCI Hot Plug Application and Design* books (available from annabooks.com) and the *PCI-X addendum bus specification* for more information.

Tables 11-1A and B below summarizes the above and other timing references to the RESET protocol.

Name	Reference # in Figure 11-1	Parameter	Min	Max	Units	Notes
trst	T2	RST# Asserted Time After Power Stable	1		ms	1
trst-clk	T3	RST# Deasserted Time After CLK Stable	100		µs	1
	T1	Stable power levels per PWR_GOOD	100		ms	
trst-off	T6	RST# deasserted to Output Float Delay		40	ns	1, 2,4
trrsu	T7	REQ64# to RST# setup time	10		CLK signal line periods	5
trhfa	Not shown in Fig. 11-1	RST# deasserted to first configuration transaction	2 ^{25}		CLK signal line periods	5
trhff	Not shown in Fig. 11-1	RST# deasserted to first assertion of FRAME#	5		CLK signal line periods	5
trrh	T8	RST# to REQ64# hold time	0	50	ns	5
tfail	T5	RST# Asserted After Power Rails Unstable		500	ns	
tfail	T5	RST# Asserted After 5 V rail is below 3.3 V rail by 300 mv		100	ns	
	Not shown in Fig. 11-1	RST# Slew Rate	50		MV/ns	3

Table 11-1-A: PCI RST# Signal Line Timing Considerations

Notes
1.   RST# is asserted and deasserted asynchronously with respect to CLK. signal line. The CLK signal line
      is stable when all of the thigh, tcyc, and tlow parameters are met See Chapter 12: *Signal Line Timing
      and Electrical Requirements* for more information.
2.   All output drivers must be floated when RST# is active.
3.   The minimum RST# slew rate applies only to the rising (deassertion) edge of the reset signal, and
      ensures that system noise cannot render an otherwise monotonic signal to appear to bounce in the
      switching range.
4.   For purposes of Active/Float timing measurements, the Hi-Z or "off" state is defined to be when the
      total current delivered through the component pin is less than or equal to the leakage current
      specification.
5.   See below for further discussion.

Name	Reference # in Figure 11-1	Parameter	Min	Max	Units	Notes
trst	T2	RST# Asserted Time After Power Stable	1		ms	1
trst-clk	T3	RST# Deasserted Time After CLK Stable	100		µs	1
tpvrh	T1	Stable power levels per PWR_GOOD	100		ms	
trst-off	T6	RST# deasserted to Output Float Delay		40	ns	1, 2,4
trrsu	T7	REQ64# to RST# setup time	10		CLK signal line periods	6
trhfa	Not shown in Fig. 11-1	RST# deasserted to first configuration transaction	2 26		CLK signal line periods	5, 6
trhff	Not shown in Fig. 11-1	RST# deasserted to first assertion of FRAME#	5		CLK signal line periods	5, 6
trrh	T8	RST# to REQ64# hold time	0	50	ns	6
tfail	T5	Reset Asserted After Power Rails Unstable		500	ns	
tfail	T5	RST# Asserted After 5 V rail is below 3.3 V rail by 300 mv		100	ns	
tprsu	Not shown in Fig. 11-1	Initialization pattern setup to RST# deasserted	10		CLK signal line periods	6
tprh	Not shown in Fig. 11-1	Initialization pattern hold from to RST# deasserted	0	50	ns	5,6
trlcx	Not shown in Fig. 11-1	RST# asserted to change in CLK signal line frequency	0			6
	Not shown in Fig. 11-1	RST# Slew Rate	50		MV/ns	3

Table 11-1-B: PCI-X RST# Signal Line Timing Considerations

Notes

1. RST# is asserted and deasserted asynchronously with respect to CLK. signal line. The CLK signal line is stable when all of the thigh, tcyc, and tlow parameters are met See Chapter 12: *Signal Line Timing and Electrical Requirements* for more information.
2. All output drivers must be floated when RST# is active.
3. The minimum RST# slew rate applies only to the rising (deassertion) edge of the reset signal, and ensures that system noise cannot render an otherwise monotonic signal to appear to bounce in the switching range.
4. For purposes of Active/Float timing measurements, the Hi-Z or "off" state is defined to be when the total current delivered through the component pin is less than or equal to the leakage current specification.
5. In addition, the initialization pattern is required to be held no later than two CLK signal line periods before the assertion of the FRAME# signal line and tri-stated no later than one CLK signal line period before the assertion of the FRAME# signal line.
6. See below for further discussion.

After the RST# signal line is deasserted, there is period of time that a PCI or PCI-X resource may not be ready to participate in a bus transaction. For example, a PCI or PCI-X resource may have to complete an internal initialization before being able to respond as a target. There are two time periods defined immediately after the deassertion of the RST# signal line: trhff and trhfa. The period of time between the deassertion of the RST# signal line to the end of the trhff period is defined as 5 CLK signal line periods. The period of time between the deassertion of the RST# signal line to the end of the trhfa period is 2^{25} CLK signal line periods for a PCI bus segment and 2^{26} CLK signal line periods for a PCI-X bus segment.

The interpretation of the trhff period is as follows:

■ No bus transactions (assertion of the FRAME# signal line) are permitted prior to the end of the trhff period.

■ If the PCI or PCI-X resource is between the HOST CPU and the boot ROM (not expansion ROM) or is the boot ROM itself, it is required to be ready to support bus transactions immediately after the end of the trhff period.

■ If a PCI or PCI-X resource is not ready to support a bus transaction at the end of the trhff period, its internal state machine must remain in reset until all of the following conditions are met:

■ The RST# signal line is deasserted.

■ The PCI or PCI-X resource is ready to respond to bus transactions.

■ The bus segment is in the idle state (FRAME# and IRDY# signal lines are both deasserted).

The interpretation of the trhfa period is as follows:

■ Initialization software in the HOST CPU is allowed to begin bus transactions after the end of the trhff period and before the end of the trhfa period. Consequently, the following must be considered:

■ All PCI and PCI-X resources should attempt to complete initialization before the end of the trhfa period, but are not required to do so with one exception: If a PCI or PCI-X resource is between the HOST CPU and the boot ROM (not expansion ROM) or is the boot ROM itself, it must be ready to support bus transactions at the end of the trhff period and before the end of the trhfa period.

■ Within this trhfa period and after the end of the trhff period, the initialization software in a PCI or PCI-X bus master must accept Master Abort or Retry terminations from the PCI or PCI-X resources it is addressing with bus transactions. Other considerations are:

   ■ Prior to the completion of the internal initialization and prior to the end of the trhfa period, the PCI and PCI-X resources must complete the bus transaction addressing it with a Master Abort or Retry termination if not ready to accept bus transactions (with the exception of the boot ROM discussed above).

   ■ If the initialization software knows in advance that all PCI and PCI-X resources will complete their internal initialization prior to the end of the trhfa period, the software can begin configuration access cycles prior to the end of the trhfa period.

■ PCI and PCI-X resources should complete internal initialization and be ready to accept a bus transaction by the end of the trhfa period. If the internal initialization of a PCI or PCI-X resource is not completed by the end of the trhfa period, the resource must respond to bus transactions addressing it with a Retry termination.

■ The "PCI 16 clock", "PCI 8 clock", "PCI-X 16 clock", and "PCI-X 8 clock" rules do not apply during the trhfa period. Also, "Master Latency" and Maximum Retry Timer protocols do not apply during the trhfa period.

The PCI-X addendum specification defines an initialization pattern on the TRDY#, STOP#, DEVSEL# signal lines. During RESET the initialization pattern defines the bus segment as PCI or PCI-X compliant. The initialization pattern also defines the frequency of the CLK signal line. For a PCI-X bus segment, the initialization pattern and when the change in the CLK signal line occurs is defined by the tprsu, tprh, and trlcx periods during RESET (See Table 11-1-B). See Subchapter 11.3: *Bus Segment Interoperability* for more information.

The tprsu and tprh periods define the timing relationship of the RST#4 signal line and the TRDY#, STOP#, DEVSEL# signal lines (collectively called "initialization pattern") during RESET as follows:

■ After the RST# signal line is asserted, trst establishes the minimum time the RST# signal line remains asserted (T2). At the end of the trst minimum time the RST# signal can be deasserted. The initialization pattern must be valid a minimum setup period (tprsu) relative to the earliest deassertion point of the RST# signal line. After the RST# is deasserted the initialization pattern is held for the time defined by tprh. The adherence to the tprh maximum time is required because the initialization pattern is encoded onto the TRDY#, STOP#, and DEVSEL# signal lines, and used as part of the bus transaction protocol.

The PCI-X addendum specification defines changes in the CLK signal line frequency during RESET. The PCI local bus specification defined that the CLK signal line had to be at a stable frequency a minimum time before the RST# signal line is deasserted (trst-clk). The PCI-X addendum specification also defines the trst-clk period, and also defines the trlcx period as follows:

- The minimum time from the RST# signal line asserted to the change in the CLK signal line frequency is trlcx.

11.1 POWER

The PCI local bus specification and the PCI-X addendum do not define the sequence of power rail activation or deactivation, or the rate of change. All bus segments (independent of whether 3.3 volt or 5 volt signaling is implemented) must provide power to all 5, 12, -12, and 3.3 volt power pins. As previously discussed, there are some issues relative to 3.3 Vaux. See the *PCI Bus Power Management* and *PCI Hot Plug Application & Design* books (available at annabooks.com) and the *PCI-X addendum bus specification* for more information.

Each add-in card connector must be able to provide a minimum of 500 milliamps at 12 +/- 5% volts and a minimum of 100 milliamps at –12 +/- 5% volts. There is a maximum current limit for the 5 V and 3.3 V power pins on each connector. For 5 V +/- 5% the maximum is 5 amps. For 3.3 V +/- 10% the maximum is 7.6 amps. The actual available maximum current is bus segment dependent.

The total power to be supplied to each connector will vary depending upon the value of the PRSNT1# and PRSNT2# pins on each connector according to the following protocol:

- No power—no add-in card attached. Both PRSNT1# and PRSNT2# are open.

- Maximum of 25 watts when PRSNT1# is grounded and PRSNT2# is open by add-in card.

- Maximum of 15 watts when PRSNT1# is open and PRSNT2# is grounded by add-in card.

■ Maximum of 7.5 watts when PRSNT1# is grounded and PRSNT2# is grounded by add-in card.

> In addition to the above information about the add-in card power requirements, the PRSNT1# or PRSNT2# pins also indicate the existence of an add-in card in the connector. As noted in the above bullet, when both PRSNT1# or PRSNT2# pins are open no add-in card is installed.

The above wattages represent the maximum power from all power rails. In the worst case condition, it may not be possible for the platform power supply to provide the maximum power to all connectors. Consequently, PCI and PCI-X add-in cards that consume more than 10 watts under full operation should have a power-saving state. In the power-saving state, the configuration address space and bootstrap functions should be fully operational. Add-in cards installed in platforms with advanced power management may be required to report (via registers) their respective power requirements before exiting the power-saving state. Power may also be reduced with lower CLK signal line frequencies

> Unless an add-in card is designed as some sort of special power source, no add-in card should ever supply power TO the bus segment.

11.2 SIGNAL LINE INITIALIZATION

Chapter 5: *Signal Line Definition* describes the value of the signal lines during RESET (RST# signal line is asserted). Of special concern is the REQ64# signal line. For a PCI or PCI-X resource that becomes a PCI or PCI-X bus master and requests a 64 data bit bus transaction requires a 64 data bit bus segment. The REQ64# signal line is connected to all PCI and PCI-X resources and connectors that are attached to a 64 data bit bus. Those connectors that are not attached to a 64 data bit bus segment have their respective REQ64# signal lines driven to a logical "1" by pull-up resistors. The central resource asserts the REQ64# signal lines relative to the rising edge of the RST# signal line. The sampling of the asserted REQ64# signal line during this period indicates to all PCI and PCI-X resources that they can become a PCI or PCI-X bus master and execute 64 data bit bus transactions. The setup time (T7) is 10 x CLK signal line periods, and the hold time (T8) is a minimum of 0 nanoseconds and a maximum of 50 nanoseconds (see Figure 11-1).

Another signal line that has special meaning during RESET is the MM66EN. As discussed in Chapter 5: *Signal Line Definition* and other places in the book, the

M66EN signal line establishes the support of a 66 MHz CLK signal line frequency.

The PCI-X addendum specification has expanded information provided during RESET. In conjunction with the M66EN signal line, the PCIXCAP signal line defines bus segment compliance to either the PCI local bus specification or the PCI-X addendum specification. In the case of PCI-X addendum specification compliance, during RESET the TRDY#, DEVSEL#, and STOP# signal lines provide additional information about bus segment operation. See the next subchapter for more information.

11.3 BUS SEGMENT INTEROPERABILITY

The phrases "33 MHz", "66 MHz", "100 MHz", and "133 MHz" are sometimes used in this book. These are the generic names for add-in cards, devices, or bus segments that can operate with the maximum CLK signal line frequencies of 33.3, 66.6, 100, or 133.2 MHz, respectively.

A platform can be built with all its bus segments compliant only to the PCI local bus specification, or with all bus segments compliant only to the PCI-X addendum specifications, or with a mixture of bus segments in terms of compliance to either the PCI local bus specification or the PCI-X addendum bus specification.

A bus segment compliant to only the PCI local bus specification cannot operate with PCI-X bus transactions. Consequently, any PCI-X add-in cards or attached devices must be able to operate with PCI bus transactions when installed into a bus segment compliant only to PCI local bus specification (which is a requirement of a PCI-X compliant add-in card or device).

A bus segment compliant to the PCI-X addendum specification must be able to operate with either PCI bus transactions or PCI-X bus transactions. If all of the add-in cards and attached devices are compliant to the PCI-X addendum specification, only PCI-X bus transactions will be executed. If one of the add-in cards or any attached device is only PCI local bus specification compliant, only PCI bus transactions will be executed. Consequently, any PCI-X add-in cards or attached devices must be able to operate with PCI bus transactions (that is a requirement of a PCI-X compliant add-in card or device). A PCI-X add-in card or attached device must be compliant to PCI 33 MHz with 32 data bits as a minimum. A PCI-X add-in card or attached device is not required to be compliant to PCI 66 MHz or the PCI or PCI-X 64 data bit extension.

As previously discussed in the book, there are some restrictions to PCI and PCI-X add-in cards and devices relative to PCI or PCI-X compliance and signaling voltage levels as follows:

- PCI 33 MHz add-in cards or devices can support either 5 or 3.3 volt signaling. They can be built as 5 volt only signaling, 3.3 volt only signaling, or universal I/O.

- PCI 66 MHz add-in cards or devices are 3.3 volt signaling only. They can be built as 3.3 volt only signaling or universal I/O. They can also be implemented as a 5 volt only signaling with operation restricted to PCI 33 MHz.

- PCI-X 66 MHz add-in cards or devices are 3.3 volt signaling only. They can be built as 3.3 volt only signaling or universal I/O. They can also be implemented as a 5 volt only signaling with operation restricted to PCI 33 MHz .

- PCI-X 133 MHz add-in cards or devices are 3.3 volt signaling only. They can be built as 3.3 volt only signaling or universal I/O. They can also be implemented as a 5 volt only signaling with operation restricted to PCI 33 MHz.

> PCI 3.0 local bus specification places an additional restriction on the four bullets above. The preceding bullets assert that add-in cards keyed as 5 volt only, 3.3 volt only, or universal I/O signaling add-in cards are permitted, which is true for PCI 2.2. The PCI 3.0 local bus specification DOES NOT permit add-in cards keyed for 5 volt only signaling. Devices that reside on the bus segment are required to follow the same signaling voltage restrictions as add-in cards.

The determination that a bus segment will support either a PCI or PCI-X bus transaction is determined by the PCIXCAP signal line. For a PCI-X bus segment, the PCIXCAP signal lines are bussed together, attached to a signal pull-up resistor to Vcc, and attached to voltage level comparitor circuit. (See the PCI-X addendum specification Section 14 appendix for more information.) For a PCI add-in card or device, this signal line is attached to ground. For PCI-X add-in cards or devices that can operate at 133 MHz, this signal line is open. For a PCI-X add-in card or device that can operate only at 66 MHz, this signal line is pulled down to ground with a 10K resistor (providing a non-zero voltage).

In addition, the M66EN signal line will be monitored by platform circuitry to further determine the bus transaction protocol of the bus segment. Collectively, platform circuitry uses this information to provide the initialization pattern (will be discussed in the next section). Table 11-2 lists a summary of the possibilities as viewed on the bus segment. If a logical combination of M66EN and PCIXCAP signal line is not listed, it is not defined. Also note the frequency ranges possible for the CLK signal line.

(REF Letter) BUS SEGMENT DESIGNED FOR	M66EN	PCIXCAP	Protocol used with CLK Signal Line Frequency PCI - 33 = PCI with DC to 33.3 MHz PCI - 66= PCI with 33.3+ to 66.6 MHz PCI-X - 66 = PCI-X with 50 to 66.6 MHz PCI-X - 133 = PCI-X with 66.6+ to 133.2 MHz		
			PCI resources operate with protocol of		PCI-X resources operate with protocol of
			Add-in card built for 5V Signaling Only	Add-in card built for 3.3 V or Universal I/O Signaling	Add-in card built for 3.3 V or Universal I/O Signaling (Notes)
(A) PCI	"1"	"0" ground	NA	PCI – 66 Univ. I/O = 3.3 V (2)	PCI – 66 Univ. I/O = 3.3 V (2)
(B) PCI	"0"	"0" ground	PCI – 33 (3)	PCI – 33 Univ. I/O = 3.3/5 V	PCI – 33 Univ. I/O = 3.3 V or 5 V (1)
(C) PCI-X	"1"	"0" ground	NA	PCI – 66 Univ. I/O = 3.3 V (2)	PCI – 66 Univ. I/O = 3.3 V (2)
(D) PCI-X	"0"	"0" ground	PCI – 33 (3)	PCI – 33 Univ. I/O = 3.3/5 V	PCI – 33 Univ. I/O = 3.3 V or 5 V (1)
(E) PCI-X	"1"	"0/1" non-zero voltage with pull-down to ground	NA	NA	PCI-X – 66 Univ. I/O = 3.3 V
(F-1) PCI-X	"1"	"1"	NA	NA	PCI-X –133 operated at 100 MHz Univ. I/O = 3.3 V
(F-2) PCI-X	"1"	"1"	NA	NA	PCI-X –133 Univ. I/O = 3.3 V

Table 11-2: Bus Segment Interoperability

Notes:

(1)   The abitlity for a PCI-X add-in card to support 5 V only signaling in PCI mode is optional. For compliance to revision 3.0 of the PCI local bus specification, add-in cards with the 5 volt only signaling are not permitted.

(2)   Support of PCI 66 by a PCI or PCI-X add-in card is optional.

(3)   For compliance to revision 3.0 of the PCI local bus specification, a 5 volt only signaling add-in cards are not supported.

As discussed above, the bus segment platform circuitry drives the initialization pattern. The initialization pattern is encoded onto the TRDY#, DEVSEL# and STOP# signal lines during RESET (see earlier subchapters of this chapter). There is one additional piece of information that the platform circuitry must consider: For a PCI-X 133 MHz bus segment it is virtually impossible to support a connector on a bus segment. If a specific bus segment supports two connectors, and has all PCI-X 133 MHz resources, the CLK signal line should run at 100 MHz. If there are any PCI resources or PCI-X 66 MHz resources on the bus segment, 100 MHz and 133 MHz operation are not possible.

As discussed above, there is no such thing as a 100 MHz PCI-X add-in card or device. There is only the opportunity to operate the bus segment with a 100 MHz CLK signal line frequency for loading (two connectors, etc.) considerations.

As previously discussed in this chapter, the TRDY#, DEVEL# and STOP# signal lines encode the initialization pattern during RESET. The initialization pattern establishes the CLK signal line frequency and bus transaction protocol (*i.e.*, PCI or PCI-X) for the bus segment. Table 11-3 summarizes this information. In Table 11-2 there is a "reference letter" in the first column. The associated row in Table 11-2 relates to the row in Table 11-3 with the same reference letter in its first column. In the case of reference letters "F-1" and "F-2" in Table 11-2, the associated rows identifies a PCI-X-133 protocol. Depending on the number of connectors and other factors, the bus segment will implement the PCI-X-133 with a 100 MHz CLK signal line frequency (F-1) versus implementing PCI-X-133 with a 133 MHz CLK signal line frequency (F-2).

All possible initialization patterns (assertion/deassertion) not listed in Table 11-3 for TRDY#, DEVSEL#, and STOP# are reserved.

The M66EN and PCIXCAP signal lines achieve logical "1" (Table 11-2 and 11-3) by the resource leaving the signal line open and relying on the pull-up resistor to Vcc.

(REF Letter) BUS SEG. DES. FOR	M66EN	PCIXCAP	CLK Min/Max Freq. MHz [Tran. Protocol]	Driven on bus segment system at rising edges of RST# to establish clock frequency and bus transaction protocol		
				DEVSEL#	STOP#	TRDY#
(A) PCI	"1"	"0" ground	33+/66 [PCI]	Deasserted	Deasserted	Deasserted
(B) PCI	"0"	"0" ground	DC/33 [PCI]	Deasserted	Deasserted	Deasserted
(C) PCI-X	"1"	"0" ground	33+/66 [PCI]	Deasserted	Deasserted	Deasserted
(D) PCI-X	"0"	"0" ground	DC/33 [PCI]	Deasserted	Deasserted	Deasserted
(E) PCI-X	"1"	"0/1" non-zero voltage with pull-down to ground	50/66 [PCI-X]	Deasserted	Deasserted	Asserted
(F-1) PCI-X	"1"	"1"	66+/100 [PCI-X]	Deasserted	Asserted	Deasserted
(F-2) PCI-X	"1"	"1"	100+/133 [PCI-X]	Deasserted	Asserted	Asserted

Table 11-3: Bus Segment Initialization Pattern

CHAPTER 12

SIGNAL LINE TIMING AND ELECTRICAL REQUIREMENTS

This chapter consists of the following subchapters:

12.0 OVERVIEW

The PCI local bus specification provides well-defined electrical specifications. Although some of these specifications may seem like an extra burden for the designer, these items are necessary for promoting interoperability between PCI components and add-in cards. The PCI electrical specifications have been written with total bus segment operation in mind.

The electrical specification has attempted to address a wide variety of potential market applications without overburdening the user that has just one solution in mind. This is demonstrated by the add-on nature of the 64 bit extension or use of +3.3 volt logic. Although most I/O buses currently use 5 volt TTL-like logic, PCI has anticipated (and promotes) a shift to 3.3 volt logic. Unfortunately, these two logic families do not mix well together, requiring different electrical specifications on the bus segment. The focus of the bus segment is the voltage level used for signaling: 5 volt and 3.3 volt. For a PCI bus segment operating with a 66 MHz CLK signal line, the signaling is restricted to 3.3 volts.

> 64 data bit PCI resources that are attached only to a 32 data bit bus segment must insure that the 64 data bit related signal lines do not oscillate (AD[63::32], C/BE#[7::4], and PAR64 signal lines). Each PCI resource can drive these signal lines as outputs (stable level), or, if an input, can be biased to a stable level. These and other solutions are allowed provided that the input leakage current specification is not violated. External resistors on an add-in card are not allowed. The PCI resources that are attached to a 64 data bit bus or connector rely on pull-up resistors on the bus segment to drive the aforementioned signal lines to a logical "1".

PCI-X SPECIFIC

The PCI-X addendum specification defines the same basic electrical requirements as the PCI local bus specification, with modifications. The modifications are required to accommodate the higher CLK signal line frequencies. The signaling voltage level for signal lines compliant with the PCI-X addendum specification is restricted to only 3.3 volts.

One of the unique elements of a PCI-X compliant device (component or add-in card) is the requirement to operate as either PCI or PCI-X compliant. When operating in compliance with the PCI local bus specification, the PCI-X device is required to operate according to the PCI local bus specification's electrical requirements. If the operation is compliant to the PCI 33 MHz implementation, the PCI-X compliant device may be designed to operate with 5 volt signaling.

12.1 DISTINCTION BETWEEN ADD-IN CARD VOLTAGES

The PCI local bus specification has two separate logic signaling levels: 3.3 volts and 5 volts. These names roughly follow the logic signaling levels used by logic families with 3.3 volt and 5 volt power supplies. It is important to understand that logic signaling levels refer only to the voltages used for communication on the PCI bus segment. The power supplies used for powering PCI resources may or may not correlate to the signaling levels on the PCI bus segment. In fact, it is possible to have a PCI resource that requires a 3.3 volt power supply and operates in the 5 volt signaling environment, and vice versa. The 3.3 and 5 volt signaling environments are not compatible with each other; therefore, all PCI resources on a PCI bus segment must implement either the 3.3 volt or 5 volt signaling.

> The balance of this chapter will use the bus segment viewpoint with only one signaling voltage supported on a bus segment that is independent of the signaling voltage of other bus segments.

A PCI bus segment can be designed for either the 5 volt signaling or the 3.3 volt signaling environment, but not both. To keep signaling voltages distinct, the connectors for PCI add-in cards are keyed differently for 5 volt and 3.3 volt signaling environments.

The two types of bus segment connectors are:

- **5 Volt Connector:** Allows either a 5 Volt or Dual Voltage Add-in card (also known as "universal add-in card") to be inserted via a mechanical connector key.

- **3.3 Volt Connector:** Allows either a 3.3 Volt or Dual Voltage Add-in card (also known as "universal add-in card") to be inserted via a mechanical connector key.

PCI add-in cards can be designed for either the 5 volt signaling environment, the 3.3 volt signaling environment, or both (a dual voltage or universal card, as mentioned above). Each of these three add-in card possibilities has a connector that is keyed to fit into its appropriate PCI bus segment. The mechanical keying in the connector (see Chapter 13: *Connector, Platform and Add-in Card Design, and Mechanical Considerations*) insures that add-in cards can only be installed in an appropriate PCI bus segment connector. The add-in cards can obtain power from either the 5 volt or 3.3 volt power supply pins on the connector.

The three types of add-in cards are:

- **5 Volt Add-In Card**: The I/O buffers of the component attached to the PCI signal lines adhere to the 5 volt signaling environment.

- **3.3 Volt Add-In Card**: The I/O buffers of the component attached to the PCI signal lines adhere to the 3.3 volt signaling environment.

- **Dual Voltage Add-In Card** (Universal Add-In Card): The I/O buffers of the components attached to the PCI signal lines assume the signaling environment of the bus segment. The dual voltage add-in card determines the signaling environment of the platform from connector-dependent power supply signals (defined as I/O Designated Power Pins). See Chapter 13: *Connector, Platform and Add-in Card Design, and Mechanical Considerations.*

> The I/O Designated Power Pins can be attached to either 3.3 volts or 5 volts (depending on the platform); consequently, the I/O buffers of a dual voltage add-in card must be able to operate with either the 3 volt or the 5 volt signaling environment, and may use either the 3.3 volt or the 5 volt power supply. See Chapter 5: *Signal Line Definition* for more information.

> **Rev. 2.2 of the PCI local bus specification has redefined a reserved pin to support 3.3V auxiliary power (3.3 Vaux). The purpose of the pin is to provide power for PCI resources that require power when power is not available from the other power pins (3.3 V, 5.0V, +5V (I/O), and +3.3V (I/O)). See Subchapter 12.10 for more information.**

PCI bus segments that can operate with a 66 MHz CLK signal line will only support connectors that support 3.3 volt and universal I/O add-in cards.

All of the above discussions for PCI connectors and add-in cards also apply to PCI-X connectors and add-in cards, with one exception. A PCI-X compliant add-in card does not support 5 volt signaling. A PCI-X add-in card designed for 5 volt signaling can only operate as PCI compliant (33 MHz) with no opportunity to ever work in the PCI-X compliant mode.

12.2   COMPONENT ELECTRICAL SPECIFICATIONS

INTRODUCTION

> **All electrical specifications and parameters assume packaged components. That is, measurements or simulations should not be obtained from an unpackaged die. All PCI and PCI-X electrical measurements are made at package pins unless otherwise noted.**

The PCI bus segment has two electrical characteristics that each motivate a different approach to specifying I/O buffer characteristics. First, a PCI bus segment is a CMOS bus, which means that steady state currents (after switching transients have died out) are very minimal. In fact, the majority of the DC drive current is spent on pull-up resistors. Second, PCI is based on reflected wave rather than incident wave signaling. This means that bus drivers are sized to only switch the bus half way to the required high or low voltage. The electrical wave propagates down the bus, reflects off the unterminated end and back to the point of origin, thereby doubling the initial voltage excursion to achieve the required voltage level. The bus driver is actually in the middle of its switching range during this propagation time, which lasts up to 10 nsec.

PCI bus drivers spend this relatively large proportion of bus cycle time in transient switching, and the DC current is minimal, so the typical approach of specifying buffers based on their DC current sourcing capability is not useful. PCI bus drivers are specified in terms of their AC switching characteristics, rather than DC drive. Specifically, the voltage to current relationship (V/I curve) of the driver through its active switching range is the primary means of specification. These V/I curves are targeted at achieving acceptable switching behavior in typical configurations of six loads attached directly to the bus segment and two add-in card connectors, or two loads attached directly to the bus segment and four add-in card connectors. That is, combination of components directly attached to the bus segments and add-in cards (via connectors) equals 10 loads for a 33 MHz CLK signal line frequency. However, it is possible to achieve different or larger configurations depending on the actual equipment practice, layout arrangement, loaded impedance of the motherboard, and so forth. A PCI bus segment operating with a 66 MHz CLK signal line frequency will support decreased loading.

A PCI-X bus segment is also a CMOS bus with incident wave signaling. There are a few differences in the timing, electrical, and further loading restrictions. As of the print date of this book, the PCI SIG is still simulating the effects of loading with one add-in connector at 133 MHz, two add-in connectors at 100 MHz, and four add-in connectors at 66 MHz. Please check with www.PCISIG.com for the final loading results.

COMPONENT SPECIFICATION

This chapter specifies the electrical and timing parameters for PCI and PCI-X components, *i.e.*, integrated circuit devices. Both 5 volt and 3.3 volt rail-to-rail signaling environments are defined. The 5 volt environment is based on absolute switching voltages in order to be compatible with TTL switching levels. The 3.3 volt environment, on the other hand, is based on Vcc relative switching voltages, and is an optimized CMOS approach. The intent of the electrical specification is that components connect directly together, whether on the planar or on an add-in card, without any external buffers or other "glue".

These specifications are intended to provide a design definition of PCI and PCI-X components' electrical compliance and are not, in general, intended as actual test specifications. Some of the elements of this design definition cannot be tested in any practical way, but must be guaranteed by design characterization. It is the responsibility of component designers and ASIC vendors to devise an appropriate combination of device characterization and production tests, correlated to the parameters herein, in order to guarantee that PCI and PCI-X components comply with this design definition. All component specifications have reference to a packaged component, and therefore include package parasitics. Unless specifically stated otherwise, component parameters apply at the package pins, not at the bare silicon pads or at card edge connectors.

The intent of this specification is that components operate within the "commercial" range of environmental parameters. However, this does not preclude the option of other operating environments at the vendor's discretion.

PCI and PCI-X output buffers are specified in terms of their V/I curves. Limits on acceptable V/I curves provide for a maximum output impedance that can achieve an acceptable first step voltage in typical configurations, and for a minimum output impedance that keeps the reflected wave within reasonable bounds. Pull-up and pull-down sides of the buffer have separate V/I curves, which are provided with the parametric specification. The effective buffer strength is primarily specified by an AC drive point, which defines an acceptable first step voltage, both high going and low going, together with required currents to achieve that voltage in typical configurations. The DC drive point specifies steady state conditions that must be maintained, but in a CMOS environment these are minimal, and do not indicate real output drive strength.

It is possible to use weaker output drivers that don't comply with the V/I curves or meet the timing parameters in this book, if they are set up to do continuous stepping as described in the PCI local bus specification. However, this practice is strongly discouraged as it creates violations of the input setup time at all inputs, as well as having significant negative performance impacts. In any case, all output drivers must meet the turn off (float) timing specification.

DC parameters must be sustainable under steady state (DC) conditions. AC parameters must be guaranteed under transient switching (AC) conditions, which may represent up to 33% of the PCI or PCI-X CLK signal line period. The sign on all current parameters (direction of current flow) is referenced to a ground *inside* the component; that is, positive currents flow into the component while negative currents flow out of the component.

The RST# signal line has unique requirements not covered by the general signal line discussion below. See Chapter 11: *Reset, Power, and Signal Line Initialization* for more information. Also, the PME# signal line has unique requirements not covered by the general signal line discussion below. See the *PCI Bus Power Management* and *PCI Hot Plug Application & Design* books (available at annabooks.com) for more information.

12.3 5V SIGNALING ENVIRONMENT

INTRODUCTION

The 5V signaling environment is basically industry standard TTL input thresholds with rail to rail output levels This environment is intended to be implemented with

CMOS technology although any technology could be used that meets the specifications. Since the major current consumption of CMOS logic occurs during transitions, output drive capability is specified using V/I curves and AC specifications.

5V DC SPECIFICATIONS

The 5 volt signaling protocol is only defined by the PCI local bus specification.

The timings and voltage levels are defined according to the compliance level of the bus segment. A bus segment that is operating with PCI bus transactions must follow all the timing and voltage levels according to the PCI local bus specification. A bus segment that is operating with PCI-X bus transactions must follow all the timing and voltage levels specified by the PCI-X addendum specification. If the same PCI-X bus segment is operating with PCI bus transactions, it must follow all of the timing and voltage levels according to the PCI local bus specification.

The DC specifications are steady state parameters. That is, they do not contain any information about timing or switching. DC specifications are needed to insure that devices in the same logic family can reliably communicate with each other. The output voltage levels, input switching thresholds, and static parasitic electrical parameters (capacitance and inductance) are defined. The following table outlines the DC parameters for 5V signaling:

Symbol and Parameter	Conditions	Min	Max	Units (Notes)
V_{cc} Voltage Supply		4.75	5.25	V
V_{ih} Input High Voltage		2.0	$V_{cc}+0.5$	V
V_{il} Input Low Voltage		-0.5	0.8	V
I_{ih} Input High Leakage Current	$V_{in} = 2.7$		70	µA (1)
I_{il} Input Low Leakage Current	$V_{in} = 0.5$		-70	µA (1)
V_{oh} Output High Voltage	I_{out} = -2 mA	2.4		V
V_{ol} Output Low Voltage	I_{out} = 3 or 6 mA		0.55	V (2)
C_{in} Input Pin Capacitance			10 or 16	PF (3)
C_{clk} CLK Pin Capacitance		5	12	PF
C_{idsel} IDSEL Pin Capacitance			8	PF (4)
L_{pin} Pin Inductance			20	NH (5)
I_{off} PME# input leakage current	$V_O <= 5.25$ volts V_{CC} off or floating		1	µA (6)

Table 12-1: DC Specifications for 5 Volt Signaling

NOTES:

(1)   Includes all leakage currents associated with a bidirectional buffer including the tri-state condition.

(2)   3 milliamps is for signal lines *without* pull-up resistors. 6 milliamps is for signal lines *with* pull-up resistors. The signal lines that implement pull-up resistors are: FRAME#, TRDY#, IRDY#, DEVSEL#, STOP#, SERR#, PERR#, LOCK#, INTx#, AD[63::32], C/BE[7::4]#, PAR64, REQ64#, and ACK64#. Pull-up resistors are only on the bus segment and not the add-in cards.

(3)   10 pF for components mounted on add-in cards (except CLK signal line). Up to16 pF for components mounted on the bus segment. This precludes use of high capacitance packages on add-in cards.

(4)   Lower capacitance allows for a non-resistive attachment of IDSEL to AD[xx].

(5)   Recommended but not required. High inductance packages may produce undesirable signal integrity. See spec. sheet of component.

(6)   Maximum leakage into PME# signal line when power is not supplied to Vcc. Also, the device is not requesting a power management event. See the *PCI Bus Power Management* and *PCI Hot Plug Application & Design* books (available at annabooks.com) for more information.

The above table is paraphrased from *PCI Local Bus Specification* Rev. 2.2.

When PCI or PCI-X 64 data bit resources are attached to a 32 data bit PCI or PCI-X bus segment or connector, they must insure that 64 data bit related signal lines do not oscillate. Each PCI or PCI-X resource can drive the AD[63::32] AD[63::32], C/BE[7::4], and PAR64 signal lines as outputs (stable level), or as inputs can be biased to a stable level. These and other solutions are allowed, provided the input leakage current specification is not violated. External resistors on add-in cards are not allowed. PCI or PCI-X resources attached to a 64 data bit bus segment can rely on pull-up resistors to Vcc on the bus segment to drive these signal lines to a logical "1".

5V AC SPECIFICATIONS

The 5 volt signaling protocol is only defined by the PCI local bus specification.

The timings and voltage levels defined are according to the compliance level of the bus segment. A bus segment that is operating with PCI bus transactions must follow all the timing and voltage levels according to the PCI local bus specification. A bus segment that is operating with PCI-X bus transactions must follow all the timing and voltage levels specified by the PCI-X addendum specification. If the same PCI-X bus segment is operating with PCI bus transactions, it must follow all of the timing and voltage levels according to the PCI local bus specification.

A PCI bus segment is designed to signal from one component to another with a *reflected wave* technique. When a signal is launched onto the bus, it is required to propagate to all extremes of the bus segment with only one half of the required logic threshold voltage amplitude. As the physical extremes of the bus segment wire are encountered, the signal *reflects* and propagates back to all points on the bus segment wire again. If the bus is implemented correctly, all points on the bus segment wire will obtain valid logic voltage threshold levels by the end of the second propagation. This system bus propagation parameter is defined as Tprop and will be described in greater detail in the timing section.

For the reflected wave technique to work properly, there must be enough instantaneous current from an output buffer to develop the initial half amplitude voltage step on a bus segment wire loaded with PCI devices. On the other hand, too much current from the output buffer will create excessive reflections and may require too much time for the bus segment wire to settle. The AC table and the V/I curves shown in this section are the specification mechanisms used to constrain the output buffer currents.

In addition to developing the initial half amplitude voltage step without too little or too much current drive, a PCI output buffer must also meet all of the following requirements:

- The minimum and maximum propagation times of the output buffer must be met. This parameter is defined as Tval and will be described further in the timing section.

- The slew rate (rate of output voltage change as a function of time), must be maintained within limits. This keeps the magnitude of any bus reflections under control. These parameters are defined as $slew_r$, and $slew_f$, and are described in the AC table.

- Clamp devices to the lower voltage supply are required to limit excessive voltage excursions. These clamps are intended to absorb some of the reflected energy on the bus. The clamp parameters are defined in the 5V AC table.

The information contained in Tables 12-1 and 12-2 refers to the V/I curves in Figure 12-1.

Symbol and Parameter	Conditions	Min	Max	Unit (Notes)
	$0 < V_{out} <= 1.4$	-44		ma (1)
I_{oh}	$1.4 < V_{out} < 2.4$	$-44 + (V_{out}1.4)/0.024$		ma (1,2)
Switching Current High	$3.1 < V_{out} < V_{cc}$		EQ A on V/I curve	ma (1,3)
I_{oh} Test Point	$V_{out} = 3.1$		-142	ma (3)
	$V_{out} => 2.2$	95		MA (1)
I_{ol}	$2.2 > V_{out} > 0.55$	$V_{out}/0.023$		ma (1)
Switching Current Low	$0.71 > V_{out} > 0$		EQ B on V/I curve	ma (1,3)
I_{ol} Test point	$V_{out} = 0.71$		206	ma (3)
I_{cl} Low Clamp Current	$-5 < V_{in} <= -1$	$-25 + (Vin+1)/0.015$		mA
slew$_r$ Output Rise Slew Rate	0.4V to 2.4V	1	5	V/ns (4)
slew$_f$ Output Fall Slew Rate	2.4V to 0.4V	1	5	V/ns (4)

Table 12-2: AC Specifications for 5 Volt Signaling

NOTES:

(1) Refer to the V/I curves in Figure 12-1. This parameter does not apply to the CLK and RST# signal lines. For the REQx# and GNTx# signal lines, only half the specified output current is needed (since they are point to point signals). The I_{oh} specification does not apply to open drain outputs. The open drain signal lines are: SERR#, PME#, and INTx#.

(2) This segment of the minimum portion of the V/I curve is drawn from the AC drive point directly to the DC drive point rather than to the voltage rail (Vcc). This allows for the possibility of an N-channel pull-up structure in the output buffer.

(3) Maximum current requirements must be met as drivers pull beyond the first step voltage (AC drive point). Equations defining these maximums (EQ A and EQ B) are provided with the respective V/I diagrams in Figure 12-1. The equation defined maximums should be met by design. In order to facilitate component testing, a maximum current test point is defined for the pull up and pull down V/I curve of the output driver.

(4) This parameter is the cumulative or average edge rate across the specified rise or fall voltage range. The rise slew rate does not apply to open drain outputs (see list in Note 1). The minimum slew rate (slowest signal edge) and maximum slew rate (fastest signal edge) must be met by all PCI components. Note that in revision 2.0 of the PCI specification the max slew rate was optional; consequently, there may be components with rise and fall times that are faster. To determine the maximum slew rate, it is recommended that the test load shown below be used to determine compliance.

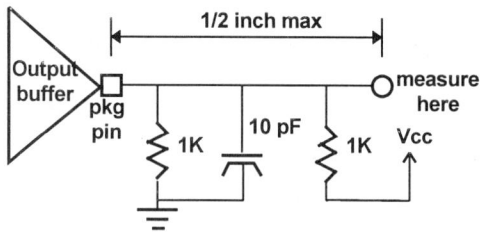

Max slew rate test load

The preceeding table is paraphrased from the *PCI Local Bus Specification* Rev. 2.2.
0

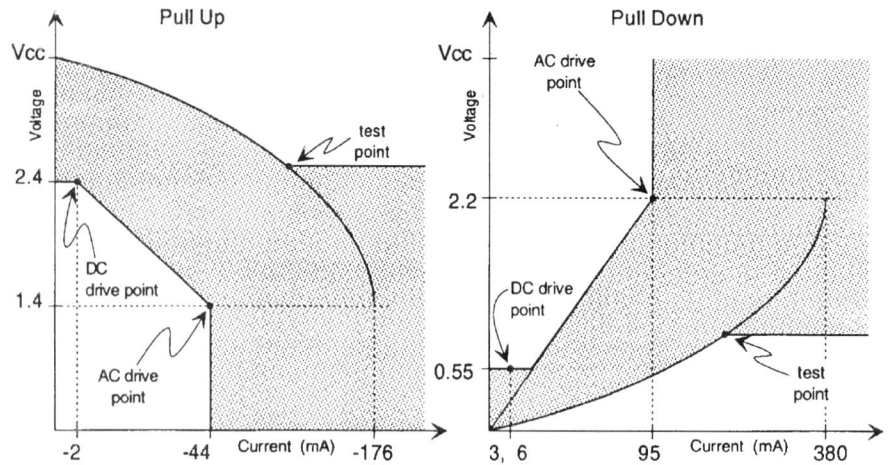

Equation A:

$$I_{oh} = 11.9*(V_{out}\text{-}5.25)*(V_{out}+2.45)$$

$$\text{for } Vcc > Vout > 3.1v$$

Equation B:

$$I_{ol} = 78.5*V_{out}*(4.4\text{-}V_{out})$$

$$\text{for } 0v < Vout < 0.71v$$

Figure 12-1: V/I Curves for 5V Signaling

The above figure is copied from *PCI Local Bus Specification Rev. 2.2*, reprinted with permission of the PCI Special Interest Group.

There are three particular points of interest on each V/I curve:

- The DC drive point
- The AC drive point
- The Test point

The **DC drive point** is the quiescent static voltage at the output of the PCI buffer. This point is also specified in Table 12-1 (DC Specifications) as V_{ol} and V_{oh}.

The **AC drive point** is the *minimum* instantaneous current needed to switch all points on the bus with one reflection. This parameter is specified in Table 12-2 (AC Specifications).

The **test point** is the *maximum* instantaneous current that any buffer is allowed to produce. Too much instantaneous current can create signal integrity problems (excessive ringing and slow settling times). This parameter is also specified in Table 12-2 (AC Specifications).

The V/I curves and associated parameters assume a bus configuration of six PCI components on the PCI bus segment, plus two PCI add-in card slots ... OR ... two PCI components on the PCI bus segment, and four PCI components in add-in slots. The 22 ohm load line shown on each V/I curve roughly represents the impedance of a heavily loaded PCI bus segment. Theoretically, if PCI bus segments actually appeared as resistive loads, buffers would not generate currents in excess of those shown at the load line.

Note that each V/I curve current axis is not drawn to scale. If plotted to scale, the 22 ohm load line will fall on the opposite side of the AC drive point.

The curves in Figure 12-1 are defined for worst case conditions as follows:

- Minimum pull-up curve is at min. Vcc and max. operating temperature.
- Minimum pull-down curve is at max. Vcc and max. operating temperature.
- Maximum curve test points are at max. Vcc and min. operating temperature.

PCI devices' inputs need to be clamped to ground. The clamping of the inputs to a 5 V power rail with a diode is optional. The clamping of the inputs of a 5 volt signaling device to 3.3 V power rail is never permitted. See further discussion in the next section. A PCI-X device that will operate in the PCI compliant mode at 5 volt signaling has the same requirements.

5V AC DEVICE PROTECTION

Since the PCI bus segment is a reflected wave non-terminated environment, it is possible that voltage excursions at the input of devices may exceed the power supply rails. Some logic technologies have intrinsic immunity to large voltage excursions, while others can incur device damage. Because it is known that reflecting signal voltages on a PCI bus segment wire can exceed the power rails (both positive and negative excursions), the PCI local bus specification recommends an over voltage test for inputs of all PCI devices. This over voltage test environment is shown in Figure 12-2. The waveforms in Figure 12-2 are not for production testing but are design goals.

The purpose of the test is to help determine long term reliability. The conditions of the test are defined as follows (refer to Figure 12-2):

- A zero impedance voltage source must provide the waveforms shown as an open circuit voltage.

- The appropriate resistor is inserted between the voltage source and the device under test (DUT).

- The upper diode clamp is optional, but if used it must be attached to the V/IO or the 5 volt supply pins. It can never be attached to the 3.3 volt supply pin. Note: if the basic technology of the PCI device is based on 3.3 volt technology, the upper clamping diode will be required. Also, it should be noted that other alternative clamping approaches to the 3.3 volt supply pin or ground are possible.

- Whenever possible, the bus segment designers should limit the wire impedance to limit ringing.

- The test waveform in Figure 12-2 is worst case with the strongest driver, max. and min. configuration with no internal clamps.

All PCI input, bi-directional, and tri-state pins should be able to withstand continuous exposure to the test conditions.

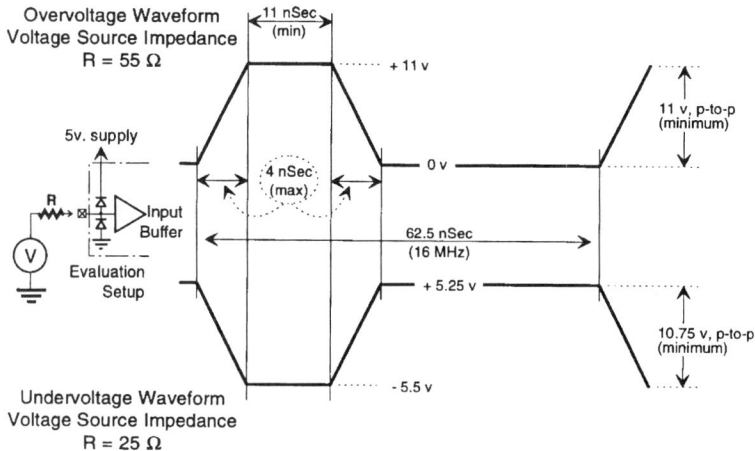

Figure 12-2: Maximum AC Waveforms for 5 Volt Signaling

The above figure is copied from *PCI Local Bus Specification Rev. 2.2*, reprinted with permission of the PCI Special Interest Group.

See Subchapter 12.9: *Clamping Issues* for further discussions about device protection.

12.4: 3.3V COMPONENT ELECTRICAL SPECIFICATIONS

INTRODUCTION

The 3.3V signaling environment not only differs from the 5V environment in voltage levels, but also in the way the voltages are specified. A scheme is used that specifies all of the important voltages as being proportional to the power supply voltage. This V_{cc} relative scheme is applied to all DC and AC voltage specifications in the 3.3V environment. This environment is intended to be implemented exclusively with CMOS technology.

Like the 5V signaling environment, output drive capability is specified using an AC drive point and the test point on V/I curves. Unlike the 5 volt environment, the 3.3 volt environment requires both upper and lower power rail clamp devices. These clamps are one important reason why the 5 volt and 3.3 volt signaling environments are incompatible.

3.3V DC SPECIFICATIONS

> The 5 volt signaling protocol is only defined by the PCI local bus specification. The 3.3 volt signaling protocol is defined by both the PCI local bus specification and the PCI-X addendum specification.
>
> The timings and voltage levels defined are according to the compliance level of the bus segment. A bus segment that is operating with PCI bus transactions must follow all the timing and voltage levels in the PCI local bus specification. A bus segment that is operating with PCI-X bus transactions must follow all the timing and voltage levels specified in the PCI-X addendum specification. If the same PCI-X bus segment is operating with PCI bus transactions, it must follow all of the timing and voltage levels according to the PCI local bus specification.

The DC specifications are steady state parameters. That is, they do not contain any information about timing or switching. DC specifications are needed to insure that devices in the same logic family can reliably communicate with each other. The output voltage levels, input switching thresholds, and static parasitic electrical parameters (capacitance and inductance) are defined. The following table outlines the DC parameters for 5 volt signaling:

Note that the switching thresholds (V_{ih} and V_{il}), have changed from the 2.0 revision of the PCI specification:

Symbol and Parameter	Conditions	Min	Max	Units (Notes)
V_{cc} Voltage Supply		3.0	3.6	V
V_{ih} Input High Voltage		$0.5V_{cc}$	$V_{cc}+0.5$	V
V_{il} Input Low Voltage		-0.5	$0.3V_{cc}$	V (7)
V_{ipu} Input Pull-Up		$0.7V_{cc}$		V (1)
I_{il} Input Low Leakage Current	$0 < V_{in.} < V_{cc}$		±10	µA (2)
V_{oh} Output High Voltage	$I_{out} = -500\ \mu A$	$0.9V_{cc}$		V
V_{ol} Output Low Voltage	$I_{out} = 1500\ \mu A$		$0.1V_{cc}$	V
C_{in} Input Pin Capacitance			10 or 16	pF (3)
C_{clk} CLK Pin Capacitance		5	12	pF (8)
C_{idsel} IDSEL Pin Capacitance			8	pF (4)
L_{pin} Pin Inductance			20	nH (5)
I_{off} PME# input leakage current	$V_0 <= 3.6$ volts V_{cc} off or floating		1	µA (6)

Table 12-3: PCI and PCI-X DC Specifications for 3.3 Volt Signaling for All CLK Signal Line Frequencies

NOTES:

(1) Guaranteed by design. The minimum voltage to which pull-up resistors are calculated to pull a floated network. Input buffers sensitive to static power consumption should assure minimum conducting current at this input voltage.

(2) Includes all leakage currents associated with a bidirectional buffer including the tri-state condition.

(3) For PCI the maximum is 10 pF for components mounted on add-in cards, or up to 16 pF for components mounted on the PCI bus segment. This precludes use of high capacitance packages on add-in cards. For PCI-X the maximum is 8pF and is the maximum for all signal lines.

(4) Lower capacitance allows for a non-resistive attachment of IDSEL to AD[xx].

(5) For PCI this value is recommended but not required. High inductance packages may produce undesirable signal integrity. See spec. sheet of component. For PCI-X this value is required, and it must be 15 nH.

(6) This is the maximum leakage current when no power is applied to the Vcc of the PCI or PCI-X resource. It is assumed that no power management event is pending and the signal line is not being asserted.

(7) For PCI-X this is $0.35V_{cc}$.

(8) For PCI-X the maximum is 8pF.

The above table is paraphrased from *PCI Local Bus Specification* Rev. 2.2, reprinted with permission of the PCI Special Interest Group.

When PCI or PCI-X 64 data bit resources are attached to a 32 data bit PCI or PCI-X bus segment or connector, they must insure that the 64 data bit related signal lines do not oscillate. Each PCI or PCI-X resource can drive the AD[63::32] AD[63::32], C/BE[7::4], and PAR64 signal lines as outputs (stable level), or as inputs can be biased to a stable level. These and other solutions are allowed, provided the input leakage current specification is not violated. External resistors on add-in cards are not allowed. PCI or PCI-X resources attached to a 64 data bit bus segment can rely on pull-up resistors to Vcc on the bus segment to drive these signal lines to a logical "1".

3.3V AC SPECIFICATIONS

For an overview discussion of AC specifications, see the section on 5V AC Specifications. The AC table and the V/I curves shown in this section are the specification mechanisms used to constrain the 3.3V output buffer currents.

In addition to developing the initial half amplitude voltage step without too little or too much current drive, a PCI or PCI-X output must also meet all of these requirements:

- The minimum and maximum propagation time of the output buffer must be met. This parameter is defined as Tval and will be described further in the timing section.

- The slew rate (rate of output voltage change as a function of time), must be maintained within limits. This keeps the magnitude of any bus reflections under control. These parameters are defined as $slew_r$, and $slew_f$ and are described in the AC table.

- Input clamp devices are required on both the upper and lower voltage supply rails to limit excessive voltage excursions. These clamps are intended to absorb some of the reflected energy on the bus. The clamp parameters are defined in the 3.3V AC table.

The information contained in Tables 12-3 and 12-4 refers to the V/I curves in Figure 12-3.

The AC specifications are divided into two tables: PCI and PCI-X for readability.

Symbol and Parameter	Conditions	Min	Max	Units (Notes)
	$0 < V_{out} <= 0.3 V_{cc}$	$-12 V_{cc}$		mA (1, 3)
I_{oh}	$0.3 V_{cc} < V_{out} < 0.9 V_{cc}$	$-17.1 (V_{cc} - V_{out})$		mA (1)
Switching Current High	$0.7 V_{cc} < V_{out} < V_{cc}$		EQ C on V/I curve	(1, 2)
I_{oh} Test Point	$V_{out} = 0.7 V_{cc}$		- $32 V_{cc}$	mA (2)
	$V_{cc} > V_{out} => 0.6 V_{cc}$	$16 V_{cc}$		mA (1, 3)
I_{ol}	$0.6 V_{cc} > V_{out} > 0.1 V_{cc}$	$26.7 / V_{out}$		mA (1)
Switching Current Low	$0.18 V_{cc} > V_{out} > 0$		EQ C on V/I curve	mA (1, 2)
I_{ol} Test point	$V_{out} = 0.18 V_{cc}$		$38 V_{cc}$	mA (2)
I_{cl} Low Clamp Current	$-3 < V_{in} <= -1$	$-25 + (Vin + 1)/0.015$		mA
I_{ch} High Clamp Current	$V_{cc} + 4 > V_{in} => V_{cc} + 1$	$25 + (Vin - V_{cc} - 1)/0.015$		mA
Slew$_r$ Output Rise Slew Rate	$0.2 V_{cc}$ to $0.6 V_{cc}$	1	4	V/ns (4)
Slew$_f$ Output Fall Slew Rate	$0.6 V_{cc}$ to $0.2 V_{cc}$	1	4	V/ns (4)

Table 12-4-A: PCI AC Specifications for 3.3 Volt Signaling For DC to 33.3 MHz CLK Signal Line Frequencies

Notes:

(1) Refer to the V/I curves in Figure 12-3. This parameter does not apply to the CLK and RST# signals. For the REQx# and GNTx# signals, only half the specified output current is needed. The Ioh parameter does not apply to open drain outputs. The open drain signal lines are: SERR#, PME#, and INTx#.

(2) Maximum current requirements must be met as drivers pull beyond the initial first step voltage (AC drive point). Equations defining these maximums (EQ C and EQ D) are provided with the respective V/I diagrams in Figure 12-3. The equation defined maximums should be met by design. In order to facilitate component testing, a maximum current test point is defined for the pull up and pull down V/I curve of the output driver.

(3) Refer to the V/I curves in Figure 12-3. This condition correlates to the AC drive point on the pullup or pulldown V/I curve.

(4) This parameter is the cumulative or average edge rate across the specified rise or fall voltage range. The rise slew rate does not apply to open drain outputs (See list in Note (1). The minimum slew rate (slowest signal edge) and maximum slew rate (fastest signal

edge) must be met by all PCI components. Note that in revision 2.0 of the PCI specification the max slew rate was optional; consequently, there may be components with rise and fall times that are faster. To determine the maximum slew rate, it is recommended that the test load shown below be used to determine compliance.

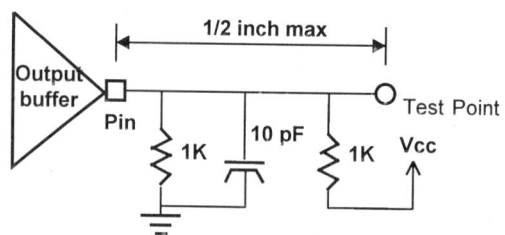

Max slew rate test load

The preceeding table is paraphrased from the *PCI Local Bus Specification Rev. 2.2*, reprinted with permission of the PCI Special Interest Group.

Symbol and Parameter	Conditions	Min	Max	Units (Notes)
I_{oh} Switching Current High AC	$V_{out}=0.3V_{cc}$	$-12V_{cc}$		mA (1)
	$V_{out}=0.7V_{cc}$		$-32V_{cc}$	
I_{ol} Switching Current Low AC	$V_{out}=0.6V_{cc}$	$16V_{cc}$		mA (1)
	$V_{out}=0.18V_{cc}$		$38V_{cc}$	
V_{oh}	$I_{out}>-0.5$ ma	$0.9V_{cc}$		V
V_{ol}	$I_{out}>1.5$ ma		$0.1V_{cc}$	V
I_{cl} Low Clamp Current	$-3<V_{in}<=-1$	$-25+(V_{in}+1)/0.015$		mA
I_{ch} High Clamp Current	$V_{cc}+4>V_{in} =>$ $V_{cc}+1$	$25+(V_{in}-V_{cc}-1)/0.015$		mA
$Slew_r$ Output Rise Slew Rate	$0.3V_{cc}$ to $0.6V_{cc}$	1	4	V/ns (2
$Slew_f$ Output Fall Slew Rate	$0.6V_{cc}$ to $0.3V_{cc}$	1	4	V/ns (2)

Table 12-4-B: PCI AC Specifications for 3.3 Volt Signaling Above 33.3 MHz to 66.6 MHz CLK Signal Line Frequencies

Notes:

(1)   The switching current and drivers for the REQx# and GNTx# signal lines can be ½ the size of the other signal lines specified in the table. This parameter does not apply to the CLK and RST# signals.The Ioh parameter does not apply to open drain outputs. The open drain signal lines are SERR#, PME#, and INTx#.

(2)   This parameter is relative to the cumulative edge rate in the range and not the instantaneous rate.The test load for this measurement is shown below. Optionally, the unloaded output test as specified by Rev 2.0 of the PCI local bus specification may be used. These parameters do not apply to open drain outputs. The open drain signal lines are SERR#, PME#, and INTx#.

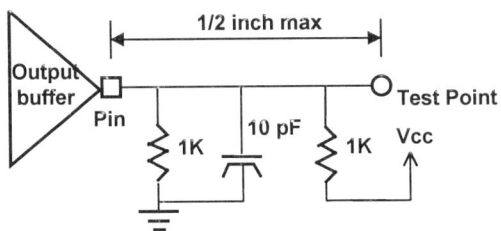

Max slew rate test load

The preceeding table is paraphrased from the *PCI Local Bus Specification Rev. 2.2*, reprinted with permission of the PCI Special Interest Group.

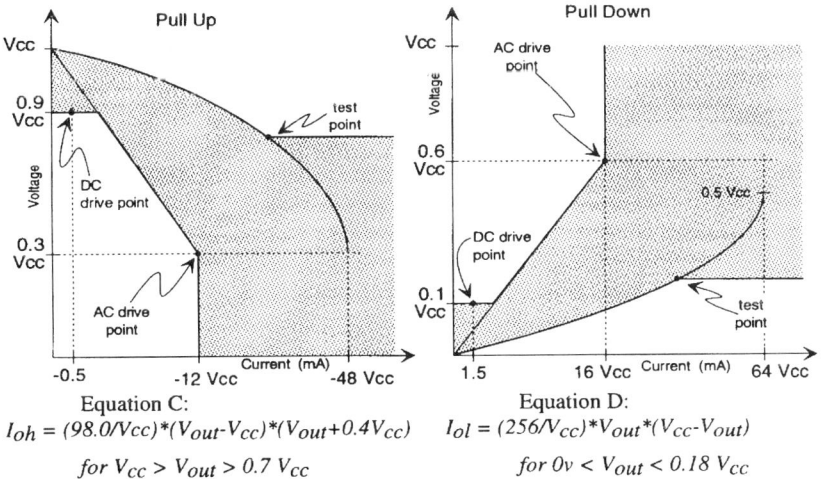

Equation C:

$$I_{oh} = (98.0/Vcc)*(V_{out}-V_{cc})*(V_{out}+0.4V_{cc})$$

$$for\ V_{cc} > V_{out} > 0.7\ V_{cc}$$

Equation D:

$$I_{ol} = (256/V_{cc})*V_{out}*(V_{cc}-V_{out})$$

$$for\ 0v < V_{out} < 0.18\ V_{cc}$$

Figure 12-3: V/I Curves for 3.3 Volt Signaling

The prefix "numbers" of Vcc in the above figure are multipliers. For example, -12Vcc means –12x(3.3) = -39.6 ma.

The above figure is partly copied from *PCI Local Bus Specification Rev. 2.2*, reprinted with permission of the PCI Special Interest Group.

There are three particular points of interest on each V/I curve:

- The DC drive point
- The AC drive point
- The Test point

The **DC drive point** is the quiescent static voltage at the output of the PCI buffer. This point is also specified in Table 12-3 (DC Specifications) as V_{ol} and V_{oh}.

The **AC drive point** is the *minimum* instantaneous current needed to switch all points on the bus with one reflection. The AC drive point must current be reached within the output delay time. This parameter is specified in Table 12-4 (AC Specifications).

The **test point** is the *maximum* instantaneous current that any buffer is allowed to produce. Too much instantaneous current can create signal integrity problems (excessive ringing and slow settling times). This parameter is also specified in Table 12-4 (AC Specifications).

The V/I curves and associated parameters assume a bus configuration of six PCI components on the PCI bus segment plus two PCI add-in cards slots ... OR ... two PCI components on the PCI bus segment plus four PCI components in add-in slots. The 22 ohm load line shown on each V/I curve roughly represents the impedance of a heavily loaded PCI bus segment. Theoretically, if PCI bus segments actually appeared as resistive loads, buffers would not generate currents in excess of those shown at the load line.

Note that each V/I curve current axis is not drawn to scale. If plotted to scale, the 22 ohm load line will fall on the opposite side of the AC drive point.

The curves in Figure 12-1 are defined for worst case conditions as follows:

- Minimum pull-up curve is at min. Vcc and max. operating temperature.
- Minimum pull-down curve is at max. Vcc and max. operating temperature.
- Maximum curve test points are at max. Vcc and min. operating temperature.

Symbol and Parameter	Conditions (notes)	Min	Max	Units (Notes)
I_{oh} Switching Current High	$0 < V_{cc} - V_{out} \leq 3.6$ Volts		$-74\ (V_{cc} - V_{out})$	mA
	$0 < V_{cc} - V_{out} \leq 1.2$ Volts	$-32\ (V_{cc} - V_{out})$		mA (1)
	1.2 Volts $< V_{cc} - V_{out} \leq 1.9$ Volts	$-11\ (V_{cc} - V_{out})$ -25.2 Volts		mA (1)
	1.9 Volts $< V_{cc} - V_{out} \leq 3.6$ Volts	$-1.8\ (V_{cc} - V_{out})$ -42.7 Volts		mA (1)
I_{ol} Switching Current Low	$0 < V_{out} \leq 3.6$ Volts		$100\ V_{out}$	mA
	$0 < V_{out} \leq 1.3$ Volts	$48\ V_{out}$		mA (1)
	1.3 Volts $< V_{out} \leq 3.6$ Volts	$5.7\ V_{out} + 55$		mA (1)
I_{cl} Low Clamp Current	-3 Volts $< V_{in} \leq -0.8875$ Volts	$-40 + (V_{in} + 1) / 0.005$		mA
	-0.8875 Volts $< V_{in} \leq -0.625$ Volts	$-25 + (V_{in} + 1) / 0.0015$		
I_{ch} High Clamp Current	-0.8875 Volts $\leq V_{in} - V_{cc} < 4$ Volts	$-40 + (V_{in} - V_{cc} - 1) / 0.005$		mA
	0.625 Volts $\leq V_{in} - V_{cc} < 0.8875$ Volts	$25 + (V_{in} - V_{cc} - 1) / 0.015$		
$Slew_r$ Output Rise Slew Rate	$0.2V_{cc} - 0.6V_{cc}$	1	6	V/ns (2)
$Slew_f$ Output Fall Slew Rate	$0.6V_{cc} - 0.2V_{cc}$	1	6	V/ns (2)

Table 12-4-C: PCI-X AC Specifications for 3.3 Volt Signaling For All CLK Signal Line Frequencies

Notes:

(1) The switching current and drivers for the REQx# and GNTx# signal lines can be ½ the size of the other signal lines specified in the table. This parameter does not apply to the CLK and RST# signals.The Ioh parameter does not apply to open drain outputs. The open drain signal lines are SERR#, PME#, and INTx#.

(2) This parameter is relrtive to the cumulative edge rate in the range and not the instaneous rate. The test load for this measurement is shown below. Optionally, the unloaded output test as specified by Rev 2.0 of the PCI local bus specification may be used. These parameters do not apply to open drain outputs. The open drain signal lines are SERR#, PME#, and INTx#.

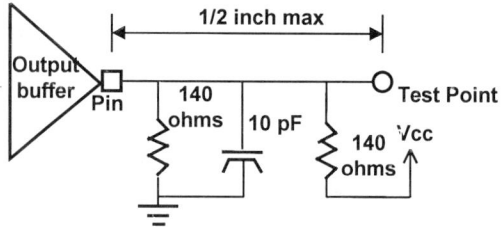

Max slew rate test load

Figures 12-4-A to D define the output drive current limits for the PCI and PCI-X 3.3 volt signaling environment.

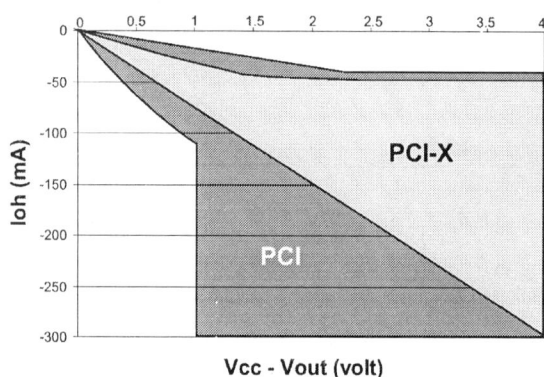

Figure 12-4-A: PCI and PCI-X Pull-Up Output Buffer I/V Curves

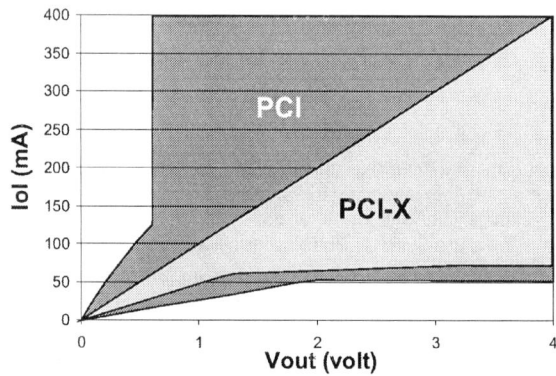

Figure 12-4-B: PCI and PCI-X Pull-Down Output Buffer I/V Curves

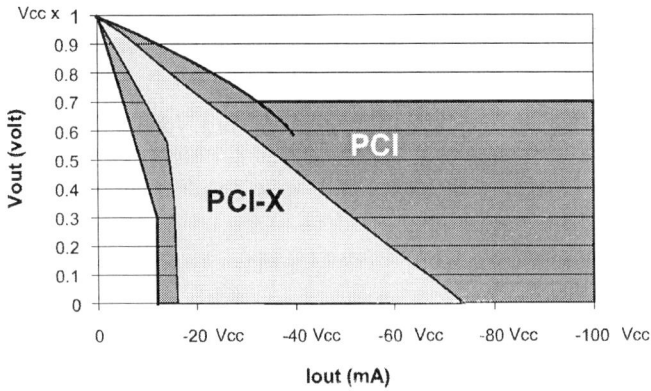

Figure 12-4-C: PCI and PCI-X Pull-Up Output Buffer I/V Curves

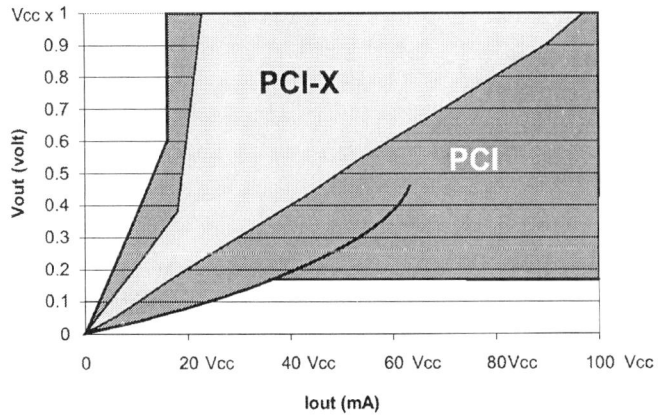

Figure 12-4-D: PCI and PCI-X Pull-Down Output Buffer I/V Curves

PCI and PCI-X devices' inputs need to be clamped to ground. The clamping of the inputs to 3.3 V power rail with a diode is also required. See further discussion in the next section

3V AC DEVICE PROTECTION

Since the PCI and PCI-X bus segments constitute a reflected wave non-terminated environment, it is possible that voltage excursions at the input of devices may exceed the power supply rails. Some logic technologies have intrinsic immunity to large voltage excursions, while others may incur device damage. Because it is known that reflecting signal voltages on a PCI bus wire can exceed the power rails (both positive and negative excursions), the PCI specification recommends an over voltage test for all inputs of PCI devices. This over voltage test environment is shown in Figure 12-5.

The purpose of the test is to help determine long term reliability. The conditions of the test are defined as follows (refer to Figure 12-5):

- A zero impedance voltage source must provide the waveforms shown as an open circuit voltage.

- The appropriate resistor is inserted between the voltage source and the device under test (DUT).

- Whenever possible, the motherboard designers should limit the wire impedance to limit ringing.

> **All PCI and PCI-X input, bi-directional, and tri-state pins should be able to withstand continuous exposure to the above test conditions.**

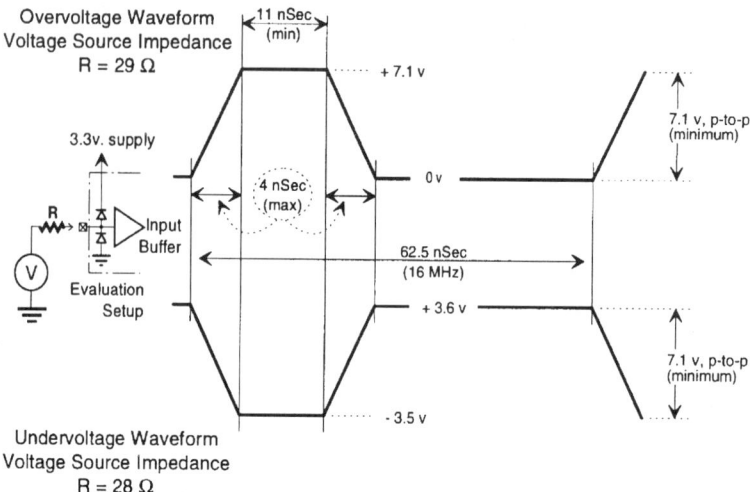

Figure 12-5: Maximum PCI and PCI-X AC Waveforms for 3.3 Volt Signaling

The above figure is copied from *PCI Local Bus Specification Rev. 2.2*, reprinted with permission of the PCI Special Interest Group.

> **See Subchapter 12.9:** *Clamping Issues* **for further discussions about device protection.**

12.5 CLOCK SIGNAL LINE TIMING

INTRODUCTION

> The generic names "33 MHz", "66 MHz", "100 MHz", and "133 MHz" are sometimes used in this book. These are the generic names for an add-in card, device, or bus segment that can operate with the maximum CLK signal line frequency of 33.3, 66.6, 100, or 133.2 MHz, respectively.

All PCI and PCI-X bus segment signal lines are synchronized to the rising edge of CLK except for RST#, INTx#, and PME# signal lines. The SERR# signal line is asserted synchronized with the CLK signal line, but deasserts asynchronous to the rising edge of the CLK signal line. Of course static signal lines like M66EN, PCIXCAP, etc. are not part of clocking discussion.

A 33 MHz PCI bus segment will have a minimum clock period of 30 ns. The PCI local bus specification requires that PCI devices in such a bus segment to operate from a frequency from DC up to 33.3 MHz. PCI devices that can reside on an add-in card must tolerate the CLK signal line frequency dynamically changing. If the device is only to reside directly on the bus segment (that is non add-in card), the CLK signal line frequency is assumed fixed after RESET. A 66 MHz PCI bus segment will have a minimum clock period of 15 ns. A 66 MHz PCI bus segment is required to operate with the CLK signal line at 33.3 MHz or less if the M66EN signal line is deasserted. Consequently, there is one range for the CLK signal line frequency in a 33 MHz PCI bus segment and two ranges for the CLK signal line frequency in a 66 MHz PCI bus segment.

For a PCI-X bus segment there are three frequency ranges: 66, 100, and 133 MHz. Unlike a PCI bus segment, the CLK signal line frequency on a PCI-X bus segment (unless operated in the PCI 33 MHz mode) cannot dynamically change. The CLK signal line frequency is established during RESET and cannot change after RESET. As discussed in See Chapter 11: *Reset, Power, and Signal Line Initialization*, the PCI-X bus segment and attached devices are required to operate as PCI 33 MHz and 66 MHz entities.

The details are as follows:

- For a PCI bus segment with a 33 MHz CLK signal line, the base frequencies are from DC to 33.3 MHz (33.MHz PCI bus segment or M66EN signal line deasserted on a 66.MHz PCI bus segment).
  - The CLK signal line frequency can change dynamically after the RST# signal line is deasserted.

- The CLK signal line cannot change its frequency when the RST# signal line is asserted.

- Minimum low and high times for the CLK signal line must be maintained at all times

- The CLK signal line edges must be monotonically increasing and decreasing.

- At frequencies below 16 MHz, the CLK signal line parameters and the support of the devices is by design and not by testing.

- At DC frequency the CLK signal line is held only at logical "0" (low voltage).

As stated above, devices residing only on the bus segment (also known as "motherboard" or "platform") are not required to support dynamic frequency changes of the CLK signal line. That is, it is assumed that the bus segment designer knows if the CLK signal line will be dynamically changing frequency and thus knows if the devices residing on the bus segment will have a need to support dynamic frequency changes. Designers of devices used on add-in cards have no way to control or know the bus segment the add-in cards are installed into. Consequently, add-in card devices must tolerate dynamic frequency changes.

- For a PCI bus segment with a 66 MHz CLK signal line, the base frequencies are from above 33.3 MHz to 66.6 MHz (M66EN signal line asserted).

  - The CLK signal line frequency cannot change dynamically after the RST# signal line is deasserted, other than the frequency range according to the SSC protocol (see the next section for more information).

  - The CLK signal line base frequency only changes when the RST# signal line is asserted (66 MHz reduced to 33 MHz when the M66EN signal line is asserted).

  - Minimum low and high times of the CLK signal line must be maintained at all times.

  - The CLK signal line edges must be monotonically increasing and decreasing.

> A PCI device that is designed to operate with a PCI 66 MHz CLK signal line frequency is also required to operate with a PCI 33 MHz CLK signal line frequency as outlined above (M66EN signal line dasserted). When this device operates with the 33 MHz CLK signal line frequency it is required to adhere to all of the requirements outlined above for a 33 MHz CLK signal line frequency.

■ For a PCI-X bus segment with a 66 MHz CLK signal line, the base frequencies are from 50 MHz to 66.6 MHz. For a PCI-X bus segment with a 100 MHz CLK signal line, the base frequencies are from above 66.6 MHz to 100 MHz. For a PCI-X bus segment with a 133 MHz CLK signal line, the base frequencies are from above 100 MHz to 133.2 MHz. (M66EN signal line asserted ... See Chapter 11: *Reset, Power, and Signal Line Initialization* for more information.)

  ■ The CLK signal line frequency cannot change dynamically after the RST# signal line is deasserted, other than the frequency range according to the SSC protocol (see the next section for more information).

  ■ The CLK signal line base frequency only changes when the RST# signal line is asserted.

  ■ Minimum low and high times of the CLK signal line must be maintained at all times.

  ■ The CLK signal line edges must be monotonically increasing and decreasing.

> A PCI-X device that is designed to operate with a PCI-X 66 MHz, 100 MHz, or 133 MHz CLK signal line frequency is also required to operate with a PCI 33 MHz or PCI 66 MHz CLK signal line frequency as outlined above. When this device operates with PCI 33 MHz or 66 MHz CLK signal line frequency it must adhere to all of the requirements outlined above for a 33 or 66 MHz CLK signal line frequency, respectively.
>
> A PCI-X device that is designed to operate with a PCI-X 133 MHz CLK signal line frequency is also required to operate with a PCI-X 66 MHz or PCI-X 100 MHz CLK signal line frequency as outlined above. When this device operates with PCI-X 66 MHz or PCI-X 100 MHz CLK signal line frequency it must adhere to all of the requirements outlined above for a 66 or 100 MHz CLK signal line frequency, respectively.

A PCI-X device that is designed to operate with a PCI-X 100 MHz CLK signal line frequency is also required to operate with a PCI-X 66 MHz CLK signal line frequency as outlined above. When this device operates with a PCI-X 66 MHz CLK signal line frequency it must adhere to all of the requirements outlined above for a 66 MHz CLK signal line frequency.

TEST & MEASUREMENT

The CLK signal line on PCI and PCI-X bus segments must be generated and distributed carefully on the platform and on add-in cards to maintain low clock skew (tcskew). As outlined below, all devices on a specific bus segment must receive the CLK signal line rising edge and falling edge signal within specific tsckew values over the different CLK signal line frequencies. All of the CLK signal line timings are measured at the package pins of the components (devices). In the case of add-in cards, compliance with the CLK signal line timings are measured on the add-in card as the component (device), not at the connector slot on the bus segment.

Outlined in Tables 12-5 and 12-6 and Figure 12-6 are the timing requirements for the CLK signal line on a specific bus segment. The PCI/PCI and PCI-X/PCI-X BRIDGES typically use a phase lock loop to generate the CLK signal line of a lower LEVEL bus segment from a higher LEVEL bus segment. However, the platform can be designed where some or all of the bus segments are provided their CLK signal lines from the same single central clock generator. For CLK signal line frequencies approaching 66.6 MHz and above, the CLK signal line techniques such as radial distribution, matched signal lengths, controlled impedance, low skew clock buffers, and termination may be necessary to insure low skew.

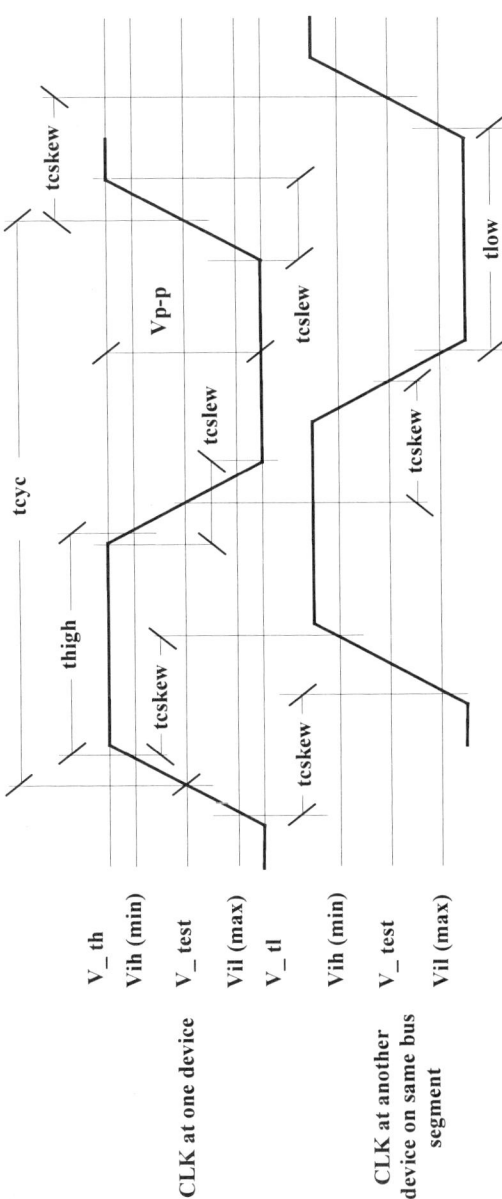

Figure 12-6: PCI and PCI-X CLK Signal Line Waveforms

SYMBOL	PARAMETER	DC to 33.3 MHz CLK Signal Line Freq.		Above 33.3 to 66.6 MHz CLK Signal Line Freq.	
		MIN nsec	MAX nsec	MIN Nsec	MAX nsec
tcyc (2)	Cycle Time	30	Infinite	15	30
thigh	High Time	11		6	
tlow	Low Time	11		6	
tckslew (1)	Clock Slew	1 V/nsec	4 V/nsec	1.5 V/nsec	4 V/nsec
tckskew	Clock Skew		2		1

Table 12-5-A: PCI CLK Signal Line Timing for DC to 33.3 MHz and Above 33.3 MHz to 66.6 MHz Frequencies

Notes:

(1) Measured at the device's package pin for minimum Vp-p of the CLK signal line. For above 33.3 MHz the measurement of tcslew is with the circuit below.

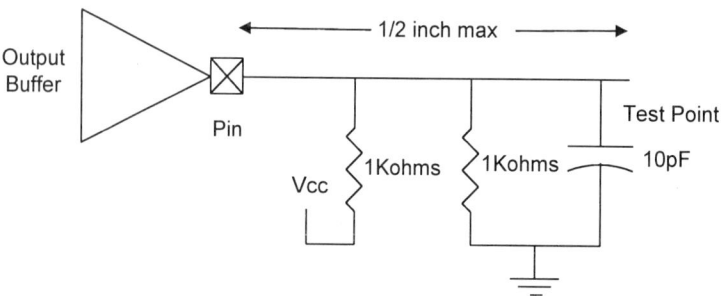

(2) The minimum and maximum periods stated cannot be violated by CLK signal line jitter. For example, 15 nsec minimum period is for a 66.6 MHz maximum frequency. When jitter is considered, the minimum period of 15 nsec is required to be maintained; thus the actual nominal minimum period must be adjusted to include the jitter. Consequently, the actual nominal maximum CLK signal line frequency is slightly less that 66.6 MHz.

SYMBOL	PARAMETER	Above 66.6 to 133.2 MHz to CLK Signal Line Freq.		50 to 66.6 MHz CLK Signal Line Freq.	
		MIN Nsec	MAX nsec	MIN Nsec	MAX nsec
tcyc (2)	Cycle Time	7.5	20	15	20
thigh	High Time	3		6	
tlow	Low Time	3		6	
tcslew(1)	Clock Slew	1.5 V/nsec	4 V/nsec	1.5 V/nsec	4 V/nsec
tcskew	Clock Skew		0.5		0.5

Table 12-5-B: PCI-X CLK Signal Line Timing for 50 MHz to 66.6 MHz and Above 66.6 MHz to 133.2 MHz Frequencies

Notes:

(1) Measured at the device's package pin for minimum V p-p of the CLK signal line with the following setup.

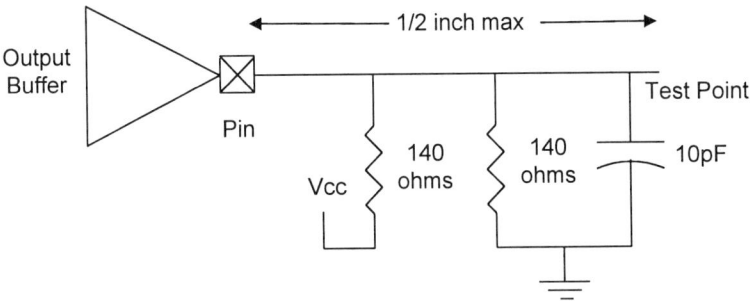

(2) The minimum and maximum periods stated cannot be violated by CLK signal line jitter. For example, 15 nsec minimum period is for a 66.6 MHz maximum frequency. When jitter is considered, the minimum period of 15 nsec is required to be maintained; thus the actual nominal minimum period must be adjusted to include the jitter. Consequently, the actual nominal maximum CLK signal line frequency is slightly less that 66.6 MHz.

Tables 12-6-A and 12-6-B define the measurement points for CLK signal line.

SYMBOL	5 V Signaling (Volts)	3.3 V Signaling (Volts)
V_th	2.4	0.6 x Vcc
V_tl	0.4	0.2 x Vcc
V_test	1.5	0.4 x Vcc
Vih	2.0	0.5 x Vcc
Vil	0.8	0.3 x Vcc
Vp-p (1)	2.0 min.	0.4xVcc min.

Table 12-6-A: PCI CLK Signal Line Test and Measurement Conditions

Note:
(1) Measured from V_th and V_tl

SYMBOL	3.3 V Signaling (Volts)
V_th	0.6 x Vcc
V_tl	0.2 x Vcc
V_test	0.4 x Vcc
Vih	0.5 x Vcc
Vil	0.35 x Vcc
Vp-p (1)	0.4xVcc min.

Table 12-6-B: PCI-X CLK Signal Line Test and Measurement Conditions

Note:
(1) Measured from V_th and V_tl

12.6 SPREAD SPECTRUM CLOCKING

According to FCC regulations, the platform's electromagnetic interference (EMI) will be measured at 6db (FCC Class B) above the EMI limits for a system's platform included in a chassis. To meet these requirements, the CLK signal line may be varied within a frequency range using a technique called Spread Spectrum Clocking (SSC). The gradual change of the CLK signal line frequency will effectively remove base frequency EMI "spikes" and will result in an estimated 10 db reduction in EMI. The effect of gradual change of the CLK signal line frequency relative to a base frequency is called modulation.

For a PCI bus segment (or a PCI-X bus segment operating in PCI compliant mode) SSC is defined for the CLK signal line frequency range from above 33.3 MHz to 66.3 MHz. (defined as the base frequency). The SSC is not defined for the base frequencies of DC to 33.3 MHz.

For a PCI-X bus segment operating as PCI-X compliant, the SCC technique is defined for the CLK signal line frequency range from 50 MHz to 133.2 MHz.

The protocol for implementing SSC is as follows:

■ The SSC is defined for components on the system's platform and add-in cards.

■ The base frequency of the PCI clock is the maximum value allowed.

  ■ The SSC frequency range is plus 0.0% of the base frequency and minus 1.0% of the base frequency (the "SCC frequency range" is also known as "frequency spread").

■ If the clock is generated by a PLL, the PLL tracking must maintain the CLK signal line frequency within the SSC frequency range.

■ The effective modulation for SSC is 30 KHz to 33 KHz

■ The modulation does not have to be linear. Linear is defined as a constant rate of change of the frequency.

■ If a PLL is the clock source for SSC, all of the tracking tolerances must remain within the plus 0.0% of the base frequency and minus 1.0% of the base frequency of the SSC protocol.

■ The value of clock skew defined for the CLK signal line must include the skew caused by SSC tracking of the PLL.

12.7 NON-CLOCK SIGNAL LINE TIMING

INTRODUCTION

As previously discussed, all PCI and PCI-X bus segment signal lines are synchronized to the rising edge of CLK except for the RST#, INTx#, and PME# signal lines. Also, the SERR# signal line is asserted synchronized with the CLK signal line, but deasserts asynchronously to the rising edge of the CLK signal line. This subchapter will detail the timing relation between the CLK signal line and the non-clock signal line synchronized to the CLK signal line.

The PCI bus segment is based on register to register transfer. Figure 12-7 shows a 33 MHz PCI bus segment. Figure 12-8 shows an above 33.3 MHz to 66.6 MHz PCI bus segment. Some important parameters for specifying a PCI register to register transfer are:

■ Cycle time (tcyc). The period of one clock cycle; the total amount of time available to complete a transfer.

■ Clock to data valid time (tval). CLK and data measured at component pins.

■ Clock skew (tcskew). The uncertainty of the rising edge of the clock at any PCI component package pin.

■ Bus propagation time (tprop). This is the time needed for the electrical signal to propagate from one PCI component to all other PCI components.

■ Input setup time (tsu). The time data must arrive at the receiving register before the PCI clock arrives.

■ Input hold time (th). The time data must remain at the receiving register after the PCI clock arrives. Not shown in the figures ... for 33 MHz and above 33.3 MHz to 66.6 MHz.

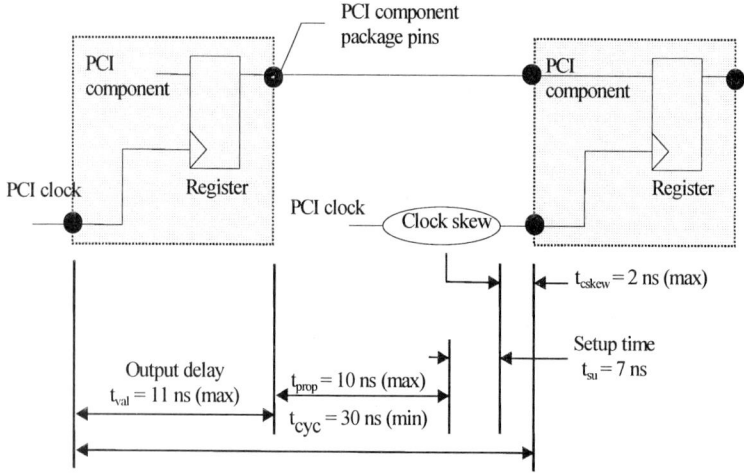

Figure 12-7: PCI Bus Segment Timing Parameters for 33.3 MHz CLK Signal Line Frequencies

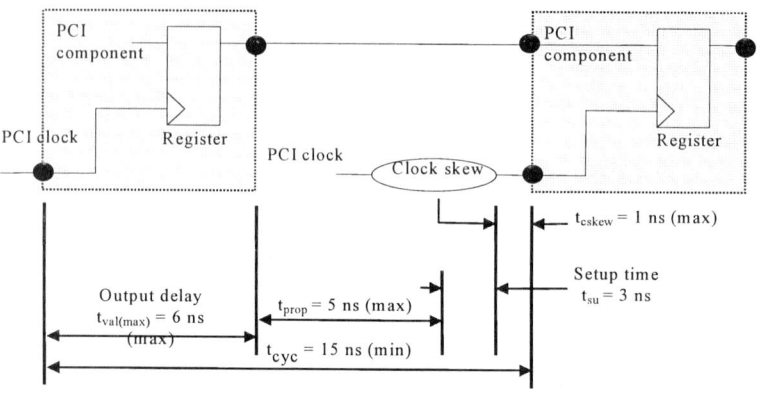

Figure 12-8: PCI Bus Segment Timing Parameters for Above 33.3 MHz to 66.6 MHz CLK Signal Line Frequencies

The parameters outlined in Figures 12-7 and 12-8 are further discussed in this subchapter. There are similar timing considerations for a PCI-X bus segment. The timing parameters are listed in this section. Applying these values yields a range of tprop values on a PCI-X bus segment. A PCI-X bus segment with 133MHz, 100

MHz, and 66 MHz CLK signal lines frequencies provide tprop values of 9, 4.5, and 2 nsec., respectively.

TEST & MEASUREMENT

All of the signal line timings are measured at the package pins of the components (devices). In the case of add-in cards, compliance with the CLK signal line timings are measured on the add-in card as the component (device), not at the connector slot on the bus segment.

The timing details for the signal lines on a PCI bus segment are outlined in Table 12-7-A and Figure 12-9 (voltage levels are defined in Table 12-8-A). The tval3r and tval3f (min) (collectively tval3) can be reduced to 1.0 ns for above 33 MHz to 66 MHz CLK signal line frequency. Unfortunately, to maintain compatibility with 33 MHz devices on the bus segment, tval3 (min) must remain at 2.0 ns. Alternatively, the M66EN signal line can be used to "program" a different value of tval3 (min) for above 33 MHz to 66 MHz operation.

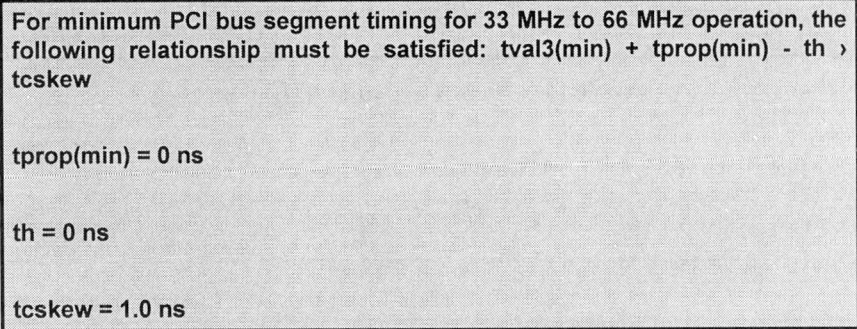

For minimum PCI bus segment timing for 33 MHz to 66 MHz operation, the following relationship must be satisfied: tval3(min) + tprop(min) - th › tcskew

tprop(min) = 0 ns

th = 0 ns

tcskew = 1.0 ns

The timing details for the signal lines on a PCI-X bus segment are outlined in Table 12-7-B and Figure 12-9 (voltage levels are defined in Table 12-8-B).

SYMBOL (Notes)	PARAMETER	DC to 33.3 MHz CLK Signal Line Freq. 5 and 3.3 Volt Signaling (Notes)		Above 33.3 to 66.6 MHz CLK Signal Line Freq. 3.3 Volt Signaling (Notes)	
		MIN nsec	MAX nsec	MIN nsec	MAX nsec
tval tval3f tval 3r (1)	Output Delay	2 (2)(6)	11 (2)(3)	2 (6)	6 (3)
tval tval3f tval3r point to point (1)	Output Delay	2 (2)(6)	12 (2)(3)	2(6)	6 (3)
tsu	Input Setup	7		3	
tsu point to point	Input Setup	10,12 (5)		5	
th	Input Hold	0		0	
ttri_d (7)	TRI to Drive	2		2	
td_tri (4)(7)	Drive to TRI		28		14

Table 12-7-A: PCI Signal Line Timing

Notes:

(1)   Tval is for 5 volt signaling, and tval3r and tval3f are for 3.3 volt signaling.

(2)   For 5 volt signaling use a 0pF equivalent load for minimum measurements. Use 50pF load for maximum measurement.

(3)   For 3.3 volt signaling use the following test setup for tval3r maximum.

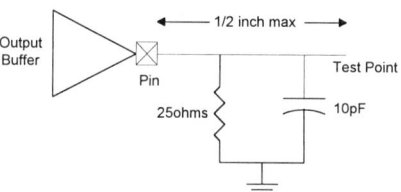

For 3.3 volt signaling use the following test setup for tval3f maximum.

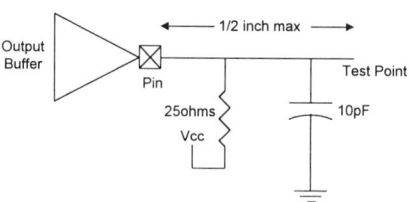

(4) All signal lines exept for CLK signal line are floated when RST# is asserted.

(5) GNTx# signal line is 10 ns. and REQx# is 12 ns.

(6) For 3.3 volt signaling use the following test setup measured at the pin (not test point) for tval3f and tval3r minimum.

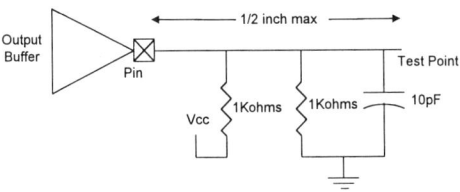

Also, see shaded the box above Table 12-7A.

(7) Tri-state current is defined as less than or equal to the leakage current.

SYMBOL (Notes)	PARAMETER	66.6 MHz CLK Signal Line Freq. 3.3 Volt Signaling (Notes)		Above 66.6 MHz to 133 MHz CLK Signal Line Freq. 3.3 Volt Signaling (Notes)	
		MIN nsec	MAX nsec	MIN nsec	MAX nsec
tval3f tval3r	Output Delay	0.7 (1)	3.8 (2) (3)	0.7 (1)	3.8 (2) (3)
tval3f tval 3r point to point (4)	Output Delay	0.7 (1)	3.8 (2) (3)	0.7 (1)	3.8 (2) (3)
tsu	Input Setup	1.7		1.2	
tsu point to point (4)	Input Setup	1.7		1.2	
th	Input Hold	0.5		0.5	
ttri_d (6)	TRI to Drive	0		0	
td_tri (5) (6)	Drive to TRI		7		7

Table 12-7-B: PCI-X Signal Line Timing

Note:

(1) The minimum numbers are measured at package pin (not test point) with the following test circuit for tval3r and tval3f

873

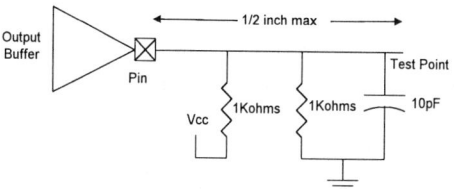

(2)   The maximum numbers are measured at test point with the following test circuit for tval3f

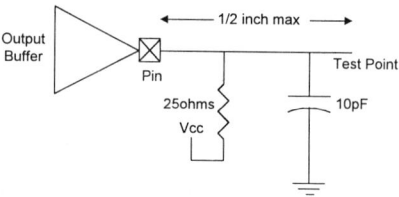

(3)   The maximum numbers are measured at test point with the following test circuit for tval3r

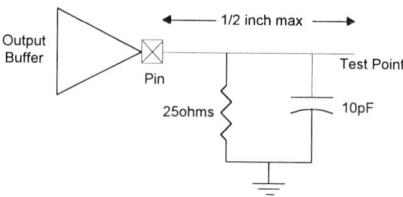

(4)   Only applies to REQx# and GNTx# signal lines.

(5)   All signal lines exept for the CLK signal line are floated when RST# is asserted.

(6)   Tri-state current is defined as less than or equal to the leakage current.

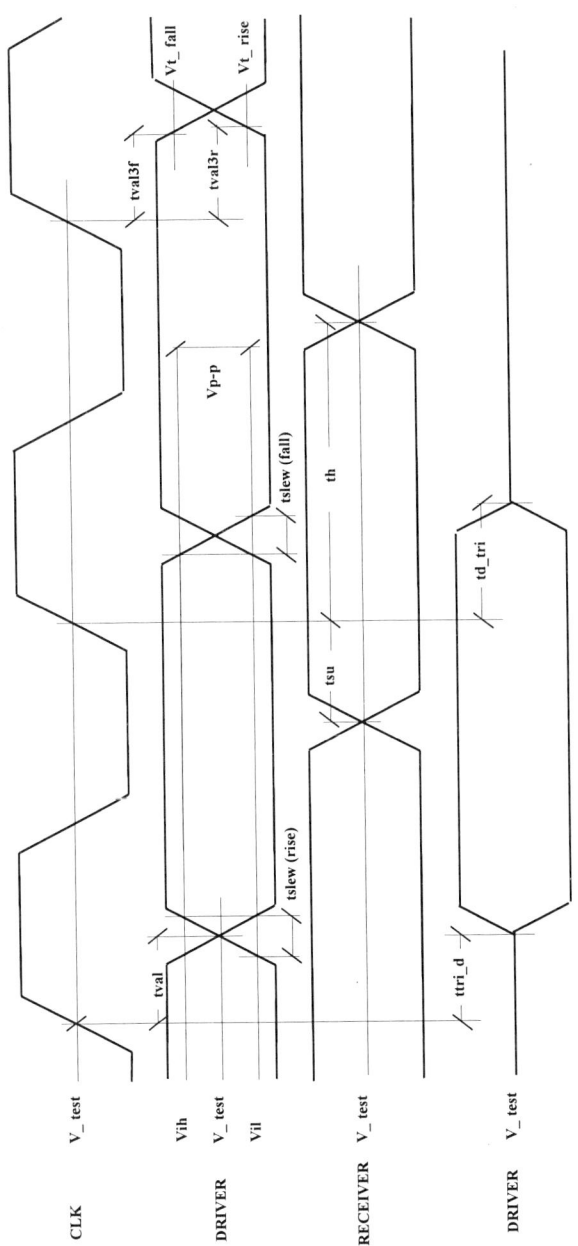

Figure 12-9: Non-Clock Signal Line Timing Relationships

SYMBOL	5 V Signaling (Notes)	3.3 V Signaling (Notes)
	Volts	Volts
V_th	2.4 (4)	0.6 x Vcc (1)
V_tl	0.4 (4)	0.2 x Vcc (1)
V_test	1.5	0.4 x Vcc
Vih	2.0	0.5 x Vcc
Vil	0.8	0.3 x Vcc
Vt_fall	-	0.615 x Vcc
Vt_rise	-	0.285 x Vcc
Input Signal Edge Rate	1 V/ns	1 V/ns (2) and 1.5 V/ns (3)
Vp-p	2.0 max.	0.4xVcc max. (1)

Table 12-8-A: PCI Signal Line Test and Measurement Conditions

Notes:

(1)   Measured from with 0.1 x Vcc of overdrive (over Vih and Vil) with no more than the Vp-p specified.

(2)   The Input Signal Slew Rate is 1 V/ns for DC to 33.3 MHz CLK signal line and measured between Vil and Vih.

(3)   The Input Signal Slew Rate is 1.5 V/ns for above 33.3 MHz to 66.6 MHz CLK signal line measured between 0.3Vcc and 0.6Vcc with the following test setup.

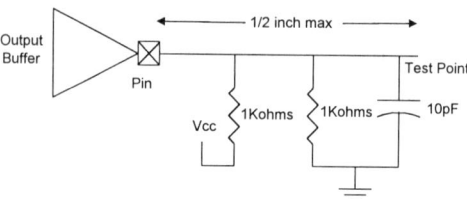

(4)   Measured from with 400mv of overdrive (over Vih and Vil) with no more than the Vp-p specified.

SYMBOL	3.3 V Signaling (Notes)
	Volts
V_th (1)	0.6 x Vcc
V_tl (1)	0.25 x Vcc
V_test	0.4 x Vcc
Vih	0.5 x Vcc
Vil	0.35 x Vcc
Vt_fall	0.615 x Vcc
Vt_rise	0.285 x Vcc
Input Signal Slew Rate	1.5 V/ns (2)
Vp-p	0.4xVcc max. (1)

Table 12-8-B: PCI-X Signal Line Test and Measurement Conditions

Notes:

(1)   Measured with 0.1 x Vcc of overdrive with no more than the Vp-p specificed.

(2)   Input Signal Slew Rate is measured between Vih and Vil.

SIGNAL LINE PROPAGATION ON A BUS SEGMENT

INTRODUCTION

As discussed in the previous section, the CLK signal line is required to have a maximum skew between its rising edge at one device and its rising edge at another device on the same bus segment. Associated with the CLK signal line skew is the propagation speed (measured in nanoseconds as tprop) of the rising and falling edges of signal lines along the bus segment. If the CLK signal line frequency is lowered to allow for longer or more heavily loaded bus segments, the tprop values are the only timing value that can be increased.

The tprop is the value of the actual "flight time" of a signal line on the bus segment. That is, the time a signal leaves the driving pin to when a full amplitude signal arrives at all receivers. The bus segment design must insure the tprop time as follows:

- The tprop time must be less than 10 nanoseconds for PCI bus segments operating at DC to 33.3 MHz.

- The tprop time must be less than 5 nanoseconds for PCI bus segments operating at above 33.3 MHz to 66.6 MHz.

- The tprop time must be less than 9 nanoseconds for PCI-X bus segments operating at 50 MHz to 66.6 MHz.

- The tprop time must be less than 4.5 nanoseconds for PCI bus segments operating at above 66.6 MHz to 100 MHz.

- The tprop time must be less than 2.0 nanoseconds for PCI bus segments operating at above 100 MHz to 133.2 MHz.

- The minimum tprop delay for a PCI bus segment is 0 nanoseconds and for a PCI-X bus segment is 0.3 nanoseconds.

PCI SPECIFIC

For the 5 volt signaling operation on a PCI bus segment, the value for tprop is measured with 0 pF test load for minimum values and 50 pF test load for maximum values. Because the wave being propagated requires reflection at the end of the bus segment, passive termination at the end of a long bus segment is not possible. Consequently, only active devices are possible (such as diodes).

The calculation for maximum tprop in Figures 12-10-A and 12-10-B for 5 volt signaling is determined by two methods. The method that provides the largest value is the one to be used. The two methods are as follows:

- Measure tprop between the buffer's waveform as if it was driving the test load as it intersects V_test to the intersection point when the waveform driving the bus intersects V_test for the last time (V_test may be crossed none or several times before the last crossing) (See Figure 12-10-A).

OR

- Input Signal Edge Rate (line in the figures that represent the slew rate) is positioned where Vih and Vil is crossed for the last time (Vih and Vil may be crossed none or several times before the last crossing) by the waveform when the buffer is actually driving the bus for rise and fall, respectively. Measure tprop between the buffer's waveform as if it was driving the test load as it passes V_test to the intersection point of the Input Signal Edge rate line as it crosses V_test (See Figure 12-10-B).

The calculation for maximum tprop for 3.3 volt signaling (for a 33 MHz CLK signal line) is the same as discussed above for 5 volt signaling. The only differences are as follows:

- Use Vt_fall or Vt_rise instead of V_test at the beginning of the tprop measurement. Use V_test at the end of the tprop measurement. See Figures 12-10-A and 12-10-B.

- The load for the measurements is shown in the notes of Table 12-7-A.

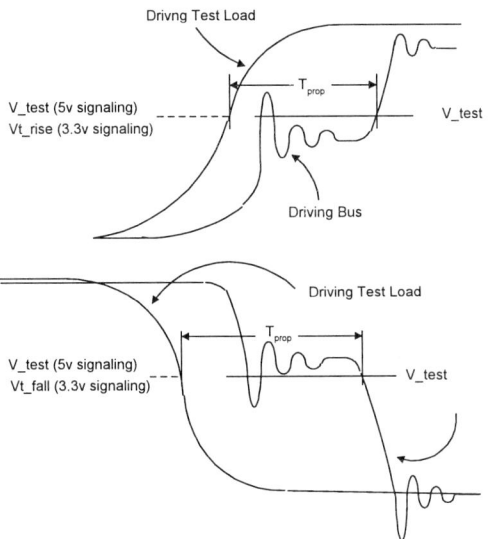

Figure 12-10-A: Measurement of t$_{prop}$ for PCI 5 and 3.3. Volt Signaling at 33.3 MHz CLK Signal Line Frequency

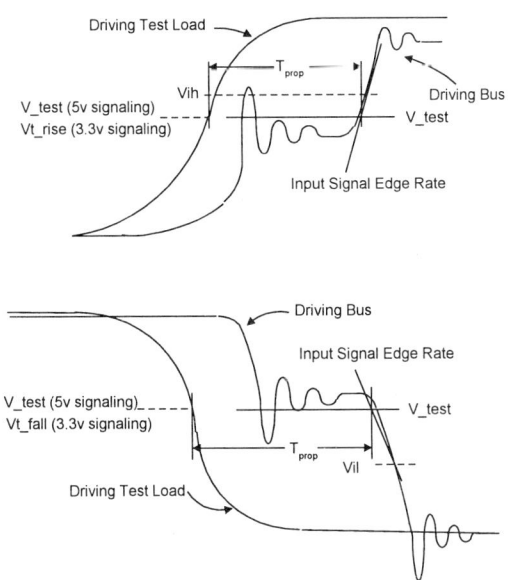

Fig 12-10-B: Measurement of t$_{prop}$ for PCI 5 and 3.3. Volt Signaling at 33.3 MHz CLK Signal Line Frequency

For PCI, the calculation for maximum tprop in Figures 12-11-A through 12-11-F for 3.3 volt signaling (for above 33MHz to 66 MHz CLK signal line) is determined by two methods. The method that provides the largest value is the one to be used. In Figures 12-11-A to 12-11-F the waveform associated with the load will actually be delayed by a propagation delay. The two methods are as follows:

■   Measure tprop between the buffer's waveform as if it was driving the test load as it intersects Vt_rise or Vt_fall to the intersection point when the waveform driving the bus intersects V_test for the last time (V_test may be crossed none or several times before the last crossing) (See Figures 12-11-A and 12-11-D.)

OR

■   Input Signal Edge Rate (line in the figures that represent the slew rate) is positioned where Vih and Vil is crossed for the last time (Vih and Vil may be crossed none or several times before the last crossing) by the waveform when the buffer is actually driving the bus for rise and fall, respectively. Measure tprop between the buffer's waveform as if it was driving the test load as it passes Vt_rise or Vt_fall to the intersection point of the Input Signal Edge rate line as it crosses V_test. (See Figs. 12-11B, 12-11C, 12-11E, and 12-11F.)

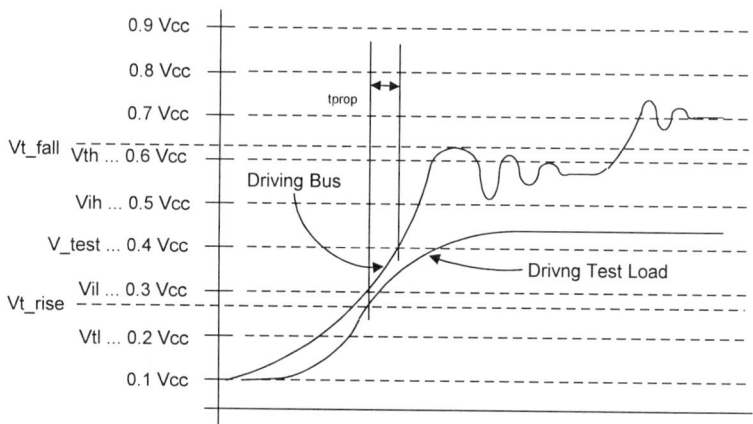

Figure 12-11-A: Measurement of tprop for PCI 3.3 Volt Signaling for Above 33.3 MHz to 66.6 MHz CLK Line Frequencies and PCI-X for all CLK Signal Line Frequencies

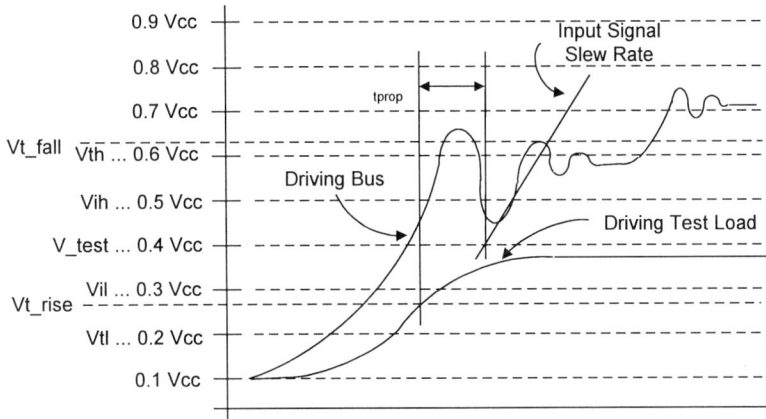

Figure 12-11-B: Measurement of tprop for PCI and PCI-X 3.3 Volt Signaling for Above 33.3 MHz to 66.6 MHz CLK Line Frequencies and PCI-X for all CLK Signal Line Frequencies

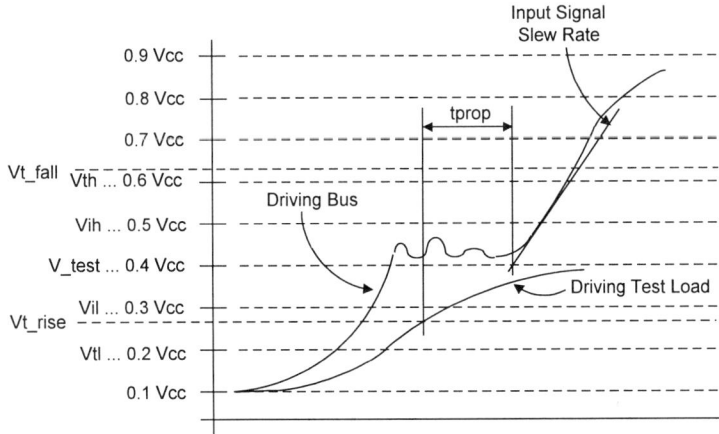

Figure 12-11-C: Measurement of tprop for PCI and PCI-X 3.3 Volt Signaling for Above 33.3 MHz to 66.6 MHz CLK Line Frequencies and PCI-X for all CLK Signal Line Frequencies

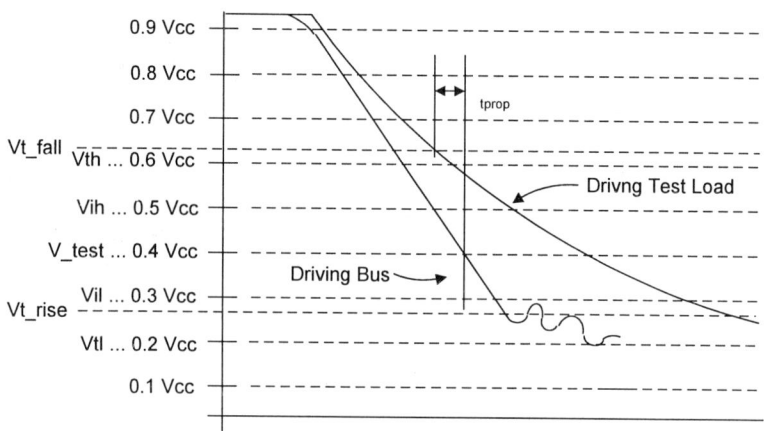

Figure 12-11-D: Measurement of tprop for PCI 3.3 Volt Signaling for Above 33.3 MHz to 66.6 MHz CLK Line Frequencies and PCI-X for all CLK Signal Line Frequencies

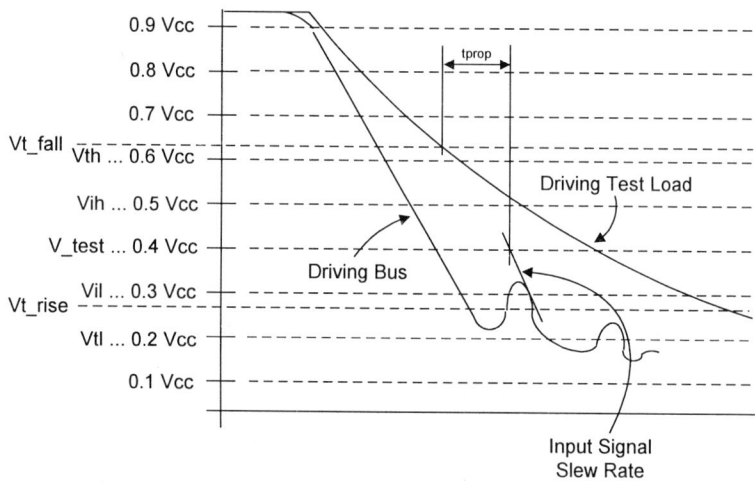

Figure 12-11-E: Measurement of tprop for PCI 3.3 Volt Signaling for Above 33.3 MHz to 66.6 MHz CLK Line Frequencies and PCI-X for all CLK Signal Line Frequencies

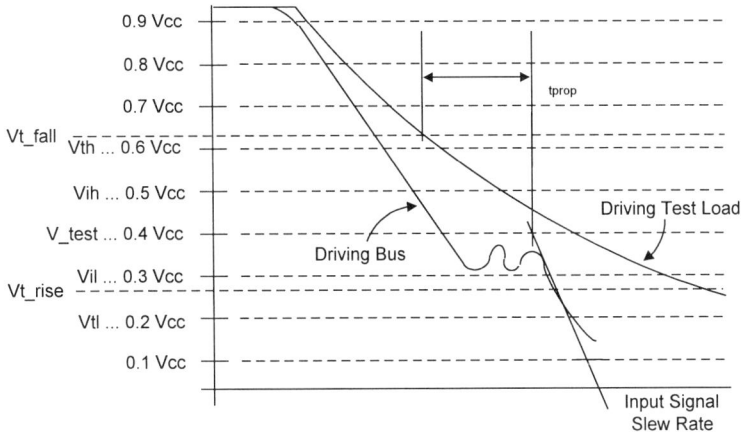

Figure 12-11-F: Measurement of tprop for PCI 3.3 Volt Signaling for Above 33.3 MHz to 66.6 MHz CLK Line Frequencies and PCI-X for all CLK Signal Line Frequencies

PCI-X SPECIFIC

The maximum tprop value for PCI-X is measured in the same fashion described above for PCI 3.3 volt signaling.

As previously discussed, the PCI-X addendum specification defines a minimum tprop value of 0.3 nsec. For PCI X 3.3 volt signaling, for minimum tprop the test load in Figure 12-12 is used. The tprop is measured from the first time the signal passes vt_rise or Vt_fall with the test load to the first time it crosses Vih (max) or Vil (min) on the bus segment, respectively (see Figures 12-13-A and 12-13-B).

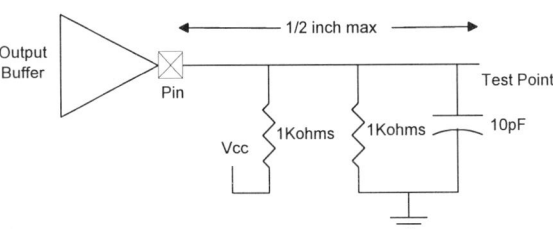

Figure 12-12: Test Load of tprop minimum for PCI-X

883

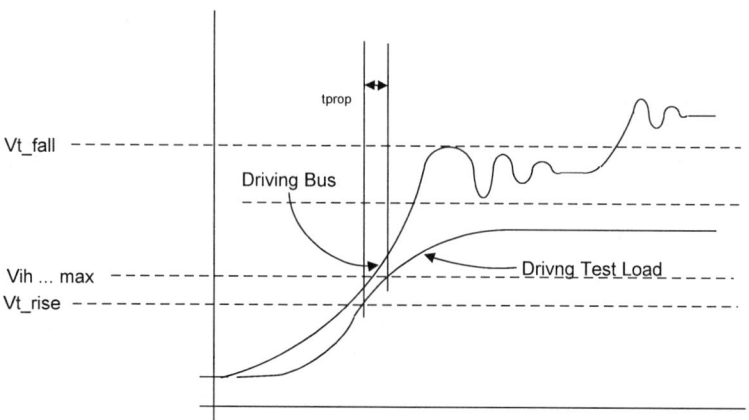

Figure 12-13-A: Measurement of tprop minimum for PCI-X

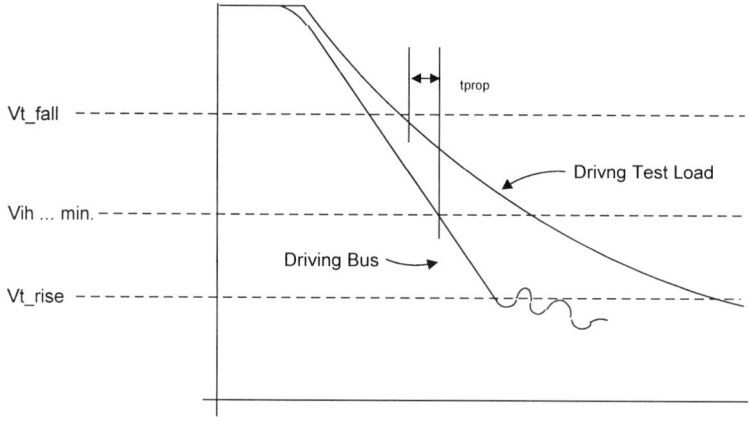

Figure 12-13-B: Measurement of tprop minimum for PCI-X

TRI-STATE SIGNALS

At times, the signal lines are not always driven, and are tri-stated. Referring to Figure 12-9, the driving event ttri_d and tri-stating event td_tri of the signal line are also referenced to the rising edge of the CLK signal line.

> Throughout the book, the driving and tri-stating of signal lines are identified by *D* and *T*, respectively. The FRAME#, IRDY#, TRDY#, DEVSEL#, REQ64#, ACK64#, STOP#, PERR#, and LOCK# signal lines (specified as bi-directional drive tri-state in Chapter 5: *Signal Lines*) must be driven by an active driver for one CLK signal line period before they are tri-stated.

OTHER SIGNAL LINE TIMING CONSDIERATIONS

Not discussed above is the timing of the RST# signal line relative to the CLK signal line or any other signal lines. The timing of the RST# signal line relative to other signal lines is discussed in Chapter 11: *Reset, Power, and Signal Line Initialization.*

VENDOR PROVIDED SPECIFICATION

During the development of PCI and PCI-X systems, many vendors will do board-level electrical simulation of PCI components. This will ensure that system implementations are manufacturable and that components are used correctly. To help facilitate this effort, as well as provide complete information, component vendors should make the following information available to developers. It is recommended that component vendors make this information electronically available in the IBIS model format.

- Pin capacitance for all pins.

- Pin inductance for all pins.

- Output V/I curves under switching conditions. Two curves should be given for each output type used: one for driving high, the other for driving low. Both should show best-typical-worst curves. Also, "beyond-the-rail" response is critical, so the voltage range should span -5 to 10V for 5 volt signaling and -3 to 7V for 3.3 volt signaling.

- Input V/I curves under switching conditions. A V/I curve of the input structure when the output is tri-stated is also important. This plot should also show best-typical-worst curves over the range of 0 to Vcc.

- Rise/fall slew rates for each output type.

- Complete absolute maximum data, including operating and non-operating temperature, DC maximums, etc.

In addition to this component information, connector vendors should make available accurate simulation models of PCI connectors.

12.8 SIGNAL LINE RESISTOR AND CAPACITOR CONSIDERATIONS

> In the following discussion, the assumption is that unless otherwise noted all resistors and capacitors are on the backplane that comprises the bus segment. Resistors and capacitors that are mounted on the add-in card (or internal to a device) are noted. Also see Chapter 13: *Connector, Platform, and Add-in Card Design* for more information.
>
> For capacitor requirements specific to the power lines, see Chapter 13: *Connector, Platform, and Add-in Card Design* for more information.

As outlined in Chapter 5: *Signal Lines* some of the signal lines have pull-up resistors. Table 12-9 summarizes the values of these resistors. The PCI and PCI-X signal lines that require bus segment pull-up resistors are FRAME#, TRDY#, IRDY# DEVSEL#, STOP#, SERR#, PERR#, LOCK#, INTx#, and PME#.

If implemented, AD[63::32], C/BE[7::4]#, and PAR64# signal lines have unique requirements. A PCI or PCI-X bus resource that supports 64 data bit accesses may be attached to a bus segment that only supports 32 data bit bus transactions. Consequently, the AD[63::32], C/BE#[7::4], and PAR64 signal lines will not be attached to pull-up resistors to Vcc on the bus segment. In order to prevent these signal lines from floating and possibly oscillating, the component must drive these signal lines as outputs or, if in the input state, they must be biased. Solutions that violate the input leakage current specification, or in the case of add-in cards external pull-up resistors are *not* allowed. When the 64 data bit resource resides on a bus segment that supports 64 data bit bus transactions, the AD[63::32], C/BE#[7::4], and PAR64 signal lines will be attached to pull-up resistors to Vcc on the bus segment. See Chapter 5: *Signal Line Definition* for more information.

There are other considerations for PCIXCAP, M66EN, REQ64#, and ACK64# signal lines, and PRSNT1# and PRSNT2# pins on the connector discussed below.

Each signal line of a specific name is bussed together with others of the same name and attached to a single pull-up resistor to Vcc according to Table 12-9.

SIGNALING VOLTAGE	Typical value OHMS (3)	Min. OHMS (1)	Max. OHMS (2)
5	2.7K	963	$[(V_{CC}\text{-} min)\text{-}2.7]/[\#loads \times I_{ih}]$
3.3	8.2K	2.42K	$[(V_{CC}\text{-} min)\text{-}(0.7 \times V_{CC})]/[\#loads \times I_{ih}]$

Table 12-9: PCI and PCI-X Pull-Up Resistor Values

Notes:

(1)   Min pull-up resistance = [(Vcc max)-Vol]/[Iol +(16 x Iil)], where the max # loads=16.

(2)   For the equations in the column, substitute Ioff for Iih when calculating the pull-up resistor value for the PME# signal line.

(3)   The typical value is derated by 10% for nominal values

The above table is paraphrased from *PCI Local Bus Specification Rev. 2.2*, reprinted with permission of the PCI Special Interest Group.

Other resistor and capacitor considerations for both PCI and PCI-X bus segments are as follows:

- The central resource in the platform may need pull-up resistors on the REQx# signal lines. The specification for REQx# signal line pull-up resistors is bus segment platform independent. These signal lines are not bussed together. The GNTx# signal lines are individually driven by the central resource and are not bussed.

- The M66EN signal line (pin 49B) is grounded on 33 MHz PCI bus segments and 33 MHz PCI add-in cards and devices.

  - For PCI 66 MHz and PCI-X bus segments, the M66EN signal line of the connectors or devices on a specific bus segment are bussed together and attached to Vcc with a 5K +/- 5% pull-up resistor on the bus segment. In addition, on each add-in card and device a 0.01uF +/- 10% capacitor must be attached between the M66EN signal line. The capacitor that resides on the add-in card has a 0.25 inch maximum trace length to the connector pad. Nothing else is attached to the M66EN pin.

- The REQ64# and ACK64# pins on the connector are attached to pull-up resistors on the bus segment of the platform (no pull-up resistors are allowed on the add-in card) and are defined as part of the 32 data bit connector. On a bus segment that supports the 64 data bit extension all of the REQ64# pins are bussed together and attached to a single pull-up resistor to Vcc. Similarly, all of the ACK64# pins are bussed together and attached to a single pull-up resistor to Vcc. On a bus segment that supports only a 32 data bit PCI bus segment, each REQ64# pin must be individually attached to separate pull-up resistor to Vcc. All of the ACK64# pins are bussed together and attached to a single pull-up resistor to Vcc. On the add-in cards, the REQ64# and ACK64# connector pads are attached to the REQ64# and ACK64# signal lines, respectively. The value of the pull-up resistor is according to Table 12-9.

- For the PRSNT1# signal line on each add-in card bus segment, a 0.01uF +/- 10% capacitor must be attached between each individual add-in card connector pad and ground with less than a 0.25 inch trace. These signal lines are not bussed together on the bus segment. Optionally, if the bus segment monitors the logical value, a 5K +/- 5% pull-up resistor on each PRSNT1# pin on each add-in card connector on the bus segment is attached to Vcc.

■ For the PRSNT2# signal line on each add-in card bus segment a 0.01uF +/- 10% capacitor must be attached between each individual add-in card connector pad and ground with less than a 0.25 inch trace. These signal lines are not bussed together on the bus segment. Optionally, if the bus segment monitors the logical value, a 5K +/- 5% pull-up resistor on each PRSNT1# pin on each add-in card connector on the bus segment is attached to Vcc.

■ The SBO# and SDONE signal lines (pins 40A and 41A) have been redefined as reserved with the elimination of the bus segment cache coherency. To be compatible to earlier specifications these connector pads and pins must be left unattached and not bussed.

■ The IDSEL signal line can optionally be connected (individually) to the AD signal lines through series resistors on the bus segment. Typically, no resistors are used for a PCI bus segment. If a resistor is implemented for a PCI-X bus segment the series resistor value is 2K ohms +/-5%

■ If boundary scan is not implemented

   ■ The connector pins associated with TMS and TDI must each individually be attached to a 5K pull-up resistor to Vcc on the bus segment.

   ■ The connector pins associated with TMS must each individually be attached to a 5K pull-up resistor to Vcc on the bus segment.

   ■ The connector pins associated with TRST# are bussed on the bus segment and attached to ground with a 5K pull-down resistor.

   ■ The connector pins associated with TCLK are bussed on the bus segment and attached to ground with a 5K pull-down resistor.

   ■ The connector pin associated to TDO is left open.

   ■ If the add-in card does not support J-TAG, the add-in card must connect the TDI and TDO signal lines pins together.

Other resistor and capacitor considerations specific to PCI-X bus segments and add-in cards are as follows:

■ The PCI-X addendum specification defines the connector and pins according to the PCI local bus specification with one exception: PCIXCAP. The PCIXCAP signal line is grounded on a PCI bus segment. For a PCI-X bus segment, the PCIXCAP signal lines are bussed together, attached to a single pull-up resistor to Vcc, and attached to voltage level comparitor circuit. (See the PCI-X addendum specification Section 14 Appendix for more information.)

- For PCI add-in cards or devices this connector pad is attached to ground on the add-in card. For PCI-X add-in cards or devices that can operate at 133 MHz, this connector pad is attached to ground with a 0.01 uF capacitor. For a PCI-X add-in card or device that can operate only at 66 MHz, this connector pad is pulled-down to ground with a 10K resistor in parallel with a 0.01 uF capacitor. The capacitance is +/- 10% and the resistance is +/- 5%. The capacitor and pull-down resistor that reside on the add-in card have a 0.1 inch and 0.25 inch maximum trace length to the connector pad, respectively. Nothing else is attached to the PCIXCAP connector pad or pin.

12.9 CLAMP ISSUES

> See Subchapters 12.3: *5 Volt (5V) Signaling Environment* and 12.4: *3.3 Volt (3.3V) Signaling Environment* for further discussions about device protection.

Clamps are specified on PCI input pins to help maintain good bus signal integrity. Care must be taken when connecting devices that operate at different supply voltages to prevent parasitic DC current paths.

Input pins of a PCI integrated circuit operating in the 5 volt signaling environment must be diode clamped to ground. Inputs to circuits operating in the 3.3 volt signaling environment must be diode clamped to both the 3.3V rail and ground. The requirements for diode clamping to 5 or 3.3 volts and associated I/O buffer issues are as follows:

- Diode clamping of the 5 volt signaling I/O buffers to the 3.3 volt power rail is not allowed under any conditions.

- If 3.3 volt PCI integrated circuit components are 5 volt tolerant and are mounted on a Dual Voltage Add-in Card, the I/O buffers may be connected to either the I/O Designated Power pads or the 3.3 volt power pads.

- Diode clamps and pull-up devices must be able to withstand a short circuit condition due to power failure during one of the following two conditions. (See Chapter 11: *RESET, Power, and Signal Line Initialization* for more information.)

■ The RST# signal line must be asserted within 500 nanoseconds (tfail) from when 3.3V or 5 volts exceeds the minimum and maximum values in Table 11-1 by 500 millivolts. See Figure 11-1 in Chapter 11: *RESET, Power, and Signal Line Initialization.*

OR

■ The RST# signal line must be asserted within 100 nanoseconds (tfail). from when the 5 volt rail falls below the 3.3 volt rail by 300 millivolts or more. See Figure 11-1 in Chapter11: *RESET, Power, and Signal Line Initialization.*

The same considerations that apply to PCI 3.3 volt signaling and Dual Voltage Add-in Cards above also apply to PCI-X.

12.10   3.3 VOLT AUXILIARY POWER SOURCE

PCI local bus specification 2.2 adds an additional power pin: a 3.3 volt auxiliary power source (3.3Vaux). The purpose of 3.3Vaux is to support wake-up event logic in PCI resources by providing the power for the wake-up logic in the PCI resource. For a PCI resource on an add-in card, it is provided by the redefinition of a reserved pin (A14) to 3.3Vaux. The basic reason for the PCI device drawing power from 3.3Vaux is that the power from other power sources will have been disabled by software.

PCI resources designed to Rev. 2.1 and earlier revisions of the PCI bus specification are required to operate "normally" in bus segments whether they do or do not support the 3.3Vaux. Similarly, bus segments designed to Rev. 2.1 and earlier revisions of the PCI local bus specification are required to operate "normally" with PCI resources that either do or do not support the 3.3Vaux (except for the wake-up logic in the PCI resource). The implementation of 3.3Vaux is optional for both the bus segment and the PCI resource. It is optional for the bus segment because not all platforms support power management. It is optional for a PCI resource in two ways:

■ If the PCI resource does not have wake-up logic, it does not draw any power from 3.3Vaux (if it is provided by the system).

■ If the PCI resource does have wake-up logic, software can enable and disable drawing power from 3.3Vaux (if it is provided by the bus segment).

The PCI resource that supports wake-up logic dependent on 3.3Vaux is required to properly operate the non-wake-up without any power from the 3.3Vaux. This protocol permits a PCI resource designed for power management according to Rev. 2.2 of the PCI local bus specification to operate in systems that do not support 3.3Vaux.

Bus segments that implement both power management and 3.3Vaux are required to comply with the *PCI Bus Power Management Interface Specification Revision 1.0*. If the system supports 3.3Vaux, it must execute the power up sequence for the power pins and 3.3Vaux according to power management requirements. See the *PCI Bus Power Management* and *PCI Hot Plug Application & Design* books *(Available at annabooks.com), and PCI-X addendum bus specification* for more information.

The 3.3Vaux issues discussed above for a PCI local bus specification compliant bus segment also apply to PCI-X addendum specification compliant bus segment.

CHAPTER 13

CONNECTOR, PLATFORM, AND ADD-IN CARD DESIGN

This chapter consists of the following subchapters:

13.0   Connector Pins and Pads
13.1   Bus Segment Design
13.2   Add-in Card Design

13.0 CONNECTOR PINS AND PADS

INTRODUCTION

PCI SPECIFIC

As outlined in Chapter 12: *Signal Line Timing and Electrical Requirements*, there are three types of add-in cards (5 Volt, 3.3 Volt, and Universal I/O) and two types of connectors (5 volt and 3.3 volt). The keying of the add-in card and connector controls the specific type of add-in card that can be inserted into a specific connector type. Also, as outlined in earlier chapters, the PCI local bus specification supports 32 and 64 data bit resources. The connector assignments are outlined in Table 13-1 for the two types of connectors. Pins 1 through 62 define the two types of connectors that support 32 data bit PCI resources. The additional pins (63 through 94) support the 64 data bit extension.

The PCI add-in card pinout is the same as the connector (Table 13-1) except for the "connector key" is the "keyway". Also, the "connector pins" defined for the connector on the platform are specified as "connector pads" on the add-in card.

There are several connector pins and pads that deserve particular note:

- On the platform, pins labeled +5V(I/O) and +3.3V(I/O) are the I/O Designated Power Pins (collectively "+V(I/O)"). If the platform supports 3.3 volt signaling, the +3.3V(I/O) pins are attached to the 3.3 volt power plane. If the platform supports 5 volt signaling, the +5V(I/O) pins are attached to the 5 volt power plane. This is how a Universal I/O add-in card "knows" what type of system it is plugged into. A Universal I/O add-in card can power the I/O buffers from the +V(I/O) connector pins. The 5 Volt and 3.3 Volt add-in card can attach the I/O buffers of its components to the +V(I/O) connector pins and be sure to obtain the proper signaling environment power supply.

The PCI 3.0 local bus specification places an additional restriction on the preceding bullet. The bullet states that add-in cards keyed as 5 volt only, 3.3 volt only, or universal I/O signaling are permitted, which is true for PCI 2.2. However, the PCI 3.0 local bus specification DOES NOT permit add-in cards keyed for 5 volt only signaling. Devices residing on the bus segment must follow the same signaling voltage restrictions as add-in cards.

Pin	5V System		Universal I/O or 3.3V System	
	Side B	Side A	Side B	Side A
	32-Bit Connector Start			
1	-12V	TRST#	-12V	TRST#
2	TCK	+12V	TCK	+12V
3	GND	TMS	GND	TMS
4	TDO	TDI	TDO	TDI
5	+5V	+5V	+5V	+5V
6	+5V	INTA#	+5V	INTA#
7	INTB#	INTC#	INTB#	INTC#
8	INTD#	+5V	INTD#	+5V
9	PRSNT1#	RSVD	PRSNT1#	RSVD
10	RSVD	+5V (I/O)	RSVD	+3.3V (I/O)
11	PRSNT2#	RSVD	PRSNT2#	RSVD
12	GND	GND	KEY	KEY
13	GND	GND	KEY	KEY
14	RSVD	3.3Vaux	RSVD	3.3Vaux
15	GND	RST#	GND	RST#
16	CLK	+5V (I/O)	CLK	+3.3V (I/O)
17	GND	GNTx#	GND	GNTx#
18	REQx#	GND	REQx#	GND
19	+5V (I/O)	PME#	+3.3V (I/O)	PME#
20	AD[31]	AD[30]	AD[31]	AD[30]
21	AD[29]	+3.3V	AD[29]	+3.3V
22	GND	AD[28]	GND	AD[28]
23	AD[27]	AD[26]	AD[27]	AD[26]
24	AD[25]	GND	AD[25]	GND
25	+3.3V	AD[24]	+3.3V	AD[24]
26	C/BE[3]#	IDSEL	C/BE[3]#	IDSEL
27	AD[23]	+3.3V	AD[23]	+3.3V
28	GND	AD[22]	GND	AD[22]
29	AD[21]	AD[20]	AD[21]	AD[20]
30	AD[19]	GND	AD[19]	GND
31	+3.3V	AD[18]	+3.3V	AD[18]
32	AD[17]	AD[16]	AD[17]	AD[16]
33	C/BE[2]#	+3.3V	C/BE[2]#	+3.3V
34	GND	FRAME#	GND	FRAME#
35	IRDY#	GND	IRDY#	GND

Table 13-1: PCI and PCI-X Connector Pinout.

Pin	5V System		Universal I/O or 3.3V System	
	Side B	Side A	Side B	Side A
36	+3.3V	TRDY#	+3.3V	TRDY#
37	DEVSEL#	GND	DEVSEL#	GND
38	PCIXCAP (2)	STOP#	PCIXCAP (2)	STOP#
39	LOCK#	+3.3V	LOCK#	+3.3V
40	PERR#	RSVD (1)	PERR#	RSVD (1)
41	+3.3V	RSVD (1)	+3.3V	RSVD (1)
42	SERR#	GND	SERR#	GND
43	+3.3V	PAR	+3.3V	PAR
44	C/BE[1]#	AD[15]	C/BE[1]#	AD[15]
45	AD[14]	+3.3V	AD[14]	+3.3V
46	GND	AD[13]	GND	AD[13]
47	AD[12]	AD[11]	AD[12]	AD[11]
48	AD[10]	GND	AD[10]	GND
49	Ground	AD[09]	M66EN	AD[09]
50	Key	Key	GND	GND
51	Key	Key	GND	GND
52	AD[08]	C/BE[0]#	AD[08]	C/BE[0]#
53	AD[07]	+3.3V	AD[07]	+3.3V
54	+3.3V	AD[06]	+3.3V	AD[06]
55	AD[05]	AD[04]	AD[05]	AD[04]
56	AD[03]	GND	AD[03]	GND
57	GND	AD[02]	GND	AD[02]
58	AD[01]	AD[00]	AD[01]	AD[00]
59	+5V (I/O)	+5V (I/O)	+3.3V (I/O)	+3.3V (I/O)
60	ACK64#	REQ64#	ACK64#	REQ64#
61	+5V	+5V	+5V	+5V
62	+5V	+5V	+5V	+5V
	32-Bit Connector End			
	Key	Key	Key	Key
	Key	Key	Key	Key
	64-Bit Connector Start			
63	RSVD	GND	RSVD	GND
64	GND	C/BE[7]#	GND	C/BE[7]#
65	C/BE[6]#	C/BE[5]#	C/BE[6]#	C/BE[5]#
66	C/BE[4]#	+5V (I/O)	C/BE[4]#	+3.3V (I/O)
67	GND	PAR64	GND	PAR64
68	AD[63]	AD[62]	AD[63]	AD[62]
69	AD[61]	GND	AD[61]	GND

Table 13-1: PCI and PCI-X Connector Pinout (continued)

Note: (1) Prior to Rev. 2.2 of the PCI local bus specifcation these pins were the SDONE and SBO# signal lines. They are left unatatched.

      (2) For PCI add-in card or a bus segment, this pin is grounded. For a PCI-X add-in card or a PCI-X bus segment this pin is PCIXCAP signal line.

Pin	5V System		Universal I/O or 3.3V System	
	Side B	Side A	Side B	Side A
70	+5V (I/O)	AD[60]	+3.3V (I/O)	AD[60]
71	AD[59]	AD[58]	AD[59]	AD[58]
72	AD[57]	GND	AD[57]	GND
73	GND	AD[56]	GND	AD[56]
74	AD[55]	AD[54]	AD[55]	AD[54]
75	AD[53]	+5V (I/O)	AD[53]	+3.3V (I/O)
76	GND	AD[52]	GND	AD[52]
77	AD[51]	AD[50]	AD[51]	AD[50]
78	AD[49]	GND	AD[49]	GND
79	+5V (I/O)	AD[48]	+3.3V (I/O)	AD[48]
80	AD[47]	AD[46]	AD[47]	AD[46]
81	AD[45]	GND	AD[45]	GND
82	GND	AD[44]	GND	AD[44]
83	AD[43]	AD[42]	AD[43]	AD[42]
84	AD[41]	+5V (I/O)	AD[41]	+3.3V (I/O)
85	GND	AD[40]	GND	AD[40]
86	AD[39]	AD[38]	AD[39]	AD[38]
87	AD[37]	GND	AD[37]	GND
88	+5V (I/O)	AD[36]	+3.3V (I/O)	AD[36]
89	AD[35]	AD[34]	AD[35]	AD[34]
90	AD[33]	GND	AD[33]	GND
91	GND	AD[32]	GND	AD[32]
92	RSVD	RSVD	RSVD	RSVD
93	RSVD	GND	RSVD	GND
94	GND	RSVD	GND	RSVD
64-Bit Connector End				

NOTE:

1.   Pins marked '+5V (I/O)' or '+3.3V (I/O)' on the system board are connected to 'V (I/O)' (3.3V or 5V) on the expansion (universal) add-in card.

Table 13-1: PCI and PCI-X Connector Pinout (continued)

The table and figure are copied from PCI Local Bus Specification Rev. 2.2, reprinted with permission of the PCI Special Interest Group.

■ All pins marked as RSVD (reserved) are not bussed together on the bus segment and are not attached to anything other than the connector.

■ The REQ64# and ACK64# pins on the connector are attached to pull-up resistors on the bus segment of the platform (no pull-up resistors are allowed on the add-in card) and are defined as part of the 32 data bit connector. On a bus segment that supports the 64 data bit extension (including connector), all of the REQ64# pins are bussed together and attached to a single pull-up resistor to Vcc. Similarly, all of the ACK64# pins are attached to a single pull-up resistor. On a bus segment that supports only a 32 data bit bus segment, these pins must be individually attached to separate pull-up resistors to Vcc. All of the ACK64# pins are bussed together and attached to a single pull-up resistor to Vcc. On the add-in cards, the REQ64# and ACK64# pins are attached to the REQ64# and ACK64# signal lines, respectively. See Chapter 12: *Signal Line Timing and Electrical Requirements* for more information.

■ PME# pins are bussed together on the bus segment and are monitored by a platform resource. See Chapter 5: *Signal Line Definition* for more information. Also see Chapter 12: *Signal Line Timing and Electrical Requirements* for more information.

■ M66EN pins are bussed together on the bus segment and are monitored by a platform resource. See Chapter 5: *Signal Line Definition* for more information. Also see Chapter 12: *Signal Line Timing and Electrical Requirements* for more information.

■ The PRSNT1# and PRSNT2# pins are not bussed together on the bus segment and identify the power (wattage) requirements of the add-in card. Please see Chapter 11: *RESET, Power, and Signal Line Initialization* for more information. Also see Chapter 12: *Signal Line Timing and Electrical Requirements* for more information.

■ To support the J-TAG boundary scan, the TDI and TDO signal lines are available on the connector. If the add-in card does not support J-TAG, the add-in card must connect these two pins together. See Chapter 12: *Signal Line Timing and Electrical Requirements* for more information.

PCI-X SPECIFIC

The PCI-X addendum specification defines the connector and pins according to the PCI local bus specification with one exception: PCIXCAP. The PCIXCAP signal line is grounded on a PCI bus segment. For a PCI-X bus segment the PCIXCAP signal lines are bussed together, attached to a signal pull-up resistor to Vcc, and attached to voltage level comparitor circuit. (See PCI-X addendum specification Section 14 *Appendix* for more information on this circuit.) See Chapter 11: *RESET, Power, and Signal Line Initialization* for more information. Also, see Chapter 12: *Signal Line Timing and Electrical Requirements* for more information.

13.1 BUS SEGMENT DESIGN

LAYOUT

The layout of the platform has several requirements:

- The layout of the CLK signal line on the bus segment must meet the clock skew requirements defined in Chapter 12: *Signal Line Timing and Electrical Requirements*. The clock skew is measured between any two PCI or PCI-X resources on the bus segment. The layout of this signal line on the bus segment must also consider the CLK signal traces on the add-in card as described in the following section.

- The layout of the other PCI and PCI-X signal lines on the platform must meet the propagation delay defined in Chapter 12: *Signal Line Timing and Electrical Requirements*. The layout of these signal lines on the bus segment must also consider associated traces on the add-in card as described in the following section.

- Any PCI or PCI-X signal line that can be shared by other PCI resources on the bus can have several PCI-compliant loads (Chapter 2: *PCI and PCI-X System Architectural Overview* for details). The pull-up resistors required for some of the signal lines are placed on the platform with the values outlined in Chapter 12: *Signal Line Timing and Electrical Requirements*. Consideration must be made to include add-in card requirements as described in the following section.

- The PCI local bus specification and PCI-X addendum specification do not define a specific bus segment impedance for the signal line traces. The bus segment impedance and layout must support a round trip time within the propagation delay defined in Chapter 12: *Signal Line Timing and Electrical Requirements*. The loaded impedance of the bus segment must allow the PCI and PCI-X output drivers to meet the V/I curves specified in Chapter 12. Consideration must be made to include add-in card requirements as described in the following section. To accommodate components and bus segment layouts that do not comply with these requirements, the CLK signal line frequency can be reduced. It is the responsibility of the bus segment designer to insure proper operation of all PCI and PCI-X resources under this consideration.

- Ideally, the bus segment should have six layers: one for 3.3 volts, one for 5 volts, one for ground, and three for non-power signal lines. For cost considerations, however, a four layer board may be more practical. In this case, two layers can be used for non-power signal lines (usually the outer layers), one layer for ground, and one layer as a power plane. If both 3.3

and 5 volts are required, the power plane must be split. When the power plane is split, the non-power signal lines should be routed on the layer adjacent to the ground layer. If non-power signal lines are routed on the layer adjacent to the split power plane layer, care must be taken to keep the signal lines entirely on the 3.3 or the 5 volt section of the split power plane. If the non-power signal line must cross between the 3.3 and 5 volt sections, the two sections must be coupled by a 0.01 uF +/- 10% high-speed capacitor for every four non-power signal lines. This capacitor must be within 0.25 inches of the point where the non-power signal lines cross the split. These requirements reflect the concern that the split in the plane disrupts the AC return path for the non-power signal lines, creating an impedance discontinuity.

The 12 and -12 volt power supply lines must be distributed as large traces, usually on the non-power signal line layers.

RESISTORS AND DECOUPLING CAPACITORS

In addition to the capacitors to connect a split power plane, there are requirements for other capacitors on the power lines on the add-in cards as discussed in the next subchapter.

The other resistor and capacitor requirements for the other signal lines are discussed in Chapter 12: *Signal Line Timing and Electrical Requirements* .

13.2 ADD-IN CARD DESIGN

LAYOUT

The add-in cards have specific layout requirements relative to the distance between the PCI or PCI-X component and the connector pad. These are summarized in Table 13-2 below. These requirements apply to all signal lines with the following exceptions:

- Traces to the interrupt and JTAG pads are not constrained by length requirements.
- Maximum trace length (at 20 milli-inch thickness) of 0.25 inches from the connector pad to the 3.3 or 5 volt power planes. See further discussion below.

PARAMETER	PCI		PCI-X	
	MIN	MAX	MIN	MAX
CLK Signal Line Length	2.4 inches	2.6 inches	2.4 inches	2.6 inches
32 Data Bit Signal Line Length		1.5 inches	0.75 inches	1.5 inches
64 Data Bit Extension Signal Line Length		2.0 inches	1.75 inches	2.75 inches
RST# Signal Line Length			0.75 inches	3.0 inches
Add-in Card Unloaded Impedance	60 ohms (1)	100 ohms	51.3 ohms	62.7 ohms
Signal Line Propagation	150 ps/inch	190 ps/inch	150 ps/inch	190 ps/inch

Table 13-2: PCI and PCI-X Add-in Card Trace Requirements

Note (1): The 60 ohm value is for a device with more than 8 pf input capacitance (Cin). If the device input capacitance is 8 pf or less, the value is 51 ohms.

Additional layout considerations are as follows:

■ Any signal line that can be shared by other PCI or PCI-X resources on the bus segment can only have one PCI or PCI-X compliant load. No pull-up resistors, other discrete devices, or non-compliant PCI or PCI-X components may be attached. A PCI/PCI bridge component must be used as a buffer if the add-in card requires circuitry that would violate these restrictions. The one exception to these requirements is the use of a resistor between the AD and IDSEL signal lines. The capacitance of each PCI or PCI-X compliant component must be less than 10 pF.

■ The load of a connector is equivalent to one PCI or PCI-X load. Thus, for an add-in card only one PCI or PCI-X component is attached to each signal line (with exceptions note above) connector pad. If more than one PCI or PCI-X compliant load is required by the collective circuitry, the add-in card must have a bridge chip between the connector pad and the collective circuitry.

■ Ideally, the add-in card should be six layers: one for 3.3 volts, one for 5 volts, one for ground, and three for non-power signal lines. For cost considerations, a four layer board may be more practical. In this case, two layers may be used for non-power signal lines (usually the outer layers), one layer for ground, and one layer (power plane) for 5 or 3.3 volts. If both 3.3 and 5 volts must be available, the power plane must be split. When the power plane is split, the non-power signal lines should be routed on the layer adjacent to the ground layer. If non-power signal lines are routed on the layer adjacent to the split power plane layer, care must be taken to keep the signal lines entirely on 3.3 to the 5 volt section of the split power plane. If the non-power signal line must cross between the 3.3 and 5 volt sections, the two sections must be coupled by a 0.01 uF +/- 10% high-speed capacitor for every four non-power signal lines. This capacitor must be within 0.25 inches of point where the non-power signal lines cross the split. These requirements reflect the concern that the split in the plane disrupts the AC return path for the non-power signal lines, creating an impedance discontinuity.

> **The 12 and -12 volt power supply lines must be distributed as large traces, usually on the non-power signal line layers.**

> **The PCI-X addendum specification expanded the discussion of the add-in card layout requirement for multi-layer boards. See Appendix 15 of the specification for more information.**

Figure 13-1 outlines the trace layout for a PCI or a PCI-X compliant component relative to the connector pads. Note that the component pin assignments are in the same order as specified in the connector pin assignments.

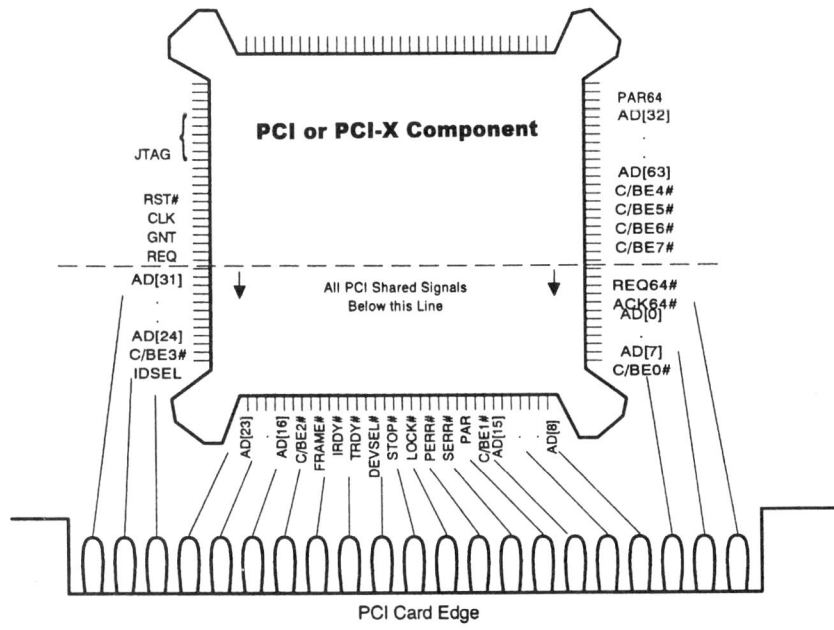

Figure 13-1: Suggested Pinout for PQFP PCI or PCI-X Component

RESISTORS AND DECOUPLING CAPACITORS

There are other resistor and capacitor requirements for add-in cards. See Chapter 12: *Signal Line Timing and Electrical Requirements* for more information.

For the power lines, there are capacitor requirements for the add-in cards as follows (in addition to the capacitors required to connect split power planes as discussed above).

- For the Universal I/O add-in card, the +V(I/O) connector pads (I/O Designated Power Pads) must individually decoupled to the ground layer with one 0.047 µF +/- 10% capacitor per connector pad. Several 0.047 µF capacitors may be combined into a larger capacitor. The trace length between the capacitor and the connector pad is no more than .25 inches (minimum width of 0.02 inches). Several connector pads can share a larger capacitor provided the trace length and width requirements are maintained.

- All unused 3.3 volt and 5 volt connector pads must be individually decoupled to the ground layer with one 0.01 µF +/- 10% capacitor per connector pad. The trace length between the capacitor and the connector pad is no more than .25 inches (minimum width of 0.02 inches). Several connector pads can share a larger capacitor provided the trace length and width requirements are maintained.

CHAPTER 14

LATENCY AND PERFORMANCE

This chapter consists of the following subchapters:

14.0   Latency
14.1   Performance

14.0 LATENCY

INTRODUCTION

There are three basic elements relative to latency for a PCI or PCI-X resource to become PCI or PCI-X bus master and transfer data (or at least attempt to do so) at the beginning of a bus transaction: Arbitration Latency, Acquisition Latency, and Target Latency. The sum of these latencies is the Total Latency.

In order to get a full picture regarding latency, this discussion will center on a bridge between the PCI or PCI-X bus master and the target. Consequently, the latency issues of porting through a bridge can be considered. The latency issues of a PCI or PCI-X bus master directly accessing the target (not through a bridge) is a subset of the issues in this discussion.

In this chapter the phrases "bus transaction", "bus segment", and "bridge" without the preceding words of "PCI" or "PCI-X". This chapter is focusing on the bus master and it is implied that a PCI bus master is accessing a PCI target on a PCI segment through a PCI/PCI BRIDGE. Similarly, it is implied that a PCI-X bus master is accessing a PCI-X target on a PCI-X segment through a PCI-X/PCI-X BRIDGE.

ARBITRATION LATENCY

The Arbitration Latency is dependent on the arbitration algorithm of the central arbiter and the priority of the PCI or PCI-X resource requesting bus segment ownership ("next" PCI or PCI-X bus master). It reflects the time required for the central arbiter to assert the GNTx# signal line of a PCI or PCI-X resource ("next" PCI or PCI-X bus master) relative to the assertion of the REQx# signal line ("next" PCI or PCI-X bus master) to request bus segment ownership. The algorithm and priority components of the Arbitration Latency vary according to the PCI or PCI-X resource and central arbiter of the bus segment. See Chapter 9: *Bus Segment Ownership* for more information.

ACQUISITION LATENCY

Once the central arbiter determines the "next" PCI or PCI-X bus master, it will award bus segment ownership by asserting the appropriate GNTx# signal line to the "next" PCI or PCI-X bus master. The delay between the "next" PCI or PCI-X bus master sampling the asserted GNTx# signal line on the rising edge of the CLK signal line and the target sampling the asserted FRAME# signal line on the rising edge of the CLK signal line for the "next" bus transaction defines Acquisition Latency. As discussed in Chapter 9: *Bus Segment Ownership*, in addition to the assertion of the GNTx# signal line of the "next" PCI or PCI-X bus master there is also the requirement that the "present bus transaction is completed before beginning the "next" bus transaction. That is, once a PCI or PCI-X resource is granted bus ownership as the "next" PCI or PCI-X bus master it must wait for the completion of the "present" bus transaction before executing the "next" bus transaction.

COMPLETION OF "PRESENT" BUS TRANSACTION ... PCI AND PCI-X

The completion of the "present" bus transaction executed by the "present" PCI or PCI-X bus master is controlled by two elements of the bus transaction protocol: Latency Timer and bus transaction termination. The Latency Timer element prevents the "present" PCI or PCI-X bus master from executing an infinitely long bus transaction when another ("next") PCI or PCI-X bus master wants to own the bus segment and execute a bus transaction. The bus transaction termination element prevents the "present" PCI or PCI-X bus master and target from excessively extending the "present" bus transaction.

As previously discussed in this book, the Latency Timer element is a programmable timer for each PCI or PCI-X bus master and reloads with the assertion of the FRAME# signal line. The timer counts each rising edge of the CLK signal line when the FRAME# signal line is asserted and expires within 256 or fewer CLK signal line periods. The Latency Timer insures that each PCI or PCI-X bus master has a minimum time slot for it to own the bus segment, but places an upper limit on how long a PCI or PCI-X bus master will own the bus segment. The Latency Timer (LT) protocol is as follows:

- If the associated GNTx# signal line is deasserted prior to the expiration of the LT , there are two possible results:

- The "present" PCI or PCI-X bus master is allowed to retain bus segment ownership until the present SINGLE bus transaction is complete

OR

- The "present" PCI or PCI-X bus master is allowed to retain bus segment ownership and execute subsequent microaccesses of a BURST bus transaction until the burst is complete or the Latency Timer expires ... whichever occurs first. The expiration of the LT when the GNTx# signal line is deasserted requires the BURST bus transaction to be immediately completed. The immediate completion of a BURST bus transaction does not always mean the very next microaccess. For example, there may be Cacheline boundary issues for PCI MWI transactions. Also, an additional microaccess of a PCI BURST bus transaction is allowed to be executed if the FRAME# and IRDY# signal lines are both asserted when the GNTx# signal line is deasserted and the Latency Timer expires. Also, as discussed in this book, there are PCI-X bus transaction completion protocols that will "temporarily" delay the immediate completion of bus transactions.

- If the associated GNTx# signal line is asserted when the LT expires, the "present" PCI or PCI-X bus master is allowed to complete the "present" bus transaction without any requirement to complete it "immediately" When the "present" bus transaction completes the "present" PCI or PCI-X bus master can reload the LT and begin another bus transaction if the associated GNTx# signal line is still asserted.

- The LT protocol is only implemented and required for PCI or PCI-X BURST bus transactions that can burst more than two microaccesses. That is, more than an initial microaccess and a subsequent microaccess. The LT protocol does not apply to SINGLE bus transactions or BURST bus transactions of two microaccesses or less.

> When the FRAME# signal line is asserted at the beginning of the bus transaction, the timer is reloaded and the counting begins. When the FRAME# signal line is deasserted, the completion of the bus transaction is forthcoming; consequently, the timer counting is stopped. The PCI or PCI-X bus master is the only PCI or PCI-X resource that knows that a Latency Timer has expired.

> The Latency Timer protocol DOES NOT apply to the completion of special transactions because the protocol for the special transaction requires a fixed quick completion.

The other element of bus transaction termination relates to rules that control how quickly a PCI or PCI-X bus master and target permit the SINGLE bus transaction or a microaccess of a BURST bus transaction to be completed. The bus transaction termination element (independent of the Latency Timer) consists of "Master Latency", "16 clock", and "8 clock" rules. The worst case consideration is that the "present" PCI or PCI-X bus master has just begun a bus transaction when another PCI resource wants to become the "next" PCI or PCI-X bus master.

COMPLETION OF "PRESENT" BUS TRANSACTION ... PCI SPECIFIC

> The "Master Latency" is only defined for the PCI bus master. The PCI-X bus master must assert the IRDY# signal line at a fixed time in the bus transaction.

The "Master Latency" rule requires that the PCI bus master assert the IRDY# signal line within eight CLK signal line periods from when the FRAME# signal line was first asserted. That is, the IRDY# signal line will be sampled asserted on the ninth rising edge of the CLK signal line relative to the first rising edge of the CLK signal line when the FRAME# signal line was asserted. The "Master Latency" rule also requires (during subsequent microaccesses of a PCI BURST bus transaction) that the IRDY# signal line be asserted on the ninth rising edge of the CLK signal line relative to the first rising edge of the CLK signal line when the IRDY# and TRDY# signal lines are both asserted in the previous microaccess.

> The "Master Latency" rule applies to all bus transactions except the special transaction. Special transactions have a specific protocol which supercedes the "Master Latency" rule.

If the target cannot complete a PCI SINGLE bus transaction or the initial microaccess of a PCI BURST bus transaction within sixteen CLK signal line periods from the assertion of the FRAME# signal line (TRDY# or STOP# signal line must be asserted on the seventeenth rising edge of the CLK signal line measured from the first rising edge of the CLK signal line when the FRAME# signal line is asserted), the "PCI 16 clock" rule applies. For a write transaction, the data is either accepted by the target (with or without posting) or a Retry termination is executed within the confines of the "PCI 16 clock" rule. For a read transaction, the target must provide the data or execute Retry termination within the confines of the "PCI 16 clock" rule. The target must implement the "PCI 16 clock" rule relative for a PCI SINGLE bus transaction or the initial microaccess of a PCI BURST bus transaction. Adherence to the "PCI 16 clock" rule may require the target to execute a Retry termination. In summary, the "PCI 16 clock" rule APPLIES to the PCI SINGLE bus transactions and initial microaccess of PCI BURST bus transactions of the following:

- Memory transactions

- I/O transactions

- Configuration transactions

- Interrupt acknowledge transactions

The "PCI 16 clock" rule DOES NOT apply to the above bus transactions during the initialization time (RST# signal line deasserted to 2^{25} CLK signal line periods later), when executing from BOOT ROM, or when copying expansion ROM to memory.

The present revision of the PCI local bus specification states that only SINGLE interrupt acknowledge transactions are executed. Earlier revisions implied that a BURST interrupt acknowledge transaction was defined.

The "PCI 16 clock" rule does not apply to special transactions because there is no specific target to assert the DEVSEL# signal line.

See Chapter 8: *Master and Target Termination* for more information.

The target must implement the "PCI 8 clock" rule with the subsequent microaccesses of a PCI BURST bus transaction. The net effect of the "PCI 8 clock" rule is to place limits on the length of a PCI BURST bus transaction. The restrictions do not apply to a PCI SINGLE bus transaction or to the initial microaccess of a PCI BURST bus transaction. The "PCI 8 clock" rule simply forces the target to execute a Disconnect termination request under the following conditions:

- All subsequent microaccesses of a BURST bus transaction are governed by the "PCI 8 clock" rule.

- The initial microaccess is completed when the IRDY# and TRDY# signal lines are both asserted at a CLK signal line rising edge. The target will begin counting on the subsequent CLK rising edge and continues counting until one of the following occurs:

■ If the TRDY# signal line is asserted simultaneously with a count value of eight or less, the bus transaction is allowed to complete with Completion termination whenever the IRDY# signal line is asserted

OR

■ If the TRDY# signal line is not asserted when the count value reaches eight, the STOP# signal line must be asserted (TRDY# or STOP# signal line will be sampled asserted on the ninth rising edge of the CLK signal line relative to the first rising edge of the CLK signal line when the IRDY# and TRDY# signal lines are both asserted in the previous microaccess). The assertion of the STOP# signal line results in a Disconnect termination without data.

In summary, the "PCI 8 clock" rule APPLIES to subsequent microaccesses of PCI BURST bus transactions of the following:

■ Memory transactions

■ I/O transactions

■ Configuration transactions

■ Interrupt acknowledge transactions

The "PCI 8 clock" rule DOES NOT apply for the above bus transactions during the initialization time (RST# signal line deasserted to 2^{25} CLK signal line periods later), when executing from BOOT ROM, or when copying expansion ROM to memory.

The present revision of the PCI local bus specification states that only SINGLE interrupt acknowledge transactions are executed. Earlier revisions implied that a BURST interrupt acknowledge transaction was defined.

The "PCI 8 clock" rule does not apply to special transactions in that there is no specific target to assert the DEVSEL# signal line.

See Chapter 8: *Master and Target Termination* for more information.

COMPLETION OF "PRESENT" BUS TRANSACTION ... PCI-X SPECIFIC

If the target cannot complete a PCI-X SINGLE bus transaction or the initial microaccess of a PCI-X BURST bus transaction within sixteen CLK signal line periods from the assertion of the FRAME# signal line (encoded in the combination of DEVSEL#, TRDY#, and STOP# signal line on the seventeenth rising edge of the CLK signal line measured from the first rising edge of the CLK signal line when the FRAME# signal line is asserted), the "PCI-X 16 clock" rule applies. The PCI-X addendum specification defines the "PCI-X 16 clock" rule protocol in a similar fashion as the PCI local bus specification defined the "PCI 16 clock" rule, EXCEPT it does not apply to the execution of Retry termination. The "PCI-X 16 clock" rule only applies to the execution of Disconnect at Next ADB and Single Phase Disconnect terminations. In summary, the "PCI-X 16 clock" rule APPLIES to the SINGLE bus transactions and initial microaccess of BURST bus transactions of the following:

- Memory transactions

- I/O transactions (Only SINGLE bus transactions are defined)

- Configuration transactions (Only SINGLE bus transactions are defined)

- Interrupt acknowledge transactions (Only SINGLE bus transactions are defined)

- Split completion transactions

> The "PCI-X 16 clock" rule DOES NOT apply for the above bus transactions during the initialization time (RST# signal line deasserted to 2^{27} CLK signal line periods later), when executing from BOOT ROM, or when copying expansion ROM to memory.
>
> The "PCI-X 16 clock" rule does not apply to special transactions in that there is no specific target to assert the DEVSEL# signal line.

See *Chapter 8: Master and Target Termination* for more information.

The target must implement the "PCI-X 8 clock" rule with the PCI-X SINGLE bus transaction and the initial microaccess of a PCI-X BURST bus transaction when the PCI-X 16 clock" rule does not apply and the target cannot transfer data. The net effect of the "PCI-X 8 clock" rule is to place limits on the length of a SINGLE bus transaction and the initial microaccess of a PCI-X BURST bus transaction. The PCI-X addendum specification requires the target to complete a PCI-X SINGLE bus transaction or the initial microaccess of a PCI-X BURST bus transaction within eight CLK signal line periods ("PCI-X 8 clock" rule) from the assertion of the FRAME# signal line. If the target is not able to terminate (encoded in the combination of DEVSEL#, TRDY#, and STOP# signal lines) on the ninth rising edge of the CLK signal line measured from the first rising edge of the CLK signal line when the FRAME# signal line is asserted, the target must terminate the bus transaction with a Retry, Target Abort, or Split Response termination. Otherwise the target must provide data access on or before the aforementioned the ninth rising edge of the CLK signal line or execute a bus transaction termination per the "PCI-X 16 clock" rule. In summary, the "PCI-X 8 clock" rule to the SINGLE bus transactions and initial microaccess of BURST bus transactions of the following:

- Memory transactions

- I/O transactions (Only SINGLE bus transactions are defined)

- Configuration transactions (Only SINGLE bus transactions are defined)

- Interrupt acknowledge transactions (Only SINGLE bus transactions are defined)

- Split completion transactions

The "PCI-X 8 clock" rule DOES NOT apply for the above PCI-X bus transactions during the initialization time (RST# signal line deasserted to 2^{27} CLK signal line periods later), when executing from BOOT ROM, or when copying expansion ROM to memory.

The "PCI-X 8 clock" rule does not apply to special transactions in that there is no specific target to assert the DEVSEL# signal line.

See Chapter 8: *Master and Target Termination* for more information.

COMPLETION OF "PRESENT" BUS TRANSACTION ... PCI AND PCI-X MISCELLANEOUS

A PCI/PCI bridge operates as a PCI bus master on each specific bus segment; consequently, the "Master Latency" rule applies to each bridge. Also, a bridge operates as a PCI or PCI-X bus master on each specific bus segment; consequently, the Latency Timer protocol and the "16 clock" and "8 clock" rules apply to each bridge.

All of the above considerations contribute to the Acquisition Latency. That is, the "present" PCI or PCI-X bus master completes the "present" bus transaction in order to provide bus segment ownership to the "next" PCI or PCI-X bus master.

TARGET LATENCY

Once the FRAME# signal is sampled asserted, the remaining latency component is Target Latency. As outlined above, the "16 clock" rule applies to the latency for the first data access and the "8 clock" rule applies to the subsequent data accesses (if a BURST cycle is executed). The time associated with the "Master Latency" rule falls within the confines of the two "8 clock" and "16 clock" rules.

TOTAL LATENCY

The Total Latency of a PCI or PCI-X bus master accessing a target is the total of the aforementioned three latencies. It should be obvious that there are multiple variables that affect the elapsed time for each of the above latencies. In addition, there may be multiple bridges and bus segments between the bus master and target; this contributes more variables to the elapsed total time. Also, for each bus segment the total latency is affected by the number of active bus masters vying for bus segment ownership.

Part of the interest in the Total Latency is related to how long it takes to transfer data between a PCI or PCI-X bus master and a target. For a PCI or PCI-X bus master, the ability to empty a buffer (write data to a target) is a concern relative to buffer sizing. For a target, the ability to read data is important if data is flowing into it from another port (for example, a serial port). The latency time associated with the actual transfer of data is further complicated by the Delayed Transaction and Split Response Transaction protocols.

The end result of all of the above issues is that the Total Latency is very difficult to predict. Even when the total latency issues have be addressed, the data may not be immediately transferred. The PCI local bus specification has suggested several total latency calculations and associated considerations. See sections 3.5.4.1 to 3.5.4.3 of the PCI local bus specification.

> Because the worst case Total Latency cannot be guaranteed, all PCI and PCI-X resources should be able to gracefully recover if the total latency they were designed for has been exceeded.

TOTAL LATENCY AND THE LEGACY BUS MASTER

As outlined above, the PCI and PCI-X bus segments have latency issues that make some level of predicting the maximum Total Latency difficult. The prediction is further complicated when a LEGACY bus segment is supported by the platform. Of particular concern is when an ISA bus master accesses a PCI or PCI-X resource through a PCI/LEGACY or PCI-X/LEGACY BRIDGE. The protocol of an ISA bus master allows it to retain ownership of the ISA bus segment and thus the associated PCI and PCI-X bus segments indefinitely. Also, Retry termination is not possible with a bus transaction associated with an ISA bus transaction executed by the ISA bus master (or ISA DMA controller). Finally, there is no ISA bus master preemption protocol or ability for the PCI/LEGACY LEGACY or PCI-X/LEGACY BRIDGE to terminate an ISA bus transaction. The EISA bus also prevents the PCI/LEGACY LEGACY or PCI-X/LEGACY BRIDGE from terminating an EISA bus transaction, but it does have a preemption protocol that restricts an EISA bus transaction to 64 BCLK signal line periods (7680 nanoseconds at a BCLK = 8.33 MHz).

14.1 PERFORMANCE

The previous subchapter outlined the amount of time required for a PCI or PCI-X bus master to obtain ownership of the bus segment and begin the access to a target. As discussed above, there are other elements that may prevent the immediate transfer of data; consequently, the time to begin data transfer into/out of target buffers will vary widely. Putting all of these issues aside, once a PCI or PCI-X bus master owns the bus segment and begins the transfer of data, the number of bytes transferred per unit time is a measure of performance (maximum transfer rate). With multiple PCI and PCI-X bus masters on a bus segment, the maximum transfer rate reflects the performance of the bus segment and not the performance of a specific PCI or PCI-X bus master. The maximum transfer rate does provide design goals for optimum performance when a PCI or PCI-X bus master does transfer data.

The maximum transfer rates discussed below are the theoretical limits without any consideration for bus segment ownership changes. That is, it reflects a single PCI or PCI-X bus master continuously owning the bus segment. Also, the theoretical limits reflect the performance between a PCI or PCI-X bus master and a target on same bus segment (either or both resources may be a bridge). The maximum transfer rates are calculated for SINGLE and BURST bus transactions for both read and write. These calculations provide the performance range of the bus segment.

The PCI protocol defines SINGLE and BURST bus transactions, some of which can be executed with the Fast Back-to-Back protocol. The PCI-X protocol also defines SINGLE and BURST bus transactions but does not support the Fast Back-to-Back protocol. See Chapter 6: *Detailed Bus Transaction Operation* for more information.

The maximum transfer rates for a **33.3 MHz CLK** signal line are as follows:

PCI NON FAST BACK-TO-BACK

- **Serial SINGLE reads**—33 Megabytes/sec at 32 data bits or 66 Megabytes/sec at 64 data bits.

- **Serial SINGLE writes**—44 Megabytes/sec at 32 data bits or 88 Megabytes/sec at 64 data bits.

- **BURST reads and writes**—133.2 Megabytes/sec at 32 data bits or 266.4 Megabytes/sec at 64 data bits.

PCI FAST BACK-TO-BACK

- **Serial SINGLE writes**—66.7 Megabytes/sec at 32 data bits or 133.3 Megabytes/sec at 64 data bits.

- **Serial BURST writes**—133.2 Megabytes/sec at 32 data bits or 266.4 Megabytes/sec at 64 data bits.

The maximum transfer rates for a **66.6 MHz CLK** signal line are as follows:

PCI NON FAST BACK-TO-BACK

- **Serial SINGLE reads**—66 Megabytes/sec at 32 data bits or 128 Megabytes/sec at 64 data bits.

- **Serial SINGLE writes**—88 Megabytes/sec at 32 data bits or 176 Megabytes/sec at 64 data bits.

- **BURST reads and writes**—266 Megabytes/sec at 32 data bits or 532 Megabytes/sec at 64 data bits.

PCI FAST BACK-TO-BACK

- **Serial SINGLE writes**—133.4 Megabytes/sec at 32 data bits or 266.6 Megabytes/sec at 64 data bits.

- **Serial BURST writes**—266 Megabytes/sec at 32 data bits or 532 Megabytes/sec at 64 data bits.

The maximum transfer rates for a **66.6 MHz CLK** signal line are as follows:

PCI-X

- **Serial SINGLE reads and write** —33.3 Megabytes/sec at 32 data bits or 66.6 Megabytes/sec at 64 data bits.

- **BURST reads and writes**—266 Megabytes/sec at 32 data bits or 532 Megabytes/sec at 64 data bits.

The maximum transfer rates for a **133.2 MHz CLK** signal line are as follows:

PCI-X

- **Serial SINGLE reads and write** —66.6 Megabytes/sec at 32 data bits or 133.2 Megabytes/sec at 64 data bits.

- **BURST reads and writes**—532 Megabytes/sec at 32 data bits or 1064 Megabytes/sec at 64 data bits.

The above calculations are without Dual Address Command (DAC). The inclusion of the DAC in a PCI bus transaction will reduce the maximum transfer rates for SINGLE read bus transactions by 20%. The inclusion of the DAC in a PCI bus transaction will reduce the maximum transfer rates for SINGLE write bus transactions by 25% and 33.3% for non Fast Back-to-Back and Fast Back-to-Back, respectively. The inclusion of the DAC in a PCI-X bus transaction will reduce the maximum transfer rates for SINGLE bus transactions by 11.1%.

The PCI local bus specification permits BURST bus transactions for memory, I/O, configuration, interrupt acknowledge, and special transactions. If the bus transaction ports through a bridge, only the memory bus transactions can implement BURST bus transactions.

The PCI-X addendum bus specification permits BURST bus transactions only for memory transactions

---

The PCI local bus specification and the PCI-X addendum specification define the I/O, configuration, interrupt acknowledge, and special bus transactions as only 32 data bit transfers.

The PCI local bus specification allows 64 data bit I/O targets can be implemented, but there is no benefit to requiring the increased complexity. Thus it is strongly recommended that 64 data bit I/O targets are not implemented. For the purposes of this book, I/O targets are only 32 data bits in size. If a 64 data bit I/O target Is implemented, the 64 data bit protocol applied to memory targets would also apply to I/O targets.

CHAPTER 15

MECHANICAL SPECIFICATION

This chapter consists of the following subchapters:

15.1 Overview

15.2 PCI Expansion (also known as Add-in) Card Physical Dimensions and Tolerances

15.3 PCI-X Extensions

The text and figures in this chapter are copied from PCI Local Bus Specification Rev. 2.2, and are reprinted with permission of the PCI Special Interest Group.

15.1 OVERVIEW

> The PCI 3.0 local bus specification places an additional restriction on the mechanical attributes of an add-in card. The following discussion assumes that a bus segment permits add-in cards keyed as 5 volt only, 3.3 volt only, or universal I/O signaling, which is true for PCI 2.2. However, the PCI 3.0 local bus specification DOES NOT permit add-in cards keyed for 5 volt only signaling. Devices residing on the bus segment must follow the same signaling voltage restrictions as add-in cards. See Chapter 11: *Reset, Power, and Signal Line Initialization* for more information.

The PCI expansion card is based on a raw card design (see Figures 15-1 and 15-6) that is easily implemented in existing cover designs from multiple manufacturers. The card design adapts to ISA, EISA, and MC systems. PCI expansion cards have two basic form factors: standard length and short length. The standard length card provides 49 square inches of real estate. The fixed and variable height short length cards were chosen for panel optimization to provide the lowest cost for a function. The fixed and variable height short length cards also provide the lowest cost to implement in a system, the lowest energy consumption, and allow the design of smaller systems. The interconnection for the expansion card has been defined for both the 32-bit and 64-bit interfaces.

PCI cards and connectors are keyed to manage the 5 volt to 3.3 volt transition. The basic 32-bit connector contains 120 pins. The logical numbering of pins, shows 124 pin identification numbers, but four pins are not present and are replaced by the keying location. In one orientation, the connector is keyed to accept 5 volt system signaling environment boards; turned 180° the key is located to accept 3.3 volt system signaling environment boards. Universal add-in cards, cards built to work in both 5 volt and 3.3 volt system signaling environments, have two key slots so that they can plug into either connector. A 64-bit extension, built onto the same connector molding, extends the total number of pins to 184. The 32-bit connector subset defines the system signaling environment. 32-bit cards and 64-bit cards are inter-operable within the system's signaling voltage classes defined by the keying in the 32-bit connector subset. A 32-bit card identifies itself for 32-bit transfers on the 64-bit connector. A 64-bit card in a 32-bit connector must configure for 32-bit transfers.

Maximum card power dissipation is encoded on the PRSNT1# and PRSNT2# pins of the expansion card. This hard encoding can be read by system software upon initialization. The system's software can then make a determination whether adequate cooling and supply current is available in that system for reliable operation at start-up and initialization time. Supported power levels and their encoding are defined in Chapter 12: *Signal Line Timing and Electrical Requirements*.

The PCI expansion card includes a mounting bracket for card location and retention. The backplate is the interface between the card and the system that provides for cable escapement. The card has been designed to accommodate PCI brackets for both ISA/EISA and MC systems. See Figures 15-8 and 15-9 for the ISA/EISA assemblies and Figure 15-10 and 15-11 for the MC assemblies. Bracket kits for each card type must be furnished with the PCI card so that end users may configure the card for their systems. The ISA/EISA kit contains a PCI bracket, four 4-40 screws, and a card extender. The assembled length of the PCI expansion board is that of an MC card. The extender fastens to the front edge of the PCI card to provide support via a standard ISA card guide. The MC bracket kit contains a riveted MC bracket-bracket brace assembly and two pan head 4-40 screws.

The component side of a PCI expansion card is the opposite of ISA/EISA and MC cards. The PCI card is a mirror image of ISA/EISA and MC cards. A goal of PCI is to enable its implementation in systems with a limited number of expansion card slots. In these systems, the PCI expansion board connector can coexist, within a single slot, with an ISA/EISA or MC card. These slots are referred to as *shared slots*. Shared slots allow the end user to install a PCI, ISA/EISA, or MC card. However, only one expansion board can be installed in a shared slot at a time. For example, shared slots in PCI systems with an ISA expansion bus can accommodate an ISA or a PCI expansion board; shared slots in PCI systems with an MC expansion bus can accommodate an MC or PCI expansion board; etc.

The PCI local bus specification Rev 2.2 has added a low profile card. The mechanical specifications for this new expansion (add-in) card will be discussed later.

The PCI-X addendum specification has adopted the mechanical requirements of the 3.3 volt PCI expansion (add-in) cards. Any PCI-X specific extensions are discussed in Subchapter 15.3.

15.2 PCI EXPANSION (ADD-IN) CARD PHYSICAL DIMENSIONS AND TOLERANCES

The maximum component height on the primary component side of the PCI expansion card is not to exceed 0.570 inches (14.48 mm). The maximum component height of the back side of the card is not to exceed 0.105 inches (2.67 mm). Datum A on the illustrations is used to locate the PCI card to the planar and to the frame interfaces; the back of the frame and the card guide. Datum A is carried through the locating key on the connector.

See Figures 15-1 through 15-18 for PCI expansion card physical dimensions.

> The following figures are from Rev. 2.2 of the PCI bus specification, and are reprinted with permission of the PCI SIG.

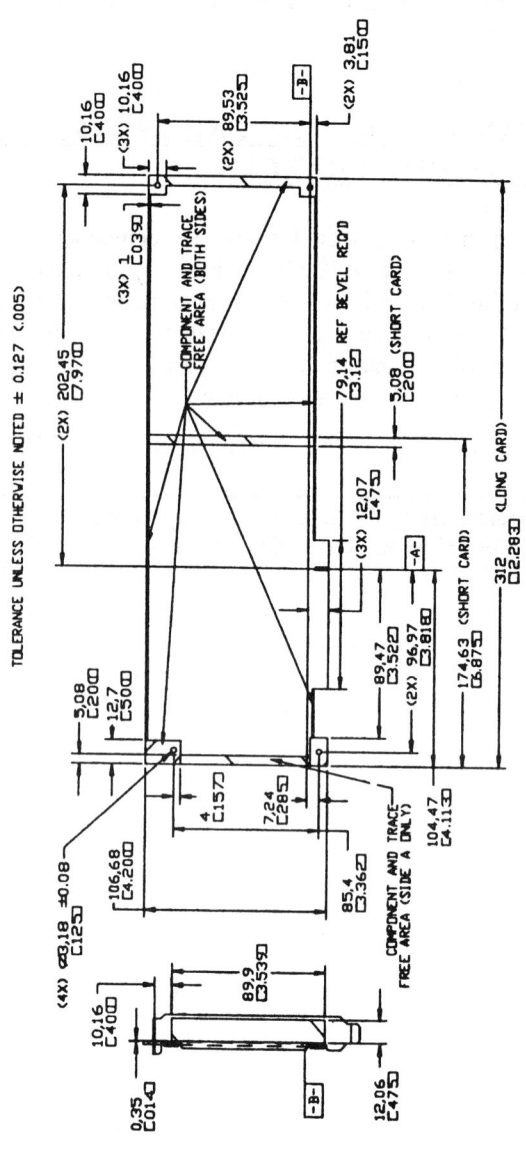

Figure 15-1: PCI Raw Card (5 volt)

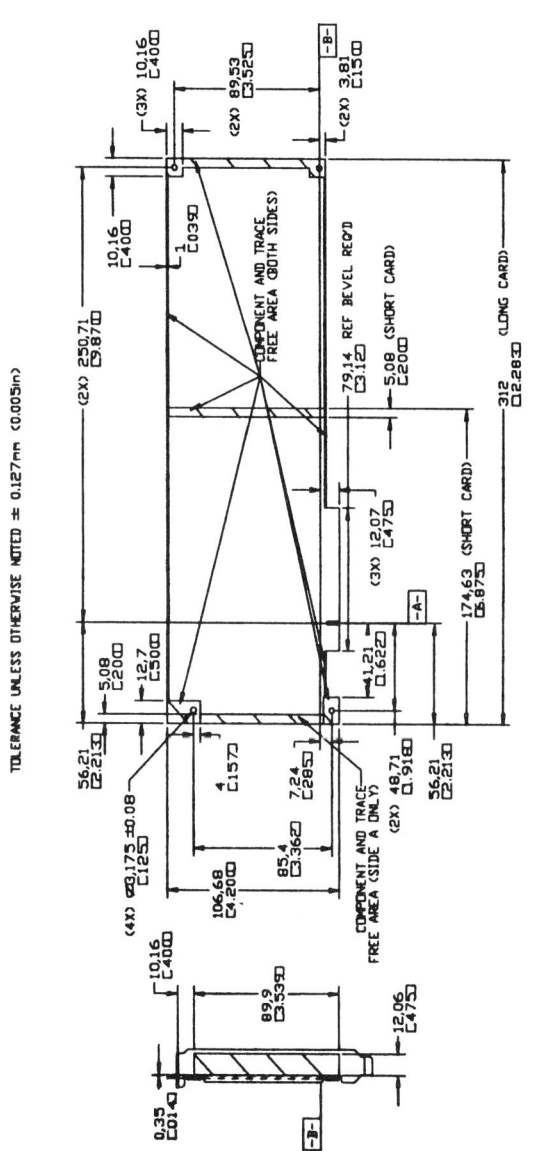

Figure 15-2: PCI Raw Card (3.3 Volt and Universal)

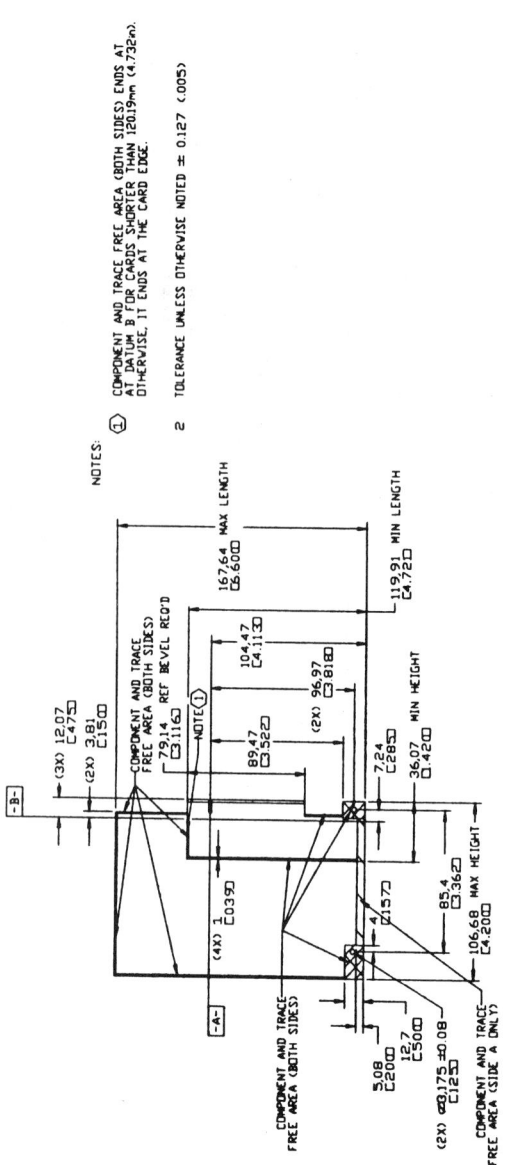

Figure 15-3: PCI Raw Variable Height Short Card (5V, 32-bit)

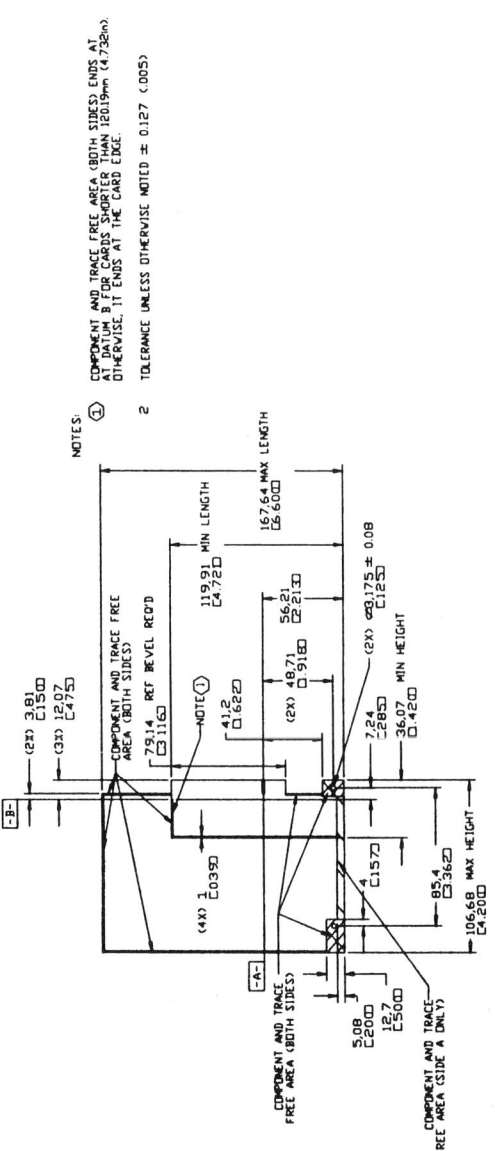

Figure 15-4: PCI Raw Variable Height Short Card (3.3V, 32-bit)

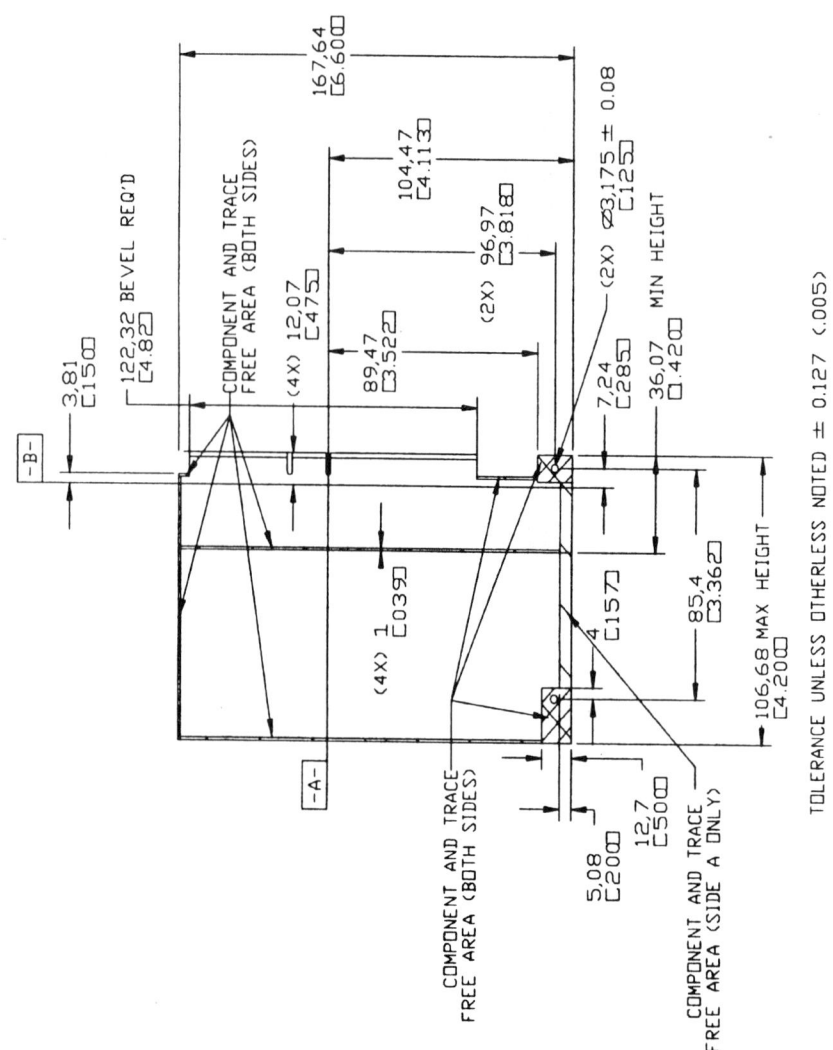

Figure 15-5: PCI Raw Variable Height Short Card (5V, 64-bit)

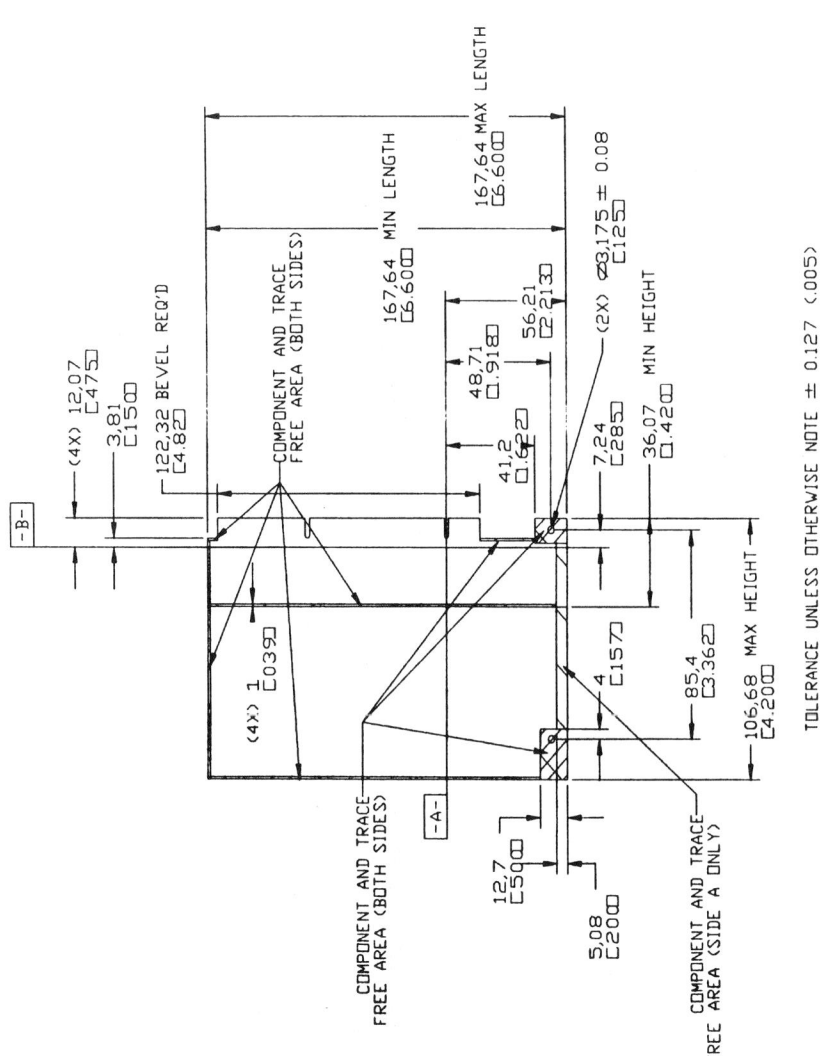

Figure 15-6: PCI Raw Variable Height Short Card (3.3V, 64-bit)

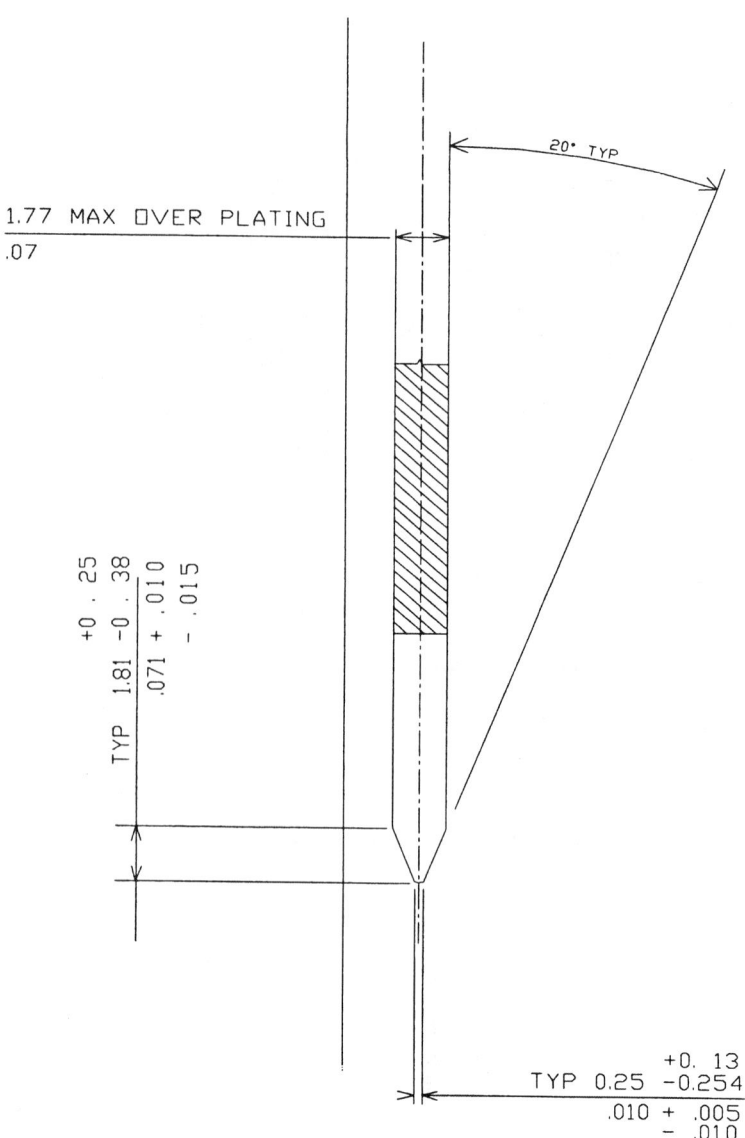

Figure 15-7: PCI Card Edge Connector Bevel

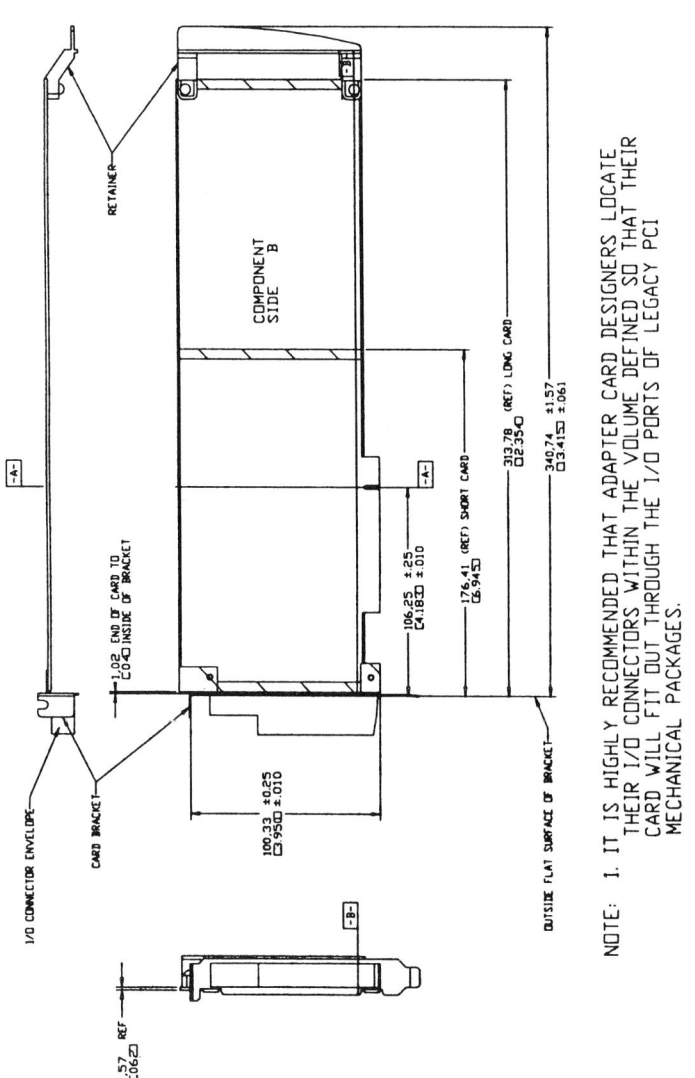

Figure 15-8: ISA Assembly (5V)

927

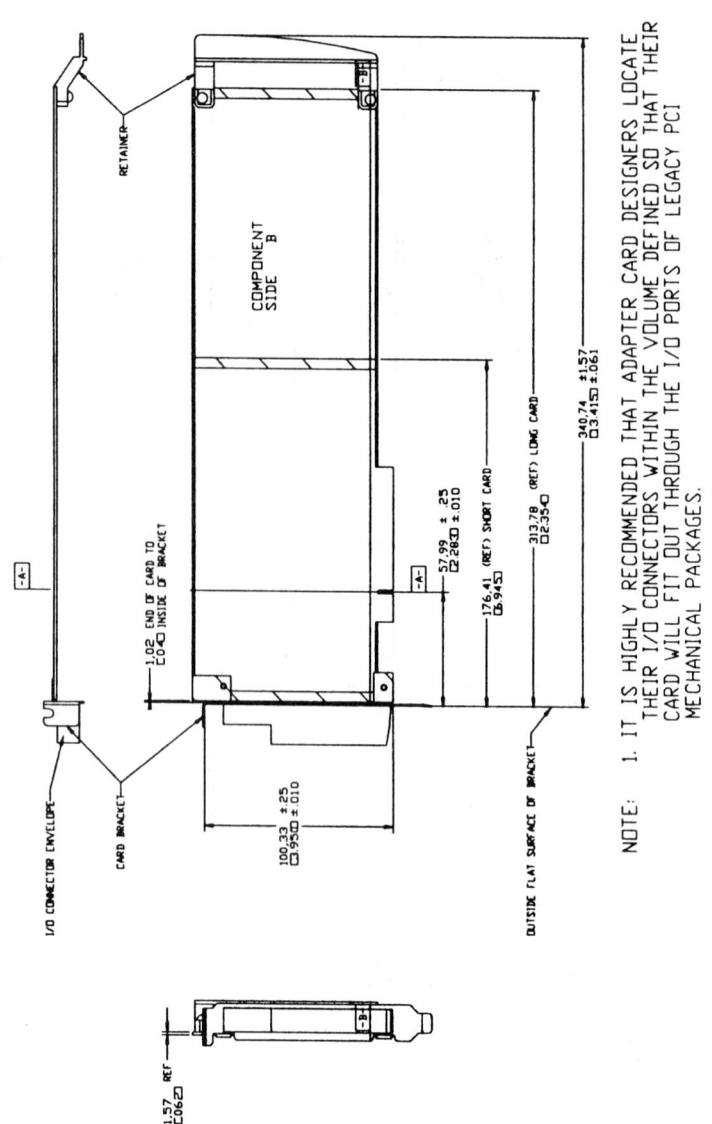

Figure 15-9: ISA Assembly (3.3 volt and Universal)

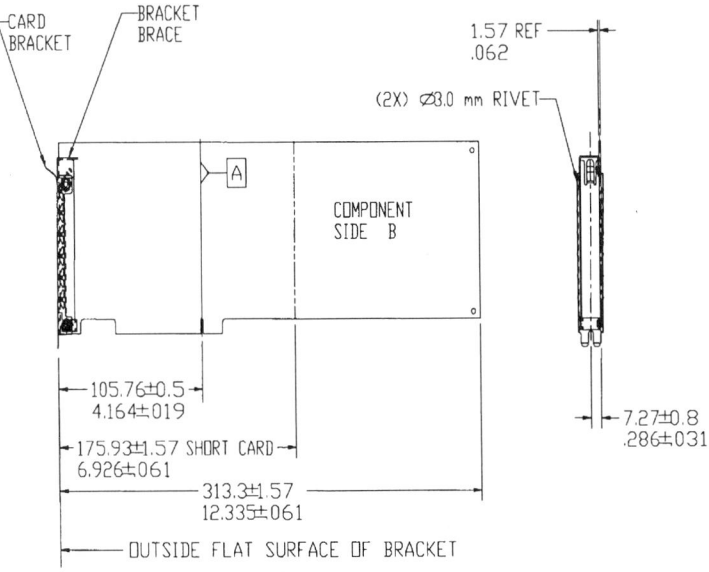

Figure 15-10: MC Assembly (5 volt)

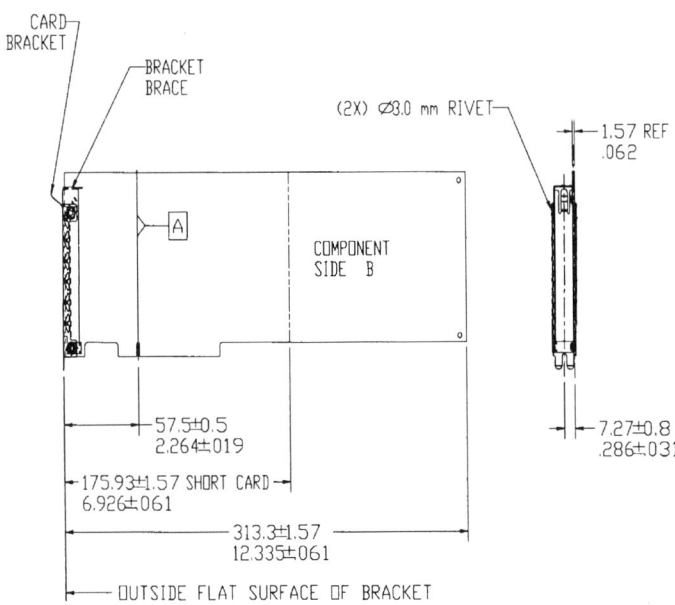

Figure 15-11: MC Assembly (3.3 volt)

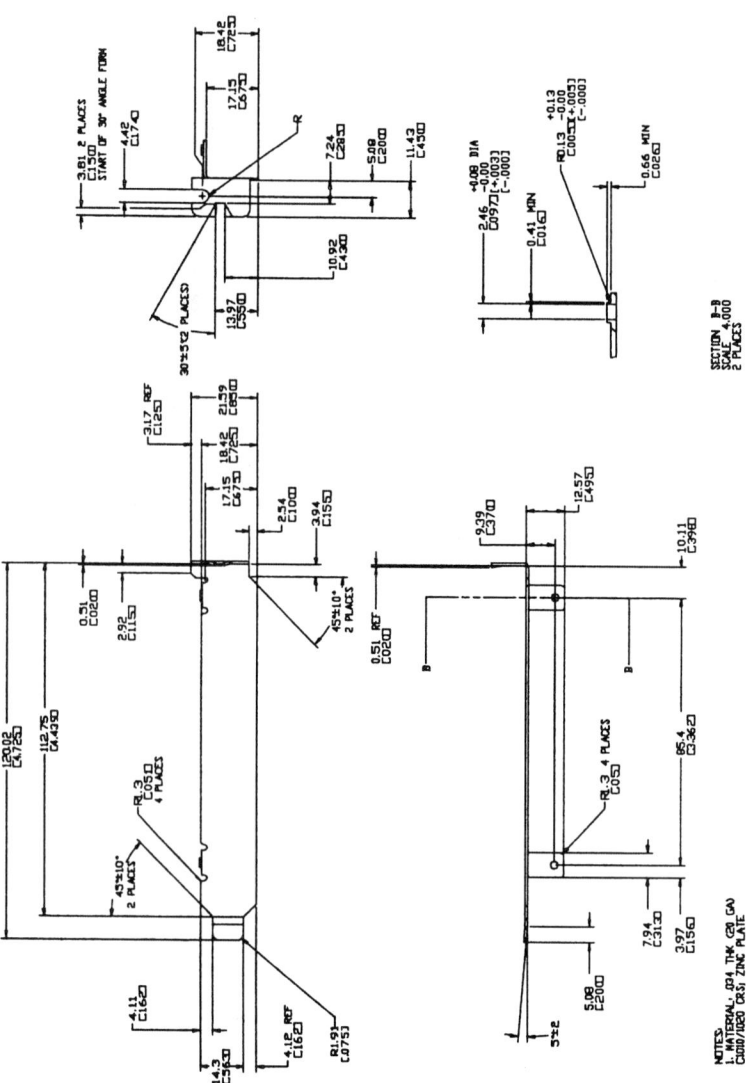

Figure 15-12: ISA Bracket

Note: It is highly recommended that adapter card designers implement I/O brackets which mount on the backside of PCI cards as soon as possible to reduce their exposure to causing EMC leakage in systems. It is also highly recommended that system designers initiate requirements that include the use of this new design by their adapter card suppliers.

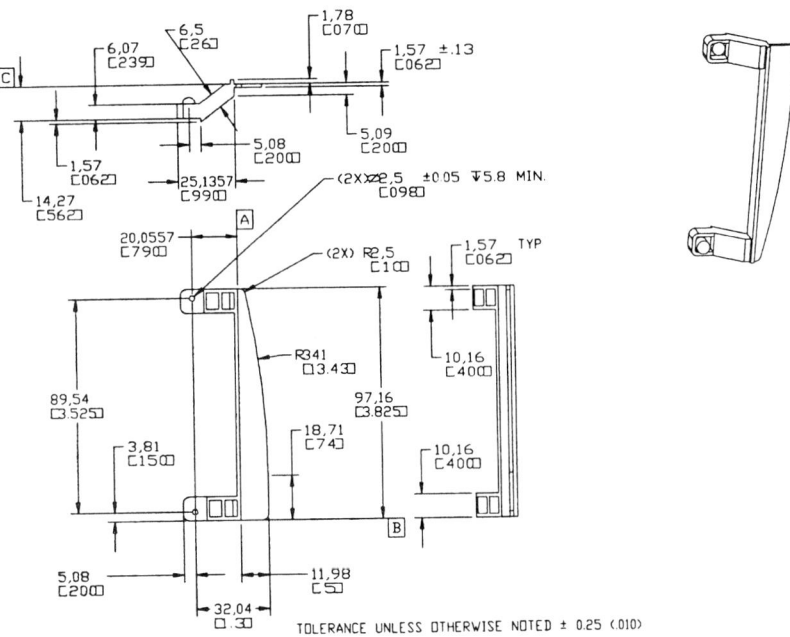

Figure 15-13: ISA Retainer

CONTINUED USE OF THE ISA RETAINER DESCRIBED IN REVISION 2.1 OF THIS
SPECIFICATION IS PERMITTED, BUT IT IS HIGHLY RECOMMENDED THAT ADAPTER CARD
DESIGNERS IMPLEMENT THIS DESIGN AS SOON AS POSSIBLE TO AVOID INSTALLATION
PROBLEMS WHEN LARGE I/O CONNECTORS ARE PRESENT.

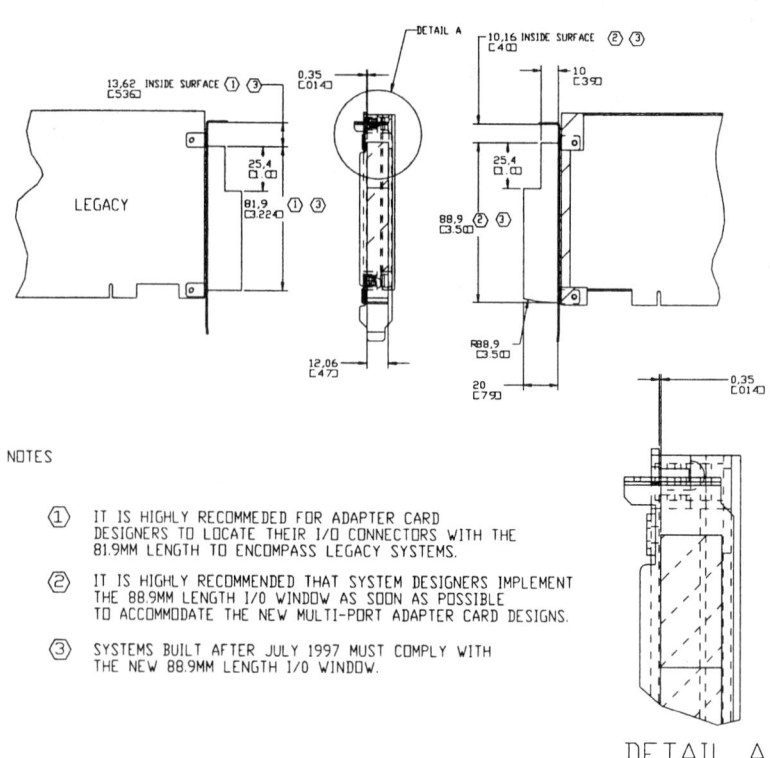

NOTES

① IT IS HIGHLY RECOMMEDED FOR ADAPTER CARD DESIGNERS TO LOCATE THEIR I/O CONNECTORS WITH THE 81.9MM LENGTH TO ENCOMPASS LEGACY SYSTEMS.

② IT IS HIGHLY RECOMMENDED THAT SYSTEM DESIGNERS IMPLEMENT THE 88.9MM LENGTH I/O WINDOW AS SOON AS POSSIBLE TO ACCOMMODATE THE NEW MULTI-PORT ADAPTER CARD DESIGNS.

③ SYSTEMS BUILT AFTER JULY 1997 MUST COMPLY WITH THE NEW 88.9MM LENGTH I/O WINDOW.

Figure 15-14: I/O Window Height

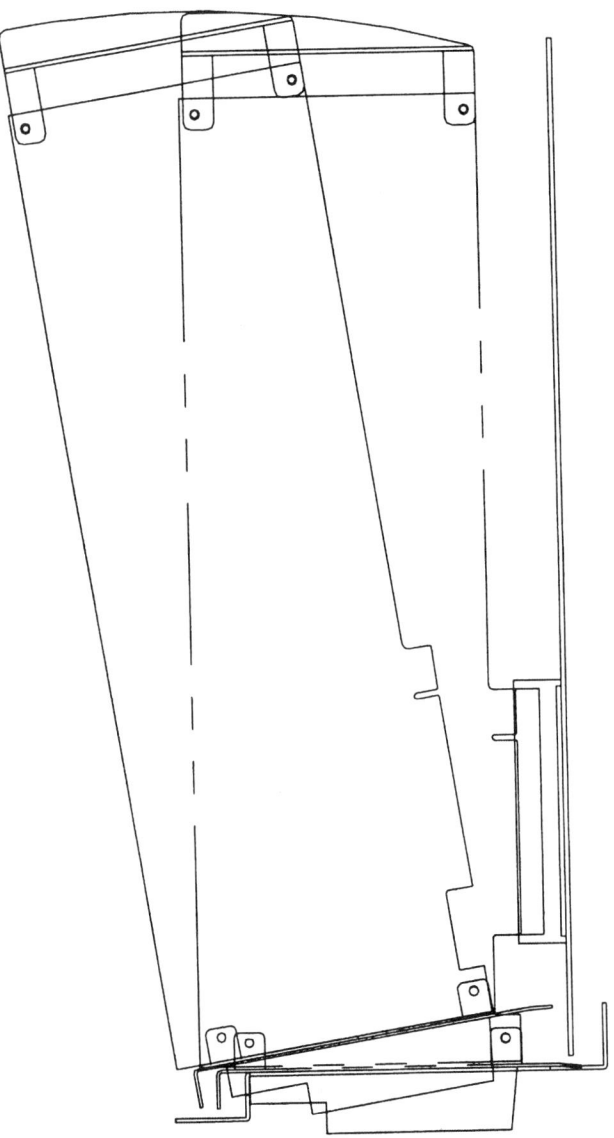

Figure 15-15: Adapter Installation with Large I/O Connector

933

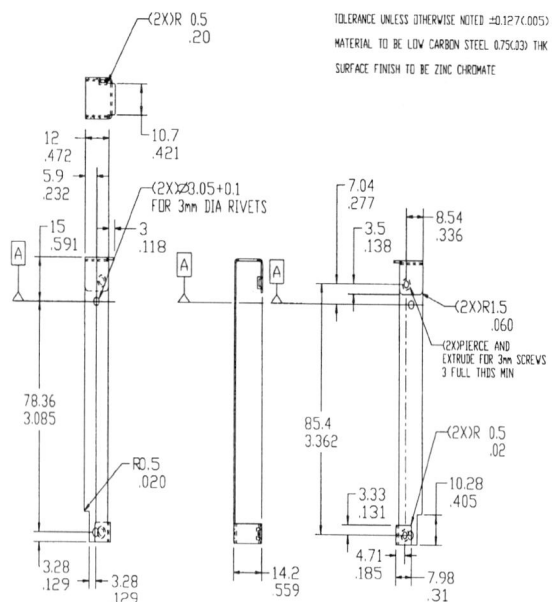

Figure 15-16: MC Bracket Brace

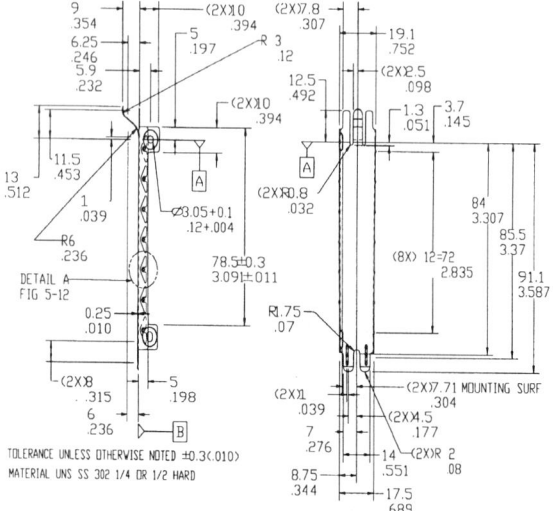

Figure 15-17: MC Bracket

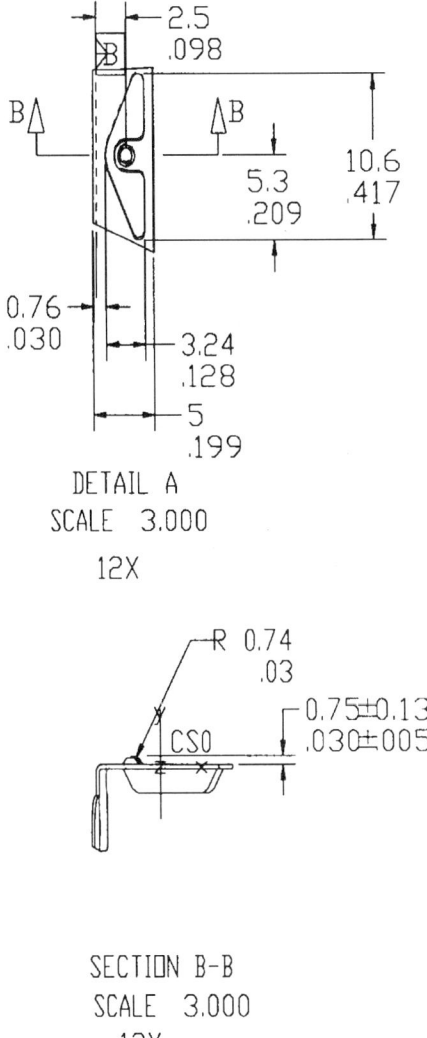

DETAIL A
SCALE 3.000
12X

SECTION B-B
SCALE 3.000
12X

Figure 15-18: MC Bracket Details

CONNECTOR PHYSICAL DESCRIPTION

The connectors that support PCI expansion cards are derived from those on the MC bus. The MC connectors are well defined and have proven value and reliability. There are four connectors that can be used depending on the PCI implementation. The differences between connectors are 32 bit and 64 bit, and the 5 volt and 3.3 volt signaling environments. A key differentiates the signaling environment voltages. The same physical connector is used for the 32-bit signaling environments. In one orientation the key accepts 5 volt boards. Rotated 180°, the connector accepts 3.3 volt signaling boards. The pin numbering of the connector changes for the different signaling environments to maintain the same relative position of signals on the connector (see Figures 15-20, 15-21, 15-23 and 15-25 for board layout details).

In the connector drawings, the recommended board layout details are given as nominal dimensions. Layout detail tolerancing should be consistent with the connector supplier's recommendations and good engineering practice.

See Figures 15-19 through 15-25 for connector dimensions and layout recommendations. See Figures 15-26 through 15-32 for card edge connector dimensions and tolerances. Tolerances for cards are given so that interchangeable cards can be manufactured.

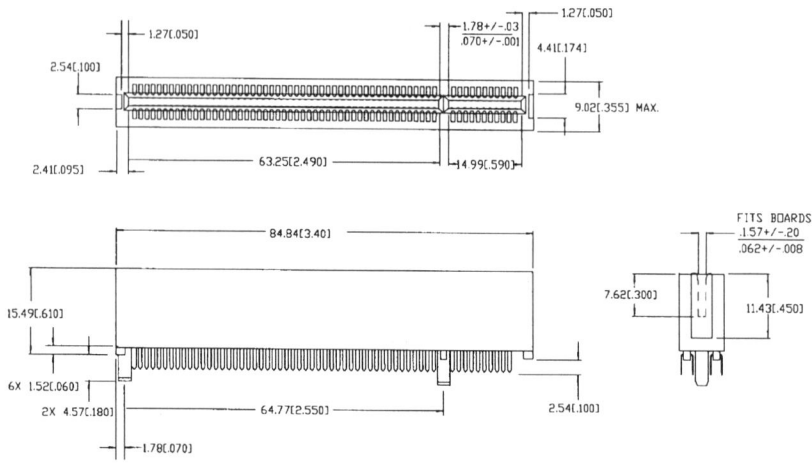

Figure 15-19: 32-bit Connector

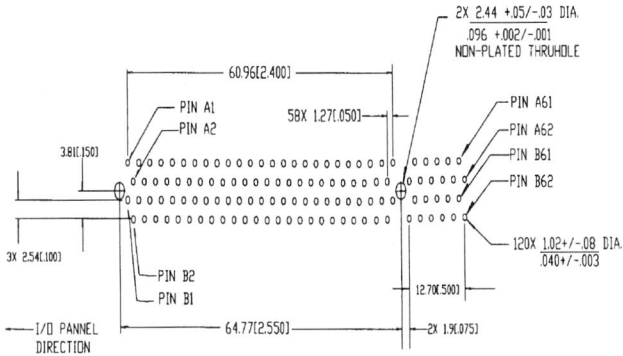

Figure 15-20: 5 Volt/32-bit Connector Layout Recommendation

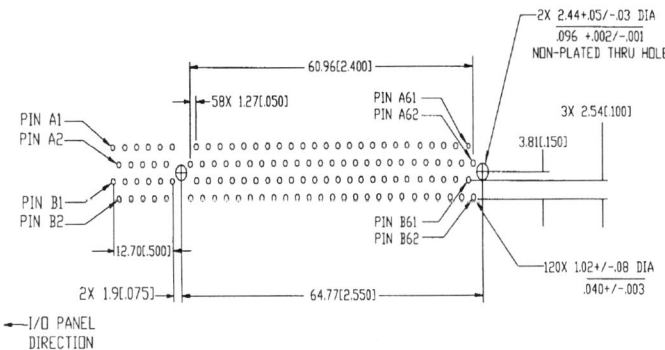

Figure 15-21: 3.3 Volt/32-bit Connector Layout Recommendation

937

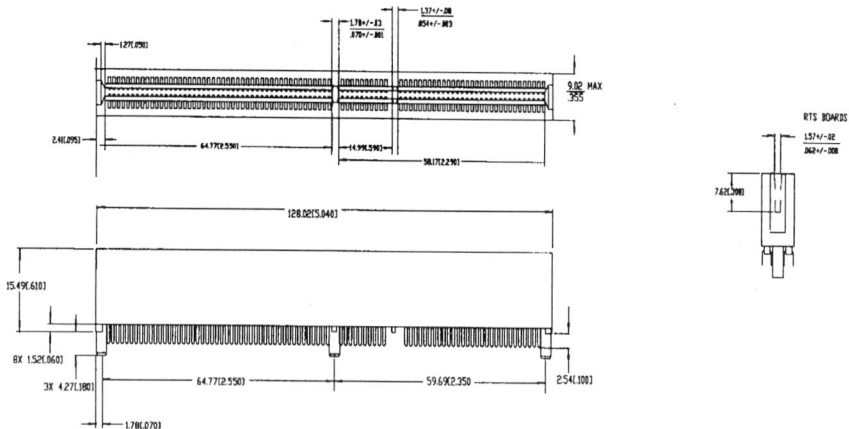

Figure 15-22: 5V/64-Bit Connector

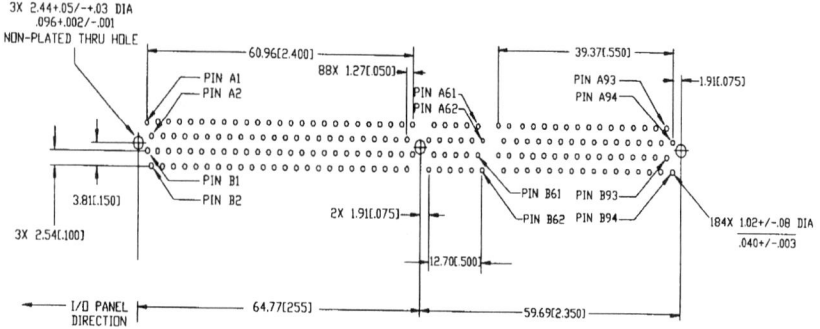

Figure 15-23: 5 Volt/64-Bit Connector Layout Recommendation

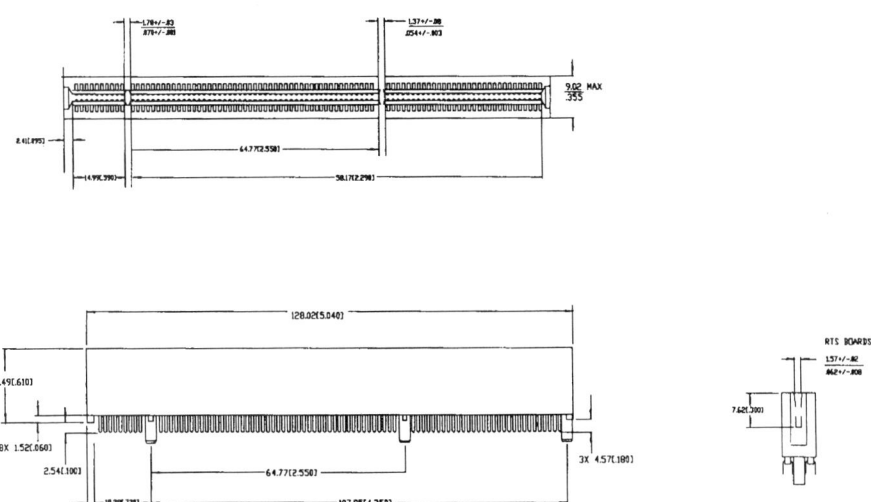

Figure 15-24: 3.3 Volt/64-Bit Connector

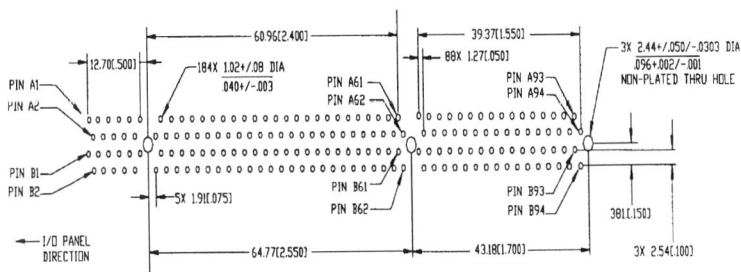

Figure 15-25: 3.3 Volt/64-Bit Connector Layout Recommendation

939

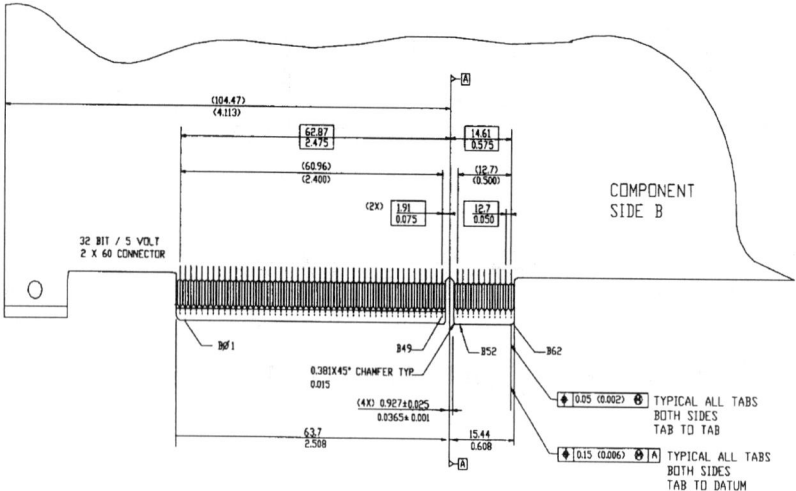

Figure 15-26: 5 Volt/32-Bit Card Edge Connector Dimensions and Tolerances

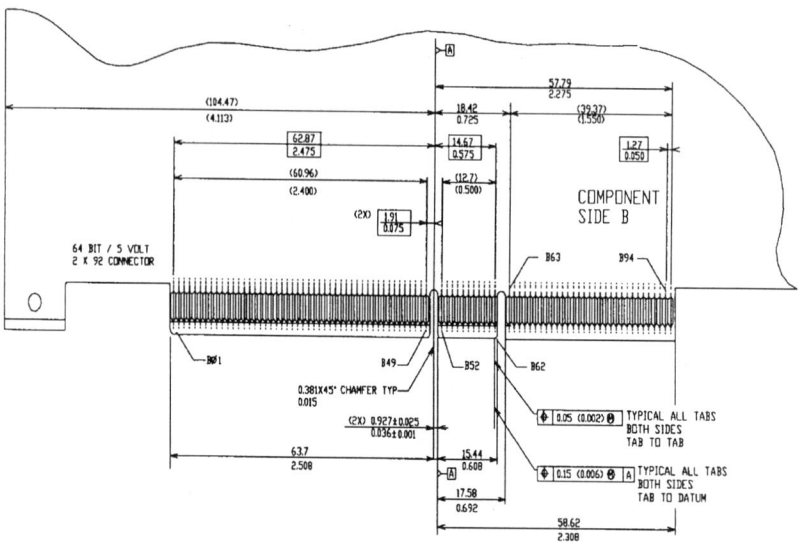

Figure 15-27: 5 Volt/64-Bit Card Edge Connector Dimensions and Tolerances

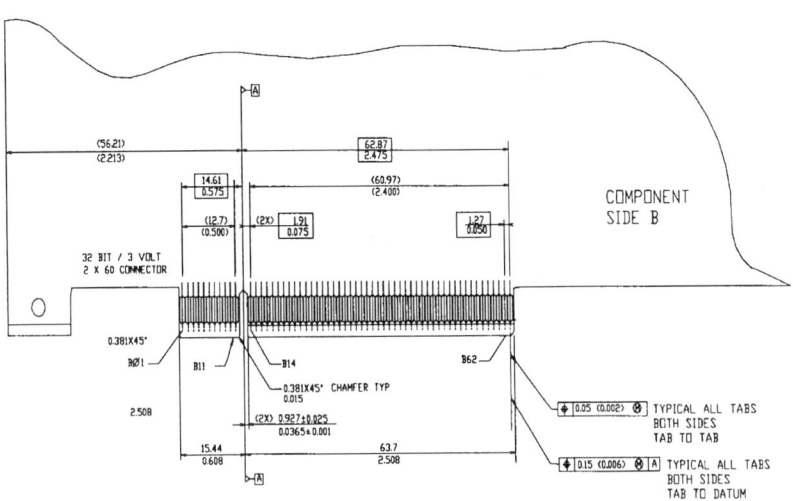

Figure 15-28: 3.3 Volt/32-Bit Card Edge Connector Dimensions and Tolerances

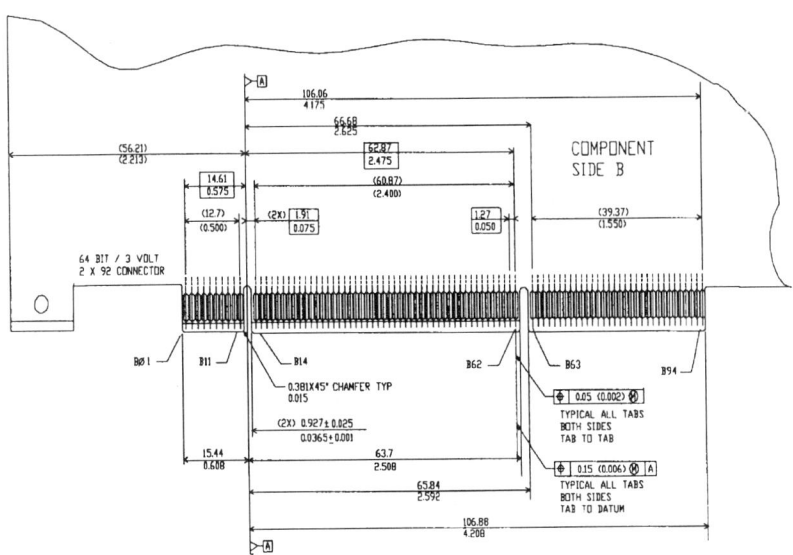

Figure 15-29: 3.3 Volt/64-Bit Card Edge Connector Dimensions and Tolerances

941

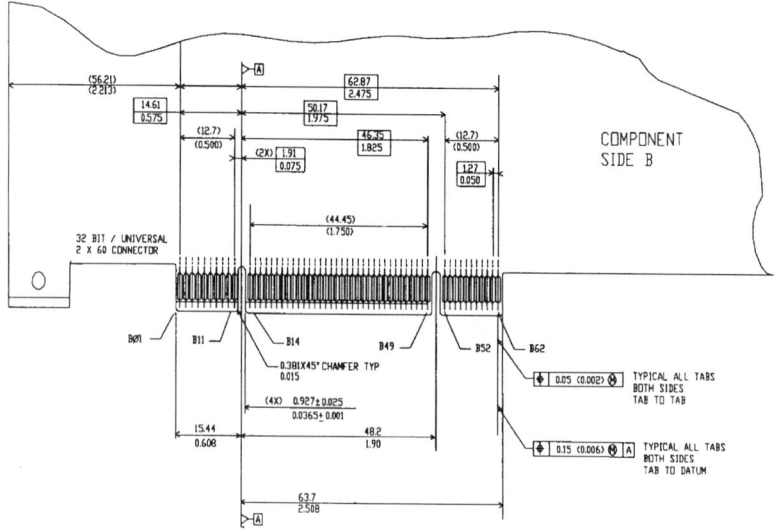

Figure 15-30: Universal 32-Bit Card Edge Connector Dimensions and Tolerances

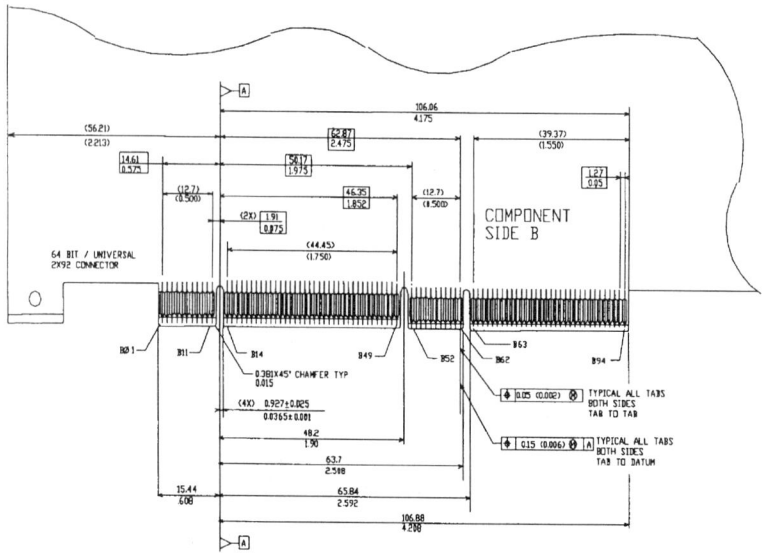

Figure 15-31: Universal 64-Bit Card Edge Connector Dimensions and Tolerances

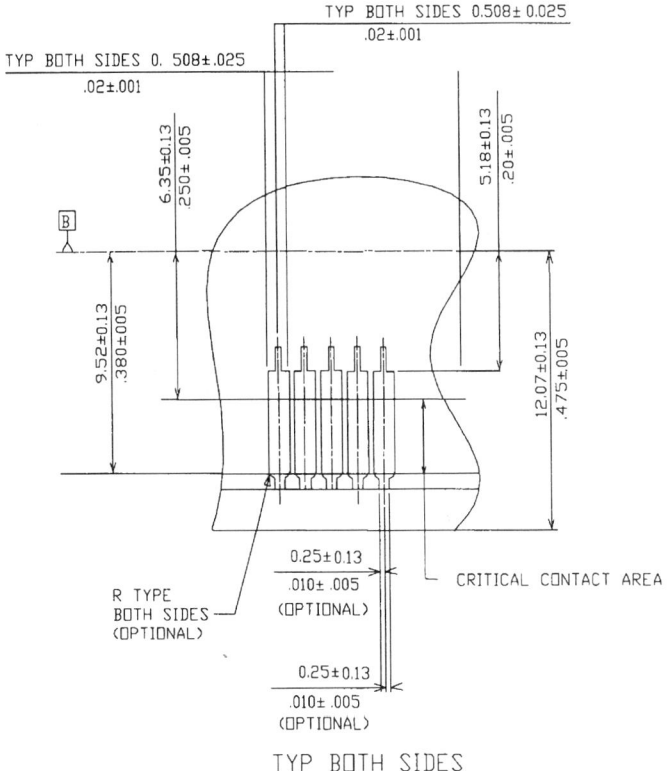

Figure 15-32: PCI Card Edge Connector Contacts

CONNECTOR PHYSICAL REQUIREMENTS

The vendors listed in Table 15-1 supply PCI expansion connectors. Other connectors may be used as long as they meet the specification in this document.

Description	AMP P/N	Burndy P/N	Foxconn P/N
32-bit, 5 volt	646255-1	CEE2X60S-V3Z14W	TBD
32-bit 3.3 volt	646255-1	CEE2X60S-V3Z14W	TBD
64-bit, 5 volt	TBD	TBD	TBD
64-bit, 3.3 volt	TBD	TBD	TBD

Table 15-1: PCI Connectors

The specification makes no recommendation about the suitability of parts from these or any other vendors for a particular application.

943

Part	Materials
Connector Housing	High-temperature thermoplastic, UL flammability rating 94V-0, color: white.
Contacts	Phosphor Bronze
Contact Finish	0.000030 inch minimum gold over 0.000050 inch minimum nickel in the contact area. Alternate finish: gold flash over 0.000040 inch (1 micron) minimum palladium or palladium-nickel over nickel in the contact area.

Table 15-2: Connector Physical Requirements

CONNECTOR PERFORMANCE SPECIFICATION

Parameter	Specification
Durability	100 mating cycles without physical damage or exceeding low-level contact resistance requirement when mated with the recommended card cage.
Mating Force	Average 6 oz (1.7N) maximum per opposing contact pair using MIL-STD-1344, Method 2013.1 and gauge per MIL-C-21097 with profile as shown in add-in board specification.
Contact Normal Force	75 grams minimum

Table 15-3: Connector Mechanical Performance Requirements

Parameter	Specification
Contact Resistance	(low signal level) 30 milliohms maximum initial, 10 milliohms maximum increase through testing. Contact resistance, test per MIL-STD-1344, Method 3002.1.
Insulation Resistance	1000 Megohms minimum per MIL-STD-202, Method 302, Condition B.
Dielectric Withstand Voltage	500 VAC RMS per MIL-STD-1344, Method D3001.1, Condition 1.
Capacitance	2 pF maximum, at 1 MHz.
Current Rating	1 A, 30° C rise above ambient.
Voltage Rating	125 volts.
Certification	UL Recognition and CSA Certification required.

Table 15-4: Connector Electrical Performance Requirements

Parameter	Specification
Operating Temperature	−40° C to +105° C
Thermal Shock	55° C to +85° C, 5 cycles per MIL-STD-1344, Method 1003.1.
Flowing Mixed Gas Test	Battelle, Class II. Connector mated with board and tested per Battelle method.

Table 15-5: Connector Environmental Performance Requirements

PLANAR IMPLEMENTATION

Two types of planar implementations are supported by the PCI expansion card design: expansion connectors mounted on the planar and expansion connectors mounted on a riser card. For illustrative purposes, only the planar mounted expansion connectors are detailed here. The basic principles may be applied to riser card designs. See Figures 15-33, 15-34, and 15-35 for planar details for ISA, EISA, and MC cards, respectively. The planar drawings show the relative locations of the PCI 5 volt and 3.3 volt connector datums to the ISA, EISA, and MC connector datums. Both 5 volt and 3.3 volt connectors are shown on the planar to concisely convey the dimensional information. Normally, a given system would incorporate either the 5 volt or the 3.3 volt PCI connector, but not both. Standard card spacing of 0.8 inches for ISA/EISA and 0.85 inches for MC allows for only one shared slot per system. If more PCI expansion slots are required, while using existing card spacing, additional slots must be dedicated to PCI. Viewing the planar from the back of the system, the shared slot is located so that dedicated ISA, EISA, or MC slots are located to the right and dedicated PCI slots are located to the left.

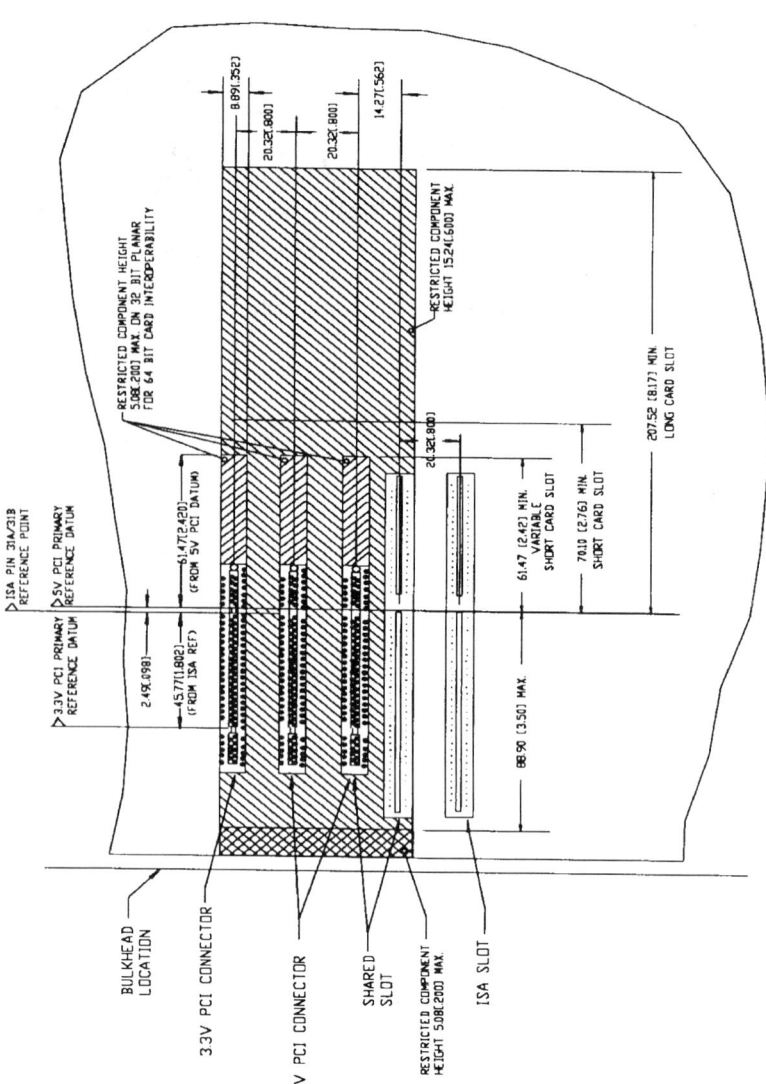

Figure 15-33: PCI Connector Location on Planar Relative to Datum on the ISA Connector

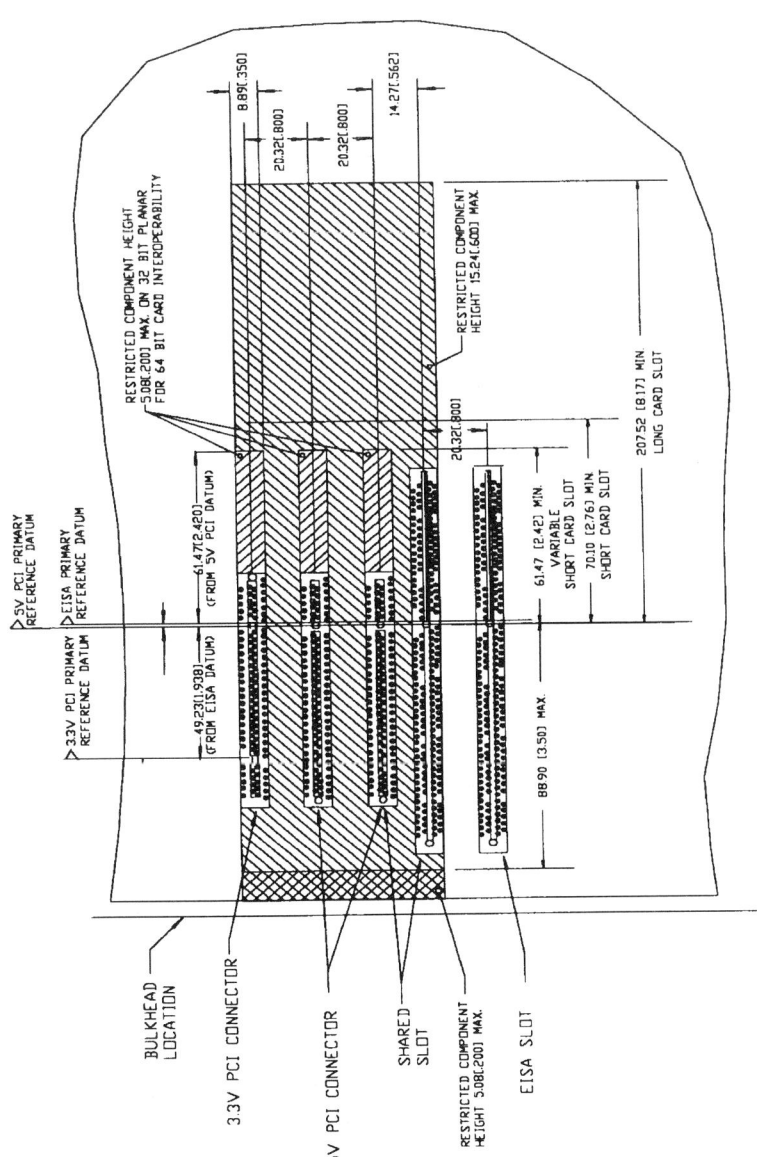

Figure 15-34: PCI Connector Location on Planar Relative to Datum on the EISA Connector

947

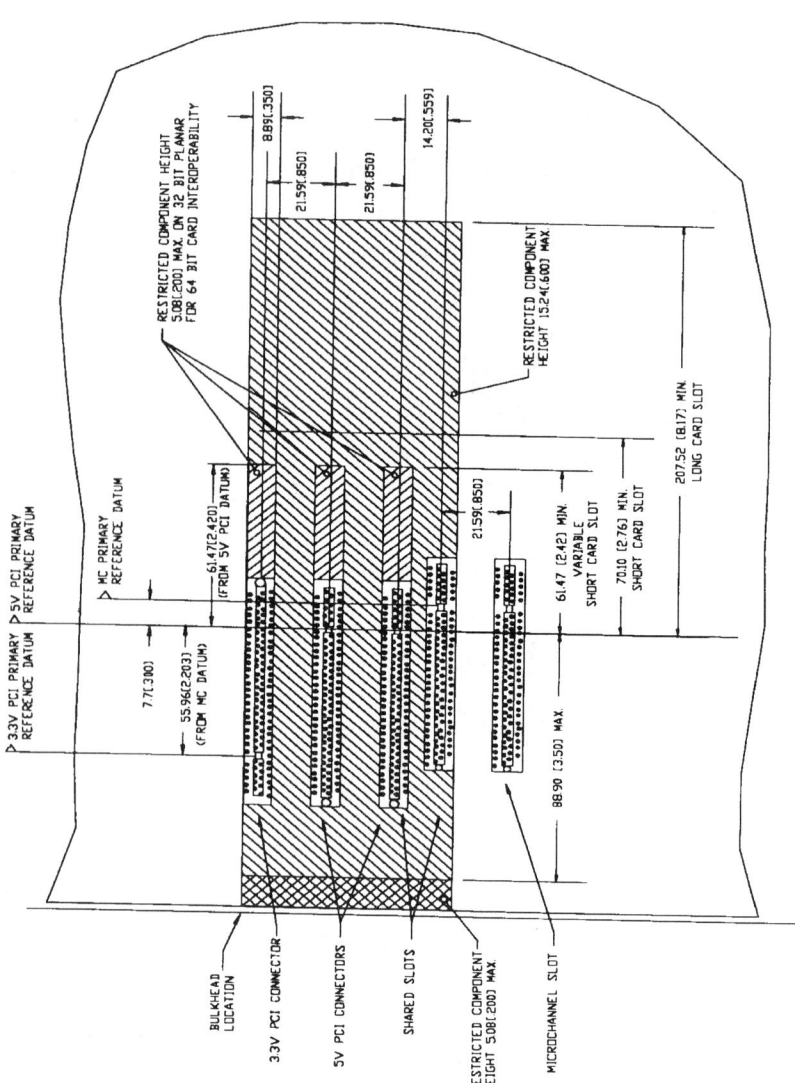

Figure 15-35: PCI Connector Location on Planar Relative to Datum on the MC Connector

Rev. 2.2 of the PCI bus specification allows for back-to-back installation of PCI add-in cards on an LPX riser card configuration. To eliminate interference fits on back-to-back add-in cards, a specific PCI connector (riser connector) has been defined for use on the riser card. The riser card connector information is provided in Figures 15-36 to 15-42. Some key elements are:

- The riser card connector is 0.075" taller than a standard PCI connector.

- The riser card connector is keyed differently than a standard PCI connector to eliminate confustion in mounting the connector into a riser card versus a system baseboard.

- The use of the riser connector permits the add-in cards to be spaced 0.800 inches apart.

- The length of the CLK signal line for a riser connector is 0.075 inches longer. The designer must consider this increased length when considering techniques to minimize CLK signal line skews to each add-in card.

- The 0.75 nH increase in lead inductance is not considered enough to affect riser connector performance versus the standard PCI connector.

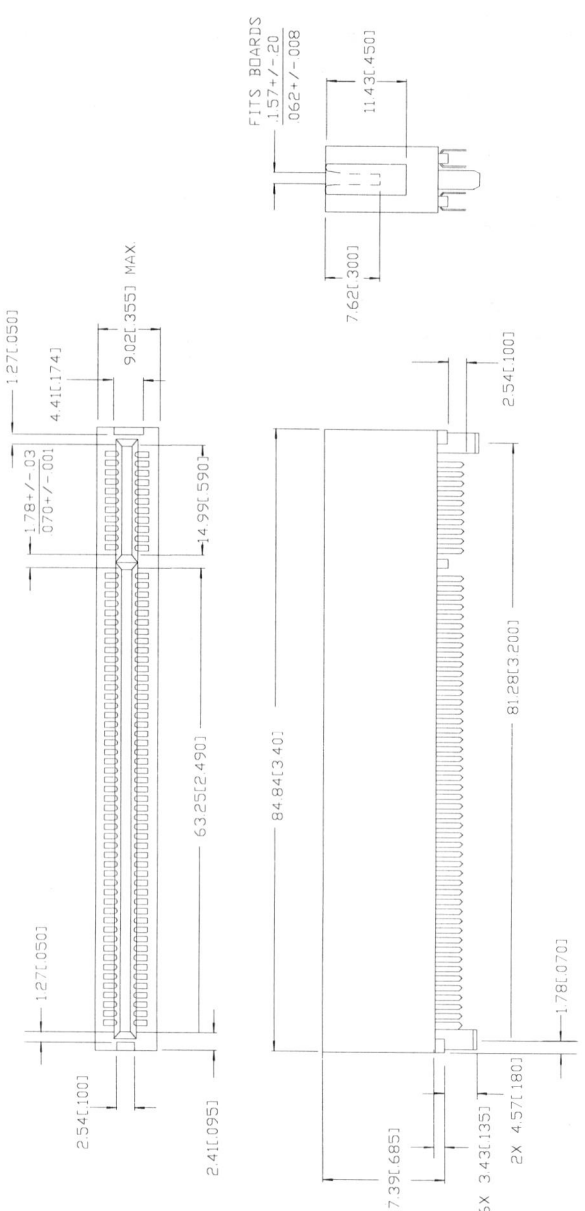

Figure 15-36: 32-bit PCI Riser Connector

Note: It is highly recommended that LPX system chassis designers use the PCI riser connector when implementing riser cards on LPX systems and using adapter card slots on 0.800" spacing. It is also highly recommended that LPX system chassis designers use the taller riser style of ISA and EISA connectors when combining PCI and ISA/EISA.

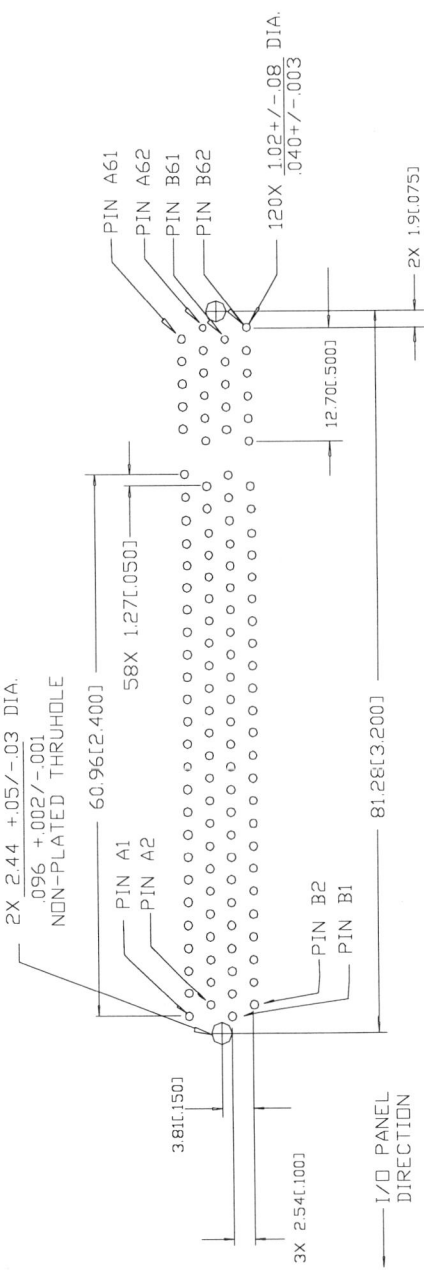

Figure 15-37: 32-bit/5V PCI Riser Connector Footprint

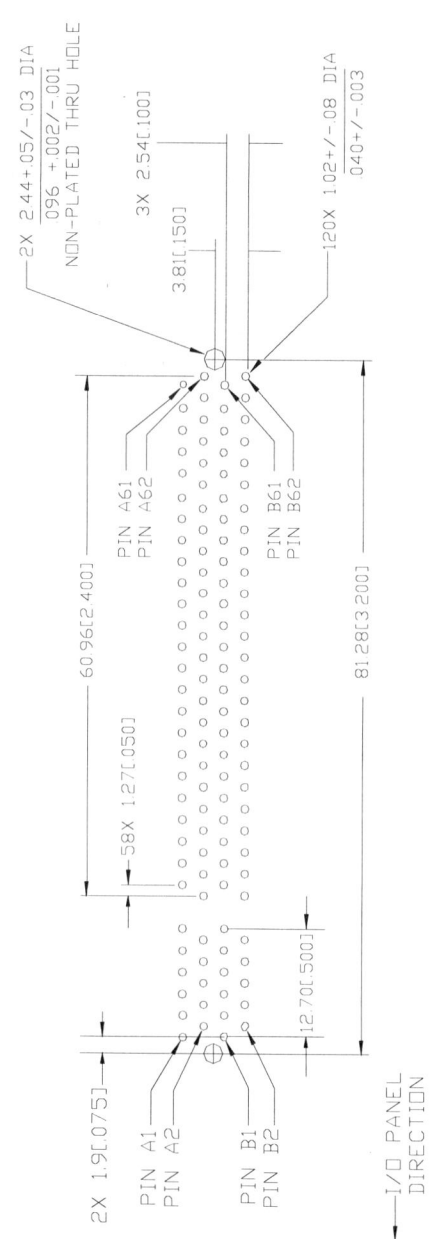

Figure 15-38: 32-bit/3.3V PCI Riser Connector Footprint

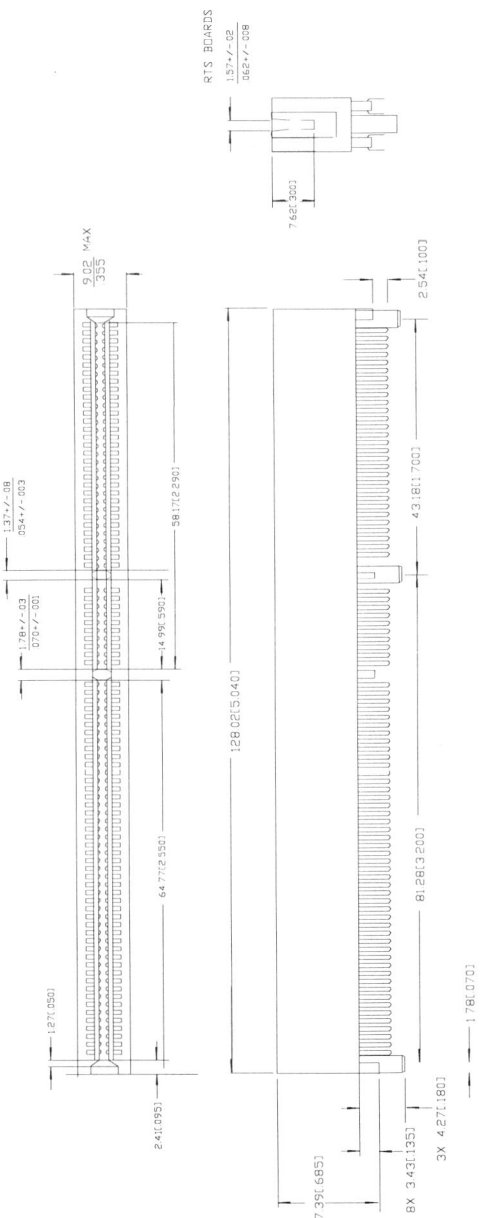

Figure 15-39: 64-bit/5V PCI Riser Connector

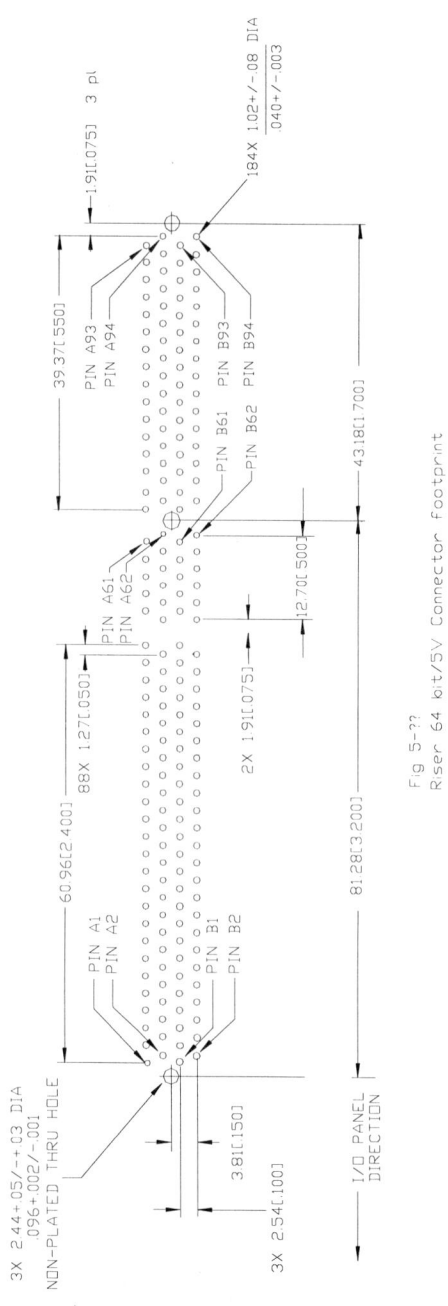

Figure 15-40: 64-bit/5V PCI Riser Connector Footprint

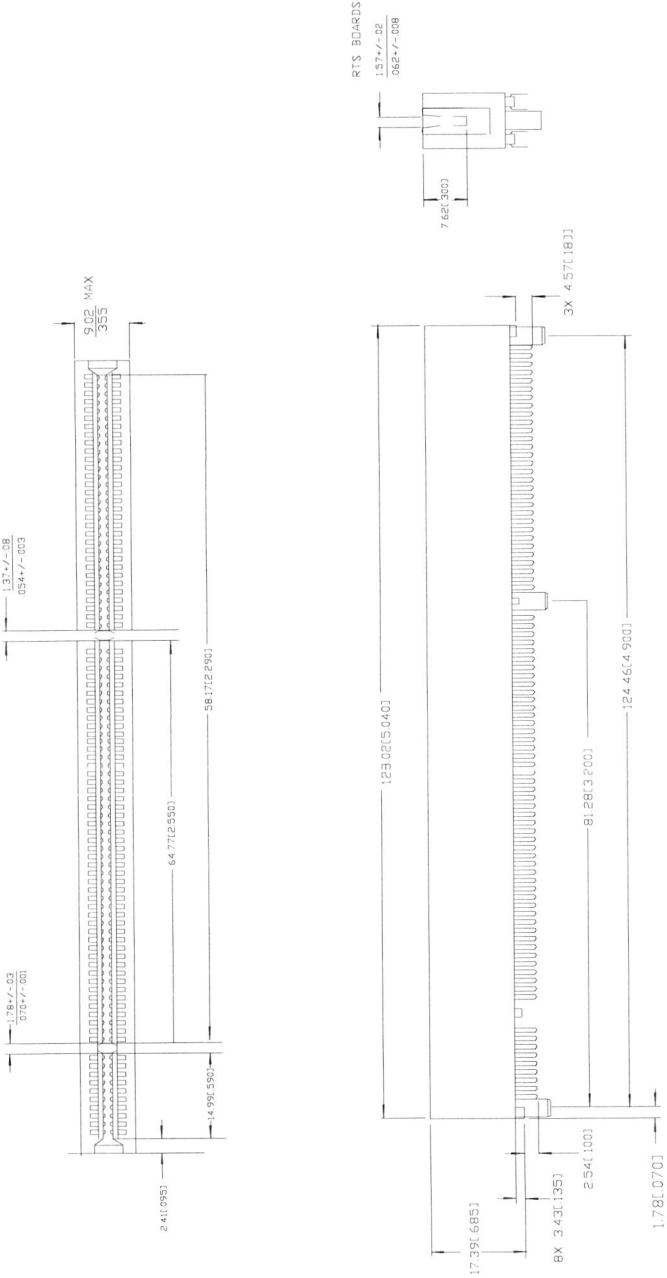

Figure 15-41: 64-bit/3.3V PCI Riser Connector

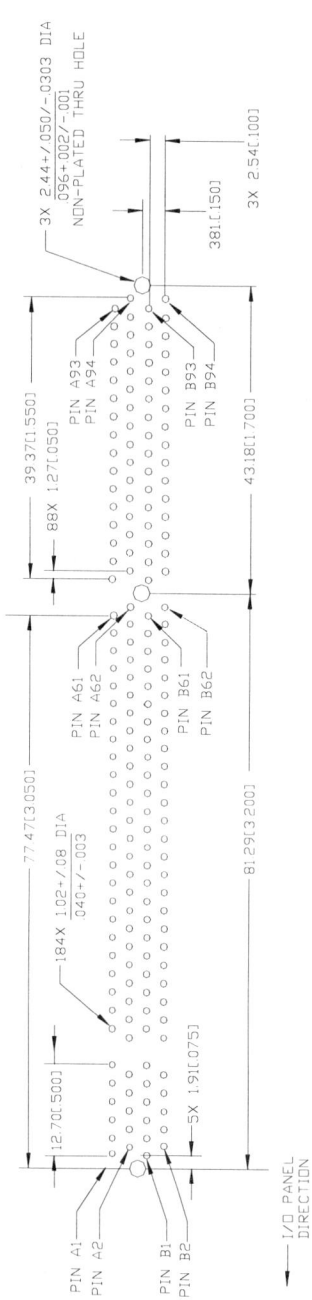

Figure 15-42: 64-bit/3.3V PCI Riser Connector Footprint

LOW PROFILE PCI CARDS

Low profile PCI allows the design of small footprint, low profile systems while still offering expandability and upgradeability to the end user. There are two defined card lengths for low profile PCI: MD1 and MD2. MD1 defines the shortest 32-bit card length available, 119.91 mm (4.721 inches). MD2 defines the maximum length of low profile PCI cards, 167.64 (6.600 inches). Any low profile PCI card that is longer than the MD1 definition is considered an MD2 card form factor. The two card lengths allow system designers to support either all low profile PCI cards, which include MD1 and MD2, or limit their design to support only MD1 cards. Low profile PCI MD1 cards provide 4.8 square inches of board real estate and may be very limiting to adapter card vendors. Low profile PCI is intended for use in the smallest system designs. See Figures 15-43 through 15-45 for low profile PCI expansion card physical dimensions.

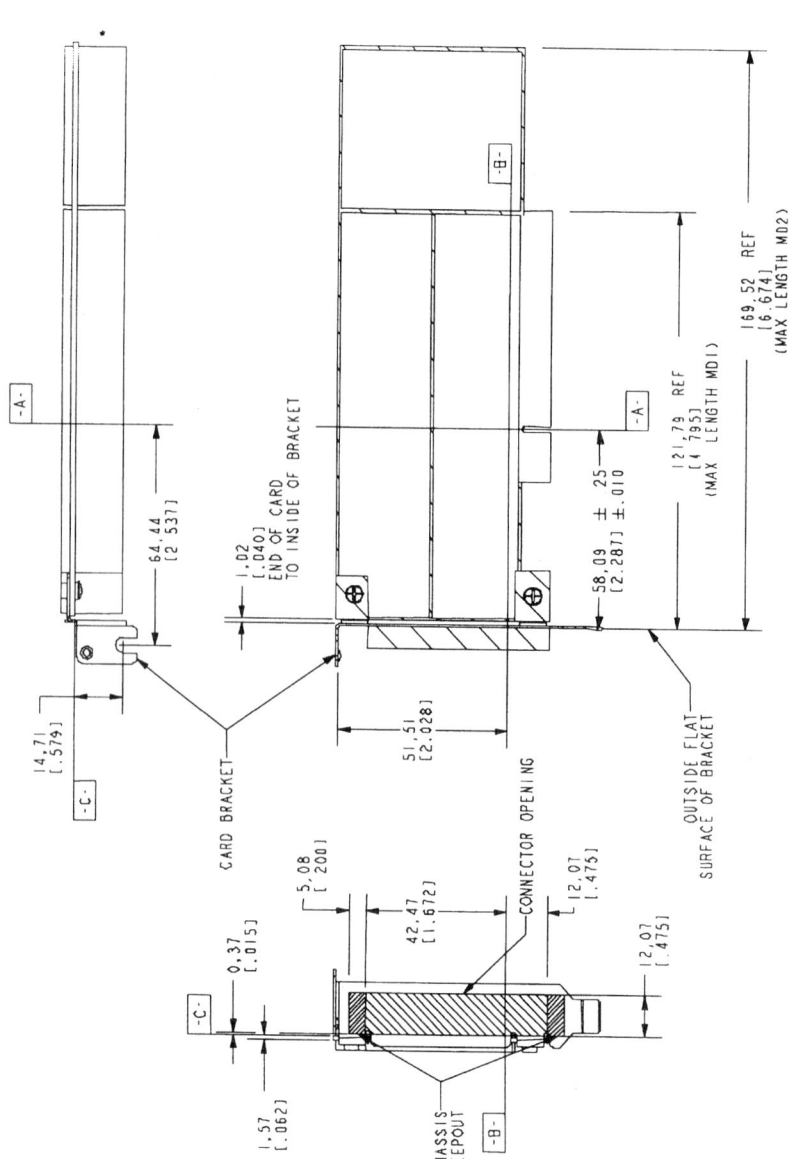

Figure 15-43: Low Profile PCI Card Assembly (3.3V, 32-bit)

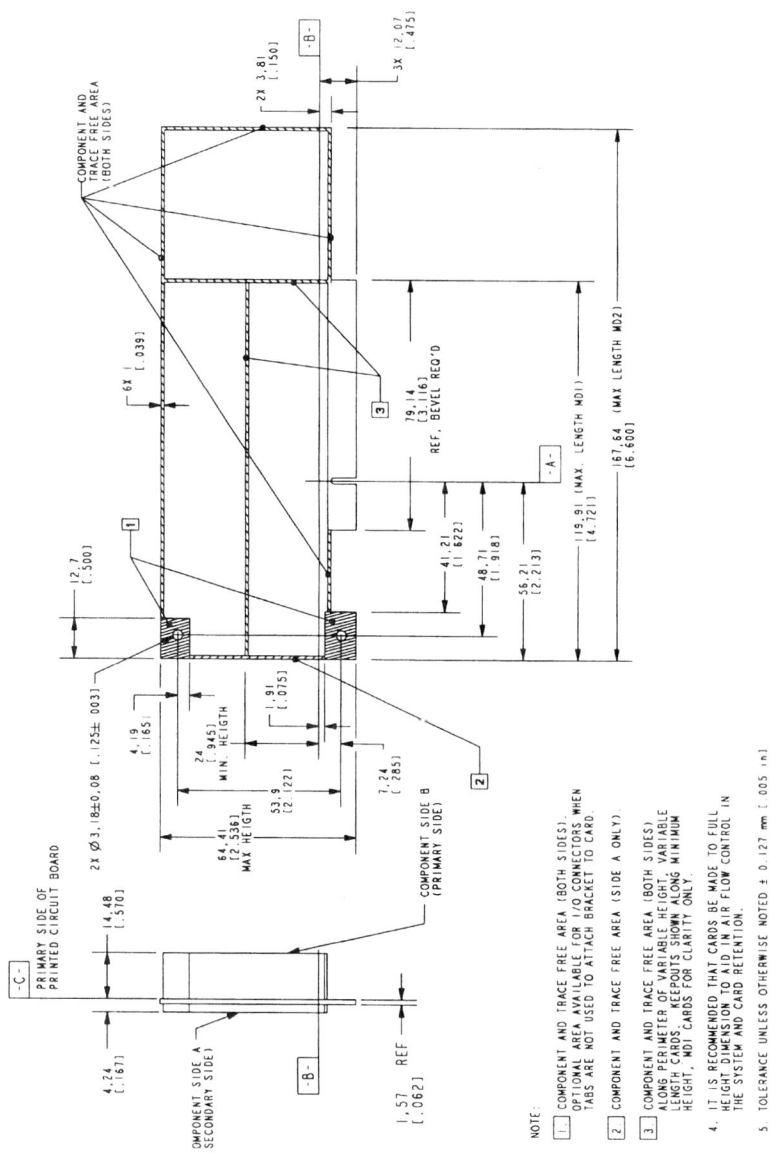

Figure 15-44: Low Profile PCI Raw Variable Height Card (3.3V, 32-bit)

959

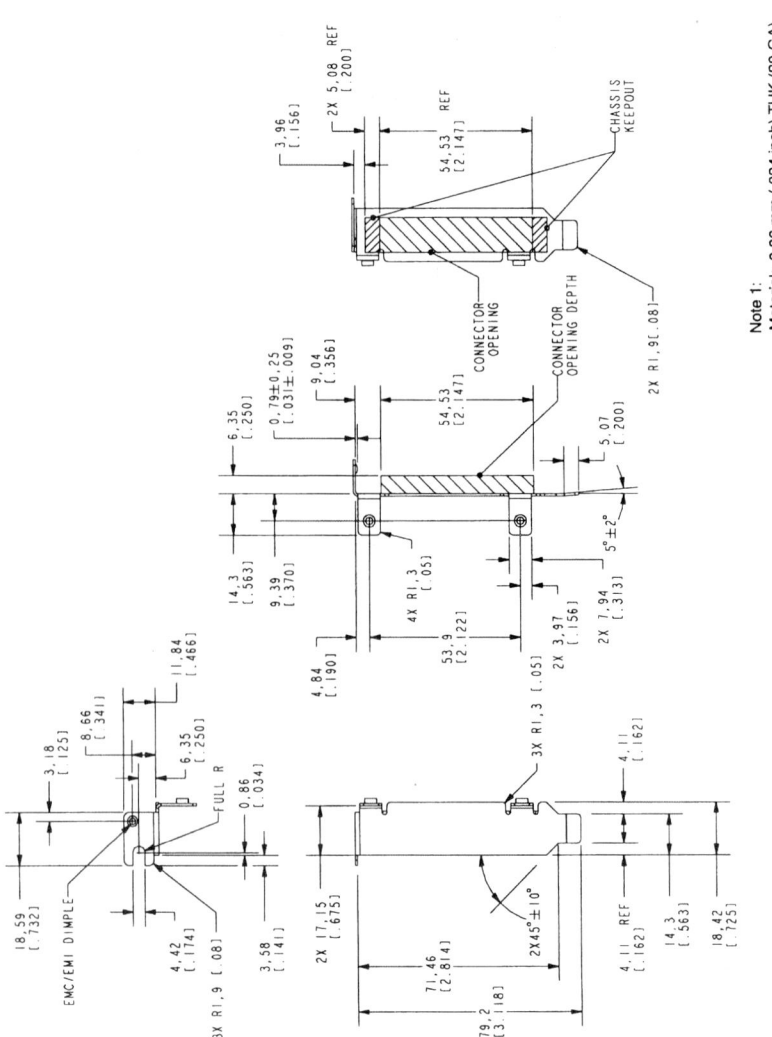

Figure 15-45: Low Profile PCI Bracket

15.3 PCI-X EXTENSIONS

The text and figures in this section are copied from PCI-X Addendum to the PCI Local Bus Specification, and are reprinted with permission of the PCI Special Interest Group.

The PCI-X mechanical specification is identical to the conventional PCI 3.3V mechanical specification, except for identification requirements. The following mechanical form factor requirements are the same as for conventional PCI:

Add-in Card Requirements:

■ Raw Card dimensions and form factors

   ■ Standard length

   ■ Short length (fixed and variable height)

   ■ Low Profile PCI

   ■ Mini PCI

■ Card edge connector dimensions and tolerances defined for both 32-bit and 64-bit interfaces

■ 3.3V or universal keying

■ Mounting brackets

■ Card thickness

■ Height requirement for both the component side and the backside

System Slot Requirements

■ 64-bit and 32-bit 3.3V slot connectors

■ Slot spacing

■ Board and system mounting

IDENTIFICATION REQUIREMENTS

PCI system and add-in cards capable of operating in PCI-X mode are required to identify that the system or the add-in card is capable of operating in the PCI-X mode.

SYSTEM REQUIREMENT

A system that includes one or more PCI slots capable of operating in PCI-X mode must indicate to the user which of the two maximum operating frequencies supported by PCI-X add-in cards the slot is optimized for. For example, a system that includes a slot operating at 60 MHz in PCI-X mode would indicate that the slot is optimized for PCI-X 66 add-in cards. A system that includes slots operating at 100 MHz in PCI-X mode would indicate that the slots are optimized for PCI-X 133 add-in cards. The method by which the system indicates this is not specified.

ADD-IN CARD REQUIREMENTS

Add-in cards capable of operating in PCI-X mode must be clearly marked to indicate their capabilities using one of the following methods:

- Silkscreen image
- Adhesive label

The following rules apply to this PCI-X identification marking:

- At least one marking must appear on either the component side or backside of the card.
- Marking must be a faithful reproduction of the image shown in Figure 15-46.

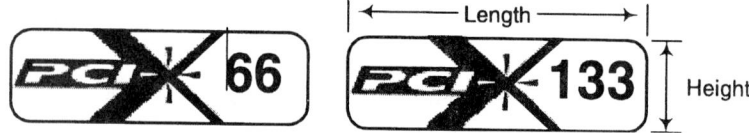

Figure 15-46: PCI-X Add-in Card Identification Marking Requirment

A PCI-X identification marking is permitted to be any size, but must be clearly legible. The recommended minimum height and length for the adhesive and the silkscreen add-in card marking is 0.25" for its height and 0.75" for its length. This minimum height and length guideline is the same for all PCI form factors including standard, Low Profile, and Mini PCI cards.

PCI-X identification marking must use high contrast colors. For example, for adhesive labels black ink on white background or for silkscreen marking a white silkscreen image on a green raw card. Furthermore, the silkscreen marking must be bordered.

Figure 15-46 shows the requirement for PCI-X 66 MHz and 133 MHz add-in card identification marking. Notice that the PCI-X identification logo uses a solid color, rather than the gray scale fading on the standard PCI-X logo.

If a side of an add-in card does not utilize a silkscreen process, the add-in card identification marking is permitted to appear on that side on an external copper layer. External copper layer marking must meet all other marking requirements.

PLACEMENT OF MARKING

Markings are permitted at any location on either the component side or backside of the PCI add-in card. Marking is recommended to be placed near the top edge of standard length, short length, and Low Profile PCI add-in cards, to allow visibility of the marking when the card is seated in a PCI slot. Figure 15-49 illustrates placement of the marking while the card is seated in a PCI slot.

Figure 15-47 illustrates PCI-X markings on standard and Low Profile PCI add-in cards. Figure 15-48 illustrates PCI-X markings on Type I, Type II, and Type III Mini PCI add-in cards.

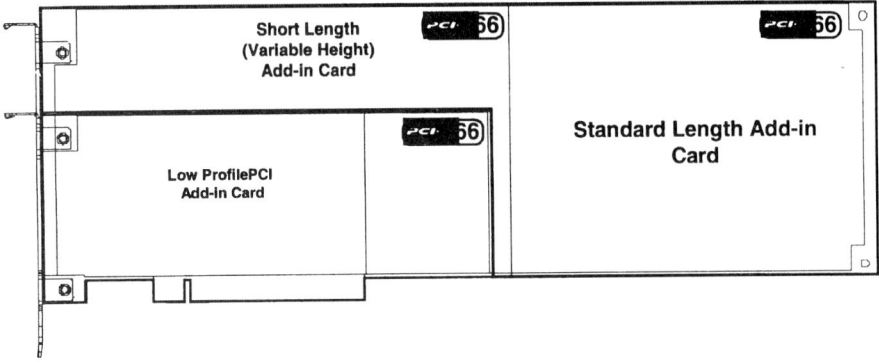

Figure 15-47: 32-bit 3.3V Low Profile, Short (Variable Height) and Standard Length Add-in Card with PCI-X Marking

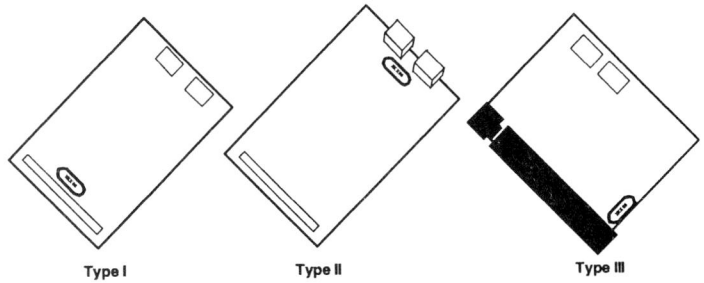

Figure 15-48: Mini PCI Type I, Type II, and Type III Add-in Cards with PCI-X Marking

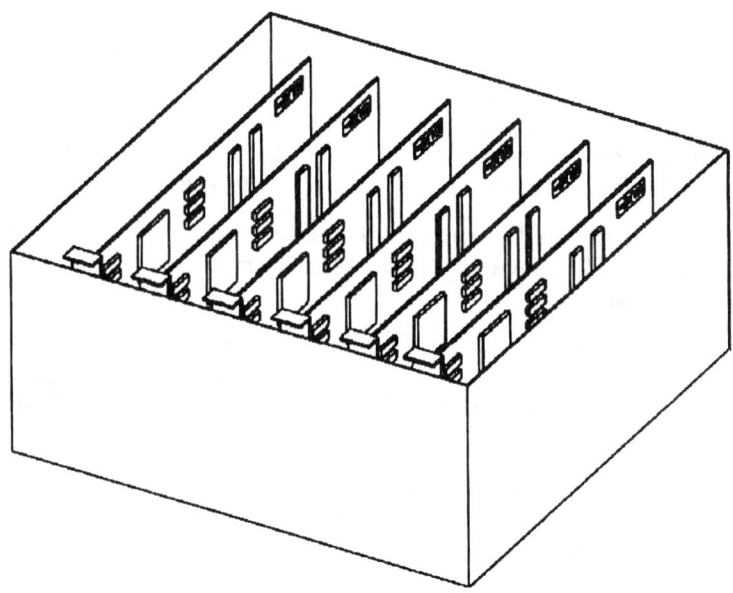

Figure 15-49: Multiple Add-in Cards in Slots

CHAPTER 16

SYSTEM RESOURCES

This chapter consists of the following subchapters:

16.0 OVERVIEW OF SYSTEM RESOURCES

Computer systems contain hardware peripherals and unique components that provide the individual functions of the system. These peripherals and components are usually either mounted directly onto the platform or are added to the system by inserting an add-in card into one of the platform's expansion slots. In the case of peripherals such as the speaker, serial port, floppy diskette, fixed disk, and keyboard, each peripheral has at least one individual hardware device that manages the configuration and control of the peripheral. For example, the Intel 8254 Programmable Timer chip is normally integrated on the system platform. This integrated circuit includes three independent timers. Traditionally, each of the timer circuits supplies the ISA compatible system with a different function: Timer 0 initiates the system time-of-day update sequence, Timer 1 is used for dynamic RAM refresh, and Timer 2 can be used to generate sounds via the speaker peripheral connected to the system.

It is not enough, however, to electrically connect the 8254 Programmable Timer (or for that matter any other device) to its associated circuitry on the system platform in order to obtain the chip's functions. Devices such as the 8254 Programmable Timer must be programmed by software to configure each of the timers individually to provide the specified functionality.

A software program consists of a set of instructions that are executed by the microprocessor. Programs that configure and manage the operation of peripherals instruct the microprocessor to send and/or receive data from the controller devices. Consequently, the microprocessor, and in certain cases the devices independent of the microprocessor, must have a way of communicating with each other. It is through the use of the system resources that this communication is accomplished.

System resources are segregated into four distinct classes. The division of these system resource classes is based on the type of hardware functions provided as well as the global interface requirements each class must adhere to in order to be considered ISA compatible. The four system resource classifications are memory address space, input/output (I/O) ports, interrupts, and direct memory access (DMA).

Software programs use memory address space and I/O ports to communicate with hardware devices. In contrast, devices that control peripherals generate hardware interrupts to communicate to the microprocessor that the peripheral needs to send or receive data within the system. Finally, DMA resources permit the direct transfer of large data streams between system components while consuming very little microprocessor bandwidth.

> **Most devices do not require all four system resource types. Rather, a subset of the four types is used. For example, ISA compatible system serial ports are assigned an interrupt and a range of eight contiguous I/O port addresses. They do not use the memory address space or DMA channel resources.**

To function properly, each device in the computer system must have a unique set of system resources dedicated to it. Typically, when two or more devices are assigned the same system resources, one or more of the devices will not function properly. Erroneously assigning two or more devices the same system resource is referred to as a system resource conflict. The result of a system resource conflict is usually a loss of functionality and/or reliability within the system. In some instances the entire system's operation is impaired.

> **Typically, unique system resources are assigned to individual devices. However, in some instances system resources such as IRQs can be shared.**

Older system platforms and add-in cards are assigned system resources by either moving jumpers or modifying switch settings. Newer system platforms and add-in cards have replaced these manual operations with software programs that configure the hardware for operation. Plug and Play devices such as PCI devices take the system device configuration and management process to a new level. The fundamental premise of Plug and Play devices is that the user is only required to add the device to the system. The System BIOS, device drivers and/or operating system will automatically detect and configure the Plug and Play devices in the system while avoiding any system resource conflicts. To achieve this goal it is imperative to have an understanding of system resources.

To this end, this chapter addresses:

- The four classes of system resources: memory address space, Input/Output ports, interrupts, and DMA channels.
- How system resources are accessed by the system hardware.

This information will also aid the reader in understanding the constraints the system power-up initialization software has in attempting to determine which system resources arc bcing utilized during the current system initialization sequence. In addition, by understanding the basics of system resources, the reader will be able to grasp the concepts behind assigning unused system resources to PCI devices during the initialization of the system. Both of these topics are addressed in Chapter 20, *PCI Device Configuration.*

16.1 MEMORY ADDRESS SPACE

In a computer system, Random Access Memory (RAM), and Read-Only Memory (ROM), are devices which provide the storage space for software program code and data. In an ISA compatible system, the placement of ROM and RAM devices within the four gigabyte address space is pre-defined. This division of memory address locations between ROM and RAM is due in part to the inherent characteristics of the Intel microprocessors. In addition, system designers chose to maintain backward compatibility to the original PC in order to support IBM PC compatible software. The way ROM and RAM address space is partitioned in an ISA compatible system has a great impact on PCI based systems, as will be seen in the discussion on PCI ROM initialization.

Table 16.1 shows the memory address space in a typical ISA compatible system with an Intel 80386 or higher microprocessor.

> Observe that while the microprocessor can access every address in this memory map, there is no guarantee that a physical ROM or RAM device exists behind every address, except where noted.

THE SYSTEM BIOS ROM AND THE RESTART VECTOR

Notice in Table 16-1 that the System BIOS ROM is accessible to the microprocessor just below the fourth gigabyte memory address region immediately after a system power-up or after a hard RESET to the microprocessor occurs. This is because address lines A20 through A31 in Intel 32 bit microprocessors are driven high for code fetches immediately after one of these resets occurs. In addition, Intel microprocessors set the 16 bit Instruction Pointer

(IP) to a fixed starting value of FFF0h. This forces the microprocessor to fetch its first instruction from physical address FFFFFFF0h.

Memory Address	Length	Contents
FFFF0000–FFFFFFFF	64K	System BIOS ROM (system initialization and boot code) when decoded immediately after power-up or hard RESET to the microprocessor
100000–FFFF0000	4G–1.06M	System RAM from 1M to 4 Gigabytes minus 64K
F0000–FFFFF	64K	System BIOS ROM (system initialization and boot code) when decoded in Real Mode
E0000–EFFFF	64K	System ROM BIOS (system initialization and boot code) or Available for adapter ROM BIOS, device drivers, memory managers
C8000–DFFFF	96K	Available for adapter BIOS ROMs, device drivers, memory managers
C0000–C7FFF	32K	Available for adapter BIOS ROMs (typically EGA/VGA Video BIOS ROM), device drivers, memory managers
B8000–BFFFF	32K	CGA Video RAM
B0000–B7FFF	32K	Monochrome Video RAM
A0000–BFFFF	128K	EGA/VGA Video RAM
80000–9FFFF	128K	System RAM from 512K to 640K or available to ISA compatible add-in cards. This functionality is device dependent.
00000–7FFFF	512K	System RAM from 0K to 512K

Table 16-1: ISA System Memory Layout

Placing the code start vector at a fixed address is very advantageous to both System BIOS ROM programmers and hardware designers. For System BIOS ROM programmers, the address of the first instruction to be executed after a system power-up or hard RESET to the microprocessor occurs is a known constant. This permits start-up code specifically designed to handle these two events to be located at a known location. Hardware designers have the advantage of decoding the System BIOS ROM device at the extreme high end of memory address space. This is a key factor in keeping the memory address space between addresses 1M and 4G unobstructed.

Due to the design of the system hardware, the top 64K of system ROM can be decoded starting at both memory address F0000h and FFFF0000h. The first iAPX intersegment control transfer instruction executed by the Intel microprocessor will disable address lines A20 through A31 from being driven during code fetches. This will place the microprocessor into true x86 Real Mode where only the first twenty bits of memory address space (zero to one megabyte) are accessible to the microprocessor. To permit the system ROM code to initially execute in Real Mode, the first instruction executed in an ISA compatible System BIOS ROM is always a FAR JMP instruction. This maintains backward compatibility to the Intel 8088 (PC) and 8086 (PC/XT) microprocessors that are only capable of decoding the first twenty bits of memory address space.

> Note that many chipsets provide the ability to disable the decode of the System BIOS ROM at the 4G region. Therefore, run-time access of the System BIOS code in this region depends on the System BIOS manufacturer.

Below is a partial display of the System BIOS ROM code. It shows the FAR JMP instruction that the microprocessor fetches from the system ROM code start vector at memory address FFFFFFF0h. The data was obtained by running the DEBUG.EXE program under DOS Version 6.0 on an PS/ValuePoint computer system. By typing d F000:FFF0 L 5 the program displays the five bytes located in ROM at physical memory address FFFF0h. The data obtained from running the DEBUG.EXE program has been transposed to the figure below for greater readability.

OFFSET:	0	1	2	3	4	5	6	7	8	9	A	B	C	D	E	F
F000:FFF0	EA	5B	E0	00	F0											

Figure 16-1: Code Bytes at the System Start Vector

All ISA compatible systems contain the identical bytes of code shown. The five-byte instruction executed by the microprocessor is:

> JMP FAR F000:E05B

Once the first far jump has been executed, the microprocessor is placed in the Real ADDRESS mode compatible with the Intel 8088 and 8086 microprocessor based IBM compatible PC and XT computer series. The microprocessor can only access the first megabyte of system memory address space. Instead of fetching and executing its code instructions from the 64K memory address block at FFFF0000h, the microprocessor begins fetching and executing instructions from the 64K memory address block starting at F0000h. The code segment (CS) register value after the first far jump is F000h. The instruction pointer (IP) register value at this point is E05Bh. All instructions executed after this CS:IP pair are System BIOS dependent. What the System BIOS does after this initial jump instruction is also discussed in Chapter 20: *PCI Device Configuration.*

SYSTEM RAM

System RAM is divided into three categories that are discussed below. The categories are *conventional RAM, shadow RAM,* and *extended RAM.* These categories are defined by which memory address region within the four gigabyte address range the RAM occupies.

Intel microprocessors support several instructions that software programs can use to read data from or write data to system memory. These include bit manipulation instructions such as BTR (Bit Test and RESET), data transfer instructions such as PUSHA (Push All registers onto stack) and string manipulation instructions such as MOVSB (Move String Byte-by-Byte). Figure 16-2 shows a sample program that will copy the System BIOS ROM date from its fixed memory vector at 0FFFF5h to a RAM buffer in conventional memory using the MOVSB, PUSH and POP instructions. The INT software instruction is explained later in this chapter during the discussion on interrupts.

```
        TITLE copydate.asm
        DOSSEG
        .MODEL medium
        .STACK 100H

        .CODE
START:  PUSH  DS           ; Copy microprocessor DS and ES
                           ;register
        PUSH  ES           ; contents to RAM based stack
        CLD                ; Set Direction flag to increment mode
        MOV  AX, 0F000H    ;Set DS:SI to base of date string located
        MOV  DS, AX        ; in System BIOS ROM
        MOV  SI, 0FFF5H ;
        MOV  AX, 0000H     ; Set ES:DI to base of RAM buffer
        MOV  ES, AX        ; located in RAM
        MOV  DI, 8000H     ;
        MOV  CX, 8H        ; Use CX register as loop counter for
                           ; the copy
DATE_LP: MOVSB             ; Copy one byte at a time
        LOOP DATE_LP       ; Repeat until done

        POP  ES            ; Restore original DS and ES register
        POP  DS            ; contents using RAM based stack data

        MOV  AX, 4C00H     ; Call DOS
        INT  21H           ; with the exit function
        END  START
```

Figure 16-2: Software Program Memory Manipulation Example

SYSTEM CONVENTIONAL RAM

Once the first far jump instruction is completed, the System BIOS code begins its Power-On Self Test, or POST. It is during POST that the system is tested and initialized in preparation for bootstrapping an operating system. A key component of POST is the test and initialization of the RAM physically present in the system. ISA compatible systems that use the INTEL 80286 microprocessor or one of its successors are always guaranteed a minimum of 512K of RAM. This RAM is based at physical memory address 00000h. In addition, the next 128K address space above 512K is normally assigned to the RAM address space. Enabling the decode of this memory address region as RAM is a function of the system memory controller. The RAM that constitutes the first 640K of system memory is known as conventional memory. The System BIOS reserves a portion of conventional memory for POST and run-time operation. Figure 16-3 shows the standard memory address regions used by the System BIOS and DOS level programs in the conventional memory address space.

Memory Address	Length	Contents
9FC00–9FFFF	1K Bytes	System Extended BIOS Data Segment
00500–9FBFF	637.75K Bytes	Used by DOS, device drivers, terminate and stay ready (TSR) programs and DOS applications
00400–004FF	256 Bytes	System BIOS Data Segment
00300–003FF	256 Bytes	System BIOS Stack
00000–002FF	768 Bytes	BIOS Interrupt Vector Table

Figure 16-3: Standard ISA Conventional RAM Map

SYSTEM SHADOW RAM

Because of component and manufacturing costs, it is common to include RAM which spans the entire first megabyte of system memory instead of just the first 640K of address space. System RAM above 640K and below one megabyte is typically ignored for two reasons: (1) because the memory region from A0000h through BFFFFh is assigned to video memory, and (2) because the memory region from C0000h through FFFFFh is assigned to adapter BIOS ROMs and the System BIOS ROM. However, many system memory controllers contain the capability to decode either the system RAM or ROM devices between memory addresses C0000h and FFFFFh. Physical RAM within this range of addresses is known as *shadow RAM*.

System BIOSs often copy the software programs contained in the system and adapter ROMs to shadow RAM. This is done to improve system performance because the microprocessor can access system RAM significantly faster than it can ROM devices that reside on a slower bus and that have a slower access time than

971

dynamic RAM. A System BIOS will usually shadow itself in RAM from address F0000h to FFFFFh to speed up the Power–On Self Test and bootstrap process. In addition, the System BIOS may shadow the video BIOS from ROM to shadow memory, typically starting at location C0000h, to improve video output performance.

Figure 16-4 illustrates the system memory address space relationship between the system shadow RAM and the ISA ROM region in relationship to the microprocessor. Programming of device specific registers within the memory controller determines whether the CPU reads from ROM or shadow RAM in the ISA compatible address space between C0000h and FFFFFh.

> A common misconception is that an option ROM's code is accessible in RAM address space by simply programming the memory controller to read from RAM at the option ROM's corresponding address space. However, this is not the case. Shadow RAM is programmable and, like an option ROM, must be initialized with data before it is accessed for the purpose of executing valid code.

Special commands specific to the system memory controller permit the microprocessor to perform the following tasks:

- Read from ROM, Write to ROM (shadowing disabled)
- Read from ROM, Write to RAM (ROM to RAM copy mode enabled)
- Read from RAM, Write to ROM (shadowing enabled and RAM write protected)

PCI based systems must incorporate a memory controller with ROM shadowing capabilities. The reason for this is because expansion BIOSs located in ROMs mounted on compliant PCI add–in boards do not directly map into the memory address region between C0000h and F0000h. However, PCI adapter BIOSs can only execute out of this memory address region in an ISA compatible system. It is the responsibility of the System BIOS to copy PCI adapter BIOSs to shadow RAM.

> There are two common methods used to shadow a PCI BIOS. The first method involves copying the PCI BIOS from ROM directly to the ISA Compatibility Region address space. Not all memory controllers support reading from ROM and writing to shadow RAM at the same time. It is, however, the fastest and most code efficient.

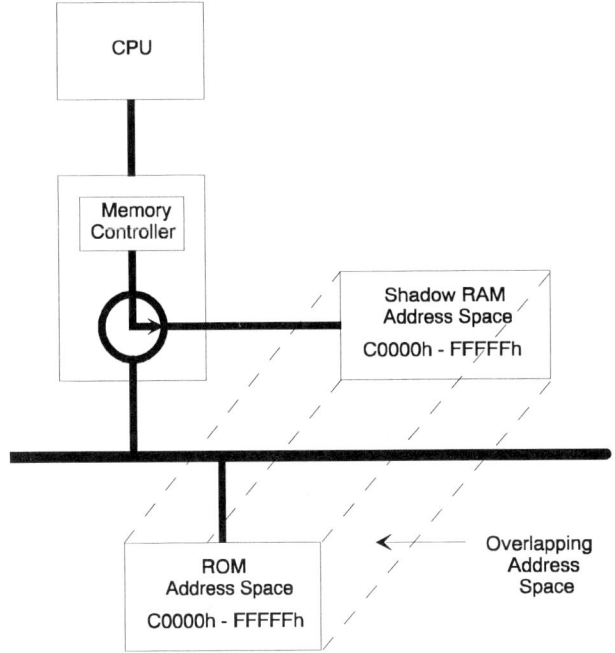

Figure 16-4: Overlapping Shadow RAM and ROM Memory Space

The second method uses a method known as double buffering. The PCI option ROM code is read from ROM and written to system RAM. The option ROM code is then read from system RAM and written to shadow RAM. While not as fast or efficient as the first method, this method is system memory controller device independent.

For an example of how the shadow RAM functions are controlled by a PCI device, see the discussion on the Programmable Attribute Map registers (address offset 59h-5Fh) of the 82434LX PCI device in the Intel 82430 PCIset Cache/Memory Subsystem manual.

SYSTEM EXTENDED RAM

Memory addresses above FFFFFh, or one megabyte, are not accessible to the microprocessor in Real ADDRESS mode. RAM in this region is known as Extended memory because it extends beyond the one megabyte boundary. Extended memory is required for programs that need more RAM than the 640K of conventional memory to execute.

The microprocessor must be programmed to operate in Protected mode in order to use extended memory. Once this is done the microprocessor can access memory anywhere within the entire four gigabyte region.

The System BIOS will begin testing and initializing extended memory at memory address 100000h. It will continue until it either detects a failure during the testing or finds the last byte of contiguous memory. The System BIOS maintains the size of the extended memory it validates in the system. This is important because DOS and typical extended memory drivers will only use the amount of contiguous extended RAM memory reported by the System BIOS.

> It is possible and sometimes desirable to have non–contiguous extended memory within a DOS based system. For example, video frame buffers consist of RAM. If this memory is appended to the top of the system extended RAM it might be interpreted as additional extended memory by the System BIOS during system RAM testing and initialization. Other run–time programs that size memory would also make the same determination.

For PCI device initialization, it is extremely important to identify where all of the extended RAM is located within the system. The reason is two–fold. First, the top of the physical extended memory located on the platform must be identified in order to append extended memory located on the PCI Bus to it. Second, a contiguous region of memory address space above one megabyte that contains no physical ROM or RAM must be identified for the purpose of shadowing PCI expansion BIOSs. This is explained in greater detail in Chapter 20, *PCI Device Configuration.*

16.2 INPUT/OUTPUT PORTS

Input/Output (I/O) ports are used in ISA compatible systems to enable the microprocessor to communicate with and control other system hardware. Starting with the Intel 80386 microprocessor family software programs can read or write I/O Ports via 8-, 16-, or 32-bit accesses. The individual devices, along with the hardware implementation, determine which type of accesses are permitted. See Appendix D for a discussion of ISA Aliasing and Appendix E for a discussion of the effects of ISA aliasing on the PCI architecture.

> Note that certain other hardware devices such as the 8237 DMA controller chip have the ability to communicate with other devices via I/O Ports independent of the microprocessor.

Intel microprocessors support two instructions that software programs can use to read data from or write data to an I/O Port. The IN software instruction moves data from an I/O Port into the microprocessor. The OUT software instruction transfers data from the microprocessor to the I/O Port. Figure 16–5 shows a sample program that will transfer the byte–wide seconds value from the system Real–Time Clock to the microprocessor. The INT software instruction is explained later in the discussion on interrupts.

```
        TITLE readrtc.asm
        DOSSEG
        .MODEL medium
        .STACK 100H

        .CODE
START:  OUT 70H, 00H  ; I/O Port 70H is the index register for the RTC
                      ; Select RTC offset 00H, the Seconds field
        IN    AL, 71H ; I/O Port 71H is the data register for the RTC
                      ; Transfer the Seconds count to the CPU
        MOV AX, 4C00H ; Call DOS
        INT 21H       ; with the exit function
        END START
```

Figure 16-5: Software Program I/O Port Manipulation Example

Table 16.2 illustrates the standard implementation of I/O Ports for ISA compatible systems. Note that I/O Ports 0000h through 00FFh are used to address devices mounted on the platform. I/O Ports 0100h through 03FFh typically address devices mounted on add–in cards. These add–in cards become part of the system when they are installed in expansion slots on the platform.

16.3 INTERRUPTS

ISA compatible systems support exception, hardware, and software interrupts. The purpose of interrupts is to suspend the execution of the software program that the microprocessor is currently executing and execute an interrupt handler. An interrupt handler is simply a software routine that services the function identified by the interrupt type or number. During system initialization and the subsequent bootstrapping/execution of a Real Mode operating system, 256 individual interrupt types are supported. These interrupts are numbered 0 through 255 (FFh). Each interrupt type may have an associated software program that is executed each time the interrupt is invoked. The starting address, or vector, of each of the interrupt routines is stored in a table in RAM. This table is called the interrupt vector table.

Address	Description
000–01F	DMA Controller #1 (8237)
020–03F	Master Interrupt Controller (8259)
040–05F	Programmable Interrupt Timer (8254)
060–06F	Keyboard (8042)
070–07F	Real Time Clock (MC146818)
080–09F	DMA Page Register
0A0–0BF	Slave Interrupt Controller (8259)
0C0–0DF	DMA Controller #2 (8237)
0F0–0F1	Math Coprocessor
0F8–0FF	Math Coprocessor
170–177	Fixed Disk Controller #2
1F0–1F8	Fixed Disk Controller #1
200–207	Game Port
278–27F	Parallel Port
2F8–2FF	Serial Communications
300–31F	Prototype Card
360–36F	Network
370–377	Floppy Diskette Controller #2
378–37F	Parallel Port
3B0–3BF	Monochrome Display Adapter and parallel Port
3C0–3CF	VGA EGA Video
3D0–3DF	Color Graphics Adapter
3F0–3F7	Floppy Diskette Controller #1
3F8–3FF	Serial Communications

Table 16-2: Standard ISA Compatible I/O ADDRESS Ports

The interrupt vector table stores the starting address of each interrupt in a 4–byte table entry. The lower word of each vector contains the value for instruction pointer (IP) and the upper word contains the code segment (CS) for its associated routine. The total length of the interrupt vector table is 1024 bytes (256 vectors x 4 bytes). The table is based at physical offset 0000:0000 in system memory.

The last entry in the table is at address 0000:03FC. Table 16–3 illustrates the standard implementation of the interrupt vector table during the Real Mode operation of DOS. All values in the table are in hexadecimal notation except for the IRQ numbers, which are in decimal notation. Also, notice that vectors 1Dh, 1Eh, 1Fh, 41h and 46h are not pointers to interrupt handlers. They are pointers to various tables of information used by the System BIOS and the operating system.

Refer to the Intel data books and sheets for a description on how to process interrupts in microprocessor modes other than Real Mode.

INT	Vector Address	Function	Type
00	000–003	Divide by Zero or Divide Overflow	Exception
01	004–007	Single Step	Exception
02	008–00B	Nonmaskable (NMI)	Exception
03	00C–00F	Breakpoint	Exception
04	010–013	Numeric Overflow	Exception
05	014–017	Print Screen	Software
06	018–01B	Reserved	Software
07	01C–01F	Reserved	Software
08	020–023	IRQ0: System Time–of–Day	IRQ 0
09	024–027	IRQ1: Kbd Controller Output Buffer Full	IRQ 1
0A	028–02B	IRQ2: Cascade Input from slave 8259	IRQ 2
0B	02C–02F	IRQ3: Serial Communications	IRQ 3
0C	030–033	IRQ4: Serial Communications	IRQ 4
0D	034–037	IRQ7: Parallel Port	IRQ 7
0E	038–03B	IRQ6: Diskette Controller	IRQ 6
0F	03C–03F	IRQ5: Parallel Port	IRQ 5
10	040–043	Video	Software
11	044–047	Equipment Check	Software
12	048–04B	Determine System RAM Size	Software
13	04C–04F	Diskette/Fixed Disk	Software
14	050–053	Serial Communications	Software
15	054–057	Cassette/Miscellaneous Extended Functions	Software
16	058–05B	Keyboard	Software
17	05C–05F	Printer	Software
18	060–063	Resident ROM BASIC/Bootstrap Failure	Software
19	064–067	Bootstrap System	Software
1A	068–06B	Time of Day/PCI	Software
1B	06C–06F	Keyboard Break Key	Software
1C	070–073	Timer Tick (called after each INT 08)	Software
1D	074–077	Pointer to Video parameter Table	Table
1E	078–07B	Pointer to Diskette parameter Table	Table
1F	07C–07F	Pointer to Graphic Characters Table	Table
20	080–083	Exit program running under DOS	Software
21	084–087	DOS Functions	Software
22	088–08B	Pointer to DOS Exit Program Routine	Software
23	08C–08F	Pointer to DOS Control–Break Routine	Software
24	090–093	Pointer to DOS Fatal Error Function	Software
25	094–097	Read Diskette/Fixed Disk	Software

Table 16-3: BIOS/DOS Interrupt Vector Table

26	098–09B	Write Diskette/Fixed Disk	Software
27	09C–09F	Terminate and Stay Resident	Software
28–32	0A0–0CB	Reserved	Software
33	0CC–0CF	Mouse Driver Functions	Software
34–40	0D0–0FF	Reserved	Software
41	104–107	Pointer to Fixed Disk Table 1	Software
42–45	108–117	Reserved	Software
46	118–11B	Pointer to Fixed Disk Table 2	Software
47–49	11C–127	Available to Programs	Software
4A	128–12B	Alarm	Software
4B–5B	12C–16F	Available to Programs	Software
5C	170–17C	NETBIOS	Software
5D–66	174–19B	Available to Programs	Software
67	19C–19F	EMS Functions	Software
68–6F	1A0–1BF	Available to Programs	Software
70	1C0–1C3	IRQ8: Real Time Clock	IRQ 8
71	1C4–1C7	IRQ9: IRQ2 Redirect	IRQ 9
72	1C8–1CB	IRQ10: Available to the system	IRQ 10
73	1CC–1CF	IRQ11: Available to the system	IRQ 11
74	1D0–1D3	IRQ12: Mouse or Available to the system	IRQ 12
75	1D4–1D7	IRQ13: Math Coprocessor	IRQ 13
76	1D8–1DB	IRQ14: AT Fixed Disk Controller	IRQ 14
77	1DC–1DF	IRQ15: Available to the system	IRQ 15
78–7F	1E0–1FF	Reserved	Software
80–85	200–217	BASIC	Software
86–F0	218–3C3	BASIC Interpreter (When BASIC is running)	Software
F1–FF	3C4–3CF	Reserved	Software

Table 16-3: BIOS/DOS Interrupt Vector Table (Continued)

PROCESSING INTERRUPTS

Servicing hardware and software interrupts is a two–stage process when the microprocessor type is within the 80x86 family of microprocessors:

STAGE 1

Stage 1 is performed under complete control of the microprocessor. A programmer has no control of the microprocessor's actions at this time. The purpose of Stage 1 is to ensure that the software program that was interrupted can continue once the interrupt has been serviced.

1. The execution of the current software program by the CPU is temporarily suspended.

2. The current state of the microprocessor flags register is pushed onto the stack. This allows the interrupt handler to modify the microprocessor flags freely without affecting the interrupted software program.

3. The code segment (CS) of the interrupted program is pushed onto the stack.

4. The address of the next instruction (IP) to be executed by the interrupted program is pushed onto the stack.

5. Hardware interrupts are disabled to ensure that the interrupt handler has the opportunity to service the current interrupt.

6. The microprocessor jumps to the memory location specified by the segment: offset values obtained from the interrupt vector table. The interrupt type determines which vector is loaded. Because each vector in the table is four bytes in length, the microprocessor automatically multiplies the interrupt type by four to obtain the correct index into the interrupt vector table for the required vector.

STAGE 2

Stage 2 is the responsibility of the programmer. Once the microprocessor loads the CS:IP pair of the interrupt handler, the next instruction it executes is the first instruction of the interrupt handler. The purpose of Stage 2 is to perform the function requested by the interrupt.

1. The current state of the microprocessor registers used by the interrupt handler, except for registers that will contain output parameters, is pushed onto the stack. This ensures that the interrupted software program will resume with the exact microprocessor state it had when it was interrupted.

2. The interrupt handler can service the call. Note that hardware interrupts should be enabled as soon as possible using the iAPX STI instruction. This will ensure that time critical events, such as the timer interrupt (IRQ0) which occurs 18.2 times a second, can transpire normally. Output parameters, if any, are loaded into the microprocessor registers at this time.

3. The entry state of the microprocessor registers that were saved by the interrupt handler are restored from the stack.

4. The interrupt handler executes the IRET instruction. This instruction will restore the microprocessor flags register to the value it contained on entry to the interrupt handler. In addition, it also forces a FAR return to the

CS:IP address pushed onto the stack by the microprocessor when the interrupt occurred.

5.   The execution of the previously suspended software program by the CPU is resumed.

INTERRUPT CHAINING

Note that the system initialization software is responsible for programming the interrupt vector table with its vectors first. However, because the interrupt vector table is in system RAM, other programs such as expansion ROM programs, operating systems, TSRs and device drivers are allowed to replace the current interrupt vector entries with addresses which point to their own routines. The program that replaces or "hooks" an interrupt vector is responsible for preserving the previous interrupt vector data. Each time a hooked interrupt routine is invoked, the interrupt handler should check to ensure that the interrupt function or device is one that it services. If not, the current interrupt handler has the responsibility of invoking the previous interrupt handler via the preserved vector.

This methodology allows several different programs to hook one specific interrupt during system operation. For example, this capability allows a video expansion ROM BIOS to take over the INT 10h vector from the System BIOS during the system initialization in order to manipulate its video controller properly when video function requests are serviced. In turn, a video driver has the capability of replacing the video expansion ROM BIOS with its vector in order to increase the video capabilities of the system.

Figure 16-6 contains a partial example of a Real Mode interrupt vector table's data. The data was obtained by running the DEBUG.EXE program under DOS Version 6.0 on an IBM PS/ValuePoint computer system. By typing $d \ \ 0:0$ the program displays the interrupt vector data starting with interrupt type 00, the divide by zero exception interrupt handler. The data obtained from running the DEBUG.EXE program has been transposed to the figure below for greater readability.

Observe the vector data for interrupt type 11h, the Equipment Check interrupt. Located at bytes 44-47 in the table, the vector contains F000:F84D. The segment address of F000 indicates that this interrupt is serviced by the system ROM BIOS code, which is always located in system memory from address F0000h to FFFFFh. In contrast, note that the two-byte segment address at memory location 0000:0002 is 0116, not F000. This indicates that at least one other program has hooked the type 00 interrupt's vector because the code segment value is not F000. Such is the case for the majority of the interrupt vectors.

OFFSET:	0	1	2	3	4	5	6	7	8	9	A	B	C	D	E	F
0000:0000	8A	10	16	01	F4	06	70	00	16	00	96	09	F4	06	70	00
0000:0010	F4	06	70	00	FB	07	6A	1C	43	EB	00	F0	EB	EA	00	F0
0000:0020	00	00	F1	1E	25	0D	6A	1C	97	EA	00	F0	6F	00	96	09
0000:0030	97	EA	00	F0	97	EA	00	F0	B7	00	96	09	F4	06	70	00
0000:0040	0F	00	FC	1E	4D	F8	00	F0	41	F8	00	F0	BA	02	6A	1C
0000:0050	39	E7	00	F0	00	00	B3	1E	F8	02	6A	1C	2B	06	6A	1C
0000:0060	00	E0	00	F0	C7	18	06	15	6E	FE	00	F0	EE	06	70	00
0000:0070	98	01	F1	1E	A4	F0	00	F0	22	05	00	00	D6	29	00	C0

Figure 16-6: Interrupt Vector DATA Example

EXCEPTION INTERRUPTS

Exception interrupts occur automatically when the system detects an error condition. Intel defined this class of interrupts to handle the class of events that are not controlled by the programmer via software interrupts or by the hardware designer via hardware interrupts. Consequently, any computer system that incorporates an Intel 80x86 microprocessor should provide interrupt handlers for exception interrupts.

An example of a Real Mode exception is the Divide by Zero error. This exception occurs when (a) the microprocessor detects a division operation with a divisor of 0 or (b) the result of a legal division operation cannot fit into the accumulator register (AL, AX, EAX). A type 00 interrupt is invoked when either of these events occurs.

SOFTWARE INTERRUPTS

Software interrupts are under the control of the programmer. In addition, software interrupts do not actually interrupt the microprocessor because they are intentionally included in software programs. From a programming viewpoint, software interrupts simply permit a caller to invoke a subroutine without knowing the address of the function called. The invocation is accomplished using the iAPX INT instruction. The caller specifies the interrupt type with the INT instruction. In addition to specifying the interrupt type, the caller also has the advantage of specifying input parameters required by the routine called. These parameters are passed to the interrupt handler via the x86 microprocessor registers. As stated above, during Stage 1 of processing the interrupt the microprocessor automatically multiplies the interrupt type by four to obtain the correct index into the interrupt vector table for the required vector. The microprocessor then performs the tasks outlined in Stage 2.

Figure 16-7 below is a sample program to illustrate the use of software interrupts under DOS. It will set the system time to 9:30 A.M.

```
        TITLE settime.asm
        DOSSEG
        .MODEL medium
        .STACK 100h

        .CODE
START:  MOV  AH, 2DH    ; AH <= DOS INT 21H set time function
        MOV  CH, 09     ; CH <= hour
        MOV  CL, 30     ; CL <= minutes
        MOV  DH, 00     ; DH <= seconds
        MOV  DL, 00     ; DL <= hundredths of seconds
        INT  21H        ; Call the DOS set system time function
        MOV  AX, 4C00H  ; Call DOS
        INT  21H        ;   with the exit function
        END  START
```

Figure 16-7: Software Interrupt Programming Example

The advantage of software interrupts within the ISA compatible system architecture is readily apparent. There is a standard set of interrupts along with their associated interrupt handlers defined for both the ISA compatible System BIOS and DOS. In most instances, these interrupt handlers relieve the applications programmer from having to know about the low level hardware implementation of a particular system. For example, in the sample program above, the caller does not need to know what underlying system hardware is used to maintain the system time to be able to set the time. In addition, the caller is not required to know how to program the hardware to set the correct time. Finally, the code size of the application is greatly reduced because interrupt handlers bear the code burden that services each function.

HARDWARE INTERRUPTS

Physical devices within the system initiate hardware interrupts. These devices may be located physically on the platform or located on an add–in board. In both cases, a special signal from the device is connected to an interrupt request (IRQ) line of a system interrupt controller. The primary function of hardware interrupts is to relieve the CPU from having to poll devices waiting for hardware events to happen. In other words, microprocessor bandwidth to process external hardware events is consumed only when the hardware interrupt is detected and serviced.

Unlike software interrupts that are under programmer control, hardware interrupts may be generated by system events in a random fashion. For instance, when a key is pressed on the keyboard or when a mouse is moved, a hardware interrupt request is generated. Multiple hardware interrupts may occur simultaneously. The system interrupt controllers are responsible for detecting that a device has requested service, prioritizing the interrupt, and generating a request to the CPU to execute the interrupt handler specific to the interrupt request. The only control the programmer has over an interrupt generated by hardware is what the system does when the interrupt occurs.

Beginning with the implementation of the Intel 80286 microprocessor, ISA compatible systems use two 8259 programmable interrupt controllers or their equivalent to manage hardware interrupts. These controllers serve as priority arbiters for the devices connected to them. During system initialization, the system ROM BIOS code will initialize the 8259 controllers. This code sets the priority of the interrupt inputs as well as the interrupt vectors that will be used by the microprocessor in response to a hardware interrupt.

Each 8259 has input pins to support up to eight hardware interrupt sources. The master (or primary) 8259 inputs are labeled IRQ0 through IRQ7. The slave (or secondary) 8259 inputs are labeled IRQ8 through IRQ15. This would seem to indicate that 16 hardware interrupts are available to the system. However, the slave 8259 is cascaded to the master 8259 via the master's IRQ2 input line. This reduces the number of available hardware interrupts to fifteen because IRQ2 is not used by external devices to generate an interrupt request. It also gives higher priority to all devices connected to the slave 8259 than IRQ3 through IRQ7 of the master 8259. This is because the master 8259 is programmed so that IRQ0 has the highest priority and IRQ7 has the lowest. Similarly, IRQ8 on the slave 8259 has the highest priority and IRQ15 has the lowest.

When two or more hardware interrupts occur simultaneously, priority is arbitrated. The IRQ with the highest priority level is serviced first by the microprocessor. Processing of any pending lower level IRQ is delayed until all higher IRQ levels serviced.

The master 8259 is programmed so that IRQ0 will generate an interrupt type 08. This base interrupt type value forces IRQ1 through IRQ7 to generate interrupt types 09 through 0F respectively. The slave 8259 is programmed so that IRQ8 will generate an interrupt type 70. This base interrupt type value forces IRQ9 through IRQ15 to generate interrupt types 71 through 77 respectively.

When a hardware interrupt request is being serviced by the microprocessor, the interrupt type is placed on the microprocessor's data bus by the 8259. This value is read by the microprocessor. As stated above, during Stage 1 of processing the interrupt the microprocessor automatically multiplies the interrupt type by four to obtain the correct index into the interrupt vector table for the required vector. The microprocessor then performs the tasks outlined in Stage 2.

Processing slave 8259 interrupt requests is more complex than servicing the master's. When an interrupt request is detected by the slave 8259, it in turn generates an IRQ2 interrupt request to the master 8259. The master 8259 then checks to see if either an IRQ0 (Timer Interrupt) or IRQ1 (Keyboard Interrupt) request is pending. If not, the IRQ2 request for servicing is granted by the master 8259. The master then issues a hardware–generated command to the slave 8259 to place the interrupt type associated with the IRQ line being serviced onto the microprocessors data bus. The microprocessor then completes the interrupt servicing.

Table 16-4 illustrates the typical use of the hardware IRQs. The priority level of each IRQ (IRQ0 has the highest, IRQ7 has the lowest), its interrupt type, the physical address of its vector table entry and the function of the hardware interrupt are shown.

DIRECT INVOCATION OF REAL MODE INTERRUPTS

The system ROMs in ISA compatible systems contain fixed memory addresses that point to certain interrupt handlers, specific System BIOS code and System BIOS–specific tables. These entry points are used to maintain backward compatibility to the PC and XT computer systems. Table 16–5, The System ROM Compatibility Table, contains a list of the compatible fixed entry points.

| IRQs | | Type | Vector Address | Function |
Master	Slave			
0		08	020–023	Timer
1		09	024–023	Keyboard
2		0A	028–02B	Cascade Input from slave 8259
	8	70	1C0–1C3	Real Time Clock
	9	71	1C4–1C7	IRQ2 Redirect
	10	72	1C8–1CB	Available to the system
	11	73	1CC–1CF	Available to the system
	12	74	1D0–1D3	Mouse or Available to the system
	13	75	1D4–1D7	Math Coprocessor
	14	76	1D8–1DB	Fixed Disk Controller
	15	77	1DC–1DF	Available to the system
3		0B	02C–02F	Serial Communications
4		0C	030–033	Serial Communications
5		0D	034–037	Parallel Port
6		0E	038–03B	Diskette Controller
7		0F	03C–03F	Parallel Port

Table 16-4: Hardware Interrupt Priority Levels

Fixed Address	System BIOS Function	Type
FE05Bh	System BIOS POST entry point	BIOS Code
FE2C3h	NMI handler entry point	Handler
FE3FEh	INT 13h Fixed Disk Service entry point	Handler
FE401h	Fixed Disk Drive parameter Table	Table
FE6F2h	INT 19h Boot Strap Service entry point	Handler
FE6F5h	Configuration DATA Table	Table
FE729h	DATA Transmission Rate generator Table	Table
FE739h	INT 14h Serial Communications Service entry point	Handler
FE82Eh	INT 16h Keyboard Service entry point	Handler
FE987h	INT 09h Keyboard Service entry point	Handler
FEC59h	INT 13h Floppy Disk Service entry point	Handler
FEFC7h	Floppy Disk Controller parameter Table	Table
FEFD2h	INT 17h parallel Printer Service entry point	Handler
FF045h	INT 10h Video Service Functions 00 through 0Fh entry point	Handler
FF065h	INT 10h Video Service entry point	Handler
FF0A4h	MDA and CGA Video parameter Table	Table
FF841h	INT 12h Memory Size Service entry point	Handler
FF84Dh	INT 11h Equipment List Service entry point	Handler
FF859h	INT 15h Systems Service entry point	Handler
FFA6Eh	Low order 128 of the 300x200 and 640x200 graphics fonts	Table
FFE6Eh	INT 1Ah Time of Day/PCI entry point	Handler
FFEA5h	INT 08h System Timer Interrupt Handler entry point	Handler
FFEF3h	Initial Interrupt Vector offsets loaded by POST	BIOS Code
FFF53h	IRET Instruction for Dummy Interrupt Handler	BIOS Code
FFF54h	INT 05h Print Screen Service entry point	Handler
FFFF0h	Power–On entry point	BIOS Code
FFFF5h	ROM Date (ASCII). Eight characters in mm/dd/yy format	BIOS Code
FFFFEh	System Model ID	BIOS Code

Table 16-5: System ROM Compatibility Table

INT 1AH FIXED MEMORY ADDRESS

One fixed memory address, the INT 1Ah entry point, is critical to the successful implementation of a PCI–based system. The reason is that the INT 1Ah interrupt handler was selected to be used as the System BIOS interface between the PCI based hardware and software. See Chapter 19: *PCI System BIOS Software Interface* for an in-depth discussion of the PCI INT 1Ah interface. The INT 1Ah

985

interrupt handler is the PCI BIOS interface for both Real Mode and 16 bit Protected Mode microprocessor operation. The 32 bit Protected Mode PCI BIOS interface is a separate entity, mainly because of its 32 bit attributes. It does not use the INT 1Ah interrupt handler routine. See Chapter 19: *PCI System BIOS Software Interface* for the discussion on the 32 bit Protected Mode PCI BIOS interface.

Because the INT 1Ah instruction is native to 8086 Real Mode operation, the software programmer can choose to use the INT 1Ah instruction or call the entry point directly to access the PCI/Time of Day interrupt services. However, executing Real Mode interrupt handlers using the iAPX INT instruction in 16 bit Protected Mode is not possible when the Real Mode interrupt descriptor table is in use. Note Table 16–6. In Real Mode, the microprocessor's segment registers contain 16 bit paragraph addresses, ranging from 0000h to FFFFh. In Protected Mode, each segment register holds a selector. Selectors are 16 bit values that specify a segment descriptor. Segment descriptors specify the segment's base address, size and usage attributes. Recall that Real Mode interrupt vectors contain a 16 bit segment address and a 16 bit offset address. Consequently, a protection fault would be generated if a 16 bit Protected Mode program executed a Real Mode interrupt handler using the iAPX INT instruction because the microprocessor would attempt to load an invalid selector into the code segment register.

There is, however, a method to execute the INT 1Ah interrupt handler without using the iAPX INT instruction in 16 bit Protected Mode. As Table 16–6 illustrates, the register size for both Real Mode and 16 bit Protected Mode is 16 bits. This means that in both modes the 16 bit IP (code Instruction Pointer) and SP (Stack Pointer) registers are used.

Attribute	Real Mode	16–Bit Protected Mode
Reference 16 bit Segment	Yes	No
Reference 16 bit Selector	No	Yes
Segment Base Address Limit	16 bit (1Mb)	24 bit (16Mb)
Segment Size Limit (64K)	16 bit (64K)	16 bit (64K)
Operand and Address Size	16 bit	16 bit
Interrupt Descriptor Table (IDT)	Fixed at 00000h	Protected Mode IDT

Table 16-6: Addressing Attributes for Real Mode and 16-Bit Protected Mode.

Because the two modes use 16 bit code and stack references, the 16 bit Protected Mode code can call the INT 1Ah entry point directly. When doing so, the following should be taken into account (assume that the code is currently executing in protected mode):

1. The 16 bit Protected Mode calling routine is required to place the contents of the Flags Register onto the stack prior to executing the call. The PUSHF iAPX instruction is typically used to accomplish this.

2. The call to the System BIOS INT 1Ah PCI interrupt handler at physical address FFE6Eh must be typed FAR.

3. The code segment descriptor should have a base of F0000h and a limit of 64k.

4. The System BIOS INT 1Ah PCI interrupt handler will use the caller's stack.

5. If the INT 1Ah interrupt handler was hooked by an application prior to the 16 bit protected mode call, the hooked code will not be executed.

6. The INT 1Ah interrupt handler will execute a FAR return to the caller by using the iAPX IRET instruction. This instruction automatically restores the contents of the Flags Register.

16.4 DMA CHANNELS

DMA is currently not implemented by the PCI Specification. This discussion is included in this section on system resources for completeness.

Beginning with the implementation of the Intel 80286 microprocessor, ISA compatible systems use two 8237 Direct Memory Access (DMA) controller chips or their equivalent. These controllers can transfer large amounts of data directly between physical I/O devices such as the floppy diskette or hard disk and main memory without the assistance of the CPU.

The figure below displays the function and type of each DMA channel.

Channel	Function	Type
0	Memory refresh. This function recharges RAM cells.	8–Bit
1	Available to the system.	8–Bit
2	Diskette operations.	8–Bit
3	Available to the system.	8 bit
4	DMA controller cascade line. Not available to the system.	
5	Available to the system.	16– Bit
6	Available to the system.	16–Bit
7	Available to the system.	16–Bit

Figure 16-8: DMA Channels

16.5   ACCESSING SYSTEM RESOURCES

The microprocessor controls most of the computer system through software programs. This control is made possible by the implementation of three distinct buses in the ISA architecture. These three buses are the control bus, address bus and data bus. These buses provide the communication path between the microprocessor and the individual devices in the system. Figure 16–9 shows a simple diagram of the bus connections between the system microprocessor and hardware devices.

CONTROL BUS

Starting with the Intel 80386 microprocessor family, software programs can access of up to four gigabytes of system memory. This memory consists of Read–Only Memory (ROM) and Random Access Memory (RAM). ROM and RAM system memory address values range from 0 to FFFFFFFFh, or 4,294,967,295 unique byte-wide addresses.

I/O port address values range from 0 to FFFFh, or 65,535 unique byte–wide addresses.

Notice that the address region assigned to the I/O port memory address space is also assigned to the lowest sixty–four kilobyte address region of RAM in ISA compatible systems. However, because of the signals generated on the control bus, the four gigabytes of system memory address space and the 64 kilobytes of I/O port memory address space are not affiliated. When the microprocessor communicates with an I/O port, it generates a unique pattern of signals on the control bus which are recognized by hardware devices that implement I/O ports.

For RAM or ROM device accesses, a different set of control signals are generated. It is the responsibility of both the computer system's hardware along with the individual devices accessible to the microprocessor to decode the control bus signals.

ADDRESS BUS

While the decode of the control bus signals directs the memory access to either RAM, ROM or an I/O port, it is the address bus that communicates to the system hardware which unique address is to be either read or written. The memory addresses that the microprocessor can physically access are determined by the address decoding logic hardware. Each time a memory address is read or written, this decode logic routes the access to the selected device. Because of the address decoding in conjunction with the operation of the control bus, system RAM, ROM and I/O are made exclusive and cannot be accessed at the same time.

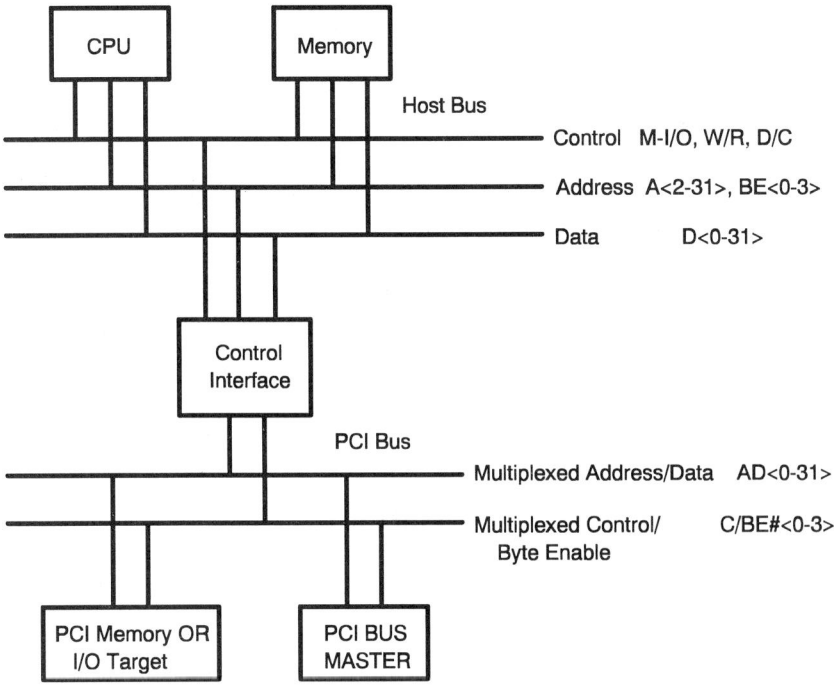

Figure 16-9: General Architecture of PC/AT with PCI bus

DATA BUS

During a memory read cycle, the data bus holds the information, or data, retrieved from the memory. RAM, ROM and I/O ports may be read. During a memory write cycle, the data bus holds the data to write to memory. However, only RAM and I/O ports (that are designated writeable) may be written. ROM devices are read–only. Attempts to write read–only memory should not adversely affect system operation.

16.6 SYSTEM RESOURCES EXAMPLE

To complete the discussion on system resources, an example of how they are used in the system as well as the interaction between the individual components is now presented. The sequence required to update the System BIOS Time–of–Day count was chosen for this example because it demonstrates the connectivity between different system resources as well as the System BIOS and operating system level software. Refer to Figure 16-10 as the example is explained.

SYSTEM CLOCK

The System Clock provides the 8254 Programmable Timer with a fixed input clock rate of 1.9318 MHz. This frequency is the same on all ISA compatible systems. The microprocessor frequency, which is considerably higher, has no effect on the clock rate of the 8254 Timer chip. The System Clock is unique in that the device does not consume any system resources. It also does not require any special programming. Once system power is applied, this device starts oscillating at the correct frequency. The output of the System Clock is continuously fed to the 8254 Programmable Timer's clock input signal.

8254 PROGRAMMABLE TIMER

The 8254 Programmable Timer chip contains three independent timer circuits, or channels. The three timers are identical. However, each timer is used to supply a different function. This discussion is limited to Timer 0.

The 8254 Timer is uninitialized when power is applied to the system. The System BIOS must program the 8254 Timer for correct operation. Each channel of the 8254 Timer can be programmed to operate in one of six modes. The microprocessor uses four I/O ports to communicate with the 8254 Timer. These I/O port resources are not shareable with any other device in the system. In addition, they should never be assigned to any other device in the system. The I/O port addresses assigned to the 8254 Timer are as follows:

I/O Port	Function
40h	Timer 0
41h	Timer 1
42h	Timer 2
43h	8254 Timer Command Register

Recall that I/O port addresses in the range 00h through 00FFh are used to address devices mounted on the platform, which is where the 8254 Timer is located.

The microprocessor uses I/O ports 40h and 43h to program the 8254 Timer to pulse its output line 18.2 times per second. The 8254 will run continuously in this mode without any further intervention on the part of the microprocessor. The output line of Timer 0 is connected directly to the IRQ0 input line of the 8259 Interrupt Controller chip. Each time the Timer 0 output is pulsed, it generates a hardware interrupt request to the 8259 chip.

8259 INTERRUPT CONTROLLER

As explained in Subchapter 16-3, there are two 8259 Interrupt Controllers in an ISA compatible system. These are referred to as the master and slave interrupt controllers. Their purpose is to manage the system's hardware interrupts.

Both 8259 Interrupt Controllers are also initialized when power is applied to the system. The System BIOS must program each interrupt controller for correct operation. The microprocessor uses I/O ports 20h and 21h to communicate with the master 8259 Interrupt Controller. It uses I/O ports A0h and A1h to communicate with the slave 8259 Interrupt Controller. These I/O port resources are not shareable. In addition, they should never be assigned to any other device in the system. Once each interrupt controller is programmed for ISA compatible operation, it will run continuously in this mode without any further intervention on the part of the microprocessor.

When the 8254 Timer 0 output is pulsed, it generates a hardware interrupt request to the master 8259 Interrupt Controller via its IRQ0 input line. This is the highest priority hardware interrupt in the system. If a different hardware interrupt is currently being serviced, IRQ0 will be serviced next. This is regardless of any other pending hardware interrupts such as the keyboard or fixed disk types. In addition, this hardware interrupt resource is not shareable. Hardware system designers should never use IRQ0 for any other purpose than to generate the time-of-day interrupt request.

> Recall that hardware interrupts can be disabled using the iAPX CLI instruction or via the 8259 Interrupt Controller's interrupt mask register. Be careful not to disable interrupts for a long period of time in your software or the system time-of-day will become invalid.

The master 8259 Interrupt Controller will execute a series of hand–shakes with the microprocessor while the IRQ0 interrupt is being processed. During this time the microprocessor is instructed by the master 8259 Interrupt Controller to fetch the interrupt vector that services IRQ0.

FETCH INTERRUPT VECTOR

Fetching the interrupt vector that services IRQ0 is important for two reasons. First, because the microprocessor was asynchronously interrupted by a device in the system. In this case, the microprocessor is being requested to halt its current process and provide software support for the system time-of-day function. Second, because up until this point, only I/O port and hardware interrupt system resources have been used. Fetching the interrupt vector requires the utilization of a third type of system resource, system RAM.

Recall that the Real Mode interrupt vector table is located in system RAM from physical address 0000:0000 through 0000:03FF. Also remember that the master 8259 Interrupt Controller is programmed to request service from the Type 8 interrupt handler when an IRQ0 is generated. The vector for this handler is at physical address 0000:0020. Once the microprocessor fetches the vector from the interrupt vector table, the INT 8h interrupt handler is called.

INT 8H INTERRUPT HANDLER

The INT 8h interrupt handler is responsible for registering the number of times the output of Timer 0 of the 8254 Programmable Timer pulses while the system power is on. Each time this routine is invoked, the value contained in the four–byte system memory resource located at physical address 0040:006C is incremented by one. This is the system time-of-day-count.

INT 1AH INTERRUPT HANDLER

The INT 1Ah interrupt handler is responsible for servicing the system Real Time Clock functions. Software programs can use the INT 1Ah interrupt handler to read (function 0) and set (function 1) the system time–of–day count at physical address 0040:006C.

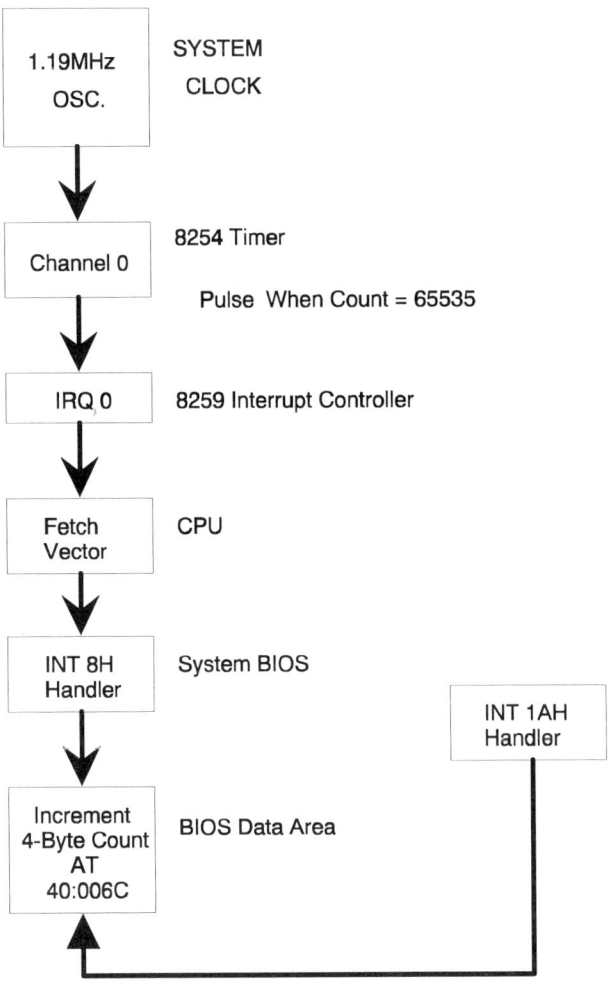

Figure 16-10: BIOS Time-of-Day Count; Update Sequence

16.7 CHAPTER SUMMARY

The system resources example just presented reinforces several concepts that have been introduced in this chapter. First, communication between the devices in the system rarely occurs without the use of system resources. System memory and I/O port resources are used to transfer data between devices. Hardware interrupts relieve the CPU from having to poll devices waiting for hardware events to occur.

In addition, the management of system resources is of primary importance. In the example, there is a seamless interaction between several devices despite the fact that certain devices use only I/O ports while others use memory, etc. Assign system resources judiciously to guarantee that the desired results are achieved.

System resources that are assigned to standard ISA devices such as the 8254 Programmable Timer should be protected. These types of resources are usually non-shareable. When the system resources have been assigned, avoid using them for anything else in the system or catastrophic system failures may occur.

CHAPTER 17

PCI CONFIGURATION ADDRESS SPACE

This chapter consists of the following subchapters:

17.0 OVERVIEW

Run-time transactions on a PCI bus are typically executed using standard memory and I/O address space accesses. However, a separate address space is provided for configuring PCI devices. This address space is called PCI Configuration Address Space. Except for PCI HOST Bus bridges, all PCI devices are required to support PCI Configuration Address Space. Support of all other bus transactions is optional.

> PCI configuration space is required to be accessible at all times during system operation, not just during device initialization.

This chapter discusses various aspects of PCI configuration address space. See Chapters 18 and 19 for a description of the two defined configuration address space templates chip designers can utilize in PCI device implementations.

17.1 FEATURES

Because PCI configuration register space is a unique address space within the system, exclusive access to the PCI configuration registers is guaranteed. This feature permits PCI targets to be accessed before they have been mapped into memory or I/O address space. Being able to access a PCI device's configuration registers prior to enabling the device to respond to memory or I/O address transactions is the key ingredient behind PCI's Plug and Play functionality. Some of the other major features of the PCI configuration address space that enhance every PCI device's Plug and Play capabilities are:

- PCI devices are detected.

- Individual PCI device functions are identified.

- PCI devices identify their system resource requests.

- PCI devices are assigned their system resource requests.

- PCI device responses to memory and I/O accesses are enabled or disabled.

- PCI device responses to errors are enabled or disabled.

- Expansion ROM initialization mapping.

- Programming of interrupt routing information to each PCI function.

The ability to identify each PCI device and dynamically assign system resources to them enables configuration software to construct optimized system memory and I/O address space maps that remain resource conflict free.

> Except for the VGA compatible class of devices, PCI devices cannot request specific system resources. PCI device system resource assignments are required to be fully relocatable. PCI device specific software must be capable of utilizing the system resources assigned to it. Vendors that hard-wire PCI configuration space registers with fixed values are non-compliant.

Another important feature of PCI configuration address space is geographical addressing of PCI devices. Accesses to a PCI device's configuration address space registers are made by specifying the device's bus number, device number and function number. The bus number is specified using eight bits. Thus, valid PCI bus numbers are zero through 255. PCI device numbers permit multiple PCI devices connected to the same PCI bus to be uniquely identified. Device numbers are specified using five bits. Therefore, 32 unique device numbers per PCI bus are available. However, as described in the hardware section of this book, electrical loading can severely limit the number of physical devices that can actually be connected to a PCI bus. Three bits are utilized to identify which function within a PCI device. Consequently, each PCI device can contain between one and eight functions, inclusive, in the same physical package. Every PCI function must support PCI configuration space accesses per the requirements specified in the section on access rules later in this chapter.

17.2 FUNCTIONS

The three major intended uses for PCI configuration space are summarized as follows:

- To permit device detection and control of PCI devices.
- To initialize PCI devices.
- To support catastrophic error handling functions.

As an example, the following is an overview of some of the PCI configuration space registers and their functional usage.

CONFIGURATION

Each function within a device is required to implement the following PCI configuration space registers:

- **Vendor ID**   identifies the device's manufacturer
- **Device ID**   identifies the manufacturer's assigned part number
- **Revision ID**   identifies the revision of the part
- **Class Code**   identifies a PCI device's generic function
- **Header Type**   identifies a PCI function's predefined header type

This information can be used by all levels of software to determine such things as when and if to enable a device. For example, when multiple VGA devices are detected in a system, only one should be enabled for video output during execution of the System BIOS POST. Detection of PCI VGA devices is easily accomplished using the Class Code register.

INITIALIZATION

Each function within a device can implement registers that request system resources such as I/O and memory address space, as well as interrupts. In addition, configuration software can program each individual PCI device function with system resource assignments. These two tasks are accomplished by implementing the following PCI configuration space registers:

- **Base Address**   identifies a request for either I/O or memory
- **Interrupt Pin**   identifies a request for an interrupt line
- **Interrupt Line** programmed with an interrupt line number

This information is used by configuration software to initialize the device with non-conflicting resources. For example, a device may require exactly one megabyte of memory address space to perform its function. Configuration software can easily detect this resource request and initialize the device with the appropriate resource using a base address register.

CATASTROPHIC ERROR HANDLING

PCI devices can support two error reporting signals: SERR# and PERR#. PERR# is used to report parity errors. It must be supported by all PCI add-in cards. It is implemented as an output signal on targets. Bus masters must implement PERR# as both an input and output. SERR# is used as a last recourse for reporting serious errors. It is used to report Address Parity errors, Data Parity errors during a special transaction, and any other critical errors. These functions are accomplished by implementing the following PCI configuration space registers:

- **Command**   controls parity and system error responses
- **Status**   records the assertion of SERR# and PERR#

17.3 FORMAT

The PCI configuration register address space is designed to accommodate many different types of computer systems. These include RISC architectures as well as Intel x86 implementations. To meet the requirements of these various architectures, the architects of the PCI configuration space implemented a template approach to PCI configuration address space. This template consists of a block of 256-byte-wide contiguous I/O addresses into which all of the PCI configuration registers are mapped. The block of addresses is divided into a Configuration Space Header region and a Device Dependent region. Refer to Figure 17-1 for a block level diagram of the PCI configuration address space.

> PCI device vendors need support only those registers that are applicable within each region of the PCI configuration space. Note that all PCI Configuration Space Registers must be readable.

HEADER REGION

Every PCI compliant device must support a predefined PCI Configuration Space Header Region and strictly adhere to its organization. The purpose of the PCI Configuration Space Header registers is twofold:

1. To uniquely identify the PCI device.
2. To permit generic control of all PCI compliant devices.

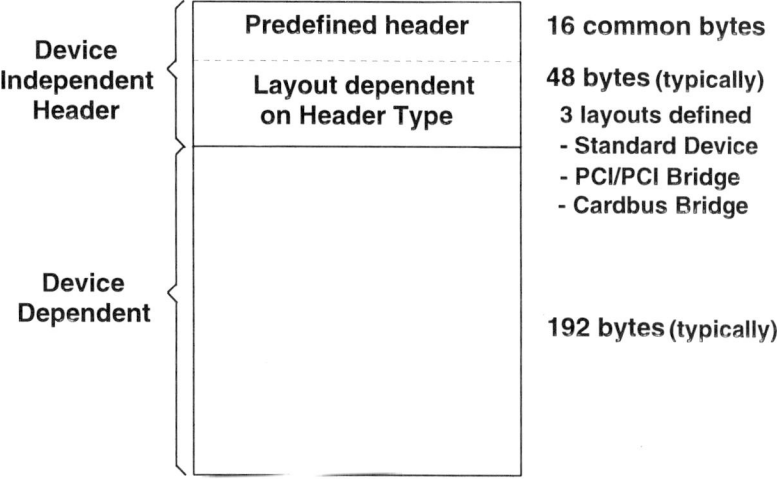

Figure 17-1: PCI Configuration Space Format

Note that while many registers in the predefined PCI Configuration Space Header region must be supported, programmer control over the individual bits in the registers is not required to be implemented. For example, the Command Register must be implemented by all PCI devices. However, the Bus Master Control bit (bit 2 of the Command Register), does not have to be programmable for devices that are not bus masters. In this case it is recommended that:

1. The bit attribute is read only; writes should have no affect on the bit.
2. The state of the bit is set to the value (0 or 1) that is optimum for the PCI device. In most instances, the value will be 0, the disabled state.

The PCI Local Bus Specification treats the predefined header as a monolithic 64 byte structure. This structure is subdivided into two regions: the PCI Device Independent Region and the PCI Device Header Type Region.

> **Note that all device dependent registers must be located after the predefined header in the PCI configuration space.**

PCI DEVICE INDEPENDENT REGION

The PCI Device Independent Region occupies the first 16 bytes of the PCI Configuration Space Header Region. This region is identical in function and layout for all PCI devices. The intended use of this region is twofold: device identification and generic control. Of these first 16 bytes, the PCI Local Bus Specification states that the Vendor ID, Device ID, Command, Status, Revision ID, Class Code and Header Type registers are required to be supported by all PCI compliant devices. All other PCI Device Independent registers can be implemented as reserved registers. Remember that reserved registers must return a value of zero when read.

PCI DEVICE HEADER TYPE REGION

The second part of the predefined PCI Configuration Space Header region is the Header Type Region. The layout and use of these remaining bytes (starting at offset 10h) in the PCI Configuration Space Header Region are defined according to the value encoded in the lower seven bits of the PCI Header Type register. This register is located at offset 0EH within the PCI Device Independent Region. Currently there are three defined PCI device header types. Type00h supports standard PCI devices. See Chapter 18 for a description of the Type 00h template. Type 01h supports PCI/PCI Bridges. See Chapter 19 for a description of the Type 01h template. Type 02h supports CardBus Bridges. A description of the CardBus Bridge template is not included in this book. A description can be found in the *PC Card Standard* document. Information on this document is located at http://www.pc-card.com.

DEVICE DEPENDENT REGION

The PCI configuration space Device Dependent region consists of the last 192 bytes of the PCI configuration space. PCI device vendors are only permitted to implement device specific registers in this region.

This area of PCI configuration space can be used for any device functionality that is not typically accessed during runtime. The most likely use of this region is device specific configuration.

PCI device designers should avoid placing run-time control and status in this area because of the longer access times that can occur when accessing PCI configuration address space.

REGISTER AND BIT IMPLEMENTATION

A PCI function is required to respond to any access to its PCI configuration space. The reason is that PCI devices must assert DEVSEL on any access to all 256 bytes of its configuration address space. This is regardless of whether the register accessed is implemented or not. Within this 256 byte region there can be reserved, required, and optional registers and bits. While the definition of the PCI configuration address space can change with the various template types, the implementation standards associated with the individual registers and bits does not.

On write operations, a PCI device can choose to throw away the data. On read operations, a PCI device can return any value, subject to the required and reserved register rules.

RESERVED REGISTERS AND BITS

Reserved registers and bits do not perform any function. Reserved registers and bits are reserved for future PCI Special Interest Group use. Because of this they cannot be used for any other purpose. Reserved registers and bits must not be writeable, and must always return zero when read.

REQUIRED REGISTERS AND BITS

When the PCI Local Bus Specification states that a register is required, it means that it cannot be treated as a reserved register. Required registers or bits must have the capability or encoding provided in the specification.

In some cases this can make a register or bit behave exactly like a reserved register or bit (*i.e.*, not writeable, returns zero on reads). For example, in most devices the Header Type register is hard–coded to zero because zero is the correct value for the device. Also, older PCI devices may return a Base Class Code of zero, which was a valid value at the time the device was implemented.

OPTIONAL REGISTERS AND BITS

When the PCI Local Bus Specification states that a register or bit is optional it means that the device designer can choose to implement the register as reserved or to implement it with the capability/encoding defined in the PCI Local Bus Specification.

> In some cases optional registers become required if the device has a certain capability. For instance, any device that needs to generate interrupts must implement the Interrupt Line register as an eight bit Read/Write register. If a device does not generate interrupts, the Interrupt Line register can be treated as reserved (i.e., not writeable, returns zero when read).

REGISTER AND BIT IMPLEMENTATION SUMMARY

In summary, Reserved Registers or bits must be read–only and return zero when read. Required registers or bits must be implemented to the capabilities/encoding defined in the PCI Local Bus Specification. Optional registers or bits must follow the capability/encoding defined in the specification or be treated as reserved.

17.4 ACCESS RULES

The objective of a PCI configuration access is to permit the Host CPU to access a specific register in a specific PCI target located on a specific PCI bus. The PCI Bus Specification defines two separate bus transactions for accessing PCI configuration address space registers. These are the PCI configuration read and write transactions.

READING PCI CONFIGURATION SPACE

The following rules pertain to reading PCI configuration space:

- PCI targets are required to return data when their configuration space is read.
- Read accesses of reserved or unused configuration registers must terminate normally.
- Reserved bit values are undefined.
- Data values read are the values the device is actually using.
- A value of zero must be returned for read accesses of reserved or unused Configuration Space Register bits.

WRITING PCI CONFIGURATION SPACE

The following rules pertain to writing PCI configuration space:

- PCI devices must treat write operations to Reserved Registers in configuration space as NO-OPs. The data must not be written to the device. The transaction must complete normally.

- Reserved bit states must be preserved when writing PCI configuration registers. Use a Read/Modify/Write implementation when writing registers with reserved bits. This ensures software transparency in the event a reserve bit(s) is implemented in the future.

17.5 MULTI-FUNCTION DEVICES

A multi-function device is a single piece of silicon that incorporates between two and eight functions. For example, a device may contain two functions. One function may provide a SCSI connection and the other an Ethernet connection. Each individual function must implement a separate set of PCI Configuration Space Registers.

> **The multiple functions within a device share the device's PCI interface.**

The first function within a multi-function device must respond as function zero. One reason for this is that configuration software only reads function zero when scanning the system for the presence of PCI devices. The remaining functions can be assigned a unique value between two and seven.

Multi-function devices should ignore configuration space accesses to functions that are not implemented. For instance, a device with two functions, 0 and 4, should not respond (*i.e.*, assert DEVSEL) when functions 1, 2, 3, 5, 6, and 7 are accessed. It is important that when the Vendor ID field of an unimplemented function is read the value returned is 0FFFFh.

SHARING CONFIGURATION SPACE REGISTERS

Certain PCI configuration space registers can be shared when implementing multifunction devices. Sharing registers can reduce the gate count and complexity of a device. For instance, Vendor IDs are typically (but not always) the same for different functions in a device. Device ID and Revision ID registers may also be shared.

> **The guideline to use for sharing registers within a multi-function device is that the register is read-only and has the same value in each function.**

Registers that have writeable bits normally are not shared. For instance, all functions must implement unique Command, Status, Latency Timer, Interrupt Line and Base Address Registers so that the writeable bits within the registers can be individually controlled. An exception to this rule is the Cacheline Size register. The Cacheline Size register can be shared because this is a fixed value throughout the system.

17.6 PCI DEVICE DETECTION

To determine if a device is present on the PCI bus, do the following:

1. Read the Vendor ID register of Function 0. If a value other than FFFFh is read, the device is present.

2. Determine if the device is a single function or multi–function device: Read the Header Type register, located at offset 0Eh of the PCI configuration space Header. If bit [7] is set to '0', it is a single function device. If bit [7] is set to '1', it is a multi-function device.

3. If the device is a multi–function device, for each function, one through seven, read the Vendor ID register of Function [1, .., 7]. If a value other than FFFFh is read, the function is present.

> **Use the Header Type register, Bit 7, to determine whether the device is multi-function or not. If the device is a single-function component, be aware that it may not decode AD10::AD8. This will force all eight functions of the device to return the same values. Consequently, if the software is not written with this in mind, it could report the presence of eight functions when there is actually only one. This is one case where the hardware does not protect the software.**

17.7 CONFIGURATION MECHANISMS

Earlier it was stated that the objective of a PCI configuration access is to permit the Host CPU to read or write a specific register in a specific PCI target on a specific PCI bus. In this section the details of how a PCI configuration access is accomplished are introduced.

The PCI Bus Specification defines two mechanisms for accessing PCI configuration address space. These are known as PCI Configuration Mechanism

#1 and PCI Configuration Mechanism #2. Only PCI Configuration Mechanism #1, which was defined in PCI Bus Specification 2.0, is discussed in this section.

> **PCI Configuration Mechanism #2 is only defined in the later PCI Bus Specifications for backward compatibility. PCI Configuration Mechanism #1 should be implemented in all PCI devices designed to revision 2.0 or later of the PCI Bus Specification. In addition, any devices that support PCI Configuration Mechanism #2 and are turned should be upgraded to support PCI Configuration Mechanism #1.**

The reason the PCI access mechanisms were defined is because the Intel x86 and other processor families do not possess the ability to perform PCI read and write transactions. Consequently, a method is required to convert Host CPU bus read and write transactions into PCI configuration address space read and write transactions. The typical way to accomplish this is to integrate the conversion mechanism in a Host/PCI bridge. The Host/PCI bridge must recognize certain Host CPU I/O and memory transactions as PCI configuration accesses and convert them to PCI configuration transactions on the Host/PCI bridge's PCI bus.

> **The PCI Bus Specification does not define access mechanisms for non-x86 architectures.**

PCI CONFIGURATION MECHANISM #1

PCI Configuration Mechanism #1 uses two DWORD I/O addresses. These DWORD locations are referred to as the CONFIG_ADDRESS register and the CONFIG_DATA register, located at I/O locations 0CF8h and 0CFCh respectively. These addresses were selected because they do not conflict with other devices in the system The reason there is no conflict is that the 0CF8h and 0CFCh DWORD locations are reserved for the system board by the EISA specification. The description of these registers follows in this section. Section 17-9 describes how PCI Configuration Mechanism #1 is used in a system.

CONFIG_ADDRESS REGISTER

The CONFIG_ADDRESS register is a 32-bit read/write register. This register is located at location CF8h in I/O address space. The reset state of this register is zero. This disables any access to the PCI Bus. The CONFIG_ADDRESS register serves as an index to one of 64 DWORDS within PCI configuration address space. In essence, the value in the CONFIG_ADDRESS register opens a 4-byte "window" through which data can be read or written via the CONFIG_DATA register on a byte, word, or dword boundary. Note that reads and writes to the CONFIG_ADDRESS register must be full DWORD I/O transactions. Non-DWORD transactions are treated as normal I/O accesses; consequently, they are not to be forwarded to PCI configuration address space. Figure 17-2 illustrates the layout of the CONFIG_ADDRESS Register.

> The Host/PCI bridge is required to return the actual data latched in the CONFIG_ADDRESS register whenever the Host CPU executes a dword I/O read of the register.

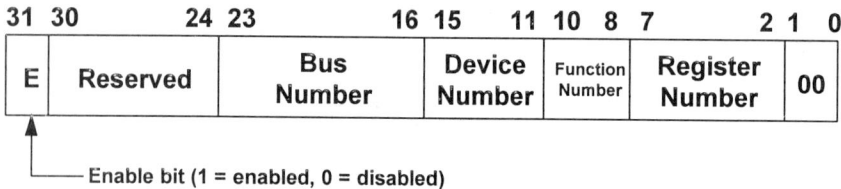

Figure 17-2: CONFIG_ADDRESS Register Layout

Bit	Definition
1::0	**Reserved** Non-zero values written to these bits by the Host CPU are ignored. The HOST /PCI bridge and PCI/PCI bridges use this field to differentiate the two access types. The devices behind the PCI bridge currently translating the configuration space access interpret this bit to determine if it is valid to claim the transaction. The definitions of a Type 0 and a Type 1 access configuration space transaction are as follows: Type 0 transaction — Indicates that the target of the transaction is a device connected to the bus behind the bridge currently translating the configuration space access. Any PCI device behind the bridge can claim the transaction. However, PCI/PCI bridges may only claim the transaction if their configuration space is being accessed. Type 1 transaction — Indicates that the target of the transaction is a device connected to another bus behind the bridge currently translating the configuration space access. Only PCI/PCI bridges may claim the transaction
7::2	**Register Number (encoded value)** Specifies which aligned DWORD to access in a target's configuration address space (1 of 64).
10::8	**Function Number (encoded value)** Specifies which function to access within the target device (1 of 8).
15::11	**Device Number (encoded value)** Specifies the target's PCI device number (1 of 32). This register's value is based on the access type as follows: Type 0 transaction — This field is decoded and 1 of 32 AD lines is asserted to select a unique device. Type 1 transaction — This field is mapped directly to AD[15::11].
23::16	**Bus Number (encoded value)** Specifies the target's bus number (1 of 256). Bus = 0 — The target of the configuration transaction is directly connected to the compatible Host/PCI bridge. Bus <>0 — The Host/PCI bridge generates a Type 1 configuration access transaction. The bus number is mapped directly to AD[23::16].
30::24	**Reserved** These bits are not ported to the AD lines. The bits must return zero when read.
31	**Configuration Space Access Enable Bit** Bit 31 is set by the Host CPU to activate the configuration access. The value in this bit is not ported to the AD lines. When set, any read or write of CONFIG_DATA register results in a PCI configuration access. The values this bit represents are: 0 Execute a standard I/O transaction on the PCI bus. 1 Translate subsequent Host Bus I/O access to the CONFIG_DATA register into a PCI configuration transaction on the PCI bus.

Table 17-1: CONFIG_ADDRESS Register Bit Definition

CONFIG_DATA REGISTER

The CONFIG_DATA register is a 32-bit read/write register. This register is located at location CFCh in I/O address space. The reset state of this register is zero. The CONFIG_ADDRESS register opens a "window" into PCI configuration address space through which one of 64 PCI configuration address registers can be accessed. The CONFIG_DATA register points to the register address specified by the CONFIG_ADDRESS. The CONFIG_DATA register is accessed to perform a byte, word or dword read or write transaction of the selected register. The Host/PCI bridge interprets the size of the transaction, byte, word or dword, using the Host bus byte enable signals. Figure 17-3 illustrates the layout of the CONFIG_DATA register.

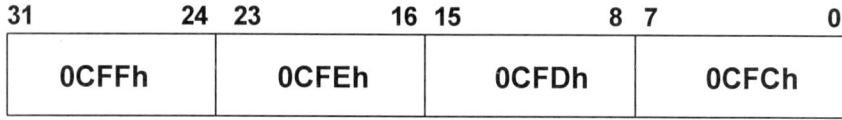

Figure 17-3: CONFIG_DATA Register Layout

CONFIGURATION MECHANISM #1 EXAMPLE

Assume that software wants to write byte 53h in function 04h of device 02h with a value of 23h on PCI bus 01h. This example shows the effects of the writes on the CONFIG_ADDRESS and CONFIG_DATA registers.

CF8h, CONFIG_ADDRESS is programmed using an I/O DWORD write with 80_01_14_53:

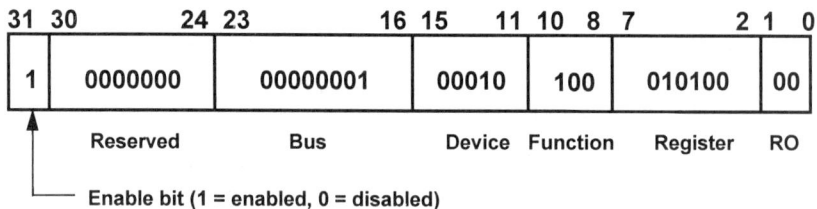

Figure 17-4-A: CONFIG_ADDRESS Register Example

Recall that the access type bits, bits zero and one, are ignored by the Host/PCI bridge. This automatically aligns the register value on a dword boundary. The value that is latched in the Host/PCI bridge is actually 80_01_14_50. When the the enable bit is set in the CONFIG_ADDRESS access to CFCh, the CONFIG_DATA register, is enabled. If the enable bit was not set the I/O space byte write to CFCh would be passed unchanged through the Host/PCI bridge as a normal I/O address space access.

When the the enable bit is set in the CONFIG_ADDRESS register, the register field selects a "window" to one of sixty-four dwords (aligned on a dword boundary) in a PCI target's configuration address space. In this example, registers 50h through 53h are made accessible. The Host bus byte enable signals indicate which byte(s) within the window to access. In this case the byte write to register 53h of the target requires that I/O address space byte CFFh is driven with the value 23h. Bytes CFCh, CFDh and CFEh are treated as don't cares

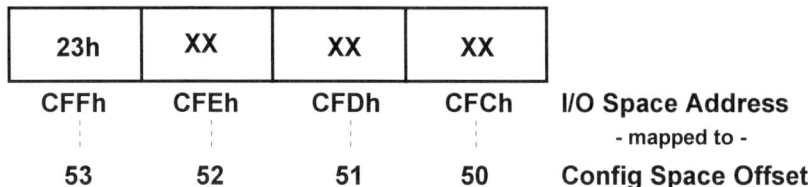

Figure 17-4-B: CONFIG_DATA Register Example

17.8 ACCESS TYPES

Two access types are defined for accessing PCI configuration address space. They are referred to as Type 0 and Type 1 accesses. These access types are defined specifically to support hierarchical PCI buses.

The bit definitions of Type 0 and Type 1 accesses follow in this section. Section 17-9 gives an example of a Type 0 access occurring using PCI Configuration Mechanism #1.

TYPE 0 ACCESS

When a PCI bridge receives a configuration address space transaction command, it must indicate to the devices on the PCI bus behind the bridge whether the access is intended for a device on that bus or for a device on another bus behind the bridge. The Type 0 access indicates that the target of the transaction is connected to the bridge currently translating the configuration space access. Figure 17-5 illustrates how a Host/PCI bridge translates a PCI configuration space address transaction from the Host CPU bus into a Type 0 access on a PCI bus 0.

> **If no device on the local bus claims the Type 0 configuration access, the cycle must terminate with a Master-Abort.**

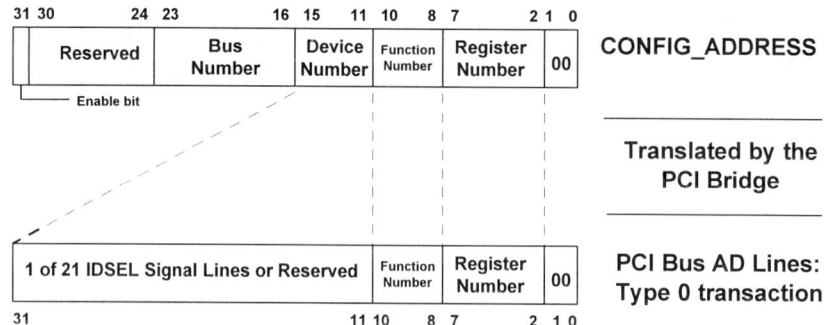

Figure 17-5: Type 0 Access Address Format

AD Bit	Definition
1::0	**Access Type (encoded value)** 00 - indicates that this is a Type 0 access. Type 0 accesses are not forwarded across PCI/PCI bridges. Any PCI device can claim a Type 0 access. However, a PCI/PCI bridge ignores a Type 0 access unless its configuration space is the target of the transaction.
7::2	**Register Number (encoded value)** Ported directly to AD[7::2]. Bits [7::2] specify which aligned DWORD to access in a target's configuration address space (1 of 64).
10::8	**Function Number (encoded value)** Ported directly to AD[10::8]. Bits [10::8] specify which function to access within the target device (1 of 8).
15::11	**Device Number (encoded value)** Each PCI device is connected to a single address line on the PCI bus via the device's IDSEL input pin. The PCI bridge asserts one IDSEL after decoding the Device Number value into the AD [31::11] signal lines. In this way, one of 21 targets on a single PCI bus can be chip selected. Note that AD[10::0] are not used as ID selects. This is because they are required to specify the access type, register and function number of the target. Only one IDSEL line can be asserted at a time. Note that there is no fixed correlation between IDSEL AD[31::11] signal lines and device numbers (per PCI Specification).

Table 17-2: Type 0 Access Address Register Bit Definition

1010

23::16	**Bus Number (encoded value)** Selects 1 of 256 geographically assigned busses to access. . This field is not required for a Type 0 access since the target PCI bus has been located. The AD lines that correspond to bits in this field are instead used as IDSEL (Initialization Device Select) signal lines. Note that the PCI bus number must be 00h for a Type 0 Host/PCI Bridge access transaction to be generated.
30::24	**Reserved** These bits are not ported to the AD lines. The bits must return zero when read. The AD lines that correspond to bits in this field are used as IDSEL (Initialization Device Select) signal lines during a Type 0 access.
31	**Configuration Space Access Enable Bit** Bit 31 is set by the Host CPU to activate the configuration access. The value in this bit is not ported to the AD lines. When set, any read/write of CONFIG_DATA register results the Host/PCI bridge generating a PCI configuration space access. AD[31] is used as an IDSEL (Initialization Device Select) signal line during a Type 0 access.

Table 17-2: Type 0 Access Address Register Bit Definition (continued)

TYPE 1 ACCESS

When a PCI bridge receives a configuration address space transaction command, it must indicate to the devices on the PCI bus behind the bridge whether the access is intended for a device on that bus or for a device on another bus behind the bridge. The Type 1 access indicates that the target of the transaction is a device connected to another bus behind the bridge currently translating the configuration space access.

Figure 17-6 illustrates how a Host/PCI bridge translates a PCI configuration space address transaction from the Host CPU bus into a Type 1 access on PCI bus 0. Note that a Type 1 access will be generated by all PCI/PCI bridges in the target's hierarchy until the PCI/PCI bridge connected to the target's bus is located. The PCI/PCI bridge with the target's bus will generate a Type 0 transaction so that the transaction can complete.

Only PCI/PCI bridges should claim a Type 1 configuration access. All other PCI devices should ignore the access.

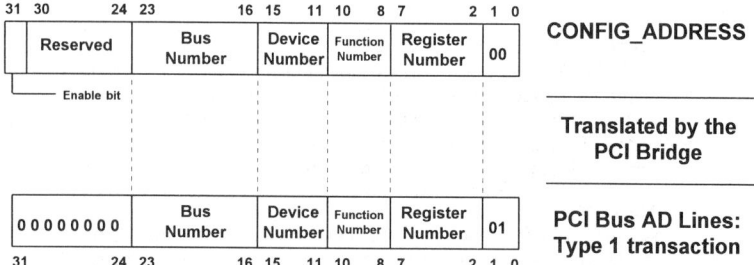

Figure 17-6: Type 1 Access Address Format

AD Bit	Definition
1::0	**Access Type (encoded value)** 01 - indicates that this is a Type 1 access. 00 is returned if these bits are read by the Host CPU when executing a read of I/O port address 0CFCh, the CONFIG_DATA register. PCI/PCI bridges are the only devices that can claim a Type 1 access. All other PCI devices ignore the access.
7::2	**Register Number (encoded value)** This value is ported directly to AD[7::2]. Bits [7::2] specify which aligned DWORD to access in a target's configuration address space (1 of 64).
10::8	**Function Number (encoded value)** This value is ported directly to AD[10::8]. Bits [10::8] specify which function to access within the target device (1 of 8).
15::11	**Device Number (encoded value)** Remember that the PCI bridge only decodes the Device Number into an IDSEL signal during a Type 0 access. In the Type 1 access, the encoded Device Number value is passed straight through the bridge to the AD lines of the bridge's secondary bus.
23::16	**Bus Number (encoded value)** These bits are ported directly to the AD[23::16]signal lines. They select 1 of 256 geographically assigned busses to access. Note that the bus number must be different from the PCI bridge's subordinate bus number in order for a Type 1 Host/PCI Bridge access transaction to be generated.
30::24	**Reserved** These bits are not ported to the AD lines. The bits must return zero when read. Bits [30::24] must be driven to a stable level in order to maintain parity. They contain no valid data.
31	**Configuration Space Access Enable Bit** The value in this bit is not ported to the AD lines. Bit 31 is set by the Host CPU to activate the configuration access. This bit is driven by the PCI bridge to a logical 0 during a Type 1 access. When set, any read/write of CONFIG_DATA register results the Host/PCI bridge generating a PCI configuration space access.

Table 17-3: Type 1 Access Address Register Bit Definition

17.9 CONFIGURATION SPACE ACCESS EXAMPLES

PCI configuration space transactions are initiated by software commands issued to the Host CPU. Depending on the hardware implementation, either a Configuration Mechanism #1 or Configuration Mechanism #2 is used by the Host/PCI bridge to translate the Host CPU Bus signals into a valid PCI configuration space transaction. The PCI bus on which the target resides determines whether the Host/PCI bridge generates a Type 0 or Type 1 access on PCI Bus 0. Remember that PCI Bus 0 is always connected to the compatible Host/PCI bridge. This section includes the following examples to illustrate the concepts of PCI configuration address space transactions:

- ■ **Target: Host/PCI Bridge Configuration Address Space**
- ■ **Target: Bus 00h PCI Device**

TARGET: HOST/PCI BRIDGE CONFIGURATION ADDRESS SPACE

Figure 17-7 illustrates a system implementation in which bus 00h is the only PCI bus in the system. PCI bus 00h is connected to the Host/PCI bridge. In this example, the PCI/Host bridge configuration address register 04h of function 0, device 0, is accessed with a write transaction. The data to be written to register four is 07h.

> This type of access constitutes a special case for most host bridges. Since the PCI configuration space address and data registers (0CF8h and 0CFCh) are integrated within the host bridge, the bridge can "capture" all Bus 00h/Device 00h accesses. The bridge is not required to forward these accesses to the physical PCI Bus 00h.

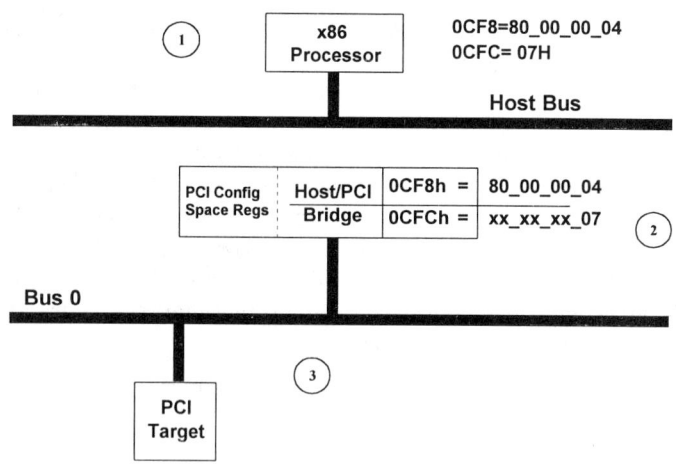

Figure 17-7: Target: Host/PCI Bridge

[1] Host CPU and Bus

1. The Host CPU generates two I/O address space transactions using Configuration Mechanism #1. The first transaction is an I/O write. A dword value is written to register 0CF8h, the CONFIG_ADDRESS register. This Host bus write transaction specifies the PCI bus is 00h, device is 0, function is 0, and the register to write to the PCI target's configuration address space is 04h.

2. The second transaction is an I/O write. A byte value is written to register 0CFCh, the CONFIG_DATA register. In this example the Host bus write transaction specifies a byte-wide value of 07h to be written into configuration space at offset 04h of the PCI/Host bridge. Note that the data written to the CONFIG_DATA register is not latched.

[2] Host/PCI Bridge

1. The Host/PCI bridge is required to latch all dword writes to the CONFIG_ADDRESS register. In this example, the Host/PCI bridge latches the value 80000004h. Bit 31, the configuration space enable bit, is set. This bit indicates that the Host/PCI bridge should translate the access into a configuration transaction The Host/PCI bridge decodes the values latched in the bus number field, AD bits [23::16], and device number field, AD bits [15::11]. The selected bus number is 00h. The device number is also 0. Because the Host/PCI bridge understands that it is device 0 and that bus 00h is its subordinate bus, as soon as the data is written to CONFIG_DATA, the HOST/PCI bridge permits the write of

the data, 07h in this example, to its own function 0 configuration space at offset 04h.

[3] PCI Bus 00h

1. Since the target of the configuration address space write is the Host/PCI bridge, it is not necessary for the Host/PCI bridge to generate a PCI configuration space access on PCI Bus 00h. If it does not, the IDSEL signal assigned to the Host/PCI bridge will never go active on PCI Bus 00h.

TARGET: BUS 00H PCI DEVICE

Figure 17-8 illustrates a system implementation in which bus 00h is the only PCI bus in the system. Bus 00h is connected to the Host/PCI bridge. The Host/PCI bridge is PCI device 0. Assume that the Host/PCI bridge is Device 0 and that its IDSEL input signal line is AD[16]. There are two PCI devices connected to Bus 00h. Device 1's IDSEL signal line is connected to AD[17]. Device 5's IDSEL signal line is connected to AD[21]. In this example, PCI Device 1's configuration address register 04h of function 0 is accessed with a read transaction. Refer to Figures 17-8 and 17-9 while reading about the address phase definition of this Type 0 access of PCI configuration space.

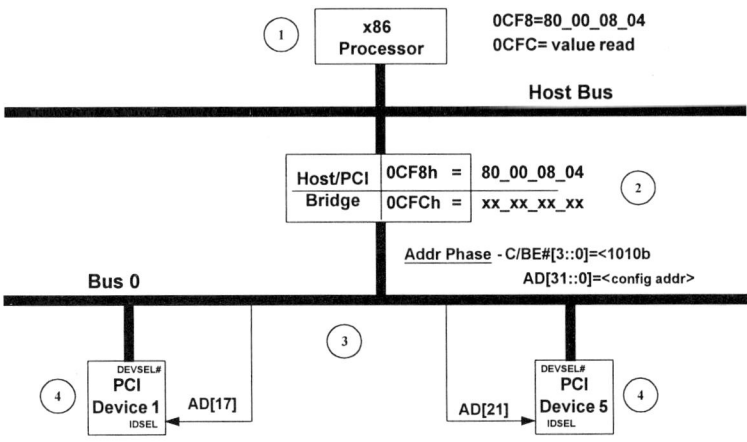

Figure 17-8: Target: Bus 00h PCI Device/Address Phase

[1] Host CPU

1. The Host CPU generates two I/O address space transactions using Configuration Mechanism #1. The first transaction is an I/O write. It is a dword value targeted for register 0CF8h, the CONFIG_ADDRESS

register. This Host CPU bus write transaction specifies PCI bus 00h, device 1, function 0, and register 04h.

2. The second transaction is an I/O read. A byte value read is targeted for register 0CFCh, the CONFIG_DATA register. In this example the Host bus read transaction specifies a byte-wide value of 04h to be read from function 0 of device 1's configuration space at offset 04h.

[2] Host/PCI Bridge: Address Phase

The Host/PCI bridge is required to latch all dword writes to the CONFIG_ADDRESS register. In this example, the Host/PCI bridge latches the value 80000804h. Bit 31, the configuration space enable bit, is set. This bit indicates that the Host/PCI bridge should translate the access into a configuration transaction on the PCI bus. The Host/PCI bridge decodes the values latched in the bus number field, AD bits [23::16], and device number field, AD bits [15::11]. The selected bus number is 00h. The device number is 1. Consequently, as soon as the data read is initiated using a byte I/O read command to CONFIG_DATA on the Host CPU bus, the HOST/PCI bridge generates a Type 0 access. See Figure 17-10 for a pictorial representation of the Type 0 access generated by the HOST/PCI bridge. At this point, the CONFIG_DATA register still contains invalid data for this transaction.

[3] PCI Bus 00h AD[31::0]: Address Phase

Note that all byte lanes and byte enables (C/BE#3::0) must be driven during the address phase. Otherwise, a parity error will occur.

Bits 1::0 Access Type

These bits are set to 00b by the Host/PCI bridge because AD bits [23::16], bus number, equaled zero.

Bits 7::2 Register Number

These bits select the aligned 32-bit dword (04h in this example) to access. The bits are ported directly to AD[7::2] on bus 00h.

Bits 10::8 Function Number

These bits select the PCI target's function 0 256-byte configuration address space. AD[10::8] on bus 00h.

Bits 31::11 Device Number translated to IDSEL

These bits select the PCI target. In this example, device 1 is the target of the configuration access. Its IDSEL input pin is connected to AD[17]. The Host/PCI bridge decodes the five bit device number field. The result of the decode is that 1 of the upper 21 AD[31::11] lines is asserted by the Host/PCI bridge. Remember that only one IDSEL line can be asserted at any given time during the address phase of a PCI configuration space transaction. The IDSEL signal is used as PCI device chip select during PCI read and write transactions.

> Note that the Bus Number field, AD[23::16], is no longer required when a PCI bridge generates a Type 0 access. The target bus has been identified by the bridge. This allows the bits to be freed up for use as IDSEL signal lines.

> Bit 31, the enable bit, was initially set by Host CPU to activate the configuration transaction. It is no longer required once the Host/PCI bridge initiates the transaction. This allows the bit 31 to be freed up for use as an IDSEL signal line.

C/BE#[3::0]: Address Phase

During the address phase the Host/PCI bridge asserts the C/BE#[3::0] command signals based on whether the access is a PCI configuration read or a write. In this example, C/BE#[3::0] is set 1010b to indicate a configuration read. If this were a configuration write the value would be 1011b.

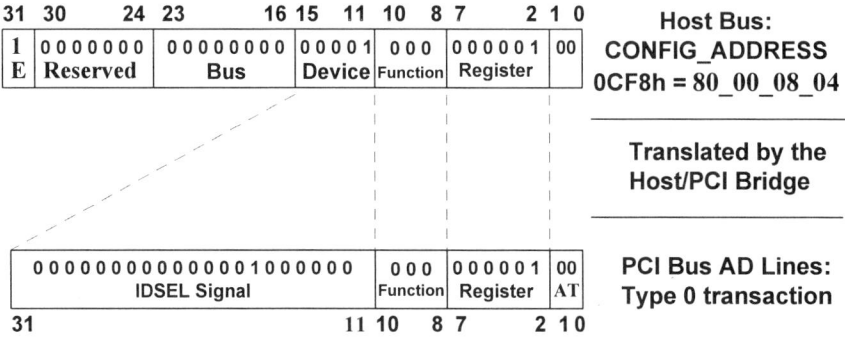

Figure 17-9: Type 0 Access on Bus 00h

> Note that because there are 32 address bus signal lines, there are 32 possible devices. However, in this implementation, there are only 21 address signal lines available for IDSEL chip select lines. In this example, the bridge will decode only 15 IDSELs, starting with PCI device 1 connected to AD[17]. The Host/PCI bridge consumes AD[16].

[4] PCI Device 1 and 5: Address Phase

1. Both PCI targets are required to latch the address during the address phase. This is because the address phase is only one PCI clock in duration. Because device 1 is selected, AD[17] only is asserted.

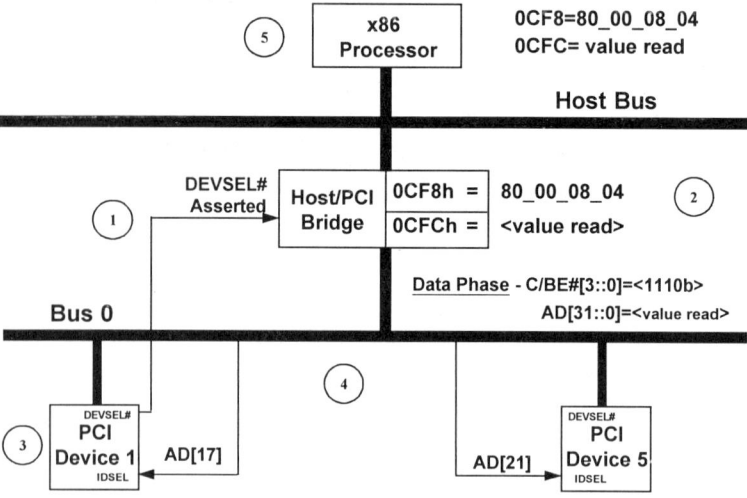

Figure 17-10: Target: Bus 00h PCI Device/Data Phase

Refer to Figure 17-10 while reading about the data phase definition of this Type 0 access of PCI configuration space.

[1] PCI Device 1 and 5: Data Phase

1. DEVSEL# is asserted by device 1 because its IDSEL line AD[17] is asserted. Device 1 has now claimed the configuration space transaction. Note that Device 5 ignores the transaction because its IDSEL line AD[21] is deasserted.

> It is typical for Bus Masters to assert all four byte enable lines (C/BE#[3::0] = 0000b) on a read access, regardless of the required byte enable(s) for the transfer.

[2] Host/PCI Bridge: Data Phase

1. During the data phase, after a device claims the transaction, the Host/PCI bridge asserts the C/BE#[3::0] byte enable signals to identify the valid byte lanes for the current transaction. It may use 1110b. In this example, this indicates that only the first byte within Device 1, Function 0, at offset 4 (even DWORD boundary) will be transferred.

> **Note that all byte lanes and byte enables (C/BE#[3::0]) must be driven to an asserted or deasserted state during the data phase. Otherwise, a parity error will occur.**

[3] PCI Device 1: Data Phase

1. Once the Host/PCI bridge asserts the required CBE#[3::0] byte enable signals device 1 responds by filling the byte lanes on the AD bus with the data obtained from device 1's configuration space.

[4] PCI Bus 00h AD[31::0]: Data Phase

1. The AD bus contains the data obtained from device 1's configuration space.

[5] Host CPU and Host/PCI Bridge: Data Phase

1. Once the Host/PCI Bridge and the Target complete the data phase transaction device 1 deasserts its DEVSEL# signal.

2. The value read from Device 1 is then read from the CONFIG_DATA register by the Host CPU, thus completing the entire transaction.

17.10   PCI-X AND CONFIGURATION ADDRESS SPACE TRANSACTIONS

Just as in conventional Type 0 PCI configuration address space transactions, PCI-X Type 0 transactions execute on a single bus segment. Type 0 transactions are not forwarded across a PCI-X bridge device. The following rules apply to PCI-X Type 0 configuration address space transactions:

■ Configuration address space transactions are required to include the target *device number* in AD[15:11] during the address phase of the transaction.

■ Configuration address space transactions are required to include the target *device bus number* in AD[7:0] during the attribute phase of the transaction.

■   A target of a Type 0 PCI-X configuration address space *write* transaction must store its *device number* and *bus number* in its internal registers.

Just as in conventional Type 1 PCI configuration address space transactions, PCI-X Type 1 transactions are forwarded across a PCI-X bridge device. The following rules apply to PCI-X Type 1 configuration address space transactions:

■   Type 1 PCI-X configuration address space transactions flow through the PCI bus hierarchy in the same manner as conventional PCI Type 1 transactions.

■   Type 1 transactions are ultimately converted to Type 0 transactions or Special Cycle transactions in the same manner as conventional PCI.

The PCI-X Status register contains two fields, one for recording the function's Device Number (bits [7::3]) and one for recording the function's Bus Number (bits [15::8]). Each PCI-X function is required to update these two fields each and every time the function is accessed with a PCI configuration address space write transaction. These registers are read-only and are read for diagnostic purposes only. After power-up (RST# asserted) all bits in these fields are set to '1'. After RST# is deasserted, system software forces the automatic initialization of these two fields during the PCI Bus enumeration process. After the enumeration process is complete, any subsequent change to the number assigned to a PCI bus segment operating in PCI-X mode requires that software executes a PCI configuration address space write transaction to each device on that bus to update these registers.

17.11   CHAPTER SUMMARY

In this chapter several important aspects of PCI configuration address space are discussed. The major features and functions are introduced. The format is presented. See Chapters 18 and 19 for complete definitions of the two Header Type structures defined for PCI configuration address space. Rules for reading and writing PCI configuration address space are also introduced in this chapter. The configuration mechanism that permits software to access a PCI device's configuration space is explained. The two different access types are also defined. Finally, examples describing at the bit level how configuration address space is accessed during the address and data phase of a transaction are included to give greater insight into the various aspects PCI configuration address space.

CHAPTER 18

PCI HEADER TYPE 00H

18.0 PCI HEADER TYPE 00H

The Type 00h PCI Configuration Space Header Region is the predefined header format for all PCI devices except PCI to PCI Bridges. A Type 00h PCI Configuration Space Header Region consists of 64 bytes. The first 16 bytes are the PCI Device Independent Region. The remaining 48 bytes are assigned to the PCI Device Header Type Region. Consequently, 64 bytes are assigned to the predefined PCI Configuration Space Header Region and 192 bytes to the Device Dependent region of the PCI configuration register space. For additional details about PCI configuration space device header types, refer to the description of the PCI Header Type register, found later in this section. In addition, refer to Table 18-1 and Figure 18-1 for pictorial representations of the Type 00h PCI Device Header Region.

> A Type 00h PCI Device Header Type Register (offset 0EH) specifies that the PCI Device Header Type Region consists of 48 bytes. When new header types are defined, they may specify fewer or more registers for this region.

Note that individual PCI devices need only implement the registers required to support their functionality. For example, some devices may not support an expansion ROM. Consequently, the Expansion ROM Base Address Register (DWORD at offset 30H), of the PCI Configuration Header Region is not implemented. In this case, the register is treated as reserved. As stated in Chapter 17, all bits in this register must be hardwired to zero.

The remainder of this section contains a description of each register in a Type 00h PCI Configuration Header region. Each register description contains the following:

- Name of the register
- Address location within the PCI device of the register
- Byte width of the register
- Read/Write attribute assigned to the register
- Valid value range of the register
- Register's global function definition
- Individual bit definitions of the register

Default values for each register are vendor and device specific and therefore are not specified.

Figure 18-1 is a pictorial view of the 64 byte register layout of Type 00h PCI Configuration Space Header. All PCI compliant devices that implement a Type 00h header must support this layout. Fields that utilize more than one byte in this structure follow little–endian ordering. For example, the least significant byte of the two-byte Vendor ID field is contained in the bottommost byte of the field.

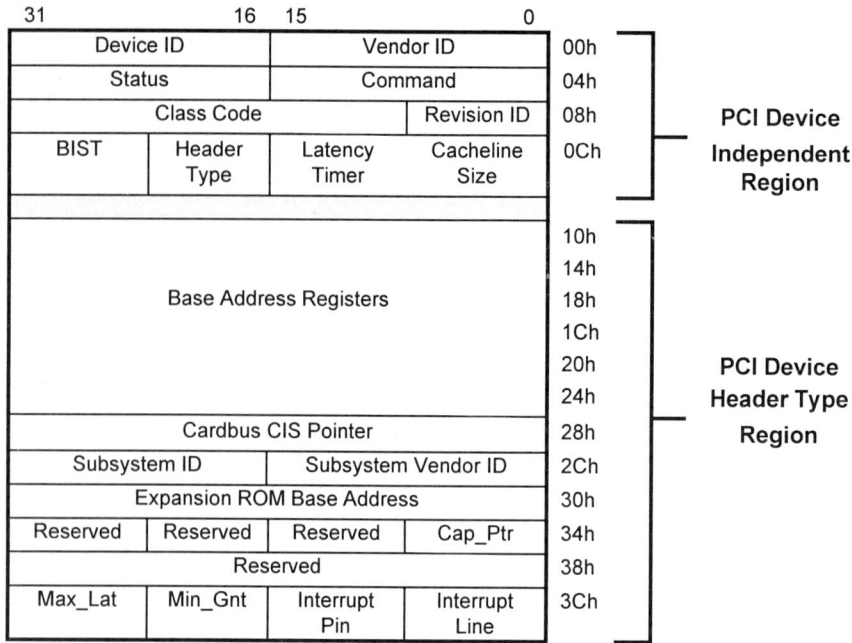

Figure 18-1: Type 00h PCI Configuration Space Header Region

For quick reference, Table 18-1 contains a list of the Type 00h PCI Configuration Space Header Region registers with their corresponding offset from the base of the structure.

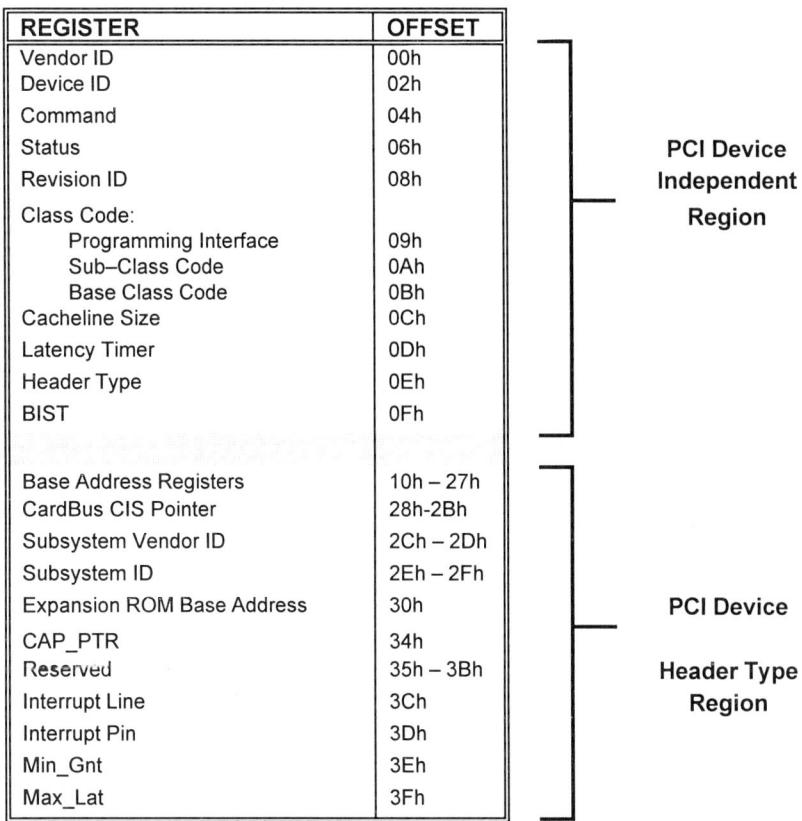

REGISTER	OFFSET	
Vendor ID	00h	
Device ID	02h	
Command	04h	
Status	06h	PCI Device
Revision ID	08h	Independent
Class Code:		Region
Programming Interface	09h	
Sub–Class Code	0Ah	
Base Class Code	0Bh	
Cacheline Size	0Ch	
Latency Timer	0Dh	
Header Type	0Eh	
BIST	0Fh	
Base Address Registers	10h – 27h	
CardBus CIS Pointer	28h-2Bh	
Subsystem Vendor ID	2Ch – 2Dh	
Subsystem ID	2Eh – 2Fh	
Expansion ROM Base Address	30h	PCI Device
CAP_PTR	34h	
Reserved	35h – 3Bh	Header Type
Interrupt Line	3Ch	Region
Interrupt Pin	3Dh	
Min_Gnt	3Eh	
Max_Lat	3Fh	

Table 18-1: Type 00h PCI Configuration Space Header Region

Vendor ID	
Offset:	00h
Width:	2 Bytes
Valid Values:	0000h–FFFEh
Description:	This register is used to identify the manufacturer of the device. The PCI Special Interest Group assigns vendor identifiers to ensure uniqueness. For example, a value of 8086h will always be read from the Vendor ID register of any PCI device manufactured by Intel Corporation.

Bit	Type	Function
15::0	RO	**Vendor ID** This register contains a unique 16 bit value assigned to each vendor. This number enables each PCI device's manufacturer to be uniquely identified.

Table 18-2: Vendor Identification Register

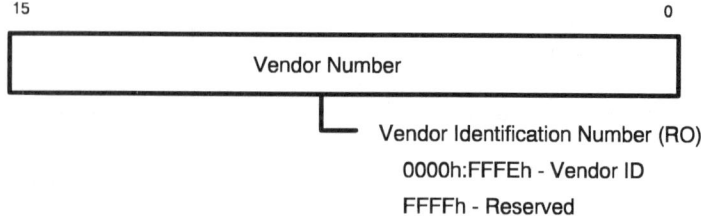

Figure 18-2: Vendor Identification Register

The platform hardware is responsible for ensuring that a value of FFFFh is returned when an attempt is made to read the vendor identifier of a non-existent PCI device. Consequently, the Vendor ID register is the one that should be used when attempting to determine whether a PCI device exists in a system. Because FFFFh is an invalid value for Vendor ID, that value will be returned only when no device is present.

Device ID	
Offset:	02h
Width:	2 Bytes
Valid Values:	0000h–FFFFh
Description:	This register identifies the device with a unique number. The value is assigned by the vendor of the device. 　　Vendors may choose to assign device IDs such that devices in one family that are backward compatible with earlier members of the family are easily recognized by software device drivers. For instance, assume a vendor built a SCSI device with some base functionality and assigned an identification number of 0AA0h to the device. Later the vendor develops the next generation part which has all the capabilities of the first part, but has extensions that make it perform better if they are used. The vendor assigned an identification number of 0AA1h to this device. A device driver for the original part would continue to work for the new part if the driver looked for an identification number of 0AAxh when trying to locate its device. The current device driver wouldn't take advantage of new features. However, the problem of immediately providing a new driver for the latest device would be solved.

Avoid assigning a Device ID of either 0000h or FFFFh, because zero indicates a Reserved Register and FFFF a *no response*.

Bit	Type	Function
15::0	RO	**Device ID** The value in this register is the PCI device identifier that is assigned by a vendor.

Table 18-3: Device Identification Register

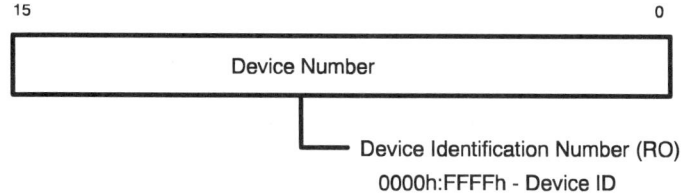

Device Identification Number (RO)
0000h:FFFFh - Device ID

Figure 18-3: Device Identification Register

Command	
Offset:	04h
Width:	2 Bytes
Valid Values:	N/A. This field is a collection of bits, not a range of values. The register should not be viewed as values, but as individual bits.
Description:	This register controls the device's ability to generate and respond to PCI bus accesses. Note that a value of zero in this register logically disconnects the device from the PCI bus.

> All PCI devices are required to respond to PCI configuration accesses, even when bits 2:0 of the command register are set to zero.

Bit	Type	Function
0	RW	**I/O Space Control** 0 Disables a device's response to I/O space accesses (**RST#** state). 1 Enables a device's response to I/O space accesses. This bit must be implemented if the device implicitly or explicitly requests I/O space.
1	RW	**Memory Space Control** 0 Disables a device's response to memory space accesses (**RST#** state). 1 Enables a device's response to memory space accesses. This bit must be implemented if the device implicitly or explicitly requests memory space.
2	RW	**Bus Master Control** 0 Disables a device's ability to generate PCI bus accesses (**RST#** state). 1 Enables a device's ability to generate PCI bus accesses. Any device that can be a master (*i.e.*, asserts FRAME#) must implement this bit.
3	RW	**Special Cycle Control** 0 Device ignores all Special Cycle operations (**RST#** state). 1 Device monitors Special Cycle operations. Devices that always ignore Special Cycle's are not required to implement this bit.
4	RW	**Memory Write and Invalidate Control** 0 Device will use Memory Write (**RST#** state). 1 Bus master devices can generate the Memory Write and Invalidate command. Devices that can never generate Memory Write and Invalidate commands are not required to implement this bit.

Table 18-4: Command Register

5	RW	**VGA Palette Snoop Control**
		0 Positively respond to write accesses to the palette registers. VGA compatible and graphics devices should initialize this bit to this state on RESET.
		1 Snoop write accesses to the palette registers. The device does not respond to palette register writes. Non–VGA graphics controllers that need palette information should initialize this bit to this state on RESET.
		This bit is required for VGA compatible devices. Other devices are not required to implement this bit. See Appendix C for details.
6	RW	**Parity Error Response**
		0 Device ignores detected parity errors (**RST#** state).
		1 Device responds to detected parity errors.
		1 Devices that implement parity checking are required to support this bit.
		2 Devices will generate parity even if parity checking is disabled.
		3 Any device that doesn't check parity (and as a result will never get a parity error) can hardwire the bit to zero.
7	RW	**Stepping Control**
		0 Disable ADDRESS/DATA STEPPING. Hardwire this bit to zero if ADDRESS/DATA STEPPING is not implemented.
		1 Enable ADDRESS/DATA STEPPING. Hardwire this bit to one if ADDRESS/DATA STEPPING is always performed.
		Bit 7 must be read/writeable if the device can either enable or disable ADDRESS/DATA STEPPING. The **RST#** state of this bit is one.
8	RW	**System Error Control**
		0 Disable the SERR# output driver (**RST#** state).
		1 Enable the SERR# output driver.
		1 Devices which implement SERR# must support this bit.
		2 This bit and bit 6 must be set to one to report address parity errors.
9	RW	**Fast Back–to–Back Control**
		0 Fast back–to–back transactions are only allowed to the same agent (**RST#** state).
		1 Enable fast back–to–back transactions.
		1 This bit is optional. It has the read/write attribute when implemented.
		2 Software (typically the System BIOS) may set this bit to one only if all targets are capable of fast back–to–back transactions.
15::10	RO	**Reserved**

Table 18-4: Command Register (continued)

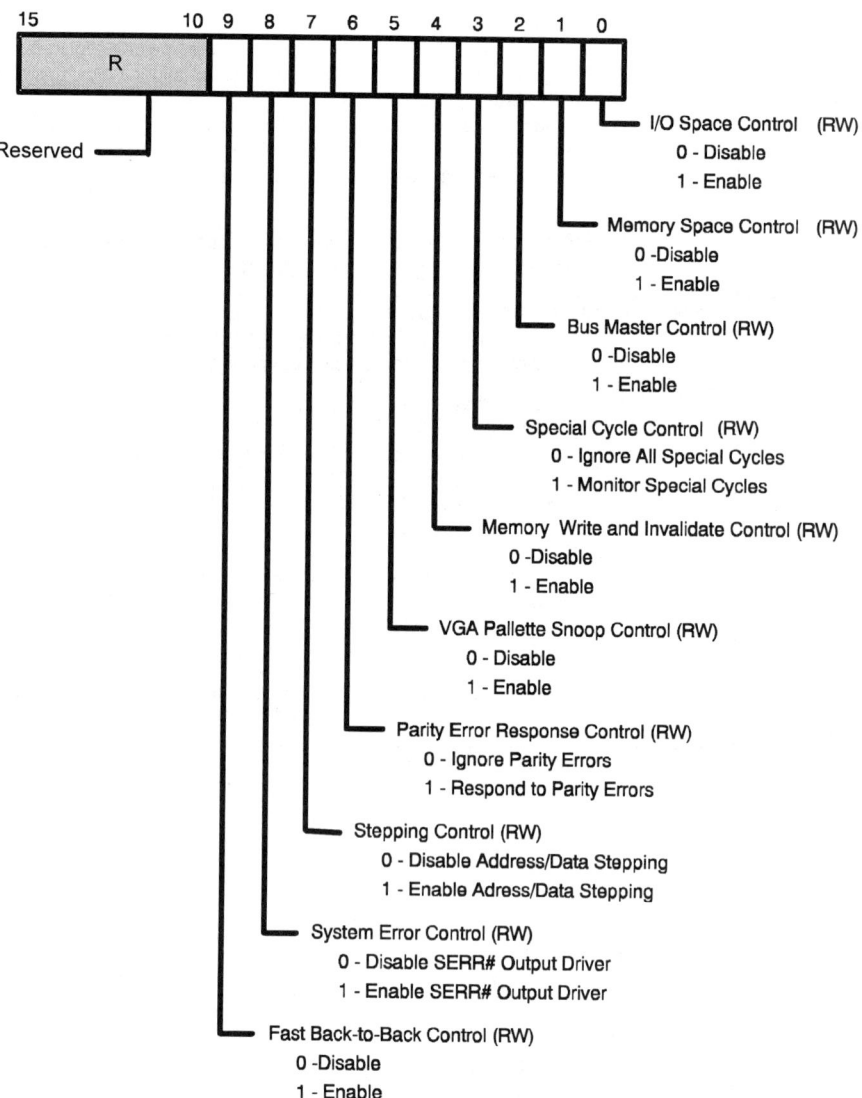

Figure 18-4: Command Register

PCI-X AND THE COMMAND REGISTER

PCI-X devices include the standard PCI configuration address space header. The registers in this header will function as specified in the *PCI Local Bus Specification, Revision 2.2*, when the device is running in conventional mode. The following apply to devices running in PCI-X mode:

■ Bit [9], Fast Back-to-Back Control, is ignored by the device in PCI-X mode.

■ Bit [7], Stepping Control, is ignored by the device in PCI-X mode.

■ Bit [4], Memory Write and Invalidate Control, is ignored by the device in PCI-X mode.

■ Bit [2], Bus Master Control, is ignored by the device in PCI-X mode when initiating Split Completions.

Status	
Offset:	06h
Width:	2 Bytes
Valid Values:	N/A. This field is a collection of bits, not a range of values. The register should not be viewed as values, but as individual bits.
Description:	This register records events that occur on the PCI bus. The following rules apply to this register:

1   Reads of this register occur normally.

2   Writes to this register may clear bits to zero but never set them to one.

3   There are several bits with the attribute type RWC in the Status Register Table below. These are individual bits that are cleared to zero if the bit has the write attribute and its bit location is written with a data value of one.

4   The function of the device determines which bits will be implemented.

The Status Register is typically not used by device drivers. Rather, it is intended to record events that (a) tend to be catastrophic and (b) are not part of normal operation.

System monitoring software can use the Status Register to determine precisely what happened if a catastrophic error occurs. In addition, the system monitoring software can keep statistics on PCI specific events.

Bit	Type	Function
3::0	RO	**Reserved**
4	RO	**Capabilities List** 0 This PCI function does not support PCI capabilities. 1 This PCI function supports PCI capabilities. See Chapter 24, *PCI Capabilities*, for more information.
5	RO	**66MHz Capable Status** 0 The device is capable of running at 33MHz. 1 The device is capable of running at 66MHz. This bit is optional.
6	RO	**User Definable Features Status** 0 The device does not support User Definable Features. 1 The device supports User Definable Features. This bit is optional. It must be set when a device function has device specific configuration selections that must be presented to the user. See Appendix B for a complete descripton of requirements for setting this bit. Bit 6 has been changed to a Reserved bit in PCI Specification 2.2.
7	RO	**Fast Back–to–Back Status** 0 The target is not capable accepting fast–back–to–back transactions that address different targets. 1 The target is capable accepting fast–back–to–back transactions that address different targets. This bit is optional.
8	RWC	**Master Data Parity Error** 0 No data parity errors have occurred. (**RST#** state). 1 All three of the following conditions must be met: a. **PERR#** was asserted by the bus master (on a read) or the bus master observed **PERR#** asserted (on a write). b. The agent which set the bit was the bus master during the transaction when the error occurred. c. Parity Error Response (bit 6 of the bus master's Command Register) is enabled. This bit is only implemented by Bus Masters.

Table 18-5: Status Register

Bit	Type	Function
10::9	RO	**Device Select Timing Status** 00 Device asserts DEVSEL# in the *fast* timing mode for any bus command. 01 Device asserts DEVSEL# in the *fast or medium* timing mode for any bus command. 10 Device asserts DEVSEL# in the *fast, medium, or slow* timing mode for any bus command. 11 Reserved. Configuration read and write cycles do not apply to the above definition. For example, if a device performs FAST decode for all memory and I/O accesses, but medium decode for configuration accesses, the device should set this register to fast.
11	RWC	**Signaled Target Abort Status** 0 Target device did not terminate a transaction with a Target Abort (**RST#** state). 1 Target device terminated a transaction with a Target Abort. Devices incapable of terminating a transaction with a target are not required to implement this bit.
12	RWC	**Received Target Abort Status** 0 A Target Abort did not terminate a bus master's transaction (**RST#** state). 1 A Target Abort terminated a bus master's transaction. All bus master devices are required to implement this bit.
13	RWC	**Received Master Abort Status** 0 A bus Master Abort did not terminate a transaction (**RST#** state). 1 Set by a bus master whose transaction was terminated by a bus Master Abort. 1 All bus master devices are required to implement this bit. 2 A Master Abort on a Special Cycle transaction should not cause this bit to be set.
14	RWC	**Signaled System Error Status** 0 Device did not generate a system error on the SERR# line. 1 Device generated a system error on the SERR# line. Devices which cannot assert SERR# are not required to implement this bit.
15	RWC	**Detected Parity Error Status** 0 Device did not detect a parity error (**RST#** state). 1 Device detected a parity error. Devices will set this bit regardless of the state of Parity Error Response (bit 6 of the Command Register).

Table 18-5: Status Register (continued)

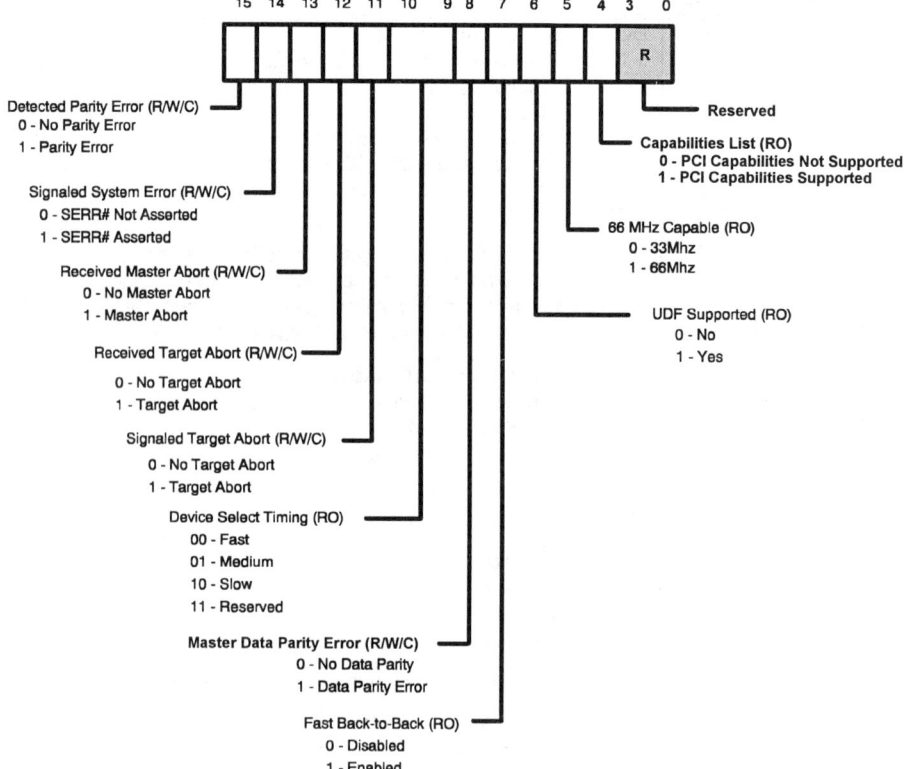

Figure 18-5: Status Register

PCI-X AND THE STATUS REGISTER

PCI-X devices include the standard PCI configuration address space header. The registers in this header will function as specified in the *PCI Local Bus Specification, Revision 2.2,* when the device is running in conventional mode. The following apply to devices running in PCI-X mode:

- Bit [4], **Capabilities List**, is always set to a value of '1' in all PCI-X mode capable devices. The reason for this is because the PCI-X Capabilities List item is always included in the PCI Capabilities Linked List. This bit is set to a value of '1' regardless of whether the device is operating in conventional mode or PCI-X mode.

- Bit [7], **Fast Back-to-Back Status**, can have any value when the device operates in PCI-X mode. The reason is because devices operating in PCI-X mode never use fast back-to-back timing, and thus will ignore this bit.

- Bit [8], **Master Data Parity Error**, is controlled under the same conditions as a conventional PCI device. However, the conditions under which this bit is set when the device is running in PCI-X mode are as follows:

  - When the **Initiator** (requestor or PCI-X bridge):

    - Of a completed read transaction immediately calculates a data parity error.

    - Of a read transaction that is terminated with a Split Response, calculates a data parity error in the Split Response.

    - Of a write that is completed, immediately observes PERR# asserted three clocks after one or more of its data phases.

    - Of a write that is terminated with Spit Response observes PERR# asserted three clocks after the data phase.

  - When the **Target** (requestor or PCI-X bridge):

    - Of a Split Completion calculates a data parity error in either read data or a Split Completion Message.

    - Receives a Split Completion Message that indicates a data parity error occurred on one of the device's non-posted write transactions.

- Bits [10::9], **Device Select (DEVSEL) Timing**, indicates the device's conventional mode DEVSEL# timing as specified in the PCI Local Bus Specification, Revision 2.2. This is regardless of whether the device is operating in PCI-X mode or conventional mode.

- Bit [15], **Detected Parity Error**, operates the same in PCI-X mode as it does in conventional mode. This bit is set by the device whose parity checking logic calculated the data parity error.

PCI-X DATA PARITY ERROR HANDLING

Systems that run in PCI-X mode have two options when it comes to recovering from errors. The first option is for PCI-X devices, device drivers, and system software that are designed to recover data parity errors. The second option is for devices and system software that are not designed to recover data parity errors. The second option requires the assertion of the **SERR#** signal line when an error occurs. Forcing a system to do one of the above eliminates the assumption that data parity errors are always a system wide catastrophic event.

DATA PARITY ERROR RECOVERY VIA SOFTWARE AND DEVICE CONTROL

PCI-X devices are allowed to recover from a data parity error only under the control of software. This is accomplished by the following actions:

- The **Data Parity Error Recovery Enable** bit, bit [0] of the **PCI-X Command** register, is set to '0' when **RST#** is asserted. In this state the device will assert **SERR#** when the PCI-X function's **Status** register **Master Data Parity Error** bit, bit [8], is set to '1'.

- The operating system loads a device driver that supports data parity error recovery.

- The device driver or system software sets the **Data Parity Error Recovery Enable** bit to '1' to enable the device to recover from a data parity error.

- The device driver sets the **Data Parity Error Recovery Enable** bit to '1'. This allows the device to attempt to recover from a data parity error under software control.

- During a transaction that results in a data parity error, the PCI-X device that set its **Master Data Parity Error** bit notifies its device controlling software of the error. The recovery software acts according to the error recovery requirements specified by the operating system vendor. For example, the recovery software could take one of the following actions in the event of a data parity error:

  - Take the device/card off line
  - Terminate system operation
  - Reschedule the failing transaction
  - Reinitialize the device/card and continue operation

> The operating system vendor is ultimately responsible for defining the complete paradigm for how the system recovers from data parity errors. As part of this paradigm, the operating system vendor is required to specify how device-controlling software such as a device driver responds to a data parity error. For example, the operating system could specify that it will completely handle the error, leaving the device controlling software with nothing to do. Alternatively, the operating system could require the device controlling software to take actions necessary for recovery.

SERR# AND DATA PARITY ERRORS

There are instances where PCI-X devices or system software are not capable of recovering from a data parity error. If a data parity error occurs under this circumstance the following must occur:

- The **Data Parity Error Recovery Enable** bit, bit [0] of the **PCI-X Command** register, is set to '0' when **RST#** is asserted. In this state the device will assert **SERR#** when the PCI-X function's **Status** register **Master Data Parity Error** bit, bit [8], is set to '1'. This bit is left in its default state.

- During a transaction that results in a data parity error, the PCI-X device sets its **Master Data Parity Error** bit.

- **SERR#** is asserted.

- A system-specific software program is invoked as a result of the **SERR#** assertion.

- Due to the catastrophic exception, the system-specific software program will attempt to gracefully halt the system.

Revision ID	
Offset:	08h
Width:	1 Byte
Valid Values:	00h–FFh
Description:	This register identifies the revision level of the device. The value is assigned by the vendor of the device. This register is typically used to indicate different steppings of the same device.

> **Plug and Play software does not use this field for device identification purposes. The System BIOS and device drivers can use this field to isolate code execution to particular revisions of the device.**

Bit	Type	Function
7::0	RO	**Revision ID** This value reflects the version level of the device.

Table 18-6: Revision Identification Register

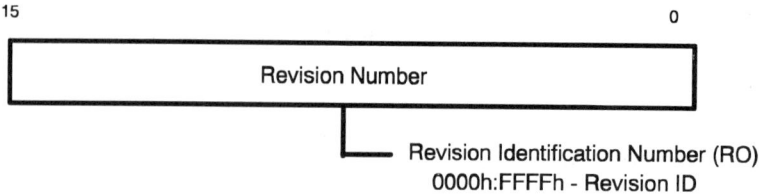

15   0

Revision Number

Revision Identification Number (RO)
0000h:FFFFh - Revision ID

Figure 18-6: Revision Identification Register

Class Code	
Offset:	09h
Width:	3 Bytes
Valid Values:	Programming Interface (09h): Base Class specific Sub–Class Code (0Ah): Base Class specific Base Class Code (0Bh): 00h–0Ch, FFh
Description:	This register identifies the generic function of the device and the register level programming interface of the device (if applicable to the class of the device). The figure below shows the current definitions for the Base Class field of this register. **See Appendix A for a complete definition of this register.**

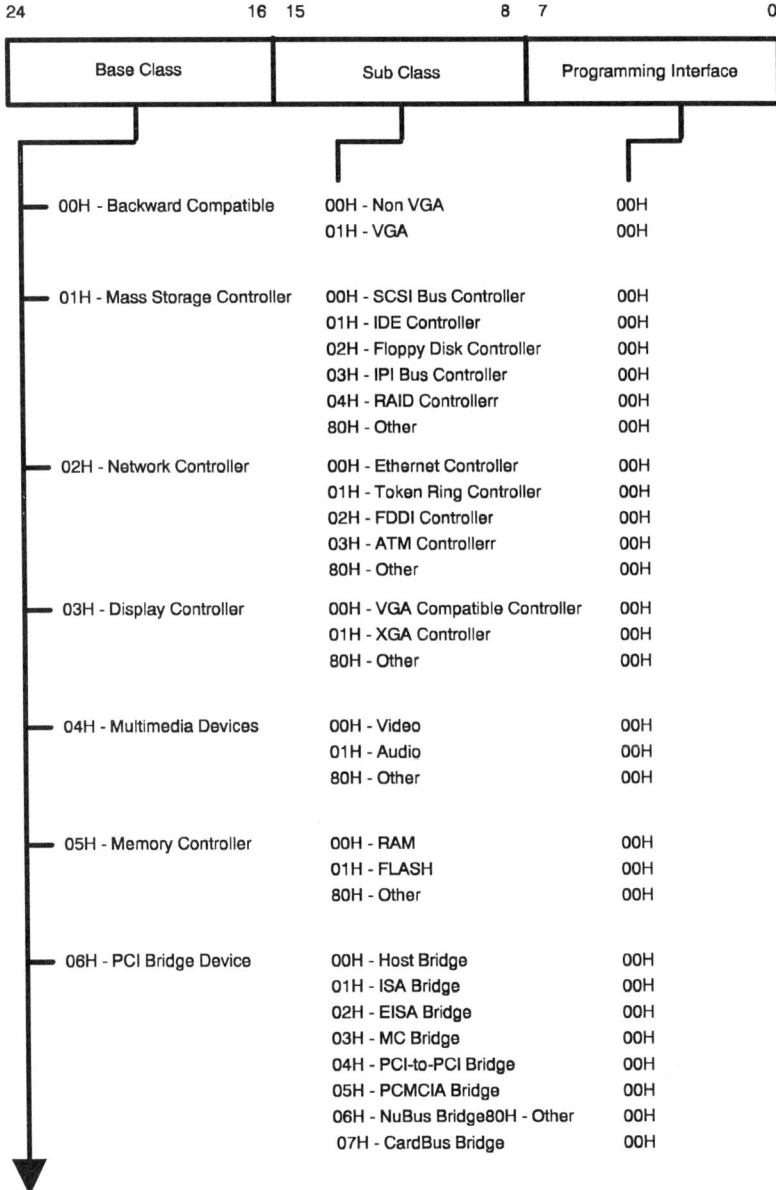

Figure 18-7: Class Code Register

Note: See Appendix A for a more up-to-date and complete definition of the defined register.

1037

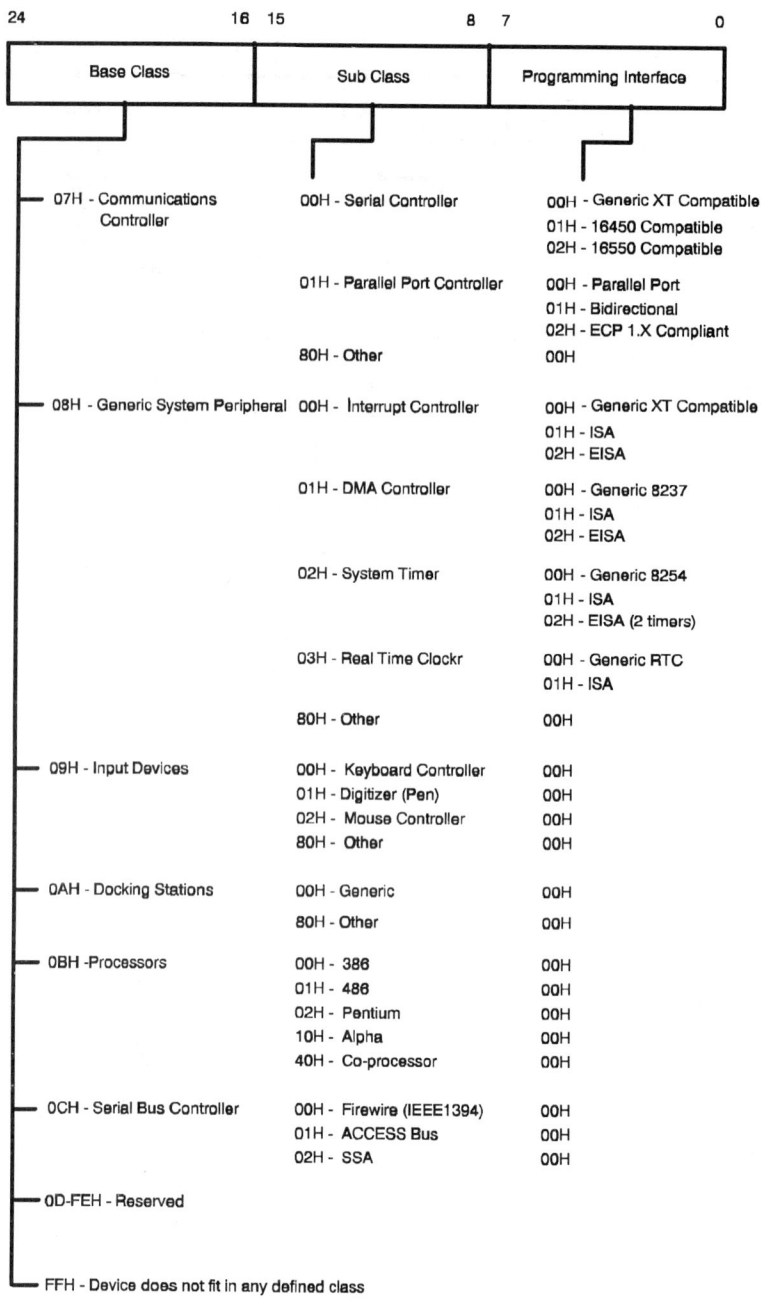

Figure 18-7: Class Code Register (continued)

Note: See Appendix A for a more up-to-date and complete definition of the defined register.

Cacheline Size	
Offset:	0Ch
Width:	1 Byte
Valid Values:	0000h–FFFFh
Description:	This register specifies the cacheline size in units of DWORDs.
	Bus master devices must support this register if the PCI function can generate a Memory Write and Invalidate command. In addition, bus masters use this register's contents to determine which command (Read, Read Line or Read Multiple) to use to access memory.
	Slave devices must support this register if the PCI function allows memory bursting using cacheline wrap addressing mode. This permits the function to detect when a burst sequence wraps to the beginning of the cacheline.
	A value of zero indicates that the system cache (if it exists) is not caching the device's memory.

Bit	Type	Function
7::0	RW	**Cacheline Size**
		00h – Memory target is configured as non-cacheable.
		01H:0FFh – Cacheline size value in DWORDs.
		Slave devices must support this register if the PCI function allows memory bursting using cacheline wrap addressing mode. This permits the function to detect when a burst sequence wraps to the beginning of the cacheline.
		A value of zero indicates that the system cache (if it exists) is not caching the device's memory.
		1 Bus Masters that generate the Memory Write and Invalidate command are required to implement this register.
		2 Devices that provide cacheable memory are required to implement this register.
		3 The number of cachelines supported by a given PCI function is determined by the PCI device's design. The PCI function should behave as if a value of '0' were written to the Cacheline Size register whenever unsupported values are written to the register.

Table 18-8: Cacheline Size Register

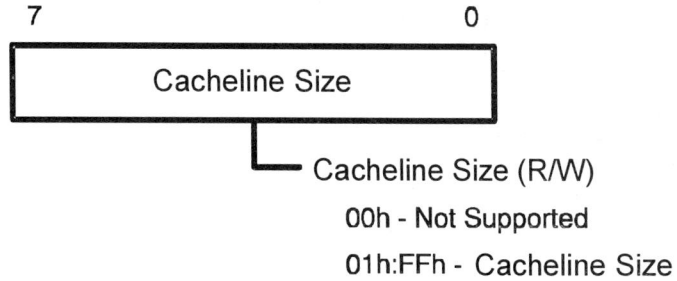

Figure 18-8: Cacheline Size Register

PCI-X AND THE CACHELINE SIZE REGISTER

This register is optional for devices that run in PCI-X mode. If it is implemented, the register must comply with the **Cacheline Size** register implementation and programming requirements as specified in the *PCI Local Bus Local Bus Specification, Revision 2.2*.

> The Cacheline Size register can be used to aid in the optimization of cache operations for a PCI-X function that bursts data to system memory. The function should align the start of the transaction to the beginning of a cacheline and ensure that the length of the transaction is a multiple of the value contained in the Cacheline Size register.

Latency Timer	
Offset:	0DH
Width:	1 Byte
Valid Values:	00h–FFh
Description:	This register specifies the Master Latency Timer value for a PCI Master when the device is on the PCI bus.
	A reasonable implementation of this register is to only implement the top five bits. This means that field can only be modified in increments of 8, but this is acceptable.
	A typical way for a System BIOS to configure this register is to just choose an appropriate value and use that value for all devices. 32 (approximately 1 μsec) is a reasonable value. Higher level software, *i.e.*, an OS heuristic, can use the knowledge of how the system is being used (server, desktop, multimedia) as well as MIN_GNT and MAX_LAT values to adjust the timers appropriately.

Bit	Function
7::0	**Read Only Implementation:** Bus Masters incapable of bursting for more than two DATA PHASES may implement this register with a Read Only attribute. The register must contain a fixed value of 16 or less. **Read/Write Implementation:** Bus Masters capable of bursting for more than two DATA PHASES must implement this register with a Read/Write attribute. **RST#** should clear this register.

Table 18-9: Latency Timer Register

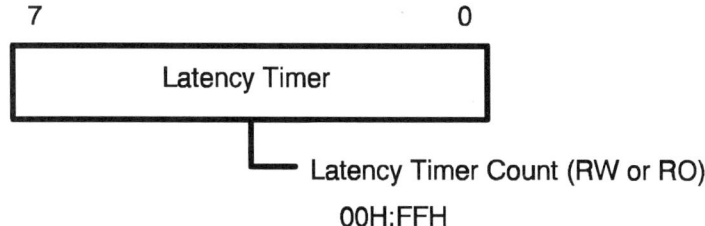

Figure 18-9: Latency Timer Size Register

PCI-X AND THE LATENCY TIMER REGISTER

PCI-X devices include the standard PCI configuration address space header. The registers in this header will function as specified in the *PCI Local Bus Specification, Revision 2.2*, when the device is running in conventional mode. The following apply to devices running in PCI-X mode:

- Initiators running in PCI-X mode have a Latency Timer default value of 64 for devices that adhere to either the Type 00h or Type 01h configuration address space header types. The Latency Timer default value for conventional mode PCI devices is 00h.

- The initiator's Latency Timer register is loaded with the preset value each time the initiator starts a new transaction.

- After the preset value is loaded, the Latency Timer counts down the number of clocks that FRAME# is asserted.

- Initiators are required to disconnect the current transaction as soon as possible if GNT# is deasserted and the Latency Timer expires.

> The *PCI-X Addendum to the PCI Local Bus Specification, Revision 1.0a*, strongly recommends that the PCI-X default value for the Latency Timer not be changed. The authors feel this is the optimum setting to ensure good bus efficiency, effective sharing of the bus, and practical arbitration latencies in the majority of cases.

Header Type	
Offset:	0Eh
Width:	1 Byte
Valid Values:	00h or 80h
Description:	This register identifies the layout of bytes beginning at offset 10h in the PCI configuration space. In addition, this register specifies whether the device is a single or multi–function device. Configuration software such as a System BIOS should validate this register's value prior to doing anything with the device.

> **If configuration software finds a header type that it does not know about, it should disable the device. This is done by setting the bottom three bits in the Command Register to zero. Leave the device alone once this is done.**

Bit	Type	Function
6::0	RO	**Header Layout Code** 000000B Device supports the layout of configuration registers 10h through 3Fh as defined in Figure 18-1. 000001B Device supports the layout of PCI to PCI Bridge configuration registers 10h through 3Fh as defined in Figure 19-1. 000010B Device supports the layout of a PCI Cardbus bridge. 03h-7Fh Reserved.
7	RO	**Multi–Function Status** 0 Device has one function. 1 Device contains between two and eight functions.

Table 18-10: Header Type Register

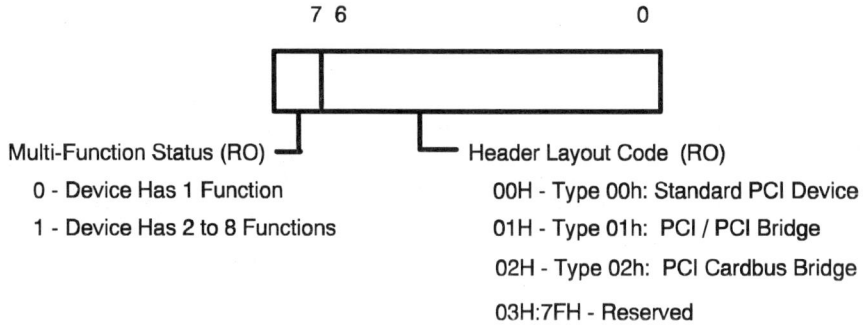

Figure 18-10: Header Type Register

BIST (Built–In Self Test)	
Offset:	0Fh
Width:	1 Byte
Valid Values:	Device dependent. See description below.
Description:	This register is used to control the invocation of a PCI device's BIST and to report the status of the BIST. Devices that do not support BIST must return a value of 00h when this register is read.

> POST code may choose to run a device's BIST at cold boot. When a device is running its BIST it should not generate any cycles to the PCI bus.

Bit	Type	Function
3::0	RO	**BIST Completion Status**
		00h Device test passed.
		01h:0Fh Device test failed. Vendors may define up to 15 device specific failure codes in these bits.
5::4	RO	**Reserved**
		Device must return zero in these two bit fields.
6	RW	**BIST Start Control Bit**
		0 Device resets this bit after BIST completes.
		1 Invoke the device's BIST. Software should fail the device if this bit is not RESET to zero within two seconds after the BIST is invoked.
		Hard code this bit to 0, RO, if BIST is not implemented.
7	RO	**BIST Support Status**
		0 Device does not support BIST.
		1 Device supports BIST.

Table 18-11: BIST Register

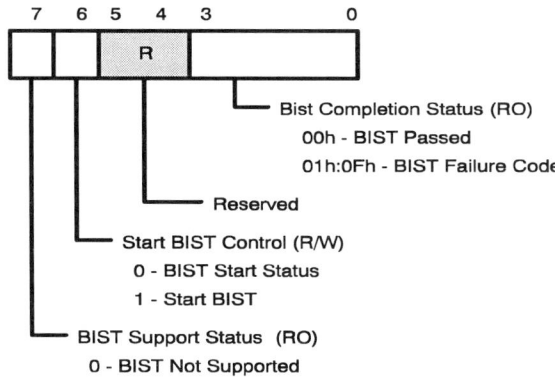

Figure 18-11: BIST Register

I/O and Memory Base Address Registers	
Offset:	10h (first register location)
Width:	I/O: 32 bit word length
	Memory: 32 bit or 64 bit word length
Valid Values:	Device dependent
Description:	This register set allows a PCI device's I/O and memory functions to be dynamically mapped into a system's memory and I/O address spaces. Depending on the system implementation, this dynamic mapping may be accomplished by the System ROM BIOS during POST or later by other system software such as a device driver or operating system.
	PCI devices with a Type 00h configuration space header contain twenty–four bytes dedicated for memory and I/O base address assignments. Because the first base address register location is 10h, the second base address register may either be located at 14h or 18h. The offset location of the any base address register other than zero depends on the size of the previous one. In other words, the word length of preceding base address register determines the offset addresses of the remaining base address registers.
	PCI devices with a Type 01h configuration space header contain 8 bytes dedicated for memory and I/O base address. The rules stated in the previous paragraph also apply to devices with Type 01h configuration space Headers.

> Note that there is no specification for the order in which registers request blocks of I/O or memory. Any combination is permissible. For example, a device may request a block of memory followed by a request for two blocks of I/O, followed by another request for a block of memory.
>
> There may also be gaps in the register implementations. For instance, in a Type 00h configuration space header a device may implement a register at offset 10h, leave the registers at offsets 14h and 18h unimplemented, and implement another register at offset 1Ch.
>
> These registers do not provide a mechanism that allows the device to request specific addresses in the address space.
>
> PCI devices should always allow control functions to be mapped into memory space.

I/O BASE ADDRESS IMPLEMENTATION

For I/O base address registers, there are two ways to decrease the number of bits in the address decoder. The first method is to claim more address space than is actually needed. For example, a device that has 16 bytes of registers may decide to claim 128 bytes of address space, thus saving three bits in the decoder.

The second way to decrease the number of bits in the address decoder is to take advantage of the Intel x86 architecture. This architecture only has a 64K I/O space. Hence, there is no need to implement the top 16 bits of the 32 bit I/O base register. These bits can be hardwired to zero. However, a full 32 bit decode must still be performed. Note that the decode for the top 16 bits can be accomplished using a simple NAND gate.

The first method should be avoided since I/O space is typically tight. In no case should a PCI device designed to operate in a ISA compatible system request more than 256 bytes of I/O space per each I/O base address register. The major reason is the ISA aliasing issue, which is discussed in Appendices D and E.

To assign a value to an I/O base address register, software should do the following:

1. Write a value of 1 to all bits within this register.

2. Confirm that bit 0 of this register contains a value of 1, indicating an I/O request.

3. Starting at bit location 2, search for the first bit set to a value of 1. This bit is the binary weighted size of the total contiguous block of I/O address space requested. For example, if bit 8 is the first bit set, the device is requesting a 256 byte block of I/O address space.

4. Write the start address of the I/O space block assigned to this register.

Bit	Type	Function
0	RO	**Address Space Indicator** 0 N/A for I/O—see Memory Base Address Implementation. 1 Base address register is requesting I/O space.
1	RO	**Reserved** This bit must return zero when read.
31::2	RW	**I/O Base Address** Start address of an I/O space region assigned to this device.

Table 18-12: I/O Base Address Register

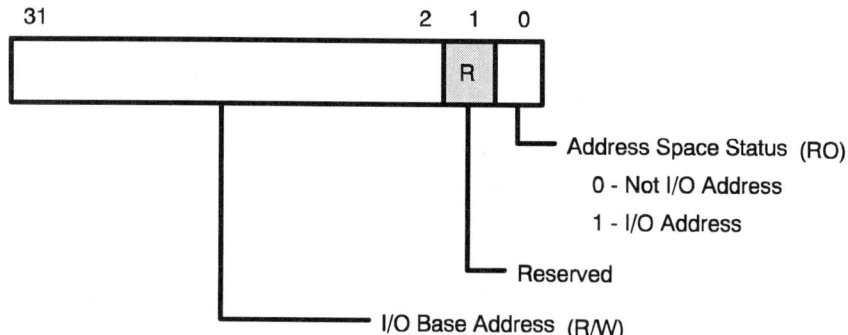

Figure 18-12: I/O Base Address Register

MEMORY BASE ADDRESS IMPLEMENTATION

Memory base address decoders can decrease the number of address bits by claiming more space than is needed. Hardwiring upper order address bits is not allowed (unless the device is requesting space at an address below one megabyte - see the definition for Base Address Memory Type bits in Table 18-13).

To assign a value to a memory base address register software should do the following:

1. Write a value of 1 to all bits within this register.

2. Confirm that bit 0 of this register contains a value of 0, indicating a memory request.

3. Starting at bit location 4, search upwards for the first bit set to a value of 1. This bit is the binary weighted size of the total contiguous block of memory requested. For example, if bit 15 is the first bit set, the device is requesting a 32 kilobyte block of memory.

4. Write the start address of the memory block assigned to this register. This memory address region must not conflict with any other memory space utilized within the system. In addition, it must comply with the definition contained in bits 1 and 2 of this register.

Bit	Type	Function
0	RO	**Address Space Indicator** 0 Base address register is requesting memory space. 1 N/A for Memory—see I/O Base ADDRESS Implementation.
2::1	RO	**Memory Type** 00 Base address is 32 bits wide. Set the base address anywhere within the 32 bit memory space. 01 Base address is 32 bits wide. Set the base address below 1Mb in memory space. The upper 12 bits in this register can be hardwired to zero, but must still participate in address decode. Configuration software must handle this case. 10 Base address is 64 bits wide. Set the base address anywhere within the 64 bit memory space. 11 Reserved.
3	RO	**Prefetchable** 0 Memory is not prefetchable. 1 A device can mark its memory range as prefetchable if the following conditions are met: 1 The device returns all bytes on reads regardless of the byte enables. 2 Reads to this memory space create no side effects. 3 Host BRIDGEs can merge CPU writes (i.e. take multiple byte and/or word accesses from the CPU and merge them into single DWORD writes on PCI) into this range without errors. Linear frame buffers on graphics devices are an example of prefetchable memory. They behave like system memory. However, linear frame buffers do not participate in PCI's caching protocol. Host BRIDGEs can make performance optimizations on memory ranges that support prefetching.
31::4	RW	**32–Bit Memory Base Address** 32 bit start address of a memory space region assigned to this device. Bits 2:1 must be set to a value of either 00 or 01.
63::4	RW	**64–Bit Memory Base Address** 64 bit start address of a memory space region assigned to this device. Bits 2:1 must be set to a value of 10.

Table 18-13: Memory Base Address Register

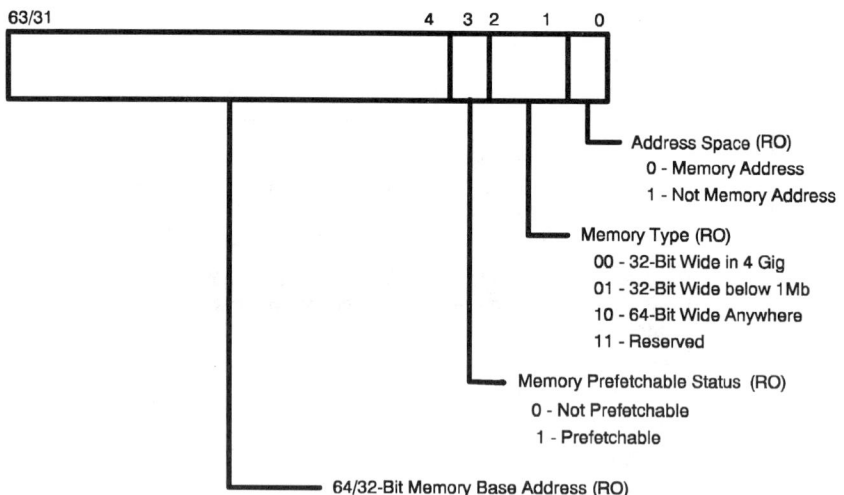

Figure 18-13: Memory Base Address Register

MEMORY AND I/O BASE ADDRESS REGISTER GUIDELINES

Power-up system software such as the PC/AT compatible System BIOS is responsible for initializing memory and I/O base address registers with system resources in a resource conflict free manner. However, depending on the system configuration, certain system resources (most likely I/O) may be depleted before all base address registers have been initialized. Base address registers that do not get a system resource assigned will be initialized with a value zero. In addition, depending on the type of resource that failed to be assigned, the associated memory or I/O control bit in the PCI function's Command Register will be set to disabled (zero). Note that some System BIOS vendors go as far as to reset the I/O, Memory, and Bus Master control bits in a device's Command Register (bits 2::0) when any memory or I/O allocation failure occurs. This gives device specific software two quick methods for determining what memory and I/O system resource allocations failed for their device.

Device specific executables such as device drivers and add-in card BIOSs should never assign system resources to their device. System resource conflicts could result, rendering the system inoperable. Allocating system resources is the task of power-up system software and operating systems.

When a resource allocation fails for a given PCI device, the power-up system software should attempt to allocate memory and I/O system resources to the remaining base address registers that have requested resources. This permits PCI devices that map their control functions into both memory and I/O to use the space that was successfully assigned. The other space should remain disabled and unused.

> **The Command Register control bit for either the memory or I/O address space that is disabled by the power-up system software or an operating system should not be enabled by device specific software. This could result in system resource conflicts, depending on the programmed values of the control bits associated base address registers.**

If a device uses the "claim more than needed" technique for minimizing decoder bits (in either memory or I/O), there is no requirement for how the device should behave if it is accessed in the "unused" portion of a claimed range. As an example, take a device that has 256 bytes of registers mapped to memory but claims 4K of memory space. When software accesses any of the 256 bytes, the device is expected to respond appropriately for those bytes. Accesses to any other part of the 4K range can behave anyway the device finds appropriate. For instance, it may be easiest to alias the 256 bytes throughout the 4K range. Another possibility is to just return garbage whenever the "unused" portion is accessed.

PCI-X AND THE BASE ADDRESS REGISTERS

The following rules apply to I/O ranges assigned through base address registers:

- PCI-X devices are discouraged from using I/O address space.
- As with conventional PCI, I/O ranges are always assigned via 32-bit based address registers.
- If the device uses a base address register to request a range of I/O address space, it is required to also use another base address register to request memory address space mapped to the same resource.

> **System configuration software will only assign memory address space resources to the device when the requested I/O space is not available.**

The following rules apply to memory address ranges assigned through base address registers:

- All assigned memory address ranges must be unique for each PCI function in the system.

1049

■   Each assigned memory address range must be aligned to a unique ADB.

■   All requested and assigned memory address ranges must be 128 bytes or larger.

■   Except for **Expansion ROM Base Address** registers, all functions that incorporate memory base address registers are required to support 64-bit addressing, as defined in the *PCI Local Bus Local Bus Specification, Revision 2.2.*

PCI-X devices typically set the Prefetchable bit in memory base address registers. Exceptions are when the PCI function does not work with write merging or if the assigned memory range includes addresses with read side effects.

CardBus CIS Pointer

Offset:	28h
Width:	4 Bytes
Valid Values:	See Below
Description:	This register is optional. It is also read-only.

This register is used by devices that want to share silicon between CardBus and PCI. CardBus cards use the Card Information Structure (CIS). This structure contains specific information about the card. The information contained in this register identifies the location of the CIS start address in the system.

The Card Information Structure can be located in one of the following address spaces:

Configuration Space
The CIS must be located in the device dependent region of the PCI device; that is, after the PCI device's predefined header.
Memory Space
The CIS can be accessed using the value of one of the memory Base Address registers.
Expansion ROM
The CIS is stored in an expansion ROM image.

Each configuration space of a multi-function card must have its own CIS. The CIS will be pointed to by the CIS Pointer located in its own configuration space.

Bit	Type	Function
31::3	RO	**Address Space Offset Value** This value specifies the offset into the address space indicated by the Address Space Indicator field at which the CIS begins.

Space Indicator	Address Space Offset Value
0	The CIS start address is located in PCI device dependent configuration address space. This address space offset is stored in bits [31:3] of the CardBus CIS Pointer register. See Figure 18-14A.
1 thru 6	The CIS start address is located in the system memory address space addressable by the selected Base Address Register. Add the value in bits [31::3] of this register to the value programmed into the selected Base Address Register to obtain the CIS start address. See Figure 18-14A.
7	To obtain the start address of the CIS within the expansion ROM, do the following: 1. Obtain the ROM image number from bits [31::28]. 2. Starting at ROM image 0, located at Address Space Offset (bits [27::3] value + 0h), scan the expansion ROM until the start of the ROM image number specified in bits [31::28] is reached. See Section 23.3 for information on how to scan a PCI Expansion BIOS. PCI expansion ROMS may contain multiple images. Bits [31:28] of CardBus CIS Pointer register contain the image number within the expansion ROM that contains the CIS. Valid values are: 00h <= image <= 0Fh To obtain the start address of the CIS within the ROM, add the value programmed into the expansion ROM Base Address register with the offset of the expansion ROM image and the value contained in bits [27::3]. See Figure 18-14B.

Table 18-14: CardBus CIS Pointer Register

2::0	RO	**Address Space Indicator**
		This 3-bit field identifies the address space in which the Card Information Structure is located.
		0 The Card Information Structure resides in device-dependent PCI configuration space.
		1 The Card Information Structure resides in the memory space addressed by the Memory Base Address register located at offset 10h in the predefined header.
		2 The Card Information Structure resides in the memory space addressed by the Memory Base Address register located at offset 14h in the predefined header.
		3 The Card Information Structure resides in the memory space addressed by the Memory Base Address register located at offset 18h in the predefined header.
		4 The Card Information Structure resides in the memory space addressed by the Memory Base Address register located at offset 1Ch in the predefined header.
		5 The Card Information Structure resides in the memory space addressed by the Memory Base Address register located at offset 20h in the predefined header.
		6 The Card Information Structure resides in the memory space addressed by the Memory Base Address register located at offset 24h in the predefined header.
		7 The Card Information Structure resides in an expansion ROM.

Table 18-14: CardBus CIS Pointer Register (continued)

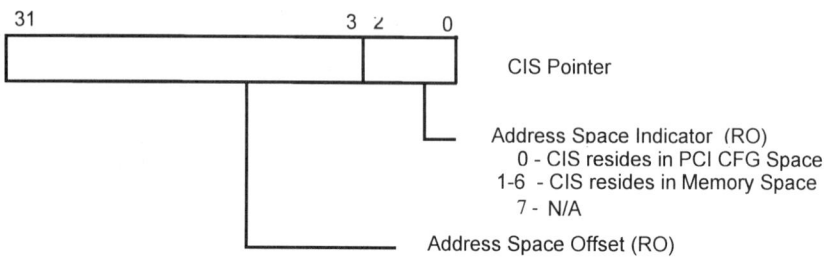

Figure 18-14A: CardBus CIS Pointer Register - Memory/PCI CFG Space Based

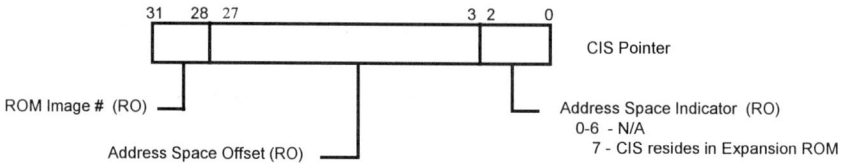

Figure 18-14B: CardBus CIS Pointer Register - ROM Based

Expansion ROM Base Address Register

Offset:	30h
Width:	4 Bytes
Valid Values:	Device dependent
Description:	This register allows a PCI device's expansion ROM to be mapped into a system's physical address space. Depending on the system implementation, this dynamic mapping may be accomplished by the System ROM BIOS during POST or later by other system software such as a device driver or operating system.
	See Chapter 23,*PCI Device Configuration*, for a description of how this register is implemented in a system.

Bit	Type	Function
0	RW	**Expansion ROM Decode Enable** 0 Disable decode the Expansion ROM within System memory address space. 1 Enable decode of the Expansion ROM within System memory address space. Bit 1 of this device's Command Register, the Memory Space Control bit, has precedence over this bit. It must be set to a value of 1 for this bit to enable the expansion ROM address decode.
10::1	RO	**Reserved**
31::11	RW	**Expansion ROM Base Address** Start address of the expansion ROM memory space region assigned to this device. This is where the expansion ROM code will appear in system memory when bit 0 of this register contains a value of 1 and bit 1 of this device's Command Register contains a value of 1. Because the Expansion ROM Base Address may share a decoder with the I/O and Memory Base Address Register, device independent software should not access any other base address register of this device while the expansion ROM decode for this device is enabled.

Table 18-15: Expansion ROM Base Address Register

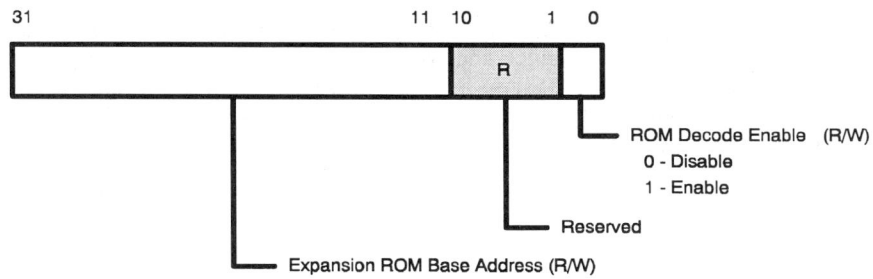

Figure 18-15: Expansion ROM Base Address Register

To assign an expansion ROM base address to this register software should do the following:

1. Write a value of 1 to bits 11 through 31 of this register.

2. Starting at bit location 11, search upward for the first bit set to a value of 1. This bit is the binary weighted size of the total contiguous block of memory address space requested. For example, if bit 16 is the first bit set, the device is requesting a 64 kilobyte block of memory address space.

3. Write the start address of the memory space block assigned to this register. This memory space region must not conflict with any other memory address space utilized within the system. Otherwise, data reads from the ROM may be corrupted.

Expansion ROM Base Address registers may share an address decoder with other Base Address registers. This reduces the number of address decoders on a device. While this feature permits each base address register to hold a unique value at the same time, it does place constraints on software:

A device–independent software program should only set Bit 0, the Expansion ROM Decode Enable bit, to 1 when it is copying the expansion ROM code to the shadow memory. For example, when a PC/AT System BIOS copies a PCI ROM image to the ISA compatibility region between C0000h and EFFFFh. Also POST code should RESET Bit 0 to zero before calling the initialization function of any relocated expansion ROM code. This is because the option ROM code may try to access the device using one or more of the device's standard base address registers. Because of the decoder implementation, the registers may not be accessible if the expansion ROM register is left enabled.

Some System BIOSs may leave a valid address in the Expansion ROM Base Address register after the device has been initialized. This is done to allow device dependent software to access the device's ROM during run-time operation. Other System BIOSs may clear this register to prevent run-time usage of the ROM. Device specific code, such as a device driver, may set the Expansion ROM Decode Enable bit to one (after ensuring a valid address is written to it) to obtain some device specific information out of the ROM. During the time the ROM image is mapped into physical address space, the standard base address registers must not be accessed.

Capabilities Pointer Register	
Offset:	34h
Width:	1 Byte
Valid Values:	40h–FEh
Description:	This register contains an address pointer to a register located in the PCI function's Device Dependent region. The register pointed to is the head of a linked list of data structures that define the function's PCI capabilities, such as AGP or PCI Power Management. See Chapter 24 for a complete definition of this register.

> **Register 34h is qualified by Bit 4 of Register 06h, the Status Register. If Bit 4 is set to '0', the CAP_PTR register is not valid. If Bit 4 is set to '1', the CAP_PTR register is valid if its value is within the legal range.**

Bit	Type	Function
7::0	RO	**PCI Capabilities Pointer** Pointer to the head of a linked list of data structures that define the function's PCI capabilities.

Table 18-16: Capabilities Pointer Register

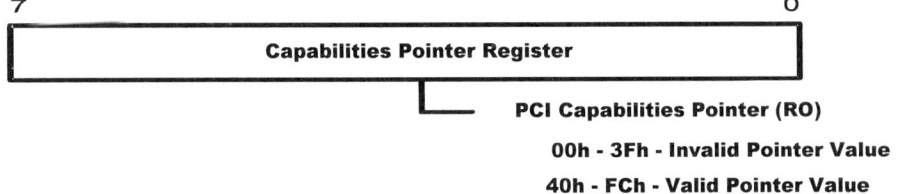

Figure 18-16: Capabilities Pointer Register

1055

Interrupt Line	
Offset:	3Ch
Width:	1 Byte
Valid Values:	00h–FFh
Description:	This register identifies which interrupt request line of a system interrupt controller the PCI device's interrupt line is connected to. Device drivers as well as other device dependent software query this register to determine the interrupt request line assigned to their device. This value is system architecture specific. For ISA compatible systems, valid encodings are shown below. The PCI Specification does not provide encodings for other system architectures. 00h = IRQ0 01h = IRQ1 — 0Eh = IRQ14 0Fh = IRQ15 Note that these encodings specify the physical pin on the system interrupt controller that the interrupt line is connected to. These encodings do not specify the interrupt vector that is generated by the interrupt controller. Other values are reserved.

Bit	Type	Function
7::0	RW	**Interrupt Line Value** 00h:FEh Interrupt line number that the device is connected to. FFh Device interrupt line is not connected to a system interrupt controller.

Table 18-17: Interrupt Line Register

POST software is responsible for routing the device's interrupt line to a system interrupt controller. This routing is dependent upon the specific hardware implementation. In addition, POST code will update this register with the interrupt line value assigned to the device. Software other than POST may read this register to determine which interrupt line the PCI device is connected.

Device-specific executables including device drivers and add-in card BIOSs should never assign system resources such as an IRQ to their device. System resource conflicts could result, rendering the system inoperable. Allocating system resources is the task of power-up system software and operating systems.

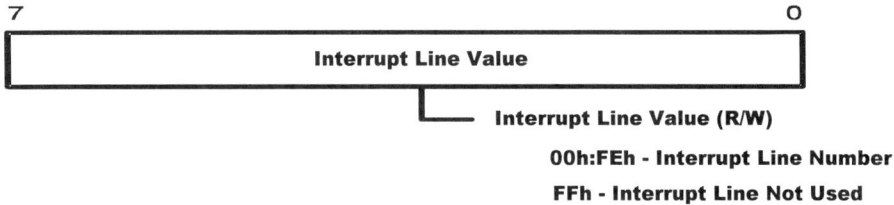

Figure 18-17: Interrupt Line Register

Interrupt Pin	
Offset:	3Dh
Width:	1 Byte
Valid Values:	00h–04h
Description:	This register identifies which interrupt pin, INTA# through INTD#, a device function uses. This register assists in the proper initialization of the Interrupt Line register. Once initialization software knows which interrupt pin(s) the device uses, the Interrupt Line register(s) can be initialized appropriately.

Bit	Type	Function
7::0	RO	**Interrupt Pin Value**
		00h Interrupt pin is not used by the device.
		01h Device function uses interrupt pin INTA#.
		02h Device function uses interrupt pin INTB#.
		03h Device function uses interrupt pin INTC#.
		04h Device function uses interrupt pin INTD#.
		05h:FFh Reserved

Table 18-18A: Interrupt Pin Register

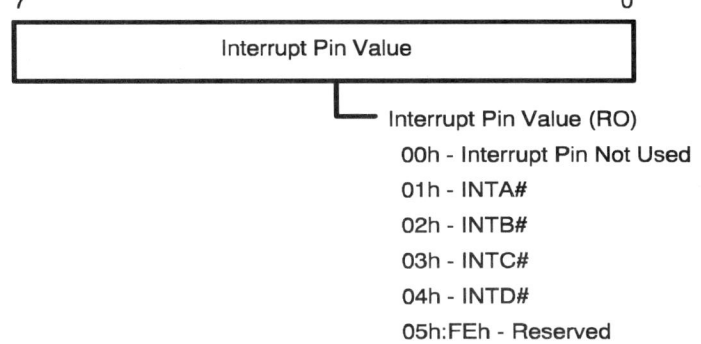

Figure 18-18: Interrupt Pin Register

SINGLE-FUNCTION DEVICE

A Single-Function Device can have only one interrupt pin. If the device has an interrupt pin it must be connected to the INTA# of the add-in board connector (if the device is on an add–in board).

MULTI-FUNCTION DEVICE

A multi–function device can have zero, one, or more interrupt pins. If it has one interrupt pin and both functions use it, both functions must have 01h in their Interrupt Pin registers. The interrupt pin must be connected to the INTA# of the add–in board connector (if the device is on an add-in board).

If the multi–function device has two interrupt pins, function 0 should have 01h in its Interrupt Pin register, and function 1 should have 02h in its interrupt pin register. If the device is located on an add–in card, the two interrupt pins must be connected to INTA# and INTB#, respectively, of the card connector. Vendors of devices with multiple interrupt pins must clearly label these pins so that integrators can properly connect them to the pins on the add–in board connector. Table 18-18-B below lists the valid interrupt pin encodings.

Number of Interrupt Pins	Number of Functions	Valid Interrupt Pin Encodings	Comments
0	1 to 8	00h	Interrupt line register in all functions should have the value 00h, indicating that no interrupt pins are used.
1	1 to 8	00h	Use this encoding in any functions that don't use the interrupt pin.
		01h	Use this encoding in any functions that use the interrupt pin.
2	2 to 8	00h	Use this encoding in any functions that don't use the interrupt pin.
		01h	Use this encoding in any functions that use the interrupt pin corresponding to INTA#.
		02h	Use this encoding in any functions that use the interrupt pin corresponding to INTB#.
3	3 to 8	00h	Use this encoding in any functions that don't use the interrupt pin.
		01h	Use this encoding in any functions that use the interrupt pin corresponding to INTA#.
		02h	Use this encoding in any functions that use the interrupt pin corresponding to INTB#.
		03h	Use this encoding in any functions that use the interrupt pin corresponding to INTC#.
4	4 to 8	00h	Use this encoding in any functions that don't use the interrupt pin.
		01h	Use this encoding in any functions that use the interrupt pin corresponding to INTA#.
		02h	Use this encoding in any functions that use the interrupt pin corresponding to INTB#.
		03h	Use this encoding in any functions that use the interrupt pin corresponding to INTC#.
		04h	Use this encoding in any functions that use the interrupt pin corresponding to INTD#.

Table 18-18-B: Interrupt Pin Register: Valid Encodings

From the table above, devices must have at least as many functions as interrupt pins. Functions in a device can share an interrupt pin allowing fewer interrupt pins than functions in the device.

Note that each function in a device can use at most one interrupt.

MIN_GNT	
Offset:	3Eh
Width:	1 Byte
Valid Values:	00h–FFh
Description:	This register specifies the burst period (assuming a clock rate of 33MHz) required by the device. The value is specified in 250 nanoseconds (1/4 microsecond) increments. This value is used to determine Latency Timer values.

Bit	Type	Function	
7::0	RO	**Min_Gnt Value**	
		00h	Do not use this register for calculating Latency Timer values.
		01h:FFh	Number of 250 nanosecond units required for a burst period.

Table 18-19: Min_Gnt Register

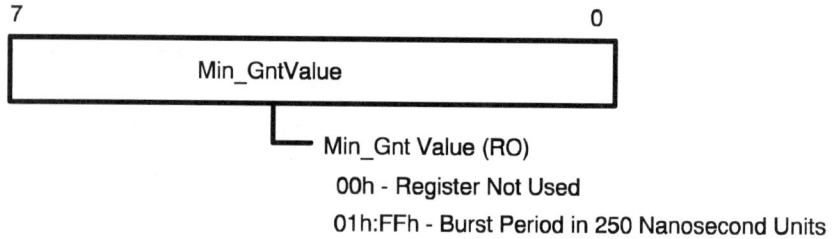

Figure 18-19: Min_Gnt Register

MAX_LAT	
Offset:	3Fh
Width:	1 Byte
Valid Values:	00h–FFh
Description:	This register specifies how often (assuming a clock rate of 33MHz) the device needs to gain access to the PCI Bus. The value is specified in 250 nanoseconds (1/4 microsecond) increments. This value is used to determine Latency Timer values.

Bit	Type	Function
7::0	RO	**Max_Lat Value** 00h Do not use this register for calculating Latency Timer values. 01h:FFh How often the device needs to gain access to the PCI Bus in 250 nanosecond units.

Table 18-20: Max_Lat Register

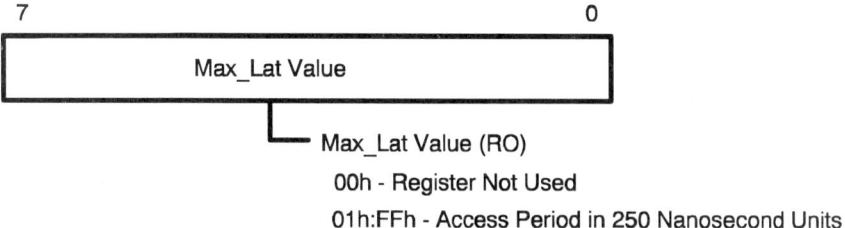

Figure 18-20: Max_Lat Register

The MIN_GNT and MAX_LAT registers are used to help tune the performance of the system. This tuning is accomplished by adjusting Latency Timer values throughout the system. The values in these registers provide a measure of how much of the PCI bus bandwidth the device requires. As an example, consider a device whose MIN_GNT value is 02h (0.5 μsecs) and whose MAX_LAT value is 14h (5 μsecs). These values say that for every 5 μsecs, the device needs .5 μsecs on the bus, or 10% of the bus bandwidth (at 33 MHz).

PCI-X AND THE MIN_GNT AND MAX_LAT REGISTERS

These registers are optional for devices that run in PCI-X mode. If they are implemented, the registers must comply with the **Min_Gnt and Max_Lat** register implementations and programming requirements as specified in the *PCI Local Bus Local Bus Specification, Revision 2.2*.

CHAPTER 19

PCI HEADER TYPE 01H

19.0 PCI HEADER TYPE 01H

The primary function of a PCI/PCI Bridge device is to permit transactions to occur between a PCI master on one PCI bus and a PCI target on another PCI bus. As with all compliant PCI devices, PCI/PCI Bridge devices must support the 256 byte configuration space requirement of the PCI Local Bus Specification.

The Type 01H PCI Configuration Space Header Region is the predefined header format for PCI/PCI Bridge devices. A Type 01H PCI Configuration Space Header Region consists of 64 bytes. The first 16 bytes are the PCI Device Independent Region. The remaining 48 bytes are assigned to the PCI Device Header Type Region. Consequently, 64 bytes are assigned to the predefined PCI Configuration Space Header Region and 192 bytes to the Device Dependent region of the PCI configuration register space. For additional details about PCI configuration space device header types, refer to the description of the PCI Header Type register, found later in this section. In addition, refer to Table 19-1 and Figure 19-1 for pictorial representations of the Type 01H PCI Device Header Region.

> A Type 01H PCI Device Header Type Register (offset 0EH) specifies that the PCI Device Header Type Region consists of 48 bytes. When new header types are defined, they may specify fewer or more registers for this region.

Note that individual PCI devices need only implement the registers required to support their functionality. For example, some PCI/PCI Bridge devices may not support an expansion ROM. Consequently, the Expansion ROM Base Address Register (DWORD at offset 38H), of the PCI Configuration Header Region is not implemented. In this case, the register is treated as reserved. As stated in Chapter 17, all bits in a reserved register must be hardwired to zero.

The remainder of this section contains a description of each register in a Type 01H PCI Configuration Header region. Each register description contains the following:

- Name of the register
- Address location within the PCI device of the register
- Byte width of the register
- Read/Write attribute assigned to the register

- Valid value range of the register
- Register's global function definition
- Individual bit definitions of the register

Default values for each register are vendor and device specific and therefore are not specified.

Figure 19-1 is a pictorial view of the 64 byte register layout of Type 01H PCI Configuration Space Header. All PCI compliant devices that implement a Type 01H header must support this layout. Fields that utilize more than one byte in this structure follow little–endian ordering. For example, the least significant byte of the two-byte Vendor ID field is contained in the bottommost byte of the field.

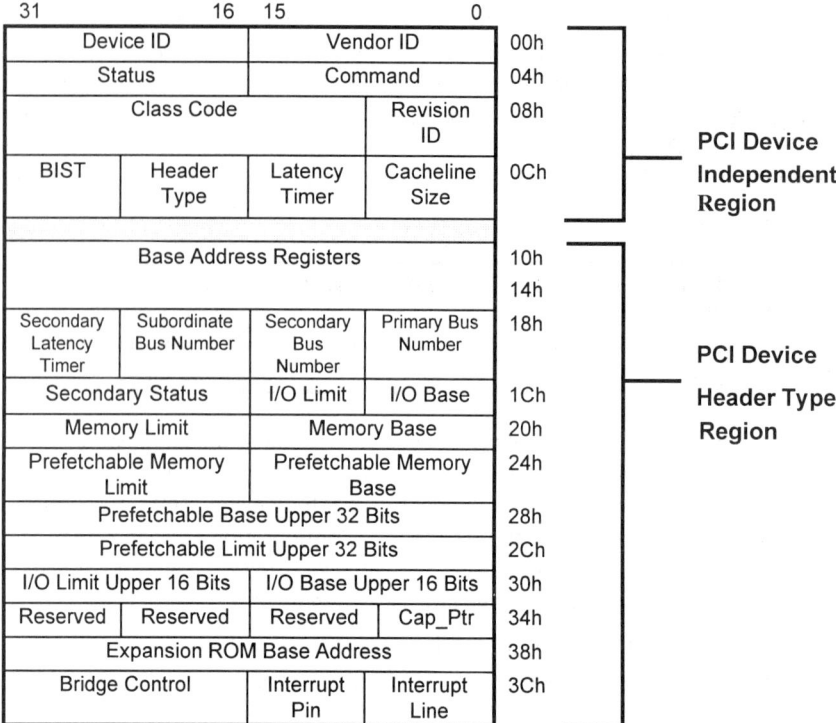

Figure 19-1: Type 01h PCI Configuration Space Header Region

For quick reference, Table 19-1 contains a list of the Type 01h PCI Configuration Space Header Region registers with their corresponding offset from the base of the structure.

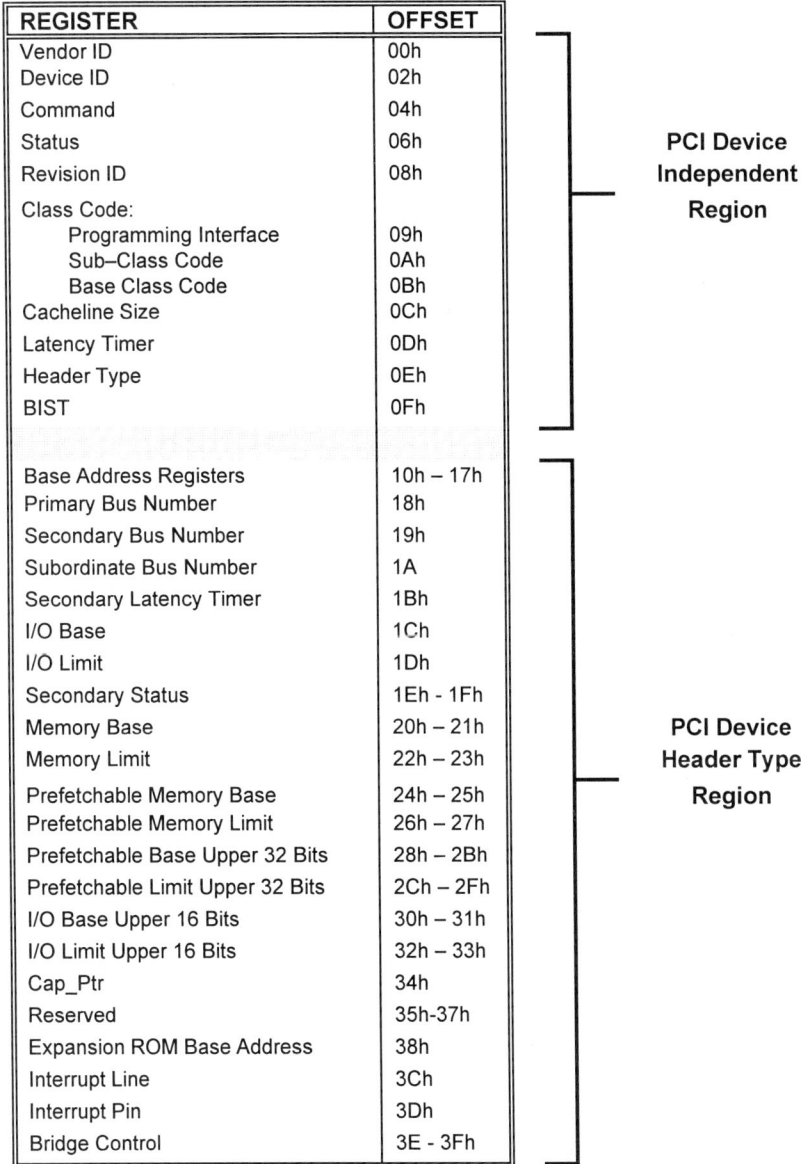

REGISTER	OFFSET	
Vendor ID	00h	
Device ID	02h	
Command	04h	
Status	06h	**PCI Device**
Revision ID	08h	**Independent**
Class Code:		**Region**
Programming Interface	09h	
Sub–Class Code	0Ah	
Base Class Code	0Bh	
Cacheline Size	0Ch	
Latency Timer	0Dh	
Header Type	0Eh	
BIST	0Fh	
Base Address Registers	10h – 17h	
Primary Bus Number	18h	
Secondary Bus Number	19h	
Subordinate Bus Number	1A	
Secondary Latency Timer	1Bh	
I/O Base	1Ch	
I/O Limit	1Dh	
Secondary Status	1Eh - 1Fh	
Memory Base	20h – 21h	**PCI Device**
Memory Limit	22h – 23h	**Header Type**
Prefetchable Memory Base	24h – 25h	**Region**
Prefetchable Memory Limit	26h – 27h	
Prefetchable Base Upper 32 Bits	28h – 2Bh	
Prefetchable Limit Upper 32 Bits	2Ch – 2Fh	
I/O Base Upper 16 Bits	30h – 31h	
I/O Limit Upper 16 Bits	32h – 33h	
Cap_Ptr	34h	
Reserved	35h-37h	
Expansion ROM Base Address	38h	
Interrupt Line	3Ch	
Interrupt Pin	3Dh	
Bridge Control	3E - 3Fh	

Table 19-1: Type 01H PCI Configuration Space Header Region

Vendor ID	
Offset:	00h
Width:	2 Bytes
Valid Values:	0000h–FFFFh
Description:	This register is used to identify the manufacturer of the device. The PCI Special Interest Group assigns vendor identifiers to ensure uniqueness. For example, a value of 8086H will always be read from the Vendor ID register of any PCI device manufactured by Intel Corporation.

The platform hardware is responsible for ensuring that a value of FFFFh is returned when an attempt is made to read the vendor identifier of a nonexistent PCI device. Consequently, the Vendor ID register is the one that should be used when attempting to determine whether a PCI device exists in a system. Because FFFFh is an invalid value for Vendor ID, that value will be returned only when no device is present.

Bit	Type	Function
15:0	RO	**Vendor ID** This register contains a unique 16 bit value assigned to each vendor. This number enables each PCI device's manufacturer to be uniquely identified.

Table 19-2: Vendor Identification Register

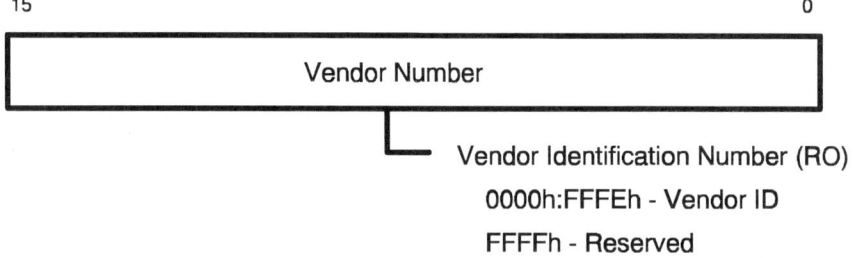

Figure 19-2: Vendor Identification Register

Device ID	
Offset:	02h
Width:	2 Bytes
Valid Values:	0000h–FFFFh
Description:	This register identifies the device with a unique number. The value is assigned by the vendor of the device.
	Vendors may choose to assign device IDs such that devices in one family that are backward compatible with earlier members of the family are easily recognized by software device drivers. For instance, assume a vendor built a SCSI device with some base functionality and assigned an identification number of 0AA0h to the device. Later the vendor develops the next generation part which has all the capabilities of the first part, but has extensions that make it perform better if they are used. The vendor assigned an identification number of 0AA1h to this device.
	A device driver for the original part would continue to work for the new part if the driver looked for an identification number of 0AAxh when trying to locate its device. The current device driver wouldn't take advantage of new features. However, the problem of immediately providing a new driver for the latest device would be solved.

Bit	Type	Function
15:0	RO	**Device ID** This number enables each PCI device's manufacturer to be uniquely identified.

Table 19-3: Device Identification Register

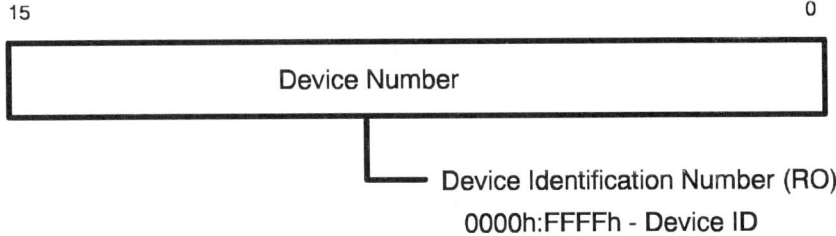

Figure 19-3: Device Identification Register

Avoid assigning a Device ID of either 0000h or FFFFh, because zero indicates a Reserved Register and FFFFh a *no response*.

Command	
Offset:	04h
Width:	2 Bytes
Valid Values:	N/A. This field is a collection of bits, not a range of values. The register should not be viewed as values, but as individual bits.
Description:	This register controls the device's ability to generate and respond to PCI bus accesses. Note that a value of zero in this register logically disconnects the device from the PCI bus.

All PCI devices are required to respond to PCI configuration accesses, even when bits 2:0 of the Command register are set to zero.

Bit	Type	Function
0	RW	**I/O Space Control** This bit controls the PCI/PCI Bridge's response to I/O accesses on the bridge's primary interface. Internal registers within the bridge itself can be the targets of an I/O transaction as well as registers of devices behind the bridge. Hard wire this bit to return '0' if the bridge, along with all devices behind the bridge, do not support an I/O address range BAR or I/O mapped BAR. Implement this bit as a read/write bit if the bridge or at least one device behind the bridge supports an I/O address range or I/O mapped BAR. When the I/O Space Control bit is disabled after previously being enabled, internal transaction buffers are in an unknown state. The actual buffer states when this action occurs are design dependent and are chosen by the device developer. Consequently, software must assume data has been lost and must act accordingly if the bit is re-enabled. **Read Only Implementation:** 0 I/O Space Control not supported. **Read/Write Implementation:** 0 Ignore I/O transactions on the primary interface (**RST#** state). 1 Enable response to I/O transactions on the primary interface.

Table 19-4: Type 01h Command Register

Bit	Type	Function
1	RW	**Memory Space Control** This bit controls the PCI/PCI Bridge's response to memory accesses on the bridge's primary interface. Internal registers within the bridge itself can be the targets of a memory transaction as well as registers of devices behind the bridge. This bit must be implemented as a read/write bit because the bridge must support at least one memory address range. When the Memory Space Enable Control bit is disabled after previously being enabled, internal transaction buffers are in an unknown state. The actual buffer states when this action occurs are design dependent and are chosen by the device developer. Consequently, software must assume data has been lost and must act accordingly if the bit is re-enabled. 0 Ignore all memory transactions on the primary interface (**RST#** state). 1 Enable response to memory transactions on the primary interface
2	RW	**Bus Master Control** This bit controls the bridge's ability to operate as a bus master on the primary interface on behalf of a bus master on the secondary interface for memory or I/O transactions. This bit does not affect the ability of a bridge to forward or convert PCI configuration address space transactions from the secondary interface to the primary interface of the PCI bridge device. When the Bus Master Control bit is disabled after previously being enabled, internal transaction buffers are in an unknown state. The actual buffer states when this action occurs are design dependent and are chosen by the device developer. Consequently, software must assume data has been lost and must act accordingly if the bit is re-enabled. 0 Do not initiate memory or I/O transactions on the primary interface. Also disable all resonses to memory or I/O on the secondary interface. (**RST#** state). 1 Enable the bridge to operate as a master on the primary interface for memory and I/O transactions forwarded from the bridge's secondary interface.
3	RO	**Special Cycle Control** 0 PCI/PCI bridge devices cannot respond as a target to special cycle transactions. Consequently, this bit is read only and must return a zero read. (**RST#** state).

Table 19-4: Type 01h Command Register (continued)

Bit	Type	Function
4	RW	**Memory Write and Invalidate Control** 0 PCI/PCI bridge devices cannot initiate a memory write and invalidate command unless it is operating on behalf of another master whose transaction has crossed the bridge. The initiating master has the control to determine which memory write command to use. Consequently, this bit is read only and must return a zero read. (**RST#** state). **Read Only Implementation:** 0 The bridge can only forward a Memory Write and Invalidate transaction for another bus master. The bridge cannot originate the actual transaction. **Read/Write Implementation:** 0 The bridge is not permitted to convert a Memory Write transaction to a Memory Write and Invalidate transaction for another bus master (RST# state). 1 The bridge is permitted to convert a Memory Write transaction to a Memory Write and Invalidate transaction for another bus master.
5	RW	**VGA Palette Snoop Control** This bit is optional. It controls the bridge's response to VGA-compatible palette write accesses. The definition of this bit for PCI/PCI bridges is different from the the *PCI Local Bus Specification.* **Read Only Implementation:** 0 VGA palette snooping is not supported. **Read/Write Implementation:** 0 Ignore VGA palette accesses on the primary bridge (**RST#** state). 1 Enable response to VGA palette writes on the primary interface. I/O writes with address bits AD[9::0] = 3C6h, 3C8h and 3C9h (inclusive of ISA aliases - AD[15::10] are not decoded) must be positively decoded on the primary side and forwarded to the secondary interface. Note that the bridge on the secondary interface must not respond to these three addresses.
6	RW	**Parity Error Response** This bit controls the PCI/PCI Bridge's response address and data parity errors on the bridge's primary interface. If the bit is set to '0', the bridge ignores any detected parity errors and proceeds as if they had not occurred. This bit is required. 0 Device ignores detected parity errors (RST# state). 1 Device responds to detected parity errors.

Table 19-4: Type 01h Command Register (continued)

Bit	Type	Function
7	RW	**Wait Cycle Control** This bit controls address/data stepping by the bridge. The primary and secondary interfaces are affected. **Read Only Implementation:** 0 The PCI/PCI bridge never performs stepping. **Read/Write Implementation:** 0 Address/Data stepping is disabled. 1 Address/Data stepping is enabled (**RST#** state). Bit 7 must be read/writeable if the device can either enable or disable ADDRESS/DATA STEPPING. The **RST#** state of this bit is one.
8	RW	**System Error Control** This bit controls the enable for the SERR# driver on the primary interface. 0 Disable the SERR# output driver on the primary interface (RST# state). 1 Enable the SERR# output driver on the primary interface. 1 Devices which implement SERR# must support this bit. 2 This bit and bit 6 must be set to one to report address parity errors.
9	RW	**Fast Back–to–Back Control** This bit controls the ability of the bridge to generate fast back-to-back transactions to different devices on the primary interface. **Read Only Implementation:** 0 The bridge cannot initiate fast back-to-back transactions on the primary interface. **Read/Write Implementation:** 0 The bridge cannot initiate fast back-to-back transactions on the primary interface (RST# state). 1 The bridge can initiate fast back-to-back transactions on the primary interface. 1 This bit is optional. It has the read/write attribute when implemented. 2 Software (typically the System BIOS) may set this bit to one only if all targets are capable of fast back–to–back transactions.
15::10	RO	**Reserved**

Table 19-4: Type 01h Command Register (continued)

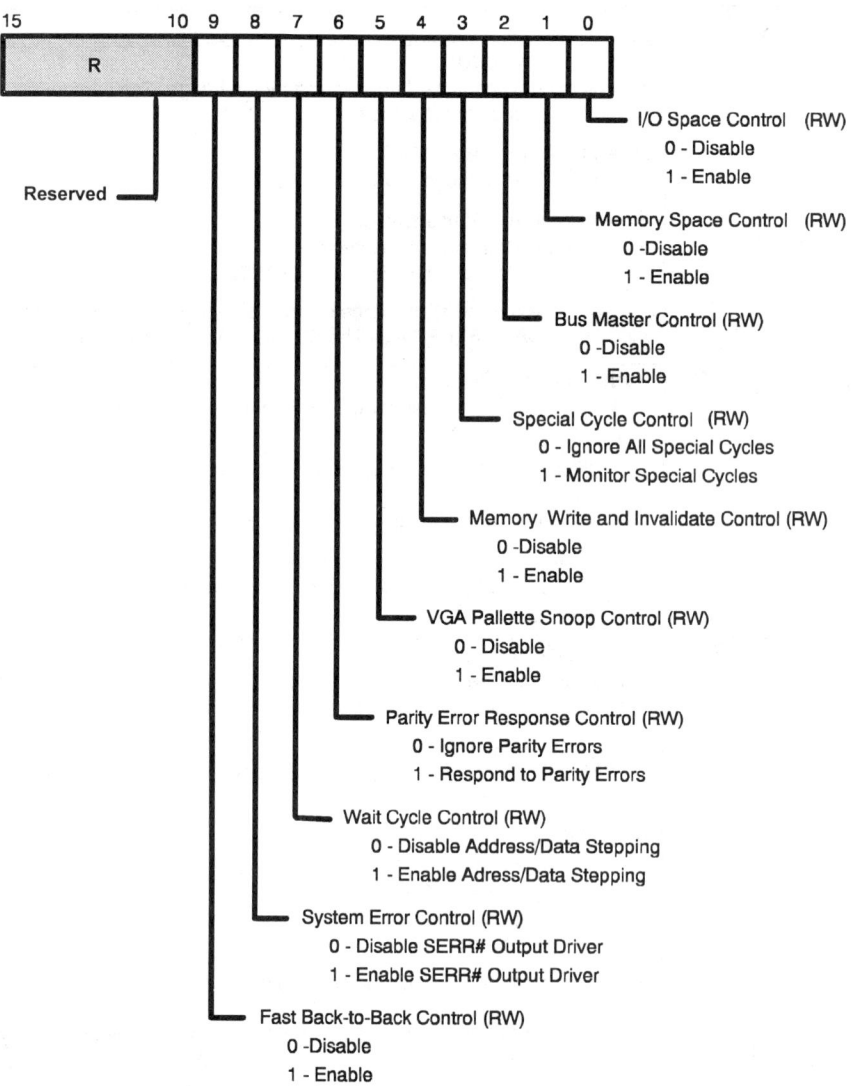

Figure 19-4: Type 01h Command Register

PCI-X AND THE COMMAND REGISTER

Operating in conventional PCI mode, a PCI-X bridge's **Command** register adheres to the conventional Type 01h configuration address space definition for this register. If the primary interface of a PCI-X bridge device is operating in PCI-X mode, the following apply:

- Bit [9], **Fast Back-to-Back Control**, is ignored by the device in PCI-X mode.

- Bit [7], **Wait Cycle Control,** is ignored by the device in PCI-X mode.

- Bit [4], **Memory Write and Invalidate Control**, is ignored by the device in PCI-X mode.

- Bit [2], **Bus Master Control**, is ignored by the device in PCI-X mode when initiating Split Completions.

Status	
Offset:	06h
Width:	2 Bytes
Valid Values:	N/A. This field is a collection of bits, not a range of values. The register should not be viewed as values, but as individual bits.
Description:	This register records events that occur on the PCI bus. The following rules apply to this register:

1 Reads of this register occur normally.

2 Writes to this register may clear bits to zero but never set them to one.

3 There are several bits with the attribute type RWC in the Status Register Table below. These are individual bits that are cleared to zero if the bit has the write attribute and its bit location is written with a data value of one.

4 The function of the device determines which bits will be implemented.

The Status register bit definitions are compliant with the PCI Local Bus Specification. However, these bits only apply to the primary interface of a PCI/PCI bridge.

The Status Register is typically not used by device drivers. Rather, it is intended to record events that (a) tend to be catastrophic and (b) are not part of normal operation.

System monitoring software can use the Status Register to determine precisely what happened if a catastrophic error occurs. In addition, the system monitoring software can keep statistics on PCI specific events.

Bit	Type	Function
3::0	RO	**Reserved**
4	RO	**PCI Capabilities** 0 This PCI function does not support PCI capabilities. 1 This PCI function does support PCI capabilities. This bit is optional.
5	RO	**66MHz Capable Status** 0 The primary interface of the bridge cannot operate at 66Mhz. 1 The primary interface of the bridge is able to operate at 66Mhz. This bit is optional.
6	RO	**Reserved**
7	RO	**Fast Back–to–Back Status** 0 The primary interface of the bridge cannot decode fast back-to-back transactions from the same master but to different targets (RST# state). 1 The primary interface of the bridge can decode fast back-to-back transactions from the same master but to different targets. This bit is optional. A PCI/PCI Bridge is required to support fast back-to-back transactions as a target from the same master.
8	RWC	**Master Data Parity Error Status** 0 A parity error was not detected during a transaction in which the bridge was the master (RST# state). 1 A parity error was detected during a transaction in which the bridge was the master. All three of the following conditions must be met: a. The bridge was the bus master agent on the bridge's primary interface at the time of the transaction. b. **PERR#** was asserted by the bridge due to a read transaction or detected **PERR#** asserted due to a write transaction. c. Parity Error Response (bit 6 of the PCI/PCI Bridge's Command register) is enabled (set to '1').
10::9	RO	**Device Select Timing Status** 00 Device asserts DEVSEL# in the *fast* timing mode for any bus command. 01 Device asserts DEVSEL# in the *fast or medium* timing mode for any bus command. 10 Device asserts DEVSEL# in the *fast, meduim, or slow* timing mode for any bus command. 11 Reserved.

Table 19-5: Status Register

Bit	Type	Function
		All timing encodings are specific to the primary interface DEVSEL#. Configuration read and write cycles do not apply to the above definition. For example, if a device performs FAST decode for all memory and I/O accesses, but medium decode for configuration accesses, the device should set this register to fast.
11	RWC	**Signaled Target Abort Status** The bridge can respond as the target of a transaction on its primary interface. If the bridge terminates the transaction with a Target-Abort under this circumstance this bit is set to a '1'. 0 A Target-Abort was not signaled by the bridge on its primary interface (RST# state). 1 A Target-Abort was signaled by the bridge on its primary interface.
12	RWC	**Received Target Abort Status** The bridge can be the bus master of a transaction on its primary interface. If the bridge terminates the transaction with a Target-Abort under this circumstance this bit is set to a '1'. 0 A Target-Abort was not signaled by the bridge on its primary interface (RST# state). 1 A Target-Abort was signaled by the bridge on its primary interface.
13	RWC	**Received Master Abort Status** The bridge can be the bus master of a transaction on its primary interface. If the bridge detects a Master-Abort under this circumstance this bit is set to a '1'. 0 A Master-Abort was not detected by the bridge on its primary interface (RST# state). 1 A Master-Abort was detected by the bridge on its primary interface.
14	RWC	**Signaled System Error Status** 0 The bridge did not assert SERR# on its primary interface (RST# state). 1 The bridge asserted SERR# on its primary interface.
15	RWC	**Detected Parity Error Status** 0 An address or data parity error was not detected by the bridge on its primary interface (RST# state). 1 The bridge detected an address or parity error on its primary interface. This bit is set to '1' when any of the following three conditions are true: a. As a potential target, the bridge detects an address parity error. b. As the target of a write transaction, the bridge detects a data parity error. c. As the master of a read transaction, the bridge detects a data parity error. Devices will set this bit regardless of the state of Parity Error Response (bit 6 of the Command Register).

Table 19-5: Status Register (continued)

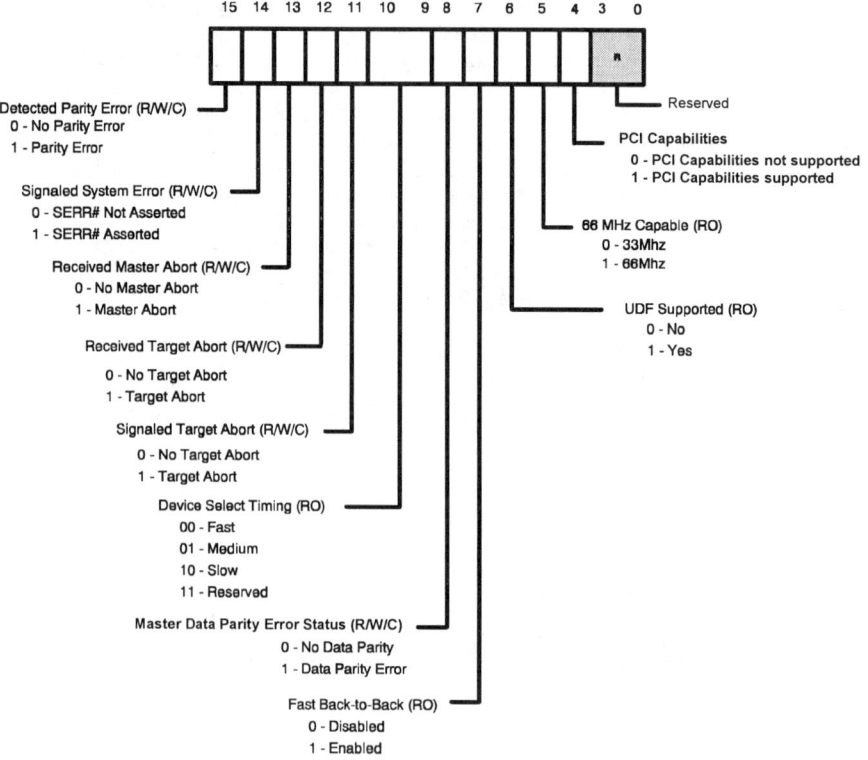

Figure 19-5: Status Register

PCI-X AND THE STATUS REGISTER

Operating in conventional PCI mode, a PCI-X bridge's **Status** register adheres to the conventional Type 01h configuration address space definition for this register. If the primary interface of a PCI-X bridge device is operating in PCI-X mode, the following apply:

■   Bit [4], **Capabilities List**, is always set to a value of '1' in all PCI-X mode capable devices. The reason for this is because the PCI-X

Capabilities List item is always included in the PCI Capabilities Linked List. This bit is set to a value of '1' regardless of whether the device is operating in conventional mode or PCI-X mode.

■ Bit [7], **Fast Back-to-Back Status**, can have any value when the device operates in PCI-X mode. The reason is because devices operating in PCI-X mode never use fast back-to-back timing, and thus ignore this bit.

■ Bit [8], **Master Data Parity Error**, is controlled under the same conditions as a conventional PCI device. However, the conditions under which this bit is set when the device is running in PCI-X mode are as follows:

- When the **Initiator** (requestor or PCI-X bridge):

    ■ Of a completed read transaction immediately calculates a data parity error.

    ■ Of a read transaction that is terminated with a Split Response, calculates a data parity error in the Split Response.

    ■ Of a write that is completed, immediately observes **PERR#** asserted three clocks after one or more of its data phases.

    ■ Of a write that is terminated with Spit Response observes **PERR#** asserted three clocks after the data phase.

- When the **Target** (requestor or PCI-X bridge):

    ■ Of a Split Completion calculates a data parity error in either read data or a Split Completion Message.

    ■ Receives a Split Completion Message that indicates a data parity error occurred on one of the device's non-posted write transactions.

■ Bits [10::9], **Device Select (DEVSEL) Timing**, indicates the device's conventional mode **DEVSEL#** timing as specified in the PCI Local Bus Specification, Revision 2.2. This is regardless of whether the device is operating in PCI-X mode or conventional mode.

■ Bit [15], **Detected Parity Error**, operates the same in PCI-X mode as it does in conventional mode. This bit is set by the device whose parity checking logic calculated the data parity error.

Revision ID

Offset:	08h
Width:	1 Byte
Valid Values:	00h–FFh
Description:	This register identifies the revision level of the device. The value is assigned by the vendor of the device.
	This register is typically used to indicate different steppings of the same device.

> Plug and Play software does not use this field for device identification purposes. The System BIOS and device drivers can use this field to isolate code execution to particular revisions of the device.

Bit	Type	Function
7::0	RO	**Revision ID**
		This value reflects the version level of the device.

Table 19-6: Revision Identification Register

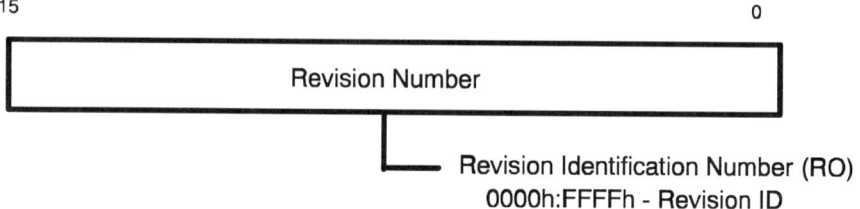

Figure 19-6: Revision Identification Register

Class Code			
Offset:	09h		
Width:	3 Bytes		
Valid Values:	**Field**	**Value**	**Definition**
	Programming Interface (09h):	00h	PCI/PCI Bridge
		01h	Subtractive Decode PCI/PCI Bridge
	Sub–Class Code (0Ah):	04h	PCI/PCI Bridge
	Base Class Code (0Bh):	06h	Bridge Device
Description:	This register identifies the generic function of the device and the register level programming interface of the device (if applicable to the class of the device). The Class Code register consists of three contiguous byte wide field: (09h) – Base Class register, (0Ah) – Sub-Class register and (09h) – Programming Interface register. **See Appendix A for a complete definition of the Class Code Register.**		
	A bridge with Class Code of 060400h supports the PCI-PCI Bridge Architecture Specification. A bridge with Class Code of 060401h also supports the PCI-PCI Bridge Architecture Specification. In addition, the 060401h bridge also supports subtractive decoding on its primary interface.		
	Subtractive decoding can be dynamically controlled through a device-specific PCI configuration address space control bit. The definition of the bit is:		
	0 Subtractive decoding is disabled; Set the programming interface register to a value of 00h		
	1 Subtractive decoding is enabled; the device supports subtractive decoding on the primary interface Set the programming interface register to a value of 01h		

Table 19-7: Class Code Register

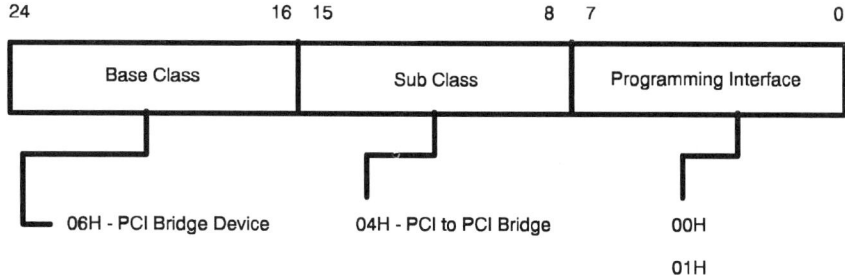

Figure 19-7: Class Code Register

Cacheline Size Register	
Offset:	0Ch
Width:	1 Byte
Valid Values:	0000h–FFFFh
Description:	This register specifies the cacheline size in units of DWORDs.
	PCI/PCI Bridges support this register if the PCI function can generate a Memory Write and Invalidate command. In addition, the bridge uses this register's contents to determine which command (Read, Read Line or Read Multiple) to use to access memory.

> The number of cachelines supported by a given PCI function is determined by the PCI device's design. PCI/PCI Bridges that originate or forward memory Write and Invalidate transactions must implement the Cacheline register as a read/write register. PCI/PCI Bridges that do not originate or forward memory Write and Invalidate transactions or support enhanced read commands must implement the Cacheline register as a read only register that returns a value of '0' when read.

Bit	Type	Function
7::0	RW	**Cacheline Size Register** **Read Only Implementation** 00h The bridge does not originate or forward Memory Write and Invalidate transactions. It also does not support any enhanced memory read commands (Memory Read Line and Memory Read Multiple). **Read/Write Implementation** 00h The bridge does not originate or forward Memory Write and Invalidate transactions. Enhanced memory read commands (Memory Read Line and Memory Read Multiple) support is disabled. (**RST#** state). 01H- The bridge can originate or forward Memory Write and 0FFh Invalidate transactions. Enhanced memory read commands (Memory Read Line and Memory Read Multiple) support is enabled.
		1 Bus Masters that generate the Memory Write and Invalidate command are required to implement this register.
		2 Devices that provide cacheable memory are required to implement this register.

Table 19-8: Cacheline Size Register

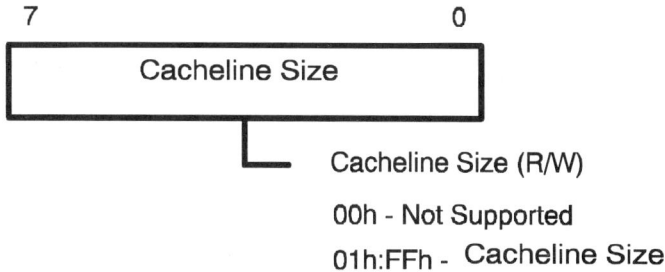

Figure 19-8: Cacheline Size Register

PCI-X AND THE CACHELINE SIZE REGISTER

Operating in conventional PCI mode, a PCI-X bridge's **Cacheline Size** register adheres to the conventional Type 01h configuration address space definition for this register. If either interface of a PCI-X bridge device is operating in conventional PCI mode, that interface's operation is the same as described above. If either interface is operating in PCI-X mode, the contents of the **Cacheline** register are ignored by that interface.

Latency Timer	
Offset:	0DH
Width:	1 Byte
Valid Values:	00h–FFh
Description:	This register specifies, in the number of PCI bus clocks, the value of the Latency Timer register for a PCI/PCI Bridge. A PCI/PCI Bridge is allowed to hardwire the Latency Timer register to a value of 16 or less if the bridge is incapable of burst transfers of more than two data phases on its primary interface. On the other hand, the PCI/PCI Bridge is required to implement the Latency Timer register as a read/write register if it is capable of burst transfers of more than two data phases on its primary interface.
	If the PCI/PCI Bridge implements this register as a read/write register, the granularity in this register can be limited to 8 PCI clocks by hardwiring the register's lowest three bits to '0'. In this case the bridge's Latency Timer is programmed in increments of 8 PCI bus clocks.

Bit	Function
7::0	**Read Only Implementation:** A PCI/PCI Bridge incapable of burst transfers of more than two data phases on its primary interface is allowed to hardwire the Latency Timer register to a value of 16 or less. **Read/Write Implementation:** PCI/PCI Bridges capable of bursting for more than two data phases on its primary bus must implement this register as a read/write register. After a reset, the default value of this timer is required to be '0'.

Table 19-9: Latency Timer Register

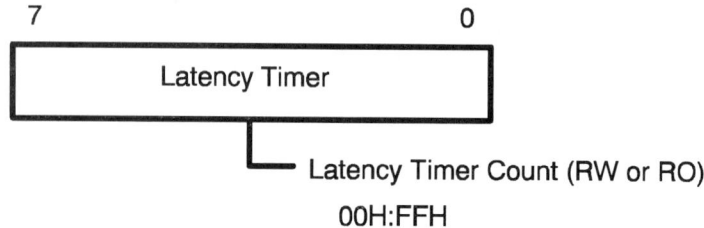

Figure 19-9: Latency Timer Register

PCI-X AND THE LATENCY TIMER REGISTER

Operating in conventional PCI mode, a PCI-X bridge's **Latency Timer** register adheres to the conventional Type 01h configuration address space definition for this register. If the primary interface of a PCI-X bridge device is operating in PCI-X mode, the value of the **Latency Timer** register must be 64.

Header Type	
Offset:	0Eh
Width:	1 Byte
Valid Values:	01h or 81h
Description:	This register identifies the header type of the PCI device as a PCI/PCI bridge. In addition, this register specifies whether the device is a single or multi–function device. Configuration software such as a System BIOS should validate this register's value prior to doing anything with the device.

> If configuration software finds a header type that it does not know about, it should disable the device. This is done by setting the bottom three bits in the Command Register to zero. Leave the device alone once this is done.

Bit	Type	Function
6::0	RO	**Header Layout Code**
		000000B Device supports the layout of configuration registers 10h through 3Fh as defined in Figure 18-1.
		000001B Device supports the layout of PCI/PCI Bridge configuration registers 10h through 3Fh as defined in Figure 19-1.
		000010B Device supports the layout of a PCI Cardbus bridge.
		03h-7Fh Reserved.
7	RO	**Multi–Function Status**
		0 Device has one function.
		1 Device contains between two and eight functions.

Table 19-10: Header Type Register

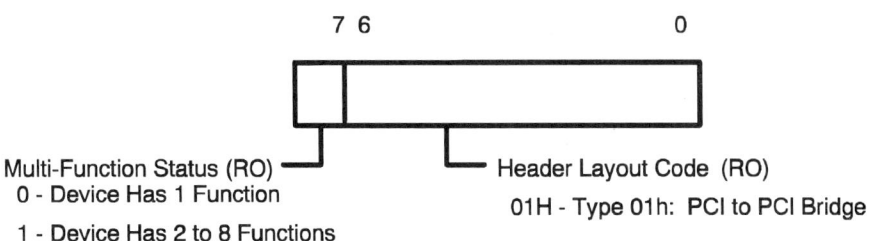

Figure 19-10: Header Type Register

BIST (Built–In Self Test)

Offset: 0Fh

Width: 1 Byte

Valid Values: Device dependent. See description below.

Description:

This register is used to control the invocation of a PCI device's BIST and to report the status of the BIST. PCI/PCI Bridges that do not support the optional BIST function must implement the register as read-only. In this case, a value of 00h must be returned when the register is read.

A PCI/PCI Bridge that implements the BIST register must comply with the following:

- A bridge whose BIST is in progress must not interfere with the normal execution of any other device on the bridge's primary bus.
- During BIST, except for PCI configuration address space accesses to the PCI/PCI Bridge's BIST register, the bridge is not permitted to respond as a target to a transaction.
- During BIST, the PCI/PCI bridge is not permitted to forward any transaction to either its primary or secondary bus.
- The effect that a PCI/PCI bridge's BIST operation has on its secondary bus is not specified.

During a PCI/PCI Bridge's BIST execution:

- Software should not attempt to access any register within the PCI/PCI Bridge except for the BIST register itself.
- Software should not access any of the bridge's secondary devices. The behavior of all devices on the bridge's secondary bus is not guaranteed during this time.

> Software is required to reinitialize both the PCI/PCI Bridge and all of its downstream devices once the bridge's BIST operation is complete.

Bit	Type	Function
3::0	RO	**BIST Result** 00h — Device test passed. 01h:0Fh — Device test failed. Vendors may define up to 15 device specific failure codes in these bits.
5::4	RO	**Reserved** Device must return zero in these two bit fields.
6	RW	**Start BIST** 0 — Device resets this bit after BIST completes. 1 — Invoke the device's BIST. Software should fail the device if this bit is not RESET to zero within two seconds after the BIST is invoked. Hard code this bit to 0, RO, if BIST is not implemented.
7	RO	**BIST Capable** 0 — Device does not support BIST. 1 — Device supports BIST.

Table 19-11: BIST Register

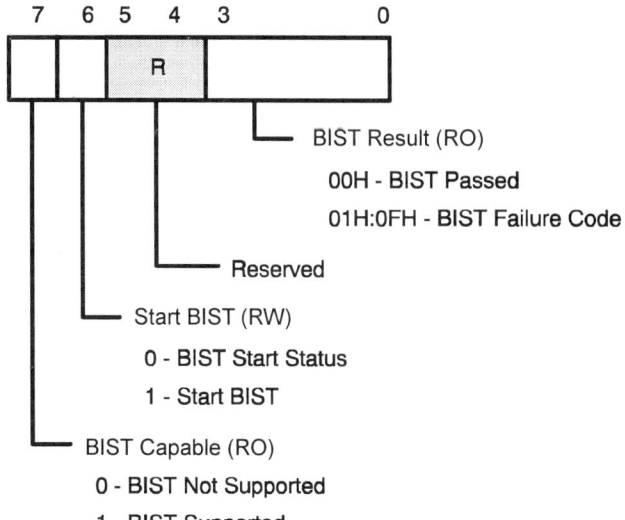

Figure 19-11: BIST Register

I/O and Memory Base Address Registers

Offset:	10h (first register location)
Width:	I/O: 32 bit word length
	Memory: 32 bit or 64 bit word length
Valid Values:	Device dependent
Description:	The Base Address register bit definitions are compliant with the PCI Local Bus Specification.

The Base Address register bit definitions are compliant with the PCI Local Bus Specification.

This register set allows a PCI/PCI bridge device's internal (device specific) bridge registers to be dynamically mapped into I/O and memory space. Depending on the system implementation, this dynamic mapping may be accomplished by the System ROM BIOS during POST or later by other system software such as a device driver or operating system.

PCI devices with a Type 01H configuration space header contain 8 bytes dedicated for memory and I/O base address. This means that a PCI/PCI Bridge can implement either one or two Base Address Registers, depending on the word length and type of the register.

Note that there is no specification for the order in which registers request blocks of I/O or memory. Any combination is permissible.

These registers do not provide a mechanism that allows the device to request specific addresses in the address space.

PCI devices should always allow control functions to be mapped into memory space.

I/O BASE ADDRESS IMPLEMENTATION

For I/O base address registers, there are two ways to decrease the number of bits in the address decoder. The first method is to claim more address space than is actually needed. For example, a device that has 16 bytes of registers may decide to claim 128 bytes of address space, thus saving three bits in the decoder.

The second way to decrease the number of bits in the address decoder is to take advantage of the Intel x86 architecture. This architecture only has a 64K I/O space. Hence, there is no need to implement the top 16 bits of the 32 bit I/O base register. These bits can be hardwired to zero. However, a full 32 bit decode must still be performed. Note that the decode for the top 16 bits can be accomplished using a simple NAND gate.

The first method should be avoided since I/O space is typically tight. In no case should a PCI device designed to operate in an ISA compatible system request more than 256 bytes of I/O space per each I/O base address register. The major reason is the ISA aliasing issue, which is discussed in Appendices E and F.

To assign a value to an I/O base address register, software should do the following:

1. Write a value of 1 to all bits within this register.

2. Confirm that bit 0 of this register contains a value of 1, indicating an I/O request.

3. Starting at bit location 2, search for the first bit set to a value of 1. This bit is the binary weighted size of the total contiguous block of I/O address space requested. For example, if bit 8 is the first bit set, the device is requesting a 256 byte block of I/O address space.

4. Write the start address of the I/O space block assigned to this register.

Bit	Type	Function
0	RO	**Address Space Indicator** 0 N/A for I/O—see Memory Base Address Implementation. 1 Base address register is requesting I/O space.
1	RO	**Reserved** This bit must return zero when read.
31::2	RW	**I/O Base Address** After reset, this register's contents are undefined. Enumeration software programs this register to determine the size and alignment for an I/O Base address range. The software then programs this register with an assigned physical start address for the I/O address range.

Table 19-12: I/O Base Address Register

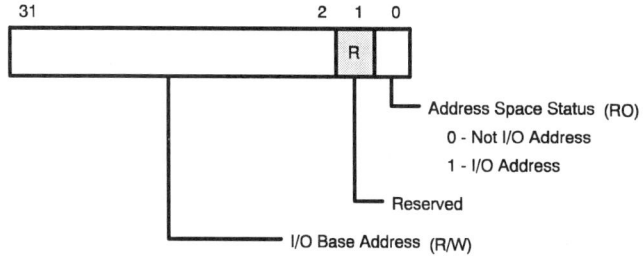

Figure 19-12: I/O Base Address Register

MEMORY BASE ADDRESS IMPLEMENTATION

Memory base address decoders can decrease the number of address bits by claiming more space than is needed. Hardwiring upper order address bits is not allowed (unless the device is requesting space at an address below 1 megabytes - see the definition for Base Address Memory Type bits in Table 19-13).

Bit	Type	Function
0	RO	**Address Space Indicator** 0 Base address register is requesting memory space. 1 N/A for Memory—see I/O Base ADDRESS Implementation.
2::1	RO	**Memory Mapping Type** 00 Base address is 32 bits wide. Set the base address anywhere within the 32 bit memory space. 01 Not allowed The upper 12 bits in this register can be hardwired to zero, but must still participate in address decode. Configuration software must handle this case. 10 Base address is 64 bits wide. Set the base address anywhere within the 64 bit memory space. 11 Reserved. Prior revisions did support the '01' encoding, which requested a memory range below the first physical 1MB boundary. For PCI/PCI bridges, the bridge must be capable of operation downstream from another bridge, which precludes this definition.
3	RO	**Prefetchable** Encodes the attributes of the requested memory address range as follows: 0 Memory is not prefetchable. Read side effects may occur. 1 Memory address range is prefetchable and byte merging of write transactions is allowed (take multiple byte and/or word accesses from the CPU and merge them into a single DWORD write on PCI). Prefetchable memory has no side effects on read transactions. It returns all bytes, regardless of the byte enable values.
31::4	RW	**32–Bit Memory Base Address** After reset, this register's contents are undefined. Enumeration software programs this register to determine the size and alignment for a 32-bit Memory Base address range. The software then programs this register with an assigned physical start address for the memory address range. Bits [2::0] are set to '000'.
63::4	RW	**64–Bit Memory Base Address** After reset, this register's contents are undefined. Enumeration software programs this register to determine the size and alignment for a 64-bit Memory Base address range. The software then programs this register with an assigned physical start address for the memory address range. Bits [2::0] are set to '100'.

Table 19-13: Memory Base Address Register

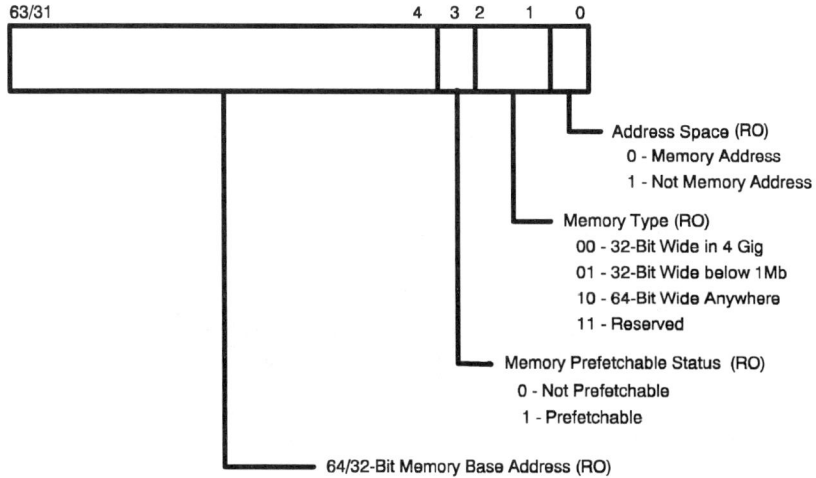

Figure 19-13: Memory Base Address Register

To assign a value to a memory base address register, software should do the following:

1. Write a value of 1 to all bits within this register.

2. Confirm that bit 0 of this register contains a value of 0, indicating a memory request.

3. Starting at bit location 4, search upwards for the first bit set to a value of 1. This bit is the binary weighted size of the total contiguous block of memory requested. For example, if bit 15 is the first bit set, the device is requesting a 32 kilobyte block of memory.

4. Write the start address of the memory block assigned to this register. This memory address region must not conflict with any other memory space utilized within the system. In addition, it must comply with the definition contained in bits 1 and 2 of this register.

MEMORY AND I/O BASE ADDRESS REGISTER GUIDELINES

Power-up system software such as the PC/AT compatible System BIOS is responsible for initializing memory and I/O base address registers with system resources in a resource conflict free manner. However, depending on the system configuration, certain system resources (most likely I/O) may be depleted before all base address registers have been initialized. Base address registers that do not get a system resource assigned will be initialized with a value zero. In addition, depending on the type of resource that failed to be assigned, the associated memory or I/O control bit in the PCI function's Command Register will be set to disabled (zero). Note that some System BIOS vendors go as far as to reset the I/O, Memory, and Bus Master control bits in a device's Command Register (bits 2::0 = 0) when any memory or I/O allocation failure occurs This gives device specific software two quick methods for determining what memory and I/O system resource allocations failed for their device.

Device-specific executables such as device drivers and add-in card BIOSs should never assign system resources to their device. System resource conflicts could result, rendering the system inoperable. Allocating system resources is the task of power-up system software and operating systems.

When a resource allocation fails for a given PCI device, the power-up system software should attempt to allocate memory and I/O system resources to the remaining base address registers that have requested resources. This permits PCI devices that map their control functions into both memory and I/O spaces to use the space that was successfully assigned. The other space should remain disabled and unused.

The Command Register control bit for either the memory or I/O address space that is disabled by the power-up system software or an operating system should not be enabled by device specific software. This could result in system resource conflicts, depending on the programmed values of the control bit's associated base address registers.

If a device uses the "claim more than needed" technique for minimizing decoder bits (in either memory or I/O), there is no requirement for how the device should behave if it is accessed in the "unused" portion of a claimed range. As an example, take a device that has 256 bytes of registers mapped to memory but claims 4K of memory space. When software accesses any of the 256 bytes, the device is expected to respond appropriately for those bytes. Accesses to any other part of the 4K range can behave any way the device finds appropriate. For instance, it may be easiest to alias the 256 bytes throughout the 4K range. Another possibility is to just return garbage whenever the "unused" portion is accessed.

PCI-X AND THE BASE ADDRESS REGISTERS

Operating in conventional PCI mode, a PCI-X bridge's Base Address registers adhere to the conventional Type 01h configuration address space definition for these registers. If the PCI-X bridge's primary interface is operating in PCI-X mode, the **Memory Base Address** registers (other than the **Expansion ROM** register) must support 64-bit addressing, as defined in the *PCI Local Bus Local Bus Specification, Revision 2.2*.

> **PCI-X devices typically set the Prefetchable bit in memory base address registers. The exception is when the PCI function is assigned a memory range that includes addresses with read side effects.**

Primary Bus Number	
Offset:	18h
Width:	1 Byte
Valid Values:	See Below
Description:	The Primary Bus Number register is a read/write register. Configuration software programs this register with the number of the PCI bus that the primary interface of the bridge is connected to. The PCI bridge uses this register to decode type 1 configuration transactions on the secondary interface that should be converted to Special Cycle transactions on the primary interface.

> In all cases except one, the PCI/PCI Bridge is required to implement this register as a read/write register. The exception is when a PCI/PCI bridge is connected by design or implementation to PCI bus segment 0. In this case, the bridge's Primary Bus Number register can be read-only and return a value of '0'.

Bit	Type	Function
7::0	RW	**Primary Bus Number** The number of the PCI bus that the primary interface to which the bridge is connected. The value of this register after reset must be 00h.

Table 19-14: Primary Bus Number Register

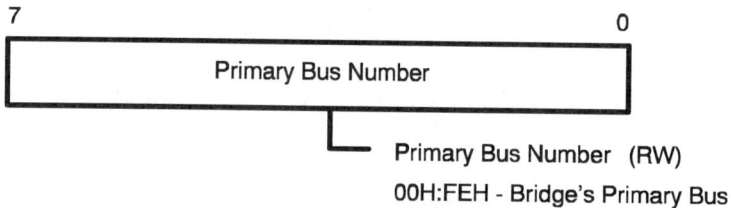

Figure 19-14: Primary Bus Number Register

Secondary Bus Number	
Offset:	19h
Width:	1 Byte
Valid Values:	See Below
Description:	The Secondary Bus Number register is a read/write register. Configuration software programs this register with the number of the PCI bus that the secondary interface of the bridge is connected to. Configuration software programs the value in this register. The bridge uses this register to determine when to respond to type 1 configuration transactions on the secondary interface.

Bit	Type	Function
7::0	RW	**Secondary Bus Number** The number of the PCI bus to which the secondary interface of the bridge is connected. The value of this register after reset must be 00h.

Table 19-15: Secondary Bus Number Register

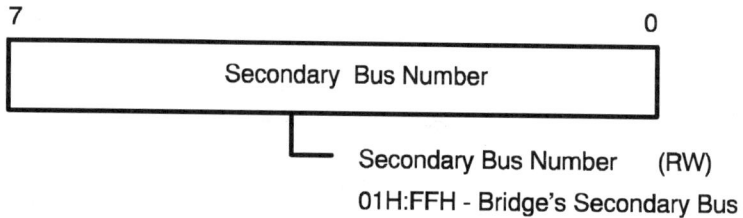

Figure 19-15: Secondary Bus Number Register

1092

PCI-X AND THE SECONDARY BUS NUMBER REGISTER

Operating in conventional PCI mode, a PCI-X bridge's **Secondary Bus Number** register adheres to the conventional Type 01h configuration address space definition for this register. If either interface of a PCI-X bridge device is operating in PCI-X mode, the following requirements apply:

■ The **Secondary Bus Number** register's value should not be changed by system software while secondary devices have incomplete Split Transactions anywhere in the system.

■ After the **Secondary Bus Number** register's value is changed, at least one PCI configuration address space write transaction must be executed on each device attached to the bridge's secondary bus. This ensures that each secondary device's **PCI-X Bridge Status** register's **Device Number** field (bits [7:3]) and **Bus Number** field (bits [15:8]) reflects the current system configuration.

Subordinate Bus Number	
Offset:	1Ah
Width:	1 Byte
Valid Values:	See Below
Description:	The Subordinate Bus Number register is a read/write register. Configuration software programs this register with the number of the highest numbered PCI bus that is behind (or subordinate to) a bridge. The bridge uses this register to determine when to respond to type 1 configuration transactions on the primary interface and to pass them on to the secondary interface.

Bit	Type	Function
7::0	RW	**Subordinate Bus Number** Contains the highest numbered PCI bus that is behind (or subordinate to) a bridge. The value of this register after reset must be 00h.

Table 19-16: Subordinate Bus Number Register

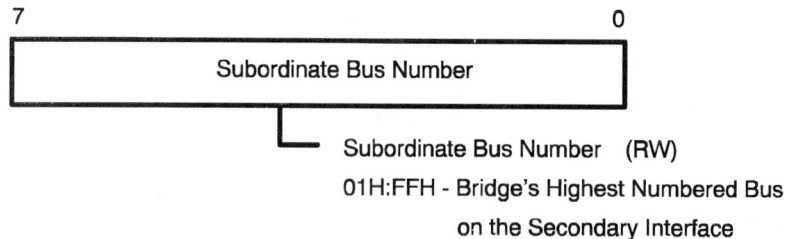

Figure 19-16: Subordinate Bus Number Register

Secondary Latency Timer	
Offset:	1Bh
Width:	1 Byte
Valid Values:	00h–FFh
Description:	This register's definition is the same as the Latency Timer register at offset 0Dh in the predefined header region. The Latency Timer at offset 0Dh is only applicable to the primary interface of a PCI bridge. The Secondary Latency Timer register is only applicable to the secondary interface.
	This register specifies the Master Latency Timer value for a PCI Master when the device is on the PCI bus.
	A reasonable implementation of this register is to only implement the top five bits. This means that field can only be modified in increments of 8, but this is acceptable.
	A typical way for a System BIOS to configure this register is to just choose an appropriate value and use that value for all devices. 32 (approximately 1 µsec) is a reasonable value. Higher level software, *i.e.*, an OS heuristic, can use the knowledge of how the system is being used (server, desktop, multimedia) as well as MIN_GNT and MAX_LAT values to adjust the timers appropriately.

Bit	Function
7::0	**Read Only Implementation:** Bus Masters incapable of bursting for more than two DATA PHASES may implement this register with a Read Only attribute. The register must contain a fixed value of 16 or less.
	Read/Write Implementation: Bus Masters capable of bursting for more than two DATA PHASES must implement this register with a Read/Write attribute. **RST#** should clear this register.

Table 19-17: Secondary Latency Timer Register

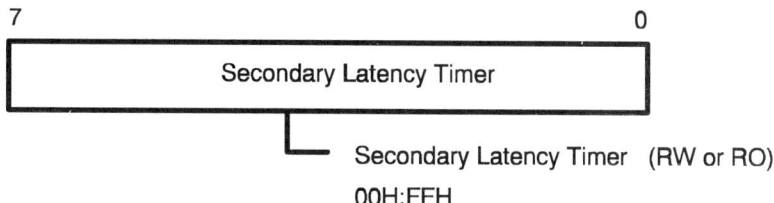

Figure 19-17: Secondary Latency Timer Register

I/O Base	
Offset:	1Ch
Width:	1 Byte
Valid Values:	See Below
Description:	The I/O Base register defines the bottom address (inclusive) of an I/O address range. This range is used by the PCI/PCI bridge to determine when to forward I/O transactions from one interface to the other. This register is optional. Consequently, the I/O Base register can be either a read/write or read only register. If a bridge supports an I/O address range then this register must be initialized by configuration software.

Bit	Type	Function
7::0	RO	**Read Only Implementation:** The register must return a value of zero. **Read/Write Implementation:**
3::0	RO	These bits encode the I/O addressing capability of the PCI/PCI bridge as follows: 0000b 16 Bit I/O addressing 0001b 32 Bit I/O addressing 02h-Fh Reserved
7::4	RW	0h-0Fh These bits correspond to address bits AD[15::12] for I/O address decoding.
		The lower 12 address bits, AD[11::0], are not implemented in the I/O Base register. The bridge always assumes that these bits are zero. Consequently, PCI/PCI bridge devices consume a minimum of 4K of I/O address space when the I/O Base register is implemented.

Table 19-18: I/O Base Register

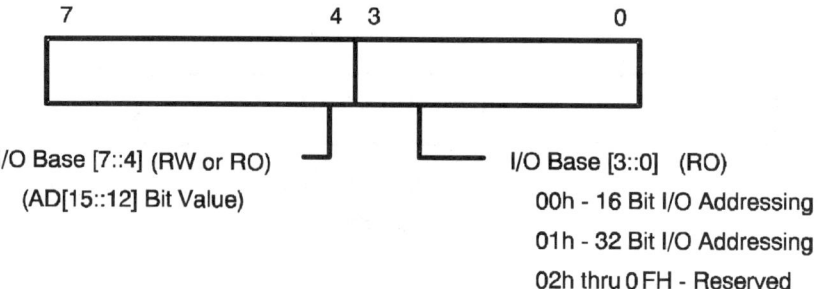

Figure 19-18: I/O Base Register

PCI/PCI BRIDGE I/O BASE REGISTER

Configuration software such as a System BIOS or operating system is responsible for allocating system resources. When initializing PCI/PCI bridges, the resource allocation algorithm must account for the I/O address space that the bridge itself consumes, as well as the I/O resources that are requested by devices below (on the secondary interface) of the bridge. These devices may be other bridges as well as single and multifunction PCI devices such as LAN, and SCSI.

> With only 64K of I/O address space, it is easy to see how this resource can be depleted in a fully loaded system. This is a major reason why PCI devices should implement memory base address registers that support memory mapped I/O.

Once the configuration software has determined how much I/O address space is required for a bridge and its secondary interface components, it will allocate a previously unassigned amount of contiguous I/O address space to the bridge device. The base of the allocated I/O address space is the value programmed into the I/O Base Register. The base address for this register will always be aligned on a 4K boundary. The reason is because the bridge assumes that the lower 12 address bits, AD[11::0], of the I/O Base Address are zero. When assigning I/O address resources to the bridge and its secondary interface components, the configuration software will use the range of I/O addresses between the values contained in the I/O Base registers and the I/O Limit registers (inclusive).

16 BIT I/O ADDRESSING

PCI/PCI bridges support 16 bit I/O address decoding when I/O Base register bits [3::0] contain a value of 0h. The bridge assumes that that the upper 16 address bits, AD[31::16], of the I/O base are 0000h. The I/O Base Upper 16 Bits and the

I/O Limit Upper 16 Bits registers are implemented as read only and return zero when read

> The I/O address range supported by the bridge will be restricted to the first 64 Kbytes of PCI I/O address space (0000 0000h to 0000 FFFFh) when using 16 Bit I/O addressing. However, the bridge must still perform a full 32 bit decode of the I/O address as required by the PCI Local Bus Specification (*i.e.*, check that AD[31::16] = 0).

32 BIT I/O ADDRESSING

PCI/PCI bridges support 32 bit I/O address decoding when I/O Base register bits [3::0] contain a value of 01h. The upper 16 bits of the 32 bit I/O Base address, corresponding to AD[31::16], are contained in the I/O Base Upper 16 Bits register. The I/O address range supported by the bridge may be located anywhere in the 4 Gigabyte PCI I/O address space.

> Note that the 4 Kbyte alignment and granularity restrictions still apply.

I/O Limit	
Offset:	1Dh
Width:	1 Byte
Valid Values:	See Below
Description:	The I/O Limit register defines the top address (inclusive) of an I/O address range. This range is used by the PCI/PCI bridge to determine when to forward I/O transactions from one interface to the other. This register is optional. Consequently, the I/O Limit register can be either a read/write or read only register. If a bridge supports an I/O address range then this register must be initialized by configuration software.

Bit	Type	Function
7::0	RO	**Read Only Implementation:** The register must return a value of zero. **Read/Write Implementation:**
3::0	RO	These bits encode the I/O addressing capability of the PCI/PCI Bridge as follows: 0h 16 Bit I/O addressing 01h 32 Bit I/O addressing 02h-Fh Reserved
7::4	RW	0h-0Fh These bits correspond to address bits AD[15::12] for I/O address decoding. The lower 12 address bits, AD[11::0], are not implemented in the I/O Limit register. The bridge always assumes that these bits are FFFh. Consequently, the top of a PCI/PCI bridge device's I/O address range will be at the top of a 4K aligned address block when the I/O Limit register is implemented.

Table 19-19: I/O Limit Register

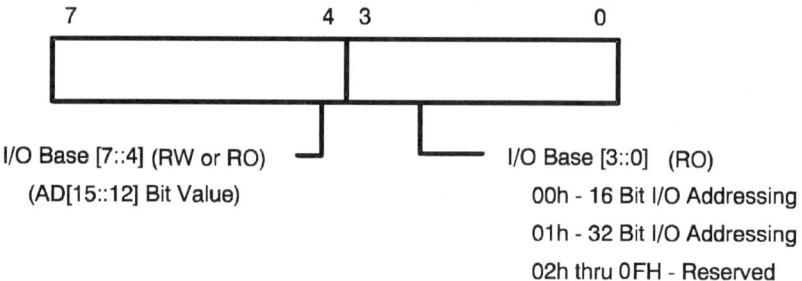

Figure 19-19: I/O Limit Register

Secondary Status

Offset:	1Eh
Width:	2 Bytes
Valid Values:	N/A. This field is a collection of bits, not a range of values. The register should not be viewed as values, but as individual bits.
Description:	This register records events that occur on the PCI bus. The following rules apply to this register:

1   Reads of this register occur normally.

2   Writes to this register may clear bits to zero but never set them to one.

3   There are several bits in the Status Register Table below bits with the attribute type RWC. These are individual bits that are cleared to zero if the bit has the write attribute and its bit location is written with a data value of one.

4   The function of the device determines which bits will be implemented.

The Secondary Status register bit definitions are compliant with the PCI Local Bus Specification. However, these bits only apply to the secondary interface of a **PCI/PCI** bridge.

   The Secondary Status Register is typically not used by device drivers. Rather, it is intended to record events that (a) tend to be catastrophic and (b) are not part of normal operation.

> Bit 14 of the Status register, offset 06h in the PCI/PCI bridge's configuration space, is the Signaled System Error bit. In the Secondary Status register, the bit is defined as the Received System Error bit. This is the major difference between the two status registers.
>
> A PCI/PCI bridge never asserts SERR# on the secondary interface. The bridge will assert SERR# on the primary interface if SERR# is asserted on the secondary interface. Note that the SERR# Enable bit in the Command register, offset 04h, and the Secondary SERR# bit in the Bridge Control register, offset 3Eh, must be enabled to allow the secondary interface SERR# to be reported.

Bit	Type	Function
4::0	RO	**Reserved**
5	RO	**66MHz Capable Status** 0 The secondary interface of the bridge is incapable of 66MHz operation. 1 The secondary interface of the bridge is capable of 66MHz operation. This bit is optional.
6	RO	**Reserved**
7	RO	**Fast Back–to–Back Status** 0 The bridge's secondary interface is incapable of decoding fast–back–to–back transactions to different targets. 1 The bridge's secondary interface is capable of decoding fast–back–to–back transactions to different targets. This bit is optional.
8	RWC	**Master Data Parity Status** 0 No data parity errors have been detected on the secondary interface. (**RST#** state). 1 A data parity error has been detected on the secondary interface. All three of the following conditions must be met: a. The bridge asserted **PERR#** (read transaction) or detected **PERR#** asserted (write transaction). b. The agent which set the bit was the bridge, as bus master during the transaction on the secondary interface when the error occurred. c. **Parity Error Response** bit in the Bridge Control register is set to '1'. This bit is only implemented by Bus Masters.
10::9	RO	**Device Select Timing Status** These two bits encode the timing of the secondary interface **DEVSEL#**. This encoding indicates the slowest response time the bridge will use to assert **DEVSEL#** on its secondary interface when the bridge responds a target to any PCI transaction but a PCI configuration address space read or write. 00 Device asserts **DEVSEL#** in the *fast* timing mode for any bus command. 01 Device asserts **DEVSEL#** in the *medium* timing mode for any bus command. 10 Device asserts **DEVSEL#** in the *slow* timing mode for any bus command. 11 Reserved.

Table 19-20: Secondary Status Register

		Configuration read and write cycles do not apply to the above definition. For example, if a device performs FAST decode for all memory and I/O accesses, but medium decode for configuration accesses, the device should set this register to fast.
11	RWC	**Signaled Target Abort Status** 0 A Target Abort was signaled by the bridge on its secondary interface. (**RST#** state). 1 A Target Abort was signaled by the bridge on its secondary interface. The bridge must implement this bit.
12	RWC	**Received Target Abort Status** 0 A Target Abort was not detected by the bridge on its secondary interface. (**RST#** state). 1 A Target Abort was detected by the bridge on its secondary interface. The bridge must implement this bit.
13	RWC	**Received Master Abort Status** 0 A Master Abort was not detected by the bridge on its secondary interface. 1 A Master Abort was detected by the bridge on its secondary interface.
14	RWC	**Received System Error Status** 0 SERR# assertion not detected on the secondary interface. 1 SERR# assertion detected on the secondary interface.
15	RWC	**Detected Parity Error Status** 0 Bridge did not detect an address or data parity error on its secondary interface. (**RST#** state). 1 Bridge did detect an address or data parity error on its secondary interface. Bridges will set this bit regardless of the state of Parity Error Response (bit 0 of the Bridge Control egister).

Table 19-20: Secondary Status Register (continued)

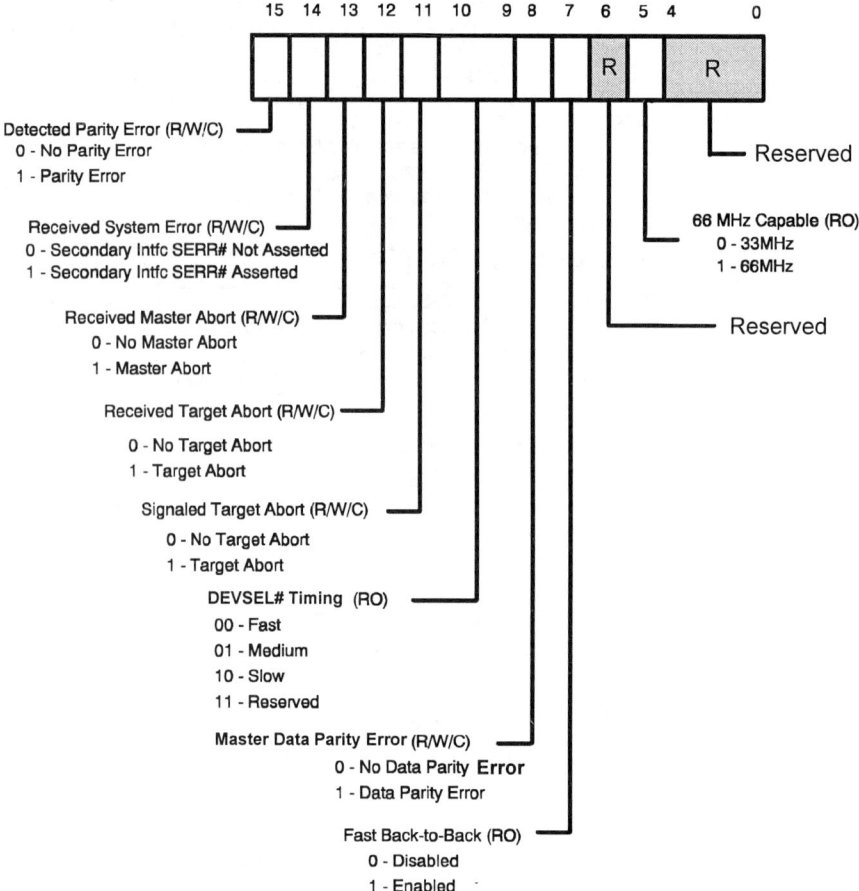

Figure 19-20: Secondary Status Register

Memory Base		
Offset:	20h	
Width:	2 Bytes	
Valid Values:	See Below	
Description:	The Memory Base register defines the base address (inclusive) of a memory mapped I/O address range. This range is used by the PCI/PCI bridge to determine when to forward I/O transactions from one interface to the other.	

Bit	Type	Function
15::4	RW	These bits correspond to address bits AD[31::20] for decoding a 32 bit address.
		The bridge does not implement AD[19::0] in the Memory Base register. The bridge assumes that these lower 20 bits are zero. This aligns the Memory Base register value on a 1 Megabyte boundary.
3::0	RO	These bits return zero when read.

Table 19-21: Memory Base Register

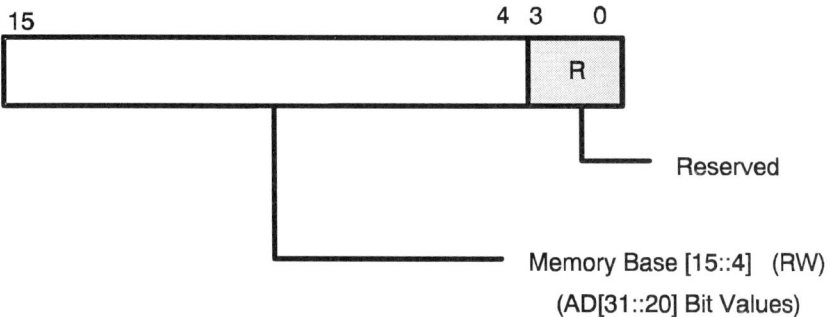

Figure 19-21: Memory Base Register

Memory Limit		
Offset:	22h	
Width:	2 Bytes	
Valid Values:	See Below	
Description:	The Memory Limit register defines the top address (inclusive) of a memory mapped I/O address range. This range is used by the PCI/PCI bridge to determine when to forward I/O transactions from one interface to the other.	

Bit	Type	Function
15::4	RW	These bits correspond to address bits AD[31::20] for decoding a 32 bit address.
		The bridge does not implement AD[19::0] in the Memory Limit register. The bridge assumes that these lower 20 bits are FFFFh. This aligns the top of the memory address range at the top of a 1 Megabyte aligned address block.
3::0	RO	These bits return zero when read.

Table 19-22: Memory Limit Register

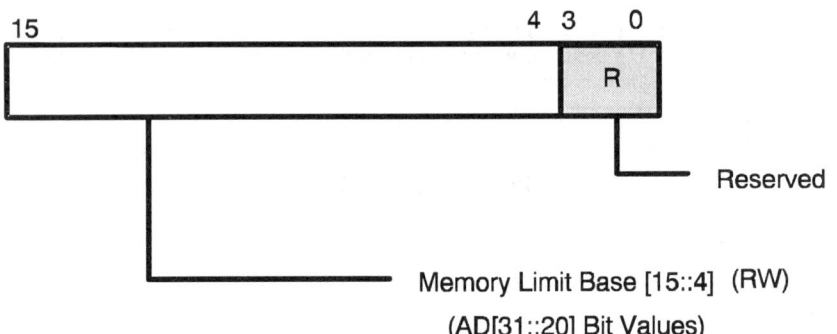

Figure 19-22: Memory Limit Register

Prefetchable Memory Base	
Offset:	24h
Width:	2 Bytes
Valid Values:	See Below
Description:	The Prefetchable Memory Base register defines the base address (inclusive) of a prefetchable memory address range. This range is used by the PCI/PCI bridge to determine when to forward memory transactions from one interface to the other. This register is optional. Consequently, the Prefetchable Memory Base register can be either a read/write or read only register. If a bridge supports a prefetchable memory address range, then this register must be initialized by configuration software.

Bit	Type	Function
15::0	RO	**Read Only Implementation:** The register must return a value of zero.
3::0	RO	**Read/Write Implementation:** These bits encode the prefetchable memory addressing capability of the PCI/PCI bridge as follows: 0000b 32 Bit addressing 0001b 64 Bit addressing 02h-Fh Reserved If bits [3::0] contain 01h, the bridge supports 64 bit addresses. The upper 32 bits of the Prefetchable Memory Base register are contained in the Prefetchable Base Upper 32 Bits register.
15::4	RW	0h- These bits correspond to address bits AD[31::20] of a 32 FFF0h bit address. The bridge does not implement AD[19::0] in the Prefetchable Memory Base register. The bridge assumes that these lower 20 bits are zero. This aligns the Prefetchable Memory Base register value on a 1 megabyte boundary.

Table 19-23: Prefetchable Memory Base Register

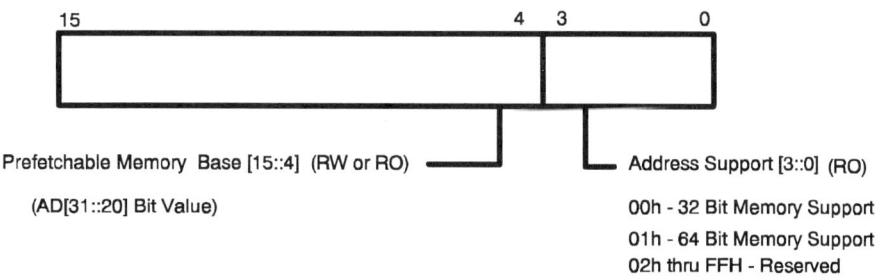

Prefetchable Memory Base [15::4] (RW or RO)

(AD[31::20] Bit Value)

Address Support [3::0] (RO)

00h - 32 Bit Memory Support
01h - 64 Bit Memory Support
02h thru FFH - Reserved

Figure 19-23: Prefetchable Memory Base Register

PCI-X AND THE PREFETCHABLE MEMORY BASE REGISTER

Operating in conventional PCI mode, a PCI-X bridge's **Prefetchable Memory Base** register adheres to the conventional Type 01h configuration address space definition for this register. This register is required if the primary interface of a PCI-X bridge device is operating in the PCI-X mode.

Prefetchable Memory Limit	
Offset:	26h
Width:	2 Bytes
Valid Values:	See Below
Description:	The Prefetchable Memory Limit register defines the top address (inclusive) of a prefetchable memory address range. This range is used by the PCI/PCI bridge to determine when to forward memory transactions from one interface to the other. This register is optional. Consequently, the Prefetchable Memory Limit register can be either a read/write or read only register. If a bridge supports a prefetchable memory address range, then this register must be initialized by configuration software

Bit	Type	Function
15::0	RO	**Read Only Implementation:** The register must return a value of zero.
3::0	RO	**Read/Write Implementation:** These bits encode the prefetchable memory addressing capability of the PCI/PCI bridge as follows: 0000b 32 Bit addressing 0001b 64 Bit addressing 02h-Fh Reserved If bits [3::0] contain 01h, the bridge supports 64 bit addresses. The upper 32 bits of the Prefetchable Memory Limit register are contained in the Prefetchable Limit Upper 32 Bits register.
15::4	RW	0h- These bits correspond to address bits AD[31::20] of a 32 FFF0h bit address. The bridge does not implement AD[19::0] in the Prefetchable Memory Limit register. The bridge assumes that these lower 20 bits are FFFFFh. This aligns the top of the Prefetchable Memory Limit register at the top of a 1 Megabyte aligned address block.

Table 19-24: Prefetchable Memory Limit Register

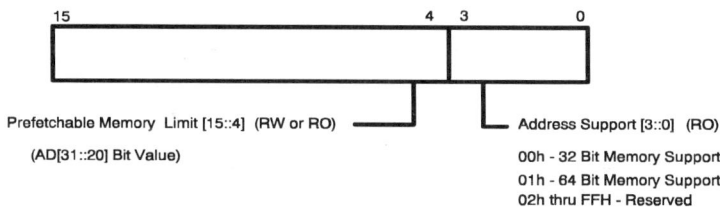

Figure 19-24: Prefetchable Memory Limit Register

PCI-X AND THE PREFETCHABLE MEMORY LIMIT REGISTER

Operating in conventional PCI mode, a PCI-X bridge's **Prefetchable Memory Limit** register adheres to the conventional Type 01h configuration address space definition for this register. This register is required if the primary interface of a PCI-X bridge device is operating in the PCI-X mode.

Prefetchable Base Upper 32 Bits	
Offset:	28h
Width:	4 Bytes
Valid Values:	See Below
Description:	The Prefetchable Base Upper 32 Bits register defines the upper 32 bits of the base of a prefetchable 64 bit memory address range. This range is used by the PCI/PCI bridge to determine when to forward memory transactions from one interface to the other. This register is optional. Consequently, the Prefetchable Base Upper 32 Bits register can be either a read/write or read only register. If a bridge supports a 64 bit prefetchable memory address range, then this register must be initialized by configuration software.

Bit	Type	Function
31::0	RO	**Read Only Implementation:** Configured as read only if the bridge does not implement a Prefetchable Memory Base register or the Prefetchable Memory Base register indicates support for 32 bit addressing. The register must return a value of zero.
31::0	RW	**Read/Write Implementation:** Specifies the upper 32 bits of a 64 bit Prefetchable Memory Base address. The bits in this register correspond to AD[63::32].

Table 19-25: Prefetchable Base Upper 32 Bits Register

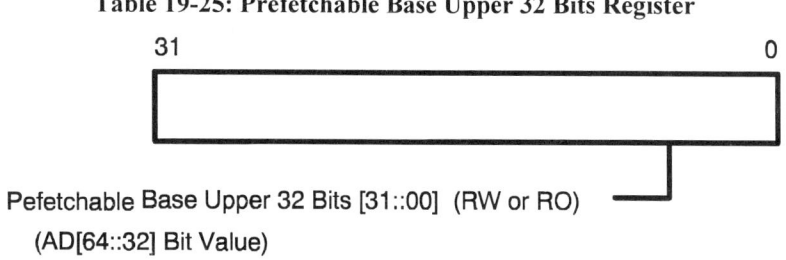

Figure 19-25: Prefetchable Base Upper 32 Bits Register

PCI-X AND THE PREFETCHABLE BASE UPPER 32 BITS REGISTER

Operating in conventional PCI mode, a PCI-X bridge's **Prefetchable Base Upper 32 Bits** register adheres to the conventional Type 01h configuration address space definition for this register. This register is required if the primary interface of a PCI-X bridge device is operating in the PCI-X mode.

Prefetchable Limit Upper 32 Bits	
Offset:	2Ch
Width:	4 Bytes
Valid Values:	See Below
Description:	The Prefetchable Limit Upper 32 Bits register defines the top address (inclusive) of a prefetchable 64 bit memory address range. This range is used by the PCI/PCI bridge to determine when to forward memory transactions from one interface to the other. This register is optional. Consequently, the Prefetchable Limit Upper 32 Bits register can be either a read/write or read only register. If a bridge supports a 64 bit prefetchable memory address range, then this register must be initialized by configuration software.

Bit	Type	Function
31::0	RO	**Read Only Implementation:** Configured as read-only if the bridge does not implement a Prefetchable Memory Base register or the Prefetchable Memory Base register indicates support for 32 bit addressing. The register must return a value of zero.
31::0	RW	**Read/Write Implementation:** Specifies the upper 32 bits of a 64 bit Prefetchable Memory Limit address. The bits in this register correspond to AD[63::32].

Table 19-26: Prefetchable Limit Upper 32 Bits Register

Pefetchable Limit Upper 32 Bits [31::00]   (RW or RO)
(AD[64::32] Bit Value)

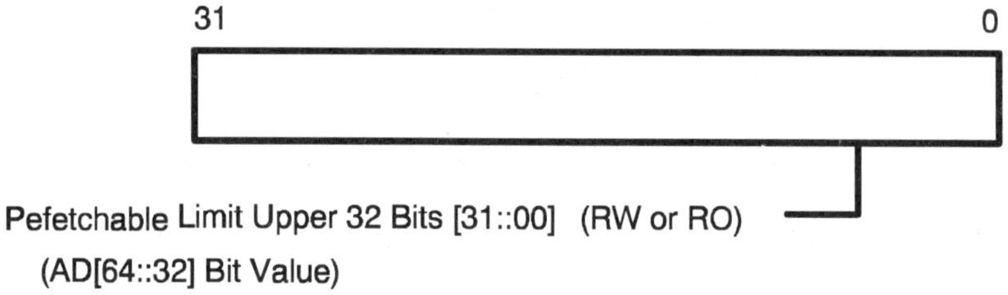

Figure 19-26: Prefetchable Limit Upper 32 Bits Register

PCI-X AND THE PREFETCHABLE LIMIT UPPER 32 BITS REGISTER

Operating in conventional PCI mode, a PCI-X bridge's **Prefetchable Limit Upper 32 Bits** register adheres to the conventional Type 01h configuration address space definition for this register. This register is required if the primary interface of a PCI-X bridge device is operating in the PCI-X mode.

I/O Base Upper 16 Bits	
Offset:	30h
Width:	2 Bytes
Valid Values:	See Below
Description:	The I/O Base Upper 16 Bits register defines the upper 16 bits of the base of a 32 bit I/O address range. This range is used by the PCI/PCI bridge to determine when to forward I/O transactions from one interface to the other. This register is optional. Consequently, the I/O Base Upper 16 Bits register can be either a read/write or read only register. If a bridge supports a 32 bit I/O address range, then this register must be initialized by configuration software.

Bit	Type	Function
15::0	RO	**Read Only Implementation:** Configured as read only if the bridge does not implement an I/O Base register or the I/O Base register indicates support for 16 bit addressing. The register must return a value of zero.
15::0	RW	**Read/Write Implementation:** Specifies the upper 16 bits of a 32 bit I/O Base address. The bits in this register correspond to AD[31::16].

Table 19-27: I/O Base Upper 16 Bits Register

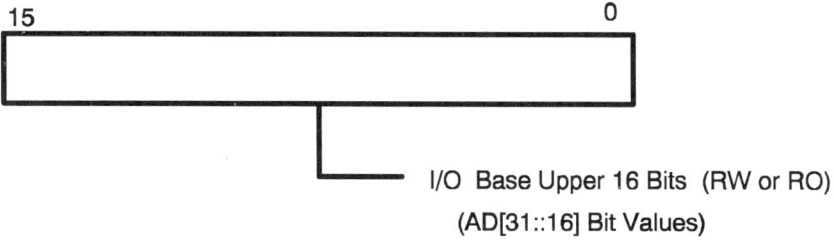

I/O Base Upper 16 Bits (RW or RO)
(AD[31::16] Bit Values)

Figure 19-27: I/O Base Upper 16 Bits Register

I/O Limit Upper 16 Bits	
Offset:	32h
Width:	2 Bytes
Valid Values:	See Below
Description:	The I/O Limit Upper 16 Bits register defines the top address (inclusive) of a 16 bit I/O address range. This range is used by the PCI/PCI bridge to determine when to forward memory transactions from one interface to the other. This register is optional. Consequently, the I/O Limit Upper 16 Bits register can be either a read/write or read only register. If a bridge supports a 32 bit I/O address range, then this register must be initialized by configuration software.

Bit	Type	Function
15::0	RO	**Read Only Implementation:** Configured as read only if the bridge does not implement an I/O Base register or the I/O Base register indicates support for 16 bit addressing. The register must return a value of zero.
15::0	RW	**Read/Write Implementation:** Specifies the upper 16 bits of a 32 bit I/O Limit address. The bits in this register correspond to AD[31::16].

Table 19-28: I/O Limit Upper 16 Bits Register

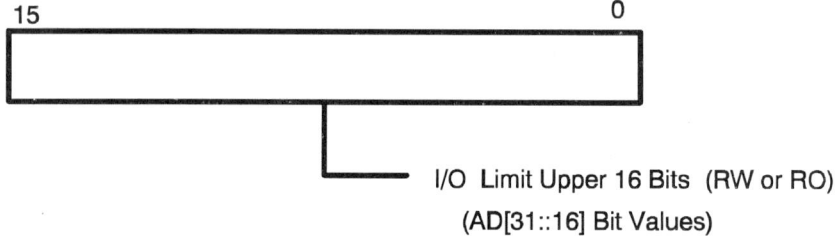

I/O Limit Upper 16 Bits (RW or RO)
(AD[31::16] Bit Values)

Figure 19-28: I/O Limit Upper 16 Bits Register

Capabilities Pointer	
Offset:	34h
Width:	1 Byte
Valid Values:	40h–FEh
Description:	This register contains an address pointer to a register located in the PCI function's Device Dependent region. The register pointed to is the head of a linked list of data structures that define the function's PCI capabilities, such as AGP or PCI Power Management. See Chapter 24 for a complete definition of this register.

> Register 34h is qualified by Bit 4 of Register 06h, the Status Register. If Bit 4 is set to '0', the CAP_PTR register is not valid. If Bit 4 is set to '1', the CAP_PTR register is valid if its value is within the legal range.

Bit	Type	Function
7::0	RO	**PCI Capabilities Pointer** Pointer to the head of a linked list of data structures that define the function's PCI capabilities.

Table 19-29: Capabilities Pointer Register

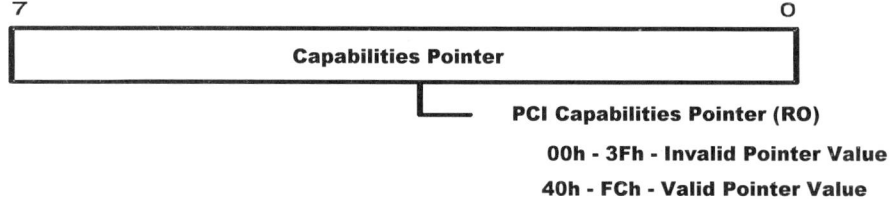

7   **Capabilities Pointer**   O

PCI Capabilities Pointer (RO)

00h - 3Fh - Invalid Pointer Value

40h - FCh - Valid Pointer Value

Figure 19-29: Capabilities Pointer Register

Expansion ROM Base Address Register	
Offset:	38h
Width:	4 Bytes
Valid Values:	Device dependent
Description:	The Expansion ROM Base Address register bit definitions are compliant with the PCI Local Bus Specification. This register allows a PCI device's expansion ROM to be mapped into a system's physical address space. Depending on the system implementation, this dynamic mapping may be accomplished by the System ROM BIOS during POST or later by other system software such as a device driver or operating system. See Chapter 23, *PCI Device Configuration*, for a description of how this register is implemented in a system.

Bit	Type	Function
0	RW	**Expansion ROM Decode Enable** 0 Disable decode the Expansion ROM within System memory address space. 1 Enable decode of the Expansion ROM within System memory address space. Bit 1 of this device's Command Register, the Memory Space Control bit, has precedence over this bit. It must be set to a value of 1 for this bit to enable the expansion ROM address decode.
10::1	RO	**Reserved**
31::11	RW	**Expansion ROM Base Address** Start address of the expansion ROM memory space region assigned to this device. This is where the expansion ROM code will appear in system memory when bit 0 of this register contains a value of 1 and bit 1 of this device's Command Register contains a value of 1. Because the Expansion ROM Base Address may share a decoder with the I/O and Memory Base Address Register, device independent software should not access any other base address register of this device while the expansion ROM decode for this device is enabled.

Table 19-30: Expansion ROM Base Address Register

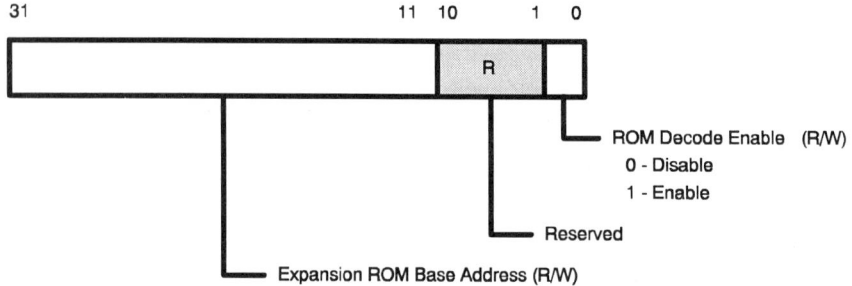

Figure 19-30: Expansion ROM Base Address Register

To assign an expansion ROM base address to this register, software should do the following:

1. Write a value of 1 to bits 11 through 31 of this register.

2. Starting at bit location 11, search upward for the first bit set to a value of 1. This bit is the binary weighted size of the total contiguous block of memory address space requested. For example, if bit 16 is the first bit set, the device is requesting a 64 kilobyte block of memory address space.

3. Write the start address of the memory space block assigned to this register. This memory space region must not conflict with any other memory address space utilized within the system. Otherwise, data reads from the ROM may be corrupted.

Expansion ROM Base Address registers may share an address decoder with other Base Address registers. This reduces the number of address decoders on a device. While this feature permits each base address register to hold a unique value at the same time, it does place constraints on software:

A device–independent software program should only set Bit 0, the Expansion ROM Decode Enable bit, to 1 when it is copying the expansion ROM code to the shadow memory. For example, when a PC/AT System BIOS copies a PCI ROM image to the ISA compatibility region between C0000h and EFFFFh. Also, POST code should RESET Bit 0 to zero before calling the initialization function of any relocated expansion ROM code. This is because the option ROM code may try to access the device using one or more of the device's standard base address registers. Because of the decoder implementation the registers may not be accessible if the expansion ROM register is left enabled.

Device specific code, (*i.e.*, a device driver) may set this bit to one (after locating a non–conflicting address space and doing the appropriate mapping) to obtain some device specific information out of the ROM.

Interrupt Line	
Offset:	3Ch
Width:	1 Byte
Valid Values:	00h–FFh
Description:	This register identifies which interrupt request line of a system interrupt controller the PCI device's interrupt line is connected to. Device drivers
	as well as other device dependent software query this register to determine the interrupt request line assigned to their device.
	This value is system architecture specific. For ISA compatible systems, valid encodings are shown below.

00h =   IRQ0
01h =   IRQ1
         —

0Eh =   IRQ14
0Fh =   IRQ15

Note that these encodings specify the physical pin on the system interrupt controller that the interrupt line is connected to. These encodings do not specify the interrupt vector that is generated by the interrupt controller. Other values are reserved.

Bit	Type	Function
7::0	RW	**Interrupt Line Value**
		00h:FEh Interrupt line number that the device is connected to.
		FFh Device interrupt line is not connected to a system interrupt controller.
		POST code is responsible for either setting the value in this register to the interrupt signal it is connected to. Alternatively, POST sets this register to a value of 0FFh when an interrupt pin is not implemented.

Table 19-31: Interrupt Line Register

POST software is responsible for routing the device's interrupt line to a system interrupt controller. This routing is dependent upon the specific hardware implementation. In addition, POST code will update this register with the interrupt line value assigned to the device. Software other than POST may read this register to determine which interrupt line the PCI device is connected.

Device specific executables including device drivers and add-in card BIOSs should never assign system resources such as an IRQ to their device. System resource conflicts could result, rendering the system inoperable. Allocating system resources is the task of power-up system configuration software and operating systems.

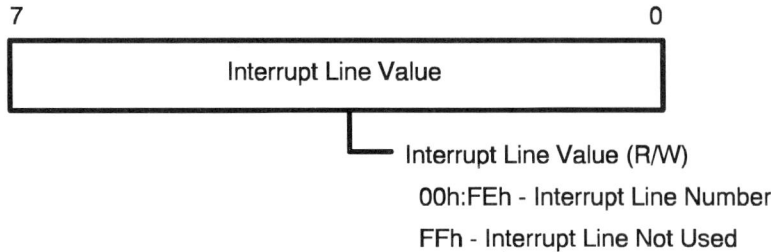

Figure 19-31: Interrupt Line Register

Interrupt Pin	
Offset:	3Dh
Width:	1 Byte
Valid Values:	00h–04h
Description:	The Interrupt Pin register bit definitions are compliant with the PCI Local Bus Specification.
	This register identifies which interrupt pin, INTA# through INTD#, a device function uses. This register assists in the proper initialization of the Interrupt Line register. Once initialization software knows which interrupt pin(s) the device uses, the Interrupt Line register(s) can be initialized appropriately.

Bit	Type	Function
7::0	RO	**Interrupt Pin Value**
		00h Interrupt pin is not used by the device.
		01h Device function uses interrupt pin INTA#.
		02h Device function uses interrupt pin INTB#.
		03h Device function uses interrupt pin INTC#.
		04h Device function uses interrupt pin INTD#.
		05h:FFh Reserved

Table 19-32: Interrupt Pin Register

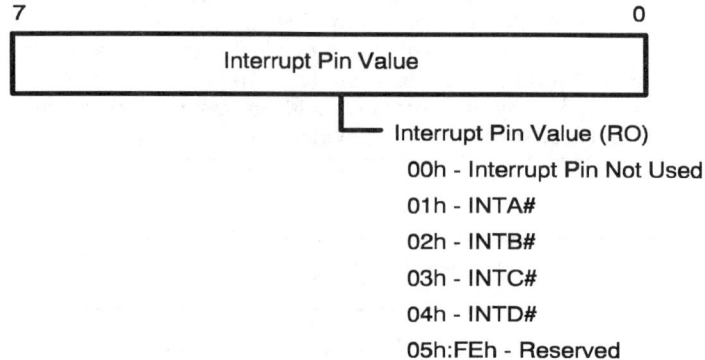

Figure 19-32: Interrupt Pin Register

Bridge Control	
Offset:	3Eh
Width:	2 Bytes
Valid Values:	N/A. This field is a collection of bits, not a range of values. The register should not be viewed as values, but as individual bits.
Description:	This register provides extensions to the Command register, offset 04h, that are specific to PCI/PCI bridges. Certain bits within this register affect the operation of both the primary and secondary interfaces of PCI/PCI bridges; other bits are applicable only to the secondary interface. These bits provide the same controls to the secondary interface as the Command register provides for the primary interface.

Bit	Type	Function
0	RW	**Parity Error Response Enable** Controls the bridge's response to parity detected on the secondary interface. 0 Ignore address and data parity errors on the secondary interface. (**RST#** state) 1 Enable parity error reporting and detection on the secondary interface.
1	RO	**SERR# Enable** Controls the forwarding of secondary interface SERR# assertions to the primary interface. 0 Disable forwarding secondary SERR# to primary interface's SERR# (**RST#** state) 1 Disable forwarding secondary SERR# to primary interface's SERR# (**RST#** state) The bridge can only detect the assertion of SERR# on the secondary interface if the SERR# Enable bit in Command register is set.
2	RW	**ISA Enable** 0 Forward all I/O addresses in the address range as defined by the I/O Base and I/O Limit registers. 1 Block forwarding of the top 768 bytes of each 1K I/O in the address range as defined by the I/O Base and I/O Limit registers. This applies to the first 64k of PCI I/O address space. I/O addresses in the defined range will not be forwarded to the secondary interface if this bit is set. Conversely, the secondary interface can forward I/O addresses in the top 768 bytes of each 1K to the primary interface.
3	RW	**VGA Enable** This bit modifies the PCI/PCI bridge's response to VGA compatible addresses. 0 Do not forward VGA compatible I/O and Memory addresses from the primary interface to the secondary interface. (**RST#** state) 1 Forward VGA compatible I/O and Memory addresses from the primary interface to the secondary interface. This will be done regardless of the state of the ISA Enable bit and the bridge's I/O and memory address ranges.
4	RO	**Reserved**
5	RW	**Master Abort Mode** 0 Do not report master aborts. The bridge will return FFFF FFFFh on reads. Data is discarderd on writes. (**RST#** state). 1 Report master aborts. SERR# will be detected if enabled. Target abort will be signaled if possible.

Table 19-33: Bridge Control Register

6	RW	**Secondary Bus Reset**
		Assert the **RST#** signal pin on the secondary interface.
		0 Do not assert the secondary interface **RST#** signal pin. (**RST#** state).
		1 Assert the secondary interface **RST#** signal pin.
7		**Fast Back to Back Enable**
		Controls ability of the bridge to generate Fast Back to Back transactions to different devices on the secondary interface.
	RO	**Read Only Implementation:**
		0 Fast Back to Back transactions not supported. Return 0 when this bit is read.
	RW	**Read/Write Implementation:**
		0 Disable Fast Back to Back transactions on the secondary interface. (**RST#** state).
		1 Enable Fast Back to Back transactions on the secondary interface.
		Bridges capable of generating Fast Back-to-Back cycles must implement this as a read/write bit. Configuration software should only set this bit if all devices on the secondary interface are capable of Fast Back-to-Back operation.
8	RW	**Primary Discard Timer**
		Selects the number of PCI clocks that the bridge will wait for a master on the primary interface of the bridge to repeat a Delayed Transaction request.
		0 The Primary Discard Timer counts 2^{15} PCI clock cycles. (**RST#** state).
		1 The Primary Discard Timer counts 2^{10} PCI clock cycles.
9	RW	**Secondary Discard Timer**
		Selects the number of PCI clocks that the bridge will wait for a master on the secondary interface of the bridge to repeat a Delayed Transaction request.
		0 The Secondary Discard Timer counts 2^{15} PCI clock cycles. (**RST#** state).
		1 The Secondary Discard Timer counts 2^{10} PCI clock cycles.
10	RW	**Discard Timer Status**
		When either the Primary Discard Timer or Secondary Discard Timer count expires and a Delayed Completion is discarded from a queue in the bridge, this bit is set to '1' to indicate the condition.
		0 No Discard Timer error (**RST#** state).
		1 Discard Timer error occured.

Table 19-33: Bridge Control Register (continued)

11	RW	**Discard Timer SERR# Enable** When either the Primary or Secondary Discard Timer count expires and a Delayed Completion is discarded from a queue in the bridge, and this bit is set to '1', the bridge asserts **SERR#** on the primary interface.
		0 **SERR#** is not asserted in the event the Primary Discard Timer or the Secondary Discard Timer expired. (**RST#** state).
		1 **SERR#** is asserted on the bridge's primary interface in the event the Primary Discard Timer or the Secondary Discard Timer expired and a delayed Transaction is discarded from the queue in the bridge.
15::12	RO	**Reserved**

Table 19-33: Bridge Control Register (continued)

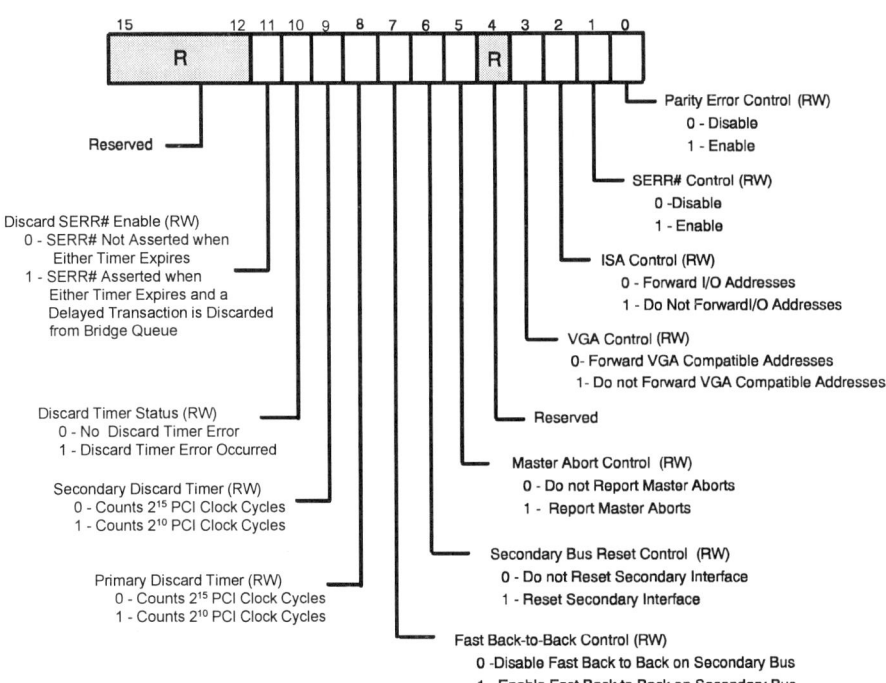

Figure 19-33: Bridge Control Register

PCI-X AND THE BRIDGE CONTROL REGISTER

Operating in conventional PCI mode, a PCI-X bridge's **Bridge Control** register adheres to the conventional Type 01h configuration address space definition for this register. If the PCI-X bridge device is operating in PCI-X mode, the **Discard Timer** control bits are ignored by the appropriate interface.

CHAPTER 20

PCI BRIDGES

This chapter consists of the following subchapters:

20.0 OVERVIEW

As stated in Chapter 17, *PCI Configuration Address Space*, PCI based systems utilize three independent address spaces. These are memory, I/O and PCI configuration address spaces. A bridge's principal function is to map these various address spaces from one bus into the address spaces of another bus, thus allowing for interbus communication.

In a PCI based system, the bus types that are interfaced to one another may be the same or different. For example, a PCI/PCI bridge provides the interface between two PCI buses. Conversely, a PCI legacy bridge interfaces a PCI bus to either an ISA, EISA or Micro Channel bus. The bus types that a bridge interfaces are specific to the hardware design of the bridge. This chapter contains information relating to four different types of PCI bridges: the Host/PCI, Peer Host/PCI, PCI/PCI and the Legacy bridge.

Two of the PCI bridge types, the PCI/PCI bridge and the Peer Host/PCI bridge, provide the ability to implement multiple PCI buses in a single system. Multiple PCI bus designs allow systems to be optimized in a variety of configurations. For instance, hierarchical PCI buses may be utilized to provide expansion capability beyond the electrical load limits of one PCI bus and for isolating high bandwidth devices from other devices within the system. Peer Host/PCI bridges permit PCI buses to be implemented as peers of one another on the Host CPU bus. PCI/PCI bridges allow PCI buses to be integrated in a hierarchical fashion in order to provide greater I/O expansion capabilities. Advantages and trade-offs for both bridge types are discussed later in this chapter.

> **Interbus operations are affected by several issues such as different data sizes between buses, cache coherency and memory write posting. See Chapter 3, *Bridges and Interbus Operations*, for a discussion on this important subject.**

20.1 PCI BRIDGE BUS TERMINOLOGY

Before continuing, it is important to be familiar with certain PCI bridge bus terminology. Figure 20-1 illustrates these terms. The PCI bridge used in this example is a PCI/PCI bridge; however, the terminology applies to all PCI bridges.

HOST CPU

The primary CPU in a system. It typically runs the operating system software. Note that some systems may incorporate multiple Host CPUs that share a common bus interface and use common I/O resources.

PRIMARY BUS

The first of two PCI buses that are connected to a PCI bridge. A PCI bridge's primary bus is the PCI bus closest to the Host CPU in the hierarchy.

SECONDARY BUS

The second of two buses that are connected to a PCI bridge. A PCI bridge's secondary bus is the bus furthest from the Host CPU in the hierarchy.

SUBORDINATE BUS

A subordinate bus is any bus behind (on the secondary side) of a PCI bridge.

UPSTREAM TRANSACTION

PCI bus transactions may flow in either of two directions. An upstream transaction is initiated by a bus master on the secondary bus side of a PCI bridge. The transaction flows through the PCI bridge towards the Host CPU.

DOWNSTREAM TRANSACTION

A downstream transaction is initiated by a bus master on the primary bus side of a PCI bridge. The transaction flows through the PCI bridge away from the Host CPU.

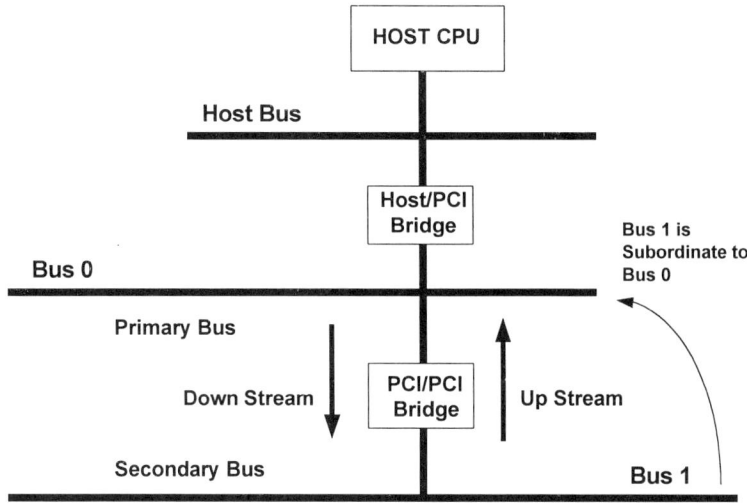

Figure 20-1: PCI Bridge Terminology

20.2 PCI BRIDGE COMPONENT ARCHITECTURE

A PCI bridge allows transactions between a master on one PCI bus and a target on another bus. The initiator of a transaction may reside on either the primary or secondary interface of a PCI bridge. Thus, the target interface on one bus is connected to the master interface on another bus. To handle transactions that can occur on either interface, the bridge must incorporate the following components as shown in the high level architecture drawing in Figure 20-2. All components except PCI configuration address space registers are discussed in this section. The PCI configuration address space registers implementations are specific to each type of PCI bridge and are therefore explained in each PCI bridge type discussion.

- Primary Master Interface
- Secondary Target Interface
- Primary Target Interface
- Secondary Master Interface

- Optional Data Buffers
- PCI Configuration Address Space Registers

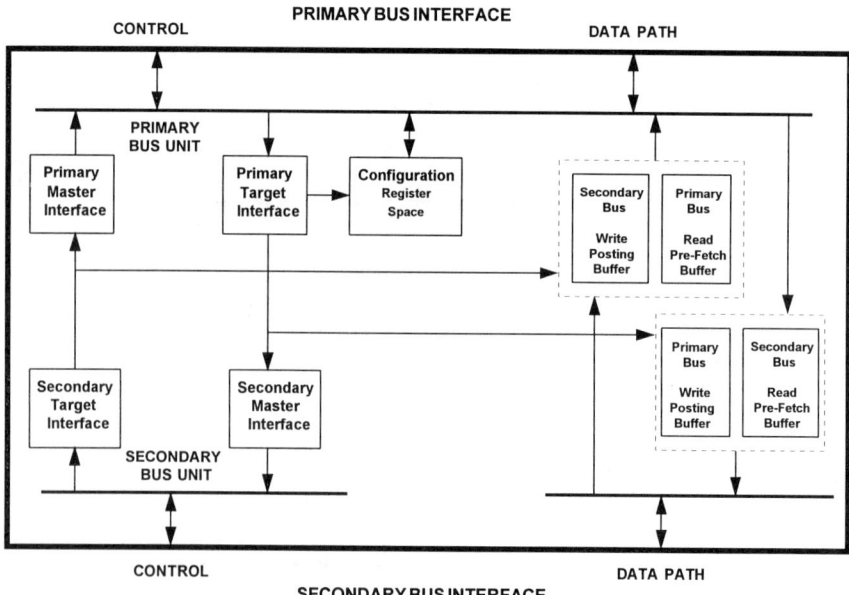

Figure 20-2: PCI Bridge Component Architecture

PRIMARY BUS UNIT

The primary bus unit contains the interface logic that manages the primary bus side of a PCI bridge. The primary bus unit consists of the Primary Master Interface and the Primary Target Interface of the PCI bridge.

SECONDARY BUS UNIT

The secondary bus unit contains the interface logic that manages the secondary bus side of a PCI bridge. The secondary bus unit consists of the Secondary Master Interface and the Secondary Target Interface of the PCI bridge.

PRIMARY MASTER INTERFACE

The Primary Master Interface accepts commands from the Secondary Target Interface and forwards them to a target upstream.

SECONDARY TARGET INTERFACE

The Secondary Target Interface accepts commands initiated by a master on the secondary interface and forwards them to Primary Master Interface.

PRIMARY TARGET INTERFACE

The Primary Target Interface accepts commands initiated by a master on the primary interface and forwards them to the Secondary Master Interface.

SECONDARY MASTER INTERFACE

The Secondary Master Interface accepts commands from the Primary Target Interface and forwards them to a target downstream.

PRIMARY AND SECONDARY DATA BUFFERS

In order to increase system performance designers can implement write posting and read pre-fetch buffers in a bridge. The bridge design may incorporate data buffers that temporarily store read and write data from transactions that route from the primary bus interface to the secondary bus interface or from the secondary bus interface to the primary bus interface.

Primary and secondary data buffers are optional for PCI bridge designs.

WRITE POSTING BUFFER

A write posting data buffer temporarily stores data that is being transferred from one bus to another when either a Memory Write or Memory Write and Invalidate bus command is used. For example, data writes initiated by Host-to-PCI, Host-to-main memory or PCI-to-main memory transactions can be write posted if the bridge supports this feature.

> Posted write data must be written or flushed before a read transaction can be serviced. However, to prevent a deadlock, the bridge must be capable of accepting write data in either the Primary or Secondary Write Posting Buffer without having to first flush the other buffer's posted data.

READ PRE-FETCH BUFFER

Read prefetch buffers store more data than was requested by the immediate transaction. For instance, the Host CPU might request a single byte of PCI data. The bridge could read additional data from memory and also store this extra data in its read pre-fetch buffer. This is done to increase performance. The assumption made is that the additional data will be read on subsequent transactions. The data read is held in the read pre-fetch buffer until it is invalidated or read. Host reads from PCI targets and PCI reads of main memory are examples of data that can be stored in the read pre-fetch buffer.

> According to the PCI Local Bus Specification, reliable prefetching of data can occur when either the Memory Read Line or Memory Read Multiple PCI bus command are used.
>
> All PCI bridges support the Memory Read PCI bus command. However, many Host/PCI bridges do not support the Memory Read Line or Memory Read Multiple commands. This is because typical Host CPU architectures do not comprehend the concept of prefetching of data. To permit prefetching of memory data, these bridges are required to implement Prefetchable Memory Base and Limit registers. Configuration software programs these registers with a range of memory that can be prefetched.
>
> For example, when a Host/PCI bridge detects a read access from prefetchable main memory that is initiated by a PCI bus master, it is allowed to convert the Memory Read command to a the Memory Read Line or Memory Read Multiple PCI bus command. The Host/PCI bridge prefetchable read buffer posts the data read. The Host/PCI bridge can then drive the data onto the PCI bus using a burst transaction to increase performance.

PRIMARY BUS WRITE POSTING BUFFER

In the case of the primary bus write posting data buffer, the bridge accepts the data to be written on its secondary bus from the bridge's primary bus. The bridge's primary bus is free to perform other bus transactions once the bridge acknowledges receipt of the data. The posted data is written to the bridge's secondary PCI bus at a later time, when the PCI bus is available.

SECONDARY BUS WRITE POSTING BUFFER

A secondary bus write posting data buffer permits a bus master's data write from a secondary bus to the primary bus to be posted in the bridge. The bridge's secondary bus is free to perform other bus transactions once the bridge acknowledges receipt of the data. The posted data is written at later time, when the target is available.

PRIMARY BUS READ PRE-FETCH BUFFER

The primary bus read pre-fetch buffer contains data read from a target on the bridge's secondary side. The data stored in the buffer is more than was originally requested by the transaction initiator. This data is transferred to the bridge's primary bus.

SECONDARY BUS READ PRE-FETCH BUFFER

The secondary bus read pre-fetch buffer contains data read from a target on the bridge's primary side. The data stored in the buffer is more than was originally requested by the transaction initiator. This data is transferred to the bridge's secondary bus.

20.3 HOST/PCI BRIDGE

A Host/PCI bridge is responsible for transferring Host CPU transactions to a target residing on a PCI bus. In addition, the PCI host bridge is also responsible for translating PCI bus transactions intended for main memory or devices that reside on the Host CPU bus into the appropriate Host bus cycles. As a PCI device, a Host/PCI bridge can be a PCI bus master when initiating Host-to-PCI transactions. Conversely, a Host/PCI bridge can also be a PCI bus target when servicing a PCI bus master's access to main memory or the Host CPU bus.

Transactions initiated by the Host CPU are divided into two basic categories: normal run-time transactions and PCI configuration address space transactions. Run-time transactions on a PCI bus are typically executed using standard memory and I/O address space accesses. PCI device configuration address space transactions are accomplished using PCI configuration address space. See Chapter 17, *PCI Configuration Address Space*, for a complete discussion of Host/PCI bridge configuration address space transactions. Figure 20-3 shows a simple Host/PCI bridge topology.

Note that for ease of discussion, a stand-alone Host/PCI bridge is assumed. This is not a specification requirement. Host/PCI bridges may be packaged with other independent functions such as a memory controller or even with a processor.

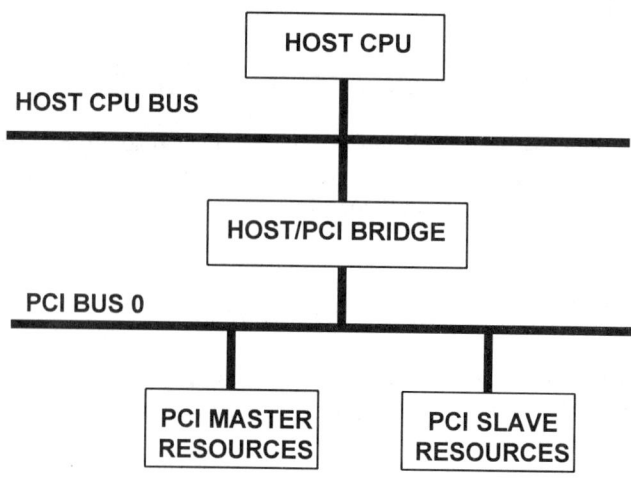

Figure 20-3: Host/PCI Bridge Topology

PCI CONFIGURATION ADDRESS SPACE REGISTERS

Host/PCI bridges, like all other PCI devices, are required to support PCI configuration address space. As with all PCI devices, this allows a specific implementation of a Host/PCI bridge function to support up to 256 8-bit configuration registers. The complexity of a particular Host/PCI bridge's feature set determines how many registers are actually required. Host/PCI bridges utilize variations of the PCI configuration address space Type 00h template shown in Figure 20-4. See Chapter 18, *PCI Header Type 00h*, for a complete description of the Type 00h template. The three PCI configuration address space regions of a Host/PCI bridge are discussed below.

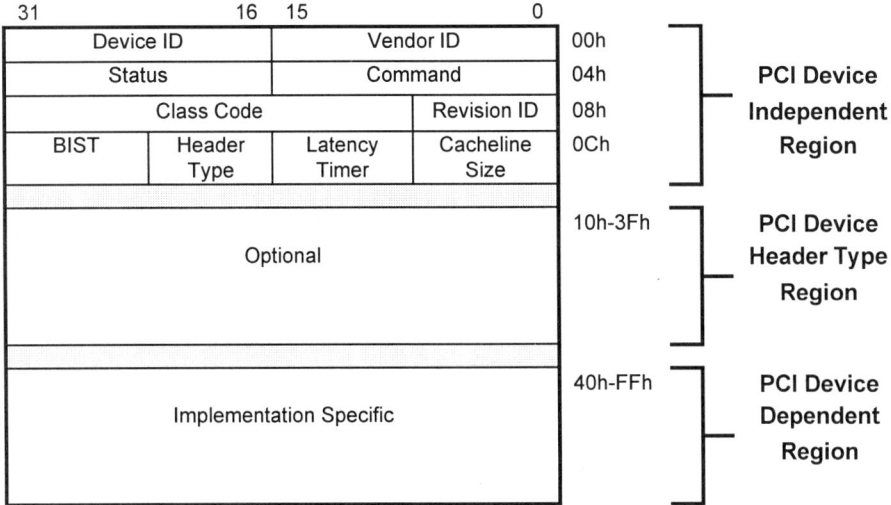

Figure 20-4: Type 00h PCI Configuration Space Header Region

PCI HEADER REGION

The PCI Local Bus Specification treats the predefined header as a monolithic 64 byte structure. This structure is subdivided into two regions: the PCI Device Independent Region and the PCI Device Header Type Region.

> Note that all device dependent registers must be located after the predefined header in the PCI configuration space.

PCI DEVICE INDEPENDENT REGION

The PCI Device Independent Region occupies the first 16 bytes of the PCI Configuration Space Header Region. This region is identical in function and layout for all PCI devices. The purpose for this region is device identification and generic control. For this discussion the registers of particular interest in this region are the PCI Command, Status, Class Code, Header Type and Master Latency registers.

PCI COMMAND REGISTER

The 16-bit Command register at offset 04h controls the Host/PCI bridge device's ability to generate and respond to PCI bus accesses. Note that a value of zero in this register logically disconnects the device from the PCI bus. Table 20-1 contains descriptions of individual bits in a Host/PCI bridge Command register that are typically implemented. Note that a Host/PCI bridge's Command register is a subset of the Type 00h PCI Configuration Space Header Region Command register that is discussed in Chapter 18: *PCI Header Type 00h.*

> **PCI bridge devices are required to respond to PCI configuration accesses, even when bits 2:0 of the Command register are set to zero.**

PCI STATUS REGISTER

The 16-bit Status register at offset 06h reports the status of PCI transactions. In addition, it reports the DEVSEL# timing of the Host/PCI bridge.

Table 20-2 contains descriptions of individual bits in a Host/PCI bridge Status register that are typically implemented. Note that a Host/PCI bridge's Status register is a subset of the Type 00h PCI Configuration Space Header Region Status register that is discussed in Chapter 18, *PCI Header Type 00h.*

REGISTER LEVEL PROGRAMMING INTERFACE REGISTER

This 8-bit register at offset 09h identifies the register level programming interface of a device. Host/PCI bridge devices do not have a defined register level programming interface. Consequently, the read-only value in this register is hard-wired to 00h.

SUB-CLASS CODE REGISTER

This 8-bit register at offset 0Ah identifies the specific function of the device as being a Host/PCI bridge device. Hence, the read-only value in this register is hard-wired to 00h.

BASE CLASS CODE REGISTER

This 8-bit register at offset 0Bh identifies the generic function of the device as being a PCI bridge device. Therefore, the read-only value in this register is hard-wired to 06h.

Bit	Type	Function
0	RW	**I/O Space Control** 0 Disables the bridge's response to I/O space accesses. 1 Enables the bridge's response to I/O space accesses. Host/PCI bridges usually do not respond to PCI I/O transactions. Consequently, PCI bus master accesses to I/O space on the Host CPU bus is disabled. Expect to find this bit hard-wired to 0 in most implementations.
1	RW	**Memory Space Control** 0 Disables the bridge's response to memory space accesses. 1 Enables the bridge's response to memory space accesses. When this bit is 1, PCI bus masters can access main memory.
2	RW	**Bus Master Control** 0 Disables the bridge's ability to generate PCI bus. 1 Enables the bridge's ability to generate PCI bus accesses. Host/PCI bridges typically do not allow their bus master capability on the PCI bus to be disabled. Consequently,. expect to find this bit hard-wired to 1 in most implementations.
5::3	RO	**Reserved**
6	RW	**Parity Error Response** 0 The Host/PCI bridge ignores detected parity errors. 1 The Host/PCI bridge responds to detected parity errors.
7	RO	**Reserved**
8	RW	**System Error Control** 0 Disable the SERR# output driver. 1 Enable the SERR# output driver. Typically, this bit and bit 6 must be set to one to report errors.
15::9	RO	**Reserved**

Table 20-1: Typical Host/PCI Bridge Command Register

Bit	Type	Function
7::0	RO	**Reserved**
8	RWC	**Data Parity Status** 0 No data parity errors have occurred. 1 All three of the following conditions must be met: a. PERR# was asserted by the bridge or the bridge sampled PERR# asserted. b. The bridge was the bus master during the transaction when the error occurred. c. Parity Error Response (bit 6 of the bridge's Command Register) is enabled.
10::9	RO	**Device Select Timing Status** 00 Bridge asserts DEVSEL# in the *fast* timing mode for any bus command. 01 Bridge asserts DEVSEL# in the *medium* timing mode for any bus command. 10 Bridge asserts DEVSEL# in the *slow* timing mode for any bus command. 11 Reserved. Configuration read and write cycles do not apply to the above definition. For example, if a bridge performs FAST decode for all memory and I/O accesses, but *medium* decode for configuration accesses, the device should set this register to *fast*.
11	RO	**Reserved**
12	RWC	**Received Target Abort Status** 0 A Target Abort did not terminate a bus master's transaction. 1 A Target Abort terminated the bridge's bus master transaction.
13	RWC	**Received Master Abort Status** 0 Bridge did not terminate a Host-to-PCI (bridge as bus master) transaction with a Master Abort. 1 Bridge terminated a Host-to-PCI (bridge as bus master) transaction with a Master Abort. The transaction is not a Special Cycle. 1 All bus master devices are required to implement this bit. 2 A Master Abort on a Special Cycle transaction should not cause this bit to be set.
14	RWC	**Signaled System Error Status** 0 Bridge did not assert the SERR# line. 1 Bridge asserted the SERR# line.
15	RO	**Reserved**

Table 20-2: Status Register

HEADER TYPE REGISTER

Bits 6::0 of this 8 bit register at offset 0Eh identify the layout of PCI configuration address space registers 10h through 3FH. Bit 7 identifies whether this is a single function device (bit 7=0) or a multi-function device (bit 7=1).

> Of the first 16 bytes in the PCI configuration address space, the PCI Local Bus Specification states that the Vendor ID, Device ID, Command, Status, Revision ID, Class Code and Header Type registers are required to be supported by all PCI compliant devices. Some Host/PCI bridge documentation specifies this register as RESERVED. Per the PCI Local Bus Specification, reserved registers must return a value of 00h when read. By default these Host/PCI bridges support PCI configuration address space Header Type 00h and are single function devices.

MASTER LATENCY REGISTER

This 8-bit register at offset 0Dh controls the amount of time the Host/PCI bridge can burst data on the PCI bus. When the Host/PCI bridge becomes the PCI bus master (FRAME# is asserted), the Master Latency Timer (MLT) counter is enabled and begins counting. The MLT counter value represents the guaranteed time slice that the Host/PCI bridge can keep the PCI bus. If the Host/PCI bridge transaction completes prior to the expiration of the MLT count, the counter is ignored. If the MLT count expires before the Host/PCI bridge transaction completes, the Host/PCI bridge must terminate the transaction as soon as its GNT# is removed.

PCI DEVICE HEADER TYPE REGION

The second part of the predefined PCI Configuration Space Header region is the Header Type Region. The layout and use of these remaining bytes (starting at offset 10h) in the PCI Configuration Space Header Region are defined according to the value encoded in the lower seven bits of the PCI Header Type register. This register is located at offset 0Eh within the PCI Device Independent Region. Typical Host/PCI bridges return 00h when this register is read.

PCI DEVICE DEPENDENT REGION

The PCI configuration space Device Dependent region consists of the last 192 bytes of the PCI configuration space. PCI device vendors are only permitted to implement device specific registers in this region.

This area of PCI configuration space should be used for any device functionality that is not typically accessed during runtime. The most likely use of this region is device specific configuration. The PCI System Design Guide gives several examples of registers that could be implemented for a Host/PCI bridge. For instance, a Disconnect Counter register for burst operations, system memory and I/O mapping range control registers, and a Subordinate Bus Number register to indicate the last PCI bus number in the Host/PCI bridge's hierarchy.

> PCI device designers should avoid placing run–time control and status in this area because of the longer access times that can occur when accessing PCI configuration address space.

SYSTEM MEMORY ADDRESS SPACE

Chapter 16, *System Resources*, introduced the Intel x86 processor memory address space generic to PC compatible computers as an example of a system memory map. The addition of PCI to the system complicates the system memory map. Additional hardware and software is required to ensure a consistent and resource conflict free system. A major portion of the complications is resolved by correctly designing and implementing, both in the hardware and software, a Host/PCI bridge. For example, when the Host CPU executes a memory read or write transaction on the Host CPU bus, it is the Host/PCI bridge that must determine whether or not to forward the transaction to the PCI bus. This is achieved by implementing system memory address space range control registers in the Host/PCI bridge's device dependent PCI configuration address space registers. These registers can be programmed by configuration software to either decode or not decode the system memory address spaces assigned to PCI targets.

In one scenario, a minimal register set can be programmed to direct the Host/PCI bridge's primary bus unit to respond to and forward all memory addresses that are unused by the Host CPU bus and main memory accesses to the PCI bus. Conversely, the Host/PCI bridge's secondary bus unit will respond to and forward all memory addresses that are not within the boundaries of the PCI memory range control registers to the Host/CPU bus and main memory. This is one example. In another, the primary bus unit could respond to address ranges assigned to the PCI bus; the secondary bus unit would then respond and forward accesses to addresses outside this range to the Host CPU bus and main memory.

The number of system memory range control registers can vary. Systems that have complex memory maps require a greater level of discrete control over the memory map, and thus require more registers. In addition, when designing the Host/PCI bridge, designers should also account for address size, either 32-bit or 64-bit, as well as any attributes that could be associated with particular system memory ranges. These include read-only and cacheable attributes.

In the event that the target of a transaction does not exist, the system is required to respond in a manner such that normal operation may continue, regardless of which bus the transaction was attempted. For example, the system hardware is required to return FFFFh to the Host CPU when the Vendor Identification register of a non-existent PCI device is read.

SYSTEM I/O ADDRESS SPACE

Chapter 16, *System Resources*, also introduced the Intel x86 processor I/O address space generic to PC compatible computers as an example of a system I/O map. The addition of PCI to the PC compatible system adds a further level of complication for controlling the system I/O map. The Host/PCI bridge is required to forward I/O transactions that originate on the Host CPU bus to the PCI bus.

A complication arises from the fact that PCI I/O space supports a full 32-bit address range. However, Intel x86 processors only use the first 64K of I/O address space. The Host/PCI bridge is therefore required to drive the upper 16 bits of the I/O address to zero when forwarding I/O transactions to the PCI bus. The lower 16 bits of the I/O address must remain unchanged.

HOST/PCI BRIDGE STATE AFTER RESET

The Host/PCI bridge should come out of reset in a state that permits all devices required by the boot process to be visible via I/O and system memory address space. In PC compatibles this means that I/O addresses assigned to video and boot devices such as floppy and hard disks must be passed through the Host/PCI bridge without any software initialization of the Host/PCI bridge. All other memory and I/O address space accesses should be disabled. In addition, non-boot related features such as data buffering and error detection must be disabled.

All Host/PCI bridge PCI configuration address space configuration registers must be accessible after a reset. These registers must reflect the reset state of the bridge.

HOST/PCI BRIDGE INITIALIZATION

The Host CPU is typically responsible for configuring the Host/PCI bridge. During the execution of the System BIOS POST, configuration software is required to perform tasks such as sizing main memory. Based on the amount discovered and other information about the system memory address map, the memory range control registers in the Host/PCI bridge's PCI configuration address space are programmed with acceptable values. In addition, the configuration software will enable memory accesses and data buffering, as well as system and parity error detection via registers in the Host/PCI bridge's PCI configuration address space. Depending on the feature set of the Host/PCI bridge, configuration software will have additional tasks beyond those mentioned in order to initialize the system for operation.

20.4 PCI/PCI BRIDGE

A PCI/PCI bridge provides the electrical interface between two PCI buses. PCI/PCI bridges allow transactions to occur between a PCI bus master on one PCI bus with a PCI target on another PCI bus. The PCI/PCI bridge has several advantages. First, PCI bus electrical loading limits can be overcome. The PCI/PCI bridge presents only one electrical load to its primary bus. In turn, it allows for more PCI devices or slots to be attached to its secondary bus, providing additional expansion capabilities. Note that devices located on a PCI/PCI bridge's secondary bus do not present a load on the PCI/PCI bridge's primary bus.

Integrating PCI/PCI bridges in a system thus results in a hierarchy of multiple buses within the system. This hierarchical PCI bus structure can also increase system performance when the majority of bus traffic is I/O between PCI devices and not between PCI devices and main memory. System performance is also increased because the two PCI buses connected by a PCI/PCI bridge operate independently of each other.

> The PCI System Design Guide states only one guideline when choosing a peer or hierarchical implementation: avoid more than two levels of hierarchy in hierarchical designs.

> When the majority of PCI bus traffic is between PCI devices and main memory, consider using a Peer Host/PCI bridge to increase system performance. Note that Peer Host/PCI bridges typically cost more than PCI/PCI bridges. This infers that a tradeoff between cost, performance and expansion must be considered when designing a PCI based system.

PLATFORM TOPOLOGY

Figure 20-5 shows a PCI/PCI bridge topology that is fully integrated on a platform. Observe that the number assigned to each PCI bridge corresponds to the PCI bus immediately subordinate to the bridge. Configuration software assigns the bus numbers to each bridge. As will be shown later, this numbering scheme permits software to operate in a transparent fashion across multiple PCI buses.

ADD-IN CARD INTEGRATION

PCI/PCI bridges are unique in that they can be integrated on add-in cards as well as platforms. Embedding a PCI/PCI bridge on an add-in card enables adding one or more devices to the system while only increasing the electrical load on the add-in slot's PCI bus by a factor of one. Note that the PCI/PCI bridge's secondary PCI bus is full PCI. The standard rules that apply to integrated PCI/PCI bridges on a platform apply to add-in cards with PCI/PCI bridges as well. Figure 20-6 depicts this type of implementation.

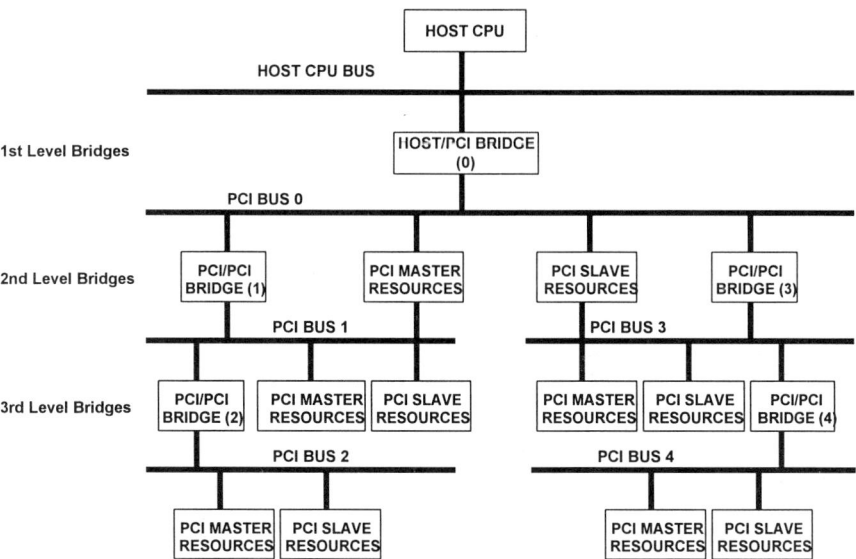

Figure 20-5: PCI/PCI Bridge Platform Topology

It is important to recognize that the number of PCI buses along with the number of devices that can be connected to each bus, is not the only factor that limits a system's expansion capabilities. The system power supply must also be capable of delivering the required power to meet the system's total requirements.

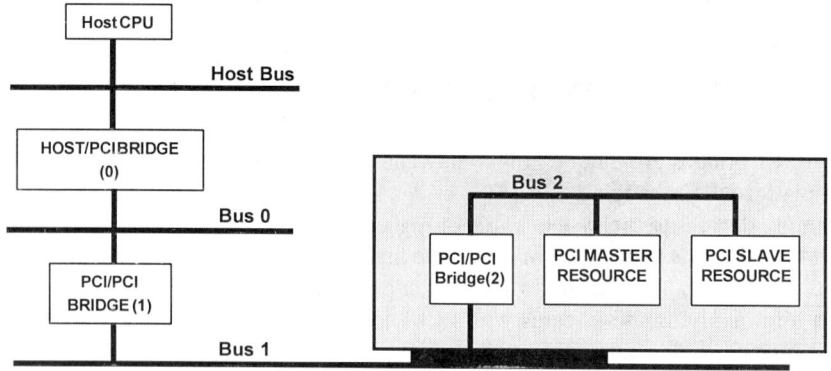

Figure 20-6: PCI/PCI Bridge Embedded on Add-in Card

PCI CONFIGURATION ADDRESS SPACE REGISTERS

PCI/PCI bridge PCI configuration address space must be accessible from the primary bus interface of the device. As with all PCI devices, each PCI device function within a PCI/PCI bridge can support up to 256 8-bit configuration space address registers. The complexity of a particular PCI/PCI bridge's feature set determines how many registers are actually implemented. PCI/PCI bridges utilize the PCI configuration address space Type 01h template presented in Figure 20-7. Refer to Chapter 19, *PCI Header Type 01h*, for a complete discussion of a PCI/PCI bridge's PCI configuration address space. A subset of the PCI/PCI bridge PCI configuration address space registers are described below because they are germane to the remainder of this discussion of PCI/PCI bridges.

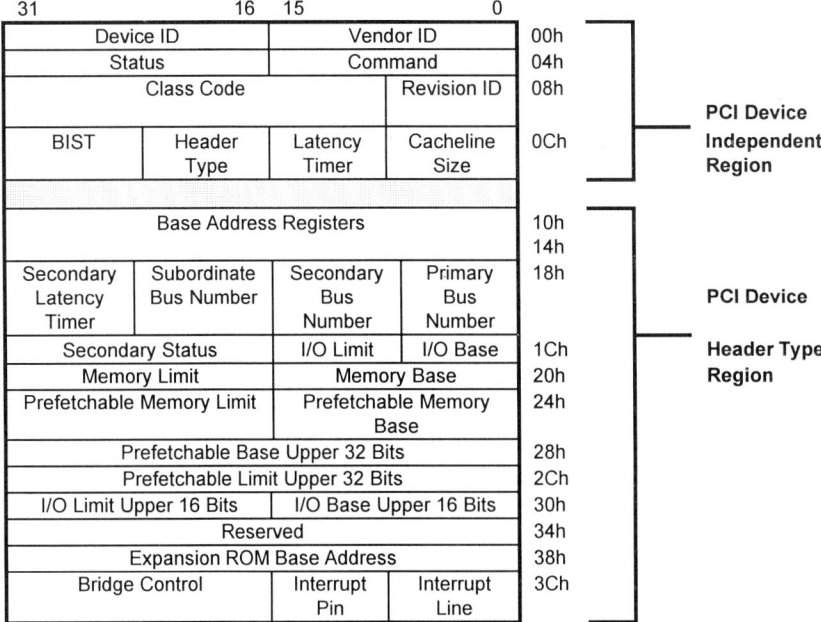

Figure 20-7: Type 01h PCI Configuration Space Header Region

PCI HEADER REGION

Again, the PCI Local Bus Specification treats the predefined header as a monolithic 64 byte structure. This structure is subdivided into two regions: the PCI Device Independent Region and the PCI Device Header Type Region.

PCI DEVICE INDEPENDENT REGION

The PCI Device Independent Region occupies the first 16 bytes of the PCI Configuration Space Header Region. This region is identical in function and layout for all PCI devices. The purpose for this region is device identification and generic control. The PCI device independent region registers described in the Host/PCI Bridge discussion of PCI configuration address space also apply to the PCI/PCI bridge. Consequently, in this section the only the Header Type and Class Code registers are considered. The reason is that they are different for a PCI/PCI bridge.

REGISTER LEVEL PROGRAMMING INTERFACE REGISTER

This 8-bit register at offset 09h identifies the register level programming interface of a device. PCI/PCI bridge devices do not have a defined register level programming interface. Consequently, the read-only value in this register is hard-wired to 00h.

SUB-CLASS CODE REGISTER

This 8-bit register at offset 0Ah identifies the specific function of the device as being a PCI/PCI bridge device. Hence, the read-only value in this register is hard-wired to 04h.

BASE CLASS CODE REGISTER

This 8-bit register at offset 0Bh identifies the generic function of the device as being a PCI bridge device. Therefore, the read-only value in this register is hard-wired to 06h.

HEADER TYPE REGISTER

The lower seven bits of this read-only 8-bit register located at offset 0Eh defines the register layout of addresses 10h through 3Fh in PCI configuration address space. This value is a 01h to indicate that the header type used is the PCI/PCI bridge layout. Bit seven indicates the multi-function status of the PCI/PCI bridge. A one in bit seven indicates that the bridge contains multiple PCI functions. A zero in bit seven indicates that the bridge is a single function PCI device.

PCI DEVICE HEADER TYPE REGION

The second part of the predefined PCI Configuration Space Header region is the Header Type Region. The layout and use of these remaining bytes (starting at offset 10h) in the PCI Configuration Space Header Region are defined according to the value encoded in the lower seven bits of the PCI Header Type register. This register is located at offset 0Eh within the PCI Device Independent Region. PCI/PCI bridges use Header Type 01h. There are several registers in this region that are used for routing and controlling bridge transactions. These are briefly described below in preparation for the discussion on initializing PCI/PCI bridges. In addition, Header Type region registers and bits specific to memory and I/O address space are also described in their respective sub-sections below.

PRIMARY BUS NUMBER REGISTER

The Primary Bus Number is located at offset 18h in the Type 01h PCI Device Header Type Region. Its read/write value is the number of the PCI bus to which the primary interface of the PCI/PCI bridge is connected. The PCI/PCI bridge uses this register to decode Type 1 configuration transactions on the secondary interface that should be converted to special cycle transactions on the primary interface.

SECONDARY BUS NUMBER REGISTER

The Secondary Bus Number is located at offset 19h in the Type 01h PCI Device Header Type Region. Its read/write value is the number of the PCI bus to which the secondary interface of the PCI/PCI bridge is connected. The PCI/PCI bridge uses this register to determine when to respond to Type 1 configuration transactions on the secondary interface of a hierarchical PCI bus. The PCI/PCI bridge will forward the Type 1 access to its secondary bus when the Secondary Bus Number matches the bus number driven during the Type 1 address cycle.

SUBORDINATE BUS NUMBER REGISTER

The Subordinate Bus Number is located at offset 1Ah in the Type 01h PCI Device Header Type Region. Its read/write value is the highest PCI bus number in the range of PCI buses beneath the physical secondary interface of a given PCI/PCI bridge. A PCI/PCI bridge uses the value of this register to determine when to claim Type 1 configuration transactions. When the bus number of a Type 1 configuration transaction is between a PCI/PCI bridge's Secondary Bus Number and Subordinate Bus Number register values, inclusive, the bridge will claim the transaction.

If the PCI/PCI bridge's Subordinate Bus Number register value is the same as its Secondary Bus Number value, the PCI bus connected to the PCI/PCI bridge's secondary interface is the last in the branch. When the PCI/PCI bridge claims a Type 1 transaction in this case, the PCI/PCI bridge converts the transaction to a Type 0 transaction. The Type 0 transaction is then forwarded to the PCI/PCI bridge's secondary interface.

If the PCI/PCI bridge's Subordinate Bus Number register value is not the same as its Secondary Bus Number value, the PCI bus connected to the PCI/PCI bridge's secondary interface is not the last in the branch; the PCI bus connected to the PCI/PCI bridge's secondary interface has at least one PCI/PCI bridge attached to it. In this case, when the PCI/PCI bridge claims a Type 1 transaction it must determine whether to convert the transaction to a Type 0 transaction before forwarding it. The PCI/PCI bridge will convert the transaction only if the Type 1 transaction's bus number matches the PCI/PCI bridge's Secondary Bus Number value. Otherwise, the Type 1 transaction is simply forwarded to the PCI/PCI bridge's secondary interface unchanged.

SYSTEM MEMORY ADDRESS SPACE

PCI/PCI bridges can support both prefetchable and memory mapped I/O (non-prefetchable) memory. These two types of memory are discussed in this section.

MEMORY MAPPED I/O

Memory mapped I/O can produce side effects when read. This type of memory is typically not prefetchable. Special rules apply to a PCI/PCI bridge when using the various memory read bus commands to access this memory region. In addition, PCI configuration address space supports registers and control bits to manage memory mapped I/O. These items are discussed below.

READING MEMORY MAPPED I/O

The following rules apply when reading data from a memory mapped I/O range assigned to a PCI/PCI bridge. These rules apply to accesses that originate on either the primary or secondary bus of the bridge.

Bus Command	**Rule**
Memory Read	Bridge will not prefetch data.
Memory Read Line	Bridge is allowed to prefetch data. If prefetching is not supported, this command can be aliased to the PCI Memory Read bus command.
Memory Read Multiple	Bridge is allowed to prefetch data. If prefetching is not supported, this command can be aliased to the PCI Memory Read bus command.

PCI/PCI bridges are not required to support memory mapped I/O data prefetching. A PCI/PCI bridge that can prefetch memory mapped I/O is required to support an enable/disable control bit for this feature if it is implemented. This bit can be implemented in the bridge's PCI configuration address space device dependent region. The purpose of this bit is to permit disabling of memory mapped I/O data prefetching in the event unexpected side effects occur.

PCI CONFIGURATION ADDRESS SPACE

The aperture for the memory mapped I/O region is maintained in programmable PCI configuration address space registers that reside in the Type 01h PCI Device Header Type Region. These are programmed by configuration software. The PCI/PCI bridge decodes the memory ranges programmed in these registers to determine when and if a memory transaction should be forwarded from one PCI bus interface to the other. Note that the memory mapped I/O PCI configuration address space base and limit registers are required.

> **A PCI/PCI bridge does not perform any address decoding. PCI based systems use a flat addressing model.**

MEMORY BASE REGISTER

The 16-bit Memory Base register is located at offset 20h in the Type 01h PCI Device Header Type Region. Its read/write value defines the 32-bit base address (inclusive) of a memory mapped I/O address range. A PCI/PCI bridge does not implement AD[19::0] for the Memory Base register. The bridge assumes that these lower 20 bits are zero. This aligns the Memory Base register value on a 1 megabyte boundary. This implementation enables a 16-bit register to represent the 32-bit memory mapped I/O memory base address. Memory address bits AD[31::20] correspond to bits 15::4 of the Memory Base register. Bits 3::0 of this register are read only, reserved and will always return zero when read.

MEMORY LIMIT REGISTER

The 16-bit Memory Limit register is located at offset 22h in the Type 01h PCI Device Header Type Region. Its read/write value defines the 32-bit top address (inclusive) of a memory mapped I/O address range. A PCI/PCI bridge does not implement AD[19::0] for the Memory Limit register. The bridge assumes that these lower 20 bits are a value of FFFFFh. This ensures that the granularity and size of the Memory Limit register value is always one megabyte. This implementation enables a 16-bit register to represent the 32-bit memory mapped I/O memory limit address. Memory address bits AD[31::20] correspond to bits 15::4 of the Memory Base register. Bits 3::0 of this register are read only, reserved and will always return zero when read.

PREFETCHABLE MEMORY

Prefetchable memory has no side effects when read. With this type of memory the PCI/PCI bridge can read more data than the current bus master requested. The data is stored in the bridge's read prefetch buffers. Special rules apply to a PCI/PCI bridge when using the various memory read bus commands to access this memory region. In addition, PCI configuration address space supports registers and control bits to help manage prefetchable memory. These items are discussed below.

READING PREFETCHABLE MEMORY FROM A SECONDARY BUS

The following rules apply when reading prefetchable data from the secondary bus of a PCI/PCI bridge when the access originated on the bridge's primary bus:

Bus Command	**Rule**
Memory Read	Bridge is allowed to prefetch data .
Memory Read Line	Bridge is allowed to prefetch data.
Memory Read Multiple	Bridge is allowed to prefetch data.

READING PREFETCHABLE MEMORY FROM A PRIMARY BUS

The following rules apply when reading prefetchable data from the primary bus of a PCI/PCI bridge when the access originated on the bridge's secondary bus:

Bus Command	**Rule**
Memory Read	Bridge is not allowed to prefetch data .
Memory Read Line	Bridge is allowed to prefetch data.
Memory Read Multiple	Bridge is allowed to prefetch data.

PCI CONFIGURATION ADDRESS SPACE

The aperture for the prefetchable memory region is maintained in programmable PCI configuration address space registers that reside in the Type 01h PCI Device Header Type Region. These are programmed by configuration software. The PCI/PCI bridge decodes the memory ranges programmed in these registers to determine when and if a memory transaction should be forwarded from one PCI bus interface to the other.

> A PCI/PCI bridge does not perform any address decoding. PCI based systems use a flat addressing model.

PREFETCHABLE MEMORY BASE REGISTER

The 16-bit Prefetchable Memory Base register is located at offset 24h in the Type 01h PCI Device Header Type Region. The value programmed in the register defines the base address of a prefetchable memory address range that the PCI/PCI bridge uses to determine when and if to forward prefetchable memory address transactions from one interface to another. This register is optional. Consequently, the Prefetchable Memory Base register can be either a read only or a read/write register. If a bridge supports a prefetchable memory address range, then this register must be initialized by configuration software.

When prefetchable memory is not supported by the PCI/PCI bridge, the register is reserved, read-only, and must return a value of zero when read.

When prefetchable memory is supported by the PCI/PCI bridge the Prefetchable Memory Base register is read-writeable. The bit definition for bits 15::0 of this register is as follows:

Bits	Type	Function
3::0	RO	These bits encode the prefetchable memory addressing capability of the PCI to PCI Bridge as follows. If bits [3::0] contain 0001b, the bridge supprts 64 bit addresses. The upper 32 bits of the Prefetchable Memory Base register are contained in the Prefetchable Base Upper 32 Bits register.
		0000b 32 Bit addressing 0001b 64 Bit addressing 02h-Fh Reserved
15::4	RW	0h-FFF0h The top 12 bits correspond to address bits AD[31::20] of a prefetchable memory base address. The bridge does not implement AD[19::0] in the Prefetchable Memory Base registers. The bridge assumes that these lower 20 bits are zero. This aligns the Prefetchable Memory Base register value on a 1 Megabyte boundary.

PREFETCHABLE MEMORY LIMIT REGISTER

The 16-bit Prefetchable Memory Limit register is located at offset 26h in the Type 01h PCI Device Header Type Region. The value programmed in the register defines the top address (inclusive) of a prefetchable memory address range that the PCI/PCI bridge uses to determine when and if to forward prefetchable memory address transactions from one interface to another. This register is optional. Consequently, the Prefetchable Memory Limit register can be either a read only or a read/write register. If a bridge supports a prefetchable memory address range, then this register must be initialized by configuration software.

When prefetchable memory is not supported by the PCI/PCI bridge the register is reserved, read-only, and must return a value of zero when read.

When prefetchable memory is supported by the PCI/PCI bridge the Prefetchable Memory Limit register is read-writeable. The bit definition for bits 15::0 of this register is as follows:

Bits	Type	Function
3::0	RO	These bits encode the prefetchable memory addressing capability of the PCI to PCI Bridge as follows. If bits [3::0] contain 01h, the bridge supports 64 bit addresses. The upper 32 bits of the Prefetchable Memory Limit register are contained in the Prefetchable Limit Upper 32 Bits register.
		0000b 32 Bit addressing 0001b 64 Bit addressing 02h-Fh Reserved
15::4	RW	0h-FFF0h The top 12 bits correspond to address bits AD[31::20] of a prefetchable memory limit address. The bridge does not implement AD[19::0] in the Prefetchable Memory Limit registers. The bridge assumes that these lower 20 bits are FFFFFh. This aligns the top of the Prefetchable Memory Limit register at the top of a 1 Megabyte aligned address block.

PREFETCHABLE BASE UPPER 32-BITS REGISTER

The 32-bit Prefetchable Base Upper 32-Bits register is located at offset 28h in the Type 01h PCI Device Header Type Region. It specifies the upper 32 bits of a 64-bit Prefetchable Memory Base address. This register is optional. Consequently, the Prefetchable Base Upper 32-Bits register can be either a read only or a read/write register. If a bridge supports a 64-bit prefetchable memory address range this register must be initialized by configuration software.

When prefetchable memory is not supported by the PCI/PCI bridge or the Prefetchable Memory Base register indicates support for 32 bit addressing, this register is reserved. It is read-only and must return a value of zero when read.

When 64-bit prefetchable memory is supported by the PCI/PCI bridge, the bits in the Prefetchable Base Upper 32-Bits correspond to AD[63::32] of the 64-bit prefetchable memory base address.

PREFETCHABLE LIMIT UPPER 32-BITS REGISTER

The 32-bit Prefetchable Limit Upper 32-Bits register is located at offset 2Ch in the Type 01h PCI Device Header Type Region. It specifies the upper 32 bits of a 64 bit Prefetchable Memory Limit address. This register is optional. Consequently, the Prefetchable Limit Upper 32-Bits register can be either a read only or a read/write register. If a bridge supports a 64-bit prefetchabie memory address range this register must be initialized by configuration software.

When prefetchable memory is not supported by the PCI/PCI bridge or the Prefetchable Memory Limit register indicates support for 32 bit addressing this register is reserved. It is read-only and must return a value of zero when read.

When 64-bit prefetchable memory is supported by the PCI/PCI bridge, the bits in the Prefetchable Limit Upper 32-Bits correspond to AD[63::32] of the 64-bit prefetchable memory limit address.

> The prefetchable memory address range is allowed to cross 4 gigabyte boundaries when the 64-bit address range is supported.

FORWARDING MEMORY TRANSACTIONS

The Memory Mapped I/O Base and Limit and the Prefetchable Memory Base and Limit registers specify an address range used by a PCI/PCI bridge to determine when to forward the following transactions across the bridge:

- Memory Read
- Memory Read Line
- Memory Read Multiple
- Memory Write
- Memory Write and Invalidate

The base address range for these two memory regions is always one megabyte aligned. In addition, the minimum size and the granularity is always one megabyte.

MEMORY TRANSACTION CONTROL

A PCI/PCI bridge's responses to memory transactions are controlled by the following PCI configuration address space Command and Bridge Control register bits. See the discussion in Chapter 19: *PCI Header Type 01h*, that pertains to these two registers for additional information.

MEMORY ENABLE BIT

Bit 1 of the Command register, the Memory Enable bit must be set to enable the primary interface of the bridge to respond to memory mapped I/O and prefetchable memory transactions. When this bit is zero, the bridge ignores memory mapped I/O and prefetchable memory transactions on the primary interface.

> VGA compatible addresses are not forwarded when this bit is zero, regardless of the state of the VGA Control bit in the Bridge Control register.

BUS MASTER ENABLE BIT

Bit 2 of the Command register, the Bus Master Enable bit, controls the bridge's ability to operate as a bus master on the primary interface on behalf of a bus master on the secondary interface for memory transactions. When this bit is set, the bridge is enabled to act as a master on the primary interface. When this bit is zero, the bridge is cannot initiate transactions on the primary interface. In addition, the bridge cannot forward memory transactions from the secondary interface to the primary interface.

> Configuration commands that are either forwarded or converted by the PCI bridge device are not affected by this bit.

VGA ENABLE BIT

Bit 3 of the Bridge Control register, the VGA Enable bit, controls the bridge's response to VGA compatible memory addresses. This address range is A0000h to BFFFFh.

When this bit is set, VGA compatible memory addresses are forwarded from the primary interface to the secondary interface. Secondary interface to primary interface transactions of VGA compatible memory addresses are blocked by the PCI/PCI bridge.

> Forwarding will be done regardless of the state of the VGA Palette Snoop bit, ISA Enable bit and the bridge's programmed memory base and limit address range registers. However, the Memory Enable bit must also be set for this bit to control VGA compatible memory addresses.

When this bit is zero, VGA compatible memory addresses are not forwarded from the primary interface to the secondary interface unless they are defined in one of the bridge's programmable memory address ranges.

DOWNSTREAM MEMORY TRANSACTIONS

Downstream transactions occur when a PCI/PCI bridge forwards a transaction from the bridge's primary interface to its secondary interface. For a downstream memory transaction to occur, the PCI/PCI bridge must decode a memory address within the base and limit of either the memory mapped I/O or prefetchable memory range. Figure 20-8 illustrates this rule.

UPSTREAM MEMORY TRANSACTIONS

Upstream transactions occur when a PCI/PCI bridge forwards a transaction from the bridge's secondary interface to its primary interface.

For a PCI/PCI bridge to forward an upstream memory mapped I/O memory transaction, two conditions must be met. First, the PCI/PCI bridge must decode the memory address specified in the transaction. This address must fall outside the memory mapped I/O range designated in the region's base and limit range registers. Second, the memory address specified in the transaction must be outside the region designated in the PCI/PCI bridge's prefetchable memory base and limit range registers. Figure 20-8 illustrates these rules.

For a PCI/PCI bridge to forward an upstream prefetchable memory transaction, two conditions must be met. First, the PCI/PCI bridge must decode the memory address specified in the transaction. This address must fall outside the prefetchable range designated in the region's base and limit range registers. Second, the memory address specified in the transaction must be outside the region designated in the PCI/PCI bridge's memory mapped I/O range base and limit range registers. Figure 20-8 illustrates these rules.

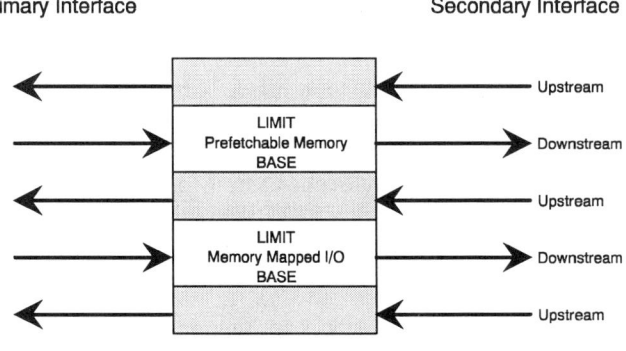

Figure 20-8: PCI/PCI Bridge Memory Transactions

DISABLING MEMORY ADDRESS RANGES

To turn off a memory mapped I/O or prefetchable memory range, set the memory limit address register to a value less than that of its respective memory base address register.

> Disabling both memory mapped I/O and prefetchable memory in this manner inhibits the PCI/PCI bridge from forwarding memory transactions initiated on the primary interface to the bridge's secondary interface. In this case, however, all memory transactions initiated on the secondary interface will be forwarded to the bridge's primary interface.

SYSTEM I/O ADDRESS SPACE

PCI/PCI bridges can support either 16 or 32 bit I/O addressing. I/O address space is controlled by the bridge in a manner similar to the memory base and limit registers.

PCI CONFIGURATION ADDRESS SPACE

The aperture for the I/O address space region is maintained in programmable PCI configuration address space registers that reside in the Type 01h PCI Device Header Type Region. These are programmed by configuration software. The PCI/PCI bridge decodes the I/O range programmed in these registers to determine when and if an I/O transaction should be forwarded from one PCI bus interface to the other.

I/O BASE REGISTER

The 8-bit I/O Base register is located at offset 1Ch in the Type 01h PCI Device Header Type Region. The value programmed in the register defines the base address of an I/O address range that the PCI/PCI bridge uses to determine when and if to forward I/O address transactions from one interface to another. This register is optional. Consequently, the I/O Base register can be either a read only or a read/write register. If a bridge supports an I/O address range, this register must be initialized by configuration software.

When the I/O Base address register is not supported by the PCI/PCI bridge, the register is reserved, read-only, and must return a value of zero when read.

When the I/O Base address register is supported by the PCI/PCI bridge, the I/O Base address register is read-writeable. The bit definition for bits 7::0 of this register is as follows:

Bits	Type	Function
3::0	RO	These bits encode the I/O addressing capability of the PCI to PCI Bridge as follows. If bits [3::0] contain 0001b, the bridge supports 32 bit addresses. The upper 16 bits of the I/O Base register are contained in the I/O Base Upper 16 Bits register.
		0000b 16-Bit I/O addressing 0001b 32-Bit addressing 02h-Fh Reserved
7::4	RW	0h-0Fh The top 4 bits correspond to address bits AD[15::12] of an I/O base address. The lower 12 address bits, AD[11::0], are not implemented in the I/O Base register. The bridge always assumes that these bits are zero. Consequently, each PCI/PCI bridge device consumes a minimum of 4K of I/O address space, aligned on a 4K boundary, when the I/O Base register is programmed.

The PCI Local Bus Specification requires that the PCI/PCI bridge performs a 32-bit decode of the I/O address when 16-bit I/O decode is implemented. The upper 16 bits of the address, AD[31::16] should be zero in this case. PCI I/O base address space is limited to the range 0000h to FFFFh inclusive.

The 32-bit I/O address range supported by a bridge can be located anywhere in the four gigabyte PCI I/O address space. The base address is required to be aligned on a 4K boundary.

I/O LIMIT REGISTER

The 8-bit I/O Limit register is located at offset 1Dh in the Type 01h PCI Device Header Type Region. The value programmed in the register defines the top address (inclusive) of an I/O address range that the PCI/PCI bridge uses to determine when and if to forward I/O transactions from one interface to another. This register is optional. Consequently, the I/O Limit register can be either a read only or a read/write register. If a bridge supports an I/O address range, then this register must be initialized by configuration software.

When an I/O address range is not supported by the PCI/PCI bridge this register is reserved, read-only and must return a value of zero when read.

When an I/O address range is supported by the PCI/PCI bridge the I/O Limit register is read-writeable. The bit definition for bits 7::0 of this register is as follows:

Bits	Type	Function
3::0	RO	These bits encode the I/O addressing capability of the PCI to PCI Bridge as follows. If bits [3::0] contain 01h, the bridge supports 32 bit I/O addresses. The upper 16 bits of the I/O Limit register are contained in the I/O Limit Upper 16 Bits register.
		0000b 16 Bit addressing
		0001b 32 Bit addressing
		02h-Fh Reserved
7::4	RW	0h-0Fh The top 4 bits correspond to address bits AD[15::12] of of an I/O limit address. The lower 12 address bits, AD[11::0], are not implemented in the I/O Limit register. The bridge always assumes that these bits are FFFh. Consequently, each PCI/PCI bridge device consumes a minimum of 4K of I/O address space, aligned on a 4K boundary, when the I/O limit register is programmed.

I/O BASE UPPER 16 BITS REGISTER

The 16 bit I/O Base Upper 16 Bits register is located at offset 30h in the Type 01h PCI Device Header Type Region. It specifies the upper 16 bits of a 32 bit I/O Base address. This register is optional. Consequently, the I/O Base Upper 16 Bits register can be either a read only or a read/write register. If a PCI/PCI bridge supports a 32 bit I/O address range this register must be initialized by configuration software.

When an I/O address range is not supported by the PCI/PCI bridge or the I/O Base register indicates support for 16 bit addressing, this register is reserved. It is read-only and must return a value of zero when read.

When a 32 bit I/O range is supported by the PCI/PCI bridge, the bits in the I/O Base Upper 16 Bits correspond to AD[31::16] of the range's 32 bit I/O Base address.

I/O LIMIT UPPER 16 BITS REGISTER

The 16 bit I/O Limit Upper 16 Bits register is located at offset 32h in the Type 01h PCI Device Header Type Region. It specifies the upper 16 bits of a 32 bit I/O

Limit address. This register is optional. Consequently, the I/O Upper 16 Bits register can be either a read only or a read/write register. If a bridge supports a 32 bit I/O address range this register must be initialized by configuration software.

When an I/O address range is not supported by the PCI/PCI bridge or the I/O Base register indicates support for 16 bit addressing, this register is reserved. It is read-only and must return a value of zero when read.

When a 32 bit I/O address range is supported by the PCI/PCI bridge, the bits in the I/O Limit Upper 16 Bits correspond to AD[31::16] of the range's 32 bit I/O Limit address.

FORWARDING I/O TRANSACTIONS

The I/O Base and Limit registers specify an address range used by a PCI/PCI bridge to determine when to forward the following transactions across the bridge:

- I/O Read
- I/O Write

The base address range for an I/O region is always 4K aligned. In addition, the minimum size and the granularity of the region are both always 4K.

I/O TRANSACTION CONTROL

A PCI/PCI bridge's response to I/O transactions are controlled by the following PCI configuration address space Command and Bridge Control register bits. See the discussion in Chapter 19, *PCI Header Type 01h*, that pertains to these two registers for additional information.

I/O ENABLE BIT

Bit 0 of the Command register, the I/O Enable bit must be set to enable the primary interface of the bridge to respond to I/O transactions. When this bit is zero, the bridge ignores I/O and prefetchable memory transactions on the primary interface.

> **VGA compatible addresses are not forwarded when this bit is zero, regardless of the state of the VGA Control bit in the Bridge Control register.**

BUS MASTER ENABLE BIT

Bit 2 of the Command register, the Bus Master Enable bit, controls the bridge's ability to operate as a bus master on the primary interface on behalf of a bus master on the secondary interface for I/O transactions. When this bit is set, the bridge is enabled to act as a master on the primary interface. When this bit is zero, the bridge is cannot initiate transactions on the primary interface. In addition, the bridge cannot forward I/O transactions from the secondary interface to the primary interface.

> **Configuration commands that are either forwarded or converted by the PCI bridge device are not affected by this bit.**

VGA PALETTE SNOOP ENABLE BIT

Bit 5 of the Command register, the VGA Palette Snoop Enable bit, controls the bridge's response to VGA compatible palette accesses. The I/O addresses are 3C6h, 3C8h and 3C9h. This bit is optional.

> **The VGA I/O addresses include the ISA alias address for each port. This is because AD[15::10] are not decoded.**

If the VGA Palette Snoop Enable bit is not implemented, the bit is read-only and returns zero when read.

If a PCI/PCI bridge supports the VGA Palette Snoop Enable bit the bit is read-writeable.

When this bit is set, VGA palette accesses are forwarded from the primary interface to the secondary interface. Secondary interface to primary interface transactions of the palette snoop I/O addresses are blocked by the PCI/PCI bridge.

When this bit is zero, VGA palette accesses on the primary interface are ignored.

ISA ENABLE BIT

Bit 2 of the Bridge Control register, the ISA Enable bit, controls the bridge's response to ISA I/O addresses. This bit is only applicable to I/O Base and Limit registers with I/O addresses that lie in the first 64K of PCI I/O address space.

When this bit is set, forwarding of the top 768 bytes of each 1K I/O in the address range as defined by the PCI/PCI bridge's I/O Base and I/O Limit registers from the primary interface to the secondary interface is blocked. Only the lower

256 bytes of each 1K block can be forwarded. This effectively limits the usable number of I/O addresses within a any 4K block to only 1K for downstream transactions.

For any 4K block, the usable base addresses for the 256 bytes are:

- 0 x000 - 0 x0FFh
- 0 x400 - 0 x4FFh
- 0 x800 - 0 x8FFh
- 0 xC00 - 0 xCFFh

Figure 20-9 is a pictorial view of the effects of each 1K of I/O within the first 64K of I/O address space (inclusive) when the ISA Enable bit is set. Note that blocking of I/O addresses only affects transactions that are initiated on the primary interface.

> **Upstream I/O transactions that fall within the upper 768 bytes of each 1K of I/O address space are forwarded to the primary interface, regardless of whether or not the address falls within the I/O Base and I/O Limit range.**

When this bit is zero, all I/O transactions in the address range as defined by the PCI/PCI bridge's I/O Base and I/O Limit registers are forwarded downstream from the primary interface to the secondary interface.

> **See the appendices on ISA Aliasing for more information.**

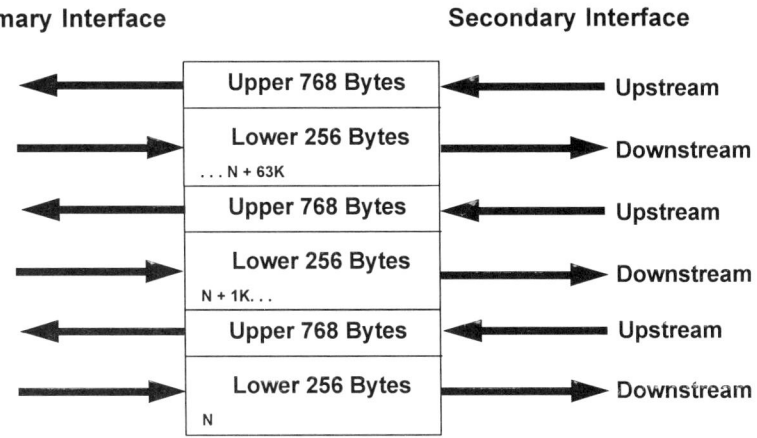

Figure 20-9: Individual 1K Blocks of I/O When ISA Enable Bit = 1

VGA ENABLE BIT

Bit 3 of the Bridge Control register, the VGA Enable bit, controls the bridge's response to VGA compatible I/O addresses. This I/O address range is 3B0h to 3BBh and 3C0h to 3DFh.

> **The VGA I/O addresses include the ISA alias address for each port. This is because AD[15::10] are not decoded.**

When this bit is set, VGA compatible I/O addresses are forwarded from the primary interface to the secondary interface. Secondary interface to primary interface transactions of VGA compatible I/O addresses are blocked by the PCI/PCI bridge.

> **The PCI function's Command Register I/O Enable bit must be set to allow its VGA Enable Bit to control VGA compatible I/O addresses. When both of these bits are set, forwarding of VGA compatible I/O addresses will be done regardless of the state of the VGA Palette Snoop bit, ISA Enable bit, and the bridge's programmed I/O base and limit address range registers.**

When this bit is zero, VGA compatible memory addresses are not forwarded from the primary interface to the secondary interface unless they are defined in the bridge's programmable I/O address range.

DOWNSTREAM I/O TRANSACTIONS

Downstream transactions occur when a PCI/PCI bridge forwards a transaction from the bridge's primary interface to its secondary interface. For a downstream I/O transaction to occur, the I/O transaction must be initiated on the primary interface the PCI/PCI bridge. If the bridge decodes an I/O address within the range programmed in its I/O Base and I/O Limit registers, it will forward the transaction to its secondary bus. Figure 20-10 illustrates this rule. In this example, 4K of I/O address space was assigned to the PCI/PCI bridge. The 4k range from 6000h to 9FFFh is programmed into the bridge's I/O Base and I/O Limit registers. Any downstream transaction that falls within this I/O range is positively decoded by the bridge and forwarded to the secondary interface.

UPSTREAM I/O TRANSACTIONS

Upstream transactions occur when a PCI/PCI bridge forwards a transaction from the bridge's secondary interface to its primary interface. For an upstream I/O transaction to occur, the I/O transaction must be initiated on the secondary interface the PCI/PCI bridge. If the bridge decodes an I/O address that lies outside the range programmed in its I/O Base and I/O Limit registers, it will forward the transaction to its primary bus. Figure 20-10 illustrates this rule. In this example, 4K of I/O address space has been assigned to the PCI/PCI bridge. The 4k range from 6000h to 9FFFh is programmed into the bridge's I/O Base and I/O Limit registers. Any upstream transaction that falls outside of this I/O range is decoded by the bridge and forwarded to the primary interface.

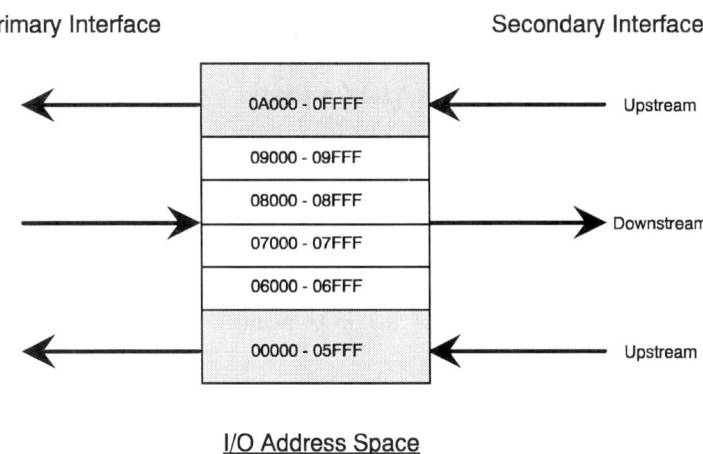

Figure 20-10: PCI/PCI Bridge I/O Transactions

DISABLING I/O ADDRESS RANGES

To turn off an I/O address range, set the I/O limit address register to a value less than that of its respective I/O base address register.

> Disabling the I/O range in this manner inhibits the PCI/PCI bridge from forwarding any I/O transactions initiated on the primary interface to the bridge's secondary interface. In this case, however, all I/O transactions initiated on the secondary interface will be forwarded to the bridge's primary interface.

PCI/PCI BRIDGE STATE AFTER RESET

Immediately after reset, a PCI/PCI bridge's read-writeable registers should be initialized to zero. This disables features such as data buffering within the bridge and error detection on both PCI interfaces. Device dependent features should be disabled after reset. All memory and I/O address space accesses should be disabled because the I/O, Memory and Bus Master command bits within the

Command register are reset to zero as well as all address range registers. Also, PCI/PCI bridges are required to park the secondary bus. In addition, the Primary, Secondary and Subordinate Bus Number registers are set to 00h. This infers that only PCI Bus 00h, which is connected to the primary PCI Host bridge, will decode PCI configuration address space transactions. With all devices in the hierarchical topology effectively disconnected from the Host CPU, the system is prepared to be initialized for run-time operation.

PCI/PCI BRIDGE INITIALIZATION

After reset, the only PCI devices accessible to the Host CPU are the primary Host/PCI bridge and any PCI devices that reside on PCI Bus 00h. This is enough to permit the system to be configured. Two major initialization functions are performed on PCI/PCI bridge devices. The first is the assigning of the Primary, Secondary and Subordinate Bus Number values to each PCI/PCI bridge. The second function the allocation of the I/O, memory and memory mapped I/O address spaces.

PCI BUS ENUMERATION

The PCI to PCI Bridge Architecture Specification does not define when and in what order the PCI bus numbers are assigned. The only requirement is that the bus number assigned to a bus behind a PCI/PCI bridge must be greater than the bridge's primary bus number and less than or equal to the value assigned to the bridge's Subordinate Bus Number. This permits PCI configuration address space transactions to propagate correctly.

Refer to Figure 20-5 for this discussion on PCI Bus enumeration. There are several different ways to enumerate the hierarchical bus topology. Below is one high level algorithm to give the reader insight into the process and its complexity. Also, see Chapter 23: *PCI Device Configuration*, for information on initializing non-PCI/PCI bridge devices.

1.   After reset, the Primary Bus Number, Secondary Bus Number, and Subordinate Bus Number of each PCI/PCI bridge should be reset to zero. Consequently, only PCI devices located on PCI bus zero can be accessed.

2.   Using the Class Code Register, the system configuration software searches PCI bus zero devices for PCI/PCI bridges. The class code criteria is Base Class=06h, Sub Class=04h, and Programming Interface=00h. The Find PCI Class Code routine is an excellent choice for this step. See Chapter 22, *PCI*

System BIOS Software Interface. Note that there is no requirement for the Find PCI Class Code function to scan a bus starting with the lowest device number. In this example, there is no guarantee that what is enumerated as PCI Bridge (3) in Figure 20-5 will not in an actual implementation be enumerated as PCI Bridge (1). The key point here is that device initialization software drivers should make no assumptions as to a particular System BIOS or OS order of scanning for devices in a PCI based system.

3. When a PCI/PCI bridge is found, the configuration software assigns the bridge its actual Primary Bus Number and Secondary Bus Number register values. If this were the first PCI/PCI bridge detected in Figure 20-5, the Primary Bus Number register value assigned to PCI/PCI Bridge (1) is 00h; the Secondary Bus Number register value is 01h. The Subordinate Bus Number register value, unless it is known, should be set to FFh to permit propagation of PCI configuration address space transactions.

4. The configuration software then searches for any PCI/PCI bridges on the Secondary Bus of PCI/PCI Bridge (1). It finds a PCI/PCI Bridge (2) and assigns its Primary Bus Number register a value of 01h. The Secondary Bus Number register value is 02h. The Subordinate Bus Number register value is set to FFh

5. The search is continued on PCI Bus 02h for more PCI/PCI bridges. None is found. The configuration software assigns PCI Bridge (2) with a Subordinate Bus Number register value of 02h, because that is the most subordinate bus in its hierarchy. Note that for PCI Bridge (2), the Subordinate Bus Number value and the Secondary Bus Number value are identical.

6. The Configuration software backs up the branch to PCI bus 01h. The search is continued on PCI Bus 01h for more PCI/PCI bridges. None is found. The configuration software assigns PCI Bridge (1) with a Subordinate Bus Number register value of 02h, because that is the most subordinate bus in its hierarchy.

7. The Configuration software backs up the branch to PCI bus 00h. The search is continued on PCI Bus 00h for more PCI/PCI bridges. One is found. The configuration software assigns PCI Bridge (3) a Primary Bus Number register a value of 00h. The Secondary Bus Number register value is 03h. The Subordinate Bus Number register value is set to FFh

8. The configuration software then searches for any PCI/PCI bridges on the Secondary Bus of PCI/PCI Bridge (3). It finds a PCI/PCI Bridge (4) and assigns its Primary Bus Number register a value of 03h. The Secondary Bus Number register value is 04h. The Subordinate Bus Number register value is set to FFh

9. The search is continued on PCI Bus 04h for more PCI/PCI bridges. None is

found. The configuration software assigns PCI Bridge (4) with a Subordinate Bus Number register value of 04h, because that is the most subordinate bus in its hierarchy. Note that for PCI Bridge (4), the Subordinate Bus Number value and the Secondary Bus Number value are identical.

10.   The Configuration software backs up the branch to PCI bus 03h. The search is continued on PCI Bus 03h for more PCI/PCI bridges. None is found. The configuration software assigns PCI Bridge (3) with a Subordinate Bus Number register value of 04h, because that is the most subordinate bus in its hierarchy.

11.   The Configuration software backs up the branch to PCI bus 00h. The search is continued on PCI Bus 00h for more PCI/PCI bridges. None is found. If supported, the configuration software assigns the Host/PCI bridge's Subordinate Bus number register a value of 04h. PCI bus enumeration is now complete.

Figure 20-11 depicts the Primary Bus Number, the Secondary Bus Number and the Subordinate Bus Number register values programmed in each PCI/PCI bridge after the configuration process in the above example was complete.

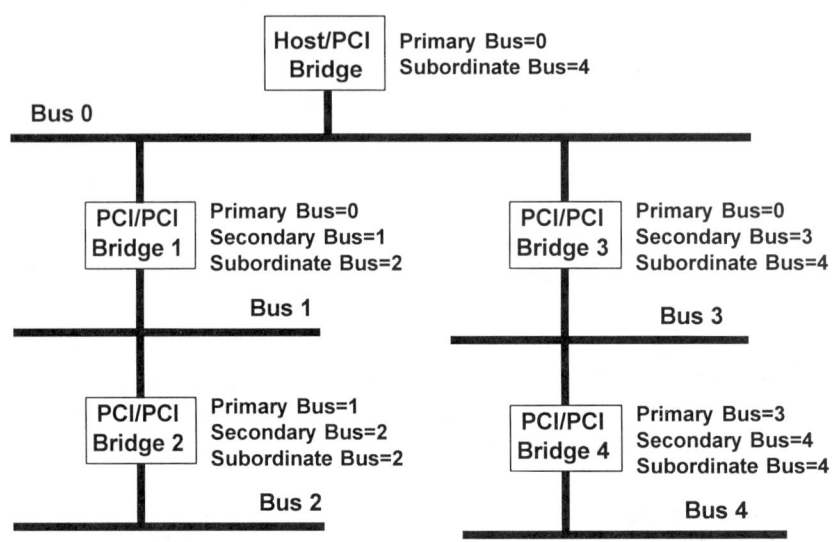

Figure 20-11: PCI/PCI Bridge Bus Enumeration Example

ALLOCATING PCI BUS ADDRESS SPACE

> Most PCI/PCI Bridges have only one "window" for each address space. Consequently, down any given tree branch in a hierarchical bus implementation, the total amount of required resources assigned must encompass the entire window for a given address space attribute type. This is a PCI/PCI bridge Architecture Specification requirement.

There are two typical methods that are used for allocating memory and I/O address space in a PCI based system. The first method, Static Resource Allocation, assigns a predetermined amount of address space to each tree branch in the hierarchy. For example, in Figure 20-5 each branch beneath the Host/PCI bridge could be assigned half the system resources. In a 32 bit system the first two gigabytes of prefetchable memory address space could be assigned to PCI Bridge (1)'s branch, the remaining two gigabytes of prefetchable memory address space could be assigned to PCI Bridge (3)'s branch, and so on. The advantage of this method is that it minimizes power-up configuration software and is not complex. This method is suitable for "closed" systems where a single configuration is implemented and explicit resources have to be assigned to specific devices.

The second common method used for allocating memory and I/O address space in a PCI based system is Dynamic Resource Allocation. In this process all tree branches are traversed. A tally of requested resources requirements is made for each branch. The configuration software then dynamically assigns a contiguous amount of address space to each branch based on the total amount requested. Each device in a specific branch is assigned resources from its branch's system resource pool.

Refer to Figure 20-12 for an example of allocating three megabytes of prefetchable memory. The branch shown is one of several branches in the system. A system resource usage scan is performed on the branch. Device 1 on PCI Bus 1 (Bridge 1) requires 1 megabytes and Device 1 on PCI Bus 02h (Bridge 2) requires 2 megabytes of prefetchable memory address space. Combined they request 3 megabytes. In order to be able to perform a single address decode on the branch for either device the two allocated spaces must be contiguous. Configuration software assigns a contiguous pool of prefetchable memory address space to the branch. The three megabytes of memory address space is then divided between the device on PCI bus 01h, that requires 1 megabyte of memory address space and the device on PCI bus 02h, that requires 2 megabyte of memory address space. As shown in Figure 12, each PCI/PCI bridge's prefetchable memory base and limit registers must be programmed with the correct values that ensures the contiguous address space between bridges. Note that if the Host/PCI bridge supports the prefetchable memory base and limit registers, its values will be the same as PCI/PCI Bridge (1)'s.

Assume that the base of the contiguous three megabytes is A0 00 00 00h. The limit of the contiguous three megabytes is A0 2F FF FFh. Figure 20-12 demonstrates how the three megabytes of prefetchable memory address space would be divided between the different PCI resources.

20.5 LEGACY BRIDGE

A Legacy or Standard PCI bridge is very similar in architecture to a typical Host/PCI bridge with its PCI configuration address space registers, data buffers and primary and secondary bus units. The Legacy bridge is a true PCI agent. The major difference between a Legacy bridge other bridge types is that its secondary bus unit interfaces with an ISA, EISA or MCA bus. It is the Legacy Bridge that permits access to the standard PCI compatible resources, such as interrupt controllers, hardware timers, and DMA. Figure 20-13 illustrates a simple Legacy PCI bridge topology.

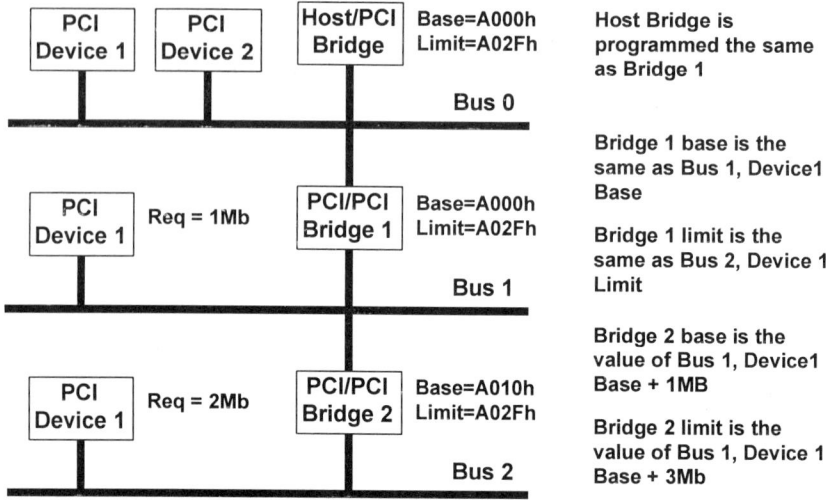

Figure 20-12: PCI/PCI Bridge Address Allocation Example

LEGACY PCI BRIDGE STATE AFTER RESET

Like the Host/PCI bridge, a Legacy bridge should come out of reset in a state that permits all devices required by the boot process to be visible via I/O and system memory address space. In PC compatibles this means that I/O addresses assigned to video and boot devices such as the floppy disk must be passed through to the Legacy PCI bridge without any software initialization of the Host/PCI bridge or Legacy bridge. In addition, memory address transaction between A0000h and FFFFFh should initially be forwarded to the Legacy bridge. All other memory and I/O address space accesses should be disabled. In addition, non-boot related features such as data buffering and error detection must be disabled.

> All Legacy PCI bridge PCI configuration address space configuration registers must be accessible after a reset. This means that the Legacy bridge should be connected to the primary Host/PCI bridge via PCI bus 00h. These registers must reflect the reset state of the bridge.

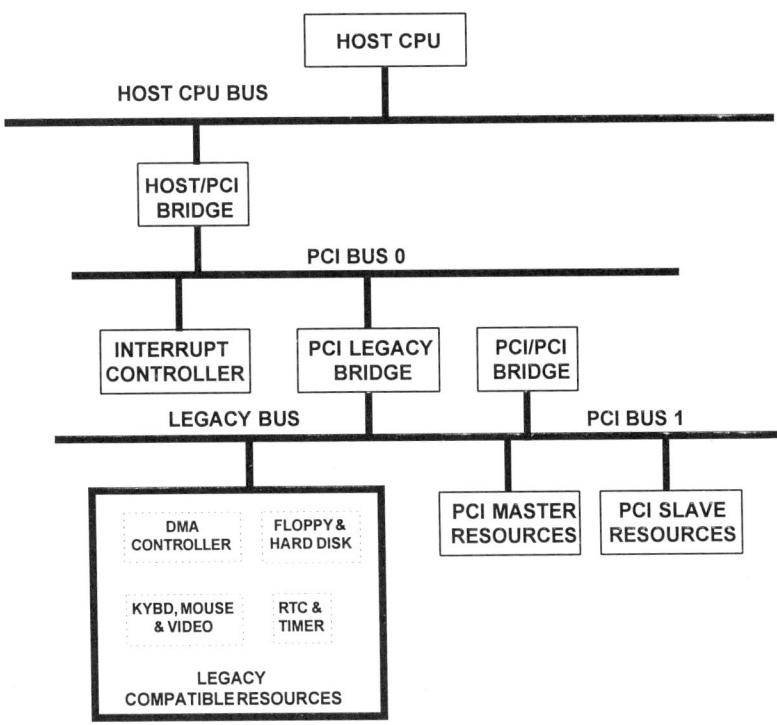

Figure 20-13: Legacy PCI Bridge Topology

LEGACY PCI BRIDGE INITIALIZATION

The Host CPU is typically responsible for configuring the Legacy PCI bridge. During the execution of the System BIOS POST, configuration software is required to perform tasks such as sizing main memory. Based on the amount discovered and other information about the system memory address map, the memory range control registers in the Legacy PCI bridge's PCI configuration address space are programmed with acceptable values. In addition, the configuration software will enable memory accesses and data buffering, as well as system and parity error detection via registers in the Legacy PCI bridge's PCI configuration address space. Depending on the feature set of the Legacy PCI bridge, configuration software will have additional tasks beyond those mentioned in order to initialize the system for optimal operation.

20.6 PEER HOST/PCI BRIDGE

A Peer Host/PCI bridge is very similar in functionality to a typical Host/PCI bridge. Therefore, in this section only the major differences between the two bridge types are discussed. Figure 20-14 shows a simple Peer Host/PCI bridge topology. What is most noticeable in the figure is the second Host/PCI bridge that is connected to the Host CPU bus. This implementation was obviously designed by a group of hardware engineers who thought it would be fun to drive their corresponding BIOS engineers into a state of mental imbalance while attempting to configure both devices.

There are two major items to note about a Peer Host/PCI bridge implementation. First, unlike PCI/PCI bridges, Peer Host/PCI bridges cannot be added to the system via PCI expansion slots. This is important because the System BIOS must be designed up front to contain the proper configuration software support for this type of implementation. Single Host/PCI bridge implementations do not require this special code. This brings us to the second point. While initializing each Peer Host/PCI bridge, the System BIOS must divide the system resources between the Peer Host/PCI bridges.

> Why use Peer Host/PCI bridges? The reason is the higher performance gain over a comparable PCI/PCI bridge implementation. The performance gain is the result of the parallel operation of the Peer Host/PCI bridges. The extra delay of a transaction passing through a second bridge is avoided. Server platforms are an ideal candidate for a Peer Host/PCI bridge implementation because of their higher performance requirements as compared to desktop platforms.

Why not use Peer Host/PCI bridges? The major reason is that they typically cost more to implement. Peer Host/PCI bridges interface to the Host CPU bus. This means that their primary bus unit must be capable of running at the Host CPU's bus speed. Also, additional pins may be required to interface to such things as non-multiplexed address and data buses. This requires extra pins which in turn could increase cost.

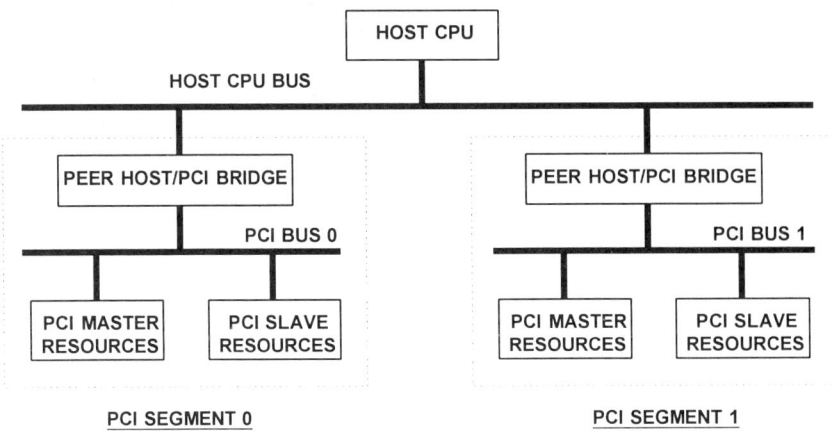

Figure 20-14: Peer Host/PCI Bridge Topology

PCI CONFIGURATION ADDRESS SPACE REGISTERS

Peer Host/PCI bridges, like all other PCI devices, are required to support PCI configuration address space. As with all PCI devices, this allows a specific implementation of a Peer Host/PCI bridge function to support up to 256 8-bit configuration registers. The complexity of a particular Peer Host/PCI bridge's feature set determines how many registers are actually required. Peer Host/PCI bridges utilize variations of the PCI configuration address space Type 00h template shown in Figure 20-3.

PCI HEADER REGION

The PCI Local Bus Specification treats the predefined header as a monolithic 64 byte structure called the Header Region. This structure is subdivided into two regions: the PCI Device Independent Region and the PCI Device Header Type Region. The entire discussion of Host/PCI bridge PCI configuration address space

Header Region is applicable to Peer Host/PCI bridges. Note that Peer Host/PCI bridge implementations may support more or fewer registers than those described in the Host/PCI bridge discussion. Also, bit implementations may vary as well.

PCI DEVICE DEPENDENT REGION

The PCI configuration space Device Dependent Region consists of the last 192 bytes of the PCI configuration space. PCI device vendors are only permitted to implement device-specific registers in this region.

This area of PCI configuration space can be used for any device functionality that is not typically accessed during runtime. The most likely use of this region is device-specific configuration. The major difference between a Host/PCI bridge and a Peer Host/PCI bridge in this PCI configuration address space region is that the Peer Host/PCI bridge is required to support a Bus Number register and a Subordinate Bus Number register. These two registers allow configuration software to differentiate between each of the Peer Host/PCI bridges for configuration purposes. These registers are optional for a Host/PCI Bridge.

BUS NUMBER REGISTER

When accessing PCI configuration address space, recall that PCI devices are addressed geographically by specifying a bus, device, and function number. To achieve independent access to each Peer Host/PCI bridge in the system at power-up or reset, each bridge is assigned a predetermined bus number that is programmed by the hardware into the 8-bit Bus Number register. This value represents the geographical bus number of the PCI bus directly behind each Peer Host/PCI bridge. This register should be read/writeable in order to allow configuration software to reprogram the registers as required during the PCI bus enumeration process.

One of the Peer Host/PCI bridges must be assigned a bus number value of 00h after a hardware reset or cold boot. Other Peer Host/PCI bridges should be assigned bus number values that are non-contiguous with 00h. These values must be initialized by hardware before execution of the System BIOS configuration software. In addition to eliminating system resource conflicts when accessing each bridge, this allows for the easy detection of PCI/PCI bridges that may exist in the geographical hierarchy between the individual Peer Host/PCI bridges. For instance, a default value of 80h for the second of two Peer Host/PCI bridges in a system is acceptable. This is because the value is easily programmable and it is well out of the possible range of PCI/PCI bridges that the primary Peer Host/PCI bridge hierarchy can support. See the example in the discussion of the Subordinate Bus Number register for additional information.

SUBORDINATE BUS NUMBER REGISTER

This 8-bit register is programmed by configuration software with the number of the last PCI bus in a particular bridge's hierarchy. Figure 20-14 is an example of a very simple Peer Host/PCI implementation. Note that there is always a minimum of two PCI buses in a Peer Host/PCI system. The primary PCI bus in the system will always reside behind one of these bridges and be assigned a value of 00h, the first PCI Bus number. This value will be programmed into the correct Peer Host/PCI bridge's Subordinate Bus Number register. Because there are only two PCI buses in Figure 20-14, the configuration software will program the second Peer Host/PCI bridge's Subordinate Bus Number register with a value of 01h when it performs its PCI bus enumeration function.

To further illustrate the role of the Subordinate Bus Number register, assume that a PCI/PCI bridge is attached to Bus 0, either directly or via an add-in card in a PCI slot. Because PCI buses are programmed in a hierarchical fashion, the bus behind the PCI/PCI bridge would be assigned a value of 01h. This means that the second Peer Host/PCI bridge's Subordinate Bus Number value would be programmed with a value of 02h by the configuration software during PCI bus enumeration.

PCI CONFIGURATION ADDRESS SPACE ACCESSES

Assuming that the correct bus number and subordinate bus number values have been assigned, discrete access to each Peer Host/PCI bridge is relatively simple. When an access to the CONFIG_ADDRESS register is initiated by the Host CPU, one of the Peer Host/PCI bridges will respond to the access. How this is done is device specific. However, it must be done so that the correct bridge can respond to the transaction.

When an access is made to the CONFIG_DATA register, each Peer Host/PCI bridge compares the value of the PCI bus field written by the Host CPU against its own Bus Number value. If a match is detected, the bridge with the selected bus number executes a Type 0 configuration access on its PCI bus. If neither bridge's Bus Number register value matches the one to be accessed, a range check is made by each bridge to determine which bridge contains the bus in its hierarchy. This is done using the Peer Host/PCI bridge's Bus Number and Subordinate Bus Number values. The Peer Host/PCI bridge with the matching range generates a Type 1 configuration access to forward the transaction to the selected bus.

The last PCI bus number in the system is important for device drivers and operating systems for device and system configuration purposes. It is important to note that the System BIOS PCI bus enumeration software uses two standard values when specifying the last PCI bus in the system. The first value is the actual number of the last physically present PCI bus in the system. The second value is the last valid value for a PCI bus; this value is FFh, which represents 256 PCI buses, 0 through 255. The primary goals of PCI bus enumeration are to ensure that each PCI bus is assigned a unique value and that a consistent hierarchical topology is achieved with all bus numbers assigned in ascending order. This guarantees that all PCI configuration address space transactions are forwarded to the correct bus and device in a manner transparent to software.

In a typical two Peer Host/PCI bridge implementation such as the one shown in Figure 20-14, the primary Peer Host/PCI Bus Number register value is 00h. Its Subordinate Bus Number register value will reflect the last physical PCI bus in its hierarchy, or PCI bus 00h through N. The second Peer Host/PCI Bus Number register value is assigned the value N+1. Its Subordinate Bus Number register value will either reflect the last physical PCI bus in its hierarchy, or be programmed with a value of FFh.

Other than the primary bridge, device drivers typically cannot detect Peer Host/PCI bridges in a system without special knowledge of the platform's hardware. And as shown above, the primary Peer Host/PCI bridge's Subordinate Bus Number register value does not reflect the last PCI bus in the system. In order to guarantee software transparency in any PCI system, use the System BIOS Get PCI BIOS Present Status routine, function B101h, to obtain the last PCI bus number and other vital information specific to the PCI system. Refer to Chapter 22, PCI System BIOS Software Interface, for more information on this routine.

SYSTEM MEMORY ADDRESS SPACE

Peer Host/PCI bridges are also similar in functionality to a Host/PCI bridge when decoding system memory transactions generated by the Host CPU. However, because there is more than one host PCI bridge connected to the Host CPU bus, special hardware must be implemented to ensure that transactions are forwarded to the correct PCI bus. Designers have wide latitude as to how system memory transactions are decoded and forwarded. For instance, in the case of a two Peer Host/PCI bridge implementation, one bridge device may contain programmable range mapping registers that specify the address range the bridge will positively decode. The second bridge could positively decode only those memory ranges not claimed by the other and not intended for main memory. This minimizes the number of registers required by both Peer Host/PCI bridges. More complex memory maps may require that both bridges contain programmable range mapping registers. In addition, advanced programmable range mapping registers could be programmed in such a way as to support either memory or I/O ranges. In any case, the system memory map is divided between the two bridges. Regardless of the programmable range mapping register implementation, it is highly recommended that configuration software be allowed to allocate large blocks of contiguous memory to both bridges to meet the resource requirements of PCI devices in each bridge's hierarchy.

> There is no requirement to divide the system memory resources evenly between Peer Host/PCI bridges.
>
> Remember that when designing the Peer Host/PCI bridge, designers should also account for address size, either 32-bit or 64-bit, as well as any attributes that could be associated with particular system memory ranges. These include read-only and cacheable attributes.

SYSTEM I/O ADDRESS SPACE

Where system I/O address space is concerned, the Peer Host/PCI bridge is under the same constraints as the Host/PCI bridge, with one exception. Because more than one PCI host bridge is connected to the Host CPU bus, the system I/O resources must typically be divided between both bridges. Again, programmable range mapping registers located in the bridge's PCI configuration address space can handle this task.

> System I/O is an extremely limited resource in PC compatible computers. Dividing the system I/O address space between two or more Peer Host/PCI bridges limits the amount available to each PCI bus in the system. It is highly recommended that PCI device designs that request system I/O also request memory mapped I/O regions as well. This can be done using two or more of the six Base Address registers in a function's PCI configuration address space. Device drivers must be written in such a manner that they could use either system resource to perform their function.

> There is no requirement to divide the system I/O resources evenly between Peer Host/PCI bridges. In fact, intelligent configuration software may not assign any I/O resources to a Peer Host/PCI bridge that does not require I/O in its PCI bus hierarchy.

PEER HOST/PCI BRIDGE STATE AFTER RESET

Just like a Host/PCI bridge, Peer Host/PCI bridges should come out of reset in a state that permits all devices required by the boot process to be visible via I/O and system memory address space. In PC compatibles this means that I/O addresses assigned to video and boot devices such as floppy and hard disks must be passed through the Peer Host/PCI bridge without any software initialization of the Host/PCI bridge. All other memory and I/O address space accesses should be disabled. In addition, non-boot related features such as data buffering and error detection should be disabled.

> All Peer Host/PCI bridge PCI configuration address space configuration register must be accessible after a reset. These registers must reflect the reset state of the bridge.

PEER HOST/PCI BRIDGE INITIALIZATION

The Host CPU is typically responsible for configuring the Peer Host/PCI bridges. During the execution of the System BIOS POST, configuration software is required to perform tasks such as sizing main memory. Based on the amount discovered and other information about the system memory address map, the memory range control registers in the Peer Host/PCI bridge's PCI configuration address space are programmed with acceptable values. In addition, the configuration software will enable memory accesses and data buffering, as well as system and parity error detection via registers in the Peer Host/PCI bridge's PCI configuration address space. Configuration software will also determine the hierarchical bus structure of each PCI segment. Once this is done, each bridge's Bus Number and Subordinate Bus Number register is then programmed with the optimal value for the PCI bus configuration. Depending on the feature set of the Peer Host/PCI bridge, configuration software will have additional tasks beyond those mentioned in order to initialize the system for operation.

CHAPTER 21

OVERVIEW OF SYSTEM BIOS

This chapter consists of the following subchapters:

21.0 INTRODUCTION

As stated in Chapters 1 and 2, the ROM–based system initialization and run–time software contained in all personal computers must be modified to manage the automatic configuration of PCI devices. To aid in the comprehension of the required modifications (these are discussed in Chapters 22 and 23), this chapter presents an overview of an unmodified System BIOS program.

THE SYSTEM BIOS ROM

The System BIOS ROM is the only ROM device required in all x86 PC compatible systems. This ROM contains a minimum of two software components. The first component is a software program called Power On Self Test, or POST. This is executed first each time the computer is turned on or reset. The second required component of an ISA compatible System ROM BIOS is known as System BIOS.

POST OVERVIEW

While there are many System BIOS vendors, the fundamental tasks performed by each POST software program remains the same. The POST software is responsible for checking for the presence or absence of devices within the system, initializing those devices that require software initialization, testing the system hardware, reporting the system configuration and diagnostic status, and finally loading (or bootstrapping) an operating system.

SYSTEM BIOS OVERVIEW

The x86 PC Compatible System BIOS is the portion of code in a system ROM BIOS that contains software programs that are available during POST and the operating system run-time. This is in contrast to the POST, which is not used during run-time operations.

> The System BIOS ROM may contain other software programs such as a Setup or Configuration Utility. These software programs are beyond the scope of this discussion. In addition, the System BIOS may be implemented in more than one ROM memory device.

21.1 INVOKING POST

POST is typically invoked by one of four methods:

1. Applying power to the computer system will automatically invoke the POST. This is accomplished by the microprocessor jumping to the address located at the reset vector, which is located at physical address FFFF0h. Refer to Chapter 16, the section entitled *The System BIOS ROM and the Restart Vector,* for additional information.

2. Many computers have a reset button or switch. It is normally located on the front panel of the computer. When activated, the POST is invoked as described in method one.

3. Simultaneously pressing the <CTRL> <ALT> <DEL> keys on the keyboard in the DOS environment will halt execution of the current software program and transfer control to the start of the POST program. This is known as a *warm* reset. Be aware that multi–tasking software may trap warm resets and handle them without invoking the System BIOS POST.

4. Software programs can jump to the microprocessor reset vector located at physical address FFFF0h. When this method is used, the POST is invoked as described in method one.

21.2 POST DEVICE INITIALIZATION AND TESTING

The initialization and testing of the various system components in an x86 PC compatible system is not a simple two–stage process wherein all components are first initialized and then tested. Rather, it is a sequence of individual component initialization and testing processes.

The early component tests and initializations involve those system components that are mission–critical to the operation of the computer system. If a failure is detected during this stage of the POST it is considered fatal and code execution is halted. For example, if the system ROM BIOS checksum test fails, the System BIOS code is considered unreliable. In this case, code execution is halted instead of risking the possibility of damaging any system component by executing faulty code.

The later POST component tests and initializations involve those system components that, while perhaps are critical to the overall operation of the computer system, do not warrant terminating the code execution process. For instance, should the system cache memory fail to pass its initialization and test process the overall system performance would be degraded. However, the operation of the system would not be hindered.

POST ERROR HANDLING

The POST errors that occur prior to video initialization are reported via the system speaker. A unique sequence of beeps is output, usually through Channel 2 of the 8254 Programmable Timer chip, for each type of failure. Each System BIOS vendor documents their own beep code sequences.

The POST errors that occur after video initialization are reported via the computer CRT. Some System BIOSs print failure numbers that have to be referenced via documentation to determine the failure. Other System BIOSs may go so far as to place exhaustive failure and help screen messages on the CRT. A sequence of beeps may also be output to the system speaker when a failure occurs. Each System BIOS vendor documents their own failure reporting codes and messages.

POST TESTS

Below is a description of Power-On Self Tests performed by a typical x86 PC compatible System BIOS. Note that the sequence of the tests, and the test descriptions themselves, may vary among System BIOS vendors. While perhaps not exhaustive, this will provide helpful insight into the POST initialization and testing phase.

POST TEST	DESCRIPTION
Microprocessor	The microprocessor built–in self–test status is examined for pass/fail. The individual microprocessor registers are tested by writing various values to them. These values are read back and verified. A minimal set of iAPX instructions may be executed and their operations verified.
System BIOS Checksum	A checksum is performed on the System BIOS ROM contents.
CMOS RAM	The CMOS RAM battery is checked for operational status. A checksum test of the standard CMOS RAM is performed. If a system has greater than 64 bytes of CMOS RAM, the extended CMOS RAM may be tested.
DMA Controller	The DMA controller registers are tested, then initialized.
Keyboard Controller	The keyboard controller has a self–test command. The System BIOS issues this command and then checks the result.
Interrupt Controller	The two interrupt controllers are tested, then initialized.
System Timer	Each timer channel is tested for proper operation. Upon test completion, each timer channel is initialized to its standard run–time operating mode.
Memory Refresh	Ensures that the system RAM is being refreshed properly. This usually includes testing timer channel 1.
First 64K	The first 64K of system RAM is tested. This typically includes a parity test for this region. The System BIOS will set up a stack in this region after the test passes.
Video	The system video device is identified, tested and initialized.
Cache Memory	The cache memory subsystem is tested. A failure results in the cache being disabled.
Protected Mode	The ability to switch into and out of Protected Mode is tested.
Address Lines	All system memory address lines are tested.
System RAM	All of system RAM is tested with various data patterns. This test also checks the system data lines.
Parallel and Serial Ports	Each port detected is tested and initialized.
Keyboard	The keyboard has a self–test command. The System BIOS issues this command and then checks the result. The keyboard interface is also tested.
Floppy	Usually a Seek is executed and verified. This also tests and initializes the Floppy controller.
Hard Disk	Usually a Seek is executed and verified. This also tests and initializes the Hard Disk controller.

Table 21-1: System BIOS POST Tests

21.3   POST STACK AND DATA INITIALIZATION

The System BIOS reserves a portion of the system RAM for itself. This dynamic memory is used for a stack, storing information about the system, and the Real Mode interrupt vector table. These areas are initialized after the first 64K system RAM test is performed by the System BIOS. See *Chapter 16: System Resources* for additional information.

STACK

The microprocessor stack segment register [SS] is usually initialized to 30h. The stack pointer register [SP] is initialized to 100h. This sets the top of stack to physical address 400h. This translates into 256 bytes of stack space available for program execution. Because the System BIOS executes in Real Mode (except for the Protected Mode and Extended Memory tests), each time 16 bits of data are placed (pushed) on the stack the [SP] register is decremented by two bytes. For instance, a near call would place the contents of the 16 bit instruction pointer [IP] register onto the stack. If [SP] contained the top of stack value prior to the call, the [SP] register value after the call would be 3FEh.

In Chapter 16, *System Resources*, the Real Mode interrupt vector table was described as having a physical memory base address of 0000:0000. Its length is 1K, or 400 hex bytes. The ISA–compatible system Real Mode stack uses the top 256 bytes (100h) of the interrupt vector table for its stack region. By convention, the highest interrupt vector implemented will never extend into the stack region. This reduces the actual number of available interrupt vectors to 192.

INTERRUPT VECTOR TABLE

Shortly after the first 64K of RAM is tested, the System BIOS will initialize the Real Mode Interrupt Vector Table with segment:offset address pairs that point to System BIOS service routines. The base of the Real Mode Interrupt Vector Table is always located at physical address 0000h in system RAM. There are 256 Real Mode interrupt vectors. Each segment:offset address pair is four bytes. Thus, the first 1K of system RAM, or 0000h-03FFh, is allocated to Interrupt Vector Table. Notice that the location of the standard System BIOS stack overlaps the Interrupt Vector Table.

SYSTEM BIOS DATA AREA

During the testing and initialization phase of the POST, the System BIOS stores information about the system environment in an area referred to as the BIOS Data Area. The structure of this area is predefined. This area is based at physical address 400h. Every x86 PC compatible System BIOS reserves 256 bytes of system memory (400h-4FFh) for the BIOS Data Area. The data stored in this region is used to control the operation of the system.

> **Because this information is stored in system RAM, any program can access and modify the contents of the BIOS Data Area.**

It is beyond the scope of this book to list the structure of the entire BIOS Data Area. However, to demonstrate how this area is used, included below is a partial display containing data stored in the first 16 bytes of the BIOS Data Area and their System BIOS usage. The data shown in Figure 21-1-A was obtained by running the DEBUG.EXE program under DOS Version 6.0 on an IBM PS/ValuePoint computer. The first 16 bytes are displayed by typing *d 40:0 L F*. The data obtained from running the DEBUG.EXE program has been transposed to the figure below for greater readability. Note that, depending on the system configuration, the values displayed below may change.

OFFSET:	0	1	2	3	4	5	6	7	8	9	A	B	C	D	E	F
40:0	F8	03	00	00	00	00	00	00	78	03	00	00	00	00	5F	03

Figure 21-1-A: Partial Contents of the System BIOS Data Area

Figure 21-1-B shows the structure definition and use of the first 16 bytes of the BIOS Data Area. The BIOS interrupt service routine for the system serial ports is INT 14h. For the system parallel ports, the BIOS interrupt service routine is INT 17h. Note that only one serial port and one parallel port were detected, tested and initialized by the System BIOS. In addition, the contents of the serial and parallel ports structure elements are I/O port addresses. The contents of the Extended BIOS Data Area Segment contain a system RAM address. Also, there is no BIOS interrupt service routine associated with the Extended BIOS Data Area Segment.

21.4   POST EXPANSION ROM BIOS INITIALIZATION

Expansion ROM BIOSs are software programs typically located on add–in cards. They may sometimes be integrated into the System BIOS ROM. The purpose of these software programs is to either augment or replace the System BIOS service routines. For example, VGA video add-in cards always contain a ROM BIOS. During its initialization, the VGA ROM BIOS software will usually replace the System BIOS INT 10h interrupt vector with a segment:offset pair pointing to the VGA ROM BIOS INT 10h service routine.

Offset (from 40:0)	BIOS Service	Description	Contents
00h	INT 14h	Serial Port 1 (LSB)	03F8h (I/O address):
01h	INT 14h	Serial Port 1 (MSB)	Serial Port 1 present
02h	INT 14h	Serial Port 2 (LSB)	0000h:
03h	INT 14h	Serial Port 2 (MSB)	No Serial Port 2
04h	INT 14h	Serial Port 3 (LSB)	0000h:
05h	INT 14h	Serial Port 3 (MSB)	No Serial Port 3
06h	INT 14h	Serial Port 4 (LSB)	0000h:
07h	INT 14h	Serial Port 4 (MSB)	No Serial Port 4
08h	INT 17h	Parallel Port 1 (LSB)	0378h: (I/O address):
09h	INT 17h	Parallel Port 1 (MSB)	Parallel Port 1 present
0Ah	INT 17h	Parallel Port 2 (LSB)	0000h:
0Bh	INT 17h	Parallel Port 2 (MSB)	No Parallel Port 2
0Ch	INT 17h	Parallel Port 3 (LSB)	0000h:
0Dh	INT 17h	Parallel Port 3 (MSB)	No parallel Port 3
0Eh	POST	Ext. BIOS Data Area Segment (LSB)	035Fh (memory address)
0Fh	POST	Ext. BIOS Data Area Segment (MSB)	Ext. BIOS segment

Figure 21-1-B: Partial Contents of the System BIOS Data Area

EXPANSION ROM BIOS DETECTION

Expansion ROM BIOSs may appear on any even 2K boundary between physical addresses C0000h and EF800h.

> This allows 64K of code space for System BIOS run–time operation. The actual top of memory where an expansion ROM BIOS could reside is system dependent. For example, some System BIOSs have a size of 128K. In this case the last even 2K boundary an expansion ROM could reside at is DF800h.

The address that the POST starts searching for expansion ROM BIOSs depends on whether a video device with a ROM BIOS is detected and initialized during the Post Device Initialization And Testing phase. If such a device is initialized by the POST during this time, the search for other ROM extensions will usually commence at physical address C8000h. This is because ISA video expansion BIOSs typically consume 32K of address space at run-time. Depending on the System BIOS implementation, the search for non-video ROM extensions will commence at physical address C0000h or C8000h if no video device is detected in the system.

The POST detects an expansion ROM BIOS by searching for a predefined header that all ISA compatible system expansion ROMs must support. A partial structure definition of the expansion ROM header is as follows:

Offset	Description	Value	Size
00h	Expansion ROM identification byte #1	55h	1 Byte
01h	Expansion ROM identification byte #2	AAh	1 Byte
02h	Size of expansion ROM BIOS code in 512–byte blocks.		1 Byte
03h	Start of the expansion ROM BIOS initialization code. Normally contains a FAR return or 3–byte JMP instruction.		4 Bytes

Figure 21-2: Partial Expansion BIOS Header

EXPANSION ROM BIOS VERIFICATION

Once an expansion ROM BIOS signature has been detected, the System BIOS must verify the expansion ROM BIOS is valid. It does this by reading the contents of offset 02h of the Expansion ROM BIOS Header. This byte indicates the length in 512-byte blocks of the ROM BIOS image. The System BIOS will perform a byte-wide checksum of the expansion ROM BIOS starting at offset zero and ending with the last byte of the last 512-byte block of the ROM BIOS image. The expansion ROM BIOS is considered to be valid if the checksum equals zero.

EXPANSION ROM BIOS INITIALIZATION

When a valid expansion ROM BIOS is located, the System BIOS executes a FAR CALL to offset three of the expansion ROM BIOS. For example, in the case of a video expansion BIOS detected at physical address C0000h, the System BIOS would call address C000:0003.

Once invoked, the expansion ROM BIOS initialization routine will test and initialize the devices that it manages. It also has the option of hooking the existing interrupt vector(s) that service its device type. The expansion ROM BIOS will execute a FAR return to the System BIOS when it is done initializing.

Some expansion ROM BIOSs use the microprocessor [BP] register to return completion status to the System BIOS. A status of [BP]=0000h indicates success. A non-zero status indicates failure. This information is System BIOS dependent. Because not all expansion ROM BIOS vendors use this completion status mechanism, the status indicator is generally useless. As a caution, if your software calls expansion ROM, remember to preserve the [BP] register prior to the call.

21.5 BOOTSTRAPPING AN OPERATING SYSTEM

The last function performed by the POST is to load an operating system. Note that the operating system type is not relevant to the boot process. It can be a non-DOS type.

INT 19H BOOTSTRAP LOADER

The POST will execute the INT 19h software interrupt. This service routine will attempt to load an operating system from a floppy diskette or hard disk or network device. If the boot sequence passes, the operating system will assume control of the computer system. If the INT 19h boot process fails (usually due to a no-disk or non-bootable disk condition), the INT 18h software interrupt service routine is invoked.

INT 18H SERVICE ROUTINE

Network expansion ROM BIOSs may also hook the INT 18h interrupt vector when the system is configured to boot from a network. If this is the case, an attempt will be made to boot from the network. If the network boot fails or if the INT 18h interrupt vector was not hooked by a bootable device, a message will be displayed on the CRT and/or a beep code is issued. These will inform the user that the boot process failed and may also contain a request for a bootable device.

21.6 SYSTEM BIOS

The System BIOS ROM may contain other software programs such as a Setup or Configuration Utility. These software programs are beyond the scope of this discussion. In addition, the System BIOS may be implemented in more than one ROM memory device.

The System BIOS provides a system-independent programming interface for the upper layers of software to easily access and control the system hardware. All of the System BIOS level interrupt service routines and device drivers described in Chapter 16 are part of the System BIOS. POST and operating system level software use the functions of the System BIOS that communicate with the system components such as hard disks, floppy drives, parallel and serial ports to perform their hardware related tasks.

The majority of the System BIOS software interfaces to the system hardware were originally specified by IBM Corporation in its PC, XT, and AT technical reference manuals. All x86 PC compatible System BIOSs provide the software interfaces for the machine class as defined in these reference manuals. In addition, various System BIOS vendors often define private software interfaces that are not made available for public use. For example, manufacturing and test software use private software interfaces for production reliability testing of subsystems such as the cache, memory and communication ports. This allows system independent software (in this example, test software that can be reused on various types of systems without modifying the software) to access system dependent hardware.

21.7 CHAPTER SUMMARY

The basic functions of the System BIOS, particularly the POST functions, are presented in this chapter. A description of non-PCI device testing and initialization is given that will be used as a reference in the following chapters when PCI device initialization and testing are discussed.

In addition, the initialization of reserved segments of system memory was given. PCI device initialization has a direct impact on these reserved memory segments.

Also, expansion ROM BIOS initialization of non-PCI devices was covered. While there are some similarities between LEGACY type expansion ROM BIOSs and PCI expansion ROM BIOSs, there are differences that require major reconstruction of the System BIOS, expansion ROM BIOS detection, and initialization code.

Finally, the ISA compatible System BIOS method for loading an operating system was presented. This is one area where little has changed between a LEGACY style System BIOS and a PCI-aware System BIOS.

With an understanding of the information presented in this and the previous chapters, the reader is now prepared to delve into the intricacies surrounding the implementation of a PCI-aware System BIOS.

CHAPTER 22

PCI SYSTEM BIOS SOFTWARE INTERFACE

This chapter consists of the following subchapters:

22.0 INTRODUCTION

Chapter 2: *PCI System Architectural Overview,* presented a high-level design of a Plug and Play system. Within the System BIOS section of the design is a partition entitled Plug and Play Device Services. Each Plug and Play device class such as PCI will have an associated set of device service routines. These services are similar to the ones described in Chapter 16: *System Resources,* in the section on software interrupts.

As with the services described in Chapter 16, the major function of the Plug and Play Device Services is to provide a hardware independent programming interface that allows software to manipulate the computer's hardware. These device services are used by the System BIOS during the POST. They are also used by the System BIOS and operating system level software at run-time. The PCI software interface supports multiple microprocessor operating and addressing modes. This chapter describes the Plug and Play device service routines specific to the PCI device class.

PCI SYSTEM BIOS INTEGRATION

Accessing PCI configuration space and generating special cycles at the lowest hardware level is typically platform dependent. This is due in part to the hardware dependencies associated with individual PCI chip sets and in part to an individual platform's PCI hardware implementation. For example, some chip sets only support PCI Configuration Access Mechanism #1 while others only support PCI Configuration Access Mechanism #2. Because of hardware dependencies as well as the requirement to allow system level PCI based software to be platform independent, the computer's System BIOS is the most sensible location to install PCI software support. Placing PCI software support in the System BIOS minimizes code size and coding effort in the following three programming areas:

■ The computer's System BIOS itself can use the PCI BIOS extensions when detecting and initializing PCI devices. The defined extensions are also portable from product to product because once written and debugged, they require no further modifications. Only the code that interfaces directly with the hardware needs to be modified to accommodate the specific PCI hardware implementation.

■ PCI based adapter BIOSs can utilize the PCI BIOS extensions during the Power-On Self Test (POST) phase of the system to correctly identify and initialize their PCI hardware. By using the PCI BIOS extensions, this initialization code remains platform independent. This ensures that the add-in board's PCI software interface is transparent to the system platform. It will work in a variety of manufacturer's systems.

■ PCI based system level software can utilize the PCI BIOS extensions during the run-time phase of the system to correctly identify and initialize their PCI hardware. Like the PCI add-in boards, this initialization code remains platform independent, thus ensuring that the application software will also work in a variety of manufacturer's systems.

PCI configuration registers can always be accessed directly by software programs. Programmers should be cautious when using direct access programming because software transparency may be reduced between PCI based systems.

The System BIOS x86 Real Mode and 16/32 bit Protected Mode PCI software interfaces are initialized and available by the time PCI expansion BIOSes are scanned during POST. Note that during run time, use the specific PCI applications programming interface provided by the operating system for PCI Configuration Space accesses whenever possible.

X86 OPERATING MODE SUPPORT OVERVIEW

The PCI BIOS software extensions support the 16 bit Real Mode, 16 bit Protected Mode and 32 bit Protected Mode operating modes of the x86 architecture. This represents a major departure from the standard x86 PC compatible System BIOS.

REAL MODE PCI SYSTEM BIOS

Standard x86 PC compatible computer System BIOSs traditionally only support system level software with a 16 bit Real Mode interface that utilizes the software interrupt method described in Chapter 16. To maintain compatibility with this implementation and to provide ease of use, the PCI BIOS software interface includes support for 16 bit Real Mode extensions that are also invoked using the software interrupt process.

16 BIT PROTECTED MODE PCI SYSTEM BIOS

16 bit Protected Mode is also supported by the PCI System BIOS. The System BIOS code that supplies the Real Mode PCI System BIOS support is usually the same code that is executed when 16 bit Protected Mode extensions are invoked. The only difference is how the extensions are invoked. The Real Mode extensions are typically invoked using the iAPX software interrupt mechanism. However, due to the nature of 16 bit Protected Mode, users must call the INT 1Ah entry point directly, as described in Chapter 16.

Real Mode users have the option of using the software interrupt method or calling the INT 1Ah fixed entry point directly.

---

32 BIT PROTECTED MODE PCI SYSTEM BIOS

The PCI System BIOS supports 32 bit Protected Mode software extensions. Because of the nature of the 32 bit Protected Mode, these extensions are supported by a different set of code than its 16 bit counterparts. In addition, a different software interface is supplied to specifically support the 32 bit Protected Mode callers.

The PCI-specific System BIOS software extensions and the different methodologies used to access them are discussed in the remainder of this chapter.

22.1 PCI SYSTEM BIOS SOFTWARE EXTENSIONS

INTRODUCTION

The PCI BIOS software extensions consist of a limited set of routines that allow software programmers to access and manage PCI based hardware in a platform independent manner. These software extensions include services for locating a PCI device, support for PCI special cycles, and methods for accessing the configuration space. This subchapter describes the defined PCI BIOS extensions and their microprocessor register usage. Note that the description of each function applies to both the 16 bit and 32 bit PCI software extensions.

PCI INTERRUPT ROUTINE FUNCTION IDENTIFIER

PCI has been assigned a software function identifier that is used with the system INT 1Ah interrupt service routine. Its value is B1h. This value should always be passed to the 16 bit PCI BIOS interrupt services entry point via the x86 microprocessor [AH] register when invoking PCI software functions.

> **32 bit Protected Mode users must use a special 32 bit calling interface to access PCI System BIOS extensions. This calling interface does not require the [AH] microprocessor register to contain B1h upon invocation. However, System BIOSs may validate [AH] = B1h for 32 bit calls. Therefore, to be safe, initialize the [AH] Register prior to making 32 bit calls.**

PCI SUBFUNCTION IDENTIFIERS

In addition, each of the defined PCI software functions has been assigned a unique subfunction identifier. These subfunction identifiers are always passed in the x86 [AL] register. The System BIOS uses both the PCI function and subfunction identifier when a PCI software function request is made in order to fully qualify the function request and to invoke the correct System BIOS code to properly service the request.

CLASS DEFINITIONS FOR PCI EXTENSIONS

Currently there are twelve defined PCI BIOS extensions. These extensions are divided into one of three classes, according to their specific purpose. These classes are:

- PCI Resource Identification Extensions
- PCI Support Extensions
- PCI configuration space Access Extensions

PCI EXTENSIONS LIST

The table below is a list of the PCI BIOS software functions along with their respective subfunction code and class type. For completeness, the PCI software function identifier is also included in the table.

PCI EXTENSIONS COMPLETION STATUS

All routines use the Carry Flag (bit 0 of the Flags register), and the microprocessor [AH] Registers to return status to the caller. The routine was successful if the Carry Flag bit and the [AH] Register equal zero upon return to the caller. Note that some of the System BIOS extensions, such as the GENERATE A PCI SPECIAL CYCLE, return extended status ([AH] will be non–zero in these instances) in the [AH] Register.

PCI Function	AH	AL	Class
PCI Function ID	B1h		
Get PCI BIOS Present Status		01h	Resource Identification
Find a PCI Device		02h	Resource Identification
Find a PCI Class Code		03h	Resource Identification
Generate A PCI Special Cycle		06h	PCI Support
Read a PCI Configuration Byte		08h	Configuration space
Read a PCI Configuration Word		09h	Configuration space
Read a PCI Configuration Dword		0Ah	Configuration space
Write a PCI Configuration Byte		0Bh	Configuration space
Write a PCI Configuration Word		0Ch	Configuration space
Write a PCI Configuration Dword		0Dh	Configuration space
GET PCI Interrupt Routing Options		0Eh	PCI Support
SET PCI Hardware Interrupt		0Fh	PCI Support

Table 22-1: PCI Software Function List

Callers can optimize their status check code by using either the microprocessor [AH] Register or the Carry Flag bit after the execution of a specific extension; typically both do not have to be checked to verify the completion status.

PCI EXTENSIONS COMPLETION CODE LIST

The table below is a list of the predefined completion codes for PCI BIOS software functions. They will be returned to the caller in the [AH] microprocessor register, and will be referenced in all the PCI functions described below.

PCI Function Return Code	AH
SUCCESSFUL	00h
FUNCTION_NOT_SUPPORTED	81h
BAD_VENDOR_ID	83h
DEVICE_NOT_FOUND	86h
BAD_REGISTER_NUMBER	87h
SET_FAILED	88h
BUFFER_TOO_SMALL	89h

Table 22-2: PCI Function Return Code List

Get PCI BIOS Present Status

PURPOSE:	This function returns the following information to the caller:	
	1	Existence of a PCI BUS and PCI System BIOS Services.
	2	PCI BIOS interface level.
	3	Hardware mechanism type used to access PCI configuration space.
	4	PCI Special Transaction support status.

ENTRY:	[AH]	0B1h
	[AL]	01h

EXIT:	[AH]	Return Code:
		00h = Successful. PCI BIOS Services are present. This field must be qualified by the contents of [EDX].
	[AL]	Hardware mechanism type to access PCI configuration space.

Bits	Value	Description
0	0	Configuration Mechanism #1 not supported
	1	Configuration Mechanism #1 supported
1	0	Configuration Mechanism #2 not supported
	1	Configuration Mechanism #2 supported
3:2	0	Reserved (return value is always zero)
4	0	Special Cycle not supported via Config. Mechanism #1
	1	Special Cycle supported via Config. Mechanism #1
5	0	Special Cycle not supported via Config. Mechanism #2
	1	Special Cycle supported via Config. Mechanism #2
7:6	0	Reserved (return value is always zero)

[BH]	PCI BIOS Interface Level Major Version Number in BCD format
[BL]	PCI BIOS Interface Level Minor Version Number in BCD format
[CL]	Number of the last PCI bus in the system
[EDX]	PCI signature string in ASCII. The value of each byte is as follows:

Bits	Hex Value	ASCII Value
7::0	50h	'P'
15::8	43h	'C'
23::16	49h	'I'
31::24	20h	'∧'

[CF]	PCI BIOS Services present status. This bit is qualified by the contents of [EDX].
	0 = PCI BIOS Services are present.
	1 = PCI BIOS Services are not present.

SPECIAL NOTES:

1. This routine will indicate that a PCI BUS and PCI System BIOS Services exist if:

    1. [AH] = 00h AND [EDX] = 'PCI$_\wedge$'

    OR

    2. [CF] = 00h AND [EDX] = 'PCI$_\wedge$'

    OR

    3. [CF] = 00h AND [AH] = 00h AND [EDX] = 'PCI$_\wedge$'

2. PCI configuration space can be accessed by two separate hardware mechanisms. These are referred to as Configuration Access Mechanism #1 and Configuration Access Mechanism #2. See Chapter 17 for more information. Platforms typically only support one of the two mechanisms. Note that both mechanisms can be supported on the same platform. To ensure that software operates transparently in either environment, it is recommended that the PCI BIOS software functions always be used to access configuration space.

3. Each PCI bus in the system is assigned a number. The BUS Numbers start at zero. For example, if three PCI buses are detected by the System BIOS POST, a value of 02h will be returned in the [CL] register.

4. The PCI BIOS software interface described in this chapter is Version 2.1. System BIOSs written to this function specification will return a of 02h in the [BH] register and 10h in the [BL] register.

PCI RESOURCE IDENTIFICATION EXTENSIONS

There are three PCI Resource Identification Extensions. This class of PCI subfunctions permits the caller to determine if the platform System BIOS contains PCI BIOS software support and to query the system for the presence of specific PCI devices.

Find a PCI Device		
PURPOSE:	This function returns the geographical bus, device, and function number of a PCI device that has a specific Device Identifier and Vendor Identifier.	
ENTRY:	[AH]	0B1h
	[AL]	02h
	[CX]	PCI Device Identifier (0-65535)
	[DX]	PCI Vendor Identifier (0-65534)
	[SI]	Index (0.N) i.e., which instance of the device to search for
EXIT:	[AH]	Return Code:
		00h = Successful. A PCI device was found
		83h = Routine was called with a Bad_Vendor_ID
		86h = A PCI Device_Not_Found
	[BH]	PCI Bus number (0-255) where device is located
	[BL]	PCI Device/Function Numbers in the following format:
		Bits Description
		2::0 Function Number
		7::3 Device Number
	[CF]	Function Completion Status
		0 = Successful
		1 = Error

SPECIAL NOTES:

1. Although the Carry Flag will contain completion status, do not use it. Instead, interpret the [AH] microprocessor register for the routine's actual return status.

2. Return Code 83h, BAD_VENDOR_ID, will only be returned if the caller invoked this function with a value of FFFFh in the [DX] register.

3. This function is extremely useful for callers that wish to quickly locate all devices in the system that contain the same Device ID and Vendor ID. See the suggested algorithm below:

    1. Set the [SI] register to zero to search for the first device.
    2. Call this function. If return code in [AH] equals 86h, then no more devices. Go to Step 5.
    3. Increment the Index input parameter, [SI] register. At least one device found.
    4. Go to Step 2.
    5. Done.

The PCI bus order in which devices are scanned is not specified. For instance, when [SI] is set to zero, the service routine could start the scan for the first device on the last PCI bus, and not necessarily PCI Bus 00h. In addition, the order in which an individual PCI bus is scanned for devices is not specified. The PCI bus could be scanned starting with the highest device identification number or the lowest. And finally, the routine could return the highest function number of a multi-function device first or the last. Device dependent software should make no assumptions as to the order that device information is returned in with this routine. This also applies to the Find A PCI Class Code routine as well.

Find a PCI Class Code

PURPOSE:		This function returns the geographical bus, device, and function of a PCI device that has a specific Class Code.
ENTRY:	[AH]	0B1h
	[AL]	03h
	[ECX]	PCI Device Class Code (Bits 0-23)
	[SI]	Index (0.N) i.e., which iteration of the Class Code to search for
EXIT:	[AH]	Return Code:
		00h = Successful. A PCI device was found.
		86h= A PCI Device_Not_Found with the specified Class Code
	[BH]	PCI Bus number (0-255) where device is located
	[BL]	PCI Device/Function Numbers in the following format:
		Bits Description
		2::0 Function Number
		7::3 Device Number
	[CF]	Function Completion Status
		0 = Successful
		1 = Error

SPECIAL NOTES:

1.   This function is extremely useful for callers that wish to quickly locate all devices in the system that contain the same Class Code. See the suggested algorithm below:

    1.   Set the [SI] register to zero to search for the first device with the specified Class Code.

    2.   Call this function. If return code in [AH] equals 86h then no more devices. Go to Step 5.

3. Increment the Index input parameter, [SI] register. At least one device found.
4. Go to Step 2.
5. Done.

PCI SUPPORT EXTENSIONS

There are three PCI Support Extensions. This class of PCI subfunctions permits the caller to generate PCI bus specific operations.

Generate a PCI Special Transaction		
PURPOSE:	This function allows the caller to broadcast PCI Special Transaction data to a specified bus in the system.	
ENTRY:	[AH]	0B1h
	[AL]	06h
	[BH]	PCI Bus number (0-255) to broadcast data to
	[EDX]	Special Transaction DATA.
EXIT:	[AH]	Return Code:
		00h = Successful.
		81h = This PCI Function_Not_Supported
	[CF]	Function Completion Status
		0 = Successful
		1 = Error

SPECIAL NOTES:

1. PCI Configuration Access Mechanism #2 cannot generate a Special Cycle on any PCI bus except Bus zero.

2. This function should return successful if the operation was done. Otherwise the [AH] Register will contain 81h indicating that the function is not supported.

Get PCI Interrupt Routing Options

PURPOSE: This function returns the PCI interrupt routing options available on the platform. The PCI interrupt routing options define how the platform is able to route individual hardware interrupt lines to PCI devices and PCI Slots.

This function also returns a bit–map containing the current hardware interrupt line (IRQ) assignments that are exclusive to PCI devices.

ENTRY:

[AH]	0B1h
[AL]	0Eh
[BX]	0000h

16–Bit Real Mode parameters:

[DS]	Segment for BIOS data. The base address value in [DS] must resolve to F0000h. The limit value for [DS] must equal 64K.
[ES]	Segment to caller's data structure.
[DI]	16 bit offset address to caller's data structure.

16–Bit Protected Mode parameters:

[DS]	Selector for BIOS data. The base address value in [DS] must resolve to F0000h. The limit value for [DS] must equal 64K.
[ES]	Selector to caller's data structure.
[DI]	16 bit offset address to caller's data structure.

32–Bit Protected Mode parameters:

NOTE: For 32 bit code, see Section 22.3.

[DS]	Selector for BIOS data.
[ES]	Selector to caller's data structure.
[EDI]	32 bit offset offset address to caller's data structure.

EXIT:

[AH]	Return Code:
	00h = Successful.
	81h = This PCI Function_Not_Supported
	89h = Buffer too small.
[BX]	IRQ bitmap. Indicates which IRQs are exclusively dedicated to PCI devices. A '0' bit indicates the that the corresponding IRQ is not exclusive to PCI. A '1' bit indicates the IRQ is exclusive to PCI.
[ES]	Segment or Selector to caller's data structure.
[DI] or [EDI]	16 or 32 bit offset offset address to caller's data structure.
[CF]	Function Completion Status
	0 = Successful
	1 = Error

SPECIAL NOTES:

1.   Description of the caller's data structure:

Get PCI Interrupt Routing Options is called with a FAR pointer to a data structure. The base of this data structure will be pointed to by ES:DI for 16 bit callers and ES:EDI for 32 bit callers. The caller will use this data structure to pass two fields to this function. These fields are defined as follows:

Buffer Size (Offset 00)

■   On entry, this field contains size of the caller's buffer. This is a 2 byte value.

■   If the caller's buffer size is greater than or equal to the actual table size, the System BIOS will update this field with the actual size in bytes of the IRQ routing table.

■   If the System BIOS returns a size of zero in this field then the system does not have any PCI add-in card slots or any integrated PCI devices that use an IRQ.

> If the system has at least one PCI add-in card slot then the returned data will contain the IRQ routing information for that slot.

■   The System BIOS must update this field with the required buffer size if the caller's buffer is too small to contain the IRQ routing data.

> A buffer size of 256 bytes should avoid this problem. This value assumes: 16 devices times the length of one IRQ routing table entry, which is 16 bytes.

DATA Buffer (Offset 02)

■   This field contains a far pointer to the caller's buffer. Upon successful completion, this buffer will be initialized with the system IRQ hardware routing information for each integrated PCI device and PCI add-in card slot in the system.

For each of the microprocessor operating modes, the structure elements will be as follows:

Structure Field	Mode		
	16 Bit Real	**16 Bit Protected**	**32 Bit Protected**
Buffer Size	2 Bytes	2 Bytes	2 Bytes
DATA Buffer Segment/Selector	2 Byte Segment	2 Byte Selector	2 Byte Selector
DATA Buffer Offset	2 Bytes	2 Bytes	4 Bytes

2.   Description of the System BIOS PCI IRQ Routing Table:

The System BIOS knows the PCI IRQ routing options for the integrated PCI devices and add–in card slots. The routing options are returned to the caller in table format via the buffer pointed to by the caller's data structure. The data in the table consists of individual IRQ routing table entries. Each entry describes how the platform is able to route hardware interrupt lines to individual PCI devices and PCI add–in card slots. One IRQ routing table entry is required for each integrated PCI device that uses an IRQ and for each PCI add–in card slot. See Table 22–3 for the structure definition of an IRQ routing table entry.

> Note that the information in this table is static because it reflects platform capabilities. The table contents will always be the same.

The fields within an IRQ routing table entry are defined as follows:

PCI bus number

- PCI bus that the device or slot resides on.

PCI Device Number

- PCI Device Number (upper 5 bits) of the integrated device or slot.

Link Values

- The Link Value field provides a way of specifying which PCI Interrupt Pins are wire–ORed together on the platform.

- Interrupt Pins that are wired together must have the same 'link' value in their table entries.

  - Values for the 'link' field are arbitrary except for a value of zero.

    > A value of zero indicates that the PCI Interrupt Pin has no connection to the interrupt controller. This is typically used for integrated devices that only have an INTA# pin. In this case, INTB#, INTC#, and INTD# pin Link Values would be assigned zero.

IRQ Bit–Map

- This field defines (in a bit– map format) which of the standard PC/AT IRQs the associated PCI interrupt pin can be routed to. Note that entries with the same 'link' value must have the same IRQ Bit–Map value.

  ### Bit–Map Definition:

  Bit 0 corresponds to IRQ0, bit 1 to IRQ1, bit 15 to IRQ15.

  0 –   indicates no routing is possible
  1 –   indicates a routing is possible

Slot Number

- This field indicates if the table entry is for an integrated PCI device or a PCI add–in card slot:

Zero   – Integrated PCI device

Non–Zero   – PCI add–in card slot number.

See Figure 22–1 for an example of how to number platform add–in card slots.

> **Add–in slot numbering is platform vendor specific. Software such as a networking program can use the Slot Number information to inform the user as to which particular external chassis slot a specific network device is located. Consequently, it is critical to physically integrate the slots on the platform in a manner that permits an internal platform slot number to correspondence to an external chassis slot number.**
>
> **This is not always easy to accomplish. It is a common practice with server platforms to integrate two physical slots on a platform such that they share a single external slot. While the platform slots can be enumerated sequentially, the external chassis slots might not be. This could lead to confusion when the software attempts to use the IRQ routing table information to identify an external chassis slot number that does not have a 1:1 correspondence.**
>
> **One final note: it is recommended that add–in card slot numbers be silk–screened onto the platform for ease of internal identification and reference.**

3.   Description of the IRQ Bit–Map return value:

This parameter is contained in the microprocessor [BX] register. The caller must initialize this input parameter to 0000h prior to invoking this routine. Upon return [BX] will contain a 16 bit word that indicates which IRQs are solely dedicated to PCI. These IRQs are not available for use by devices on other device class buses such as the ISA bus.

> **Any IRQs that can be used by both PCI and otherbus types such as ISA or EISA should not appear in this bit-map valueas per the bit-map definition below.**

Bit–Map Definition:

Bit 0 corresponds to IRQ0, bit 1 to IRQ1, bit 15 to IRQ15.

0 – IRQ can be routed to both PCI and non-PCI devices in the system

1 – IRQ can only be routed to PCI devices in the system

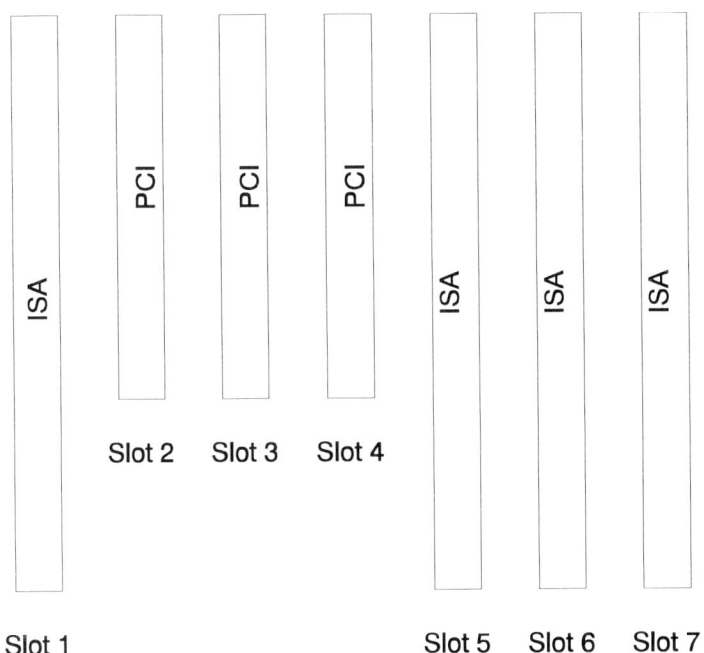

Figure 22-1: Slot Numbering Example

Offset	Size	Description
0	Byte	PCI bus number
1	Byte	PCI Device number (in upper 5 bits)
2	Byte	Link Value for INTA#
3	Word	IRQ Bit–Map for INTA#
5	Byte	Link Value for INTB#
6	Word	IRQ Bit–Map for INTB#
8	Byte	Link Value for INTC#
9	Word	IRQ Bit–Map for INTC#
11	Byte	Link Value for INTD#
12	Word	IRQ Bit–Map for INTD#
14	Byte	Slot Number
15	Byte	Reserved

Table 22-3: IRQ Routing Table Entry Structure Definition

Set PCI Hardware Interrupt		
PURPOSE:		This function allows the caller to request that a specific hardware interrupt line (IRQ) be connected to a specified interrupt pin of a PCI device.
		This function is intended for use by PnP operating systems and system wide configuration utilities. Expansion ROM initialization code and device drivers should never call this function.
ENTRY:	[AH]	0B1h
	[AL]	0Fh
	[BH]	PCI bus number (0-255) where device is located
	[BL]	PCI Device/Function Numbers in the following format:

Bits   Description
2::0   Function Number
7::3   Device Number

	[CL]	PCI device's Interrupt Pin Number to connect to IRQ line. Values are:

0AH =   INTA#
0BH =   INTB#
0CH =   INTC#
0DH =   INTD#

	[CH]	Interrupt Line number (0–15), to connect to PCI device Interrupt Pin. This value corresponds directly to IRQ0–IRQ15 (*i.e.*, 0 = IRQ0, 1 = IRQ1,..15 = IRQ15.).

16–Bit Real Mode parameters:

	[DS]	Segment for BIOS data. The base address value in [DS] must resolve to F0000h. The limit value for [DS] must equal 64K.

16–Bit Protected Mode parameters:

	[DS]	Selector for BIOS data. The base address value in [DS] must resolve to F0000h. The limit value for [DS] must equal 64K.

32–Bit Protected Mode parameters:

NOTE: For 32 bit code, see section 22.3.

	[DS]	Selector for BIOS data.
EXIT:	[AH]	Return Code:

00h =   Successful
81h =   This PCI Function_Not_Supported
88h =   The set hardware interrupt operation failed

	[CF]	Function Completion Status

0 =   Successful
1 =   Error

SPECIAL NOTES:

1.   The caller is responsible for:

■   All error checking. No resource conflict should exist between the specific hardware interrupt line assigned to the PCI device and any other hardware interrupt resource in the system.

■   Ensuring that the specified interrupt is configured properly (level triggered) in the interrupt controller.

■   Updating PCI configuration space (i.e. Interrupt Line register at offset 3Ch) for all affected devices.

> The return status of this function should be verified for a successful completion prior to updating any Interrupt Line register.

2.   This function returns the SET_FAILED status if the requested interrupt cannot be assigned to the specified PCI device.

3.   This function will set the platform hardware to comply with the caller's request prior to returning to the caller if the requested interrupt can be assigned to the specified PCI device.

4.   Changing the IRQ routing for one device will also change the IRQ routing for other devices whose INTx# pins are WIRE–ORed together (i.e. they have the same 'link' field. See the Get PCI Interrupt Routing Options call).

5.   The IRQ line mapping affected by this routine has no affect on the PCI interrupt mapping of next system boot. No routing information is stored by this function for later use.

PCI CONFIGURATION SPACE ACCESS EXTENSIONS

There are six PCI configuration space Access Extensions. This class of PCI subfunctions permits the caller to perform read and write operations in PCI configuration space.

Read A PCI Configuration Register Byte		
PURPOSE:		This function allows the caller to read a single byte from the configuration space of a specified PCI device.
ENTRY:	[AH]	0B1h
	[AL]	08h
	[BH]	PCI bus number (0-255) where device is located
	[BL]	PCI Device/Function Numbers in the following format:
		Bits Description
		2::0 Function Number
		7::3 Device Number
	[DI]	Configuration Space Register Number to read (0-255)
EXIT:	[AH]	Return Code:
		00h = Successful
	[CL]	Byte Value read from the PCI Configuration space Register
	[CF]	Function Completion Status
		0 = Successful
		1 = Error

SPECIAL NOTE:

The PCI BIOS Specification, Revision 2.0, incorrectly states that return code 87h, Bad_Register_Number, is a valid return code. This is not the case for byte–wide read operations in the PCI configuration space. Each byte can be individually read.

1198

Read a PCI Configuration Register Word

PURPOSE:	This function allows the caller to read two contiguous bytes from the configuration space of a specified PCI device.

ENTRY:	[Ah]	0B1h
	[AL]	09h
	[BH]	PCI bus number (0-255) where device is located
	[BL]	PCI Device/Function Numbers in the following format:

                      Bits   **Description**
                      2::0   Function Number
                      7::3   Device Number

	[DI]	Configuration Space Register Number to read (0, 2, 4,.. 254)

EXIT:	[AH]	Return Code:
		00h = Successful
		87h = Function called with Bad_Register_Number
	[CX]	Word Value read from the PCI configuration space
	[CF]	Function Completion Status
		0 = Successful
		1 = Error

SPECIAL NOTE:

The Register Number parameter, [DI], must be a multiple of two (*i.e.*, bit 0 must be set to 0). The PCI BIOS function should return a value of 87h in the [AH] register and set the Carry Flag if this condition is not met.

1199

Read A PCI Configuration Register Dword

PURPOSE: This function allows the caller to read four contiguous bytes from the configuration space of a specified PCI device.

ENTRY: [AH]   0B1h
[AL]   0Ah
[BH]   PCI bus number (0-255) where device is located
[BL]   PCI Device/Function Numbers in the following format:

Bits	Description
2::0	Function Number
7::3	Device Number

[DI]   Configuration Space Register Number to read (0, 4, 8,.. 252)

EXIT: [AH]   Return Code:
00h =   Successful
87h =   Function called with Bad_Register_Number
[ECX]   Dword Value read from the PCI configuration space

[CF]   Function Completion Status
0 =   Successful
1 =   Error

SPECIAL NOTE:

The Register Number parameter, [DI], must be a multiple of four (*i.e.*, bits 0 and 1must be set to 0). The PCI BIOS function should return a value of 87h in the [AH] register and set the Carry Flag if this condition is not met.

Write a PCI Configuration Register Byte

PURPOSE: This function allows the caller to write a single byte value to the
Configuration Space Register of a specified PCI device.

ENTRY: [AH]   0B1h
[AL]   0Bh
[BH]   PCI bus number (0-255) where device is located
[BL]   PCI Device/Function Numbers in the following format:

Bits   Description
2::0   Function Number
7::3   Device Number

[CL]   Byte Value to Write
[DI]   Configuration Space Register Number to Write (0-255)

EXIT: [AH]   Return Code:
00h =   Successful

[CF]   Function Completion Status
0 =   Successful
1 =   Error

SPECIAL NOTE:

The PCI BIOS Specification, Revision 2.0, incorrectly states that return code 87h,
Bad_Register_Number, is a valid return code. This is not the case for byte–wide write
operations in the PCI configuration space. Each byte can be individually written.

1201

Write a PCI Configuration Register Word		
PURPOSE:	This function allows the caller to write a word value to two contiguous bytes of configuration space of a specified PCI device.	
ENTRY:	[AH]	0B1h
	[AL]	0Ch
	[BH]	PCI bus number (0-255) where device is located
	[BL]	PCI Device/Function Numbers in the following format:
		Bits Description
		2::0 Function Number
		7::3 Device Number
	[CX]	Word Value to Write
	[DI]	Configuration Space Register Number to Write (0, 2, 4,.. 254)
EXIT:	[AH]	Return Code
		00h = Successful.
		87h = Function called with Bad_Register_Number
	[CF]	Function Completion Status
		0 = Successful
		1 = Error

SPECIAL NOTE:

The Register Number parameter must be a multiple of two (*i.e.*, bit 0 must be set to 0). The PCI BIOS function should return a value of 87h in the [AH] Register and set the Carry Flag if this condition is not met.

Write a PCI Configuration Register DWORD		
PURPOSE:	This function allows the caller to write a DWORD value to four contiguous bytes of configuration space of a specified PCI device.	
ENTRY:	[AH]	0B1h
	[AL]	0Dh
	[BH]	PCI bus number (0-255) where device is located
	[BL]	PCI Device/Function Numbers in the following format:
		Bits Description
		2::0 Function Number
		7::3 Device Number
	[ECX]	Dword Value to Write
	[DI]	Configuration Space Register Number to Write (0, 4, 6.. 252)
EXIT:	[AH]	Return Code
		00h = Successful.
		87h = Function called with Bad_Register_Number
	[CF]	Function Completion Status
		0 = Successful
		1 = Error

SPECIAL NOTE:

The Register Number parameter must be a multiple of four (*i.e.*, bits 0 and 1 must be set to 0). The PCI BIOS function should return a value of 87h in the [AH] Register and set the Carry Flag if this condition is not met.

22.2 16–BIT PCI SYSTEM BIOS SOFTWARE INTERFACE

The 16 bit PCI BIOS Software Interface is provided through extensions added to the ISA compatible INT 1Ah software interrupt handler. The initial function of this interrupt handler was to provide time–of–day services. However, a new function identifier, B1h, has been assigned to the System BIOS to identify requests for PCI BIOS services when an iAPX INT 1Ah instruction is executed. The individual PCI BIOS subfunctions have also been assigned unique identifiers in order to allow the caller to specify which PCI BIOS function is to be serviced.

> **Using the INT 1Ah handler to service PCI based software also represents a major departure from the standard ISA System BIOS. Traditionally, all programming extensions to the ISA System BIOS have been serviced through the INT 15h Miscellaneous Extended Functions software interrupt handler.**

The 16 bit PCI BIOS Software extensions operate in either the real mode, virtual–86 mode or 16:16 protected mode of the microprocessor. The PCI System BIOS extensions are under all the conditions and restraints of the ISA software interrupt mechanism that is discussed in Chapter 16. In addition, other restrictions apply. The requirements for invoking and returning from 16 bit PCI BIOS functions are listed below:

- The caller must pass parameters to the interrupt handler in the microprocessor's registers.

- Return parameters are placed in the microprocessor's registers. All other registers are preserved.

- Both the microprocessor [AH] Register and the Carry Flag (bit zero of the microprocessor Flags register) indicate the PCI BIOS function interrupt handler completion status.

- The PCI BIOS function interrupt handler will not enable hardware interrupts. The Interrupt Enable bit (bit nine of the microprocessor Flags register) is not modified.

- All PCI BIOS functions are re-entrant.

- The caller to the PCI System BIOS function must provide a minimum of 1024 bytes of stack.

- The caller must ensure that microprocessor privilege levels are set so that the PCI BIOS functions can access I/O address space without generating a protection fault.

- 16 bit Protected Mode users must invoke Real Mode PCI System BIOS extensions by simulating an iAPX INT 1Ah instruction. This is performed by pushing the Flags Register onto the stack and calling the System BIOS fixed entry point at physical address FFE6Eh. See Chapter 16: *System Resources* for details.

The microprocessor Code Segment [CS] and Data Segment [DS] should be set as follows prior to calling the INT 1Ah entry point:

[CS] Must have a base of F0000h
Segment size must be at least 64K
May be execute only

[DS] Should have a base of F0000h
Segment size must be at least 64K
May be read only

■ Real Mode users have the option of using the software interrupt method or simulating the call the INT 1Ah interrupt handler.

The figure below is a partial sample program that illustrates the invocation of a 16 bit PCI BIOS function using the INT 1Ah software interrupt handler. It will request the System BIOS to find an 82378IB System I/O (SIO) PCI device in the system using the Find PCI Device routine discussed in Section 22.1.

```
      .
      .
MOV   AH,  0B1h    ; AH <= PCI Function ID
MOV   AL,  02h     ; AL <= Find PCI Device identifier
MOV   CX,  0484h   ; CX <= SIO Device ID
MOV   DX,  8086h   ; DX <= SIO Vendor ID
MOV   SI,  00      ; SI <= command to find first SIO
           ;device
INT   1Ah          ; Call the PCI BIOS function
      .
      .
```

Figure 22-2: 16 Bit PCI BIOS Software Interrupt Programming Example

22.3 32 BIT PCI SYSTEM BIOS SOFTWARE INTERFACE

The 32 bit PCI BIOS Software Interface is more complicated than its 16 bit counterpart. The reason is that the microprocessor is in 32 bit protected mode. The Interrupt Descriptor Table that was based at physical memory address zero is no longer valid because it relies upon the microprocessor's 16 bit operating mode to compute the physical address of an interrupt vector's entry point. In addition, recall that a typical ISA System BIOS does not support a 32 bit software interface for application programs. Consequently, the 32 bit PCI BIOS support had to be developed from scratch.

BIOS32 SERVICE DIRECTORY

As Intel architecture microprocessors become more and more powerful, operating systems and device drivers running on those microprocessors have evolved into full–featured 32 bit programs to take advantage of the advanced capabilities. These programs still need to access System BIOS functions. However, doing this in the traditional Real Mode manner is often not realistic. The BIOS32 Service Directory was defined to allow 32 bit operating systems to determine what 32 bit BIOS functions are supported by the System BIOS. The BIOS32 Service Directory is a routine that maintains a database of all 32 bit BIOS software service types, such as PCI, supported by the platform's System BIOS.

Finding and using a specific 32 bit BIOS service involves three steps which are further defined below:

1. Determine the existence of the BIOS32 Service Directory

2. Determine the existence of a specific 32–Bit BIOS Service

3. 32–Bit BIOS Service Invocation

BIOS32 SERVICE DIRECTORY INSTALLATION CHECK

Standard x86 PC Compatible System BIOSs typically do not support a 32 bit software interface. Therefore, applications which require 32 bit BIOS function support must first ascertain whether this support is present in the System BIOS of the machine they are currently running on. This will allow application programs the ability to gracefully handle the *32 bit BIOS support not present* condition. The verification process also prevents unpredictable results from occurring if an attempt is made to access a 32 bit BIOS service when it is not supported by the System BIOS.

In Chapter 16 it was shown that a standard x86 PC compatible system ROM is allocated the physical address space from E0000h through FFFFFh. An x86 PC Compatible PCI based System BIOS will contain a contiguous 16 byte data structure within this address range. This data structure must be aligned on a 16 byte boundary. Embedded in this data structure is all of the information an application program requires to verify the existence of a System BIOS that supports 32 bit BIOS services. The fields of the data structure are defined in Table 22-4 below.

> The software application is responsible for handling the condition "BIOS32 Service Directory structure not found".

Offset	Size	Description

00h	4 bytes	BIOS32 signature string in ASCII. The value of each byte follows:
		Offset Hex Value ASCII Value
		  0 5Fh '_'
		  1 33h '3'
		  2 32h '2'
		  3 5Fh '_'

04h	4 bytes	Entry point for the BIOS32 Service Directory. This is a 32 bit physical address.
08h	1 byte	Revision level of the BIOS32 Service Directory data structure. This version has revision level 00h.
09h	1 byte	The length of this data structure in 16–byte units. This data structure is 16–bytes long so this field contains 01h.
0Ah	1 byte	Checksum byte. The contents of this field forces the checksum of the complete data structure to add up to 0.
0Bh	5 bytes	Reserved. Must be zero.

Table 22-4: BIOS32 Service Directory Structure

> This data structure only confirms the existence of the BIOS32 Service Directory. It does not confirm the existence of 32 bit software services such as the 32 bit PCI BIOS extensions.

Below is a suggested algorithm for a procedure that applications can implement to verify the existence of the BIOS32 Service Directory:

1. Save registers.

2. Scan physical address E0000h for the BIOS32 signature string "_32_".

3. If found go to Step 10.

4. Add 16 to the last physical address that did not contain "_32_".

5. Compare the physical address obtained in Step 3 with FFFF0h.

6. If the physical address obtained in Step 4 equals FFFF0h then 32 bit BIOS support is not available. Save status and go to step 13.

   Stop here because the last 16 bytes of the System BIOS cannot contain the structure. This is because physical address FFFF0h contains a hard coded jump instruction to the start of the platform System BIOS code.

7. Scan the current physical address for "_32_".

8. If found go to Step 10.

9. Go to Step 4.

10. Perform a byte–wide checksum of the 16 bytes beginning at the current physical address (i.e., add the contents of bytes xxxx0h through byte xxxxFh).

11. If the byte checksum value obtained in Step 10 is 00h then 32 bit BIOS support is available in the platform System BIOS. Save status and go to Step 13.

12. Go to Step 4.

13. Done. Restore registers and return status to the caller.

> There may be more than one occurrence of the BIOS32 signature string "_32_" in the E0000h – FFFFFFh region. Verify that the data checksums correctly to ensure that this is indeed the BIOS32 Service Directory data structure.

32 BIT BIOS SERVICES INSTALLATION CHECK

Offset 4 of the BIOS32 Service Directory Structure contains the entry point to the BIOS32 Service Directory routine. Support for specific 32 bit services such as PCI can be determined by calling the BIOS32 Service Directory. The BIOS32 Service Directory is invoked by doing a CALL FAR to the entry point provided in the BIOS32 Service Directory data structure. All parameters to the BIOS32 Service Directory routine are passed in registers.

Each 32 bit BIOS software service type is assigned a unique Service Identifier. This Service Identifier is a parameter passed in a microprocessor register to the BIOS32 Service Directory routine. The routine compares this value against valid Service Identifiers in its database and returns an exist status to the caller. If the exist status is true for the specific Service Identifier, the caller is also returned information about the physical location and entry point of the service. The Service Identifier for PCI is the ASCII string "$PCI", or 49435024h. Note that the "$" is the least significant byte in the string.

> Software programs should check the System BIOS for 32 bit PCI software support only if the existence of the BIOS32 Service Directory has first been confirmed.

The definition of the BIOS32 Service Directory routine software is as follows:

CALLER REQUIREMENTS

There are specific requirements for invoking the BIOS32 Service Directory routine. These are listed below:

- The caller must pass parameters to the BIOS32 Service Directory routine in the microprocessor's registers.

- The System BIOS implementor must assume that the microprocessor [CS] (Code Segment) is execute–only.

- The System BIOS implementor must assume that the microprocessor [DS] (Data Segment) is read–only.

- As a minimum, the microprocessor [CS] and [DS] descriptors must be set up to encompass the 4K physical page that contains the BIOS32 Service Directory entry point as well as the next contiguous 4K physical page.

- The microprocessor [CS] and [DS] selectors must be assigned the same base address.

BIOS32 Directory Service		
PURPOSE		Verify if 32-bit service routines are present in the System BIOS for a specific class of devices such as PCI
ENTRY:	[EAX]	Service Identifier. This is a four character string used to specifically identify which 32 bit BIOS Service is being sought.
	[EBX]	The low order byte ([BL]) is the BIOS32 Service Directory function selector. Currently only one function is defined (with the encoding of zero) which returns the values provided below
		The upper three bytes of [EBX] are reserved and must be zero on entry.
EXIT:	[AL]	Return code:
		00h = Service corresponding to Service Identifier is present.
		80h = Service corresponding to Service Identifier is not present
		81h = Unimplemented function for BIOS Service Directory (i.e. BL has an unrecognized value).
	[EBX]	Physical address of the base of the BIOS service.
	[ECX]	Length of the BIOS service.
	[EDX]	Entry point into BIOS service. This is an offset from the base provided in EBX.

- The caller must provide the BIOS32 Service Directory routine with at least 1024 bytes of stack space.

- Return parameters are placed in the microprocessor's registers. All other registers are preserved.

■   The caller must ensure that microprocessor privilege levels are set so that the BIOS32 Service Directory routine can access I/O address space without generating a protection fault.

■   The caller must execute an iAPX FAR CALL to the BIOS32 Service Directory entry point.

As an example, assume that the following BIOS32 Service Directory Structure exists in a System BIOS:

BIOS32 Service Directory Structure				Offset
'_'	'2'	'3'	'_'	00
00	0E	00	00	04
00	CE	01	00	08
00	00	00	00	0C

This structure indicates:

■   The 32 bit PCI software support is present in the platform System BIOS.

■   The physical address of the BIOS32 Directory Service is E0000h.

At this point, the presence of 32 bit BIOS software services has been determined. The next step is to access the BIOS32 Service Directory with a query for whether 32 bit PCI BIOS services are present in the System BIOS. The figure below is a partial sample program that illustrates the invocation of the BIOS32 Service Directory routine. Assume that the CS and DS descriptor 32 bit base addresses are set to 00000000h and their segment limits are set to one megabyte. This permits code and data accesses from physical address 00000000h through 000FFFFFh.

```
; Assume EDX contains the value 000E0000h
          .
          .
          .
       MOV  EAX, 49435024h   ; EAX <= PCI Service
                      ;Identifier
       MOV  EBX, 0000h       ; EBX <= Function selector 0
       CALL FAR PTR EDX      ; FAR CALL to Directory entry
                 ;address
          .
          .
          .
```

Figure 22-3: Partial BIOS32 Service Directory Programming Example

Assume that the return values after making this call are as shown in the table below.

Reg	Value	Description
[AL]	00h	32 bit PCI Service is present.
[EBX]	E0000h	Physical address of the base of the 32 bit PCI BIOS service.
[ECX]	10000h	Length of the 32 bit PCI BIOS service.
[EDX]	8000h	The entry point to the 32 bit PCI BIOS service. This value is an offset from the base of the PCI service.

These return values provide the following information:

■ The physical address of the base of the 32 bit PCI BIOS service is E0000h.

■ The length of the 32 bit PCI BIOS service is specified as 64K or 10000h. Although the actual code length is not this great, it makes it easier for the caller to set up the protected mode descriptors for accessing the services.

■ The 32 bit PCI BIOS service entry point is located at physical address E8000h.

32 BIT PCI BIOS SERVICE INVOCATION

The caller can use the returned values in the EBX and ECX registers to easily create both the CS and DS segment descriptors These descriptors contain the proper base address and segment limit that permit calls to the 32 bit PCI BIOS functions. To invoke a 32 bit PCI BIOS function after the descriptors and segment registers have been initialized, simply set up the microprocessor registers in the same manner as was for the 16 bit PCI BIOS functions. Then execute an iAPX FAR CALL to the entry point of the 32 bit PCI BIOS software services to execute the desired PCI software function.

CALLER REQUIREMENTS

The specific requirements for invoking the 32 bit PCI BIOS routines are listed below:

■ At a minimum, the microprocessor [CS] and [DS] descriptors must be set up to encompass the physical ranges specified by return values in the BIOS32 Service Directory Call.

■ The microprocessor [CS] and [DS] selectors must be assigned the same base address.

■ The System BIOS implementor must assume that the microprocessor [CS] (Code Segment) is execute-only.

■ The System BIOS implementor must assume that the microprocessor [DS] (Data Segment) is read-only.

- The caller must provide the PCI BIOS routines with at least 1024 bytes of stack space.

- The caller must ensure that microprocessor privilege levels are set so that the PCI BIOS routines can access I/O address space without generating a protection fault.

- The caller must execute an iAPX FAR CALL to the PCI BIOS entry point.

22.4 CHAPTER SUMMARY

In this chapter PCI System BIOS extensions were introduced. These software extensions allow software programmers to access and manage PCI based hardware in a platform independent manner. Each routine's purpose and register usage was described. In addition, the specific calling interfaces for both 16 bit Real Mode and 16/32 bit Protected Mode were discussed. Remember to perform all the checks described in this chapter prior to attempting 32 bit Protected Mode accesses to PCI System BIOS functions.

Note that several important guidelines and restrictions for invoking the PCI System BIOS extensions were introduced. These will aid the reader in producing more robust software when implementing System BIOS or higher level software.

CHAPTER 23

PCI DEVICE CONFIGURATION

This chapter consists of the following subchapters:

23.0 INTRODUCTION

Chapter 21 discusses the System BIOS section of the Plug and Play system architecture that deals with PCI Plug and Device Services. These services are used by both the System BIOS during POST and run–time as well as by the operating system level software at run–time to access the PCI hardware within the system.

In this chapter the remainder of the Plug and Play System BIOS software architecture as it pertains to the PCI Bus is discussed. The concepts required for dynamically configuring PCI devices during the power–up system initialization sequence are addressed. In addition, operating system level software concepts will be addressed when applicable. Note that to make the discussion more practical and to reinforce concepts discussed in the previous chapters, an ISA bus is assumed to be integrated in the system along with a single PCI bus. In addition, the discussion will assume a single microprocessor system. Although the x86/ISA bus architecture is used in the following examples, the discussion is broad enough to adapt to any computer system architecture.

For ease of understanding, this discussion is aligned with the basic program flow that an ISA compatible system's BIOS follows to initialize the system components in preparation for bootstrapping an operating system:

■   System Reset

■   Before-Video System Initialization

■   Video Sub–System Initialization

■   After-Video Initialization

■   System Boot

In addition to the above, PCI Expansion ROM BIOS Initialization is also discussed in this chapter. This topic is directly related to PCI device configuration. Because of its complexity and the desire to position this information in one easy to reference location, this topic is contained in a separate subchapter.

> Note that throughout this chapter the PCI Configuration Manager, that is described in Chapter 2, is said to perform certain functions. Keep in mind that while only the PCI Configuration Manager may be referenced, the functions described may be carried out as a result of the PCI Configuration Manager calling the PCI Device Initialization Functions, etc.

23.1 SYSTEM RESET

As we wrote in Chapter 21: *Overview of the System BIOS*, there are four typical ways to force the microprocessor to execute code starting at the system restart vector:

■   Applying power to the computer system.

■   Depressing the system front panel reset button or switch (if installed).

■   Simultaneously pressing the <CTRL> <ALT> <DEL> keys on the keyboard.

■   Jumping to the microprocessor reset vector located at physical address FFFF0h via software instructions.

Once at the reset vector, certain conditions must be met by the different BRIDGEs in a PCI-based system.

1.   After a hard reset, all BRIDGEs except the compatibility BRIDGE and the LEGACY bus BRIDGE must be in the disabled state. The disabled state includes:

   a. The BRIDGE does not respond to I/O space accesses.

   b. The BRIDGE does not respond to memory space accesses.

   c. The BRIDGE does respond to Configuration space accesses.

2.   After any type of reset the compatibility BRIDGE must be in a state that permits the System Boot ROM to be accessed.

3.   When main memory is the only type of device on the HOST bus, the compatibility BRIDGE must respond to all accesses in I/O address space and to the memory address space between 000A0000h and 000FFFFFh.

This ensures that the microprocessor is able to fetch code from the System BIOS ROM. This ROM resides on the LEGACY bus.

NOTE

A compatibility BRIDGE is a HOST BRIDGE that supports PC–compatible functionality by controlling the read/write attributes of the system memory between addresses 00080000h and 000FFFFFh. This region is referred to as the ISA Compatibility Region.

Typical System BIOS configuration utilities contain an option that the user can set to indicate whether the System BIOS POST should only initialize the PCI devices that will be used for input (typically keyboard), output (typically video), and booting (typically a hard drive or network device). When this option is enabled, all other PCI devices detected by the System BIOS POST may or may not be assigned system resources; they are all, however, disabled via their PCI Configuration Space Command register. The operating system is expected to complete the PCI device initialization sequence. If the option is not enabled, the System BIOS POST will perform the entire PCI device initialization.

This BRIDGE is used to enable the shadow RAM mapping of expansion ROMs and the system ROM in the memory address region between 000C0000h and 000FFFFFh.

A LEGACY bus BRIDGE is one that actually provides the PC–compatible functionality.

This BRIDGE incorporates PC–compatible functions compatible with devices such as the 8259 interrupt controllers, the 8254 timers, and 8237 DMA controllers.

RST#

RST# is an asynchronous signal on the PCI bus. Its function is to generate a hard reset to each device on the PCI bus(s). The result is that the sequencer of each PCI device is forced to a known, power-up type state.

RST# can be activated in several ways. First, the signal is always asserted during the system power-up sequence. Second, a HOST compatibility BRIDGE can and should provide a way for software to assert **RST#**. Finally, specific

1215

hardware capable of asserting **RST#** can be incorporated onto the platform. This circuitry is under software control.

Asserting **RST#** after any type of reset is required for proper system operation. This action will halt all PCI device operations that were in progress at the time of the reset. These operations include networking device data transfer cycles and PCI video output. Asserting **RST#** guarantees that these type of operations will not commence until after the PCI devices have been initialized, either by the System BIOS or a device driver. If **RST#** is not asserted after a reset occurs, the system could become inoperable. For example, if the PCI networking device was not reset, it would attempt to continue its previous data transfer operations once the device was enabled. This could lead to data corruption in the system address space.

Some PCI based systems do not have the ability to control **RST#** through any of the methods described above except for the system power–up reset. Because of this the following is recommended for all System BIOS and add–in card vendors:

- The System BIOS must reset the bus master (bit 2), memory space (bit 1) and I/O space (bit 0) control bits of each PCI device's Command Register as early in POST as possible. This will disable the PCI device functions. This includes the Command Register of each function within a multi– function device.

- If a device has an associated option ROM, the option ROM code (when it's INIT function is called) must reset its device(s) in a device specific manner.

- If a device has an associated option ROM, the option ROM code (when its INIT function is called) may enable its bus master (bit 2) bit by setting it to 1.

- If a device does not have an associated option ROM, the device's device driver must reset its device(s) in a device specific manner.

- The device's device driver may enable its bus master (bit 2) bit by setting it to 1 after resetting its associated PCI device(s).

PCI DEVICE BIST OPERATIONS

The Built-In Self Test (BIST) register is located at offset 0Fh of the PCI configuration space predefined header. This register is optional. The purpose of the BIST register is to control the testing of a PCI device and perform status checking on the BIST operation. The usefulness of this register is questionable. For example, if the device was inoperative it is doubtful that its configuration space could be written to even initiate the BIST.

If both the System BIOS and the PCI device support the PCI configuration space BIST register, invoke the BIST after **RST#** and before the video device initialization occurs. The following are guidelines for testing a PCI device via its BIST register:

1. The System BIOS should test all devices that support the BIST register, regardless of whether they are boot devices or not.

2. The System BIOS should wait a minimum of two seconds for BIST completion to occur.

3. The System BIOS should guarantee that the lower three bits (bus master, memory space and I/O space control bits)of the Command Register in PCI configuration space are disabled for any PCI device that fails its BIST.

4. The System BIOS should not attempt to initialize any PCI device that fails its BIST.

5. The System BIOS should not call the associated option ROM of a PCI device that fails its BIST.

6. The System BIOS should report failed devices to the user during POST any time after the video device has been initialized (assuming the video device does not fail its BIST).

7. Device drivers, applications software and the operating system should not attempt to configure and use a PCI device that fails its BIST.

23.2 PRE-VIDEO PCI DEVICE INITIALIZATION

OVERVIEW

Typically, only components required to enable the operation of video are initialized at this time. This includes testing and initializing the first 64K bytes of system memory in order to set up a stack. The stack is required for calling the video BIOS. If a fatal error occurs prior to video device initialization, beep codes are issued to the system speaker to identify the failure. It is at this point that any PCI bus(s) and register initialization must take place in preparation for the possible configuration of a PCI video device.

Figure 2-4 shows the design of a Plug and Play system that encompasses both the System BIOS and the operating system. Note in Figure 2-4 that the entry point for all Plug and Play device class configuration is the POST Global Device Class Configuration Manager. All Plug and Play device initialization in this model is accomplished by the System BIOS calling the POST Global Device Class Configuration Manager with a specific initialization request. Notice how easy it is in Figure 2-4 for the System BIOS to bypass any and all Plug and Play device initialization code. As will be seen, this is a very important feature of a Plug and Play enabled System BIOS.

EARLY PCI INITIALIZATION

One of the tasks performed by the System BIOS before video initialization occurs is to call the POST Global Device Class Configuration Manager with the *Early Plug and Play Device Initialization* request. This permits the POST Global Device Class Configuration Manager to invoke the early device initialization code for each Plug and Play device class. In the case of PCI, the POST Global Device Class Configuration Manager will call the PCI Configuration Manager with the *Early PCI Device Initialization* request. The PCI Configuration Manager will call PCI Device Initialization functions to accomplish the early PCI device initialization. Note that the PCI 16/32–bit functions are available because the system stack is initialized at this point. However, depending on the implementation, the System Resource Manager may or may not be functional this early in POST. The System BIOS must accommodate either scenario.

PCI BUS COUNT

One of the PCI initialization tasks that should be performed early is to determine how many PCI buses exist in the system. The number of the last PCI bus must be stored by the System BIOS for both POST and run–time reference. For example, this is one of the parameters returned to the caller when INT 1Ah, function B101, Get_PCI_Bios_Present_Status, is invoked. See *Chapter 22: PCI System BIOS Software Interface* for a description of this function.

CONFIGURATION SPACE

Depending on the hardware implementation, certain PCI registers located in the 64–byte predefined Configuration Space Header may require early POST time initialization. The System Resource Manager does not need to be functional at the time these specific PCI registers and bits are initialized because specific system resources are not required. Consequently, this initialization can be accomplished early in POST. Some of the registers that may need to be initialized at this time are:

Offset	Register
06h	Status
0Ch	Cacheline Size
0Dh	Latency Timer

STATUS REGISTER

The Status Register is located at offset 06h of the predefined PCI Configuration Space Header. The Status Register records system wide events that occur on the PCI bus. This register is a collection of bits. Several bits in the Status Register have the attribute type RWC. These are individual bits that are cleared to zero if the bit has the write attribute and its bit location is written with a data value of one. It is recommended (but not required) that the System BIOS clear any set status bits in this register prior to booting an operating system. The Status Register may be initialized by writing the value FFFFh to it.

CACHELINE SIZE REGISTER

The Cacheline Size register is located at offset 0Ch of the predefined Configuration Space Header. This register specifies the system Cacheline size in 32 bit words. This value is fixed by the hardware implementation. System BIOS vendors can specify this value with an equate.

> For Intel 80486 class machines the value programmed into this register is 04h (16 byte Cacheline size). For Intel Pentium class machines the value programmed into this register is 08h (32 byte Cacheline size).

This register is implemented in any device that can generate a Memory Write and Invalidate bus cycle or in any device that provides cacheable memory to the system.

> A Cacheline size value of 00h has a special meaning. For master devices it indicates that the Memory Write and Invalidate command should not be used. Instead use Memory Write.
>
> For cacheable memory devices, the value 00h indicates that the system cache (if it exists) is not caching that device's memory and therefore the SBO# and SDONE signals may be ignored.

LATENCY TIMER REGISTER

The Latency Timer register is located at offset 0Dh of the predefined Configuration Space Header. The Latency Timer register specifies the Master Latency Timer value for a PCI Master when the device is on the PCI bus. A typical way for a System BIOS to configure this register is to just choose an appropriate value and use that value for all devices. 32 (approximately 1 μsec at 33 MHz) is a reasonable value.

> **Higher level software, i.e. an OS heuristic, can use the knowledge of how the system is being used (server, desktop, multimedia) as well as MIN_GNT and MAX_LAT values to adjust the Latency Timer appropriately.**

23.3 GENERIC PCI EXPANSION BIOS INITIALIZATION

A PCI device may have an expansion BIOS associated with it. For example, devices such as video and SCSI usually have an associated expansion BIOS either integrated on an add-in card or on the platform itself. The actual expansion BIOS code is stored in a ROM device. The expansion BIOS code is responsible for the initialization of the specific device it is associated with. In addition, some expansion BIOSs contain a system boot function. Understanding the initialization process of PCI expansion BIOSs is essential to understanding PCI device initialization.

PCI EXPANSION ROM

In Chapter 21: *Overview of the System BIOS*, the structure of an ISA compatible expansion ROM BIOS was presented. PCI has extended the ISA definition to increase the functionality of the expansion ROM contents to support new requirements and features. Below is a comparison of the ISA expansion ROM definitions.

EXPANSION ROM ACCESSES

ISA

ISA expansion ROMs can be accessed with either a byte (8 bit) or word (16 bit) access. The ISA expansion BIOS must reside in the ISA Compatibility Region within the physical address range C0000h and EFFFFh. All ISA expansion BIOSs must be visible to the microprocessor at initialization time. In addition, each ISA expansion BIOS must begin on a 2K boundary.

PCI

PCI expansion ROMs must be accessible with any combination of byte-enables. This includes byte (8 bit), word (16 bit), and DWORD (32 bit) accesses. PCI expansion BIOSs that reside within a PCI add-in card ROM device are never executed in place. They are copied from the PCI ROM to shadow RAM within the ISA Compatibility Region.

> The reason that the PCI expansion BIOS must always be copied to system RAM is because of the PCI device ROM decoder implementation. The decoder that is used to make the PCI expansion BIOS appear in the system address space may also be used for one of the other PCI configuration space Base Address Registers. If the PCI expansion BIOS were executed in place the other Base Address Register could not be accessed. PCI expansion BIOS initialization code must have access to all of its device's Base Address Registers (not including the Expansion ROM Base Address Register).

PCI expansion BIOSs that are integrated on the platform itself are typically stored in the System BIOS ROM. When the PCI expansion BIOS is integrated on the platform the System BIOS is responsible for preventing system conflicts.

> The System BIOS is still required to copy the PCI expansion BIOS to shadow RAM and to invoke the expansion BIOS initialization code.

> PCI add-in card expansion BIOSs should never be hardwired to a fixed address. There is no guarantee that an ISA LEGACY BIOS does not map to the same address space. For example, PCI and ISA video BIOSs that are based at physical address C0000h would cause a system conflict.

MULTIPLE IMAGE SUPPORT

ISA

ISA expansion ROMs contain only one expansion BIOS. There is no mechanism for supporting an ISA expansion ROM with multiple images. The ISA image must start on a 2K boundary in order for the System BIOS to detect its presence.

PCI

PCI expansion ROMs may contain several different code images. Each code image can be designed to support a specific platform, a different microprocessor, or a different function within a multifunction device. This allows add-in card manufacturers to support different hardware architectures with a single version of a physical expansion ROM. See Figure 23-1 for a description.

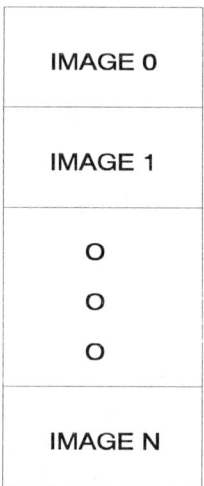

Figure 23-1: PCI Expansion ROM Structure

> The first image in a PCI add-in card ROM must start at offset 00h in the ROM. Subsequent images (if any) must start on a 512-byte boundary.
>
> PCI expansion BIOSs that are integrated on the platform itself are typically stored in the System BIOS ROM. There are no boundary requirements for integrated PCI expansion BIOSs.

PCI EXPANSION BIOS LAYOUT

As shown above, the PCI expansion ROM may contain multiple expansion BIOS images. This section discusses the contents and organization of a single generic PCI image. The data contained in each PCI expansion BIOS ROM includes two PCI device class specific sections. The first section is the PCI Expansion ROM header. This header is designed for compatibility with existing expansion BIOS headers such as the one used by ISA expansion BIOSs. The second section is the

PCI data structure. This structure contains information specific to the PCI expansion BIOS as well as to the PCI device that is supported by the expansion BIOS.

EXPANSION ROM HEADER

ISA

In Chapter 21: *Overview of the System BIOS*, the structure of an ISA compatible expansion BIOS header was discussed. This structure has the format shown in Figure 23-2. See Chapter 21 for details.

Offset	Description	Value	Length
00h	Expansion ROM identification byte #0	55h	1 Byte
01h	Expansion ROM identification byte #1	AAh	1 Byte
02h	Size of expansion ROM BIOS code in 512–byte blocks.	xx	1 Byte
03h	Start of the expansion ROM BIOS initialization code. Normally contains a 3–byte JMP instruction.	xx	3 Bytes

Figure 23-2: Partial ISA Expansion BIOS Header

PCI

The structure of a PCI expansion ROM header is defined to permit compatibility with existing expansion BIOS header structures. The PCI expansion ROM header must be located at the beginning of the PCI expansion BIOS image. That is, the image begins with Expansion ROM identification byte #0. Figure 23-3 shows the format of the PCI expansion ROM header.

Offset	Description	Value	Length
00h	Expansion ROM identification byte #0	55h	1 Byte
01h	Expansion ROM identification byte #1	AAh	1 Byte
02h–17h	Reserved (processor architecture unique data)	xx	16h Bytes
018h–19h	Pointer to PCI data structure	xx	2h Bytes

Figure 23-3: Partial PCI Expansion ROM BIOS Header

IDENTIFICATION BYTES (BYTES 00H–01H)

The Expansion ROM identification bytes identify the start of an expansion BIOS. The value at byte 00h is always 55h. The value at byte 01h is always AAh.

1223

RESERVED BYTES (BYTES 02H–17H)

This region is reserved for extensions to the standard PCI ROM header. The architecture of the system in which the PCI expansion BIOS will function determines the specific extensions that may be added. For an example, see the discussion on PC Compatible PCI Expansion ROMs later in this chapter.

POINTER TO PCI DATA STRUCTURE (BYTES 18H–19H)

This is the offset address of the PCI data structure within the current expansion BIOS image. The offset is calculated from Expansion ROM identification byte #0 of the current PCI expansion BIOS image. The address is in little endian format. For example, if the offset address of the structure is 4300h, byte 18h will contain 00h and byte 19h will contain 43h.

> The PCI data structure must be located within the first 64K of the PCI expansion BIOS image. The base address of the structure must be DWORD aligned.

PCI DATA STRUCTURE

The PCI data structure contains information specific to the PCI expansion BIOS and the device it supports. Figure 23-4 shows the format of the PCI data Structure. The offset values are from the beginning of the data structure. The length values are the number of bytes each field is assigned.

> The PCI data structure must be aligned on a DWORD boundary (0000h, 0004h, 0008h, etc.).

Offset	Length	Description
0	4	Data structure signature, the string "PCIR"
4	2	Vendor Identification
6	2	Device Identification
8	2	Reserved, starting with Revision 2.2 of the PCI Local Bus Specification; otherwise, the Pointer to Vital Product Data
A	2	PCI data structure Length
C	1	PCI data structure Revision
D	3	Class Code
10	2	Image Length
12	2	Revision Level of Code/DATA
14	1	Code Type
15	1	Indicator
16	2	Reserved.

Figure 23-4: Partial Expansion ROM BIOS Header

SIGNATURE STRING

The signature string is used to identify and validate the PCI data structure. It is used instead of a checksum. The signature string "PCIR". "P" is inserted at offset 0 of the structure, "C" at offset 1, "I" at offset 2 and "R" at offset 3.

VENDOR IDENTIFICATION

This field contains the Vendor ID of the PCI device that the image is to be used for. This field (along with the Device Identification field) is one of the criteria for selecting the proper image.

DEVICE IDENTIFICATION

This field contains the Device ID of the PCI device that the image is to be used for. This field (along with the Vendor Identification field) is one of the criteria for selecting the proper image.

POINTER TO VITAL PRODUCT DATA

This field is reserved by Revision 2.2 of the PCI Local Bus Specification. Starting with Revision 2.2, Vital Product Data is specified as a New PCI Capability. See Appendix K, Vital Product Data, for more information. For PCI devices designed to a specification earlier than Revision 2.2, this is the offset address of the Vital Product DATA (VPD) structure within the current expansion BIOS image. The offset is calculated from Expansion ROM identification byte #0 of the current PCI expansion BIOS image. The address is in little endian format. For example, if the VPD structure is at offset 4300h in the image, byte 18h will contain 00h and byte 19h will contain 43h. A value of 0000h in bytes 8 and 9 of the PCI data structure indicates that no Vital Product DATA is contained in the expansion BIOS image.

> **Vital Product DATA must be within the first 64K of the PCI expansion BIOS image.**

PCI DATA STRUCTURE LENGTH

The PCI data structure Length declares the length of the PCI data structure. The length of the structure is calculated from offset 0 of the structure, which is the first byte of the Signature field. This field is in little endian format and is in units of bytes.

PCI DATA STRUCTURE REVISION

The PCI Data Structure Revision identifies the revision level of the PCI Data Structure definition. The current revision level is 00h. This value should be placed at offset 0Ch of the PCI Data Structure.

CLASS CODE

Each PCI device contains a 24 bit device class code field. This device identification field is located at offset 09h of the PCI device's configuration space. The values in this field are placed into the PCI Data Structure at offset 0Dh (device programming interface), 0Eh (sub-class code), and 0Fh (base class code) of the PCI Data Structure. This information permits software to easily identify the function(s) supported by the expansion BIOS image.

IMAGE LENGTH

The Image Length declares the length of the current expansion BIOS image. This field is in little endian format and is in units of 512 bytes. This information is used to calculate the address of the next PCI expansion BIOS image (if any) in the PCI expansion ROM device.

REVISION LEVEL

The Revision Level field contains the revision level of the expansion BIOS code in the current image. Layout and interpretation of this field is vendor specific.

CODE TYPE

The Code Type field identifies the type of code contained in the current image of the PCI expansion ROM device. This field is used as part of the selection criteria for finding the proper image for a device. The following code types have been assigned:

Type	Description
0	Intel x86, PC–AT compatible
1	Open Firmware standard for PCI
2	Hewlett-Packard PA RISC
3-FF	Reserved

Open Firmware is a processor architecture and system architecture independent standard. The standard addresses the implementation of device specific option ROM code. See the IEEE1275-*1994 Standard for Boot (Initialization, Configuration) Firmware Core Requirements and Practices* for documentation on Open Firmware. Also *see PCI Bus Binding to IEEE 1275-1994* for applying the Open Firmware standard to the PCI Local Bus.

INDICATOR

Bit	Description
6::0	Reserved for future use
7	0-Another PCI expansion BIOS image follows the current image
	1-This is the last PCI expansion BIOS image in the ROM device

PCI expansion BIOSs that are integrated with the platform instead of the with PCI device (as in the case of add–in cards) will set bit [7] of the indicator field to '1'. It is permissible to integrate an expansion ROM BIOS that contains more than one expansion BIOS image in it on a platform. However, the System BIOS will require additional code to handle this type of implementation. This implementation is beyond the scope of this discussion.

PCI EXPANSION BIOS INVOCATION

PCI Expansion BIOSs may either be located in a PCI add-in card ROM device or integrated in a ROM device on the Platform. Each of these implementations requires special, yet distinct handling. The PCI add-in card and integrated expansion BIOS initialization functions may be performed as two distinct operations, or combined.

All system resources requested by a PCI device must be assigned prior to invoking the PCI device's expansion BIOS code. The only exception to this rule is in the case of PCI video device initialization. See Subchapter *23.5: Video Sub–System Initialization* for details.

In addition, the device must have both the I/O (bit 0) and Memory (Bit 1) of the configuration space Command Register set to 1 (if possible; some devices do not implement read/write capability for these bits) prior to the PCI expansion BIOS invocation phase.

ADD-IN CARD PCI EXPANSION BIOS DETECTION AND SELECTION

The PCI Configuration Manager (see Figure 2-4) is responsible for locating and invoking the PCI expansion BIOS associated with a device on a PCI add-in card. The steps below describe the generic process for detecting and selecting a PCI expansion BIOS image. Specific details on this subject for PC compatibles are found in the *PC Compatible PCI Expansion ROM* section later in this chapter. Note that the System Resource Manager must be functional at this time. The steps for locating and invoking a PCI expansion BIOS associated with a device on a PCI add-in card are as follows:

1. Test the PCI device to determine if the Expansion ROM Base Address Register at offset 30h of the device's configuration space has been implemented. Do this by:

   a. Writing FFFFFFFEh to the register. (Use PCI BIOS function B10Ch.)

   b. Reading the DWORD contents of the register. (Use PCI BIOS, function B10Ah.)

   c. If the value read is 00000000h, the register is not implemented. Go to DONE.

Certain types of PCI devices may indicate that there is an expansion ROM associated with the device when in reality one is not physically present. For example, consider network devices. Usually, the only time an expansion BIOS is required for network device initialization is when the device will be used for booting an OS. To save cost, if the device is not used for booting an OS, the associated ROM containing the boot initialization code is not included.

The System BIOS can only determine that a ROM image may be associated with a given device by performing the above test. The PCI specification provides no mechanism for determining if an expansion ROM actually is or is not supposed to be physically present. This presents a dilemma for the System BIOS during POST as well as PCI-aware operating systems and applications programs. There is no way to determine whether a hardware or software failure has indeed occurred when an attempt is made to access the ROM image or whether the image was intentionally excluded from the configuration. Be aware that how the different levels of software handle this situation is vendor-specific. For example, one System BIOS vendor may display a warning message on the CRT indicating a possible failure each time a ROM image is not located for a device that claims it has one; another vendor may choose to ignore the situation altogether.

---

2. The upper 21 bits read from the Expansion ROM Base Address Register indicate the address range required for mapping the PCI expansion ROM code into the system's physical address space.

    The PCI Configuration Manager makes a request to the System Resource Manager for an unused contiguous memory space within the memory address map that will accommodate the PCI device's expansion ROM address requirement. The address allocated by the System Resource Manager is written to the Expansion ROM Base Address Register.

    This process ensures that no system resource conflict occurs when the PCI device's expansion ROM is mapped into the system memory address space.

3. The PCI Configuration Manager turns on the Memory Space bit (bit 0) of the PCI device's configuration space Command Register (offset 4).

    > The Memory Space bit in the Command Register has precedence over the expansion ROM's address decode Enable bit. PCI devices must only respond to expansion ROM accesses when the Memory Space bit and the expansion ROM's address decode enable bit are both set to '1'.

4. The PCI Configuration Manager enables the PCI device's expansion ROM address decode enable bit. This is bit 0 of the Expansion ROM Base Address Register. The PCI expansion ROM is now physically mapped to the system address space obtained in Step 2.

    > PCI devices are permitted to share a decoder between the Expansion ROM Base Address Register and a Base Address Register. When the expansion ROM address decode is enabled the decoder is used to access the PCI ROM expansion BIOS. The Base Address Register is disabled. For this reason, device independent software should never access any other Base Address Register of a PCI device whose expansion ROM address decode is enabled.

5. The PCI Configuration Manager checks the first two bytes contained in the expansion ROM image for the expansion ROM identification signature, AA55h.

    If the value read is not AA55h, the PCI expansion ROM is not present. Go to Step 14, UNMAP ROM.

> **This will occur if a PCI device is integrated on a platform and the device implemented the Expansion ROM Base Address Register.**

6. The expansion ROM is present. The PCI Configuration Manager obtains the Pointer to the PCI Data Structure from bytes 18h and 19h of the current expansion BIOS image.

7. The PCI Configuration Manager checks the first four bytes contained in the PCI Data Structure for the PCI Data Structure Signature, the string "PCIR".

    If the value read is not *PCIR*, the PCI expansion ROM image is invalid. Go to Step 14, UNMAP ROM.

8. The PCI Configuration Manager compares the value of the Vendor Identification field in the PCI device's configuration space with the Vendor Identification field in the expansion BIOS's PCI Data Structure. If the values do not match, the expansion BIOS does not match the PCI device. Go to Step 12, NEXT IMAGE.

9. The PCI Configuration Manager compares the value of the Device Identification field in the PCI device's configuration space with the Device Identification field in the expansion BIOS's PCI Data Structure. If the values do not match, the expansion BIOS does not match the PCI device. Go to Step 12, NEXT IMAGE.

10. The PCI Configuration Manager verifies that the expansion BIOS's PCI data structure code type value is appropriate for the system. If the value is not appropriate, the expansion BIOS does not match the PCI system. Go to Step 12, NEXT IMAGE.

11. At this point a valid PCI expansion BIOS image has been found. The PCI Configuration Manager PCI copies the expansion BIOS image to system RAM. In the case of PC compatibles, the image is copied to shadow RAM in the ISA Compatibility Region.

    Go to Step 14, UNMAP ROM

12. **NEXT IMAGE-**The PCI Configuration Manager vectors here if an expansion BIOS image is detected in the PCI expansion ROM that does not match the PCI device to be initialized. The PCI Configuration Manager reads the Indicator field of the expansion BIOS's PCI data structure. If bit 7 is set to 1 there are no more expansion BIOS images in the expansion ROM. Go to Step 14, UNMAP ROM.

13. The PCI Configuration Manager reads the Image Length field of the expansion BIOS's PCI data structure. This value is multiplied by 512 to obtain the length in bytes of the current expansion BIOS image. The result of the multiplication operation is added to the base address value of the current expansion BIOS image. The result of the addition operation is the base address of the next expansion BIOS image within the PCI expansion ROM. Go to Step 5 and repeat the search for a valid image.

14. **UNMAP ROM**-The PCI Configuration Manager disables the PCI device's expansion ROM address decode by writing a DWORD value of 00000000h to the Expansion ROM Base Address Register. The PCI expansion ROM is no longer physically mapped to the system address space obtained in Step 2. If no valid image was found go to Step 16, DONE.

15. The PCI Configuration Manager PCI calls the expansion BIOS initialization code. The PCI expansion BIOS initialization code will return to the PCI Configuration Manager when the device initialization is complete.

> This step assumes that the PCI device has been allocated system resources prior to the invocation of the expansion BIOS initialization code.

16. DONE.

INTEGRATED PCI EXPANSION BIOS INVOCATION

PCI devices may be integrated on platforms. An integrated PCI device may require expansion BIOS initialization. To satisfy this configuration, a PCI expansion BIOS can be integrated in a ROM device on the platform. The System BIOS contains the information on which PCI devices have been integrated with the platform as well as the location of any integrated PCI expansion BIOSs.

The PCI Configuration Manager (see Figure 2-4) is responsible for invoking PCI expansion BIOSs associated with PCI devices that are integrated on a platform. The PCI Configuration Manager skips this section if there are no integrated PCI expansion BIOSs to be initialized. Note that the System Resource Manager must be functional at this time. The steps for invoking PCI expansion BIOSs associated with PCI devices that are integrated on a platform are as follows:

1231

1. For the First/Next integrated PCI expansion BIOS in the system, the PCI Configuration Manager obtains the following information from the System BIOS device specific code:

    a. The location of the integrated PCI expansion BIOS.

    b. The Vendor Identification number that corresponds to the PCI expansion BIOS.

    c. The Device Identification number that corresponds to the PCI expansion BIOS.

    d. The Device/Function number of the device that corresponds to the PCI expansion BIOS.

    e. The Bus number of the device that corresponds to the PCI expansion BIOS.

2. The PCI Configuration Manager copies the PCI expansion BIOS image to system RAM. In the case of PC compatibles, the image is copied to shadow RAM in the ISA Compatibility Region.

3. The PCI Configuration Manager PCI calls the expansion BIOS initialization code. The PCI expansion BIOS initialization code will return to the PCI Configuration Manager when the device initialization is complete.

4. Go to Step 1 and repeat until no more integrated PCI BIOSs to initialize.

23.4   PC COMPATIBLE PCI EXPANSION BIOS INITIALIZATION

PCI expansion ROM images that are used in PC compatible systems require extensions to both the PCI ROM Header and to the PCI Configuration Manager ROM initialization code. These extensions apply to any image that specifies Intel x86, PC-AT compatible in the Code Type field of the PCI data structure and to any platform that is PC compatible.

PC COMPATIBLE PCI EXPANSION BIOS IMAGE

Figure 23-5 is a pictorial representation of a PC compatible PCI Expansion BIOS Image. The layout of the image incorporates an extended PCI Expansion ROM Header (discussed below) in addition to the standard PCI data structure. The image also has three lengths associated with it. These lengths are the Image

Length, Initialization Length and Run-Time Length. These features are combined to make the PC compatible PCI Expansion BIOS highly optimized for PC compatible system architectures.

IMAGE LENGTH

The Image Length is the total length of the PCI expansion BIOS image. The Image Length must be greater than or equal to the Initialization Length. The Image Length is contained in the 'Image Length' field of the PCI data structure.

> **The total length of the PCI expansion BIOS image is not required to be checksummed.**

INITIALIZATION LENGTH

The Initialization Length is the portion of the image that contains both the PCI expansion BIOS initialization code and run–time code. The PCI Configuration Manager copies this portion of the image from the ROM device to shadow RAM in the ISA Compatibility Region. The shadow RAM is left writeable after the copy to allow the PCI expansion BIOS to have a scratch pad and to permit the initialization code to update the Run-Time checksum. The PCI Configuration Manager will then call the entry point to the PCI expansion BIOS initialization code that is located at offset 3 of the PC Compatible PCI ROM Header of the image.

> **The Initialization Length must be greater than or equal to the Run-Time Length of the PCI expansion BIOS image. The expansion ROM vendor must include in the image a byte-wide checksum of the PCI expansion BIOS. The checksum is calculated by adding all bytes in the Initialization Length. The checksum must equal 00h.**

> **Minimize the size of the Initialization Length. This increases the possibility of fitting the PCI expansion BIOS into the unused address space of the ISA Compatible Region.**

RUN-TIME LENGTH

The Run-Time Length is the portion of the image that contains the PCI expansion BIOS run-time code. This is the amount of code that will be used after the system is booted with an operating system.

> PCI Expansion BIOSs should always adjust their Run-Time Size down to the smallest value possible. This consumes as little as possible of the ISA Compatibility Region (a very limited system resource). The Run-Time Length must be less than or equal to the Initialization length of the PCI expansion BIOS image. If the PCI expansion BIOS initialization code does adjust its Run-Time Size, the Run-Time Length checksum must equal zero. The checksum must be stored in the Run-Time portion of the image.

PCI DATA STRUCTURE LOCATION

The PCI expansion BIOS run-time image must contain the PCI data structure. However, if the PCI expansion BIOS image only contains initialization code, the initialization image must contain the PCI data structure.

PC COMPATIBLE PCI ROM HEADER EXTENSIONS

Two fields, illustrated in Figure 23-5, are added to the PCI Expansion ROM Header to make it PC compatible. At offset 02h a field is added to declare the initialization size for the PCI expansion BIOS image. Offset 03h contains the entry point for the PCI expansion BIOS initialization code.

Offset	Description	Value	Length
00h	Expansion ROM identification byte #0	55h	1 Byte
01h	Expansion ROM identification byte #1	AAh	1 Byte
02h	Initialization size of the PCI expansion ROM BIOS code in 512–byte blocks.	xx	1 Byte
03h	Start of the PCI expansion ROM BIOS initialization code. Normally contains a 3 byte JMP instruction.	xx	4 Bytes
06h–17h	Reserved (processor architecture unique data)	xx	12h Bytes
018h–19h	Pointer to PCI data structure	xx	2h Bytes

Figure 23-5: PC Compatible PCI Expansion BIOS Header

PCI ADD-IN CARD EXPANSION BIOS INVOCATION

The actions that the PCI Configuration Manager takes to initialize a PC compatible add-in card PCI expansion BIOS are divided into three areas. These areas deal with the activities that take place before the PCI expansion BIOS is invoked, during the PCI expansion BIOS initialization, and after the PCI expansion BIOS initialization completes. These areas are discussed below.

Note that all system resources requested by a PCI device must be assigned prior to invoking the PCI device's expansion BIOS code. The only exception to this rule is in the case of PCI video device initialization. See *Subchapter 23.5: Video Sub–System Initialization*, for details.

In addition, the device must have both the I/O (bit–0) and Memory (Bit 1) of the configuration space Command Register set to 1 (if possible, some devices do not implement read/write capability for these bits) prior to the PCI expansion BIOS invocation phase.

BEFORE THE EXPANSION BIOS IS INVOKED

The PCI Configuration Manager performs the following steps before invoking each PC compatible PCI expansion BIOS integrated within the ROM device of a PCI add-in card:

1. If the PCI expansion BIOS image is contained in a PCI add–in card ROM device, this step assumes that Steps 1 through 10 of the *Add–In Card PCI Expansion BIOS Invocation* section of this chapter have been performed.

2. The PCI Configuration Manager asks the System Resource Manager to allocate a region of memory address space within the ISA Compatibility Region large enough to hold the Initialization image of the PCI expansion BIOS.

    If the request is denied, the PCI expansion BIOS Initialization image is too large to fit into the unused ISA Compatibility Region memory address space. A message may be printed to the CRT to notify the user.

The device is NOT disabled in this case. The reason is that another expansion BIOS may have already initialized the device.

If the image is too large to copy into shadow RAM, go to the DONE (Step 5) in the *After the Expansion BIOS Is Called* section.

3. The PCI Configuration Manager asks the System Resource Manager to allocate an unused region of memory within the 4 gigabyte address space large enough to satisfy the alignment request of the PCI device's Expansion ROM Base Address Register.

If the request is denied, the PCI Device requested a block of memory that cannot be granted by the System Resource Manager. A message may be printed to the CRT to notify the user. Go to the Step 5, DONE, in the *After the Expansion BIOS Is Invoked* section.

> **A device's Expansion ROM Base Address Register should never request more than a 16 Megabyte memory area. Systems may not be able to satisfy requests larger than this.**

4. The PCI Configuration Manager checksums the expansion BIOS Initialization image within the PCI expansion ROM using the method described for ISA expansion BIOSs in Section 21.4. The length of the Initialization image is stored in the byte at offset 2 of the PCI compatible PCI Expansion ROM Header. The value at offset 2 is the number of 512 byte blocks in the initialization image.

If the Initialization portion of the PCI expansion BIOS image fails to checksum to zero the expansion BIOS initialization code will not be invoked. Go to the DONE (Step 5) in the *After The Expansion BIOS Is Called* section if the expansion BIOS fails to checksum.

> **The System Resource Manager may have allocated an extended memory address region to the PCI Device's Expansion ROM Base Address Register. The x86 microprocessor must be in either Protected Mode or Flat Mode to read the PCI add-in card expansion BIOS.**

5. The PCI Configuration Manager configures the system memory controller to make the shadow RAM region allocated in Step 3 writeable. The code required for this operation is device dependent and specific to a given platform.

6. The PCI Configuration Manager copies the PCI expansion BIOS image from the PCI add-in card ROM device to the shadow RAM region allocated in Step 3.

> **For efficiency, the PCI Configuration Manager may use DWORD reads of the PCI ROM device during the copy.**

7. This step is optional. It is used for additional error checking.

    The length of the Initialization image is stored in the byte at offset 2 of the PC-AT compatible PCI Expansion ROM Header. The PCI Configuration Manager checksums the expansion shadow RAM BIOS Initialization image (see the checksum procedure for ISA expansion BIOSs in Chapter 21).

IF THE CHECKSUM OPERATION FAILS:

    The PCI Configuration Manager either removes the entire image from shadow RAM or erase the Expansion ROM identification byte #0 and #1 signature from the shadowed image. The address space is either allocated to a different expansion PCI BIOS or made available to the operating system after boot.

    The PCI Configuration Manager configures the system memory controller to make the shadow RAM region allocated in Step 3 non–readable and non-writeable.

    Set ERROR status and go to Step 8.

8. Unmap ROM

    The PCI Configuration Manager disables the PCI device's expansion ROM address decode by writing a DWORD value of 00000000h to the Expansion ROM Base Address Register. The PCI expansion ROM is no longer physically mapped to the system address space.

    If ERROR, go to the DONE (Step 5) in the *After the Expansion BIOS Is Called* section.

9. The PCI Configuration Manager calls the PCI expansion BIOS initialization code at offset 3 of the PCI compatible PCI Expansion ROM Header. The PCI Configuration Manager must pass the PCI expansion BIOS initialization code three parameters:

    [AH]-*Number* of the PCI Bus where the device to be initialized resides.

    [AL]-*Device Number* (upper 5 bits) and *Function Number* (lower 3 bits) of the device to be initialized.

EXPANSION BIOS INITIALIZATION

The Initialization function of a PCI expansion BIOS is responsible for initializing an I/O device(s) and preparing the expansion BIOS for Run-Time operation. The PCI Configuration Manager copies the PCI expansion BIOS initialization image to shadow RAM within the ISA Compatibility Region. This region ranges from C0000h to EFFFFh.

A key element in the PCI expansion initialization is that the PCI Configuration Manager must leave the shadow RAM where the expansion BIOS has been copied to writeable while the BIOS initialization function is executing. This opens up a range of possibilities to PCI expansion BIOS vendors. Single parameters as well as tables can be created/adjusted on the fly. This and other information may be stored for use by the BIOS or device drivers at run–time. This data will not be destroyed because the shadow regions where PCI BIOSs are installed are write–protected after the initialization function returns to the PCI Configuration Manager.

> PCI expansion BIOSs often hook real mode interrupt vectors. It is recommended that the Segment Offset address pairs of the hooked vectors be stored within the shadow RAM region to which the PCI expansion BIOS is assigned.

> The PCI expansion BIOS initialization code must never attempt to use shadow RAM that was not allocated to it. For example, assume that an expansion BIOS is 8K, and that it will be based at C8000h–C9FFFh (8K). However, the memory controller is only capable of manipulating shadow RAM on a 16K granularity. When the expansion BIOS initialization function is invoked the shadow RAM region between C8000h and CBFFFh (16K) is writeable. Another expansion BIOS may be based at CA000h–CBFFFh (8K). If the BIOS based at C8000h wrote any data into an address between CA000h–CBFFFh, that BIOS would be corrupted. There is a high probability that the system will crash when the code between CA000h–CBFFFh is attempted to be executed.

Another feature of the PCI initialization function is that the expansion BIOS can adjust its size field. This will conserve memory in the ISA Compatibility Region. This is possible because the shadow RAM is writeable at initialization time. This means that the Initialization Size and Run-Time Size can be different. There are three requirements that must be met when the expansion BIOS size is adjusted:

1. The size field at offset 2 of the PCI expansion BIOS Header must be updated to reflect the Run-Time image size.

2. The Run-Time size must be less than (or equal to) the Initialization Size.

> There is no requirement that the Run-Time size of a PCI expansion BIOS be adjusted down from the Initialization Size. However, the Run-Time Size should never be set greater than the Initialization Size. A Run-Time size that equals 00h indicates that the PCI expansion BIOS did not install a run–time image. This is the only mechanism that PCI expansion BIOS vendors should use to declare that there is no Run-Time BIOS image for the device. When a Run-Time Size is set to 00h, the expansion BIOS does not have to checksum its BIOS.

3. The Run-Time BIOS must checksum to zero as described in Chapter 21.

As an example of a PCI expansion BIOS initialization, consider the case where there are two identical PCI devices in the system. These are the only PCI devices in the system. Each device has an identical expansion ROM BIOS associated with it. The initialization size of the expansion BIOS is 16K. The first expansion BIOS is copied to shadow RAM based at C8000h–CC000h (16K). The PCI Configuration Manager passes the bus location and device/FUNCTION Number of the device to its expansion BIOS. The expansion BIOS can determine the device associated with it. The expansion BIOS can then use the FIND_DEVICE PCI routine to locate all of the other devices in the system that it can support. The expansion BIOS can then initialize its own device as well as all other devices in the system that it can service. The expansion BIOS can build a table of its device system configuration table in shadow RAM. This table can be used at run–time. Finally, the expansion BIOS can adjust its size, say to 8K, for run–time operation. This makes the first expansion BIOSs run–time size address region from C8000h– C9FFFh (8K). The expansion BIOS returns to the PCI Manager when its initialization function is complete.

The PCI Configuration Manager adjusts the system memory map to account for the change in the expansion BIOSs size (how this is accomplished is explained in the *After the Expansion BIOS Is Called* section). Now assume that the next BIOS to be initialized is the second PCI expansion BIOS. The second 16K BIOS image will be copied to address region CA000h–CDFFFh (16K). The PCI Configuration Manager passes the bus location and device/FUNCTION Number of the device to its expansion BIOS. By using a device specific mechanism, the second PCI expansion BIOS detects that its device has already been initialized. The BIOS initialization code understands that only one image of itself has to be in shadow RAM. The second expansion BIOS therefore sets its Run-Time Size to 00h and simply returns to the PCI Configuration Manager. The PCI Configuration Manager adjusts the system memory map to account for the disappearance of the second expansion BIOS. The next BIOS that fits would be copied to shadow RAM at CA000h.

AFTER THE EXPANSION BIOS IS CALLED

The PCI Configuration Manager performs the following steps after invoking each PC compatible PCI expansion BIOS initialization code integrated within the ROM device of a PCI add-in card:

1. When the device initialization is complete, the PCI expansion BIOS initialization code returns to the PCI Configuration Manager.

2. The PCI Configuration Manager configures the system memory controller to make the shadow RAM region allocated in Step 3 read–only. The code required for this operation is device dependent and specific to a given platform.

3. The PCI Configuration Manager checks the byte value of the Run-Time Length at offset 2 of the shadowed PCI expansion BIOS image:

   A. If the Run-Time Length equals 00h, the PCI expansion BIOS did not install a run-time image. This is the **only** mechanism that PCI expansion BIOS vendors should use to declare that there is no Run-Time BIOS image for the device.

   > A typical example of this is when a SCSI BIOS only detects a CD ROM device. Current SCSI BIOSs do not support CD ROM devices. Consequently, there is no reason for the SCSI BIOS to remain in system memory.

   The PCI Configuration Manager:

   1. Asks the System Resource Manager to deallocate the memory address space that the PCI expansion BIOS was allocated.

   2. Configures the system memory controller to make the shadow RAM region allocated in Step 3 writeable.

   3. Then either removes the entire image from shadow RAM or erases the Expansion ROM identification byte #0 and #1 signature, AA55h, from the shadowed image. The freed address space is either allocated to a different expansion PCI BIOS or made available to the operating system after boot.

   4. Configures the system memory controller to make the shadow RAM region allocated in Step 3 non–readable and non–writeable.

   5. DONE. Optional error message may be printed to the CRT.

B. If the Run-Time Length is greater than the Initialization Length the system is unstable.

> This is considered a CATASTROPHIC error. It should NEVER happen. One reason is because the PCI expansion BIOS code may have overwritten a previously installed expansion BIOS. An error message will be printed. In addition, the System BIOS vendor can take one of several actions if this occurs: Halt, Continue-on-error, etc.

4. The Run-Time image is checksummed.

    If the checksum operation fails:

    The PCI Configuration Manager either removes the entire image from shadow RAM or erases the Expansion ROM identification byte #0 and #1 signature from the shadowed image. The address space is either allocated to a different expansion PCI BIOS or made available to the operating system after boot.

    The PCI Configuration Manager configures the system memory controller to make the shadow RAM region allocated in Step 3 non-readable and non-writeable only if the region is not used by another device.

    Set ERROR status and go to Step 5.

5. DONE. Optional error message may be printed to the CRT.

PCI INTEGRATED EXPANSION BIOS INITIALIZATION

The PCI Configuration Manager performs the following when invoking the initialization code of a PCI expansion BIOS integrated with the platform:

1. If the PCI expansion BIOS image is integrated on the platform, this step corresponds to Step 3 of the *Integrated PCI Expansion BIOS Invocation* section of this chapter.

2. The PCI Configuration Manager asks the System Resource Manager to allocate a region of memory address space within the ISA Compatibility Region large enough to hold the Initialization image of the PCI expansion BIOS. If the request is denied, the PCI expansion BIOS Initialization image is too large to fit into the unused ISA Compatibility Region memory address space. A message may be printed to the CRT to notify the user. In this case go to Step 9, Done.

3. The PCI Configuration Manager configures the system memory controller to make the shadow RAM region allocated in Step 3 writeable. The code required for this operation is device dependent and specific to a given platform.

4. The PCI Configuration Manager copies the PCI expansion BIOS image from the memory location specified by the System BIOS to the shadow RAM region allocated in Step 2.

5. The PCI Configuration Manager checksums the expansion BIOS Initialization image within the shadow RAM using the method described for ISA expansion BIOSs in Chapter 21. The length of the Initialization image is stored in the byte at offset 2 of the PCI compatible PCI Expansion ROM Header. If the checksum operation fails:

    The PCI Configuration Manager either removes the entire image from shadow RAM or erases the Expansion ROM identification byte #0 and #1 signature from the shadowed image. The address space is allocated to a different expansion PCI BIOS or made available to the operating system after boot.

    The PCI Configuration Manager configures the system memory controller to make the shadow RAM region allocated in Step 3 non–readable and non–writeable.

    Set error status and go to step 9, Done.

6. The PCI Configuration Manager calls the PCI expansion BIOS initialization code at offset 3 of the PCI compatible PCI Expansion ROM Header. The PCI Configuration Manager must pass the PCI expansion BIOS initialization code three parameters:

    [AH]-BUS Number of the PCI device to be initialized.

    [AL]-Device Number (upper 5 bits) and Function Number (lower 3 bits) of the device to be initialized.

7. The PCI expansion BIOS initialization code is executed as described in the Expansion BIOS Initialization section

8. The remainder of the PCI integrated expansion BIOS initialization is the same as the After the Expansion BIOS Is Called section. Reference it for details.

9. DONE

    Print error message if error occurred.

23.5 VIDEO SUB-SYSTEM INITIALIZATION

OVERVIEW

The power-up video device is detected and initialized during the Video Sub-System Initialization. As a minimum the system may have a monochrome device, VGA compatible device or combination of both. In a system that supports more than one type of bus, such as the ISA and PCI combination used in this discussion, the initialization sequence for video is more complex because the System BIOS must determine which video device to enable. An initialization sequence that handles both PCI and non-PCI video devices is presented. This initialization sequence gives precedence to video devices on the ISA bus. This is because LEGACY ISA add-in cards do not come up disabled at power-up, while all PCI compliant devices (except the compatibility BRIDGE and the LEGACY bus BRIDGE) power-up in a disabled state.

VIDEO DEVICE LOCATIONS

Video devices can be located in several different areas in an ISA/PCI based system as follows:

1. ISA add-in card slot: Monochrome device installed.

2. ISA add-in card slot: VGA compatible device installed.

3. Integrated on the ISA bus on the platform: VGA compatible device installed.

4. One or more PCI add-in card slots: VGA compatible device installed.

5. Integrated on the PCI bus on the platform: VGA compatible device installed.

6. A combination of one ISA monochrome add–in video card, one ISA VGA compatible add-in video card along with one or more PCI VGA compatible video devices. The PCI video devices may be integrated on the platform, installed in add-in card slots, or a combination of both.

The fundamental question is: Which VGA compatible video device should the system use?

VIDEO DEVICE SELECTION

The System BIOS is responsible for the selection and initialization of the VGA compatible video device that the system will use during the POST and bootstrapping process. A precisely defined method for the video device selection is required. This method must handle LEGACY (a standard ISA VGA compatible device in this example) and Plug and Play video devices. The video device selection algorithm presented in this section uses the following assumptions.

1. VGA compatible video devices always have precedence over monochrome video devices. Except for implementations such as serial port video redirection, monochrome video devices are the POST and bootstrapping video device only if a VGA device is not detected in the system.

> **The video device used for the POST and bootstrapping video is referred to as the primary video device.**

2. LEGACY video devices (such as ISA VGA compatible video devices) always have precedence over Plug and Play video devices. This is because the best way to avoid system resource conflicts is to give precedence to those devices which cannot be programmatically disabled and whose exact system resource consumption cannot be determined.

3. Add–in video devices always have precedence over video devices integrated onto the platform. The reason is that it requires special effort to add a video card to the system when video is available from the platform. Under normal circumstances a user would not install a video card in this situation unless its video output was desired.

> **Because of the dynamic configuration capabilities of PCI devices, the Setup Utility can have an option that permits the user to select off-board vs. on-board PCI video as the default power-up video device.**

4. The System BIOS previously reset the bus master (bit 2), memory space (bit 1) and I/O space (bit 0) control bits of each PCI video device's Command Register to 0 prior to the video device check. This ensures that no PCI video device is active on a PCI bus.

5. The System BIOS only searches for a Plug and Play VGA compatible video device if it determines that no LEGACY VGA compatible video device is present in the system.

6. The System BIOS will attempt to initialize and use the first Plug and Play VGA compatible video device detected in the system. All other Plug and Play VGA compatible video devices in the system remain uninitialized until the non-Plug and Play video devices are initialized. At that time, non-boot video devices are initialized along with non-video devices. This ensures that system resources are properly allocated to all non-boot PCI video devices found in the system. This is performed to allow video device drivers to function with non-video boot devices after boot.

7. The expansion BIOS of the primary Plug and Play VGA compatible video device such as PCI is always based at physical address C0000h.

> In some systems the active VGA video BIOS can be located at either physical address C0000h or E0000h. In regard to Plug and Play VGA compatible video devices such as PCI, this capability extends beyond the scope of this discussion.

8. The LEGACY ISA expansion ROM BIOS never exceeds a size of 32K.

> The manner in which platform PCI slots are assigned is key to achieving a clean video solution. Hardware designers that integrate PCI video onto the platform should assign the device select lines so that the PCI add–in slots are assigned to either all higher or all lower device selects than the integrated PCI video device. The integrated PCI video device select line should never be interleaved with the PCI add–in card select lines.
>
> By assigning the PCI device select lines in this manner the System BIOS can easily search up from the lowest device found on the bus or search down from the highest device found on the bus for the first video PCI device found. By using this method, the System BIOS can handle on-board and add-in PCI video devices with little or no special casing software.
>
> It is recommended that integrated devices be placed on PCI Bus 0 with a device select line lower than the one assigned to the first PCI add-in card slot. This will avoid potential problems on both single PCI bus systems as well as multiple PCI bus implementations.

1245

ADD–IN ISA VIDEO DEVICE DETECTION AND INITIALIZATION

It is relatively easy to detect whether an ISA VGA compatible device is present in the system when all other VGA compatible devices are disabled. The standard ISA video expansion ROM BIOS is assumed to always be based at physical address C0000h.

The System BIOS can verify that a valid expansion ROM is present at this address by following the guidelines in Chapter 21: *Overview of System BIOS*. See the *Post Expansion* section entitled *Expansion ROM BIOS Detection*.

If a valid expansion ROM BIOS is found at physical address C0000h, the System BIOS will assume that it is an ISA VGA compatible video BIOS. The System BIOS will invoke the initialization code of the video BIOS. For an expansion of how this is performed, see Chapter 21, the *POST Expansion ROM BIOS Initialization* section.

Once the video BIOS has completed its initialization sequence, the system will have video output from the ISA VGA compatible device. INT 10h video requests will be serviced by the ISA Video BIOS instead of the System BIOS from this point on.

INTEGRATED ISA VIDEO DEVICE INITIALIZATION

Some platforms have an integrated ISA VGA compatible video device. If this device is enabled, then it will be the one selected by the System BIOS to provide video output to the system CRT. The location of an integrated video expansion ROM BIOS that supports the on–board ISA video device complicate matters.

The location of the video expansion ROM BIOS that supports the integrated LEGACY ISA video device is system dependent. Special handling may be required by the System BIOS in order to locate and initialize an integrated LEGACY ISA video BIOS. Below is a list of some of the different methods that platform designers use to integrate the ISA video device onto the platform. Note that the System BIOS should give precedence to an ISA add-in video card. In this case the integrated video device should be disabled and the integrated video BIOS should not be invoked.

1. The system platform incorporates a ROM device that contains the ISA video BIOS code. This ROM device is decoded beginning at physical address C0000h. The System BIOS invokes the LEGACY ISA VGA BIOS initialization code at address C0000h.

2. The video BIOS code is integrated into the ROM device(s) that also contains the System BIOS code. The system platform incorporates a chip set capable of mapping the section of the System BIOS ROM that contains the video BIOS code directly to physical address C0000h. The System BIOS invokes the LEGACY ISA VGA BIOS initialization code at address C0000h after the mapping has been enabled.

3. The video BIOS code is integrated into the ROM device(s) that also contains the System BIOS code. However, the system platform does not incorporate a chip set capable of mapping the section of the System BIOS ROM that contains the video BIOS code directly to physical address C0000h. The System BIOS copies the video BIOS code from the System ROM to the 32K of shadow RAM based at physical address C0000h. The System BIOS invokes the LEGACY ISA VGA BIOS initialization code at address C0000h after the shadow function is completed.

4. The video BIOS code is integrated into the ROM device(s) that also contains the System BIOS code. This code is located at a fixed location that is visible at all times to the microprocessor. (*e.g.*, physical address E0000h). The System BIOS special cases this implementation and invokes the LEGACY ISA VGA BIOS initialization code at E0000h instead of C0000h.

There are deviations on the above methods. However, regardless of the implementation, the System BIOS is responsible for locating the LEGACY ISA video device and calling the video BIOS initialization code.

Finally, the System BIOS must bypass the code that detects and initializes a Plug and Play video device as the POST and bootstrapping video device whenever a LEGACY video device is detected and initialized first.

ADD-IN PCI VIDEO DEVICE DETECTION AND INITIALIZATION

In the case of Plug and Play video device initialization, the System BIOS first determines that no LEGACY video device is installed in the system. Once the determination is made that no LEGACY video device is installed, it is valid for the System BIOS to request that a Plug and Play video device be searched for and, if found, initialized as the primary video device.

In the example system, only LEGACY ISA and PCI video devices can be installed in the system. Note that if more than one class of Plug and Play devices is integrated into the system (and both device classes support video devices) the video device detection and initialization algorithm requires a slight modification. The System BIOS vendor must extend the example hierarchical video device detection and initialization scheme so that each Plug and Play device class in turn has the opportunity to install its video device. Figure 23-6 shows a flow chart of an implementation that supports two Plug and Play device classes.

The PCI primary video device initialization code will likely be performed separately from all other PCI device initialization code. The reason is that it is highly desirable to have screen output operational prior to any non-video PCI device initialization. This is because configuration information and error reporting are infinitely easier when screen output is functional.

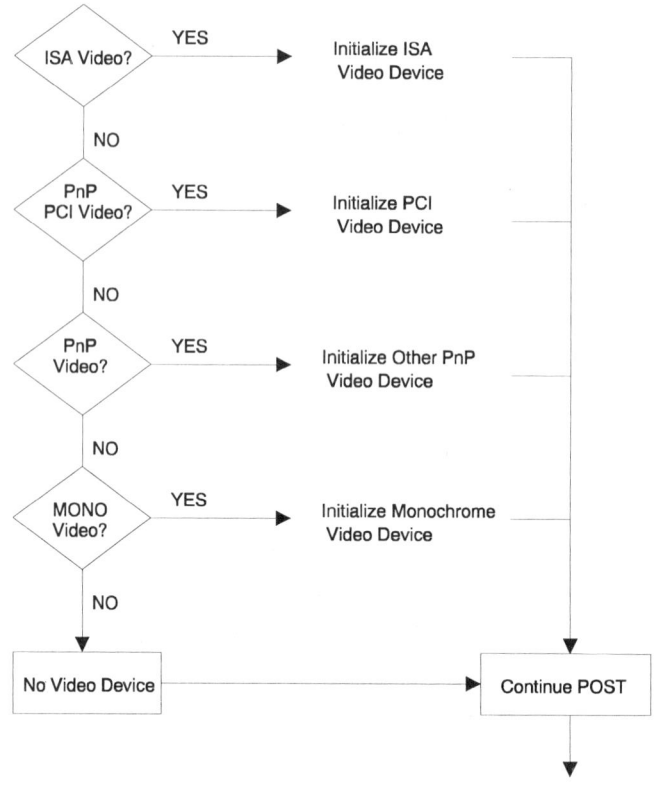

Figure 23-6: Video Selection Hierarchy

This discussion assumes that in all cases the PCI video device BIOS size is 32K. Like all PCI expansion BIOSs, the PCI video BIOS must be copied to shadow RAM. In most PCI based systems the shadowed PCI video BIOS will be absolutely located at physical address C0000h-C7FFFh.

To locate and initialize a PCI video add–in card in an ISA/PCI only based system according to Figure 2-4 the following will be performed:

1. The System BIOS calls the POST Global Device Class Configuration Manager.

2. The POST Global Device Class Configuration Manager calls the PCI Configuration Manager with the *Initialize PCI Video Device* request.

3. The PCI Configuration Manager calls the PCI Device Initialization Function that is responsible for PCI video initialization.

4. By invoking the Get_PCI_Bios_Present_Status INT 1Ah PCI Function, the PCI Video Device Initialization Function can obtain the number of the last PCI Bus to search. This function returns the number of the last PCI bus in the system. In this example, the value returned will be 00h, indicating that the system contains one PCI bus.

5. Depending on the system implementation, the PCI Video Device Initialization Function will either begin its scan for a video device at the highest PCI bus number and PCI Device Number or at the lowest PCI bus number and PCI Device Number. This search includes multi–function devices.

> **The Find Device and/or Find PCI Class Code INT 1Ah PCI Functions can be used to quickly locate a PCI video device.**

6. Once an add–in card PCI video device has been found, its BIOS will be installed as described in the subchapter PCI Expansion ROM BIOS Initialization of this chapter.

> **Plug and Play video devices are guaranteed the use of standard VGA system resources at video BIOS initialization time. Other system resources such as a video frame buffer address or interrupt line may not be assigned until later and thus are not guaranteed at this time.**

7. The PCI Video Device Initialization Function returns status to the System BIOS declaring that PCI software has initialized the primary video

device. The System BIOS then knows to halt the search for the primary video device.

INTEGRATED PCI VIDEO DEVICE INITIALIZATION

PCI based platforms may include an integrated PCI VGA compatible video device. Like the integrated ISA video device, the System BIOS must incorporate special software to handle this configuration. Again, note that the System BIOS will typically give precedence to an ISA or PCI add-in video card over an integrated video device for the reasons described earlier in this chapter.

INTEGRATED PCI VIDEO BIOS LOCATION

The physical location of the video expansion BIOS that supports the integrated PCI video device is system dependent. The most common implementations place the PCI video BIOS in the System ROM device along with the System BIOS code.

VIDEO DEVICE INITIALIZATION

The process used to locate and initialize an integrated PCI device is identical to steps 1 through 5 that are used to locate and initialize a PCI video add–in card. In fact, when the PCI Video Device Initialization Function locates a video device, it does not know if the device even has a BIOS that can be manipulated via PCI configuration space. If the first PCI video device located is the integrated device, the PCI Video Device Initialization Function will discover that there is no video BIOS associated with the device. In this case PCI Video Device Initialization Function will query the device dependent code for the location of an integrated PCI video BIOS. The query is carried out by comparing the PCI video device vendor identification number and device identification number against the vendor identification number and device identification number associated with the integrated PCI video BIOS. If the compare is positive, the integrated PCI video BIOS will be installed as described in the subchapter PCI Expansion ROM BIOS Initialization of this chapter that discusses integrated BIOSs. The PCI Video Device Initialization Function will return status to the System BIOS declaring that PCI software has initialized the primary video device.

HANDLING A NO-BIOS CONDITION

In the event that there is not a match between the PCI video device and the integrated PCI video BIOS the PCI Video Device Initialization Function will still return status to the System BIOS declaring that PCI software has initialized the primary video device. This is because the System BIOS cannot determine what the user's intentions are. For instance, the user may have inserted a PCI video add–in card into the system that does not have a video BIOS associated with it. In any case, the assumption is made that a run–time device driver will initialize the PCI video device during the operating system boot sequence.

> The no match algorithm presented above may vary among System BIOS vendors. This situation might be a good candidate for a Setup Utility option that would allow the user to stop the search in this event or continue looking for another video device.

23.6 SYSTEM RESOURCE REGISTRATION

SYSTEM RESOURCE MAP

Figure 2-4 contains an element called the System Resource Map. The System Resource Map is a list of all allocated (assigned) system resources in a given system. This information is used to allocate the remaining system resources to devices that have not been assigned resources. The System Resource Map data is stored in non-volatile system memory. This memory is typically either CMOS RAM or a Flash ROM device. The format of the data as well as how the storage devices are programmed with the data is beyond the scope of this document. As Figure 2-4 shows, both the System Resource Manager (System BIOS Level-- POST) and Disk Based Configuration Utilities (Operating System Level--Run-Time) access the System Resource Map for the purpose of allocating system resources. To ensure a system that is free of resource conflicts, a System Resource Map that is stored in non-volatile memory must be implemented in the system.

SYSTEM RESOURCE MANAGER

In a Plug and Play environment, the System BIOS is responsible for resource management during POST. Figure 2-4 contains an element called the System Resource Manager. The System Resource Manager is responsible for allocating (assigning) and deallocating (removing) system resource assignments to/from devices in the system. During POST, the System Resource Manager maintains the list of all currently allocated system resources in the System Resource Map.

ALLOCATION REQUEST PHASE

System resource allocation requests can be one of two types. The first type of request is non-specific. When this type of request is used, the device requiring the resource does not care which resource is assigned. The second type of request is a specific request. The device requiring the resource needs a specific resource assigned to it.

During the request phase of a resource allocation cycle the System Resource Manager executes extensive error checking on the request. An error will occur if the resource is not available (the System Resource Map indicates that the resource is assigned to another device or the resource type is exhausted beyond the device's requirement) or if the request is non–compliant (the system resource request is not within the bounds of acceptable limits for the specific device class-for example, a PCI device requesting more than 256 contiguous bytes of I/O space with one request).

ALLOCATION GRANT PHASE

During the grant phase of a resource allocation cycle the System Resource Manager updates its list (registers the system resource assigned to a device in the System Resource Map) of allocated resources to account for the resource assignment. The System Resource Manager then returns the resource allocation to the caller.

DEALLOCATION REQUEST PHASE

System resource de-allocation requests must be specific requests. This means that the caller must provide the correct type of the resource to deallocate, the exact base address (if I/O, DMA, or Memory) and amount (size) of the assigned resource, or, as in the case of IRQs, the reference value of the assigned resource. If the parameters are correct, the System Resource Manager will remove the resource from the System Resource Map. This 'frees' the resource. Depending on the hardware implementation the freed resource may be assigned to other devices within the system.

MANAGING SYSTEM RESOURCES

To successfully manage system resources, the System BIOS must be aware of three things:

- What are the actual system resources available in the system. These include hardware interrupts, I/O ports, system memory and DMA channels.

- What are the different types and attributes of the system resources. For example, some interrupts in a PC compatible system may be shareable while others are not.

- At a given moment, which system resources have been allocated (assigned to devices).

RESOURCE TYPES

The System BIOS is aware of all system resources that are or may be consumed by the platform. This awareness encompasses both LEGACY and Plug and Play devices integrated on the platform. These resources are divided into two categories: fixed and dynamic.

FIXED RESOURCES

PC Compatible platforms contain several fixed resources that are consumed by the platform. These resources are not configurable and must be assigned to the platform for successful operation. The System BIOS is aware of all fixed system resources that must be allocated to the platform. For example, in a PC compatible system IRQ0 and IRQ2 are always consumed by the platform. These and other fixed platform resources may not be assigned to any other device in the system. During POST the System BIOS must ask the System Resource Manager to allocate (assign and register) all fixed system resources to the platform (see Figure 2-4). This activity occurs prior to assigning dynamic system resources to any PCI device. In addition, platform fixed resource requests are always specific system resource requests. Note that in a properly configured system, no resource conflicts should occur when performing fixed system resource allocations.

DYNAMIC RESOURCES

Dynamic system resources are resources that may or may not be consumed by the system. For example, the platform may contain an integrated device that provides a serial port function. This serial port may be assigned one of several I/O port ranges as well as one of several IRQs. Depending on the implementation, the System BIOS can execute either a specific or non-specific request for each resource allocation.

Note that devices such as serial ports are typically configurable when it comes to assigning system resources to them. These devices may be enabled or disabled, depending on the system configuration. The System BIOS is responsible for determining if the various devices (serial ports, parallel ports, IDE controllers, etc.) are enabled. If the devices are enabled, the System BIOS, in conjunction with the System Resource Manager, must assign system resources to the devices for successful operation. Again, the System Resource Manager must maintain a list of allocated system resources.

LEGACY VS. PLUG AND PLAY DEVICES

The System BIOS is aware of all system resources that are requested by Plug and Play devices. The geographical location of Plug and Play devices (platform vs. add–in card) is not relevant. The reason is that the System BIOS can identify each Plug and Play device in the system as well as identify the device's system resource requirements.

In contrast, identifying add-in card LEGACY devices and their system resource requirements is, in most instances, beyond the capability of the System BIOS. To avoid system resource conflicts, an operating system with the required functionality or a Disk Based Configuration Utility (shown in Figure 2-4), can be used to allocate system resources to LEGACY devices. The operating system or the disk-based utility is capable of accessing the System Resource Map to obtain the system resource allocation data. They use this information to recommend/allow specific system resource assignments for LEGACY devices. If system resource assignments are made, the System Resource Map is updated to reflect the latest changes.

SUMMARY

System resources used by both the platform and LEGACY add–in cards should be registered in the System Resource Map. This should be performed prior to the dynamic configuration of Plug and Play devices. Proper system resource registration ensures that no conflicts will occur when allocating the remaining system resources to Plug and Play devices.

23.7   AFTER-VIDEO PCI DEVICE INITIALIZATION

OVERVIEW

The remainder of system memory is tested and initialized. Device initialization continues. If a device has an associated ROM, the ROM will be called by the System BIOS to permit the ROM to configure the system for its device. In a PCI based system all non-PCI devices should be configured and initialized first. This ensures that no resource conflicts will occur when PCI devices are assigned their system resources. A method for initializing PCI devices while avoiding system resource conflicts is presented. Again, only one PCI Bus is assumed. In addition, this discussion assumes that the PCI Configuration Manager is responsible for initializing all PCI devices in the system.

PCI DEVICE INITIALIZATION

There are several steps involved in initializing a PCI device. First, the device has to be detected. Then its resource requirements must be determined. System resources must be allocated to the device. Finally, the device must be enabled for system operation. This section discusses how to initialize one PCI device.

VENDOR ID CHECK

The first requirement for initializing a PCI device is to locate the device. To determine if a PCI device is present on the PCI bus, do the following:

1.   Read the Vendor ID register of Function 0. If a value other than FFFFh is read, then the device is present.

2.   Determine if the device is a single function or multi–function device: Read the Header Type register, located at offset 0Eh of the PCI Configuration Space Header. If bit seven is not set it is a Single-Function Device; otherwise it is a multi–function device.

3.   If the device is a multi–function device, for each function, one through seven: Read the Vendor ID register of Function [1..., 7]. If a value other than FFFFh is read, then the function is present.

ASSIGN SYSTEM RESOURCES

See Chapter 19: *Header Type 00h* for an in-depth discussion of each of the PCI Configuration Space Registers mentioned below. In addition, only valid system resource requests are assumed for this discussion.

ALGORITHM

The PCI device has been located on Bus 0. The PCI Configuration Manager now performs a three-step process to assign system resources to the device in a device independent manner:

1. Determine the system resource requirements.

2. Request the System Resource Manager to allocate the required resources.

3. Program the PCI device with the allocated system resources.

In the event that a PCI device cannot be assigned all of the resources it requests, the PCI Configuration Manager will attempt to assign as many resources as possible. However, the PCI Configuration Manager will leave the device disabled. An expansion BIOS or device driver associated with the PCI device may be able to function with the resources that were assigned. However, the expansion BIOS or device driver must first initialize the device.

HARDWARE INTERRUPT LINE

The PCI Configuration Manager reads the PCI device's Interrupt Pin register. If the value of the register is zero, the PCI device does not request a hardware interrupt. If the value of the register is between one and four, the PCI device is requesting that a hardware interrupt be assigned to one of its interrupt pin lines.

1. The interrupt pin mappings are as follows:

    1   INTA#

    2   INTB#

    3   INTC#

    4   INTD#

2. The PCI Configuration Manager calls the System Resource Manager with a request for an IRQ line. The PCI Configuration Manager passes the Interrupt Pin register value to the System Resource manager along with the BUS Number and device/FUNCTION Number of the device.

3. The System Resource Manager determines which hardware interrupt line to assign to the device based on the capabilities of the platform's IRQ line mapping functions.

4. The System Resource Manager calls a PCI Device Initialization Function to perform the actual hardware mapping of the IRQ line to the PCI device.

5. The System Resource Manager returns a value between 0 and 15 to the PCI Configuration Manager. This value indicates which of the 15 PC compatible IRQ lines the PCI device is now mapped to.

6. This assumes that the system reserves at least one hardware interrupt line for PCI device initialization.

   The PCI Configuration Manager programs the PCI device's Interrupt Line register.

7. DONE.

BASE ADDRESS REGISTERS

For each Base Address Register starting at offset 10h of the PCI configuration space:

1. According to Chapter 19's specifications, the PCI Configuration Manager determines if the PCI device is requesting I/O or Memory Space, how many bytes of the resource are requested, and in the case of memory, which system memory address space the request is for.

2. The PCI Configuration Manager calls the System Resource Manager with a request for the system resource that the device requires. The PCI Configuration Manager passes the memory or I/O type, and length requested value to the System Resource Manager along with the BUS Number and device/FUNCTION Number of the device.

3. The PCI Configuration Manager programs the PCI device's Base Address Register with the value returned by the System Resource Manager.

4. DONE.

LATENCY TIMER

This register specifies the Master Latency Timer value for a PCI Master when the device is on the PCI bus. A typical way for PCI Configuration Manager to configure this register is to just choose an appropriate value and use that value for all devices. 32 (approximately 1 μsec) is a reasonable value.

PRIMARY VGA DEVICE CHECK

The PCI Configuration Manager checks each PCI video device it encounters in the system to determine if the device is the primary VGA device. It does this by reading the Class Code Register. If the byte value in the Base Class register (offset 0Bh of configuration space) is either 03h or 00h (with a Sub-Class register, offset 0Ah, value of 01h), the device is a video device. If the device is the primary VGA device, the PCI Configuration Manager leaves the device enabled. If the device is not the primary VGA device, the PCI Configuration Manager ensures that the device is disabled. Note that all non-primary PCI VGA devices are assigned the system resources they requested.

COMMAND REGISTER

For each control bit in the PCI device's configuration space Command Register:

Bit	Action
0	I/O Space Access bit is set to 1. Some devices hardwire this bit to 0 if the device does not utilize I/O address space.
1	Memory Space Access bit is set to 1. Some devices hardwire this bit to 0 if the device does not utilize memory address space.
2	The Master Enable bit is set to 0. A PCI device expansion BIOS or device driver is responsible for enabling Bus Master capabilities.
3	Special Cycles Operation is set to 1. This allows the device to monitor special cycle operations.
4	Memory Write and Invalidate may be set. This function is supported by some bus master devices. The System BIOS is responsible for the enable/disable of Memory Write and Invalidate.
5	VGA Palette Snoop may be set. VGA devices must support this bit. See Appendix C.
6	Parity Error Response may be set. This permits the device to respond to parity errors. The System BIOS is responsible for the enable/disable of Parity Error Response.
7	Wait Cycle control may be set. The System BIOS is responsible for the enable/disable of Wait Cycle control
8	SERR# Enable may be set to 1. The System BIOS is responsible for the enable/disable of SERR#.
9	Fast Back-to-Back Enable is set to 1 if all targets can do fast back-to-back transactions to different devices. A value of 0 indicates that fast back-to-back transactions are only allowed to the same agent. Bit 7 of a PCI device's Status Register indicates if the device is capable of fast back-to-back transactions.

STATUS REGISTER

The PCI device's Status Register is written with all 1's. This action clears all pending status flags.

23.8 BOOT DEVICE INITIALIZATION

Through system device enumeration, Plug and Play operating systems have the capability of determining the type and number of devices within the system. To a large extent, the Plug and Play operating systems will have the capability of initializing all non-primary boot devices in the system. These devices include serial ports, parallel ports and so on. This means that a Plug and Play capable System BIOS only needs to configure the primary boot devices prior to bootstrapping the operating system. These devices are the input devices, such as keyboard, output device, such as graphics controller and monitor, and operating system boot device such as floppy, hard drive or LAN.

When bootstrapping an operating system, the major problem for a Plug and Play capable System BIOS is that there is no way for the System BIOS to determine which type of operating system will be loaded: Plug and Play capable or non–Plug and Play capable. The System BIOS is responsible for the platform and add–in card initialization in the case of a non-Plug and Play operating system. A Plug and Play capable operating system is responsible for initializing all non-primary boot devices once it is loaded.

It is recommended that a user option in the Setup Utility program be installed for handling both of the above scenarios. This option would give the user the choice of which method to use for device initialization. Note that because there are fewer devices that the System BIOS is required to initialize, the system typically takes less time to boot under the Plug and Play operating system configuration.

23.9 PCI DEVICE DRIVERS

PCI device drivers have two requirements that extend beyond standard or existing device drivers. First, PCI device drivers must be able to use any system resource assigned to their devices. This is because PCI devices are not assigned hardwired resources. For example, a LEGACY ISA SCSI device may only be able to use either IRQ9 or IRQ11. The selection of which IRQ to use is typically based on a jumper setting or configuration utility option setting. The corresponding PCI device can be assigned any IRQ that the system hardware is capable of mapping to the PCI device. PCI device drivers are required to read their Configuration Space Registers to obtain their device's system resource mapping information. PCI device drivers must use the resources assigned to their devices.

> A PCI device driver should never attempt to assign resources to its device. This could cause the system to become unstable or crash.
>
> In a non-Plug and Play boot scenario the System BIOS Resource Manager is responsible for allocating all system resources to PCI devices.
>
> In a Plug and Play boot scenario the Operating System Device Class Configuration Manager is responsible for allocating all system resources to PCI devices.

The second requirement that PCI device drivers have that extends beyond standard or existing device drivers is that they must support shareable hardware interrupts. This is because a single hardware interrupt can be assigned to more than one PCI device at a time.

23.10 CHAPTER SUMMARY

This chapter presents several different aspects concerning the detection and initialization of PCI devices. PCI devices are capable of true Plug and Play operation. This chapter referenced Figure 2-4, the system Plug and Play pictorial figure, very heavily. Keep in mind that the device and system initialization algorithms presented here are designed to give the reader a working understanding of PCI device initialization from the System BIOS, operating system, and device driver points of view. In an actual implementation some concepts presented in this chapter, such as how the video sub-system is implemented, may be performed differently.

CHAPTER 24

PCI CAPABILITIES

This chapter consists of the following subchapters:

24.0 INTRODUCTION

Beginning with *PCI Local Bus Specification 2.2*, a standard method has been defined for allowing PCI bus features, such as power management, to be detected and controlled. Through this mechanism, software can quickly identify PCI functions that support these additional capabilities. Once this identification occurs, system software is able to control the PCI device based on its specific feature set of PCI capabilities. This chapter begins by enumerating the PCI capabilities that are currently defined. It then provides an overview of the generic PCI capabilities architecture. Finally, this chapter presents a summary of several specific PCI capabilities.

CAPABILITIES IDS

The following table contains the current definitions for PCI Capability IDs as of this book's printing date (early 2001):

ID	Capability
00h	Reserved
01h	PCI Power Management is implemented in compliance with the *PCI Power Management Interface Specification.*
02h	AGP (Accelerated Graphics Port) features are implemented in compliance with the *Accelerated Graphics Port Interface Specification.*
03h	VDP (Vital Product Data) is implemented in compliance with the *PCI Bus Local Specification*.
04h	PCI slot identification is implemented in compliance with the *PCI to PCI Bridge Architecture Specification*.
05h	MSI (Message Signaled Interrupts) is implemented in compliance with the *PCI Bus Local Specification*.
06h	CompactPCI Hot Swap insertion and extraction is implemented in compliance with the *CompactPCI Hot Swap Specification PICMG 2.1.*
07h	PCI-X is implemented in compliance with the *PCI-X Addendum to the PCI Local Bus Specification*.
08h	Reserved for AMD
09h	Vendor Specific
0Ah	Debug Port
0Bh	CompactPCI Hot Central Resource Control
0Ch	PCI Hot-Plug
0Dh-0FFh	**Reserved**

Table 24-1: Capability IDs

The PCI Special Interest Group (PCI SIG) is responsible for assigning Capability ID codes.

Note that the following PCI capabilities are not discussed due to lack of available documentation (specifications not published at the time of this book) or because they are beyond the scope of this book: 06h - CompactPCI Hot Swap, 08h - AMD, 0Ah - CompactPCI Hot Central Resource Control, and 0Ch - PCI Hot Plug.

24.1 GENERAL OVERVIEW OF PCI CAPABILITIES

This section describes how to:

- Identify PCI functions that support PCI capabilities.
- Locate the list of PCI capabilities supported by a given PCI function.
- Identify the PCI capabilities supported by a given PCI function.

PCI CAPABILITIES CHECK

System software cannot assume that PCI devices support capabilities such as power management, slot identification, message signaled interrupts, and so forth. The reason that the assumption cannot be made is because many existing PCI devices were designed according to PCI Specification 2.1 or lower, and therefore do not comply with PCI capabilities such as the one described in the *PCI Bus Power Management Interface Specification*. Consequently, software must utilize a methodology for detecting compliance with the PCI capability specifications. Note that this methodology is consistent with all PCI devices, regardless of class type. Detecting the presence of PCI capabilities requires a status check of each PCI function.

> **Individual functions within a multi-function PCI device can support different sets of PCI capabilities.**

With the understanding that the introduction of additional capabilities is ongoing for PCI, an extensible paradigm is required to detect and control new capabilities. The acceptable model could not consume large portions of PCI configuration address space. In addition, to speed software execution, an interface that permits quick detection of the capabilities is required. To permit fast detection, a previously reserved bit was selected to allow the global detection of capabilities in a PCI function. This bit is referred to as the **Capabilities List** bit, or **CAP_LIST** bit. The actual bit utilized is bit [4] of the PCI configuration address space **Status** register. The **Status** register is located at offset 06h in the PCI configuration address space Device Header Type Region. Note that bit [4] is ideally suited for its task because it is located in a register common to all PCI devices, regardless of the PCI header type. The purpose of the **Capabilities List** bit is to indicate the presence or absence of a linked list of PCI capabilities. The linked list of PCI capabilities is called the Capabilities List. If present, the Capabilities List is located in the Device Dependent Region of a function's PCI configuration address space. Thus, with a single PCI configuration address space register read, software can easily distinguish between PCI functions that support PCI capabilities and those that do not. Table 24-2 illustrates the bit's new definition.

> **When set, the Capabilities List bit indicates that the PCI function supports at least one PCI capability. PCI functions can support multiple capabilities.**

Bit	Type	Function
3::0	Read Only	See the latest *PCI Local Bus Specification* (available from the PCI SIG) or the discussion of the PCI configuration address space **Status** register in this book for the definitions of bits [3::0] of the **Status** register.
4	Read Only	**Capabilities List** 0 PCI function does not support capabilities. 1 PCI function supports capabilities.
15::5	--	See the latest *PCI Local Bus Specification* (available from the PCI SIG) or the discussion of the PCI configuration address space **Status** register in this book for the definitions of bits [15::5] of the **Status** register.

Table 24-2: Status Register – Capabilities List Bit

CAPABILITY POINTER REGISTER READ

In a typical function's PCI configuration address space, many device-dependent registers are unused. This makes the Device Dependent Region the ideal area to store the linked list of data structures that support PCI capabilities within a given PCI function. However, recall that the register layout of the Device Dependent Region is not identical for every device. To maintain software transparency between PCI functions, a standard method is required to permit the identification of the start location of the **Capabilities List** stored in the Device Dependent Region. The method chosen is to store the start location of each PCI function's capabilities linked list in the predefined PCI Device Header Type Region of its PCI configuration address space. Recall that each PCI function contains 256 contiguous bytes of PCI configuration address space. Consequently, only one byte-wide register is required to point to the first item in the **Capabilities List**. The register that stores this one-byte pointer to the linked list is called the **Capabilities Pointer** register, or **CAP_PTR** register.

> Each PCI capability is supported by a specific set of registers. Each set of registers forms a structure that supports one unique capability. These structures are stored in a linked list called the Capabilities List.

The location of the **Capabilities Pointer** register in the PCI configuration address space is dependent on the PCI header type. For standard PCI devices and PCI/PCI Bridges, the pointer's location is offset 34h; for CardBus Bridges, this location is 14h. These registers were previously reserved. In any PCI device, the **Capabilities Pointer** register offset will always be a value of less than 40h. Table 24-3 illustrates the **Capabilities Pointer** register definition.

Bit	Type	Function
7::0	Read Only	**Capabilities Pointer (Cap_Ptr)** This register contains the DWORD offset of the first byte in the Capabilities Linked List.

Table 24-3: Capabilities Pointer Register

The start location of the Capabilities List (the value contained in the Capabilities Pointer register) must be DWORD aligned. In addition, the value of the linked list's start location must be between 40h and FCh for all currently defined PCI header types. The reason is because offset 40h in PCI configuration address space is the start location of the Device Dependent region and FCh is its last DWORD aligned offset.

To be *PCI Local Bus Specification 2.2* compliant, the lower two bits of the Capabilities Pointer register must be reserved and return zero when read. Note that these lower two bits may be implemented in a future version of the specification. To accommodate both the current and possible future implementations, software should mask the lower two bits of the Capabilities Pointer register after reading it to obtain the pointer to the head of the Capabilities List.

Also note that the Capabilities Pointer register might not be treated as a PCI reserved register when the Capabilities List bit value is '0'. In this case, the register's default value is '00h' after a PCI reset occurs. If this register is written, subsequent reads could return indeterminate values. Consequently, software should not write to the Capabilities Pointer register under any circumstance.

Always use the PCI function's Status register's Capabilities List bit as a qualifier for the Capabilities Pointer register's value.

CAPABILITIES ID SCAN

The final step in detecting whether or not a PCI function supports a specific PCI capability or not is to scan the Capabilities List for a structure that contains the data specific to the desired PCI capability. Before explaining how to perform the scan, the general composition of the Capabilities List should be understood. The Capabilities List consists of one or more predefined structures. Each structure is specific to the PCI capability it supports. The general layout of these capability structures is discussed first. Once this is done, how the structures are assembled into a linked list in PCI configuration address space is explained. Finally, how to scan the linked list is demonstrated.

CAPABILITY STRUCTURE LAYOUT

The layout of each structure linked in the Capabilities List serves two purposes. The first purpose is to permit detection of the start address of a structure that supports a specific PCI capability. The second function of the layout is to allow for a variable number of contiguous registers to support each unique PCI capability. Each type of capability structure consumes only the number of registers needed to meet the interface requirements of the capability. Consequently, the size of each type of capability structure may vary in length. This reduces the overall number of registers consumed within each structure. One alternative to the chosen implementation would have been to define a single fixed length structure that could satisfy the worst-case capability structure size. The inevitable negative result in doing this would have been wasted registers in the PCI function's Device Dependent Region.

Architecturally, a capability structure is divided into two unique regions. The first region of the capability structure is common to all structures; it is capability independent. The second part of the capability structure is specific to each type of PCI capability and is therefore capability dependent. Figure 24-1, PCI Capability Structure Layout, illustrates the two regions of a generic capability structure. The capability independent and dependent regions are described below.

Offset 00h of each capability structure must be DWORD aligned. In addition, all bytes associated with the data structure must be contiguous within the PCI function's PCI configuration address space. Optional PCI configuration address space registers and bits that are not implemented in a capability structure should be treated as reserved. Reserved registers and bits must be read only and must return a value of zero when read.

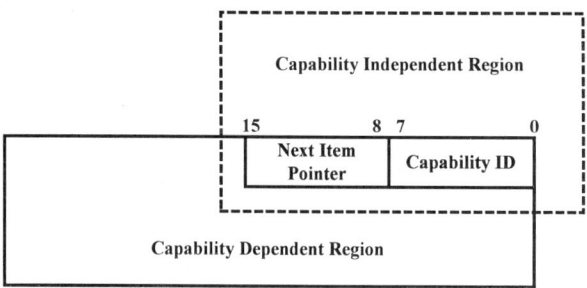

Figure 24-1: PCI Capability Structure Layout

CAPABILITY STRUCTURE INDEPENDENT REGION

The function of the capability independent region is to permit the software detection of a specific PCI capability and the end (tail) of the Capabilities Linked List. The capability independent region of the structure consists of two bytes. The first byte is the **Capability ID** register. It is located at offset 0 of every capability structure. This register identifies one and only one PCI capability that the PCI function supports. For example, the PCI power management **Capability ID** is '01b' while AGP has a **Capability ID** of '10b'. The second byte, located at offset 1 of the each capability structure, is the **Next Item Pointer** register. This register points to the location of the next capability structure in the linked list. If the structure being accessed by software is the last structure in the Capabilities List, the **Next Item Pointer** register will contain a data value of 00h. Together, the **Capability ID** and the **Next Item Pointer** registers form the linked list infrastructure for connecting each member of the Capabilities List.

> To be *PCI Local Bus Specification 2.2* compliant, the lower two bits of each Next Item Pointer register must be reserved and return zero when read. Note that these lower two bits may be implemented in a future version of the specification. To accommodate both the current and possible future implementations, software should mask the lower two bits of each Next Item Pointer register after reading it to obtain the start address of the next PCI capability structure in the Capabilities List.

CAPABILITY STRUCTURE DEPENDENT REGION

The capability structure dependent region consists of a set of registers contiguous with the structure's independent region. These registers are used to implement the features of a specific PCI capability.

> The register requirements for the capability dependent region, such as the number of registers needed, each register's bit definition, the layout of the registers, and so forth, to support the interface of each capability, depends on the actual PCI capability itself.

CAPABILITIES LIST

Now that the capability structure layout is understood, all that remains is to create a linked list with multiple capability structures. Once the list is built, how to traverse the linked list searching a specific structure's **Capability ID** is presented. Figure 24-2 illustrates a Capabilities List. While keeping in mind that the Capabilities List resides in a PCI function's Device Dependent Region of PCI configuration address space, note the following:

- The **Capability Pointer (CAP_PTR)** register's value always points to the first structure (head) in the linked list.

- Each capability structure must be DWORD aligned.

- Capability structures may be stored in any order.

- Capability structures do not have to be contiguous with one another.

- The first byte of each capability structure in the linked list contains that structure's **Capability ID.**

- The second byte of each capability structure, **Next Item Pointer** register, contains an absolute offset that points to the start of the next capability structure in the linked list.

- The data value in the **Next Item Pointer** register must be DWORD aligned.

- The number of registers following the **Next Item Pointer** register in a capability structure is dependent on the type of PCI capability supported and thus may vary from structure to structure.

- The last capability structure in the linked list (tail) indicates its position in the list by containing the data value 00h in its **Next Item Pointer** register.

- The capability dependent region can contain optional or reserved registers and bits.

- Using only the registers in the Capability List, the list can only be traversed from head to tail.

DETECTING A PCI CAPABILITY

All the pieces required to determine whether a specific PCI capability is present have now been introduced. All that is left is to present is a method by which software can use a PCI function's hardware interface to scan for the presence of a PCI capability. The following is an algorithm for such a scan operation. Note that error checking is highly suggested but not required to successfully complete a scan.

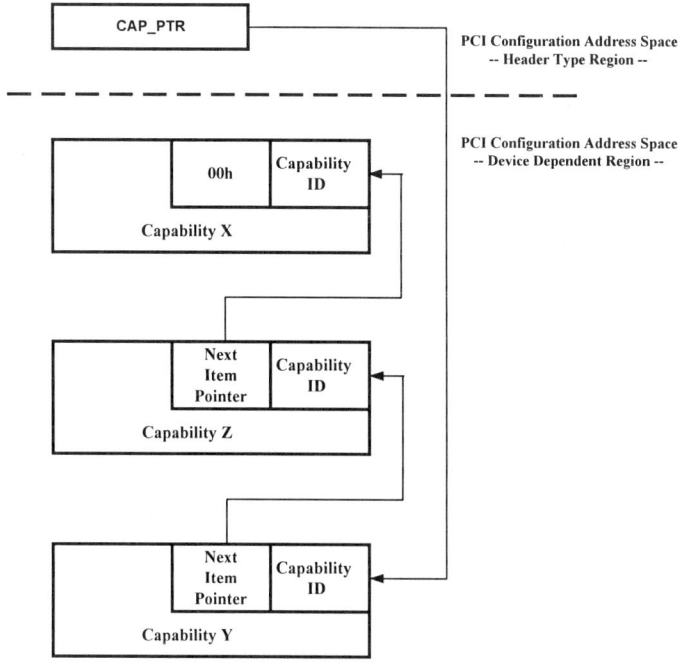

Figure 24-2: Capabilities List Example

For a given PCI function:

1. Read the PCI **Status** register at offset 06h in PCI configuration address space.

2. Test bit [4], the **Capabilities List** bit, of the PCI function's **Status** register.

   Bit [4] = '0'   Set a flag to indicate that this function does not support PCI capabilities and proceed to DONE

   Bit [4] = '1'   PCI capabilities are supported - proceed to the next step.

3. Read the **Capability Pointer** register – note that the absolute offset of this register is PCI Header Type dependent.

4. Mask bits [1::0] of the data value contained in the register just read

5. Compare the masked data value read in step 4 with 40h.

   Value < 40h   Set a flag to indicate that the register contains an invalid value (points to wrong PCI configuration address space region) and proceed to DONE.

Value >= 40h   Proceed to the next step.

6.   The register contains the value of an absolute offset in PCI configuration address space. This offset points to a specific structure's Capability ID in the linked list. Read the contents of the register pointed to.

7.   Compare the contents of the register just read with the capability ID value being scanned for.

Value = 'ID'   Set a flag to indicate that the function supports specified capability and proceed to DONE.

Value <> 'ID'   Proceed to the next step.

8.   Read the value contained in the **Next Item Pointer** register of the current capability structure.

Value = '00h'   Set a flag to indicate that the PCI function does not support the specified capability (end of linked list found) and proceed to DONE.

Value <> '00h' Go to Step 4 and repeat scan.

9.   DONE.

24.2 PCI POWER MANAGEMENT

This section describes the PCI Power Management Capability interface. This interface permits individual PCI functions to be power managed in a standardized manner by an operating system at the system, bus, and device level.

Figure 24-3 and Table 24-4 illustrate the layout and design of the PCI power management capability data structure. Note that the PCI Bus Power Management Interface Specification refers to this structure as the Power Management Register Block. The structure is eight bytes in length.

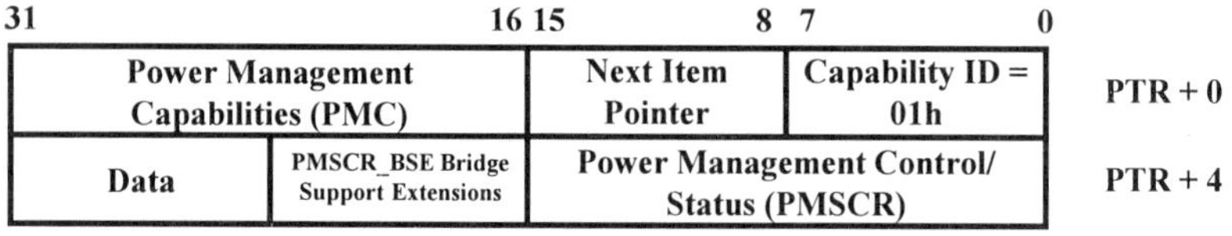

31		16 15	8 7	0	
Power Management Capabilities (PMC)		Next Item Pointer	Capability ID = 01h		PTR + 0
Data	PMSCR_BSE Bridge Support Extensions	Power Management Control/ Status (PMSCR)			PTR + 4

Figure 24-3: PCI Power Management Capability Structure Layout

Offset	Bits	Register/Field	Attributes	Description
0	7::0	Capability ID	Required Read Only	Identifies PCI Power Management as the capability of the structure with a value of 01h.
1	15::8	Next Item Pointer	Required Read Only	Provides the absolute offset to the next item in the Capabilities Linked List (00h if last structure)
2	31::16	PMC	Required Read Only	Enumerates the PCI function's power management capabilities
4	47::32	PMCSR	Required Read/Write	(1) Control PCI function's power management state (2) Enable power management events (3) Monitor power management events
6	55::48	PMCSR_BSE	Required for PCI-PCI Bridges Read Only	Support PCI-PCI bridge specific functionality
7	63::56	Data	Optional Read Only	Report state dependent operating data

Table 24-4: PCI Power Management Capability Structure Definition

CAPABILITY IDENTIFIER REGISTER

Capability Identifier

Offset:	00h of the PCI Power Management Capability Structure
Width:	1 Byte
Valid Values:	00h-FFh

> A value of 01h indicates the structure supports the power management capability as defined in the *PCI Bus Power Management Interface Specification.* This specification can be obtained from the PCI Special Interest Group at http://www.pcisig.com.

Description:	This register identifies the specific capability supported by a structure member of a PCI Capabilities Linked List.

Bit	Type	Function
7::0	Read Only	**Capability Identifier** This value identifies a capability supported by a PCI function. Capability IDs are assigned by the PCI SIG.

Table 24-5: Capability Identifier Register

NEXT ITEM POINTER REGISTER

Next Item Pointer
Offset: 01h of the PCI Power Management Capability Data Structure Width: 1 Byte Valid Values: 00h, 40h-FCh (must be DWORD aligned) Description: This register identifies the absolute offset of the start of the next structure member of a Capabilities Linked List. A value of 00h indicates this structure is the last one in the list.

Bit	Type	Function
7::0	Read Only	**Next Item Pointer** This value identifies the start location of the next item (capability data structure) in a PCI function's Capabilities Linked List.

Table 24-6: Next Item Pointer Register

POWER MANAGEMENT CAPABILITIES REGISTER

Power Management Capabilities (PMC)
Offset: 02h of the PCI Power Management Capability Data Structure Width: 2 Bytes Valid Values: N/A. This register is a collection of bits, not a range of values. The register should not be viewed as values, but as individual bits. Description: The bits in this register contain information about the PCI function's power management capabilities and features.

Bit	Type	Function
2::0	Read Only	**Version** 000 **Reserved** 001 The PCI function complies with Revision 1.0 of *the PCI Power Management Interface Specification.* 010 The PCI function complies with Revision 1.1 of the *PCI Power Management Interface Specification.* 011 **Reserved** to 111
3	Read Only	**PME Clock** 0 PCI clock is not required for the PCI function to generate **PME#**. 1 PCI clock is required for the PCI function to generate **PME#**. This field must return "0" if PME# generation is not supported in any power state.
4	Read Only	**Reserved**
5	Read Only	**Device Specific Initialization Bit - DSI** 0 No special initialization of the PCI function is required after a PCI function transitions to the $D0_{unitialized}$ State from another power state; the generic class device driver can use the PCI function imediately after the transition. 1 Additional, special initialization of the PCI function is required after a PCI function transitions to the $D0_{unitialized}$ State from another power state. The initialization sequence is device specific. The generic class device driver should only use the PCI function after the special initialization sequence is complete. Operating systems are not required to use this bit. For example, Microsoft Windows 9x and Windows 2000 use the function's device driver capabilities instead of this bit to manage PCI functions.

Table 24-7: Power Management Capabilities Register

8::6	Read Only	**AUX Current Bits**
		If the PCI function supports the Data register:
		• "000b" must be returned when this field is read
		• Software must read the **Data** register to obtain **3.3Vaux** requirements because it has precedence over this field
		If the PCI function does not support PME# generation from the $D3_{cold}$ **power state (PMC register bit [15] = 0):**
		• "000b" must be returned when this field is read
		3.3Vaux powers logic that must remain active while the rest of the system is not powered. These three bits indicate the PCI function's maximum required **3.3Vaux** current while in power state $D3_{cold}$.
		Bits [8::6] are applicable when the function meets the following requirements:
		• Power management events are supported in $D3_{cold}$
		• Function can draw power from the **3.3Vaux** supply
		• The **Data** register is not supported

Aux Current Bits			3.3 Vaux Maximum Current 3.4 in Milliamps
8	7	6	
1	1	1	375
1	1	0	320
1	0	1	270
1	0	0	220
0	1	1	160
0	1	0	100
0	0	1	55
0	0	0	0 (The function has its own auxiliary power source)

9	Read Only	**D1_Support**
		0 The **D1** power management state is not supported.
		1 The **D1** power management state is supported.
		PCI functions that do not support the D1 power management state must return a value of "0" for this bit. Otherwise, side effects may occur.

10	Read Only	**D2_Support**
		0 The **D2** power management state is not supported.
		1 The **D2** power management state is supported.
		PCI functions that do not support the D2 power management state must return a value of "0" for this bit. Otherwise, side effects may occur.

Table 24-7: Power Management Capabilities Register
(continued)

15::11	Read Only	**PME_Support**	
		Bit [11] xxxx1b	PME# can be asserted from the *D0* State.
		Bit [12] xxx1xb	PME# can be asserted from the *D1* State.
		Bit [13] xx1xxb	PME# can be asserted from the *D2* State.
		Bit [14] x1xxxb	PME# can be asserted from the $D3_{hot}$ State.
		Bit [15] 1xxxxb	PME# can be asserted from the $D3_{cold}$ State.
		This is a five bit field. PME# can be asserted in any power state where its associated bit value is a "1". A value of "0" will be returned for each bit whose power state cannot assert PME#.	

Table 24-7: Power Management Capabilities Register
(continued)

When bit [15] is set, the function indicates that PME# can be asserted from the $D3_{cold}$ State. Recall that Vcc is not applied to any function in this state. Therefore, an auxiliary power source must be present to supply the required 3.3Vaux power. The function must guarantee that the power source is available before this bit can be set. Consider the following PCI device implementations:

System Board Devices:

The system designer can guarantee that auxiliary power is always available to the function.

Add-in Card Devices:

Bit [15] is only set to '1' when voltage is detected on the 3.3Vaux auxiliary power pin, otherwise the bit is set to '0'.

CardBus Devices:

CardBus functions can receive auxiliary power on the same pins that supply Vcc to the device. Refer to the *PCI Style Power Management Interface Specification for CardBus Cards* white paper for more information on how CardBus auxiliary power is managed.

POWER MANAGEMENT CONTROL/STATUS REGISTER

Power Management Control/Status (PMCSR)	
Offset:	04h of the PCI Power Management Capability Data Structure
Width:	2 Bytes
Valid Values:	N/A. This field is a collection of bits, not a range of values. The register should not be viewed as values, but as individual bits.
Description:	The bits in this register perform three basic functions:
	1 - Manage a PCI function's power states
	2 - Enable power management events
	3 - Monitor power management events

Bit	Type	Function		
1::0	Read/Write	**Power State Bits**		**Power Management State**
		1	**0**	
		0	0	$D0$ power management state
		0	1	$D1$ power management state
		1	0	$D2$ power management state
		1	1	$D3_{hot}$ power management state
		This is a two bit field. Software can read this field to determine the current power state of the PCI function. Software can write this field to set the PCI function to a new power state. When software attempts to write an unsupported, optional power state the following must occur: - the write operation must complete normally on the bus - the write data must be discarded - no power management state change should occur		
7::2	Read Only	**Reserved**		

Table 24-8: Power Management Control/Status Register (PMCSR)

8	Read/Write	**PME_En (a power management event support bit)**
		When PCI function does not support PME# generation from any device power state (PMC bits [15::11] - "00000b")
		0 This bit can be hardwired to always return "0" when read.
		When PCI function does not support PME# generation from $D3_{cold}$
		0 Always return "0" because the PCI function cannot assert **PME#**.
		This field must return a value of "0" if PME# generation is not supported by the D3cold power state. In this context, "0" is the default state for bit [8].
		When PCI function does support PME# generation from $D3_{cold}$
		0 Disable the PCI function's ability to generate **PME#**.
		1 Enable the PCI function's ability to assert **PME#**.
		The state of bit [8] is indeterminate at the time of the initial load of an operating system. When PME# generation is supported by the D3cold power state, system software must write bit [8] with a value of "0" each time the operating system is initially loaded. This action disables the PCI function's ability to assert PME#.
12::9	Read/Write	**Data_Select**
		0000b- Each value of the **Data_Select** field selects a unique 1111b set of data that software can read via the PCI Power Management Capability Structure's **Data** register (offset 7). This data is stored in the Power Consumption and Dissipation Table. The **Data_Select** field can index to 1 of 16 values in this table via the **Data** register.
		This is a four bit field. Which information that is reported via the Data_Scale field (bits [14::13]) and the Data register (offset 07h) is selected by these bits. This field and the Data_Scale field are required when the Data register is implemented. If the Data register is not implemented, this field, the Data_Scale field and the Data register are reserved and must return a value of zero when read. See the Data register description for additional information.

Table 24-8: Power Management Control/Status Register (PMCSR) (continued)

14::13	Read Only	**Data_Scale** 00b- 11b Each bit combination specifies the scaling factor to be used to interpret the value read from the PCI Power Management Capability Structure's **Data** register (offset 07h).
		This is a two bit field. The value of the Data_Select (bits [12::9]) field determines the value and meaning of this field. This field and the Data_Select field are required when the Data register (offset 07h) is implemented. If the Data register is not implemented, this field, the Data_Select field and the Data register are reserved and must return a value of zero when read. See the Data register description for additional information.
15	Read/Write/ Clear	**PME_Status (a power management event support bit)** **When PCI function does not support PME# generation from D3$_{cold}$** 0 Always return "0" because **PME#** is never asserted by the PCI function.
		This field must return a value of "0" if PME# generation is not supported by the D3cold power state. In this context, "0" is the default state for bit [15].
		When PCI function does support PME# generation from D3$_{cold}$ 0 **PME#** is not asserted by the PCI function. 1 **PME#** is asserted by the PCI function.
		The state of bit [15] is indeterminate at the time of the initial load of an operating system. When PME# generation is supported by the D3cold power state, the system software must write bit [15] with a value of "1" each time the operating system is initially loaded. This action will set bit [15] to a value of "0", which stops the PCI function from asserting the PME# signal (if the PCI function was in the process of doing so).
		Writing a value of "0" to bit [15] has no effect.

**Table 24-8: Power Management Control/Status Register
(PMCSR) (continued)**

POWER MANAGEMENT EVENT SUPPORT BITS

The **PME_En** (bit [8]) and **PME_Status** (bit [15]) fields of the **PMCSR** register contain bits that support power management events. Fields that support PCI functions that can generate power management events from the *D3$_{cold}$* power management state have the following characteristics:

■   Field bit states are not affected by power on reset.

- Field bit states are not affected by a transition from the D3cold to the D0uninitialized State.

- Typically, the use of an auxiliary power source or non-volatile storage cells preserves the state of the bits.

- System software or the System BIOS during initial power up or an initial operating system load must clear the bits to '0'.

PME# GENERATION FROM D3$_{COLD}$

A PCI function can support **PME#** generation from the *D3$_{cold}$ State*. In this case, a hardware reset does not affect a function's PME Context when this transition occurs, because the PCI function itself may be responsible for generating the wakeup event that forced the system back to the *D0 State*. In other words, the PME Context contained in the **PMCSR** register's **PME_En** (bit [8]) and **PME_Status** (bit [15]) fields is not affected by the hardware reset. Preserving the function's PME Context allows the system software to properly determine that the PCI function caused the wakeup event. The system software can then service the event properly.

If a PCI function supports PME# generation in the *D3$_{cold}$ State*, during the initial load of the operating system the software is required to explicitly initialize all PME Context. This includes setting the PMCSR register's PME_En (bit [8]) and PME_Status (bit [15]) fields to "0".

If a PCI function does not support PME# generation in the *D3$_{cold}$ State*, all PME Context must be initialized with the assertion of a hardware reset.

PCI/PCI BRIDGE SUPPORT EXTENSIONS REGISTER

PCI-PCI Bridge Support Extensions (PMCSR_BSE)	
Offset:	06h of the PCI Power Management Capability Data Structure
Width:	1 Byte
Valid Values:	N/A. This field is a collection of bits, not a range of values. The register should not be viewed as values, but as individual bits.
Description:	The bits in this register support PCI bridge specific functionality. This register is required for all PCI-PCI bridges that comply with Revision 1.0 or later of the PCI Power Management Interface Specification.

Bit	Type	Function
5::0	RO	**Reserved**
6	RO	**B2_B3# (B2/B3 support for *D3hot*)** 0 Power is removed from the secondary bus of the bridge (State ***B3***) 1 The PCI clock of the secondary bus of the bridge is stopped (State ***B2***) **Default State:** Set by external strap or internally hardwired. Bit [6] is qualified by bit [7] of the PMCSR_BSE register. Bit [7], BPCC_En, must have a value of "1" for bit [6] to have meaning. When programmed to the D3hot power state, the state of this bit defines which actions the function is required to perform.
7	RO	**BPCC_En (Bus Power/Clock Control Enable)** 0 The bus power/clock control policies are disabled. 1 The bus power/clock control policies are enabled. **Default State:** Set by external strap or internally hardwired. The bridge's PMCSR register Power State field (bits [1::0]) cannot be used by system software to control the power or clock of the PCI bridge's secondary bus when this bit has a value of "0".

Table 24-9: PCI/PCI Bridge Support Extensions Register (PMCSR_BSE)

DATA REGISTER

Data Register	
Offset:	07h of the PCI Power Management Capability Data Structure
Width:	1 Byte
Valid Values:	N/A. This field is a collection of bits, not a range of values. The register should not be viewed as values, but as individual bits.
Description:	This register is used by software to read a PCI function's state dependent data. Consequently, the **Data** register in effect provides a 'window' into the data sheet for the PCI function. The only data currently defined by Revision 1.1 of the *PCI Power Management Interface Specification* to be read from the **Data** register pertains to power consumption and power dissapation. Other data may be defined in a future version of the specification.

> The Data_Select (bits [12::9]) and the Data_Scale (bits [14::13]) fields of the PMCSR register are required when the Data register is implemented. If the Data register is not implemented, the Data_Select field, Data_Scale field and the Data register are reserved and must return a value of zero when read. See the PMCSR register description for additional information about the Data_Select and Data_Scale fields.

Bit	Type	Function
7::0	Read Only	**Data** This register is used to access a PCI function's state dependent data. The specific data is requested by programming the **PMCSR** register's **Data_Select** field. The value read is scaled by the value specified in the **PMCSR** register's **Data_Scale** field.

Table 24-10: Data Register

INTERPRETING THE DATA REGISTER

When defining a PCI function's Power Management Capability Data Structure, implementing the **Data** register is optional. If the register is not implemented, it is defined as a reserved PCI register; as such the register must return a value of zero when read. In this case, the bits specific to the **Data_Select** (bits [12::9]) and **Data_Scale** (bits [14::13]) fields of the **PMCSR** register (offset 04h) are defined as PCI reserved bits - they too must return a value of zero when read.

If the **Data** register is implemented, it must be compliant with the *PCI Bus Power Management Interface Specification*. The specification defines the layout of the data that can be read as well as the method by which the data is accessed via the **Data** register. This information is described below.

POWER CONSUMPTION AND DISSIPATION TABLE

Power consumption and dissipation data is currently the only state dependent information that is available from the **Data** register. This data can be used by system software to develop a dynamic system wide power management paradigm. Table 24-11 illustrates the layout of the data as defined by the PCI Bus Power Management Interface Specification.

> There are no requirements for how the data returned in the Data register is actually stored. Data that is fixed can be stored in a static look up table. On the other hand, if a PCI function supports many different options that affect the values reported, a serial EPROM or strapping option can be used to load the appropriate data values at reset into a storage area.

Value in Data_Select	Data Reported	Data_Scale Interpretation	Units/Accuracy
0	*D0* Power Consumed	0 = Unknown	Watts
1	*D1* Power Consumed		
2	*D2* Power Consumed		
3	*D3* Power Consumed	1 = 0.1x	
4	*D0* Power Dissipated		
5	*D1* Power Dissipated	2 = 0.01x	
6	*D2* Power Dissipated		
7	*D3* Power Dissipated	3 = 0.001x	
8	Common logic power consumption (Multi-function PCI devices. Function 0 only)		
9-15	Reserved (Function 0 of a multi-function PCI device)	Reserved	TBD
8-15	Reserved (Single function PCI devices, and other functions (greater than function 0) within a multi-function PCI device)	Reserved	TBD

Table 24-11: Power Consumption and Dissipation Table

DATA TEST ENVIRONMENT

Information returned in the **Data** register must be obtained by using the following test parameters:

■ Bus Frequency: 33MHz/66MHz.

■ Vcc: 5.25 VDC or 3.3 VDC (if 5 VDC is not supported).

■ Temperature: 70°C.

If the PCI function is 66MHz capable, use 66MHz characterization to obtain the worst case data values.

POWER MEASUREMENT DEFINITION

Power measurements defined for values "0" through "8" of the Power Consumption and Dissipation Table are defined as follows:

Dynamic Range	Resolution
0W - 25.5W	.1W
0W - 2.55W	.01W
0W - 255mW	.001W

Table 24-12: Power Measurement Values

POWER CONSUMED VALUES

The information obtained from the Power Consumed fields (**Data_Select** values "0" through "3") of the Power Consumption and Dissipation Table is used for managing the power source, such as a power supply or battery, of the PCI function. The following rules apply to the data values reported by the Power Consumed fields:

■ The value reported must be the sum of all power consumed by the PCI function from the PCI power planes through the PCI connector pins.

■ Power supplied to external devices by a PCI card must also be included in the final sum for each device power state.

■ Battery or other external power source supplied to the PCI function should not be included when calculating the total power consumed.

PCI functions must report the maximum power consumed by each individual supported device power state.

POWER DISSIPATED VALUES

The information obtained from the Power Dissipated fields (Data_Select values "4" through "7") of the Power Consumption and Dissipation Table is used for managing a system's thermal behavior. The following rules apply to the data values reported by the Power Dissipated fields:

- The value reported is the amount of heat generated by the PCI function in a given device power state when installed in a closed chassis.

- Battery or other external power source supplied to the PCI function should be included when calculating the total heat released.

- Power supplied to external devices by a PCI card must not be included in the final amount for each device power state.

> PCI functions must report the maximum heat generated by each individual device power state that is supported.

READING THE DATA REGISTER

The following is a suggested approach for reading the **Data** register of the PCI power management capability structure and interpreting its values:

1. Write function 0's **PMCSR** register (offset 04h), **Data_Select** field (bits [12::9]) with the value that corresponds to the data to be read. This specifies the data that will be returned when reading function 0's **Data** register (offset 07h). See Table 24-11, Power Consumption and Dissipation Table, for a list of valid values for the **Data_Select** field.

2. Read function 0's **Data** register (offset 07h).

   - If function 0's optional **Data** register is not implemented, the value read will be zero. Go to Done.

3. Read function 0's **PMCSR** register (offset 04h), **Data_Scale** field (bits [14::13]). This is the device specific scaling factor used to obtain the power consumption data as follows:

   0 = Unknown

   1 = 0.1x

   2 = 0.01x

3   = 0.001x

4.   Multiply function 0's **PMCSR** register (offset 04h of the PCI Power
      Management Data Structure), **Data_Scale** field (bits [14::13]) scaling
      factor by the value read from function 0's **Data** register.

      -    If function 0's optional **Data** register is implemented, the
           resultant value is the common logic power consumption in
           watts per the scaling factor.

5.   DONE.

As an example, specify that the ***D1*** power dissipated value data is to be read
from the **Data** register by programming the **PMCSR** register's read/write
Data_Select field with a value of "0101b". Read the binary value from the **Data**
register. With a **Data_Scale** value of "01b", the ***D1*** power dissipation is reported
in scaling factor of one-tenth of one watt. Multiply the value read by the scaling
factor to obtain the desired value.

MULTI-FUNCTION DEVICE POWER CONSUMPTION

A multi-function device that supports power management according to the *PCI
Power Management Specification 1.0* or later has a unique requirement: the power
consumed by the common logic shared by each function must be reported
separately from the power consumed by each specific function.

A multi-function device can only report its common logic power consumption
via its function 0 within PCI configuration address space. To determine a multi-
function device's power consumption, write its function 0 **PMCSR** register (offset
04h), **Data_Select** field (bits [12::9]) with a value of 1000b. This specifies that the
value returned when reading function 0's **Data** register (offset 07h) will be the
multi-function's common logic power consumption. Then follow the algorithm
given for reading and interpreting the PCI power management capability structure
Data register.

> If a multi-function device supports power management per the PCI Power Management Specification 1.0 or later and function 0's Data register is implemented, then the Data_Select and Data_Scale fields of function 0's PMCSR register must also be implemented. If the Data register is not implemented, then function 0's Data register, along with its PMCSR register Data_Select and Data_Scale fields must return a value of zero when read.

PCI/PCI BRIDGE POWER CONSUMPTION

PCI/PCI bridges connect one PCI bus to another PCI bus. PCI/PCI bridges can be incorporated on the platform itself and/or on add-in cards. PCI/PCI bridges can also be multi-function devices. Each function within the PCI/PCI bridge must report its own power consumption. In addition, individual functions incorporated in each device located on the secondary bus of a PCI/PCI bridge must report only the power that the function consumes. This maintains a power reporting structure based at the PCI function level, regardless of the PCI device type. As a result, software can easily determine the power consumption of the PCI subsystem when devices are implemented behind PCI/PCI bridges.

24.3 ACCELERATED GRAPHICS PORT (AGP)

The Accelerated Graphics Port (AGP) is a bus that enables high performance graphics. See the *Accelerated Graphics Port Interface Specification* for information on how to program and manage the AGP feature. This section describes the AGP Capability interface.

Figure 24.4 and Table 24.13 illustrate the layout and design of the AGP capability data structure.

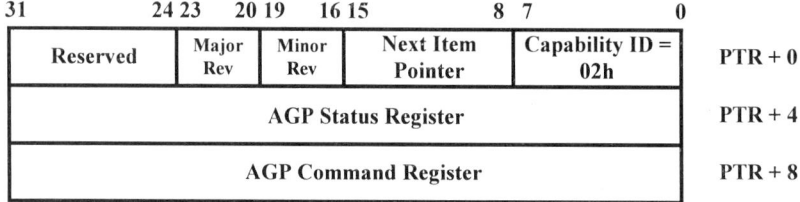

Figure 24-4: AGP Capability Structure Layout

Offset	Bits	Register/Field	Attributes	Description
0	7::0	Capability ID	Required Read Only	Identifies AGP as the capability of the structure with a value of 02h.
1	15::8	Next Item Pointer	Required Read Only	Provides the absolute offset to the next item in the Capabilities Linked List (00h if last structure)
2	19::16	Minor	Required Read Only	Minor revision number of the AGP interface specification that this device adheres to
2	23::20	Major	Required Read Only	Major revision number of the AGP interface specification that this device adheres to
3	31::24	Reserved	Required Read Only	Must return 00h when read
4	63::32	Status	Required Read Only	Reports AGP status for this PCI function
7	96::64	Command	Required Read Only	Permits control for the AGP capability of this PCI function

Table 24-13: AGP Capability Structure Definition

CAPABILITY IDENTIFIER REGISTER

Capability Identifier	
Offset:	00h of the AGP Capability Structure
Width:	1 Byte
Valid Values:	00h-FFh
	A value of 02h indicates the structure supports the AGP capability as defined in the *Accelerated Graphics Port Interface Specification.* This specification is available at http://www.agpforum.org.
Description:	This register identifies the specific capability supported by a structure member of a PCI Capabilities Linked List.

Bit	Type	Function
7::0	Read Only	**Capability Identifier** This value identifies a capability supported by a PCI function. Capability IDs are assigned by the PCI SIG.

Table 24-14: Capability Identifier Register

NEXT ITEM POINTER REGISTER

Next Item Pointer	
Offset:	01h of the AGP Capability Data Structure
Width:	1 Byte
Valid Values:	00h, 40h-FCh (must be DWORD aligned)
Description:	This register identifies the absolute offset of the start of the next structure member of a Capabilities Linked List. A value of 00h indicates this structure is the last one in the list.

Bit	Type	Function
7::0	Read Only	**Next Item Pointer** This value identifies the start location of the next item (capability data structure) in an AGP device's Capabilities Linked List.

Table 24-15: Next Item Pointer Register

MINOR REVISION REGISTER

Minor Revision	
Offset:	02h, Bits [3::0] of the AGP Capability Data Structure
Width:	4 Bits
Valid Values:	0000b-1111b
Description:	This register identifies the minor revision number of the AGP interface specification that this device adheres to.

Bit	Type	Function
19::16	Read Only	**Minor Revision** This value identifies the minor revision number of the AGP interface specification that this device adheres to.

Table 24-16: Minor Revision Register

MAJOR REVISION REGISTER

Major Revision	
Offset:	02h, Bits [7::4] of the AGP Capability Data Structure
Width:	4 Bits
Valid Values:	0000b-1111b
Description:	This register identifies the major revision number of the AGP interface specification that this device adheres to.

Bit	Type	Function
23::20	Read Only	**Major Revision** This value identifies the major revision number of the AGP interface specification that this device adheres to.

Table 24-17: Major Revision Register

AGP STATUS REGISTER

AGP Status	
Offset:	04h of the AGP Capability Data Structure
Width:	4 Bytes
Valid Values:	N/A. This register is a collection of bits, not a range of values. The register should not be viewed as values, but as individual bits.
Description:	The bits in this register contain information AGP device's capabilities and features.

Bit	Type	Function
2::0	Read Only	**Rate** Bits [2::0] indicate the data transfer rates supported by this AGP device. The device is required to report all transfer rates that it supports. The **Rate** field applies to the **AD** and **SBA** busses.<table><tr><td>**2**</td><td>**1**</td><td>**0**</td><td>**Transfer Rate**</td></tr><tr><td>0</td><td>0</td><td>0</td><td>NA</td></tr><tr><td>0</td><td>0</td><td>1</td><td>1X transfer rate supported</td></tr><tr><td>0</td><td>1</td><td>0</td><td>2X transfer rate supported</td></tr><tr><td>0</td><td>1</td><td>1</td><td>1X and 2X transfer rate supported</td></tr><tr><td>1</td><td>0</td><td>0</td><td>4X transfer rate supported</td></tr><tr><td>1</td><td>0</td><td>1</td><td>1X and 4X transfer rate supported</td></tr><tr><td>1</td><td>1</td><td>0</td><td>2X and 4X transfer rate supported</td></tr><tr><td>1</td><td>1</td><td>1</td><td>1X, 2X, and 4X transfer rate supported</td></tr></table>
3	Read Only	**Reserved**

4	Read Only	**FW** 0 Fast Write transactions are not supported. 1 Fast Write transactions are supported.
5	Read Only	**4G** 0 Memory addresses greater than 4 GB are not supported. 1 Memory addresses greater than 4 GB are supported.
8:6	Read Only	**Reserved**
9	Read Only	**SBA** 0 Side Band Addressing is not supported. 1 Side Band Addressing is supported.
23::10	Read Only	**Reserved**
31::24	Read Only	**RQ** The **RQ** field indicates the maximum number of AGP commands that the AGP graphics accellerator can enqueue in its target's request queue. Register values range from 00h, which indicates a depth of 1 entry, to 0ffh, which indicates a depth of 256 entries.

Table 24-18: AGP Status Register

FW (FAST WRITE) FIELD

Fast write transactions permit the core logic to write data to an AGP graphics accelerator at a very high transfer rate. Both the master and the target must be operating in either the 2x or 4x data transfer mode. Fast write transactions are optional for both the core logic (master) and the AGP graphics accelerator (target).

SBA (SIDE BAND ADDRESS) FIELD

The AGP Sideband Address Port is a dedicated 8-bit wide port that permits an AGP graphics accelerator, acting as the master, to send transaction requests to core logic, the target. When SBA is used, the **AD** and **C/BE** buses are not used to transmit transaction requests. This frees the AD bus to be used solely for transferring data. Note that supporting SBA is optional for AGP graphics accelerators; however, all core logic devices that support AGP are also required to support SBA.

RQ (REQUEST) FIELD

The **RQ** field indicates the maximum number of AGP commands that the AGP graphics accelerator can enqueue in its target's request queue. Register values range from 00h, which indicates a depth of 1 entry, to 0ffh, which indicates a depth of 256 entries.

AGP COMMAND REGISTER

AGP Command	
Offset:	04h of the AGP Capability Data Structure
Width:	4 Bytes
Valid Values:	N/A. This field is a collection of bits, not a range of values. The register should not be viewed as values, but as individual bits.
Description:	The bits in this register permit the control of an AGP device's capabilities and features. All bits in this register are set to "0" after reset is asserted.
	Except for the AGP_ENABLE bit, avoid modifiying this register during runtime, as the results are unpredictable.

Bit	Type	Function
2::0	Read Write	**Data_Rate** Bits [2::0] indicate the maximum desired data transfer rate by this A.G.P device. Only one bit may be set. Both the AGP master and target devices must have the same bit set. Data_Rate Bits <table><tr><td>**2**</td><td>**1**</td><td>**0**</td><td>**Data Transfer Rate**</td></tr><tr><td>0</td><td>0</td><td>0</td><td>NA</td></tr><tr><td>0</td><td>0</td><td>1</td><td>1X transfer rate is maximum supported</td></tr><tr><td>0</td><td>1</td><td>0</td><td>2X transfer rate is maximum supported</td></tr><tr><td>0</td><td>1</td><td>1</td><td>NA</td></tr><tr><td>1</td><td>0</td><td>0</td><td>4X transfer rate is maximum supported</td></tr><tr><td>1</td><td>0</td><td>1</td><td>NA</td></tr><tr><td>1</td><td>1</td><td>0</td><td>NA</td></tr><tr><td>1</td><td>1</td><td>1</td><td>NA</td></tr></table>
3	Read Only	**Reserved**
4	Read Write	**FW Enable** 0 Memory write transactions initiated by the core logic to the AGP master follow the standard PCI protocol. 1 Memory write transactions initiated by the core logic to the AGP master follow the Fast Write protocol.
5	Read Write	**4G** **Master** 0 Master cannot initiate AGP requests to memory addresses greater than 4 GB. 1 Master can initiate AGP requests access memory addresses greater than 4 GB.

Table 24-19: AGP Command Register

		Target 0 NA 1 When bit [5], **4G**, is set to '1' and bit [9], **SBA**, is set to '0', the target can accept AGP DAC commands. When bit [5], **4G**, is set and bit [9], **SBA are** set to '1', the target can accept Type 4 SBA commands and utilize A[35::32] for a Type 3 command.
7::6	Read Only	**Reserved**
8	Read Write	**AGP_Enable** **Master** 0 Master cannot initiate AGP operations. 1 Master can initiate A.G.P. operations. Asserting AGP_Reset sets the AGP_Enable bit to '0'. **Target** 0 Target ignores AGP transactions. 1 Target accepts AGP transactions. Before the AGP master is enabled, the AGP target must be configured and enabled. No assumptions by the device can be made in regard to the sequence in which the individual AGP Command register fields are programmmed. The exception is the AGP_Enable bit, which must be set last. Note that if all Command register fields are programmed concurrently using a single 32-bit write transaction, that the AGP_Enable bit can bet set at the time as well.
9	Read Write	**SBA_Enable** 0 Side Band Addressing is not enabled. 1 Side Band Addressing is enabled.
23::10	Read Only	**Reserved**
31::24	Read Write	**RQ_Depth** **Master** RQ-Depth field is required to be programmed with the maximum number of AGP commands that the AGP master can enqueue in the target. Register values range from 00h, which indicates a depth of 1 entry, to 0ffh, which indicates a depth of 256 entries The value of RQ_Depth must be equal to or less than the value reported in the RQ field of the target's AGP Status register. **Target** RQ-Depth field is reserved.

Table 24-19: AGP Command Register (continued)

All bits in the AGP Command register are initialized to a value of "0" at reset. Except for the AGP_Enable bit, the behavior of an AGP device is indeterminate when its Command register is modified during runtime. During runtime operation the AGP_Enable bit can be set to '0' to prevent the AGP master from initiating AGP transactions or set to allow the master to initiate AGP transactions.

FW (FAST WRITE) ENABLE FIELD

Fast write transactions permit the core logic to write data to an AGP graphics accelerator at a very high transfer rate. Both the master and the target must be operating in either the 2x or 4x data transfer mode. Fast write transactions are optional for both the core logic (master) and the AGP graphics accelerator (target). During system initialization, the operating system reads the values contained in both the master and target's AGP **Status** register **FW** fields. The operating system then programs the master and target's AGP **Command** register **FW_ENABLE** fields based on its predefined algorithm for the values read from the **Status** registers and the master and target's AGP **Command** register's **Data_Rate field** settings.

SBA (SIDE BAND ADDRESS) ENABLE FIELD

The AGP Sideband Address Port is a dedicated 8-bit wide port that permits an AGP graphics accelerator, acting as the master, to send transaction requests to core logic, the target. When **SBA** is used, the **AD** and **C/BE** buses are not used to transmit transaction requests to the target. This frees the **AD** bus to be used solely for transferring data. Note that supporting SBA is optional for AGP graphics accelerators; however, all core logic devices that support AGP are also required to support SBA. During system initialization the operating system reads, the values contained in both the master and target's AGP **Status** register **SBA** fields. The operating system then programs the master and target's AGP **Command** register's **SBA_ENABLE** fields based on its predefined algorithm for the values read from the AGP **Status** registers.

RQ (REQUEST) DEPTH ENABLE FIELD

The **RQ** field indicates the maximum number of AGP commands that the AGP graphics accelerator can enqueue in its target's request queue. Register values range from 00h, which indicates a depth of 1 entry, to 0ffh, which indicates a depth of 256 entries. During system initialization the operating system reads the values contained in both the master and target's AGP **Status** register **RQ** fields. The operating system then programs the master's AGP **Command** register **RQ_Depth** fields with the smaller of the two values read. This prevents queue overruns. Note that the master is responsible for preventing overruns in the target's request queue.

> **RQ_Depth is a reserved field for targets.**

24.4 VITAL PRODUCT DATA (VPD)

PCI Local Bus Specification 2.2 requires the **Device ID**, **Vendor ID**, **Revision ID**, and **Class Code** registers to be implemented in each PCI function's Configuration Space Header. In addition, the **Subsystem ID** and **Subsystem Vendor ID** registers are also required for PCI functions implemented with a Header Type 00H. The **Device ID**, **Vendor ID**, **Revision ID**, and **Class Code** registers are read-only; the **Subsystem ID** and **Subsystem Vendor ID** registers are read-writeable. These latter two registers are dynamically programmed during the power-on cycle before software can read them. These six registers are used to identify and configure each PCI function. However, these registers are not sufficient to provide all of the data needed to completely identify a system component. Additional information is required to enable extensible software operations such as system configuration and tracking, intelligent installation of software upgrades based on each system component, more robust remote diagnostics, component defect tracking, and even identifying components that are and are not covered under the manufacturer's warranty with information such as part number and serial number. The ultimate goal of this information is to permit each PCI component to operate seamlessly in a Plug and Play environment and to reduce the total cost of ownership of the system itself. The Vital Product Data (VPD) PCI capability provides a mechanism for accessing this additional information.

VPD STORAGE MEDIA

PCI Local Bus Specification 2.2 does not specify the storage media for Vital Product Data. Designers are unrestricted when implementing hardware to support VPD.

> Note that *PCI Local Bus Specification 2.1* required that the Vital Product Data be stored in the first 64K of an expansion ROM image. Backward compatibility to support ROM-based VPDs is required for existing boards by Revision 2.2 of the PCI Bus Specification. Therefore, when the Revision 2.2 VPD implementation is supported, software is required to check expansion ROMs for VPD.

However, the specification does make provisions for distinct read-only and read-writeable storage within the selected media. For example, consider an EEPROM that is half read-only and half read-writeable. This device is able to store static information, such as device-specific initialization data and a board's part and serial numbers, in the read-only portion of the EEPROM. Dynamic vendor and system specific data such as failure events can be stored in and retrieved from the read-writeable segment of the EEPROM. *PCI Local Bus Specification 2.2* does not specify how the read-writeable region of the VPD storage media is used or how to manage the available read-writeable space. It only specifies the format for storing VPD in this region.

> **Writes to the read-only data region of the VPD storage media will result in a no-op transaction. In addition, read-writeable data must be preserved when system power is removed.**

MULTIPLE DEVICE SUPPORT

Add-in boards may incorporate multiple PCI devices. The designer has three choices:

- ■ Do not support VPD.
- ■ Support VPD using a single device or function.
- ■ Support VPD in all of the devices.

PCI devices that are incorporated on system boards can optionally support VPD.

> **Some devices or functions may indicate that they support VPD. However, these devices or functions may not have the associated storage media to hold the VPD content. When software accesses VPD Address zero of a device or function in this configuration, hardware will return 00000000h in the *VPD Data* field. This indicates that VPD information cannot be obtained through that particular device or function. See the *ACCESSING VPD* section below for more information on the *VPD Data* field.**

Figure 24-5 and Table 24-20 illustrate the layout and design of the VPD capability data structure. Note that all fields are required.

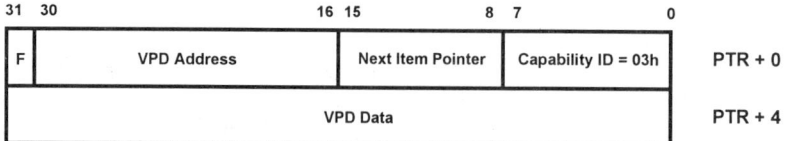

Figure 24-5: VPD Capability Structure Layout

Offset	Bits	Register/Field	Attributes	Description
0	7::0	Capability ID	Required Read Only	Identifies VPD as the capability of the structure with a value of 03h.
1	15::8	Next Item Pointer	Required Read Only	Provides the absolute offset to the next item in the Capabilities Linked List (00h if last structure).
2	30::16	VPD Address Field	Required Read/Write	Address to access within the VPD storage area. **Initial value of *VPD Address* at power-up is not defined.**
3	31	Flag Field	Required Read/Write	Semaphore that indicates when a data transfer between the VPD storage media and the VPD Data field is complete.
4	63::32	VPD Data	Required Read/Write	VPD information is transferred between the four-byte address specified by *VPD Address* and this field. **Initial value of *VPD Data* at power-up is not defined.**

Table 24-20: VPD Capability Structure Definition

CAPABILITY IDENTIFIER REGISTER

Capability Identifier	
Offset:	00h of the VPD Capability Structure
Width:	1 Byte
Valid Values:	00h-FFh
	A value of 03h indicates the structure supports the VPD capability as defined in the *PCI Local Bus Specification*. This specification can be obtained from the PCI Special Interest Group at http://www.pcisig.com.
Description:	This register identifies the specific capability supported by a structure member of a PCI Capabilities Linked List.

Bit	Type	Function
7::0	Read Only	**Capability Identifier** This value identifies a capability supported by a PCI function. Capability IDs are assigned by the PCI SIG.

Table 24-21: Capability Identifier Register

NEXT ITEM POINTER REGISTER

Next Item Pointer	
Offset:	01h of the VPD. Capability Data Structure
Width:	1 Byte
Valid Values:	00h, 40h-FCh (must be DWORD aligned)
Description:	This register identifies the absolute offset of the start of the next structure member of a Capabilities Linked List. A value of 00h indicates this structure is the last one in the list.

Bit	Type	Function
7::0	Read Only	**Next Item Pointer** This value identifies the start location of the next item (capability data structure) in a PCI function's Capabilities Linked List.

Table 24-22: Next Item Pointer Register

VPD ADDRESS FIELD

VPD Address Field	
Offset:	02h of the VPD Capability Structure
Width:	15 Bits
Valid Values:	00h-7Fh
Description:	This field is programmed with the start address of an area within the VPD storage to either read from or write to.

Bit	Type	Function
30::16	Read/Write	**VPD Address Field** Specifies the address of the least significant byte of a 4-byte data area within the VPD to read from or write to.

Table 24-23: VPD Address Field

VPD ADDRESS FIELD

VPD Address is 15 bits in length. This field is an index pointer into the VPD. The field is used in conjunction with **Flag** field and the **VPD Data** register to transfer four bytes of data at a time to or from the VPD storage media. Note that the value written to **VPD Address** only specifies the least significant byte offset within VPD that data will be transferred to or from. For example, if a value of 21h were written to this field, 21h would be the least significant byte accessed, followed by offsets 22h, 23h and offset 24h.

FLAG FIELD

Flag Field	
Offset:	03h of the VPD Capability Structure
Width:	1 Bit
Valid Values:	0b or 1b
Description:	This field is a semaphore that indicates when a data transfer between the VPD storage media and the VPD Data field is complete.

Bit	Type	Function
31	Read/Write	**Flag Field** Semaphore used in VPD Data read and write operations **Reading VPD** 0 Software sets this bit to '0' to specify a read operation 1 Hardware sets this bit to a '1' to indicate 4 bytes of data have been transferred from the VPD storage media to the *VPD Data* field **Writing VPD** 0 Hardware set this bit to a '0' to indicate 4 bytes of data have been transferred from the *VPD Data* field to the VPD storage media 1 Software sets this bit to '0' to specify a write operation

Table 24-24: Flag Field

FLAG FIELD

Data can be read from any location within the VPD. Data can be written to read-writeable locations with the VPD **F**, or the **Flag** Field, is a semaphore that indicates when a data transfer between the VPD storage media and the **VPD Data** register is complete.

VPD DATA REGISTER

VPD Address	
Offset:	04h of the VPD Capability Structure
Width:	4 Bytes
Valid Values:	00000000h-FFFFFFFFh
Description:	This register is programmed with the data either read from or written to an area within the VPD storage media.

Bit	Type	Function
63::32	Read/Write	**VPD Data** Specifies four bytes of data to read from or written to an area within the VPD.

Table 24-25: VPD Data

VPD DATA REGISTER

VPD Data is 32 bits in length. The field is used in conjunction with **Flag** and **VPD Address** fields to either read data from or write data to the VPD storage media. The data value written to **VPD Address** specifies the least significant byte of the offset within VPD that data will be transferred to or from. For VPD read operations, the least significant byte of data read from the VPD storage media (as specified by **VPD Address**) will be written to the least significant byte of the **VPD Data** register, followed by the remaining three bytes. For VPD write operations, the least significant byte of data to be written to the VPD storage media (as specified by **VPD Address**) will be written to the least significant byte of the **VPD Data** field, followed by the remaining three bytes.

READING VPD

Use the following steps to read data from the VPD storage media:

1.	Simultaneously write the **VPD Address** (bits [30::16]) and **Flag** (bit [31]) fields:

- The least significant byte address of the VPD data to be read is written to the **VPD Address** field.

- A zero is written to the **Flag** field, bit [31]. A zero indicates that a read operation is specified.

2. Software monitors the **Flag** field, bit [31]:

- When hardware has set this field to a one, four bytes of data have been transferred from the VPD storage media to the **VPD Data** register.

Once a VPD read operation has been initiated, do not write to the VPD Address or Flag fields before the Flag field is set to a one by the hardware. Doing so will produce unpredictable results for the original read operation.

WRITING VPD

Use the following steps to write data to the VPD storage media's read-writeable region:

1.	Write the **VPD Data** register, bits [63::32] with four bytes of data to be transferred to the VPD storage media.
2.	Simultaneously write the **VPD Address**, bits [30::16] and the **Flag**, bit [31], fields:
	- The least significant byte address of the VPD storage media to be programmed is written to **VPD Address** field.
	- A one is written to the **Flag** field, bit [31]. A one indicates that a write operation is specified.
3.	Software monitors the **Flag** field, bit [31]:
	- When hardware has set this field to a zero, four bytes of data have been transferred from the **VPD Data** register to the VPD storage media.

Once a VPD write operation has been initiated, do not write to the VPD Address field or VPD Data register before the Flag field is set to a zero by the hardware. Doing so will produce unpredictable results for the write operation to the VPD storage media.

VPD DATA CONSTRUCTS

VPD content is maintained in the VPD storage media by using a predefined set of contiguous data structures. These structures fall into two categories. The first category is the Tag Data Structure. This type of structure is used to "wrap" one or more predefined categories of data together. The second category of data structures is the Keyword Data Structure. Each keyword data structure contains information unique to the specific keyword field of the data structure. Tag data structures can contain one or more keyword data structures. Both types of data structures are described below.

TAG DATA STRUCTURES

The format of TAG data structures is specified in the *Plug and Play ISA Specification, Version 1.0a*. The two data structures used for VPD are referred to as Small and Large Resource Data Types. Figures 24-6 and 24-7 illustrate the structure layouts. Both figures are reproduced from *Plug and Play ISA Specification, Version 1.0a*. Tables 24-26 and 24-27 give the bit definitions for each structure's fields.

Offset	Field		
Byte 0	Tag Bit[7]	Tag Bit [6::3]	Tag Bit [2::0]
	Type = 0	Small item name	Length = n bytes
Bytes 1 to n	Actual Information		

Figure 24-6: Small Resource Data Type Tag Bit Layout

Bit	Field	Description
2::0	Length	Specifies the length of the data structure in bytes.
6::3	Item Name	The unique Small Resource numeric id assigned to the data structure. Note that a unique alpha character name is also associated with each **Item Name**.
7	Type	A value of zero indicates that this is a Small Resource Data Type.
n::8	Data	The actual data that can be stored in a specified Small Resource Data Type.

Table 24-26: Small Resource Data Type Tag Bit Definition

Offset	Field
Byte 0	Value = 1xxxxxxxB (Type = 1, Large item name = xxxxxxx).
Byte 1	Length of data items bits [7::0] (lsb).
Byte 2	Length of data items bits [15::8] (msb).
Bytes 3 to n	Actual data items.

Figure 24-6: Large Resource Data Type Tag Bit Layout

Bit	Field	Description
6::0	Item Name	The unique Large Resource numeric id assigned to the data structure. Note that a unique alpha character name is also associated with each **Item Name**.
7	Type	A value of one indicates that this is a Large Resource Data Type.
15::8	Length (lsb)	The length of the Large Resource Data Type is stored in a word value. Bits [15::8] contain the least significant byte of the length.
23::16	Length (msb)	The length of the Large Resource Data Type is stored in a word value. Bits [23::16] contain the most significant byte of the length.
n::24	Data	The actual data that can be stored in a specified Large Resource Data Type.

Table 24-27: Large Resource Data Type Tag Bit Definitions

VPD SMALL AND LARGE RESOURCE DATA TAGS

Vital Product Data is associated with four specific Small and Large Resource Tags. The following is a description of these tags. Also, note that the order of the tags listed in Table 24-28 is the order that the data structures in the VPD would be stored in, starting at offset 00H of the VPD with the Identifier String tag structure.

TAG Name	Numeric ID	Resource Type	Description
Identifier String	0x02	Large	This item is required to be the first item stored in the VPD media. This structure contains the alphanumeric product name of the device.
VPD-R	0x10	Large	This item contains (wraps) read-only VPD keyword data structures.
VPD-W	0x11	Large	This item contains (wraps) read-writeable VPD keyword data structures.
End Tag	0x0F	Small	This item is required to be last in the list. It identifies the end of the VPD in the storage media.

Table 24-28: VPD Resource Data Type Tag Definitions

The Identifier String and End tags were defined previously. The VPD-R and VPD-W tags were defined for implementation with Revision 2.2 of the *PCI Local Bus Specification*.

Revision 2.1 of the *PCI Local Bus Specification* also used certain tags for VPD. See the specification for more information.

Tags that are not recognized by software can be ignored.

VPD KEYWORD DATA STRUCTURES

Figure 24-8 illustrates the **VPD Keyword** structure layout. Table 24-29 gives the bit definitions for each field of the structure.

Offset	Field
Byte 0	Least significant character of the two-byte **Keyword**.
Byte 1	Most significant character of the two-byte **Keyword**.
Byte 2	Length of data .
Bytes 3 to n	Actual data items.

Figure 24-8: VPD Keyword Data Structure Layout

Keywords that are not recognized by software can be ignored.

Bit	Field	Description
15::0	Keyword	Mnemonic consisting of two ASCII characters that uniquely identifies the information in the **Data** field.
23::15	Length	Length value in bytes of the data that follows the three byte header of the structure. The three byte header is not included in the length value.
n::24	Data	The actual data that can be stored in a specified keyword data structure.

Table 24-29: VPD Keyword Data Structure Bit Definitions

VPD KEYWORDS

Vital Product Data is associated with specific keywords. These keywords are defined using ASCII characters. The keywords are used in the **Keyword** data field when defining the VPD **Keyword** data structures. VPD keywords are defined for both the read-only and read-writeable regions of the VPD storage media. The following is a description of the VPD keywords.

> All unspecified VPD keyword values are reserved by the PCI Special Interest Group (PCI SIG). Contact the PCI SIG to obtain new definitions. The PCI SIG reserves the right to update the current VPD keyword list at any time.

VPD READ ONLY KEYWORDS

Table 24-30 contains the read-only VPD keywords definitions. Note that the **VPD-R** tag contains (wraps) read-only VPD keyword data structures.

Keyword	Name	Description
CP	Extended Capability	Allows a PCI capability to be identified in the Vital Product Data. Recall that the VPD does not have the capability for dynamic control/status. Consequently, the device's capability control/status registers are located elsewhere in the PCI device, namely in the device's address space. The **Data** field of the **CP** keyword data structure specifies where in the device's address space the control/status registers are located. The **Data** field of the **CP** keyword data structure has a length of four bytes. The first byte contains the **Capability ID**. The second byte contains the zero-based index of the base address register within the address space in which the the control/status registers reside. The last two bytes contain a 16-bit offset from offset zero of the base address. The start location for the control/status registers of the PCI Capability begins at this offset.

EC	EC Level of the Board	The Engineering Change level of this board, specified in alphanumeric characters.
MN	Manufactu rer ID	Extension to the **Vendor ID** and/or **Subsystem Vendor ID**. Use this keyword structure to add a greater level of detail as to the source of the device.
PN	Board Part Number	Extension to the **Device ID** and/or **Subsystem ID**. Use this keyword structure to add a greater level of detail in regards to the identification of the device.
SN	Serial Number	The unique serial number of this board, specified in alphanumeric characters.
RV	Checksum and Reserved	The **RV** keyword data structure should be the last VPD keyword structure located within the **VPD-R** tag. The first byte in the **Data** field of the **RV** keyword data structure is a checksum byte. The checksum is calculated by summing the bytes from VPD address zero to the checksum byte, inclusive. If the summed value equals zero, the VPD checksum is good. The value in the **Length** field of the **RV** keyword structure is added to its offset location value in the VPD. The result is the location of the last read-only byte in the VPD storage media. All bytes from the second data byte of the structure to the last read-only byte inclusive are reserved and should return zero when read.
Vx	Vendor-Specific	Vendor-specific item defined with alphanumeric characters. Multiple vendor-specific items can be defined. However, each item requires a unique set of alphanumeric characters. Valid second keyword characters (x) are 0-Z. For example, V0, V1..V9, VA, VB..VZ.

Table 24-30: VPD Read-Only Keywords

VPD READ-WRITEABLE KEYWORDS

Table 24-31 contains the read-writeable VPD Keywords definitions. Note that the **VPD-W** tag contains (wraps) read-writeable VPD keyword data structures.

> **The VPD read-writeable region is not check summed.**

Keyword	Name	Description
RW	Remaining Read-writeable Area	The **RW** keyword data structure describes the unused portion of the VPD read-writeable storage media. Product vendors are required to initialize this data structure. Initialization data is based on the size of the VPD read-writeable region or the space remaining after the last Vx or Yx data structure. One or more Vx or Yx keyword data are required.
Vx	Vendor-Specific	Vendor- specific item defined with alphanumeric characters. Multiple vendor-specific items can be defined. However, each item requires a unique set of alphanumeric characters. Valid second keyword characters (x) are 0-Z. For example, V0, V1..V9, VA, VB..VZ.
YA	Asset Tag Identifier	**YA** is a system specific data structure defined with alphanumeric characters. It contains the system asset identifier. This value is provided by the system owner.
Yx	System Specific	**Yx** is a system specific data structure defined with alphanumeric characters. Multiple system specific items can be defined. However, each item requires a unique set of alphanumeric characters. Valid second keyword characters (x) are 0-9 and B-Z. For example, V0, V1..V9, VB, VC..VZ.

Table 24-31: VPD Read-writeable Keywords

VPD EXAMPLE

Offset	Item	Value
0	Large Resource Type: *ID String Tag* (0x02)	0x82
1	Length	0x17
3	Data	"EdSo Cat Nip Controller"
26	Large Resource Type: *VPD-R Tag* (0x10)	0x90
27	Length	0x0063
29	VPD Keyword	"PN"
31	Length	0x0E
32	Data	"42464653590007"
46	VPD Keyword	"EC"
48	Length	0x08
49	Data	"45430007"
57	VPD Keyword	"SN"
59	Length	0x08
60	Data	"00087636"
68	VPD Keyword	"MN"
70	Length	0x04
71	Data	"8617"
75	VPD Keyword	"CP"
77	Length	0x04
78	Data	0x006401FE

82	VPD Keyword	"RV"
84	Length	0x2B
85	Data	Checksum
86	Data	Reserved (0x00)
128	Large Resource Type: *VPD-W Tag* (0x11)	0x91
129	Length	0x007E
131	VPD Keyword	"YB"
133	Length	0x12
134	Data	"Last Tested 122597"
156	VPD Keyword	"RW"
158	Length	0x60
159	Data	Reserved (0x00)
255	Small Resource Type: *End Tag* (0x0F)	0x78

Table 24-32: VPD Example

24.5 SLOT IDENTIFICATION

As described in Chapter 17, *PCI Configuration Address Space*, PCI devices are accessed by software using logical addressing versus physical addressing. Each PCI device in a system is uniquely identified using the combination of a PCI bus number, device number and function number. With this information, the hardware is able to assert the **IDSEL** signal line (one **IDSEL** signal line per device on a given bus) to select, or logically address, a unique device and function during PCI configuration space access transactions.

A platform or PCI expansion chassis' add-in card slots are assigned and physically connected to a unique **IDSEL** signal line in the same manner as integrated devices. Thus, PCI devices integrated on add-in cards are logically addressed in the same fashion as PCI devices integrated on a platform or expansion chassis.

In certain circumstances, it is desirable for system software to be able to identify a physical slot in the main chassis (contains the platform with the primary CPU) or expansion chassis (a group of PCI slots that can be connected to or disconnected from the main chassis), for instance, to identify the unique physical location of a defective add-in card that needs to be removed and replaced. Solely using a PCI device's bus, device, and function number to locate the specific physical slot of an add-in card on which the device resides in is not feasible. The reason is because a system's PCI bus numbers will increase by one when adding a PCI-PCI bridge or decrease by one when removing a PCI-PCI bridge from either the main or expansion chassis. PCI devices that were initially assigned to one PCI bus may subsequently be assigned a new bus number after the bridge is installed or removed and PCI bus re-enumeration is accomplished. Consequently, a consistent method to permit software to translate the logical address of a PCI device into a physical slot is required. The mechanism provided for accomplishing this task is the PCI Slot Identification Capability, that is described in this section.

> The PCI Slot Identification Capability only applies to bridges. A PCI bridge can be designed to provide external expansion from the main chassis to another chassis or from one expansion chassis to another expansion chassis. These types of bridges are required to support the Slot Identification Capability. For PCI bridges that do not support external expansion, the Slot Identification Capability is optional.

Figure 24-9 and Table 24-33 illustrate the layout and design of the Slot Identification Capability data structure. Note that all fields are required.

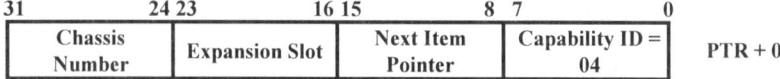

31 24	23 16	15 8	7 0	
Chassis Number	Expansion Slot	Next Item Pointer	Capability ID = 04	PTR + 0

Figure 24-9: Slot Identification Capability Structure Layout

Offset	Bits	Register/Field	Attributes	Description
0	7::0	Capability ID	Required Read Only	Identifies Slot Identification as the capability of the structure with a value of 04h.
1	15::8	Next Item Pointer	Required Read Only	Provides the absolute offset to the next item in the Capabilities Linked List (00h if last structure).
2	23::16	Expansion Slot	Required Read Only	Contains information used by system software to calculate the unique physical slot number of a device installed in a PCI expansion chassis. **This register is initialized by hardware when RST# is asserted.**
3	31::24	Chassis Number	Required Read/Write	Contains the physical chassis number for the slots on this bridge's secondary interface. **This register is either initialized to zero by hardware when RST# is asserted or its contents are non-volatile.**

Table 24-34: Slot Identification Capability Structure Definition

CAPABILITY IDENTIFIER REGISTER

Capability Identifier	
Offset:	00h of the Slot Identification Capability Structure
Width:	1 Byte
Valid Values:	00h-FFh
	A value of 04h indicates the structure supports the Slot Identification Capability as defined in the *PCI-to-PCI Bridge Architecture Specification*. This specification can be obtained from the PCI Special Interest Group at http://www.pcisig.com.
Description:	This register identifies the specific capability supported by a structure member of a PCI Capabilities Linked List.

Bit	Type	Function
7::0	Read Only	**Capability Identifier** This value identifies a capability supported by a PCI function. Capability IDs are assigned by the PCI SIG.

Table 24-35: Capability Identifier Register

NEXT ITEM POINTER REGISTER

Next Item Pointer	
Offset:	01h of the Slot Identification Capability Data Structure
Width:	1 Byte
Valid Values:	00h, 40h-FCh (must be DWORD aligned)
Description:	This register identifies the absolute offset of the start of the next structure member of a Capabilities Linked List. A value of 00h indicates this structure is the last one in the list.

Bit	Type	Function
7::0	Read Only	**Next Item Pointer** This value identifies the start location of the next item (capability data structure) in a PCI function's Capabilities Linked List.

Table 24-36: Next Item Pointer Register

EXPANSION SLOT REGISTER

Expansion Slot	
Offset:	02h of the Slot Identification Capability Structure
Width:	1 Byte
Valid Values:	00h-FFh
Description:	This register contains information used by system software to calculate the unique physical slot number of a device installed in a PCI expansion chassis.

Bit	Type	Function
4::0	Read Only	**Expansion Slots Provided** A binary value that indicates the number of PCI expansion slots located directly on the secondary interface of this bridge. If no PCI slots are present on the secondary bus, this field is intialized to zero. Also, PCI expansion slots located on bridges attached to the secondary interface of this bridge are not counted.
5	Read/Write	**First in Chassis** 0 This is not a parent bridge 1 Parent Bridge – this bridge is the first bridge in an expansion chassis (contains the lowest primary bus number or the lowest device number of all bridges with the same primary bus number) Software uses bit [5] to determine the existence of an expansion chassis. Software knows that the bridge requires a unique chassis number when this bit is set.
7::6	Read Only	**Reserved**

Table 24-37: Expansion Slot Register

EXPANSION SLOT REGISTER

The **Expansion Slot** register contents are used by system software to calculate the unique physical slot number of a device installed in a PCI expansion chassis. The *PCI-to-PCI Bridge Architecture Specification* contains a software-based slot numbering mechanism. Implementers can choose to use this method or supply a proprietary method for the logical address to physical slot translation. Either way, a translation mechanism is required when a PCI/PCI bridge utilizes the PCI Slot Identification capability.

The *PCI-to-PCI Bridge Architecture Specification* defines the main chassis as the one that contains the CPU that initializes the PCI configuration address space of the system. The specification also defines a group of PCI slots that can be connected to and disconnected from the main chassis as residing in an expansion chassis. An expansion chassis must use a slot numbering mechanism.

Note that not all PCI-PCI bridges are required to support the PCI Slot Identification capability. The capability is only required for the first bridge in a PCI expansion chassis and for any additional bridges in an expansion chassis that have additional expansion slots on their secondary bus. Other bridges that are integrated on the main chassis' platform or on add-in cards are not required to implement this feature.

The PCI system initialization software assumes that no PCI expansion slots are present on the bridge's secondary bus when the software does not detect an Expansion Slot register.

INITIALIZATION

Hardware initializes the **Expansion Slot** register after **RST#** is asserted. The register's default value is established by the hardware design and is system specific.

The *PCI-to-PCI Bridge Architecture Specification* does not specify the default value of the Expansion Slot register after a RST# is asserted. However, the specification does require that the Expansion Slot register's value is valid by the time the PCI system initialization software reads the register. Designers are free to implement any method to accomplish this requirement.

CHASSIS NUMBER REGISTER

Chassis Number	
Offset:	03h of the Slot Identification Capability Data Structure
Width:	1 Byte
Valid Values:	01h-FFh
	Chassis number '0' is not valid for this register. This value is reserved for the main chassis. Also, chassis numbers do not have to be sequential; however, each expansion chassis number must be different from every other one in the system.
Description:	This register contains the physical chassis number associated with the physical slots on this bridge's secondary interface.

Bit	Type	Function
7::0	Read/Write	**Chassis Number** This value identifies the physical chassis number associated with the physical slots on an expansion bridge's secondary interface.

Table 24-38: Chassis Number Register

CHASSIS NUMBER REGISTER

The **Chassis Number** register contains the physical chassis number associated with the physical slots on an expansion bridge's secondary interface. The PCI-to-PCI Bridge Architecture Specification places the following requirements on the **Chassis Number** register:

- The register should not be programmed with a value of '0' because this value is reserved for the main chassis.

- If a chassis contains more than one bridge that implements the PCI Slot Identification capability, all bridges in the chassis must be programmed with the same chassis number. This is regardless of whether the bridge supports PCI expansion slots on its secondary bus.

- PCI system initialization software must assign a different chassis number to each expansion chassis that contains PCI expansion slots.

- Unless the register contents are stored in system non-volatile memory, the **Chassis Number** register must be initialized to a value of '00h' when a reset occurs. Each time the bridge is reset the **Chassis Number** register will be re-programmed by PCI system initialization software.

- PCI system initialization software is required to write a non-zero value into the register when it either detects that the register is initialized by the hardware to '00h' or if the non-zero value of the register conflicts with another expansion chassis' number.

> It is recommended that the contents of the Chassis Number register be maintained by non-volatile memory. Doing so provides the advantage of allowing multiple expansion chassis in a system to be rearranged without the chassis number being modified. Using the non-volatile implementation, a Chassis Number register's contents will only be modified in the event another chassis in the system is detected with the same chassis number. System designers are free to implement any method that stores and retrieves the chassis number.

24.6 MESSAGE SIGNALED INTERRUPTS (MSI)

For PCI, there are now three methods defined to support interrupts: **INTx#** signal lines, polling, and Message Signaled Interrupts. The **INTx#** signal lines are active low which permits sharing of a single **INTx#** signal line among several PCI resources that can request interrupt service. The receipt of a hardware interrupt request via a shared **INTx#** signal line requires the software to read the configuration address space and possibly other registers of the PCI resources sharing the associated **INTx#** signal line to determine the interrupt source. Another method of interrupt support is polling. This is simply the software reading the configuration address space and possibly other registers of PCI resources to determine which resource requires interrupt service.

Revision 2.2 of the *PCI Local Bus Specification* has added the third method to support interrupts. It is called Message Signaled Interrupts (MSI). MSI is entirely based on memory write access cycles from the PCI resource requesting the interrupt (source) to the PCI resource that will service the interrupt (destination). Thus, MSI defines a protocol known as peer-to-peer. The MSI protocol permits the destination to be any appropriately designed PCI resource or the interrupt controller on PCI bus 0 (the PCI resource that receives the **INTx#** signal lines) if one is developed that supports MSI. This section describes the Message Signaled Interrupt Capability.

> Only one MSI Capability is allowed per PCI function. In addition, each function within a multi-function PCI device is required to implement its own MSI Capability structure.

PCI functions can either support a 32 bit or 64 bit message addresses. The MSI data structure is ten bytes in length to support a 32 bit message address or fourteen bytes in length to support a 64 bit message address. Table 24-39 illustrates a 32 bit

Message Address (MA) structure while Table 24-40 defines a 64 bit Message Address (MA) structure. Figures 24-10 and 24-11 show the layout and general design of the PCI Message Signaled Interrupt (MSI) capability data structure for 32 and 64 bits.

Offset	Bits	Register/Field	Attributes	Description
0	7::0	Capability ID	Required Read Only	Identifies Message Signaled Interrupts as the capability of the structure with a value of 05h.
1	15::8	Next Item Pointer	Required Read Only	Provides the absolute offset to the next item in the Capabilities Linked List (00h if last structure).
2	31::16	Message Control	Required Read/Write	Provides system software the ability to control the MSI capability.
4	63::32	Message Address	Required Read/Write	32 bit system specified message address.
8	79::64	Message Data	Required Read/Write	System specified data.

Table 24-39: 32 Bit MA Message Signaled Interrupt Capability Structure Definition

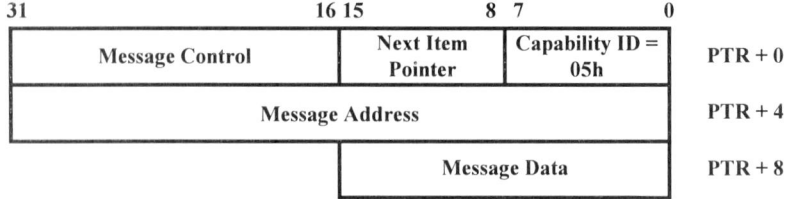

Figure 24-10: 32 Bit MA Message Signaled Interrupt Capability Structure Layout

Offset	Bits	Register/Field	Attributes	Description
0	7::0	Capability ID	Required Read Only	Identifies Message Signaled Interrupts as the capability of the structure with a value of 05h.
1	15::8	Next Item Pointer	Required Read Only	Provides the absolute offset to the next item in the Capabilities Linked List (00h if last structure).
2	31::16	Message Control	Required Read/Write	Provides system software the ability to control the MSI capability.
4	63::32	Message Address	Required Read/Write	Lower 32 bit system specified message address.
8	95::64	Message Upper Address	Required Read/Write	Upper 32 bits of the 64-bit system specified message address (optional). Can be programmed to zero by system software.
12	111::96	Message Data	Required Read/Write	System specified data.

**Table 24-40: 64 Bit MA Message Signaled Interrupt Capability
Structure Definition**

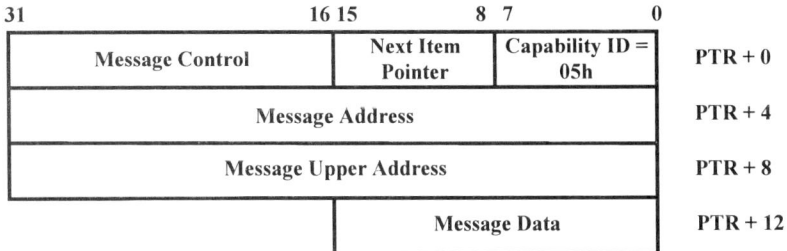

**Figure 24-11: 64 Bit MA Message Signaled Interrupt Capability
Structure Layout**

CAPABILITY IDENTIFIER REGISTER

Capability Identifier	
Offset:	00h of the Message Signaled Interrupt Capability Structure
Width:	1 Byte
Valid Values:	00h-FFh
	A value of 05h indicates the structure supports Message Signaled Interrupts Capability as defined in the *PCI Local Bus Specification*. This specification can be obtained from the PCI Special Interest Group at http://www.pcisig.com.
Description:	This register identifies the specific capability supported by a structure member of a PCI Capabilities Linked List.

Bits	Type	Function
7::0	Read Only	**Capability Identifier** This value identifies a capability supported by a PCI function. Capability IDs are assigned by the PCI SIG.

Table 24-41: Capability Identifier Register

NEXT ITEM POINTER REGISTER

Next Item Pointer	
Offset:	01h of the Message Signaled Interrupt Capability Data Structure
Width:	1 Byte
Valid Values:	00h, 40h-FCh (must be DWORD aligned)
Description:	This register identifies the absolute offset of the start of the next structure member of a Capabilities Linked List. A value of 00h indicates this structure is the last one in the list.

Bit	Type	Function
7::0	Read Only	**Next Item Pointer** This value identifies the start location of the next item (capability data structure) in a PCI function's Capabilities Linked List.

Table 24-42: Next Item Pointer Register

MESSAGE CONTROL REGISTER

Message Control	
Offset:	02h of the Message Signaled Interrupts Capability Structure
Width:	2 Bytes
Valid Values:	N/A. This field is a collection of bits, not a range of values. The register should not be viewed as values, but as individual bits.
Description:	The bits in this register allow system software to control MSI as well as indicate the function's capabilities.

Bit	Type	Function
0	Read/Write	**MSI Enable** 0 MSI is disabled and cannot be used to request service. The function is allowed to use its INTx# pin (if implemented). 1 The function is allowed to use MSI to request service. The function is not allowed to use its INTx# pin (if implemented). A reset will set this bit to "0", disabling MSI. System software sets this bit to a "1" to enable MSI. Device drivers should never set this bit to a "0" in order to mask the function's service request.
3::1	Read Only	**Multiple Message Capable** This field specifies the number of requested messages. The number must be aligned to a power of two. For example, set the bit value of this field to "011" if either five, six, seven or eight messages are required. The encoding of the **Multiple Message Capable** bits is as follows: 3 2 1 # of Messages Requested 0 0 0 1 0 0 1 2 0 1 0 4 0 1 1 8 1 0 0 16 1 0 1 32 1 1 0 Reserved 1 1 1 Reserved

Table 24-43: Message Control Register

6::4	Read/Write	**Multiple Message Enable**
		This field specifies the number of messages allocated by system software. The number of enabled messages must be equal to or less than the number of requested messages specified by bits [3::1]. For example, system software can set the bit value of this field to either "010", "001" or "000" to allocate four, two or one messages, respectively, when the number of requested messages is four.
		A device will be allocated at least one message when MSI is enabled (Message Control register, bit [0]=1).
		The encoding of the **Multiple Message Enable** bits is as follows:

6	5	4	# of Messages Allocated
0	0	0	1 (reset state)
0	0	1	2
0	1	0	4
0	1	1	8
1	0	0	16
1	0	1	32
1	1	0	Reserved
1	1	1	Reserved

7	Read Only	**64-Bit Address Capable**
		0 PCI function cannot generate a 64 bit message address.
		1 PCI function can generate a 64 bit message address.
15::8	Read Only	**Reserved**

Table 24-43: Message Control Register (continued)

MESSAGE ADDRESS REGISTER

Message Address	
Offset:	04h of the Message Signaled Interrupts Capability Structure
Width:	4 Bytes
Valid Values:	System Specific
Description:	This register's value specifies the DWORD aligned address for the MSI memory write transaction. AD[31::02] are driven with the target address while AD[01::00] are driven to zero during the address phase of the write transaction.

Bit	Type	Function
1::0	Read Only	**Reserved** This field will return 00b when read. Memory writes have no effect on bits [1::0].
31::2	Read/Write	**Message Address** This field is programmed with the lower DWORD of the message destination address of the MSI. It is DWORD aligned. Message Control register bit [0], MSI Enable, must be set to '1' for this register to be functional.

Table 24-44: Message Address Register

MESSAGE UPPER ADDRESS REGISTER

Message Upper Address (Optional)	
Offset:	08h of the Message Signaled Interrupts Capability Structure
Width:	4 Bytes
Valid Values:	System Specific
Description:	This register's value specifies the upper 32 bits of a 64 bit message address driven during the address phase of a MSI memory write transaction. The **Message Upper Address** register is only implemented if a device supports 64 bit messaging.

Bit	Type	Function
31::0	Read Write	**Message Upper Address** This field is programmed with the upper 32 bits of the message destination address, AD[63::32], of the MSI. It is DWORD aligned. Message Control register bit [0], MSI Enable, and bit [7], 64 Bit Addess Capable, must both be set to '1' for this register to be functional. If the value of this register is set to zero by system software, the device will only drive AD[31::2] with the contents of the Message Address register to address the target during the address phase of the write transaction.

Table 24-45: Message Upper Address Register

MESSAGE DATA REGISTER

Message Data	
Offset:	08h of the MSI Capability Data Structure if 32-bit message address
	0Ch of the MSI Capability Data Structure if 64-bit message address
Width:	2 Bytes
Valid Values:	System Specific
Description:	This register's value specifies a system specific encoded message that is transmitted by the device during the data phase of a MSI memory write transaction.

Bit	Type	Function
31::0	Read Write	**Message Data**
		This field is programmed with the encoded data to be transmitted to the target during the data phase of a MSI. Encoding is achieved by modifying certain bits in the *Message Data* register. Up to 32 unique messages can be generated in the manner described below.
		The actual bits that can be modified in the **Message Data** register is a function of both the **Multiple Message Capable** field, bits [3::1], and the **Multiple Message Enable** field, bits [6::4], of the **Message Control** register. The **Multiple Message Capable** field is read only and defines the number of messages requested by a function. System software reads this field. Based on the system's requirements, the system software will write to the **Multiple Message Enable** field to indicate the number of messages allocated to the function. This value is aligned to a power of two.
		The number of allocated messages must be equal to or less than the number of requested messages.
		The value of the **Multiple Message Enable** field determines how many of the bits of the **Message Data** register can be modified to generate specific messages. For example, when the **Multiple Message Enable** field is programmed with a value of '010', four unique messages (00b, 01b, 10b and 11b) can be supported by the function. In this example, system software can generate a specific message by setting bits[1::0] of the **Message Data** register to the desired value; bits [15::2] of the **Message Data** register are not permitted to be modified when the **Multiple Message Enable** field is programmed with a value of '010'.

Table 24-46: Message Data Register

		Message Control register bit [0], MSI Enable, must be set to '1' to permit the device to drive AD[15::0] during the data phase of the memory write transaction.
		The Message Data register cannot be modified when the Multiple Message Enable field is programmed with a value of '000'. As a result, a device will always be allocated at least one message when MSI is enabled.
		AD[31::16] are driven to zero during the data phase of the memory write transaction.
		All byte enables, C/BE[3::0] are asserted during the data phase of the memory write transaction.
		The Message Data register must be a DWORD aligned, WORD write.

Table 24-46: Message Data Register (continued)

MSI OPERATION

System software is responsible for detecting, configuring and controlling a PCI function's MSI capability. Below is a summary of MSI operation. See the *PCI Local Bus Specification* for additional information.

CONFIGURING THE MSI CAPABILITY

Provided a PCI function supports MSI, system software must configure the function's MSI capability to operate within system specifications as follows:

- System software determines how many MSI messages the PCI function has requested by reading the **Multiple Message Capable** field, bits [3::1], of the **Message Control** register. Because the number of requested messages is aligned to a power of two, a PCI function that wants to support an odd number of messages must round the request up to the next valid boundary as specified in bits [3::1]. For example, if a PCI function requires 5 messages, read-only bits [3::1] will be set to "011b", which indicates that 8 messages are requested.

A PCI function is not allowed to request more messages than it can utilize.

- Based on the value of the **Multiple Message Capable** field, system software allocates all or a subset of the messages requested by programming the **Multiple Message Enable** field, bits [6::4], of the

1321

Message Control register. The actual number of messages enabled is system specific. The number of allocated messages that a PCI function is programmed to support is aligned to a power of two. For example, if a PCI function requests five messages, read-write bits [6::4] can be set to "011b", "010", "001", or "000" to indicate that the number of allocated messages is 8, 4, 2, or 1, respectively. Consequently, as a minimum, PCI functions are always allocated at least one message when MSI is enabled via the **MSI Enable** field, bit [0] of the **Message Control** register. Note that when the number of allocated messages is 1 (**Multiple Message Enable** field, bits [6::4], programmed to "000") system software is not allowed to modify the **Message Data** register contents.

> A PCI function is required to gracefully handle the case where it is allocated fewer messages than it actually requested.

■ System software must initialize the system specific MSI message destination address by programming the PCI function's **Message Address** register and, optionally, its **Message Upper Address** register:

■ If the read-only **64-Bit Address Capable field**, bit [7], of the **Message Control** register is '0', only the **Message Address** register is programmed with the system specific MSI message destination address. In this case the PCI function only supports 32 bit address space for the message destination address.

■ If the read-only **64 Bit Address Capable field**, bit [7], of the **Message Control** register is '1', both the **Message Address** register and the **Message Upper Address** register are programmed with the system specific MSI message destination address. Note that the **Message Upper Address** register can be programmed with a value of zero. In this case the PCI function will only generate a 32 bit address during the address phase of the MSI write transaction (only AD [31::0] are driven with the contents of the Message Address register). As a result, the PCI function can support a message destination address that resides in either 32 bit or 64 bit address space.

■ System software programs the **Message Data** register with a system specific message.

CONTROLLING THE MSI CAPABILITY

System software sets the **MSI Enable** field, bit [0], of the **Message Control** register to a '1'. This simultaneously enables the PCI function's MSI functionality and disables **INTx#** pin operation. At this point, the PCI function can generate an MSI. System software specifies the message to be sent by writing the **Message Data** register.

> How a PCI function uses multiple MSI messages is device dependent.

MSI SPECIFIC DEVICE DRIVERS

A PCI device is capable of generating back-to-back MSI messages of the same type. At least the first message is guaranteed to be serviced in this case. If subsequent back-to-back messages of the same type are required to be serviced, the device driver must contain code to prevent the PCI device from generating another MSI message until the previous MSI message has been serviced. If subsequent back-to-back messages of the same type are not required to be serviced, the device driver does not have to contain code to prevent the PCI device from generating a MSI message until the previous one is serviced. In addition, for PCI functions that support more than one unique message, the device driver is required to service each and every unique message without a device driver handshake.

> A PCI function's device driver is not required to read its device prior to servicing its MSI.

PCI-X CONSIDERATIONS

HARDWARE

- If the PCI-X device can generate interrupts it must support MSI and a 64 bit message address.

- Some systems do not support MSI. In this case, PCI-X devices used in these systems must also implement hardware interrupt pins.

SOFTWARE

- Software must not assume that message capable PCI devices have an associated hardware interrupt pin.

- Software can be written to transparently support both polling of PCI-X devices in systems that do not support MSI as well as supporting messages in those systems that do support MSI.

- The requester of an MSI transaction is required to set **No Snoop** in the Requester Attributes to '0' during the attribute phase of a transaction.

■ The requester of an MSI transaction is required to set the **Relaxed Ordering** bit in the Requester Attributes to '0' during the attribute phase of a transaction.

24.7 PCI-X (HEADER TYPE 00H)

This section describes the PCI-X Header Type 00H Capability interface. The PCI-X Header Type 00H interface applies to devices that are not PCI-X bridge functions. This interface permits system software to detect and manage individual PCI functions that incorporate the PCI-X feature.

> Multi-function PCI devices are required to include The PCI-X capability structure in the Capabilities List of each PCI function within the device. In addition, the PCI-X capability structure must be accessible regardless of whether the device is operating PCI-X mode or conventional PCI mode.

Figure 24-12 and Table 24-47 illustrate the layout and design of the PCI-X Header Type 00H capability data structure. The structure is eight bytes in length.

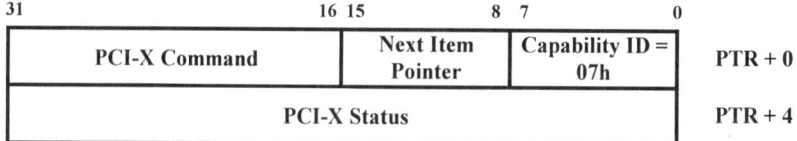

31	16	15	8	7	0	
PCI-X Command		**Next Item Pointer**		**Capability ID = 07h**		PTR + 0
PCI-X Status						PTR + 4

Figure 24-12: PCI-X Capability Structure Header Layout (Type 00H)

Offset	Bits	Register/Field	Attributes	Description
0	7::0	Capability ID	Required Read Only	Identifies PCI-X as the capability of the structure with a value of 07h.
1	15::8	Next Item Pointer	Required Read Only	Provides the absolute offset to the next item in the Capabilities Linked List (00h if last structure)
2	31::16	PCI-X Command	Required Read/Write	Permits control of the function's PCI-X modes and features
4	63::32	PCI-X Status	Required Read/Write	Identifies the function's PCI-X capabilities and current operating mode

Table 24-47: PCI-X Capability Structure Definition (Header Type 00H)

CAPABILITY IDENTIFIER REGISTER

Capability Identifier	
Offset:	00h of the PCI-X Header Type 00H Capability Structure
Width:	1 Byte
Valid Values:	00h-FFh
	A value of 07h indicates the structure supports the PCI-X capability as defined in the *PCI-X Addendum to the PCI Local Bus Specification*. This specification can be obtained from the PCI Special Interest Group at http://www.pcisig.com.
Description:	This register identifies the specific capability supported by a structure member of a PCI Capabilities Linked List.

Bit	Type	Function
7::0	Read Only	**Capability Identifier** This value identifies a capability supported by a PCI function. Capability IDs are assigned by the PCI SIG.

Table 24-48: Capability Identifier Register

07h, the PCI-X Header Type 00H Capability ID, is also the value used for the PCI-X Header Type 01H capability. Software must determine which PCI header type it is managing. How to accomplish this is described below.

PCI configuration address space offset 0Eh is the Header Type register. System software can use this register to determine if a PCI-X device is a bridge and whether the device is a single or multi-function device.

Bits [6::0] of the Header Type register are used by system software to determine the layout of the predefined header of a PCI device as follows:

00h – Type 00h Configuration Space Header

01h – Type 01h Configuration Space Header – PCI/PCI Bridge

02h – Type 02h Configuration Space Header – CardBus Bridge

Bit [7] of the Header Type register is also used by system software to determine if a PCI device is a single or multi-function device, as follows:

'0' - indicates a single function device

'1' indicates a multi-function device

NEXT ITEM POINTER REGISTER

Next Item Pointer	
Offset:	01h of the PCI-X Header Type 00H Capability Structure
Width:	1 Byte
Valid Values:	00h, 40h-FCh (must be DWORD aligned)
Description:	This register identifies the absolute offset of the start of the next structure member of a Capabilities Linked List. A value of 00h indicates this structure is the last one in the list.

Bit	Type	Function
7::0	Read Only	**Next Item Pointer** This value identifies the start location of the next item (capability data structure) in a PCI function's Capabilities Linked List.

Table 24-49: Next Item Pointer Register

PCI-X COMMAND REGISTER (HEADER TYPE 00H)

PCI-X Command	
Offset:	02h of the PCI-X Header Type 00H Capability Structure
Width:	2 Bytes
Valid Values:	N/A. This field is a collection of bits, not a range of values. The register should not be viewed as values, but as individual bits.
Description:	The bits in this register permit the function's PCI-X features and modes to be controlled.

Bit	Type	Function
0	Read/Write	**Data Parity Error Recovery Enable** 0 If the device is in PCI-X mode and the **Master Data Parity Error** bit (bit [8] of the PCI function's **Status** registor) is set, the PCI device will assert the **SERR#** signal, providing **SERR#** enabled. 1 Set by the device driver, the device is enabled to attempt recovery from data parity errors. State after **RST#** is 0.

Table 24-50: PCI-X Command Register (Header Type 00H)

1	Read/Write	**Enable Relaxed Ordering** 0 When the device initiates transactions that do not require strong write ordering, the device is not allowed to set the Relaxed Ordering bit in the transaction's Requester Attributes. 1 When the device initiates transactions that do not require strong write ordering, the device is allowed to set the Relaxed Ordering bit in the transaction's Requester Attributes. Devices that never set the Relaxed Ordering attribute bit can implement bit [1] as read-only and set to '0'. State after **RST#** is 1 (if bit is read/write).
3::2	Read/Write	**Maximum Memory Read Byte Count** The value programmed into this field sets the maximum byte count the device uses upon initiating a Sequence with one of the burst memory read commands. This field enables system software to tune the system's performance. See the definition of bits [22::21] of the PCI-X Status register for more details. <table><tr><th colspan="2">Bits</th><th>Maximum</th></tr><tr><td>3</td><td>2</td><td>Byte Count</td></tr><tr><td>0</td><td>0</td><td>512</td></tr><tr><td>0</td><td>1</td><td>1024</td></tr><tr><td>1</td><td>0</td><td>2048</td></tr><tr><td>1</td><td>1</td><td>4096</td></tr></table> This field may be modified during run-time. To understand the ramifications of modifying this field, see Chapter 13 of the PCI-X Addendum to the PCI Local Bus Specification. State after **RST#** is 00.

Table 24-50: PCI-X Command Register (Header Type 00H)
(continued)

6::4	Read/Write	**Maximum Outstanding Split Transactions** The value programmed into this field sets the maximum number of split transactions the device is permitted to have outstanding at one time. This field enables system software to tune the system's performance. See the definition of bits [25::23] of the PCI-X Status register for more details.

	Bits		**Maximum Outstanding**
6	**5**	**4**	**Split transactions**
0	0	0	1
0	0	1	2
0	1	0	3
0	1	1	4
1	0	0	8
1	0	1	12
1	1	0	16
1	1	1	32

This field may be modified during run-time.

This field can be implemented as read-only by Host bridges.

Hardware sets the value of this field after **RST#** with the value equal to the maximum number of split transactions that the device is designed to have outstanding when the **Maximum Memory Read Byte Count** field is set to '00', or 512 bytes.

15::7	Read Only	**Reserved**

Table 24-50: PCI-X Command Register (Header Type 00H)
(continued)

PCI-X STATUS REGISTER (HEADER TYPE 00H)

PCI-X Status	
Offset:	04h of the PCI-X Header Type 00H Capability Structure
Width:	4 Bytes
Valid Values:	N/A. This field is a collection of bits, not a range of values. The register should not be viewed as values, but as individual bits.
Description:	The bits in this register identifies the function's PCI-X capabilities and current operating mode.

Bit	Type	Function
2::0	Read Only	**Function Number** The value in this field indicates this function's number. This is the number the function responds to during a Type 0 PCI configuration address space transaction. Valid values are 0 though 7, which correspond to the possible values of the Function Number field (**AD[10::8]**) during a Type 0 transaction. The PCI function uses the Function Number as part of its Requestor ID and Completer ID. This field is read for diagnostic purposes only.
7::3	Read Only	**Device Number** The value in this field indicates the number of the PCI device that contains this function. This is the number specified in the Device Number field (**AD[15::11]**) during a Type 0 PCI configuration address space transaction. Valid values for this field are 1h though 1Fh. The actual device number is determined by how the device is connected to the system hardware. The device is required to update the Device Number field of this function with the contents of AD[15::11] of the PCI configuration write transaction's address phase. This field must be updated regardless of which register in the function was the target of the configuration write transaction. The following must occur for a PCI configuration write to this function: 1. The transaction uses the PCI Configuration Write command. 2. The IDSEL signal line is asserted during the address phase of the transaction. 3. AD[1::0] are set to 00b, specifying a Type 0 configuration transaction. 4. AD[10::8] of the PCI configuration address contains the appropriate function number. The PCI function uses the Device Number as part of its Requestor ID and Completer ID. The value of this field will always be non-zero. The reason is because 00h is reserved for the source bridge. This field is read for diagnostic purposes only.

Table 24-51: PCI-X Status Register (Header Type 00H)

		State after **RST#** is 1Fh
15::8	Read Only	**Bus Number** The value in this field indicates the number of the PCI bus segment that the device that contains this function resides on. The bus number of a PCI configuration write transaction is contained in **AD[7::0]** during the attribute phase of the transaction. Valid values for this field are 1h though FFh.
		The device is required to update the Bus Number field of this function with the contents of AD[7::0] of the PCI configuration write transaction's attribute phase. This field must be updated regardless of which register in the function was the target of the configuration write transaction. The following must occur for a PCI configuration write to this function: 1. The transaction uses the PCI Configuration Write command. 2. The IDSEL signal line is asserted during the address phase of the transaction. 3. AD[1::0] are set to 00b, specifying a Type 0 configuration transaction. 4. AD[10::8] of the PCI configuration address contains the appropriate function number. The PCI function uses the Device Number as part of its Requestor ID and Completer ID. This register is read for diagnostic purposes only.
		State after **RST#** is 1Fh
16	Read Only	**64-bit Device** 0 Bus width is 32 bits 1 Bus width is 64 bits The value in this field is used by system management software. The software reads this bit and uses its value to help identify which PCI slot in the system should be used for an add-card.
		This bit is set to '1' when the PCI function is part of a device integrated on an add-in card, the device on the add-in card is electrically connected directly to the PCI slot and not through a bridge, and the following requirements are met: 1. The function implements a 64-bit AD interface. 2. The device implements a 64-bit AD interface. 3. The add-in card implements a 64-bit PCI connector. When the device is subordinate to a bridge on an add-in card or the device is integrated on the system board as opposed to an add-in card inserted into a PCI slot, the bit may contain a value of either '0' or '1'.

Table 24-51: PCI-X Status Register (Header Type 00H)
(continued)

17	Read Only	**133MHz Capable** 0 66MHz is the maximum operating frequency of the device 1 133MHz is the maximum operating frequency of the device The value in this field is used by system management software. The software reads this bit and uses its value to help identify which PCI slot in the system should be used for an add-card. In addition, software can use this bit to determine if the add-in card would work properly if the bus it was connected to in a hot plug system were changed to PCI-X 133 mode. This bit indicates whether the device is capable of 133MHz operation in PCI-X 133 mode when the function is part of a device integrated on an add-in card and the device on the add-in card is connected directly to the PCI slot and not through a bridge. When the device is subordinate to a bridge on an add-in card or the device is integrated on the system board as opposed to an add-in card inserted into a PCI slot, the bit may contain a value of either '0' or '1'. If the device is integrated on a add-in card, the add-in card's PCIXCAP pin is required to be consistent with this bit.
18	Read/Write/ Clear	**Split Completion Discarded** 0 No Split Completion has been discarded 1 A Split Completion has been discarded This bit is set when a requester would not accept a Split Completion. When this occurs, the device is forced to discard the Split Completion. This bit remains set to '1' until it is cleared to '0' by software writing a '1' to this bit's location. State after **RST#** is 0.
19	Read/Write/ Clear	**Unexpected Split Completion** 0 No unexpected Split Completion has been received 1 An unexpected Split Completion has been received This bit is set when an unexpected Split Completion with this device's Requester ID is received. This bit remains set to '1' until it is cleared to '0' by software writing a '1' to this bit's location. State after **RST#** is 0.
20	Read Only	**Device Complexity** 0 Simple device 1 Bridge device

Table 24-51: PCI-X Status Register (Header Type 00H)
(continued)

22::21	Read Only	**Designed Maximum Memory Read Byte Count** The value of this field specifies the maximum byte count (or a greater value) that the function is designed to use. This value is applicable when the device initiates a Sequence with one of the burst memory read commands.
		Bits **22 21** **Maximum** **Byte Count** 0 0 512 0 1 1024 1 0 2048 1 1 4096
		The smallest value that correctly indicates the capability of the device must be reported. If system software sets the Maximum Memory Read Byte Count register in the PCI-X Command register to a different value than the one specified in this field, the device will use the smaller value.
25::23	ReadOnly	**Designed Maximum Outstanding Split Transactions** The value of this field is either equal to or greater than the maximum number of split transactions the function is permitted to have outstanding at one time.
		Bits **25 24 23** **Maximum Outstanding** **Split transactions** 0 0 0 1 0 0 1 2 0 1 0 3 0 1 1 4 1 0 0 8 1 0 1 12 1 1 0 16 1 1 1 32
		The smallest value that correctly indicates the capability of the function must be reported. If system software sets the Maximum Outstanding Split Transaction register in the PCI-X Command register to a different value than the one specified in this field, the device will use the smaller value.
28::26	ReadOnly	**Designed Maximum Cumulative Read Size** The value of this field is either equal to or greater than the maximum cumulative size of all burst memory read transactions that the function is designed to have outstanding at one time.

Table 24-51: PCI-X Status Register (Header Type 00H)
(continued)

		Bits			Max. Outstanding	Bytes
		28	**27**	**26**	**ADQs**	**(ref)**
		0	0	0	8	1 KB
		0	0	1	16	2 KB
		0	1	0	32	4 KB
		0	1	1	64	8 KB
		1	0	0	128	16 KB
		1	0	1	256	32 KB
		1	1	0	512	64 KB
		1	1	1	1024	128 KB
		The smallest value that correctly indicates the capability of the function must be reported				
29	Read/Write/ Clear	**Received Split Completion Error Message** 0　　No Split Completion error message has been received 1　　A Split Completion error message has been received This bit is set when the device receives a Split Completion Message with the Split Completion Error Attribute bit set. This bit remains set to '1' until it is cleared to '0' by software writing a '1' to this bit's location. State after **RST#** is 0.				
31::30	Read Only	**Reserved**				

Table 24-51: PCI-X Status Register (Header Type 00H)
(continued)

24.8 PCI-X (HEADER TYPE 01H)

This section describes the PCI-X Header Type 01H Capability interface. The PCI-X Header Type 01H interface applies to PCI bridge devices that incorporate a Type 01h PCI configuration address space header region as well as the PCI-X Capabilities List item. This PCI capability permits system software to detect and manage individual PCI functions that incorporate the PCI-X bridge features.

> A PCI-X bridge can be part of a multi-function PCI device. In this case, each function within the PCI device is required to include the PCI-X capability structure in the Capabilities List. In addition, the PCI-X capability structure must be accessible regardless of whether the device is operating PCI-X mode or conventional PCI mode.

Figure 24-13 and Table 24-52 illustrate the layout and design of the PCI-X Header Type 01H capability data structure. The structure is eight bytes in length.

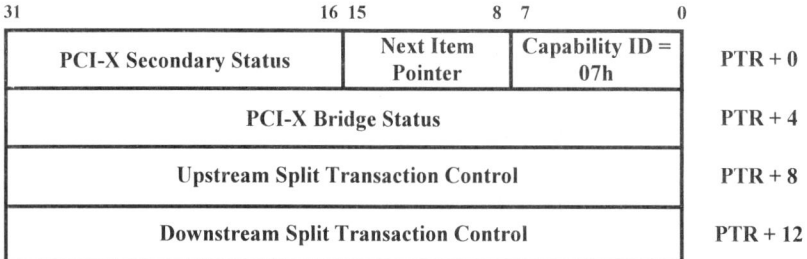

Figure 24-13: PCI-X Capability Structure Layout
(Header Type 01H)

Offset	Bits	Register/Field	Attributes	Description
0	7::0	Capability ID	Required Read Only	Identifies PCI-X as the capability of the structure with a value of 07h.
1	15::8	Next Item Pointer	Required Read Only	Provides the absolute offset to the next item in the Capabilities Linked List (00h if last structure)
2	31::16	PCI-X Status	Required Read/Write	Permits control of the function's PCI-X modes and features
4	63::32	PCI-X Status	Required Read/Write	Identifies the function's PCI-X capabilities and current operating mode
8	95::64	Upstream Split Transaction Control	Required Read/Write	Identifies the function's PCI-X capabilities and current operating mode
12	127::96	Downstream Split Transaction Control	Required Read/Write	Identifies the function's PCI-X capabilities and current operating mode

Table 24-52: PCI-X Capability Structure Definition
(Header Type 01H)

CAPABILITY IDENTIFIER REGISTER

Capability Identifier	
Offset:	00h of the the PCI-X Header Type 01H Capability Structure
Width:	1 Byte
Valid Values:	00h-FFh
	A value of 07h indicates the structure supports the PCI-X capability as defined in the *PCI-X Addendum to the PCI Local Bus Specification*. This specification can be obtained from the PCI Special Interest Group at http://www.pcisig.com.
Description:	This register identifies the specific capability supported by a structure member of a PCI Capabilities Linked List.

Bit	Type	Function
7::0	Read Only	**Capability Identifier** This value identifies a capability supported by a PCI function. Capability IDs are assigned by the PCI SIG.

Table 24-53: Capability Identifier Register

07h, the PCI-X Header Type 01H Capability ID, is also the value used for the PCI-X Header Type 00H capability. Software must determine which PCI header type it is managing. How to accomplish this is described below.

PCI configuration address space offset 0Eh is the Header Type register. System software can use this register to determine if a PCI-X device is a bridge and whether the device is a single or multi-function device.

Bits [6::0] of the Header Type register are used by system software to determine the layout of the predefined header of a PCI device as follows:

00h – Type 00h Configuration Space Header

01h – Type 01h Configuration Space Header – PCI//PCI Bridge

02h – Type 02h Configuration Space Header – CardBus Bridge

Bit [7] of the Header Type register is also used by system software to determine if a PCI device is a single or multi-function device as follows:

'0' - indicates a single function device

'1' indicates a multi-function device

NEXT ITEM POINTER REGISTER

Next Item Pointer	
Offset:	01h of the PCI-X Header Type 01H Capability Structure
Width:	1 Byte
Valid Values:	00h, 40h-FCh (must be DWORD aligned)
Description:	This register identifies the absolute offset of the start of the next structure member of a Capabilities Linked List. A value of 00h indicates this structure is the last one in the list.

Bit	Type	Function
7::0	Read Only	**Next Item Pointer** This value identifies the start location of the next item (capability data structure) in a PCI function's Capabilities Linked List.

Table 24-54: Next Item Pointer Register

PCI-X SECONDARY STATUS REGISTER (HEADER TYPE 01H)

PCI-X Secondary Status	
Offset:	02h of the PCI-X Header Type 01H Capability Structure
Width:	2 Bytes
Valid Values:	N/A. This field is a collection of bits, not a range of values. The register should not be viewed as values, but as individual bits.
Description:	The bits in this register report the PCI-X bridge function's secondary bus status information.

Bit	Type	Function
0	Read Only	**64-bit Device** 0 Bus width of the bridge's secondary **AD** interface is 32 bits wide. 1 Bus width of the bridge's secondary **AD** interface is 62 bits wide.
1	Read Only	**133MHz Capable** This bit indicates that an operating frequency of 133MHz in PCI-X mode is allowed on the bridge's secondary interface 0 Maximum frquency is 66MHz 1 Maximum frquency is 133MHz

Table 24-55: PCI-X Secondary Status Register
(Header Type 01H)

2	Read/Write/ Clear	**Split Completion Discarded** 0 No Split Completion has been discarded 1 A Split Completion has been discarded The bridge sets this bit because a requester would not accept a Split Completion that was moving towards the bridge's secondary interface. When this occurs, the bridge is forced to discard the Split Completion. This bit remains set to '1' until it is cleared to '0' by software writing a '1' to this bit's location. State after **RST#** is 0.
3	Read/Write/ Clear	**Unexpected Split Completion** 0 No unexpected Split Completion has been received 1 An unexpected Split Completion has been received This bit is set when an unexpected Split Completion with a Requester ID that equals the bridge's secondary bus number, device number 00h, and function number 0 is received on the bridge's secondary bus interface. This bit remains set to '1' until it is cleared to '0' by software writing a '1' to this bit's location. State after **RST#** is 0.
4	Read/Write/ Clear	**Split Completion Overrun** 0 Bridge has accepted all split completions 1 The bridge's buffers were full. The bridge has terminated the Split Completion with a Retry or Disconnect at Next ADB. Algorithms that optimize the setting of the **Downstream Split Transaction Commitment Limit** register use this bit. This bit remains set to '1' until it is cleared to '0' by software writing a '1' to this bit's location. State after **RST#** is 0.
5	Read/Write/ Clear	**Split Request Delayed** 0 Bridge has not delayed split request 1 Bridge has not delayed split request This bit is set when the bridge is prevented from forwarding a transaction on its secondary bus due to not enough room within the limit specified in the **Transaction Commitment Limit** field in the **Downstream Split Transaction Control** register. Algorithms that optimize the setting of the **Downstream Split Transaction Commitment Limit** register use this bit. This bit remains set to '1' until it is cleared to '0' by software writing a '1' to this bit's location.

Table 24-55: PCI-X Secondary Status Register
(Header Type 01H) (continued)

8::6	ReadOnly	**Secondary Clock Frequency**
		System configuration software needs to know the mode and (in PCI-X mode) frequency the bridge set the secondary bus to the last time secondary **RST#** was asserted.

	Bits		**Maximum Clock**	**Minimum Clock**
8	**7**	**6**	**Frequency (MHz) (ref)**	**Period (ns)**
0	0	0	Conventional Mode	N/A
0	0	1	66	15
0	1	0	100	10
0	1	1	133	7.5
1	0	0	Reserved	Reserved
1	0	1	Reserved	Reserved
1	1	0	Reserved	Reserved
1	1	1	Reserved	Reserved

		This information was also used to create the PCI-X initialization pattern on the bridge's secondary bus the last time RST# was asserted.
15::9	Read Only	**Reserved**

Table 24-55: PCI-X Secondary Status Register
(Header Type 01H) (continued)

PCI-X BRIDGE STATUS REGISTER (HEADER TYPE 01H)

PCI-X Bridge Status	
Offset:	04h of the PCI-X Header Type 01H Capability Data Structure
Width:	4 Bytes
Valid Values:	N/A. This field is a collection of bits, not a range of values. The register should not be viewed as values, but as individual bits.
Description:	The bits in this register identifies the PCI-X bridge function's capabilities and current operating mode on the bridge's primary bus.

Bit	Type	Function
2::0	Read Only	**Function Number** The value in this field indicates this function's number. This is the number the function responds to during a Type 0 PCI configuration address space transaction. Valid values are 0 though 7, which correspond to the possible values of the Function Number field (**AD[10::8]**) during a Type 0 transaction. Along with the Bus Number and Device Number fields, the PCI-X Bridge function uses the Function Number field to create the Completer ID when responding with a Split Completion to a read of an internal bridge register. This field is read for diagnostic purposes only.
7::3	Read Only	**Device Number** The value in this field indicates the number of the PCI device that contains this bridge function. This is the number specified in the Device Number field (**AD[15::11]**) during a Type 0 PCI configuration address space transaction. Valid values for this field are 1h though 1Fh. The actual device number is determined by how the device is connected to the system hardware. The bridge is required to update the Device Number field of this function with the contents of AD[15::11] of the PCI configuration write transaction's address phase. This field must be updated regardless of which register in the function was the target of the configuration write transaction. The following must occur for a PCI configuration write transaction to this bridge function: 1. The transaction uses the PCI Configuration Write command. 2. The IDSEL signal line is asserted during the address phase of the transaction. 3. AD[1::0] are set to 00b, specifying a Type 0 configuration transaction. 4. AD[10::8] of the PCI configuration address contains the appropriate function number. Along with the Bus Number and Function Number fields, the PCI-X Bridge function uses the Device Number field to create the Completer ID when responding with a Split Completion to a read of an internal bridge register. This field is read for diagnostic purposes only. State after **RST#** is 1Fh

Table 24-56: PCI-X Bridge Status Register (Header Type 01H) (continued)

15::8	Read Only	**Bus Number** This field is actually an additional location from which the contents of the **Primary Bus Number** register in the Type 01h PCI Configuration Address Space header can be read. Along with the Device Number and Function Number fields, the PCI-X Bridge function uses the Bus Number field to create the Completer ID when responding with a Split Completion to a read of an internal bridge register. This register is read for diagnostic purposes only.
16	Read Only	**64-bit Device** 0 Bus width is 32 bits 1 Bus width is 64 bits The value in this field is used by system management software. The software reads this bit and uses its value to help identify which PCI slot in the system should be used for an add-card. This bit is set to '1' when the bridge function is part of a device integrated on an add-in card, the device on the add-in card is electrically connected directly to the PCI slot and not through a bridge, and the following requirements are met: 1. The bridge function implements a 64-bit AD interface on its primary side. 2. The device implements a 64-bit AD interface on its primary side. 3. The add-in card implements a 64-bit PCI connector. When the bridge is subordinate to another bridge on an add-in card or the bridge is integrated on the system board as opposed to an add-in card inserted into a PCI slot, the bit may contain a value of either '0' or '1'.
17	Read Only	**133MHz Capable** 0 66MHz is the maximum operating frequency of the device 1 133MHz is the maximum operating frequency of the device The value in this field is used by system management software. The software reads this bit and uses its value to help identify which PCI slot in the system should be used for an add-card. In addition, software can use this bit to determine if the add-in card would work properly if the bus it was connected to in a hot plug system were changed to PCI-X 133 mode. This bit indicates whether the bridge's primary interface is capable of 133MHz operation in PCI-X 133 mode when the bridge function is part of a device integrated on an add-in card. The device on the add-in card must be electrically connected directly to the PCI slot and not through a bridge. When the bridge is subordinate to another bridge on an add-in card or the bridge is integrated on the system board as opposed to an add-in card inserted into a PCI slot, the bit may contain a value of either '0' or '1'.

Table 24-56: PCI-X Bridge Status Register (Header Type 01H)
(continued)

1340

18	Read/Write/ Clear	**Split Completion Discarded** 0 No Split Completion has been discarded 1 A Split Completion has been discarded This bit is set when a requester on the bridges primary bus would not accept a Split Completion. When this occurs, the bridge is forced to discard the Split Completion. This bit remains set to '1' until it is cleared to '0' by software writing a '1' to this bit's location. State after **RST#** is 0.
19	Read/Write/ Clear	**Unexpected Split Completion** 0 No unexpected Split Completion has been received 1 An unexpected Split Completion has been received This bit is set when an unexpected Split Completion with a Requester ID that is equal to the bridge's primary bus number, device number and function number is received on the bridge's primary bus. This bit remains set to '1' until it is cleared to '0' by software writing a '1' to this bit's location. State after **RST#** is 0.
20	Read/Write/ Clear	**Split Completion Overrun** 0 Bridge has accepted all split completions 1 The bridge's buffers were full. The bridge has terminated the Split Completion with a Retry or Disconnect at Next ADB. Algorithms that optimize the setting of the **Upstream Split Transaction Commitment Limit** register use this bit. This bit remains set to '1' until it is cleared to '0' by software writing a '1' to this bit's location. State after **RST#** is 0.
21	Read/Write/ Clear	**Split Request Delayed** 0 Bridge has not delayed split request 1 Bridge has not delayed split request This bit is set when the bridge is prevented from forwarding a transaction on its secondary bus due to not enough room within the limit specified in the **Transaction Commitment Limit** field in the **Upstream Split Transaction Control** register. Algorithms that optimize the setting of the **Upstream Split Transaction Commitment Limit** register use this bit. This bit remains set to '1' until it is cleared to '0' by software writing a '1' to this bit's location.
31::22	Read Only	**Reserved**

Table 24-56: PCI-X Bridge Status Register (Header Type 01H)
(continued)

PCI-X UPSTREAM SPLIT TRANSACTION CONTROL REGISTER (HEADER TYPE 01H)

PCI-X Upstream Split Transaction Control	
Offset:	08h of the PCI-X Header Type 01H Capability Data Structure
Width:	4 Bytes
Valid Values:	N/A. This register is a collection of fields, not a range of values. The register should not be viewed as values as individual bits.
Description:	The fields in this register control the behavior of the bridge function's buffers for forwarding Split Transactions from a secondary bus requestor to a primary bus completer.

Bit	Type	Function
15::0	Read Only	**Split Transaction Capacity** A bridge is permitted to store Split Completions for memory reads in a separate buffer from Split Completions for I/O and PCI configuration address space reads and writes. When a separate buffer for storing memory reads is implemented this register indicates the size of the buffer. The size reported is in the number of ADQs for storing Split Completions for memory reads for requestors on the secondary bus that are addressing completers on the primary bus. Bridges that use the same buffer to store memory read, I/O and PCI configuration address space read and write Split Completions, this register indicates the size of this buffer in units of ADQs.
31::16	ReadWrite	**Split Transaction Commitment Limit** A bridge is permitted to store Split Completions for memory reads in a separate buffer from Split Completions for I/O and PCI configuration address space reads and writes. When a separate buffer for storing memory reads is implemented, this register indicates the cumulative Sequence size for all memory read transactions forwarded by the bridge from requestors on the secondary bus that are addressing completers on the primary bus. Bridges that use the same buffer to store memory read, I/O and PCI configuration address space read and write Split Completions, this register indicates the size of all upstream Split Transactions of these types that the bridge is permitted to commit to at one time. **Outstanding Commitments Rules:** 1. The size of the commitment limit is in units of ADQs. 2. If the value in this register is set to 0FFFFh, the bridge does not track the outstanding commitment. 3. Do not set this register to a value of 0FFFFh if the system requires an accurate limitation of Split Transactions.

Table 24-57: PCI-X Upstream Split Transaction Control Register (Header Type 01H)

4. If the system does require an accurate limitation of Split Transactions and this register is set to a value of 0FFFFh, the system should first change the value from 0FFFFh. The system should then place all devices that initiate traffic that crosses the bridge in this direction to a quiescent state.

5. One case to note is where the bridge is programmed with a value of 0FFFFh, and the value is subsequently changed to a non-0FFFFh value. All currently outstanding commitments must complete before the bridge can accurately track outstanding commitments.

6. When this register is programmed with a value of 0FFFFh, the bridge is permitted to forward all Split Requests of any size. This is regardless of the amount of buffer space available.

Software Rules:

1. Software is allowed to program this register to any value greater than or equal to the **Split Transaction Capacity** register.

2. System software is allowed to change the value in this register at any time.

3. The bridge will use the most recently programmed value each time the bridge forwards a Split Transaction.

4. No algorithm is specified for programming this register' value.

5. System software may use any method for selecting the value of this register.

6. A system-level configuration routine should control the programming of this register.

Unspecified results will occur is the programmed value of this register is less than the value of the Split Transaction Capacity register.

State after **RST#** is the same as the **Split Transaction Capacity** register.

Table 24-57: PCI-X Upstream Split Transaction Control Register (Header Type 01H) (continued)

PCI-X DOWNSTREAM SPLIT TRANSACTION CONTROL REGISTER (HEADER TYPE 01H)

PCI-X Upstream Split Transaction Control	
Offset:	12h of the PCI-X Header Type 01H Capability Data Structure
Width:	4 Bytes
Valid Values:	N/A. This register is a collection of fields, not a range of values. The register should not be viewed as values as individual bits.
Description:	The fields in this register control the behavior of the bridge function's buffers for forwarding Split Transactions from a primary bus requestor to a secondary bus completer.

Bit	Type	Function
15::0	Read Only	**Split Transaction Capacity** A bridge is permitted to store Split Completions for memory reads in a separate buffer from Split Completions for I/O and PCI configuration address space reads and writes. When a separate buffer for storing memory reads is implemented, this register indicates the size of the buffer. The size reported is in the number of ADQs for storing Split Completions for memory reads for requestors on the primary bus that are addressing completers on the secondary bus. Bridges that use the same buffer to store memory read, I/O and PCI configuration address space read and write Split Completions, this register indicates the size of this buffer in units of ADQs.
31::16	ReadWrite	**Split Transaction Commitment Limit** A bridge is permitted to store Split Completions for memory reads in a separate buffer from Split Completions for I/O and PCI configuration address space reads and writes. When a separate buffer for storing memory reads is implemented, this register indicates the cumulative Sequence size for all memory read transactions forwarded by the bridge from requestors on the primary bus that are addressing completers on the secondary bus. Bridges that use the same buffer to store memory read, I/O and PCI configuration address space read and write Split Completions, this register indicates the size of all downstream Split Transactions of these types that the bridge is permitted to commit to at one time. **Outstanding Commitments Rules:** 1. The size of the commitment limit is in units of ADQs. 2. If the value in this register is set to 0FFFFh, the bridge does not track the outstanding commitment. 3. Do not set this register to a value of 0FFFFh if the system requires an accurate limitation of Split Transactions.

Table 24-58: PCI-X Downstream Split Transaction Control Register (Header Type 01H)

| | | 4. | If the system does require an accurate limitation of Split Transactions and this register is set to a value of 0FFFFh, the system should first change the value from 0FFFFh. The system should then place all devices that initiate traffic that crosses the bridge in this direction to a quiescent state. |

4. If the system does require an accurate limitation of Split Transactions and this register is set to a value of 0FFFFh, the system should first change the value from 0FFFFh. The system should then place all devices that initiate traffic that crosses the bridge in this direction to a quiescent state.

5. One case to note is where the bridge is programmed with a value of 0FFFFh, and the value is subsequently changed to a non-0FFFFh value. All currently outstanding commitments must complete before the bridge can accurately track outstanding commitments.

6. When this register is programmed with a value of 0FFFFh, the bridge is permitted to forward all Split Requests of any size. This is regardless of the amount of buffer space available.

Software Rules:

1. Software is allowed to program this register to any value greater than or equal to the **Split Transaction Capacity** register.

2. System software is allowed to change the value in this register at any time.

3. The bridge will use the most recently programmed value each time the bridge forwards a Split Transaction.

4. No algorithm is specified for programming this register' value.

5. System software may use any method for selecting the value of this register.

6. A system-level configuration routine should control the programming of this register.

Unspecified results will occur is the programmed value of this register is less than the value of the Split Transaction Capacity register.

State after **RST#** is the same as the **Split Transaction Capacity** register.

Table 24-58: PCI-X Downstream Split Transaction Control Register (Header Type 01H) (continued)

24.9   VENDOR SPECIFIC

This section describes the PCI Vendor Specific Capability interface. This PCI capability permits device vendors to implement a PCI capability for vendor specific purposes.

Figure 24-14 and Table 24-59 illustrate the layout and design of the Vendor Specific capability data structure. The structure length is defined by the device vendor and is variable.

> Note that the byte that immediately follows the Next Item pointer register is required. This byte is defined as a length field. The function of the Length field is to provide the number of bytes in a given PCI function's Vendor Specific capability. The value of the Length field **must** include the first two bytes of the Vendor Specific capability structure, the Capability ID register and the Next Item pointer register. In addition to meeting the requirements of the Length field, this structure must adhere to the PCI Capability requirements described in Section 1.

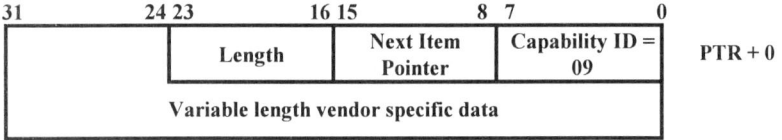

Figure 24-14: Sample Vendor Specific Capability Structure Layout

Offset	Bits	Register/Field	Attributes	Description
0	7::0	Capability ID	Required Read Only	Identifies Vendor Specific as the capability of the structure with a value of 09h.
1	15::8	Next Item Pointer	Required Read Only	Provides the absolute offset to the next item in the Capabilities Linked List (00h if last structure)
2	23::16	Length	Required Read Only	Length in bytes of this Vendor Specific Capability.
3	N::24	Vendor Specific	Variable	Implementation is vendor specific.

Table 24-59: Vendor Specific Capability Structure Definition

CAPABILITY IDENTIFIER REGISTER

Capability Identifier
Offset: 00h of the Vendor Specific Capability Structure Width: 1 Byte Valid Values: 00h-FFh
A value of 09h indicates the structure supports the PCI capability as defined in the *PCI Local Bus Specification*. This specification can be obtained from the PCI Special Interest Group at http://www.pcisig.com.
Description: This register identifies the specific capability supported by a structure member of a PCI Capabilities Linked List.

Bit	Type	Function
7::0	Read Only	**Capability Identifier** This value identifies a capability supported by a PCI function. Capability IDs are assigned by the PCI SIG.

Table 24-60: Capability Identifier Register

NEXT ITEM POINTER REGISTER

Next Item Pointer
Offset: 01h of the Vendor Specific Capability Structure Width: 1 Byte Valid Values: 00h, 40h-FCh (must be DWORD aligned) Description: This register identifies the absolute offset of the start of the next structure member of a Capabilities Linked List. A value of 00h indicates this structure is the last one in the list.

Bit	Type	Function
7::0	Read Only	**Next Item Pointer** This value identifies the start location of the next item (capability data structure) in a PCI function's Capabilities Linked List.

Table 24-61: Next Item Pointer Register

LENGTH REGISTER

Length	
Offset:	02h of the Vendor Specific Capability Structure
Width:	1 Byte
Valid Values:	Vendor specific.
Description:	This register contains the length in bytes of this Vendor Specific Capability. The first two bytes of this structure, the Capability ID and the Next Item Pointer register, are included in the total number of bytes that make up this capability structure.

Bit	Type	Function
7::0	Read Only	**Length** This value speicies the total number of bytes that make up this vendor specific PCI capability.

Table 24-62: Vendor Specific Length Register

24.10 DEBUG PORT

This section describes the Debug Port Capability interface. This interface is intended to permit individual PCI functions to be controlled during a debug session by diagnostic specific software. The implementation and usage model of the debug port is device specific. Other bus classes, notably USB, implement this capability as well.

Figure 24-15 and Table 24-63 illustrate the layout and design of the Debug Port capability data structure.

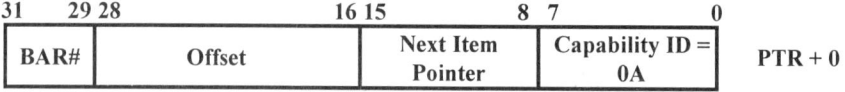

31 29 28	16 15	8 7	0	
BAR#	Offset	Next Item Pointer	Capability ID = 0A	PTR + 0

Figure 24-15: Debug Port Capability Structure Layout

Offset	Bits	Register/Field	Attributes	Description
0	7::0	Capability ID	Required Read Only	Identifies **Debug Port** as the capability of the structure with a value of 0Ah.
1	15::8	Next Item Pointer	Required Read Only	Provides the absolute offset to the next item in the Capabilities Linked List (00h if last structure).
2	31::16	Debug Port	Required Read Only	Contains two sub-fields. The first is an offset within a **Base Address Register** (**BAR**) that identifies the first byte of the **Debug Port** registers. The second sub-field identifies to which one of up to six possible **BARs** in the PCI configuration address space that the **Debug Port** registers are mapped.

Table 24-63: Debug Port Capability Structure Definition

CAPABILITY IDENTIFIER REGISTER

Capability Identifier	
Offset:	00h of the Debug Port Capability Structure
Width:	1 Byte
Valid Values:	00h FFh
Description:	This register identifies the specific capability supported by a structure member of a PCI Capabilities Linked List.

Bit	Type	Function
7::0	Read Only	**Capability Identifier** This value identifies a capability supported by a PCI function. Capability IDs are assigned by the PCI SIG.

Table 24-64: Capability Identifier Register

NEXT ITEM POINTER REGISTER

Next Item Pointer	
Offset:	01h of the Debug Port Capability Data Structure
Width:	1 Byte
Valid Values:	00h, 40h-FCh (must be DWORD aligned)
Description:	This register identifies the absolute offset of the start of the next structure member of a Capabilities Linked List. A value of 00h indicates this structure is the last one in the list.

Bit	Type	Function
7::0	Read Only	**Next Item Pointer** This value identifies the start location of the next item (capability data structure) in a PCI function's Capabilities Linked List.

Table 24-65: Next Item Pointer Register

DEBUG PORT

The **Debug Port** field contains two sub-fields, **Offset** and **BAR#**. Together, the **Offset** and **BAR#** fields point to the base address in memory where the **Debug Port** starts. The value of the first sub-field, **Offset**, is an offset within the physical address space assigned to the **Base Address** register specified in the **BAR#** field. This value identifies the start address of the **Debug Port** registers within the specified **BAR's** assigned memory address space. The second sub-field, **BAR#**, identifies to which one of the six possible **Base Address** registers within a function's PCI configuration space that the **debug port** register(s) are mapped.

Only memory BARs can be used for the Debug Port.

Valid values for **BAR#** are '1' through '6'. The value is independent of whether the **BAR's** width is 32 bit or 64 bit. These values correspond to the six possible **Base Address** registers in PCI configuration address space as follows:

BAR#	Offset
1	10h
2	14h
3	18h
4	1Ch
5	20h
6	24h

Table 24-66: BAR# Field Mapping

OFFSET FIELD

Offset	
Offset:	Bits [28::16] of the Debug Port Capability Data Structure
Width:	13 Bits
Valid Values:	Any DWORD aligned value from 0h up to and including 1000h (4K).
Description:	The byte offset within the specified **BAR** at which the **Debug Port** starts.

Bit	Type	Function
28::16	Read Only	The byte offset, up to 4K, at which the **Debug Port** starts within the memory address space assigned to the specified **BAR**. The offset must be DWORD aligned.

BAR# FIELD

Offset	
Offset:	Bits [31::29] of the **Debug Port** Capability Data Structure
Width:	3 Bits
Valid Values:	01h-06h
Description:	The **BAR** within PCI configuration address space that contains the **Debug Port**.

Bit	Type	Function
31::29	Read Only	One of up to six possible **Base Address** registers within PCI configuration address space into which the **Debug Port** registers are mapped. Only memory **BARs** can be used.

EXAMPLE DEBUG PORT ADDRESS MAPPING

If the BAR# field, bits [31::29] of the Debug Port capability structure, contains the value '010b', the Debug Port registers are mapped to BAR 2. This BAR is located at offset 14h in a function's PCI configuration address space. If BAR 2 is programmed with a value of C0000000h and the Offset field is programmed with 100h, the base address of the Debug Port registers is located at C0000100h.

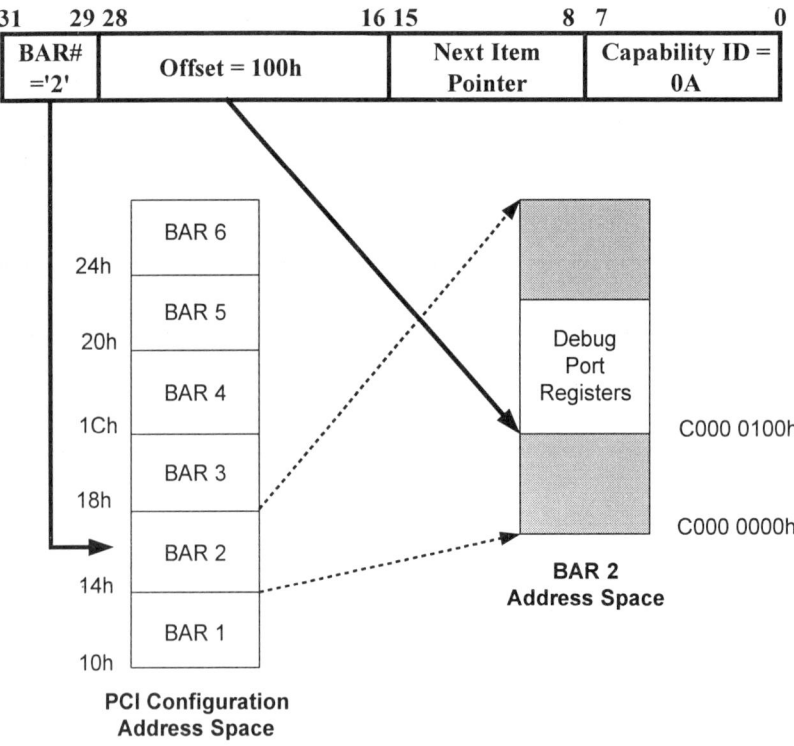

Figure 24-16: Debug Port Address Mapping Example

PCI CLASS CODE REGISTER ENCODING

The PCI Class Code Register is segregated into three contiguous byte wide fields starting at offset 09H of the PCI Configuration Header region.

This Class Code Register has two uses. The first is to generically identify the function that the device performs or provides. The second use is to allow generic device drivers to work with devices from multiple vendors. For instance, a standard VGA device driver will work with any device whose Class Code indicates it is VGA.

> Be aware that the PCI Special Interest Group will define new values for the Class Code Register as the need arises. This register is currently read only. However, its use will probably be extended to have some writeable bits for specific encodings.

The definition of each byte is as follows:

Offset 0B	Base Class Code
	PCI devices are classified according to the function they perform. This value identifies the functional class of the device.
Offset 0Ah	Sub–Class Code
	This value identifies the specific function of a device within its Class Code.
Offset 09h	Programming Interface
	This value specifies a register level programming interface. This interface allows device independent software to interact with the device. Note that currently most devices do not support a register level programming interface.

Table A-1: Class Code Register Definitions

BASE CLASS DEFINITIONS

The following table describes the current definitions for the Base Class Code field (offset 0Bh) of the Class Code Register:

Base Class	Description
00h	Backward Compatible Base Class
01h	Mass Storage Controller
02h	Network Controller
03h	Display Controller
04h	Multimedia Device
05h	Memory Controller
06h	Bridge Device
07h	Simple Communication Controllers
08h	Base System Peripherals
09h	Input Devices
0Ah	Docking Stations
0Bh	Processors
0Ch	Serial Bus controllers
0Dh	Wireless Controllers
0Eh	Intelligent I/O Controllers
0Fh	Satellite Communication Controllers
10h	Encryption and Decryption Controllers
11h	Data Acquisition and Signal Processing Controllers
12h – FEh	Reserved
FFh	Undefined Base Class

Table A-2: Base Class Register Definitions

SUB CLASS AND PROGRAMMING INTERFACE DEFINITIONS

The following sections describe the current definitions for the Sub–Class field and Programming Interface field for each Base Class value. Values not defined are reserved for future use.

BACKWARD COMPATIBLE BASE CLASS

Devices built prior to when the Class Code field was defined have a value of 00h. New devices will use Base Class Codes 01h through 06h or 0FFh. It is recommended that existing devices with a Base Class code of 00h switch to the value which correctly identifies the device's function.

Base Class	Sub–Class	Programming Interface	Description
00h	00h	00h	All non–VGA compatible devices with a Base Class value of 00h will contain these values.
	01h	00h	All VGA compatible devices with a Base Class value of 00h will contain these values.

Table A-3-A: Base Class 00h

MASS STORAGE CONTROLLER BASE CLASS

Use this Base Class for all mass storage controller devices. Note that no standard programming interfaces are defined. Refer to the PCI SIG document *PCI IDE Controller Specification* and the document *Programming Interface for Bus Master IDE Controller* for more information on the IDE sub-class. Both documents may be obtained from the PCI SIG.

Base Class	Sub–Class	Prog. Intfc.	Description
01h	00h	00h	SCSI Bus Controller
	01h	xxh	IDE Controller
	02h	00h	Floppy Disk Controller
	03h	00h	IPI Bus Controller
	04h	00h	RAID Controller
	80h	00h	Other Mass Storage Controller

Table A-3-B: Base Class 01h

NETWORK CONTROLLER BASE CLASS

Use this Base Class for all network controller devices. Note that no standard programming interf2aces are defined.

Base Class	Sub–Class	Prog. Intfc.	Description
02h	00h	00h	Ethernet Controller
	01h	00h	Token Ring Controller
	02h	00h	FDDI Controller
	03h	00h	ATM Controller
	04h	00h	ISDN Controller
	80h	00h	Other Network Controller

Table A-3-C: Base Class 02h

DISPLAY CONTROLLER BASE CLASS

Use this Base Class for all display controller devices. The VGA code (030000h) indicates that the device is VGA compatible. A device with this class code will work with any generic VGA device driver. The programming interface field is used to describe the video controller's compatibility modes. Devices can support multiple video interfaces. The bit map defines which interfaces the controller supports.

Base Class	Sub–Class	Prog. Intfc.	Description
03h	00h	00000000b	VGA Compatible Controller. Memory addresses A00000h-BFFFFFh. I/O addresses 3B0h-3BBh, 3C0h-3DFh and all aliases of these addresses.
		00000001b	8514 Compatible Controller. I/O addresses 2E8h and its aliases, 2EAh-2EFh.
	01h	00h	XGA Controller
	02h	00h	3D Controller
	80h	00h	Other Display Controller

Table A-3-D: Base Class 03h

MULTIMEDIA DEVICE BASE CLASS

Use this Base Class for all multimedia devices such as video capture devices and video codecs.

Base Class	Sub–Class	Prog. Intfc.	Description
04h	00h	00h	Video Device
	01h	00h	Audio Device
	02h	00h	Computer Telephony Device
	80h	00h	Other Multimedia Device

Table A-3-E: Base Class 04h

MEMORY CONTROLLER BASE CLASS

Use this Base Class for all memory controller devices. PCI add-in memory will be defined in the future. Note that no standard programming interfaces are defined.

Base Class	Sub–Class	Prog. Intfc.	Description
05h	00h	00h	RAM
	01h	00h	Flash
	80h	00h	Other Memory Device

Table A-3-F: Base Class 05h

BRIDGE DEVICE BASE CLASS

Use this Base Class for all PCI BRIDGE devices. Note that no standard programming interfaces are defined.

Base Class	Sub–Class	Prog. Intfc.	Description
06h	00h	00h	Host Bridge
	01h	00h	ISA Bridge
	02h	00h	EISA Bridge
	03h	00h	MC Bridge
	04h	00h	PCI to PCI Bridge
		01h	Subtractive Decode PCI/PCI Bridge. Programming Interface code 01h indicates that the PCI/PCI bridge supports subtractive decoding. In addition, this PCI/PCI bridge is also required to support all currently defined functions of a PCI/PCI bridge.
	05h	00h	PCMCIA Bridge
	06h	00h	NuBus Bridge
	07h	00h	CardBus Bridge
	08h	00h	RACEway Bridge: operation mode is Transparent Mode
		01h	RACEway Bridge: operation mode is End-point Mode
	80h	00h	Other Bridge Device

Table A-3-G: Basc Class 06h

BASE CLASS 07H

Use this Base Class for all types of simple communication controllers. Several sub-class values are defined, some of these having specific well-known register-level programming interfaces.

Base Class	Sub–Class	Prog. Intfc.	Description
07h	00h	00h	Generic XT Compatible Serial Controller
		01h	16450 Compatible Serial Controller
		02h	16550 Compatible Serial Controller
		03h	16650 Compatible Serial Controller
		04h	16750 Compatible Serial Controller
		05h	16850 Compatible Serial Controller
		06h	16950 Compatible Serial Controller
	01h	00h	Parallel Port
		01h	Bi-directional Parallel Port
		02h	ECP 1.X Compliant Parallel Port
		FEh	IEEE 1284 Target Device (not a controller)
		03h	IEEE 1284 Controller
	02h	00h	Multiport Serial Controller
	03h	00h	Generic Modem
		01h	Hayes Compatible Modem, 16450 Compatible Interface
		02h	Hayes Compatible Modem, 16550 Compatible Interface
		03h	Hayes Compatible Modem, 16650 Compatible Interface
		04h	Hayes Compatible Modem, 16750 Compatible Interface
	80h	00h	Other Communications Device

Table A-3-H: Base Class 07h

BASE CLASS 08H

Use this Base Class for all types of generic system peripherals. Note that each of the defined sub-class values has a specific well-known register-level programming interface.

Base Class	Sub–Class	Prog. Intfc.	Description
08h	00h	00h	Generic 8259 PIC
		01h	ISA PIC
		02h	EISA PIC
		10h	I/O APIC Interrupt Controller
		20h	I/O(x) APIC Interrupt Controller
	01h	00h	Generic 8237 DMA Controller
		01h	ISA DMA Controller
		02h	EISA DMA Controller
	02h	00h	Generic 8254 System Timer
		01h	ISA System Timer
		02h	EISA System Timers (2 Timers)
	03h	00h	Generic RTC Controller
		01h	ISA RTC Controller
	04h	00h	Generic PCI Hot-Plug Controller
	80h	00h	Other System Peripheral

Table A-3-I: Base Class 08h

BASE CLASS 09H

Use this base class for all types of input devices.

Base Class	Sub–Class	Prog. Intfc.	Description
09h	00h	00h	Keyboard Controller
	01h	00h	Digitizer (Pen)
	02h	00h	Mouse Controller
	03h	00h	Scanner Controller
	04h	00h	Gameport Controller (generic)
		10h	Gameport Controller (conforms to 'legacy' game ports)
	80h	00h	Other Input Controller

Table A-3-J: Base Class 09h

Gameport controllers have a defined register level programming interface. Gameport programming interface 10h is defined as follows:

If an I/O resource is assigned to a Base Address register in this function, the register's functions are required to conform to legacy game ports as follows:

Offset 00h of the assigned I/O resource:

1359

```
Read:    return joystick information


Write:   start the RC timer


Offset 01h of the assigned I/O resource:


Alias the byte at offset 00h


Offset 02h through n of the assigned I/O resource:


The function of these bytes are vendor-specific.
```

BASE CLASS 0AH

Use this base class for all types of docking stations. Note that no specific register-level programming interfaces are defined.

Base Class	Sub–Class	Prog. Intfc.	Description
0Ah	00h	00h	Generic Docking Station
	80h	00h	Other Type of Docking Station

Table A-3-K: Base Class 0Ah

BASE CLASS 0BH

Use this base class for all types of processors. Several sub-class values are defined corresponding to different processor types or instruction sets. Note that no specific register-level programming interfaces are defined.

Base Class	Sub–Class	Prog. Intfc.	Description
0Bh	00h	00h	386
	01h	00h	486
	02h	00h	Pentium
	10h	00h	Alpha
	20h	00h	Power PC
	30h	00h	MIPS
	40h	00h	Co-processor

Table A-3-L: Base Class 0Bh

BASE CLASS 0CH

Use this base class for all types of serial bus controllers. Note that no specific register-level programming interfaces are defined.

Base Class	Sub–Class	Prog. Intfc.	Description
0Ch	00h	00h	Firewire (IEEE 1394)
		10h	Firewire (IEEE 1394)
	01h	00h	ACCESS.bus
	02h	ooh	SSA
	03h	00h	Universal Serial Bus (USB) that follows the Universal Host Controller Interface specification (UHCI)
		10h	Universal Serial Bus (USB) that follows the Open Host Controller Interface specification (OHCI)
		80h	Universal Serial Bus with no specific programming interface
		FEh	USB device (not host controller)
	04h	00h	Fibre Channel
	05h	00h	SMBus (System Management Bus)

Table A-3-M: Base Class 0Ch

BASE CLASS 0DH

Use this base class for all types of wireless controllers. Several sub-class values are defined. Note that no specific register-level programming interfaces are defined.

Base Class	Sub–Class	Prog. Intfc.	Description
0Dh	00h	00h	IrDA compatible controller
	01h	00h	Consumer IR controller
	10h	00h	RF controller
	80h	00h	Other type of wireless controller

Table A-3-N: Base Class 0Dh

BASE CLASS 0EH

Use this base class for Intelligent I/O controllers. The *Intelligent I/O Architecture* specification is available at ftp.intel.com/pub/IAL/I2O/

Base Class	Sub–Class	Prog. Intfc.	Description
0Eh	00h	xxh	Intelligent I/O (I$_2$O) Architecture Specification 1.0
		00h	Message FIFO at offset 40h

Table A-3-O: Base Class 0Eh

BASE CLASS 0FH

Use this base class for all types of satellite communications controllers.

Base Class	Sub–Class	Prog. Intfc.	Description
0Fh	00h	00h	TV
	01h	00h	Audio
	03h	00h	Voice
	04h	00h	Data

Table A-3-P: Base Class 0Fh

BASE CLASS 10H

Use this base class for all types of encryption and decryption controllers. Several sub-classes are defined. Not that no specific register-level programming interfaces are required.

Base Class	Sub–Class	Prog. Intfc.	Description
10h	00h	00h	Network and Computing En/Decryption
	01h	00h	Entertainment En/Decryption
	80h	00h	Other En/Decryption

Table A-3-Q: Base Class 10h

BASE CLASS 11H

Use this base class for all types of data acquisition and signal processing controllers. Several sub-classes are defined. Not that no specific register-level programming interfaces are required.

Base Class	Sub–Class	Prog. Intfc.	Description
11h	00h	00h	DPIO modules
	80h	00h	Other data acquisition and signal processing controllers

Table A-3-R: Base Class 11h

UNDEFINED BASE CLASS

Specific device class not defined.

> Vendors should NOT arbitrarily use this class if a device does not correspond to one of the defined device classes. When in doubt, contact the PCI Special Interest Group for aid in determining the proper Base Class to use for a new device. A new Base Class code may be created if needed.

Base Class	Sub–Class	Prog. Intfc.	Description
FFh	00h	00h	Undefined Class

Table A-3-S: Base Class FFh

USER DEFINABLE CONFIGURATION ITEMS

This appendix (reprinted from the PCI Bus Local Specification 2.1 with permission) describes the mechanism to support the configuring of PCI adapters that have User Definable Features (UDFs) using system configuration mechanisms (such as the EISA Configuration Utility). UDFs are defined to be device configuration items that are dependent on the environment into which the device is installed and whose settings can not be automatically determined by hardware or system software. For example, the token ring speed setting for token ring network devices will be dependent on the specific token ring network into which the device is installed. Therefore, the default value of these configuration items may prevent successful system boot given the environment in which it is installed and the user may be required to insure a proper configuration. UDFs do not apply to devices that have a common compatible default configuration, such as VGA compatible graphics adapters, since a successful system boot can be achieved using the device's default configuration.

> Note that Appendix B is included for reference only. Support for UDF functionality has been removed, starting with PCI Bus Local Specification 2.2. New PCI devices that are designed to meet PCI Bus Local Specification 2.2 or later should not implement UDF functionality. PCI Bus Local Specification 2.2 requires that the UDF Feature Status Bit, bit [6], of each function's PCI Configuration Address Space Status Register, offset 06h, be Reserved and return a value of '0' when read.

OVERVIEW

Device UDFs are described in a text based file that is supplied with an adapter. This file will be referred to as a PCI Configuration File, or PCF. The PCF will specify to the system configuration mechanism the device specific user definable features (UDFs). Adapters that do not support device specific UDFs are not required to supply a PCF. Adapter vendors are required to supply a separate PCF for each adapter function that supports device specific UDFs.

The PCF can be supplied with an adapter via a 1.44 MB diskette formatted with the PC/MS-DOS File Allocation Table (FAT) format. The filename for the file containing the PCF should be XXXXYYYY.PCF, where XXXX is the two byte Vendor ID as specified in the device's configuration space header (represented as hexadecimal digits), and YYYY is the two byte Device Id as specified in the device's configuration space header (represented as hexadecimal digits). The file must be in the root directory on the diskette.

A function on an adapter is required to indicate that it has user definable features via the UDF_Supported bit. This read only UDF_Supported bit resides in the Status Register and will be set when a device function has device specific configuration selections that must be presented to the user. Functions that do not support user selectable configuration items would not implement this bit, and therefore return a 0 when read.

For devices where the UDF_Supported bit is set, system startup and/or configuration software will then recognize the function on the adapter as one that supports user definable features. Systems are not required to be capable of interpreting a PCF. For such systems, the user will need to rely on a vendor supplied device specific configuration utility if the user requires the ability to alter user definable features of that device.

Systems that choose to support interpreting PCFs are also responsible for supplying non-volatile storage (NVS) to hold the device specific configuration selected by the user. In this scenario, system Power-On-Self-Test (POST) software will at system boot time copy the appropriate values for each PCI adapter from the non-volatile storage to the appropriate configuration space registers for each function. The mechanism for interpreting a PCF, presenting the information to the user and storing the selections in the non-volatile storage is system specific. Note that when sizing NVS for a given system, the number of adapters supported, the number of functions per adapter, and the number of bytes of configuration information per function must be analyzed. In addition, the system will need to store enough overhead information such that POST knows what address of which device/function each configuration byte will be written to, masked appropriately as specified in the PCF. It is recommended that system non-volatile storage be sized such that an average of 32 bytes of configuration data (potentially non-contiguous) will be written to each adapter device function. In addition, vendors should design adapters such that they do not require more than 32 bytes of configuration information per function as a result of PCF specified configuration options.

PCF DEFINITION

NOTATIONAL CONVENTION

The PCF contains ISO Standard 8859-1 character set text, commonly referred to as Code Page 850. The text includes keywords that aid the system configuration mechanism's interpretation of the PCF information, as well as provides generic text representing device specific information. All text is case insensitive, unless otherwise noted. White space, including spaces, tabs, carriage returns, and linefeeds, is ignored outside of quoted strings. All PCF selections must be for device specific configuration options and be targeted for the device specific portion (192 bytes) of the function's configuration space. The PCF cannot be used for requesting allocation of system level resources such as interrupt assignments, or memory, I/O or expansion ROM address allocations. The PCF can not request writes to the PCI Configuration Space Header (addresses less than 40h). This must be enforced by the system configuration mechanism.

System configuration software will use the PCF to present to the user the device specific configuration options. User selections will be stored in system non-volatile storage, presumably as values to be written to device specific configuration space addresses. POST software will use the information stored in non-volatile memory to write appropriate configuration settings into each device's configuration space. The device's logic can use the information as loaded in configuration space, or require their expansion ROM logic or device driver SW to copy the device specific configuration space values into appropriate I/O or memory based device registers at system initialization. In addition, the device can choose to alias the device specific configuration space registers into appropriate I/O or memory based device registers if needed. Any configuration information required to be accessible after device initialization should not be accessible exclusively via configuration space.

VALUES AND ADDRESSES

A *value* or *address* can be given in hexadecimal, decimal, or binary format. The radix, or base identifier, is specified by attaching one of the following characters to the end of the *value* or *address*:

H or h - Hexadecimal

D or d - Decimal

B or b - Binary

The radix character must be placed immediately after the value, with no space in between. If no radix is specified, decimal is assumed.

Example: 1FOOh

Hexadecimal numbers beginning with a letter must have a leading zero.

Example: 0C000h

TEXT

Text fields contain information that is to be presented to the user. These fields are free form and are enclosed in quotation marks. These text fields can be tailored to a specific international market by using the Code Page 850 character set to support international languages (see the LANG statement description below). Text field maximum lengths are given for each instance. Text fields can contain embedded tabs, denoted by \t, and embedded linefeeds, denoted by \n. Quotation marks and backslashes can also be placed in the text using \" and \\ respectively.

Embedded tabs are expanded to the next tab stop. Tab length is eight characters (tab stops are located at 9, 17, 25, etc.).

INTERNAL COMMENTS

Comments can be embedded in the PCF for annotational purposes. Comments are not presented to the user. Comments can be placed on separate lines, or they can follow other PCF statements. Comments begin with a semi-colon (;) and are terminated with a carriage return.

SYMBOLS USED IN SYNTAX DESCRIPTION

This description of the PCF syntax uses the following special symbols:

[ ]   The item or statement is optional.

x|y   Either x or y is allowed.

PCI CONFIGURATION FILE OUTLINE

A PCF is structured as follows:

Device Identification Block

Function Statement Block(s)

[Device Identification Block

Function Statement Block(s)]

The Device Identification Block identifies the device by name, manufacturer, and ID. The PCF must begin with this block.

The Function Statement Blocks define the user presentable configuration items associated with the device.

The Device Identification Block and Function Statement Block set can optionally be repeated within the PCF file to support multiple languages.

DEVICE IDENTIFICATION BLOCK

The Device Identification Block within the PCF is defined as follows:
    BOARD
    ID="XXXXYYYY"
    NAME="*text*"
    MFR="*text*"
    SLOT=PCI
    [VERSION=value]
    [LANG=XXX]

The BOARD statement appears at the beginning of each PCF. This statement, along with the other required statements, must appear before the optional statements contained in brackets [ ]. The statements should occur in the order shown.

ID is a required statement containing the vendor and device IDs, XXXXYYYY, where XXXX is the two byte vendor ID as specified in the device's configuration space header (represented as hex digits), and YYYY is the two byte device ID as specified in the device's configuration header (represented as hex digits). The ID must contain eight characters and must be placed in quotation marks.

NAME is a required statement that identifies the device. Vendor and product name should be included. A maximum length of 90 characters is allowed. The first 55 characters are considered significant (that is, only the first 55 characters will be shown if truncation or horizontal scrolling is required).

MFR is a required statement that specifies the board manufacturer. A maximum length of 30 characters is allowed.

SLOT=PCI is a required statement that identifies the device as PCI. This is included to assist configuration utilities that must also parse EISA or ISA CFG files.

VERSION is an optional statement that specifies the PCF standard that this PCF was implemented to. The syntax described by this appendix represents version 0. This statement allows future revisions of the PCF syntax and format to be recognized and processed accordingly by configuration utilities. Version 0 will be assumed when the VERSION statement is not found in the Device Identification Block.

LANG is an optional statement that specifies the language used within the quote enclosed text found within the given Device Identification Block/Function Statement Block set. When no LANG statement is included, then the default language is English. XXX can have the following values:

CZE	Czech
DAN	Danish
DUT	Dutch
ENG	English (default)
FIN	Finnish
FRE	French
GER	German
HUN	Hungarian
ITA	Italian
NOR	Norwegian
POL	Polish
POR	Portuguese
SLO	Slovak
SPA	Spanish
SWE	Swedish

FUNCTION STATEMENT BLOCK

Function Statement Blocks define specific configuration choices to be presented to the use. A Function Statement Block is defined as follows:

```
FUNCTION="text"
[HELP="text"]
Choice Statement Block
    .
    .
    .
[Choice Statement Block]
```

The FUNCTION statement names a function of the device for which configuration alternatives will be presented to the user. A maximum of 100 characters is allowed for the function name.

HELP is an optional text field containing additional information that will be displayed to the user if the user requests help while configuring the function. This text field can contain a maximum of 600 characters.

Each Choice Statement Block names a configuration alternative for the function, and lists the register addresses, sizes, and values needed to initialize that alternative. Each Function Statement Block must contain at least one Choice Statement Block. The first choice listed for a given function will be the default choice used for automatic configuration.

CHOICE STATEMENT BLOCK

CHOICE = "*text*"
[HELP="*text*"]
INIT Statement

.

.

.

[INIT Statement]

CHOICE statements are used to indicate configuration alternatives for the function. Each FUNCTION must have at least one CHOICE statement, and can have as many as necessary. A maximum of 90 characters is allowed for the choice name.

HELP is an optional text field containing additional information that will be displayed to the user if the user requests help with the CHOICE. This text field can contain a maximum of 600 characters.

A Choice Statement Block can contain one or more INIT statements. INIT statements give the register addresses and values needed to initialize the configuration alternative named by the CHOICE statement.

INIT STATEMENTS

INIT=PCI(*address*) [BYTE|WORD|DWORD] *value*

INIT statements provide the register addresses and values needed to initialize the device's vendor specific registers.

The PCI keyword is used to indicate that this is a PCI INIT statement. This is included to assist configuration utilities that must also parse EISA or ISA CFG files.

Address is the register's offset in the PCI configuration space. This address value must be within the 192 bytes of device specific configuration space (offsets 64-255).

An optional BYTE, WORD, or DWORD qualifier can be used to indicate the size of the register. The default is BYTE.

Value gives the value to be output to the register. Bit positions marked with an 'r' indicate that the value in that position is to be preserved. The 'r' can only be used as a bit position in a binary value, or as a hex digit (4 bit positions) in a hex value. The length of the value must be the same as the data width of the port: 8, 16, or 32 bits.

Examples:

```
INIT = PCI(58h) 11110000b
INIT = PCI(5Ah) 0000rr11b
INIT = PCI(0A6h) WORD R8CDh
INIT = PCI(48h) WORD RR0000001111RR11b
```

SAMPLE PCF

```
BOARD
ID="56781234"       ; Vendor is 5678h, Device is 1234h
         ; Filename would be "56781234.PCF"
NAME=         "Super Cool Widget PCI Device"
MFR=          "ABC Company"
SLOT=         PCI
VERSION=      0

FUNCTION="Type of Widget Communications"
HELP="This choice lets you select which type of
communication you want this device to use."
  CHOICE="Serial"
    INIT=PCI(45h)         rrr000rrb  ;Default size is
BYTE
    INIT=PCI(8Ch)         DWORD      0ABCDRRRRh
  CHOICE="Parallel"
    INIT=PCI(45h)         rrr010rrb
    INIT=PCI(8Ch)         DWORD      1234abcdh
  CHOICE="Cellular"
    INIT=PCI(45h)         rrr100rrb
    INIT=PCI(8Ch)         DWORD      5678abcdh

FUNCTION="Communication Speed"
  CHOICE="4 Mbit/Sec"  INIT=PCI(56h) WORD R12Rh
  CHOICE="16 Mbit/Sec"  INIT=PCI(56h) WORD R4CRh
  CHOICE="64 Gbit/Sec"  INIT=PCI(56h) WORD R00Rh

FUNCTION="Enable Super Hyper Turbo Mode"
HELP="Enable Super Hyper Turbo Mode only if the 64
Gbit Speed has been selected."
  CHOICE="No"    INIT=PCI(49h)       rrrrr0rrb
  CHOICE="Yes"   INIT=PCI(49h)       rrrrr1rrb

FUNCTION="Widget Host ID"
  CHOICE="7"     INIT=PCI (9Ah)      rrrrr000b
  CHOICE="6"     INIT=PCI (9Ah)      rrrrr001b
  CHOICE="5"     INIT=PCI (9Ah)      rrrrr010b
  CHOICE="4"     INIT=PCI (9Ah)      rrrrr011b
```

VGA PALETTE SNOOPING

Some graphics controllers that are not VGA compatible, take the output from a VGA controller and map it onto their display as a way to provide boot information and VGA compatibility. However, the color information coming from the VGA controller references the palette table inside the VGA controller. In order for the graphics controller to generate the proper colors, it has to know what is in the VGA controller's palette. To do this the non-VGA graphics controller watches for write accesses to the VGA palette registers, and snoops the data.

In PCI based systems where the VGA controller is on the PCI bus and a non-VGA graphics controller is on the ISA bus, write accesses to the palette will not show up on the ISA bus if the PCI VGA controller responds to the writes. In this case the PCI VGA controller should not respond to the write (does not assert DEVSEL#), should only snoop the data, and should permit the access to be forwarded to the ISA bus. The non-VGA ISA graphics controller can then snoop the data on the ISA bus.

The value of bit 5 in the command register of the PCI VGA device determines whether or not the PCI VGA controller responds to the palette write, or whether it just snoops the data. Non-VGA PCI graphics controllers that need to have VGA palette information must also implement bit 5 in the Command Register to control whether or not to respond or snoop the palette access.

Table C–1 shows how to interpret the Snoop Enable bit in the command register. The table applies to both PCI VGA controllers and non-VGA graphics controllers that need to have VGA palette information. This bit only affects the behavior on <u>write</u> accesses to the palette registers. PCI VGA controllers always respond to read accesses to the palette; non-VGA graphics controllers always ignore read accesses to the palette.

Snoop Enable (Bit 5 in Command)	Description
0	Positively respond to write accesses to the palette registers. VGA controllers should initialize this bit to this state on RESET.
1	Snoop write accesses to the palette registers. Non-VGA graphics controllers that need palette information should initialize this bit to this state on RESET.

Table C-1: Snoop Enable Bit

APPENDIX D

ISA ALIASING

IBM PC AND COMPATIBLES

Intel x86 microprocessors support a 64K I/O address space. However, the original IBM PC platform design only routed ten address lines, SA[0::9], to the expansion slots for decoding I/O address space. For I/O address space the upper five address lines SA[10::15] were not connected and were treated as "don't cares" by add-in cards. This effectively limited the I/O address space to 1K (ten address bits). The I/O address range for ten address bits is 0000h to 03FFh.

The result of limiting the I/O address space decode to the first ten address lines is that this 1K block of I/O address space is repeated 64 times in the address space. This is because the upper five address lines are ignored by add-in devices during I/O bus cycles. Aliasing SA[10::15] are ignored by add–in devices during I/O bus cycles. For example, an add–in device located at I/O address 300h (address lines SA[8::9] are active) that only decodes address lines SA[0::9] will respond to I/O addresses 300h, 1300h, 2300h, 700h, 1700h, 2700h, 0B00h, 1B00h, 2B00h, 0F00h, 1F00h, 2F00h, and so on for a total of sixty–four combinations within the I/O address space. In each instance, address lines SA[8::9] are active, regardless of the state of address lines SA[10::15]. The device assigned I/O port address 300h will respond to any of these addresses. Therefore, I/O port addresses are said to be aliased because devices assigned to an I/O port address between 0000h and 03FFh, or the first 1K of I/O port address space, will respond to multiple addresses above that range.

Of the first 1K of I/O port address space IBM reserved the first 256 bytes of I/O address space (0000h-00FFh) were for platform devices such as interrupt and DMA controllers. The upper 768 bytes (0100h-03FFh) were left free to assign to add-on devices. The defacto standard in the PC industry is to only make a combination of address lines SA[0::7] active when accessing platform devices. The figure below shows how the original IBM PC platform decoded I/O port addresses.

IBM XT AND COMPATIBLES

When IBM introduced their XT model, they increased the number of I/O address lines routed to the expansion slots to 16 allowing access to the full 64K I/O address space. This was largely to overcome the problem of only having 1K of address space in which to map devices. But unfortunately there were (and still are) a large number of add-in cards that only decoded 10 bits. Using the example above, the device that claimed the 10 bit address 300h would continue to claim all the 16 bit aliases of that address making them useless for other devices. Also, platform devices were still doing a 10 bit decode. So even though the number of address lines was increased, the usable address space remained the same.

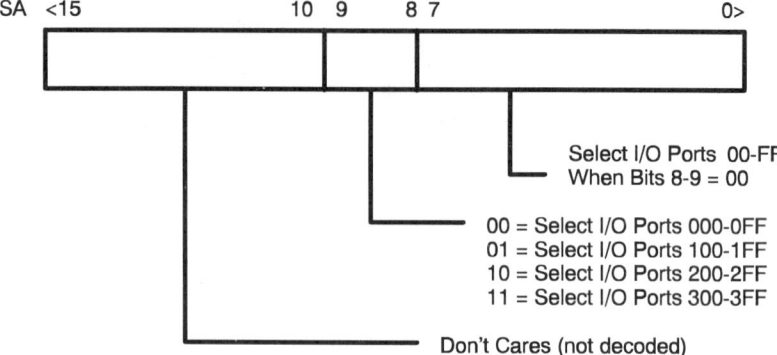

Figure D-1: PC Ten Bit I/O Decode

To overcome the limited address space, add-in card vendors started claiming some address in the first 1K, and then using that address as aliases for unique registers in the device. For example a device may claim the address 0300h for one of its registers and then use the address 1300h (an alias) for another register with a different function. The register at address 300h could be used as an address register, while the register at 1300h may be a data register. Using this technique a device could claim one byte in the 10 bit address space, and implement up to 63 others in the aliases of that address. Many high-function add-in cards use this technique to provide more registers, while consuming small amounts of the 10 bit address space.

IBM AT AND COMPATIBLES

When IBM introduced the AT model, ISA aliasing was once again affected. A full 16 bit I/O address space decode of platform devices was implemented. This means that aliases of platform devices (*i.e.*, addresses where SA[8::9] = 00) can be used for add-in cards. In fact in EISA machines these aliases are used to uniquely address cards in add-in slots.

PRESENT DAY IMPLEMENTATIONS

As a result of this history, the currently defined I/O address map of AT–class machines is such that in each of the unique 64 1K segments the upper 768 bytes of each segment are used by ISA devices (including their aliases) and the lower 256 bytes of each segment are available for use. Effectively, this means that 3/4 of the *total* I/O address space is consumed by ISA devices.

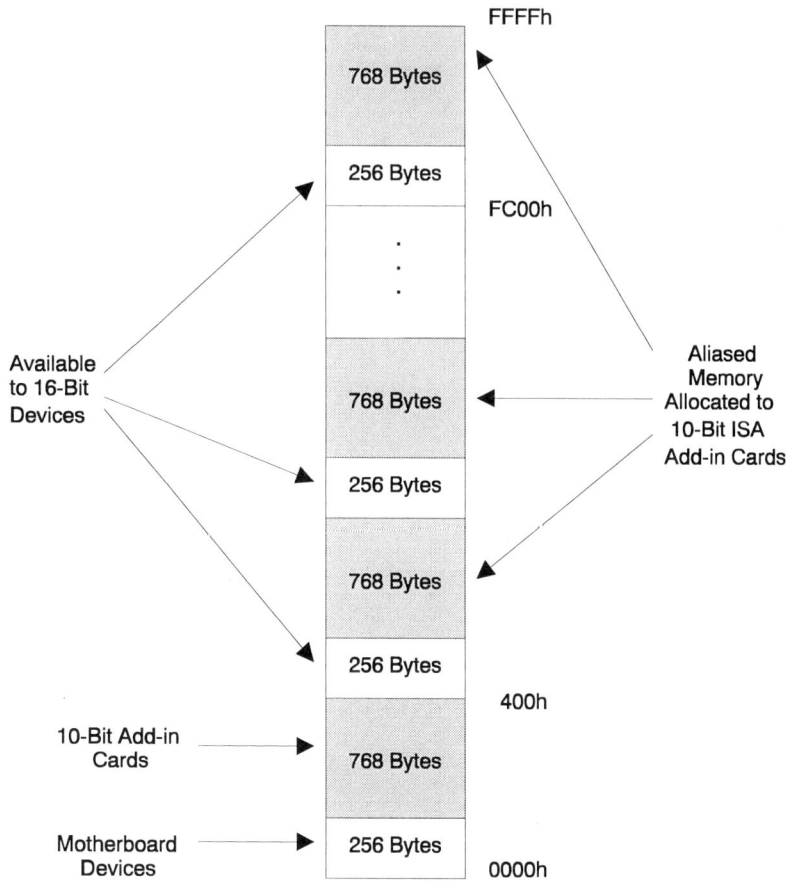

Figure D-2: 64K I/O Decode Map

However, 10 bit add-in cards still assume that an I/O address is for a platform device whenever an I/O address is on the bus with address lines SA[8::9] set to zero. This leaves the upper 63 1K segments for assigning unique I/O addresses to add-in devices in a manner that will not conflict with add-in cards that only decode the first ten address lines. In all cases this requires that address lines SA[8::9] =00 and at least one address line in the range SA[10::15] is set to one. As the figure illustrates, this means that only the lower 256 bytes of each 1K segment are available in order to avoid I/O address space conflicts.

> **Present day implementations now assign the first 4K of I/O address space to platform devices.**

PCI AND ISA ALIASING

The typical PCI system architecture has an interesting impact on the ISA address aliasing problem. I/O addresses emitted by the processor first go to the PCI bus where a PCI device can claim the access. If no PCI device claims the access, the access is then forwarded (using subtractive decode) to the expansion bus (*i.e.*, ISA). If configuration software places a PCI device at the same address as an ISA device *(or any of the ISA aliases),* the ISA device will never see I/O accesses to it. The device on the expansion bus will appear to be broken. As a result, both the design of the PCI device as well as PCI configuration software must account for ISA aliasing to permit the computer system to be configured with no conflicts.

PCI DEVICE DESIGN

PCI devices should never request more than 256 bytes of contiguous I/O address space in one base address register. If more than 256 bytes is requested, it is impossible to assign an address that won't conflict with a possible ISA alias.

> A PCI BIOS is responsible for ensuring that the system resources are assigned in a conflict free manner. Therefore, assume that a PCI BIOS will disable any PCI device requesting more than 256 contiguous bytes of I/O address space.

CONFIGURATION SOFTWARE DESIGN

Configuration software should configure PCI devices such that no conflicts exist. This can be performed in one of two ways. In the first method the configuration software can explicitly know what ISA devices are in the system, what addresses and aliases those devices use, and then configure PCI devices so that no conflicts occur. The major problem with this method is that the automatic detection of ISA devices as well as determining what resources they consume is very difficult. Typically this method can only be accomplished with user input.

The second method is to pre-allocate 3/4 of the address space to ISA devices and their aliases. PCI devices are placed in the remaining spaces. Essentially any I/O address that is greater the 4K (to avoid platform ISA devices) and where SA[8::9] = 00 (to avoid ISA aliases) is a valid address for PCI devices. This technique provides for sixty 256 byte-wide addresses where PCI devices can be mapped without conflicting with platform or ISA devices. This is the preferred method for allocating I/O address space in a PCI based system.

Figure E-1 is an illustration of the I/O port address line assignments for PCI devices.

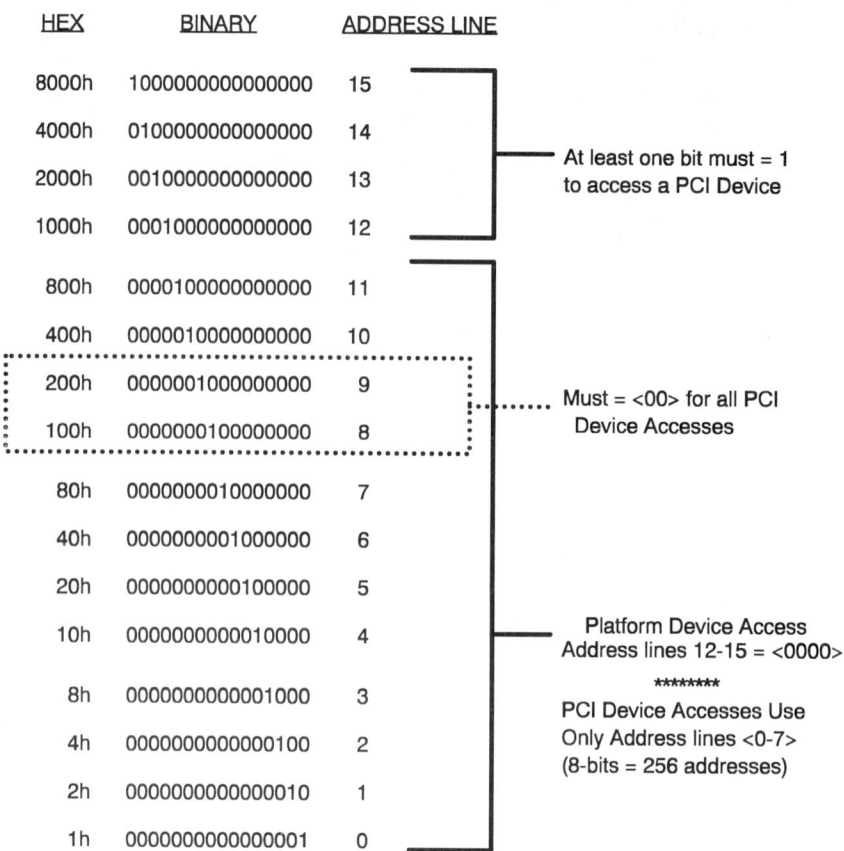

Figure E-1: PCI I/O Address Line Map

PCI AND I/O PORTS 0000H THROUGH 03FFH

The effects of assigning a given range of I/O ports within the 0000h through 03FFh range to the PCI bus in an ISA/PCI based system are as follows:

1. If PCI devices are assigned some of the I/O port addresses between 0000h and 00FFh, the ISA bus will never see the addresses. Some

system platform devices may not respond. This may result in a non–functional system.

2. If PCI devices are assigned all of the I/O port addresses between 0000h and 00FFh, the ISA bus will never see the addresses. No system platform devices will respond. This will result in a non–functional system.

3. If PCI devices are assigned some of the I/O port addresses between 0100h and 03FFh, the ISA bus will never see the addresses. Some add–in ISA devices may not respond. How the system will react cannot be determined.

4. If PCI devices are assigned all of the I/O port addresses between 0100h and 03FFh, the ISA bus will never see the addresses. No add–in ISA devices will respond. How the system will react cannot be determined.

5. If PCI devices are assigned all I/O port addresses between 0000h and 03FFh, the ISA bus will never see this range of addresses. The system platform and all add–in ISA devices will never respond. This will result in a non–functional system.

GUIDELINES FOR PCI AND ISA ALIASING

To avoid the effects of ISA Aliasing in a PCI based system, do the following:

1. Follow the current PC/AT compatible defacto standard. Recognize that the first 4K of I/O address space should only be decoded by the platform ISA bus.

2. Remember that ISA add–in devices only decode the first ten address lines of I/O port address space. Do not assign the I/O address space between 0100h and 03FFh to any PCI device. An ISA bus device assigned to the same I/O port address space as a PCI Device will not respond if you do.

3. Because of items one and two, never assign I/O port address space 0000h through 0FFFH to the PCI bus. Do not assign this I/O port address space to anything but the ISA bus.

4. The PCI bus should never respond to an aliased I/O port address that would prevent any device on the platform ISA bus from responding to I/O port address space 0100h through 03FFh. This means that address lines SA[8::9] will never be active when the PCI bus claims an I/O port access. In effect, this limits the size of the I/O port address space for any PCI device to 256 contiguous bytes. Only I/O port address bits SA[0::7] and SA[10::15] may be active during an I/O port access claimed by the

PCI bus. For example, the first valid 256 byte range of I/O address space that can be assigned to the PCI bus is 1000h through 10FFh. In this instance address line SA[12] is active for all I/O port accesses in this region. The next valid 256 byte range of I/O address space that can be assigned to PCI is 1400h through 14FF. For this region address lines SA[10] and SA[12] are active for all I/O port accesses. Because there are 64K of I/O port addresses, decoding the lower 256 bytes of I/O port address space within a specific 1K block can be repeated 63 times; once for each 1K block of I/O address space above the first 1K block. However, the first 4K are assigned to the platform; this leaves only [60 times 256] byte-wide I/O ports that can be assigned to PCI devices.

5. To summarize, the base address of any PCI device's I/O port region is defined by the contents of address lines SA[0::7] combined with SA[10::15]. At least one of the SA[12::15] address lines should be active for a PCI device to claim the I/O port access. If none of the SA[10::15] address lines is active, then the I/O port access should be forwarded to the ISA bus. In addition, a PCI device should never be assigned more than 256 contiguous bytes of I/O port address space. There is a possibility of preventing an ISA add-in device from functioning if this occurs because at least one of the SA[8::9] address lines will be active.

COMMON PROBLEMS TO AVOID

This appendix lists some of the common problems that have been observed in early versions of PCI devices. Component designers and add-in card vendors should take care to avoid these problems.

DEVICE ASKS FOR MORE THAN 256 BYTES OF I/O SPACE.

A PCI device should never request more than 256 bytes of I/O space. This is because of the address aliasing characteristics of ISA add-in cards (see Appendix C). A PCI device that does request more that 256 bytes will likely be left disabled in any system that contains ISA devices.

EXPANSION ROM IS NOT RELOCATABLE.

One of the key features of PCI that enables Play and Play behavior is the ability to relocate Expansion ROM code (so the user doesn't have to make any decisions) and to tightly pack the code for optimum use of the Expansion ROM area (0C0000h–0E8FFFh). VGA devices must also provide relocatable Expansion ROMs even though the code will eventually be relocated to 0C0000h. This is to allow easy detection of VGA devices on other buses, as well as allowing multiple display devices on PCI (two-headed graphics system).

EXPANSION ROM PUTS SECOND LOAD ON BUS.

The PCI Specification is very clear that add-in cards can have only one electrical load on each PCI signal pin. And yet designs appear where the controller device is attached to the AD lines, and an Expansion ROM is also attached to the AD lines. Designs like this cause subtle timing problems in the system and are very difficult to isolate.

DEVICE'S CONFIGURATION SPACE IS NOT ACCESSIBLE AS BYTES OR WORDS.

Configuration space must be accessible as bytes, words, and DWORDS. Many POST code algorithms depend on this when accessing the predefined header portion of configuration space. For instance, when POST wants to clear the Status Register (at offset 06h) it does a word write with all bits set. If the device only supports DWORD accesses, this operation will cause the Command byte (at offset 04h) to be modified as well. Similarly in the Expansion ROM Base address register, the address is written in one operation (typically DWORD) and then the enable is modified with a byte operation. If the device only supports DWORD accesses to configuration space, this byte write will corrupt the address information.

DEVICE COMES UP ENABLED.

All add-in devices on PCI must power–up in the disabled state. There are no exceptions for any class of devices. Even devices that are used in the boot process must come up disabled, and the BIOS will enable them after resources have been assigned and the device has been selected to perform the boot operation.

UNIMPLEMENTED FUNCTIONS IN MULTIFUNCTION DEVICE RESPOND TO CONFIG ACCESSES.

Most PCI multifunction devices do not implement a complete set of eight functions. Typically the number of functions implemented is less than four. When the System BIOS is checking to see how many functions the device contains, it is important that the device not respond when reads are made to unimplemented functions configuration space. If the device does respond the BIOS will falsely detect functions, operating systems will start unnecessary and incorrect drivers and system behavior will become erratic.

BASE ADDRESS REGISTERS NOT FULLY WRITABLE.

The PCI Specification requires PCI devices to be fully relocatable in the address spaces. Devices cannot decode fixed addresses. Similarly when a Base Address Register is implemented, all bits in the upper part of the register (down to some alignment and size) must be writeable. A device should never hardwire any address bits in a Base Address Register to one. For instance, it is not correct for a device designer to decide that the device operates best when assigned to I/O addresses 3F0h or 1F0h, hardwire bits 8::4 in the Base Address

Register to 1, make bit 9 writeable and hardwire all other address bits to 0. This will have the effect of mapping the device to 3F0h when all 1's are written to the Base Address Register and mapping the device to 1F0h when all 0's are written to the register. However, virtually all BIOSs will break when their POST code tries to determine the size and alignment requirements for this device.

USING RESERVED PINS ON THE CONNECTOR.

Reserved pins on the PCI connector are off limits. Platform designs should never use these pins, and add–in cards should never use these pins. Both platform designs and add–in card designs should leave these pins as "no-connects". The PCI Special Interest Group controls these pins and will decide when and if these pins are assigned a specific function.

3.3V PINS NOT TIED TOGETHER AND DECOUPLED.

The PCI Specification requires that 5V only add–in cards decouple the unused 3.3V pins to the ground plane. Decoupling should average at least 0.01 υF per 3.3V pin, and should occur within 0.25 inches of the pin pad. More details on the decoupling requirements can be found in Section 13.2, Add-in Card Design.

EXPANSION BIOS CODE GOES DIRECTLY TO HARDWARE TO ACCESS CONFIG SPACE.

Expansion BIOS code should always use the PCI BIOS functions to access PCI configuration space. Expansion BIOS code should not assume, or try to determine, which configuration space access mechanism is implemented and then manipulate the hardware directly to access configuration space. Direct access of the hardware mechanism increases the code size of the expansion BIOS (because both mechanisms have to be supported) and may also cause problems if the hardware mechanism is not truly compliant.

EXPANSION BIOS CODE CHANGES OTHER DEVICE'S CONFIGURATION SETTINGS.

Some devices that have problems with certain PCI features (*e.g.*; bursting) have their expansion ROM code disable the feature in the platform chip set. This should not be done. Add-in boards that do this will cause systems to mysteriously have lower performance. Also more and more chip sets are appearing in systems and each of these have a device specific method for enabling/disabling platform features. It is impossible for expansion BIOS code to be aware of all chip sets so eventually the card will be added into a system where the feature is not disabled and the card will cause the system to fail. Bottom line is that Expansion ROM code should only modify the specific device that was added in.

TARGET INSERTS TOO MANY WAIT STATES BEFORE RETURNING FIRST DATA.

The PCI Specification is rather lenient about (in fact it doesn't specify) how many wait states the target (or the master) is allowed to insert between the ADDRESS PHASE and the first DATA PHASE of a bus transaction. Some devices abuse this leniency by inserting fifty or more wait states. While this is not technically illegal it is clearly ill-behaved especially when there are protocol mechanisms where this bus hogging can be eliminated. Target devices that cannot deliver data within a reasonable amount of time (16 clocks) after the ADDRESS PHASE should retry the access by asserting the STOP# signal. This allows the bus to be used by other PCI agents while the target clears up the condition that was causing the large number of wait states. (The master will retry the transaction when it gets granted the bus.) Note that some targets (if they are inherently slow on reads) may choose to automatically retry the access while they go fetch the read data. When the master tries the access again the target can then deliver the data with few wait states.

VGA DEVICES DON'T IMPLEMENT PALETTE SNOOP BIT CORRECTLY.

Some VGA devices operate correctly only when the Palette Snoop bit (bit 5 in the Command Register) is in a certain state. This is not the correct behavior in that VGA devices should continue to function no matter what the state of the Palette Snoop bit. See Chapter 21 for more details on the meaning and usage of the Palette Snoop bit.

IRQ ROUTING TABLE EXAMPLE

DEVICE NUMBERS

A PCI based system can contain a maximum of 256 PCI buses. Each PCI bus can contain between 1 and 32 unique devices. Each PCI device or slot on a given PCI bus is assigned a unique Device Number. This unique PCI Device Number is an encoded number assigned to each device by tying the device's Initialization Device Select line (IDSEL) to one of the AD[31:0] system address lines. An IDSEL line is used as a device select line during PCI configuration read and write transactions. See Chapter 4: *Functional Interaction between PCI Resources* for details on the IDSEL signal.

For purposes of this example, assume that the first (lowest) system address line assigned to a PCI device's IDSEL line is system address line AD[16]. The corresponding Device number would be 0. The maximum number of devices on this particular bus is 16 because only AD[31::16] are used as shown in Table G-1.

Table G-1 contains an example of physical PCI Device Number assignments for a single PCI bus system. Note that the 82430 HOST/PCI BRIDGE and the SIO ISA BRIDGE are used in this example. Also, the slot numbers are defined according to Figure G-1.

Address Line	Device Number	Integrated PCI Device/Slot
16	00h	82434 (PCMC)
17	01h	On-board IDE controller
18	02h	82378IB (SIO)
19	03h	N/C
20	04h	N/C
21	05h	N/C
22	06h	PCI/System Slot 2
23	07h	N/C
24	08h	N/C
25	09h	N/C
26	0Ah	N/C
27	0Bh	N/C
28	0Ch	PCI/System Slot 4
29	0Dh	N/C
30	0Eh	PCI/System Slot 3
31	0Fh	N/C

Table G-1: Physical PCI Device Number Assignment Example

Notice that the Single PCI platform mounted and three PCI slot assignments are not assigned contiguous PCI device numbers. Also, since PCMC and SIO PCI devices do not require an IRQ resource, the IRQ Routing Table will not contain entries for these devices.

PCI INTERRUPT PIN ROUTING

Before the IRQ Routing Table structure entry for each PCI device can be filled in, the specific routing for each interrupt pin to the PCI mappable IRQ lines must be determined. Figure G-2 is an example of how a platform can route PCI interrupt pins to hardware interrupt request lines. Note that the actual routing of PCI interrupt pins is platform dependent. The major components of the interrupt pin routing in this example are the Hardware Interrupt Lines, the IRQ Router and the Interrupt Pin Routes.

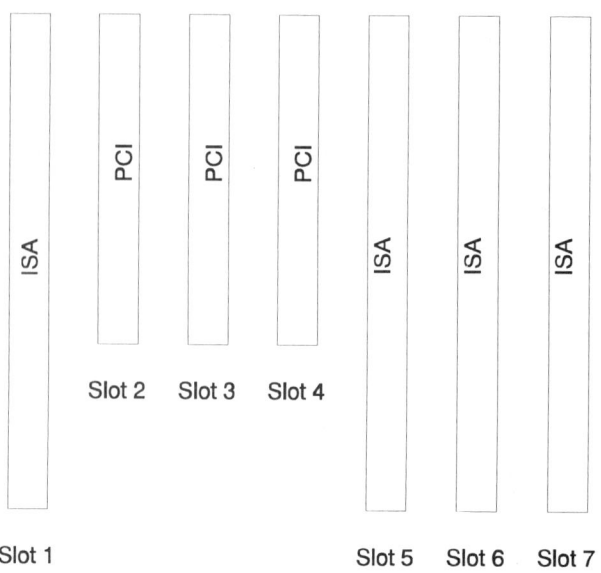

Figure G-1: Slot Numbering Example

HARDWARE INTERRUPT LINES

The Hardware Interrupt Line (or IRQ) signals are outputs of the IRQ Router. They are inputs to the 8259-compatible hardware interrupt controllers. In this example, five IRQ lines are available for mapping to PCI devices. When a device requires servicing, it will signal the request to one of the hardware interrupt lines. See *Chapter 16: System Resources*, for details on interrupt requests and servicing.

> **Note that the IRQ numbers and quantity of Hardware Interrupt Lines available for mapping to PCI devices is platform dependent. It is recommended that this number should be three or greater.**

IRQ ROUTER

The IRQ Router may be either a single device or group of hardware components. The function of the IRQ Router is to connect an interrupt pin of a PCI device to a specific hardware interrupt line. Once the connection is made and interrupts are enabled, the device can request servicing by generating a hardware interrupt. The inputs to the IRQ Router are called Interrupt Pin Routes. The IRQ Router allows the Interrupt Pin Routes to be mapped to any of its outputs.

> **IRQ Routers vary in complexity from full crossbar switches to hardwired connections. The IRQ router should always allow selection from at least three Hardware Interrupt Lines.**

INTERRUPT PIN ROUTES

Each PCI slot supports four interrupt pin signals. These signals are INTA#, INTB#, INTC#, and INTD#. Each of these four signals on each slot should be routed to an input of the IRQ Router in order to permit the connection to a hardware interrupt line. The physical paths of the various interrupt pin signals to the IRQ Router are the Interrupt Pin Routes.

> **Note that the number of Interrupt Pin Routes available for mapping to PCI devices to Hardware Interrupt Line signals is platform dependent. This number ranges from one to as many interrupt pins as there are in the system. A reasonable number of Interrupt Pin Routes for a desktop system is four.**

Figure G-2 illustrates the concept of interrupt line balancing of PCI add-in card slots. In the IRQ Routing Table example there are three physical add-in card slots. These slots are associated with PCI device numbers 06h (Slot 2), 0Ch (Slot 4) and 0Eh (Slot 3). Notice that there is not a straight 1-to-1 connection of the interrupt pins between these slots. In other words, all interrupt pin A#s are not connected together, interrupt pin B#s are not connected together, and so forth. Interrupt Pin Route 0 consists of a connection of interrupt pin C# of Slot 2, interrupt pin B# of Slot 3, and interrupt pin A# of Slot 4 Wiring the individual Interrupt Pin Routes in this way allows the IRQ line load to be distributed to prevent the possibility of one IRQ line servicing all of the slots.

For example, consider the case where:

■ All slot interrupt pin A#s are wired together on one Interrupt Pin Route, all INTB#s from another Interrupt Pin Route, all INTC#s, etc.

■ Each PCI slot contains an add–in card

■ Each add-in card uses its INTA#

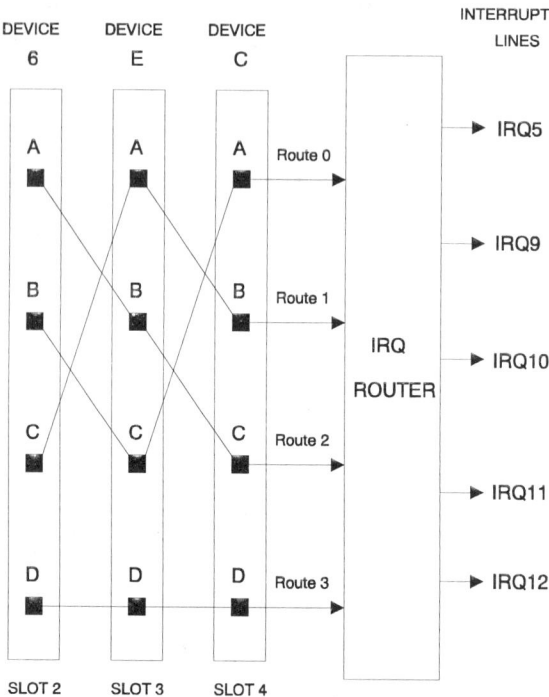

Figure G-2: Interrupt Pin Routing Example

In this case, even though the platform supports multiple Interrupt Pin Routes, the add-in cards are forced to share one interrupt line because of the way the Interrupt Routes were wired. This would place an unnecessary latency factor on servicing the interrupts of the PCI add-in devices.

In Figure G-2, Interrupt Pin Routes 1 and 2 are wired in a manner similar to Interrupt Pin Route 0. However, for purposes of illustration, note how Interrupt Pin Route 3 has the interrupt pin D# signal of all three add–in slots wired together. The impact to interrupt servicing to a system with this configuration depends on the number and types of multi-function devices inserted into the PCI add-in card slots at any given time.

INTERRUPT LINE MAPPING

Ultimately, either POST or operating system level software is responsible for mapping each Interrupt Pin Route to a specific Hardware Interrupt Line. Factors that influence the decision of which IRQ line to use for a specific Interrupt Pin Route are whether a LEGACY device already consumes a specific IRQ line that can be mapped to a PCI as well as IRQ line priority levels.

Offset	Size	Value	Description	Comments
0	Byte	00h	PCI bus number	PCI Bus #0
1	Byte	08h	PCI Device number (in upper 5 bits)	IDSEL connected to AD[17] Bus Device = 1
2	Byte	0FFh	Link Value for INTA#	Unique Link ID
3	Word	0100000000000000b	IRQ Bit–Map for INTA#	Route to IRQ 14 only
5	Byte	00h	Link Value for INTB#	No routing possible
6	Word	0000h	IRQ Bit–Map for INTB#	N/A
8	Byte	00h	Link Value for INTC#	No routing possible
9	Word	0000h	IRQ Bit–Map for INTC#	N/A
11	Byte	00h	Link Value for INTD#	No routing possible
12	Word	0000h	IRQ Bit–Map for INTD#	N/A
14	Byte	00h	Slot Number	00h = platform device
15	Byte	00h	Reserved	Not used

Table G-2: IRQ Routing Table with No Links Example

SINGLE ROUTED PCI DEVICE

Table G-2-A is one of four IRQ routing entries in the IRQ Routing Table that would be returned for the system shown in Figure G-2. Table G-2-A is an example of how to define the IRQ routing table structure for a device that does not have a link to any other PCI device. This means that no other PCI interrupt pins are wire-ORed with this device's interrupt pin.

> Note that the order of IRQ routing entries in an IRQ Routing Table is arbitrary.

MULTIPLE ROUTED PCI DEVICE

Table G-1 shows that the example system also has three PCI add–in card slots. These PCI slots are labeled Slot 2, Slot 3, and Slot 4 as shown in Figure G-1. The IRQ Routing Table entries for these three slots are shown in Tables G-2-B through G-2-D below. These tables are a continuation of the IRQ Routing Table example started in Table G-2-A.

PCI DEVICE 06H:

Offset	Size	Value	Description	Comments
0	Byte	00h	PCI bus number	PCI Bus #0
1	Byte	30h	PCI Device Number (in upper 5 bits)	IDSEL connected to AD[22] Device Number = 6h
2	Byte	012h	Link Value for INTA#	Wired to Interrupt Pin Route 2
3	Word	1000111000100000b	IRQ Bit–Map for INTA#	Route to IRQ 5, 9, 10, 11, or 15
5	Byte	11h	Link Value for INTB#	Wired to Interrupt Pin Route 1
6	Word	1000111000100000b	IRQ Bit–Map for INTB#	Route to IRQ 5, 9, 10, 11, or 15
8	Byte	10h	Link Value for INTC#	Wired to Interrupt Pin Route 0
9	Word	1000111000100000b	IRQ Bit–Map for INTC#	Route to IRQ 5, 9, 10, 11, or 15
11	Byte	13h	Link Value for INTD#	Wired to Interrupt Pin Route 3
12	Word	1000111000100000b	IRQ Bit–Map for INTD#	Route to IRQ 5, 9, 10, 11, or 15
14	Byte	02h	Slot Number	Slot = 2
15	Byte	00h	Reserved	Not used

Table G-2-B: IRQ Routing Table Example

Recall that, except for a value of zero, values for the link fields are arbitrary. The values used in Tables G-2-B through G-2-D were selected based on the Interrupt Pin Route numbers shown in Figure G-2 as follows:

Link Value	Represents
10h	Interrupt Pin Route 0
11h	Interrupt Pin Route 1
12h	Interrupt Pin Route 2
13h	Interrupt Pin Route 3

This method makes it easy to identify specific link values of each slot. Example: to assign the link value of interrupt pin A# of PCI slot 1 (PCI Device Number 06h) determine which Interrupt Pin Route slot 1's interrupt pin A# signal is wired to. As Figure G-2 shows, the Interrupt Pin Route for this case is 2. Thus, the assigned link value for the INTA# signal of slot 1 is 12h. Similarly, INTB# of slot 1 is wired to Interrupt Pin Route 1. Its assigned link value is 11h. And so on.

PCI DEVICE 0EH:

Offset	Size	Value	Description	Comments
0	Byte	00h	PCI bus number	PCI Bus #0
1	Byte	70h	PCI Device Number (in upper 5 bits)	IDSEL connected to AD[30] Device Number = 0Eh
2	Byte	011h	Link Value for INTA#	Wired to Interrupt Pin Route 1
3	Word	1000111000100000b	IRQ Bit–Map for INTA#	Route to IRQ 5, 9, 10, 11, or 15
5	Byte	10h	Link Value for INTB#	Wired to Interrupt Pin Route 0
6	Word	1000111000100000b	IRQ Bit–Map for INTB#	Route to IRQ 5, 9, 10, 11, or 15
8	Byte	12h	Link Value for INTC#	Wired to Interrupt Pin Route 2
9	Word	1000111000100000b	IRQ Bit–Map for INTC#	Route to IRQ 5, 9, 10, 11, or 15
11	Byte	13h	Link Value for INTD#	Wired to Interrupt Pin Route 3
12	Word	1000111000100000b	IRQ Bit–Map for INTD#	Route to IRQ 5, 9, 10, 11, or 15
14	Byte	03h	Slot Number	Slot = 3
15	Byte	00h	Reserved	Not used

Table G-2-C: IRQ Routing Table Example

PCI DEVICE 0CH:

Offset	Size	Value	Description	Comments
0	Byte	00h	PCI bus number	PCI Bus #0
1	Byte	60h	PCI Device Number (in upper 5 bits)	IDSEL connected to AD[28] Device Number = 0Ch
2	Byte	010h	Link Value for INTA#	Wired to Interrupt Pin Route 0
3	Word	1000111000100000b	IRQ Bit–Map for INTA#	Route to IRQ 5, 9, 10, 11, or 15
5	Byte	12h	Link Value for INTB#	Wired to Interrupt Pin Route 2
6	Word	1000111000100000b	IRQ Bit–Map for INTB#	Route to IRQ 5, 9, 10, 11, or 15
8	Byte	11h	Link Value for INTC#	Wired to Interrupt Pin Route 1
9	Word	1000111000100000b	IRQ Bit–Map for INTC#	Route to IRQ 5, 9, 10, 11, or 15
11	Byte	13h	Link Value for INTD#	Wired to Interrupt Pin Route 3
12	Word	1000111000100000b	IRQ Bit–Map for INTD#	Route to IRQ 5, 9, 10, 11, or 15
14	Byte	04h	Slot Number	Slot = 4
15	Byte	00h	Reserved	Not used

Table G-2-D: IRQ Routing Table Example

IRQ BIT-MAP RETURN VALUE

To illustrate what the Get IRQ Routing Options function would return for the IRQ Bit-Map value (in the microprocessor [BX] register) assume that the system is configured such that:

- Interrupt Route 0 is connected to IRQ9
- Interrupt Route 1 is connected to IRQ15
- Interrupt Route 2 is connected to IRQ9
- Interrupt Route 3 is not connected to any IRQ

In this case the value returned for IRQ Bit–Map is 1000000100000000b. This indicates that IRQ9 and IRQ15 are the only IRQs that can be used exclusively by PCI. All other IRQs can be used by other devices in the system.

INDEX

W

X

Notes

Notes